May 10–12, 2017
Banff, Alberta, Canada

AF690323

Association for Computing Machinery

Advancing Computing as a Science & Profession

GLSVLSI'17

Proceedings of the
Great Lakes Symposium on VLSI 2017

Sponsored by:

ACM SIGDA

Supported by:

Cādence, University of Calgary - Schulich School of Engineering, University of Alberta, & IEEE Young Professionals

Association for
Computing Machinery

Advancing Computing as a Science & Profession

The Association for Computing Machinery
2 Penn Plaza, Suite 701
New York, New York 10121-0701

Copyright © 2017 by the Association for Computing Machinery, Inc. (ACM). Permission to make digital or hard copies of portions of this work for personal or classroom use is granted without fee provided that copies are not made or distributed for profit or commercial advantage and that copies bear this notice and the full citation on the first page. Copyright for components of this work owned by others than ACM must be honored. Abstracting with credit is permitted. To copy otherwise, to republish, to post on servers or to redistribute to lists, requires prior specific permission and/or a fee. Request permission to republish from: permissions@acm.org or Fax +1 (212) 869-0481.

For other copying of articles that carry a code at the bottom of the first or last page, copying is permitted provided that the per-copy fee indicated in the code is paid through www.copyright.com.

Notice to Past Authors of ACM-Published Articles
ACM intends to create a complete electronic archive of all articles and/or other material previously published by ACM. If you have written a work that has been previously published by ACM in any journal or conference proceedings prior to 1978, or any SIG Newsletter at any time, and you do NOT want this work to appear in the ACM Digital Library, please inform permissions@acm.org, stating the title of the work, the author(s), and where and when published.

ISBN: 978-1-4503-4972-7 (Digital)

ISBN: 978-1-4503-5470-7 (Print)

Additional copies may be ordered prepaid from:

ACM Order Department
PO Box 30777
New York, NY 10087-0777, USA

Phone: 1-800-342-6626 (USA and Canada)
+1-212-626-0500 (Global)
Fax: +1-212-944-1318
E-mail: acmhelp@acm.org
Hours of Operation: 8:30 am – 4:30 pm ET

Printed in the USA

Foreword

Welcome to the 27th edition of the *Great Lakes Symposium on VLSI (GLSVLSI) 2017,* held at Lake Louise, Alberta, Canada. GLSVLSI is a premier venue for the dissemination of manuscripts of the highest quality in all areas related to VLSI, devices, and system-level design. The venue of this year's GLSVLSI is Lake Louise in the heart of the Canadian Rockies, which is a glacial lake in Banff National Park. The lake's emerald color and beautiful scenery attracts millions of visitors to the location in the summer. The lake is frozen over in the winter, making it one of the largest natural skating rings in the world.

Lake Louise water comes from the Victoria glacier which is visible from the hotel venue. Several hiking trails and ski hills can be accessed from the Lake Louise area. The conference venue, Fairmount Chateaux Lake Louise, is a luxury hotel that was built at the turn of the 20th century by the Canadian Pacific Railway one of their grand railway Hotels. Banff national park is a gem in the Canadian Rockies and has been declared by UNESCO as a World Heritage Site. The park was established in 1885 and consists of Alpine trails, numerous glaciers, dense forests and natural hot springs. Banff national park hosts more than three million tourists annually who come to enjoy the natural beauty and the amenities of the parks. The park is located 110 km west of the city of Calgary, Canada's third largest municipality, and the engineering capital of Canada. Calgary has a vibrant economy with many innovators and entrepreneurs who work in the energy sector. We believe that the natural beauty of the area combined with the engineering and the entrepreneurial mindset of Calgary makes Lake Louise a great location for this high-quality symposium on VLSI, and that you will enjoy the beautiful surroundings as well as the symposium program over the three days of this year's GLSVLSI.

GLSVLSI 2017 starts on Wednesday May 10th 2017, with an exciting line up of speakers on a broad range of issues including VLSI Design, hardware security, new methods in computer-aided design (CAD) and network-on-chips (NoCs), low-power systems and emerging memory designs, bio chips and biological systems and emerging computing applications. Overall, there are 10 regular sessions, 4 special sessions, and 2 poster sessions in the technical program. Seven outstanding papers have been selected as candidates for the best paper award and will be presented in different technical sessions (as marked in the program).

We have four special sessions during the three days of the conference. In the first special session on Wednesday, we will explore Low Power Computing based on Non-Volatile Memories. This is followed by two special sessions on Thursday on the Three-Dimensional Integrated Circuit (3D IC) Security and Logic Obfuscation for IoT Security. On Friday, the fourth special session on Efficient IoT Systems will be held.

As for the technical meeting, GLSVLSI 2017 had outstanding statistics: 197 papers were submitted, including authors from 27 different countries, of which 48 papers were accepted as full papers for oral presentation at the symposium (with a 24.4% acceptance rate). Including papers presented as poster, a total of 72 papers will be included in the symposium and published in the symposium proceedings. Special sessions add another 16 exciting papers to the proceedings of the symposium.

In addition to great technical talks, we have organized several keynote talks from recognized experts. On Wednesday we will open the conference with a talk from Dr. Leland Chang who will speak about Cognitive Data Centric Systems. Dr. Niraj K. Jha will talk about Internet of Medical Things on Thursday morning. On Thursday at lunch Dr. Andrew Putnam will discuss FPGAs in the Datacenter - Combining the Worlds of Hardware and Software Development. On Friday, Dr. Alex Jones will deliver another keynote talk on Green Computing: New Challenges and Opportunities. In addition, we have organized a session on innovation on Friday afternoon. Dr. Alex Bruton who is a professor of entrepreneurship at the University of Calgary, will give a talk on ideation and the entrepreneurship mindset. This will be followed by an innovation challenge where participants will work on developing ideas using EDA and embedded systems tools.

The social events of GLSVLSI 2017 include two special events this year. The first event consists of a reception cocktail on Wednesday evening at the Chateau Lake Louise. Then, on Thursday May 11th, a hiking trip is planned to walk around Lake Louise. The 1-hour hiking trip will be followed by the conference banquet.

We would like to thank all the members of the Technical Program Committee and the secondary reviewers, who have done a rigorous and thorough job in evaluating the submissions and determining the final high-quality technical program of GLSVLSI 2017. The track chairs have done outstanding work in ensuring that each submitted paper was consistently reviewed and helped prepare the final program. In addition, we extend our strong appreciation for the hard work and excellent service that the members of the Organizing Committee (Houman Homayoun, Emre Salman, Theocharis Theocharides, Tali Moreshet, Danella Zhao, Weisheng Zhao, Aida Todri-Sanial, and Brett Meyer) have contributed while organizing the proceedings, special sessions, web presence, registration, finances, publicity and the organization of the event and to make this edition of GLSVLSI a great success.

We thank Department of Electrical and Computer Engineering and Schulich School of Engineering for their gracious support and tremendous assistance in the organization of GLSVLSI. Our corporate sponsors include Cadence, IEEE Southern Alberta Section Young Professionals.

We trust that you will find GLSVLSI 2017 highly rewarding and exciting in terms of the technical quality, networking opportunities, as well as the content and diversity of the talks and sessions.

Laleh Behjat and Jie Han
General Co-Chairs

Miroslav Velev and Deming Chen
Program Co-Chairs

Table of Contents

Session 3: Strategies for In-Memory Computing

Session 4: Circuits, Architectures, and System Level Issues for Many-Core Processors

Session 5: CAD for the Nano Era

Special Session 1: Low Power Computing based on Non-Volatile Memories

Special Session 2: Three-Dimensional Integrated Circuit (3D IC) Security

Special Session 3: Logic Obfuscation for IoT Security: A New Arms Race?

Special Session 4: Efficient IoT Systems: The Power of Heterogenous Integration

Poster Session I

Poster Session II

27th ACM Great Lakes Symposium on VLSI, Lake Louise, Alberta, Canada, May 10 – 12, 2017

General Chairs: Laleh Behjat (University of Calgary, Canada)
Jie Han (University of Alberta, Canada)

Program Chairs: Miroslav N. Velev (Aries Design Automation, USA)
Deming Chen (University of Illinois, USA)

Web Chair: Theocharis Theocharides (University of Cyprus, Cyprus)

Registration Chair: Tali Moreshet (Boston University, USA)

Proceedings Chair: Houman Homayoun (George Mason University, USA)

Finance Chair: Danella Zhao Old Dominion University, USA)

Publicity Chairs: Aida Todri-Sanial (CNRS, LIRMM, France)
Brett Meyer (McGill University, Canada)
Weisheng Zhao (Beihang Univrsity, China)

Special Sessions Chair: Emre Salman (Stony Brook University, USA)

Steering Committee: Jose Ayala (Univ. Complutense Madrid, Spain)
Iris Bahar (Brown University, USA)
Sanjukta Bhanja (University of South Florida, USA)
Erik Brunvand (University of Utah, USA)
Yehea Ismail (American Uniersity in Cairo, Egypt)
Alex K. Jones (University of Pittsburgh, USA)
Hai (Helen) Li (University of Pittsburgh, USA)
Fabrizio Lombardi (Northeastern University, USA)
Enrico Macii (Politecnico di Torino, Italy)
Martin Margala (University of Massachusetts)
Gang Qu (University of Maryland, USA)
Ken Stevens (University of Utah, USA)
Yuan Xie (University of California, Santa Barbara, USA)
Zhiyuan Yan (Lehigh University, USA)
Hai Zhou (Northwestern University, USA)

GLSVLSI'17 Program Committees

Track 1: VLSI Design

Chair: Vasilis Pavlidis (University of Manchester, UK)
Co-chair: Srinivas Katkoori (University of South Florida, USA)

Committee:
Iraklis Anagnostopoulos (Southern Illinois University, USA)
Bishnu Das (Indian Institute of Technology, Roorkee, India)
Joseph Friedman (University of Texas, Dallas, USA)
Pierre-Emmanuel Gaillardon (University of Utah, USA)
Dhruva Ghai (Oriental University, India)
Ann Gordon-Ross (University of Florida, USA)
Rajendran Jeyavijayan (University of Texas, Dallas, USA)
Selcuk Kose (University of South Florida, USA)
Akash Kumar (Dresden University of Technology, Germany)
Vivek Nandakumar (University of California, Santa Barbara)
Partha Pande (Washington State University, USA)
Sudeep Pasricha (Colorado State University, USA)
Francesco Regazzoni (ALaRI - USI, Switzerland)
Anirban Sengupta (Indian Institute of Technology, Indore, India)
Saket Srivastava (University of Lincoln, UK)
Nan Wang (California State University at Fresno, USA)
Yong Zou (Synopsys, USA)

Track 2: VLSI Circuits, and Power Aware Design

Chair: Sumeet Gupta (Penn State University, USA)
Co-chair: Yu Wang (Tsinghua University, China)

Committee:
Tosiron Adegbija (University of Arizona, USA)
Jose Ayala (Complutense University of Madrid, Spain)
Jianwei Dai (Intel, USA)
Bassem Fahs (RPI, USA)
Deliang Fan (University of Central Florida, USA)
Swaroop Ghosh (Penn State University, USA)
Vinayak Honkote (Intel, USA)
Mehdi Kamal (University of Tehran, Iran)
Liang Men (University of Arkansas, USA)
Ioannis Savidis (Drexel University, USA)
Upasna Vishnoi (Marvell Semiconductor, USA)
Tian Xia (University of Vermont, USA)
Bei Yu (Chinese University of Hong Kong, China)
Qiaoyan Yu (University of New Hamshire, USA)
Joseph Zambreno (Iowa State University, USA)

Track 3: Computer-Aided Design (CAD)

Chair: Wei Zhang (Hong Kong University of Science and Technology, Hong Kong)
Co-chair: Wenjing Rao (University of Illinois at Chicago, USA)

Committee:
Xiang Chen (George Mason University, USA)
Daniel Große (University of Bremen, Germany)
Siew Kei Lam (Nanyang Technological University, Singapore)
Shuai Li (Cadence Design Systems, U.S.A)
Weichen Liu (Chongqing University, China)
Mirko Loghi (Universita di Udine, Italy)
Ilia Polian (University of Passau, Germany)
Donghwa Shin (Yeungnam University, Korea)
Sharad Sinha (Nanyang Technological University, Singapore)
Hamed Tabkhi (University of North Carolina Charlotte, USA)
Amit Trivedi (University of Illinois at Chicago, USA)
Jia Wang (Illinois Institute of Technology, USA)
Yanzhi Wang (Syracuse University, USA)
Yaoyao Ye (Shang Hai Jiao Tong University, China)

Track 4: Testing, Reliability, and Fault-Tolerance

Chair: Nicola Nicolici (McMaster University, Canada)
Co-chair: Chih-Tsun Huang (National Tsing Hua University, Taiwan)

Committee:
Al Crouch (Consultant, USA)
Giorgio di Natale (LIRMM, France)
Masahiro Fujita (University of Tokyo, Japan)
Yu Huang (Mentor Graphics, USA)
Naghmeh Karimi (University of Maryland, Baltimore County, USA)
Rene Krenz-Baath (Hamm-Lippstadt University, Germany)
Peilin Song (IBM Research, USA)
Matteo Sonza Reorda (Politecnico di Torino, Italy)
Pouya Taatizadeh (Dialog Semiconductor, Germany)
Nur Touba (University of Texas at Austin, USA)
Spyros Tragoudas (Southern Illinois University, USA)
Andreas Veneris (University of Toronto, Canada)
James Wingfield (AMD, USA)
Zeljko Zilic (McGill University, Canada)

Track 5: Emerging Computing, and Post-CMOS Technologies

Chair: Mehdi Tahoori (Karlsruhe Institute of Technology, Germany)
Co-chair: Garrett S. Rose (University of Tennessee, Knoxville, USA)

Committee:
Pascal Benoit (LIRMM, France)
Jayita Das (Intel, USA)
Miao Hu (Hewlett-Packard Labs, USA)
Sachhidh Kannan (Intel, USA)
Duo Liu (Congquing University, China)
Dimin Niu (Samsung, USA)
Fabian Oboril (Intel, Germany)
Guillaume Prenat (CEA-Spintec, France)
Fei Qiao (Tsinghua University, China)
Aida Todri-Sanial (LIRMM, France)
Ioana Vatajelu (TIMA Labs, France)
Lan Wei (University of Waterloo, Canada)
Wujie Wen (Florida International University)
Weisheng Zhao (Beihang University, China)

Track 6: Hardware Security

Chair: Gang Qu (University of Maryland, USA)
Co-chair: Guru Venkataramani (George Washington University, USA)

Committee:
Domenic Forte (University of Florida, USA)
Yier Jin (University of Central Florida, USA)
Ramesh Karri (New York University, USA)
Mehran Kermani (Rochester Institute of Technology, USA)
Yongqiang Lyu (Tsinghua University, China)
Ken Mai (Carnegie Mellon University, USA)
James Plusquellic (University of New Mexico, USA)
Hassan Salmani (Howard University, USA)
Avesta Sasan (George Mason University, USA)
Marten van Dijk (University of Connecticut, USA)
Sheng Wei (University of Nebraska-Lincoln, USA)
Yuan Xie (University of California, Santa Barbara, USA)
Jing Ye (Institute of Computing Technology, CAS, China)
Jiliang Zhang (Northeastern University, China)
Yuliang Zhou (Huawei Technologies, China)

Track 7: Biochips, and Biological Systems

Chair: Krishnendu Chakrabarty (Duke University, USA)
Co-chair: Robert Wille (Johannes Kepler University Linz, Austria)

Committee:
Mirela Alistar (Hasso-Plattner Institute, Germany)
Emre Araci (Santa Clara University, USA)
Jonathan Babb (MIT, USA)
Jacob Beal (Raytheon BBN Technologies, USA)
Philip Brisk (University of California, Riverside, USA)
Douglas Densmore (Boston University, USA)
Tsung-Yi Ho (National Tsinghua University, Taiwan)
Kai Hu (Oracle, USA)
Bing Li (Technical University of Munich, Germany)
Jan Madsen (Technical University of Denmark, Denmark)
Paul Pop (Technical University of Denmark, Denmark)
Fei Su (Intel, USA)
Bo Yuan (City University of New York, City College, USA)

GLSVLSI 2017 Sponsors & Supporters

Sponsors:

Supporters:

Cognitive Data-Centric Systems

Leland Chang
IBM T. J. Watson Research Center
Yorktown Heights, NY, USA
lelandc@us.ibm.com

ABSTRACT

With rapid growth in the availability of massive amounts of data and the development of new machine learning and deep learning techniques, significant opportunities exist in the application of computing to learn from data, build models, and discover insights – cognitive tasks that can augment human expertise in a broad range of industries. Computing systems must evolve to efficiently meet these needs by leveraging innovation in heterogeneous systems infrastructure and information technology consumption models that are increasingly driven by cloud-based delivery. These new systems must be designed to accommodate the entirety of the overall workflow, including not just machine learning and analytics tasks, but also data management and manipulation. In a convergence with systems for classical modeling and simulation (HPC and technical computing), cognitive workloads can benefit dramatically from hardware acceleration. As decades of sustained CMOS technology scaling begins to slow, the specificity and optimality of hardware accelerators will be a key enabler for system-level performance while simultaneously presenting challenges in composing systems that seamlessly integrate traditional CPUs, multiple accelerators, and different memories. This talk will discuss cognitive data-centric systems for the next era of computing, in which balanced heterogeneous systems are delivered through the cloud.

Keywords

Cognitive computing; Hardware acceleration; Heterogeneous systems.

Permission to make digital or hard copies of part or all of this work for personal or classroom use is granted without fee provided that copies are not made or distributed for profit or commercial advantage and that copies bear this notice and the full citation on the first page. Copyrights for third-party components of this work must be honored. For all other uses, contact the Owner/Author. Copyright is held by the owner/author(s).
GLSVLSI '17, May 10-12, 2017, Banff, AB, Canada
ACM 978-1-4503-4972-7/17/05.
http://dx.doi.org/10.1145/3060403.3060491

BIOGRAPHY

Leland Chang is the Senior Manager of VLSI Design at the IBM T. J. Watson Research Center, where he leads a team driving the transition of new research concepts into next-generation POWER server and System Z mainframe products, including system architecture and microprocessor design implementation as well as roadmap definition and applications analysis. With a technical background spanning semiconductor technology, circuit design, system architecture, and software algorithms, his key contributions have included the FinFET structure for CMOS scaling, 8T-SRAM and high-speed register files for embedded memory scaling, integrated voltage regulators with new passive device technologies, and system design for emerging workloads such as machine learning and deep learning. He received the B. S., M. S., and Ph.D. degrees in electrical engineering and computer sciences from the University of California, Berkeley, has authored more than 75 technical articles and 115 patents, and is currently the memory subcommittee chair for the ISSCC technical program committee.

Green Computing: New Challenges and Opportunities

Alex K. Jones
University of Pittsburgh
3700 O'Hara Street
1238 Benedum Hall
akjones@pitt.edu

ABSTRACT

As individuals and researchers approach the challenge of green computing it is natural to consider the energy consumption of computational devices and their supporting systems during their use phase (i.e., after they are deployed into service). This includes reducing energy consumption in processors, memory systems, peripheral devices, cooling systems and a host of other components that are used in deployed systems. However, for computing to be truly green, all phases of the system life-cycle, from manufacturing to disposal, must be considered. In particular there is limited awareness to the considerable fraction of the total life-cycle environmental impacts of computing systems that result from the fabrication of the integrated circuits (ICs) that are used in those devices. Studies have shown that the energy and environmental costs of IC fabrication can actually significantly outpace use-phase sustainability metrics and environmental impacts. With trends towards more exotic, thus, more environmentally unfriendly, fabrication approaches at deeply scaled nodes, life-cycle thinking for next generation computing systems that includes traditional optimization of operational energy-efficiency as well as minimizing impacts from IC fabrication is critical. In this talk I will present a new cadre of tools and methodologies to holistically evaluate energy consumption and other environmental impacts from computing. Based on these tools, I will discuss new interdisciplinary research directions and educational opportunities that emerge towards achieving more sustainable computing.

CCS Concepts/ACM Classifiers

•Social and professional topics → Sustainability; **•Hardware → Impact on the environment**; *VLSI design manufacturing considerations; VLSI system specification and constraints;*

Author Keywords

Sustainability; life cycle assessment (LCA); embodied energy; dark silicon; technology scaling; emerging memory; reliability; approximate computing; indifference analysis

Permission to make digital or hard copies of part or all of this work for personal or classroom use is granted without fee provided that copies are not made or distributed for profit or commercial advantage and that copies bear this notice and the full citation on the first page. Copyrights for third-party components of this work must be honored. For all other uses, contact the Owner/Author.
Copyright is held by the owner/author(s).
GLSVLSI '17, May 10-12, 2017, Banff, AB, Canada
ACM 978-1-4503-4972-7/17/05.
http://dx.doi.org/10.1145/3060403.3066859

BIOGRAPHY

Professor Alex K Jones is a MCSI Faculty Fellow in Sustainability and Director of Computer Engineering at the University of Pittsburgh. In addition to sustainable computing, his research interests include compilers, computer architectures, electronic design automation, and reliability. He is the author of more than 140 publications in these areas. His research is funded by the U.S. National Science Foundation, DARPA, CCC, the NSF CHREC center, and industry. Dr. Jones' contributions have resulted in several awards including an ACM/SIGDA Distinguished Service Award, a seminal paper award from FCCM in addition to multiple best paper awards and nominations, a University of Pittsburgh Innovator Award, and the 2017 Carnegie Science Award. Recently, Dr. Jones led an effort in visioning for the electronic design automation community funded by the Computing Community Consortium (CCC). Dr. Jones is also actively involved in efforts to improve the scientific method for experiments in computers science and engineering, to develop methods reproducible research, and a centralized hub for computer architecture simulators, emulators, benchmarks and experiments. He serves on many journal editorial boards and conference committees including in area of sustainability, the IEEE Transactions on Sustainable Computing and the IEEE International Green and Sustainable Computing Conference. In his spare time he performs as the principal clarinetist with the Pittsburgh Philharmonic and Aeolian Winds and enjoys skiing and Tae Kwon Do.

REFERENCES

[1] A. K. Jones *et al.*, "Considering fabrication in sustainable computing," in *Proc. of ICCAD*, 2013, pp. 206-210.

[2] D. Kline, Jr., N. Parshook, X. Ge, E. Brunvand, R. Melhem, P. K. Chrysanthis, and A. K. Jones. "Holistically Evaluating the Environmental Impacts in Modern Computing Systems." in *Proc. of the IEEE International Green and Sustainable Computing Conference (IGSC)*. 2016.

[3] I. Bayram, E. Eken, D. Kline Jr., N. Parshook, Y. Chen, and A. K. Jones. "Modeling STT-RAM Fabrication Cost and Impacts in NVSim." in *Proc. of the IEEE International Green and Sustainable Computing Conference (IGSC)*. 2016.

FPGAs in the Datacenter – Combining the Worlds of Hardware and Software Development

Andrew Putnam
Microsoft
Andrew.Putnam@microsoft.com

ABSTRACT

The Catapult project has brought the power and performance of FPGA-based reconfigurable computing to Microsoft's hyperscale datacenters, accelerating major production cloud applications such as Bing web search and Microsoft Azure, and enabling a new generation of machine learning and artificial intelligence applications. Catapult is now deployed in nearly every new server across the more than a million machines that make up the Microsoft hyperscale cloud.

The presence of ubiquitous and programmable silicon in the datacenter ushers in a new era where the discipline and rigor of the VLSI community are combining with the speed and agility of the software community to form new opportunities in a blend development styles and techniques.

In this talk, I will describe the next generation of the Catapult configurable cloud architecture, and the tools and techniques that have made Catapult successful to date. I will also discuss areas where traditional hardware and software development flows fall short, and ways in which the VLSI community can branch into new opportunities in software and computing.

CCS Concepts/ACM Classifiers

Computer systems organization → Reconfigurable computing; Computer systems organization → Cloud computing; Applied computing → Data centers, Networks → Data center networks; Hardware → Reconfigurable logic and FPGAs;

Author Keywords

Catapult; SmartNIC; Configurable Cloud

Permission to make digital or hard copies of part or all of this work for personal or classroom use is granted without fee provided that copies are not made or distributed for profit or commercial advantage and that copies bear this notice and the full citation on the first page. Copyrights for third-party components of this work must be honored. For all other uses, contact the Owner/Author.
Copyright is held by the owner/author(s).
GLSVLSI '17, May 10-12, 2017, Banff, AB, Canada
ACM 978-1-4503-4972-7/17/05.
http://dx.doi.org/10.1145/3060403.3066860

BIOGRAPHY

Andrew Putnam is a Principal Research Hardware Development Engineer in a collaboration between Microsoft Azure and Microsoft Research NExT. He received a dual B.A/B.S. from the University of San Diego in 2003, and an M.S. and Ph.D. in Computer Science and Engineering from the University of Washington in 2006 and 2009 respectively. His research focuses on reconfigurable computing, future datacenter design, and computer architecture, with an emphasis on seeing research through from concept to prototype to technology transfer. He was a founding member of the Microsoft Catapult project, which was the first to put Field Programmable Gate Arrays (FPGAs) into production hyperscale datacenters, doubling the capacity of each server for web search, and creating the fastest network in the cloud.

Internet-of-Medical-Things

Niraj K. Jha
Department of Electrical Engineering, Princeton University
jha@princeton.edu

ABSTRACT

We have arrived at the dawn of the Internet-of-Things (IoT) era. 25 billion devices (things or physical objects) are already connected to the Internet, and this number is expected to grow to 50 billion by 2020. IoT is a network of physical objects. These objects contain sensors, actuators, and processing elements that enable us to gather data, monitor the health of the object, make intelligent decisions, and optimize processes. IoT is expected to have a potential economic impact of \$3-6 trillion per year by 2025, with \$1-2.5 trillion of this economic impact (its largest fraction) coming from smart healthcare applications. These applications will be enabled by a personal healthcare system consisting of implantable and wearable medical sensors and devices connected to a personal health hub (e.g., a smartphone or smartwatch) that is connected to the Internet.

In this talk, we will explore this Internet-of-Medical-Things from two angles: energy-efficient inference and security. We will first explore energy-efficient inference on sensor nodes. This exploits sparsity, which is characteristic of a signal that allows us to represent information efficiently. We will look at an approach that enables efficient representations based on sparsity to be utilized throughout a signal processing system, with the aim of reducing the energy and/or resources required for computation, communication, and storage. Such intelligent sensor nodes can be expected to be an important building block of IoT. We will then show how wearable medical sensors, which are being increasingly used as part of a body-area network to provide proactive healthcare, can be used in a completely different domain: continuous authentication, through monitoring of the biological aura of the person. Unfortunately, as with any other technology, along with the upside, we also have the downside of IoT – if the security challenges facing IoT are not addressed, it may just become an Internet-of-Things-to-be-Hacked. Hence, in the last part of the talk, we will focus on the security of a body-area network that consists of implantable/wearable medical devices and a health hub. We will also explore physiological side channels that leak information about our health condition.

CCS Concepts/ACM Classifiers

Security and privacy → Biometrics; Embedded systems security; Computing methodologies → Supervised learning; Hardware → Signal processing systems.

Permission to make digital or hard copies of part or all of this work for personal or classroom use is granted without fee provided that copies are not made or distributed for profit or commercial advantage and that copies bear this notice and the full citation on the first page. Copyrights for third-party components of this work must be honored. For all other uses, contact the Owner/Author. Copyright is held by the owner/author(s).
GLSVLSI '17, May 10-12, 2017, Banff, AB, Canada
ACM 978-1-4503-4972-7/17/05.
http://dx.doi.org/10.1145/3060403.3066861

Author Keywords

Body-area network; energy efficiency; inference; IoT; medical devices; security; sparsity.

BIOGRAPHY

Niraj K. Jha received his B.Tech. degree in Electronics and Electrical Communication Engineering from Indian Institute of Technology, Kharagpur, India in 1981 and Ph.D. degree in Electrical Engineering from University of Illinois at Urbana-Champaign in 1985. He is a Professor of Electrical Engineering at Princeton University. He has served as an Associate Director for the Princeton Andlinger Center for Energy and the Environment. He is a Fellow of IEEE and ACM. He has co-authored five books, among which are "Switching and Finite Automata Theory, 3rd ed." and "Testing of Digital Systems" that are textbooks being used around the world. He has served as the editor-in-chief of IEEE Transactions on VLSI Systems and on the editorial boards of several other IEEE Transactions. He is an author or co-author of more than 430 papers among which are 14 award-winning papers. His research interests include smart healthcare, machine learning, computer security, IoT, energy-efficient design, IC design automation, FinFETs, and monolithic 3D IC design.

Designing Really Big Value Ideas

Dr. Alex Bruton
The Innographer
Calgary, Canada
alex@theinnographer.com

ABSTRACT

Why did an engineering firm perform no better at some basic innovation tasks than a class of grade 6 and 7 students? Why are many of us not good at coming up with good ideas, even though we think we are? What keeps us, our students, and our employees from getting better at it? And what can we do about all that?

In this interactive and visually engaging talk, Dr. Bruton will tackle questions such as these by sharing some compelling examples and a simple, powerful model for innovation literacy. He'll urge us to stop competing with each other (or having our organizations hire consultants to compete with each other) in order to spread the Post-It-Notes-on-the-wall-because-they're-cool and the let's-get-the-keywords-into-the-annual-report notions of ideation, innovation, and entrepreneurial thinking. And he'll offer ideas and solutions that enable and inspire action.

Expect an explicit theory-informed connecting of the dots to and between many of the popular tools and approaches used by leading startups, innovation strategy consultants, and educational institutions, such as: design thinking; idea modeling; lean startup's build-test-learn process and minimum viable product (MVP); business design; the business model canvas; and customer development.

Expect to receive and practice using a practical toolset for the deliberate design of really big value ideas – ideas that are at the same time highly impactful *and* imminently feasible for your and your teams to carry out.

And expect to be inspired and enabled with those DIY tools to do it again for yourself and your teams, either on your own whiteboards or on the back of the next napkin your run into.

Author Keywords

Ideation; innovation; creativity; tools; design thinking.

BIOGRAPHY

Dr. Alex Bruton, P.Eng., MBA, helps people (learn to) innovate. He's spoken and led workshops around the world, including an invited talk at Google, and he's been recognized as Entrepreneurial Educator of the Year in Canada. He's been an engineer, a manager, a several time entrepreneur, and a professor - among other exciting roles. Today he's the founder and president of a practical open education and innovation design firm that helps people become more innovative and entrepreneurial, and a tenured faculty member at the University of Calgary's Schulich School of Engineering.

Permission to make digital or hard copies of part or all of this work for personal or classroom use is granted without fee provided that copies are not made or distributed for profit or commercial advantage and that copies bear this notice and the full citation on the first page. Copyrights for third-party components of this work must be honored. For all other uses, contact the Owner/Author(s). Copyright is held by the owner/author(s).
GLSVLSI'17, May 10–12, 2017, Banff, AB, Canada.
ACM ISBN 978-1-4503-4972-7/17/05.
http://dx.doi.org/10.1145/3060403.3066909

Design of a Low-Power Non-Volatile Programmable Inverter Cell for COGRE-based Circuits

Pilin Junsangsri, Fabrizio Lombardi
Department of Electrical & Computer Engineering
Northeastern University
Boston, MA USA 02115
junsangsri.p@husky.neu.edu, lombardi@ece.neu.edu

Salin Junsangsri, Martin Margala
Department of Electrical and Computer Engineering
University of Massachusetts
Lowell, MA USA 01854
salin_junsangsri@student.uml.edu, martin_margala@uml.edu

ABSTRACT
This paper proposes a low-power non-volatile programmable inverter cell (NVPINV) that can be used with a COGRE (i.e. a compactly organized generic reconfigurable element) circuit to store the correct information for programming when establishing the desired logic function. The programmable data in the cell is read from a non-volatile SRAM (NVSRAM); two RMs (racetrack memories) are utilized as non-volatile elements. The RM is selected as non-volatile memory element due to its capability for independent operations (read and write), thus making possible a parallel execution of the programming process. The NVSRAM operates as a programmable circuit, i.e. a programmable circuit under control as either a buffer, or an inverter. The cell is extensively analyzed in terms of its operations with respect to different figures of merit, such as delay, power dissipation and power delay product (PDP). Simulation results show that in addition to low-power operation, the proposed NVPINV cell provides significant advantages (such as low delay and non-volatile storage) compared to an SRAM based Look-Up-Table (LUT) implementation.

CCS Concepts: • Hardware~Non-volatile memory • Hardware~Programmable logic elements • Hardware~Memory and dense storage

Keywords: Non-volatile memory; Racetrack Memory; FPGA; Programmable inverter; Emerging Technology.

1. INTRODUCTION
Field Programmable Gate Arrays (FPGAs) are programmable chips that can be configured for fast prototyping of digital circuits; the resources (mostly in a form of Look-Up-Tables (LUTs)) can be reconfigured multiple times. The configuration of a FPGA is established through a stream of configuration bits (received serially) that set all resources to the desired state, usually through a scan chain [1]. Many logic functions do not fully require the entire LUT, thus a substantial inefficiency in utilization is often encountered; moreover, the number of configuration bits required for a LUT is large.

[2] has proposed a novel logic structure referred to as COGRE (i.e. a compactly organized generic reconfigurable element). A COGRE implementation consists of a 2-input binary NAND tree in which a programmable inverter cell is placed at every primary input/output as well as between gates. Figure 1 shows 5-input and 6-input COGRE circuits [2]. Each programmable inverter can operate as either a buffer, or an inverter according to the different requirements of a design [2, 3]. A LUT is often implemented by SRAM cells; however, a SRAM is volatile, so additional off-chip non-volatile storage (often flash memories) is required to store the FPGA configuration data during power-off [4, 5]. Data transfer between the FPGA and the external non-volatile memory is often very slow ((based on serial data transfer), so resulting in a loss of performance for the start-up operation. Moreover, the off-chip stored configuration data is vulnerable to external attacks, thus posing a security concern for many applications [6].

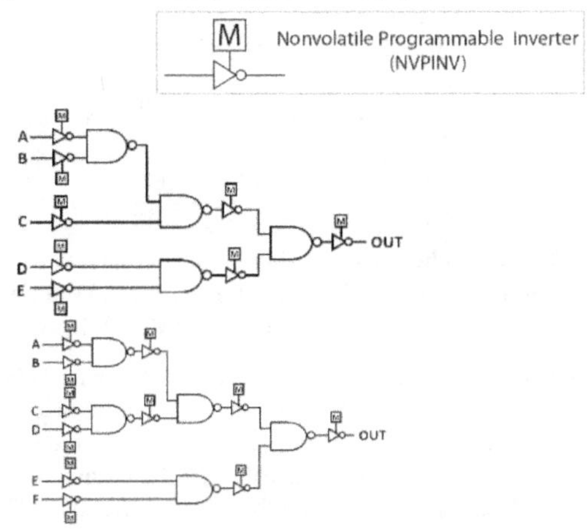

a) *b)*

Figure 1. COGRE circuits a) 5-input type b) 6-input type [2, 3]

Non-volatile memories (NVMs) have gained considerable attention for FPGAs [6, 7]. Among NVMs, the racetrack memory (RM) has been advocated as a promising candidate for future non-volatile memories. RM is based on the current-induced domain wall motion in magnetic nanowires [8][9][10]. A hybrid cell made of a CMOS circuit and a RM has the potential to provide substantial advantages over a flash memory for non-volatile storage. Features such as fast switching time, lower (read) power consumption, good endurance and excellent retention [11] make the RM very attractive for many applications requiring both stand-alone and embedded memories [8]. CMOS integration and fast data access can be achieved [8] by combining the RMs with magnetic tunnel junction (MTJ) nanopillars as (read and write) heads. Moreover, the peripheral circuits of the RMs (for shift as well as read/write) have an excellent operational compatibility with the transfer of programming data through a chain, as commonly occurring in FPGAs.

In this paper, perpendicular magnetic anisotropy (PMA) based racetrack memories [12] are utilized as non-volatile memory elements. A non-volatile programmable inverter (NVPINV) using two PMA-based RMs is proposed for use with COGRE; this cell ensures a non-volatile and fast programming of the logic circuit of

Permission to make digital or hard copies of all or part of this work for personal or classroom use is granted without fee provided that copies are not made or distributed for profit or commercial advantage and that copies bear this notice and the full citation on the first page. Copyrights for components of this work owned by others than ACM must be honored. Abstracting with credit is permitted. To copy otherwise, or republish, to post on servers or to redistribute to lists, requires prior specific permission and/or a fee. Request permissions from Permissions@acm.org.
GLSVLSI '17, May 10-12, 2017, Banff, AB, Canada
© 2017 ACM. ISBN 978-1-4503-4972-7/17/05…$15.00
DOI: http://dx.doi.org/10.1145/3060403.3060405

COGRE. An extensive evaluation of the cell is pursued to establish different figures of merit; the low-power dissipation of the proposed cell with differently sized COGRE circuits is also assessed and compared to an SRAM-based LUT implementation.

2. REVIEW

The racetrack memory (RM) is a novel technology for a Magnetic RAM (MRAM); it is based on controlling the domain wall (DW) motion in ferromagnetic nanowires [13][14][15]. Data is stored in the form of a magnetization direction between two artificial potentials (or constrictions) to pin the DW (so, no current pulse is applied) [12]. The distance between two constrictions can be extremely small (in the range of few nanometers), so attaining an extremely high density and compact storage (in excess of a GB within a small die) at device level. The scalability potential of a RM is one of the most pronounced advantages compared to other non-volatile memories [12]. A RM consists of three parts: the write head, the read head and the propagation part. The write head nucleates a local domain in the magnetic stripe by spin-transfer torque (STT). The read head detects the data stored in the racetrack cell using the tunnel magneto-resistance (TMR) effect [8]. The propagation part controls the motion of the domain wall and drives the stored data from the write to the read heads. The basic cross sectional structure of a RM is shown in Figure 2.

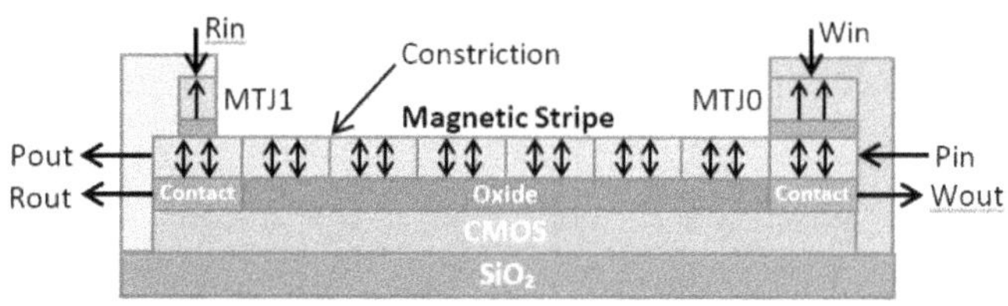

Figure 2. The cross-section structure of a racetrack memory; nodes Rin and Rout are for reading, Win and Wout for writing, and Pin and Pout for the shift operation [12].

A CoFeB magnetic stripe is separated by constriction to store data; two CoFeB/MgO MTJs are used as write and read heads. CMOS circuits are required to write, read, or shift data in the cell and generate the corresponding voltages; the number of stored bit data in the cell is equal to the number of constrictions. The widths of the write and read heads are different; for the write operation, a lower resistance with a larger width is required to reduce the rate of the oxide barrier breakdown, as one of the most significant constraints in a high-speed STT switching mechanism [12]. The high resistance of the MTJ with a smaller width is exploited when reading, because it can greatly improve data sensing [9][12]. The CMOS circuitry dominates the area of a RM, because the magnetic stripe is implemented at the back-end through a 3D integration in a manner similar to a MRAM [12]. It should be noted that RMs have separate paths for writing and reading data, a feature that is very useful for the FPGA application considered in this manuscript.

3. PROPOSED CELL

The proposed NVPINV cell consists of two shared RMs (denoted by RL and RR), 18 MOSFETs; the shift and control circuits are shared among the arrays of NVPINVs. In terms of operations and as per device characteristics, four circuits can be distinguished: a write circuit, a read circuit, a logic circuit and, a shift circuit. The connections between these circuits are illustrated in Figure 3. Racetrack Memories (RM) are used as non-volatile storage elements and MOSFETs are used as controlled elements. The write, read, logic and shift circuits are shown in Figures 4 through 7.

The proposed cell exploits the shift capabilities in the operation of the RMs as shown in Figure 3. Configuration data is initially loaded through an I/O port of the FPGA in a serial fashion; using a chain, it is then parallelized and stored in all COGRE programmable cells in a non-volatile form (i.e. the RMs); then the shift operation is performed to move the configuration data from the write to the read circuits.

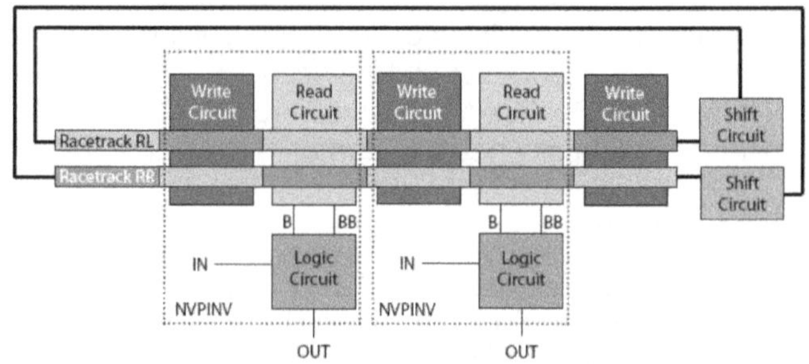

Figure 3. Connections between the RMs and the circuits (write, read, logic and shift) of the proposed NVPINV cell

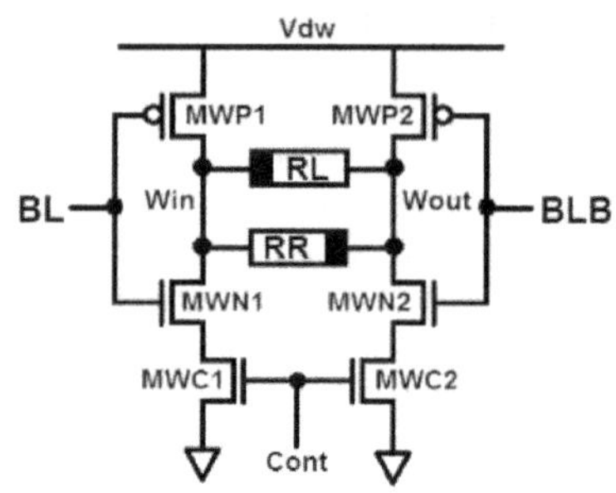

Figure 4. Write circuit [16] of the proposed RM-based NVPINV cell

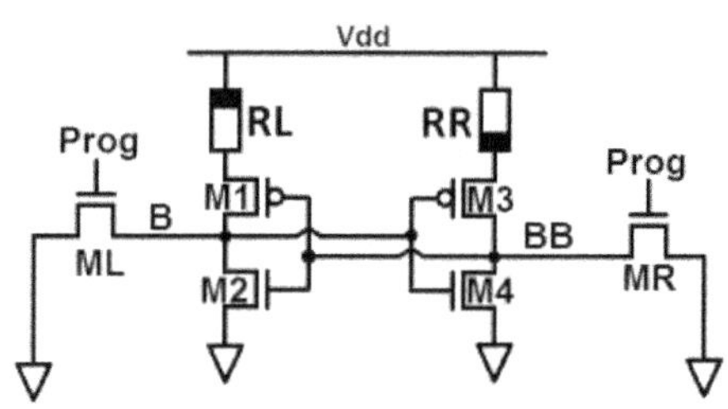

Figure 5. Read circuit of the proposed RM-based NVPINV cell

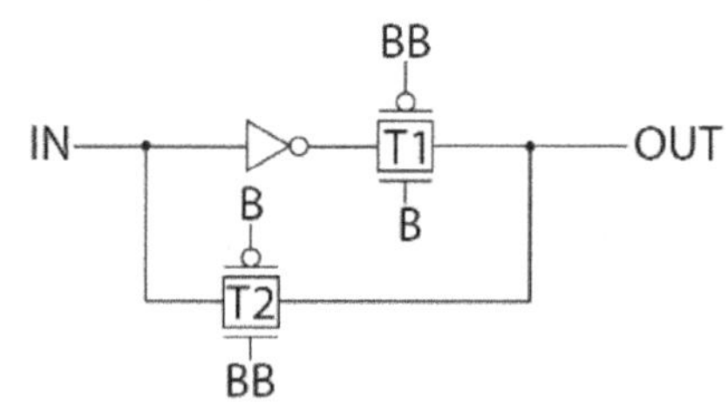

Figure 6. Logic circuit of the proposed RM-based NVPINV cell

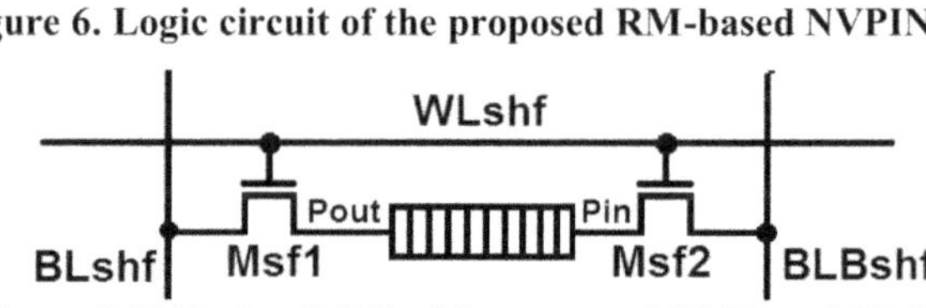

Figure 7. Shift circuit [16] of the proposed RM-based NVPINV cell

When an application is evoked or on power-up, the configuration data (now stored internally to the FPGA chip) is read from the RMs, such that all programmable devices are set to the desired state (for a COGRE circuit, they correspond to the inverter or buffer state of the NVPINVs between gates). In a traditional (non-volatile) FPGA, this process is usually executed sequentially, i.e.

the programming of the resources can be performed through an internal scan chain [1] connecting the logic resources to the I/O port. By utilizing the proposed NVPINV cells, the RMs allow the configuration data (that is internally stored in non-volatile form) to be loaded in parallel (i.e. simultaneously in multiple cells) through a read operation, as presented in more detail next.

3.1 Write operation

Data in the proposed NVPINV cell is stored in nonvolatile form in the two racetracks RL and RR. The circuit in Figure 4 [16] is used to write data into RL and RR; as per the characteristics of a racetrack device, the write operation is executed provided the write current is larger than its critical value [12, 17]. A large voltage difference is required across a PMA-based racetrack cell to write data [16]. The write voltage (V_{dw}) is larger than V_{DD} [15, 16]. During the write operation, the write voltage appears at BL and BLB while the control voltage (V_{Cont}) must be equal to V_{dw} for turning ON the transistors MWC1 and MWC2 [16]. The data stored in the proposed cell varies depending on the voltages at BL and BLB. When the voltages of BL and BLB are V_{dw} and GND (GND and V_{dW}), MWP1 and MWN2 are OFF (ON), while MWN1 and MWP2 are ON (OFF); hence, the voltage difference across RL is negative (positive), while the voltage difference across RR is positive (negative). So, RL and RR change from low to high state and high to low state (high to low state and low to high state) respectively, and a '1' ('0') is written as data.

3.2 Read Operation

This circuit for the proposed NVPINV (Figure 5) reads data from the racetrack devices and sends it to the logic circuit (Figure 6). The logic circuit behaves as either a buffer or an inverter depending on its control data, i.e. the voltages at nodes B and BB. If the voltages at nodes B and BB are at GND and V_{DD}, the transmission gate T2 is ON and the transmission gate T1 is OFF; so the output voltage (node OUT) is the same as the input voltage (node IN) and the proposed NVPINV behaves as a buffer. However, if the voltages at nodes B and BB are at V_{DD} and GND respectively, the transmission gate T1 is ON and the transmission gate T2 is OFF; so the output voltage (node OUT) has the inverted value of the input (node IN) and the proposed NVPINV behaves as an inverter.

The operation of the proposed read circuit operates only at power-up or after the shift operation. During the shift operation, the voltage of line prog is at V_{DD}. Transistors ML and MR are ON, i.e. the voltage at lines B and BB are not stable and cannot be read. Once the shift circuit completes its operation, the read operation starts. The voltage at line prog is at GND so transistors ML and MR are OFF; the voltages at nodes B and BB vary depending on the data stored in the racetrack devices. If racetracks RL and RR are in state '0' (high resistance) and '1' (low resistance) respectively, the voltages at nodes B and BB are GND and V_{DD}, so the logic circuit of the proposed RM-NVPINV behaves as a buffer. However, if the racetracks RL and RR are in state '1' and state '0' respectively, the voltages at nodes B and BB are V_{DD} and GND. The logic circuit of the proposed RM-NVPINV behaves as an inverter.

As per the characteristics of the RMs (Figure 2), the heads for the write and read operations are disjoint and they operate separately. Since the write circuit is not employed during the read operation, the proposed circuit can perform the write operation when the data in the NVPINV cell is read. Data is shifted from the write circuit to the read circuit via the corresponding shift operation [16] and its data is subsequently copied back to the SRAM following the shift operation. This independence in operations can be used for programming purposes.

3.3 Shift Operation

This operation shifts the data from the write head to the read head or vice versa. The shift circuit in Figure 7 [16] is used for the shift operation of the proposed NVPINV; it shifts the domain wall of the RM. Due to the low shift resistance of a RM, the voltage difference across the shift terminals is very small. To increase the shift voltage, the supply voltage of the shift circuit must be increased (V_{dsf}); the width to length ratio of the transistors (W/L) must also be increased. The shift operation is performed by connecting the proposed shift circuit to the terminals Pin and Pout of the RM. As the direction of the shift operation is either forward or backward, then two transistors are needed to control this operation in the racetrack memory. If only one transistor is utilized, then a negative supply voltage is required, thus requiring additional circuitry to generate this voltage through a supply regulator. To reduce the complexity of the shift operation, two transistors are employed.

During the shift operation, the voltage at WLshf is at the supply voltage value of the shift operation (V_{dsf}). The voltages at lines BLshf and BLBshf are varied depending on the shift direction, i.e. the shift direction is to the left (right) when the voltages at the bitlines BLshf and BLBshf are GND and V_{dsf} (V_{dsf} and GND).

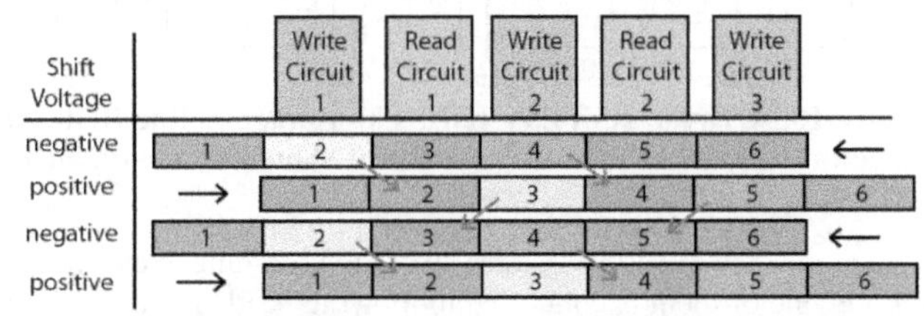

Figure 8. Racetrack index at each write and read heads when racetrack is shifted forward and backward respectively

Operation of a racetrack is based on an index (with the capability of shifting forward or backward); so, a racetrack cell can be shared between NVPINV cells. For complete utilization of the racetrack devices, another write circuit is added at the end of each row of proposed NVPINV cells. In Figure 8, write circuit 3 is added to the NVPINV row; so there is a racetrack index that does not connect to any write or read head. This extra index is used as a "spare" to insure that every write and read heads are connected to the racetrack devices for the shift operation; by this arrangement, a racetrack device can be shifted only by a single index in a forward or backward direction. Based on this scheme, read circuit 1 (Figure 8) is connected only to index 2 or index 3 of the racetrack memories, while read circuit 2 is connected only to index 4 or index 5 of the racetrack memories. Index 1 and index 6 of the RMs are never connected to a read head, so index 1 and index 6 are not used for the NVPINV cell.

To efficiently utilize the racetrack devices, a control circuit is needed; the control circuit selects the appropriate circuits for a write operation. Consider Figure 8; if a racetrack is shifted left (the shift voltage is negative), the programming data is stored by using the write circuit that is located to the left of its read circuit. The write circuit that is located to the right of the read circuit is used to write the data if the racetrack is shifted to the right (the shift voltage is position). Therefore, data is not written to the heads with indices 1 and 6 of the racetrack memory (Figure 8).

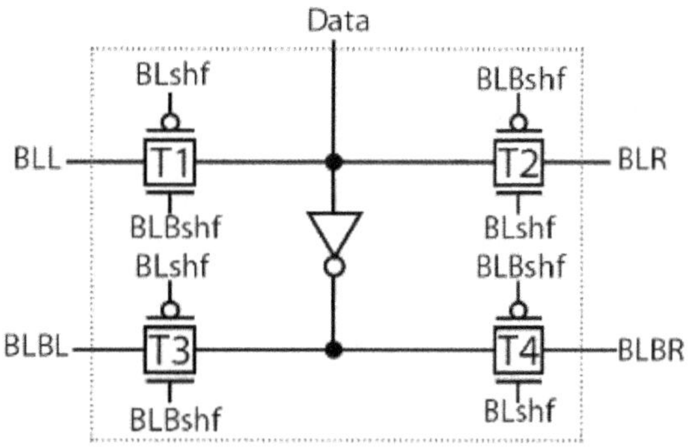

Figure 9. Control circuit of NVPINV array

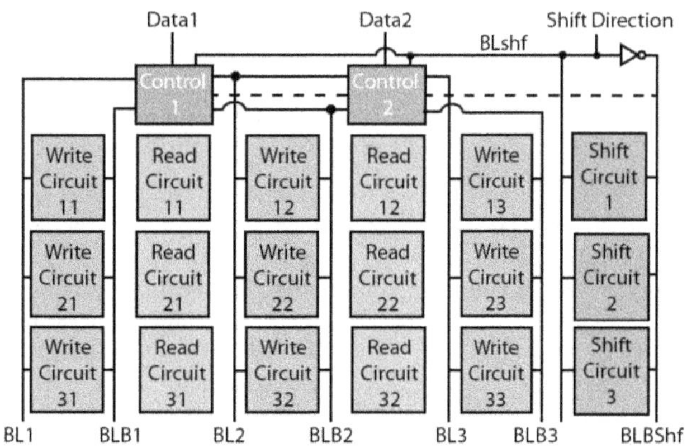

Figure 10. Array of NVPINV cells. The voltage at line BLBShf is connected to both control circuits as shown by the dashed line

Moreover, each NVPINV stores two programming data for the cell, i.e. one of them is connected to its write head, and the second one is connected to its read head. These programming data are used in a NVPINV when its index is shifted from its write head to the read head.

Figure 9 shows the control circuit of the proposed NVPINV array. The input at node Data corresponds to the programming data of the NVPINV. The voltages of the transmission gates (T1-T4) for controlling lines BL and BLB are shown on the left and right columns; node BLL (BLBL) is the voltage at line BL (BLB) on the left column, while node BLR (BLBR) is the voltage at line BL (BLB) on the right column. The shift directions (shift voltages at nodes BLShf and BLBShf) are used for the control circuit. The shift direction voltage is at the supply voltage value during the shift operation. Recall that V_{dsf} is the supply voltage value at line BLshf; if BLshf is at V_{dsf} (GND) while the voltage at line BLBshf is at GND (V_{dsf}), the racetrack is shifted to the right (left). Transmission gates T2 and T4 of the control circuits are then ON (OFF) while T1 and T3 of the control circuits are OFF (ON). The write circuits to the right (left) of the read circuits are then used to write data from the input programming voltage to the racetrack. Figure 10 shows the connection between an array of NVPINV cells and the control circuits.

4. RESULTS AND COMPARISON

This section presents the simulation results of the proposed NVPINV cell. HSPICE is used as a simulation tool. The model of [17] is employed for the racetrack memories. The simulation parameters of [17] are used for simulating a PMA RM; the physical parameters of the RMs are listed in Table 1. As for the MOSFETs, HP-CMOS at a feature size of 22nm [18] and a supply voltage (V_{DD}) of 0.8V are used; the CMOS-based interface circuits of a RM are designed and operated as detailed in [16]. The width of PMOS transistor is 2.5 times the width of the NMOS transistor. The performance of the proposed NVPINV cell is assessed as follows.

Table 1. Macromodel Parameter For Racetrack [17]

Parameter	*Value*	*Parameter*	*Value*	*Parameter*	*Value*
a (m)	$65*10^{-9}$	M_s (Oe)	15800	T (K)	300
b (m)	$65*10^{-9}$	H_k (Oe)	$1.734*10^{3}$	PP	0.52
c (m)	$1*10^{-6}$	tsl (m)	$1.3*10^{-9}$	t_{ox} (nm)	$8.5*10^{-10}$
thick_f (m)	$1.3*10^{-9}$	μ_B	$9.27*10^{-28}$	Phibas (eV)	0.4
P	0.72	TMR	1.2	FAA	332.253
Jc0 (A/m^2)	$0.62*10^{12}$	Surface (Square)	a*b	Surface (Ellipse)	πab/4
Fa (m^3/C)	$30*10^{-12}$	K_b (J/K)	$1.38*10^{-23}$	V_h (V)	0.5
α	0.025	rau (Ω·m)	$100*10^{-9}$	e (C)	$1.6*10^{-19}$
γ (Hz/Oe)	$1.76*10^{7}$	CC	0.577		

4.1 Write Operation

This operation utilizes the write circuit in Figure 4 [16] for the heads and is performed with V_{dw}=2V while the width to length ratio of the MOSFETs in the write circuit is given by 15. Figure 11 shows the signals of the write circuit for its operation. The simulation results for the write delay, the power dissipation, and the power delay product (PDP) are presented in Table 2. Figure 11 shows the signals of the write circuit [16]; the data stored in RL and RR is overwritten if the voltage at Cont is the same as the write voltage (i.e. V_{dw}). Table 2 show the simulation results of the write circuit [16] for the delay, power dissipation and PDP. The results in Table 2 show that for the write operation, the delay and the power dissipation (and therefore the PDP) of the proposed cell are nearly independently of the data value, i.e. they are very close; this occurs, because RL and RR are connected in parallel and the voltage drops across them are similar in value.

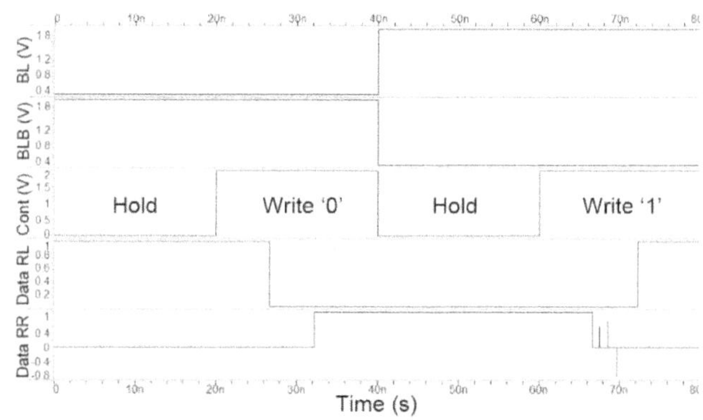

Figure 11. Signals of the write circuit [16] for write operation

Table 2. Delay, power dissipation, and power delay product (PDP) of the proposed cell when the write operation is executed

Operation	*Delay (ns)*	*Power Dissipation (mW)*	*PDP ($*10^{-12}$ s·W)*
Write '0'	12.27	1.6663	20.446
Write '1'	12.274	1.6663	20.453

4.2 Read Operation

For the read operation, the data stored in the racetrack devices is represented by the voltages at B and BB. The proposed NVPINV cell operates as either an inverter, or a buffer depending on the control voltages (B and BB). The read delay is measured after the shift operation until the output voltage of the NVPINV (i.e. the voltage at node OUT) has a stable value. Figure 12 presents the transient simulation of the proposed NVPINV when a '0' (RL is in state '0' and RR is in state '1') and '1' (RL is in state '1' and RR is in state '0') are stored in the racetrack cells. As shown in Figure 12, when a '0' ('1') is stored in the racetrack cell, the voltage at B is at GND (V_{DD}) and the proposed circuit behaves as a buffer (inverter).

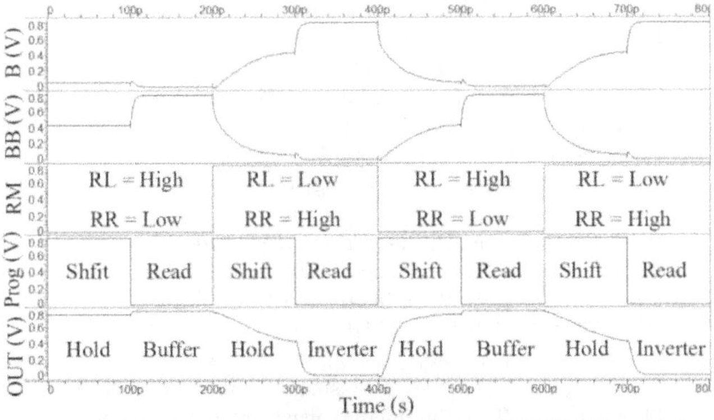

Figure 12. Signals of the proposed RM-based NVPINV cell when executing the read operation

Table 3. Delay, power dissipation, and power delay product (PDP) of the proposed cell when the read operation is executed

Operation	*Delay (ps)*	*Power Dissipation (µW)*	*PDP (*10^{-17} s·W)*
Buffer (V_{IN} = 0)	7.4402	21.361	15.893
Buffer (V_{IN} = V_{DD})	4.4195	25.171	11.124
Inverter (V_{IN} = 0)	10.793	12.275	13.249
Inverter (V_{IN} = V_{DD})	17.441	9.5438	16.645

Table 3 presents the simulation results of the proposed cell for the read operation. The simulation results of Table 3 show that read delay of the proposed cell when operating as an inverter is larger than as a buffer. When the proposed cell operates as a buffer, a transmission gate is connected between the input and output nodes. If the proposed cell operates as an inverter, an inverter and a transmission gate are connected between the input and output nodes. The delay of the proposed NVPINV when operating as an inverter is higher than when operating as a buffer. Moreover, the results in Table 3 also show that the delay of the proposed cell when the output voltage is at GND is higher than when the output voltage is at V_{DD}. At 22nm, the driving capability of the PMOS (in which the width is 2.5 times of the NMOS width) is better than the NMOS. The delay when the output is at V_{DD} is lower than when the output is at GND.

4.3 Shift Operation

This operation shifts the data from the write head to the read head of the racetrack devices. In this simulation, the shift voltage (V_{dsf}) is selected at 2V while the width to length ratio of the MOSFETs in the shift circuit is given by 15.

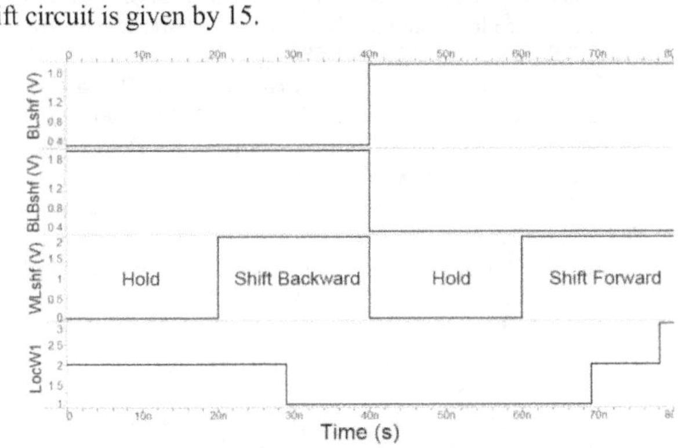

Figure 13. Shift operation of RM when the proposed propagation circuit is employed [16]

So the shift operation requires the voltage at WLshf to be V_{dsf} (Figure 13). The racetrack is shifted left (right) when the voltage at BLshf is GND (V_{dsf}) and the voltage at BLBshf is V_{dsf} (GND). The delay of the proposed circuit for shifting a track is 9.2ns, while the power dissipation and power delay product (PDP) are 718.23µW and 6.6077pJ respectively.

4.4 Control Circuit

This section evaluates the performance of the control circuit of the proposed NVPINV array. As shown in Figure 10, the control circuit selects the write circuits based on the shift directions. During simulation, the supply voltage of the control circuit is at 2V, so the same as the shift and the write supply voltages (also in this case, the width to length ratio of the MOSFETs in the control circuit is given by 15).

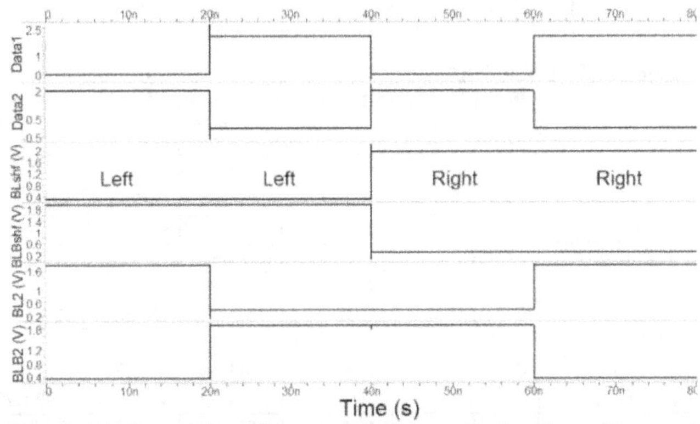

Figure 14. Operation of two control circuits for the voltages at BL2 and BLB2 of Figure 10

As shown in Figure 14, the voltages at BL2 and BLB2 depend on the shift directions (i.e. the voltages at lines BLshf and BLBshf). When the voltages at BLshf and BLBshf are at GND and V_{dw} (V_{dw} and GND), the write circuits on the left of the control circuits are selected. As on Figure 10, the voltages at BL2 and BLB2 are varied as per the control 2 circuit (data 2) in the first 2 steps and the control 1 circuit (data1) in the next 2 steps. The delay of the control circuit is 6.1083ps, while the power dissipation and power delay product (PDP) are 6.9543mW and 42.476fJ respectively.

4.5 COGRE Delay

The performance of COGRE when the proposed NVPINV cells are employed as programmable inverters is evaluated next; so, the worst case delay of a 2-input NAND gate (using HP-CMOS at a feature size of 22nm) is 10.59ps, while the worst case delay of the proposed NVPINV cell for the read operation is 17.441ps. Table 5 presents the worst case delay of a COGRE circuit at different number of inputs (i.e. n). As expected, the delay increases when n increases.

Table 5. Worst Case Delay of n-Inputs COGRE when the read operation is executed

Worst Case delay of COGRE	*Number of Inputs, n*			
	5	*6*	*7*	*8*
Number of NAND Gates	4	5	6	7
Number of NPINV Cells	8	11	13	15
Worst Case Delay (ps)	181.888	244.801	290.273	335.745

4.6 Comparison

In this section, the power dissipation of COGRE at different number of inputs is compared with the power dissipation of the corresponding SRAM-based LUT (i.e. with 2^n SRAM cells of single output). The COGRE with n inputs consists of NAND gates as well as the NVPINVs for operating such logic structure; [2] and [19] have shown efficient COGRE logic designs. However, the results of [2, 19] are not fully applicable to power dissipation, because power consumption is significantly affected by programmable inverters, as proposed in this paper.

Table 6. Power dissipation of COGRE and SRAM-based LUT when the write operation is executed

Power Dissipation (mW)		*Number of Inputs (n)* 5	6	7	8
Write '0'	COGRE	13.330	18.329	21.662	24.995
	LUT	0.478	0.956	1.911	3.822
Write '1'	COGRE	13.330	18.329	21.662	24.995
	LUT	0.481	0.963	1.9252	3.850
Average	COGRE	9.046	12.538	15.078	17.937
	LUT	0.48	0.959	1.918	3.836

Table 7. Power dissipation of COGRE and SRAM-based LUT when the read operation is executed

Power Dissipation (μW)		*Number of Inputs (n)* 5	6	7	8
Buffer ($V_{IN} = 0$)	COGRE	**170.888**	**234.97**	**277.69**	**320.415**
	LUT	207.21	414.42	828.838	1657.677
Buffer ($V_{IN} = V_{DD}$)	COGRE	201.368	**276.88**	**327.223**	**377.565**
	LUT	**190.68**	381.36	762.73	1525.45
Inverter ($V_{IN} = 0$)	COGRE	**98.20**	**135.025**	**159.575**	**184.125**
	LUT	190.68	381.36	762.73	1525.45
Inverter ($V_{IN} = V_{DD}$)	COGRE	**76.35**	**104.98**	**124.07**	**143.157**
	LUT	207.21	414.42	828.838	1657.677
Average	COGRE	**136.70**	**187.965**	**222.14**	**256.3157**
	LUT	198.946	397.89	795.78	1591.565

Tables 6 and 7 show the power dissipation of an n-inputs COGRE and an n-inputs SRAM-based LUT (bold entries identify the best performance). As expected for the write operation, the power dissipation of the proposed COGRE circuit is larger than for a SRAM-based LUT due to the higher voltage that is required for the RMs (and hence the non-volatile feature). However, the write operation is only utilized once the configuration data is acquired, i.e. it occurs only once for configuring the entire circuit and FPGA. For the power dissipation of the read operation, a COGRE using the proposed cells consumes substantially less power than a SRAM-based LUT; this improvement increases when increasing the number of inputs (n).

5. CONCLUSION

This paper has proposed a racetrack-based non-volatile programmable inverter (NVPINV) cell that can be used with a COGRE circuit for low-power operation. The proposed NVPINV cell operates as a programmable circuit, i.e. either as a buffer, or an inverter depending on the programmable data. Two racetrack devices (RM) have been used as non-volatile storage elements; they store the programmable data of the proposed NVPINV, while the MOSFETs are used as control elements. One of the significant advantages of a racetrack device is its operational capabilities of independent read and write, thus making possible a parallel execution of the programming process. The proposed low-power NVPINV provides significant advantages such as low delay and non-volatile storage. Simulation results in this paper show that during the read operation, a COGRE with the proposed RM-based NVPINV cells has a power dissipation significantly lower than an SRAM-based LUT implementation.

6. REFERENCES

[1] S. Kilts, "Advanced FPGA Design: Architecture, Implementation, and Optimization", Wiley-IEEE Press, 2007.

[2] Y. Yasuhiro, Y. Ichinomiya, M. Amagasaki, M. Iida, and T. Sueyoshi, "COGRE: A Configuration Memory Reduced Reconfiguration Logic Cell Architecture for Area Minimization," Proc. Int. Conf. on FPL and Applications, pp. 304-309, 2010.

[3] Q. Zhao, Y. Ichinomiya, Y. Okamoto, M. Amagasaki, M. Iida, T. Sueyoshi, "A Robust Reconfigurable Logic Device Based on Less Configuration Memory Logic Cell" Proc. International Conference on Field-Programmable Technology (FPT), pp. 162-169, Beijing, 2010.

[4] W. Wang, T. T Jing, B. Butcher, "FPGA based on integration of memristors and CMOS devices," Circuits and Systems (ISCAS), Proceedings of 2010 IEEE International Symposium on, pp. 1963-1966, May 30 2010-June 2 2010

[5] X. Xue, W. Jian, Y. Xie, Q. Dong, R. Yuan, Y. Lin "Novel RRAM Programming Technology for Instant-on and High-security FPGAs," 2011 IEEE 9th International Conference on ASIC (ASICON), pp. 291-294, 2011.

[6] O. Turkyilmaz, S. Onkaraiah, M. Reyboz, F. Clermidy, C. A. Hraziia, J. Portal, M. Bocquet, "RRAM-based FPGA for "normally off, instantly on" applications," Proc. IEEE/ACM International Symposium on Nanoscale Architectures, pp. 101-108, 4-6 July 2012

[7] N. Sakimura, T. Sugibayashi, R. Nebashi, N. Kasai, "Non-volatile Magnetic Flip-Flop for Standby-Power-Free SoCs," IEEE Journal of Solid-State Circuits, vol.44, no.8, pp. 2244-2250, Aug. 2009

[8] Y. Zhang, W. Zhao, J.-O. Klein, D. Ravelsona, C. Chappert "Ultra-High Density Content Addressable Memory Based on Current Induced Domain Wall Motion in Magnetic Track" IEEE Trans. Magn. Vol. 48, No. 11, November 2012, pp. 3219-3222

[9] C. Chappert, A. Fert, F. Nguyen Van Dau "The emergence of spin electronics in data storage" Nature materials Vol. 6, pp. 813-823, 2007

[10] S. Mangin, D. Ravelosona, J. A. Katine, M. J. Carey, B. D. Terris, E.E. Fullerton "Current-induced magnetization reversal in nanopillars with perpendicular anisotropy" Nature Materials Vol.5, pp. 210-215, 2006

[11] S. Ghosh "Design Methodologies for High Density Domain Wall Memory" IEEE/ACM Nanoarch 2013 pp. 30-31, July 2013, NY USA

[12] Y. Zhang, W. S. Zhao, D. Ravelosona, J.-O. Klein, J. V. Kim "Perpendicular-magnetic-anisotropy CoFeB racetrack memory" Journal of Applied Physics 111, 093925, 2012

[13] W. S. Zhao, Y. Zhang, H.-P. Trinh, J-O. Klien, C. Chappert, R. Mantovan, A. Kamperti, R.P. Cowburn, R. Trypiniotis, M. Klaui, J. Heinen, B. Ocker, D. Ravelsona "Magnetic Domain-Wall Racetrack Memory for high density and fast data storage" ICSICT 11st, pp. 1-4, Oct 2012

[14] M. Hayashi, L. Thomas, R. Moriya, C. Rettner, S. S. P. Parkin "Current-Controlled Magnetic Domain-Wall Nanowrie Shift Register" Science Vol. 320, No. 5873, pp. 209-211, 2008

[15] S. S. P. Parkin, M. Hayashi, L. Thomas "Magnetic Domain-Wall Racetrack Memory" Science Vol. 320 No. 5873 pp.190-194, 2008

[16] P. Junsangsri, J. Han, F. Lombardi, "Circuits for a Perpendicular Magnetic Anisotropic (PMA) Racetrack Memory" IEEE Transactions on Multi-Scale Computing Systems, vol. 1, no. 3, pp. 127-137, 2015.

[17] P. Junsangsri, J. Han, and F. Lombardi "HSPICE Macromodel of a PMA Racetrack Memory," Proc IEEE NMDC, pp. 97-101, Anchorage, September 2015.

[18] Predictive Technology Model : http://ptm.asu.edu, 2016

[19] M. Iida, M. Amagasaki, Y. Okamoto, Q. Zhao, T. Sueyoshi, "COGRE: A Novel Compact Logic Cell Architecture for Area Minimization" IEICE Trans. INF&SYST. Vol. 95-D, No. 2, February 2012

VaLHALLA: Variable Latency History Aware Local-carry Lazy Adder

Ali Murat Gok
Electrical Engineering and Computer Science Dept.,
Northwestern University, Evanston, IL 60208, USA
amg@u.northwestern.edu

Nikos Hardavellas
Electrical Engineering and Computer Science Dept.,
Northwestern University, Evanston, IL 60208, USA
nikos@northwestern.edu

ABSTRACT
Current low-energy adder designs fail to address subtraction or signed operations, are imprecise, or have large overheads. These overheads include overlapping sub-adders, relatively complex carry speculation mechanisms and bulky error correction circuits, all of which consume considerable amount of energy. In this paper, we address all these problems and introduce Variable Latency History Aware Local-carry Lazy Adder (VaLHALLA). VaLHALLA employs sliced non-overlapping sub-adders and speculates the carry-ins for each slice by exploiting the temporal operand correlation of each instruction location (i.e., it considers both operand history and instruction locale). VaLHALLA achieves accurate results at lower energy-delay-product than competing designs.

Keywords
Power efficiency; Variable latency adders; Speculative adders

1. INTRODUCTION
The breakdown of Dennard scaling [6] and the advent of dark silicon [8] have elevated power consumption to a first-class design constraint [13]. Several techniques have been proposed to lower the power consumption, including dynamic voltage and frequency scaling [17], near-threshold computing, sleep states [5], approximate computing [7] and specialized cores (accelerators) [4]. In the quest to achieve higher power and energy efficiency, a significant amount of recent work focuses directly on decreasing the power consumption of functional units, and in particular, adders [10,16].

One of the most common methods is to slice the full bit range of an adder into smaller bit ranges ("slices") and run them in parallel. This architecture provides two potential benefits: (a) a reduction in the total number of gates which leads to lower power consumption, due to the superlinear relationship between bitwidth and hardware complexity, and (b) running smaller slices in parallel decreases the total delay of the circuit. This reduced delay can then be utilized to decrease power consumption by scaling down each slice's supply voltage to the lowest setting that allows the slice to still fit within the same cycle time [14]. However, running the slices in parallel generates complications in carry propagation, as the slices break the carry chain. The natural solution is to supply each slice with a speculative carry-in. Slice organization, carry propagation and the carry generation mechanisms for each slice constitute the main differences between current low-power adders.

Most low-power adders are categorized into two groups: approximate and variable latency speculative adders. The main difference between the two groups is on how mispredictions of carry-ins are handled. Approximate adders [10] finish the operation in a single cycle. However they lead to inaccuracies since they do not possess error correction mechanisms and wrong results are supplied whenever a carry-in is mispredicted. The main focus of approximate adders is to increase the accuracy in the output while constraining the execution to a single cycle. In contrast to approximate adders, variable latency speculative adders [16] always provide the correct output in one or two cycles. If all slices' carry-ins are speculated correctly, the operation completes in a single cycle. Otherwise, a carry misprediction is detected and a second cycle is employed to correct the output. Variable latency speculative adders focus on decreasing the number of two-cycle operations by increasing the accuracy of the carry-in speculation mechanism.

Unfortunately, the majority of previously proposed low-power adders only support unsigned addition and disregard signed operations or subtraction [9], and hence cover only a small portion of a real workload's instructions. In addition, even the most sophisticated prior attempts to increase the accuracy of carry speculation fall short of delivering on their promise. Some of the previous techniques exploit the correlation of arithmetic operations in real workloads (i.e., the temporal correlation of add instruction results) and use the prior operation to predict the carry-ins for the current one. However, consecutive add operations in the dynamic instruction stream interleave adds from different program locations, and are much less correlated than consecutive add operations from the same line of code. We contend that to improve the accuracy of carry-in speculation, low-power adders should exploit the correlation of consecutive invocations of the same static instruction.

In this paper we address both shortcomings of existing designs and propose VaLHALLA (Variable Latency History Aware Local-carry Lazy Adder), a variable latency adder design that:

- Exploits for the first time (to the best of our knowledge) spatial and temporal PC-based correlation in a low-power adder.
- Provides full support for real-world workloads (64-bit signed and unsigned addition and subtraction).
- Exhibits lower power and energy consumption and lower energy-delay product compared to the current state of the art.

Permission to make digital or hard copies of all or part of this work for personal or classroom use is granted without fee provided that copies are not made or distributed for profit or commercial advantage and that copies bear this notice and the full citation on the first page. Copyrights for components of this work owned by others than the author(s) must be honored. Abstracting with credit is permitted. To copy otherwise, or republish, to post on servers or to redistribute to lists, requires prior specific permission and/or a fee. Request permissions from Permissions@acm.org.
GLSVLSI '17, May 10 - 12, 2017, Banff, AB, Canada
Copyright is held by the owner/author(s). Publication rights licensed to ACM.
ACM 978-1-4503-4972-7/17/05…$15.00
DOI: http://dx.doi.org/10.1145/3060403.3060437

This work was supported by NSF awards CCF-1218768 and CCF-1453853

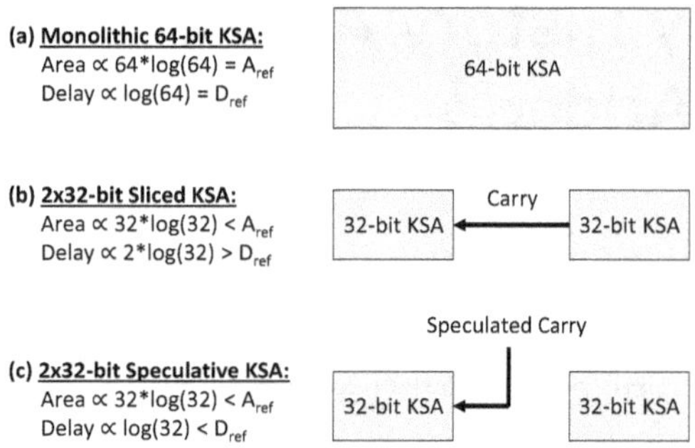

Figure 1. Hardware and delay scaling for KSA.

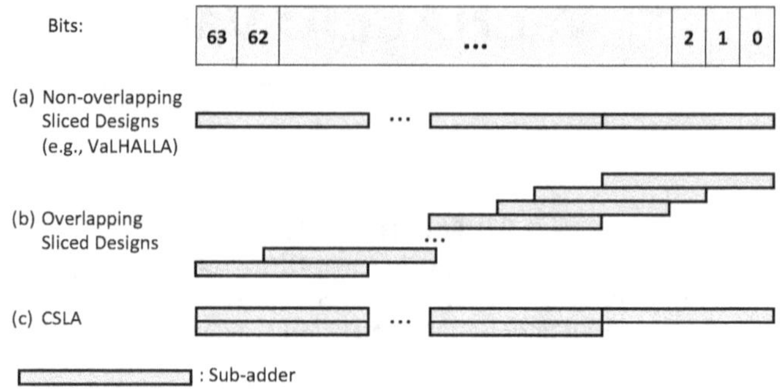

Figure 2. Sliced adder configurations.

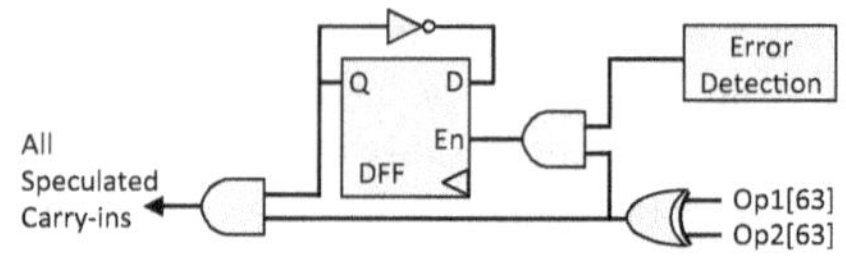

Figure 3. CASA [12] carry speculation technique.

2. BACKGROUND

2.1 Voltage Scaling

Voltage scaling (VS) exploits the trade-off between supply voltage and circuit delay [14] in circuit optimization. VS exchanges the existing slack in the timing budget for a reduction in the supply voltage to lower power consumption.

2.2 Hardware Scaling and Sliced Designs

Most traditional adder designs have a superlinear relationship between their bitwidth and hardware complexity. For example, the hardware complexity of a Kogge-Stone adder (KSA) scales in the order of $N \times logN$ and its delay scales in the order of $logN$, where N is the bitwidth of the adder. This illustrates a trade-off between hardware complexity and delay. As an example, it is possible to build a 64-bit adder from two 32-bit KSAs by concatenating one after another (Figure 1.b). This sliced approach decreases total area at the cost of increasing delay since the upper slice needs to wait for the lower one. On the other hand, if carry speculation is employed (Figure 1.c), both slices can run at the same time and attain both lower area and lower delay compared to the reference 64-bit KSA. However, speculated carries introduce inaccurate results when one or more of the carry-ins is speculated incorrectly.

Similar to KSA, most modern adders possess a similar trade-off between hardware complexity and delay, and face similar design choices in a sliced design. An example of a sliced adder configuration with non-overlapping slices is shown in Figure 2.a. Many of the current low-power adder designs employ slices with overlapping bit ranges (Figure 2.b), as "peeking" at the high-order bits of the lower slice may increase the accuracy of the carry speculation. However, this comes at the cost of employing more slices.

2.3 Carry Select Adder (CSLA)

The classical CSLA design [1] (Figure 2.c) resembles current low-power adders with its sliced design. However, CSLA slices do not overlap in terms of their bit ranges. Every slice in CSLA except the lowest one employs two sub-adders, one for each possible carry-in. Each one of the two slices in a bit range computes assuming a different carry-in. When the lower slice finishes its computation and produces a carry-out, that carry-out is matched against the two carry-ins used by the higher-order slice to determine which one of the two results is the correct result for the computation at hand.

2.4 Correlation-Aware Speculative Adders

Correlation-Aware Speculative Adder (CASA) [12] is a state-of-the-art speculative adder based on ACA [10]. CASA employs a new carry speculation technique in which the carry-ins of all slices are speculated to be 1 if the operand signs differ, and 0 otherwise. To improve accuracy, CASA uses a DFF as a dynamic prediction mechanism. The output of this DFF is used as an enable signal for the sign difference (Figure 3). This way CASA exploits the correlation between two temporally consecutive ADD/SUB operations.

3. THE ENERGY BENEFITS OF SLICING

To determine the potential benefit of employing a sliced design, we perform a limit study on the energy consumption of adders with non-overlapping slices (Figure 2.a) by exploring the trade-offs between bitwidth, number of sub-adders, hardware complexity, circuit delay and carry speculation accuracy. We assume a 64-bit adder design with 1 (i.e., conventional), 2, 4, or 8 non-overlapping slices, where each slice employs one sub-adder. We synthesize sub-adders of different bitwidths (8, 16, 32, or 64 bits) using the Synopsys Design Compiler. We feed these sub-adders with random vectors as inputs and with speculative carry-ins, and report the energy consumption of the overall adder for each configuration in Figure 4. To decouple the impact of slicing from the choice of supporting circuit design, only the sub-adders are taken into consideration for the energy and delay analysis. The rest of the circuit (e.g., error detection or carry generation circuitry) is assumed to have no delay or energy consumption.

The smallest possible energy consumption occurs when all the speculated carries are the correct ones and every slice computes only once. This case is indicated as "Best Case", where only one sub-adder is utilized for each slice. On the other hand, the largest energy consumption occurs when all the speculated carries are the

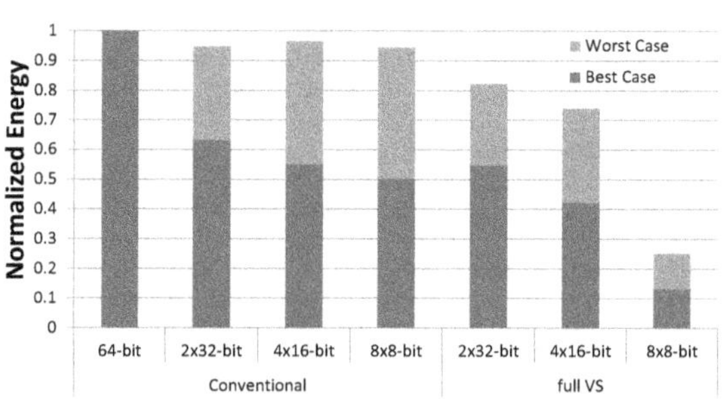

Figure 4. Limit study of the energy savings of sliced adders.

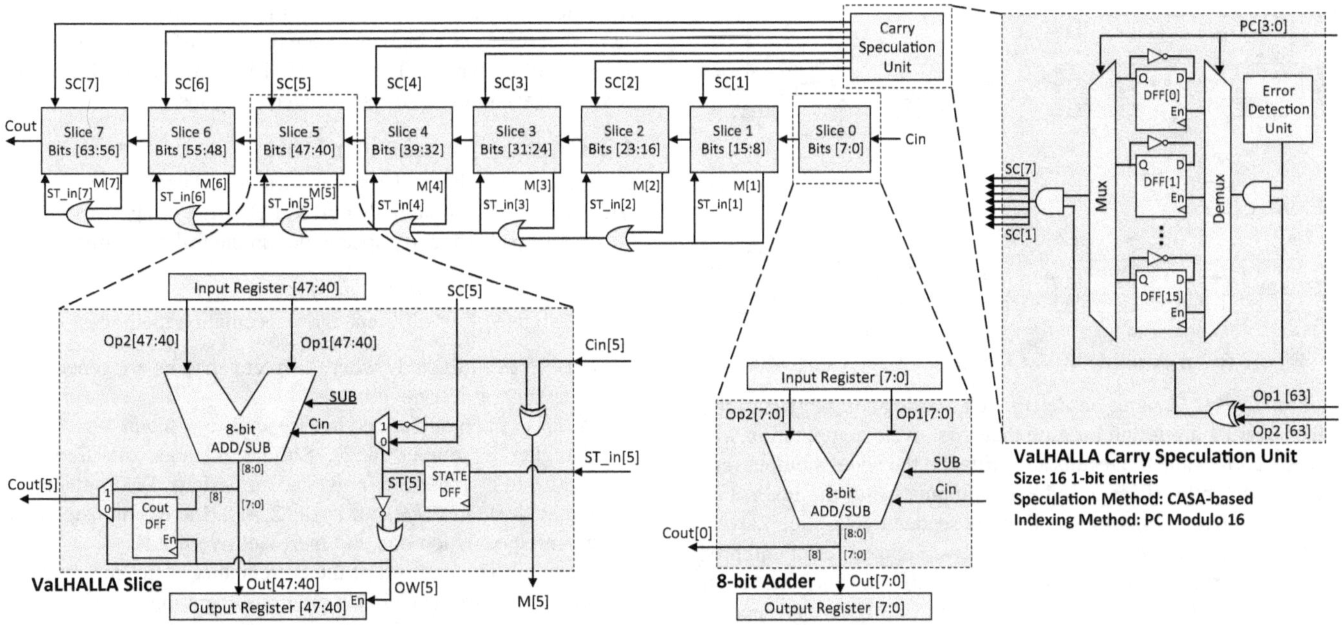

Figure 5. Example of a VaLHALLA adder design with 8x8-bit configuration. Slice 0 is a standard 8-bit adder, whereas all other slices are designed specifically for VaLHALLA. Slice 5 is shown in detail as an example of such slices.

wrong ones, and all sub-adders (except the lowest-order one) require an extra computation (this time with the correct carry-in). This case is indicated as "Worst Case". To investigate the potential for additional power savings, we apply voltage scaling to the sub-adders by decreasing their supply voltages until they have reached the same delay as the reference 64-bit single-slice adder. The resulting energy consumptions are given in Figure 4 as "Full VS".

It is possible to achieve significant power and energy savings by employing smaller sub-adders, as the actual power consumption will not necessarily be the worst case, but somewhere between the worst and best cases. The overall energy consumption directly depends on the carry-in speculation accuracy. Employing the minimum possible number of sub-adders to decrease the power consumption is one of the main ideas behind VaLHALLA, which is also a non-overlapping sliced design (Figure 2.a). As Figure 4 shows, employing voltage scaling with 2 or 4 slices shows a potential to save 18–58% of the adder energy per operation. Pushing to 8 slices, however, results in small enough sub-adders (just 8 bits) that allow the supply voltage to scale to 60% of the reference voltage, leading to 75–87% potential energy savings. While best-case savings are probably unachievable as only the sub-adders are considered in the analysis, they are however indicative of the high potential of sliced adder designs, and of VaLHALLA in particular.

4. VALHALLA

VaLHALLA is a CSLA-inspired design that employs multiple non-overlapping slices with only one sub-adder per slice. VaLHALLA performs an operation by computing for only one set of speculated carries in the first cycle of its operation and writing the results in its output register, optimistically expecting that no more work will be necessary (hence its designation as "lazy"). If additional work is needed to obtain the correct result, it is performed at an additional second cycle. Thus, VaLHALLA is a variable-latency "lazy" adder.

In most cases all carry-ins are speculated correctly and a second cycle of operation is not required. When a slice produces a carry-out at the end of the first cycle, VaLHALLA detects whether the next slice computed with the correct carry-in. If the carry-out of slice k does not match the carry-in used in slice $k+1$ during the first cycle, VaLHALLA employs a second cycle during which slice $k+1$ re-computes using the inverse of the previously speculated carry, i.e., the inverse of the carry-in that slice $k+1$ used during the first cycle. At that time, however, it is unknown whether the carry-out produced by slice $k+1$ at the end of the first cycle was the correct carry-in for the subsequent slice $k+2$. Thus VaLHALLA cannot determine whether slice $k+2$ also needs to re-compute. In fact, a carry mismatch at slice $k+1$ spreads towards the higher slices, causing all of them to conservatively require a second cycle of computation. At the end of the second cycle all correct carry-ins are known, which allows VaLHALLA to either keep the results already in the output register for a slice (i.e., the slice computation in the first cycle was the correct one) or overwrite them with the slice's result obtained at the second cycle of computation. Because only the necessary subset of slices re-computes (the slices higher than the first carry mismatch), VaLHALLA avoids unnecessary computations and exhibits significant power savings over CSLA. Figure 5 details the architecture of VaLHALLA.

Figure 6 illustrates a simple example where a 32-bit addition is performed using four 8-bit slices, where all of the carry-ins are speculated to be zeros. *SC[k]* denotes the speculated carry-in provided to slice *k*. *Cin[k]* denotes the carry-in used by slice *k* during that cycle. *Cout[k]* denotes the carry-out generated by slice *k* during that cycle. Because the carry-in of slice 0 is determined only by the type of the operation (addition or subtraction), it always gets the correct carry and computes correctly. At the end of the first cycle, there is no carry mismatch between *Cout[0]* and *Cin[1]*, also guaranteeing that slice 1 computed correctly. However, there is a mismatch between *Cout[1]* and *Cin[2]*, thus slice 2 in cycle 1 computed assuming the wrong carry in and should re-compute. Although there is no mismatch between *Cout[2]* and *Cin[3]*, slice 3 still needs the second cycle of computation because the correct-

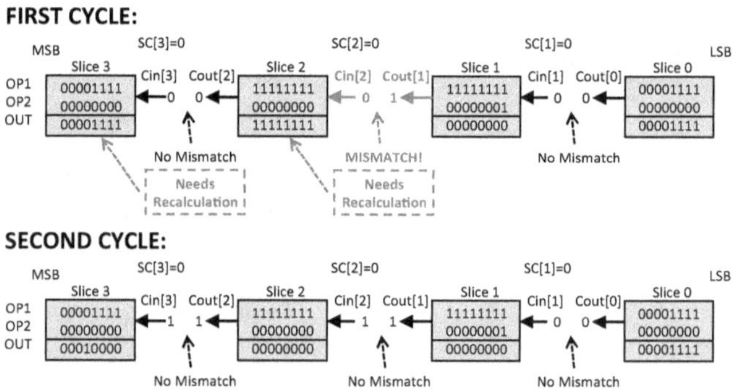

Figure 6. An example of VaLHALLA's 2-cycle operation

ness of *Cout[2]* cannot be determined. During the second cycle, slices 0 and 1 are idling because their first-cycle computation was already correct and the results are written in the adder's output register. Meanwhile, slices 2 and 3 re-compute using the inverse of their respective *SC*'s. At the end of the second cycle, slice 2 overwrites the output register with the newly-computed result and produces the **correct** *Cout[2]*. Similarly, *Cout[2]* and *Cin[3]* match in the second cycle, so slice 3's results from cycle 1 were erroneous. Thus, the output register is overwritten with the correct newly-computed value of slice 3, concluding the operation. If *Cout[2]* and *Cin[3]* had not match in the second cycle, slice 3's computation would have been deemed correct the first time and no further action (i.e., a second cycle for slice 3) would have been necessary.

4.1 VaLHALLA Slice Design

The design of VaLHALLA slices is illustrated in Figure 5. Each slice except the lowest-order one has a 1-bit DFF STATE register that keeps track of whether the slice is performing the first or the second cycle (STATE=0 or 1, respectively). When a new operation is assigned to the integer ALU, all STATE registers in it are reset to 0 to indicate that this is the first cycle of operation. After the first cycle, the STATE register of slice *i* is updated by OR-ing the mismatch signals of the current and all previous slices *i, i-1, ..., 1* and then stays at that value until a new operation is assigned:

$$\mathrm{STATE}[i] \leftarrow M[i] \mid M[i-1] \mid \ldots \mid M[1] \tag{1}$$

During the first cycle every slice is in state 0. Consequently, the speculated carry *SC* is used for computation and the output register is overwritten with the generated output. Every slice *i* generates its own mismatch signal *M[i]* by comparing the used carry-in *Cin[i]* with the carry-out of the lower slice *Cout[i-1]*. Then these mismatch signals are used to determine the states of the slices for the next cycle. If all mismatch signals are 0, then the operation completed correctly in a single cycle. If there is at least one mismatch signal set, then the second cycle is employed. During the second cycle, slices in state 0 wait idle, whereas slices in state 1 compute using the inverse of the carry-in used they used in the first cycle. At the end of the second cycle, correct carries gradually arrive from the lower to higher slices and VaLHALLA determines whether to overwrite the output register for each slice or not. To facilitate this operation, VaLHALLA retains the carry-out that a slice generates in the first cycle in a DFF, and also provides a direct path to propagate the carry-out from the sub-adder. This design ensures that the correct carries will arrive during the second cycle.

As Figure 4 indicates, employing a larger number of smaller slices increases the potential for energy savings. However, at the same time it increases energy and delay overheads for the rest of the circuit. More importantly, it increases the misprediction rate, as with more slices there is a higher chance that at least one carry-in speculation will be wrong. Thus, VaLHALLA strives to achieve high prediction accuracy for the speculated carry-ins.

4.2 Carry Speculation Unit

The Carry Speculation Unit provides speculated carries to VaLHALLA slices. To obtain the best VaLHALLA design we explored the design space for carry speculation in the following dimensions:

4.2.1 Carry Speculation Methods

We investigated four different carry speculation methods:

- *Perfect:* A limit study where correct carry-ins are generated at no energy or delay overheads.
- *Peek(k):* Each sub-adder is extended to *k* lower bits without changing its output range. Similar methods are frequently employed by other low-power adder designs. We implemented and evaluated *Peek(k)* for *k* = 1, 2, 4, 8. Increasing *k* decreases the misspeculation rate, but increases overheads.
- *Previous:* The carry-in of the current slice is the correct carry-out of the lower slice in the previous operation.
- *CASA-based*: Carry-ins are generated based on the difference between the operand signs, similar to CASA (Section 2.4).

4.2.2 Spatio-Temporal PC-Based Correlation

In real workloads, the dynamic instruction stream includes several instances of the same static instruction (i.e., an instruction at a specific PC). Consecutive operations stemming from the same line of code have a higher chance to have correlated operands and thus similar internal carries. For example, consider a static instruction which increments a loop iterator whose value ranges from 0 to 100, and we are using the Previous carry speculation method. All the dynamic instances executed from this static instruction will have their operands and outputs between 0 and 101, which means all the internal slice carry-ins in an 8-slice design and all higher operand bits will be zero. However, it is very unlikely that instances of this instruction will appear in the dynamic instruction stream consecutively without intervening add/subtract operations from other locations in the executing code. A single addition in the body of the loop would interleave with the increments of the loop iterator, and the operands of the loop-body instruction can be entirely outside the range of values used for the loop iterator. The Previous carry speculation method normally holds the carries of only the immediately preceding arithmetic operation observed by the functional unit, which may be irrelevant for the operation currently at hand.

VaLHALLA addresses this issue by using PC-based correlation. Instead of memory for a single carry bit per slice, VaLHALLA remembers an array of carries (Figure 5), each coming from the last invocation of a different static instruction. The register file that holds these carries for each slice is indexed using bits from the PC, allowing dynamic instructions that are instances of the same static instruction to interact with the same set of carry registers.

To the best of our knowledge, this is the first time that PC-based (spatial) correlation is used in a low-power adder design. VaLHALLA utilizes the history of carries generated by the same static instruction over time, hence it is a "history-aware" adder that predicts "local carry-ins" (i.e., carry-ins from the same instruction). Because the register file has finite size, it is possible that multiple static instructions map into the same register set (alias). Larger reg-

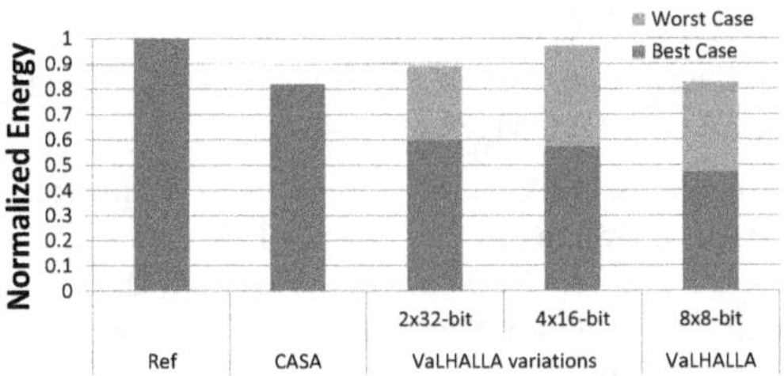

Figure 7. Potential for energy savings.

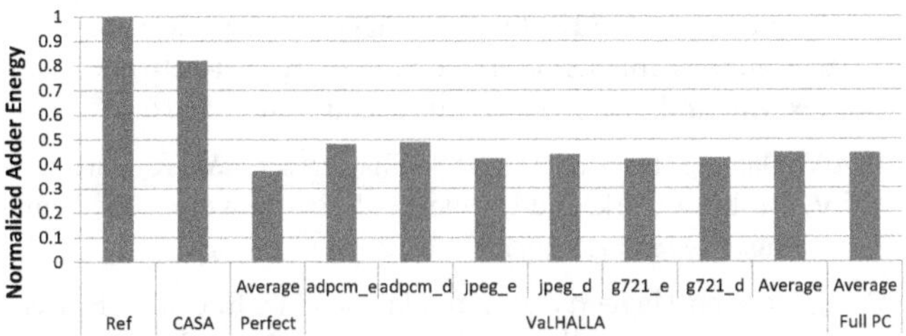

Figure 8. Normalized adder energy.

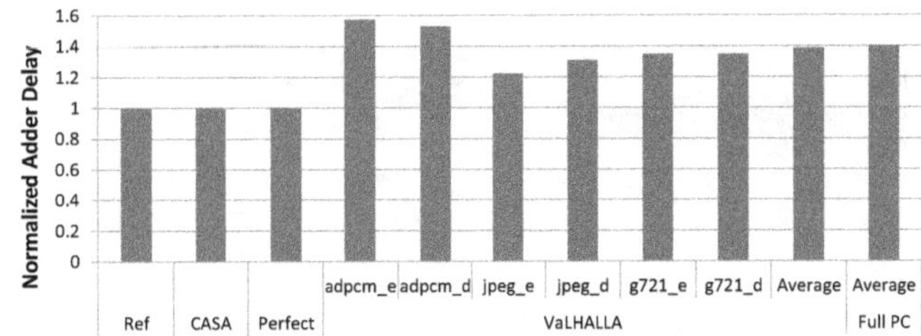

Figure 9. Normalized adder delay.

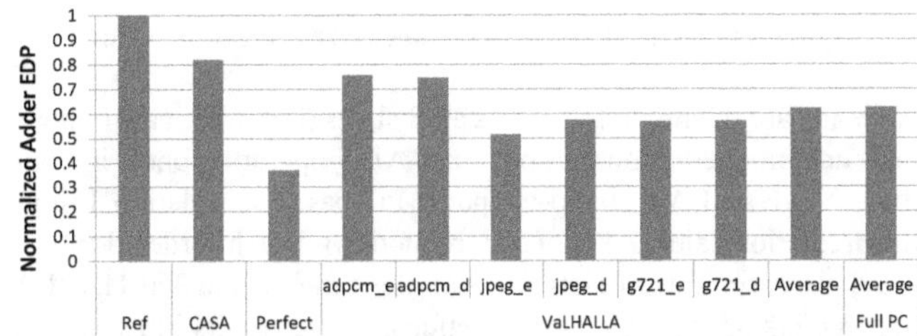

Figure 10. Normalized adder energy-delay product (EDP).

ister files would decrease aliasing. To arrive at an optimal design, we explored power-of-2 register file sizes from 2 to 128 entries per slice, as well as an infinitely-sized register file that removes all instruction aliasing with no latency or energy overheads.

4.2.3 PC-Based Register File Indexing Methods

To exploit PC-based correlation, the register file holding the carry-ins for a slice needs to be indexed by some combination of PC bits. Assuming a register file with 2^N entries, we evaluate the following two methods to index the register file:

- *PC Modulo:* index by *PC[N-1:0]*
- *PC Xor Hash:* index by $PC[N\text{-}1{:}0] \oplus PC[2N\text{-}1{:}N]$

We explore the design space of VaLHALLA along all these dimensions to arrive at a near-optimal design.

5. METHODOLOGY

We model all adder designs (reference, CASA and VaLHALLA) in Verilog. We synthesize them using Synopsys Design Compiler with the same optimization parameters and the Synopsys SEAD 90nm library and obtain gate-level netlists. We convert these gate-level netlists into HSpice netlists and perform analog HSpice simulations of the resulting circuits to characterize their energy and delay. We characterize the performance of the adder designs by modeling them in gem5 [2] simulations that run a range of Mediabench [11] audio and video applications. Such media applications are among the most popular applications today [3]. CASA outperforms ACA and VLSA adders [12], thus we only compare VaLHALLA against the current state of the art, CASA.

Using this methodology, we perform a design space exploration across slice configurations, carry speculation methods, register file sizes and indexing methods, in search of the optimal VaLHALLA configuration. We simulate both in-order and out-of-order (OoO) x86 architectures with 6 integer ALUs. Space limitations prevent us from discussing the design space exploration in detail. The optimal configuration across our search space is a 64-bit VaLHALLA adder comprising 8x8-bit slices, CASA-based carry speculation, and a 4- or 16-entry register file (each register is 1 bit) for in-order or OoO x86 architectures, respectively. The register file in the optimal designs is indexed by the PC modulo method.

Because of its high relevance to modern processor designs, and due to space constraints, the rest of this paper discusses only the optimal VaLHALLA design for OoO processors. For readability, in the rest of the paper VaLHALLA refers to this optimal configuration.

6. EVALUATION

We demonstrate the potential energy savings of VaLHALLA in Figure 7. *Ref* represents the reference adder, which is a conventional 64-bit adder synthesized by Synopsys Design Compiler, whereas *CASA* represents a state-of-the-art carry-speculative approximate adder [12]. While the optimal VaLHALLA design employs eight 8-bit slices (Section 5), Figure 7 additionally shows two variations of VaLHALLA (2x32-bit and 4x16-bit slices) to demonstrate the exact benefits of the optimal VaLHALLA design over alternative slice bitwidths. The reference adder uses nominal supply voltage, whereas the other adders employ voltage scaling to decrease their supply voltages as much as possible as long as their delay does not exceed the reference adder's delay.

Best cases indicate the lowest possible energy consumption when the operation requires only one cycle to complete. Worst cases indicate the highest possible energy requirement when the second cycle is employed and all the slices (except the lowest one) need to re-compute for a second cycle. Energy consumptions of real workloads fall in between the best and the worst cases. High-accuracy carry speculation will bring the design closer to the best case.

In Figures 8, 9 and 10 we report normalized energy, delay and energy-delay product (EDP) for various adder types and applications. *Perfect* represents a limit study with an ideal carry speculation unit that always generates the correct carry-ins at zero energy cost. *Full PC* represents another limit study where the carry speculation unit is the same as in VaLHALLA, with the exception that it employs an ideal infinite-size register file indexed by the full PC that consumes zero power. Consequently it eliminates all aliasing among dynamic instructions, allowing them to enjoy the full effects of temporal correlation.

We find that temporal correlation alone (i.e., the previous carry speculation method) exhibits 53% average misprediction rate for an 8-sliced OoO design. A misprediction occurs when one or more

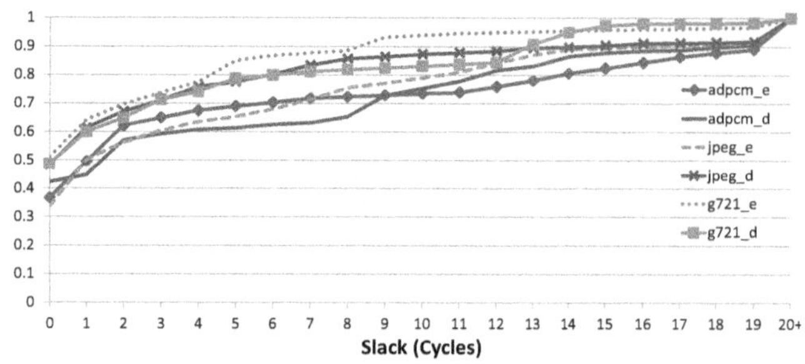

Figure 11. CDF of slack in consecutive ALU operations

carry-ins are mispredicted across all 8 slices (i.e., we measure not a per-slice misprediction rate but a per-ALU-operation one). In contrast, VaLHALLA's spatio-temporal PC-based correlation brings misprediction rate to 39% (1.4x reduction). For in-order designs, previous carry mispredicts 60% of the time, while VaLHALLA mispredicts only 35% (1.7x reduction). These results illustrate the accuracy potential of PC-based spatio-temporal correlation.

The area overhead of VaLHALLA consists of two 1-bit registers in each slice, 16 1-bit registers in the Carry Speculation Unit, a 16-to-1 mux/demux and a few combinational gates (Figure 5). The total area overhead over the reference design is 10.4%.

VaLHALLA consumes 55% less energy than Ref and 46% less energy than CASA (Figure 8), but mispredictions increase the average adder delay (i.e., the average number of cycles the adder is occupied per operation, Figure 9). However, the energy savings are significantly higher than the delay increase, which allows VaLHALLA to exhibit 24% and 38% lower average EDP than CASA and Ref respectively. When the full processor is considered and modeled using McPAT and gem5, including the execution overhead of VaLHALLA (1% for IO and 5% for OoO architectures), VaLHALLA saves 3x the energy saved by CASA. The total processor energy savings of VaLHALLA is 2% for the OoO processor we model, which employs only 6 ALUs. Applying VaLHALLA on ALU-intensive circuits (e.g., NVIDIA GTX-1080 Ti has 3584 ALUs) would yield significantly higher processor energy savings.

While the average adder delay can significantly increase due to misspeculated carries, the effect on the application runtime is drastically smaller because (a) processors typically employ multiple ALUs, and thus their execution delay overlaps, (b) only a fraction of the total executed instructions are additions or subtractions, and (c) modern OoO cores can overlap the additional delay with useful work if there is slack [15] between an ALU operation and the use of its result. We observe that 49–66% of ALU operations in our workload suite have at least 1 cycle of slack (Figure 11).

7. CONCLUSION

VaLHALLA is a variable-latency adder suitable for real-world applications that (unlike most other low-power adder designs) supports signed and unsigned addition and subtraction. VaLHALLA is a sliced adder with non-overlapping slices that employs only one sub-adder per slice, and exploits for the first time spatio-temporal PC-based correlation to increase the accuracy of carry-in speculations. We explored the design space of VaLHALLA and arrived at an optimized design that consumes 46% less energy per operation on average than the current state of the art (CASA), leading to 24% lower EDP. Compared to a conventional 64-bit adder, VaLHALLA saves 55% energy and exhibits 38% lower EDP.

8. REFERENCES

[1] O. J. Bedrij. Carry-select adder. *IRE Transactions on Electronic Computers*, pages 340–344, 1962.

[2] N. Binkert, B. Beckmann, G. Black, S. K. Reinhardt, A. Saidi, A. Basu, J. Hestness, D. R. Hower, T. Krishna, S. Sardashti, R. Sen, K. Sewell, M. Shoaib, N. Vaish, M. D. Hill, and D. A. Wood. The gem5 simulator. *SIGARCH Comput. Archit. News*, 39(2):1–7, 2011.

[3] Cisco. The zettabyte era—trends and analysis, white paper, document id:1465272001812119. http://www.cisco.com/c/en/us/solutions/collateral/service-provider/visual-networking-index-vni/vni-hyperconnectivity-wp.html, June 2016.

[4] W. Dally, J. Balfour, D. Black-Shaffer, J. Chen, R. Harting, V. Parikh, J. Park, and D. Sheffield. Efficient embedded computing. *Computer*, 41(7):27–32, 2008.

[5] S. Dawson-Haggerty, A. Krioukov, and D. E. Culler. Power optimization: a reality check. Technical Report UCB/EECS-2009-140, University of California, Berkeley, 2009.

[6] R. Dennard, V. Rideout, E. Bassous, and A. LeBlanc. Design of ion-implanted mosfet s with very small physical dimensions. *IEEE Journal of Solid-State Circuits*, 9(5), 1974.

[7] H. Esmaeilzadeh, A. Sampson, L. Ceze, and D. Burger. Neural acceleration for general-purpose approximate programs. In *Proceedings of the 45th Annual IEEE/ACM International Symposium on Microarchitecture*, 2012.

[8] N. Hardavellas, M. Ferdman, B. Falsafi, and A. Ailamaki. Toward dark silicon in servers. *IEEE Micro*, 31(4):6–15, 2011.

[9] J. Hu and W. Qian. A new approximate adder with low relative error and correct sign calculation. In *Proceedings of Design, Automation and Test in Europe*, 2015.

[10] A. B. Kahng and S. Kang. Accuracy-configurable adder for approximate arithmetic designs. In *Proceedings of the 49th ACM/EDAC/IEEE Design Automation Conference*, 2012.

[11] C. Lee, M. Potkonjak, and W. H. Mangione-Smith. Mediabench: A tool for evaluating and synthesizing multimedia and communications systems. In *Proceedings of the 30th Annual International Symposium on Microarchitecture*, 1997.

[12] G. Liu, Y. Tao, M. Tan, and Z. Zhang. Casa: Correlation-aware speculative adders. In *Proceedings of the International Symposium on Low Power Electronics and Design,* 2014.

[13] T. Mudge. Power: A first-class architectural design constraint. *Computer*, 34(4):52–58, 2001.

[14] J. M. Rabaey. *Digital Integrated Circuits: A Design Perspective*. Prentice-Hall, Inc., Upper Saddle River, NJ, USA, 1996.

[15] G. Tziantzioulis, A. M. Gok, S. M. Faisal, N. Hardavellas, S. Ogrenci-Memik, and S. Parthsarathy. Lazy pipelines: Enhancing quality in approximate computing. In *Proceedings of Design, Automation and Test in Europe,* 2016.

[16] A. K. Verma, P. Brisk, and P. Ienne. Variable latency speculative addition: A new paradigm for arithmetic circuit design. In *Proceedings of Design, Automation and Test in Europe,* 2008.

[17] B. Zhai, D. Blaauw, D. Sylvester, and K. Flautner. Theoretical and practical limits of dynamic voltage scaling. In *Proceedings of the 41st Design Automation Conference,* 2004.

Energy Efficient Magnetic Tunnel Junction Based Hybrid LSI Using Multi-Threshold UTBB-FD-SOI Device

Hao Cai, You Wang, Lirida A.B. Naviner
Télécom-ParisTech, Université Paris-Saclay
75013, Paris, France
hao.cai, you.wang,
lirida.naviner@telecom-paristech.fr

Wang Kang, Weisheng Zhao
Fert Beijing Institute, BDBC and School of Electronic and Information Engineering,
Beihang University,Beijing 100191, China
wang.kang,
weisheng.zhao@buaa.edu.cn

ABSTRACT

The energy scalability of ultra-low power nonvolatile (NV) large-scale integration (LSI) is explored in this paper. Multi-threshold computing (super/near/sub-V_t) in hybrid CMOS/magnetic tunnel junction (MTJ) circuits are investigated based on SPICE-compatible MTJ model and fully depleted silicon on insulator (FD-SOI) devices. Ultra-low supply voltage operation bottlenecks associated with performance loss, parametric variations and function failure are studied in differential pair-based sensing circuit, MTJ writing/control circuit and other building blocks. A case study is performed with three typical NV-flip-flops (NV-FF), which are implemented with 28nm FD-SOI low V_t (LVT) device and forward back-bias. Results show that MTJ writing/control circuit must operate at nominal supply (super-V_t) region to guarantee MTJ switching; sensing circuit is configured with near-V_t operation (0.6V) with robustness consideration, whereas other parts could be implemented with near/sub-V_t computing to achieve ultra-low power consumption and energy efficient operations.

Keywords

Nonvolatile LSI, ultra-low power, near/sub-threshold computing, 28nm UTBB-FD-SOI, magnetic tunnel junction, forward back-bias

1. INTRODUCTION

The next-generation internet of things (IoT) era interacts technologies that span the whole way from the data centers to electronic devices. There is a growing need to design ultra-low power, high security and reliable computing architectures while maintaining high performance [1]. As a promising candidate, spintronic device (e.g., magnetic tunnel junction, MTJ) based nonvolatile large-scale-integration (NV-LSI) presents solution for ultra-low power IoT development [2–4].

Permission to make digital or hard copies of all or part of this work for personal or classroom use is granted without fee provided that copies are not made or distributed for profit or commercial advantage and that copies bear this notice and the full citation on the first page. Copyrights for components of this work owned by others than ACM must be honored. Abstracting with credit is permitted. To copy otherwise, or republish, to post on servers or to redistribute to lists, requires prior specific permission and/or a fee. Request permissions from permissions@acm.org.

GLSVLSI '17, May 10-12, 2017, Banff, AB, Canada
© 2017 ACM. ISBN 978-1-4503-4972-7/17/05...$15.00
DOI: http://dx.doi.org/10.1145/3060403.3060413

Beyond the 65 nm node, CMOS technology scaling down no longer delivers the energy gains as before [5]. It drives the requirement of enhanced electrostatic control of the channel with thin film devices like FinFET [6] and ultra-thin body and ultra-thin BOX fully depleted silicon on insulator (UTBB-FD-SOI) [7, 8]. Recently, emerging NV-memories and circuits, e.g., NV arithmetic logic units [4, 9] and NV flip-flops (NV-FF) [10–13] have been developed, which allow zero leakage during circuit retention mode.

Transistor threshold voltage (V_t) plays a fundamental role in device electrical characterization and stands as a significant parameter. Near-Vt and sub-Vt circuit operations have been presented as the efficient way to reduce power [5, 7]. They also provide high transcendence for given drain current and similar nMOS and pMOS current density ($I_{on}/\mu m$). low supply voltage V_{dd} STT-MRAMs have been reported in [14–19]. The proposed near-V_t (NTV) and even sub-V_t computing in NV-LSI circuits can lead to performance loss, increased variability and failure rate that is similar to previous NTV computing circuits [5].

In order to overcome these barriers in hybrid CMOS/MTJ NV-LSI design, V_{dd} allocation and multi-V_t FD-SOI devices with back-bias are combined to form an ultra-low power design scenario. The rest of paper is organized as follows. Section 2 introduces FD-SOI basics. Section 3 presents the ultra-low power methodology by using multi-scale transistor operation regions in NV-LSI circuits. Section 4 evaluates three NV-FFs performance with the proposed supply method. Finally, conclusions are drawn in Section 5.

2. FD-SOI BACK-BIAS

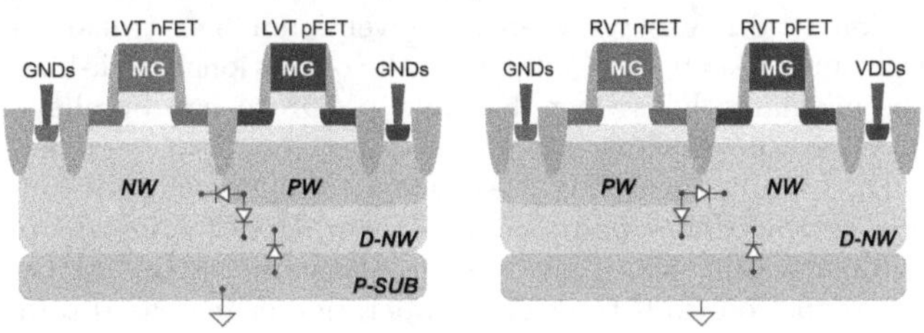

Figure 1: Cross-sectional view of FD-SOI LVT and RVT transistors.

FD-SOI device enlarges the physically-described range of back-plane polarizations. The buried-oxide under the thin silicon film enables transistor back-plane as a second gate allowing to form another channel at the poly-silicon/metal oxide interface [8, 20]. Figure 1 shows the cross-sectional view of LVT (low-power V_t) and RVT (regular V_t) transistor. The back-bias voltage (V_B) range of LVT and RVT transistor is given by:

$$LVT: \quad V_{Bp} = -V_B, \; V_{Bn} = V_B, \; V_B \in [-0.3V, 3V] \quad (1)$$

$$RVT: V_{Bp} = V_{dd} - V_B, V_{Bn} = V_B, V_B \in [-3V, 0.3V + V_{dd}/2] \quad (2)$$

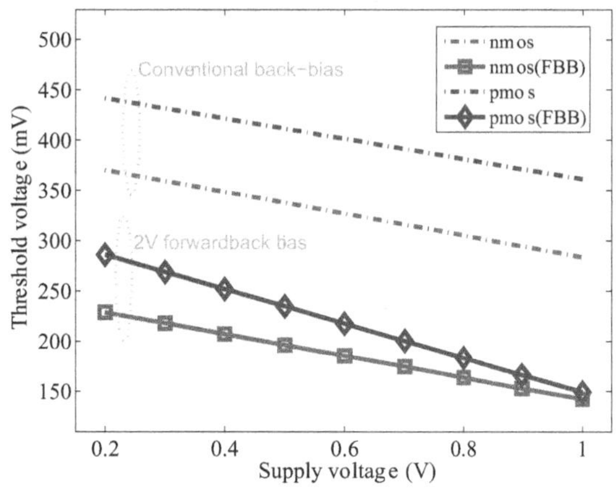

Figure 2: Threshold voltage adjustment versus supply voltage scaling. LVT FD-SOI transistor with W/L=80nm/30nm, V_{ds}=V_{gs}=V_{dd}.

A theoretical forward V_{BB} up to +3V (breakdown node) can be applied into performance adjustment of nMOS device (absolute values for pMOS device), which changes the electrostatic control of the transistors and shifts their V_t. Thus, more drive current can be obtained at the expense of increased leakage current (forward back-bias, FBB), or reduced leakage with reduced performance (reverse back-bias, RBB). For practical considerations (e.g., breakdown node, additional power), in this work 2V FBB is selected as a reference boundary to optimize transistor performance [21, 22].

FD-SOI device allows operation in an ultra wide voltage range (UWVR) with outstanding power efficiency especially in sub/near-V_t regime [5, 7]. As shown in Figure 2, the additional forward back-bias enlarges the near-V_t operation region to 0.28V V_{dd}, whereas conventional bias transistor is around V_{dd}=0.4V. Compare with conventional back-bias, the mismatch between nMOS and pMOS V_t can be alleviated with forward back bias.

Due to advanced CMOS technology scaling along with increased variability and standby energy, the effectiveness of voltage scaling has diminished to the point where further V_{dd} reduction leads to incorrect operation or increased total energy. In this work, we propose to use FD-SOI intrinsic characteristics to enhance transistor performance at near-V_t and sub-V_t regions. However, circuits with near/sub-V_t operation have a higher susceptibility to parametric variation comparing to the nominal counterpart. The FD-SOI process offers better tolerance of very low channel doping concentration, so that random dopant fluctuations can be significantly reduced [23].

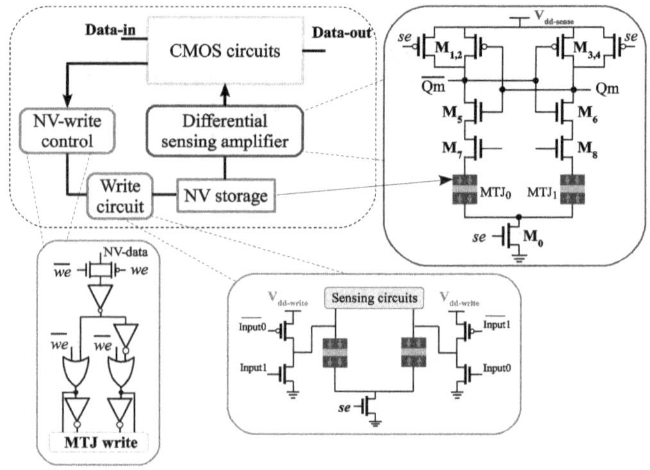

Figure 3: Multi-scale computing in NV-LSI circuits with super-V_t (red), near-V_t (blue) and sub-V_t (green) implementations.

3. NV-LSI WITH MULTIPLE OPERATION

3.1 Hybrid NV-LSI

The hybrid NV-LSI is composed of writing circuit, control circuit, sensing circuit and other standard CMOS building blocks. Figure 3 shows the schematic of main building blocks in NV-LSI, including differential pair-based SA, differential NV writing circuit and MTJ storage. During the writing phase (se='0'), PCSA works at pre-charge phase so that the data 'Q' is stored in the MTJs when write enable is set to '1'. During the sensing phase (se='1'), the writing part is disabled and PCSA is activated to drive reading currents on both sides flowing to the ground. A differential current will be created because of the resistance difference between MTJ_0 and MTJ_1. The output will be pulled to V_{dd} while the other one will be pulled down to the ground.

In this work, a SPICE-compatible MTJ compact model for hybrid NV-LSI is used to simulate static and dynamic behaviors [24]. Planar FD-SOI technology at 28nm node is applied to NV-LSI design with multiple operation regions. The process variation of MTJ device is caused by the limited fabrication precision, which results in uncorrected errors [25, 26], due to the deviations of oxide barrier thickness (t_{ox}), free layer thickness (t_{sl}) and TMR ratio. Inter-die and within-die process variations in FD-SOI low power (LVT) family transistor are evaluated. Simulations are performed with Cadence *spectre* analog design environment (ADE). Variability induced writing/sensing fault probability is estimated with 500 samples Monte-Carlo simulation by Cadence ADE-XL.

3.2 Super-V_t writing

STT-MTJ stochastic effect has deep impact on the reliability of CMOS/MTJ circuits [27]. Its switching mechanism has been demonstrated intrinsically stochastic due to the thermal fluctuation of magnetization [28]. Due to the phenomena of stochastic effect, the switching errors occur frequently, e.g., writing operation may fail to store the right data in MTJ and sensing operation may erroneously cause unexpected switching. In order to guarantee MTJ switch-

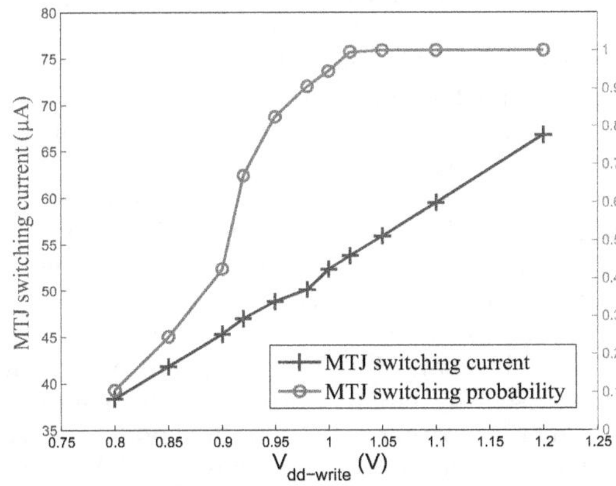

Figure 4: Nonvolatile data writing: MTJ switching current and probability.

ing, average switching time (τ) and a above critical switching current (I_{c0}) are required:

$$I_{c0} = \alpha \frac{\gamma e}{\mu_B g}(\mu_0 M_s) H_k V \tag{3}$$

$$\frac{1}{\tau} = [\frac{2}{C + ln(\frac{\pi^2 \zeta}{4})}] \frac{\mu_B P_{ref}}{em_m(1 + P_{ref}P_{free})}(I - I_{c0}) \tag{4}$$

where E is the barrier energy, H_k is the effective anisotropy field, μ_0 is permeability of free space, M_s is the saturation magnetization, α is the magnetic damping constant, γ is the gyromagnetic ratio, e is the elementary charge, μ_B is the Bohr magneton, V is the volume of the free layer, g is the spin polarization efficiency factor, k_B is the Boltzmann constant, C is the Euler's constant, ζ is the thermal stability factor, m_m is the magnetization moment, and P_{ref} and P_{free} are the tunneling spin polarizations [27].

A typical 4 transistor-2 MTJ differential (4T-2M) differential write circuit is illustrate in Figure 3. MTJ writing and sensing operations are controlled with the tail transistor (M_0). Besides, the NV writing control unit is composed by several transmission and logic gates which provide input signal for 4T-2M write circuit.

As shown in Figure 4, write supply scaling significantly impacts MTJ switching current and probability, even with large W/L ratio transistors (pMOS W/L=1000nm/30nm, nMOS W/L=500nm/30nm). The near-I_{c0} (40 μA) current has increased probability to cause MTJ stochastic behavior or writing fault, which reduces switching probability and the entire NV-LSI reliability performance. Due to large W/L ratio transistors usage in MTJ write circuit, The back-bias method shows very limited impact to MTJ writing performance [13]. As mentioned in previous section, back-bias can be used to adjust nMOS/pMOS V_t mismatch ($V_{tp} \simeq V_{tn}$). The writing signal propagation delay is optimized with the 1V V_{dd} and 2V FBB implementation.

3.3 Near/sub-V_t in differential pair-based SA

A remarkable transistor V_t reduction can be realized when applying FBB in the differential pair-based SA circuit, Fig 5 shows the V_t dependence on V_{dd} scaling (absolute value of V_t in pMOS) in the sensing circuit. nMOS in pass-transistor

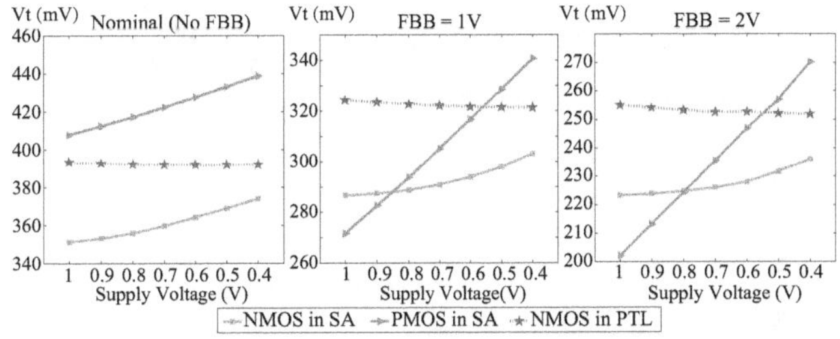

Figure 5: Transistor V_t configuration in SA and PTL under different forward back-bias voltages (absolute value of V_t in pMOS).

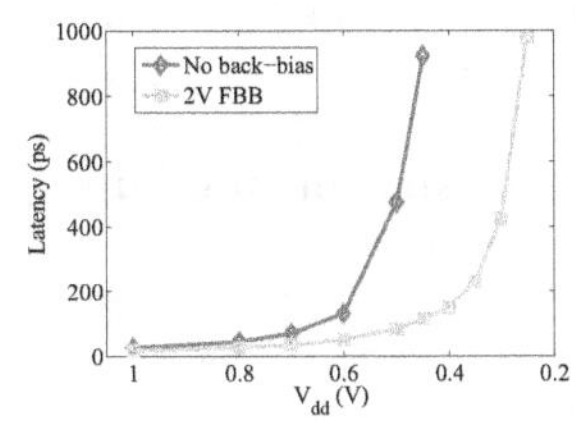

(a) sensing latency

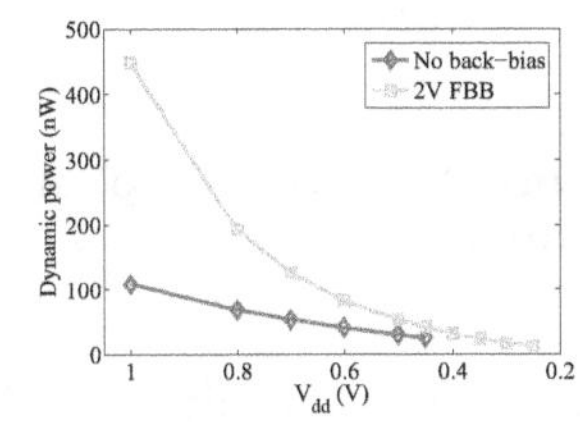

(b) dynamic power

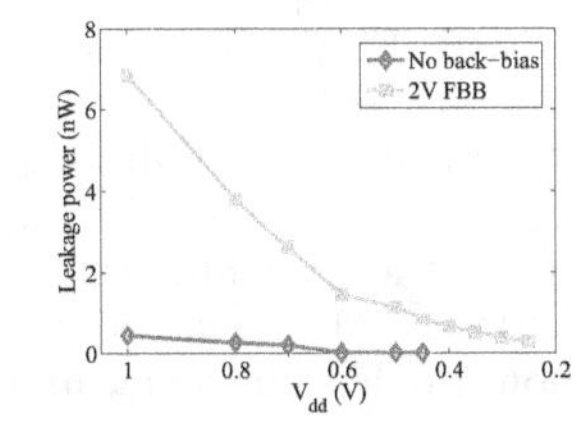

(c) leakage power

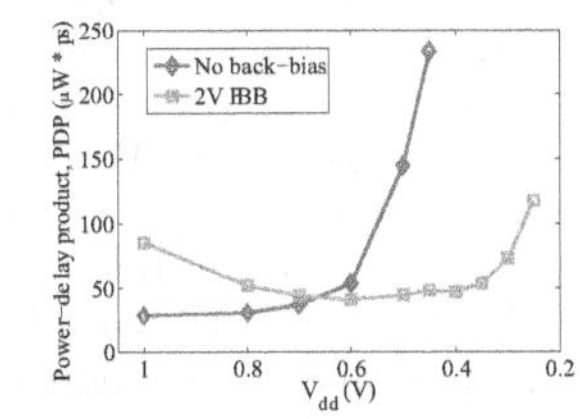

(d) power-delay product

Figure 6: Differential pair-based SA performance with V_{dd} scaling down. Forward back-bias is effective to compensate performance loss in sensing latency, dynamic/leakage power compensation.

stack is less sensitive to V_{dd} scaling compared to transistors in cross-coupled latch.

In differential pair-based SA, one possible V_t scenario is to introduce sub-V_t operation in cross-coupled latch (SA) and driver circuit (to reduce sub-V_t leakage currents), whereas releasing V_t requirement in pass-transistor logic (PTL) stack [29]. The PTL stack performance can be optimized. Figure 6 shows the performance of differential pair-based sensing circuit, which includes sensing delay, average dynamic power, leakage power and power-delay product. The power overhead of generating the FBB voltage is decreased with respect to supply scaling. In the near-V_t operation region, the usage of 2V back-bias reduces 82.3% sensing latency, with the tradeoff of 1.74x dynamic power and 64x leakage power consumption. As the non-volatile device (MTJ) based memory and circuit allows zero leakage during circuit retention mode, the leakage penalty could be overcome. Figure 6(d) shows the power-delay product of sensing circuit. The near-V_t region (0.5V-0.6V) with 2V FBB is assigned the most efficient along the supply scaling.

The effect of process variations and transistor mismatch is another important figure of merit in near/sub V_t circuits. MTJ process variation is included in this work to investigate the robustness of hybrid MTJ/CMOS circuits. In order to

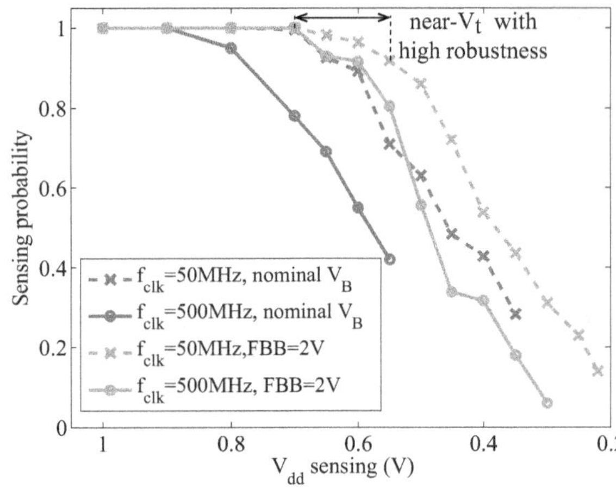

Figure 7: Sensing probability versus sensing supply scaling.

enhance the variability in performance, sensing circuit W/L ratio is optimized (W/L=320nm/30nm). Figure 7 shows the sensing probability of MTJ based differential pair-based SA with standard back-bias and 2V FBB. Simulation results show that sensing probability is highly dependent on V_{dd}. In near-V_t region (e.g., V_{dd}=0.55V), sensing probability can be enhanced by using back-bias method, as well as lowering operation frequency. Table 1 presents the V_t configuration of each transistor. We propose to design MTJ sensing circuit with near-V_t operation for power-delay efficiency and robustness consideration.

Table 1: Reduced V_t with 2V FBB in near-V_t region

	M_{1-4}	M_{5-6}	M_{7-8}	M_0
Transistor function	SA	SA	PTL	I_{tail}
Op. region in [29]	sub-V_t	sub-V_t	near-V_t	sub-V_t
Aver. V_t reduction	38.4%	37.7%	36.2%	35.9%
Proposed op. region	near-V_t	near-V_t	near-V_t	near-V_t

With the guaranteed MTJ writing and robust sensing performance, further supply scaling (sub-V_t operation region) can be applied into the CMOS blocks of hybrid circuits. In NV-FF circuits, sub-V_t CMOS FF core achieves ultra-low power consumption, as it will be described in the next section.

4. A CASE STUDY ON NV-FF

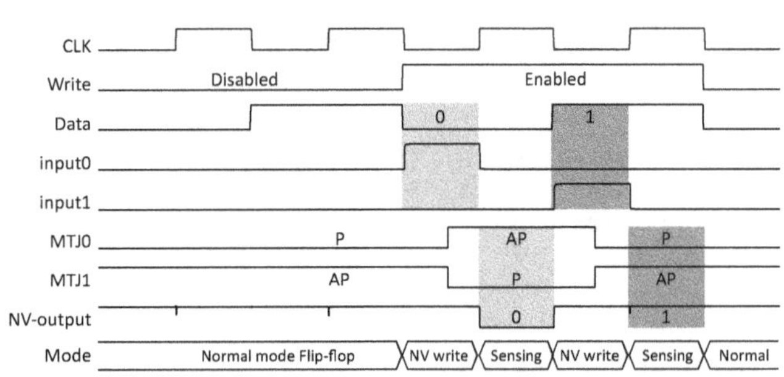

Figure 8: NV-FF write/sense control signal.

Based on the results above, a multi-V_t scenario is proposed for ultra-low power NV-LSI: writing/control circuits are designed with super-V_t (1V nominal supply), near-V_t operation in differential pair-based sensing circuit. We conduct a case study on NV-FF to explore sub-/near-V_t operation in other CMOS building blocks of NV-LSI.

NV-FF broadly refers to integrate nonvolatile storage into conventional CMOS-FF core, with the advantage of infinite endurance and zero standby leakage. It can be used to preserve internal data into NV memories, and recall them after the NV-LSI system activation. A typical NV-FF is composed of one classical CMOS-FF, one writing circuit, NV storages and sensing circuit, with respect to normal flip-flop/latch mode, write mode, standby mode and sensing mode. Once standby-mode is required in NV-LSIs, data backup into MTJ must be performed before system power-off. Figure 8 shows the NV-FF operation mode with writing and sensing enable signal.

CMOS FF core is the essential building block in NV-FF. During normal flip-flop/latch mode and sensing mode, FF core performance dominates the efficiency of the whole NV-LSI. In this work, three NV-FF topologies are investigated (see Fig. 9), including classic master-slave (MSFF) [10–12, 19], transmission gate pulsed latch (TGPL) [30] based NVFF and differential sense amplifier (SAFF) based NV-FF [13, 31]. Owing to its simple structure and superior density., the conventional MSFF with tri-state inverters remains the mainstream in NV-FF design. This foundry qualified FF topology is with high area efficiency, guaranteed cell yield and reliability with nominal supply.

Table 2: CMOS FF core performance comparison, with 1V/27°C, f_{clk}=50 MHz.

	MSFF	TGPL[1)]	SAFF
Clk-to-Q latency (ps)	38.1	30.1	37.3
Dynamic power (nW)	237.4	266.8	147.5
Process variation[2)] (σ/μ)	9.76	4	7.85
$Nr.$ of transistor	22	24	20
1 bit layout area (μm^2)	5.16[3)]	5.75	5.39

[1)] Implementation with a pulsed generator.
[2)] Process variation is evaluated with clock-to-output delay.
[3)] Measured from 28nm FD-SOI standard cell library.

Table 3: Near/sub-V_t CMOS FF core performance.

	MSFF	TGPL	SAFF
V_{dd} = 0.3V	near-V_t	near-V_t	sub-V_t
Clk-to-Q latency (ps)	354.1	247.6	427.5
Dynamic power (nW)	36.04	30.66	22.3
V_{dd} = 0.25V	sub-V_t	sub-V_t	sub-V_t
Clk-to-Q latency (ps)	711.32	2220	1420
Dynamic power (nW)	25.03	28.03	19.38
Max. sub-V_t margin (mV)	39	57	12.5

One of the main weaknesses of classical MSFF is that the positive setup time in the master latch and output latency in the slave latch cause large FF latency, so that MSFF is not suitable to be placed at the circuit critical path [32]. Another

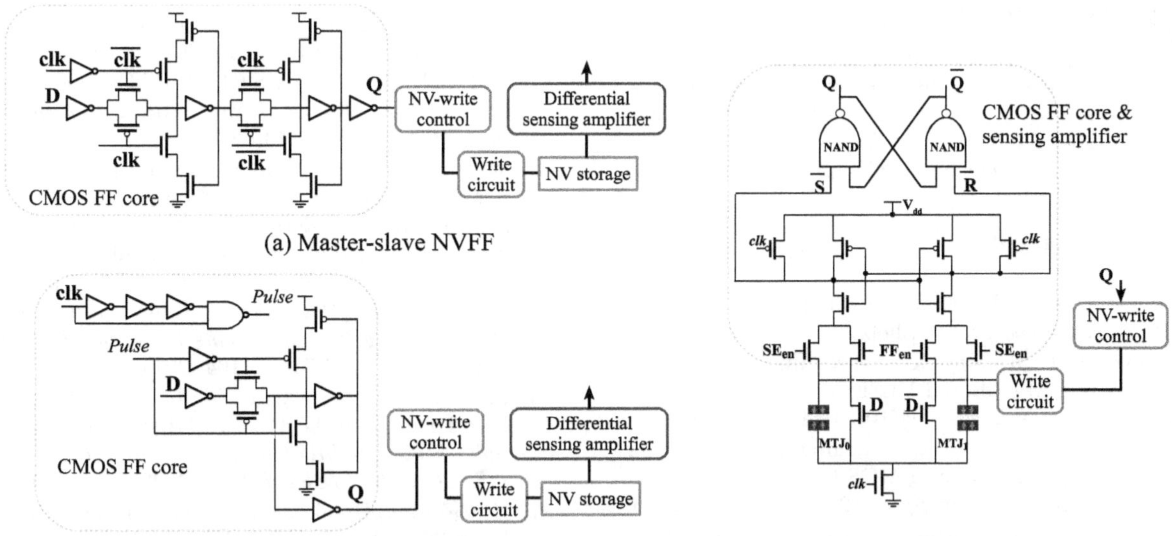

(a) Master-slave NVFF

(b) TGPL NVFF

(c) SA-NVFF

Figure 9: NVFFs with different CMOS FF cores. (a) master-slave (MS) NVFF. (b) transmission gate pulsed latch (TGPL) based NV-FF. (c) differential sense amplifier (SAFF) based NV-FF.

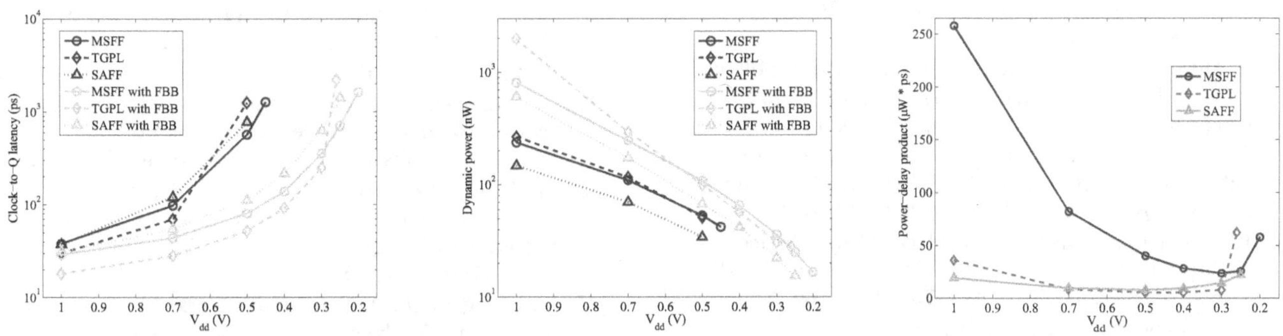

(a) CMOS FF core latency

(b) Average dynamic power

(c) Power-delay product

Figure 10: TGPL is faster than other two topologies. Both TGPL and SAFF achieve the power-delay efficient in near-V_t and sub-V_t operation regions.

problem is that MSFF hard clock edge property leads to high sensitivity to clock skew. The time borrowing between clock phases is impossible in MS topology. Table 2 summarizes the CMOS FF cores performance with 1V/27°C, 50 MHz clock frequency.

Figure 10(a) shows the clk-to-Q latency of each CMOS FF core along V_{dd} scaling. TGPL is faster than other topologies. MSFF has the ultra-low operation voltage at 0.2V supply thanks to robust FD-SOI devices. With 2V forward back-bias voltage, ultra-wide operation range can be realized in circuit design. Their average dynamic power consumption are demonstrated in Figure 10(b). SAFF shows the most power efficient among the three CMOS FF core candidates. The power-delay product (with 2V FBB) is shown in Figure 10(c), both TGPL and SAFF topology achieves the efficient operation in near-V_t and sub-V_t operation regions. Each CMOS FF core benefits the low power from near/sub-V_t operation. Notice that 0.3V below supply voltage shows limits of efficient FF core design. Table 3 summarizes the near/sub-V_t CMOS FF core performance.

5. CONCLUSION

In this paper, an ultra-low power scenario was proposed for hybrid CMOS/MTJ NV-LSI. The proposed solution includes super-V_t (with 1V nominal supply) MTJ writing and control circuits, besides near-V_t operation in differential pair-based sensing circuit, as well as near/sub-V_t operation in other CMOS circuits. Low V_t FD-SOI device with forward back-bias was used to enhance NV-LSI latency, power and robustness. The 1V MTJ writing guaranteed MTJ switching, 0.6V near V_t sensing operation showed a 81% dynamic power reduction, with the tradeoff of 6.2% increased sensing error rate. The investigation of NV-FF compared the performance of three types of NV-FFs. Sub-V_t operation has been realized in CMOS FF core which achieved at least power-latency tradeoff.

6. ACKNOWLEDGMENTS

This work is supported by STmicroelectronics Nano2017-SOBER. The authors gratefully acknowledge the International Collaboration Project 2015DFE12880 and B16001, Beijing Municipal of Science and Technology (Grant No. D15110300320000) for their financial support of this work.

7. REFERENCES

[1] J. de Boeck. IoT: The impact of things. *2015 Symp. on VLSI Technology*, 50–61, Feb 2015.

[2] T. Hanyu *et al.*. Standby-Power-Free Integrated Circuits Using MTJ-Based VLSI Computing. *Proceedings of the IEEE*, 104(10):1844–1863, 2016.

[3] W. Kang *et al.*. Spintronics: Emerging ultra-low power circuits and systems beyond MOS technology. *ACM J. Emerg. Technol. Comput. Syst.*, 12(2):Article 16, 2015.

[4] H. Cai *et al.*. Robust Ultra-Low Power Non-Volatile Logic-in-Memory Circuits in FD-SOI Technology. *Circuits and Systems I: Regular Papers, IEEE Trans. on*, 2016, doi: 10.1109/TCSI.2016.2621344.

[5] R. G. Dreslinski *et al.*. Near-Threshold Computing: Reclaiming Moore's Law Through Energy Efficient Integrated Circuits. *Proceedings of the IEEE*, 98(2):253–266, 2010.

[6] D. Hisamoto *et al.*. FinFET-a self-aligned double-gate MOSFET scalable to 20 nm. *IEEE Transactions on Electron Devices*, 47(12):2350–2325, 2000.

[7] S.A. Vitale *et al.*. FDSOI Process Technology for Subthreshold-Operation Ultralow-Power Electronics. *Proceedings of the IEEE*, 98(2):333–342, 2010.

[8] J.P. Noel *et al.*. Multi-VT UTBB FDSOI Device Architectures for Low-Power CMOS Circuit. *IEEE Trans. on Elec. Dev.*, 58(8):2473–2482, Aug 2011.

[9] G. Di Pendina *et al.*. A hybrid magnetic/ complementary metal oxide semiconductor process design kit for the design of low-power non-volatile logic circuits. *Journal of Applied Physics*, 111:07E350, 2012.

[10] K. Ryu *et al.*. A Magnetic Tunnel Junction Based Zero Standby Leakage Current Retention Flip-Flop. *Very Large Scale Integr. Syst., IEEE Trans. on*, 20(11):2044–2053, 2012.

[11] S. Daisuke *et al.*. Magnetic-tunnel-junction based low-energy nonvolatile flip-flop using an area-efficient self-terminated write driver. *Journal of Applied Physics*, 117(17):17B504, 2015.

[12] D. Chabi *et al.*. Ultra Low Power Magnetic Flip-Flop Based on Checkpointing/Power Gating and Self-Enable Mechanisms. *Circ. and Sys. I: Regular Papers, IEEE Trans. on*, 61(6):1755–1765, 2014.

[13] H. Cai *et al.*. Multiplexing sense amplifier based magnetic flip-flop in 28nm FDSOI technology. *Nanotechnology, IEEE Trans. on*, 14(4):761–767, 2015.

[14] C. W. Smullen *et al.*. Relaxing non-volatility for fast and energy-efficient STT-RAM caches. *High Performance Computer Architecture (HPCA), 2011 IEEE 17th Inter. Symp. on*, 50–61, Feb 2011.

[15] R. Patel *et al.*. Field driven STT-MRAM cell for reduced switching latency and energy. *Circ. and Sys. (ISCAS), 2014 IEEE Intl. Symp. on*, 2173–2176, 2014.

[16] Y. Umeki *et al.*. A 0.38-V operating STT-MRAM with process variation tolerant sense amplifier. *IEEE Asian Solid-State Circ. Conf. (A-SSCC)*, 249–252, Nov 2013.

[17] R. Patel *et al.*. 2T-1R STT-MRAM memory cells for enhanced on/off current ratio. *Microelectronics Journal*, 45(2):133–143, 2014.

[18] Y. Shuto *et al.*. 0.5V operation and performance of nonvolatile SRAM cell based on pseudo-spin-FinFET architecture. *Simulation of Semiconductor Processes and Devices, Inter. Conf. on*, 305–308, 2014.

[19] I. Kazi *et al.*. Energy/Reliability Trade-Offs in Low-Voltage ReRAM-Based Non-Volatile Flip-Flop Design. *Circuits and Systems I: Regular Papers, IEEE Trans. on*, 61(11):3155–3164, 2014.

[20] P. Flatresse *et al.*. Ultra-wide back-bias range LDPC decoder in 28nm UTBB FDSOI technology. *Solid-State Circuits Conf. Digest of Tech. Papers (ISSCC), 2013 IEEE Intl.*, 424–425, Feb 2013.

[21] H. Cai *et al.* Breakdown Analysis of Magnetic Flip-flop With 28nm UTBB FDSOI Technology. *IEEE Trans on Dev. and Mat. Reliability*, 16(3):376–383, 2016.

[22] H. Cai *et al.* Low power magnetic flip-flop optimization with FDSOI technology boost. *IEEE Transactions on Magnetics*, 52(8):1–7, 2016.

[23] Y. Yang *et al.*. Back-Gate Bias Dependence of the Statistical Variability of FDSOI MOSFETs With Thin BOX. *IEEE Transactions on Electron Devices*, 60(2):739–745, 2013.

[24] Y. Wang *et al.*. Compact thermal modeling of spin transfer torque magnetic tunnel junction *Microelectronics Reliability*, 55(9):1649–1653, 2015.

[25] W. Kang *et al.*. Reconfigurable Codesign of STT-MRAM Under Process Variations in Deeply Scaled Technology. *IEEE Trans. Electron Devices*, 62(6):1769–1777, 2015.

[26] Y. Wang *et al.*. A Non-Monte-Carlo Methodology for Variability Analysis of Magnetic Tunnel Junction-Based Circuits. *IEEE Trans. on Magnetic*, 53(3):1–6, 2017.

[27] Y. Wang *et al.*. Compact model of dielectric breakdown in spin-transfer torque magnetic tunnel junction. *IEEE Trans. on Electron Devices*, 63(4):1762–1767, 2016.

[28] T. Devolder *et al.*. Single-Shot Time-Resolved Measurements of Nanosecond-Scale Spin-Transfer Induced Switching: Stochastic Versus Deterministic Aspects. In *Phys. Rev. Lett.*, 100(5):057206, 2018.

[29] D. Markovic *et al.*. Ultralow-Power Design in Near-Threshold Region. *Proceedings of the IEEE*, 98(2):237–252, 2010.

[30] E. Consoli *et al.*. Conditional push-pull pulsed latches with 726fJ.ps energy-delay product in 65nm CMOS. *IEEE Intl. Solid-State Circuit Conf.*, 482–484, 2012.

[31] D. Mahalanabis *et al.*. A Nonvolatile Sense Amplifier Flip-Flop Using Programmable Metallization Cells. *IEEE J. Emerg. and Sel. Top. in Circ. and Syst.*, 5(2):205–213, 2015.

[32] M. Alioto *et al.*. Analysis and Comparison in the Energy-delay-area Domain of Nanometer CMOS Flip-flops: Part I-methodology and Design Strategies. *Very Large Scale Integr. Syst., IEEE Trans. on*, 19(5):725–736, 2011.

A Mixed-Size Monolithic 3D Placer with 2D Layout Inheritance

Xu He
School of Information Science and Technology, Hunan University
& School of Computer, National University of Defense Technology
China
dawn.hx@gmail.com

Yao Wang, Yang Guo
School of Computer, National University of Defense Technology
China
{wangyaobsz, guoyang}@nudt.edu.cn

Sorin Cotofana
Computer Engineering Laboratory
Delft University of Technology
the Netherlands
s.d.cotofana@tudelft.nl

ABSTRACT

Monolithic 3D IC is a high integration density emerging technology in the age of both "More Moore" and "More-than-Moore". In this paper, we propose a novel method of generating mixed-size 3D placement based on transforming a 2D placement result. Experimental results indicate that, when compared with the input 2D placement, the 3D placer can reduce the wirelength by 57%, and provide a four-layer 3D chip footprint of about one quarter of the 2D counterpart. Moreover, our placer can preserve the layout information from the 2D placement input, which means that the 2D placement quality can be inherited in the 3D placement results. Compared with an analytical wirelength-driven placer, our placer achieves 34% benefit on 2D layout inheritance and 12% benefit on runtime with acceptable (4%) wirelength cost.

1. INTRODUCTION

Three-dimensional Integrated Circuits (3D ICs) offer the potential to meet semiconductor industry developing requirements, such as for shorter interconnection, better performance, power reduction, and so on. In particular, 3D ICs are advocated by two design paradigms [11]: (1) "More Moore" with shrinking device nodes, and (2) "More-than-Moore" with heterogeneous integration. Monolithic 3D ICs (M3D) is an emerging technology that allows for the sequential fabrication of more device layers one on top of another. When compared with Through-Silicon-Via (TSV) based 3D, the M3D integration technology eliminates the requirement of die alignment [21]. Moreover, the Monolithic Inter-layer Vias (MIVs) used for interconnections between device layers are much smaller (<100 nm, i.e., as small as a regular local via [3]) than TSVs (around 5-10 um [8]). Therefore, M3D is regarded as an emerging alternative that provides much higher integration density, and the continuation of the historical Moore's Law value scaling trajectory.

Permission to make digital or hard copies of all or part of this work for personal or classroom use is granted without fee provided that copies are not made or distributed for profit or commercial advantage and that copies bear this notice and the full citation on the first page. Copyrights for components of this work owned by others than ACM must be honored. Abstracting with credit is permitted. To copy otherwise, or republish, to post on servers or to redistribute to lists, requires prior specific permission and/or a fee. Request permissions from permissions@acm.org.

GLSVLSI '17, May 10-12, 2017, Banff, AB, Canada
© 2017 ACM. ISBN 978-1-4503-4972-7/17/05. . . $15.00
DOI: http://dx.doi.org/10.1145/3060403.3060411

M3D ICs related research focus on fabrication techniques [3, 15], transistor-level monolithic 3D ICs [4, 17], as well as on design methodologies. Related to block level design in [22], the authors study the power-performance trade-off and propose a variation-aware floorplanning techniques to make the design more tolerant to manufacturing variations. The M3D gate-level placement issue is addressed in [21] which introduce a method to leverage existing 2D placers to mimic the generation of a flattened M3D placement and give a routability-driven cell partitioning for two-layer 3D structures.

At its turn the TSV-based 3D placement problem received. Folding-based 3D placement [8] reuses 2D placement results or tools and derives a 3D placement by folding transformations and refinements extended from [5]. Partitioning-based approaches [12, 16] minimize the usage of vertical resources, and a process of partitioning and/or floorplanning is invoked before actual placement. Another popular category is analytic placement, which is based on numerical analysis of non-linear equations to minimize wirelength, cell overlaps and other objectives. In [19, 1, 7, 16, 2], the layer assignments of circuit modules are fixed while accounting for the interconnections of modules across different layers. Some approaches [19, 10, 14] compute layer assignment of modules when optimizing placement solution.

For an existing large 2D IC design, tremendous effort has been made to optimize the placement and routing of the design for timing-closure. As the monolithic 3D technology advances, we can make a more integrated 3D design from the existing 2D design by inheriting its physical design information. In such a way, the time-to-market progress can be greatly accelerated and a lot of computing resource and design effort can be saved. In this paper, we propose a novel approach to obtain a mixed-size 3D placement by reusing existing 2D placement results. Many techniques are proposed and analyzed for both wirelength optimization and 2D layout inheritance. Experimental results indicate that the 2D placement layout circuit modules distribution is well preserved by our 3D placer which means that the 2D placement quality can be inherited in the 3D placement results. Our major contributions can be summarized as follows:

- Propose an effective 2D transformation flow to generate an initial 3D layout for mixed-size placement.

- Present an algorithm of coarse-grained cell relocation for both interconnection and 2D layout inheritance.
- Demonstrate that the distribution of circuit modules of 2D placement layout maintained very well after our 3D placement, providing potential of performance inheritance.
- Provide high quality input for other following 3D refinements, and also give a fast performance estimation when deciding to transform an existing 2D design to 3D design.

The remainder of this paper is organized as follows. In Section II, we give the problem formulation and in Section III an overview of the proposed 3D placing method. Section IV describes the initial 3D placement generation method out of an existing 2D placement. Section V introduces the bin-grained cell relocation algorithm to consider both wirelength and 2D layout inheritance. Experimental results and conclusions are given in Section VI and Section VII, respectively.

2. 3D PLACEMENT FORMULATION

Given a circuit netlist $N = (E, V)$ with nets E and nodes V, a 3D IC embodiment with k layer, and a 2D placement P, the 3D placement problem can be formulated as: Determine the physical position (x_i, y_i, z_i), z_i being the layer number, of each circuit node v_i (including macros and standard cells) without violating the non-overlap constraint.

The Half-Perimeter Wire-Length (HPWL) model is used for wirelength evaluation. We make use of the "flatten HPWL" [21] as measure for monolithic 3D ICs if all pins of nodes are projected onto a 2D placement plane. The major goal of our 3D placement is to minimize the sum of the flatten HPWL of all nets. The calculation of the flatten HPWL $w(e_k)$ of net e_k is done according to Equation (1).

$$w(e_k) = (\max_{v_i, v_j \in e_k} |x_i - x_j| + \max_{v_i, v_j \in e_k} |y_i - y_j|) \quad (1)$$

In this paper, we set the number of device layers to four, but the proposed techniques can also be applied to an arbitrarily number of layer. Because the routing information is unknown during the placement process, the e_k net MIV number is calculated as the number of layers crossed by the nodes belonging to net e_k. The MIV number $v(e_k)$ of net e_k is shown in Equation (2).

$$v(e_k) = \max_{v_i, v_j \in e_k} |z_i - z_j| \quad (2)$$

To investigate the issue of 2D layout inheritance quantitatively, we define the "extended displacement" as the displacement of nodes in the 3D placement result and the input 2D layout. Since a four-layer 3D chip has nearly one quarter area of a 2D chip, we first shrink both x and y coordinates of nodes in the 2D layout by half before computing the extended displacement. The extended displacement *displace* of node v_i is defined as:

$$displace(v_i) = |x_i - xs_i| + |y_i - ys_i|, \quad (3)$$

where (x_i, y_i) and (xs_i, ys_i) are the x/y coordinates of v_i in 3D layout and its corresponding counterpart after shrinking coordinates in 2D layout, respectively. Small extended displacements of nodes indicate that the 2D layout distribution is preserved well in the 3D placement result, which means that the 2D placement quality can be inherited well in the 3D placement result.

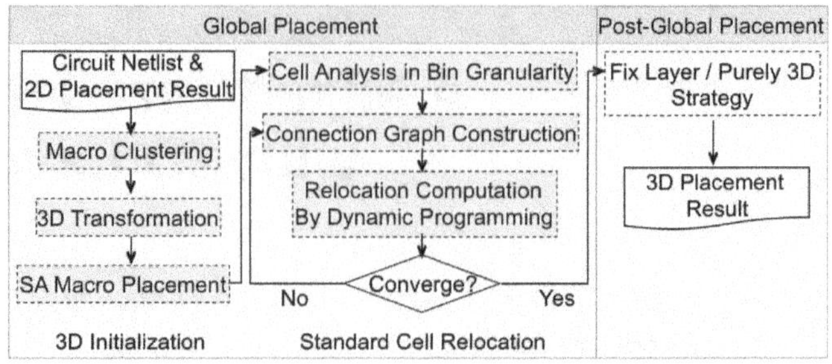

Figure 1: Mixed-Size 3D placement overview.

3. FRAMEWORK OVERVIEW OF THE PROPOSED 3D PLACER

The overall 3D placement framework is illustrated in Figure 1. The global placement stages includes two phases: (1) the Mixed-size 3D Placement Initialization, and (2) the Standard Cell Relocation. In the 3D placement initialization, we first cluster each big macro with its surrounding small macros (we call terminals to distinguish them from big macro) and form a new macro. Folding-based 3D transformation [8] is then applied to transform the input 2D placement to a 3D placement with overlap tolerance. Then, we invoke a Simulated Annealing (SA) engine to legalize the locations of all macros within each layer. The SA algorithm resolves overlaps among macros with a minimum perturbation of their positions obtained after the 3D transformation. After the macro legalization step, they are unclustered and their position fastened. In the standard cell relocation phase, we first divide each layer of the 3D chip into uniform bins. The cells in the same bin are seen as an entire, and the problem of cell relocation is converted into the problem of bin relocation. We use a connection graph to abstract the relationships between bins. The connection graph is then partitioned into several connection subtrees, and the bin relocation problem is solved in linear time by a dynamic programming technique. The bin relocation process is iterated until the improvement of the flatten HPWL is converged.

For the post-global placement stage, the FastPlace-DP techniques [20] is extended for 3D ICs. Instead of invoking a 2D detailed placer in a layer-by-layer manner as in previous 3D placers [10, 8], we implement two 3D post-global placement strategies: (1) Fix layer: it looks at all cells and nets in the 3D space but does not move cells between layers, and (2) Purely 3D: the standard cells are free to move among layers to do refinement on the flatten HPWL, and the layer number given by the global placement result will be chosen with priority.

In the following sections, we mainly discuss about the techniques in the global placement.

4. MIXED-SIZE 3D PLACEMENT INITIALIZATION

The purpose of the mixed-size 3D placement initialization is to give 3D positions to all macros and cells according to the 2D placement layout input. In addition, the overlaps between macros should be removed in this initialization stage.

4.1 Macro Clustering

Macros (including small terminals) are frequently utilized in IC designs and it is quite usual that big macros are surrounded by many small terminals in the 2D placement layout input. Two potential problems are discussed below.

Oversize scale: The number of total macros (including small terminals) are usually very large in current circuit design. A flat macro placement methodology may not be effective in producing a good quality solution within an acceptable runtime.

Disordered distribution: The surrounding terminals of a macro are usually the I/O circuits of the macro. If these terminals are treated as independent individuals, they may be distributed disorderly in the following 3D transformation phase. Consequently, the layer of the macro may be different with the one of its surrounding terminals.

Since the number of IC design macros is usually large, for efficient and scalable macro placement, a hierarchical approach is beneficial to reduce the problem size. According to the 2D placement layout input, all macros are sorted by their sizes in descending order, and they are handled one by one in the process of macro clustering. Each macro is combined with its surrounding terminals. After macro clustering, each cluster is recorded as a macro with its size equal to the minimum bounding box containing all its constituting nodes.

4.2 3D Transformation & Macro Placement

To transform the input 2D placement into a good performance 3D placement, we first apply a folding strategy called symmetric layer assignment [8] to do initialization. After the folding-based 3D transformation for four layer design, the x and y coordinates of nodes are nearly half of their original 2D coordinates, and the layer are also initially assigned by considering reducing via number for multi-layer connections.

However, a lot of overlaps may emerges, especially on top of the macros, which have to be removed during the macro placement process.

We first adjust the macro layer assignment to reduce overlaps. We handled the macros one by one in size descending order and choose the layer with minimum overlaps for each of them. The x/y coordinates of macros will not be changed during layer adjustment.

After layer adjustment, we apply an SA algorithm [24] to preform the macro legalization of each layer. The objective of the macro legalization step is to obtain a placement which resolves overlaps among the macros with minimum perturbation of the folding-based 3D transformation. Besides, all macros have to be placed in legal positions within the chip region. We note that experiments demonstrate that because the macro clustering is substantially reducing the number of macros, the SA legalization process runs very fast and provides high quality result. Finally, all macros are unclustered and fixed after the legalization step is completed.

5. STANDARD CELL RELOCATION

After the placement initialization stage, cells are placed based on a simple heuristic which results in a lot of overlaps. Thus, a cell relocation stage is necessary to further diminish the flatten HPWL and overlaps.

5.1 Connection Graph Model

Since the interconnections have already been considered and optimized in the 2D placement input and our 3D initial placement is generated from the 2D placement, it is better to maintain this 3D layout as much as possible during the cell relocation stage. Each 3D chip layer is divided into uniform bins and all cells are assigned into bins according to their center coordinates. Consequently, the cell relocation is performed at bin-grain, and the relative coordinates between cells in the same bin are conserved. In our implementation, the bin size is set to be 30x the average cell area.

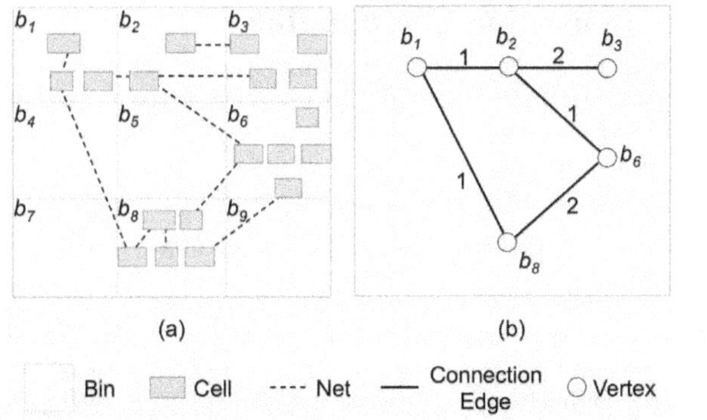

Figure 2: A connection graph G (b) generated from the netlist N in (a). The weight of each connection edge is equal to the number of nets across the bins connected by the edge.

In this way the netlist $N = (E, V)$ is collapsed into a bin-based connection graph $G = (C, B)$, each vertex $b \in B$ represents a bin and a connection $c_{b,b'} \in C$ exists between bins b and b' if, and only if, there are associated nets connecting cells from b and b'. Figure 2 presents a connection graph G example generated from the netlist N; only nets associated to cells across different bins are represented as connection edges in the connection graph G.

For each bin b, we use $pos(b)$ to denote the set of b candidate positions. Theoretically, the cells of b can be moved into any positions within the 3D chip placement region. But to reduce the complexity, only the bin positions in the "optimal region" of b are considered as potential candidates. The optimal region of b is calculated according to the median idea in [13] and all associated nets of cells in b are counted as the associated nets of b during the calculations. The b original position is also added into the set $pos(b)$, in case that b may not be successfully relocated into its optimal region.

For each bin b, we also associate a cost array o_b of size $|pos(b)|$. Each element $o_b[i]$ specifies the cost of assigning b to its candidate position i. Clearly the cost array o_b can be used to measure the overlaps. If the whitespace in the candidate position i is large enough to accomodate all cells in b, $o_b[i] = 0$; otherwise, $o_b[i] = \infty$.

For each connection $c_{b,b'}$, we associate a cost matrix $m_{b,b'}$ of size $|pos(b)| \times |pos(b')|$. Each entry $m_{b,b'}[i,j]$ gives the cost for assigning b to candidate position i and b' to candidate position j at the same time. The cost matrix $m_{b,b'}$ captures the reduction of the flatten HWPL on the simultaneous relocation of b and b'. If the flatten HPWL is decreased due to the relocation, the entry is < 0; otherwise, it is ≥ 0.

The cost of a bin relocation scheme δ which is placing each bin b into the candidate position $\delta(b) \in pos(b)$, is computed by Equation (4). Our objective is to reduce the flatten HPWL and the overlaps by identifying a minimum cost δ.

$$cost(\delta) = \sum_{b \in B} o_b[\delta(b)] + \sum_{c_{b,b'} \in C} m_{b,b'}[\delta(b), \delta(b')] \tag{4}$$

5.2 Relocation Computation

For a special case when the connection graph $G = (C, B)$ is a tree, the $cost(\delta)$ is equal to the tree cost, i.e., the summation of all connection and vertex costs. For a solution δ, we define $cost_b$ of a tree rooted at b as:

$$cost_b(\delta) = o_b(\delta(b)) + \sum_{b' \in ch(b)} (m_{b,b'}[\delta(b), \delta(b')] + cost_{b'}(\delta)), \tag{5}$$

where $ch(b)$ is the children set of the tree root b. As indicated in Equation (5), $cost_b$ has three parts: (1) the cost of bin b, (2) the connection cost between b and b' ($b' \in ch(b)$), and (3) the cost of each subtree rooted at b'.

We use $minC_b(i)$ to denote the minimum tree cost when assigning its root b at the candidate position i. The computation of $minC_b(i)$ is described in Equation (6).

As one can observe in Equation (6), the $minC_b(i)$ recurrence relation is obtained in terms of $minC_{b'}(j)$ for each optional position $j \in pos(b')$ of the subtree rooted at $b' \in ch(b)$. Based on the recurrence relation, dynamic programming can be applied to compute the minimum cost of the tree rooted at b.

The bin relocation pseudo-code is presented in Algorithm 1. We first compute $minC_b$ for each vertex b of the tree rooted at r recursively by function COMPUTE_MINCOST() (line 5-17). Note that for a leaf vertex b, $minC_b(i) = o_b(i), i \in pos(b)$ (line 10). When $minC_b(i)$ of vertex b is computed, we set $p_{b'}(i)$ of child b' to t, where t is the b' position providing the minimum $minC_b(i)$ cost (line 12-14). After $minC_r$ is computed for the root r, we obtain the minimum cost for the entire tree rooted at r. Then, we call the function SOLVE_RELOCATION() to compute the new positions of each vertex b in order to give the minimum cost of the tree. For the tree root r, its new position is set to the candidate position s, if $minC_r(s)$ is the smallest among $minC_r$ of all candidates positions of r. (line 21-22). For the non-root vertex b, its new position is set to $p_b[\delta(p^*)]$, where $\delta(p^*)$ is the new position of its parent p^* (line 24-25). For each child b' of b, when the new b position is decided, the new b' position is selected such that it provides the minimum cost for b (line 27-29).

$$\begin{aligned} minC_b(i) &= \min_{\delta(b)=i} \{cost_b(\delta)\} \\ &= \min_{\delta(b)=i} \{o_b(\delta(b)) + \sum_{b' \in ch(b)} (m_{b,b'}[\delta(b), \delta(b')] \\ &\quad + cost_{b'}(\delta))\} \\ &= o_b(i) + \sum_{b' \in ch(b)} \min_{\delta(b') \in pos(b')} \{m_{b,b'}[i, \delta(b')] \\ &\quad + cost_{b'}(\delta)\} \\ &= o_b(i) + \sum_{b' \in ch(b)} \min_{j \in pos(b')} \{ \min_{\delta(b')=j} \{m_{b,b'}[i,j] \\ &\quad + cost_{b'}(j)\}\} \\ &= o_b(i) + \sum_{b' \in ch(b)} \min_{j \in pos(b')} \{m_{b,b'}[i,j] + minC_{b'}(j)\} \end{aligned} \tag{6}$$

Theorem 1 Given a connection graph $G = (C, B)$ which is a tree, the bin relocation algorithm finds an optimal relocation in $O(|B|^3)$.

Algorithm 1 Bin Relocation by Dynamic Programming

```
Input: Connection graph G = (C, B) is a tree rooted at r.
Output: Generate solution δ with minimum cost.
1: COMPUTE_MINICOST(r)
2: SOLVE_RELOCATION(r)
3: return δ
4:
5: function COMPUTE_MINICOST(b)
6:     for b' ∈ ch(b) do
7:         COMPUTE_MINICOST(b')
8:     end for
9:     for i ∈ pos(b) do
10:        minC_b(i) = o_b(i)
11:        for b' ∈ ch(b) do
12:            Find m_{b,b'}[i,t] + minC_{b'}(t) = min_{j∈pos(b')} {m_{b,b'}[i,j] + minC_{b'}(j)}
13:            minC_b(i) += m_{b,b'}[i,t] + minC_{b'}(t)
14:            p_{b'}[i] = t
15:        end for
16:    end for
17: end function
18:
19: function SOLVE_RELOCATION(b)
20:    if b is root then
21:        Find minC_b(s) = min_{i∈pos(b)} {minC_b(i)}
22:        δ(b) = s
23:    else
24:        b* = parent(b)
25:        δ(b) = p_b[δ(b*)]
26:    end if
27:    for b' ∈ ch(b) do
28:        SOLVE_RELOCATION(b')
29:    end for
30: end function
```

Proof : The $minC_b$ of each leave vertex b are minimum. When $minC_{b'}$ for each child b' of b is optimally computed, the $minC_b$ is optimally computed by the induction formula (6). Finally, we can conclude that $minC_r$ of root r is optimally computed.

As indicated in Algorithm 1, to obtain the minimum cost the function COMPUTE_MINCOST(), each connection of G is examined once. For each connection $c_{b,b'}$, every entry of matrix $m_{b,b'}$ is checked for the $minC_b$ computation. For a tree with vertex number $|B|$, the number of tree connections is $|B| - 1$. The maximum size of the matrix $m_{b,b'}$ is $|B|^2$, since $|B|$ is also equal to the total number of 3D chip bin optional positions. Thus the complexity of computing minimum cost is in the order of $O(|B|^3)$.

To obtain the bin relocation solution δ by the function SOLVE _RELOCATION(), we first compute the position of the root r with minimum cost $minC_r$. The maximum size of $minC_r$ is equal to $|B|$. Each non-root vertex b is visited once by a top-down traversal procedure, and the position of b can be determined according to the position of $parent(b)$ directly. Therefore, the complexity of computing δ is in the order of $O(|B|)$.

In practice, the number of the candidate positions of each bin b is limited to a integer value (≤ 25 in our implementation). Therefore, the complexity of bin relocation algorithm is $O(|B|)$ when the connection graph is a tree.

For general case when the graph is not a tree, we set a weight to each connection edge $c_{b,b'}$ reflecting the number of nets across between b and b' (shown in Figure 2 (b)) and we generate a maximum spanning tree for each connected subgraph of the graph by the Kruskal algorithm [9] which has the complexity in the order of $O(|E|log|E|)$. Then, the bin relocation is processed for each subtree.

6. EXPERIMENTAL RESULTS

We implement the proposed framework in C++ and compiled with g++ 4.8.2 and make use of the ICCAD 2012 Contest [23] for the evaluations. Our experiments are done on a Linux workstation with a 3.40 GHz Intel Xeon CPU and 32 GB RAM, using one CPU core. The 3D placer result analysis is presented in the remainder of the section.

Table 1: Benchmark Characteristics

Bench mark	Net	Cell	Macro	2D Area (×E8)	3D Area (×E8)
sb1	822744	765102	52627	2.25×1.65	1.18×1.01
sb3	898001	833370	55033	2.56×1.66	1.36×0.99
sb4	567607	521466	40550	1.49×1.66	0.78×0.97
sb5	786999	677416	74365	2.48×2.28	1.27×1.31
sb7	1340418	1271887	66995	1.59×2.85	0.92×1.61
sb10	1158784	1045874	96251	2.18×3.10	1.21×1.67
sb16	697458	680450	419	1.49×1.61	0.80×0.96
sb18	468918	442405	25063	1.22×1.61	0.65×0.86
Avg.	-	-	-	1.00×1.00	0.54×0.57

ICCAD 2012 benchmark related information is listed in Table 1. The benchmark is one of the most recent benchmarks open for public access, and it is a very practical representation of circuit blocks utilized in real designs. The 2D placement results that we used as input to our 3D placer are taken from the best results of the top 4 placers in the ICCAD 2012 Contest [23].

The implemented 3D placer mainly consists of three parts: Placement Initialization (PI), Cell Relocation (CR), and 3D Post-Global Placement. For 3D post-global placement, we have implemented the two strategies mentioned in Section 3: (1) Fix layer (DP-FL), and (2) Purely 3D (DP-Pure3D). To evaluate the effectiveness of our techniques, we have built four 3D placer versions: (1) Base (PI & DP-FL), which is considered as the basic version of our 3D placer, (2) Base3D (PI & DP-Pure3D), which applies purely 3D post-global placement to assign cells into different layers, (3) CellRel (Base & CR), which includes the cell relocation technique in global placement for both overlap reduction and flatten HPWL optimization, and (4) CellRel3D (Base3D & CR), which applies both cell relocation and purely 3D post-global placement.

Furthermore, we also need a reference 3D placer as a comparison baseline for 3D related parameters, e.g., flatten HWPL. Unfortunately, to our best knowledge, there is no other 3D placer reported for the same benchmarks in literature. As so far, only a binary 3D placer "3D-Craft" [6] can be found, but it is used for LEF/DEF format in 45nm design, and our benchmarks are in bookshelf format without manufactory information. On that account, we have implemented a monolithic 3D placer "Analy3D" by modifying an analytical 2D placer according to [21] as the baseline reference. The analytical 2D placer is HPWL-driven using algorithms proposed in POLAR [18], which is one of recent top academic 2D placers. The 3D layer assignment for Analy3D is performed by an overlap-aware partitioner only, which can optimize the HPWL most without considering other performance objective. We use Analy3D for reference to estimate the HPWL cost when considering the 2D layout inheritance.

In the experiments, we use flatten HPWL and CPU runtime as metrics to evaluate placer effectiveness and performance, respectively, and the results are presented in Table 2.

As one can observe in Table 2, CellRel3D achieves the best flatten HPWL (FWL). When compared with the input 2D placement results, it reduces HPWL by 57% on average. However, the runtime of CellRel3D is the longest among the four 3D placer versions. The reason is that the standard cells can be moved among different layers, and the number of the optional cell positions is larger in DP-Pure3D than in DP-FL, thus the DP-Pure3D process takes more time to determine the cell positions. It is also indicated in Table 2 that the Flatten HPWL gap between our 3D placers and Analy3D is very small, i.e., only 4% for CellRel3D as the best scenario. But CellRel3D requires 12% less runtime than Analy3D, since our placer is based on transformation. We also have to mention that CellRel is only 3% and 7% worse in terms of HPWL but 8% and 20% faster than CellRel3D and Analy3D, respectively.

Table 2 presents the average extended displacement (Dis.) of cells for our placers and Analy3D. As one can observe, the average displacements of our placers are quite similar, and these displacements are usually generated by moving cells away from macros after placement initialization stage. As a comparison, since Analy3D does not consider the input 2D layout during placement, its average displacement is up to 34% larger than the results of our transformation-based methods. On this foundation, Figure 3 presents a visual comparison of the results from the mixed-size 3D transformation and the analytical placer Analy3D for the *superblue*18 benchmark. As one can observe, the node distribution (including macros and standard cells) within the CellRel3D placement results (see Figure 3(b)) is very similar with that within the 2D layout input. The relative macro positions are kept after the 3D tranformation. For a four-layer design, the chip footprint area is a little larger than one quarter of the input 2D chip area, since the 3D chip region needs to be expanded to contain the macros on the boundary after the 3D transformation. When compared with the CellRel3D generated layout, the Analy3D one (see Figure 3(c)) looks much more dense, because Analy3D is a HPWL-driven placer and doesn't take into consideration on the input 2D layout. Therefore, the analytical placer Analy3D fails on inheriting the layout information from the 2D placement input. We also note that if extra information, e.g., routability, is take into consideration, the Analy3D execution time increases dramatically.

Table 2 also presents an MIV number (MIV) comparison. Note that Analy3D uses overlap-aware partitioner for layer assignment, thus the Analy3D MIV number is utilized only for reference. In the placer Base, we do not change the cell's layer after initialization, thus the MIV number is equal to the MIV number of placement initialization. For the other three placers, cells can be moved among layers during the CR and DP-Pure3D processes, thus the MIV number may increase. Since in M3D IC design, MIV is much smaller than TSV, the via number is not the most important issue in M3D IC manufacturing. Therefore, the results of CellRel3D are still applicable. For those via-aware designs, i.e., using TSV manufacturing technology, we can choose CellRel for placement while maintains a fair effectiveness and good performance as illustrated in Table 2.

As a conclusion, our placers preserve the layout information from the 2D placement input, and since this information is proven to be beneficial for former 2D designs, substantial optimization effort and runtime is saved. This is a key fea-

Table 2: **Comparison of Flatten HPWL(×E8), Avg. Displacement(×E5), MIV (×E5), and CPU (×E3 s)**
(The results of 2D are obtained from top 4 contestants in ICCAD 2012 Contest [23].)

Ben ch.	2D	Base				Base3D				CellRel				CellRel3D				Analy3D			
	WL	FWL	Dis.	MIV	CPU	FWL	Dis.	MIV	CPU	FWL	Dis.	MIV	CPU	FWL	Dis.	MIV	CPU	FWL	Dis.	MIV	CPU
sb1	2.71	2.34	1.94	2.60	0.77	2.11	1.94	4.03	0.81	2.00	1.96	2.85	1.23	1.90	1.95	4.16	1.23	1.72	2.90	2.96	1.30
sb3	3.38	2.16	2.11	2.04	0.43	2.05	2.11	2.87	0.58	1.99	2.10	2.27	0.81	1.96	2.10	3.00	1.05	1.90	2.54	2.21	1.06
sb4	2.18	1.60	2.11	1.46	0.29	1.54	2.09	2.33	0.36	1.47	2.09	1.63	0.55	1.46	2.07	2.41	0.62	1.39	2.08	1.74	0.60
sb5	3.45	2.91	2.74	2.40	0.81	2.62	2.76	3.30	0.84	2.52	2.71	2.61	1.11	2.39	2.70	3.44	1.20	2.20	2.37	2.59	1.22
sb7	4.02	2.41	0.60	4.03	0.71	2.37	0.59	6.05	0.90	2.25	0.59	4.22	1.31	2.24	0.59	6.10	1.39	2.46	1.63	4.33	1.90
sb10	5.78	5.10	2.03	3.46	1.07	4.23	2.03	4.61	1.12	4.10	2.05	3.60	1.59	3.95	2.04	4.88	1.67	3.52	2.83	3.53	1.70
sb16	2.58	1.68	0.86	2.29	0.41	1.64	0.86	3.49	0.46	1.56	0.86	2.42	0.76	1.54	0.85	3.57	0.77	1.49	2.21	2.60	0.96
sb18	1.52	0.92	1.56	1.32	0.26	0.88	1.56	2.17	0.32	0.86	1.55	1.41	0.44	0.85	1.55	2.20	0.53	0.89	2.01	1.42	0.69
Avg.	1.57	1.17	1.01	0.66	0.56	1.07	1.01	0.97	0.64	1.03	1.00	0.71	0.92	1.00	1.00	1.00	1.00	0.96	1.34	0.72	1.12

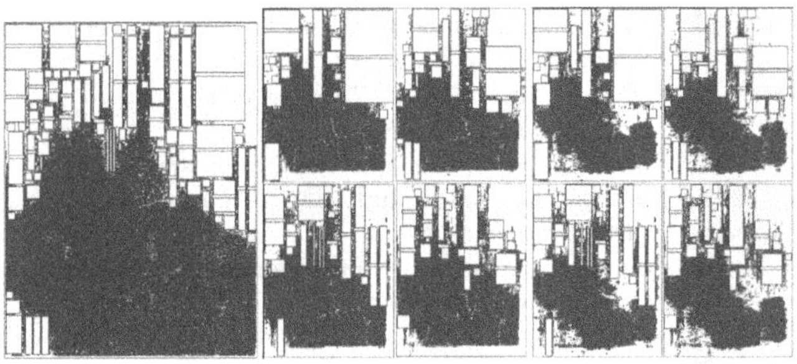
(a) Input 2D Layout (b) CellRel3D (c) Analy3D

Figure 3: An example to show the input 2D layout for superblue18 (a), the corresponding 3D layout (b) after our mixed-size 3D placer, and the result of analytical method Analy3D (c).

ture of our approach as it allows for the effective transformation of a 2D design into a 3D one, and/or for the utilization a state of the art 2D placer to generate a 3D placement.

7. CONCLUSION

In this paper, we propose a novel method of generating mixed-size 3D placement based on transforming a 2D placement result. First, we propose a mixed-size folding-based method to generating an initial 3D layout from input 2D layout. Second, an $O(N)$ algorithm of bin-based cell relocation is developed to improve both overlaps and flatten HPWL simultaneously and globally. Finally, we compare two different methods of post-global placement: (1) Fix layer, and (2) Purely 3D. The results show that , when compared with the 2D placement, the 3D placer can reduce the wirelength by 57%, and provide a four-layer 3D chip footprint of about one quarter of the 2D counterpart. Furthermore, the distribution of the input 2D layout is preserved by our 3D placer, which provides potential of performance inheritance.

8. ACKNOWLEDGMENTS

This work is supported by the National Natural Science Foundation of China under Grant No.: 61402505 and 61133007.

9. REFERENCES

[1] K. Athikulwongse and et al. Stress-driven 3D-IC placement with TSV keep-out zone and regularity study. In *ICCAD*, pages 669–674, 2010.

[2] K. Athikulwongse, M. Pathak, and S. K. Lim. Exploiting die-to-die thermal coupling in 3D IC placement. *TVLSI*, 22(10):741–746, 2012.

[3] P. Batude, M. Vinet, A. Pouydebasque, C. L. Royer, B. Previtali, C. Tabone, J. M. Hartmann, L. Sanchez, L. Baud, and V. Carron. Advances in 3D CMOS sequential integration. *IEDM*, pages 1–4, 2009.

[4] S. Bobba and et al. CELONCEL: Effective design technique for 3-D monolithic integration targeting high performance integrated circuits. In *ASPDAC*, pages 336–343, 2011.

[5] C.-C. Chang and J. Cong. An Efficient Approach to Multi-layer Layer Assignment with Application to Via Minimization. *TCAD*, 18(5):608–620, 1999.

[6] J. Cong and G. Luo. A Multilevel Analytical Placement for 3D ICs. In *ASPDAC*, pages 361–366, 2009.

[7] J. Cong, G. Luo, and Y. Shi. Thermal-aware cell and through-silicon-via co-placement for 3D ICs. In *DAC*, pages 670–675, 2011.

[8] J. Cong, G. Luo, J. Wei, and Y. Zhang. Thermal-Aware 3D IC Placement Via Transformation. In *ASPDAC*, pages 884–886, 2007.

[9] T. H. Cormen, C. E. Leiserson, R. L. Rivest, and C. Stein. *Introduction to Algorithms (Third Edition)*. The MIT Press, 2009.

[10] J. L. et al. ePlace-3D: Electrostatics based Placement for 3D-ICs. In *ISPD*, 2016.

[11] W. A. et al. "More-than-Moore" White Paper. In *ITRS, Tech. Rep.*, 2010.

[12] B. Goplen and S. Sapatnekar. Placement of 3D ICs with Thermal and Interlayer Via Considerations. In *DAC*, pages 626–631, 2007.

[13] S. Goto. An efficient algorithm for the two-dimensional placement problem in electrical circuit layout. *IEEE Transactions on Circuits and Systems*, 28(1):12–18, 1981.

[14] M. K. Hsu, V. Balabanov, and Y. W. Chang. TSV-Aware Analytical Placement for 3-D IC Designs Based on a Novel Weighted-Average Wirelength Model. *TCAD*, 32(4):497–509, 2013.

[15] S. M. Jung, H. Lim, K. H. Kwak, and K. Kim. A 500-MHz DDR High-Performance 72-Mb 3-D SRAM Fabricated With Laser-Induced Epitaxial c-Si Growth Technology for a Stand-Alone and Embedded Memory Application. *IEEE Transactions on Electron Devices*, 57(2):474–481, 2010.

[16] D. H. Kim and et al. Study of Through-Silicon-Via Impact on the 3-D Stacked IC Layout. *TVLSI*, 21(5):862–874, 2009.

[17] Y. J. Lee, D. Limbrick, and S. K. Lim. Power benefit study for ultra-high density transistor-level monolithic 3D ICs. In *DAC*, pages 1–10, 2013.

[18] T. Lin, C. Chu, J. R. Shinnerl, I. Bustany, and I. Nedelchev. POLAR: Placement based on novel rough legalization and refinement. In *ICCAD*, pages 357–362. IEEE, 2013.

[19] G. Luo, Y. Shi, and J. Cong. An Analytical Placement Framework for 3-D ICs and Its Extension on Thermal Awareness. *TCAD*, 32(4):510–523, 2013.

[20] M. Pan, N. Viswanathan, and C. Chu. An efficient and effective detailed placement algorithm. In *ICCAD*, pages 48–55. IEEE Computer Society, 2005.

[21] S. Panth, K. Samadi, Y. Du, and S. K. Lim. Placement-Driven Partitioning for Congestion Mitigation in Monolithic 3D IC Designs. *TCAD*, 34(4):540–553, 2015.

[22] S. Panth, K. Samadi, D. Yang, and S. K. Lim. Power-performance study of block-level monolithic 3D-ICs considering inter-tier performance variations. In *DAC*, pages 1–6, 2014.

[23] N. Viswanathan, C. Alpert, C. Sze, Z. Li, and Y. Wei. Iccad-2012 cad contest in design hierarchy aware routability-driven placement and benchmark suite. In *ICCAD*, pages 345–348. IEEE, 2012.

[24] N. Viswanathan, M. Pan, and C. Chu. Fastplace 2.0: An efficient analytical placer for mixed-mode designs. In *ASPDAC*, pages 221–223, 2006.

LightNN: Filling the Gap between Conventional Deep Neural Networks and Binarized Networks

Ruizhou Ding, Zeye Liu, Rongye Shi, Diana Marculescu, and R. D. (Shawn) Blanton
Department of Electrical and Computer Engineering
Carnegie Mellon University, Pittsburgh, PA, U.S.A.
{rding, zeyel, rongyes, dianam, rblanton}@andrew.cmu.edu

ABSTRACT

Application-specific integrated circuit (ASIC) implementations for Deep Neural Networks (DNNs) have been adopted in many systems because of their higher classification speed. However, although they may be characterized by better accuracy, larger DNNs require significant energy and area, thereby limiting their wide adoption. The energy consumption of DNNs is driven by both memory accesses and computation. Binarized Neural Networks (BNNs), as a trade-off between accuracy and energy consumption, can achieve great energy reduction, and have good accuracy for large DNNs due to its regularization effect. However, BNNs show poor accuracy when a smaller DNN configuration is adopted. In this paper, we propose a new DNN model, LightNN, which replaces the multiplications to one shift or a constrained number of shifts and adds. For a fixed DNN configuration, LightNNs have better accuracy at a slight energy increase than BNNs, yet are more energy efficient with only slightly less accuracy than conventional DNNs. Therefore, LightNNs provide more options for hardware designers to make trade-offs between accuracy and energy. Moreover, for large DNN configurations, LightNNs have a regularization effect, making them better in accuracy than conventional DNNs. These conclusions are verified by experiment using the MNIST and CIFAR-10 datasets for different DNN configurations.

1. INTRODUCTION

As a widely implemented machine learning model, deep neural networks (DNNs) have shown power in classification, due to their non-linear characteristics, flexible configurations and self-adaptive features [1]. Increasingly in recent years, research has focused on DNNs implemented directly in hardware for a variety of reasons stemming from design requirements or application characteristics. First, real-time classification applications (such as Siri and Google glass [2]) have great sensitivity to latency, thereby making pure hardware implementations better candidates than conventional architectures based on CPUs or GPUs. Second, neural networks implemented in custom ASICs require mostly logic with little complicated control, lending themselves to lower design effort. Third, heterogeneous architectures as a whole appear to be more suitable for DNN implementation due to the combined benefits of CPU, GPU, FPGA and ASIC-based hardware acceleration [3] [4]. In heterogeneous systems, ASICs can handle specific tasks that are required frequently, such as classification tasks in a real-time image recognition application, while CPUs and GPUs can perform the online training. However, hardware implementations of neural networks face difficulties for large scale deployment. With the increased use of DNNs, the number of layers and neurons increases significantly [5]. Google's AlphaGo adopts a 13-layer architecture, with hundreds of filters per layer [6]. Microsoft implements a 152-layer DNN for image classification [7]. An increasing number of neurons and connections in DNNs require significant energy and power, thereby limiting their wide adoption [5].

Permission to make digital or hard copies of all or part of this work for personal or classroom use is granted without fee provided that copies are not made or distributed for profit or commercial advantage and that copies bear this notice and the full citation on the first page. Copyrights for components of this work owned by others than ACM must be honored. Abstracting with credit is permitted. To copy otherwise, or republish, to post on servers or to redistribute to lists, requires prior specific permission and/or a fee. Request permissions from Permissions@acm.org.
GLSVLSI '17, May 10-12, 2017, Banff, AB, Canada
© 2017 ACM. ISBN 978-1-4503-4972-7/17/05...$15.00
DOI: http://dx.doi.org/10.1145/3060403.3060465

2. RELATED WORK

The two main factors limiting the energy efficiency of computing systems in general, and DNN architectures in particular, are memory accesses and computation. Much of the prior research has focused on the computation. Du *et al.* adopt inexact circuits for multipliers and adders with less dynamic energy consumption [3]. Li *et al.* reduce energy with memristor-based approximators [8], while Kim *et al.* propose an approximate adder to reduce energy [9]. Sarwar *et al.* use alphabet set multipliers that implement multiplication by selection, shifts and adds, reducing energy of neural networks with a pre-computed bank [10]. These works can reduce the energy consumption of DNNs, and some [3] [8] [9] are also compatible with models introduced in this paper.

There has also been significant work on reducing energy of memory accesses. Gupta *et al.* reduce accesses to memory by limiting parameter precision [11]. Furthermore, Venkataramani *et al.* propose an energy-efficient neural network design approach by reducing bit precision of resilient neurons [12], while Zhang *et al.* combine computation approximation and memory access reduction, and propose an approximate computing framework of NNs [13]. Han *et al.* compressed DNNs to reduce weight storage [14]. Hubara *et al.* proposed BNNs, which constrain the weights and activations to be binary values (+1 or -1) and achieve almost no accuracy loss for MNIST and CIFAR-10 datasets [15]. Moreover, the reported accuracy for MNIST is even better than the conventional DNN architecture, especially when the DNN configuration is very large, with many more layers and neurons than typical. On the other hand, BNNs have notably worse accuracy when the smaller Caffe example configurations for MNIST and CIFAR-10 are implemented.

In this paper, we focus on both computation and memory access energy reduction. We propose a new DNN model, LightNN, by replacing multipliers with one shift or a limited number of shifts and adds. Marchesi *et al.* proposed the idea of replacing multipliers of multi-layer perceptrons (MLP) with shifts [16]. Different from their proposed training algorithm where the weights are constrained to be power of 2 after every iteration, we maintain a set of continuous weights and only use the constrained weights in the forward pass. In addition, we test LightNNs on real datasets, and compare their accuracy, energy and area with conventional DNNs and BNNs. LightNNs are also different from Sarwar *et al.* where the weights are broken down into two parts with an equal number of shift operations [10]. Instead, LightNNs maintain weights as a whole and only constrain the total number of shifts. Furthermore, we explore the energy consumption of memory accesses. To the best of our knowledge, our work makes the following contributions:

1. Similar to prior work [3] [8]-[15], we consider the scenario where DNNs are trained in software and used for classification in hardware. Different from prior work, we propose a new neural network architecture, LightNN, which features simpler, more energy-efficient logic. Note that LightNN is ***compatible*** with prior work [3] [11] [14] since it can be adopted either standalone, or in conjunction with other approaches.
2. Compared to BNNs where all the weights are constrained to $+1$ or -1, we relax this constraint and achieve better accuracy than BNNs while still maintaining lower power and area than conventional DNNs. The advantage of this relaxation is that hardware designers can have more options to select the model according to their resource constraint. For a fixed DNN configuration, LightNNs have better accuracy at a slight energy increase than BNNs, yet are more energy efficient with only slightly less accuracy than DNNs. It is worth noting that both LightNNs and BNNs have a regularization effect, thereby achieving higher accuracy than conventional DNNs for large configurations.
3. We compare the accuracy, energy and area of conventional DNNs, BNNs and LightNNs via industrial-strength design simulation, for the MNIST and CIFAR-10 datasets. A set of guidelines for model selection *w.r.t.* accuracy and energy is provided. We also implement a non-pipeline version of conventional DNNs and LightNNs for datasets from the UCI machine learning repository [17], and confirm that LightNNs are compatible with approaches that use limited bit precision for inputs and intermediate results [11].

The rest of this paper is organized as follows. In Section 3, we first introduce conventional DNNs and BNNs, and propose LightNN with its training scheme. Experiment results are shown in Section 4, including accuracy, storage, energy and area for conventional DNNs, BNNs and LightNNs. Section 5 concludes the paper.

3. DNN ARCHITECTURE

In this section, we first describe the operation of conventional DNNs. Then, we introduce the architecture and the training scheme of BNNs. Finally, we propose the new DNN architecture, LightNN, and describe its associated training scheme.

3.1 Conventional DNNs

An artificial neural network (ANN) is called a DNN when there are more than four layers, including the input and output layers. In the *training phase* with a back-propagation algorithm [18], the loss function, such as the l_2-*norm*, *cross-entropy loss,* or *hinge loss*, is computed using output values and data labels, to update the weights used for the linear combination described above. In the *deployment (testing) phase*, the output neuron with the largest value indicates the prediction result. During deployment, the vast majority of computation resources are used for the multiplication within DNNs [3]. Therefore, prior research has focused on replacing multiplication with other types of logic operations that are more energy-efficient. One successful example is BNN.

3.2 BNNs

Two types of binarized neural networks (BNNs) have been proposed by Courbariaux *et al.* BinaryConnect [19], a type of BNN, only constrains the weights to $\mathbf{+1}$ or $\mathbf{-1}$, but leaves the inputs and intermediate results as floating point values. On the other hand, a second BNN known as BinaryNet [15], constrains both weights and intermediate results (activations) to $\mathbf{+1}$ or $\mathbf{-1}$, and only keeps the input values as floating point.

To train a BinaryConnect or BinaryNet, the classic back-propagation algorithm is adopted. The only change is that during each forward pass, the weights are copied and binarized. Then, the binarized copy of weights is used to compute the gradients. Note that the updated weights are always stored as original floating point values and only in the forward pass of training phase and during testing phase, the weights are binarized [19].

During the testing, BinaryNet is different from BinaryConnect only in that it uses a binarized activation function, thereby having binarized intermediate results. In the testing phase, a sign function $\boldsymbol{f(x) = sign(x)}$ is used as the activation function. In the training phase, hard tanh function, defined as $\boldsymbol{Htanh(x) = clip(x, -1, 1)}$, is used as a substitute for the sign function [15]. The benefit of BinaryNet is that it can further regularize the DNN and can use an XNOR operation to replace multiplications in a hardware implementation.

3.3 LightNNs

Replacing multiplications with a shift or a limited number of shifts and adds can serve as a way to build more energy-efficient DNNs and regularize them, thereby producing better accuracy. The detailed architecture and training algorithm are introduced next.

3.3.1 Model Architecture

In binary representations, any parameter w can be written as a sum of powers of two $w = sign(w) \cdot (2^{n_1} + 2^{n_2} + \cdots + 2^{n_K})$, where K is the number of 1s in w's binary representation. A multiplication of two values w and x is equal to several shifts and additions:

$$\begin{aligned} w \cdot x &= sign(w) \cdot (2^{n_1} + 2^{n_2} + \cdots + 2^{n_K}) \cdot x \\ &= sign(w) \cdot (x \ll n_1 + x \ll n_2 + \cdots + x \ll n_K) \quad (1) \end{aligned}$$

where "$x \ll n_1$" means left-shifting x by n_1 bits. For negative values of n_1, right-shifts are used instead. Assuming $n_1 > n_2 > \cdots > n_K$, smaller n values correspond to a less significant part of the result $w \cdot x$. Furthermore, logical shift units are more energy efficient than multipliers. Therefore, the computation energy consumption can be reduced by converting multiplications to approximate versions using a limited number of shifts (and adds). LightNNs change the computation logic of each neuron. A *k-ones approximation* drops the least significant powers of two in equation (1) such that the resulting value has at most k ones in its binary representation. Figure 1 illustrates a basic example that utilizes a neuron with two inputs. Two weights w_1 and w_2 are both converted to a 2-ones approximation: $w_1 \approx 2^{n_{11}} + 2^{n_{12}}$, $w_2 \approx 2^{n_{21}} + 2^{n_{22}}$. Therefore, a multiplication $w \cdot x$ is changed to two shifts and one addition. Moreover, when $k = 1$, the equivalent multiplier unit is only a shift.

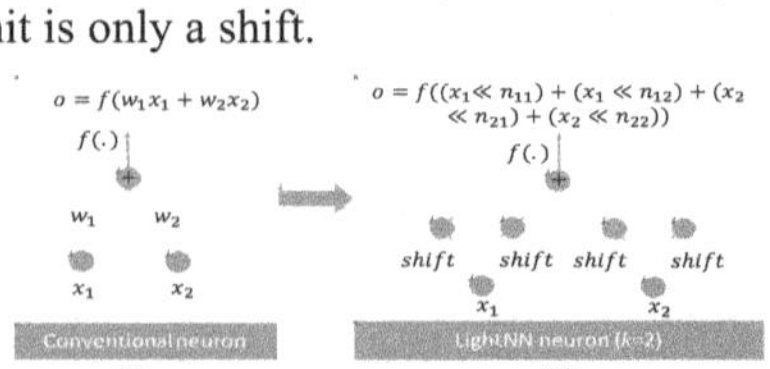

Figure 1. (a) A conventional neuron and, (b) LightNN neuron implemented using a 2-ones approximation

Furthermore, we use a stochastic rounding scheme [11]. As opposed to a *rounding-to-nearest* scheme, the *stochastic rounding* scheme finds both the nearest higher value w_h and the nearest lower value w_l, and stochastically rounds w to one of them based on a probability distribution:

$$w = \begin{cases} w_h, & with\ prob\ p \\ w_l, & with\ prob\ 1-p \end{cases},$$

where $p = \frac{w-w_l}{w_h-w_l}$. Intuitively, stochastic rounding ensures that the expected error introduced by the rounding scheme is zero.

3.3.2 LightNN Training

We adopt a training algorithm similar to that of BNNs. As shown in Algorithm 1, during each training epoch, the forward pass constrains the weights, and provides intermediate results and loss function. Then, the backward pass computes the derivatives of the loss function over the parameters. After that, the parameters are updated based on the derivatives. It is worth noting that weight constraint occurs only in the forward pass. When updating the weights, we use $\boldsymbol{w_{t-1}} - \eta\frac{\partial l}{\partial w_c}$ instead of $\boldsymbol{w_c} - \eta\frac{\partial l}{\partial w_c}$, where $\boldsymbol{w_{t-1}}$ is the real-value weights after $(t-1)$-th iterations, $\boldsymbol{w_c}$ is the constrained $\boldsymbol{w_{t-1}}$, η is the learning rate, and l is the loss function. Therefore, the weights are always accumulated in a floating point form. As stated by Courbariaux *et al.* [19], the reason to maintain high resolution for the weights is that the noise needs to be averaged out by the stochastic gradient contributions accumulated in each weight.

After a LightNN is trained, the last step is to perform the k-ones approximation for all weights. Then, the constrained weights are used for testing.

Algorithm 1. LightNN Training Epoch

Input: Training dataset $(\boldsymbol{x}, \boldsymbol{y})$, where $\boldsymbol{x}$ is input and $\boldsymbol{y}$ is label; parameters after the $(\boldsymbol{t}-\boldsymbol{1})$-th iteration: $\boldsymbol{w_{t-1}}$ (weights) and $\boldsymbol{b_{t-1}}$ (biases); DNN forward computation function $\boldsymbol{f}(\boldsymbol{x}, \boldsymbol{w}, \boldsymbol{b})$; $\boldsymbol{k}$ value used for $\boldsymbol{k}$-ones approximation $\boldsymbol{approx_k}(\cdot)$; learning rate $\boldsymbol{\eta}$.

Output: Updated weights $\boldsymbol{w_t}$ and biases $\boldsymbol{b_t}$

For each mini-batch of $(\boldsymbol{x}, \boldsymbol{y})$, **do**

1. **Constrain weights:** $\boldsymbol{w_c} = \boldsymbol{approx_k}(\boldsymbol{w_{t-1}})$
2. **Forward:** compute intermediate results and loss function $\boldsymbol{l}$ with $\boldsymbol{f}(\cdot)$, $\boldsymbol{w_c}$, $\boldsymbol{b_{t-1}}$, and mini-batch of $\boldsymbol{x}$
3. **Backward:** compute derivatives $\frac{\partial l}{\partial w_c}$ and $\frac{\partial l}{\partial b_{t-1}}$
4. **Update parameters:** $\boldsymbol{w_t} = \boldsymbol{w_{t-1}} - \boldsymbol{\eta}\frac{\partial l}{\partial w_c}$, and $\boldsymbol{b_t} = \boldsymbol{b_{t-1}} - \boldsymbol{\eta}\frac{\partial l}{\partial b_{t-1}}$

End For

3.3.3 LightNN with Binarized Activations

We can also use a binarized activation function described in Section 3.2 for LightNNs. The advantages of doing so are twofold. First, the multiplication of a weight and an input of a neuron will be limited to ± 1 multiplied by a power of two if the weights are constrained to k-ones approximations where $k = 1$. This leads to an increased likelihood of achieving energy reduction within a hardware implementation. Second, binarized activations also inherently perform a regularization, beneficial to eliminating overfitting for large DNN configurations.

4. EXPERIMENTS

In this section, we compare conventional DNNs, LightNNs, and BNNs in terms of accuracy, storage, energy consumption and area. We also present a guideline for selecting models for hardware implementations to meet the needs of different applications.

4.1 Accuracy

We first introduce the experiment set-up, including the models, datasets, DNN configurations and training approaches. Then, the accuracy results of different models are reported and compared.

4.1.1 Set-up

Models. Seven models are considered – conventional DNN, LightNN-2, LightNN-1, BinaryConnect, LightNN-2-bin, LightNN-1-bin, and BinaryNet. Table 1 describes their main characteristics. ReLU activation function is adopted in the first four models, while the last three models use the hard tanh function for training and the sign function for testing.

Datasets. We test the seven models on two datasets – MNIST and CIFAR-10. The MNIST dataset contains 70,000 gray-scale hand-written images, while CIFAR-10 contains 60,000 colored images for animals or vehicles.

DNN configurations. Both multi-layer perceptrons (MLPs) and convolutional neural networks (CNNs) are adopted for MNIST and CIFAR-10. We selected five configurations as shown in Table 2. The basic idea is to include both small and large DNN configurations, to determine how different models perform under varying configurations. **3-hidden** for MNIST and **6-conv** for CIFAR-10 are two large configurations used by Courbariaux *et al.* [15] [19]. **2-conv** for MNIST and **3-conv** for CIFAR-10 are two smaller configurations borrowed from Caffe examples [20]. **1-hidden** for MNSIT is a simple configuration adopted by prior research [10].

Training approach. The training algorithm is described in Section 3. Batch normalization and dropout techniques are adopted to accelerate training and avoid overfitting, respectively. The dataset is divided into training set, validation set, and test set. The validation set is used for selecting the best epoch. The same number of total training epochs is applied to all models and the test error of the epoch with the lowest validation error is reported. These models are trained on Theano platform [21]. We use existing open source models [22] to train conventional DNN, BinaryConnect and BinaryNet. Finally, hinge loss function and ADAM learning rule are used to train all seven models [23].

Table 1. Constraints on seven models.

Model	Weights	Activation function	Intermediate results	Inputs
Conventional DNN	floating	ReLU	floating	floating
LightNN-2	$\pm(2^{-m_1}+2^{-m_2})$, $m_1, m_2 = 0,1,\ldots,7$	ReLU	floating	floating
LightNN-1	$\pm 2^{-m}, m = 0,1,\ldots,7$	ReLU	floating	floating
BinaryConnect	+1 or -1	ReLU	floating	floating
LightNN-2-bin	$\pm(2^{-m_1}+2^{-m_2})$, $m_1, m_2 = 0,1,\ldots,7$	Sign	+1 or -1	floating
LightNN-1-bin	$\pm 2^{-m}, m = 0,1,\ldots,7$	Sign	+1 or -1	floating
BinaryNet	+1 or -1	Sign	+1 or -1	floating

Table 2. Five configurations for two datasets.

Dataset	Configuration	Detail
MNIST	**1-hidden**	One hidden layer with 100 neurons
	2-conv	Two convolution layers and two fully-connected layers
	3-hidden	Three hidden layers each with 4096 neurons
CIFAR-10	**3-conv**	Three convolution layers and one fully-connected layer
	6-conv	Six convolution layers and three fully-connected layers

Table 3. Test error and the number of parameters for all models.

		MNIST			CIFAR-10	
		1-hidden	2-conv	3-hidden	3-conv	6-conv
Number of parameters		79,510	431,080	36,818,954	82,208	39,191,690
Test error	Conventional	1.72%	0.86%	0.75%	21.16%	10.94%
	LightNN-2	1.86%	1.29%	0.83%	24.62%	8.84%
	LightNN-1	2.09%	2.31%	0.89%	26.11%	8.79%
	BinaryConnect	4.10%	4.63%	1.29%	43.22%	9.90%
	LightNN-2-bin	2.94%	1.67%	0.89%	32.58%	10.12%
	LightNN-1-bin	3.10%	1.86%	0.94%	36.56%	9.05%
	BinaryNet	6.79%	3.16%	0.96%	73.82%	11.40%

4.1.2 Results

Comparison. The test error for all configurations and datasets is reported in Table 3. For most configurations (except a few), the accuracy decreases from: conventional, LightNN-2, LightNN-1, LightNN-2-bin, LightNN-1-bin, BinaryConnect, BinaryNet. This is because when we constrain the weights and activations, the model suffers from varying levels of accuracy loss.

Regularization. Interestingly, we note that for CIFAR-10 **6-conv** configuration, the conventional DNN performs no better than other models. This shows the regularization effect of weight constraints. When the DNN is relatively large, it tends to overfit and trap within a local optimum. In this case, weight constraints serve as a regularization method to avoid overfitting [19].

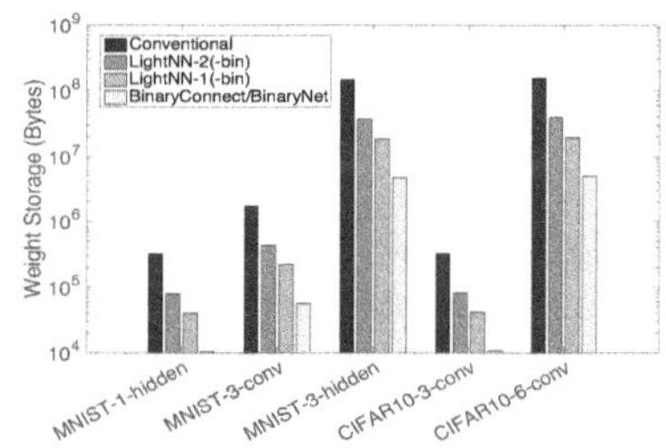

Figure 2. Storage (for weights) required by different models under varying datasets and configurations.

4.2 Storage requirements

The weight storage requirements for different models are compared in Figure 2. Since the constraint on activations does not affect weight storage, we only show four models. While it has been shown that limited bit precision can also lead to good accuracy [11], we retain the 32-bit representation for the conventional DNN as baseline. Therefore, a weight in conventional DNNs has four bytes, while in BinaryConnect and BinaryNet, it has only one bit. To store a weight $w = \pm 2^{-m}$, LightNN-1 and LightNN-1-bin need four bits: one bit for $sign(w)$ and another three bits for $|m|$. LightNN-2 and LightNN-2-bin need seven bits for a weight $w = \pm(2^{-m_1} + 2^{-m_2})$: one bit for $sign(w)$, three bits for $|m_1|$ and three bits for $|m_2|$. For easier hardware implementation, one byte is used for a weight of LightNN-2 or LightNN-2-bin. Storage affects the number of memory accesses, and is thereby essential to energy consumption, which is shown in Section 4.3.

4.3 Energy and Area

4.3.1 Set-up

For all seven models under consideration, we designed pipelined implementations with one stage per neuron. The weights and inputs are initially stored in the memory, and fetched to the pipeline stage logic to compute the output for all neurons in that layer; intermediate results are written back. A 65nm commercial standard library is adopted. The logic computations circuit of one neuron is composed using Synopsys Designware commercial IP [24] (e.g. floating point multiplication and addition). The Synopsys Design Compiler [25] is used to generate the gate-level netlist and measure the circuit area. The power consumption of one neuron circuit is calculated using Synopsys Primetime [26]. Cacti [27] is used to obtain the power of memory accesses and registers. While prior work describes approaches (such as data reuse) to optimize the CNN hardware implementation [28], we keep all the models implemented an unoptimized fashion because our main objective is to compare how constraining weights impacts both computation and memory access energy. The size of the register files is chosen to accommodate the data size required for the computation of the largest neuron.

4.3.2 Multipliers vs. equivalent multiply units

Power and area of each multiplier or equivalent multiply unit in all models under consideration are explored first. For BinaryConnect and BinaryNet, a multiply unit is simply an XNOR gate [15]. For LightNN-1 and LightNN-1-bin, it is a shift unit. Since operands (e.g., unbinarized weights, activations and inputs) are represented as single-precision float-point., the shift operation is equivalent to an integer addition for the exponent. LightNN-2 and LightNN-2-bin both rely on two shifts and an add operation. The adder required by LightNN-2 is floating point, while LightNN-2-bin only needs an integer adder to perform fixed point addition. The area and power are reported in Figure 3.

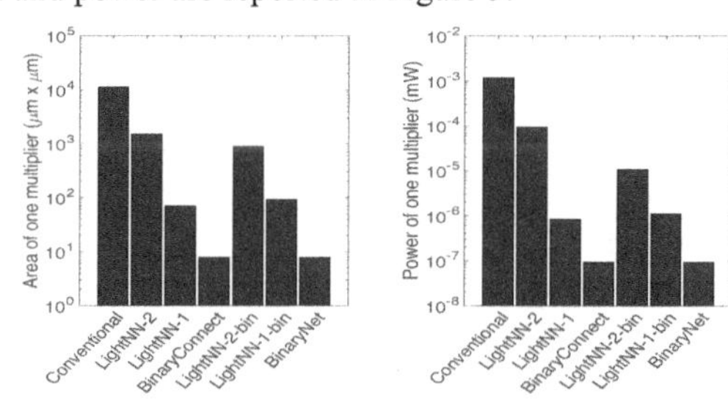

Figure 3. Area and power of an equivalent multiply unit across all models.

4.3.3 Energy comparison

Figure 4 shows the comparison of energy consumption for all seven models considered. Under the same DNN configuration, conventional DNNs and BinaryNet are always the most and least energy-consuming model, respectively. Furthermore, LightNN-2 is more energy-consuming than LightNN-1 and LightNN-2-bin, both of which consume more energy than LightNN-1-bin. When comparing LightNN-1 and LightNN-2-bin, the former has fewer bits for each weight, and therefore consumes less energy for each memory access, while the latter has more energy-efficient logic. The results in Figure 4 show that LightNN-1 has higher energy consumption than LightNN-2-bin in all configurations except MNIST **1-hidden**. The same comparison holds for the BinaryConnect and LightNN-1-bin, where BinaryConnect has more energy-consuming logic circuitry (e.g., floating point adder) while LightNN-1-bin has larger weight storage.

Although BinaryNet always has the lowest energy consumption under the same configuration, its high accuracy only occurs when the configuration is very large. For example, conventional DNN with **2-conv** can surpass BinaryNet with **3-hidden** in terms of both accuracy and energy consumption.

To explore the energy composition for each model, we report the results in Figure 5. Specifically, the various components of energy are averaged across different configurations and datasets. For the conventional DNNs with floating point circuitry, the most energy-consuming part is the computational portions, while the majority of energy in LightNN-2-bin, LightNN-1-bin and BinaryNet is consumed by memory accesses, though the absolute values are still smaller than that of conventional DNNs. We also break down the logic energy into leakage, switch and internal energy, where the switch energy is caused by switched load capacitance, and the internal energy is due to internal device switching. The leakage, switch and internal energy take 31.6%, 35.2% and 33.2% respectively, averaged on all models and configurations.

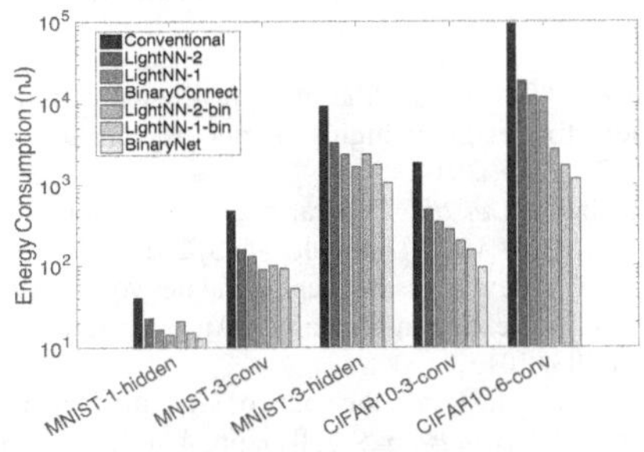

Figure 4. Comparison of energy consumption of different models under varying datasets/configurations. Energy consumption is measured for inferring a single image.

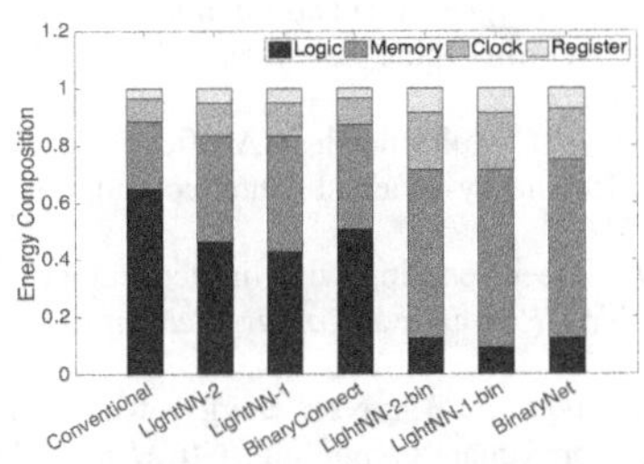

Figure 5. Energy breakdown for all models, averaged across different datasets and configurations.

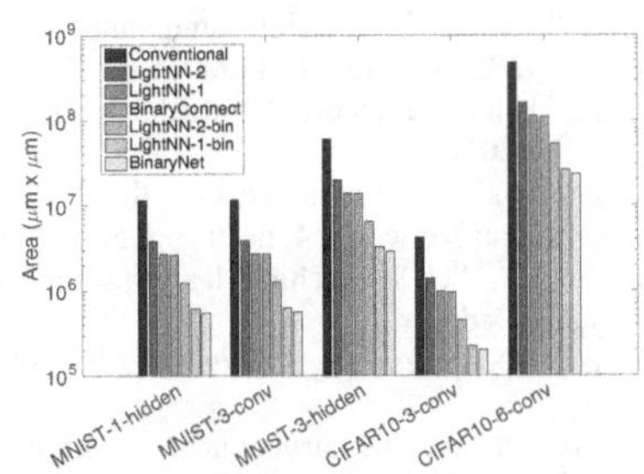

Figure 6. Comparison of area of different models under varying datasets and configurations.

4.3.4 *Area comparison*

We also compare the area of the seven models under varying configurations in Figure 6. Note that the reported area includes both logic circuits and register files. Also note that the DNN inference is implemented in a pipeline fashion, and the logic is set to handle the largest neuron count in each configuration. Since more computation modules indicate larger area, but fewer memory fetches, the absolute values for the area encompass the energy consumption reported in Figure 4. However, the comparison of different models within a configuration is still meaningful since they use the same (largest) neuron count. The models follow a consistent order (from larger area to smaller): Conventional DNNs, LightNN-2, LightNN-1, BinaryConnect, LightNN-2-bin, LightNN-1-bin, and BinaryNet.

4.3.5 *Guidelines for model selection*

An interesting question is whether there is a model that always surpasses another in terms of both accuracy and energy, under varying configurations and datasets? The answer is no. However, with constraints on accuracy or energy, some models are more preferable than others. Suppose one will implement DNN for MNIST on hardware with the constraint that energy consumption per inference is below 200nJ. In this case, the LightNN-2 model with **2-conv** configuration is selected, since it has the highest accuracy.

Does higher accuracy always require higher energy? Again, the answer is no. A comparison of different models and configurations are presented in Figure 7. Only the red triangles are the Pareto-optimal ones in terms of accuracy and energy.

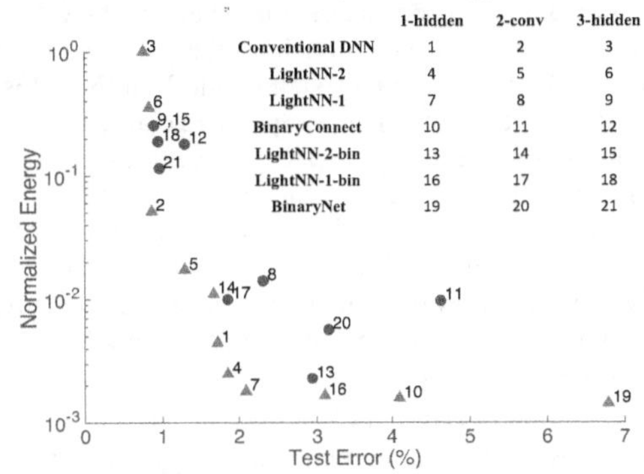

(a)

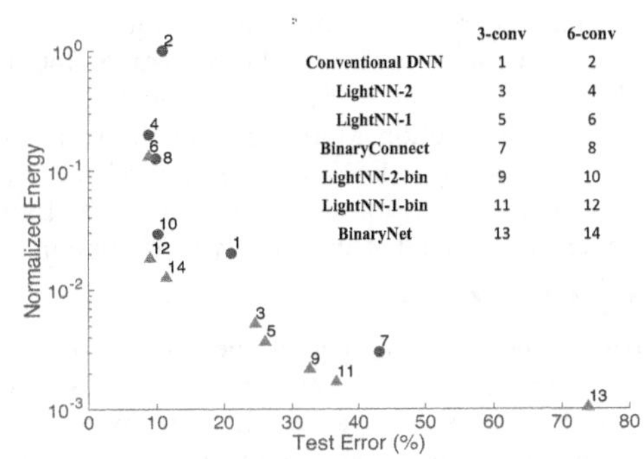

(b)

Figure 7. Normalized energy and test error of varying models and configurations for (a) MNIST and (b) Cifar-10. Red triangles are Pareto-optimal.

4.4 Non-pipeline Implementation

To further explore how LightNNs perform in a non-pipeline implementation, we implement the ANNs for five benchmarks from the UCI machine learning repository [17]: *abalone, banknote-authentication, transfusion, sinknonsink,* and *balance-scale.* They are chosen because of their small ANN configurations, making direct implementations of whole ANNs doable. The size of the datasets varies from 600 (*balance*) to 200,000 (*sinknonsink*), so a greater coverage is ensured. Instead of computing each neuron at one stage, the non-pipeline implementation builds the whole ANNs for each dataset. Moreover, to confirm that LightNNs are compatible with the use of limited bit precision for inputs and intermediate results [11], we use both 32-bit and 12-bit implementations. Similar to Section 4.3, the ANNs are implemented using Synopsys Designware commercial IP [24].

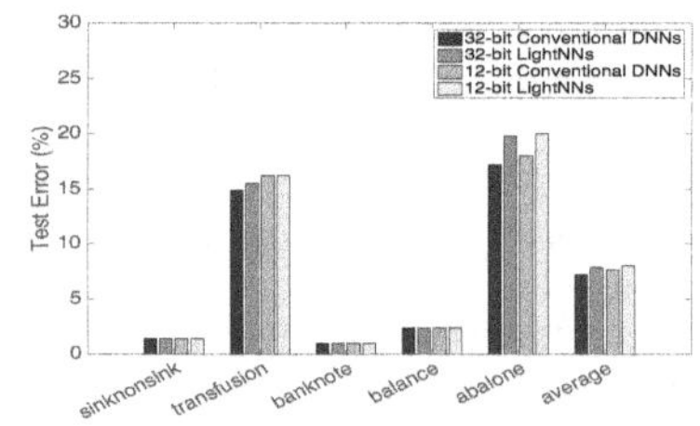

Figure 8. Test accuracy of conventional DNNs and LightNNs with 32-bit and 12-bit implementation.

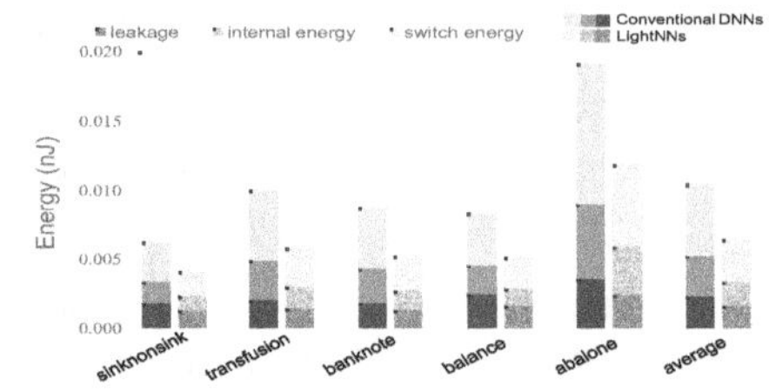

Figure 9. Energy of 12-bit conventional DNNs and LightNNs.

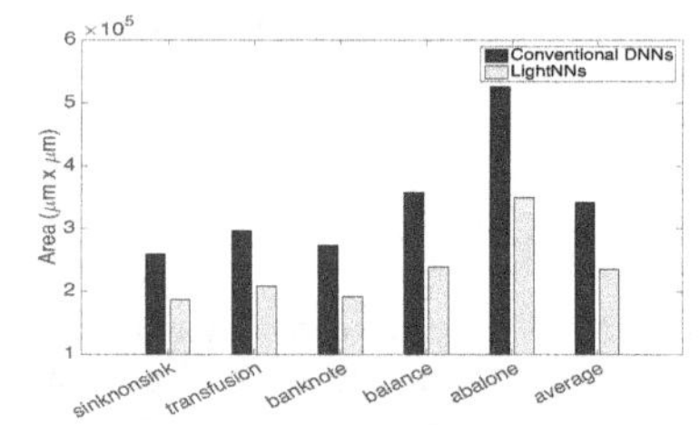

Figure 10. Area of 12-bit conventional DNNs and LightNNs.

4.4.1 Accuracy

Figure 8 shows the accuracy for the testing phase for the five benchmarks. All of them are trained with 2-ones stochastic approximation. For each benchmark, the accuracy of the 12-bit and 32-bit configurations are shown for both the conventional DNNs and LightNNs. From an accuracy standpoint, LightNNs lose only 0.66% and 0.40% accuracy when compared to conventional DNNs for 32- and 12-bit implementations, respectively. Furthermore, the accuracy results for 32- and 12-bit data confirm that the additional error incurred by limiting numerical precision is quite small [11]. Finally, the small accuracy differences between 32-bit and 12-bit LightNNs prove that they have high tolerance for limited precision, thereby showing their compatibility with prior work [11]-[13].

4.4.2 Energy and area

12-bit conventional DNNs and LightNNs for the five benchmarks are implemented and all three types of energy consumption are measured: leakage, internal, and switch energy, all shown in Figure 9. The area is also compared in Figure 10. Note that the energy and area are reported only for the logic. The use of LightNNs reduces total energy by 38.8% on average. Both leakage and dynamic energy are reduced, benefiting from the more energy efficient logic implementation. More precisely, the area of a 12-bit multiplier is reduced by 61.6% by the use of the LightNN multiplier. As a result, fewer transistors are required by LightNNs, leading to less leakage and dynamic energy consumption.

5. CONCLUSIONS

The increasing demand of neural networks for real-time classification, and the trend of heterogeneous systems leveraging the high speed of ASICs, accelerate the pace of ASIC implementations for DNNs. Due to the increasing size of DNNs, energy and area requirements have become a very challenging problem. LightNNs modify the computation logic of conventional DNNs by making reasonable approximations, and replace the multipliers with more energy-efficient operators involving only one shift or limited shift-and-add operations. In addition, LightNNs also reduce weight storage, thereby decreasing the memory access energy. Experiment results show that LightNNs fill the gap between conventional DNNs and BNNs in terms of accuracy, storage, energy and area, and provide more options for hardware designers to select DNN models based on their accuracy and resource constraints.

6. ACKNOWLEDGEMENT

This research was supported in part by NSF CCF Grant No. 1314876 and NSF CCF Grant No. 1331804.

7. REFERENCES

[1] G. P. Zhang, "Neural networks for classification: a survey." *Systems, Man, and Cybernetics, Part C: Applications and Reviews, IEEE Transactions on*, 30(4), pp. 451-462, 2000.

[2] J. Hauswald *et al.*, "DjiNN and Tonic: DNN as a service and its implications for future warehouse scale computers." *ACM ISCA*, pp. 27-40, 2015.

[3] Z. Du *et al.*, "Leveraging the error resilience of machine-learning applications for designing highly energy efficient accelerators." *ASP-DAC,* pp. 201-206, 2014.

[4] A. Yazdanbakhsh *et al.*, "Neural acceleration for GPU throughput processors." *ACM MICRO,* pp. 482-493, 2015.

[5] L. Deng *et al.*, "New types of deep neural network learning for speech recognition and related applications: An overview." *IEEE ICASSP*, pp. 8599-8603, 2013.

[6] D. Silver *et al.*, "Mastering the game of Go with deep neural networks and tree search." *Nature*, *529*(7587), pp. 484-489, 2016.

[7] K. He *et al.*, "Deep Residual Learning for Image Recognition." *CVPR. arXiv preprint arXiv:1512.03385*, 2016.

[8] B. Li *et al.*, "Memristor-based approximated computation." *IEEE ISLPED*, pp. 242-247, 2013.

[9] Y. Kim *et al.*, "An energy efficient approximate adder with carry skip for error resilient neuromorphic vlsi systems." *IEEE ICCAD,* pp. 130-137, 2013.

[10] S. S. Sarwar, *et al.*, "Multiplier-less Artificial Neurons exploiting error resiliency for energy-efficient neural computing." *IEEE DATE*, pp. 145-150, 2016.

[11] S. Gupta *et al.*, "Deep learning with limited numerical precision." *ICML, JMLR: W&CP* volume 37. *arXiv preprint arXiv:1502.02551,* 2015.

[12] S. Venkataramani *et al.*, "AxNN: energy-efficient neuromorphic systems using approximate computing." *ACM ISLPED,* pp. 27-32, 2014.

[13] Q. Zhang *et al.*, "ApproxANN: an approximate computing framework for artificial neural network." *DATE*, pp. 701-706, 2015.

[14] H. Song, *et al.*, "Learning both weights and connections for efficient neural network." *NIPS*, pp. 1135-1143, 2015.

[15] I. Hubara, *et al.*, "Binarized Neural Networks." *NIPS*. arXiv preprint arXiv:1602.02505, 2016.s

[16] M. Marchesi, *et al.*, "Fast neural networks without multipliers." IEEE transactions on Neural Networks 4, no. 1, pp. 53-62, 1993.

[17] A. Asuncion *et al.*, "UCI machine learning repository.", 2007. http://archive.ics.uci.edu/ml/

[18] Y. LeCun *et al.*, "Deep learning." *Nature*, *521*(7553), pp.436-444, 2015.

[19] M. Courbariaux, et al., "Binaryconnect: Training deep neural networks with binary weights during propagations." NIPS, pp. 3123-3131, 2015.

[20] https://github.com/BVLC/caffe/tree/master/examples

[21] http://deeplearning.net/software/theano

[22] https://github.com/MatthieuCourbariaux/BinaryNet

[23] D. Kingma, *et al.*, "A method for stochastic optimization." arXiv preprint arXiv:1412.6980, 2014.

[24] https://www.synopsys.com/designware-ip/soc-infrastructure-ip/designware-library.html

[25] Synopsys, Inc., Synopsys Design Compiler. Product Version 14.9. 2014.

[26] https://www.synopsys.com/implementation-and-signoff/signoff/primetime.html

[27] N. Muralimanohar, *et al.*, "Cacti 6.0: A tool to model large caches." HP Laboratories, pp. 22–31, 2009.

[28] R. Andri, *et al.*, "YodaNN: An ultra-low power convolutional neural network accelerator based on binary weights." *IEEE ISVLSI*, pp. 236-241, 2016.

Design of a Flash-based Circuit for Multi-valued Logic

Monther Abusultan Sunil P. Khatri
ECE Department, Texas A&M University, College Station, TX 77843.

ABSTRACT

Flash transistors serve as the technology of choice for implementing non-volatile memory. Current flash memory densities are increasing to meet storage demands. One of the key features that has resulted in increasing flash memory densities is the ability to program a flash transistor to have multiple threshold voltages. This feature has recently been exploited to implement ternary-valued logic. However, this implementation exhibited increased delays, due to the lowered V_{gs} values which result from using multiple threshold voltages. In this work, we present a circuit implementation that uses flash transistors to implement multi-valued digital circuits. The flash transistors used in our implementation only need two threshold voltages. As a result they have high V_{gs} values which improves delays significantly, and have higher write endurance as well. We evaluate our design methodology through circuit simulations, and compare our results to a CMOS standard cell based approach as well as the previously reported implementation of ternary-valued logic using flash transistors. Averaged over 20 designs, we report improvements in delay (23% lower), power (5% lower), energy (26% lower) and physical area (4% lower) compared to a CMOS standard cell based implementation. This is significant since it is hard for a new circuit approach to beat the established standard cell based approach in all the figures of merit (delay, area, power and energy. Compared to the ternary flash-based implementation, we operate at 3.15× faster than the ternary flash-based designs, while consuming more power and energy. The design approach presented in this paper targets high performance applications, unlike the TLC-based approach which targets low power and low speed applications. Also, the proposed approach scales elegantly to multi-valued logic using more than three values as well.

Keywords: Multi-valued logic; Flash-based Digital Design; Logic using Flash; Lower power; High speed; Ternary-valued;

1. INTRODUCTION

A flash transistor has four terminals (drain, gate, source and body) that are contacted. However, a flash transistor also has a buried gate (which is called *floating gate*) inside the dielectric material between the channel and the contacted gate (which is called *the control gate*). The floating gate is used as a reservoir to trap electrons when the flash transistor is programmed. Programming the flash transistors increases its threshold voltage. The flash transistor can also be "erased", which results in its threshold voltage reverting to the erased threshold voltage level. Flash transistors are programmed and erased using Fowler-Nordheim (FN) tunneling [1].

There are two approaches to implement multi-valued digital circuits. The first approach, which was introduced in [2], uses flash transistors with three V_T levels to implement ternary-valued logic functions. In [2], the structure that implements the ternary-valued logic is called a ternary logic cluster (TLC). One could implement four-valued (or more) flash-based digital circuits by using four V_T levels (or more). However, increasing the number of V_T levels would result in a very expensive delay penalty, due to the fact that the V_{gs} values of the flash devices would be lowered.

The second approach, which is presented in this paper, is based on the idea of implementing multi-valued logic using a one-hot implementation. In this implementation, instead of using multiple V_T levels to implement multi-valued logic, flash transistors will only be programmed to one of two V_T levels, the erase V_T level (we call it VT_0) and the program V_T level (we call it VT_1). This has many benefits, such as – a) using two V_T levels instead of three (or more) results in higher V_{gs} values, which improves the design's speed, b) using *single-level cells* (SLCs) which have improved write endurance as well as tolerance to read and write disturbs, compared to the *multi-level cells* (MLCs) used in [2] and c) the scheme of this paper generalizes to multi-valued logic with 4 or more values elegantly, with no V_{gs} reduction and speed penalties compared to the approach of [2].

This paper presents a multi-valued logic flash-based design approach. The circuit structure used to implement the multi-valued logic functions is called *a multi-valued flash cluster* (MVFC). The threshold voltage of the flash devices in the MVFC is controlled to implement different logic functions. This structure implements combinational logic only, and is fully compatible with the sequential logic elements used in digital designs. In this paper, we compare the MVFC design approach to both the CMOS standard cell design approach as well as a previously proposed ternary-valued flash-based design approach [2]. Our MVFC-based design approach can implement multi-valued logic functions with 4 or more values. However, we implement ternary-valued logic functions to compare with the work presented in [2].

The market need for dense and compact flash memory has fueled the advancement in flash technology. The technology node of flash devices has recently been able to track the CMOS technology node. Currently memory devices are being fabricated at sub-20nm minimum feature dimensions, similar to the minimum feature of CMOS technology nodes [3, 4, 5, 6]. In this work, we only explore our design approach with a 45nm technology because electrical characteristics of flash technology nodes below 45nm are not easily available.

We evaluate the delay, power, energy and physical area of our implementation, and compare these results to a CMOS standard cell based design approach. On average, over 20 random designs, our MVFC-based design approach yields 23% delay, 5% lower power, 26% lower energy and 4% physical area reduction, when compared with CMOS standard cell-based design approach. Additionally, our implementation operates at 3.1× the speed of TLC-based designs, which comes with an increase in power and energy. The area utilization of our MVFC-based design approach is similar to that of the TLC-based design approach (the MVFC is 1% larger than the TLC-based). Between the TLC and the MVFC approaches, a designer has a way to explore the tradeoff between delay, power and energy of the design.

The key contributions of this paper are:

- This paper presents a flash-based design approach to implement

Permission to make digital or hard copies of all or part of this work for personal or classroom use is granted without fee provided that copies are not made or distributed for profit or commercial advantage and that copies bear this notice and the full citation on the first page. Copyrights for components of this work owned by others than ACM must be honored. Abstracting with credit is permitted. To copy otherwise, or republish, to post on servers or to redistribute to lists, requires prior specific permission and/or a fee. Request permissions from permissions@acm.org.
GLSVLSI '17, May 10-12, 2017, Banff, AB, Canada
Copyright 2017 ACM. ISBN 978-1-4503-4972-7/17/05 ...$15.00
DOI: http://dx.doi.org/10.1145/3060403.3060452

multi-valued logic functions with an arbitrary number of values.

- The MVFC-based circuit approach presented in this paper achieves significant improvements in delay (0.77× of CMOS), power (0.95× of CMOS), energy (0.96× of CMOS) and physical area (0.74× of CMOS). It is rare for a new circuit methodology to beat CMOS standard-cells in all these metrics.
- The MVFC presented in this paper runs at 3.1× the speed of the TLC, with a penalty in power (7.9× the power of the TLC) and energy (2.5× the energy of the TLC).
- Unlike the TLC-based design approach in [2] which targets low power/energy applications, the MVFC design approach targets high speed applications.
- By precisely controlling the threshold voltage of the flash transistors, the proposed flash-based design approach has the ability to control speed binning (at the factory), perform age mitigation (in the field) and facilitate engineering change orders (ECOs) by precisely controlling the threshold voltage of the flash transistors.

The remainder of this paper is organized as follows. Section 2 discusses some previous work. Section 3 describes our MVFC-based implementation approach. Section 4 discusses experiments and results. We conclude in Section 5.

2. PREVIOUS WORK

Flash-based digital design approach [2, 7, 8] has recently been introduced and proven to produce appealing results compared to the popular CMOS standard cell based design approach. These flash-based digital design approaches addressed the implementation of binary logic [7, 8] and ternary-valued logic [2] using flash transistors.

In [2], the authors used a structure called *ternary logic clusters* (TLCs), which use multiple threshold voltage levels to implement ternary-valued logic functions. Although this approach has benefits, the use of using multiple threshold voltages has some drawbacks. One of the issues that arise from using multiple threshold voltages is decreased write endurance, since programming a flash transistor becomes harder and requires a longer process of V_T adjustment, thus degrading the write endurance of the device. Another issue is read and write disturbs, since the threshold voltage levels are closer to each other and hence a read or write disturb could change the threshold level of a victim cell enough to hurt the proper operation of the circuit. Finally, using multiple threshold voltages between VDD and GND reduces the V_{gs} values applied to the flash transistors which lowers the currents flowing through the flash device when its on, resulting in increased delays. Also, the TLC structure used in [2] consists of NAND flash-like pulldown stacks. Those stacks require 2 flash transistors in series per multi-valued variable. So a 4-variable TLC would require 8 series transistors. The use of long series stack results in an additional increase in the delay of the design. In our work, we address these issues by using two threshold voltage levels only (one for program and one for erase), and use pulldown stacks that only have 1 flash transistor per input variable. These changes in the design result in an increase in the speed of the multi-valued flash-based designs by more than 3× the speeds reported in [2]. However, this improvement in speed incurred an increase in power and energy. Compared to CMOS standard cells, however, the MVFCs are faster (by 23%) and consume less energy (by 26%) and power (by 5%) as well.

The authors of [7] presented a flash-based design approach to implement binary logic circuits. In their implementation, they use a *flash cluster* (FC). The FC consists of an array of NAND flash-like pulldown stacks. Each stack has 6 flash transistors (one transistors per variable). Our work achieves lowered delays compared to the FC-based designs approach, since we use only 4 flash transistors in series. The use of a shorter pulldown stack also increases the power of the MVFC design by 42%, compared to the FC. In [8], the authors applied the design approach in [7] on more complex designs at the block-level.

3. APPROACH

3.1 Overview

The focus of this paper is on the circuit details of the multi-valued flash cluster (MVFC). However, before describing the circuit details of the MVFC, we will briefly outline how a design can be mapped into a flash-based design using a network of MVFCs. Our MVFC structure is capable of implementing multi-valued logic with arbitrary number of logic values. However, we choose ternary-valued logic in order to compare the performance of our approach to that in [2]. In this paper, each MVFC implements a ternary logic function $G_{p,q}$, where p is the number of inputs and q is the number of outputs. Our simulations have shown that choosing $p = 4$ and $q = 2$ yields the best results. After describing the mapping procedure, we describe the MVFC structure, the configuration of the MVFC cell and the MVFC programming.

3.2 Flash-based Design Conversion

Multi-valued flash clusters implement q-output (multi-valued) functions with up to p multi-valued inputs ($G_{p,q}$). Therefore, to implement an entire digital design using MVFC cells, we need to represent the digital design using functions of the type $G_{p,q}$. This is done starting with a technology-independent logic netlist, and grouping the logic nodes into clusters. These clusters of logic are constructed so as to meet the criteria of the number of inputs (p or fewer) and number of outputs (q or fewer) that can be implemented by an MVFC. Note that the technology-independent logic netlist represents binary logic, and hence, we need to convert the binary logic functions into multi-valued logic functions (ternary-valued logic functions in our implementation). The process of converting binary logic functions into multi-valued logic functions is described next and is followed by a discussion on mapping of a technology-independent logic netlist into an MVFC-based design.

3.3 Multi-valued Logic Flash-based Design Conversion

In this section, we show how we convert a binary logic function into a multi-valued logic function (ternary-valued in our implementation). We perform this conversion in two steps. The first step is to implement the entire design using an interconnected network of MVFCs, and the second step is to identify the MVFC cells that implement the logic at the I/O interfaces of the digital design and appropriately configure them as shown later in this section.

In this paper we need to convert the binary functions in the logic cluster into ternary-valued logic functions to be implemented using our MVFC cell. In our implementation, we convert each binary logic function with u inputs binary (which has 2^u binary minterms) into a v-input ternary-valued logic function (which has 3^v ternary-valued minterms). This is done by mapping the 2^u binary minterms into 3^v ternary-valued minterms. Since, there is no value of $u > 0$ and $v > 0$ that results in a solution for the equation $2^u = 3^v$, we have to choose u and v such that $2^u < 3^v$ (to be able to map all the binary minterms). However, this choice will result in *unused* ternary minterms. It was found that choosing $u = 3$ and $v = 2$ results in the least number of unused ternary-valued minterms. As a result, when implementing a digital design using MVFC cells, we cluster binary logic nodes such that the numbers of inputs and outputs that are multiples of 3. This yields a ternary-valued function with inputs and outputs that are multiples of 2. This issue of unused minterms can be entirely avoided if we implement multi-valued logic with k values, where $k = 2^w$. In such a case, mapping a binary function into a multi-valued function is straightforward and can be done by encoding w binary bits in each 2^w-valued multi-valued digit. As mentioned earlier, the reason we are implementing ternary-valued logic is to compare the multi-valued implementation approach of this paper to that presented in [2], which also discusses a ternary-valued logic design approach.

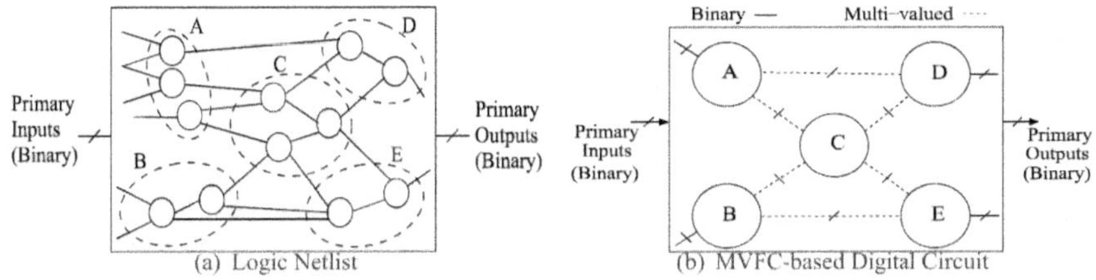

(a) Logic Netlist (b) MVFC-based Digital Circuit

Figure 1: Converting a Logic Netlist into an MVFC-based Design

From a block-level perspective, the mapping of a binary logic design into a ternary-valued logic design is shown in Figure 1. Figure 1(a) shows a binary logic netlist that consist of a network of interconnected logic nodes. We perform the conversion process by grouping the logic nodes into clusters of logic that have no more than m binary inputs and n binary outputs. The logic function representing this cluster of logic is $F_{m,n}$. Recall that in order to efficiently map a binary logic function into a ternary-valued logic, the binary logic function should have a number of inputs and outputs that are multiples of 3. These clusters of logic nodes (represented by the dashed ovals in Figure 1(a)) are then mapped into MVFCs (represented by the solid circles in Figure 1(b)). Each MVFC implements a ternary-valued logic function $G_{p,q}$, where $p = \frac{2}{3}m$ and $q = \frac{2}{3}n$. Our simulations have shown that choosing $m = 6$, $n = 3$ (which results in $p = 4$ and $q = 2$) yields the best results.

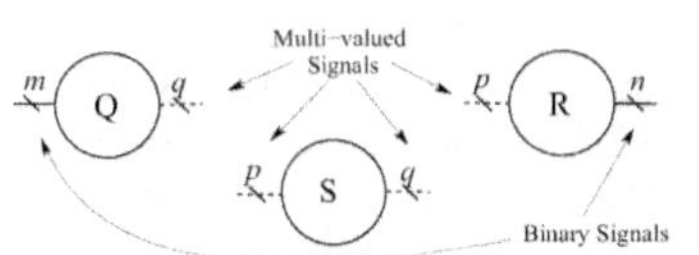

Figure 2: MVFC Types in our Implementation.

After discussing the conversion of a binary logic netlist into a network of interconnected MVFCs (each implementing a ternary-valued logic function), we will address the binary I/O interfaces, since the MVFC-based design implements parts of a whole binary system and will require to interface with binary logic. Our MVFC-based design approach can natively interface with binary logic *without* the need for adding circuits dedicated to encode the binary signals into multi-valued signals. This reduces design overhead, complexity of the design and area utilization. Figure 2 shows the types of MVFCs used in our implementation. In the figure, we represent binary signals with a solid line, and multi-valued (ternary-valued in our implementation) with dashed lines. The MVFCs used at the input interfaces of a logic design have binary input and multi-valued output (type Q) as shown in Figure 2. We use MVFCs that have ternary-valued inputs and binary outputs (type R) at the output interfaces of our multi-valued flash-based design. The remaining MVFCs used in our design approach have ternary-valued inputs and outputs (type S) and are used internally. Note that, an MVFC can have a mix of binary and ternary-valued inputs (or outputs) in order to implement clusters that have some of their inputs (or outputs) being binary and the remaining inputs (or outputs) being ternary-valued.

3.4 Multi-valued Flash Cluster Circuit Design

The flash-based design approach presented in this paper maps multi-valued logic functions (ternary-valued in our implementation) into multi-valued flash clusters (MVFCs). Figure 3 shows the structure of an MVFC. MVFCs are dynamic circuit structures that implement the cubes of a multi-valued logic function $G_{p,q}$, where p is the number of inputs and q is the number of outputs. Recall that the multi-valued logic function $G_{p,q}$ is equivalent to the binary logic function $F_{m,n}$, where $p = \frac{2}{3}m$ and $q = \frac{2}{3}n$. Each MVFC consists of an array of NAND flash-like pulldown stacks (each stack implements a cube of the multi-valued logic function $G_{p,q}$). These pulldown stacks are grouped based on their output. We call these groups *multi-valued logic arrays* (MVLAs). Since the MVFC is a dynamic circuit, the outputs of the MVFC are pre-discharged to GND using the *oPch* circuit. The oPch circuit block consists of pulldown NMOS transistors driven by the clock signal (*clk*). The oPch circuit pre-discharges the primary outputs of the MVFC as shown in Figure 3. The primary inputs of the MVFC drive the MVLAs. Also, the clock signal (*clk*) also drives precharge and evaluate transistors in the MVLAs. In our implementation, the number of primary outputs of the MVFC is 2 ($q = 2$), and the number of primary inputs is 4 ($p = 4$). The MVFCs also include the programming logic that is required to program the flash transistors in the structure to implement the desired function $G_{p,q}$.

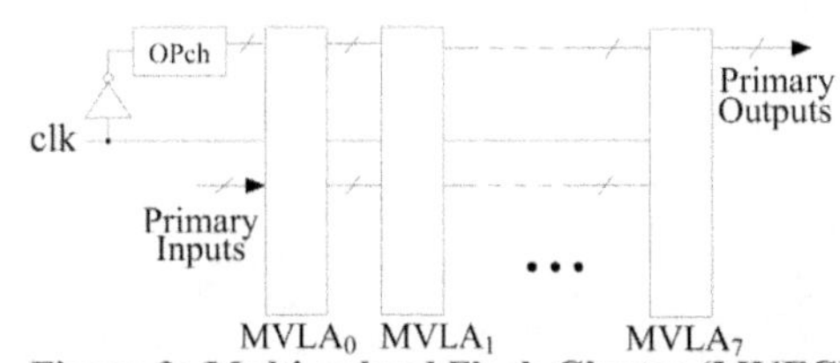

Figure 3: Multi-valued Flash Cluster (MVFC)

As mentioned earlier, each MVFC consists of a group of MVLAs, where $MVLA_k$ generates the kth output minterm of the function $G_{p,q}$. For example, let the 3 ternary-valued input cubes (represented using the multi-valued positional notation) $< 010|111|100|001 >$, $< 001|100|010|001 >$ and $< 100|010|010|100 >$ generate the output $< 010|100 >$, which is the 5th output in decimal notation. In this case, $MVLA_5$ consists of 3 pulldown stacks, where each stack implements one of the input cubes mentioned above. The number of cubes implemented in any $MVLA_k$ is called *cubes per array* (CPA_k). The values of CPA_k are determined by the logic function $G_{p,q}$. In our MVFC-based design approach, only one of the MVLAs pulls down when an input minterm is applied to the MVFC, since input minterms are not shared among different MVLAs. Finally, the outputs 2^n through $3^q - 1$ are not used, and hence, we do not implement $MVLA_{(2^n)}$ through $MVLA_{(3^q-1)}$. In our MVFC-based design approach, we only implement 2^n MVLAs (shown as $MVLA_0$, $MVLA_1$, $\cdots$, $MVLA_7$ in Figure 3, for $n = 3$.

3.5 Multi-valued Logic Array

The delay of the MVLA increases as the number of cubes in the MVLA increases. This is a result of the increase in output diffusion capacitance incurred from using a wire-or evaluation style of the MVLA. The delay of the MVLA is improved by splitting the pulldown stacks implemented in each MVLA into bundles of pulldown stacks where each bundle has a limited number of pulldown stacks (shown in Figure 4). These bundles are called *multi-valued logic bundles* (MVLBs). The circuit details of MVLBs are covered in Section 3.6. The number of maximum pulldown stacks per MVLB is called *cubes per bundle* (CPB). In our implementation, it was found through parametric sweeps that $CPB = 3$ yields the best results. CPB is a global parameter that is fixed for all MVFC-based designs. For example, assume that $MVLA_i$ has CPA_i cubes in total, then the total number of MVLBs in $MVLA_i$ is $\lceil \frac{CPA_i}{CPB} \rceil$. Note that all the MVLBs in each MVLA generate the same output, however, each one of them has its own output generation logic.

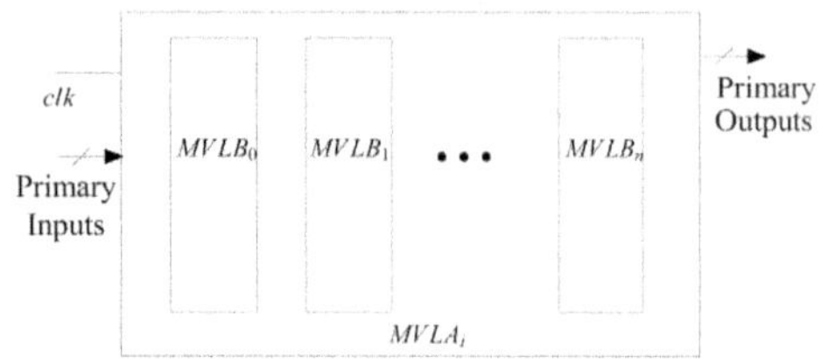

Figure 4: i^{th} Multi-valued Logic Array (MVLA$_i$) Structure.

3.6 Multi-valued Logic Bundles

In Figure 5 we show the circuit details of an MVLB. The MVLB can be split into two portions – a) the input logic, and b) the output logic.

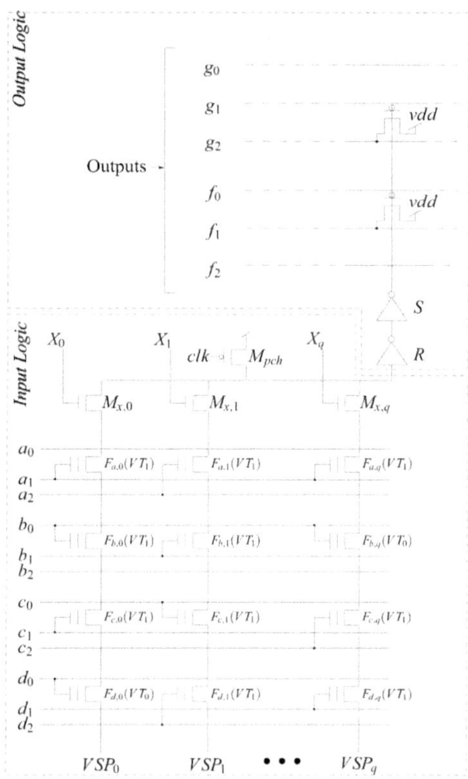

Figure 5: k^{th} Multi-valued Logic Bundle in MVLA$_i$ (MVLB$_{i,k}$)

The input logic (shown inside the bottom dashed area in Figure 5) consists of the NAND flash-like pulldown stacks. These stacks share the same output in a wire-OR configuration. Each one of the pulldown stacks implements a cube of the function $G_{p,q}$. The maximum number of cubes any MVLB can implement is *CPB*, which is an electrically determined parameter that is used to improve the quality (power, delay and area) of the MVFC-based designs. As shown in Figure 5, each pulldown stack in the MVLB has p flash transistors and 1 regular NMOS transistor (as shown in Figure 5). The multi-valued inputs of the function $G_{p,q}$ are implemented using one-hot representation. For example, since we are implementing ternary-valued logic, we represent the inputs a, b, c and d using their literals a_0, a_1 and a_2 for the input a, b_0, b_1 and b_2 for the input b, and similarly for the inputs c and d. For each input, only one of its literals will be high based on the input value. We will explain the configuration of the pull down stack using an example in Section 3.7. The flash transistors are programmed to implement cubes, while the regular NMOS transistor is used for evaluate and program purposes. The shared regular PMOS transistor shown at the top of the *input logic* block of Figure 5 (M_{pch}) serves as the precharge transistor for all pulldown structures of the MVLB. When it turns on, it pulls up $MVLBout_{i,k}$ during the precharge (low) phase of the clock signal (clk). The lines VSP_0 to VSP_q are connected to ground during operation to allow the NAND stacks to pull down when they evaluate, but also have a special purpose during programming, which will be discussed in Section 3.8. The regular NMOS transistors ($M_{x,i}$) shown at the top of each stack in Figure 5 serve two purposes. In regular operation they are used as the evaluate transistors and are off during the precharge (low) phase of clk and only turn on during the evaluate (high) phase of clk. In this way, they allow the pulldown stack to evaluate the output $MVLBout_{i,k}$. The NMOS transistors ($M_{x,i}$) are also used during the programming of the NAND flash stack. Programming will be discussed in detail in Section 3.8.

The output logic (shown inside the top dashed area in Figure 5) generates the final output of the MVFC. Each MVLB has a dedicated output logic that activates when one of the pulldown stacks of the MVLB pulls down (when the applied input minterm is contained in one of the cubes implemented by this MVLB). When the output logic is activated, it pulls up the corresponding pre-discharged output lines, generating the final output. The horizontal lines shown in the top part of Figure 5 represent one of the final one-hot output lines in the MVFC. These output lines run across the entire MVFC, as shown in Figure 3. As mentioned in Section 3.4, the output lines are pre-discharged using NMOS transistors in the oPch circuit shown in Figure 3. The output logic circuit has PMOS transistors that charge the output lines based on which output this MVLB drives. For example, if the current MVLB is part of $MVLA_5$, then the ternary-valued output generated by this MVLB is $< 010|100 >$. As a result, the output logic will connect the drains of two PMOS transistors to the lines f_1 and g_2, respectively (given that f is the most significant output bit). This is illustrated in Figure 5. The gates of these two PMOS transistors are driven by the buffered output of the NAND flash-like pulldown stacks, as shown in Figure 5. These PMOS transistors are sized to drive a load equivalent to input load of 3 MVFCs.

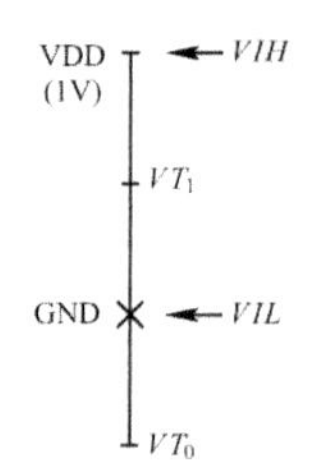

Figure 6: Threshold Voltages used in Multi-valued Flash-based Designs

3.7 MVLB Configuration

Unlike the TLC-based approach presented in [2] which uses 3 V_T levels, the MVLC-based design approach uses two V_T levels only. Figure 6 shows (on the left side), the input voltages applied to the gate of the flash devices in the MVLC. On the right side, the figure shows the V_T levels used to configure the flash transistors in the MVLC. The MVLC is configured by first determining which input cubes of the function $G_{p,q}$ are implemented by each MVLA. $MVLA_k$ implements all cubes that produce the output vector whose decimal encoding is k. Then each MVLA is split into a group of MVLBs based on the number of cubes implemented by this MVLA. The input cubes of the function $G_{p,q}$ are configured in the MVLB (shown in Figure 5) by choosing the V_T of the flash transistors in the stack corresponding to the input cube. Table 1 shows the configuration of each flash transistor for each literal. The flash transistors in the MVLC can only be configured to implement the literals $< 001 >$, $< 010 >$, $< 100 >$ and $< 111 >$. The remaining literals shown in Table 1 cannot be represented by the MVFC design approach. For example, the left-most stack of Figure 5 implements the ternary-valued cube $< abcd > = < 010|001|010|111 >$. Note that the transistor $F_{d,0}$ is driven by the literal d_0 and is programmed to a threshold voltage VT_0 which is below GND (see Figure 6). The threshold voltage VT_0 is also referred to as the *erase* threshold voltage. Therefore, this transistor is *on* irrespective of the value of the literal d_0. In other words, this transistor is *on* irrespective of the value of the input d, and hence implements the multi-valued literal of $< 111 >$ for d. In fact, the flash transistors that are programmed to VT_0 are always driven by the 0th literal of their input, only because they cannot be left floating. Now, the transistors $F_{a,0}$, $F_{b,0}$ and $F_{c,0}$ are programmed to a threshold voltage VT_1, which is between VDD and GND (see Figure 6). This means that these devices turn on only when their gate signal is high. The transistors $F_{a,0}$, $F_{b,0}$ and $F_{c,0}$ are driven by the signals a_1, b_0 and c_1 respectively. As a consequence, the left-most stack of Figure 5 implements the cube $< abcd > = < 010|001|010|111 >$.

Literal	V_T of F_x	Gate Input
001	VT_1	x_0
010	VT_1	x_1
100	VT_1	x_2
011	Not supported	N/A
110	Not supported	N/A
101	Not supported	N/A
111	VT_1	x_0
000	Invalid	N/A

Table 1: Flash Transistor Configuration F_x for each Minterm/Cube Literal.

The second stack of Figure 5 implements the cube $< 100|010|001|100 >$. Note that all of its transistors are programmed to the VT_1 threshold, which is why it implements a minterm in the p-input space of $G_{p,q}$. Finally, the rightmost stack of Figure 5 implements the cube $< 010|111|100|010 >$.

3.8 Programming the Multi-valued Flash Cluster

Figure 5 shows the MVLB circuit structure, including both the input logic and the output logic parts. The input logic is the only part that has flash transistors and requires programming. The output logic part does not contain flash transistors, and hence, does not require programming.

In an MVFC, all the flash transistors share a common bulk. As a result, the flash transistors in the MVFC are all erased together. This is performed by driving the bulk node of the MVFC to a high voltage, and floating the source and drain terminals of each flash transistor. The source and drain terminals of the flash transistors in each stack are floated by turning off the $M_{x,i}$ transistors and floating the signals VSP_i. The gates of all transistors are driven to GND. This results in the erasure of all the flash transistors in the MVFC, and resets their threshold voltage to VT_0.

For programming, assume that $F_{b,0}$ and $F_{b,1}$ need to be programmed. In this case, the b_0 and b_1 lines are driven to a programming voltage for a sufficiently long duration. The transistors $M_{x,0}$ and $M_{x,1}$ are turned on by driving X_0 and X_1 high. All other X_i are driven low. Also, the lines VSP_0 and VSP_1 are driven low and the remaining VSP_i lines are floated. This disables programming of all but the 1st and 2nd NAND stacks of the MVLB. All other inputs (i.e. $a_0, a_1, a_2, b_2, c_0, c_1, c_2, d_0, d_1$ and d_2) are driven high to a pass voltage, and the common bulk is held to GND. The duration of the programming pulse is determined based on the final desired V_T. This results in a programming of $F_{b,0}$ and $F_{b,1}$ to the desired V_T (VT_1), while the threshold voltage levels of all other transistors in the MVLB are unaltered and stay at the erase threshold voltage (VT_0).

3.9 Logic Minimization of the MVFC

We use Espresso-MV [9] to minimize the logic function ($G_{p,q}$) before implementing it in the MVFC (recall $G_{p,q}$ has p inputs and q outputs). The input minterms $\{m_j\}$ of each output minterm j are minimized separately using Espresso-MV. We ensure that Espresso-MV does not generate any unsupported input literal as shown in Table 1. If the unsupported literals are produced, they are split (for example a literal $< 101 >$ can cause a cube to be split into 2 cubes, one with literal $< 100 >$ and the other with literal $< 001 >$. The resulted minimized cover is used to configure the MVFC.

4. EXPERIMENTS

In this paper, we compare our MVLC-based design approach to the CMOS standard cell-based and the TLC-based [2] design approaches. In this section, we first present the simulation environment used in evaluating our proposed design approach. Then, we present the details of our experiments and discuss the results.

4.1 Simulation Environment

In our experiments, we evaluate the flash-based designs using flash design flows (MVFC and TLC), and CMOS-based designs using a CMOS standard cell design flow. In all three design flows, we implement the same benchmark circuits using the flash-based and the CMOS-based design approaches and compare the results obtained by each design approach. We implement all design approaches in 45nm process technology.

For the CMOS-based design approach, we use Synopsys Design Compiler [10] to synthesize and map the benchmark circuits. We use the 45nm Nangate FreePDK45 Open Cell Library [11, 12] to implement the CMOS-based designs. The mapped designs are then simulated using HSPICE circuit simulator from Synopsys [10] using a 45nm PTM model card [13]. Layout areas were computed as the sum of cell areas.

For the flash-based design approach, we used custom scripts to generate the circuits. We also used HSPICE to simulate the flash-based circuits. The CMOS devices in the flash-based designs were modeled using a 45nm PTM model card, and the flash devices used a model card that we generated using model card regression from device measurements obtained for a fabricated 45nm flash device as described in [2]. For flash-based design approaches, we verified the correct logical operation through exhaustive simulation. We generated custom layouts for the multi-valued digital circuit using Cadence Virtuoso. The layout of our MVFCs used design rules for flash devices that were compiled from the ITRS [14]. The layout area for the flash-based designs are more accurate than those for the CMOS standard cell-based designs (which are lower bounds of the true area).

We generated 20 random designs to evaluate our multi-valued digital circuit design approach. These designs implement binary logic functions of 6 inputs and 3 outputs, and were converted into multi-valued designs (ternary-valued in this paper) as described previously in Section 3.3. The logic functions implemented in the MVFCs in this paper have 4 inputs ($p = 4$) and 2 outputs ($q = 2$). The maximum number of cubes per bundle (CPB) we used in this paper is 3. The threshold voltages used for the flash transistors in our MVLC design approach were VT_0 = -0.5V and VT_1 = 0.5V. The flash-based designs were each verified to be correct by conducting exhaustive circuit simulations.

4.2 Results and Analysis

Table 2 shows the delay (including precharge delay), power, energy and physical area ratios of 20 randomly generated logic functions implemented using our MVFC-based approach compared to the CMOS-based based implementation. The delay reported in the table (D_{max} Ratio) is maximum delay of any transition seen at any primary output of the circuit. Since the flash-based implementation is dynamic, we

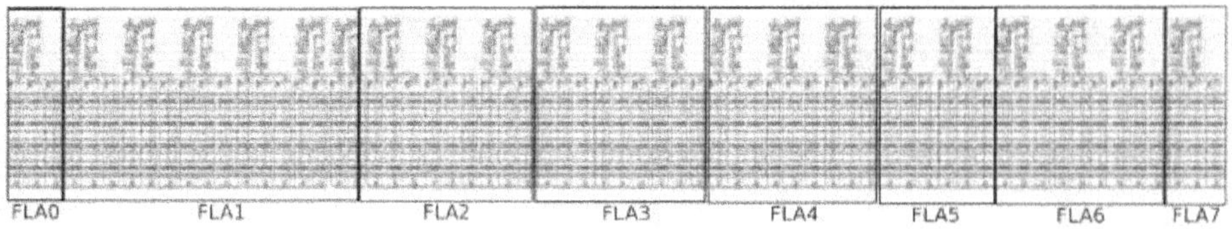

Figure 7: Layout View of an MVFC Implementing Benchmark "des00"

Design	D_{max} Ratio	P_{avg} Ratio	Eng Ratio	Cell Area Ratio
des00	0.73×	0.92×	0.68×	0.99×
des01	0.71×	0.87×	0.62×	0.86×
des02	0.77×	0.95×	0.74×	0.93×
des03	0.69×	1.01×	0.70×	0.89×
des04	0.79×	1.03×	0.82×	0.97×
des05	0.71×	0.89×	0.64×	0.94×
des06	0.88×	0.89×	0.79×	0.96×
des07	0.77×	0.98×	0.76×	0.97×
des08	0.78×	0.93×	0.73×	0.96×
des09	0.80×	0.84×	0.68×	0.93×
des10	0.83×	1.05×	0.88×	0.92×
des11	0.77×	1.04×	0.80×	0.90×
des12	0.79×	0.97×	0.77×	0.90×
des13	0.83×	1.04×	0.87×	1.02×
des14	0.73×	0.90×	0.66×	0.93×
des15	0.91×	1.05×	0.96×	1.02×
des16	0.80×	0.90×	0.72×	1.02×
des17	0.69×	0.95×	0.66×	1.02×
des18	0.75×	0.91×	0.69×	1.02×
des19	0.70×	0.97×	0.68×	1.01×
Average	0.77×	0.95×	0.74×	0.96×
Stdev	0.06×	0.07×	0.09×	0.05×

Table 2: Delay, Power, Energy and Area Ratios of Multi-valued (Ternary) Logic Circuits Relative to CMOS Standard Cell Based Circuits

accounted for the precharge delay in the reported delay shown in the table. As shown in the table, the delay of the flash-based digital circuits ranges from 0.69× to 0.91× of the CMOS standard cell-based digital circuit delay, with an average of 0.77×. Table 2 also shows power dissipation (of 0.95×) when implementing the digital circuits using our multi-valued logic compared to CMOS standard cell based implementation. We also show the energy utilization of our multi-valued implementation compared to the CMOS standard cell based implementation. On average, the energy utilization of the MVFC-based ternary-valued digital circuits is about 0.74× of the CMOS standard cell based implementation. Also, on average, digital circuits implemented using an MVFC-based design approach use 0.96× the physical area of a CMOS-based design. Figure 7, shows the representative layout of an MVFC implementing the benchmark "des00". In general, it is significant for a new circuit design approach to beat the established standard cell-based approach on all metrics (delay, area, power and energy), and so these results are significant.

The MVFC shows tremendous improvements in the delay compared the TLC [2]. The delay of the MVFC is ∼0.32× the delay of the TLC. This delay improvements in the MVFC comes with an increase in its power dissipation and energy. In average, the MVFC has ∼7.9× the power dissipation and ∼2.5× the energy consumption of a TLC. The MVFC has slightly larger physical area (1% larger) compared to the TLC. The TLC can be used for power or energy constrained designs which can tolerate much larger delays. The MVFC can be used for delay sensitive designs, and improves on standard cell designs in terms of delay, area, power and energy.

Table 2 also shows the standard deviation of the results. The standard deviation indicates that the relative results of the flash-based designs vary by 6% in delay, 7% in power, 9% in energy and 5% in physical area. The noise in these metrics is smaller than the improvements, specially for delay and energy.

Flash-based digital circuits have the ability of tuning their delay, power and energy characteristics. This is done through shifting the V_T of the flash transistors in the circuit after fabrication. The ability to shift V_T with precision offers the flash-based digital circuits huge advantages over the traditional CMOS standard-cell based circuits when it comes to speed binning at the factory, age mitigation and performing post-manufacturing ECOs. Figure 8 shows the average delay, power and energy of the flash-based digital designs as their V_T is swept. The delay in Figure 8 is the sum of the evaluate and the precharge delays. Note that shifting the V_T levels has to be limited to a range that guarantees the correct operation of the circuit. The results shown in Figure 8 are extracted after verifying the proper operation of the circuit.

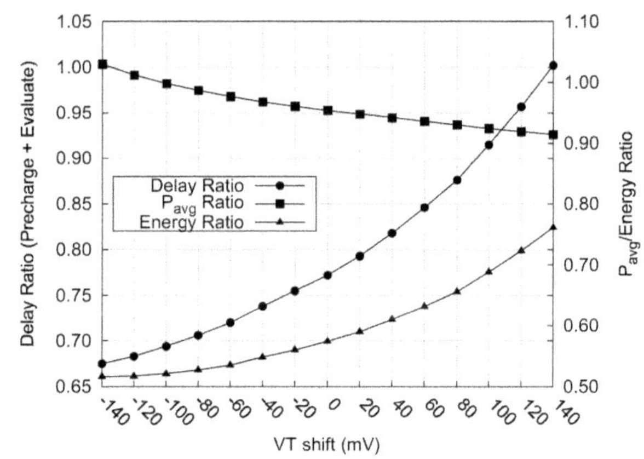

Figure 8: Delay, Power and Energy of the MVFC-based Designs as the V_T is shifted.

5. CONCLUSION

This paper presented the use of flash transistors to implement multi-valued digital circuits. We presented the details of the circuit topology that we use in our multi-valued, flash-based digital circuit approach. Our HSPICE simulations show that, averaged over 20 designs, our approach yields improved delay (∼23% lower), power (∼5% lower), energy (∼26% lower) and area (∼4% lower) characteristics compared to a traditional CMOS standard cell based approach, when averaged over 20 designs. Our approach targets high performance multi-valued, flash-based applications.

6. REFERENCES

[1] R. Fowler and L. Nordheim, "Electron emission in intense electric fields," *Proceedings of the Royal Society of London. Series A, Containing Papers of a Mathematical and Physical Character*, vol. 119, pp. 173–181, May 1928.

[2] M. Abusultan and S. P. Khatri, "A ternary-valued, floating gate transistor-based circuit design approach," in *IEEE Comp. Society Annual Symp. on VLSI (ISVLSI)*, July 2016.

[3] S. Lee *et al.*, "A 128Gb 2b/cell NAND flash memory in 14nm technology with t_{PROG}=640us and 800MB/s I/O rate," in *2016 IEEE International Solid-State Circuits Conference (ISSCC)*, pp. 138–139, Jan 2016.

[4] D. Lee *et al.*, "A 64Gb 533Mb/s DDR interface MLC NAND flash in sub-20nm technology," in *Solid-State Circuits Conference Digest of Technical Papers (ISSCC), 2012 IEEE International*, pp. 430–432, Feb 2012.

[5] K. Park *et al.*, "A 7MB/s 64Gb 3-bit/cell DDR NAND flash memory in 20nm-node technology," in *Solid-State Circuits Conference Digest of Technical Papers (ISSCC), 2011 IEEE International*, pp. 212–213, Feb 2011.

[6] J. Hwang *et al.*, "20nm gate bulk-FinFET SONOS flash," in *Electron Devices Meeting, 2005. IEDM Technical Digest. IEEE International*, pp. 154–157, Dec 2005.

[7] M. Abusultan and S. Khatri, "Implementing low power digital circuits using flash devices," in *Computer Design (ICCD), 2016 34nd IEEE International Conference on*, October 2016.

[8] M. Abusultan and S. P. Khatri, "A flash-based digital circuit design flow," in *Proceedings of the 35th International Conference on Computer-Aided Design*, ICCAD '16, November 2016.

[9] R. K. Brayton, A. L. Sangiovanni-Vincentelli, C. T. McMullen, and G. D. Hachtel, *Logic Minimization Algorithms for VLSI Synthesis*. Norwell, MA, USA: Kluwer Academic Publishers, 1984.

[10] "Synopsys website." `http://www.synopsys.com/`.

[11] J. Stine *et al.*, "FreePDK: An open-source variation-aware design kit," in *IEEE Int'l Conf. on Microelectronic Systems Education (MSE)*, pp. 173–174, June 2007.

[12] "NanGate Library Optimization website." `http://www.nangate.com/`.

[13] "PTM website." `http://ptm.asu.edu/`.

[14] "ITRS website." `http://www.itrs.net/`.

Design of Approximate Logarithmic Multipliers

Weiqiang Liu
College of EIE
Nanjing University of Aero. & Astro., Nanjing, China
liuweiqiang@nuaa.edu.cn

Jiahua Xu
College of EIE
Nanjing University of Aero. & Astro., Nanjing, China
xujiahua@nuaa.edu.cn

Danye Wang
College of EIE
Nanjing University of Aero. & Astro., Nanjing, China
wangdanye@nuaa.edu.cn

Fabrizio Lombardi
ECE Department.
Northeastern University
Boston, MA USA
lombardi@ece.neu.edu

ABSTRACT
Lower power has been a main challenge for IC design. Approximate computing provides a new approach for low power design. Logarithmic multiplier (LM) is a kind of approximate multipliers in nature. In this paper, the design of both non-iterative and iterative approximate LMs (IALM) are studied to further reduce the power consumption and improve the performance. Non-iterative approximate LMs (ALM) that use three inexact mantissa adders are presented. The proposed IALMs use set-one adder in both mantissa adders during the iteration and they also use lower-part-or adders and approximate mirror adders for the final addition. The error analysis and simulation results are also provided. It is found that the proposed approximate LMs with appropriate number of inexact bits has achieved even higher accuracy and lower power consumption compared with the conventional LMs using exact units. To be exact, compared with conventional LMs with exact units, the normalized mean error distance (NMED) of 16-bit approximate LMs is decreased by up to 18% and the power-delay product (PDP) has a reduction of up to 37%. The proposed approximate LMs are also compared with previous approximate Booth multipliers. It is found that approximate LMs are more suitable for applications allowing large errors but require less power consumption, while approximate Booth multipliers fit for applications allowing larger power but require less errors.

CCS Concepts
• Hardware→Arithmetic and datapath circuits; Logic circuits; Combinational circuits.

Keywords
Approximate Computing; Logarithmic Multiplier; Inexact Adder; Lower Power.

1. INTRODUCTION
Approximate computing [1] is a promising approach to deal with the power issue that is one of the main challenges of today's IC design. As high precision and exactness are not so strict for many applications related to human perception such as multimedia and machine learning, the power consumption and performance can be further improved by relaxing the requirement of strict accuracy. As the basic operations of an arithmetic processor, addition and multiplication are very important for achieving high performance, which have been extensively studied for approximate computing for reduction in power consumption [2, 3]. Error metrics including error rate (ER), error distance (ED), mean error distance (MED), normalized mean error distance (NMED), and maximum absolute error (MAE) have been proposed for evaluating the designs of approximate arithmetic circuits [4]. Design of approximate multipliers has been studied based on conventional multiplier schemes [3].

The multipliers using logarithmic transformation that converts multiplication into addition show approximate characteristics in nature. The first logarithmic multiplier (LM) was proposed by Mitchell [5], which performs multiplication using shifting and addition only by converting the operands to approximate logarithmic numbers. As the logarithmic transformation is approximate, inherent error in the results is unavoidable. However, the area, delay and power consumption have been improved significantly at the cost of precision. The state-of-the-art designs of LMs are trying to improve the accuracy using fine piecewise linear approximation [6, 7, 8] or iterative technique [9, 10].

However, there is little research has been conducted on the design of LMs using inexact parts and there is an interesting question that has not been answered: which is better for approximate computing, logarithmic multipliers or approximate normal binary multipliers? In this work, the inexact adders are used to replace the exact mantissa adder in the logarithmic multipliers so that the performance and power of logarithmic multipliers can be further improved. The iterative technique is also applied in the approximate LMs to improve the accuracy.

The rest of the paper is organized as follows. Section 2 reviews the conventional non-iterative and iterative logarithmic multipliers. The design of approximate logarithmic multiplier is presented in Section 3. The design of iterative approximate logarithmic multipliers is also presented in this section. Error analysis and simulation results of the approximate logarithmic multipliers are given in Section 4. The proposed approximate LMs are also compared with previous approximate Booth multipliers in this section. Section 5 concludes this paper.

2. REVIEW
2.1 Non-Iterative Logarithmic Multiplier
Assume A and B are two operands of the logarithmic multiplier, which can be expressed as follows [5]:

$$A = 2^{k_1}(1 + x_1) \tag{1}$$

$$B = 2^{k_2}(1 + x_2) \tag{2}$$

where, k_1 and k_2 are the characteristics of A and B, respectively. They represent the most significant operand bits [10]. x_1 and x_2 are the fractional parts and in a range of [0, 1]. The logarithm of a product, *i.e. P*, is equal to the sum of the logarithms of the multiplier and the multiplicand.

Permission to make digital or hard copies of all or part of this work for personal or classroom use is granted without fee provided that copies are not made or distributed for profit or commercial advantage and that copies bear this notice and the full citation on the first page. Copyrights for components of this work owned by others than ACM must be honored. Abstracting with credit is permitted. To copy otherwise, or republish, to post on servers or to redistribute to lists, requires prior specific permission and/or a fee. Request permissions from Permissions@acm.org.
GLSVLSI '17, May 10-12, 2017, Banff, AB, Canada
© 2017 ACM. ISBN 978-1-4503-4972-7/17/05…$15.00
DOI: http://dx.doi.org/10.1145/3060403.3060409

$$P = A \times B = 2^{k_1+k_2}(1 + x_1) \times (1 + x_2) \quad (3)$$

$$log_2 P = k_1 + k_2 + log_2(1 + x_1) + log_2(1 + x_2) \quad (4)$$

As $log_2(1 + x) \approx x$ when $0 \leq x < 1$, the approximate product can be calculated as follows:

$$log_2 P \approx k_1 + k_2 + x_1 + x_2 \quad (5)$$

which can be calculated by adders.

The conventional logarithmic multiplier proposed by Mitchell mainly includes four steps: leading one detection, binary to logarithm conversion, mantissa addition and logarithm to binary conversion. The structure of a 16-bit Mitchell multiplier is shown in Fig. 1. The leading one detector (LOD) finds the left-most one bit. Then the binary-logarithm converter (BLC) produces the logarithms of the original operand numbers. The multiplication is then performed by the mantissa addition in the logarithmic domain. The results are then decoded by logarithm-binary converter (LBC) into binary numbers as the final product.

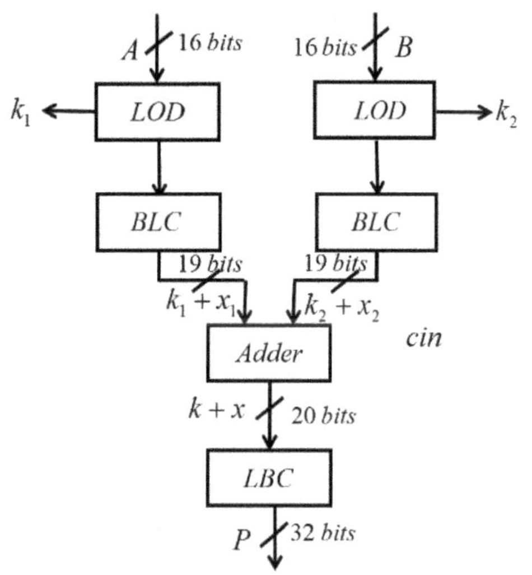

Fig. 1 A 16-bit non-iterative logarithmic multiplier structure.

2.2 Iterative Logarithmic Multiplier

Iterative approaches are usually used to improve the accuracy at the cost of duplicated hardware [10]. As mentioned above, the product of LM is approximate. The errors are introduced by ignoring the correction parts. The exact product can be rewritten as follows [5]:

$$P = 2^{k_1+k_2}(1 + x_1 + x_2) + 2^{k_1+k_2}(x_1 \times x_2), x_1 + x_2 < 1 \quad (6)$$

$$P = 2^{1+k_1+k_2}(x_1 + x_2) + 2^{k_1+k_2}(1 - x_1) \times (1 - x_2), x_1 + x_2 \geq 1 \quad (7)$$

where, $2^{k_1+k_2}(x_1 \times x_2)$ and $2^{k_1+k_2}(1 - x_1) \times (1 - x_2)$ are the correction parts. Define *U* and *V* as follows:

$$U = 2^{k_1}x_1, V = 2^{k_2}x_2, x_1 + x_2 < 1 \quad (8)$$

$$U = 2^{k_1}(1 - x_1), V = 2^{k_2}(1 - x_2), \ x_1 + x_2 \geq 1 \quad (9)$$

The correction parts can be calculated as follows:

$$P_L = U \times V \quad (10)$$

which can be calculated using the same LM structure as shown in Fig. 1. P_L is then added to the original LM product (*i.e.*, $P_H = A \times B$) to increase the accuracy of the final product.

3. APPROXIMATE LOGARITHMIC MULITPLIERS

The performance and power of logarithmic multipliers are further improved by using inexact units during the mantissa addition in this section. Three inexact adders, namely, lower-part-or adder (LOA) [11], approximate mirror adder-A3 (MAA3) [12] and set-one adder (SOA) are used. The SOA is proposed with truncated BLC in this work for approximate LMs. Both non-iterative and iterative approximate LMs are then proposed based on these inexact adders.

3.1 Non-Iterative Approximate LM (ALM)

3.1.1 ALM Using LOA (ALM-LOA)

ALM-LOA uses lower-part-or adder (LOA) [11] in the mantissa adder. A *n*-bit LOA consists of two parts, *i.e.*, an *m*-bit inexact adder and an (*n-m*)-bit exact adder (EA) (Fig. 2). The (*n-m*)-bit adder is used for the *(n-m)* most significant bits of the sum, while the m-bit adder consists of OR gates to compute the addition of the least significant *m* bits (*i.e.*, the lower *m*-bit adder is an array of *n* 2-input OR gates). The logic expressions for lower m-bit adder are as follows:

$$Sum = a \cdot b \quad (11)$$

$$Cout = ab \quad (12)$$

As the inexact adder only uses one OR-gate, its complexity and critical path have been reduced significantly, which leads to much lower power consumption. This is achieved at the cost of lower accuracy. The ER, MED and MAE are as follows:

$$ER = 1 - \left(\frac{3}{4}\right)^m \quad (13)$$

$$MED = 3 \times 2^{m-4} - \frac{1}{8} \quad (14)$$

$$MAE = 2^{m-1} \quad (15)$$

The error characteristics of approximate LMs are further studied in the next section.

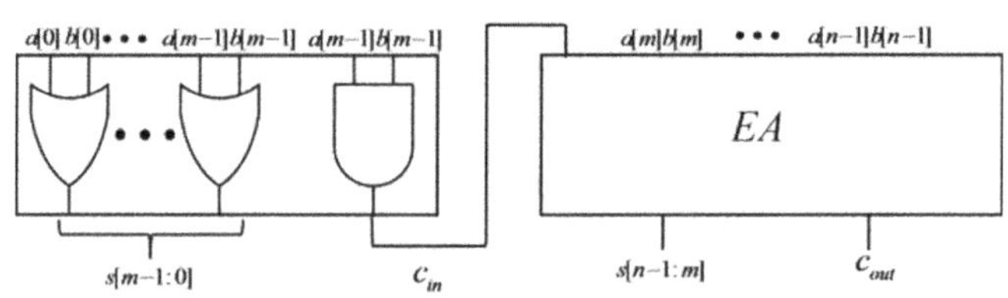

Fig. 2 The structure of LOA with *m* inexact bits.

3.1.2 ALM Using MAA3 (ALM-MAA3)

ALM-MAA3 uses the approximate mirror adder (MAA3) [12] in the mantissa adder. A *n*-bit MAA3 also consists of two parts, *i.e.*, an *m*-bit inexact adder and an (*n-m*)-bit exact adder (Fig. 3). The (*n-m*)-bit adder is used for the *(n-m)* most significant bits of the sum, while the sum of m-bit adder is actually one of its input. The logic expressions for lower m-bit adder are as follows:

$$Sum = b \quad (16)$$

$$Cout = a \quad (17)$$

Its complexity and critical path are reduced significantly and even smaller compared with LM-LOA, which also leads to lower power consumption. The ER, MED and MAE of LM-MAA3 are as follows:

$$ER = 1 - \left(\frac{1}{2}\right)^m \quad (18)$$

$$MED = 2^{m-2} \tag{19}$$

$$MAE = 2^{m-1} \tag{20}$$

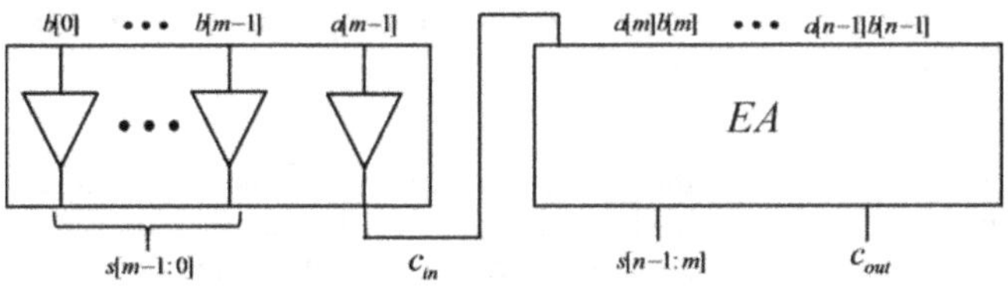

Fig. 3 The structure of MAA3 with *m* inexact bits.

3.1.3 *ALM Using SOA (ALM-SOA)*

ALM-SOA uses both the set-one adder as the mantissa adder and a truncated BLC (TBLC). A *n*-bit SOA consists of two parts, *i.e.*, an *m*-bit inexact adder and an (*n-m*)-bit exact adder (Fig. 4). The sum of m-bit adder is set to logic one. The logic expressions for lower *m*-bit adder are as follows:

$$Sum = 1 \tag{21}$$

$$Cout = ab \tag{22}$$

The SOA is firstly designed for approximate LM in this paper. As the product from LM is always smaller than its exact counterpart, SOA is proposed to compensate the negative errors. The ER, MED and MAE of LM-SOA are as follows:

$$ER = 1 - \left(\frac{1}{2}\right)^m \tag{23}$$

$$MED = \frac{2^m}{3} - \frac{1}{3 \times 2^m} \tag{24}$$

$$MAE = 2^{m-1} \tag{25}$$

As the lower significant sum bits of SOA are set to one already, it is not necessary to perform exact binary-logarithm conversion. Therefore, TBLC is used in the ALM-SOA to further reduce its complexity. The number of truncated bits is the same as number of inexact bits in SOA, *i.e., m*.

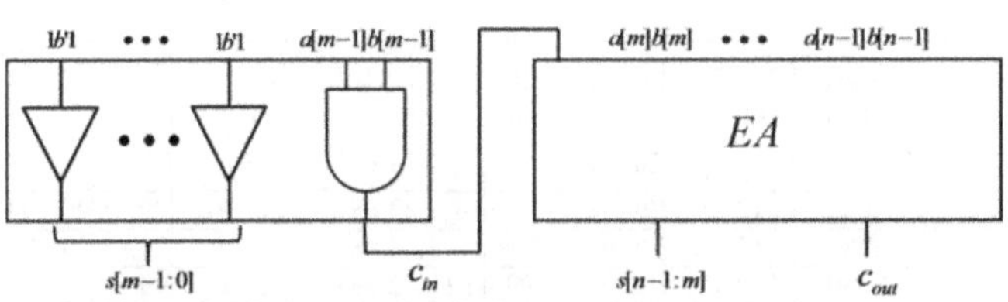

Fig. 4 The structure of SOA with *m* inexact bits.

3.2 Iterative Approximate LM (IALM)

As shown in the last section, the accuracy of ALM can be changed by applying difference number of inexact bit in the mantissa adder to achieve even more efficient design compared with conventional LMs. However, the error of ALM is large. In this section, three iterative ALMs (IALMs), namely, IALM-S (IALM using SOA and Exact Adder3), IALM-SL (IALM using SOA and LOA) and IALM-SM (IALM using SOA and MAA3), are proposed to improve the accuracy of ALM at architectural level. The proposed architecture of an iterative logarithmic multiplier is shown in Fig. 5, where Adder1, Adder2 and Adder3 can be designed approximately. For all IALMs, the numbers of inexact bits of Adder1, Adder2 and Adder3 are defined as M_1, M_2 and M_3, respectively. As the Adder2 is used for the correction parts, M_2 can be generally larger than M_1 as the corresponding bits of original product are already approximate. In Fig. 5, the Estimator is an approximate unit that is used to record the carry-in bit from Adder1 to choose the correct correction part. If *cin=0*, $\boldsymbol{x_1}$ and $\boldsymbol{x_2}$ can be used directly. If *cin=1*, the one's complement of $\boldsymbol{x_1}$ and $\boldsymbol{x_2}$ will be used instead. The inexact parts of this architecture include BLC, Adder1, Adder2, Adder3 and Estimator, which are highlighted with shaded blocks in Fig. 5.

3.2.1 *IALM Using SOA and Exact Adder3 (IALM-S)*

The architecture of the IALM-SL is shown in Fig. 5. As SOA has least complexity compared with other two inexact adders, both of the exact Adder1 and Adder2 are replaced with SOA with M_1 and M_2, respectively. TBLCs are used for both binary to logarithm conversion before Adder1 and Adder2. The numbers of its truncated bits of TBLCs are also M_1 and M_2, respectively. As the Adder3 is sensitive to error, an exact Adder3 is used in IALM-S ($M_3=0$) in this case.

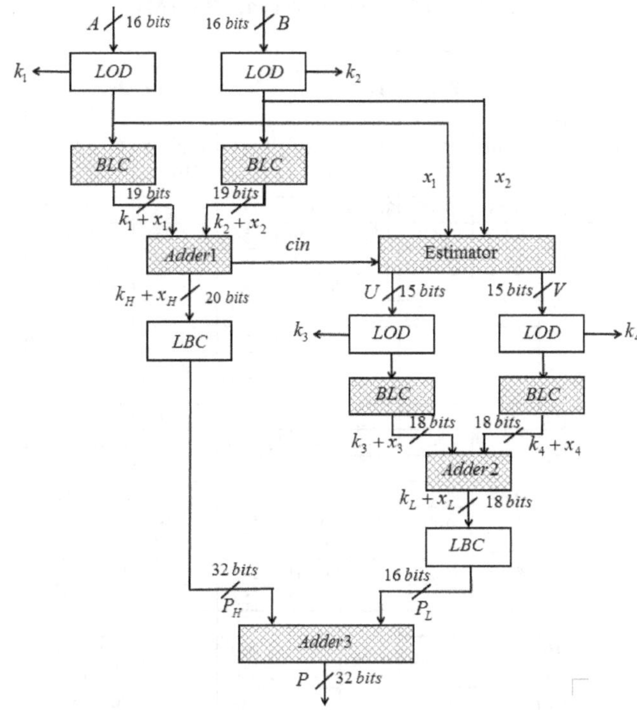

Fig. 5 The proposed architecture of 16-bit IALM.

3.2.2 *IALM Using SOA and LOA (IALM-SL)*

The architecture of the IALM-SL is similar as IALM-S, where SOAs with TBLCs are used for Adder1 and Adder2. The numbers of its truncated bits of TBLCs are the same as the number of inexact bits of SOA. The difference is Adder3 that uses LOA with different M_3. As the Adder3 is sensitive to error, SOA is avoided.

3.2.3 *IALM Using SOA and MAA3 (IALM-SM)*

In IALM-SM, the Adder1 and Adder2 are the same as IALM-SL, which are replaced with SOA. TBLCs are used for both binary to logarithm conversion. However, the Adder3 uses a MAA3 instead of LOA. SOA is also avoided to be used in Adder3 due to its low accuracy. The accuracy and power consumption of both IALM-SL and IALM-SM are heavily dependent on M_1, M_2 and M_3. The tradeoff between error and power-delay product is further studied in next section.

4. EVALUATION AND ANALYSIS

4.1 ERROR ANALYSIS

For approximate designs, several metrics have been proposed to measure the error of approximate adders and multipliers including the mean error distance (MED), the relative error distance (ED) and the normalization of MED (NMED) [4]. Several error metrics are used to fairly compare different approximate designs of various sizes:

- The NMED is defined as the normalized MED by the maximum output of the accurate design.
- RED is defined as the ED over the absolute accurate result.
- Mean RED (MRED) and P_{RED} are usually used to evaluate the error distribution of approximate multipliers. P_{RED} is the probability of obtaining a RED smaller than a specific percentage value.

Table 1. Error Characteristics of Proposed 8-bit and 16-bit Non-Iterative Approximate Logarithmic Multipliers with Different Number of Inexact Bits (M)

LM Design	M	8-bit LMs				16-bit LMs			
		NMED (10^{-2})	MRED (10^{-2})	P_{RED} (%)	ER (%)	NMED (10^{-3})	MRED (10^{-2})	P_{RED} (%)	ER (%)
LM	0	0.93	3.76	36.59	93.09	9.256	3.85	35.17	99.77
ALM-LOA	2	0.90	3.68	37.94	93.09	9.256	3.85	35.17	99.77
	4	1.01	3.91	32.23	93.09	9.253	3.84	35.19	99.77
	6	2.16	7.88	16.26	93.09	9.250	3.84	35.22	99.77
	7	4.11	14.42	13.47	93.09	9.250	3.84	35.24	99.77
	8	-	-	-	-	9.255	3.84	35.25	99.77
	9	-	-	-	-	9.277	3.85	35.21	99.77
	10	-	-	-	-	9.357	3.88	35.02	99.77
	11	-	-	-	-	9.640	3.98	33.65	99.77
	13	-	-	-	-	13.634	5.43	18.84	99.77
	15	-	-	-	-	41.636	15.10	8.15	99.77
ALM-MAA3	2	0.87	3.58	39.64	94.65	9.253	3.85	35.18	99.80
	4	1.01	3.96	31.96	95.63	9.251	3.84	35.20	99.83
	6	2.22	8.77	13.78	96.02	9.248	3.84	35.24	99.85
	7	4.15	16.79	8.17	96.11	9.247	3.84	35.26	99.86
	8	-	-	-	-	9.253	3.84	35.26	99.86
	9	-	-	-	-	9.276	3.85	35.21	99.86
	10	-	-	-	-	9.360	3.88	34.89	99.87
	11	-	-	-	-	9.650	3.99	33.20	99.87
	13	-	-	-	-	13.704	5.56	20.89	99.87
	15	-	-	-	-	41.652	16.98	6.04	99.87
ALM-SOA	2	**0.74**	**3.00**	**48.33**	97.87	9.248	3.84	35.23	99.95
	4	0.95	4.01	30.29	98.66	9.226	3.83	35.36	99.97
	6	4.31	18.57	7.59	99.09	9.160	3.80	35.77	99.97
	7	9.71	42.50	4.02	99.11	9.083	3.77	36.24	99.97
	8	-	-	-	-	8.942	3.71	37.13	99.97
	9	-	-	-	-	8.701	3.61	38.76	99.97
	10	-	-	-	-	8.347	3.46	41.54	99.97
	11	-	-	-	-	**8.055**	**3.33**	**41.92**	99.97
	13	-	-	-	-	13.186	5.36	22.06	99.97
	15	-	-	-	-	54.596	22.43	5.57	99.97

4.1.1 Error Analysis of ALMs

The error metrics of the proposed non-iterative approximate logarithmic multipliers are provided in Table 1 for 8-bit and 16-bit designs. Table 1 shows that with an increase of the number of inexact bits (*i.e.,* M) of 8-bit designs, the accuracy of all three ALMs decrease (*i.e.,* NMED, MRED and ER increase, while P_{RED} decrease). However, it is interesting to see that when M=2 for 8-bit designs, errors of all three designs are even smaller than the LM using exact units. For 16-bit designs, when M<9, all three ALMs have smaller errors compared with exact LM. For 16-bit ALM-SOA, it has smaller errors compared with exact LM even when M<11; and it has the smallest NMED and MRED when M=11. The ALM-SOA with M=11 can reduce the NMED and MRED by up to 12% and 13%, respectively, compared with LM using exact units. **This result clearly shows that ALMs using approximate parts can be even more accurate than LM using exact part, which is firstly found in this work.**

4.1.2 Error Analysis of IALMs

The error metrics of the proposed iterative approximate logarithmic multipliers are provided in Table 2 for 16-bit design. To evaluate the errors of IALM-S, an exact Adder2 (M_2=0) is used firstly. From the left-hand column, it is interesting to see the accuracy is actually improved when M_1<8 and when M_1=5 and 6 it has smallest errors. Therefore, for the right-hand side columns, M_2 is changed with these two fixed M_1 numbers. It can be seen that when M_1=5 and M_2=11, the IALM-S has the smallest NMED. It is also interesting to see the error of IALM with an exact Adder2 is much larger compared with IALM with inexact Adder2 using SOA. This is consistent with the error analysis as discussed above that IALMs using approximate parts can produce much more accurate results compared with ILMs using all exact units.

Table 2. Error Characteristics of 16-bit IALM-S

IALM-S with M_2=0					IALM-S with M_1=5					IALM-S with M_1=6				
M_1	NMED (10^{-4})	MRED (10^{-4})	P_{RED} (%)	ER (%)	M_2	NMED (10^{-4})	MRED (10^{-4})	P_{RED} (%)	ER (%)	M_2	NMED (10^{-4})	MRED (10^{-4})	P_{RED} (%)	ER (%)
0	3.50	14.93	99.98	99.158	0	3.21	13.50	99.98	99.992	0	3.21	13.38	99.98	99.993
3	3.36	14.27	99.98	99.980	3	3.20	13.46	99.98	99.996	3	3.20	13.35	99.98	99.997
5	**3.21**	13.50	99.98	99.992	6	3.17	13.31	99.98	99.996	6	3.17	13.23	99.98	99.997
6	**3.21**	13.38	99.98	99.993	8	3.11	13.01	99.98	99.996	8	3.12	13.00	99.98	99.998
7	3.50	14.47	99.98	99.996	9	3.04	12.70	99.98	99.996	9	3.06	12.74	99.98	99.998
8	4.71	19.28	99.99	99.997	10	2.94	12.29	99.98	99.997	10	2.98	12.43	99.98	99.998
9	8.22	33.38	99.99	99.998	11	**2.88**	12.08	99.98	99.997	11	**2.96**	12.39	99.98	99.998
12	77.85	289.13	44.96	99.999	12	3.21	13.51	99.98	99.997	12	3.35	14.09	99.98	99.998

Table 3. Error Characteristics 16-bit IALM-SL and IALM-SM with M_1=5 and M_2=11

IALM-SL					IALM-SM				
M_3	NMED (10^{-4})	MRED (10^{-4})	P_{RED} (%)	ER (%)	M_3	NMED (10^{-4})	MRED (10^{-4})	P_{RED} (%)	ER (%)
0	2.881	12.08	99.98	99.997	0	2.881	12.08	99.98	99.997
4	2.882	12.08	99.98	99.996	4	2.881	12.07	99.98	99.994
8	2.882	12.08	99.98	99.996	8	2.881	12.08	99.98	99.992
12	2.880	12.11	99.98	99.996	12	2.881	12.12	99.98	99.992
15	2.871	12.59	99.92	99.997	15	2.881	12.59	99.92	99.992
16	**2.869**	13.16	99.85	99.997	16	2.881	13.12	99.86	99.992
17	2.873	14.24	99.72	99.997	17	2.884	14.14	99.74	99.993
18	2.885	16.17	99.48	99.997	18	2.895	16.00	99.51	99.993
19	2.927	19.54	99.05	99.997	19	2.934	19.31	99.10	99.994
20	3.062	25.27	98.29	99.997	20	3.058	25.08	98.35	99.995
24	12.154	102.96	85.75	99.998	24	10.165	110.80	84.66	99.997

The error metrics of IALM-SL and IALM-SM are analyzed with M_1=5 and M_2=11 by changing M_3. It is clear that by using the iterative technique, the accuracy has been significantly increased compared with non-iterative LMs; their P_{RED} are all larger than 98% when M_3<24, while the P_{RED} of ALMs are all less than 50%. When M_3 <18, the NMEDs of both IALM-SL and IALM-SM are similar as IALM-S with M_1=5 and M_2=11. The smallest NMED is achieved around with M_3=16. The IALM-SL with M_1=5, M_2=11 and M_3=16 can reduce NMED by up to 18% compared with ILM with exact units. Therefore, IALM-SL and IALM-SA with M_3=15, 16 and 17 are further studied with hardware simulations in Section 4.2.2.

4.2 HARDWARE EVALUATION

The proposed ALMs including IALMs are described at gate-level in Verilog HDL and verified by Synopsys VCS. Both designs are then synthesized by the Synopsys Design Compiler using the NanGate 45 nm Open Cell Library. The average power consumption is found using the Synopsys Power Compiler with a back annotated switching activity file generated from the random input vectors.

Table 4. Hardware Results (45nm Technology) of 8-bit and 16-bit Non-Iterative Approximate Logarithmic Multipliers with Different Number of Inexact Bits (M)

LM Design	M	8-bit LMs				16-bit LMs			
		Power (μW)	Delay (ns)	Area (μm²)	PDP (fJ)	Power (μW)	Delay (ns)	Area (μm²)	PDP (fJ)
LM	0	85.60	0.69	390.22	59.06	168.12	1.00	781.24	168.12
ALM-LOA	2	68.55	0.68	316.81	46.61	183.32	0.95	848.00	174.15
	4	62.75	0.65	315.48	40.79	162.60	0.98	772.20	159.35
	6	56.67	0.60	286.75	34.00	153.18	1.01	720.59	154.71
	7	49.63	0.62	269.72	30.77	148.08	0.98	721.66	145.12
	8	-	-	-	-	147.55	0.96	701.71	141.65
	9	-	-	-	-	148.23	0.91	751.45	134.89
	10	-	-	-	-	149.32	0.88	757.03	131.40
	11	-	-	-	-	139.74	0.90	733.63	125.77
	13	-	-	-	-	139.13	0.85	738.15	118.26
	15	-	-	-	-	138.51	0.79	733.89	109.42
ALM-MAA3	2	67.79	0.67	321.59	45.42	164.08	1.02	759.43	167.36
	4	63.24	0.66	319.20	41.74	175.12	0.99	840.83	173.37
	6	50.09	0.59	258.55	29.55	161.89	0.95	786.56	153.80
	7	42.00	0.55	218.12	23.10	158.75	0.93	779.38	147.64
	8	-	-	-	-	157.51	0.92	780.98	144.91
	9	-	-	-	-	148.68	0.96	746.40	142.73
	10	-	-	-	-	149.63	0.92	747.99	137.66
	11	-	-	-	-	133.00	0.90	680.16	119.70
	13	-	-	-	-	137.36	0.88	720.59	120.88
	15	-	-	-	-	107.36	0.76	557.54	81.59
ALM-SOA	2	58.65	0.71	287.28	41.64	172.51	0.96	826.20	165.61
	4	56.02	0.60	301.12	33.61	145.86	0.97	703.57	141.48
	6	31.75	0.51	185.40	16.19	134.97	0.95	660.21	128.22
	7	16.09	0.39	108.79	6.28	122.76	0.91	636.80	111.71
	8	-	-	-	-	114.54	0.90	601.96	103.09
	9	-	-	-	-	103.64	0.90	558.33	93.28
	10	-	-	-	-	97.15	0.90	535.46	87.44
	11	-	-	-	-	89.03	0.81	515.24	72.11
	13	-	-	-	-	69.44	0.75	427.46	52.08
	15	-	-	-	-	32.14	0.52	231.42	16.71

4.2.1 Hardware Results of ALMs

The critical path delay, area, power consumption and PDP are reported in Table 4 for 8-bit and 16-bit ALMs at different values of M. With an increase of M, the power consumption and PDP of all three designs for both 8-bit and 16-bit decrease. The PDPs of approximate designs are significantly lower than for conventional LM. The critical path delay is also reduced, which leads to an overall better performance. The PDPs of ALM-SOA are much better than that of ALM-LOA and ALM-MAA3. As the NMED of ALM-SOA is the smallest when M=11, this specific design shows best tradeoff between error and power consumption for non-iterative ALMs.

4.2.2 Hardware Results of IALMs

According to the error analysis in Section 4.1.2, the IALM with M_1=5, M_2=11, and 14<M_3<18 show good error characteristics. These IALM designs are evaluated with hardware simulations as shown in Table 5.

It can be seen that the power, delay and area of both IALM-SL and IALM-SM are smaller than conventional iterative LMs with exact units. Considering their error characteristics, it is found that both the NMEDs and PDPs of approximate iterative LMs with truncated BLC, inexact Adder1, Adder2 and Adder3 are better than that of conventional iterative LMs with exact units. **This confirms that approximate design techniques can improve both performance and accuracy of iterative logarithmic multipliers.** The designs of IALM-SL with M_3=16 is the most efficient design in terms of PDP, which can reduce the PDP up to 37% compared with ILM with exact units. These approximate logarithmic multipliers are further compared with approximate Booth multipliers in the next subsection.

Table 5. Hardware Results (45nm Technology) of 16-bit IALM.

Designs	M_1	M_2	M_3	Power (μW)	Delay (ns)	Area (μm²)	PDP (fJ)
ILM	0	0	0	469.31	2.04	2089.70	957.39
IALM-SL	5	11	15	333.01	**1.82**	1538.28	606.08
	5	11	16	**328.61**	1.83	**1529.23**	**601.36**
	5	11	17	332.99	1.85	1543.86	616.03
IALM-SM	5	11	15	345.79	1.83	1602.65	632.80
	5	11	16	334.65	1.84	1534.82	615.76
	5	11	17	329.78	1.86	1525.24	613.39

4.3 COMPARISON

As designs of 16-bit ALM-SOA with M=9, 10 and 11 show good tradeoff between power consumption and accuracy, they are selected along with 16-bit IALM-SL with M_1=5, M_2=11, and 14< M_3<18 to compared with previous approximate multiplier designs that are based on accurate 16-bit binary Booth multipliers. The approximate Booth multipliers compared in this subsection include three radix-4 (R4) designs R4BM04 [13], R4ABM11 [14], R4ABM12 [15], and three radix-8 (R8) designs R8ABM1, R8ABM2-C9 and R8ABM2-C15 that are proposed in [16] with no truncation, 9-bit truncation and 15-bit truncation, respectively. R8ABM2-C9 and R8ABM2-C15 are also designed with the compensation circuits. Also in these cases, all designs are described in Verilog and synthesized by the Synopsys Design Compiler using the NanGate 45 nm Open Cell Library. The power consumption, delay, area, PDP, NMED and error rate are reported in Table 6.

It is clear from Table 6 that the non-iterative ALMs generally have much lower power consumption compared with IALMs and approximate Booth multipliers and they are also fastest. While IALMs improve accuracy significantly, the NMEDs of IALMs are one order larger compared with approximate Booth multipliers. However, the P_{RED} of IALMS are the best and they are all larger than 99.85%, which is slightly better than approximate Booth multipliers.

As shown in Fig. 6, for these three kinds of approximate multipliers, they are suitable for different application scenarios. For applications allow large error but requires small power consumption, non-iterative ALMs are the best choice; for applications require more accuracy while allow larger power consumption, the approximate multipliers based on accurate binary multipliers should be used. Although the iterative approximate logarithmic multipliers show significant improvement in terms of accuracy over non-iterative LMs, its large PDP make them less attractive compared with approximate Booth multipliers.

Table 6. Comparative Performance of 16-bit Approximate ALMs (M) and IALMs (M1, M2, M3) with Approximate Booth Multipliers.

Designs	Power (W)	Delay (ns)	Area (m^2)	PDP (fJ)	NMED (10^{-4})	P_{RED} (%)
LM (M=0)	168.1	1.00	781	168	92.56	35.17
ALM-SOA (M=10)	**97.2**	0.90	535	88	83.47	41.54
ALM-SOA (M=11)	89.0	**0.81**	**515**	**72**	80.55	41.92
ILM (0,0,0)	469.3	2.04	2090	957	3.50	**99.98**
IALM-SL (5,11,15)	333.0	1.82	1538	606	2.87	99.92
IALM-SL (5,11,16)	328.6	1.83	1529	601	2.87	99.85
IALM-SM (5,11,15)	345.8	1.83	1603	633	2.88	99.92
IALM-SM (5,11,16)	334.7	1.84	1535	616	2.88	99.86
R4ABM04 [9]	427.3	0.95	1939	406	0.53	97.72
R4ABM11 [12]	404.4	0.94	1859	380	0.22	99.17
R4ABM12 [15]	394.6	0.95	1808	374	0.23	99.10
R8ABM1 [22]	376.7	1.23	1516	463	**0.19**	99.77
R8ABM2-C9 [22]	332.6	1.22	1332	406	0.44	99.43
R8ABM2-C15 [22]	217.3	1.18	912	256	0.57	98.79

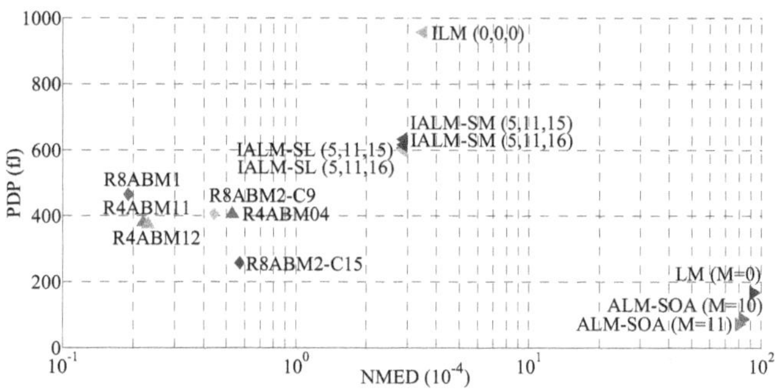

Fig. 6 The NMEDs and PDPs of 16-bit approximate LMs and Booth multipliers.

5. CONCLUSIONS

The design of both non-iterative and iterative approximate logarithmic multipliers are studied in this paper. Three kinds of inexact adders are used in the mantissa addition in the non-iterative approximate LMs, which forms ALM-LOA, ALM-MAA3 and ALM-SOA. In the design of ALM-SOA, the truncated binary-logarithm converter (TBLC) is applied without the loss of accuracy. To further improve the accuracy of approximate LMs, iterative techniques is used, in which both Adder1 and Adder2 uses TBLC and SOA, while Adder3 uses either LOA or MAA3. All approximate LMs are analyzed with various error metrics. **It is firstly found in this work that approximate LMs, *i.e.*, ALMs and IALMs, are even more accurate with appropriate number of inexact bits compared with conventional LMs and ILMs with exact units.** The proposed IALMs with approximate number of inexact bits can improve both NMED (up to 12%) and PDP (up to 37%) significantly over conventional designs.

The proposed designs are also compared with approximate multipliers that are based on accurate binary Booth multipliers. The comparison results asked an interesting question: what kind of approximate designs should the designers to choose? The answer is clear from the comparison results: **for applications allow large error but requires small power consumption, non-iterative approximate LMs are the best choice; for applications require more accuracy while allow larger power consumption, the approximate multipliers based on accurate binary multipliers should be used.** Although the iterative approximate logarithmic multipliers show significant improvement in terms of accuracy over non-iterative LMs, its large PDP make them less attractive compared with approximate Booth multipliers.

6. ACKNOWLEDGMENTS

This work is supported by grants from the National Natural Science Foundation of China (61401197) and Nature Science Foundation of Jiangsu Province (BK20151477).

7. REFERENCES

[1] Han, J. and Orshansky, M. 2013. Approximate computing: an emerging paradigm for energy-efficient design. In *Proc. 18th IEEE European Test Symposium* (27-31 May 2013), 1-6.

[2] Liu, W., Chen, L., Wang, C., O'Neill, M. and Lombardi, F., 2016 Design and analysis of floating-point adders, *IEEE Trans. Computers*, 65, 1, 308-314.

[3] Liu, W., Qian L., Wang, C., Jiang H., Han, J. and Lombardi, F., 2017. Design of approximate radix-4 Booth multipliers for error-tolerant computing", *IEEE Trans. Computers,* (Feb. 2017). (Accepted) DOI= 10.1109/TC.2017.2672976.

[4] Liang, J., Han, J. and Lombardi, F., 2013, New metrics for the reliability of approximate and probabilistic adders, *IEEE Trans. Computers*, 63, 9, 1760-1771.

[5] Mitchell, J., 1962, Computer multiplication and division using binary logarithms, *IRE Transactions on Electronic Computers*, EC-11, 4, 512-517.

[6] Nam, B., Kim, H. and Yoo, H., 2008, Power and area-efficient unified computation of vector and elementary functions for handheld 3D graphics systems, *IEEE Trans. Comput.*, 57, 4, 490-504.

[7] Gutierrez, R. and Valls, J. 2011, Low cost hardware implementation of logarithm approximation, *IEEE Trans. VLSI Systems*, 19, 12, 2326-2330.

[8] Low, J., and Jong, C., 2015, Unified Mitchell-Based Approximation for Efficient Logarithmic Conversion Circuit. *IEEE Trans. Computers*, 64, 6, 1783-1797.

[9] Sullivan, M. and Swartzlander, Jr. E., 2012, Truncated error correction for flexible approximate multiplication, in Proc. *Conference Record of the Forty Sixth Asilomar Conference on Signals, Systems and Computers* (4-7 Nov. 2012), 355–359.

[10] Ahmed, S., Kadam, S., and Srinivas, M., 2016, An Iterative Logarithmic Multiplier with Improved Precision, in Proc. *IEEE 23nd Symposium on Computer Arithmetic* (10-13 Jul. 2016), 104-111.

[11] Mahdiani, H., Ahmadi, A., Fakhraie S., and Lucas, C., 2010, Bio-inspired imprecise computational blocks for efficient VLSI implementation of soft-computing applications. *IEEE Trans. Circuits Syst. I: Reg. Papers*, 57, 4, 850-862.

[12] Gupta, V., Mohapatra, D., Park, S., Raghunathan, A., and Roy, K. 2010, IMPACT: imprecise adders for low-power approximate computing, in Proc. *IEEE/ACM International Symposium on Low Power Electronics and Design* (18-20 Aug. 2010), 409-414.

[13] Cho, K.-J., Lee, K.-C., Chung, J.-G. and Parhi, K. 2004, Design of low error fixed-width modified Booth multiplier, *IEEE Trans. VLSI Systems*, 12, 5, 522–531.

[14] Wang, J.-P., Kuang, S.-R. and Liang, S.-C. 2011, High-accuracy fixed-width modified Booth multipliers for lossy applications, *IEEE Trans. VLSI Systems,* 19, 1, 52-60.

[15] Chen, Y.-H. and Chang, T.-Y. 2012. A high-accuracy adaptive conditional-probability estimator for fixed-width Booth multipliers, *IEEE Trans. Circuits Syst. I: Reg. Papers*, 59, 3, 594-603.

[16] Jiang, H., Han, J., Qiao, F., and Lombardi, F., 2016. Approximate radix-8 Booth multipliers for low-power and high performance operation, *IEEE Trans. Computers*, 65, 8, 2638-2644.

Mitigating the Effect of Reliability Soft-errors of RRAM Devices on the Performance of RRAM-based Neuromorphic Systems

Amr M.S.Tosson
University of Waterloo
atosson@uwaterloo.ca

Shimeng Yu
Arizona State University
Shimeng.Yu@asu.edu

Mohab Anis and Lan Wei
University of Waterloo
mhanis,lan.wei@uwaterloo.ca

ABSTRACT

With the speed and power bottleneck in the conventional Von Neumann architecture, the interest in the neuromorphic systems has greatly increased in recent years. To create a highly dense communication network between the pre- and post-neurons, RRAM devices are used as synapses in the neuromorphic systems due to many advantages including their small sizes and low-power operations. However, due to RRAM reliability issues, in particular soft-errors, the performance of the RRAM-based neuromorphic systems are significantly degraded. In this article, we propose a novel framework for detecting and resolving the degradation in the system performance due to the RRAM reliability soft-errors. The read and write circuits modifications to implement the framework, and their impact on the delay and energy consumption of the neuromorphic system are also discussed in this article. Using a combination of BRIAN and SPICE simulations, we demonstrate that the proposed framework can restore the accuracy of the example RRAM-based neuromorphic system from 43% back to its target value of 91.6% with a minimal impact on the read (< 0.1% and 1.1% increase in the delay and energy respectively) and write (0% and < 0.1% increase in the delay and energy respectively) operations.

1. INTRODUCTION

The interest in the neuromorphic systems has significantly increased in recent years due to the speed and power bottleneck imposed by the separation between processing and memory units in the Von-Neumann architecture [1,2]. With the architecture of the neuromorphic system, which consists of pre- and post-neurons connected by a large connectivity network, high computationally complex operations, such as cognitive operations, can be achieved in fast and energy-efficient manners. The Resistive Random Access Memory (RRAM) crossbar arrays are used to build the high-density neural network between the pre- and post-neurons of the neuromorphic system [3,4]. This is mainly due to several attractive features of the RRAM device such as its: a) compact size , b) fast switching speed, c) low programming voltage , and d) easy integration with the Back-End Of Line (BEOL) CMOS fabrication process. The current in the RRAM device is carried by the conductive filaments (CF) made of oxygen vacancies in the oxide material which act as electron hoping sites [5].

Permission to make digital or hard copies of all or part of this work for personal or classroom use is granted without fee provided that copies are not made or distributed for profit or commercial advantage and that copies bear this notice and the full citation on the first page. Copyrights for components of this work owned by others than ACM must be honored. Abstracting with credit is permitted. To copy otherwise, or republish, to post on servers or to redistribute to lists, requires prior specific permission and/or a fee. Request permissions from permissions@acm.org.

GLSVLSI '17, May 10-12, 2017, Banff, AB, Canada
© 2017 ACM. ISBN 978-1-4503-4972-7/17/05...$15.00
DOI: http://dx.doi.org/10.1145/3060403.3060431

However, due to the stochastic nature of the oxygen vacancies, RRAM devices suffer from reliability failures which can be categorized as hard-errors (i.e errors that can not be fixed) and soft-errors (i.e errors that can be restored) failures. Hard-errors are caused by a permanent damage in the CF, after certain cycle limit ($\approx 10^{10}$ cycles [6]), resulting from the high-current used during the switching of the RRAM device between its low resistive state (LRS) and its high resistive state (HRS) with each pulse [6, 7]. In case of the neuromorphic applications, since the resistive state of the RRAM device changes slightly with each pulse ($\approx$ 1% of the full swing between LRS and HRS) [8], the hard-errors are not expected to occur [9]. On the other hand, the RRAM reliability soft-errors are caused by: a) diffusion of oxygen vacancies out of the containment of CF [10, 11], b) the excess generation/recombination of oxygen vacancies coming from the use of unbalanced programming pulses [12], and c) manufacturing defects [13]. As discussed in [9], the RRAM reliability soft-errors, resulting from the diffusion and excessive generation/recombinations of the oxygen vacancies, are the main contributors to the significant degradation in the accuracy of system. For instance, in [8], the accuracy of the system in recognizing the MNIST dataset [14] reduces from 91.6% to 43% due to those soft-errors [9].

In this work, we propose a new framework which can detect and resolve the degradation in the system performance due to the RRAM reliability soft-errors. In this framework, the lost state of the RRAM device is detected when the received number of pulses at the post-neurons drops below a preset threshold. Using the system in [8] as an example, our BRIAN [15] system-level simulations show that, using this newly proposed framework, the reliability-related degradation in the system accuracy can be restored with minimal impact on the delay and energy consumption of the system. The conventional read and write circuits are modified to implement the proposed framework. Our SPICE simulation results demonstrate that the increase in the delay and energy of the read operation are minimal (< 0.1 % and 1.1% respectively). Similarly, the increase in the energy consumption of the write operation is negligible (< 0.1%) while there is no increase in its delay.

2. PROPOSED FRAMEWORK

Fig.1 illustrates the flowchart of the proposed methodology to detect and fix the degradation in the system performance resulting from the RRAM reliability soft-errors. Although the values in Fig.1 are obtained based on the calculations done using the neuromorphic system in [8] as an example, the framework and the methodology used to get those values can be easily adjusted to adapt to any other neuromorphic systems. The framework in Fig.1 consists of two main steps:

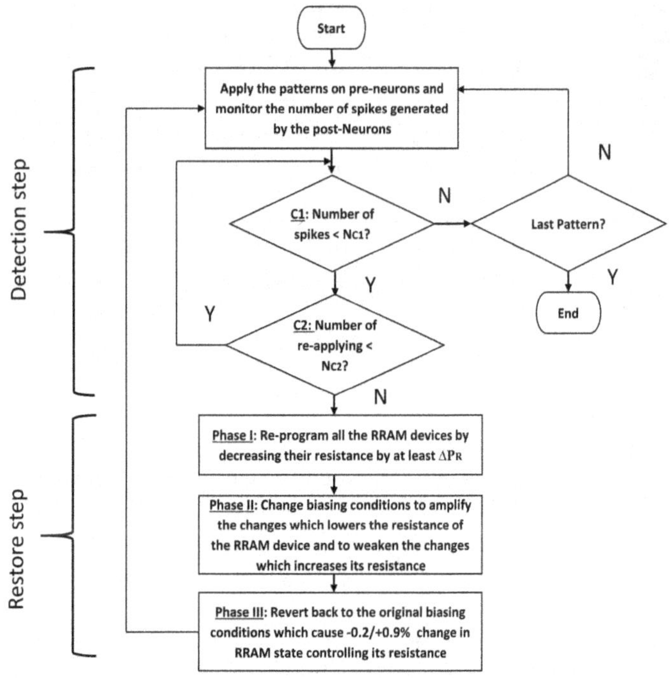

Figure 1: Flowchart of the proposed framework to detect and fix the degradation in the system performance caused by the RRAM reliability soft-errors

- **Detection Step**: The purpose of this step is to detect the degradation in the output accuracy of the system when the RRAM reliability soft-errors occur.
- **Restore Step**: This step describes the process through which the system performance can be restored to its expected accuracy percentage (91.6% in case of the system in [8]) .

2.1 Detection Step

Whenever the RRAM reliability soft-errors occur, the number of pulses at the post-neurons decrease significantly. This is dominated by the fact that those soft-errors are originated from the oxygen vacancies diffusing out of the CF containment which results in the increase of the RRAM resistance [10, 11, 13]. Accordingly, the connections between the pre- and post-neurons are weakened which reduce the number of pulses generated at post-neurons. In case of the system in [8], the authors describe that the minimum threshold for the number of pulses generated at the post-neurons is N_{C1}=5 (C1 in Fig.1). If less than 5 pulses are generated, the input pattern, corresponding to the low-number of pulses, has to be re-applied to the system. Following the spike-timing-dependent plasticity (STDP) rule [16], the RRAM resistive state changes based on the time overlap between the pulses coming from the pre- and post-neurons. By re-applying the input pattern, the overlap between the pre- and post-neurons pulses is re-introduced. Consequently, the period, during which the RRAM resistance can change, is increased. Given that the average overlap between the pre- and post-neuron pulses is 10ms for our system example and using the biasing voltages of -0.8V/0.9V on the RRAM devices [8, 9], the input pattern has to be re-applied N_{C2}=50 times in order to change the RRAM from its maximum HRS to its LRS (C2 in Fig.1). The average pulse overlap of 10ms is computed based on the fact that the maximum overlap between the pulses of the pre- and post-neurons is 20ms and the minimum overlap is as small as 10μs [8].

2.2 Restore Step

If, after N_{C2}=50 times of re-applying a pattern, the number of pulses at the post-neurons is still less than N_{C1}=5, this indicates that RRAM reliability soft-errors have occurred since the RRAM resistive state can not be changed from its HRS to its LRS by the given input pattern. In this case, the restore step is initiated. As illustrated in Fig.1, the restore step consists of three phases:

Phase I: In this phase, the resistance of all the RRAM devices is decreased by a minimum of ΔP_R (25% in our example). This is done by applying a voltage pulse of +1.1 V for a period of 20ms on the post-neurons while the pre-neurons are grounded. For the majority of RRAM devices, which are at HRS, their resistance decreases by ΔP_R while for other RRAM devices, whose resistance is lower than the HRS value, their resistance decreases by more than ΔP_R depending on their resistive state before the +1.1V pulse is applied. The ΔP_R=25% in our case is selected based on the simulation results which show that a higher or lower percentage of decrease leads to a lower restored system accuracy as illustrated in Fig.2a. If a higher percentage of ΔP_R (ΔP_R=50% in Fig.2a) is used, the connectivity between all the pre- and post-neurons is enhanced. Accordingly, for any input pattern, a large number of post-neuron pulses is generated which makes it difficult to differentiate the various applied input patterns and hence, the accuracy of the system in recognizing the MNIST dataset reduces. Oppositely, if ΔP_R is lower than 25% (ΔP_R=10% in Fig.2a), most of the devices remain in their HRS which hardly increase the number of pulses seen at the post-neurons.

Phase II: Originally, in the detection step of the framework, the biasing conditions of -0.8V/0.9V on the RRAM device cause each pulse generated by the pre- and post-neurons in response to the input patterns, to change the RRAM resistance towards its LRS/HRS by maximum of ΔP_{LRS}=0.9%/ΔP_{HRS}=0.2% respectively[8,9]. In this phase, in order to enhance the restore process, for a certain number of input patterns (N_{amp}), whenever the applied pattern decreases the RRAM resistance, this change is amplified (i.e increasing ΔP_{LRS}). Oppositely, if the applied input pattern results in an increase in the RRAM resistance, this effect is weakened (i.e decreasing ΔP_{HRS}).

To change ΔP_{HRS} and ΔP_{LRS}, the bias conditions needs to change from those values used in the detection step. By decreasing the amplitude of the pulses from the pre-neuron by 50mv (maximum amplitude become 0.75V instead of

0.8V), the resistance increase is reduced from ΔP_{HRS}=0.2% to ΔP_{HRS}=0.02%. Since the changes in ΔP_{LRS} and N_{amp} are tightly related, a proper choice for their values is required to assure optimal system performance. Assuming a constant value for ΔP_{LRS}=5%, Fig.2b demonstrates the effect of changing N_{amp} on the restored system accuracy. Similar to the change in ΔP_R in phase I, if a higher/lower value of N_{amp} is used, too many RRAM devices are in their LRS/HRS leading to a very high/low number of pulses at the post-neurons which negatively affect the system performance. Similarly, Fig.2c shows that, for a fixed value N_{amp}=800, increasing/decreasing the ΔP_{LRS} from 5% results in the degradation of the system performance. In order to investigate the relation between ΔP_{LRS} and N_{amp}, Fig.2d illustrates that, the change in optimum N_{amp} value (i.e value of N_{amp} which will restore the system accuracy back to its expected value of 91.6% for a given ΔP_{LRS}), is inversely proportional to that of ΔP_{LRS} (i.e for decreasing/increasing the value of ΔP_{LRS}, a higher/lower value for N_{amp} is required to restore the system performance). As discussed in section 4.2, choosing any combination of ΔP_{LRS} and N_{amp} from Fig.2d has minimal impact on the increase of the write energy. To increase ΔP_{LRS} from 0.9% (i.e original value of ΔP_{LRS} in Fig.2c) to 3%/5%/8%, the amplitude of the pulses from the post-neurons needs to increase by +20mV/+50mV/+60mV respectively (i.e amplitude of the post-neuron pulses becomes 0.92/0.95/0.96V instead of 0.9V respectively). However, in order not to change the write circuit design, the ΔP_{LRS}=5% is chosen as the associated change in the pulse amplitude fits the resolution of the used digitally controlled DC-DC converter as explained in section 3.1.

<u>**Phase III**</u>: After the restore operations of **Phase I** and **Phase II**, the voltage biasing conditions used in the detection step are restored for future pre- and post-neuron pulses.

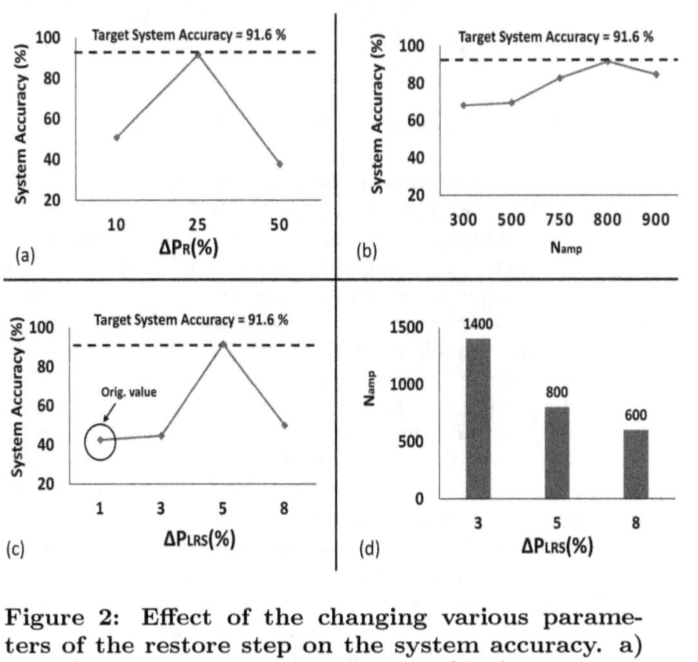

Figure 2: Effect of the changing various parameters of the restore step on the system accuracy. a) ΔP_R, b) N_{amp} for a fixed ΔP_{LRS} of 5%, c) ΔP_{LRS} for N_{amp}=800, and d) ΔP_{LRS} and the required N_{amp} to restore the system accuracy

3. READ AND WRITE CIRCUITS

The modifications to the conventional read and write circuits to implement the proposed framework in section 2, are discussed separately.

3.1 Write circuit modifications

One of the key modules of the write circuit for RRAM-based neuromorphic system is a digitally controlled low dropout DC-DC converter similar to those discussed in [17–19]. Those designs are connected to Digital-to-Analog Converter (DAC) which translates a digital input word into a proper output voltage level lower than VDD (1.2V in our case). Using the SPICE model for the HfO_x RRAM device in [5], the voltage levels of the pre- and post-neurons pulses required for the various percentage of changes in the RRAM resistive state, discussed in section 2, are in the range between [0.75-0.95]V (assuming ΔP_{LRS}=5%). The original voltage levels in our system example, described in [8, 9], are in the range between [0.8-0.9]V. Bounded by the minimum voltage level of NMOS/PMOS transistors used in the DAC, the 4-bit DACs of the DC-DC converter in [17–19] can provide 16 voltage levels from the range of VDD (1.2V) down to almost 0.4V with an accuracy as small as 50mV. Thus, in our example, the DAC-controlled DC-DC converter is capable of providing all the required voltage levels without the necessity to modify the write circuit. In case if other voltage levels are required, the DAC of the DC-DC converter needs to be redesigned. The change in the write energy consumption, resulting from using different voltage biases during the restore step, is evaluated in section 4.2.

3.2 Read circuit modifications

Fig.3 illustrates the structure of the modified read circuit, which consists of the normal integrate and fire (I&F) circuit describing the neuron operations [4, 20, 21] and two newly added modules:

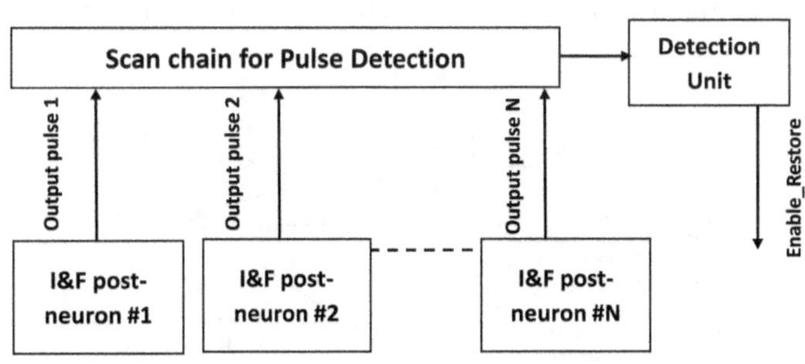

Figure 3: Schematic of the modified read circuit

- **Scan chain circuit**: This module is used to collect the pulses generated by the different neurons at various times and pass them to the detection unit to assess whether the RRAM reliability soft-errors have occurred or not based on the number of neuron pulses (condition C1 of the detection step in Fig.1).
- **Detection unit**: This module is responsible of counting the pulses coming from the scan chain in order to a) detect if the number of pulses at the post-neurons is less than 5 (indicator that RRAM reliability soft-errors have occurred as mentioned in section 2.1) and

b) find whether the restore step of the new framework, shown in Fig.1, needs to be initiated or not based on the number of times the input pattern has been re-applied (condition C2 of the detection step in Fig.1).

3.2.1 Scan chain circuit

Fig.4 shows the schematic of the scan chain circuit. Since

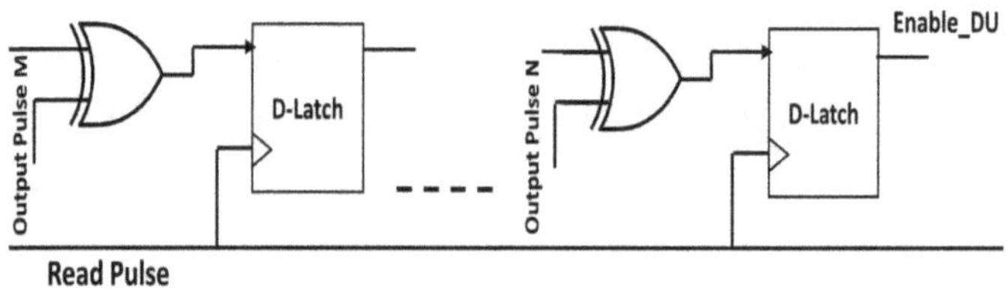

Figure 4: Scan Chain structure

pulses can occur from any neuron asynchronously, the D-Latch of each stage of the scan chain is enabled throughout the duration of the read operation (350 ms as per [8]). In our system example, given that the duration of each pulse is fixed to 20ms, our BRIAN simulations show that the post-neurons can generate pulses either simultaneously or with a minimum time split of around 10 μs. Since the delay of the entire scan chain is around 400 ns $(((Delay_{D-latch} + Delay_{XOR})$*number of stages = 1ns*400), any two pulses separated by $\geq$ 10 μs can travel through the scan chain without causing errors at the counters of the detection unit due to the overlap between the pulses. However, in case when pulses from the post-neurons are generated simultaneously, the counters at the detection unit might miscount them due to the time overlap between the pulses. The XOR gates at the input of each D-Latch in Fig.4 are added to prevent such issue. Fig.5 illustrates the worst case scenario, when two pulses from two adjacent stages (stages M-1 and M) are generated simultaneously. The parameter t_p in Fig.5 defines

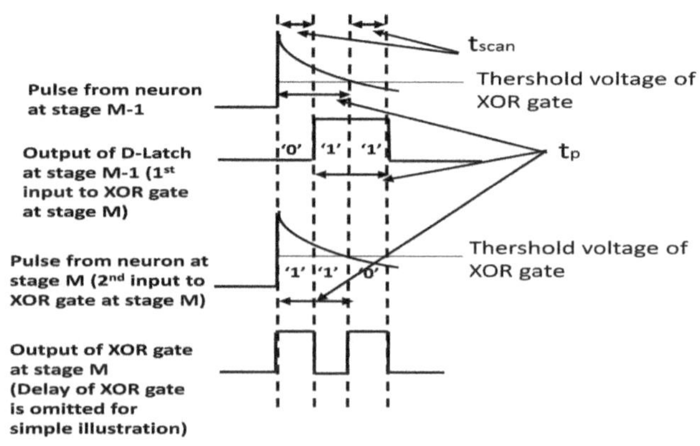

Figure 5: XOR gate output signals in case when the pulses observed at post-neurons occur simultaneously

the period of the write pulse during which the pulse amplitude is higher than the threshold voltage of XOR gate (i.e logic '1'). Although t_p is about 4ms, Fig.5 is not drawn to scale in order to focus mainly on the effect of introducing the delay of XOR and D-latch (t_{scan} = 1ns) on insuring the correct operation of the framework in worst-case scenario (when pulses from two adjacent neurons are generated simultaneously). This large delay of t_{scan} is achieved by increasing the channel length of all the transistors (i.e decreases W/L) used in scan chain design by a factor of 8. Hence, a delayed version of the same pulse is applied to the input of XOR gate at stage M which guarantees the generation of two pulses at the output of the XOR gate with a time split of 1ns. As a result, the correct number of pulses (=2) are counted.

However, the introduction of the scan chain increases the delay of the read operation as it needs to account for the worst-case scenario when a pulse is generated at the end of the read operation from the first neuron of the scan chain. In this case, the delay of the read operation is augmented by the delay of each stage of the scan chain multiplied by the number of post-neuron stages. This increase is less than 0.1% as highlighted in section 4.1.

3.2.2 Detection unit circuit

Fig.6 shows the structure of the detection unit (DU). This unit consists mainly of: a) 3-bit counter which is used to detect whether the number of received pulses from the scan chain is less than 5 or not (condition C1 of the detection step in Fig.1), and b) a 6-bit counter which is used to recognize whether the input pattern, causing the generation of less than 5 pulses, has been already re-applied for more than 50 times or not (condition C2 of the detection step in Fig.1). The OR-gate in Fig.6 disables the 3-bit counter once

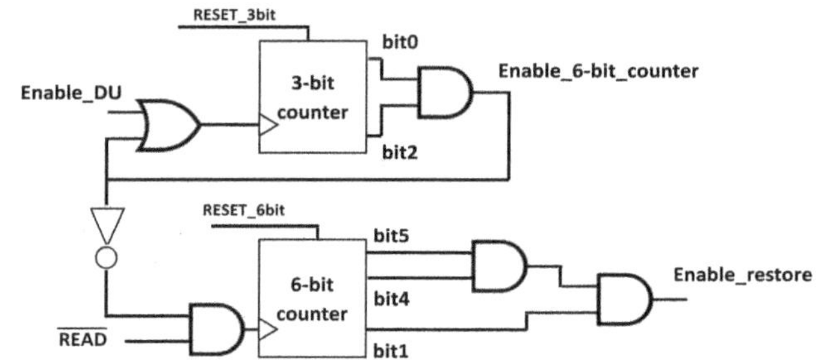

Figure 6: Detection Unit (DU) structure

5 pulses are computed from the sequence of pulses passed by the scan chain (Enable_DU signal in Fig.6) which could be as many as 200 pulses. This is needed to a) save energy consumption, b) speed-up the operation of the DU unit, and c) prevent the value of the counter to be reset when more than 8 pulses are passed by the scan chain. The output from the 3-bit counter (Enable_6-bit_counter signal in Fig.6) is then checked at the end of the read operation (by anding it with the control signal READ bar signal which is at logic '1' when the read operation is finished) to enable the 6-bit counter. If the value of the 6-bit counter reaches 50 (condition C2 in the detection step of in Fig.1), the restore step of the proposed framework, discussed in section 2, is enabled. Fig.7 demonstrates the operation of DU, in case if the number of pulses passed by the scan chain is 4 (i.e < 5). The steps S1-S3 in Fig.7 describes the sequence of the operations of the DU. After the value of the 3-bit counter is checked at the end of the read operation (S1), the 6-bit counter is incremented by 1 (S2). Since the value of the 6-bit counter has reached the limit value of 50, the restore step of the framework, shown in Fig.1, is initiated (S3). In this case, the RESET signals of the 3-bit and 6-bit counters (i.e RESET_3bit and RE-

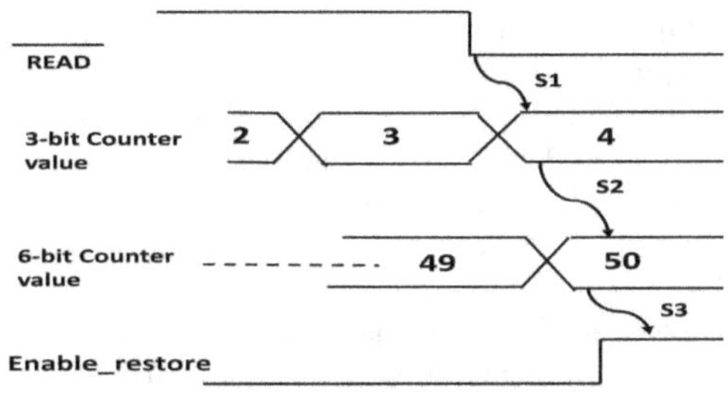

Figure 7: Waveforms for the operation of DU unit when the restore step of the framework is initiated.

SET_6bit signals in Fig.7) are also raised to re-initialize the values of the counters. If the restore step is not triggered (i.e number of times an input pattern has been re-applied is less than 50 or the number of pulses passed by the scan chain is higher than 5), only the 3-bit counter will be reset at the end of the DU operation.

It is worth mentioning that the counters used in the DU are actually asynchronous ripple counters to reduce the overhead energy consumption of the DU by removing the need to have an extra clock signal.

4. EXPERIMENTAL RESULTS

The simulation results for the modifications to the read and write circuits, required to support the various operations of newly proposed framework, are discussed in this section. Our simulation results are obtained using a combination of SPICE simulations, conducted using the compact SPICE model described in [5], and BRIAN system-level simulations on the neuromorphic system in [8].

4.1 Read circuit simulation results

As mentioned in section 3.2, the delay of the read operation is increased to account for a) the delay introduced by the scan chain and b) the worst-case scenario when a pulse, resulting from the neuron attached to the first stage of the scan chain, is generated by the end of the read operation. The percentage of increase in the delay is calculated using Equation 1:

$$T_{read,incr} = \frac{T_{read} + num_{st} * T_{scan} + T_{DU}}{T_{read}} - 1 \quad (1)$$

Where:

- T_{read}: is the duration of the read pulse which is equal to the time required for applying an input pattern to the system in [8] (350 ms)
- T_{scan}: is the delay of each stage of the scan chain.
- num_{st}: represents the number of stages of the scan chain which is equal to the number of post-neurons.
- T_{DU}: is the delay of the DU.

Our SPICE simulation results show that, for a 65nm technology, the T_{scan} and the T_{DU} are equal to 1ns and 1.2ns respectively. Given that the number of post-neurons for the neuromorphic system in [8] is 400, the percentage of increase in the read operation ($T_{read,incr}$) is less than 0.1%. This is due to the fact that the duration of the read operation is 8 order of magnitude (350ms) larger than the delay introduced by the scan chain (1ns) and the DU (1.2ns).

To compute the increase in the read energy consumption, Equation 2 is used

$$E_{read,incr} = \frac{num_{st} * (E_{read,avg} + E_{scan,avg}) + E_{DU,avg}}{num_{st} * E_{read,avg}} - 1 \quad (2)$$

Where:

- $E_{read,avg}$: refers to the average energy consumption consumed by the I&F circuits.
- $E_{scan,avg}, E_{DU,avg}$: are the average energy consumed by the scan chain and DU respectively.
- num_{st}: is the same parameter as that used in Eq.1.

Using the SPICE simulation results and substituting them in Eq.2, it is found that the increase in the energy consumption is around 1.1%. This is due to the fact that the energy drawn by each of the I&F circuit of the post-neurons is much higher compared to that of the scan chain and DU unit. The I&F circuit mainly consists of a) a Schmitt trigger and b) a shift register to count the number of pulses generated by each post-neuron to identify which neurons represent a certain digit of the MNIST dataset based on the value of the shift register. Those circuits draw large currents from the power supply leading to a large energy consumption compared to that of the scan chain and the DU ($E_{read,avg}$=0.06 mJ; $E_{scan,avg}$= 0.0007 mJ = 1.1% of $E_{read,avg}$; $E_{DU,avg}$ = 87.2μJ = 0.1% of $E_{read,avg}$).

4.2 Write circuit simulation results

As described in section 3.1, there is no introduced delay to the write operation since the same write circuit and the same write pulse, defined by the overlap between the pre- and post-neurons pulses, is used. Yet, the average increase in the energy consumption for the write operation, resulting from using different bias voltages in the restore step of the framework, can be calculated by Equation 3

$$E_{write,incr} = \frac{E_{write,avg} + E_{phaseI,avg} + E_{phaseII,avg}}{E_{write,avg}} - 1 \quad (3)$$

Where:

- $E_{write,avg}$: is the average energy consumed to modify the resistive state of the RRAM device based on the applied input pattern.
- $E_{phaseI,avg}, E_{phaseII,avg}$: describe the average energy required to complete phase I and II of the restore step of the proposed framework respectively.

Using the SPICE simulation results for the various biasing voltages required for the different percentages of change in the RRAM resistive state discussed in section 2.2, the difference in the energy consumption is minimal (< 0.1 %). This is because reducing the pulse amplitude of the pre-neurons by 50 mV, as described in Phase II of section 2.2, decreases their energy consumption by 16% which helps in lowering the overall percentage of increase of the write energy.

As described in Fig.2d, depending on the selected biasing voltages in phase II of the restore step, the optimal number of input patterns with the restore process N_{amp} varies. Fig.8 demonstrates that the impact of selecting any of the of ΔP_{LRS} and optimal N_{amp} is minimal on the write energy ($< 0.1\%$).

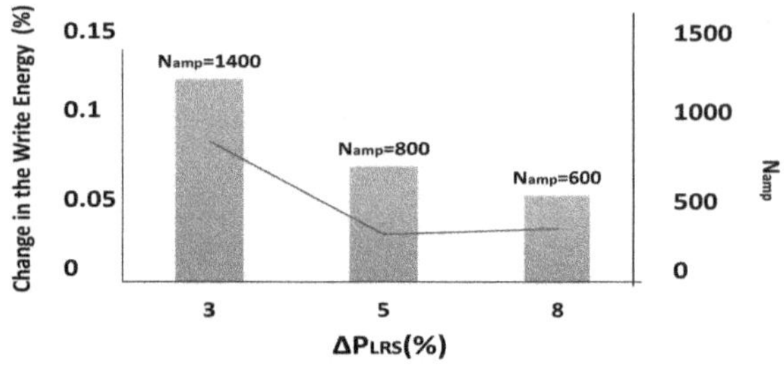

Figure 8: Effect of changing the biasing conditions of the restore step on the write energy

5. CONCLUSION

In this article, a novel framework for detecting and fixing the degradation in the RRAM-based neuromorphic system due to the RRAM reliability soft-errors is introduced. The accuracy of our example system was degraded to 43% due to the RRAM reliability failures. With the proposed framework, our BRIAN system level simulations show that the system accuracy can be restored to its original expected value of 91.6%. The required modifications to the read and write circuits to support this new framework are also discussed in this article. In our example, the SPICE simulation results demonstrate that the increase in the delay and energy consumption of the read operation is less than 0.1% and 1.1% respectively. Similarly, for the write operation, the increase in energy consumption is less than 0.1% while there is no change to its delay.

6. REFERENCES

[1] P.A.Merolla *et al.*, "A million spiking-neuron integrated circuit with a scalable communication network and interface," *Science, vol. 345, no. 6197*, pp. 668–673, 2014.

[2] Q.V.Le *et al.*, "Building high-level features using large scale unsupervised learning," in *IEEE International Conference on Acoustics, Speech and Signal Processing (ICASSP)*, pp. 8595–8598, Oct. 2013.

[3] S. Yu *et al.*, "An Electronic Synapse Device Based on Metal Oxide Resistive Switching Memory for Neuromorphic Computation," *IEEE Transactions on Electron Devices, Vol.58, no. 8*, Aug. 2011.

[4] S. Park *et al.*, "Rram-based synapse for neuromorphic system with pattern recognition function," in *IEEE International Electron Devices Meeting (IEDM)*, pp. 10.2.1–10.2.4, Dec 2012.

[5] P.-Y. Chen and S. Yu, "Compact modeling of RRAM devices and its applications in 1T1R and 1S1R array design," *IEEE Transaction on Electron Devices, Vol. 62, No. 12,*, pp. 4022 – 4028, Dec. 2015.

[6] Y.Y.Chen *et al.*, "Understanding of the Endurance Failure in Scaled $HfO2$-based 1T1R RRAM through Vacancy Mobility Degradation," in *IEEE International Electron Devices Meeting (IEDM)*, pp. 20.3.1 – 20.3.4, Dec. 2012.

[7] B. Chen *et al.*, "Physical mechanisms of endurance degradation in tmo-rram," in *2011 International Electron Devices Meeting*, pp. 12.3.1–12.3.4, Dec 2011.

[8] P.U.Diehl and M.Cook, "Unsupervised learning of digit recognition using spike-timing-dependent plasticity," *Frontiers of Computational Neuroscience, Vol.9, No.99*, Aug. 2015.

[9] A.Tosson *et al.*, "Analysis of rram reliability soft-errors on the performance of rram-based neuromorphic systems," in *submitted to 2017 IEEE Computer Society Annual Symposium on VLSI (ISVLSI)*, 2017.

[10] Y.Y.Chen *et al.*, "Postcycling LRS Retention Analysis in HfO2/Hf RRAM 1T1R Device," *IEEE Electron Device Letters, Vol. 34, No. 5*, pp. 626 – 628, May 2013.

[11] S.Ambrogio *et al.*, "Data retention statistics and modeling in HfO2 resistive switching memories," in *IEEE International Reliability Physics Symposium (IRPS)*, pp. M.Y.1 – M.Y.6, Apr. 2015.

[12] Y.Chen *et al.*, "Balancing SET/RESET Pulse for > 1010 Endurance in HfO2/Hf 1T1R Bipolar RRAM," *IEEE Transactions on Electron devices , Vol. 59, No. 12*, pp. 3243 – 3249, Dec. 2012.

[13] Y.Y.Chen *et al.*, "Improvement of data retention in HfO2 / Hf 1T1R RRAM cell under low operating current," in *IEEE International Electron Devices Meeting (IEDM)*, pp. 10.1.1 – 10.1.4, Dec. 2013.

[14] Y.LeCun *et al.*, "Gradient-based learning applied to document recognition," *Proceedings of the IEEE, Vol.86, No.11*, pp. 2278–2324, Nov. 1998.

[15] D.Goodman and R.Brette, "Brian: a simulator for spiking neural networks in python," *Frontiers in Neuroinformatics, Vol.2*, p. 5, 2008.

[16] G. Bi and M. Poo, "Synaptic Modifications in Cultured Hippocampal Neurons: Dependence on Spike Timing, Synaptic Strength, and Postsynaptic Cell Type," *The Journal of Neuroscience, Vol.18, No.24*, pp. 10464 –10472, Dec. 1998.

[17] G. Patounakis *et al.*, "A fully integrated onchip dc-dc conversion and power management system," *IEEE Journal of Solid-State Circuits, Vol. 39, No. 3*, pp. 987–994, March 2004.

[18] R.J.Milliken *et al.*, "Full on-chip cmos low-dropout voltage regulator," *IEEE Transactions on Circuits and systems -I: Regular papers, Vol. 54, No. 9*, pp. 1879–1891, Sept. 2007.

[19] J. F. Bulzacchelli *et al.*, "Dual-loop system of distributed microregulators with high dc accuracy, load response time below 500 ps, and 85mv dropout voltage," *IEEE Journal of Solid-State Circuits, Vol. 47, No. 4*, pp. 863–874, April 2012.

[20] D. Kadetotad *et al.*, "Parallel architecture with resistive crosspoint array for dictionary learning acceleration, vol.5, no.2," *IEEE Journal on Emerging and Selected Topics in Circuits and Systems*, pp. 194–204, June 2015.

[21] C. Liu *et al.*, "A spiking neuromorphic design with resistive crossbar," in *ACM/EDAC/IEEE Design Automation Conference (DAC)*, pp. 1–6, June 2015.

A Spin-Orbit Torque based Cellular Neural Network(CNN) Architecture

Yu Bai
California State University Fullerton
800 N State College Blvd.
Fullerton, CA, 92831
ybai@fullerton.edu

Sharon Hu
University of Notre Dame
Notre Dame, IN 46556
shu@nd.edu

Ronald F. DeMara
University of Central Florida
4000 Central Florida Blvd.
Orlando, FL, 32817
Ronald.Demara@ucf.edu

Mingjie Lin
University of Central Florida
4000 Central Florida Blvd.
Orlando, FL, 32817
mingjie@eecs.ucf.edu

ABSTRACT

In this paper, we propose a differential Spin Hall Effect(SHE) assisted domain wall synapse, which can generate either positive or negative synaptic weighting values without the significant cost of multiple power supply voltages, supply rails, or computationally-intensive digital hardware. The architecture of the proposed synapse utilizes reading currents flowing through two oppositely-oriented devices as weighted by device conductance. The conductance is used to encode synaptic weight and programmed by domain wall position through writing current. The ability to set the current as positively or negatively weighted results in highly-configurable functionality within a compact synapse design. The synapses are used with a soft-limiting nonlinear neuron to employ the relationship between positions and input current magnitude. We show through micro-magnetic simulation how the non-volatile physical characteristic of the domain wall calibrated synapse is used to implement a numerical integration function to realize a Cellular Neural Network(CNN). The performance of the proposed CNN design for isolated letter denoising at 0ns to 4ns demonstrates noise filtering functionality with total energy consumption during sensing of 24fJ. This compares favorably to existing spin CNN cell designs to provide a promising design approach for intrinsic neural computation.

Keywords

Spin-Orbit Torque; Cellular Neural Network; Domain Wall

1 Introduction

Recently, a significant amount of research has been carried out to develop a Cellular Neural Network(CNN) in hardware for various computational intensive workloads, such as information processing, image processing, motion detection, and some bioinformatics applications [1]. The major attractive aspects of CNN focus on: 1) CNN provides a neural-inspired parallel computing model which can be mapped onto a 2-D array of locally connected cells 2). The interconnections between cells and other synapses are space invariant, therefore it is suitable for VLSI implementation. 3). Their ability to process a continuous analog signal allows for real-time processing. Implementations of hardware-based CNN have recently emerged from research efforts. Thus, the CMOS-based CNN architecture is devoted to numerous applications. Although realization of CMOS-based CNN has received significant attention [2], there are still metrics which remain to be improved, such as energy, performance, area, and accuracy [3]. Much of the research in CMOS implemented CNN is devoted to reducing energy consumption, however, energy consumption reducing techniques for CMOS CNN is constrained due to high switching energy and leakage current of the MOSFET [4]. Therefore, it is crucial to seek out an improved hardware CNN architecture, if the performance trend is still associated with Moore's Law.

Recently, emerging devices have been explored in an effort to replace MOSFET technology for implementing ultra-low power CNN cells. Among many proposals, Tunnel-FETs(TFETs) and spintronic devices have shown to be a promising choice for the design of ultra-low power CNN cells. However, design challenges remain due to the complex architecture of the integrator and the transfer function generator. Spintronic devices are considered as an promising choice to implement the CNN cell. The paper [5] proposed a hybrid structure to implement CNN through spintronic devices and CMOS with a complete driving and sensing circuit. More than an order of magnitude energy reduction per operation can be achieved compared to the CMOS counterpart. The paper utilizes a magnetic switching according to spin orbit torque induced by spin-polarized current. However, restriction of input number of CNN cell, power consumption, and hard controlling of switching delay due to the amplitude of spin-polarized current are its drawbacks [5].

This paper explores the potential of Domain Wall(DW) device physics to naturally implement the synapse, integrator, and neuron. The dynamic relationship of CNN is achieved by utilizing emerging device physics for ultra-low power, high performance, and accuracy. The remainder of

Permission to make digital or hard copies of all or part of this work for personal or classroom use is granted without fee provided that copies are not made or distributed for profit or commercial advantage and that copies bear this notice and the full citation on the first page. Copyrights for components of this work owned by others than ACM must be honored. Abstracting with credit is permitted. To copy otherwise, or republish, to post on servers or to redistribute to lists, requires prior specific permission and/or a fee. Request permissions from permissions@acm.org.

GLSVLSI '17, May 10-12, 2017, Banff, AB, Canada
© 2017 ACM. ISBN 978-1-4503-4972-7/17/05...$15.00
DOI: http://dx.doi.org/10.1145/3060403.3060472

paper is organized as follows: Section 2 describes the background of CNN. In section 3, we introduce the physical characteristics of ferromagnetic spin-orbit torque devices. Section 4 presents overall architecture of spintronic based CNN. The detailed implementations of the CNN cell are discussed in section 5 and section 6. In section 7, we test our proposed architecture on image noise filter application using proposed CAD flow. In section 8, we compare our proposed CNN architecture with other methods. Conclusions are drawn in section 9.

2 Background

The conventional CNN with the single layer and spatially-invariant property is proposed by Chua [2]. In Figure 1(a), an array with 3×3 cells is shown. Each cell $C_{i,j}$, $(i,j) \in \{1,\ldots,k\} \times \{1,\ldots,l\}$ has synaptic connections with all predefined neighborhood cells, where $N_r(i,j)$ of radius r. The size of the neighborhood is defined as distance between the center cell and its adjacent cell. The distance is defined as equation, $m = (2r+1)^2$, where r is positive integer. For example, if $r = 1$, an array with a center cell has 8 neighbor cells.

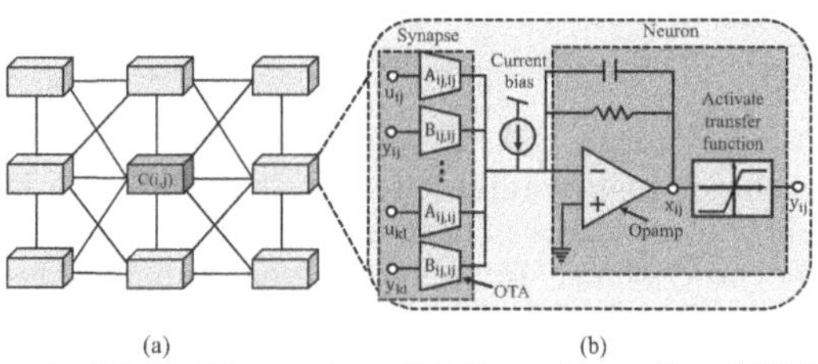

Figure 1: (a) CNN topology(b) the schematic of CNN cell

In Figure 1(b), an analog implementation of CNN cell is presented. There are three nodes in a given CNN cell C_{ij}, input u_{ij}, state x_{ij}, and output y_{ij}. The dynamic of the CNN can be expressed by an Ordinary Differential Equation(ODE) with $k \times l$ size. The dynamic equation of each CNN cell is given by Kirchhoff's Current Law(KCL):

$$C\frac{dx_{i,j}(t)}{dt} = -\frac{x_{ij}(t)}{R} + \sum_{C_{kl}\in N_r(i,j)} A_{kl,ij}y_{kl} + \sum_{C_{kl}\in N_r(i,j)} B_{kl,ij}u_{kl} + I_{ij} \quad (1)$$

where y_{kl} and u_{kl} are the output and inputs of neighboring cells, $A_{kl,ij}$ and $B_{kl,ij}$ are weighting parameters for the nearby cells, whose values are set by templates of the cell. The value of $A_{kl,ij}$ and $B_{kl,ij}$ are presented by matrices due to space invariant nature of synaptic connections interconnections. The $N_r(i,j)$ is the set of neighboring cells connected with the cell C_{ij}. I_{ij} represents the bias term. The active transfer function of CNN usually employs sigmoid transfer function to ensure fixed binary voltage levels at the output.

3 Ferromagnetic Spin-orbit Torque Devices

Comparing with a prototypical DW device, the SHE domain wall exerts a Spin-Orbit Torque(SOT) to displace the DW in the FerroMagnet(FM) and receives a charge current through a Heavy Metal(HM) underlayer, shown in Figure 2(a) [6, 7, 8, 9]. The writing current is in-plane flowing through a HM underlayer. The dynamic magnetization of the system is based on a regular FM magnetization dynamics model which is described by solving the Landau-Lifshitz-Gilbert (LLG) equation with additional information of SOT generated by spin hall effect at the FM-HM interface [9].

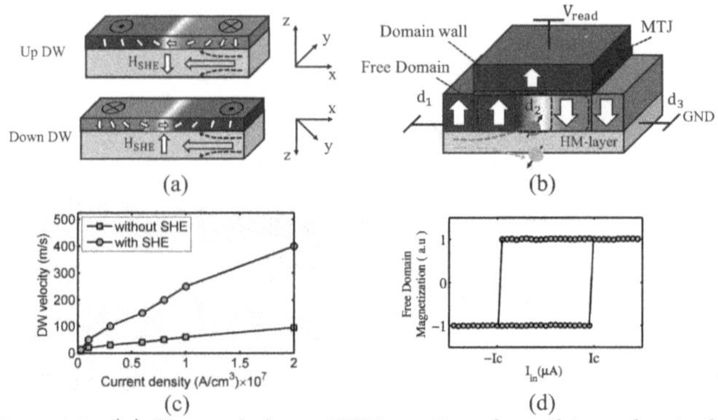

Figure 2: (a) Up and down DW motion describing physical phenomena of SHE assisted domain wall device. The domain wall is moving in Perpendicular Magnetic Anisotropy(PMA) nanowires according to flowing of the in-plane injection current through HM layer. The SOT coupling is generated and making the stabilization of chiral Neel domain wall through Dzyaloshinskii-Moriya Interaction(DMI). According to this model, a transverse spin current is generated by in-plane injection current. (b) Three-terminal DWM cell structure. (c) DW speed with and without SHE assistance. (d) DW switch characteristics. The hysteresis characteristics depends on critical current I_c of moving DW.

According to the given physical phenomena above, three terminal devices are utilized to construct the SOT spin-based CNN architecture. Figure 2(b) shows SOT neuron with three terminals based on a magnetic DW strip. The device has three magnetic domain d1, d2, and d3 associated with a Magnetic Tunnel Junction(MTJ) with fixed magnetization on the top. The free domain d2 has a free spin polarity which can be switched parallel or anti-parallel to the two fixed magnetic domains d1 and d3 through the different direction of applied current at the heavy metal layer. Therefore, the spin polarity at free domain d2 can sense direction(spin polarity is up if current is injecting to d1 and spin polarity is down if current is going out from d1) and amplitude(high current amplitude pushes d2 moving with large distance, otherwise moving with small distance). The minimum amplitude of injected current has the requirement to flip the state of domain wall d2. This phenomenon is called domain wall hysteresis, shown in Figure 2(d). The value of injected current depends on critical current density for magnetic domain motion passing through free magnetic domain d2. Thus, with help of spin hall effect, the current density with approximate value $\backsim 10^7\mathrm{A/cm}^2$ can produce more than 200m/s DW velocity, which is twice fast than the baseline DW structure with 60m/s DW velocity. The effective magnetic field of SHE assisted architecture can be expressed as, $\mathrm{H_{SHE}} = \mathrm{K}(\sigma \times \mathrm{m})$, where σ is a current dependent vector by $\sigma = j \times z$, where j is the current vector and z is direction perpendicular to the magnetization plane, m denotes the magnetization of magnetic domains. Notably, since σ is a vector, it can be in-plane or out of plane two directions. K is defined as a quality of material parameter, which is proportional to the effectiveness of the spin hall angle θ_H. Therefore, a given 100 nm long free layer with cross section area of $20 \times 2\mathrm{nm}^2$ can be pushed passing through

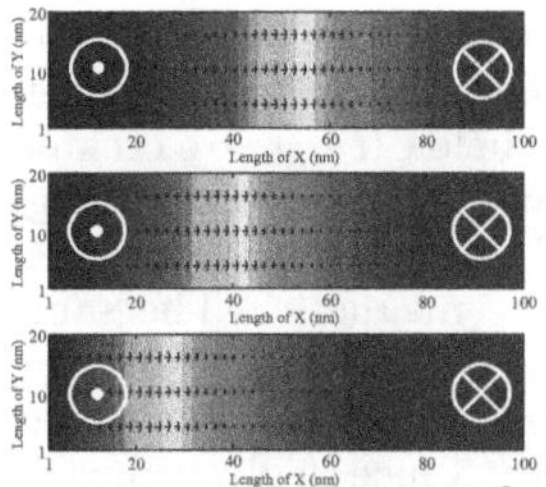

Symbol	Description	Value
α	Gilbert damping coefficient	0.3
K_{u2}	Perpendicular magnetic anisotropy constant	$0.48 \times 10^6 J/m^3$
D	Effective DMI constant -torque anisotropy constant	$-1.2 \times 10^{-3} J/m^2$
M_s	Saturation magnetization	$700KA/m$
ρ	Resistivity of Pt	$200\Omega/nm$
A	Exchanges correlation constant	$1.1 \times 10^{-11} J/m$
θ	Spin hall angle	0.07
	DW width	7.6nm
	FM thickness	0.6nm
	Heavy metal thickness	3nm
	Grid size	$4 \times 1 \times 0.6nm^3$

TABLE I: Device parameter used in the simulation.

Figure 3: Left: Mumax^3 simulation of DW motion according to injected current of 25μA flowing through the HM layer in 0.3ns. The given FM layer is 100nm in length with ferromagnet thickness 0.6nm. Right: Table I: device parameter used in the simulation.

whole length distance with less than 10μA in 0.5ns, according to the behavior shown in Figure 2(c).

In order to demonstrate a SHE assist domain wall device, the bottom-up device is simulated in Figure 3 Left. The simulation model considers device physics of current injection spin orbit torque in FM. The device parameters are obtained from previous experiment of magnetometric nano device [10, 11], shown in Table. I. Figure 3 Left show simulation results using Mumax^3 simulation interface, a GPU based micromagnetic simulation tool [12]. The results show the DW DMI stabilized motion in the device according to injected current applied on HM with 0.3ns duration. According to the speed plot in Figure 2(c), given free layer with a size of 120nm $\times$ 20nm, the injected current of 25μA will displace the domain wall by 30nm in a duration of 0.3nm.

Device variation is also considered in many research papers [13]. The device resistance depends on domain wall position, which is described through Non-Equilibrium Green's function(NEGF) transportation framework. This framework is calibrated with experimental results and presented in [9, 13]. In this case, the regular NEGF transportation framework is modified due to parallel connection of three domains, because FM with domain wall separates two fixed oppositely polarized magnetized domain. These three domains are considered parallel, anti-parallel and perpendicular DW to the pinned layer magnetization. Furthermore, the resistance range of the device is also varied by physical characteristics, such as oxide thickness t_{MgO} and relative angle θ. The variation of device resistance ΔR is a summation of variation of device resistance due to oxide thickness $R_{t_{MgO}}$ and relative angle θ, which is between magnetization of FM and the pinned layer. The equation of variation of device resistance ΔR is shown by following equations:

$$R_{t_{MgO}} \propto (e^{a_0 t_{MgO} + b_0} + \sum_{m=1}^{c} ((-1)^{m-1} V_{read}^{2m} e^{a_m t_{MgO} + b_m})^{-d} \tag{2}$$

$$R(\theta) = ((\frac{1}{R_P})(cos(\frac{\theta}{2}))^2 + \frac{1}{R_{AP}}(sin(\frac{\theta}{2}))^2)^{-1} \tag{3}$$

where R_P and R_{AP} represents resistance at parallel($\theta = 0$) and anti-parallel($\theta = \pi$) state respectively. The report of calibrating results of experimental data provides fitting parameters a_m, b_m, c, d. Based on these results, we can leverage the behavior to realize dynamic integrators.

4 Overall Architecture of Spintronic-based CNN

In this section, we introduce a new spintronic-based CNN architecture. Since the dynamic relationship of CNN is describing by a differential equation, the existing Artificial Neural Network(ANN) architecture cannot be adopted easily. In this paper, we proposed multi-layer DW architecture to implement dynamic integrator and active transfer function based on non-volatile physical characteristics of DW device. In Figure 4(a), the overall architecture of a CNN cell implemented by a magnetic DW device is shown. The voltage inputs of CNN cell($C_{i,j}, V_{in1}, \cdots, V_{inn}$) are used to implement inputs u_{kl}, y_{kl}, where $C_{kl} \in N_{C_{ij}}$. The weighting parameters $A_{kl,ij}$ and $B_{kl,ij}$ are mapped to the proposed SHE DW device. The positive and negative weight can be generated according to the proposed architecture.

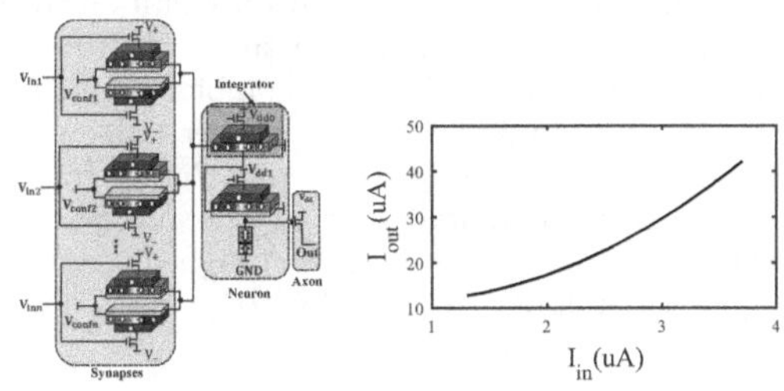

(a) (b)

Figure 4: (a) The proposed CNN cell architecture using SHE DW device(b) Output current provided by the PMOS transistor increases almost linearly with the input current.

A PMOS transistor is used for implementing axons which transmits neuron output to next stage. The output current to next stage is amplified linearly by the PMOS transistor since read current margin of the proposed spin torque neuron is small, shown in Figure 4(b). In Figure 4(b), with increasing of writing current flowing through the HM layer, the gate voltage of the axon transistor decreases as the resistance of the pull-down device in the resistive divider network decreases. The accuracy of proposed spintronic CNN needs to be taken into consideration. In general, the accuracy and robustness of spintronic CNN are degraded according to device variations. For programming variation, although there are variations with programming procedure of DW position in the proposed synapse and neuron, DW displacement still can be observed, modeled and measured by many research works [14]. The paper [15] proposed a dynamic model of DW displacement accuracy. Since the SHE DW position is very important information for the proposed CNN, the pin domain wall method at the specific location of a nanowire is used to achieve necessary bit discretization [16]. The stochastic simulation is performed to evaluate impact of resistance variation on accuracy. If the 20% 3σ variation of resistance is applied on SOT device, a negligible degradation in accuracy is observed, which is usually less than 4%. The existing on-chip or chip-in-loop learning methods are used to overcome such problems and build up a variation neuromorphic systems [17]. In the following two sections, we discuss in more detail the DW device based neural synapses and neurons.

5 Spintronic Neural Synapse

In Figure 5(a), our proposed synapse has two devices connecting in parallel. The positive and negative weight is represented by bipolar current at the output of neural synapse. To produce bipolar read current, we use two devices with different constant supply voltages. The equivalent circuit of this reading operation is shown in Figure 5(b). On each of DW device, the fixed voltage applied at read and GND ter-

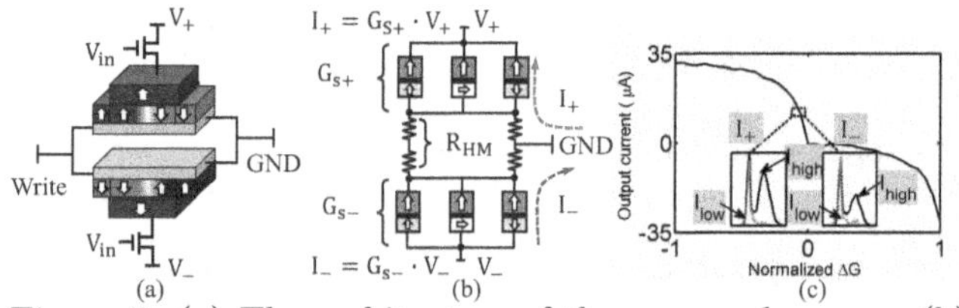

Figure 5: (a) The architecture of the proposed synapse.(b) The equivalent circuit of the proposed synapse. The two reading currents flowing through two opposite devices and weighted by device conductance. The conductance is used to encode synaptic weight and programmed by DW position through writing current. (c) Simulation results of proposed differential SHE domain wall architecture. The difference of device conductance causes different combinations of output reading current. Up and down SOT devices have two current states, high and low current I_{high} and I_{low}. In order to generate a positive weighted current, the up SOT device with lower resistance value generates higher magnitude of current I_{high} than opposite current of I_{high} from down SOT device.

minal creates a closed loop. Current I_{s+} is due to resistant of devices, which is given by the combination of parallel, anti-parallel domain and free layer domain. In Figure 5(b), the MTJ device with two arrows shows the different states of the domain. The free layer domain has magnetization along the horizontal axis. Although heavy metal has constant resistance in the reading path, it compares negligibly with tunneling oxide resistance. The device conductance of free layer is defined as $G_{P,max}$ and $G_{AP,max}$. where the magnetization of the free layer is parallel and anti-parallel to the pinned layer. Therefore, the total device conductance is given by:

$$G_{S+} = G_{P,max}(\frac{x}{L}) + G_{AP,max}(\frac{1-x}{L}) + G_{DW} \quad (4)$$

where G_{GW} is conductance of domain wall region and L is the length of the whole device. If the supplied voltage is constant, the G_{GW}, $G_{P,max}$ and $G_{AP,max}$ are constants. From the equation above, G_{S+} obeys a linear relationship with domain wall position x. Thus, the device G_{S+} can be programmed by DW position through injected current at HM layer. The weighted current is generated by a constant voltage $V_{s+,-}$ and device conductance(encodes as synaptic weights), $I_{S+} = G_{S+} \cdot V_{S+}$. In the reading operation, the hysteresis physical characteristics of DW depinning make the spintronic synapses read appropriately without any domain wall motion. The Tunneling Magnetioresistance Ratio(TMR) value can determine the ratio of synaptic weight which is encoded by device conductance. More than 1,000% TMR values are expected in ten years [18]. In artificial neural networks(ANNs), the negative weight is very important to describe an opposite relationship between the two neurons. There are two common methods to implement negative synaptic weight by emerging devices, memristor crossbar architecture [13] and memristor bridge synapse. However, for reconfigurable computing platform, these methods will incur cost of power supplies and hardware. In this paper, we propose a differential SHE assisted domain wall synapse, which can generate either positive or negative synaptic weighting value without the significant cost of multiple power supply voltages, supply rails, and computationally-intensive digital hardware. In Figure 5(b), the combination reading current depends on weighted readings from two opposite device. In the writing operation, the same writing current injects in HM layers on two devices. Thus, the positive and negative effective magnetic fields H_{SHE} are created on up and down devices, respectively. The effective magnetic fields H_{SHE} working on DW region can be observed as perpendicular to the plane of the magnetic. The same altitude and duration of injection current make DW moving with the same velocity on both devices. According to the device model, the down device conductance is given by,

$$G_{S-} = G_{P,max}(\frac{1-x}{L}) + G_{AP,max}(\frac{x}{L}) + G_{DW} \quad (5)$$

As dictated by the two device conductances G_{S-} and G_{S+} above, the currents I_+ and I_- passing through up and down SHE domain wall are generated by constant voltage V_+ and V_-. According to Kirchhoff's Current Law(KCL), the output current flowing through the load is the sum of the two input currents. Therefore, the positive or negative synaptic weight is encoded by the difference of two device conductance, shown in Figure 5(b). If up device has larger conductance than down device, the synaptic weight is positive. Otherwise, it is negative. The Figure 5(c) shows simulation results of a different combination of up and down device conductance. Therefore, the weighted output current can be generated through the specific combination of programmed device conductance.

6 All Spin Neuron

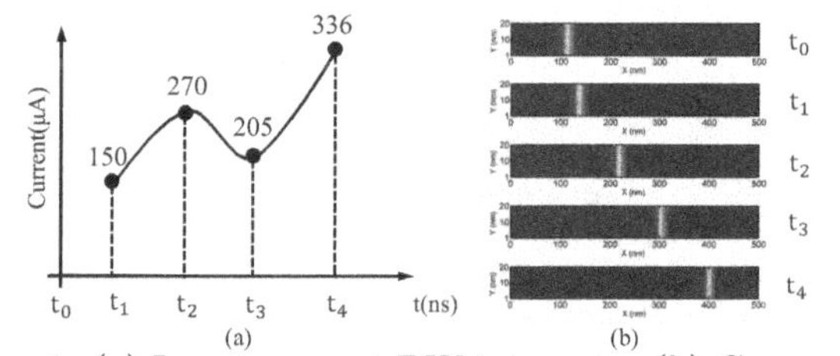

Figure 6: (a) Input wave at DW integrator.(b) Corresponding DW position simulated by Mumax^3.

The functionality of neuron is modeled as summation and active transfer function. In the CNN case, the dynamic relationship requires an integrator to sum the signal from synapses. Therefore, we propose two layers all spin neuron to implement integrator and active transfer function. The output of neuron is transmitted via the proposed axon structure which is implemented by a PMOS transistor. Figure 6 shows a simulation of the proposed integrator using a DW device. The non-volatile physical characteristic is used to implement integration needed by the CNN. In other words, the displacement of DW device depends on resultant synaptic input current and the magnitude of input current determines the displacement of DW device. The higher magnitude of synaptic current leads to greater DW displacement. If the magnitude of synaptic current is less than the critical current of DW device, no DW displacement occurs in DW device. In Figure 6, the four different magnitudes of synaptic current are applied on the DW device. The lowest magnitudes of synaptic current makes the lowest displacement, shown in t_1 of Figure 6(b), on the other hand, the highest DW displacement is made by the highest magnitude of synaptic current, shown in t_4 of Figure 6(b). The soft-limiting nonlinear transfer function in our design is implemented by single DW devices, see Figure 6. The DW2 device in Figure 6 receives output current of the integrator.

The proposed soft-limiting nonlinear neuron employs the relationship between positions and input current magnitude. With larger current pulse injection or time of integration into the DW integrator, the position of DW1 shifts and decreases DW device vertical resistance. As mentioned in previous section, in order to maintain an adequate sensing margin, the maximum vertical sensing current is $30\mu A$. Therefore, injection current is not above critical current of DW2 device and shifting DW2 device, when moving position of the DW1 is small and kept in the high resistance range. Therefore, the lower threshold $th1$ is implemented by the critical current of DW2. On another side, $th2$ is implemented by the requirement of max sensing current and length of DW device. The high magnitudes of applied current leads to high DW shifting speed, on the contrary, low magnitudes of applied current leads to low DW shifting speed. Since each DW device reads out though vertical sensing current, the horizontal DW resistance is fixed by device width and length. In our simulation, the default horizontal DW resistance R_w is equal to 294.5Ω. We now emphasis on DW device reliability issue. In order to evaluate DW device reliability due to intensive computation, we do discuss the retention time of proposed devices. The Fukami's paper reported 10-year retention time at 150^oC and 10^{14} times write endurance for Co/Ni wire. Heating effect of DW device is also analyzed in [19]. Although heating effect may affect DW device reliability, some proposed solutions based on appropriate structural optimization can reduce heating in the device.

7 Applicaction

To validate our proposed architecture and circuit design methods, we implemented the CNN array dynamics for various image processing tasks. We also quantitatively measure and compare its performance metrics, such as energy consumption with its counterpart implemented with the conventional analog based CNN architecture. Before presenting our simulation results, we first present the overall CAD flow of our mixed-model simulations. There are four essential design steps. For the cognitive application itself, we take advantage of both the MATLAB CNN training software and the technology mapping capability of the Cadence tool chain. Specifically, we start by building a rich cell library of synapses with different fan-ins. Subsequently, these design results will be read by the Cadence Spectre tool, which creates a SPICE circuit library. Such a library will then be used to evaluate the performance of our CNN implementation at the gate and system level.

The CNN system with $M \times N$ Ordinary Differential Equation(ODE) are solved by the Runge-Kutta method. Each cell contains an initial value for the information fo state, which is shown in equation 1. In our simulation framework, the initial value corresponds the initial position of the DW device. The image processing problem utilizes template parameter A, B and bias Z. In this paper, we use noise filtering image process for our application. The CNN with a fixed weight which is implemented on proposed architecture. The black and white image of letter A is treated by injecting noise with density 0.2. The image with 128×128 pixels is given to CNN and set as the initial state.

The templates of this noise filtering application is given by:

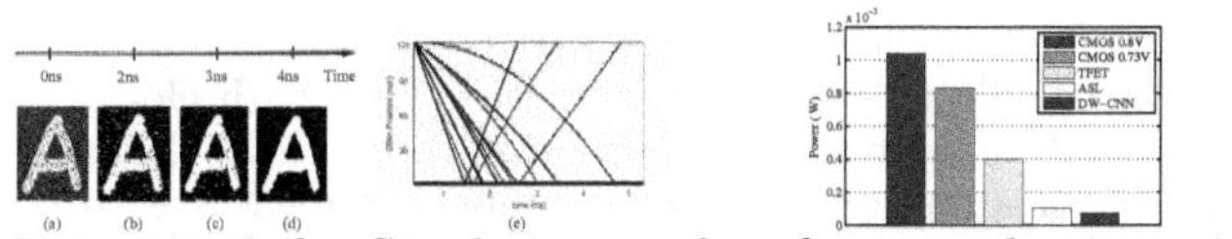

Figure 7: Left: Simulation results of proposed spintronic CNN.(a) Input noise image of letter A(b) Output image of CNN filter at 4ns(c) Output image of CNN filter at 8ns(d) Output image of CNN filter at 16ns(e) Transient response of the magnetic magnetization of CNN cell at 1ns by using created library. Right:Comparison of power consumption for different CNN cell architectures[20, 21, 1, 5]. The power consumption measurement concludes dynamic and static power of white and black pixel.

$$A = \begin{bmatrix} 0 & 0.8 & 0 \\ 1.1 & 1 & 1 \\ 0 & 1 & 0 \end{bmatrix} B = \begin{bmatrix} 0 & 0 & 0 \\ 0 & 0 & 0 \\ 0 & 0 & 0 \end{bmatrix} Z = 0$$

Since there is no intrinsic self-feedback in our proposed architecture, the middle cell of template A is set to 1 rather than 2. Compare with CMOS or TFET design, our proposed architecture doesn't have the linear feedback resistance R. In this particular application, the currents from synapse is programmed on proposed DW synapse architecture. The reading voltage on integrator V_{dd0} is set correctly in order to generate larger spin-polarized current than critical current at DW2, shown in Figure 4(a). Figure 7 shows the simulation results of proposed CNN architecture for noise filter application. In Figure 7(a)-(d), the output images are shown due to different processing time. The Figure 7(f) shows the noisy pixel is filtered by using spin torque magnetization.

8 Performance Analysis

In this section, we analyze the power consumption of proposed all spin CNN cell. A comparison between all spin CNN and other implementations is provided. Analog computations in a typical CNN cell have two energy dissipations: dynamic and static energy dissipation. Dynamic energy dissipation is defined as the requirement energy to transfer from an initial state to an equilibrium point. For example, in image processing, the equilibrium point for a pixel can be white or black. Static energy dissipation is the energy consumption when the state is stable.

Figure 7 right shows a comparison of power consumption for different CNN cell architectures. Two conventional 15nm CMOS technology based architectures are simulated and measured with different supplied voltage($0.8V$ and $0.73V$) [20, 21]. For noise filtering of a binary image, we observe that the white pixel has more power consumption than the black pixel because of asymmetric characteristics of voltage ranges. In Figure 7 Right, the conventional CMOS-based CNN cell has the highest power consumption due to large required net current at I_{eff}. The TFET CNN cell outperforms the CMOS CNN cell due to less net current I_{eff} for a transition to a white pixel by same process time. Recently, the paper using All Spin Logic(ASL) for CNN cell is proposed for potential efficiency improvements over CMOS-based design. The gain in energy efficiency allows for a CNN with low power consumption. Our proposed all spin CNN cell based on domain wall device has lower power consumption compared to other methods. The energy consumption of the proposed all spin CNN cell can be divided into three components: integrating, sensing, and resetting. For integrating component, lateral currents of 30μA on average are injected into DW devices for different weights with resistances around 200Ω. Therefore, each synapse's programming energy is calculated to be approximately 0.4fJ with clock cycle period being 1ns. For the sensing component, the total energy consumption of sensing component measures to be about 24fJ. For the resetting component, roughly 0.75fJ in energy is consumed using a 50μA current which compares favorably overall to provide a compact an energy efficient approach to realizing CNNs using emerging device technologies..

9 Conclusion

In this paper, a novel architecture of CNN is presented. In order to fully unleash the computing power of emerging devices, unconventional circuit design methodologies are utilized to to natively exploit the inherent physical property of these emerging devices, instead merely treating them simply as some "super" switches to replace CMOS transistors. In this paper, the proposed design achieves three times less energy consumption than conventional designs.

10 References

[1] I. Palit, X. S. Hu, J. Nahas, and M. Niemier, "Tfet-based cellular neural network architectures," in *Low Power Electronics and Design (ISLPED), 2013 IEEE International Symposium on*, pp. 236–241, Sept 2013.

[2] L. O. Chua and L. Yang, "Cellular neural networks: applications," *IEEE Transactions on Circuits and Systems*, vol. 35, pp. 1273–1290, Oct 1988.

[3] J. Kung, D. Kim, and S. Mukhopadhyay, "On the impact of energy-accuracy tradeoff in a digital cellular neural network for image processing," *IEEE Transactions on Computer-Aided Design of Integrated Circuits and Systems*, vol. 34, pp. 1070–1081, July 2015.

[4] A. R. Trivedi, S. Datta, and S. Mukhopadhyay, "Application of silicon-germanium source tunnel-fet to enable ultralow power cellular neural network-based associative memory," *IEEE Transactions on Electron Devices*, vol. 61, pp. 3707–3715, Nov 2014.

[5] C. Pan and A. Naeemi, "A proposal for energy-efficient cellular neural network based on spintronic devices," *CoRR*, vol. abs/1604.04584, 2016.

[6] A. Roohi, R. Zand, and R. F. DeMara, "A tunable majority gate-based full adder using current-induced domain wall nanomagnets," *IEEE Transactions on Magnetics*, vol. 52, pp. 1–7, Aug 2016.

[7] Y. Bai, B. Hu, W. Kuang, and M. Lin, "Ultra-robust null convention logic circuit with emerging domain wall devices," in *Proceedings of the 26th edition on Great Lakes Symposium on VLSI*, pp. 251–256, ACM, 2016.

[8] Y. Bai and M. Lin, "Universal random number generation with field-programmable analog array and magnetic tunneling junction (mtj) devices," in *Computer and Information Technology; Ubiquitous Computing and Communications; Dependable, Autonomic and Secure Computing; Pervasive Intelligence and Computing (CIT/IUCC/DASC/PICOM), 2015 IEEE International Conference on*, pp. 1338–1343, IEEE, 2015.

[9] A. Sengupta, Y. Shim, and K. Roy, "Simulation studies of an all-spin artificial neural network: Emulating neural and synaptic functionalities through domain wall motion in ferromagnets," *CoRR*, vol. abs/1510.00459, 2015.

[10] S. Emori, U. Bauer, S.-M. Ahn, E. Martinez, and G. S. Beach, "Current-driven dynamics of chiral ferromagnetic domain walls," *Nature materials*, vol. 12, no. 7, pp. 611–616, 2013.

[11] E. Martinez, S. Emori, N. Perez, L. Torres, and G. S. Beach, "Current-driven dynamics of dzyaloshinskii domain walls in the presence of in-plane fields: Full micromagnetic and one-dimensional analysis," *Journal of Applied Physics*, vol. 115, no. 21, p. 213909, 2014.

[12] A. Vansteenkiste and B. Van de Wiele, "Mumax: a new high-performance micromagnetic simulation tool," *Journal of Magnetism and Magnetic Materials*, vol. 323, no. 21, pp. 2585–2591, 2011.

[13] D. Fan, M. Sharad, A. Sengupta, and K. Roy, "Hierarchical temporal memory based on spin-neurons and resistive memory for energy-efficient brain-inspired computing," *arXiv preprint arXiv:1402.2902*, 2014.

[14] D. Bhowmik, M. E. Nowakowski, L. You, O. Lee, D. Keating, M. Wong, J. Bokor, and S. Salahuddin, "Deterministic domain wall motion orthogonal to current flow due to spin orbit torque," *Scientific reports*, vol. 5, 2015.

[15] F. Büttner, B. Krüger, S. Eisebitt, and M. Kläui, "Accurate calculation of the transverse anisotropy of a magnetic domain wall in perpendicularly magnetized multilayers," *Phys. Rev. B*, vol. 92, p. 054408, Aug 2015.

[16] D. Lacour, J. Katine, L. Folks, T. Block, J. Childress, M. Carey, and B. Gurney, "Experimental evidence of multiple stable locations for a domain wall trapped by a submicron notch," *Applied physics letters*, vol. 84, no. 11, pp. 1910–1912, 2004.

[17] M. Prezioso, F. Merrikh-Bayat, B. Hoskins, G. Adam, K. K. Likharev, and D. B. Strukov, "Training and operation of an integrated neuromorphic network based on metal-oxide memristors," *CoRR*, vol. abs/1412.0611, 2014.

[18] A. Hirohata, H. Sukegawa, H. Yanagihara, I. Å¡utiÄĞ, T. Seki, S. Mizukami, and R. Swaminathan, "Roadmap for emerging materials for spintronic device applications," *IEEE Transactions on Magnetics*, vol. 51, pp. 1–11, Oct 2015.

[19] M. Sharad, D. Fan, K. Aitken, and K. Roy, "Energy-efficient non-boolean computing with spin neurons and resistive memory," *Nanotechnology, IEEE Transactions on*, vol. 13, pp. 23–34, Jan 2014.

[20] D. E. Nikonov and I. A. Young, "Uniform methodology for benchmarking beyond-cmos logic devices," in *Electron Devices Meeting (IEDM), 2012 IEEE International*, pp. 25.4.1–25.4.4, Dec 2012.

[21] D. E. Nikonov and I. A. Young, "Overview of beyond-cmos devices and a uniform methodology for their benchmarking," *Proceedings of the IEEE*, vol. 101, no. 12, pp. 2498–2533, 2013.

PreNoc: Neural Network based Predictive Routing for Network-on-Chip Architectures

Michel A. Kinsy, Shreeya Khadka and Mihailo Isakov
Adaptive and Secure Computing Systems (ASCS) Laboratory
Department of Electrical and Computer Engineering
Boston University

ABSTRACT

In this paper, we introduce a neural network based predictive routing algorithm for on-chip networks which uses anticipated global network state and congestion information to efficiently route network traffic. The core of the algorithm is a multi-layer neural network machine learning approach where the inputs are level of occupancy of virtual channels, average latency for a particular router to be selected for route computation, the probability of virtual channel allocation, and the probability of winning switch arbitration at the crossbar. The algorithm lends itself to both node routing and source routing. To evaluate the **PreNoc** routing algorithm, we simulate both synthetic traffic and real application traces using a cycle-accurate simulator. In most test cases, the proposed approach outperforms current deterministic and adaptive routing techniques in terms of latency and throughput. The hardware overhead for supporting the new routing algorithm is minimal.

CCS Concepts

•**Hardware** → **Interconnect;** *Network on chip;*

Keywords

Network on chip; NoC; Adaptive Routing; Artificial Neural Network; Predictive Routing

1. INTRODUCTION

The exponential growth in transistor count has led to the integration of more processors onto a single chip. Computer systems with several distinct CPU cores on a single die are now standard with commercially available multicore designs containing 64 or more cores. Multicore and many-core systems raise new sets of design challenges, one of them being the communication infrastructure between the cores. Initially, buses were used in establishing communication between the cores and system components, but bus-based communication techniques do not scale well beyond 16 cores. As an alternative, network-on-chip (NoC) architectures have been proposed.

Permission to make digital or hard copies of all or part of this work for personal or classroom use is granted without fee provided that copies are not made or distributed for profit or commercial advantage and that copies bear this notice and the full citation on the first page. Copyrights for components of this work owned by others than the author(s) must be honored. Abstracting with credit is permitted. To copy otherwise, or republish, to post on servers or to redistribute to lists, requires prior specific permission and/or a fee. Request permissions from permissions@acm.org.

GLSVLSI '17, May 10 - 12, 2017, Banff, AB, Canada

© 2017 Copyright held by the owner/author(s). Publication rights licensed to ACM.

ISBN 978-1-4503-4972-7/17/05. . . $15.00

DOI: http://dx.doi.org/10.1145/3060403.3060406

Routing algorithms for NoC architectures can be generally classified into oblivious and adaptive. With oblivious routing, which includes deterministic routing algorithms as a subset, the path followed by a packet is statically determined. This method allows each node in the network to make its routing decisions independently from the others. By virtue of this distributed aspect, oblivious routing, such as dimension order routing, enables simple and fast router designs, and is widely adopted in early NoC-based systems.

However, oblivious algorithms perform poorly if the network state changes, as in the case of transient or permanent faults, or if the application has certain communication patterns, such as bursty data transfers. The performance reduction occurs because application and network state information are not used for computing routes. Alternatively, an adaptive routing algorithm can use state information, for example network congestion, to adjust to application phases and network changes when making routing decisions. With its dynamic load balancing, adaptive routing theoretically outperforms oblivious routing. However, in the past, adaptive routing schemes have faced the difficult challenge of balancing adaptiveness with router complexity. The vast majority of these algorithms have never been implemented because of the complexity of the router hardware that they require.

The challenge of designing adaptive routing algorithms which achieve good network load balancing, relatively short paths for packets, and modest router architecture complexity, is still relevant. Furthermore, in current multicore and many-core designs large portions of silicon are effectively "dark"– either idle for long periods of time or significantly underclocked at the nominal operating voltage. This has made adaptive routing more relevant, since oblivious routing is inadequate for dealing with the network state changes. Esmaeilzadeh et al. [4] predict that over 50% of chips will not use the ITRS scaling at 8nm technology node. Taylor [12] estimates that in few years, designs may be 93.75% dark.

In this work, we present a predictive network-on-chip routing algorithm, named **PreNoc**, that uses a neural network based learning technique to route packets for better performance and power efficiency. To achieve the best performance, adaptive routing algorithms generally need global knowledge of the current network status. However, dynamically obtaining a global and instantaneous view of the network is often impractical due to changing propagation delays. As a result, adaptive routing algorithms in practice have relied on local knowledge, which limits their effectiveness. The proposed algorithm mitigates this problem by first learning the congestion and arbitration delays in the network, then predicting the future network states and making routing decisions without requiring real-time network state information.

2. RELATED WORK

Ma et al. [10] introduced DBAR - Destination-Based Adaptive Routing. The algorithm uses both local and global network information in estimating network congestion levels. In [3], Ebrahimi et al. presented an adaptive routing algorithm based on minimal and non-minimal paths. Using local and global congestion information, the algorithm is able to estimate the latency associated with each output channel on the routing path to the destination switch. To avoid some the pitfalls associated with global network load balancing, Gratz et al. [6] proposed RCA - Regional Congestion Awareness: a lightweight adaptive routing scheme that makes path selection decisions based on the aggregated congestion information from adjacent routers. The **PreNoc** algorithm can be applied effectively to routing techniques by utilizing regional and global congestion information. Cai et al. [1] proposed a congestion prediction algorithm. It uses a hamming network to compute the link buffer congestion, finds the worst congested nodes, and then adapts to avoid congested nodes. With DyXY routing [9], packets are sent to either X or Y direction depending on the congestion conditions. It uses local information, such as the current queue length of the corresponding input port of neighboring routers to decide on the next hop. Nilsson et al [2] proposed a proximity congestion awareness technique which can be used for uniform load distribution. Information from the neighboring routers is sent from one router to its neighbors in all directions. Ramakrishna *et al.* [11] in their Global Congestion Awareness (GCA) scheme used global link state and congestion information to adapt routing to the network state. Farahnakian et al. [5] introduced a congestion aware dual-reinforcement routing algorithm where a two-way learning approach allows the source node to learn the best way to get to the destination node and from the destination node back to source node. These works have informed and influenced the design of **PreNoc** algorithm but with a key difference in path selection. In the proposed routing algorithm, path selection is done in a predictive manner as opposed to the general reactive way.

3. PREDICTIVE ROUTING ALGORITHM

To support the adaptive routing algorithms, NoC-based systems need to implement mechanisms to monitor and collect the network state data. Adaptive routing algorithms analyze this state information, for example network congestion, to make their routing decisions. In this work, we use neural networks to make routing decisions. Due to the development of more sophisticated and efficient machine learning techniques, practical neural network based adaptive routing algorithms have become more feasible.

To present **PreNoc** algorithm, the following standard definitions of network graphs are used.

DEFINITION 1. *Given a network graph $G(V,E)$, where a directed edge $(u,v) \in E$ has capacity $c(u,v)$ and buffer space $b(u,v)$. The capacities $c(u,v)$ are the available bandwidths on the edge and buffer spaces $b(u,v)$ are available buffer spaces associated with input port (u,v).*

There is a set of $N(N-1)$ source and destination pairs in the network. The set of possible flows is $F = \{f_1, f_2, ..., f_n\}$. $f_i = (s_i, t_i, d_i)$, where s_i and t_i are the source and destination, respectively, for pair i, and d_i is the demand. In this work the assumption is $s_i \neq t_i$ The flow f_i is the set of all data transfers from source s_i to destination t_i.

DEFINITION 2. *The amount of flow f_i along edge (u,v) is $f_i(u,v)$. A route is a path p_i from s_i to t_i for a flow i. Edges along this path will have $f_i(u,v) > 0$, other edges will have $f_i(u,v) = 0$. If $f_i(u,v) > 0$, then route p_i will use both bandwidth and buffer space on the edge (u,v).*

The objective function of the routing algorithm is to (1) minimize the maximum channel load (MCL) across all network links to avoid premature network saturation, and (2) control the average path length to maximize network throughput and minimize power usage.

3.1 Network State Estimation

The **PreNoc** algorithm is a hybrid approach that uses both *node routing* and *source routing*. The network state estimation is performed in a distributed fashion using local and global information. Resource sharing conflicts are at the root of network congestion, premature saturation and lower network throughput. In wormhole routers, the routing operation takes four steps or phases; namely, ① routing (RC), ② virtual channel allocation (VA), ③ switch allocation (SA), and ④ switch traversal (ST). Resource sharing conflict may arise in three of those four steps: at the buffer read and route computation level, at the virtual-channel allocation level, and at the switch arbitration level. Figure 1 shows the conventional router architecture and the three contention points, 1 through 3.

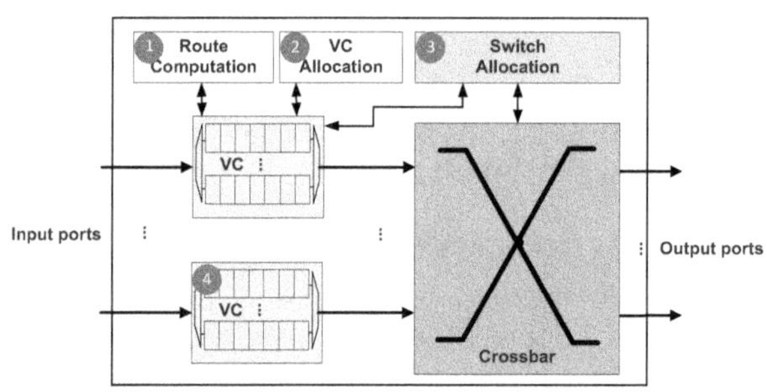

Figure 1: Conventional wormhole router and resource sharing conflict points [1-3].

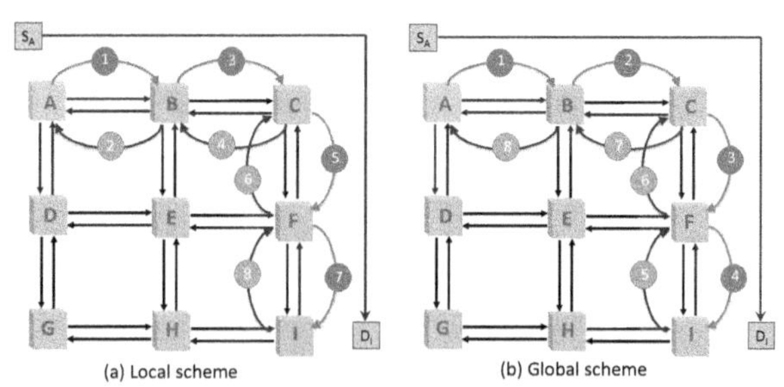

Figure 2: Cost computation protocols: local (a) and global (b).

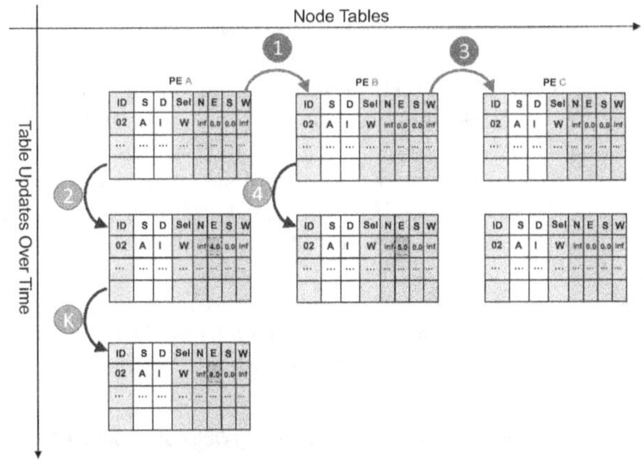

Figure 3: Routing cost tables for nodes A, B, and C and local cost updates scheme.

Initialization
Temporary calculated cost $T_{cost} = 0$;
Best routing cost $B_{cost} = \infty$;
Select direction dir = NULL ;
for $j \in i_{neighbors}$ **do**
  $T_{cost} = C_j(f(s_k, t_k, d_k))$;
  if $T_{cost} < B_{cost}$ **then**
    $B_{cost} = T_{cost}$;
    $dir = (i, j)$;
  end
end

Algorithm 1: Local Routing Cost Estimation - ψ_l

Each router node executes its own version of the **PreNoc** algorithm and stores the "best" learned routing costs to the other nodes in the network in its *routing cost table*, shown in Figure 3. The table entries are flow *ids*, source node, destination node, cost estimates per direction and the "best" cost to reach destination. Having the flow *ids* and source node in the table allows assigning different costs to the same direction depending on the flow *id* or source node. This schema represents the upper-bound size requirement for *routing cost table*. It takes into account the effects of head-off-line blocking. The table can be substantially reduced by (1) removing the source node and flow *id* distinctions – leading to $n-1$ entries per table, (2) limiting the learning range to some k hops and finally (3) applying routing constraints to the table size – for example XY-routing.

In the *node routing* mode, a node only directly calculates the routing cost to reach its adjacent neighbors, then uses the estimated costs of those neighbors to make its global prediction. The computation propagates forward to the destination then backward to the source node. Figure 2 (a) shows the different phases and Figure 3 shows the corresponding *routing cost table* updates. Initially, costs in all the tables for all the valid directions are set to zero. Although, they could be configured to some predetermined values learned off-line. To route a packet from **A** to **I**, in phase **1**, node **A** selects to go through its east link to **B**. In this illustrative example, the actual cost for routing the packet from **A** to its neighbor **B** is 4.0 which is sent from **B** to **A** as part of the routing credit message. Node **A** updates its routing cost through the east link (**E**) from 0.0 to 4.0 in phase **2**. In the following phases, node **B** forwards the packet to node **C** at a cost of 5.0 and updates its *routing cost table*. When node **A** later computes its eastbound cost, it will be 9.0.
For the *source routing*, *routing cost table* updates happen in the reverse order initiated at the destination node. It uses the global cost computation approach where the true routing cost of the packet does not arrive at node **A** until phase **8**, shown in Figure 2 (b). Although the global cost can be viewed as being less-adaptive, its routing cost estimates are exact in the beginning of the learning process.

3.2 Cost Computation

The cost computation, denoted by $C_j(f(s_i, t_i, d_i))$, is a weighted sum of the degree of goodness of considered paths from node j to destination t_i with nearest neighbors more heavily weighted than distant neighbors. The one hop cost calculation is shown in **Equation** 1 and has four key variables: (1) a_{uv_q} is the average route computation latency for VC q at the input port, p_{uv}, (2) p_{uv_q} the probability of getting through VC allocation without stall, (3) p_{uv_X} is the probability of winning arbitration at the crossbar without stall and (4) $b(u,v)$ represents the level of occupancy of virtual channels associated with the link (u,v). The weight parameters w_a, w_q, w_X and w_b measure the degree of impact of contentions 1 to 3 and amount of free buffer space at the input port. The parameters are also dynamic as they are learned at runtime via the neural network, and provide the predictive part of the algorithm. When the destination node is more than one hop away, **Equation** 2 is used to get the aggregated cost to the destination. In the equation below k represents the number of hops away from j.

$$C_j(f(s_i,t_i,d_i)) = w_a * a_{ij_q} + w_q * \frac{1}{p_{ij_q}} + w_b * b(i,j) + w_X * \frac{1}{p_{ij_X}} \quad (1)$$

$$\begin{aligned} C_{[jk]}(f(s_i,t_i,d_i)) &= w_1 * C_{j+1}(f(s_i,t_i,d_i)) \\ &+ w_2 * C_{j+2}(f(s_i,t_i,d_i)) \\ &... + w_k * C_{j+k}(f(s_i,t_i,d_i)) \end{aligned} \quad (2)$$

$$\textit{Where } w_1 \textit{ through } w_k \textit{ are weights And } w_1 \leq w_2 \leq ... \leq w_k.$$

Algorithm 1 calculates the local routing cost and Algorithm 2 performs the global recursive computation. These two algorithms are integrated to derive the hybrid local and global routing cost estimation.

3.3 Deadlock Freedom

Since the the algorithm can be used for both minimal and non-minimal routing, it is not deadlock-free by default. For deadlock freedom, the network channel dependency graph can be made acyclic by prohibiting certain turns [8]. The process of making the CDG acyclic essentially consists of removing certain routes from all possible routes in the on-chip network to guarantee deadlock-free routing. For the network performance, the routing algorithm still needs to select a route (or an optimal route) from all the allowed routes under a given Acyclic CDG (ACDG). Routing table entries at each router could be set to (1) the maximum number of edges that a packet could take in the ACDG (for example, 2-entry tables for 2-D mesh networks using dimension-order routing like XY or YX) or (2) the maximum number of edges that a packet could take in the original CDG with some default table entry value for the restricted routes generated by the

```
Initialization
Source node  src_node;
Destination node  dst_node;
Temporary calculated cost  T_cost = 0;
Best direction cost  D_cost = ∞;
Best path cost  P_cost = 0;
Select path = ∅;
Current node  cur_node = src_node;
while (cur_node != dst_node) do
    i = cur_node;
    next_hop = NULL;
    for j ∈ i_neighbors do
        T_cost = C_j(f(s_k, t_k, d_k));
        if T_cost < D_cost then
            D_cost = T_cost;
            next_hop = j;
        end
    end
    path = path ∪ (i, next_hop);
    P_cost += D_cost;
    D_cost = ∞;
    cur_node = next_hop;
end
```

Algorithm 2: Global Routing Cost Estimation - ψ_g

ACDG (for example 4-entry tables for 2-D mesh networks using dimension-order routing like XY or YX).

3.4 Predictive Model Using Neural Network

The **PreNoc** algorithm is based on the conventional hidden layers *artificial neural network* (ANN). Backpropagation is used to train the ANN in predicting the optimal path for a given flow. The process involves feed-forward computation and backpropagation from the output layer to the input layer with weight adjustments. Although, the ANN is configured to output a routing direction, its main function is to train the weight parameters w_a, w_q, w_X and w_b for the cost computation.

The input parameters to the input layer are $b(u,v)$, a_{uv_x}, where x is a VC at port (u,v)), p_{uv_x} and p_{uv_X}. For a 2D-Mesh network, there are four nodes on the output layer. Each node represents the direction for the next hop; and its output value is the routing cost associated with that direction. The weights between the layers are randomly initialized. In our experimental setup, weights are set to small values in the range of $[-0.5, 0.5]$; the learning rate and the momentum are set to 0.15 and 0.9, respectively, and the default *Sigmoid* function is $f(x) = \frac{1}{1+e^{(-l_j)}}$, where l_j is the layer node j. In active training, after each route selection (r_s), a preferred route (r_p) decision is fed back into the ANN. On the output layer the total prediction error is calculated based the *mean square error* (MSE): $E = \frac{\sum_{i=1}^{m}(r_{p_i} - r_{s_i})^2}{m}$, where m is 4 for the 2D-Mesh. We use standard backpropagation with partial derivatives.

3.5 Predictive Routing Approach

The **PreNoc** approach is a predictive scheme and defers from previous adaptive routing techniques. The routing is done in phases and in a iterative fashion. First, there is a learning phase where routers collect network state information, learn and forecast communication patterns. Second, there is a monitoring phase to validate the information learned in the first phase. In the final phase, routing tables are updated. For a user-defined period of time or number of system cycles, no learning or modification of routing paths is done. Routing during this period, named called *Oblivious Routing Phase* (ORP), is done based on the previously learned best routes and oblivious to current transient network conditions. A the end of the ORP, a new validation phase is initiated to test the robustness of routes under current network conditions. If routing performance is above the permissible threshold, the system goes into another ORP without any change to the routing tables. In the case of a degrading performance, the system performs a new learning phase, followed by a validation phase and an ORP. Figure 4 shows an illustrative view of the phases.

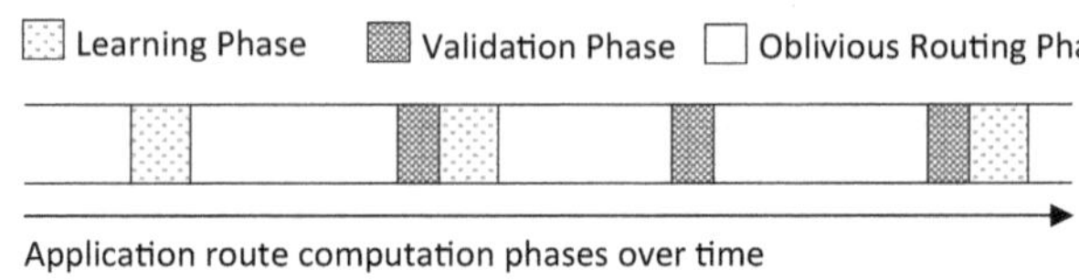

Figure 4: Phase-based hybrid adaptive-oblivious routing approach.

This intermittent aspect of the system allows for (1) the learning phase to not ping pong, (2) the learning logic to converge and stop when no learning is needed, and (3) to disable or power-gate the learning logic. In general, training of the neural networks can take a fair amount of time. Therefore, the initial training and calibration of weights can be performed offline in software to alleviate some of the latency. The online training is ongoing with user-defined break periods or ORPs.

4. MICRO-ARCHITECTURE DETAILS

The conventional wormhole router micro-architecture is modified to include three additional functional units: (1) *Router States Monitor* unit that keeps track of flits, nodes, etc. (2) a hardware engine for executing the ANN algorithm, and (3) modification of the credit message to transport router state information. Figure 5 shows the architecture of the new router.

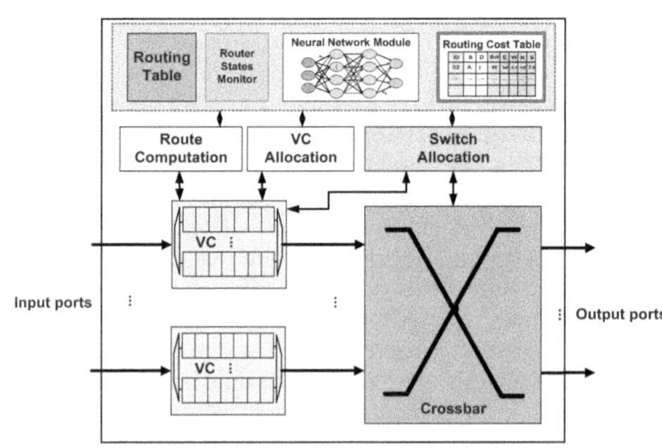

Figure 5: **PreNoc** Micro-Architecture.

Figure 6 highlights the information pieces added to the credit message. In the **PreNoc** architecture, the credit message carries: (1) the conventional credit information (CR) and then (2) the number of free buffer spaces (FB) at the port $log_2(bv \times pv)$-bit where bv is the number of buffer spaces per VC and pv is the number of VCs per port, (3) the arrival time (AT) of each header flit at the particular node in terms of cycle time is recorded and stored, (4) Latencies are calculated based on the arrival time, route computation, virtual channel allocation and switch allocation. The number of bits used for each of these message components is architecture dependent. In the prototype, 32 bits are used. Instead of sharing the network link bandwidth with program data, a secondary bufferless network is created to route the augmented credit messages. This credit network sends two types of messages: one contains the credit information when the header and the body flits are passing through the router and the second has the routing state information when the tail flit passes through the router. Tables shown in Figure 6 are stored in the *Router States Table*. Learning module including the ANN function is power-gated and can be power-down when not learning.

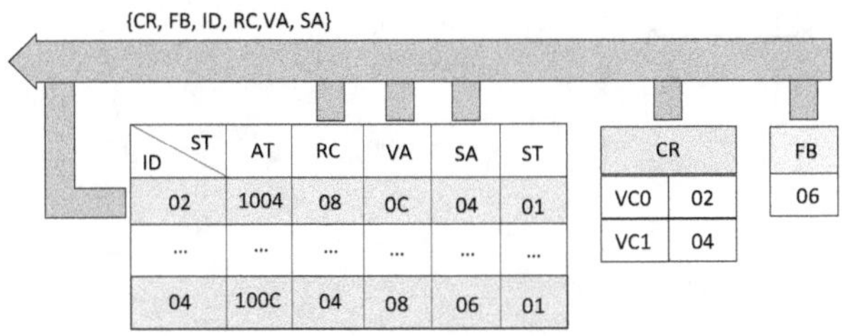

Figure 6: Augmented credit message: state table (ST), credit (CR), free buffer spaces (FB), (ST), header flit arrival time (AT), route computation latency (RC), virtual channel allocation latency (VA), and switch allocation latency (SA).

4.1 Hardware Implementation

To accurately estimate the hardware overhead and complexity of the **PreNoc** router architecture, an FPGA implementation on a Xilinx Virtex7-XC7VX980T FPGA device was performed. The router has 4 virtual channels and 8 slots per virtual channel. Table 1 shows the FPGA synthesis results. The per router register and look-up table (LUT) usage overheads are 9.2% and 9.1%, respectively.

Resource	Conventional	**PreNoc** Router	%
Regs	370829	404945	9.2
LUT	321582	350845	9.1

Table 1: FPGA implementation resource utilization.

There is no change to the critical path in the proposed modification to the router architecture. As in the conventional router, the arbitration logic controls the clock frequency. In both architectures, the clocking speed is 111.83 MHz.

5. EVALUATION

The experimental setup uses *BookSim*, a C++ based cycle-accurate on-chip network simulator [7], to implement and 8x8 2D-Mesh NoC with 4 VC per input ports, 6 buffer spaces in each VC and 8 flits per packet with an exponential distribution. To test the efficiency of our design, flows from both synthetic benchmarks and real applications are used. The synthetic benchmarks, TRANSPOSE, BIT REVERSE, and TORNADO are useful for evaluating specific communication patterns. The real application *H2.64* allows us to test for more general and uneven traffic patterns. For the H.264 application, flow bandwidths are derived from profiling results. Several video streams are run and profiled in deriving the flow demands. The injection rate variations for H.264 workload correspond to frame rates of 4 frames/second to 30 frames/second. For the comparative study, deterministic and other adaptive routing algorithms are implemented: (1) DOR routes packets first in x-direction to the correct column, then in y- direction to the destination node, (2) xy_yx: paths are switched randomly between xy and yx routes to split the traffic, and (3) Adaptive (Adap): it selects between xy and yx routes based on the least congested X or Y neighbor at the source. Simulation runs for 10000 cycles for a warm-up and executes for 100000 cycles for 10 runs. The neural network training takes on average one third of the execution cycles across all benchmarks.

Figures 7a and 7b show the throughput and average latency performance results for the different routing algorithms under the TRANSPOSE benchmark application. The **PreNoc** algorithm outperforms the DOR routing algorithm by 2.25×, the xy_yx algorithm by 1.5× and the adaptive routing by 1.2× in terms of throughput. Figures 7c and 8a present the performance results for the BIT REVERSE benchmark. The performance gab between the **PreNoc** algorithm and the other routing algorithms is smaller. The **PreNoc** algorithm outperforms the adaptive routing algorithm by 8.7% at high injection rates. Even for the less predictable TORNADO benchmark where the routing algorithms have comparable throughput performance, the **PreNoc** approach shows a better saturation point. This performance trend is validated by the H.264 Encoder application, shown in Figures 9a and 9b . The **PreNoc** approach shows a greater aptitude to create routing path diversity and avoid premature network saturation. The **PreNoc**'s performance is very stable and consistently outperforms all the other routing approaches both deterministic and adaptive in terms of both throughput and latency.

6. CONCLUSIONS

Using different network state information, the **PreNoc** algorithm is able to estimate routing costs and perform low-latency routing of traffic. A router architecture is created to support the algorithm. The hardware overhead for new router is 9.2% when compared to a conventional wormhole design. Overall the **PreNoc** algorithm generally outperforms deterministic and other adaptive routing algorithms in terms of both average packet latency and network throughput. The proposed technique performs especially well at high injection rates.

7. REFERENCES

[1] H. Cai, Y. Y. Yang, F. Qu, J. Wu, and B. Wang. *Congestion Prediction Algorithm for Network on Chip.* Telkomnika, Vol. 11, No. 12, pp. 7392-7398, 2013.

[2] J. O. E. Nilsson, M. Millberg and A. Jantsch. *Load Distribution with the Proximity Congestion Awareness in a Network-on-Chip.* In Proceedings of the Design Automation and Test in Europe Conference, pp. 1126-1127, December 2003.

[3] M. Ebrahimi, M. Daneshtalab, F. Farahnakian, J. Plosila, P. Liljeberg, M. Palesi, and H. Tenhunen. Haraq: Congestion-aware learning model for highly adaptive routing algorithm in on-chip networks. In *NOCS*, pages 19–26. IEEE, 2012.

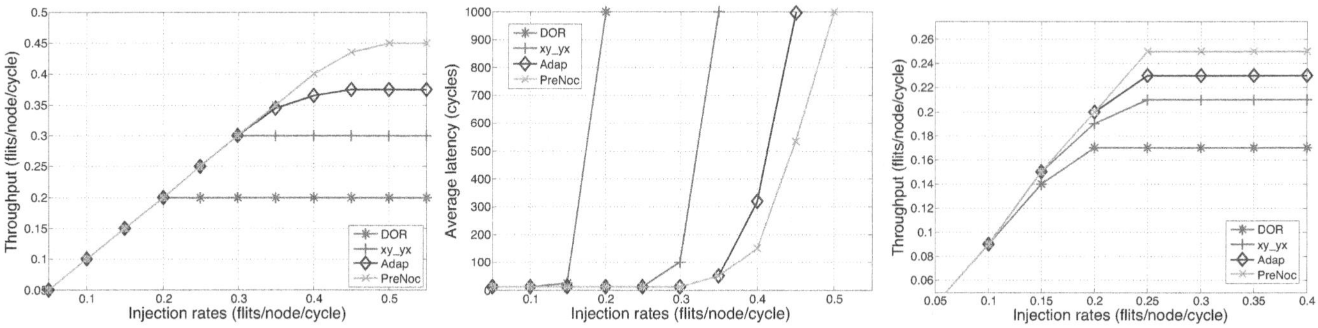

(a) Throughput results for TRANSPOSE. (b) Latency results for TRANSPOSE. (c) Throughput results for BIT REVERSE.

Figure 7: TRANSPOSE and BIT REVERSE synthetic benchmarks results.

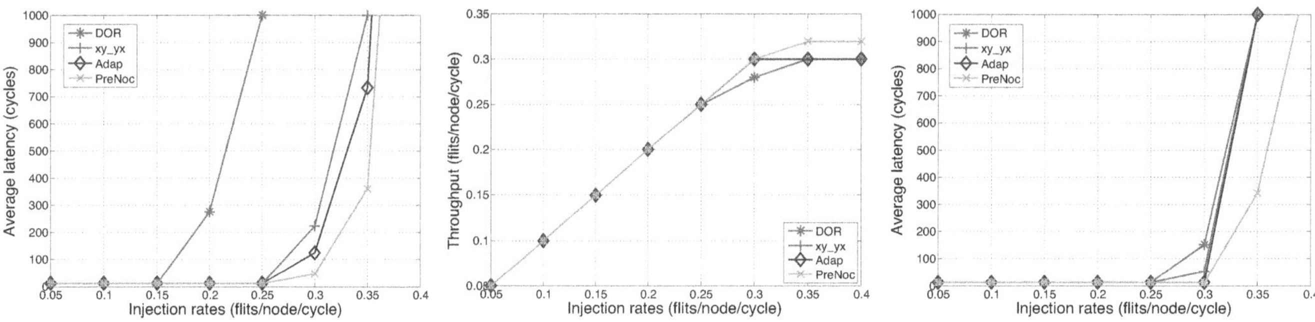

(a) Latency results for BIT REVERSE. (b) Throughput results for TORNADO. (c) Latency results for TORNADO.

Figure 8: BIT REVERSE and TORNADO synthetic benchmarks results.

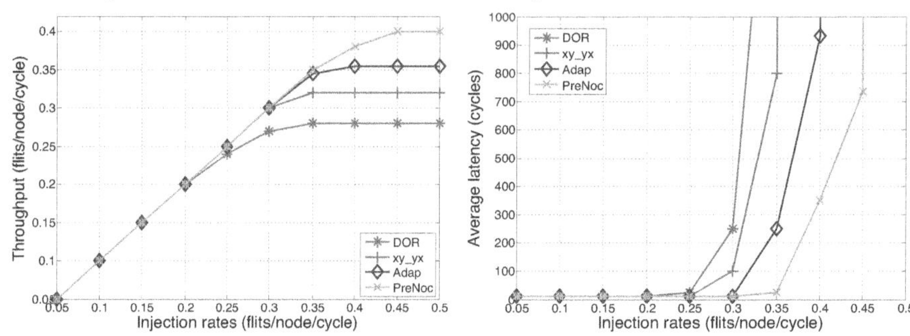

(a) Throughput results for H2.64 ENCODER. (b) Latency results for H2.64 ENCODER.

Figure 9: H2.64 ENCODER benchmark results

[4] H. Esmaeilzadeh, E. Blem, R. St Amant, K. Sankaralingam, and D. Burger. Dark silicon and the end of multicore scaling. In *Computer Architecture (ISCA), 2011 38th Annual International Symposium on*, pages 365–376. IEEE, 2011.

[5] F. Farahnakian, M. Ebrahimi, M. Daneshtalab, J. Plosila, and P. Liljeberg. Adaptive reinforcement learning method for networks-on-chip. In *Embedded Computer Systems (SAMOS), 2012 International Conference on*, pages 236–243, July 2012.

[6] P. Gratz, B. Grot, and S. Keckler. Regional congestion awareness for load balance in networks-on-chip. In *High Performance Computer Architecture, 2008. HPCA 2008. IEEE 14th International Symposium on*, pages 203–214, Feb 2008.

[7] N. Jiang, J. Balfour, D. U. Becker, B. Towles, W. J. Dally, G. Michelogiannakis, and J. Kim. A detailed and flexible cycle-accurate network-on-chip simulator, 2013.

[8] M. Kinsy, M. H. Cho, K. S. Shim, M. Lis, G. Suh, and S. Devadas. Optimal and heuristic application-aware oblivious routing. *Computers, IEEE Transactions on*, 62(1):59–73, Jan 2013.

[9] Q. Z. M. Li and W. B. Jone. *DyXY - A Proximity Congestion-Aware Deadlock-Free Dynamic Routing Method for Network on Chip.* DAC pp. 849-852, 2006.

[10] S. Ma, N. Enright Jerger, and Z. Wang. Dbar: An efficient routing algorithm to support multiple concurrent applications in networks-on-chip. *SIGARCH Comput. Archit. News*, 39(3):413–424, June 2011.

[11] M. Ramakrishna, P. V. Gratz, and A. Sprintson. Gca: Global congestion awareness for load balance in networks-on-chip. In *2013 Seventh IEEE/ACM International Symposium on Networks-on-Chip (NoCS)*, pages 1–8, April 2013.

[12] M. B. Taylor. A landscape of the new dark silicon design regime. *Micro, IEEE*, 33(5):8–19, 2013.

A Domain-Specific Language and Compiler for Computation-in-Memory Skeletons

Jintao Yu
Delft University of Technology
Mekelweg 4, 2628 CD
Delft, The Netherlands
j.yu-1@tudelft.nl

Tom Hogervorst
Delft University of Technology
Mekelweg 4, 2628 CD
Delft, The Netherlands

Razvan Nane
Delft University of Technology
Mekelweg 4, 2628 CD
Delft, The Netherlands
r.nane@tudelft.nl

ABSTRACT

Computation-in-Memory (CiM) is a new computer architecture template based on the in-memory computing paradigm. CiM can solve the memory-wall problem of classical Von Neumann-based computer systems by exploiting application-specific computational and *data-flow* patterns with the capability of performing both storage and computations of emerging resistive RAM technologies (e.g., memristors). However, to efficiently explore and design such radically new application-specific CiM architectures, we require fundamentally new algorithm specification and compilation techniques. In this paper, we introduce a domain-specific language to express not only the computational patterns of an algorithm but also its *spatial* characteristics. Furthermore, we design a compiler that is able to transform these patterns into highly-optimized CiM designs. Experiments demonstrate the functional correctness of the language and the compiler as well as an order of magnitude speedup improvement over a multicore system in both performance and energy costs.

Keywords

Domain specific language; computation-in-memory; algorithmic skeleton; memristor

1. INTRODUCTION

In classical Von Neumann-based computing systems, memory access and data transfer operations are becoming a *big bottleneck* for Big Data applications [5]. This is not only because of the limited transfer speed at which data is retrieved from and written back to memory, but also because performing a large amount of memory accesses incurs high energy costs. A solution is to design application-specific memristor-based Computation-in-Memory (CiM) architectures [9], which feature a large memristor crossbar to execute massively parallel applications. Because we can perform both computations and storage using memristors [19], no off-crossbar data transfers are required during execution, enabling CiM-based architectures to solve the memory wall bottleneck.

Application-specific CiM-based solutions can therefore result in significant performance gains over multicore systems [10]. To implement highly-optimized CiM architectures, a designer would need to explicitly *spatially program* the application-specific computational and data-flow patterns onto the crossbar. This is a new form of *Spatial Computation* paradigms [3], which map programs into completely distributed hardware. Although general purpose languages can be used for spatial computation [3], Domain-Specific Languages (DSLs) facilitate domain experts to generate optimal solutions [16]. Some DSLs have been developed for specific platforms, such as MaxJ for Data-Flow Engine [15] and ANML for Automata Processor Engines [8]. However, specifying and compiling customized application layouts for a memristor crossbar poses a new challenge. Due to the *passive nature* of the memristor, the mapping and routing results directly influences the scheduling phase [20] because data movements on the crossbar have to be controlled as well. As a result, existing DSLs for spatial computation are not applicable to memristor-based CiM architectures.

To solve aforementioned challenge, a new type of skeleton was proposed: the *CiM skeleton* [20]. Skeletons (formally referred to as *algorithmic skeletons*) are high-level software constructs used to hide the complexity of parallel computer systems from a programmer [6]. Additionally, CiM skeletons provide the scheduling, mapping, and routing information needed to program applications on the CiM architecture. In this paper, we propose a DSL and a DSL-based compilation flow to express and implement CiM skeletons. We make the following contributions:

- A skeleton-based Domain Specific Language, *CiM DSL*, to describe the low-level crossbar details of the *spatial* patterns of an algorithm.
- A compiler that generates a scheduled, mapped, and routed system from this DSL using *CiM Skeletons*.
- The verification of this compiler and comparison with a multicore system.

The paper is organized as follows. Section 2 provides background information about the CiM architecture. Section 3 and Section 4 describe the CiM DSL and the implementation of its compiler. Thereafter, Section 5 validates the compiler with multiple applications. Finally, Section 6 concludes the paper.

Permission to make digital or hard copies of all or part of this work for personal or classroom use is granted without fee provided that copies are not made or distributed for profit or commercial advantage and that copies bear this notice and the full citation on the first page. Copyrights for components of this work owned by others than ACM must be honored. Abstracting with credit is permitted. To copy otherwise, or republish, to post on servers or to redistribute to lists, requires prior specific permission and/or a fee. Request permissions from permissions@acm.org.

GLSVLSI '17, May 10-12, 2017, Banff, AB, Canada

© 2017 ACM. ISBN 978-1-4503-4972-7/17/05...$15.00

DOI: http://dx.doi.org/10.1145/3060403.3060474

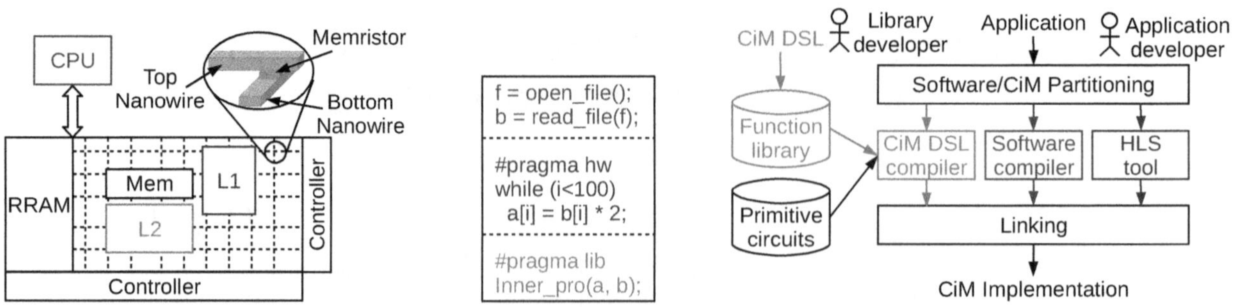

(a) CiM architecture (b) Program sample (c) CiM compilation tool-chain

Figure 1: CiM architecture and compilation tool-chain.

2. BACKGROUND

The CiM architecture is a computational template in which application-specific accelerators are instantiated and executed in-memory under the control of a CPU. Figure 1a shows a high-level view of the CPU/CiM heterogeneous system. CiM's hardware consists of two parts: a large reconfigurable crossbar of horizontal and vertical nanowires with memristors on every intersection, and a CMOS-based controller that activates voltages on the nanowires to control the memristors. Memristors can be configured as memory elements as well as computation elements [19], allowing both to be performed in the crossbar. The high density of a memristor crossbar enables this architecture to fully exploit the parallelism in embarrassingly parallel applications. Furthermore, since a CiM crossbar coexists with the general memory space (RRAM in Figure 1a), we do not have any off-chip memory accesses. This leads to significant improvements in both performance and energy consumption.

Figure 1c shows CiM's programming model. Before programmers can use application-specific accelerators in CiM, an algorithm designer is required to create the library functions (i.e., accelerators) optimized for *minimum communication maximum parallelism* on the crossbar. The algorithms are specified in the CiM DSL, using *skeleton operators* to specify not only the floorplan but also the *communication paths*[1] between the computational units. Please note that in the CiM crossbar, each corner point that changes the direction of the path needs to be explicitly controlled [18]. As a result, the scheduling is dependent on the mapping and routing. The defined CiM skeletons are used further to specify the complete algorithm that is stored in the *function library*. Subsequently, an application programmer can use this library in a different high-level language (e.g., C). Therefore, CiM DSL is designed for the library developers rather than the application developers. Functions not contained in the library are processed by a CiM High-Level Synthesis (HLS) tool. Finally, the compilation results of different tools are linked together. Figure 1a illustrates one possible compilation result of the sample program shown in Figure 1b. One circuit is generated using the library functions (colored green), and another one is generated by the CiM HLS tool (colored blue). Code that doesn't need to be executed on the CiM crossbar (colored red), is compiled regularly for the CPU. In this paper we focus only on the CiM DSL compiler.

[1]We refer to communication paths simply as paths in the remainder of the paper

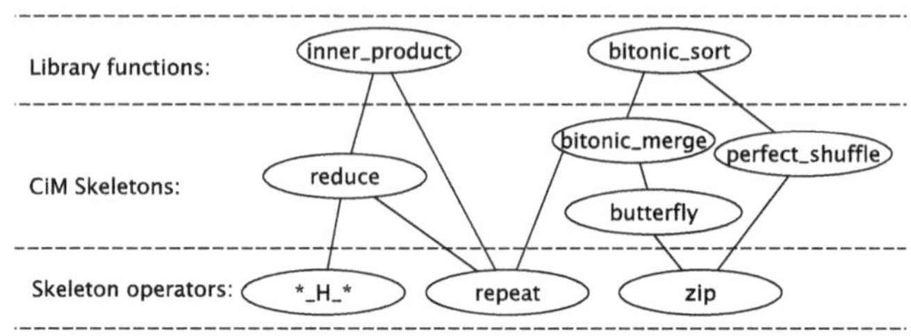

Figure 2: Dependence of CiM skeletons and library functions.

3. CIM DSL

In this section, we describe the rules of CiM DSL's syntax using one variant of Extended Backus-Naur Form (EBNF) [2]. We design the DSL with the goal to create and use CiM skeletons easily. Figure 2 shows the dependence between different CiM concepts. First, we define *skeleton language operators*, which are language constructs that are used to specify different connections between functional blocks and their relative position. Subsequently, the operators are used to define *CiM Skeletons*. Finally, both skeleton operators and CiM skeletons are used to build library functions.

3.1 Circuits and Expressions

The CiM DSL creates systems by connecting functional blocks together in expressions. The syntax related to this is as follows:

$$\begin{aligned}
Circuit_decl &::= ID\ File_name && (1)\\
Exp &::= Circuit \mid Int \mid ID\ Exp_1\ Exp_2\ ... && (2)\\
&\mid Exp_1\ Op\ Exp_2 \mid Map \mid Fold \mid Repeat && (3)\\
Op &::= *_D_* \mid *_H_* \mid *_I_* && (4)\\
Map &::= ID\ Range\ Exp && (5)\\
Fold &::= Op\ Exp && (6)\\
Repeat &::= Int\ Exp && (7)\\
Range &::= Int \mid Int\ [Ar_Op\ Int]\ Int && (8)\\
Ar_Op &::= \text{“}+\text{”} \mid \text{“}-\text{”} \mid \text{“}*\text{”} \mid \text{“}/\text{”} && (9)
\end{aligned}$$

A *circuit declaration* (Circuit_decl) declares the name of the primitive circuit used in the program and specify its

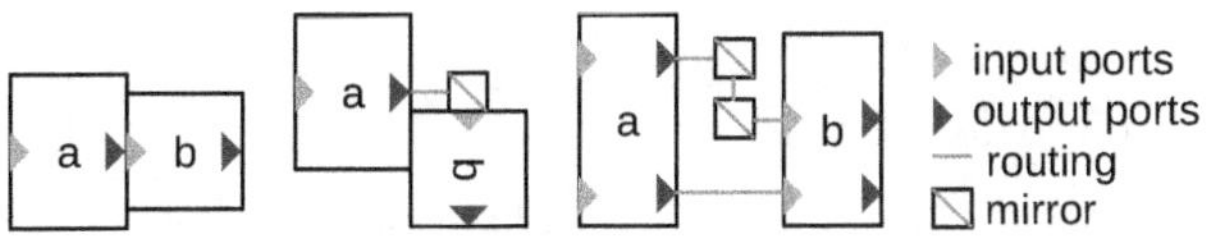

(a) *_D_* (b) *_H_* (c) *_I_*

Figure 3: Implementation of operators.

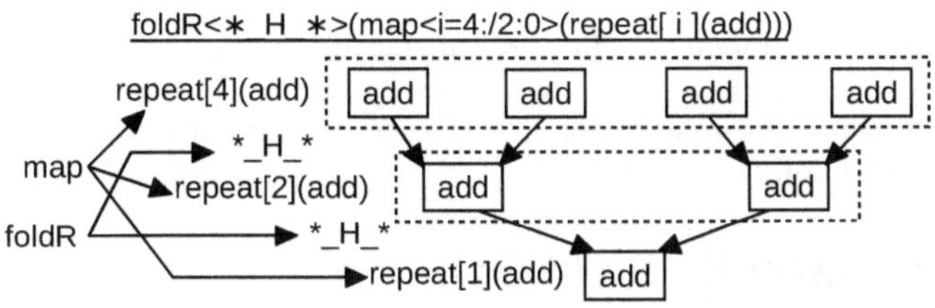

Figure 4: Expression and data-flow graph of an adder tree.

library file (Rule 1). This file contains all the circuit's information needed by the CiM compiler, including its latency, area, energy consumption, positions of input and output ports, initiation interval, and VHDL model. An *expression* can be a primitive circuit, an integer, or an instantiation of a CiM skeleton (Rule 2). To create a CiM skeleton, the user needs to specify the component name that represents the skeleton, and assign the parameters. Two expressions and an operator (Op) constitute a new expression (Rule 3). The *operators* are *_D_*, *_H_*, and *_I_*. Operators represent different mapping strategies as shown in Figure 3. The mapping is performed according to the positions of input and output ports. *_D_* puts two circuits next to each other so that an input port is directly linked with the output port. *_H_* rotates one circuit and uses a mirror in between. The mirror changes the direction of a path [18]. *_I_* links two groups of input and output ports between two components using mirrors.

Other forms of expressions include *map* (Rule 5), *fold* (Rule 6), and *repeat* (Rule 7). These expressions are useful to generate larger circuits. For example, *map* applies every number in a *range* to an expression that contains an variable. The *range* is an array of integers, which can be expressed using one to three fields (Rule 8). If the range has one field, it is a single value. If it has two fields, it is a series of incrementing integers from the first up to but not including the second value. If it has three fields, it represents a discontinuous array of integers. In this case, the arithmetic operator (*Ar_Op*) and the number in the middle indicate the intervals. The *arithmetic operators* are add ("+"), subtract ("-"), multiply ("×"), and divide ("/") (Rule 9). The bracket ([]) surrounding "*Ar_Op Int*" means they are optional.

We use an example shown in Figure 4 to explain the semantics of *repeat*, *fold*, and *map* expressions. The example is an adder tree that calculates the sum of eight values. The CiM DSL line that describes this circuit is shown at the top of the figure. *Repeat*[*n*](*add*) creates an array of *n* additions. The *map* expression duplicates the *repeat* expression following a noncontinuous array [4, 2, 1]. These duplicates are linked with *_H_* operator, which is specified by the *fold* expression. The associativity of *fold* expressions is indicated by the letter "L" or "R" at the end.

3.2 Statements and Signals

Statements connect the circuits declared in expressions to signals, to give explicit control over the data flow to and from those circuits. A *signal* is a connection path between two data locations. The relevant CiM DSL syntax is as follows:

$$\begin{aligned} Statement &::= Signal\ [Exp]\ Signal \mid Loop && (10)\\ Loop &::= ID\ Range\ Statement{+} && (11)\\ Signal &::= ID\ Range \mid Signal\ {+}{+}\ Signal && (12)\\ &\mid Zip(Signal,\ Signal) && (13) \end{aligned}$$

A statement contains an input signal, an output signal and optionally an expression (Rule 10). It will be translated into a group of primitive circuits. *Loops* can be used to compactly express a group of similar statements, which is similar to the semantics of *map* (Rule 11). The symbol "+" means the loop structure accepts one or more statements. Signals have a name and a range, and they can be built using *signal operators* "++" (Rule 12) and "zip" (Rule 13). "++" concatenates two signals sequentially and "zip" builds a single signal from the elements of two signals interleaved with one another.

Statements are allowed to specify only the connection between input and output signals, without including any component (Rule 10). This feature is useful for shuffling the signals. Listing 1 shows an example of a signal shuffle, specifically one named the butterfly pattern, which is used in a bitonic sort function.

Listing 1: Butterfly Shuffle Statement

```
zip(in[0:2:m/2], in[m/2:2:m]) ++
    zip(in[1:2:m/2], in[1+m/2:2:m]) => out[0:m];
```

3.3 Programs and Components

A complete CiM DSL program consists of one or more circuit declarations and one or more components (Rule 14). A *component* describes a library function or a CiM skeleton. The CiM DSL syntax concerning these two language constructs is as follows:

$$\begin{aligned} Program &::= Circuit\_decl^*\ Component^* && (14)\\ Component &::= ID\ Sig\_decl\ [Par\_decl]\ Statement^* && (15)\\ Sig\_decl &::= \{ID\ Int\}^*\ \{ID\ Int\}^* && (16)\\ Par\_decl &::= \{Type\ ID\}^* && (17)\\ Type &:= \text{"int"} \mid \text{"comp"} && (18) \end{aligned}$$

The head of a component contains its name (ID), signal declaration (Sig_decl), and parameter declaration (Par_decl) (Rule 15). The square brackets surrounding Par_decl means it is optional. Among all the components in a program, one and only one component should be named as "main". It represents the library function defined by the program. The *signal declaration* declares input and output signals, containing names (ID) and their sizes (Int) (Rule 16). *Parameter declaration* specifies the type and names of the parameters (Rule 17). Currently, CiM DSL supports two *types* of parameters, which are integer ("int") and components ("comp") (Rule 18). The body of a component is one or more statements (Rule 15), which link expressions with input and output signals (Rule 10).

As an example of a complete CiM DSL program, Listing 2 shows the code for matrix multiply $A_{m \times n} \times B_{n \times k}$ in CiM DSL. It is built based on the inner product function. To achieve the best performance, the primitive circuits used in the inner product are arranged following an H-tree pattern [10]. Please refer to Figure 6a for a visualization of the target layout. The inner product hardware is duplicated to calculate all the elements of the result matrix in parallel.

Listing 2: Matrix Multiply in CiM DSL

```
1  libmod add(add.lib);
2  libmod mul(mul.lib);
3  comp main<in[32] | out[16]>(){
4    in[0:32]=> matrix_multiply(4, 4, 4) =>out[0:16];
5  }
6  comp matrix_multiply<A[m*n], B[n*k] | out[m*k]>
7      (int m, int n, int k){
8    forV i=0:m do
9      A[n*i: n*i+n] ++ B[0: n*k] =>
10         row(n,k) => out[k*i:k*i+k];
11   end
12 }
13 comp row<a[n], b[n*k] | out[n]>(int n, int k){
14   forH i=0:k do
15     a[0:n]++b[n*i:n*i+n]=>inner_product(n)=>out[i];
16   end
17 }
18 comp inner_product<a[n], b[n] | out[1]>(int n){
19   zip(a[0: n], b[0: n]) => repeat[n](mul)
20       *_H_* reduce(n/2, add) => out[0];
21 }
22 comp reduce<in[2*n] | out[1]>(int n, comp c){
23   in[0: 2*n] => foldR<*_H_*>(map<i = n: /2: 0>
24       (repeat[i](c))) => out[0];
25 }
```

Line 1 and line 2 declare two primitive circuits, i.e. the adder (add) and the multiplier (mul). The keyword of this declaration is "libmod", and the name suffix of the library files is ".lib". After these declarations, the program defines five components with the key word "comp". The "main" component (line 3 to line 5) specifies that the sizes of two matrices are both four by four. The declaration of input and output ports are surrounded with a pair of angle brackets and separated with a delimiter ("|"). On the other hand, the parameter declarations are marked with parentheses (line 7, line 13, etc.). The body of components are surrounded with curly braces and consists of one or more statements. For each statement, the expression and signals are linked by "=>", which means that input locations (e.g., registers/storage locations in the crossbar) are transferred via signals to the matrix multiplication's input ports. Note the use of the "++" signal operator in lines 10 and 15 to concatenate two arrays into one, and of the "zip" signal operator in line 19 to zip the elements of two arrays into one. *matrix_multiply* and *row* components both employ a *for-loop*, which expresses a group of statements. It arranges the circuits that are obtained from the loop statements vertically (forV) or horizontally (forH). Therefore, line 15 duplicates *k inner_product* function in a row, and line 10 further extends these rows into a matrix. The *repeat* expression in lines 19 and 24 represents duplicates of a circuit, which are executed in parallel. It does not contain mapping information and will be further mapped using operators. Line 23 builds a binary tree as shown in Figure 4. The map expression duplicates a circuit using a variable (i) in the range (n:/2:0). The range is divided into three fields by colons (:). The first field (n) is the starting number. The second field (/2) is applied to n repetitively until the value reaches the third field (0). All

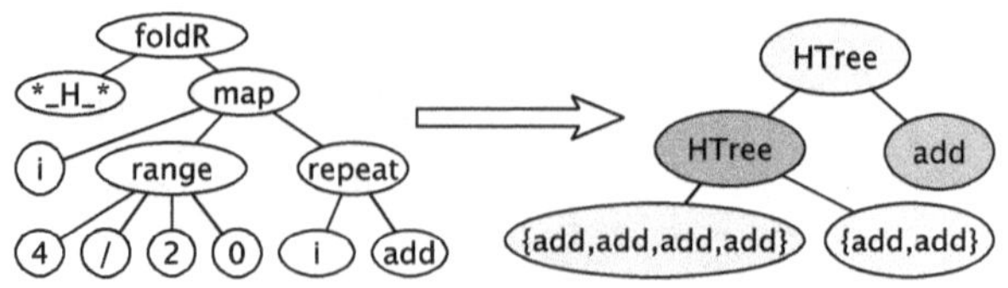

Figure 5: Dereferencing of *reduce(4, add)*.

these intermediate values, not including the third field, constitute the range. Finally, the group of circuits represented by *map* are linked with the operator specified in the *fold* expression (i.e., *_H_*).

4. IMPLEMENTATION

We developed CiM DSL compiler using Spoofax, a language workbench in the Eclipse IDE [11]. The development consists of two phases. First, we define the syntax and the name binding rules, which are used to parse user programs into an Intermediate Representation (IR). Second, we define transformation and generation rules, which annotate and transform the IR according to our defined skeleton operators, and emit the code for the desired circuits, respectively. Spoofax has good support for both phases so that the workload of developing the new DSL is significantly reduced. After defining all the rules, the CiM DSL compiler is generated by Spoofax.

A CiM DSL program is compiled into circuits following four steps, namely parsing, dereferencing, transforming, and emitting. The parsing builds an Abstract Syntax Tree (AST), which is subsequently dereferenced to eliminate language structures such as *for-loop*, *fold*, *map*, and *repeat*. During dereferencing, the loops are fully unrolled, and *fold*, *map*, and *repeat* are applied. Figure 5 shows this process for the expression in the *reduce* component in Listing 2 (line 22). In this case, we assume n is four. The left side illustrates the AST obtained after parsing, where the range is calculated into a noncontinuous array. Then, *map*, *repeat*, and *foldR* are applied successively as described in Section 3. The result of the deferencing is also an AST in which all the leaf nodes are primitive circuits, and all the internal nodes are skeleton operators. The result AST is shown in the right part of Figure 5, where the *_H_* operator is replaced by the name *HTree* that implements this pattern.

The transform process constructs circuits based on the AST that is obtained in the previous step. The circuit construction is performed using a post-order, depth-first tree traversal using the *Transform_ske* function that is dynamically dispatched according to the type of the operators. The function contains the scheduling, placement, and routing algorithms that will be applied to the circuits according to the particular CiM skeleton that it implements. Figure 7 shows an example of transforming the AST on the right of Figure 5. Its left part shows the leaf nodes of the dereferenced AST and the circuits they represent. The right part is the transformation of this AST, which is done in two steps. The lower Htree node is transformed first, which combines four adders and two adders into two group adders. Next, these two groups are transformed by the root node to form a whole circuit together with another adder. The small squares shown in this figure represent mirrors.

Finally, the code generation phase emits three types of

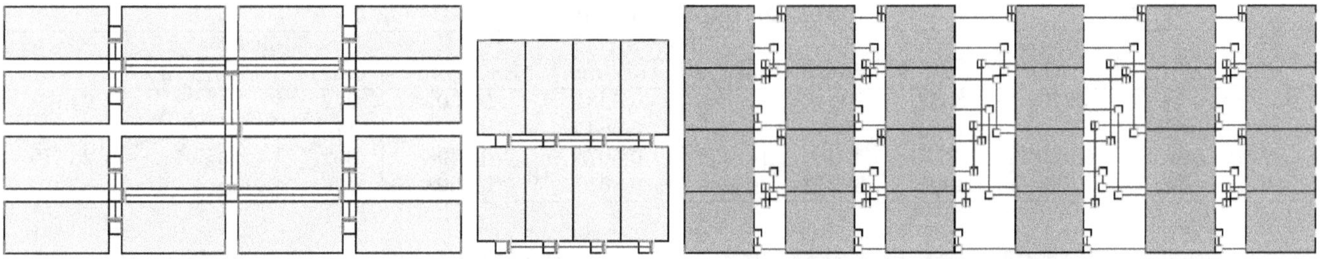

(a) Inner product (b) FIR filter (c) Bitonic sort

Figure 6: Graphic output.

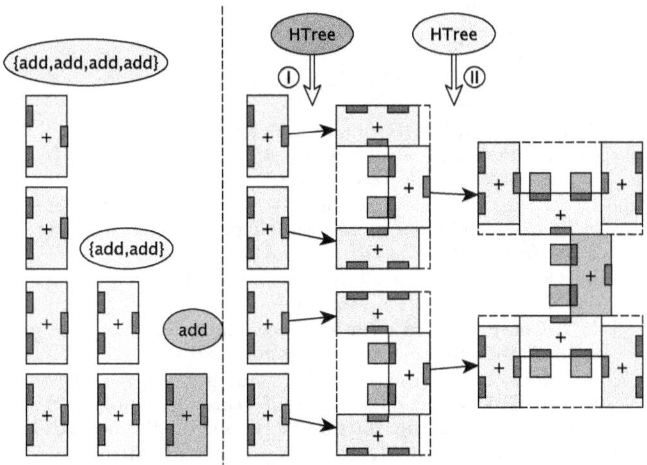

Figure 7: Transformation of *reduce(4, add)*.

files, which are VHDL, mapping constraints, and graphic outputs. The VHDL contains the port maps and an FSM, which are produced according to the mapped, routed, and scheduled Data Flow Graph (DFG) of the algorithm. This VHDL can be used for behavioral simulation. We generate graphic output to examine the placement and routing results. This output is in the C language, invoking a graphic library named *pslib* to produce a graph in postscript (.ps) format.

5. EXPERIMENTAL RESULTS

We use four functions to validate CiM DSL and its compiler, which are vector inner product, matrix multiply, Finite Impulse Response (FIR) filter, and bitonic sort. The code of the first two functions and a small part of bitonic sort is shown in Listing 2 and Listing 1. The data type used in these functions are 32-bit integer.

5.1 Compiler Outputs

The attributes of primitive circuits we used in this case study are listed in Table 1. The *adder* (Add) and the *multiplier* (Mul) are designed by previous works [12, 1]. The original design is not based on a crossbar, so the area and latency are moderately different when we adapt it to CiM. We will not discuss these changes since the hardware design is beyond the scope of this work. The *Greater than* (Gt) component, which is used in bitonic sort, cannot be found in existing works. Therefore we estimate their attributes.

Table 1: Attributes of Primitive Circuits and Copy Operation

	Latency	Width	Height	Energy	Ref.
Add	178	9	32	124.8	[12]
Mul	803	256	128	4407.8	[1]
Gt	27	128	192	93	–
Copy	3	–	–	12.8	[1]

The latency is listed in terms of Clock Cycle (CC). The area is represented by the required number of rows (Height) and columns (Width). The energy consumption of the adder and the multiplier is not given in the original papers [12, 1]. Actually, it is impossible to report accurate energy consumption at the design phase because this is input data dependent. However, we can estimate the maximum value by assuming every IMPLY or FALSE operation [12] consumes the energy of switching states. This energy varies among technologies, from 0.1 fJ [17] to 230 fJ [13]. In this paper, we use 100 fJ. We also calculated the energy consumption for copy operation following the same way. Its implementation, which is essentially two NOT operations, is taken from [1].

We generated the graphic outputs of inner product, FIR filter, and bitonic sort as shown in Figure 6. Matrix multiply is not presented because it is a matrix of inner products, which is very large but contains little information. The vector size of inner product is 16. The tap size of FIR filter is four and the input size is two. The input size of bitonic sort is eight. In Figure 6a and Figure 6b, the large and small boxes denote multipliers and mirrors respectively. The adders are tiny bars beside the mirrors. In Figure 6c, the small boxes are also mirrors while the large ones are *gts*. The red and green dashes in these figures indicate the input and output ports while the blue lines show the routing. The layouts are the same as we designed, which demonstrates the DSL works as intended.

5.2 Performance Evaluation

We enlarged the problem sizes and compared the performance of generated circuits with a multicore platform. The problem sizes and the attributes of the generated circuits are listed in Table 2. For the FIR filter, the tap size is 64 and the input size is 512. We calculated the area of the generated circuits based on the memrisor density predicted by ITRS [7], which is 2.38×10^{11} bit/cm^2. These library functions are simulated using Sniper [4], and the energy consumption is reported by McPAT [14]. The targeted multicore system is Intel Xeon X7460 processor that consists of six cores on a

Table 2: Experimental Results

	Problem size	CIM					Multicore		Speedup
		Lat/CC	Width	Height	Area/mm^2	Energy/mJ	Lat/μs	Energy/mJ	
Inner product	32768	3653	20448	73696	0.6332	0.1502	272.7	15.99	74.65
Matrix multiply	32×32	1753	19456	72704	0.5943	0.1500	174.5	21.96	99.54
FIR filter	64/512	12773	8192	147456	0.5075	0.1498	302.7	35.95	23.70
Bitonic Sort	256	1401	58240	32768	0.8019	0.0008	–	–	–

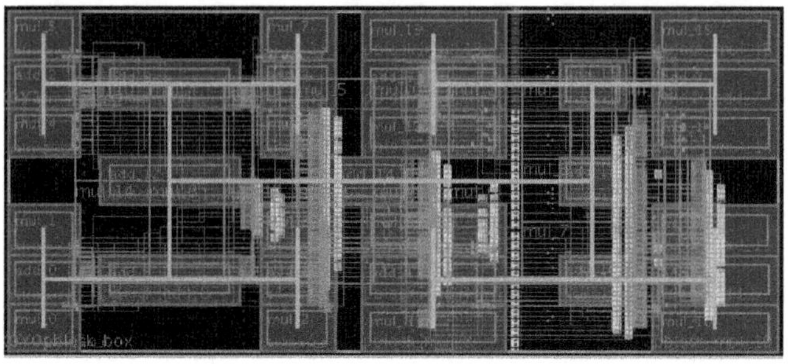

Figure 8: FPGA floorplanning for inner product.

die of 503 mm^2, running at 2.66 GHz each. These cores have 64 kB L1 cache each and share a 16 MB L3 cache. Every two cores share an L2 cache of 3 MB. The latency (Lat) and energy consumption are also listed in Table 2. The speedup of CiM's latency over multicore is calculated, which is between 23x and 99x. The area of the circuits generated by CiM compiler is very small compared with this processor. The energy consumption is less than 1% of the multicore. Please note that we do not include the CMOS controller in the energy evaluation because there is no backend synthesis tool yet for the CiM system. However, we do not expect the controller to have a big impact on the reported numbers due to its simplicity.

5.3 FPGA Prototyping

To confirm the validity of the graphical output, we built also an FPGA prototype to simulate the layout of the CiM inner product design on FPGA. We synthesized the generated area constraint file and the VHDL file with Xilinx Vivado. The implemented design of inner product is shown in Figure 8. Primitive circuits are recognizable by their yellow borders, and connections between circuit are represented by orange lines. The sizes of the adders and multipliers are different from Figure 6a. Despite this difference in visualization of the connections, we can verify that the floorplanning and interconnect information was included in the VHDL and constraint files correctly.

6. CONCLUSION

In this paper, we introduce a DSL and compiler to design programs to be run on future CiM-based systems. The skeleton-based DSL allows for the modular, high-level description of a system, and the compiler schedules, places, and routes the system using information provided by CiM skeletons. The functional correctness of the DSL is verified using VHDL files generated by the compiler, and the mapping and routing results are confirmed by generating graphical output files. This DSL can also be used for FPGA designs and it will be investigated in future work.

7. REFERENCES

[1] K. Bickerstaff and E. E. Swartzlander. *Memristor-Based Addition and Multiplication*, pages 473–486. Springer International Publishing, Cham, 2014.

[2] T. Bray, J. Paoli, C. M. Sperberg-McQueen *et al.* *Extensible markup language (XML)*. World Wide Web Consortium Recommendation, 1998.

[3] M. Budiu, G. Venkataramani, T. Chelcea *et al.* Spatial computation. ASPLOS XI, pages 14–26, New York, NY, USA, 2004. ACM.

[4] T. E. Carlson, W. Heirman, S. Eyerman, *et al.* An evaluation of high-level mechanistic core models. *ACM Trans. Archit. Code Optim.*, 11(3):28:1–28:25, Aug. 2014.

[5] C. P. Chen and C.-Y. Zhang. Data-intensive applications, challenges, techniques and technologies: A survey on big data. *Information Sciences*, 275:314 – 347, 2014.

[6] M. Cole. *Algorithmic Skeletons: Structured Management of Parallel Computation*. MIT Press, Cambridge, USA, 1991.

[7] I. R. Committee. International technology roadmap for semiconductors 2.0. Technical report, 2015.

[8] P. Dlugosch, D. Brown, P. Glendenning, *et al.* An efficient and scalable semiconductor architecture for parallel automata processing. *TPDS*, 25(12):3088–3098, Dec 2014.

[9] S. Hamdioui, L. Xie, H. A. D. Nguyen *et al.*. Memristor based computation-in-memory architecture for data-intensive applications. DATE '15, pages 1718–1725, San Jose, CA, USA, 2015. EDA Consortium.

[10] A. Haron, J. Yu, R. Nane, *et al.* Parallel matrix multiplication on memristor-based computation-in-memory architecture. HPCS '16, pages 759–766. IEEE, July 2016.

[11] L. C. Kats and E. Visser. The spoofax language workbench: Rules for declarative specification of languages and ides. OOPSLA '10, pages 444–463, New York, USA, 2010. ACM.

[12] S. Kvatinsky, G. Satat, N. Wald, *et al.* Memristor-based material implication (imply) logic: Design principles and methodologies. *VLSI*, 22(10):2054–2066, Oct 2014.

[13] S. Lee, J. Sohn, Z. Jiang *et al.* Metal oxide-resistive memory using graphene-edge electrodes. *Nature communications*, 6(8407):1–7, 2015.

[14] S. Li, J. H. Ahn, R. D. Strong *et al.* Mcpat: An integrated power, area, and timing modeling framework for multicore and manycore architectures. MICRO 42, 2009. ACM.

[15] O. Pell, O. Mencer, K. H. Tsoi *et al.* *Maximum Performance Computing with Dataflow Engines*, pages 747–774. Springer New York, New York, NY, 2013.

[16] The OpenSPL Consortium. Openspl: Revealing the power of spatial computing. Technical report, Dec. 2013.

[17] C.-L. Tsai, F. Xiong, E. Pop *et al.* Resistive random access memory enabled by carbon nanotube crossbar electrodes. *Acs Nano*, 7(6):5360–5366, 2013.

[18] L. Xie, H. A. D. Nguyen, M. Taouil *et al.* Interconnect networks for memristor crossbar. NANOARCH '15, pages 124–129. IEEE, July 2015.

[19] J. J. Yang and R. S. Williams. Memristive devices in computing system: Promises and challenges. *J. Emerg. Technol. Comput. Syst.*, 9(2):11:1–11:20, May 2013.

[20] J. Yu, R. Nane, A. Haron *et al.* Skeleton-based design and simulation flow for computation-in-memory architectures. NANOARCH '16, pages 165–170. IEEE, July 2016.

Energy Efficient In-Memory Computing Platform Based on 4-Terminal Spin Hall Effect-Driven Domain Wall Motion Devices

Shaahin Angizi, Zhezhi He and Deliang Fan
Department of Electrical & Computer Engineering, University of Central Florida, Orlando, FL 32816 USA
{angizi,elliot.he}@knights.ucf.edu, dfan@ucf.edu

ABSTRACT

In this paper, we propose an energy efficient in-memory computing platform based on novel 4-terminal spin Hall effect-driven domain wall motion devices that could be employed as both non-volatile memory cell and in-memory logic unit. The proposed designs lead to unity of memory and logic. The device to architecture level simulation results show that, with 45% area increase, the proposed in-memory computing platform achieves the write energy $\sim$ 15.6 fJ/bit which is more than one order lower than that of standard 1-transistor 1-magnetic tunnel junction counterpart while keeping the identical 1ns writing speed. In addition, the proposed in-memory logic scheme improves the operating energy by 61.3% as compared with the conventional non-volatile in-memory logic designs.

Keywords

Domain wall motion device; Spin Hall effect; In-memory computing

1. INTRODUCTION

Keeping pace with today's massive data processing, the separation of memory and computing units interconnected via buses (realizing Von-Neumann architecture) has faced serious challenges. These challenges can be identified as long memory access latency, considerable congestion at I/Os, limited memory bandwidth, and huge leakage power consumption in big data-driven (10^{18} bytes or flops) applications [1, 2]. To address above issues, in-memory computing architectures and devices have been presented to integrate memory and logic, leading to a much more energy efficient information processing platform [3].

The basic advantageous concept behind the in-memory computing is preprocessing the data and providing intermediate result for processor rather than feeding it large volume of raw data. It involves synergistic exploration spanning from device technology to architecture innovation. Fig. 1 illustrates an in-memory computing architecture with memory data organized in H-tree model [4]. It pairs each data block with in-memory logic. A local data processing scheme is employed to only provide processor intermediate results, greatly reducing the communication traffic between memory and processor and also improving the energy efficiency. From device technology perspective, there are many recent and promising researches carried out by the emerging non-volatile memories (NVMs) at nano-scale for realization of such in-memory computing platforms, such as phase-change memory (PCM) [5], resistive memory (ReRAM) [2], and spintronic memory [6, 7].

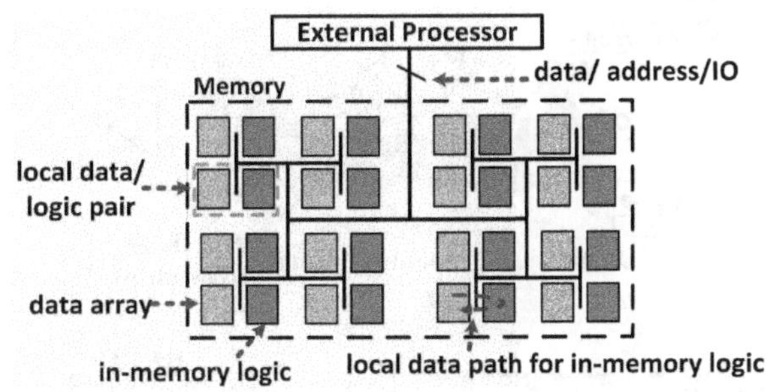

Figure 1: H-tree in-memory computing platform [4].

Unique features of spintronic devices such as instance wake-up, non-volatility, zero static power, and high integration density are difficult to achieve using today's CMOS technology [8]. Perhaps the most intriguing feature of such structures relies on their potential to redesigning existing Boolean computing architectures by utilizing a completely new class of design methods such as logic-in-memory or processor-in-memory or neuromorphic computing [9], which show orders of lower power compared to CMOS counterparts.

In this paper, we initially propose two new composite device structures employing spin Hall effect-driven domain wall motion (SHE-DWM) and Magnetic Tunnel Junction (MTJ) devices. Accordingly, we leverage them to realize an energy efficient H-tree in-memory computing platform by designing both non-volatile memory cell and in-memory logic units. In detail, the major contributions of this work are as follows: (1) Novel current mode 4T SHE-DWM and 4T SHE-Differential DWM (4T SHE-DDWM) devices are designed with completely decoupled write and read terminals, (2) An energy-efficient non-volatile memory cell with detailed interface circuits is proposed employing 4T SHE-DWM device, (3) Hybrid spin-CMOS in-memory logic designs including OR/NOR, AND/NAND, XOR/XNOR, and full adder cell are implemented using the proposed 4T SHE-DWM and 4T SHE-DDWM devices, and (4) A device to architecture level

Permission to make digital or hard copies of all or part of this work for personal or classroom use is granted without fee provided that copies are not made or distributed for profit or commercial advantage and that copies bear this notice and the full citation on the first page. Copyrights for components of this work owned by others than ACM must be honored. Abstracting with credit is permitted. To copy otherwise, or republish, to post on servers or to redistribute to lists, requires prior specific permission and/or a fee. Request permissions from permissions@acm.org.

GLSVLSI '17, May 10-12, 2017, Banff, AB, Canada
© 2017 ACM. ISBN 978-1-4503-4972-7/17/05...$15.00
DOI: http://dx.doi.org/10.1145/3060403.3060459

evaluation of proposed in-memory computing platform is accomplished.

2. FOUR-TERMINAL SPIN HALL EFFECT-DRIVEN DOMAIN WALL MOTION DEVICES

Fig. 2a and Fig. 2c illustrate the proposed device structures referred to as 4 Terminal Spin Hall Effect-driven Domain Wall Motion (4T SHE-DWM) and 4T Spin Hall Effect-driven Differential Domain Wall Motion (4T SHE-DDWM) devices, respectively. Each design is a composite stacked structure consisting of a Spin Hall Metal (SHM), a Domain Wall Motion (DWM) strip and two Magnetic Tunnel Junctions (MTJ). DWM strip (i.e. d2) is laterally connected to two anti-parallel fixed magnetic domains (d1 and d3). MTJ is formed through a MgO layer sandwiched between fixed magnetic layer - m1 or m2 and the 'free' DWM strip - d2. The only structural difference between first and second designs is the MTJ fixed layer magnetization alignment. As is clear, the first proposed design (Fig. 2a) consists of two MTJs with parallel fixed layers. However, the second design (Fig. 2c) consists of two MTJs with anti-parallel fixed layers.

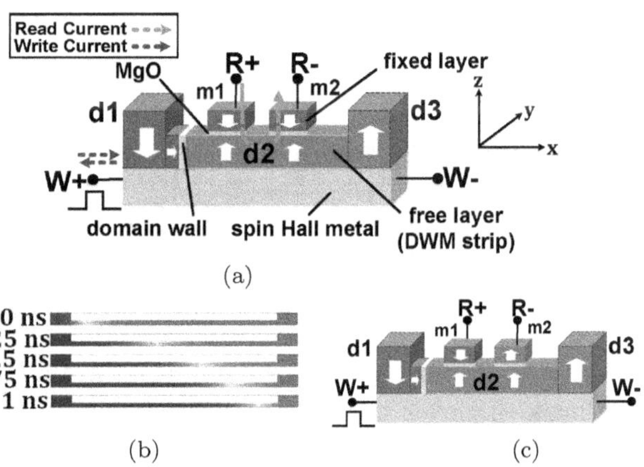

Figure 2: (a) 4T SHE-DWM device, (b) Micromagnetic simulation, (c) 4T SHE-DDWM device.

The resistance of the MTJs are depending on the free layer magnetization, namely the domain wall (DW, i.e. the transition area between two domains in the DWM strip) positions within the DWM strip. Electric manipulation of domain wall was typically accomplished by the current induced spin-transfer torque (STT) due to the coupling between local magnetic moments of the DW and spin-polarized currents [10]. Recently, it has been experimentally demonstrated that domain wall motion could be more energy efficiently achieved through Spin Hall Effect (SHE) [11]. The authors in [12] have studied deterministic magnetic reversal of a perpendicularly magnetized CoFeB layer driven by SHE torque from an in-plane current flowing in an underlying W layer along with its reliability analysis. In the proposed device structures, when charge current passes through the non-magnetic SHM (such as β-W [13], Pt, doped Cu and etc.) in lateral paths ($\pm$x), electrons with opposite spins scatter to opposite surfaces of SHM due to strong spin-orbit coupling. Thus, a spin current (I_s) perpendicular ($\pm$z) to charge current (I_c) is generated owing to the SHE [8], which will be leveraged to induce steady and fast domain wall motion.

Table 1: Device parameters used in simulation.

Symbol	Quantity	Values
α	Damping coefficient	0.3
K_u	Uniaxial anisotropy constant	$3.5 \times 10^5 J/m^3$
M_s	Saturation magnetization	$6.8 \times 10^5 A/m$
A_{ex}	Exchange stiffness	$1.1 \times 10^{-11} J/m$
t_{MgO}	MgO thickness of STD	1 nm
RA	Resistance area product	$2.38\Omega\mu m^2$
TMR_{AP}	Tunnel Magneto resistance	168%
ρ	Resistivity of magnet	$170\Omega nm$
θ_{SHM}	Spin Hall angle	0.3
$(L.W)_{MTJ}$	MTJ dimention	$20 \times 20nm^2$
$(L.W.t)_{DWM}$	DWM strip dimension	$100 \times 20 \times 1nm^3$
$(L.W.t)_{SHM}$	SHM dimension	$120 \times 20 \times 2.8nm^3$

The magnetization dynamics, m, of a nano-magnet with $N_s x$ as the number of spins per domain in x-direction in the presence of an effective magnetic field, H_{eff}, and a spin current, I_s, is modeled using the Landau–Lifshitz–Gilbert (LLG) equation as follow [8]:

$$\frac{\partial m}{\partial t} = -|\gamma|(m \times H_{eff}) + \alpha(m \times \frac{\partial m}{\partial t}) - \frac{I_s}{qN_{sx}}\frac{\partial m}{\partial x} + \xi\frac{I_s}{qN_{sx}} m \times \frac{\partial m}{\partial x} \quad (1)$$

In this equation, the first two terms denote the usual precession and damping terms, respectively. The third term is the local tracking of conduction electrons to local magnetization and the fourth term describes a phenomenological non-adiabatic spin-transfer term whose strength is described by ξ. According to SHE, the generated spin current can be written as

$$I_s = \theta_{SH}\frac{A_s}{A_c}I_c\sigma \quad (2)$$

where θ_{SH} is the spin Hall angle characterizing the strength of SHE in SHM, σ is the polarization of the electron spin and A_s and A_c are the cross-sectional areas through which spin and charge current flow, respectively.

In the proposed device structures, the free layer dimension is ($100nm \times 20nm \times 1nm$), so a Néel type DW is formed due to the small strip width (20nm). The larger thickness at the edges of the DWM strip is used to stabilize the DW at an intermediate position [8, 14]. In addition, in order to have a better controllability and thermal stability over DW movement within domain wall strip, three artificial trapping sites can be considered in the left, middle and right end of DWM strip [15]. MTJ consisting of two ferromagnetic layers (m1/m2 and d2 as shown in Fig. 2a) with a tunneling oxide (MgO) barrier sandwiched between them is employed to read the state of DWM strip. The transient micro-magnetic simulation of DW position (achieved from OOMMF [16]) is illustrated in Fig. 2b, using device dimension listed in Table 1, from 0 to 1ns. Since the magnetization of DWM strip beneath the two MTJs is fully switched at 1ns, the intrinsic threshold current (I_{th}) of this device can be considered $39.2\mu A$ within 1ns corresponding to DW velocity of $\sim 75m/s$. Fig. 3a depicts and compares the DW velocity vs. lateral current density of SHE-driven DW presented herein and conventional domain wall motion device (with same dimension without SHM layer) based on micro-magnetic simulations. It can be seen that the application of SHE induces a much higher DW velocity at the same input current density.

The proposed structures can function as 4-terminal devices with completely decoupled write and read paths. For the lateral write path ($\pm x$), the magnetization of DWM strip can be identified anti-parallel (AP) or parallel (P) to the fixed layer of MTJs (m1 and m2) by injecting a small current (larger than critical current) along SHM terminals (W+ to W- or vice-versa). Hence, the resistance states are different values based on either high (corresponding to AP configuration) or low (corresponding to P configuration) of MTJs and can be read by injecting a small sensing current through R+ to R- terminals employing a sense circuit. It is worth pointing out that the sense current ($\sim 1\mu A$) is significantly less than the DW critical depinning current so that the state of the read MTJs is not disturbed during read operation.

MTJ resistance can be expressed in terms of voltage, tunneling oxide thickness (t_{MgO}), and the angle between free layer and fixed layer magnetizations. The atomistic level experimental benchmarked simulation framework based on Non-Equilibrium Green's Function (NEGF) formalism [14] is used to evaluate the MTJ resistance. The MTJ resistance-area product vs. MgO thickness in AP and P states is plotted in Fig. 3b with a constant voltage of 50mV. It shows that resistance-area product exponentially increases with the increase of tunnel oxide thickness.

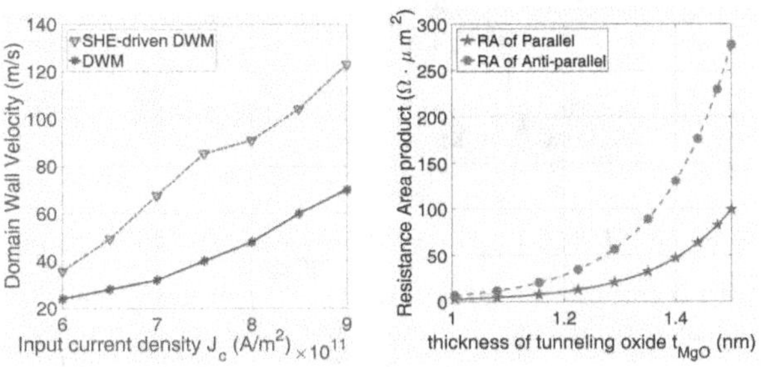

(a) (b)

Figure 3: (a) DW velocity vs. lateral current density of SHE-driven DW and conventional domain wall motion, (b) Resistance-area product vs. the thickness of tunneling oxide in AP and P states (with constant voltage of 50mV).

In order to simulate the proposed device with CMOS interface circuits in SPICE, 4T SHE-DWM device is modeled as two MTJs with variable resistance depending on DW positions (equivalent resistive network can be written as equation (3)).

$$R = R_{m1} + R_{FL} + R_{m2} = \begin{cases} 2RA_{AP}/A_{MTJ} + R_{FL} & \text{DW @ left,} \\ 2RA_P/A_{MTJ} + R_{FL} & \text{DW @ right,} \\ (RA_P + RA_{AP})/A_{MTJ} + R_{FL} & \text{DW @ middle.} \end{cases} \tag{3}$$

where R_{m1} and R_{m2} represent resistance of two read MTJs which are shown by m1 and m2, respectively, R_{FL} is the lateral free layer resistance between the two read MTJs, RA_{AP} and RA_P denote MTJ Resistance-Area (RA) product for anti-parallel and parallel configurations, respectively, obtained in the NEGF based MTJ model [14] and A_{MTJ} is the read MTJ area. As is clear in equation (3), the output resistance can have three different values based on the DW positions. The output resistance (from R+ to R-) of 4T SHE-DDWM device can also be expressed as follows:

$$R = R_{m1} + R_{FL} + R_{m2} = \begin{cases} (RA_P + RA_{AP})/A_{MTJ} + R_{FL} & \text{DW @ left or right,} \\ 2RA_P/A_{MTJ} + R_{FL} & \text{DW @ middle.} \end{cases} \tag{4}$$

It can be seen that second device only has two distinct resistance levels based on its DW positions and the output resistances are identical when the DW is positioned in the left and right end. The proposed devices will be employed as memory and in-memory logic units in following sections.

3. MEMORY CELL DESIGN BASED ON 4T SHE-DWM DEVICE

In this section, a new efficient one-bit memory cell based on 4T SHE-DWM device is designed. Note that only two resistance levels (corresponding to DW located in the left end and right end) are used in memory cell design integrated in memory array shown in Fig. 4. The read MTJ resistivity status is utilized for representation of the memory content. In this way, when DW is located at the rightmost end, the content is considered as binary "1" (low resistance) and when it is positioned at the leftmost end of domain wall strip, the content is considered as binary "0". We have considered a decoupled write and read terminals for our proposed memory cell overcoming the reliability issues associated with STT-MRAM design [8, 17].

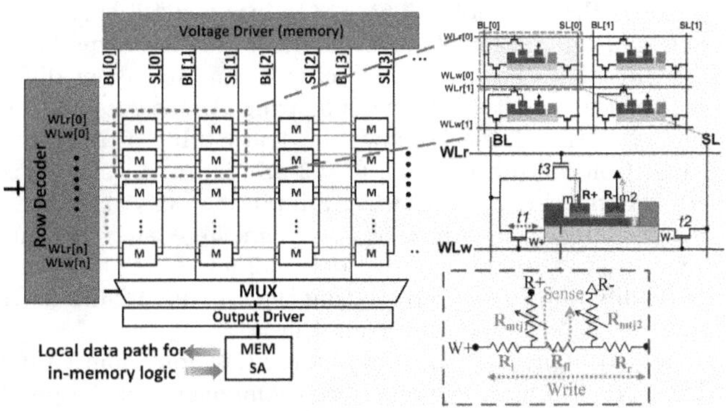

Figure 4: Proposed memory cell design and the equivalent resistive network.

As shown in Fig. 4, the write and read operations are accomplished by applying appropriate voltages to source-line (SL), the bit-line (BL), word-line write (WLw), and word-line read (WLr). In order to accomplish **read** operation, the state of m1 and m2 MTJs should be read by setting WLr to a high voltage and the read voltage (V_{read}) is applied via V_{BL}. Since m2 is grounded and WLw is low, two write access transistors (t1 and t2) are turned off and a sense current (I_{sen}) will flow from m1 to m2. Eventually, the memory cell content is determined after comparing the sensing current to a reference current by a sense amplifier (MEM SA). The sense current in read operation is unidirectional, while a bidirectional current is required to write data. In order to **write**, WLw is applied with VDD to turn on two write access transistors (t1 and t2) and a write voltage is applied across the BL or SL. For instance to write '0' (i.e. $V_{BL} - V_{SL} = V_{wr} - 0$), the write current is injected from W+ to W- and the DW will be pushed to the left end. The complete operation of the proposed memory cell in memory array shown in Fig. 4 is listed in Table 2.

Table 2: Complete operation of memory-bit cell.

Operation	WLw	WLr	BL	SL	t1	t2	t3
Read	0	VDD	I_{sen}	0	off	off	on
Write 0	VDD	0	V_{wr}	0	on	on	off
Write 1	VDD	0	0	V_{wr}	on	on	off

The equivalent resistive network of the memory cell is depicted in Fig. 4. Based on our micromagnetic simulation, a $\pm 39.2\mu A - 1ns$ current pulse can move the DW from one end to the other. The optimum access transistor size and V_{wr} is used to give the lowest failure probability, while maintaining low write energy under the given design specifications.

4. IN-MEMORY LOGIC BASED ON 4T SHE-DWM AND 4T SHE-DDWM DEVICES

4.1 Hybrid Spin-CMOS Threshold Logic Gate

In this subsection, we present a hybrid spin-CMOS threshold logic gate (TLG) design employing 4T SHE-DWM device to efficiently implement Boolean functions such as 3-input majority gate (MG), 2-input AND/NAND, and 2-input OR/NOR gates. A TLG essentially constitutes of summation of weighted inputs, followed by a thresholding operation expressed as follow [15]:

$$TLG(out) = \begin{cases} 1, & \Sigma(In_i \times W_i) \geqslant \theta \\ 0, & else \end{cases} \tag{5}$$

where In_i's are binary inputs, W_i's are scalar weights and θ is the threshold. The TLG output is "1" only if the weighted summation of binary inputs is greater or equal than the threshold. The same TLG circuit can implement different Boolean functions by reconfiguring the weights, threshold, or both. Table 3 shows the truth table of a 3-input TLG. Considering $W_i = 1$, $\theta = 2$ and input A as a "Bias" pin, different logic gates such as 3-input majority gate (MG), 2-input OR/AND gates can be implemented using the same 3-input TLG circuit. For instance, a 2-input AND gate can be readily implemented by setting Bias=0 and a 2-input OR gate can be achieved by setting Bias=1.

As shown in Fig. 5, our proposed 3-input spin-CMOS TLG circuit mainly consists of two components, corresponding to two steps of a TLG, namely weighted summation and thresholding. The TLG can be executed in the following steps: (1) Weighted summation: The operand A (or Bias), B and Cin are loaded into the corresponding 4T SHE-DWM devices using the method and circuit described in section 2. Hence, the conductance of the 4T SHE-DWM devices can be either high or low based on the operand value. After the operands are loaded, a voltage pulse (clk1, 0.4V-1ns) is applied on the R+ terminal of each weighing device, simultaneously. Thus the current coming out of R- is the weighted current, either low or high depending on operand values. For example, if "A=1", the corresponding conductance from R+ to R- is high, leading to "$I_A = high$". If "B=0", the corresponding conductance from R+ to R- is low, leading to "$I_B = low$". Then the weighted summation current ($I_{sum} = I_A + I_B + I_C$) is achieved at the common node. (2) Thresholding: I_{sum} flows into the W+ terminal of the 4T SHE-DWM thresholding device, programming the DW position (i.e. read MTJs resistance). Assuming the DW is initially located in the right end, thus the two read MTJs are in parallel states ($2R_p$). If I_{sum} is greater than the critical current (i.e. minimum current required to move the domain wall from right end to left end within 1ns), both two read MTJs switch to anti-parallel states ($2R_{AP}$). If not, two read MTJs are either both in parallel states ($2R_p$) or only m2 switches to anti-parallel state ($R_{AP} + R_p$) based on the current magnitude.

Table 3: Truth table of 3-input TLG and extracted 2-input AND/OR gates.

Inputs			3-input TLG		
A/ Bias	B	C	Σ	3-input MG	
0	0	0	0<2	0	A.B
0	0	1	1<2	0	
0	1	0	1<2	0	
0	1	1	$2 \geqslant 2$	1	
1	0	0	1<2	0	A+B
1	0	1	$2 \geqslant 2$	1	
1	1	0	$2 \geqslant 2$	1	
1	1	1	$3 \geqslant 2$	1	

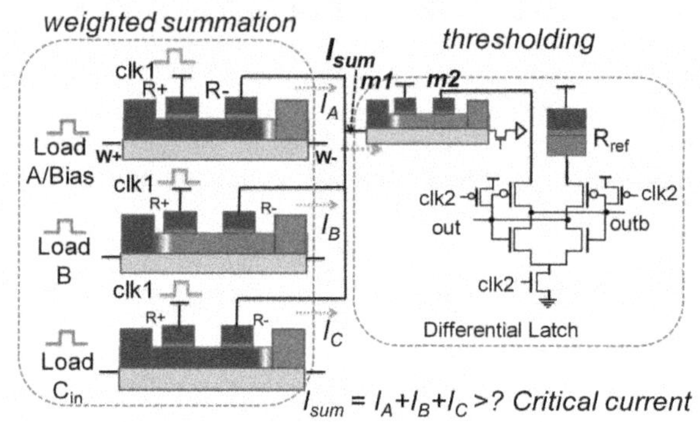

Figure 5: Hybrid spin-CMOS 3-input TLG design.

A differential latch is used to read the states of read MTJs with one current branch connecting from m1 to m2 and the other current branch through a reference MTJ (with resistance value of $1.5R_{AP} + 0.5R_p$). It is worth pointing out that proper clocking of circuit prevents backward injection of current from differential latch to weighted summation devices by removing the required potential to move the DW. In summary, the latch output (out) is high when I_{sum} is greater than the critical current ($\sim 39.2\mu A$) and vice versa. In this manner, 3-input MG and 2-input AND/OR gates can be implemented. Obviously the complementary output of differential latch (Outb as shown in Fig. 5) can be readily used for implementing NAND/NOR gates.

4.2 Hybrid Spin-CMOS XOR Design

In this subsection, we propose a compact in-memory XOR logic gate using a single 4T SHE-DDWM device as shown in Fig. 6, greatly reducing the latency, power consumption and area. In order to have a precise control of DW pinning/depinning operation and good thermal stability, three notches are manufactured within the free layer magnetic nanostrip, located in left, middle and right [18].

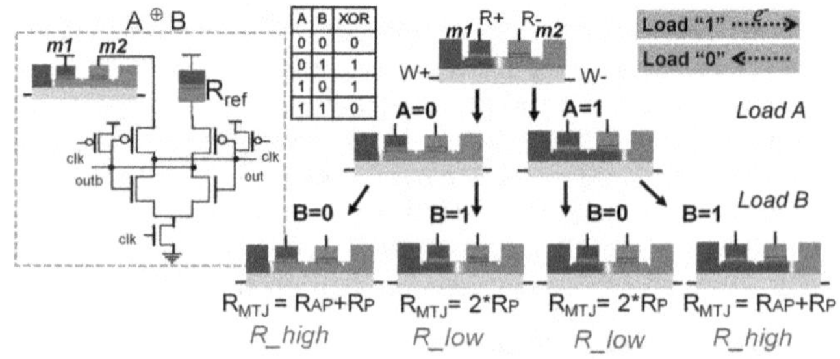

Figure 6: The proposed 2-input XOR gate based on 4T SHE-DDWM device.

Based on our micro-magnetic simulation, a $\pm 39.2\mu A -$

$0.5ns$ current pulse can move DW from one pinning site to the neighboring pinning site. We define the electron flow from W+ to W- to write "1" and electron flow from W- to W+ to write "0" as shown in Fig. 6. DW is initially located in the middle notch (corresponding to parallel configurations for both m1 and m2). Input operands are sequentially loaded to 4T SHE-DDWM device, by applying $\pm 39.2\mu A - 0.5ns$ current pulse along the lateral writing path. For instance, if "(A,B)=(0,1)", the DW firstly moves to the left pinning site due to loading "A=0". Then, the spin current due to loading "B=1" will push DW to its right neighboring pinning site. As micro-magnetic simulation shown in Fig. 6, the final DW positions for 4 possible input combinations AB=(00, 01, 10, 11) are (left, middle, middle, right) corresponding to $R = (R_{high}, R_{low}, R_{low}, R_{high})$. R_{high} and R_{low} are achieved based on m1 and m2 MTJs configurations as mentioned in equation (4). A differential latch is then used to read the two read MTJ resistance states with one current branch from m1 to m2 and the other current branch through a reference MTJ. Therefore, the latch output is (0, 1, 1, 0), successfully realizing a 2-input XOR gate.

5. PERFORMANCE EVALUATION

For performance evaluation, the MTJ is modeled using NEGF-LLG (non-equilibrium Green's function and Landau-Lifshitz-Gilbert equations) solution for spin to charge interface and calibrated with experimental data in [14, 19]. A Verilog-A model of both 4T SHE-DWM and 4T SHE-DDWM devices is developed to co-simulate with the interface CMOS circuits in SPICE to validate the functionality and evaluate performance of the proposed in-memory platform design. Note that 45nm North Carolina State University (NCSU) Product Development Kit (PDK) library [20] is used in HSPICE circuit simulation. Then, we used self-consistent modified NVSim [21] along with an in-house developed C++ code to verify the architecture level performance.

5.1 Device and Circuit Level Simulations

We evaluate and compare the device and circuit level performance of proposed in-memory computing model with the recently reported designs with respect to the logic and memory. Table 4 tabulates the quantitative comparison of proposed memory-bit cell and recently published works. The device-circuit SPICE simulation indicates that the write energy of the proposed memory cell is $\sim$ 15.6 fJ/bit which is $\times 47.6$ lower than that of standard STT-MRAM in [7] while keeping the identical 1ns writing speed and $\times 4.9$ lower than the recent differential spin Hall mram (DSH-MRAM) design [6]. It is noteworthy that in STT-MRAM cell, high write speed (1ns) design requires much larger transistor width (1.035μm) and boosted voltage (V_{wr}=1.2V) to provide sufficient write current. However, in our proposed SHE-DWM based memory cell, a much smaller transistor width and low write voltage (V_{wr}=0.4V) is enough to provide the required write current ($39.2\mu A$) for 1ns write time. Note that, the read energy and latency of these three different non-volatile memory cell designs are almost similar due to the same sensing scheme, namely reading the MTJ resistance. Our proposed memory cell also provides a decoupled write and read terminals enabling a streamlined interface circuitry design for in-memory computing.

Fig. 7 shows the SPICE transient simulation of the proposed design for realizing a 3-input TLG. Three complementary clocks with 1ns pulse width are used in the circuit simulation. For each input combination, we evaluate four distinct parameters: (1) summation of current or I_{sum} at intersection point, (2) domain wall position, (3) RMTJ (i.e. the series resistance of m1 and m2 in 4T SHE-DWM thresholding device) and (4) output indicating the differential latch output (out).

Table 4: Performance comparison of memory cells.

Memory Attributes	Proposed	DSH-MRAM [6]	STT-MRAM [7]
Bit cell TMR	166% (current sensing)	172% (voltage sensing)	205% (current sensing)
Read/Write Voltage	1.0 V/0.4 V	1.0 V/0.4 V	0.25V/1.2 V
Switching Current Density	7.5 MA/cm^2 @ 1ns	7 MA/cm^2 @ 1ns	7.4 MA/cm^2 @ 5ns
Read Frequency	1 GHZ	1 GHZ	1 GHZ
Access Transistor width	95nm	120nm	1035 nm
Write Energy/Bit	15.6 fJ @Twrite= 1ns	77 fJ @ Twrite= 1ns	744 fJ @Twrite=1ns
Read Energy/Bit @ Tread= 1ns	1.1 fJ	1.1 fJ	0.9 fJ

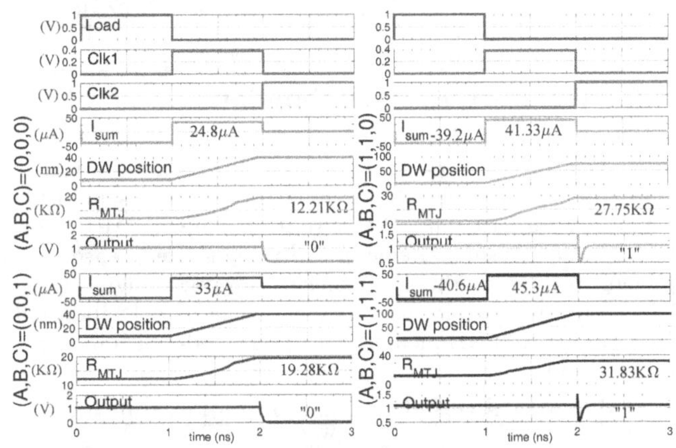

Figure 7: SPICE transient simulation of 3-input TLG.

The first clock is "load" clock, which is used to load the operand "A", "B" and "Cin" by programming the corresponding 4T SHE-DWM device conductance. Meanwhile, a reset current ($-39.2\mu A$) is also generated to initialize the DW into the right end of the 4T SHE-DWM thresholding device, ready for next cycle operation. When "Clk1" is on, a small voltage ($\sim$400 mV) is applied at the R+ terminals of 4T SHE-DWM weighing devices and I_{sum} is determined by the operand (A, B, Cin) values, leading to the change of RMTJ. As shown in the transient simulation, for operand "A", "B" and "Cin" with values of (000, 001, 110, 111), the corresponding I_{sum} are $(24.8, 33, 41.33, 45.3)\mu A$. Since the threshold current is $39.2\mu A$, the corresponding RMTJ are $(12.21, 19.28, 27.75, 31.83)k\Omega$, leading to the differential latch output as (0, 0, 1, 1) in the next "Clk2" cycle. It is worth pointing out that 2-input AND/OR gates can be implemented in the same way just by considering "A" as a "Bias" as shown in Table 3.

Comparison result between the recent in-memory non-volatile 2-input AND gates referred to as NVLs (non-volatile logic) and the CMOS counterpart is listed in Table 5. Note that, NVL1 [22] and NVL3 [23] are domain wall racetrack-based logics and NVL2 [24] is an MTJ-based logic.

The operation energy (speed) of the non-volatile logic refers to the energy (time) to write the data to the NVMs

Table 5: Performance of 2-input AND gates.

Parameters	Proposed	NVL1	NVL2	NVL3	CMOS
Operation Speed	2ns	1.12ns	1.18ns	2.14ns	62 ps
Operation Energy	26.2 fJ	67.72 fJ	125.85 fJ	504.36 fJ	6.69 fJ

and to perform the computation. As shown, the proposed in-memory computing model's logic scheme improves the operating energy by 61.3 % as compared with the best reported memory-based NVL in [22]. To evaluate the performance of proposed in-memory XOR structure in conjunction with 3-input TLG circuit, a hybrid spin-CMOS full adder is designed. Carry output can be directly obtained using 3-input TLG circuit and Sum output can be achieved using two cascaded 2-input XOR gates. A comprehensive comparison between CMOS and Diode-GSHE (Giant Spin Hall Effect) full adders presented in [25] at 22nm technology and our SHE-DWM based full adder is presented in Table 6. The performance comparison shows that the power consumption of the proposed SHE-DWM based full adder is less than the spintronic and CMOS circuits.

Table 6: Performance evaluation of FA cells.

Parameters	Proposed	CMOS [25]	Diode-GSHE [25]
Power Consumption (μW)	14.65	49.4	15.6
Complexity (transistor count)	22	42	20

5.2 Architecture Level Simulations

Fig. 8a depicts the memory array organization modeled in this work. Memory chip is divided into multiple Banks consisting of multiple Mats. Each Mat includes multiple subarrays organized in a H-tree routing manner. We exploit the external sensing scheme in [21] using shared Sense Amplifiers to improve the area efficiency of our design. Table 7 lists our proposed in-memory computing model validation for a sample 128 KB memory with 512 word-width in 45nm process node.

Table 7: Proposed memory model evaluation.

Metrics	Write	Read
Dynamic Energy	880.395pJ	890.174pJ
Mat Dynamic Energy	19.997pJ per mat	22.442pJ per mat
Subarray Dynamic Energy	4.893pJ per active subarray	5.504pJ per active subarray
Leakage Power	45.510mW per mat	
Area Overhead	18.450mm^2	

Fig. 8b shows the breakdown of area overhead of proposed in-memory computing platform in a Mat structure. As is clear, there is 45% area increase in memory die for supporting in-memory processing. The analysis shows that the proposed platform incurs 15% less area overhead in comparison to the in-memory computing model presented in [2].

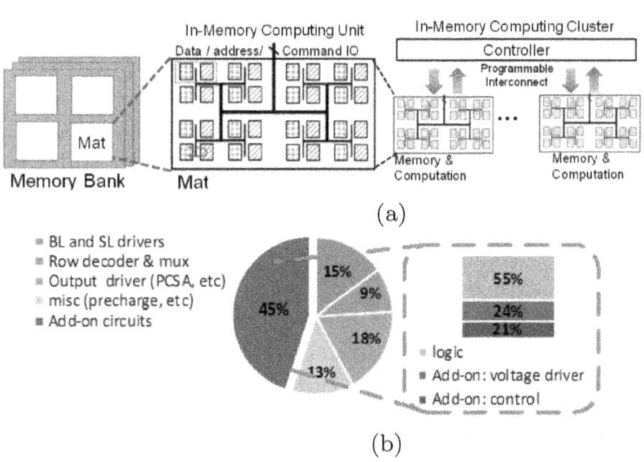

Figure 8: (a) Memory organization of proposed platform, (b) Area overhead.

6. CONCLUSION

In this paper, we proposed an ultra-energy efficient in-memory computing platform utilizing two new spin Hall effect-driven domain wall motion devices to realize both non-volatile memory cell and in-memory logic designs. The device to architecture level simulation results showed that, with 45% area increase, the proposed platform achieves the write energy $\sim$ 15.6 fJ/bit which is more than one order lower than that of standard STT-MRAM counterpart while keeping the identical 1ns writing speed. In addition, its logic scheme improves the operating energy by 61.3% as compared with the conventional nonvolatile in-memory logic designs.

7. REFERENCES

[1] D. Fan *et al.*, "Hierarchical temporal memory based on spin-neurons and resistive memory for energy-efficient brain-inspired computing," 2015.

[2] P. Chi *et al.*, "Prime: A novel processing-in-memory architecture for neural network computation in reram-based main memory," in *Proceedings of ISCA*, vol. 43, 2016.

[3] D. P. Zhang *et al.*, "A new perspective on processing-in-memory architecture design," in *Proceedings of the ACM SIGPLAN Workshop*. ACM, 2013, p. 7.

[4] Y. Wang *et al.*, "An energy-efficient nonvolatile in-memory computing architecture for extreme learning machine by domain-wall nanowire devices," *IEEE TNANO*, 2015.

[5] H.-S. P. Wong *et al.*, "Phase change memory," *Proc. IEEE*, 2010.

[6] Y. Kim *et al.*, "Dsh-mram: differential spin hall mram for on-chip memories," *IEEE Elec. Dev. Let.*, 2013.

[7] Y. Kim, S. K. Gupta, S. P. Park, G. Panagopoulos, and K. Roy, "Write-optimized reliable design of stt mram," in *Proceedings of the 2012 ACM/IEEE international symposium on Low power electronics and design*. ACM, 2012, pp. 3–8.

[8] X. Fong, *et al.*, "Spin-transfer torque devices for logic and memory: Prospects and perspectives," *IEEE TCAD*, 2016.

[9] D. Fan *et al.*, "Design and synthesis of ultralow energy spin-memristor threshold logic," *IEEE TNANO*, 2014.

[10] A. Khvalkovskiy *et al.*, "Matching domain-wall configuration and spin-orbit torques for efficient domain-wall motion," *PRB*, 2013.

[11] P. Haazen *et al.*, "Domain wall depinning governed by the spin hall effect," *Nature materials*, 2013.

[12] J. Torrejon *et al.*, "Interface control of the magnetic chirality in cofeb/mgo heterostructures with heavy-metal underlayers," *Nature communications*, 2014.

[13] C.-F. Pai *et al.*, "Spin transfer torque devices utilizing the giant spin hall effect of tungsten," *APL*, 2012.

[14] X. Fong *et al.*, "Knack: A hybrid spin-charge mixed-mode simulator for evaluating different genres of spin-transfer torque mram bit-cells," in *IEEE SISPAD*, 2011.

[15] K. Roy *et al.*, "Exploring boolean and non-boolean computing with spin torque devices," in *Proc. of ICCAD*, 2013.

[16] http://math.nist.gov/oommf/.

[17] K. Tsuchida *et al.*, "A 64mb mram with clamped-reference and adequate-reference schemes, 2010 isscc, 2010, pp. 258-259."

[18] S. J. Noh *et al.*, "Effects of notch shape on the magnetic domain wall motion in nanowires with in-plane or perpendicular magnetic anisotropy," *JAP*, 2012.

[19] S. Fukami *et al.*, "20-nm magnetic domain wall motion memory with ultralow-power operation," in *IEEE IEDM*, 2013.

[20] http://www.eda.ncsu.edu/wiki/FreePDK45.

[21] X. Dong *et al.*, "Nvsim: A circuit-level performance, energy, and area model for emerging non-volatile memory," in *Emerging Memory Technologies*. Springer, 2014.

[22] K. Huang and R. Zhao, "Magnetic domain-wall racetrack memory-based nonvolatile logic for low-power computing and fast run-time-reconfiguration."

[23] H.-P. Trinh *et al.*, "Magnetic adder based on racetrack memory," *IEEE TCASI*, vol. 60, pp. 1469–1477, 2013.

[24] K. Huang *et al.*, "Stt-mram based low power synchronous non-volatile logic with timing demultiplexing," in *NANOARC*. ACM, 2014.

[25] Y. Zhang *et al.*, "Giant spin hall effect (gshe) logic design for low power application," in *Proc. of DATE*, 2015.

Leveraging Dual-Mode Magnetic Crossbar for Ultra-low Energy In-Memory Data Encryption

Zhezhi He, Shaahin Angizi, Farhana Parveen and Deliang Fan
Depart. of Electrical & Computer Engineering, University of Central Florida, Orlando, FL 32816 USA
{Elliot.He, Angizi, Fparveen}@Knights.ucf.edu, Dfan@ucf.edu

ABSTRACT

The logic-in-memory architecture is highly promising for high-throughput data-driven applications. This paper presents a novel dual-mode magnetic crossbar architecture consisting of perpendicularly cross-coupled magnetic racetrack nanowires, which could morph between non-volatile multi-bit racetrack memory mode and in-memory data encryption mode. The proposed magnetic crossbar is able to automatically perform parallel in-memory bit-wise XOR computations of the data stored in the racetrack memories with the help of magnetic coupling physics without complex peripheral circuits, which could be leveraged to design energy efficient in-memory data encryption engine. We employ Advanced Encryption Standard (AES) algorithm to elucidate the efficiency of the proposed design. The device-to-architecture level simulation results show that the proposed architecture can achieve 70% and 17.5% lower energy consumption compared to CMOS-ASIC and recent domain wall (DW) AES implementations, respectively. In addition, the AES encryption speed increases by 29.7% compared to the DW-AES implementation.

Keywords

Magnetic crossbar, Magnetic coupling, In-memory encryption.

1. INTRODUCTION

With the onset and growth of the Internet-of-Things (IoT), there is an inundation of data in today's world. Meanwhile, most of the data are sensitive, such as health-monitoring or Bio-metric data. The demand of energy efficient and high performance cryptographic components is becoming much stronger nowadays and will keep growing rapidly in the future. However, the conventional Von-Neumann architecture and Complementary Metal-Oxide Semiconductor (CMOS) technology based computing platform fails to meet such requirements due to architecture level memory wall (long memory access latency, limited memory bandwidth, energy hungry data transfer, etc.) and device level power wall (i.e. huge leakage power consumption limits the performance growth when technology scales down) [3]. Thus, in order to cater the forthcoming data explosion, it is worth exploring innovative in-memory computing architecture and emerging device technologies beyond CMOS to overcome the above limitations for future energy efficient and high performance data encryption engine.

Recent experiments on spintronic devices have demonstrated high speed switching of nanoscale magnets with spin polarized currents [10]. Together with other characteristics, including non-volatility, zero current leakage, high integration density and compatibility with CMOS fabrication process, spintronic devices have been explored to design compact, high speed, energy efficient non-volatile memory, in-memory logic and artificial neural network [11, 18]. In this work, we propose a dual-mode magnetic crossbar architecture consisting of perpendicularly cross-coupled magnetic racetrack nanowires, which could morph between non-volatile multi-bit racetrack memory mode and in-memory data encryption mode. The proposed magnetic crossbar is able to automatically perform parallel in-memory bit-wise XOR computations of the data stored in the racetrack memories with the help of magnetic coupling physics without complex peripheral circuits, which could be leveraged to design energy efficient in-memory data encryption engine. Performance evaluation of the proposed magnetic crossbar, including speed and energy dissipation, in the application of In-memory data encryption is also examined with Advanced Encryption Standard (AES) algorithm as an example.

Permission to make digital or hard copies of all or part of this work for personal or classroom use is granted without fee provided that copies are not made or distributed for profit or commercial advantage and that copies bear this notice and the full citation on the first page. Copyrights for components of this work owned by others than ACM must be honored. Abstracting with credit is permitted. To copy otherwise, or republish, to post on servers or to redistribute to lists, requires prior specific permission and/or a fee. Request permissions from permissions@acm.org.

GLSVLSI '17, May 10-12, 2017, Banff, AB, Canada

© 2017 ACM. ISBN 978-1-4503-4972-7/17/05...$15.00

DOI: http://dx.doi.org/10.1145/3060403.3060460

2. PROPOSED MAGNETIC CROSSBAR

2.1 Magnetic Crossbar Device Structure

In this work, we propose a magnetic crossbar architecture consisting of perpendicularly coupled magnetic domain wall motion racetracks, which is able to morph between two modes: memory and computation mode. In the memory mode, all the ferromagnetic nanowires are employed as conventional magnetic racetrack memory for non-volatile multi-bit data storage [18]. In the computation mode, the proposed magnetic crossbar performs parallel in-memory bit-wise Exclusive OR (XOR) computation of the data stored in the racetrack memory, which drastically reduces energy and delay. The details of magnetic crossbar device structure is presented in the following paragraphs.

The device structure of our proposed magnetic crossbar design is shown in Fig. 1a, which mainly constitutes of equally spaced ferromagnetic nanowires both longitudinally and latitudinally. Those nanowires operate as magnetic racetrack memory, where binary data are represented by the magne-

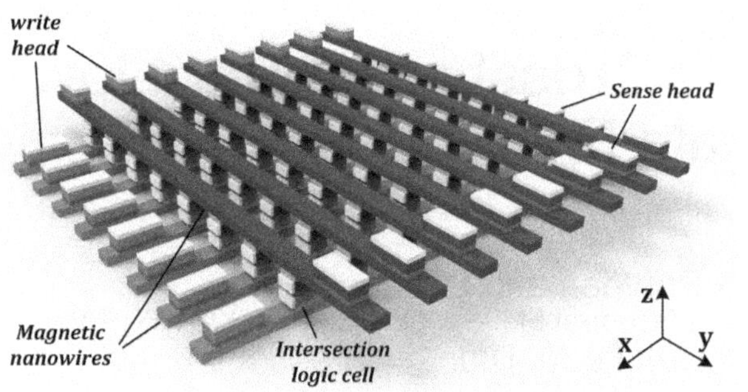

(a)

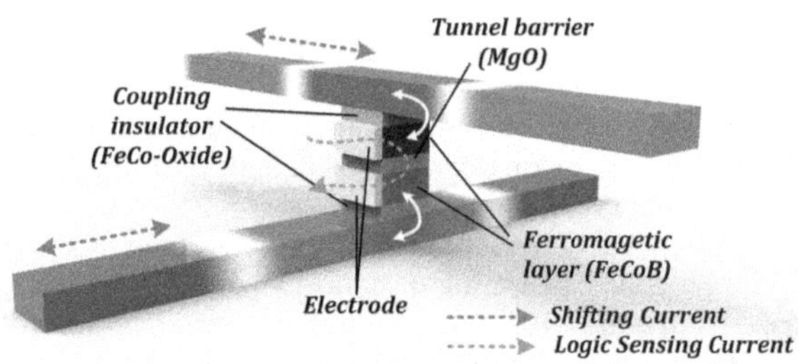

(b)

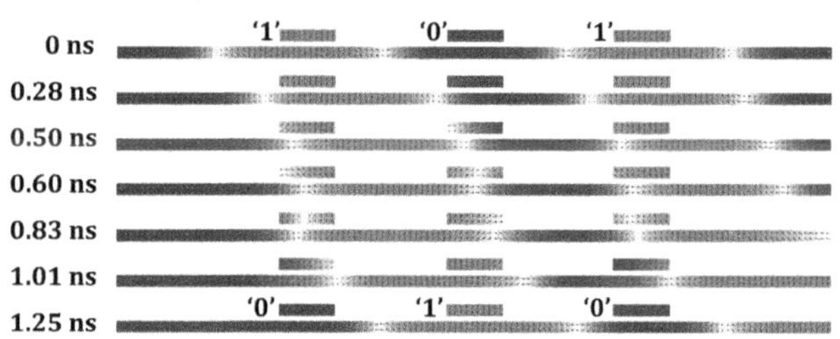

(c)

Figure 1: (a) The device structure of magnetic crossbar in the size of 8×8. (b) The XOR logic cell in the intersection of longitudinal and latitudinal domain wall nanowires. (c) The micromagnetic simulation of current induced domain wall motion and magnetic coupling effect.

tization directions and stored in the form of domain wall pair train within the nanowires [18]. In this work, we define +z oriented magnetization (in red) as binary '1', and -z oriented magnetization (in blue) as binary '0'. Write and read operations are performed through the write head (spin polarizer) and read head (sensing Magnetic Tunnel Junction) mounted on the two sides of nanowires [22]. A multilayer structure is designed at the intersection of each longitudinal and latitudinal nanowire, which consists of coupling insulator (FeCo-Oxide [19]), ferromagnetic layer (FeCoB), tunnel barrier(MgO), ferromagnetic layer (FeCoB) and coupling insulator (FeCo-Oxide), from top to bottom as shown in Fig. 1b. Owing to the magnetic coupling effect [6, 17, 19], two ferromagnetic layers are consistently staying in the identical magnetization state with corresponding top and bottom nanowire as indicated by the white arrow in Fig. 1b. When the domain wall nanowire is written with a new data followed by a domain wall pair shifting operation, the ferromagnetic layers switch their magnetization direction simultaneously due to magnetic coupling. As the transient micromagnetic simulation result shown in Fig. 1c, the initial binary bits (1, 0, 1) are stored in the bottom nanowire at 0ns. The coupled ferromagnetic layers have the same magnetization with the corresponding bottom domain wall nanowire. Through injecting lateral shifting current ($1 \times 10^{12} A/m^2$) into the bottom nanowire, the domain wall pairs start to shift from L.H.S to R.H.S, which simultaneously rotate the magnetization of the coupled top ferromagnetic layers. After 1.25ns, the domain wall pairs shift one bit right ($\sim 60nm$) within the nanowire. Meanwhile, the magnetization of all coupled ferromagnetic layers above the nanowires are flipped.

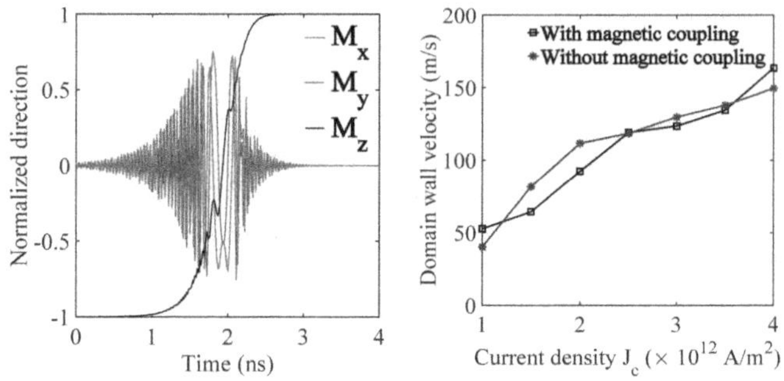

(a) (b)

Figure 2: (a)Transient magnetization simulation of the writing the domain wall pair into nanowire. (b) Domain wall motion speed versus lateral injected current density, w/ or w/o magnetic coupling effect.

In memory mode, each racetrack could work individually as a normal domain wall racetrack memory, in which the magnetization direction of each domain is used to encode data 0 and 1. Note that, these perpendicular coupled racetrack memory are electrically isolated due to the coupling layer is insulator, which avoids sneak path in the crossbar structure. The main racetrack memory operations are write, shift and read [18]. The binary bit can be written into the nanowire in the form of domain wall pair by applying a vertical writing current pulse ($J_w = 1 \times 10^{11} A/m^2$, within $\sim 2ns$) through the write magnetic tunnel junction (MTJ) head as the transient magnetization dynamics shown in Fig. 2a. Owing to the current induced domain wall motion, racetrack memory can intrinsically perform the shifting operation in an ultra low energy manner through injecting current along the nanowire as shown in Fig. 1c. Fig. 2b reveals that larger lateral shifting current can induce higher domain wall motion velocity, thus resulting in higher device operation speed. The memory read operation is achieved through shifting the data (domain wall pair) beneath the sense MTJ head mounted on the other side of nanowire. On the basis of Tunneling MagnetoResistance (TMR) effect, the sense head present high or low vertical sensing resistance with respect to the magnetization of underneath nanowire. Note that, the MTJ resistance modeling is introduced in the following simulation framework subsection.

In computation mode, the proposed magnetic crossbar design could implement an intrinsic parallel in-memory XOR computation. As shown in Fig. 1b,the ferromagnetic layers that respectively couple with the top and bottom magnetic nanowires can jointly work with the tunnel barrier layer to form a Magnetic Tunneling Junction (MTJ). In this design, the binary bit A and B located within intersection region are taken as the inputs of XOR computation, while the intersection MTJ resistance (R_{MTJ}) represents the output result ($A \oplus B$). As listed in Table. 1, when the magnetization of two ferromagnetic layers (M_A and M_B) are both up ('1') or down ('0'), the intersection MTJ cell is in parallel state with low resistance (R_P). Otherwise, when M_A and M_B are in the opposite orientation (i.e. one up and one down), the intersection MTJ cell is in anti-parallel state with high resistance (R_{AP}). Based on this description, we could see that the XOR computation is automatically implemented by the magnetic coupling physics when the data are loaded into the top and bottom domain wall nanowires with no cost of additional operations, leading to extreme energy efficient logic in-memory design. More importantly, the bitwise XOR computation of the whole data set stored in the bottom racetracks and top racetracks could be implemented simultaneously. The computed XOR outputs are then automatically stored in the intersection MTJs in the array. They could be sensed by the shared sense amplifier like a normal 1-transistor 1-MTJ memory array by enabling the corresponding access transistor as shown in Fig. 3a. Thus, this intrinsic parallel XOR operation can be extremely useful for faster and energy efficient in-memory data encryption engines designs, in which XOR operations are the dominate computation.

Table 1: The XOR logic operation

A	B	$A \oplus B$	M_A	M_B	R_{MTJ}
0	0	0	Down	Down	R_P
0	1	1	Down	Up	R_{AP}
1	0	1	Up	Down	R_{AP}
1	1	0	Up	Up	R_P

Table 2: Device and simulation parameters

Parameter	Value
Domain Wall Pair Dimension	$60 \times 20 \times 4\ nm^3$
Coupling Layer Dimension	$20 \times 20 \times 2\ nm^3$
Tunnel Barrier, t_{MgO}	$1.1\ nm$
Gilbert Damping Factor, α	0.01
Polarization, P	0.6
Exchange stiffness, A_{ex}	$1.3 \times 10^{-11}\ J/m$
Perpendicular Magnetic Anisotropy, K_u	$0.4\ MJ/m^3$
Saturation Magnetization, M_s	$6 \times 10^5\ A/m$
Mesh size, $dx \times dy \times dz$	$2 \times 2 \times 2\ nm^3$
Resistivity of coupling layer, ρ_{CL}	$1 \times 10^5\ \Omega \cdot m$
Resistance-Area product, RA_P/TMR	$5.01\ \Omega \cdot um^2$ / 168.5%

The micromagnetic simulation of our proposed magnetic crossbar design is conducted in Object Oriented MicroMagnetic Framework (OOMMF) [7] with respect to the device and simulation parameters listed in Table. 2. The real-time magnetization can be modeled by Landau-Lifshitz-Gilbert equation with spin transfer torque terms [7]:

$$\frac{d\mathbf{m}}{dt} = -|\gamma|\mathbf{m} \times H_{eff} + \alpha\left(\mathbf{m} \times \frac{d\mathbf{m}}{dt}\right) + |\gamma|\beta(\mathbf{m} \times \mathbf{m}_p \times \mathbf{m}) - |\gamma|\beta\epsilon'(\mathbf{m} \times \mathbf{m}_p) \quad (1)$$

$$\beta = |\frac{\hbar}{2\mu_0 e}|\frac{J_c P}{tM_s} \quad (2)$$

where $\hbar$ is the reduced plank constant, γ is the gyromagnetic ratio, θ_{SH} is the spin Hall angle, J_c is the charge current injected into spin Hall metal substrate, t is the thickness of magnetic nanowire, ϵ' is the second Spin transfer torque coefficient (0.04 in this work), and H_{eff} is the effective magnetic field. The long-range bilinear exchange is included as well to simulate the magnetic coupling between the ferromagnetic layer (surface-1, $20 \times 20 \times 2nm^3$) and the bottom domain wall pair (surface-2, $60 \times 20 \times 4nm^3$). The magnetic coupling energy exchange density between cell i on surface-1 and its match cell j on surface-2 can be mathematically described by [7]:

$$E_{i,j} = \frac{\sigma(1 - \mathbf{m}_i \cdot \mathbf{m}_j) + \sigma'(1 - (\mathbf{m}_i \cdot \mathbf{m}_j))}{\Delta_{i,j}} \quad (3)$$

where σ is bilinear coupling coefficient ($2.5 \times 10^4 J/m^2$ in this work), while the biquadratic exchange coefficient σ' is default as 0. m_i and m_j are the normalized magnetization directions of cell i and j. $\Delta_{i,j}$ is the discretization cell dimension oriented from cell i towards cell j. Moreover, the MTJ Resistance-Area is obtained based on an experimental benchmarked NEGF compact model [9].

2.2 Magnetic Crossbar Sensing Circuit Design

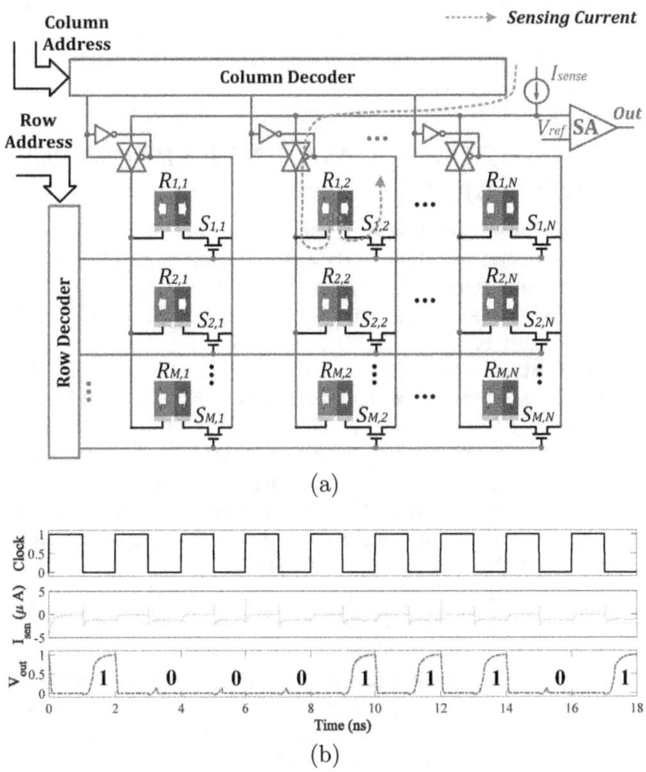

Figure 3: (a) The schematic of sensing circuit for read the parallel XOR computation result. (b) Transient simulation result of sensing circuit.

For a magnetic crossbar in a dimension of $M \times N$, two binary data set are stored in the racetrack memory, where binary data set A is stored in the bottom racetrack memories and binary data set B is stored in the top racetrack memories. Since the XOR computation result is represented by the MTJ resistance within the intersection logic cell that is electrically isolated from the top and bottom racetrack memories through coupling layer, a 1-transistor 1-MTJ array sensing circuit is proposed here to read the computation result as shown in Fig. 3a. In this work, we use 45nm NCSU PDK [1] to evaluate our magnetic crossbar in Spectre circuit simulation environment.The Sense Amplifier (SA) [12] is shared by entire MTJ array, and each MTJ cell is selected by the cascaded transistor with the row and column decoders. Such One Selector-One Resistor (1S1R) sensing scheme is utilized as the the countermeasure of sneak path issue in crossbar memory architecture [14]. Therefore, the result of bit-wise XOR computation result can be express as:

$$Out_{i,j} = A_{i,j} \oplus B_{i,j}; \qquad i \in [1, M], j \in [1, N] \qquad (4)$$

where i and j are row and column address, and $Out_{i,j}$ is the output of sense amplifier. Note that, for sensing each MTJ logic cell, a minimum 2ns clock period is required. Due to the pre-charge sense amplifier circuit structure, the output is reset to low when Clock is high. Conversely, the sense amplifier is in the sense phase while Clock signal is low, which outputs high for R_{AP} and low for R_P. As the transient waveform shown in fig. 3b (a 3×3 magnetic crossbar is used as an example), when the data array A is [1 0 1; 0 0 0; 0 1 1] and B is [0 0 1; 0 1 1; 1 1 0], the parallel bit-wise XOR result is [1 0 0; 0 1 1; 1 0 1] and resistance of corresponding MTJ XOR array R_{xor} is [R_{AP} R_P R_P; R_P R_{AP} R_{AP}; R_{AP} R_P R_{AP}].

3. IN-MEMORY DATA ENCRYPTION ENGINE DESIGN

The proposed magnetic crossbar structure could be easily employed as an in-memory data encryption engine to implement various algorithms where the dominant computations are XOR and shift operations, such as AES, PRESENT, SIMON, and KATAN [5, 21]. We take the Advanced Encryption Standard (AES) algorithm as an example and elucidate the operations of magnetic crossbar design, which reveals its benefits of energy-efficiency and high throughput for in-memory data encryption application. We first evaluate the memory mode performance of proposed magnetic crossbar. To do so, we configure the memory chip organization by dividing it into multiple Banks consisting of multiple Mats. Each Mat includes multiple sub-arrays organized in a H-tree routing manner similar to proposed memory architecture in [21]. We exploit the external sensing scheme using shared Sense Amplifiers (SA) to improve the area efficiency of our design. For the simulation, we employ modified self-consistent NVSim [8] along with an in-house developed C++ code to verify the architecture level performance and to report the accurate power and area. Table. 3 lists our proposed magnetic crossbar working in memory mode validation for a sample 128 KB memory with 512 word-width in 45nm process node.

Table 3: Proposed memory mode evaluation.

Metrics	Write	Read
Dynamic Energy	2.444nJ	1.980nJ
Mat Dynamic Energy	72.437pJ per mat	14.444pJ per mat
Subarray Dynamic Energy	18.005pJ per active subarray	3.507pJ per active subarray
Leakage Power	12.283mW per mat	
Area Overhead	13.189mm x 6.201mm = 81.780mm^2	

AES is an iterative symmetric-key cipher where both sender and receiver units use a single key for encryption and decryption. AES basically works on the standard input length of 16 bytes (128 bits) data organized in a 4×4 matrix (called the state matrix) while using three different key lengths (128, 192, and 256 bits) [20]. For 128-bit key length, AES encrypts the input data after 10 rounds of consecutive transformations. These transformations as depicted in the flow chart in Fig. 4 are enumerated as SubBytes, ShiftRows, MixColumns, and AddRoundKey.

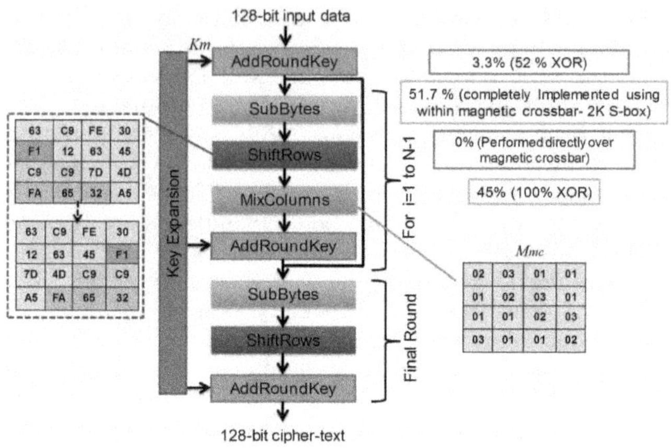

Figure 4: AES block diagram with number of required gates in each modules.

Algorithm 1 Advanced Encryption Standard

Input: $D_{IN} \leftarrow$ 128-bit input data;
Output: $D_{OUT} \leftarrow$ 128-bit cipher-text;
Initialisation :
$S_M \leftarrow$ Organize D_{IN} into 4×4 state matrix with $(S_{i,j})$ as matrix entry (one byte);
AddRoundKey stage(), described in following round loop
for $r \leftarrow 1; r <= N_r; r \leftarrow r + 1$ **do**
    for all $S_{i,j} \in S_M$ **do**
        SubBytes stage(): $S_{i,j} \leftarrow f(S_{i,j})$
    end for
    for all $S_{i,j} \in S_M$ **do**
        ShiftRows stage(): $S'_{i,j} \leftarrow S_{i,(j+i-1)mod4}$
    end for
    $S_M \leftarrow S'_M$: update state matrix
    if $r \neq N_r$ **then**
        for all $S_{i,j} \in S_M$ **do**
            MixColumns stage(): $S_{(:),j} \leftarrow M_{mc} \times S_{(:),j}$
        end for
    end if
    for all $S_{i,j} \in S_M$ and $K_{i,j} \in K_M$ **do**
        AddRoundKey stage(): $S_{ij} \leftarrow S_{i,j} \oplus K_{i,j}$,
    end for
end for
$D_{OUT} \leftarrow S_M$
return D_{OUT}

As shown in Fig. 5a, to facilitate working with input data for boosting the AES performance, we organize our memory sub-array into four 8×4 magnetic crossbars. Each magnetic crossbar exclusively saves one row of the state matrix (S_M).

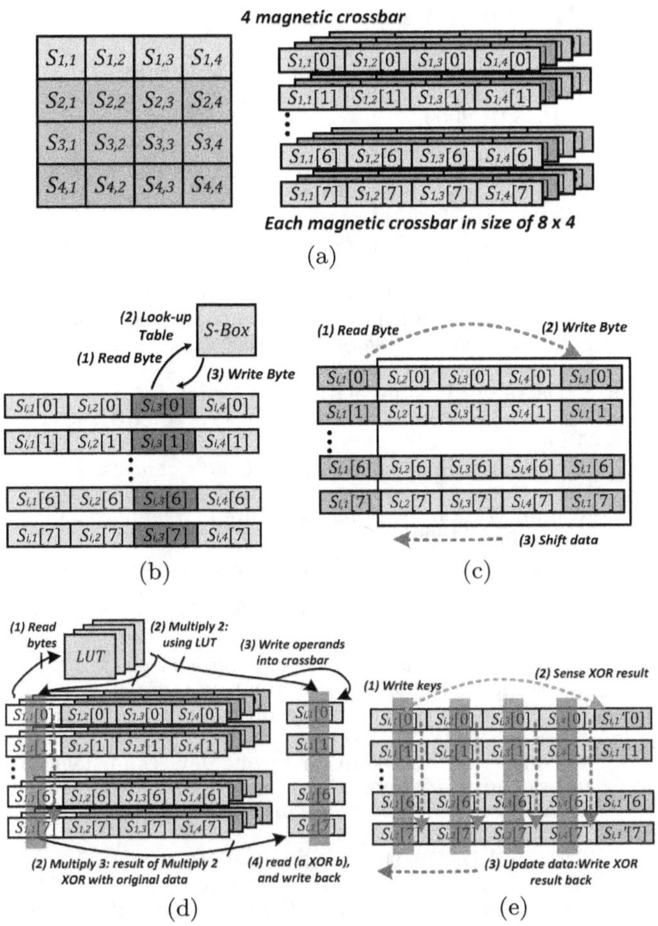

Figure 5: (a) Data mapping from state matrix to four magnetic crossbar in size of 8×4 (b) SubByte (c) ShiftRow (d) MixColumn (e) AddRoundKey

Each byte of S_M is then distributed into 8-bit, where each bit is assigned to longitudinal racetrack memory.

3.1 SubBytes

The main goal of the SubBytes stage is to diminish the correlation between the input data and output data at the byte level. Therefore, each byte of S_M will undergo a Look-up table (LUT) based transformation using S-box and will be independently updated by a nonlinear transformation f as depicted in Algorithm 1. As depicted in Fig. 5b, input of S-Box LUT (16×16 memory array with each cell stored 1 byte) is essentially a Byte which is divided into two 4-bit data patterns. Each pattern yields a row or a column index for the decoders reaching target cell in S-box. Then, the addressed data byte in S-Box is written back to the magnetic crossbar and substitutes the original data. S-box data are conventionally stored using SRAM leading to significant leakage power. However, it can be readily implemented within the proposed magnetic crossbar in the memory mode with no add-on circuits leading to a much more efficient design. In addition, the shared sense amplifiers and decoders can be used, leading to further area and power savings. To maximize the parallelism, eight SAs are required for each magnetic crossbar LUT. The number of cycles (i.e. t_{SB}) used in the SubBytes stage based on our proposed magnetic crossbar can be derived as follows:

$$t_{SB} = (t_{read} + t_{LUT} + t_{write}) \times \frac{16}{n_{LUT}} \tag{5}$$

where the t_{read}, t_{write}, and t_{LUT} are the read, write, and LUT access latency, respectively (in terms of clock cycles). The $n_{LUT} \in \{1, 2, 4, 8\}$ represents the number of LUTs that can be simultaneously accessed where its maximum value is limited to the number of bytes that can be accessed in the S_M.

3.2 ShiftRows

In the ShiftRows stage, state matrix will undergo a cyclically shift operation by a certain offset. As shown in the algorithm, the i-th row of S_M will be cyclically left shifted by i-1 bytes. Accordingly, the first row of state matrix is left unchanged. For the second to fourth rows, each byte is shifted by offsets of one to three, respectively. As discussed earlier, each magnetic racetrack in the proposed magnetic crossbar is fundamentally a shift register by which the data bits (the DW pairs) can be moved along by injecting the required current. Considering the shift, write and read operations of each racetrack are performed concurrently, the number of cycles used in the ShiftRows stage, (i.e. t_{SR}), can be achieved as follow:

$$t_{SR} = t_{read} + t_{write} + max(t_{r1}, t_{r2}, t_{r3}, t_{r4}) \tag{6}$$

Where the t_{r1} to t_{r4} denote the shift latency of first to fourth rows of S_M. To cyclically shift, the data stored in the longitudinal racetrack should be initially read and then written back to the right end of racetrack. Then, shift operation can be effectively performed according to the offset.

3.3 MixColumns

In the MixColumns stage, the state matrix will be multiplied by a preset matrix depicted in Fig. 4. The four bytes of each column of S_M are combined using an invertible linear transformation. The prerequisite operations for this stage are addition, multiplication by two (xtime2), multiplication by three (xtime3). The addition could be implemented by bit-wise XOR; xtime2 can be implemented through intrinsic domain wall shifting followed by a conditional bit-wise XOR with 0x1B; the xtime3 operation is defined as xtime2 result XOR with the original value. As mentioned in section 2, bit-wise XOR and shift operation, as the basic operations of MixColumns stage, can be efficiently executed within our proposed magnetic crossbar. As shown in Fig. 5d, to maximize the efficiency of AES performance, similar to the design in [21], we use a LUT-based transformation followed by XOR operations, where the number of clock cycle used in computation can be written as follow:

$$t_{MC} = (t_{read} + t_{LUT} + 3 \times t_{XOR} + 4 \times t_{write}) \times 4 \tag{7}$$

3.4 AddRoundKey

In the AddRoundKey stage, the subkey is combined with the state matrix. For each round, key expansion unit produces a subkey derived from the main key using Rijndael's key schedule [20]. The 16-byte round keys are organized in a similar 4×4 array (K_M) as the state matrix with $K_{i,j}$ as matrix entry. In this process, each byte of state matrix will be replaced by bit-wise XOR result of $S_{i,j}$ and $K_{i,j}$ (subkey's corresponding bit). This stage can be easily performed using the magnetic crossbar basic operations. The number of cycles consumed in this stage can be calculated as follow:

$$t_{AK} = 4 \times t_{write} + 4 \times t_{XOR} + 4 \times t_{write} \quad (8)$$

As depicted in Fig. 5e, the proposed magnetic crossbar enjoys the benefits of maximum XOR parallelism, so one complete column (32-bit) of S_M can be processed simultaneously.

3.5 AES Performance Evaluation

Table. 4 shows and compares the energy cost and speed of the basic operations performed using the proposed magnetic crossbar herein and the presented domain wall AES (DW-AES) in [21].

Table 4: Energy cost and speed comparison.

	DW-AES [21]		This work	
	Energy(fJ)	Cycles	Energy(fJ)	Cycles
Read	60	1	24	1
Write	100	1	107	1
Shift	30	1	16.3	1
XOR	260	5	24	1
LUT	280	3	244	3

The performance comparison of different AES implementations with the proposed magnetic crossbar AES is shown in Table. 5. For evaluation of AES performance in general purpose processor (GPP), we use the similar method in [21]. AES C code is firstly extracted from [15] and compiled, then cycle-accurate architecture simulator gem5 [4] is employed to take AES binary and accordingly system level processor power evaluating tool McPAT [13] is used to estimate the power dissipation. For evaluation of AES in CMOS ASIC, Synopsys Design Compiler tool is used to run an in-house developed Verilog code. Note that, the same 30MHz clock frequency is used in all the hardware implementations listed in Table. 5, while the AES C code on GPP is at 2GHz. As is clear, the magnetic crossbar significantly improves the data encryption performance by having the least energy consumption and latency in comparison to GPP-, ASIC-, CMOL- and DW-based AES implementations. This significant improvement mainly comes from our proposed massive in-memory parallelism computations.

Table 5: The performance comparison of different implementations for 128-bit AES.

Metrics	GPP [15]	ASIC [16]	CMOL[2]	DW [21]	Our work
Energy (nJ)	460	6.6	10.3	2.4	1.98
Cycles	2309	336	470	1022	718

4. CONCLUSION

In this paper, we propose a novel dual-mode magnetic crossbar design which can operate as conventional racetrack memory and in-memory data encryption engine. Ultra-low energy data encryption is achieved due to intrinsic XOR logic computation can be realized automatically through magnetic coupling physics without additional operations. The device to architecture performance evaluation using AES algorithm shows a 17.5% energy and 29.7% cycles reduction compared with similar DW-AES design. In summary, the proposed magnetic crossbar structure provides a promising approach for future post-CMOS, ultra-low energy and high throughput big data in-memory data encryption application.

5. REFERENCES

[1] Ncsu eda freepdk45, 2011.

[2] Z. Abid et al. Efficient cmol gate designs for cryptography applications. *IEEE Trans. Nanotechnol.*, 8:315–321, 2009.

[3] Y. Bi et al. Leveraging emerging technology for hardware security-case study on silicon nanowire fets and graphene symfets. In *2014 IEEE 23rd ATS*, pages 342–347. IEEE, 2014.

[4] N. Binkert et al. The gem5 simulator. *SIGARCH*, 39:1–7, 2011.

[5] D. Canniere et al. Katan and ktantan - a family of small and efficient hardware-oriented block ciphers. In *International Workshop on CHES*, pages 272–288. Springer, 2009.

[6] S. Datta et al. Non-volatile spin switch for boolean and non-boolean logic. *Appl. Phys. Lett.*, 101:252411, 2012.

[7] M. J. Donahue et al. *OOMMF User's guide.* US Department of Commerce, Technology Administration, National Institute of Standards and Technology, 1999.

[8] X. Dong et al. Nvsim: A circuit-level performance, energy, and area model for emerging non-volatile memory. In *Emerging Memory Technologies.* Springer, 2014.

[9] X. Fong et al. Knack: A hybrid spin-charge mixed-mode simulator for evaluating different genres of spin-transfer torque mram bit-cells. In *SISPAD*, pages 51–54. IEEE, 2011.

[10] X. Fong et al. Spin-transfer torque devices for logic and memory: Prospects and perspectives. *IEEE Trans. Comput.-Aided Design Integr. Circuits Syst.*, 35(1):1–22, 2016.

[11] Z. He and D. Fan. Energy efficient reconfigurable threshold logic circuit with spintronic devices. *IEEE Transactions on Emerging Topics in Computing*, 2016.

[12] Z. He and D. Fan. A low power current-mode flash adc with spin hall effect based multi-threshold comparator. In *ISPLED*, pages 314–319. ACM, 2016.

[13] S. Li et al. Mcpat: an integrated power, area, and timing modeling framework for multicore and manycore architectures. In *MICRO*, pages 469–480. ACM, 2009.

[14] E. Linn et al. Complementary resistive switches for passive nanocrossbar memories. *Nature materials*, 9:403–406, 2010.

[15] K. Malbrain. Byte-oriented-aes: a public domain byte-oriented implementation of aes in c, 2009.

[16] S. Mathew et al. 340 mv–1.1 v, 289 gbps/w, 2090-gate nanoaes hardware accelerator with area-optimized encrypt/decrypt gf (2 4) 2 polynomials in 22 nm tri-gate cmos. *IEEE J. Solid-State Circuits*, 50(4):1048–1058, 2015.

[17] D. Morris et al. mlogic: Ultra-low voltage non-volatile logic circuits using stt-mtj devices. In *Proceedings of the 49th DAC*, pages 486–491. ACM, 2012.

[18] S. S. Parkin et al. Magnetic domain-wall racetrack memory. *Science*, 320:190–194, 2008.

[19] V. Sokalski et al. Naturally oxidized feco as a magnetic coupling layer for electrically isolated read/write paths in mlogic. *IEEE Trans. Magn.*, 49(7):4351–4354, 2013.

[20] N.-F. Standard. Announcing the advanced encryption standard (aes). *FIPSP*, 197, 2001.

[21] Y. Wang et al. Dw-aes: A domain-wall nanowire-based aes for high throughput and energy-efficient data encryption in non-volatile memory. *IEEE Trans. Inf. Forensics Security*, 11, 2016.

[22] Y. Zhang et al. Perpendicular-magnetic-anisotropy cofeb racetrack memory. *J. Appl. Phys.*, 111, 2012.

Evaluating Data Resilience in CNNs from an Approximate Memory Perspective

Yuanchang Chen[1], Yizhe Zhu[4], Fei Qiao[1]*, Jie Han[2], Yuansheng Liu[3] and Huazhong Yang[1]
[1]Dept. of Electronic Engineering, Tsinghua University, China
[2]Dept. of Electrical and Computer Engineering, University of Alberta, Canada
[3]College of Robotics, Beijing Union University, China
[4]Beijing University of Posts and Telecommunications, China
qiaofei@tsinghua.edu.cn

ABSTRACT

Due to the large volumes of data that need to be processed, efficient memory access and data transmission are crucial for high-performance implementations of convolutional neural networks (CNNs). Approximate memory is a promising technique to achieve efficient memory access and data transmission in CNN hardware implementations. To assess the feasibility of applying approximate memory techniques, we propose a framework for the data resilience evaluation (DRE) of CNNs and verify its effectiveness on a suite of prevalent CNNs. Simulation results show that a high degree of data resilience exists in these networks. By scaling the bit-width of the first five dominant data subsets, the data volume can be reduced by 80.38% on average with a 2.69% loss in relative prediction accuracy. For approximate memory with random errors, all the synaptic weights can be stored in the approximate part when the error rate is less than 10^{-4}, while 3 MSBs must be protected if the error rate is fixed at 10^{-3}. These results indicate a great potential for exploiting approximate memory techniques in CNN hardware design.

Keywords

Data Resilience Evaluation; Convolutional Neural Network; Approximate Memory

1. INTRODUCTION

For many machine-learning tasks, a convolutional neural network (CNN) is a state-of-the-art technique with the processing capacity of huge data volumes and high computational demands. A number of designs [1, 2] focus on the computational part of the algorithm and aim to achieve fast efficient networks. However, efficient memory and data access are crucial for high-performance implementations of a CNN. ShiDianNao [3] focuses on minimizing memory transfers to achieve high efficiency, but it is only available for small-scale neural networks rather than large-scale ones. It is imperative to explore data storage and transmission optimization for both small and large neural networks.

Approximate memory is one of the most promising techniques to achieve efficient memory and data access in CNN hardware implementations. The main idea of approximate memory is leveraging the inherent data resilience of applications to trade off output quality for improved performance, such as energy efficiency and processing capacity. Prevalent approximate memory techniques can be divided into four categories: on-chip memory design [4, 5], off-chip memory design [6, 7], approximation in off-chip memory access [8, 9], and approximate storage in emerging devices [10, 11].

In order to apply suitable approximate memory techniques, it is important to understand data resilience in greater detail. It is required to quantitatively evaluate the data resilience of a given CNN, and identify which parts of the data are amenable to be stored in approximate memories. Motivated by the above, we propose a data resilience evaluation (DRE) framework to aid designers in adopting approximate memory techniques in CNN hardware design. The proposed DRE framework differs from previous paradigms [12, 13, 14] in one major point. All the above frameworks are established from the perspective of computation, mainly focused on the approximation in arithmetic units. Due to the fact that approximations in memory access and data transmission are distinct from that in arithmetic units, these paradigms are not applicable in approximate memory architecture design. This is the main reason for proposing the DRE framework.

The key contributions of this paper are summarized as:

- The DRE framework: Our primary contribution is a systematic framework (i.e., the DRE framework) established from the perspective of data storage in memory. It is used to quantitatively evaluate the data resilience of a given CNN and help designers to quickly estimate the potential of applying specific approximate memory techniques.
- A benchmark analysis: To verify the effectiveness of the proposed DRE framework, we characterize and analyze the inherent data resilience of several prevalent CNNs. We demonstrate the high degree of data resilience in these neural networks and emphasize the potential of approximate memory techniques.
- A design guide: Based on the analysis, we present several strategies for designers in the adoption of various

Permission to make digital or hard copies of all or part of this work for personal or classroom use is granted without fee provided that copies are not made or distributed for profit or commercial advantage and that copies bear this notice and the full citation on the first page. Copyrights for components of this work owned by others than ACM must be honored. Abstracting with credit is permitted. To copy otherwise, or republish, to post on servers or to redistribute to lists, requires prior specific permission and/or a fee. Request permissions from permissions@acm.org.

GLSVLSI'2017, May 10-12, 2017, Banff, AB, Canada.
© 2017 ACM. ISBN 978-1-4503-4972-7/17/05...$15.00
DOI: http://dx.doi.org/10.1145/3060403.3060435

approximate memory techniques in CNN hardware implementations.

The rest of the paper is organized as follows. Section 2 introduces the approximation models for prevalent approximate memory techniques and analyze the data resilience of CNN algorithms. The proposed DRE framework is presented in Section 3. Simulation results are provided in Section 4. Finally, Section 5 concludes the paper.

2. CNN DATA RESILIENCE ANALYSIS

2.1 Modeling Approximate Memory

Inherent data resilience is defined as the property of an application to produce acceptable outputs despite some of its (input and intermediate) data being approximate. Approximate memory techniques exploit the inherent data resilience of applications to trade off output quality for improved performance.

The data of a given algorithm can be partitioned into two parts: the resilient part and the sensitive part. Approximate memory techniques should be targeted towards resilient data while avoiding the sensitive ones. For the resilient part of data, it is imperative to evaluate the applicability of various approximate memory techniques. Generally, we use approximation models to abstract a wide range of approximate memory techniques so that we can make quick evaluations. The approximation models of different approximate memories greatly depend on how the techniques are utilized. Most approximate memory techniques can be modeled as random errors that are uniformly injected into resilient bits [4, 5, 6, 7, 10, 11]. For off-chip memory reduction, major approximate techniques focus on data bit-width scaling [9]. The other approximate memory techniques are usually related to the characteristics of applications [8]. Table 1 summarizes the prevalent approximation techniques and their models. By using these approximation models for resilient data subsets, we can quickly evaluate the applicability of various approximate memory techniques.

Table 1: Approximate Memory Model

Approximate Memory Technique	Approximation Model
On-chip Memory [4, 5]	Uniformly Injected Random Errors
Off-chip Memory [6, 7]	
Emerging Device [10, 11]	
Off-chip Memory Access [9]	Bit-Truncation

2.2 CNN Data Resilience

CNNs play important roles in the machine-learning domain. Many CNN hardware designs focus on fast and efficient implementations of feed-forward networks because off-line learning is sufficient for many applications. It consists of a number of layers, including convolutional layers, pooling (sub-sampling) layers and a multi-layer perceptron (MLP) which consists of several full connection layers at the top of the network. These layers are executed in sequence so that they can be considered independently. The operands of each layer includes a number of neurons (output of the previous layer) and synaptic weights obtained from early off-line training. Figure 1 shows the major data flow of a typical CNN feed-forward network example. The inherent data resilience of a CNN can be reflected in the following two aspects.

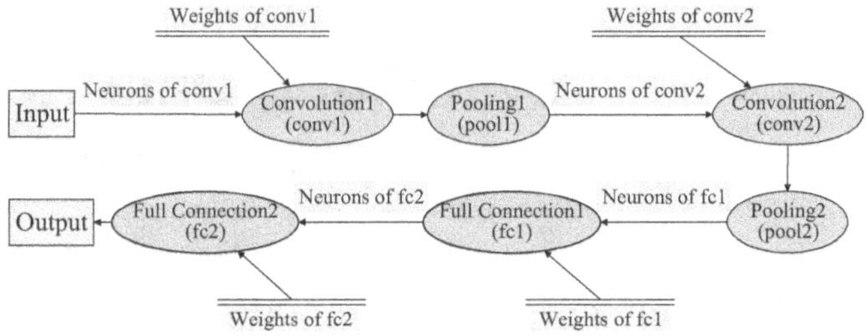

Figure 1: Data Flow of a CNN Example.

2.2.1 *Numerical Representation Requirement*

Firstly, the data resilience of CNNs is reflected in their numerical representation requirements. Many implementations use the worst-case numerical precision for all values. Most software implementations use 32-bit floating-point numbers, while hardware implementations use 16-bit/8-bit fixed-point numbers. However, the numerical representation requirement of each layer is different. The numerical representation requirement of CNNs significantly varies not only across networks but also across the layers of the same network [15]. Their operand bit-width can be decreased according to their minimum numerical requirements so that memory access and data transmission can be significantly reduced. Therefore, we use numerical representation requirement to characterize the resilience of CNN data, including neurons and weights of each layer.

2.2.2 *Random Error Tolerance*

Secondly, the data resilience of CNNs is reflected in the random error tolerance. It is described as an maximum tolerable random error rate (MTRER) injected into the resilient bits with a negligible decrease in the prediction accuracy. For most approximate memories with random errors, the difference between different accuracy levels is beyond orders of magnitude [4, 5, 6, 7, 10, 11]. Therefore, the order of magnitude of MTRER is sufficient to characterize the tolerance of random errors. From a different perspective, the random error tolerance can also be described as the number of MSBs (Most Significant Bits) that must be stored in the precise part. Given approximate cells with a specific error rate, many LSBs (Less Significant Bits) can be stored in these cells, while some MSBs must be precise (protected). The number of protected MSBs can be used to characterize the random error tolerance of a given CNN.

3. PROPOSED DRE FRAMEWORK

The proposed data resilience evaluation (DRE) framework is shown in Figure 2. It consists of three analysis modules and a characterization module. The three analysis modules are for: (1) single layer analysis; (2) comprehensive multi-layer analysis; and (3) random error tolerance evaluation. Module 1 and Module 2 implement the two steps for numerical representation requirement analysis, while Module 3 evaluates the tolerance of random errors. The whole DRE framework is realized on the Caffe [16] platform. The inputs are the network description (.prototxt), synaptic weights (.caffemodel), a representative validation data set and the

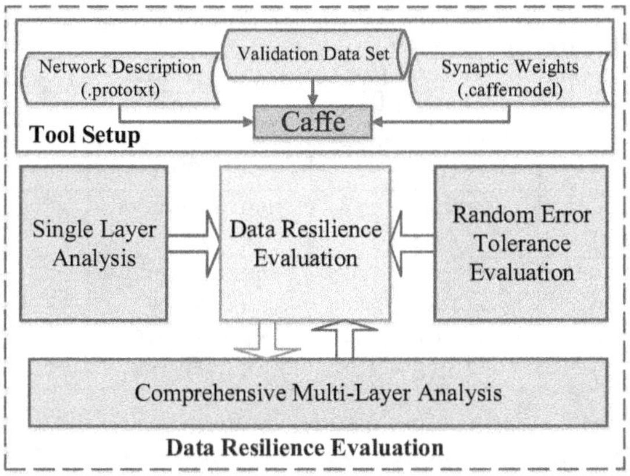

Figure 2: Overview of the DRE framework.

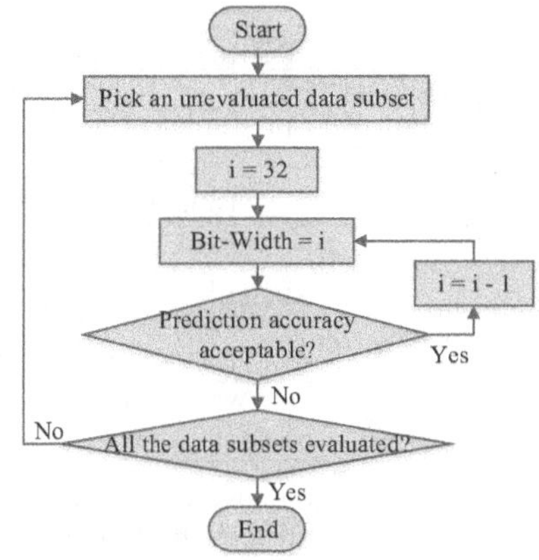

Figure 3: The Flow of Single Layer Analysis.

user-defined classification accuracy requirement. The outputs include a list of resilient data subsets, the results of evaluating the two approximation models mentioned in Section 3.2 on the resilient data subsets and their impacts on the prediction accuracy. In the sequel, we will describe the three analysis modules and the characterization module of the DRE framework in detail.

3.1 Single Layer Analysis

The first procedure of the framework is the single layer analysis. For a CNN algorithm, the control logic is highly sensitive so that it must avoid approximation. Neurons and weights of each layer are potentially resilient data subsets. The objective of the single layer analysis is to analyze and evaluate the numerical representation requirement of neurons and weights of each layer.

To explore the numerical representation requirement of a single layer, bit truncation is a commonly used technique, where approximations are introduced by reducing the data bit-width. Considering that Caffe is a 32-bit floating-point computing platform, we use 32-bit floating-point number as a baseline and the initial numerical representation in this module. The flow of this module is shown in Figure 3. We first pick a resilient data subset and transform it into the chosen numerical representation to observe the impact on the prediction accuracy of the network. If the drop in prediction accuracy is acceptable, reduce the bit-width of the chosen numerical representation by bit truncation and repeat the last step. Otherwise, the numerical representation requirement of this data subset is the chosen bit-width. Through these steps, we can derive the numerical representation requirement of the neurons and weights at each layer of CNNs. By truncating a resilient data subset into its minimum bit-width requirement, we can achieve some performance improvements in spite of a slight decrease in prediction accuracy.

3.2 Comprehensive Multi-Layer Analysis

The second procedure of the framework is a comprehensive analysis of multi-layers, which aims to derive a complete numerical representation scheme for all data subsets. This is an optimization problem with a search space of exponential scale. However, the number of neurons and synapses of each layer varies significantly. Usually, there are several dominant data subsets contributing to the total data volume. Approximate memory techniques should be targeted towards these data subsets rather than all the data in the algorithm. Therefore, the intent of this procedure is to explore a numerical representation scheme for several dominant data subsets that mainly contribute to the total data volume. Other data subsets remain using their numerical representation in 32-bit floating-point numbers.

The comprehensive analysis of multi-layers uses the same strategy as the single layer analysis. However, there are two differences. First, the judging conditions of this procedure are different from that of the single layer analysis. Not only the prediction accuracy but also the ratio of gain and loss should be considered in this procedure, while the single layer analysis only considers the former. Second, the working way of truncated operations are different from that in the single layer analysis. Truncations of different data subsets work together to influence the prediction accuracy of CNNs, while they are in isolation in the single layer analysis. The desired numerical representation scheme of a given CNN can be obtained through the procedure of Module 1 and 2.

3.3 Random Error Tolerance Evaluation

The last analysis module of the framework is for random error tolerance evaluation. Considering the fact that the approximation of many approximate memory techniques is modeled as random errors, we need to explore the random error tolerance of the neurons and weights of a given CNN. In this module, we also use the same strategy as in the single layer analysis, while the operations are random error injections other than bit truncations. Random errors with a given probability are introduced into specific resilient data subsets.

There are two parameters to evaluate the random error tolerance of the data in a CNN. The first one is the MTRER. Given a resilient data subset, the output quality is acceptable when the probability of random error is within a certain range while it is unacceptable when the probability is out of the range. The maximum probability within this range is the MTRER, which can be used to characterize the random error tolerance of this resilient data subset. On the other hand, when the probability of the random error is given, we need to determine which parts of data can be stored in such approximate cells while others must be precise. In most cases, LSBs can be stored in approximate cells while MSBs must be protected. Therefore, the amount of protect-

Table 2: Data Volume Statistics of Dominant Data Subsets

Network	Validation Data Set	Dominant Data Subsets (Major contribution to the total data volume)					
		subset1	subset2	subset3	subset4	subset5	sum
LeNet-5	MNIST	weight_fc1 (65.59%)	weight_fc2 (21.52%)	weight_conv2 (5.12%)	neuron_conv2 (1.84%)	weight_fc3 (1.79%)	95.86%
Cifar10-full	CIFAR-10	weight_conv3 (49.27%)	weight_conv2 (24.64%)	weight_fc1 (9.85%)	neuron_conv2 (7.88%)	neuron_conv1 (2.96%)	94.60%
AlexNet	ImageNet	weight_fc1 (61.50%)	weight_fc2 (27.33%)	weight_fc3 (6.67%)	weight_conv3 (1.44%)	weight_conv4 (1.08%)	98.02%
VGG-16	ImageNet	weight_fc1 (69.68%)	weight_fc2 (11.38%)	weight_fc3 (2.78%)	neuron_conv1-2 (2.18%)	weight_conv5-3 (1.60%)	87.62%

Notes: Subset weight_layer means the weights of this layer, while subset neuron_layer means the neurons of this layer. For example, weight_fc1 means the weights of layer fc1 (the first full-connection layer), while neuron_conv1 means the neurons of layer conv1 (the first convolution layer). The percentages are their contributions to total data volume.

ed MSBs can be used as a metric to evaluate the random error tolerance of these resilient bits.

3.4 Data Resilience Characterization

Data resilience evaluation goes through the whole process of the proposed DRE framework. It gives periodical evaluations as indicated in the three analysis modules and draws a concluding evaluation of data resilience for a given CNN. A periodical evaluation for single layer analysis mainly contains the bit-width requirement of each single layer and the benefits of corresponding bit-truncated operations. In a comprehensive analysis of multi-layers, we derive a complete numerical representation scheme based on the periodical evaluation in the single layer analysis. An MTRER and the amount of protected MSBs with a specific error probability are given in the random error tolerance evaluation. Additionally, the impact on prediction accuracy is also estimated during every evaluation in the above three modules.

4. SIMULATION RESULTS

The DRE framework is applied on a benchmark suite including CNNs with different scales and validation data sets with different kinds of features. The benchmark suite is shown in Table 2. We characterize the data resilience using the DRE framework and present the results in this section. Simulations are implemented on the Caffe platform [16]. The inputs of the framework include a network description (.prototxt), synaptic weights (.caffemodel), a representative validation data set and a user-defined prediction accuracy requirement. The network definitions (.prototxt) and pre-trained synaptic weights (.caffemodel) are taken from BVLC Caffe GitHub [17]. We assume that the acceptable relative reduction of prediction accuracy is 3% and use it as an example to conduct the following simulations.

4.1 Single Layer Evaluation

The intent of the proposed DRE framework is to evaluate the data resilience of dominant resilient subsets rather than all the data in the algorithm. Dominant subsets in our framework are defined as those mainly contributing to the total data volume. The dominant subsets of the benchmark suite and their contributions are shown in Table 2. It can be seen that top-5 subsets occupy a major contribution to the total data volume. The sum of the contribution of these subsets ranges from 87.62% to 98.02%. Therefore, it is

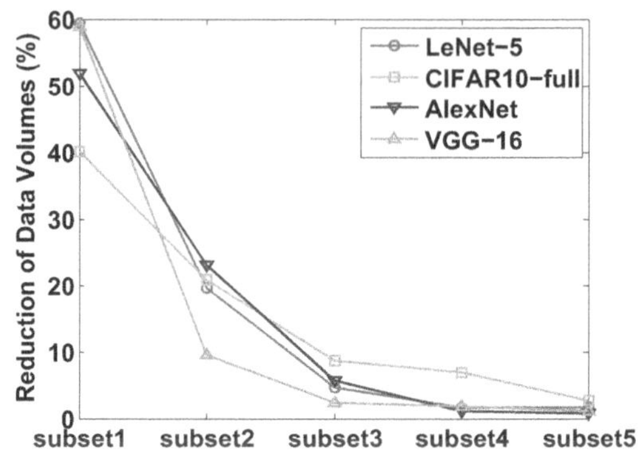

Figure 4: Benefits of single subset optimizations.

Table 3: Single Layer Bit-Width Requirements

Network	Bit-Width Requirement				
	subset1	subset2	subset3	subset4	subset5
LeNet-5	3	3	3	3	3
Cifar10-full	6	5	4	4	3
AlexNet	5	5	5	7	7
VGG-16	5	5	4	5	8

sufficient to focus approximate memory techniques on these subsets.

In this section, a bit-truncated operation is conducted on a single data subset to explore its numerical representation requirement, while other subsets remain as 32-bit floating-point numbers. The format of the target subset is first transformed from 32-bit floating-point to 32-bit fixed-point numbers. The 32-bit fixed-point numbers are then truncated into fewer bits. Table 3 shows the numerical representation requirement of the dominant data subsets in the single layer analysis. The bit-width requirements of these subsets range from 3 to 8 bits, which are far less than the original numerical representation (32-bit floating-point number) of the Caffe platform. This demonstrates a high degree of inherent resilience in these subsets. Benefits of those truncated operations (by single subset optimization) are presented in Figure 4. It can be seen that a larger reduction of data volume is obtained by the optimization of a more dominant subset. According to this observation, certain subsets can be targeted and processed (bit-truncated) with priority in the comprehensive multi-layer analysis, thereby reducing the search

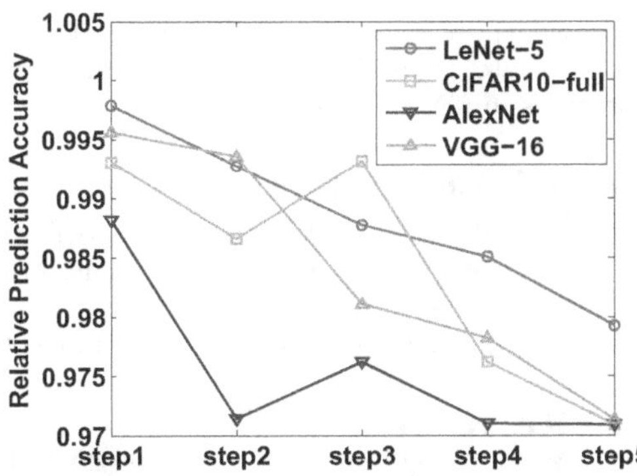

Figure 5: Trend of Prediction Accuracy.

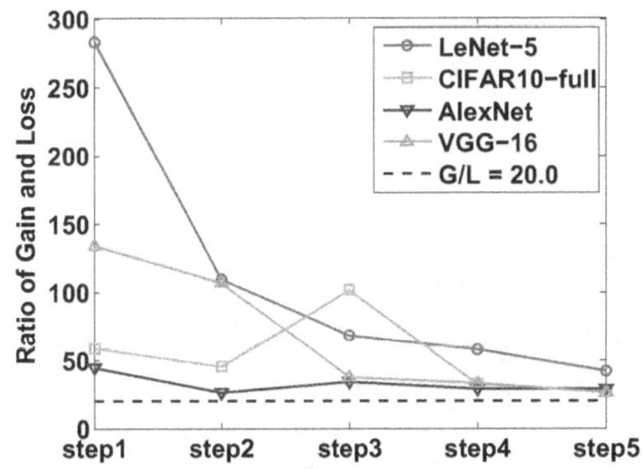

Figure 6: Ratio of Gain and Loss.

space of the optimization problem. The processing priority is determined by the size of each data subset.

4.2 Numerical Representation Scheme

The objective of the comprehensive multi-layer analysis is to derive a numerical representation scheme for dominant resilient data subsets. Truncations of each subset are conducted step by step to explore the connected bit-width requirements of these subsets. The first step in this section is to set the first dominant subset (subset1) as its bit-width requirement in a single layer evaluation. In Step i (i ranges from 2 to 5), the bit-width of subset i is scaled to reach its bit-width requirement based on the previous truncated operations. Bit-truncated operations work together to affect the output quality of a given CNN in this process. The complete numerical representation scheme is obtained through the above 5 steps, as presented in Table 4. Compared with their single layer bit-width requirements in Table 3, the combined bit-width requirements of some subsets are the same as those in the single layer analysis, while others are several (from 1 to 3) bits more. This implies that a combined operation can make a better use of the inherent data resilience. With this numerical representation scheme, the total data volume decreases on average by 80.38% with 2.69% decrease in relative prediction accuracy.

Table 4: Numerical Representation Scheme

Network	Complete Scheme					DVR[1]	RPA[2]
	S1	S2	S3	S4	S5		
LeNet-5	3	3	4	4	4	86.60%	97.93%
Cifar10-full	6	5	5	4	3	78.71%	97.09%
AlexNet	5	5	5	8	10	82.40%	97.09%
VGG-16	5	5	4	6	8	73.80%	97.13%

4.2.1 *Impact on Prediction Accuracy*

Prediction accuracy is the most important metric to measure a CNN's performance. The impact on prediction accuracy of the above steps is explored in this section, as shown in Figure 5. Basically, the prediction accuracy decreases step by step. Occasionally, it increases in a specific step, which implies that the bit-width requirement of different data subsets are interconnected with each other. Sometimes combined operations of serval subsets can achieve a better effect than single subset optimization.

[1]DVR: Data Volume Reduction.
[2]RPA: Relative Prediction Accuracy.

4.2.2 *Gain and Loss*

Gain and loss must be considered in the tradeoff of data volume reduction (DVR) benefits and accuracy loss. The gain in this section is defined as the reduction of data volume, while the loss is defined as the decline in relative prediction accuracy. The data volume reduction after step n can be calculated by (1). In (1), DVR_n represents the percentage of data volume reduction after step n, while DVC_i and BW_i represent the contribution (as shown in Table 2) and the bit-width of subset i. Figure 6 shows the trend of the ratio of gain and loss (G/L). For all the CNNs in the benchmark suite, this ratio follows a decreasing trend. However, the ratios are all larger than 20.0 after the above 5 steps. That means a small loss in relative prediction accuracy can be used to trade for larger benefits (DVR) that is over 20 times more than the loss in such context. Such tradeoff between data volume reduction and relative prediction accuracy is cost effective.

$$DVR_n = \sum_{i=1}^{n} DVC_i \times \frac{32 - BW_i}{32} \quad (1)$$

4.3 Random Error Tolerance

For most approximate memories, bit flipping is considered as the error model and the error rate varis from 10^{-8} to 10^{-1} [4, 5, 11]. The difference between different accuracy levels is in several orders of magnitude. Therefore, using the order of magnitude of MTRER is sufficient to characterize the tolerance of random errors. In the first part of this section, we assume that random errors with certain probability (from 10^{-8} to 10^{-1}) are uniformly introduced into approximate memory bit cells and all the synaptic weights of CNNs in the benchmark suite are stored in the approximate memory. Their impacts on prediction accuracy are shown in Figure 7. The relative accuracy is acceptable (i.e., greater than 97%) when the probability of random error is less than 10^{-4}. It indicates that it is feasible to use approximate memories with error rates less than 10^{-4} for the storage of synaptic weights in these CNNs. It is realizable for many approximate memory techniques to attain an error rate of bit cells below 10^{-4} [4, 5, 11].

When the injected error probability is larger than MTRER (10^{-4}), several MSBs must be protected to restrict the

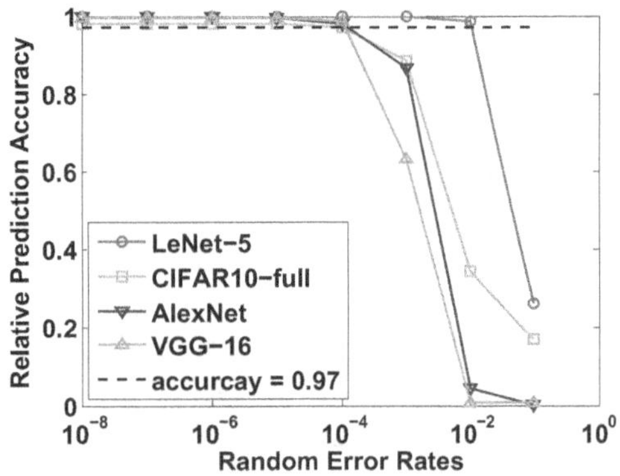

Figure 7: Accuracy with Injected Errors.

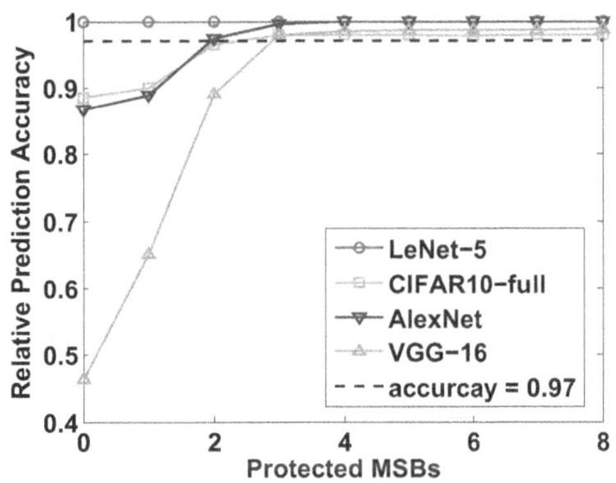

Figure 8: Accuracy with Protected MSBs [3].

magnitude of errors and to alleviate their impacts on prediction accuracy. In the second part of this section, we use fixed error probability (i.e., 10^{-3}) to explore how many MSBs should be protected while others can be stored in approximate bit cells for this error probability. Figure 8 shows the trend of prediction accuracy with various numbers of protected MSBs. It can be seen that the prediction accuracy is acceptable (i.e., greater than 97%) when the protected MSBs are more than 3 bits. Designers need to take measures to protect at least 3 MSBs to produce an acceptable output quality when using an approximate memory with a fixed error rate as 10^{-3}.

5. CONCLUSIONS

In this paper, an analytical framework is proposed for the data resilience evaluation (DRE) of CNNs. We apply the proposed DRE framework to four prevalent CNNs and demonstrate that a high degree of data resilience exists in these networks. For off-chip memory access, bit-width scaling can be used to reduce the amount of data from off-chip memory to on-chip memory. On average, the data volume can be reduced by 80.38% with a 2.69% loss in relative prediction accuracy. For approximate memory with random errors, all the synaptic weights can be stored in approximate part when the error rate is less than 10^{-4}, which is attainable in many approximate memories. When the error rate is fixed at 10^{-3}, 3 MSBs must be protected while other LSBs can be stored in the approximate part. Extensive simulations will be conducted in our subsequent work to explore appropriate approximate memory architectures for implementations in CNN hardware.

[3]The injected random error rate is 10^{-3} in this simulation.

6. ACKNOWLEDGMENTS

The authors would like to acknowledge support from National Natural Science Foundation of China under grant No. 91648116, and the Research Fund from Beijing Innovation Center for Future Chip under grant No. KYJJ2016009.

7. REFERENCES

[1] Srimat Chakradhar, Murugan Sankaradas, Venkata Jakkula, and Srihari Cadambi. A dynamically configurable coprocessor for convolutional neural networks. In *International Symposium on Computer Architecture (ISCA)*. ACM, 2010.

[2] Clément Farabet, Berin Martini, Benoit Corda, Polina Akselrod, Eugenio Culurciello, and Yann LeCun. Neuflow: A runtime reconfigurable dataflow processor for vision. In *CVPR 2011 Workshops*. IEEE, 2011.

[3] Zidong Du, Robert Fasthuber, Tianshi Chen, Paolo Ienne, Ling Li, Tao Luo, Xiaobing Feng, Yunji Chen, and Olivier Temam. Shidiannao: shifting vision processing closer to the sensor. In *International Symposium on Computer Architecture (ISCA)*. ACM, 2015.

[4] Ik Joon Chang, Debabrata Mohapatra, and Kaushik Roy. A voltage-scalable & process variation resilient hybrid sram architecture for mpeg-4 video processors. In *Design Automation Conference (DAC)*. ACM, 2009.

[5] Yuanchang Chen, Xinghua Yang, Fei Qiao, Jie Han, Qi Wei, and Huazhong Yang. A multi-accuracy-level approximate memory architecture based on data significance analysis. In *IEEE Computer Society Annual Symposium on VLSI (ISVLSI)*. IEEE, 2016.

[6] Song Liu, Karthik Pattabiraman, Thomas Moscibroda, and Benjamin G Zorn. Flikker: saving dram refresh-power through critical data partitioning. *ACM SIGPLAN Notices*, 2012.

[7] Jan Lucas, Mauricio Alvarez-Mesa, Michael Andersch, and Ben Juurlink. Sparkk: Quality-scalable approximate storage in dram. In *The Memory Forum*, 2014.

[8] Fei Qiao, Ni Zhou, Yuanchang Chen, and Huazhong Yang. Approximate computing in chrominance cache for image/video processing. In *International Conference on Multimedia Big Data (BigMM)*. IEEE, 2015.

[9] Ye Tian, Qian Zhang, Ting Wang, Feng Yuan, and Qiang Xu. Approxma: Approximate memory access for dynamic precision scaling. In *Great Lakes Symposium on VLSI (GLSVLSI)*. ACM, 2015.

[10] Jacob Nelson, Adrian Sampson, and Luis Ceze. Dense approximate storage in phase-change memory. ACM, 2011.

[11] Ashish Ranjan, Swagath Venkataramani, Xuanyao Fong, Kaushik Roy, and Anand Raghunathan. Approximate storage for energy efficient spintronic memories. In *Design Automation Conference (DAC)*. IEEE, 2015.

[12] Vinay Chippa, Anand Raghunathan, Kaushik Roy, and Srimat Chakradhar. Dynamic effort scaling: Managing the quality-efficiency tradeoff. In *Design Automation Conference (DAC)*. ACM, 2011.

[13] Woongki Baek and Trishul M Chilimbi. Green: a framework for supporting energy-conscious programming using controlled approximation. In *ACM Sigplan Notices*, volume 45, pages 198–209. ACM, 2010.

[14] Vinay K Chippa, Srimat T Chakradhar, Kaushik Roy, and Anand Raghunathan. Analysis and characterization of inherent application resilience for approximate computing. In *Design Automation Conference (DAC)*. ACM, 2013.

[15] Sajid Anwar, Kyuyeon Hwang, and Wonyong Sung. Fixed point optimization of deep convolutional neural networks for object recognition. In *International Conference on Acoustics, Speech and Signal Processing (ICASSP)*. IEEE, 2015.

[16] Yangqing Jia, Evan Shelhamer, Jeff Donahue, Sergey Karayev, Jonathan Long, Ross Girshick, Sergio Guadarrama, and Trevor Darrell. Caffe: Convolutional architecture for fast feature embedding. In *Proceedings of ACM international conference on Multimedia*. ACM, 2014.

[17] https://github.com/BVLC/caffe.

A Robust C-element Design with Enhanced Metastability Performance

Kinshuk Sharma
Texas A&M University
College Station, Texas, USA
kinshuk021@gmail.com

Sunil Khatri
Texas A&M University
College Station, Texas, USA
sunilkhatri@tamu.edu

ABSTRACT

Metastability causes unpredictable behavior in circuits which can sometimes cause circuit failure. Although much work has been done to reduce the possibility of metastability in synchronous designs, metastability in asynchronous designs has not been given significant attention to date. For asynchronous designs, metastability resolution is assumed to be handled by the handshaking protocol. However, metastability might manifest (at the electrical level) in various asynchronous circuit elements for special timing cases. One such circuit element is the C-element, which is heavily used in asynchronous circuit design. The C-element is vulnerable to metastability conditions at its output, when there is a short overlap in the input values. In this paper, a robust design of a C-element is proposed, which aims at reducing the possibility of metastability at the output by using independent paths for the pull-up and pull-down transitions. Three different popular circuit topologies for a C-element have been studied and modified with the proposed approach. Experimental results show significant improvements in signal integrity at the output of the C-element, with up to 9× improvement in the metastability window.

Keywords

asynchronous design; metastability; c-element

1. INTRODUCTION

Any binary valued circuit element that holds state (logic 0 or logic 1) is vulnerable to metastability while transitioning from one state to the other. Synchronous circuits use flip-flops or latches to hold state, and are clocked to implement control. In synchronous designs, timing violations (primarily setup and hold time violations) that can cause metastability can be avoided by design. However, at clock domain boundaries, the threat of metastability exists. *Synchronizers* are used to synchronize data from one clock domain to the other and minimize the likelihood of metastability. A significant amount of research effort has gone into avoiding metastability in synchronous circuits. Asynchronous circuits use state holding elements that operate on events and transitions instead of clocks. For asynchronous circuits it is assumed that metastability can be avoided at the protocol level, by using handshake mechanism between different events. As a result metastability has not been heavily addressed at the electrical level in asynchronous designs. This is the focus of this paper.

One such state holding element which is heavily used in asynchronous circuits is the C-element. The C-element is a logic element that computes the AND function on the events at its inputs. Here, an event is classified as a logic 0-1 or a logic 1-0 transition. The behavior of a C-element is such that the output matches the inputs if all the inputs are in the same logic state. If the states of the inputs are different the output holds its previous state. The behavior of a 2-input C-element is represented in Table 1.

Input a	Input b	Output c_{n+1}
0	0	0
0	1	c_n
1	0	c_n
1	1	1

Table 1: C-element Truth Table

As discussed earlier, any state holding element is vulnerable to metastability while transitioning from one state to another. Hence, the output of C-element is also subject to a metastable condition. In the case of a very small overlap in the input values, the output of the C-element can begin to flip its state, but may not complete the transition to the new state. This is the primary electrical cause of metastability in the C-element. One set of input transitions that could result in metastability in a C-element is shown in Figure 1, as described in [9]. These input transitions also occur in designs with dynamic logic based asynchronous micropipelines [5].

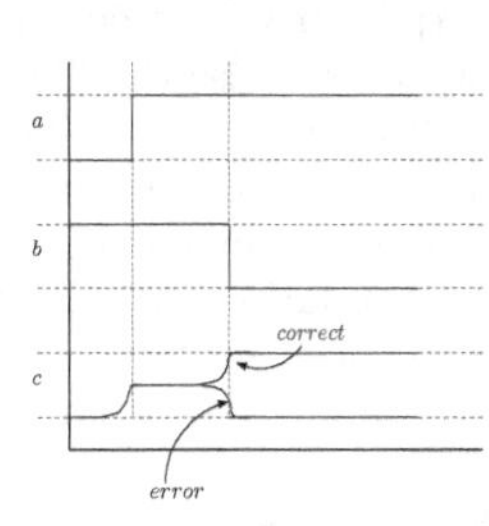

Figure 1: Input Transitions and Metastability in a C-element

In the figure, initially the input a was a stable logic 0 and the input b was a stable logic 1. The output c was holding its

Permission to make digital or hard copies of all or part of this work for personal or classroom use is granted without fee provided that copies are not made or distributed for profit or commercial advantage and that copies bear this notice and the full citation on the first page. Copyrights for components of this work owned by others than ACM must be honored. Abstracting with credit is permitted. To copy otherwise, or republish, to post on servers or to redistribute to lists, requires prior specific permission and/or a fee. Request permissions from permissions@acm.org.

GLSVLSI '17, May 10-12, 2017, Banff, AB, Canada

© 2017 ACM. ISBN 978-1-4503-4972-7/17/05...$15.00

DOI: http://dx.doi.org/10.1145/3060403.3060425

last state which happened to be a logic 0. Now, a transitions to a logic 1 and the output c starts to rise (because both the inputs are logic 1). However, after a short period, and before the output completely transitions to a stable high value, the input b falls. The output c can now get stuck in a metastable state. Several other combinations of initial output state and input transitions can cause metastability in the C-element. As a result, there is a need for a technique that avoids metastability in the C-element.

Over the years, various circuit-level implementations have been proposed to realize the functionality of the C-element. Three most popular implementations are the Martin C-element (Figure 2 (a)), the Sutherland C-element (Figure 2 (b)) and the Van Berkel C-element (Figure 2 (c)). There are other gate-level implementations of the C-element that use standard cell based design to implement a C-element as well. In our work, we will focus on the circuit-level implementations of the Martin, Sutherland and Van Berkel C-elements.

In asynchronous designs, it is hard in general to coordinate events in such a way that they do not overlap briefly. The key thing to note here is that none of the C-element implementations mentioned above address the issue of metastability electrically.

Accordingly, the goals of our work are as follows:

- To compare the metastability performance of three popular circuits to realize C-elements, namely the Martin, Sutherland and Van Berkel C-elements.
- Propose a circuit-level approach which can be adopted for all the C-elements mentioned above, to reduce the possibility of metastability at the output of the C-element.
- Qualitatively as well as quantitatively analyze the metastability behavior of the proposed solutions, and compare it with the traditional designs.
- It is important to note that our design does not guarantee the absence of metastability (no other design guarantees this either). The goal is to minimize the likelihood of metastability as far as possible.

In this paper we propose a novel circuit-level approach that minimizes the metastability conditions in a C-element. Our approach uses two independent paths for falling and rising transitions on the output of a C-element. One of these paths includes a low switchpoint (LSP) inverter while the other path includes high switchpoint (HSP) inverter. The LSP (HSP) drives a PMOS (NMOS) at its output which forms the output driver of the C-element. In this way, the likelihood of both output driver devices being ON simultaneously is reduced, which reduces the likelihood of metastability at the output. Based on our simulations, the proposed approach achieves up to 9× improvement in the *metastability window*, and up to 6× improvement in the simulated delay of a C-element. Our simulations are done at an extremely fine resolution, and have been verified to be repeatable under small variations of the timing resolution.

2. PREVIOUS WORK

Metastability conditions in synchronous circuits have been extensively addressed. However, metastability has not received similar attention in asynchronous circuits. Asynchronous circuits, with their handshake based control flow, are assumed to not suffer from metastable conditions. However, this is only true at the protocol level. In this work, we address the metastability issues in Muller C-element, which is a fundamental building block in asynchronous circuit design. The authors of [9], elaborate eight possible combinations of transitions on the inputs of a two input C-element that could cause metastability. The effort in their work is to characterize metastability in a C-element using a late transition detection scheme. The authors of [3] show, with an example of a fault-tolerant clock generation scheme, that metastability can exist in asynchronous systems in the presence of a few fault effects.

Different circuit-level implementations have been proposed to realize the functionality of the C-element. A comparison of three most popular implementations has been presented in [12]. The authors compare the performance of Martin, Sutherland and Van Berkel C-elements in terms of their propagation delay, energy consumption and area utilization. In our work, we also choose these three implementations to analyze and compare the metastability performance of different C-elements. However, our analysis is focused on the metastability behavior of different C-element implementations. The design of a latch based speed independent C-element is proposed in [8]. Different circuit implementations of C-elements are compared in [1] on the basis of their robustness to the effects of Single Event Upsets (SEUs). A comparison is made between C-elements implemented in Bulk CMOS technology and SOI technology. The key parameters compared are the delay, and the static and dynamic power of the different C-elements. However, the work in [8, 1] does not address metastability issues in C-elements. We compare the robustness of different C-elements under metastability-prone conditions at the electrical/timing level and then propose a circuit-level approach to design a more robust version of these C-elements. The authors of [14] propose a design for a multi-input C-element which has fewer restrictions on the number of inputs as compared to the traditional implementations. The work in [6] is focused on further improving the design presented in [14]. The authors of [6] discuss the possible race conditions at the output of the C-element when the inputs to the C-element arrive close to one another. In our work, we show how such situations can result in metastability at the output. The authors in [2] provide a quantitative estimate of the probability of error at the output of C-element depending on the error probabilities at the inputs.

A key observation is that metastability in C-elements has been acknowledged, studied and characterized. However, a circuit-level effort to reduce metastability in C-elements has not been made. Sutherland, in his discussion about micropipelines, lists various modules that provide the logical combination of transition events [13]. The C-element is one such module that provides the logical AND of transition events at its inputs. Its heavy use in asynchronous pipeline control motivates us to study C-element and propose a reliable design that is metastability tolerant.

3. OUR APPROACH

3.1 Traditional C-element

The three popular traditional circuit-level implementations for a C-element that we will analyze are shown in Figures 2 (a), (b) and (c). Let us begin with a brief explana-

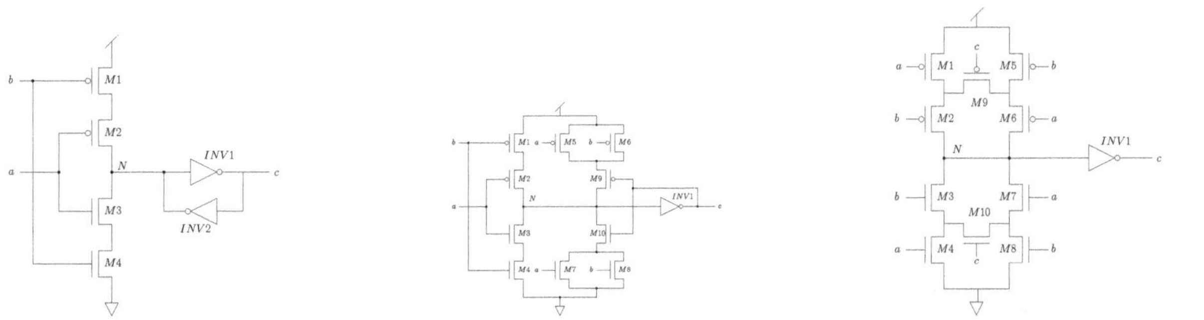

(a) Traditional Martin C-element (b) Traditional Sutherland C-element (c) Traditional Van Berkel C-element

Figure 2: Traditional C-element Designs

tion of the simplest C-element implementation, the Martin C-element (shown in Figure 2 (a)). Assume both the inputs a and b are at logic 0. In this case, the transistors $M1$ and $M2$ are turned on and the node N is pulled up to logic 1. This drives the output to a logic 0 (same as both the input values). Now, without loss of generality, if b transitions to a 1, the transistors $M2$ and $M4$ are on, and the node N stays at its last value (logic 1). The output state is maintained through the feedback inverter $INV2$. The output changes state only when both the inputs transition to a logic 1, in which case transistors $M3$ and $M4$ turn on and the node N is pulled down, which drives the output high.

The other two implementations of the C-element (Sutherland and Van Berkel) work in a similar way. The difference between these two implementations and the Martin C-element is the way the feedback structure is implemented. In the Martin C-element, the feedback inverter $INV2$ is a weak inverter (implemented with long channel devices), which allows the transistors $M1$-$M4$ to drive the node N when the output is changing state. Depending on the timing of a and b this type of feedback can result in a race condition, when the weak feedback inverter $INV2$ and the input transistors ($M1$-$M4$) try to drive conflicting values to node N. Thus, the relative strength of the feedback inverter has to be carefully selected. The Sutherland and the Van Berkel implementations of the C-element avoid such a situation by designing their feedback structure differently.

In the traditional C-element implementations, when the output is at a metastable value, a mechanism to rapidly drive the output to a rail value does not exist. Assume the output c in Figure 2 (a) is stuck at a metastable value. This will cause both the devices (NMOS and PMOS) of $INV2$ to turn on and the voltage at N will be a mid rail value (if the inputs a and b have different values). This in turn causes both devices of $INV1$ to be on. Thus, the metastable voltage loops through the feedback path, and the time to resolve the metastable voltage is unknown. A similar problem exists in the Sutherland and Van Berkel C-element implementations. However, the superior feedback structure in these two implementations makes them less prone to metastability. In our experiments, we show that when the overlap in the value of inputs is small, all the traditional C-element implementations are liable to get stuck at a metastable state which is resolved after an unpredictable amount of time.

3.2 Modified C-element

In this work, we present a circuit-level approach which works with all the 3 implementations of the C-elements discussed above, and minimizes the possibility of metastability at the output of the modified C-element. Our proposed modification for the 3 implementations of the C-elements is shown in Figures 3 (a), (b) and (c). For the sake of discussion, let us consider the design shown in Figure 3 (a) (the modified Martin C-element). As we can see, our design replaces $INV1$ of the Martin C-element of Figure 2 (a) with a structure that uses independent paths for falling and rising transitions on the output of the C-element. This structure consists of two different inverters ($INVA$ and $INVB$). These two inverters have their switchpoints shifted from the nominal value. $INVA$ is a low switchpoint (LSP) inverter and $INVB$ is a high switchpoint (HSP) inverter. When the input to $INVA$ (LSP) and $INVB$ (HSP) is a non-rail (metastable) value, the LSP and HSP have different responses, which reduces the likelihood of both output driver devices ($M5$ and $M6$) being ON simultaneously. This drastically reduces the possibility of metastability at the output of the C-element.

We need the extra pull-down inverter ($INVC$) and the NMOS transistor $M7$ because when the node N rises slowly, the output of the LSP inverter ($INVA$) switches to 0 first, turning on $M5$, while $M6$ has still not turned off. This results in a situation where both $M5$ and $M6$ are on momentarily. A similar situation occurs when the node N is falling slowly. In such a case, we pull down the output of $INVB$ by inverting the output of $INVA$ using the inverter $INVC$, and turning on the NMOS device $M7$. This turns off $M6$, and eventually only $M5$ stays on, which pulls the output to a logic 1 and resolves metastability. Thus, depending on the delay of the pull-down structure, an improved resolution time is achieved in our design. This cannot be ensured in a traditional design since there is no mechanism to actively resolve a metastable value and pull it to a stable high or low rail value.

Since the structure just described is non-inverting, the feedback structure (which replaces $INV2$ of the Martin C-element of Figure 2 (a)) consists of a pair of regular inverters.

The metastability reducing structure discussed for the Martin C-element (Figure 3 (a)) is effective for the other two C-elements as well. We use a similar structure in the Sutherland C-element (Figure 3 (b)) and the Van Berkel C-element (Figure 3 (c)).

In the Sutherland C-element, we replace $INV1$ (see Figure 2 (b)) with our metastability reducing structure. Since this structure is non-inverting, an inverter $INV3$ is introduced in the feedback path, as shown in Figure 3 (b). In the Van Berkel C-element, our metastability reducing structure replaces $INV1$ (see Figure 2 (c)). Our experimental results, which are discussed in the next section, show that

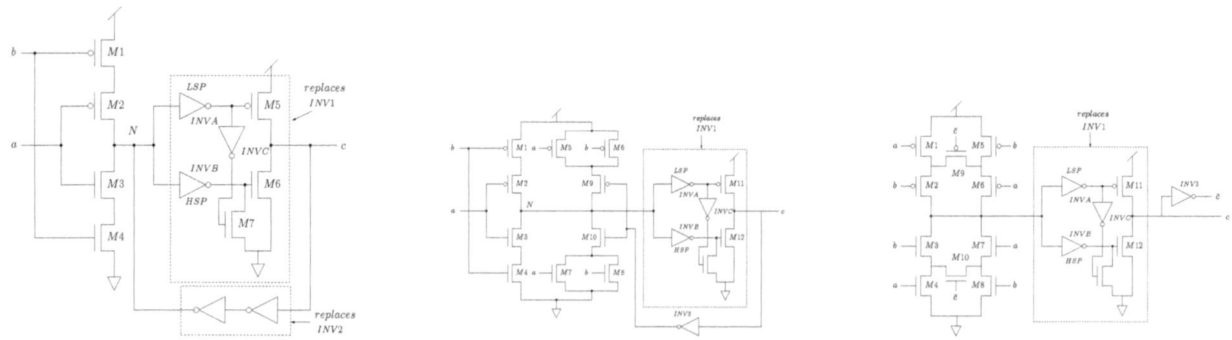

(a) Modified Martin C-element (b) Modified Sutherland C-element (c) Modified Van Berkel C-element

Figure 3: Modified C-element Designs

our modified Sutherland and Van Berkel C-element resolves metastability much faster than the traditional design.

3.3 Figures of Merit

The common performance parameter for any combinational or sequential circuit element is its delay from the input to the output. We will compare the *delay* of our designs with the traditional designs. Our simulations are done at an extremely fine resolution, and the resulting delay values have been verified to be repeatable under small variations of the timing resolution. The other common parameters that we compare are the *area utilization* and the *power consumption* of the circuits.

In addition to these traditional metrics, we define another metric that quantifies the metastability performance of a C-element. This new metric, the *metastability window*, quantitatively measures the metastability performance of any C-element. The metastability window is similar to the metric T_W as defined in [4], except that it is defined on the output, and is therefore more accurate, since the output is the node that undergoes metastability. A representative picture has been shown in Figure 4. In this figure, the input a goes through a transition from a high state to a low state at a fixed time. The input b goes through an opposite transition and the time of transition is swept. The output c, which happened to be at the high state initially, either transitions to a low state or stays high, depending on when the transition on b happens, relative to the transition on a. The metastability window is defined as the time from which the outputs in our sweep start a transition and reach 50% of the V_{dd} value, to the time when all the outputs from the sweep have settled within 10% of the power rail values. The metastability window for Figure 4, as defined above, would be either W_1 or W_2, whichever is larger. The metastability window is a representation of how long the output of the C-element stays in a metastable condition.

Other than the above metrics, we will also qualitatively analyze the signal integrity of the output of the C-element in our simulations of the circuit. Based on the qualitative and quantitative analysis, we will choose the better design.

4. EXPERIMENTAL RESULTS

To compare the metastability performance of the 3 traditional and modified C-element implementations, we simulated the proposed designs as well as the traditional designs in HSPICE [7], using a 14nm PTM [10] model card. We initially did extensive simulations to determine the sizing of the devices in our metastability reducing circuit so as to obtain

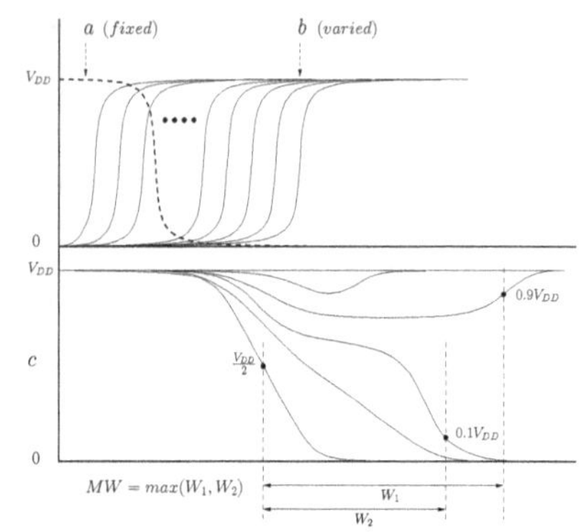

Figure 4: A Representation of Metastability Window

the best response. Based on our experiments, we selected an HSP which had a switchpoint $30mV$ above the nominal value and an LSP which had a switchpoint $30mV$ below the nominal value. The difference in their switchpoints was 7.5% of the supply voltage of $0.8V$.

To simulate the metastable condition in the C-element, we fixed the time of transition of one of the inputs (a) and swept the time of transition of the second input (b). This caused a short overlap in the input values (as shown in Figure 1). To observe metastability, sweeps of the b signal were conducted (as illustrated in Figure 4) in very fine increments of $1fs$. This input waveform set was connected to all the inputs of all the (6) implementations (3 traditional C-elements and 3 of our modified C-elements). The signal integrity at the output of each C-element was then compared. We simulated two cases; one where the output c was initially set to 0 and the transitions on the inputs marginally triggered the output to rise and vice versa.

To sweep the transition of input b while the time of transition of input a is fixed, we chose a window of $140ps$ around the time of transition of a. For some of these sweeps, the output held its previous state, for other sweeps, the output went through a complete transition, flipping to the opposite stable state, and for the remaining sweeps, the output got stuck at a metastable value. A total of 140,000 sweeps were performed

An extremely small time resolution of 1 femtosecond was used between sweeps. In theory, a finer resolution (or a small temporal shift in each of sweeps) could potentially yield different results. In practice, we experimented extensively with such changes, and determined that our choice of 1 femtoseconds between sweeps yielded substantially identical simulation results compared to finer (or shifted) sweeps.

Martin C-element			
	Our Design	Traditional Design	Impr.
c = 0	82.5 ps	315.5 ps	3.8×
c = 1	49.4 ps	460.5 ps	9.3×
Sutherland C-element			
	Our Design	Traditional Design	Impr.
c = 0	46.5 ps	160.5 ps	3.4×
c = 1	65.9 ps	154.8 ps	2.3×
Van Berkel C-element			
	Our Design	Traditional Design	Impr.
c = 0	63.2 ps	161.4 ps	2.5×
c = 1	56.9 ps	157.7 ps	2.8×

Table 2: Metastability Window Comparison

Figures 5 (a) and 6 (a) show the overlay of all the swept waveforms of the inputs a and b, the output of the traditional Martin C-element and our modified Martin C-element. Figure 5 (a) shows the case when the output c was initially set to 0 and Figure 6 (a) shows the case when c was initially set to 1. Note that since our design is inverting, the output is the compliment of a traditional C-element in all cases.

Each figure shows, from top to bottom, the input a, the input b, the output of a traditional C-element (c reg), and the output of our proposed C-element (c mod).

We see from Figures 5 (a) and 6 (a) that the output resolves to a rail value much faster in our design as compared to the traditional Martin C-Element for both the cases. The traditional Martin C-element has the risk of the output being stuck at a metastable value for a long time (up to $460ps$ in our experiments), which could cause unpredictable behavior in the combinational logic that follows the C-element. Also, we note that the metastability observed is not oscillatory [11], but rather is an artefact of slightly different circuit path delays in our design.

Figures 5 (b) and 6 (b) show similar waveforms for Sutherland C-element. We see that the traditional Sutherland C-element has much better metastability performance than the traditional Martin C-element. This is because of the difference in the feedback structure between the two C-elements. This makes the output much less metastable. However, the traditional Sutherland C-element, when compared to our modified version, is worse in terms of resolving metastability.

Figures 5 (c) and 6 (c) show the overlay of waveforms for Van Berkel C-element, for all our sweeps. As can be seen, the metastability performance of a Van Berkel C-element is similar to that of a Sutherland C-element and much better than a Martin C-element. The reason for this is similar to the one given for Sutherland C-element. Additionally, we can also see from Figures 5 (c) and 6 (c) that our design for Van Berkel C-element is better than the traditional Van Berkel C-element in resolving metastability.

In Table 2 we report across all our sweeps, the metastability window for different circuit implementations of C-elements for both, the traditional designs and our modified designs. As seen in Table 2, our design resolves the metastable output much quicker as compared to the traditional C-element implementations. We achieve improvement in the metastability window (by 2.3× to 9×) compared to the traditional implementations. This makes our design significantly more robust.

The delay of a C-element is critical in asynchronous circuit design. In Table 3, we report the simulated delay for all the implementations of the C-element, both for our modifications and the traditional designs. In all our sweeps, we simulate the C-elements in such a way that always the transition on the output c is caused by a transition on the input a. Thus we measure the delay from the transition on the

Martin C-element			
	Our Design	Traditional Design	Impr.
c = 0	157.8 ps	345.7 ps	2.2×
c = 1	80.2 ps	481.8 ps	6.0×
Sutherland C-element			
	Our Design	Traditional Design	Impr.
c = 0	78.8 ps	176.8 ps	2.2×
c = 1	83.7 ps	168.8 ps	2.0×
Van Berkel C-element			
	Our Design	Traditional Design	Impr.
c = 0	83.7 ps	171.4 ps	2.0×
c = 1	69.4 ps	168.9 ps	2.4×

Table 3: Simulated Delay Comparison

Martin C-element		
Our Design	Traditional Design	Impr.
0.765 μW	0.317 μW	−2.4×
Sutherland C-element		
Our Design	Traditional Design	Impr.
0.365 μW	0.155 μW	−2.3×
Van Berkel C-element		
Our Design	Traditional Design	Impr.
0.41 μW	0.178 μW	−2.3×

Table 4: Comparison of Average Power Consumption (Averaged over sweeps)

input a to the transition in the output c. Note that we compute the delay from the time when the transition on a crosses 50% of V_{dd} to the time when the output c has settled down within 10% of the rail values. We do not use the conventional definition of delay (50% value of a to 50% value of c) because when the output c is metastable, it reaches 50% of VDD quickly, but often stays there for a long time. In such cases, the conventional definition of the delay would not be a true representation of the actual delay of the C-element.

We can see from Table 3 that the simulated delay is better for our modified designs of a C-element (by 2× to 6×) compared to the traditional designs. The resulting delay values have been verified to be repeatable under small variations of the timing resolution.

In the next table we report the power consumption of different circuit implementations for C-elements, both for the traditional designs and our modified designs. To compute power, we define a time window (PW), in which the output (c) of a C-element goes through two different transitions. The first transition is the one where c is initially set to 1 and the sweep of transitions on one of the inputs (b) causes the output to transition to 0 for some sweeps and stay at 1 for the other sweeps. In all these sweeps we witness many cases when the output is stuck at a metastable state. The other transition on the output in our window PW is the opposite of the first transition we just described. Thus, we include both the possible metastability cases while computing power consumed by a C-element. The size of PW window for our simulations was 4ns.

To present the results of Tables 4, we first compute the average power (A) consumed by different C-element implementations being compared, for each sweep. This average power is measured over the time window PW described above. In Table 4, we report, across all our sweeps, the average value of A. It is to be noted that the average value of A for our proposed designs is more than the traditional designs (by up to 2.4×) for all the implementations of the C-element.

This is because our modifications of the C-element have extra devices that contribute in resolving metastability at the output. The power consumed by these extra devices adds to the average power consumption. However, we note that we have an up to 9× improved metastability window, and an up to 6× improved delay in our designs. This im-

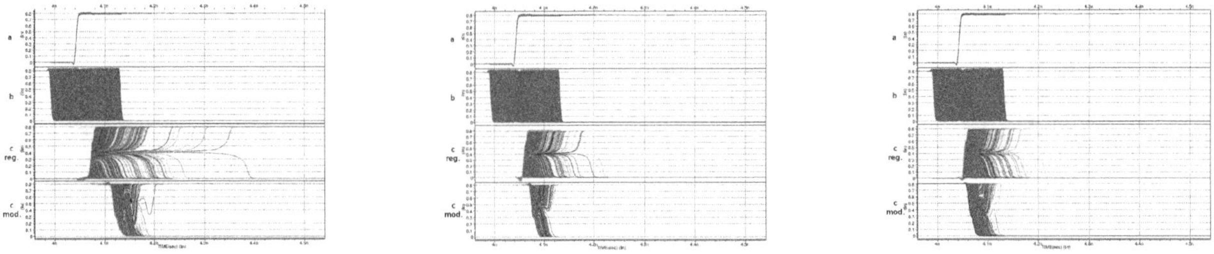

(a) Martin (b) Sutherland (c) Van Berkel

Figure 5: Overlay of c Waveform for all C-elements (c initially set to 0)

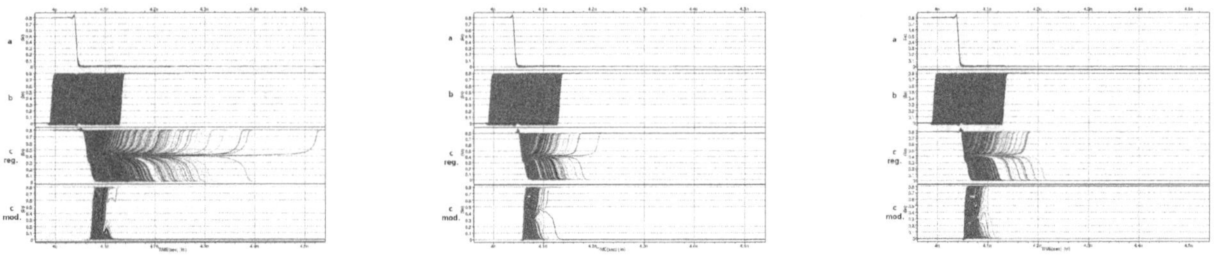

(a) Martin (b) Sutherland (c) Van Berkel

Figure 6: Overlay of c Waveform for all C-elements (c initially set to 1)

Martin C-element		
Our Design	Traditional Design	Impr.
0.0284 μm^2	0.0157 μm^2	$-1.8\times$
Sutherland C-element		
Our Design	Traditional Design	Impr.
0.0259 μm^2	0.0132 μm^2	$-1.9\times$
Van Berkel C-element		
Our Design	Traditional Design	Impr.
0.0259 μm^2	0.0132 μm^2	$-1.9\times$

Table 5: Comparison of $\sum W_i L_i$ for C-elements

provement comes at a power cost of only about 2.4×, which makes the tradeoff appealing.

The product of width (W) and length (L) of a transistor is a representative number for the on-chip area it occupies. In Table 5 we report the summation of the product (W*L) for all the devices ($\sum W_i L_i$) used in implementing different circuit implementations for the traditional and our C-elements. Is is to be noted that our C-element design uses more on-chip area (by about 1.9×) when compared to the traditional design.

We observe that our design needs more area and consumes more power as compared to the traditional design. However, these overheads usually do not impact the overall area and power consumption of an IC significantly. This is because the number of C-elements in an IC is usually limited. Robust operation of a C-element is a significantly bigger concern, as it affects the functionality and yield of an IC.

5. CONCLUSIONS

Asynchronous circuits are preferred for low power and high performance applications. In this work, we study the metastability characteristics of the C-element, which is a fundamental building block in asynchronous circuit design. The output of the C-element is prone to metastability when the input values overlap briefly. We compare the metastability response of three popular circuit implementations of the C-element. Additionally, we propose a novel circuit-level design of a robust C-element which drastically reduces the likelihood of a metastable value at the output. Our approach uses independent paths with different switchpoint inverters for rising and falling transitions on the output. Experimental results show that the proposed design achieves a significantly better metastability response as compared to the traditional design of a C-element (with up to 9× improvement in metastability window). With the improved metastability response, the delay for our design is also reduced because the output of our C-element is closer to the rails. The improved metastability response is achieved at the cost of area and power consumption.

6. REFERENCES

[1] Z. Al Tarawneh, G. Russell, and A. Yakovlev. An analysis of SEU robustness of C-element structures implemented in bulk CMOS and SOI technologies. In *Microelectronics (ICM), 2010 International Conference on*, pages 280–283. IEEE, 2010.

[2] P. Balasubramanian and H. Arabnia. Computation of error resiliency of Muller C-element. In *Computational Science and Computational Intelligence (CSCI), 2014 International Conference on*, volume 2, pages 179–180. IEEE, 2014.

[3] G. Fuchs, M. Fugger, and A. Steininger. On the threat of metastability in an asynchronous fault-tolerant clock generation scheme. In *Asynchronous Circuits and Systems, 2009. ASYNC'09. 15th IEEE Symposium on*, pages 127–136. IEEE, 2009.

[4] R. Ginosar. Metastability and synchronizers: A tutorial. In *IEEE Design and Test of Computers*, volume 28, pages 23–35, Sept-Oct 2011.

[5] N. Jayakumar, R. Garg, B. Gamache, and S. Khatri. A pla based asynchronous micropipelining approach for subthreshold circuit design. In *Proceedings of the 43rd Annual Design Automation Conference (DAC)*, pages 419–424, 2006.

[6] S. Lu. Improved design of CMOS multiple-input muller-c-elements. *Electronics Letters*, 29:1680–1682, 1993.

[7] I. Meta-Software. HSPICE user's manual. Campbell, CA.

[8] J. Murphy. Design of latch-based C-element. *Electronics letters*, 48(19):1190–1191, 2012.

[9] T. Polzer and A. Steininger. Metastability characterization for Muller C-elements. In *Power and Timing Modeling, Optimization and Simulation (PATMOS), 2013 23rd International Workshop on*, pages 164–171. IEEE, 2013.

[10] PTM. http://www.eas.asu.edu/ ptm.

[11] L. Reyneri, D. D. Corso, and B. Sacco. Oscillatory metastability in homogeneous and inhomogeneous flip-flops. *IEEE Journal of Solid-State Circuits*, 25(1):254–264, Feb 1990.

[12] M. Shams, J. C. Ebergen, and M. I. Elmasry. A comparison of CMOS implementations of an asynchronous circuits primitive: the C-element. In *Low Power Electronics and Design, 1996., International Symposium on*, pages 93–96. IEEE, 1996.

[13] I. E. Sutherland. Micropipelines. *Commun. ACM*, 32(6):720–738, June 1989.

[14] T.-Y. Wuu and S. B. Vrudhula. A design of a fast and area efficient multi-input Muller C-element. *Very Large Scale Integration (VLSI) Systems, IEEE Transactions on*, 1(2):215–219, 1993.

Circuit Level Design of a Hardware Hash Unit for use in Modern Microprocessors

Abbas Fairouz, Monther Abusultan and Sunil P. Khatri
Department of ECE, Texas A&M University, College Station TX 77843.

ABSTRACT

Modern microprocessors contain several Special Function Units (SFUs) such as specialized arithmetic units, cryptographic processors, etc. In recent times, applications such as cloud computing, web-based search engines, and network applications are widely used, and place new demands on the microprocessor. Hashing is a key algorithm that is extensively used in such applications. Hashing is typically performed in software. Thus, implementing a hardware-based hash unit on a modern microprocessor would potentially increase performance significantly. In this paper, we present the circuit design for a hardware hash unit (HU) for modern microprocessors, using a 45nm technology. Our proposed hardware hash unit is based on the use of a CAM to implement each bin of the hash function. We simulate the HU circuit and compare it with a traditional CAM design. We demonstrate an average power reduction of 5.48× using the HU over the traditional CAM. Also, we show that the HU can operate at a maximum frequency of 1.39 GHz (after accounting for process, voltage and temperature (PVT) variations and accounting for wiring parasitics). Furthermore, we present the delay, power and area trade-offs of the HU design with varying hash table sizes.

CCS Concepts

•**Hardware** → *Application specific instruction set processors;*

Keywords

Special Function Unit; Hardware Hash Unit; Modern Microprocessors; Hash Table; Hash Function; Content-Addressable Memory

1. INTRODUCTION

Today's computing systems and applications heavily utilize applications such as cloud computing, web-based search engines, social media and network applications, and demand high performance for these tasks. Most of the underlying algorithms run in software, which limits performance. Hashing is used extensively in these applications, as well as in general software algorithms and applications. Therefore, if a hardware unit for hashing was developed, it could have a significant impact in improving the performance of many applications.

A new special function unit (SFU) was proposed by [1] to speed-up hashing operations in modern microprocessors. This SFU was called a hardware hash unit (HU). The authors of [1] conducted their study at the architectural level, with no discussion on the circuit realization aspects of the design. This paper presents the circuit level details of a HU which is based on the system architecture presented in [1]. Unlike previously reported SFUs which include cryptographic units, floating point units and memory management units, the HU is intended to speed-up algorithms that uses hash table operations.

Algorithms that are hashing-intensive are generally compiled and run in software. As a result, they often entail a high CPU and memory utilization. Implementing a HU in a modern microprocessors can reduce the CPU and memory utilization of hashing-intensive algorithms, and yield a significantly improved overall system performance as shown in [1]. For example, networking applications utilize hashing algorithms to improve network packets' throughput. Also, internet protocol (IP) lookup uses hashing in order to speed-up the IP search process. Generally, hashing algorithms are designed on a per-application basis, with application-specific hash function and hash table designs.

The universal hash function of class H3 [2] is one of the best candidates for hardware hash function designs. A content-addressable memory (CAM) [3] is mostly used in fast cache memory cache applications. In a software-based hashing implementation, each bin is typically implemented as a linked list, with a search time that is $O(k)$ where k is the number of entries in the bin. In our hardware-based implementation of the HU, we choose a CAM to realize each bin. This provide $O(1)$ search time when the entry is in the CAM.

The HU design utilize a hash function of class H3 [2] and a CAM-based implementation of the hash table bins. Architectural simulations of this HU were reported by the authors of [1]. In this paper, we implement the ideas of [1] in a 45nm technology, demonstrating a HU circuit design that obtains an average power reduction of 5.48×, and a clock frequency of up to 1.39 GHz.

The key contributions of this paper are:

- We implement a hardware hash unit (HU) circuit design for modern microprocessor based on [1].
- We simulated the HU circuit design in Synopsys VCS and HSPICE [4], using a 45nm PTM [5] and verified the correctness of lookup, insert and delete hash operations. RC parasitic are extracted using Synopsys Raphael [4].
- We demonstrate an average power reduction of 5.48× using HU over the traditional CAM circuit design. The power reduction arises from the fact that our approach disables all but one bin in any clock cycle.
- Our circuit-level simulations show that the design can operate at a maximum frequency of 1.39 GHz.

The rest of the paper is organized as follows. In Section 2, we discuss related previous work. Section 3 presents our ap-

Permission to make digital or hard copies of all or part of this work for personal or classroom use is granted without fee provided that copies are not made or distributed for profit or commercial advantage and that copies bear this notice and the full citation on the first page. Copyrights for components of this work owned by others than ACM must be honored. Abstracting with credit is permitted. To copy otherwise, or republish, to post on servers or to redistribute to lists, requires prior specific permission and/or a fee. Request permissions from permissions@acm.org.

GLSVLSI '17, May 10-12, 2017, Banff, AB, Canada
© 2017 ACM. ISBN 978-1-4503-4972-7/17/05...$15.00
DOI: http://dx.doi.org/10.1145/3060403.3060451

proach and design details, while Section 4 presents and discusses our experimental results. We conclude in Section 5.

2. PREVIOUS WORK

In this work, we present a hardware-based realization of a hash function *and* a hash table.

In this paragraph, we discuss previous research in which the focus was on implementing hash function alone. Hardware hash function implementations have been proposed in [6–9]. These implementations were used to check the equivalence of a pair of large files on different nodes in a network. Networking applications often benefit from the use of hash functions. Such applications are IP addresses hashing schemes [10] and detect and authenticate messages [11]. A hashing technique has been proposed in [12] for high speed networks. In [13], the authors simulated and implemented the SHA-3 on FPGA for cryptographic network applications using a pipeline model to speed up hash operations. An efficient SHA-256 hash function implementation has been proposed in [14]. All these efforts reported work on hardware based hash functions. Other software-based hash functions have been reported as well. Real-time facial identification can benefit from the use of hashing to increase performance [15]. Image compression techniques use hashing in [16] to speed up data compression.

Unlike the techniques in the previous paragraph, our work implements both a hash function as well as a hash table in hardware and can be integrated into a modern microprocessor as an SFU.

In this paragraph, we discuss previous work in implementing hash tables. In [17], the authors proposed an online hash table implementation on an FPGA using a hash table on external DRAM. A hash join engine using hardware hash table was proposed in [18]. A hashing scheme design has been utilized in [19] for packet processing. The authors implemented the hash table as a set-associative memory module. They simulated their design with various hash function in C++. Furthermore, they proposed a multiple hash functions to reduce collision list in hash table. A key difference of [17–19] from our approach is that in [17–19], the hash table bins are not implemented using CAMs, thus sacrificing performance.

In contrast to the previous work, we present a hardware hash function and hash table SFU (with CAM-based bins), for modern microprocessors.

3. OUR APPROACH

In this section, we first discuss our circuit implementation of a Hash Unit (HU) for use as an SFU in modern microprocessors. The block diagram of the HU is shown in Figure 1. We start with a top-level discussion of the HU circuitry. Next, we discuss the Hash Function (HF) of class H3 [2] (as shown in Figure 2) and the design of the Bin Selector circuit. Then, we introduce the Control Signals Unit (CSU) circuit design as shown in Figure 3. Finally, we discuss the Hash Table (HT) circuit design as shown in Figure 4.

3.1 Hardware Hash Unit (HU)

The hash unit (HU) is an SFU that can be used in modern microprocessors to speed up hash table operations. The HU consists of 3 units: the control signals unit (CSU), the hash function (HF) and the Bin Selector, and the hash table (HT) as shown in Figure 1. This figure shows the flow of hash operation. It takes a (*key*, *value*) pair as an input and return a result based on the operation requested. There are 3 major operations, which are encoded by the W2 and W1 inputs:

- Lookup: it takes a *key* as an input and searches for it in the HT. If the *key* found, it returns the *value* associated with the *key* in the HT.
- Insert: it takes a (*key*, *value*) pair as an input. It first performs a lookup operation in the HT. If there is a match in the HT, it aborts the insert. Otherwise, it inserts the new (*key*, *value*) pair in the HT.
- Delete: it takes a *key* as the input. First, it executes a lookup operation in the HT. If the *key* is found, it deletes this entry. This is accomplished by invalidating the entry and writing a '0' to the valid bit of the entry. This is shown in Figure 4 and will be explained later.

As shown in Figure 1, the inputs and outputs of the HU are:

- Value_In: it is the *value* associated with a (*key*, *value*) pair that is input to the HT.
- Key: it is the *key* in a (*key*, *value*) pair that is input to the HT.
- EN: it is the enable signal that enables the HU.
- CLK: main clock signal.
- W2 & W1: op-code signals which encode the micro-instruction to the HT.

The outputs of the HU are the *Value_Out* and $\overline{Exist}$. The *Value_Out* signal is the output of a lookup operation. The $\overline{Exist}$ signal indicates the outcome of a lookup operation.

3.2 Hash Function (HF) and Bin Selector

The hash function (HF) takes a *key* as an input, and generates a *Bin Index*, as shown in Figure 1. The *Bin Index* is fed to a *Bin Selector* to generate several Bin_EN_i signals. The *Bin Selector* is a decoder, that decodes a *Bin Index* to generate one of many Bin_EN_i signals. The Bin_EN_i signals are one-hot. If the *Bin Index* value (in decimal) is k, then the Bin_EN_k signal is high, and all other Bin_EN_j signals are low. The HF is of class H3 [2]. It performs hash operations based on AND and XOR logic as shown in Figure 2. The AND and XOR operations result in a fast hash operation. Hashing is performed using a Q matrix which is stored in latches. This Q matrix is a random number of class H3 [2]. The Q matrix values are stored during the HU initialization. The HF can be changed for different applications, by changing the Q matrix contents.

3.3 Control Signal Unit (CSU)

The Control Signal Unit (CSU) generates the C1 and C2 signals to perform the appropriate sequence of atomic operations in the HT, as shown in Figure 1. The CSU takes 4 input signals CLK, W1, W2, and $\overline{Exist}$ and generates C1 and C2, the output control signals. The operations of the HU (encoded by (W2,W1)) require a sequence of atomic operations (encoded by (C2,C1)) to be done. For example, the insert operation (W2,W1 = 11) requires a lookup atomic operation (C2,C1 = 01) to be performed, and then possibly an insert atomic operation (C2,C1 = 11). The CSU encodes the W1, W2 and $\overline{Exist}$ signals to perform the sequence of atomic operations on the HT (indicated by the CSU outputs (C2,C1)). Table 1 illustrates the mapping between the operations and the values of (W2,W1) and the (C1,C2) signals.

Note that for every operation (i.e. every op-code on (W2,W1)), the HU has to perform a lookup operation, except for the 00 op-code (no-op operation). As a result, the delete and insert

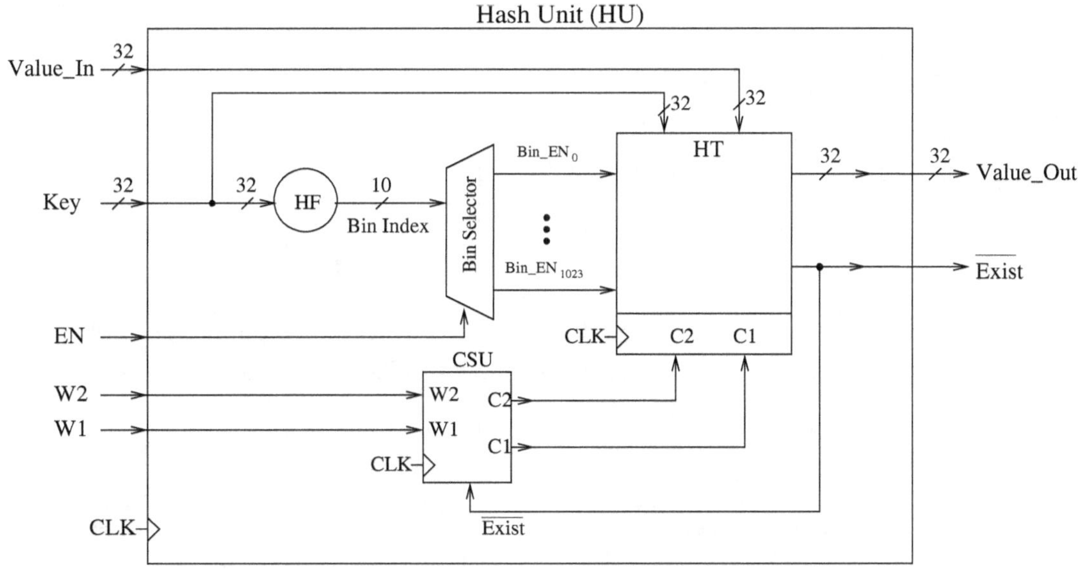

Figure 1: Hardware Hash Unit (HU) Block Diagram

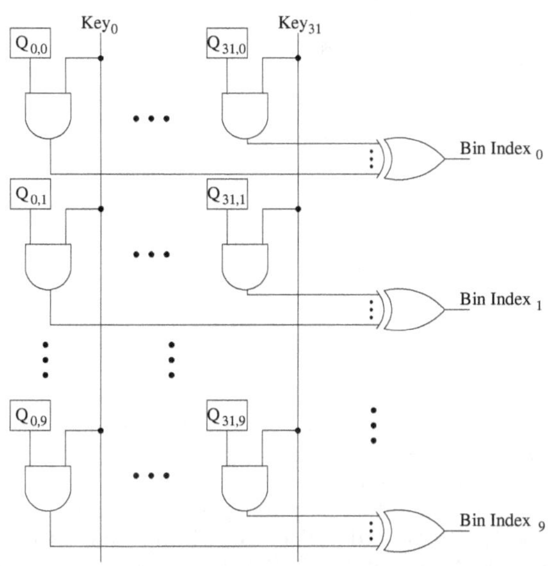

Figure 2: Hardware Hash Function (HF) of Class H3 [2]

Operation	W2	W1	$\overline{Exist}$	C2	C1
Insert	1	1	1	1	1
Delete	1	0	0	1	0
Lookup	0	1	x	0	1
no-op	0	0	x	0	0

Table 1: CSU op-codes for the HT operations

operations can take two cycles. In the first cycle, the CPU drives (W2,W1) to 11 (insert) or 10 (delete). In the second cycle, (W2,W1) are driven to 00 in both cases. For example, when the insert operation (W2,W1=11) is issued, a lookup atomic operation is performed in the first cycle by driving (C2,C1 = 01). If $\overline{Exist} = 1$ results, an insert atomic operation is performed in the next cycle by driving (C2,C1 = 11). If $\overline{Exist} = 0$, then (C2,C1 = 00) in the second cycle. Note that, in the second cycle, (W2,W1) are driven to 00. Similarly for the delete operation, the CPU will first issue a (W2,W1 = 10) op-code in the first cycle. Then, it will issue a (W2,W1 = 00) op-code in the second cycle. In the first cycle, the CSU will drive (C2,C1 = 01) to perform the lookup atomic operation. In the second cycle, the CSU generates the C2 and C1 signals based on the value of $\overline{Exist}$ signal. If $\overline{Exist} = 1$, then the CSU generates 00 for (C2,C1) and performs a no-op. Otherwise, the CSU drives 10 for (C2,C1) to delete the (*key, value*) pair in the HT. The CSU implements the state machine which produces the values of (C2,C1) based on the values of (W2,W1) and $\overline{Exist}$. This state machine is shown in Figure 3.

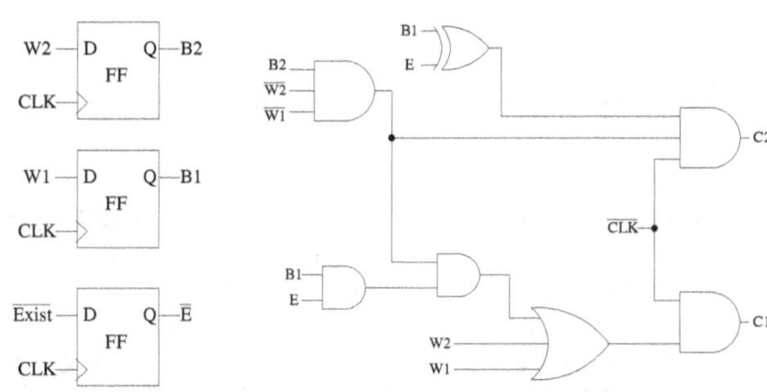

Figure 3: Control Signals Unit (CSU)

3.4 Hash Table (HT)

We design each bin of our Hash Table (HT) using a basic 9-T NOR-type CAM cell [3] to store a *key*, and a conventional 6-T SRAM cell [20] to store a *value*. Each HT bin is implemented as a CAM in order to perform fast hash operations.

The HT has 6 inputs and 2 outputs as shown in Figure 1. The inputs of the HT are: *Key*, *Value_In*, Bin_EN_i, CLK, C2, and C1. The *Key* and *Value_In* inputs are the (*key, value*) pair. The HT stores an extra *valid* bit along with the *key*, to indicate if the corresponding (*key, value*) pair is valid. This bit is written to *zero* during a delete operation. During an insert operation, it is driven to a logic 1. During a lookup, this bit must be a 1, otherwise the lookup fails. The Bin_EN_i signals are the outputs of *Bin Selector* which only enables a single bin of the HT in any clock cycle. The C2 and C1 inputs are the outputs of the CSU, which indicate the atomic operation to be performed (lookup, delete or insert) in the HT. As shown in Figure 4, there are two major blocks of memory in a HT bin. The first block is 33 CAM cells wide

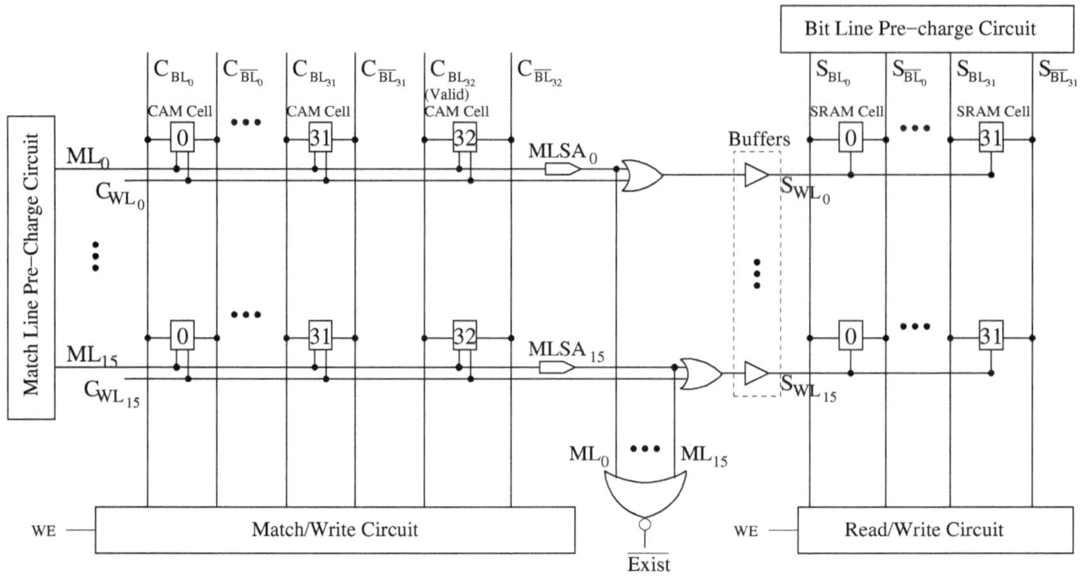

Figure 4: Hardware Hash Table (HT) for a Single Bin [1]

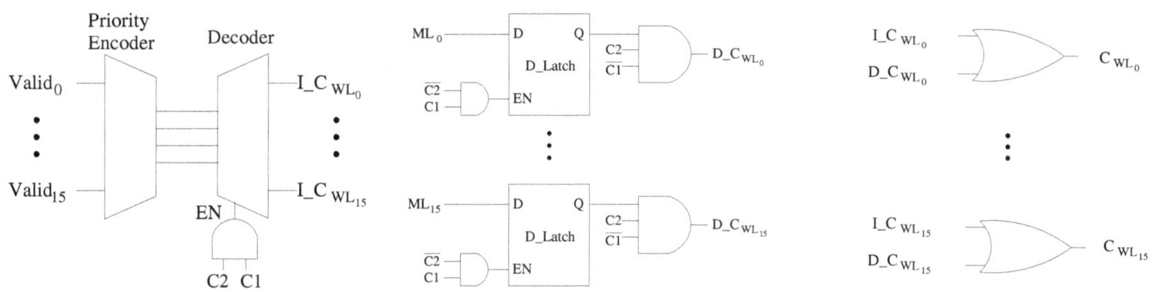

(a) Determining WL for Insertion (b) Determining WL for Deletion (c) Deriving C_{WL_i}

Figure 5: CAM Word Line Signal Generator inside HT

(32 bit of *key* and one *valid* bit) and the second is 32 SRAM cells wide (32 bit of *value*). The number of rows n represents the number of entries in a HT bin ($n = 16$ in Figure 4). There is a match line pre-charge circuit to pre-charge ML_0, ..., ML_n. Also, there is a bit line pre-charge circuit to pre-charge the SRAM bit lines (S_{BL}, $S_{\overline{BL}}$). There is a Match/Write circuit for CAM (since the polarity of C_{BL_i} and $C_{\overline{BL_i}}$ are reversed during a write to the CAM as opposed to a lookup) and a Read/Write circuit for SRAM cells (since the S_{BL_i} and $S_{\overline{BL_i}}$ lines are pre-charged during lookup and driven during a write to the SRAM). The Match/Write and Read/Write circuits are enabled by a write enable signal (WE). The WE signal is set to 1 for the delete or insert atomic operations (i.e. when (C2,C1) = 11 or 10). The *Key* input is driven on the C_{BL_i} lines using the Match/Write circuit in all HT atomic operations. In the Read/Write circuit, the *Value_In* input is driven on the S_{BL_i} lines in the insert atomic operation, while the S_{BL_i} lines are driven on the *Value_Out* output in the lookup atomic operation.

During a lookup operation, all C_{WL_i} lines are driven to a *zero* value. All ML lines are pre-charged, and at most one (say ML_i) stays *high* (indicating a match). This ML_i is amplified by the sense amplifier $MLSA_i$, and results in the $\overline{Exist}$ line being driven to a *zero* value. If no ML_i stays *high* (a mismatch condition), then $\overline{Exist}$ ends up being driven to a 1. When ML_i is *high*, then S_{WL_i} is also driven *high*, and the *value* is read out from the SRAM.

S_{WL_i} is also set *high* if C_{WL_i} is driven *high*, in a delete or insert operation (which requires the SRAM to be updated). We discuss the delete operation next.

For a delete operation, we first perform a lookup atomic operation ((C2,C1) = 01). The ML_i which is found to match during the lookup is latched in the Q_i signal of the ith D-latch in Figure 5 (b). At most one Q_i signal is high after the lookup operation. During the delete atomic operation ((C2,C1) = 10), the corresponding $D\_C_{WL_i}$ is driven *high*, which drives C_{WL_i} *high* (see Figure 5 (c)). Hence the deletion is performed on the ith row of the CAM, as required.

For an insert operation, we use a priority encoder to find the index of the first row which is not valid. Such a row can be written into since it is invalid. This is shown in Figure 5 (a). The valid bits are stored in latches as well as in the CAM cells. During the insert operation (C2,C1 = 11), we decode the index of the first invalid entry (Figure 5 (a)) and drive a single $I\_C_{WL_i}$ line *high*. This causes C_{WL_i} to be driven *high* (Figure 5 (c)), resulting in an insertion in the first invalid entry as desired.

4. EXPERIMENTAL RESULTS

In this section we present the simulation environment used to implement the proposed design of the Hash Unit. Then, we discuss the procedure we used to determine that the design operates correctly. Finally, we present the circuit-level simulation results along with a discussion.

4.1 Simulation Environment

Since our proposed hardware-based HU engine is based on the use of a CAM per bin of the HT, we compare our design with a traditional CAM of the same total size as the HU. One can conceive of a design in which the CAM of a microprocessor can be dynamically split between the cache and the HU. In such a scenario, the power and area comparison between the HU and the traditional CAM is an important figure of merit to consider.

We compare two design implementations: the HU and a traditional CAM. In the traditional CAM, the whole memory is enabled, while the HT in the HU design enables a single bin. We simulated both designs using Synopsys HSPICE [4] and 45nm PTM [5] high-performance process model card. We used custom Perl [21] scripts to generate both designs. We synthesized the HF, the *Bin Selector*, and the CSU from Verilog and simulated them in HSPICE while the HT and traditional CAM were custom designed, and simulated in HSPICE.

The ratio of the width of the pull-down NMOS device in the SRAM (and CAM) cell to the width of the NMOS access transistor of the same cell was chosen to be 1.25 [22]. Also, we choose minimum size for the pull-up transistors in the SRAM and CAM cells [22] in order to obtain minimum size, read stability and writeability.

We also generated the layout of the CAM and SRAM cells as shown in Figure 6 and Figure 7. These layouts are based on the 45nm design rules [23] and are generated using the Cadence Virtuoso [24] layout tool. We then used Synopsys Raphael [4] to extract the parasitic capacitance between wires (such as bit lines, world lines, and match lines) in the SRAM and CAM cells. We used the parasitic resistance and capacitance results in our HSPICE simulation for both the HT and traditional CAM. We sized the memory (CAM and SRAM) drivers and buffers based on the number of entries in the HT bin as well as wire parasitic. In our design, we pre-charge the bit-lines of the SRAM cells and the match lines of the CAM cells to VDD.

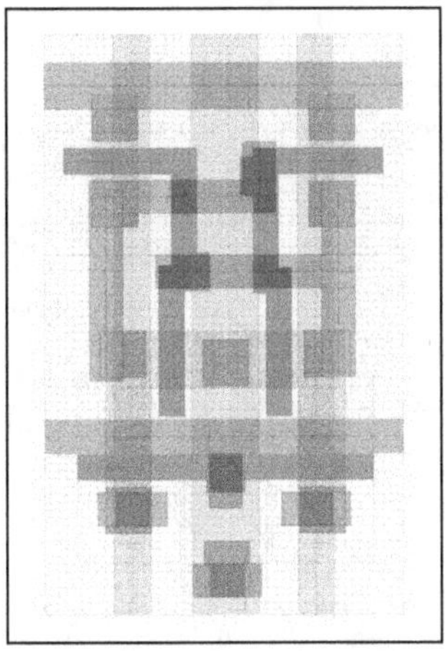

Figure 6: SRAM cell layout in 45nm design rules [23]

4.2 Design Verification

We designed the HF, the *Bin Selector*, and the CSU in structural Verilog and then generated a HSPICE netlist using Synopsys V2S [4]. Then, we exhaustively simulated and verified the logical correctness of these units using Synopsys VCS [4].

After that, we simulated the HF, Bin Selector, and CSU in HSPICE to verify their correctness, and determine their delay, power and area requirements.

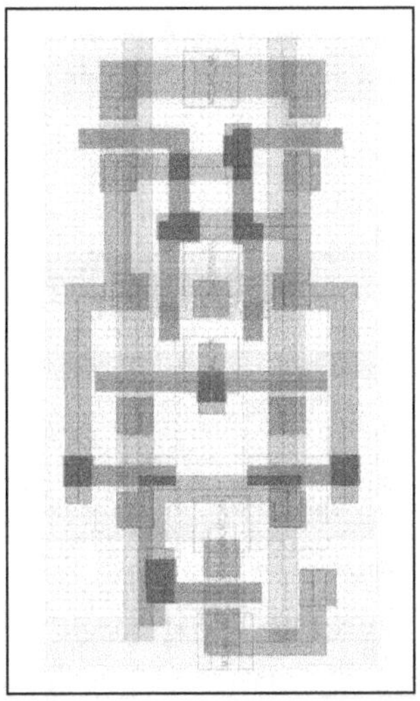

Figure 7: CAM cell layout in 45nm design rules [23]

We simulated the HT and the traditional CAM circuits with custom scripts in HSPICE to verify their correct functionality. These scripts performed lookup, delete and insert operations.

Finally, we integrated all the blocks of the HU design (HF, *Bin Selector*, CSU and HT) and verified the correctness of all operations (lookup, insert and delete) using HSPICE. The same HSPICE level verification was performed for the traditional CAM as well.

4.3 Results and Analysis

We simulated both the HU and the traditional CAM designs in HSPICE to measure their delays, dynamic power and static power.

Table 2 reports the results as the number of entries per bin are varied (Column 1). Results are shown for each operation (lookup, insert, and delete). The dynamic power increases proportionally as the number of entries per bin increases. The evaluation delay of SRAM cells in the delete operation (Column 6) is not applicable, since the delete operation writes a logic '0' to the *valid* bit of the corresponding CAM entry *only* (if the lookup atomic operation is successful). The SRAM entry is not written to in this case.

We note that the insert operation has the highest dynamic power consumption and the longest evaluation delay, compared to the lookup and delete operations, and as such, determines the worst case delay and power of the HU. For 16 entries/bin, the clock period of an insert operation (after adding a 15% guard-band due to PVT variations) is slightly lower than 720 *ps*. Hence the HU can be operated at a maximum frequency of about 1.39 *GHz*.

In Table 3, we report results for different HT sizes that were used in the architectural simulations of [1]. The different HUs utilize 12 or 16 entries per bin, with the number of bins varying from 128 to 2048.

We determine our worst case power and delay numbers assuming that one bin performs an insert operation (which was shown in Table 2 to be the slowest and most power hungry operation) and all other bins are not enabled, and consume static power.

From Table 3, we note that the area (Column 4) of the different HU designs is roughly proportional to the total HT

Entries/Bin	Operation	Pre-chg Delay (ps)		Evaluate Delay (ps)		Bin Dynamic Power (mW)
		CAM	SRAM	CAM	SRAM	
4	Insert	206.15	249.24	217.17	268.21	10.46
	Lookup			122.74	135.01	9.32
	Delete			202.73	NA	9.37
8	Insert	245.12	273.42	258.48	294.11	20.67
	Lookup			122.66	134.93	18.51
	Delete			245.90	NA	19.01
12	Insert	261.29	289.13	276.32	310.13	31.21
	Lookup			122.47	134.71	27.84
	Delete			262.81	NA	28.42
16	Insert	265.13	291.41	302.34	331.41	40.74
	Lookup			122.37	134.84	37.40
	Delete			289.27	NA	37.53

Table 2: Delay and Dynamic Power analysis of Insert, Delete, and Lookup operations in HT

HT (KB)	Bins	Entries	Area μ^2			HU Operating Speed (GHz)	Total Power (mW)			Dyn Power (mW)	
			HU	Tr.CAM	HU/Tr.CAM		HU	Tr.CAM	Tr.CAM/HU	HF+BS	CSU
8	128	16	120223.11	120117.25	1.0009×	1.39	82	389	4.74×	0.2578	0.0242
16	256	16	240347.12	240234.50	1.0005×	1.39	136	750	5.51×	0.2963	
24	512	12	360472.84	360351.74	1.0003×	1.45	224	1141	5.09×	0.3329	
32	512	16	480590.09	480468.99	1.0003×	1.39	246	1477	6.00×	0.3329	
48	1024	12	720830.96	720703.49	1.0002×	1.45	426	2261	5.31×	0.3699	
64	1024	16	961065.45	960937.98	1.0001×	1.39	464	2921	6.30×	0.3699	
96	2048	12	1441545.64	1441406.98	1.0001×	1.45	831	4501	5.42×	0.4143	
Avg.					1.00033×				5.48×		

Table 3: Area, Delay and Power analysis of HU for different configuration of HT

size (Column 1). Also, the ratio of the HU area to the area of the traditional CAM (Column 6) is almost unity, indicating that the total overhead of the HF, *Bin Selector* and CSU blocks is very small compared to the HT area. In other words, the size of the HU (on average) is only 0.033% larger than that of the traditional CAM.

Column 7 of Table 3 shows the worst case operating speed of the HU (with a 15% guard-band for PVT variations included). Note that due to the fact that we size the drivers and buffers based on the HT size, these numbers are relatively constant.

In Table 3, we note that on average, the power consumption of the HU (Column 8) is about 5.48× lower than the traditional CAM (Column 9). This is because in the HU design, exactly one bin consumes active power, and the remaining bins are static. In the traditional CAM, however, the entire CAM consumes dynamic power.

Columns 11 and 12 report the power consumption of the HF and *Bin Selector* units (Column 11) and the CSU unit (Column 12). We note that these power numbers are significantly smaller than the corresponding HT power numbers, as expected.

5. CONCLUSIONS

In this paper, we proposed the circuit design for a hardware hash unit (HU) for use as an SFU in modern microprocessors. Each bin of the HU was implemented as a CAM. We verified the correctness of all hash operations at the logic as well as the circuit level. We demonstrated an average power improvement of 5.48× for our HU design compared to a traditional CAM design. We also quantified the area, delay, and power for different HT sizes. We showed that the HU can be operated at 1.39 GHz after guard-banding for PVT variations.

References

[1] A. Fairouz, M. Abusultan, and S. P. Khatri, "A Novel Hardware Hash Unit Design for Modern Microprocessors," in *2016 IEEE 34th International Conference on Computer Design (ICCD)*, pp. 412–415, Oct 2016.

[2] M. V. Ramakrishna, E. Fu, and E. Bahcekapili, "Efficient Hardware Hashing Functions for High Performance Computers," *IEEE Transactions on Computers*, vol. 46, pp. 1378–1381, Dec 1997.

[3] K. Pagiamtzis and A. Sheikholeslami, "Content-Addressable Memory (CAM) Circuits and Architectures: A Tutorial and Survey," *IEEE Journal of Solid-State Circuits*, vol. 41, pp. 712–727, March 2006.

[4] Synopsys, Inc, "http://www.synopsys.com."

[5] Predictive Technology Model, "http://ptm.asu.edu."

[6] F. Yamaguchi and H. Nishi, "Hardware-based hash functions for network applications," in *2013 19th IEEE International Conference on Networks (ICON)*, pp. 1–6, Dec 2013.

[7] N. Hua, E. Norige, S. Kumar, and B. Lynch, "Non-crypto Hardware Hash Functions for High Performance Networking ASICs," in *Architectures for Networking and Communications Systems (ANCS), 2011 Seventh ACM/IEEE Symposium on*, pp. 156–166, Oct 2011.

[8] B. Baldwin, A. Byrne, L. Lu, M. Hamilton, N. Hanley, M. O'Neill, and W. P. Marnane, "A hardware wrapper for the SHA-3 hash algorithms," in *Signals and Systems Conference (ISSC 2010), IET Irish*, pp. 1–6, June 2010.

[9] A. Satoh, "ASIC hardware implementations for 512-bit hash function Whirlpool," in *2008 IEEE International Symposium on Circuits and Systems*, pp. 2917–2920, May 2008.

[10] R. Dobai and J. Korenek, "Evolution of Non-Cryptographic Hash Function Pairs for FPGA-Based Network Applications," in *Computational Intelligence, 2015 IEEE Symposium Series on*, pp. 1214–1219, Dec 2015.

[11] Y. k. Lai and G. T. Byrd, "Stream-Based Implementation of Hash Functions for Multi-Gigabit Message Authentication Codes," in *2006 Seventh International Conference on Parallel and Distributed Computing, Applications and Technologies (PDCAT'06)*, pp. 150–155, Dec 2006.

[12] Y. Du, G. He, and D. Yu, "Efficient Hashing Technique Based on Bloom Filter for High-Speed Network," in *2016 8th International Conference on Intelligent Human-Machine Systems and Cybernetics (IHMSC)*, vol. 01, pp. 58–63, Aug 2016.

[13] L. Ioannou, H. E. Michail, and A. G. Voyiatzis, "High performance pipelined FPGA implementation of the SHA-3 hash algorithm," in *2015 4th Mediterranean Conference on Embedded Computing (MECO)*, pp. 68–71, June 2015.

[14] F. Kahri, H. Mestiri, B. Bouallegue, and M. Machhout, "Efficient FPGA Hardware Implementation of Secure Hash Function SHA-256/Blake-256," in *2015 IEEE 12th International Multi-Conference on Systems, Signals Devices (SSD15)*, pp. 1–5, March 2015.

[15] Y. Vizilter, V. Gorbatsevich, A. Vorotnikov, and N. Kostromov, "Real-Time Face Identification via CNN and Boosted Hashing Forest," in *2016 IEEE Conference on Computer Vision and Pattern Recognition Workshops (CVPRW)*, pp. 146–154, June 2016.

[16] J. Lin and O. Morére and J. Petta and V. Chandrasekhar and A. Veillard, "Tiny Descriptors for Image Retrieval with Unsupervised Triplet Hashing," in *2016 Data Compression Conference (DCC)*, pp. 397–406, March 2016.

[17] D. Tong, S. Zhou, and V. K. Prasanna, "High-Throughput Online Hash Table on FPGA," in *Parallel and Distributed Processing Symposium Workshop (IPDPSW), 2015 IEEE International*, pp. 105–112, May 2015.

[18] B. Salami, O. Arcas-Abella, and N. Sonmez, "HATCH: Hash Table Caching in Hardware for Efficient Relational Join on FPGA," in *2015 IEEE 23rd Annual International Symposium on Field-Programmable Custom Computing Machines*, pp. 163–163, May 2015.

[19] M. Hanna, S. Demetriades, S. Cho, and R. Melhem, "Progressive Hashing for Packet Processing Using Set Associative Memory," in *Proceedings of the 5th ACM/IEEE Symposium on Architectures for Networking and Communications Systems*, ANCS '09, (New York, NY, USA), pp. 153–162, ACM, 2009.

[20] D. K. Shedge and V. Agey, "Different Types of SRAM Chips for Power Reduction: A Survey," in *2016 3rd International Conference on Computing for Sustainable Global Development (INDIACom)*, pp. 974–979, March 2016.

[21] Perl, "http://www.perl.org."

[22] M. I. Rahman, T. Bashar, and S. Biswas, "Performance evaluation and read stability enhancement of SRAM bit-cell in 16nm CMOS," in *2016 5th International Conference on Informatics, Electronics and Vision (ICIEV)*, pp. 713–718, May 2016.

[23] NCSU EDA, "http://www.eda.ncsu.edu/wiki/FreePDK45:Contents."

[24] Cadence Design Systems, Inc, "http://www.cadence.com."

DELCA: DVFS Efficient Low Cost Multicore Architecture

Shoumik Maiti
Synopsys Inc.
Chandler, AZ, U.S.A.
shoumik.maiti@synopsys.com

Sudeep Pasricha
Colorado State University
Fort Collins, CO, U.S.A.
sudeep@colostate.edu

ABSTRACT

The energy efficiency of dynamic voltage and frequency scaling (DVFS), a popular technique used for energy and thermal management, is substantially reduced in deep sub-micron (DSM) technology nodes. This can be attributed to a limited voltage scaling range in DSM nodes as well as the observation that circuits designed for highest performance are inherently power hungry and energy inefficient at other operating points. This paper proposes a DVFS efficient low-cost multicore architecture (DELCA) for dark silicon that is energy efficient and has much lower cost and faster design cycle time compared to custom designed heterogeneous or dynamically reconfigurable multicores. We also propose a runtime flexible application degree of parallelism based scheduling scheme (FlexDoP). Experimental results indicate that DELCA + FlexDoP can improve energy efficiency by 24.4% and enhance throughput by 16.5% compared to conventional multicores for a given power budget.

Keywords: DVFS; dark silicon; multicores; run time scheduling

1. INTRODUCTION

DVFS is used to achieve high energy efficiency and reduce thermal emergencies in multicore processors across all segments of computing [1]. Typically with DVFS, the supply voltage and frequency of a processor core is lowered during the non-compute-intensive phases of a workload. But the potential power and energy savings from DVFS are substantially reduced in deep sub-micron (DSM) technology nodes because *(i)* there is reduced head-room between threshold voltage (V_{th}) and nominal (NOM) operating voltage (V_{dd}), and *(ii)* gate sizes and V_{th} of underlying circuits that are optimized for highest performance do not change with operating conditions [2], [11]. The increased design guard bands required for process variations [22], [23] in DSM also significantly reduce the energy efficiency of DVFS. One possible solution to overcome the limited DVFS headroom and increase energy efficiency in DSM nodes is to increase the voltage scaling range to encompass near threshold computing (NTC) and turbo boost (TB) modes of operation [3], [13]. It has been shown that the NTC mode of operation is highly energy efficient and TB mode realizes high throughput for a given power budget. However, cores designed to operate in NTC mode (with operating voltage close to V_{th}) are not energy efficient in the NOM and TB modes because they require higher design margin to overcome sensitivity to process variations at low operating voltages [4], [5]. Other techniques to enhance the efficiency of DVFS include using heterogeneous multicores where separate cores are used for optimal performance at various modes of operation [6] or using dynamically reconfigurable cores which change their microarchitecture based on the mode of operation [7]. However, such approaches increase the intellectual property (IP) cost, development and verification time, and substantially delay time-to-market. There has thus been an increased emphasis in the semiconductor industry to develop low cost integrated circuits due to commoditization of hardware and increased pricing pressure.

The rising power density and likelihood of thermal hotspots due to technology scaling in recent years have also caused emerging multicores to be severely power limited and given rise to the dark/dim silicon phenomenon, where a significant fraction of a chip is operated in low power mode or is shut down to satisfy the chip power budget [8]. Technology scaling has also enabled packing of more processor cores on a chip, which introduces a new paradigm to optimize energy efficiency and throughput in multicores: by exploiting the degree of parallelism (DoP) of applications [9].

This paper addresses the unique challenge of designing ultra-low cost multicore processors that opportunistically use the dark silicon chip budget and DSM transistor characteristics to achieve high DVFS efficiency and also reduce the time-to-market. We propose a novel DVFS efficient low-cost multicore architecture (*DELCA*) that uses homogeneous cores for TB, NOM and low voltage (LV) modes of operation, where the cores are synthesized separately for each operating mode to achieve energy efficiency across the extended DVFS range. We select the lowest voltage of our DVFS range well below the NOM voltage but higher than NTC to reduce high design margins required for NTC operation [7]. We use the extra transistor budget due to dark silicon to provision the multicore system with banks of energy efficient cores specially synthesized for TB, NOM, and LV modes of operation and use them based on the power and performance requirements of incoming applications at runtime. With *DELCA*, there is no need to design special heterogeneous or reconfigurable cores for different modes of operation, which significantly reduces development time and IP cost. As we will see later, *DELCA* also does not require expensive per core DVFS controllers as each bank of cores operates at a fixed voltage and frequency and still achieves significant improvement in energy efficiency and throughput over conventional multicore systems. We also propose a system level flexible DoP application scheduling framework (FlexDoP) for use with *DELCA* that selects the available cores from TB/NOM/LV banks and picks the optimal DoP of incoming applications at runtime to achieve high energy efficiency and throughput for a given power budget. Our novel contributions in this paper are as follows:

- We present a CAD flow to synthesize homogeneous cores from the ground up that significantly enhances the DVFS efficiency in the extended LV to TB range of operation;
- We devise a low cost and DVFS efficient DELCA architecture targeted towards dark silicon which achieves substantial energy efficiency and throughput enhancement without the overheads of designing special heterogeneous or dynamically reconfigurable cores, or per core voltage regulators and synchronization FIFOs of fine-grained DVFS systems;
- We also design a system-level flexible DoP runtime scheduling framework (FlexDoP) for use with DELCA that selects available cores from the TB/NOM/LV banks and also selects the op-

Permission to make digital or hard copies of all or part of this work for personal or classroom use is granted without fee provided that copies are not made or distributed for profit or commercial advantage and that copies bear this notice and the full citation on the first page. Copyrights for components of this work owned by others than ACM must be honored. Abstracting with credit is permitted. To copy otherwise, or republish, to post on servers or to redistribute to lists, requires prior specific permission and/or a fee. Request permissions from Permissions@acm.org.
GLSVLSI '17, May 10-12, 2017, Banff, AB, Canada
© 2017 ACM. ISBN 978-1-4503-4972-7/17/05…$15.00
DOI: http://dx.doi.org/10.1145/3060403.3060422

timal DoP of incoming applications at runtime to enhance energy efficiency and throughput for a given power budget;

- Lastly, we quantify the benefits of DELCA + FlexDoP over conventional DVFS systems for PARSEC [10] benchmarks.

2. RELATED WORK

There are several prior works that focus on enhancing the efficiency of DVFS in multicores. Khang et al. [11] propose context aware multi-mode synthesis, micro-architectural changes, and selective block replication to achieve energy efficiency in the DVFS operating range. However context aware multi-mode design does not possess the full benefits of a ground up core synthesis targeted for different operating points. Moreover micro-architectural changes increase design and verification cost, and increase time-to-market. Gopireddy et al. [7] propose voltage scalable cores that operate in an energy efficient manner across the DVFS range by using different voltages for storage and logic elements and a pipeline architecture that dynamically reconfigures during low performance mode of operation. This variable latency pipeline also increases the development cost and time-to-market. Maiti et al. [3] and Cai et al. [13] have studied the efficiency of extended range DVFS encompassing the TB and NTC mode of operation with process variation aware thread to core mapping in multicores with fine grained voltage frequency control. But as the cores are not optimized for each mode of operation the energy savings are sub optimal and the per core voltage/frequency control increases the design cost.

Heterogeneous multicores [6] and application specific co-processors have also been proposed to improve the energy efficiency of computation. Both of these approaches increase the IP cost of a chip and design and verification overheads. Moreover application specific cores are not energy efficient for other computations beyond which they are specially designed. Chakraborty et al. [2] proposed homogenous cores synthesized for specific operating conditions in a multicore system. However their work does not consider the extended DVFS range encompassing the TB and LV mode and dark silicon transistor budget. Bokhari et al. [12] propose replication of voltage/frequency optimized routers in networks-on-chip (NoCs) and using the most energy efficient router at runtime based on traffic load. But such replication complicates wire routing and flow control. Kapadia et al. [24] and Raparti et al. [25] studied reliability issues in dark silicon DSM technology nodes.

To the best of our knowledge, this is the first work that targets the design of ultra-low cost and fast time-to-market energy efficient multicore processors for the dark silicon era. DELCA uses the dark silicon budget to add energy efficient cores synthesized for target operating points. At runtime, cores and DoP of incoming applications are selected to achieve high energy efficiency and throughput. Our approach has much lower cost and development cycle time than heterogeneous multicores or dynamic reconfigurable processors.

The rest of the paper is organized as follows. Section 3 gives the details of the CAD flow to design energy efficient homogeneous cores for an extended DVFS range. Section 4 describes our proposed *DELCA* multicore architecture. Section 5 explains the FlexDoP runtime scheduling framework for *DELCA*. Section 6 presents the experimental results and Section 7 concludes the paper.

3. HOMOGENEOUS DVFS CORE SYNTHESIS

A DVFS-capable processor core needs to work reliably at all voltage-frequency operating points in the DVFS range. In a conventional design flow, a DVFS core is synthesized to ensure that it meets the timing constraints at the highest performance (highest voltage and frequency operating point) and the lower voltage and frequency operating points in the DVFS scaling range are selected such that all the required timing constraints are met at these conditions. However the speed of each timing path scales differently with voltage. This scaling depends on the logic depth, type of threshold voltage (V_t) and gate lengths of cells in the timing path and the length of interconnects. Due to these dependencies, the critical timing path changes in each mode of operation [11]. The performance of a DVFS-capable core designed using a conventional synthesis flow is sub-optimal at lower voltage and frequency.

To obtain the best performance at all operating points, EDA vendors have developed a multi-corner multi-mode (MCMM) synthesis flow where all the design operating modes and timing constraints are made available to the synthesis tool and the design is optimized simultaneously for all operating conditions [14]. The design obtained using an MCMM synthesis flow is also not energy optimal at different operating points, compared to the DVFS-capable cores that are synthesized specifically for the operating condition, due to the mix of cell sizes and V_t which DVFS cannot alter.

Table 1: Percentage of Low V_t (LVT) cells, avg. drive strength, and power saved using targeted synthesis for various voltage/frequency operating points with a 16nm FinFET standard cell library

Operating point	Mode	% of LVT cells	Avg. drive strength	% Power saved
1.1V 4.0 GHz	TB	28.70	1.54	-
0.88V 3.0 GHz	-	9.32	1.44	17.67
0.80V 2.5 GHz	NOM	6.87	1.36	26.21
0.72V 2.0 GHz	-	5.67	1.40	38.4
0.64V 1.5 GHz	-	8.67	1.67	35.14
0.59V 1.0 GHz	LV	9.68	1.79	32.70

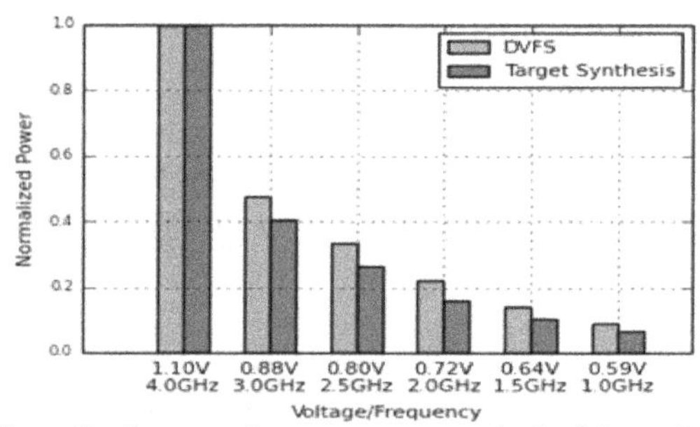

Fig. 1: Normalized power of processor core synthesized for various target operating points vs. applying DVFS on core synthesized for highest performance operating point as done in conventional synthesis flows

To highlight the inefficiency of a conventional synthesis flow for DVFS-capable cores, we have synthesized a proprietary ARM® NEON™ [15] like core used in the ARM® Cortex®-A8 [16] processor using commercial 16nm FinFET standard cell library with multi-V_t cells. We have used Synopsys® Design Compiler Graphical™ [17] to synthesize for operations across the extended DVFS range from 1.1V (TB mode) to 0.59V (LV mode) and employed Synopsys® PrimeTime PX™ [18] to analyze power.

Table 1 and Figure 1 summarize the synthesis results. Table I shows that the core synthesized for highest performance (TB mode) has a higher number of low V_t cells (28.70%) compared to the same core synthesized for lower performance LV mode (9.68%). The low V_t cells have higher leakage than standard and high V_t cells. The average drive strength (taken from standard cell library) in the high performance (TB) mode is also significantly higher than for cores synthesized for other DVFS operating points (NOM mode). Cells with higher drive strength dissipate more dynamic and leakage power than low drive strength cells. Figure 1 shows that a significant amount of power (17.67% - 38.40%) may be saved by synthesizing cores for each operating point in the DVFS spectrum, instead of applying DVFS on a core that is synthesized for highest performance, as done in conventional synthesis flows. This is due to the fact that DVFS cannot change underlying circuits. Cores synthesized for higher performance have higher drive strength cells which affects both the dynamic and leakage power. Such cores also have a considerably higher percentage of low V_t cells that increase leakage power, which is a significant portion of total power in DSM nodes.

Table 1 also shows that the average drive strength in the cores synthesized for lower performance (e.g., LV mode) is higher, to achieve the desired performance at the lower operating voltage. This is because the speed of CMOS transistors does not scale proportionally with voltage but the delay degrades much rapidly beyond a certain voltage. However the netlists in LV mode still have a significantly lower percentage of low V_t cells than the high performance TB mode that results is substantial savings in leakage power.

In summary from our synthesis experiments we conclude that significant improvements in energy efficiency may be achieved if we can include cores synthesized for each operating point in a DVFS capable multicore processor. This is the premise of our proposed DELCA architecture that is described in the next section.

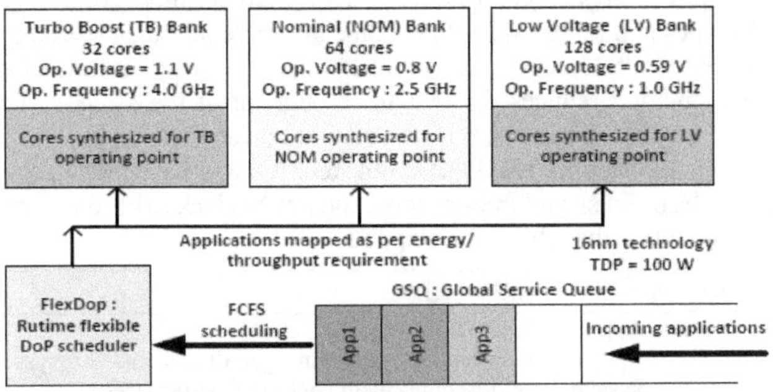

Fig. 2: Proposed DELCA + FlexDoP architecture

4. PROPOSED DELCA ARCHITECTURE

The DVFS Efficient Low Cost Multicore Architecture (*DELCA*) aims to: *(i)* increase DVFS efficiency by using energy optimal cores for each operating point; *(ii)* effectively use the dark silicon budget in deeply scaled technology nodes to provision cores for energy efficiency across different operating points while eliminating costly per-core DVFS controllers; and *(iii)* provide a lower-cost, faster time-to-market, and more energy efficient solution than expensive custom heterogeneous or dynamically reconfigurable core designs.

As discussed earlier, the increased power density in DSM technology nodes has led to the dark/dim silicon phenomenon where an increased fraction of the chip is shut-down/run at a low power mode to meet the chip thermal design power (TDP) budget. It is observed in [8] that about 50% of the chip needs to be powered off in 8nm technology to meet the power budget. While there is some improvement after transitioning to FinFET technology from planar bulk CMOS, dark silicon still accounts for a significant chip area [19]. This provides an interesting opportunity to effectively use the dark silicon budget to develop low cost DVFS-efficient multicores.

In DELCA, we propose to use replication of homogeneous cores synthesized for TB, NOM, and LV modes of operation (as described in Section 3) to substantially increase the DVFS efficiency in DSM technology nodes. We use the available dark silicon budget to provision the multicore processor with banks of homogeneous cores specially synthesized for TB, NOM, and LV modes of operation. The details of the architecture are illustrated in Fig. 2. The global service queue (GSQ) buffers all the incoming applications and a global runtime scheduler (FlexDoP, discussed in more detail in Section 5) selects the degree of parallelism (DoP) for incoming applications and maps the applications to the available cores.

The synthesis of cores for specific operating points enables DELCA multicore processors to achieve high energy efficiency across the entire DVFS range without the overhead of custom design. Several prior works have suggested the use of heterogeneous multicores and also use of dynamic reconfigurable cores to enhance the DVFS efficiency. These techniques have been widely adopted and have good use in specialized applications. However this substantially increases the IP cost and time-to-market because of increased design and verification effort for each specialized processor core and thus the approach is not suitable for low-cost applications.

It should also be noted that DELCA does not need any expensive per core voltage regulators, DVFS controllers, and synchronization FIFOs that are common in fine grained DVFS systems. Each bank (NTB/NOM/LV) works at a specific voltage and frequency and needs only a single voltage regulator and clock generator per bank. As the applications are only mapped within a single bank, there is no need to include synchronization FIFOs between the cores of banks. This further simplifies the design and reduces cost. DELCA addresses this pressing need for low-cost and faster time-to-market multicore architectures designed for energy efficiency.

Table 2: Baseline core architecture in DELCA

Parameters	Values
Core Model	Intel®-X86 Gainestown®
L1 Caches	Private 32 KB, 4-way SA, LRU
L2 Caches	Private 256 KB, 4-way SA, LRU
L3 Caches	Shared 32 MB, 16-way SA, LRU
Technology	16 nm FinFET

The choice of 3 banks is motivated by the potential percentage of dark silicon in DSM nodes [8], [19]. Higher energy savings may be obtained by adding more banks with finer voltage/frequency control but this would increase the amount of dark silicon. The number of cores in TB, NOM, and LV banks is selected based on the baseline core power at these operating modes and an available chip TDP budget of 100 Watts. Table 2 describes the baseline core architecture. The TB bank is provisioned with 32 cores, NOM bank is provided with 64 cores, and the LV bank has 128 cores. TB cores are useful to maximize throughput for time critical applications for a given power budget. These cores can also be used to execute serial applications which do not benefit from increasing DoP. The applications that benefit from moderate parallelism and have relaxed deadlines are ideal for NOM banks to achieve high throughput and good energy efficiency. The large number of cores in the LV bank in DELCA can be used to execute applications in an energy efficient and highly parallel manner, without sacrificing throughput.

From the discussion above, to fully exploit the DELCA architecture, there is a need for a runtime scheduling framework that can select the DoP of incoming applications and map them to the appropriate cores in the TB/NOM/LV banks, to achieve throughput and energy targets as well as ensuring that the dark silicon TDP budget is not violated. We propose a runtime scheduler (FlexDoP) to address this need. This scheduler is discussed in the next section.

5. FLEXDOP SCHEDULING FRAMEWORK

5.1 Motivation for DoP based scheduling

The execution of multi-threaded workloads has become common with the widespread adoption of multicore processors. Increasing the degree of parallelism (DoP or number of threads) for an application does not necessarily improve performance. At higher DoPs, the serial part of the application tends to dominate the execution time and inter-thread communication affects its energy efficiency.

To analyze the impact of DoP on application performance and energy efficiency, we profiled several PARSEC benchmarks on our baseline core architecture from Table 2. Figures 3(a)-(b) show the normalized execution time and normalized energy of five PARSEC benchmarks with DoP varying from 2 to 32 on our baseline cores. The execution time and energy of higher DoPs have been normalized with respect to the baseline DoP of 2. We used the Sniper [20] architectural simulator for this study and power numbers are obtained from the McPAT tool [21]. It can be observed that for some PARSEC benchmarks such as *blackscholes* and *canneal*, the execution time and energy reduces with increasing DoP as these applications benefit from parallelization and the minimum execution time and energy is obtained for a DoP of 32. However for other benchmarks such as *streamcluster* and *swapoptions*, the execution time and energy metrics deteriorate as DoP increases beyond a certain value, due to increased communication overheads between threads. The *streamcluster* benchmark achieves the minimum execution time at a DoP of 8 and minimum energy consumption at a DoP of 4. Similarly, *swapoptions* attains a minimum execution time and energy at DoP of 16 on the target architecture. The serial part of the application dominates in the *freqmine* benchmark where execution time and the energy progressively deteriorates with increasing DoP.

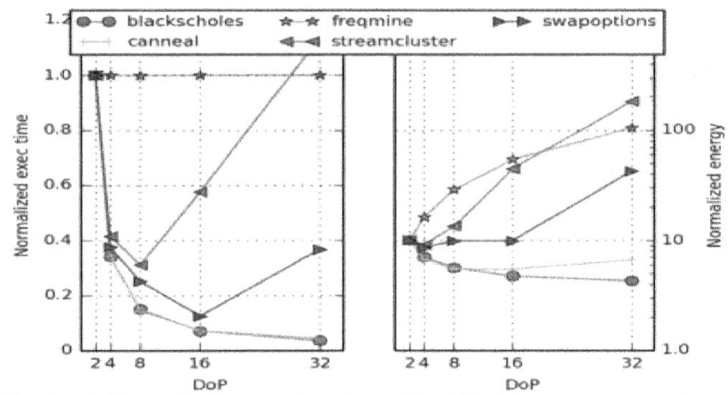

Fig. 3: (a) Normalized execution time of PARSEC benchmarks vs. DoP on baseline core architecture; (b) Normalized energy consumption of PARSEC benchmarks vs. DoP; on baseline core architecture

From these results, it can be concluded that for each application, there is an optimal DoP for highest performance and an optimal DoP for the best energy efficiency. This observation motivates us to develop the FlexDoP runtime scheduler that works on the DELCA architecture to select the DoP of incoming applications and map them to the available cores in the TB/NOM/LV banks, with the aim of achieving maximum throughput for time critical applications and minimum energy for applications that have relaxed deadlines.

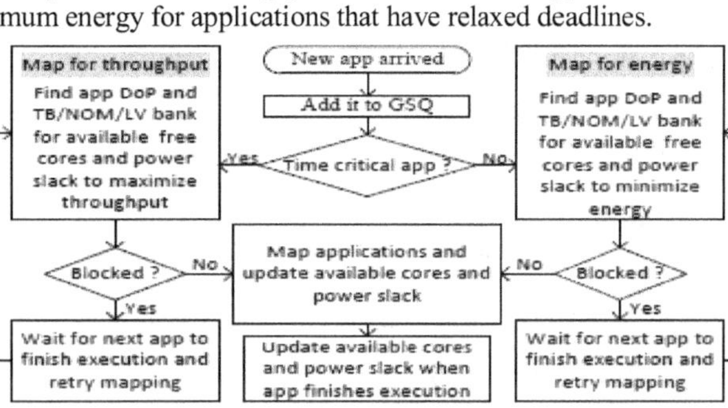

Fig. 4: FlexDoP runtime scheduler

5.2 FlexDoP Runtime Scheduling Framework

All incoming parallel applications in DELCA are buffered in the global service queue (GSQ; Figure 2). The FlexDoP runtime scheduler processes the applications from the head of service queue on a first come first serve (FCFS) basis. The applications are restricted to be scheduled in only one of the TB/NOM/LV banks, which ensures that all the threads of a job are run at the same frequency, thereby eliminating the need for synchronization between the banks. The FlexDoP runtime scheduler keeps track of the available cores in each of the three banks and also the available power slack based on the fixed TDP budget. The scheduler is assumed to have access to application profile information related to the execution time and average power dissipation of each application on the TB/NOM/LV banks of DELCA for the DoPs of 2, 4, 8, 16 and 32. Each application also has a parameter that indicates if it is time critical or not.

Figure 4 summarizes the operation of the FlexDoP scheduler. At runtime, FlexDoP picks the application at the head of the GSQ. If the application is time critical, FlexDoP finds the best combination of application DoP and the corresponding available cores from the TB/NOM/LV banks such that throughput is maximized. If the application is not time critical, FlexDoP selects the best combination of application DoP and free cores to minimize energy.

It should be noted that FlexDoP finds the best DoP for the application being mapped at runtime on the target architecture. This depends on the applications that are in progress as they impact the free cores and available power slack. FlexDoP maps the application to maximize throughput or minimize energy based on application type as soon as a valid mapping can be done that does not violate the TDP. While it may be possible to obtain better throughput or energy efficiency for the application being mapped if FlexDoP waits for more cores of certain types and power slack to become available and then selecting a different DoP. However, this typically increases the wait time of applications and reduces the overall throughput of the system. If no cores are available or there is not enough power slack to map the incoming application, FlexDoP is blocked. It waits for enough scheduled jobs to finish and free-up cores and power slack to become available such that the job can be mapped.

Algorithm 1: Map for throughput

```
inputs: App from head of GSQ
        App profile: exec. time, power info for all DoP and core types
        System State: free cores in all banks and power slack

blocked ← true , maxTpDoP ← null, maxTpBank ← null
maxThroughput ← 0, mapPower ← null
for bank in {TB,NOM,LV} :
    for dop in {2,4,8,16,32} :
        if (cores available and mapping power < power slack) :
            if (throughput for this mapping > maxThroughput) :
                maxTpDoP ← dop, maxTpBank ← bank
                blocked ← false
                maxThroughput ← throughput for this mapping
                mapPower ← power for this mapping

outputs: blocked, maxTpDoP (app DoP), maxTpBank (bank to which
         app is mapped) , mapPower (power for this mapping)
```

Algorithm 2: Map for energy

```
inputs: App from head of GSQ
        App profile: exec. time, power info for all DoP and core types
        System State: free cores in all banks and power slack

blocked ← true , minEnDoP ← null, minEnBank ← null
minEnergy ← ∞, mapPower ← null
for bank in {TB,NOM,LV} :
    for dop in {2,4,8,16,32} :
        if (cores available and mapping power < power slack) :
            if (energy for this mapping < minEnergy) :
                minEnDoP ← dop, minEnBank ← bank
                blocked ← false
                minEnergy ← energy for this mapping
                mapPower ← power for this mapping

outputs: blocked, minEnDoP (app DoP), minEnBank (bank to which
         app is mapped), mapPower (power of this mapping)
```

Algorithms 1 and 2 summarize the map for throughput and map for energy mapping schemes used by FlexDoP (Figure 4). If there are N_b banks in the system and N_d possible DoPs for applications our mapping algorithm requires $O(N_b \cdot N_d)$ comparisons to select the DoP and banks. In the case of DELCA, N_b is 3 and we assume a maximum value of N_d to be 5. Thus we need to perform at most 15 comparisons before application mapping, which makes our approach very feasible for fast runtime implementation. Our algorithm is also very scalable for higher number of core banks and application DoP counts.

6. EXPERIMENTS

6.1 Experimental setup

We evaluate a DELCA processor with three separate banks of cores (one bank each for TB, NOM, and LV modes of operation) as shown in Figure 2. The baseline core architecture is as described in Table 2, with a private L1, L2 cache per core, and a shared L3 last level cache (LLC). The cores in each bank are synthesized and hardened for their respective target operating conditions, for energy efficiency. The TB bank has 32 cores, NOM bank has 64 cores, and the LV bank has 128 cores. Each bank operates at a fixed voltage and frequency as follows: *(i)* TB core: V_{dd} = 1.1V and F = 4.0 GHz; *(ii)* NOM core: V_{dd} = 0.8V and F = 2.5 GHz and *(iii)* LV core: V_{dd} = 0.59V and F = 1.0 GHz. We also account for voltage level shifters and synchronizing FIFOs between the shared L3 cache and the banks. A 2D mesh NoC is used to communicate between the cores in each bank. The incoming applications are mapped on a single bank, so there is no communication overhead between the banks for any mapped application. The application also stays in the same bank for its entire execution and hence there is no latency due to task migration or dynamic change of voltage and frequency. To save power, unused cores are kept in deep sleep mode.

The following PARSEC [10] benchmarks are used in our simulation based analysis: *blackscholes, bodytrack, canneal, deadup, facesim, ferret, fluidanimate, freqmine, raytrace, streamcluster, swapoptions, vips* and *x264*. Each PARSEC benchmark is profiled on the base NOM cores of DELCA (Table 2) for the 16nm technology node. The execution time and power numbers on NOM cores for DoPs of 2, 4, 8, 16 and 32 are obtained using Sniper [20] micro architectural simulations and McPAT [21] respectively. The simulation time and power numbers on other cores are obtained using the frequency differences and power scaling factors obtained from synthesis experiments (similar to as discussed in section 3).

For our experiments, we generated a workload consisting of a random sequence of 1000 PARSEC benchmark applications. We varied the arrival time of the applications to simulate high, medium and low loading of the multicore system. During fast arrival (high loading) the applications arrive randomly much faster than their mean best case execution time. For medium arrival (medium loading) the applications arrive randomly at the rate of mean execution time. Similarly, for slow arrival (low loading) the applications arrive randomly much slower than their worst case execution time. For each arrival rate we have also generated three separate set of workloads of 1000 random applications where *(i)* none of the applications are time critical and all are mapped for energy efficient execution; *(ii)* 50% of the applications are time critical and are mapped for throughput and the remaining 50% are mapped for energy efficiency; and *(iii)* all applications are time critical and mapped for throughput. The dark silicon TDP budget was assumed to be 100W.

6.2 Experimental results

For comparison purposes, we created a reference system called *DVFSM* where all cores of *DELCA* are replaced by highest performance TB cores (i.e., all the cores are synthesized and hardened for the TB target operating mode). This reference system represents the approach used in conventional state-of-the-art homogenous DVFS-based systems with extended range DVFS as discussed in [3], [13]. The energy consumption and application service time of our proposed *DELCA* architecture are compared with *DVFSM* for workloads with fast/mid/slow application arrival and mixed time criticality. All application mappings are performed using the FlexDoP runtime scheduler for both *DELCA* and *DVFSM*. For a fair comparison, *DVFSM* is assumed to have the same number of cores as *DELCA*, operating at TB/NOM/LV modes and with the same TDP of 100W. The cores in *DVFSM* are not synthesized for target operating conditions (synthesized for TB mode); instead the cores use DVFS to operate at NOM/LV modes.

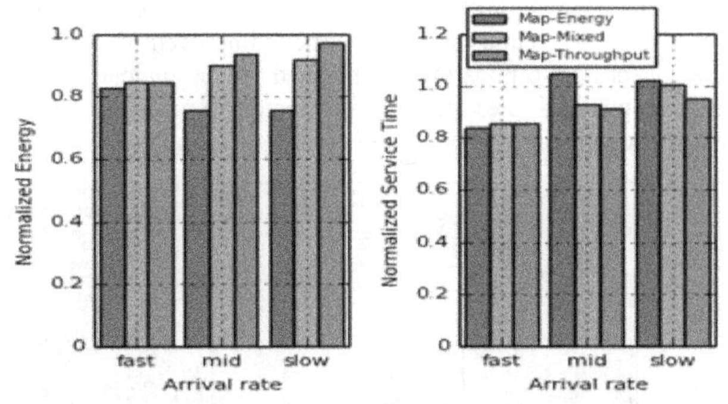

(a) (b)

Fig. 4: (a) Normalized energy of DELCA Vs DVFSM (b): Normalized Service Time of DELCA Vs DVFSM

Figure 4(a) compares the energy consumption of DELCA with that of DVFSM for the three workloads consisting of 1000 randomly selected PARSEC benchmarks, for fast, mid and slow arrival rates and mixed time criticality. The energy consumption numbers for *DELCA* in the figure are normalized with respect to that of *DVFSM*. The first bar in the clustered bar plot represents the case when all of the applications are non-time critical and mapped for energy efficiency. The second bar is for mixed time critical applications where 50% of the applications are mapped for energy efficiency and the other 50 % are mapped for throughput. All the applications in the third bar are time critical and mapped for throughput.

The cores in *DELCA* are more energy efficient than DVFSM as they are synthesized separately for different target operating conditions. When all the applications are mapped for energy, *DELCA* is 17.7% more energy efficient than DVFSM for fast application arrival rate and 24.2% and 24.4% more energy efficient than *DVFSM* for mid and low application arrival rates respectively. At a lower application arrival rate, more applications may be mapped on energy efficient NOM/LV cores in *DELCA* as they become available more frequently than for high application arrival rates. For a high application arrival rate, *DELCA* is still 15.2% more energy efficient than *DVFSM* when all applications are mapped for throughput. As TB cores are not always available when mapping for throughput and when application arrival rate is high, some applications end up using energy efficient NOM/LV cores. However when all applications are mapped for throughput for a low application arrival rate, more applications are mapped to TB cores and energy usage in *DELCA* is similar to *DVFSM*. Note that the TB mode cores are the same in *DELCA* and *DVFSM*.

Figure 4(b) compares the average service time of an application (service time is defined as the sum of wait time in the global service queue and the run time for the applications) in the *DELCA* architecture with respect to *DVFSM* for the three workloads consisting of 1000 randomly selected PARSEC benchmarks, for fast, mid and slow arrival rates and mixed time criticality. The service time numbers for *DELCA* in the figure are normalized with respect to that of *DVFSM*. The order of bars in the clustered bar graph follows the same order for application mapping as in Figure 4(a).

DELCA achieves 16.5% improvement in service time compared to *DVFSM* when all applications are mapped for energy and 14.9% improvement in service time when all applications are mapped for throughput for fast application arrival rate. During fast application arrival, the lower power of NOM/LV cores in *DELCA* compared to cores operated at NOM/LV modes via DVFS in *DVFSM* enables more applications to run simultaneously in *DELCA* for a given TDP budget. This in turn reduces the wait times and hence the total service time of the applications. It should be noted that the service improvement is achieved despite the TB/NOM/LV cores running at the same frequencies in both *DELCA* and *DVFSM*. For a medium (mid) application arrival rate, *DELCA* cores are able to cut down on the wait time of the applications and the service time is improved by 8.7% from *DVFSM* for applications that are mapped for throughput. For slow application arrival rates, there are not enough applications to run in parallel, so the service time of *DELCA* is similar to that of *DVFSM*.

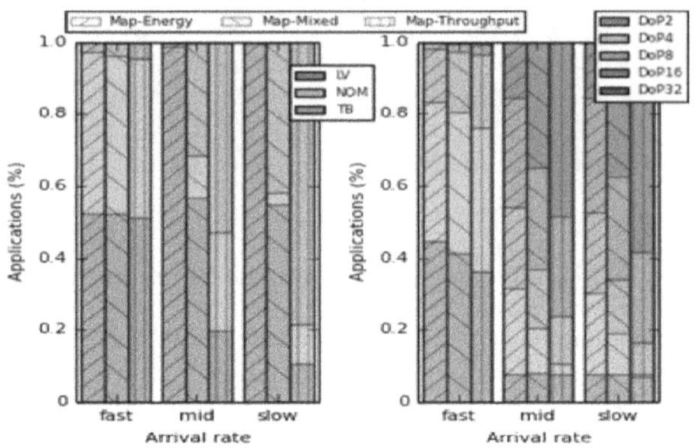

(a) (b)

Fig. 5: (a) Core usage in *DELCA* with FlexDoP scheduling (b) DoP usage in *DELCA* with FlexDoP scheduling

To gain more insights into the performance with our proposed *DELCA* architecture, we analyzed the usage of different types of cores from the TB/NOM/LV banks and the use of different application DoPs by FlexDoP for the workloads with fast/mid/slow arrival and mixed time criticality. Figure 5(a) gives the details of the core usage in *DELCA* with FlexDoP scheduling. When applications are mapped for energy, 52.5% of applications are mapped on LV cores for a fast application arrival rate and 100% of the applications are mapped on LV cores for a slow application arrival rate. This behavior is what we expect: LV cores are more preferable for energy efficient execution and more LV cores are available during mapping when applications arrive slowly. Similarly, when the applications are mapped for throughput, TB cores are preferred and as many as 78.4% of the applications are mapped on to TB cores when mapped for throughput for slow application arrival rates.

Figure 5(b) gives the details of DoP usage in *DELCA* with FlexDoP scheduling. Each application may be mapped with a DoP of 2, 4, 8, 16, or 32. For a slow application arrival rate, more cores are available during mapping and a significant fraction of the applications use higher DoPs when mapped either for energy or throughput. It can be observed that 58.3% of the applications are mapped with a DoP of 32 when mapped for throughput for a slow application arrival rate. To reduce the wait time for high application arrival rate scenarios and also due to the lower of the number of cores available during mapping, most of the applications use lower DoPs when mapped either for energy or throughput. It can be observed that 83.3% of the applications when mapped for energy and 76.2% of the applications when mapped for throughput use DoP values of 2 and 4 for fast application arrival rate scenarios.

7. CONCLUSION

Emerging multicores are severely power limited in the dark silicon era. DVFS is widely used to achieve performance goals while staying within the chip power budget. However, DVFS efficiency is steadily decreasing in DSM technology nodes due to the reduced headroom between V_{dd} and V_{th}. In addition, DVFS cannot alter the characteristics of underlying circuits designed to operate at the highest performance. There is also an increased focus in the semiconductor industry to design low cost and fast time-to-time to market multicore processors. *DELCA* addresses this unique need to develop ultra low-cost and energy efficient multicore processors that also intelligently leverages the dark silicon transistor budget. Our experimental results show that *DELCA* can achieve up to 24.4% improvement in energy efficiency and 16.5% improvement in throughput over conventional DVFS multicore architectures.

REFERENCES

[1] V. Hanumaiah et al., "Energy-efficient operation of multicore processors by dvfs, task migration, and active cooling", IEEE Trans. on Comp., Feb 2014.

[2] K. Chakraborty et al., "Architecturally Homogeneous Power-Performance Heterogeneous Multicore Systems", IEEE TVLSI, April 2013

[3] S. Maiti et al., "Process variation aware dynamic power management in multicore systems with extended range voltage/frequency scaling", MWSCAS, 2015

[4] R. Dreslinski et al., "Near-Threshold Computing: Reclaiming Moore's Law Through Energy Efficient Integrated Circuits", Proc. of IEEE, Feb. 2010

[5] S. Jain et al., "A 280mW-to-1.2V Wide-Operating-Range IA-32 Processor in 32nm CMOS", ISSCC, 2012

[6] big.LITTLE Technology: The Future of Mobile [Online] https://www.arm.com/files/pdf/big_LITTLE_Technology_the_Futue_of_Mobile.pdf

[7] Gopireddy et al., "ScalCore: Designing a core for voltage scalability", HPCA, 2016

[8] H. Esmaeilzadeh et al., "Dark silicon and the end of multicore scaling", ISCA, 2011

[9] N. Kapadia et al., "VARSHA: Variation and reliability-aware application scheduling with adaptive parallelism in the dark silicon era", DATE, 2015

[10] C. Bienna et al., "The Parsec benchmark suite: Characterization and architectural implications", PACT, 2008.

[11] A. Kahng et al., "Enhancing the Efficiency of Energy-Constrained DVFS Designs", IEEE Trans. on VLSI, Oct, 2013

[12] H. Bokhari et al., "Malleable NoC: Dark Silicon inspired adaptive Network-on-Chip", DATE, 2015

[13] E. Cai et al., "Learning-Based Power/Performance Optimization for Many-Core Systems with Extended Range Voltage/Frequency Scaling", IEEE Tran. on CAD, Aug 2016

[14] Synopsys® IC Compiler ™ User Manual [Online] http://www.synopsys.com

[15] ARM® NEON™ Core [Online] http://www.arm.com

[16] ARM® Cortex®-A8 Core [Online] http://www.arm.com

[17] Synopsys® Design Compiler Graphical™ User Manual [Online] http://www.synopsys.com

[18] Synopsys® PrimeTime PX™ User Manual [Online] http://www.synopsys.com

[19] A. Bejestan et al., "Analyzing the Dark Silicon Phenomenon in a Many-Core Chip Multiprocessor under Deeply-Scaled Process Technologies", GLSVLSI, 2015

[20] T. Carlson et al., "Sniper: Exploring the level of abstraction for scalable and accurate parallel multi-core simulations" SC, 2011

[21] S. Li et al., "The McPAT framework for multicore and manycore architectures: Simultaneously modeling power, area and timing." TACO, 2011

[22] N. Kapadia et al, "VISION: A Framework for Voltage Island Aware Synthesis of Interconnection Networks-on-Chip", GLSVLSI, 2011

[23] N. Kapadia et al, "VERVE: A Framework for Variation-Aware Energy Efficient Synthesis of NoC-based MPSoCs with Voltage Islands", ISQED, 2013

[24] N. Kapadia et al, "ARTEMIS: An Aging-Aware Run-Time Application Mapping Framework for 3D NoC based Chip Multiprocessors", NOCS, 2015

[25] V. Y. Raparti et al, "CHARM: A Checkpoint-based Resource Management Framework for Reliable Multicore Computing in the Dark Silicon Era,", ICCD, 2016

EEAL: Processors' Performance Enhancement Through Early Execution of Aliased Loads

Abhishek Rajgadia
CADSL, Department of Electrical Engineering, IIT Bombay, India
abhiraj171@gmail.com

Newton
CADSL, Department of Electrical Engineering, IIT Bombay, India
newton@ee.iitb.ac.in

Virendra Singh
CADSL, Department of Electrical Engineering, IIT Bombay, India
viren@ee.iitb.ac.in

ABSTRACT

Due to increasing speed gap between DRAM and CPU, improving the performance of memory instructions has become very critical. Load and Store instructions account for almost 20-30%. It indicates that memories have become a bottleneck in CPU's performance. Conventionally load instructions, being more critical than stores, are to be executed as early as possible. Load-Store Queues (LSQs) are used for early execution of aliased loads by forwarding them results of the executed stores. Generally memory instructions, ready to be issued from Reservation Station (RS), have their source registers available however their memory addresses are not yet known. Hence, RS cannot detect aliasing loads/stores. We propose to insert a 2nd RS after the address computation stage in the memory pipeline. The 2nd RS helps in taking data forwarding decisions based on the computed addresses of the memory instructions. If the address of a load instruction aliases with preceding store, data can be directly forwarded to it. Such forwarded loads can bypass address translation and cache access stages, leading to their early execution. Our evaluation on a 4-wide Out-of-Order (OoO) core shows that the proposed architecture outperforms the baseline architecture by up to 7.3% (avg: 2.2%) with just 0.1% area overhead and 0.05% power overhead.

Keywords

Aliased Load-Store Address Pair; Reservation Station; LSQs

1. INTRODUCTION

Since the invention of microprocessor in 1971, there has been an exponential improvement in its performance. However, in the last decade as frequency scaling has saturated due to power constraints, the pace of performance improvement of processors has slowed down [1]. DRAM's speed has also not improved much to keep the pace with CPU. Bridging the performance gap between the CPU and DRAM has become immensely important to enhance the performance of single-threaded applications.

ACM acknowledges that this contribution was authored or co-authored by an employee, contractor or affiliate of a national government. As such, the Government retains a nonexclusive, royalty-free right to publish or reproduce this article, or to allow others to do so, for Government purposes only.

GLSVLSI '17, May 10-12, 2017, Banff, AB, Canada

© 2017 ACM. ISBN 978-1-4503-4972-7/17/05...$15.00.

DOI: http://dx.doi.org/10.1145/3060403.3060445

A single-threaded application's performance can be improved executing independent instructions OoO. However, due to *true* data and memory dependencies present in the application, most of the times CPU remains idle waiting for these dependencies to get resolved. There are two types of true data dependencies that occur in a program. First is *register dependency* which occurs when an instruction writes to a register and subsequent instruction reads from the same register. Such kind of dependencies are detected at decode stage by examining the register operands of the instructions. Second is *memory dependency* which occurs when a store instruction writes to a memory location and later a load instruction reads from the same location. Such dependencies cannot be resolved at decode stage because access-addresses of memory instructions are not known while decoding. Instruction decoding of memory instruction only provides information about the registers and immediate offsets which are used at a later stage of pipeline for address computation. The addresses are calculated in memory stage of the pipeline only after instructions are issued, followed by address translation and memory access. Therefore, the instruction scheduler has no information if a load instructions can be scheduled before a preceding store instruction. If the load instruction is scheduled prior to an aliasing preceding store, it may read wrong data. Such memory-order violation leads to performance penalty. Compilers, with the capability of statically analyzing the entire program, can at times provide help in detecting aliasing loads/stores. However, even compiler cannot provide much help when the data structures used are pointers.

To avoid memory-order violations, instruction scheduler can apply a conservative approach where load and store instructions are executed inorder, however it will be a very pessimistic approach. The *load* instructions will be forced to wait till all the preceding stores are committed even if they are not dependent on the *stores*. For maximum performance, an OoO processor must detect such false dependencies and issue *load* instructions at the earliest [2]. However, at the same time it should also avoid memory-order violations with any preceding aliasing stores.

Conventionally, memory dependence predictions [3] are used which give information to the scheduler about the load instructions that are safe to schedule. Memory dependence prediction is a technique which allows load instructions to execute OoO. A memory dependence predictor uses past behaviour of load instructions to predict if a particular load instruction will alias with any prior stores. If not, the load is scheduled at the earliest. In case of incorrect prediction, memory-order violation will occur, which is detected at a later stage of the pipeline and the state of processor is recovered with a penalty of few cycles. However, memory predictors rely on past behaviors, which may change.

Our paper offers the following contributions:

1. We identify the scope of improvement in the performance of aliased loads by their early execution.
2. We present a simple yet effective micro-architecture for memory instructions to forward data from *in-flight* stores to the corresponding aliased loads.
3. Aliased loads which suffer maximum memory-order violations are identified and are handled using dynamic forwarding which reduces such violations upto 90%.

Rest of the paper is organized as follows. Section II presents the motivation behind our work. Section III elaborates on the micro-architectural changes implemented and other relevant concepts. Section IV explains the experimental framework adopted. Section V reports the experimental results. Section VI presents related work and section VII is devoted to the concluding remarks.

2. MOTIVATION

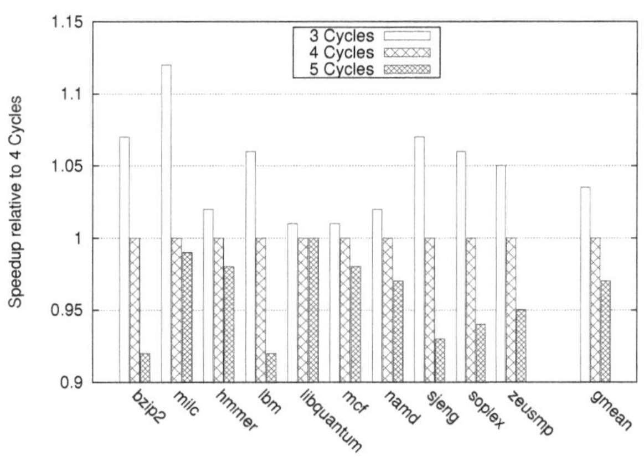

Figure 1: Effect of execution latency on performance

In load-store architecture, load and store instructions comprise of about 20-30% [4] of total instructions. Therefore, efficient execution of memory instructions is very important to improve single thread performance. Instructions do wait in RS to resolve true data dependencies and to avoid structural hazards. Memory instructions go through three stages 1) *Address Computation* 2) *Address Translation* and 3) *Memory Access.* In an OoO core only aliased memory accesses are required to be done in program order to avoid violations. Instructions should be scheduled in such a way that load instructions are executed at the earliest. One of the impediments is the load/store aliasing. A load instruction cannot be scheduled before aliased store is executed. Therefore, in order to execute load early, it is important to calculate addresses of all the earlier stores as soon as possible to check for alias.

Consider two memory instructions I1 and I2 shown below
I1: `store R3,[R2],#50`
I2: `load R1,[R2],#50`
OoO core should execute I2 at the earliest so that the dependency chain due to the load instruction I2 can get resolved early. I2 can only get executed if its operand R2 is ready and it does not alias with I1. However, I2 is aliasing with I1 as the memory location accessed by them is same. This aliasing can be detected only after *Address Computation* stage. Instruction I1 will be issued to address generation units (AGU) if both R3 and R1 are ready. If we issue both I1 and I2 when their source operand R2 is ready (only R2 is required for address computation in AGU), we will be able to detect aliasing earlier than conventional OoO processor.

As the *ready* memory instructions are waiting in RS, they can be scheduled such that their addresses can be calculated as early as possible. These calculated addresses can be used to detect aliasing load/store pairs. These computed addresses can be also used for better memory dependence predictions.

Memory predictors helps in early execution of load instructions only when it finds them not aliasing with previous pending stores. If it finds any pending aliased store, it executes stores first, holding the corresponding loads in waiting state. Such aliased loads can be executed earlier by forwarding data from the corresponding pending stores, if the addresses of loads and stores are computed earlier (to detect aliases). Loads with forwarded data do not need to access caches and Translation Lookaside Buffer (TLB) thus reducing number of cache and TLB accesses. This will also reduce stalls due to TLB misses and cache misses which are significant. However, in the conventional pipeline loads/stores have to wait in the primary RS before proceeding further to *Address Computation* stage until either their operands and data are ready or the memory predictor predicts that they will not alias. In the conventional pipeline loads can forward data from executed stores in LSQ, however stores which are in-flight are not utilized for such forwarding. For in-flight stores, neither memory predictor nor LSQ helps in early execution of corresponding aliased loads.

Memory instructions which are waiting in primary RS can be scheduled directly for *Address Computation* stage as calculated addresses can be efficiently used for finding aliases. Memory instructions with their computed address can wait in another RS (2nd RS) before their dependencies can be resolved. However, creation of 2nd RS will add an additional delay in the execution of memory instructions.

An additional cycle delay in execution of memory instruction can have serious impact on performance of processors. Our analysis on the effect of increasing or decreasing the execution latency of memory instructions by 1-cycle is done by studying 10 SPEC CPU 2006 benchmarks. The system configurations used for the study are mentioned in detail in section IV. Figure 1 shows that by decreasing the latency of execution of each memory instruction by 1-cycle, there can be improvement of up to 11.53% (average 3.45%) while increasing the execution latency by 1-cycle can cause performance loss of up to 7.57%. Thus, if we are able to decrease the execution latency of certain fraction of memory instructions, we can get significant performance gain. Improvements due to the proposed micro-architecture depends on the number of aliasing cases present in the RS. Initial study was done to find the number of such cases. Table 1 gives percentage of total instructions executed that could have bypassed the execution. As evident from our study, there is a potential for early execution of aliasing loads/stores whose dependencies can be predicted earlier in the 2nd RS to gain

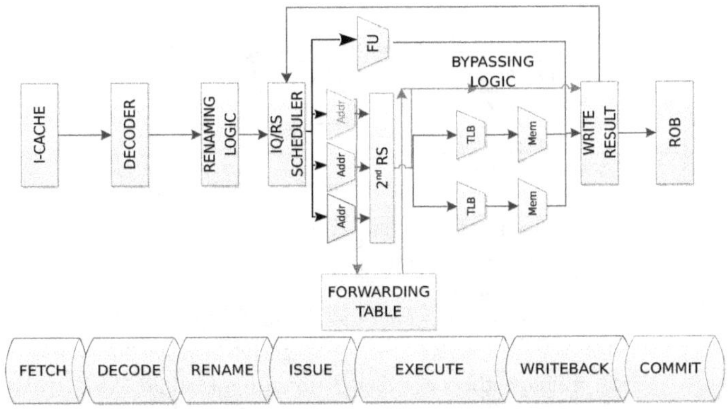

Figure 2: Proposed architecture with 2nd RS, Forwarding table and Bypass logic

performance benefits. Hence, the focus of our work is on Early Execution of Aliased Loads (EEAL).

Table 1: Potential cases for early forwarding

Benchmark	Aliasing Load/Store (%)
bzip2	2.2
mcf	1.33
lbm	0.79
milc	0.53
cactus	0.2
soplex	0.05

3. PROPOSED ARCHITECTURE

Our proposed architecture is shown in Figure 2. In order to facilitate for early address computation, we insert second RS where instructions can wait for memory access and data availability for store. There instructions from primary RS (called as RS-1) can be issued to 2nd RS (called as RS-2) as soon as operands needed for their address computation are available. After their addresses gets computed they are inserted into the RS-2. Now, these instructions present in RS-2 have their effective address known. These addresses can be used for detecting aliased loads and forwarding of data from pending store to corresponding aliased load. The advantages of RS-2 are following:

1. Since addresses are known, it can be used for forwarding data between aliased load/store pairs.

2. Due to data forwarding from stores to loads in RS-2, forwarded loads do not need to access caches and TLB thereby reducing TLB misses and cache misses.

Early Forwarding and Bypassing: In a normal OoO processor, data is forwarded from store to load in parallel to the cache access. This happens after address generation and translation. Since we have the availability of addresses of stores and loads in RS-2, we can forward data in RS-2 itself and load instruction can bypass the remaining stages of execution. The advantages of early forwarding and bypassing are as follows:

1. Loads which get forwarded data from preceding stores (called as **early-forwarded loads** from here onward) in RS-2 can bypass address translation and cache access pipeline stages. Elimination of two stages can have huge impact on performance as evident from Figure 1. It also saves power.

2. The execution units that are not used by early-forwarded loads can be used by other memory instructions. It gives an illusion of more number of execution units.

3. Memory predictor prevents issuing of loads if an aliasing preceding store is present in the RS-2 to avoid memory order violation. By early forwarding, loads do not have to suffer delay due to memory predictor.

4. Instructions dependent on early-forwarded-load can become ready early, it may have domino effect.

Forwarding Logic: Forwarding logic consists of a Forwarding table as shown in Figure 2. It has a *Valid bit*, *ROB Index*, *Data*, and *Address* per entry as shown below.

Valid	ROB Index	Address	Data

The store instructions which are issued from RS-1 are inserted into RS-2 after address computation. At the same time, the store instruction also makes an entry in the Forwarding table, indexed using LSBs of the effective address. The load instructions which are present in the RS-2, indexes into the Forwarding table using LSBs of their effective address. If the load finds a valid entry in the table at the index corresponding to it and the store is older than the load (which can be checked using ROB index), the load takes data from the table entry. When the store is issued from the RS-2, it invalidates the entry in the Forwarding table.

Dynamic Forwarding: All early-forwarded loads do not get their data from the corresponding correct stores. Correct store is the one which is the latest among the preceding aliasing stores. In case of repeated violations, it has been observed that the same static load is forwarded data from the wrong store again and again. Such cases can be identified dynamically. We can dynamically learn which loads have crossed the given threshold of wrong forwarding. This information can be communicated to the forwarding logic which will prevent early forwarding to such loads.

Bypassing Logic: The early-forwarded loads have obtained data from the Forwarding table. Hence, they do not need to perform address translation and cache/Store Queue access. Bypassing logic will send these loads directly to write-back stage, skipping the address translation and cache/store queue access. Figure 2 shows the complete architecture of the processor with RS-2, additional AGU, Forwarding table and bypassing logic. Structures bordered in red are the additional hardware added to the baseline architecture

Instruction Scheduler: The RS-2 will add additional delay for the memory instructions. As shown earlier in Figure 1, additional delay can have adverse effect on the performance. To mitigate the effect of additional stage inserted in the pipeline, instruction scheduler is changed so that all instructions do not suffer the delay. If RS-2 is empty, i.e., if there is no instruction to be scheduled for translation, the instruction coming from RS-1 after address computation is directly scheduled for translation. Thus, not all memory instructions suffer delay due to RS-2. Only those instructions which get accumulated in RS-2 due to extra AGUs get delayed which were anyways going to be scheduled later from RS-1 if there were no additional AGUs. However, such additional delays are compensated as early-forwarded loads can skip *address translation* and *cache access* stages of pipeline. In the instruction scheduler only *two* changes have been made over the conventional *Tomasulo Scheduler*

1. Directly scheduling store instruction from RS-1 to AGU when registers required for its address computation are ready.
2. If RS-2 is empty, memory instructions are directly scheduled for address translation.

In summary, the sequence followed by the memory instructions in our proposed architecture is mentioned below:

1. Load and Store instructions wait in RS-1 for their source registers to be ready. Ready loads and stores are issued from RS-1 to AGUs.
2. After their address computation in AGUs, memory instructions wait in RS-2 for further execution.
3. Store instructions make entry in the Forwarding table by indexing into it using LSBs of the address. If an entry is already present at that index, it is overwritten.
4. If there are no memory instructions waiting in RS-2, they are directly scheduled to address translation stage of the pipeline.
5. Loads waiting in the RS-2 also index into Forwarding table using LSBs of their address. If a store in the Forwarding table is older than the load and if address aliases, then the load takes data from the table.
6. If memory-order violations for a particular load increases to certain fixed threshold, early-forwarding to it is dynamically stopped.
7. All early-forwarded loads bypass address translation and cache access stages.
8. When a store gets scheduled from RS-2 to address translation stage, its corresponding entry in the Forwarding table is invalidated.
9. If the latest preceding aliasing store has already committed, the early-forwarded load can take data from wrong preceding store. The load instruction checks Store Queue for this condition and flags such violation, if any.

4. EXPERIMENTAL METHODOLOGY

4.1 Simulation Infrastructure

To simulate the proposed architecture, we used cycle accurate *gem5* [5] simulator. Power and area modeling were done using McPAT [6]. Baseline architecture, as used in [7], is a 4-wide OoO superscalar processor implementing ARM 64-bit ISA working at 2GHz. It is a 7-stage processor consisting of Fetch, Decode, Rename, Issue, Execute, Writeback and Commit stages. Detailed configuration is shown in Table 2. The baseline architecture is an aggressive architecture with 4 load/store execution units while early-forward architecture has only 2 load/store execution units. Also issue width is 6 in baseline while 4 in early-forward architecture. The memory instructions are allowed to be issued OoO based on Store Sets memory predictor [3].

Table 2: System Configuration

Parameter	Baseline	Early-fwd
Fetch width	4	
Issue width	6	4
Commit width	4	
RS	128	
Reorder Buffer	192	
Load Queue/Store Queue	32/32	
L1 inst cache	32KB, 2-way, 2-cycles	
L1 data cache	64KB, 2-way, 2-cycles	
L2 unified cache	2MB, 8-way, 20-cycles	
Branch predictor	Tournament, 4096 BTB,16 RAS	
Physical Register File	256 INT, 256 FP	
Execution units	4 INT, 2 FP units	
Memory units	4	2
Forwarding per cycle	NA	4
Extra AGU	NA	2
LFST/SSID	1024/1024	

The RS entries are freed upon issue of instructions, except memory instructions which hold the entries until completion. In early-forward architecture, entries of RS-2 are held by memory instructions until completion.

4.2 Benchmarks

For evaluation, 18 benchmarks (8 Integer and 10 Floating Point) from SPEC CPU2006 [8] benchmark suite were used. Each benchmark was fast-forwarded for 1 billion instructions and 100 million instructions were executed in detailed mode using reference inputs. All workloads were compiled for ARM 64-bit ISA using gcc 4.8.4 with full optimization (-O3).

5. RESULTS AND ANALYSIS

Figure 3 shows performance improvement compared to the aggressive baseline architecture. The graph shows normalized instructions per cycle (IPC) or speedup. The maximum performance improvement is 6.7% for *milc* and average improvement of all the benchmarks is 1.6%. There is performance enhancement as a result of early-forwarded loads which bypass TLB and cache access stages. Replay loads which now need 2-cycles to execute compared to baseline where it needs 3-cycles to execute also contribute to gain in IPC. Replay loads are those loads which are mis-speculated and needs re-execution. Such loads have their address already computed.

The early-forwarding case is also compared with a baseline having 4-wide issue with 4 load-store units (which is more closer to the proposed design) and a baseline having 4-wide issue and only 2 load-store units. Compared to the less aggressive baseline architecture, performance improvement is up to 7.32% maximum for *milc* benchmark (2.2% on average) as shown in Figure 3.

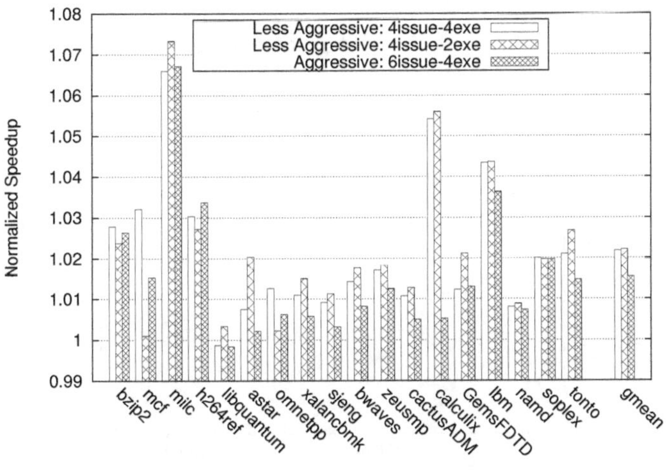

Figure 3: Performance enhancement using 2-level RS

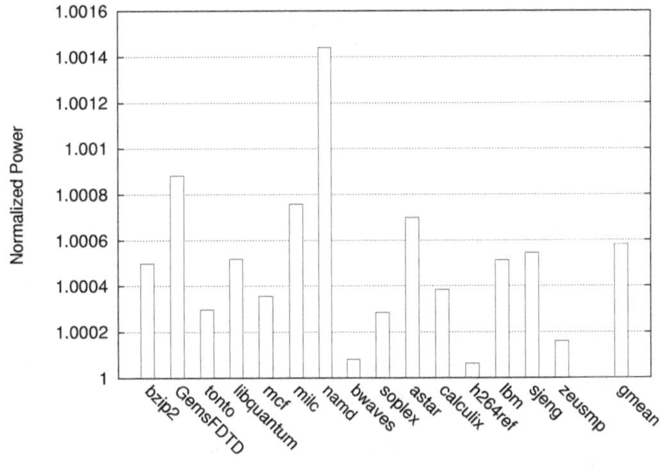

Figure 4: Power overhead with 2-level RS

5.1 Simulation data

Table 3 gives the percentage of early-forwarded loads and percentage of early-forwarded loads that got violated. On average, 2.23% of total issued loads gets early-forwarded and can bypass TLB and cache access. Maximum loads forwarded is 20.31% of total issued loads for *soplex* benchmark.

Table 3: Simulation Data

Benchmarks	% Fwd	% Fwd Violated
astar	0.00	0.00
bwaves	0.31	0.00
bzip2	4.51	0.00
cactusADM	0.00	0.00
calculix	0.11	0.00
GemsFDTD	2.38	0.00
h264ref	0.70	3.49
lbm	3.66	0.00
libquantum	1.66	0.00
mcf	0.01	1.13
milc	0.99	0.00
namd	0.59	0.14
omnetpp	0.32	1.53
sjeng	0.28	8.68
soplex	20.31	0.00
tonto	0.38	0.00
xalancbmk	3.87	0.01
zeusmp	0.01	0.00

5.2 Dynamic forwarding

As shown in Table 3, in case of *h264ref* and *sjeng*, the number of forwarded loads that got violated are 3.49% and 8.68% respectively. Analysis showed that 4 static loads in case of *h264ref* and 9 static loads in case of *sjeng* caused 90% of the violations. Dynamically such loads were identified and forwarding for them was stopped when they crossed certain threshold number of violations, 100 in this analysis. By doing so, it reduced the violations by about 90% in each case.

Figure 5 shows the IPC improvement and Figure 6 reports decrement in violations by using dynamic forwarding for *h264ref* and *sjeng* benchmarks. Performance improved by 0.5% and 0.3% by using dynamic forwarding for *h264ref* and *sjeng* benchmarks respectively.

5.3 Area and Power analysis

The extra hardware added are two AGUs, Forwarding table with 32 entries and bypassing logic. As number of stores present in RS at any time is small compared to total number instructions, Forwarding table with 32 entries is sufficient. Combined size of RS-1 and RS-2 in our proposed architecture is kept equal to the size of RS of baseline architecture for fair comparison. Small extra overhead in RS-1 is due to addition of extra ports. The area and power overhead analysis was done using McPAT [6] for 22nm technology running at 2GHz. Total area overhead is 0.1% and power overhead is 0.05% as shown is Figure 4.

6. RELATED WORK

Memory Dependence Prediction (MDP) was first proposed by Moshovos [9]. Conventionally an OoO core has a MDP to predicts if a particular load/store pair will alias. Although our approach is different than conventional memory predictors, still the focus of our work is in similar lines to that of memory dependence predictors. In [3], MDP has been proposed to issue load as early as possible, while avoiding memory-order violations. Instruction scheduler uses information about aliased loads/stores while scheduling the load instructions at the earliest. The level of aggressiveness of predictor was increased or decreased as per the characteristic of aliasing load/store pairs. Different colors have been used to represent different speculation levels as per the level of memory-order violations.

Memory-order violations can also be reduced by analyzing number of stores between a load instruction and the previous store instruction that access the same memory location, referred as Store Distance in [10]. They have used compiler to annotate instructions and pass store distance information to the micro-architecture. Their design uses store distance information to identify store upon which load depends and make safe speculations. However their technique

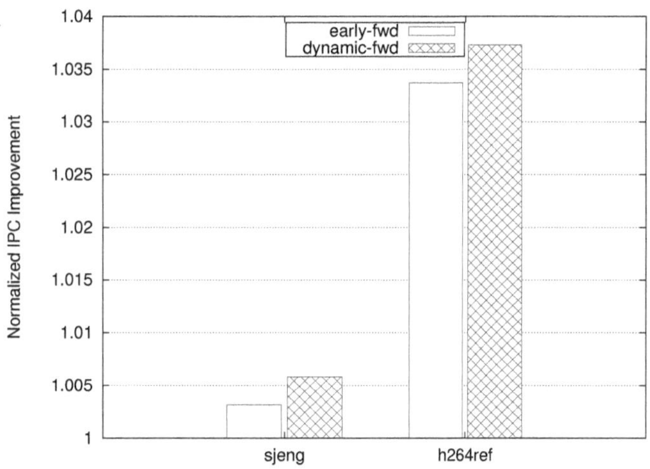

Figure 5: Performance enhancement with Dynamic Forwarding

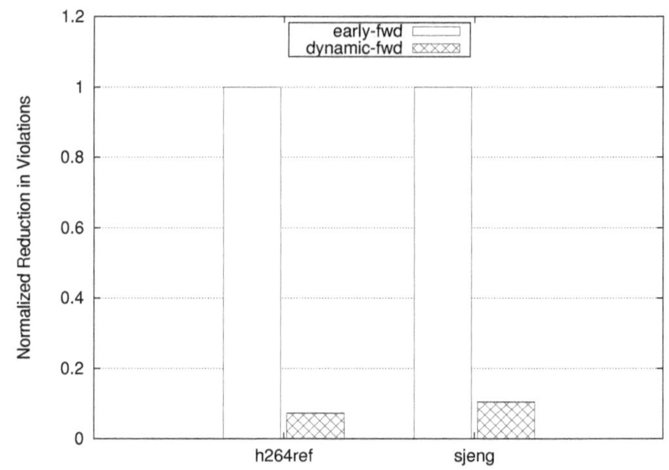

Figure 6: Violation decrement with Dynamic Forwarding

requires ISA modification as stores distances have to be encoded in load instruction. The complex design of load-store queue (LSQ) has been shown to be a bottleneck to processor's performance in [11]. A simple segmented design has been proposed in [11] to redesign the LSQ with a focus to reduce the search bandwidth demand. In [12] a storage-free MDP has been proposed. Sophisticated branch predictor has been used to predict memory dependencies, thus no separate mapped-tables have been used as in [3] to find aliased load/store pairs. However, their technique under performs when compared to [3] for some SPEC benchmarks. Our proposed technique can be used along with all the above mentioned improvisations as our technique aids MDPs by finding aliased load/store pairs using their access addresses.

7. CONCLUSION

In this work, we proposed a novel idea of using 2-level Reservation Station (RS) targeted towards improving single thread performance by early execution of aliased loads. By using 2-level RS, data can be forwarded early from store to the aliased load. We successfully decreased execution latency by early forwarding of loads and also decreased the latency for replay loads. Our analysis on SPEC CPU2006 benchmarks shows that our proposed architecture improves the performance up to 7.32% (2.2% on average) compared to less aggressive similar size baseline architecture. The power overhead is 0.05% and area overhead is 0.1%. Compared to an aggressive baseline architecture, performance improvement is up to 6.7% for *milc* benchmark (1.6% on average).

8. REFERENCES

[1] S. Borkar and A. A. Chien, "The future of microprocessors," *Communications of the ACM*, vol. 54, no. 5, pp. 67–77, 2011.

[2] S. Onder and R. Gupta, "Dynamic memory disambiguation in the presence of out-of-order store issuing," in *Proceedings of 32nd Annual International Symposium on Microarchitecture*. IEEE, 1999, pp. 170–176.

[3] G. Z. Chrysos and J. S. Emer, "Memory dependence prediction using store sets," in *ACM SIGARCH Computer Architecture News*, vol. 26, no. 3. IEEE Computer Society, 1998, pp. 142–153.

[4] J. P. Shen and M. H. Lipasti, *Modern processor design: fundamentals of superscalar processors.* Waveland Press, 2013.

[5] N. Binkert, B. Beckmann, G. Black, S. K. Reinhardt, A. Saidi, A. Basu, J. Hestness, D. R. Hower, T. Krishna, S. Sardashti, *et al.*, "The gem5 simulator," *ACM SIGARCH Computer Architecture News*, vol. 39, no. 2, pp. 1–7, 2011.

[6] S. Li, J. H. Ahn, R. D. Strong, J. B. Brockman, D. M. Tullsen, and N. P. Jouppi, "McPAT: an integrated power, area, and timing modeling framework for multicore and manycore architectures," in *Proceedings of 42nd Annual IEEE/ACM International Symposium on Microarchitecture.* IEEE, 2009, pp. 469–480.

[7] A. Perais and A. Seznec, "EOLE: Paving the way for an effective implementation of value prediction," in *ACM SIGARCH Computer Architecture News*, vol. 42, no. 3. IEEE Press, 2014, pp. 481–492.

[8] J. L. Henning, "SPEC CPU2006 benchmark descriptions," *ACM SIGARCH Computer Architecture News*, vol. 34, no. 4, pp. 1–17, 2006.

[9] A. I. Moshovos, "Memory dependence prediction," PhD dissertation, University of Wisconsin-Madison, 1998.

[10] C. Fang, S. Carr, S. Önder, and Z. Wang, "Feedback-directed memory disambiguation through store distance analysis," in *Proceedings of the 20th annual international conference on Supercomputing.* ACM, 2006, pp. 278–287.

[11] I. Park, C. L. Ooi, and T. Vijaykumar, "Reducing design complexity of the load/store queue," in *Proceedings of the 36th annual IEEE/ACM International Symposium on Microarchitecture.* IEEE Computer Society, 2003, p. 411.

[12] A. Perais and A. Seznec, "Storage-free memory dependency prediction," *IEEE Computer Architecture Letters*, 2016.

Performance-Aware Resource Management of Multi-Threaded Applications on Many-Core Systems

Daniel Olsen
Department of Electrical and Computer Engineering
Southern Illinois University, Carbondale, U.S.A

Iraklis Anagnostopoulos
Department of Electrical and Computer Engineering
Southern Illinois University, Carbondale, U.S.A

ABSTRACT

Modern computing systems employ a large number of processing elements leaving behind traditional design approaches and architectures. On the software side, this evolution in system architecture has driven rapid changes on the field of application development too, by increasing the usage of highly parallel/multi-threading and demanding applications. Thus, many-core systems raise the challenge of efficient resource management especially in cases where changes occur at run-time with a rapid pace. In this paper, a performance-aware resource management scheme for many-core architectures is presented. Particular, the developed framework takes as input parallel applications and performs an application profiling. Based on that profile information, a thread to core mapping algorithm finds (i) the appropriate number of threads that this application will have in order to maximize the utilization of the system; and (ii) the best mapping for maximizing the performance of the application. Experimental results showed that our mapping framework produces on average 23% and 18% better application turnaround time compared to another state-of-art run-time manager.

Keywords

Many-core systems; Resource management; Multi-threaded

1. INTRODUCTION AND MOTIVATION

Modern computing systems are characterized by the integration of independent homogeneous and heterogeneous processing elements in a single chip. The number of units has increased in such a way that it has formed the era of *many-core architectures* leaving behind complex superscalar and multi-core systems. This trend requires innovations both in software and hardware. Large industrial companies endorse this vision and have started to experiment and commercialize many-core computing systems. For example, Intel has already created platforms with 80, 50 and 48 processing cores [16], Tilera currently features up to 100 cores per chip and HP Inc announced "The Machine", a new heterogeneous architecture that uses small cores, photonics and memristors [14]. The industrial vision goes as far as thousand core chips [11]. This radical change of perspective, from deep-pipeline superscalar processors to many-core processors requires a global rethinking of software and hardware design approaches.

Permission to make digital or hard copies of all or part of this work for personal or classroom use is granted without fee provided that copies are not made or distributed for profit or commercial advantage and that copies bear this notice and the full citation on the first page. Copyrights for components of this work owned by others than ACM must be honored. Abstracting with credit is permitted. To copy otherwise, or republish, to post on servers or to redistribute to lists, requires prior specific permission and/or a fee. Request permissions from permissions@acm.org.

GLSVLSI '17, May 10-12, 2017, Banff, AB, Canada
© 2017 ACM. ISBN 978-1-4503-4972-7/17/05...$15.00
DOI: http://dx.doi.org/10.1145/3060403.3060426

This evolution in system architecture has driven rapid changes on the field of application development as well. Specifically, modern applications are characterized by the following features [15]: (i) They are highly parallel and compute-intensive; (ii) They are dynamic; (iii) They are variable in workload; and (iv) They impose run-time adaptivity requirements. The ability to allocate the right number of cores and to perform an efficient application mapping results in effective resource utilization and exploration of system parameters. Due to the nature of modern parallel applications, run-time resource availability may vary owed to system dynamism.

Many-core systems are designed and built in order to offer increased performance, scalability and flexibility. Traditional run-time managers are ill-suited for many-core systems and parallel applications as most of the developed methodologies were designed and implemented on top of single-core or multi-core architectures leaving underutilized the full potentials of the underlying hardware. To exploit these potential benefits, effective run-time resource management techniques are needed.

In a many-core platform, resource allocation has a spatial aspect as well. An application consists of tasks/threads that are executed in parallel and each task/thread has to be assigned to a core. In order to map applications on many-core systems, the applications need to be partitioned (parallelized) into multiple tasks/threads that can be executed concurrently on different cores [23]. Calculating a cost efficient mapping for a given application in a short amount of time is crucial. Common goals for efficient mapping techniques among others are performance maximization, minimization of inter-core communication, energy consumption, temperature, etc. Since the mapping process is an intermediate step between the request for an application to start and the actual initialization of the application, the process must be as fast as possible. Run-time resource management paradigm has been revealed as a key challenge to modern multi-core systems [1, 2] and it has become prominent due to the run-time dynamicity of modern parallel applications and platforms [3, 17]. Focusing on system's performance, a run-time thread-to-core application mapping allows the efficient usage of platform resources while meeting applications' requirements.

In this paper, a performance-aware resource management framework for parallel applications on many-core systems is presented. The proposed framework has two distinct phases: (i) A design-time; and (ii) a run-time phase. Particularly, in the design-time phase the proposed scheme takes as input parallel applications, it performs an application profiling and it classifies them based on Instructions per Cycle (IPC), temperature and power of each thread of the application. In the run-time phase, the presented framework takes an input the extracted information and employs a run-time manager which: (i) Calculates the impact of each application configuration on the system; (ii) Finds the appropriate number of threads per application in order to maximize the utilization of the system and meet the applications' requirements; (iii) Takes into consideration the status of all processing elements; and (iv) Applies an efficient thread-to-core mapping for maximizing the performance of the application under the selected number of threads.

2. RELATED WORK

Many research works have focused on run-time resource management aiming either efficient resource utilization or application optimization. The authors in [6] present a mapping in which a core is responsible to analyze the performance of the applications and find the best mapping for the tasks. Another important factor for an efficient application mapping is the topological properties of the allocated cores. Particularly, authors in [18] propose an on-the-fly application performance estimation scheme that takes into consideration the topological characteristics of the many-core platform. Topological properties are also considered in the work presented in [26] while a scheme that tries to map an application onto an optimum contiguous area of the available nodes is presented in [11]. A Divide and Conquer based distributed run-time mapping framework is presented in [2]. The authors use a matching factor value per task and assign the task to the most appropriate available processing element. A system-level run-time resource management scheme for many-core systems that focuses on the management of errors is presented in [12]. Last, authors in [1], present an agent-based framework for run-time mapping. This separation of cores into different roles/clusters has been proved as an efficient solution for many-core platforms. Authors in [17] present a distributed task mapping for parallel applications supporting also self-organization. An agent is assigned at run-time to a random core when a new application arrives having the disadvantage of a possible communication bottleneck as described in [3]. The authors extend this model in [3] and present an enhanced run-time resource management framework that takes into consideration the application speed up gain when changing the number of available resources.

Power dissipation and thermal management of a system has also been investigated in relationship to application mapping in many-core systems. A centralized thermal-aware run-time application mapping algorithm has been proposed in [28] which reduces the maximum temperature on the system while achieving low execution latency of the mapped applications. Moreover, authors in [9] have proposed a thermal aware resource management scheme that is based on information exchange between the processing elements. The authors claim that they achieve reduction in the number of on-chip hotspots. The basic idea behind the resource bargaining is a classical supply/demand model from economics. With a similar goal of thermal hot-spots reduction, distributed task migration is utilized in [10, 20] aimed at many-core microprocessors. Due to the fact that many modern many-core systems are required to take decisions fast, some approaches implement machine-learning and prediction techniques [21] such as artificial networks [13] and reinforcement learning [7] for estimating application performance and applying power optimizations respectively.

The novelty of the presented research work is threefold. Specifically, the proposed framework: (i) Employs an application profiling and classification based on Instructions per Cycle (IPC) and uniformity of IPC; (ii) Identifies the appropriate number of threads for each application in order to efficiently utilize the many-core system; and (iii) Performs an efficient performance-aware thread-to-core mapping for many-core systems while reducing the number of hotspots.

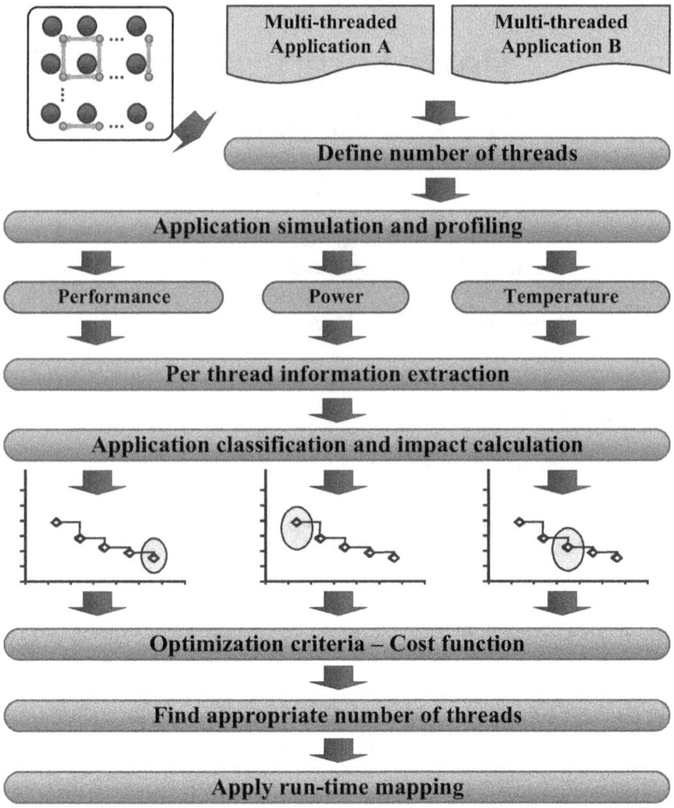

Figure 1: Overall flow of the proposed methodology

3. PROPOSED METHODOLOGY

The goal of the proposed methodology framework is to perform performance-aware mapping of application(s) on many-core systems while reducing the number of hotspots. An overview of the proposed methodology framework is presented in Figure 1. The starting point requires two inputs, the multi-threaded application(s) and the configuration of the many-core system. Then, for various number of threads, a many-core simulator is used to extract information regarding performance, power and temperature. This information is extracted at the thread level and based on it an application classification is employed. The goal of this step is to monitor, record and classify the behavior of an application in order to provide effective operation points to drive the run-time management. Applications with common characteristics can be grouped together forming a class. It is crucial to recognize the parts of the system that benefit or suffer from a specific change in order to adapt the system properly. Last, based on the properties of each class and the optimization criteria/cost function, a run-time mapping algorithm is employed in order to find: (i) The appropriate number of threads per application; and (ii) An efficient performance-aware thread-to-core mapping that satisfies the constraints of the applications.

3.1 Definitions and Problem formulation

The proposed resource management framework for many-core systems focuses on multi-threaded applications such that application threads can run in parallel on different cores. Each application $A\{TH, D_{TH}, Temp_{TH}\}$ is characterized by: (i) $TH, 1 \leq TH \leq$

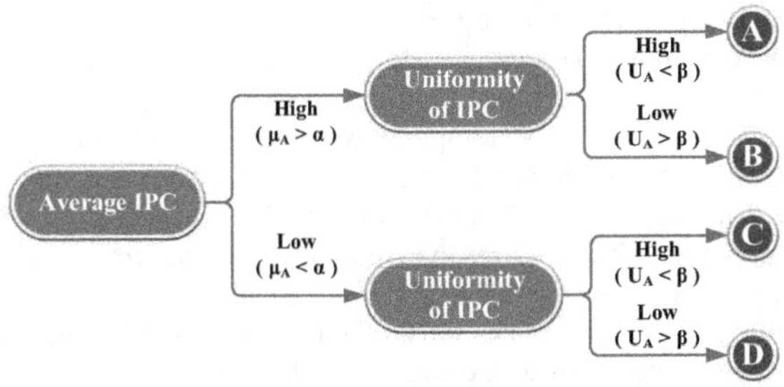

Figure 2: Proposed application classification.

$|C|$, that indicates the spawned threads of that application on a system with $|C|$ available cores; (ii) D_{TH} = that indicates the application throughput while using TH threads; and (iii) $Temp_{TH}$ that indicates the temperature of that application while using TH threads. Thus, an application that is chosen to execute with 4 threads has the format $A = \{\{TH0_A, TH1_A, TH2_A, TH3_A\}\}, D4_A, Temp4_A\}$. Each thread TH_i is an actual set $TH_i = \{IPC_{TH_i}, Temp_{TH_i}, P_{TH_i}\}$ where IPC_{TH_i} is the Instruction Per Cycle workload of the thread TH_i, $Temp_{TH_i}$ is the temperature footprint of the TH_i on a specific core and P_{TH_i} is the power consumption of the same thread.

For a given many-core platform and a set of N applications, the focus of the proposed framework is to find the number of threads, TH, for each application and the best $TH_i \rightarrow C_{PE}$ correspondence, such that the overall system maximizes its throughput. In system throughput maximization, the goals are: (i) Maximize the throughput of the applications D_i; and (ii) Keep the system under specific temperature constraints (hot-spots reduction) (Equation 1). In [8], it is demonstrated that an increase in the number of tasks with fixed execution time (i.e. an increase in system utilization) causes an increase on chip temperature.

$$max \{\sum_{j=1}^{N} D_i\} \quad (1)$$

$$s.t: \sum_{i=1}^{N}\sum_{j=1}^{K} Temp_{TH_{j_i}} \leq Temp_{Threshold}$$

Algorithm 1 Classification and thread to core mapping

```
1: Input: A{TH, D_TH, Temp_TH}
2: Class_{A_i} = ∅
3: for each TH_i ∈ A
4:     for each th_i ∈ TH
5:         Profile{A_i} ← IPC_{TH_i}
6:     Profile{A_i} ← {D_{A_i}, Temp_{A_i}, U_{A_i}, μ_{IPC_i}}
7:     Class_{A_i} ← {U_{A_i}, μ_{IPC_i}}
8: if Class_{A_i} == B or D
9:     for each TH_i ∈ A
10:        if D_{TH_i} ≥ D_Threshold && Temp_{A_i} ≤ Temp_Threshold
11:            selected_profile = [A, TH_i]
12: else
13:     selected_profile = [A, TH_{max{D}}]
14:     for each TH_i ∈ A
15:         if Temp_{A_i} ≤ Temp_Threshold
16:             selected_profile = [A, TH_i]
17: for each pe_i ∈ C_PE
18:     get IPC values
19:     sorted_C_PE = C_PE{IPC}
20: for each th_i ∈ TH_selected
21:     sorted_C_PE ← TH_i max_{IPC_{th_i}}
```

3.2 Application classification

For a given workload, an efficient run-time manager is responsible to determine on which time quantum qt the applications should run (time-sharing) and which cores they should occupy (space-sharing) by employing an efficient thread-to-core mapping. All the possible unique mappings, $map(n,k)$, of n threads to k cores is $map(n,k) = \frac{\prod_{i=0}^{i<n/k}\binom{n-k\cdot i}{k}}{(\frac{n}{k})!}$. For example, the number of possible mappings of 12 threads executed on 4 cores is $map(4,12) = 5,775$. *This vast number of combinations makes exhaustive run-time decision making infeasible.* Based on application speed-up scheme presented in [3], four classes (A, B, C and D) have been identified and the proposed framework implements the decision diagram presented in Figure 2. The criteria for classifying an application A are: (i) The average IPC value of all threads, μ_A; and (ii) U_A, the uniformity of IPC values as described as $U_A = (1 - \frac{VAR(IPC_A)}{\mu_A})$. The threshold values α and β guide the classification process. High value of IPC means high computational activity and it is considered one of the most important parameters for an increase of temperature. However, IPC alone is not a sufficient metric for resource management of modern multi-threaded applications since each thread occupies a core and can act in an independent way by creating hot-spots (local overheated areas) that can cause damage to the many-core platform. For example, suppose two applications (A and B) with 4 threads each with the following IPC values per thread: $IPC_A = \{1.5, 1.5, 1.5, 1.5\}$, $IPC_B = \{2.5, 1.2, 1.1, 1.2\}$. These two applications have the same μ_i but different U_i. The first thread of application B is responsible for creating hot-spots and requires special handling while all threads of application A have the same activity. Lines 1-7 of Algorithm 1 describe the proposed method. The input is the unclassified multi-threaded application. Then for different number of threads we extract the throughput of that application, the temperature impact for the specific number of threads, the average and the uniformity of IPC values. After having collected results for different number for threads the proposed classification scheme is employed and the class of the application is decided.

3.3 Thread-to-core mapping

Many state-of-art mapping techniques aim to maximize application performance and throughput [2]. However, they do not take into consideration the effect on the temperature and the creation of hot-spots. On the other hand, temperature-aware approaches [28] focus on the minimization of hot-spots and they try to keep temperature under specific thresholds while sacrificing the throughput of the applications.

The run-time thread-to-core mapping is employed based on the aforementioned classification. Lines 8-21 of Algorithm 1 present the proposed mapping procedure. Classes B and D are of special importance due to low uniformity of their IPC values. If an application belongs to one of these classes, the algorithm checks the profiled information in order to retrieve the impact of each thread and decides the appropriate number of threads that will be spawned for that particular application. Specifically, if there is a configuration that satisfies the time requirements and reduces the temperature and number of hot-spots, then this configuration is selected. As it will be shown in Section 4 the performance gain of these applications is small compared to the benefit that the system has if we assign less resources to them. For classes A and C, the algorithm initially chooses the configuration that maximizes the throughput of the applications and checks the temperature impact of that profile (lines 13-16). Since the uniformity of IPC in these classes is high, there is a great loss in performance if we reduce the number of

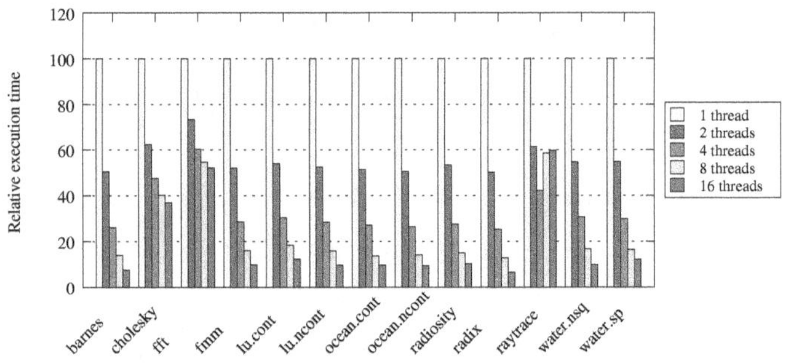

Figure 3: Relative execution time for SPLASH2 benchamrks

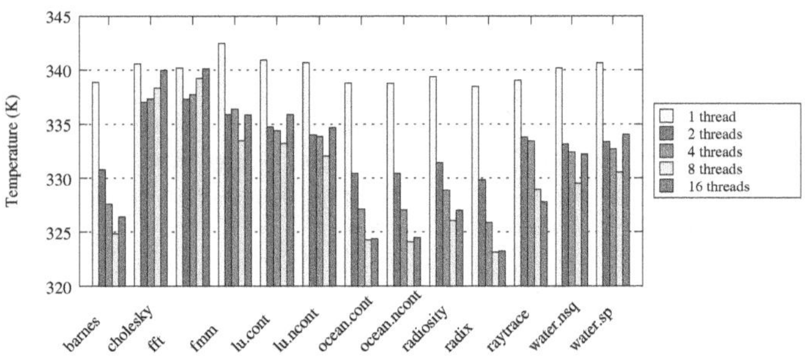

Figure 4: Temperature impact for different number of threads

threads. This happens because all threads have close IPC values meaning that they execute similar workload. Thus if the number of threads is reduced there is a great impact on the overall application performance. On the other hand, applications that belong to classes B and D do not suffer from this effect since the uniformity is very small. The proposed algorithm after deciding the number of threads per application (lines 11, 13), it checks the current status of all processing elements and sorts them according to their current workload. Then it assigns the threads based on the extracted information. The threads with the highest IPC values are mapped to the cores with the lowest current workload taking into consideration the temperature impact of the application (lines 17-21).

4. EXPERIMENTAL RESULTS

In order to evaluate the proposed methodology, we profiled the SPLASH2 benchmarks [25] for $TH = 1, 2, 4, 8, 16$ on the Nehalem architecture for $C_{PE} = 4, 8, 16$. The Sniper many-core simulator [5] was used in order to run, extract the profiles of the benchmarks and apply the proposed classification. McPAT [19] was used in order to extract information regarding power consumption and HotSpot [27] was used to generate the temperature profiles. For each application configuration we extracted the application throughput D_{TH} and temperature $Temp_{TH}$. The floorplans for the Nehalem architecture were built based on the information provided in [4]. Figure 3 depicts the relative execution time for all benchmarks while Figure 4 presents the temperature impact of each application for different number of threads. As it can be seen in Figure 3, the benchmarks have different behavior for different TH values. Specifically, the average gain in terms of execution time for having 2 threads is 45%, 67% for 4 threads, 76% for 8 threads and 81% for 16 threads. However, there are benchmarks, that they do not follow that pattern or the high number of threads does not provide any gain to the system (e.g. *raytrace*, *fft* and *cholesky*) validating the need for classification as presented in Algorithm 1. As Figure 4 depicts, temperature footprint varies as well for different application configurations. Last, Figure 5 presents the average and the variation of IPC values per core which are used to calculate the uniformity. Thus, the decision of the appropriate number of threads is also affected by that parameter as explained in Algorithm 1. Based on the information provided by Figures 3-5 SPLASH2 benchmarks are classified as follows: (i) Class A: *fmm*, *lu.cont*, *lu.ncont*, *water.nsq* and *water.sp*; (ii) Class B: *cholesky* and *fft*; (iii) Class C: *barnes*, *radix*, *ocean.cont*, *ocean.ncont* and *radiosity*; (iv) Class D: *raytrace*. Last, Figure 6(a)-(d) presents the IPC distribution and temperature profile of 4 threads for four applications that belong to different classes. All applications that belong to the same class, have similar behavior.

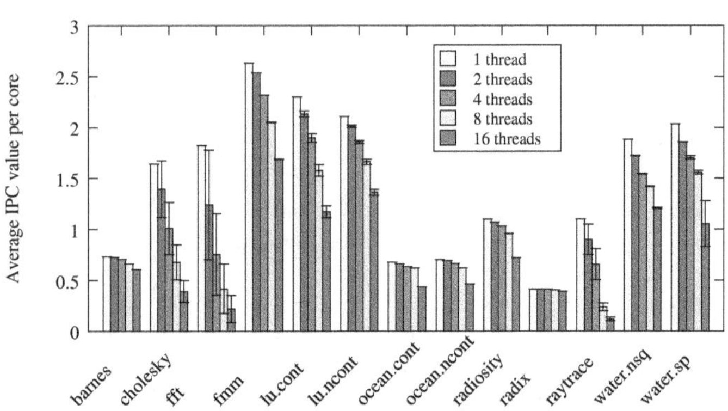

Figure 5: Average and variation of IPC values

In order to validate our approach, different scenarios, with multiple instances of applications per scenario, were simulated for a 16-core system. During the design-time phase, Sniper was used to profile and classify the parallel applications and extract traces. As the number of applications increase in each scenario, cycle-accurate many-core simulations are timewise infeasible. Thus, for the run-time evaluation, another trace-based simulator was developed on top of Sniper, that allowed us to use the traces of Sniper in order to monitor the time of application mapping. The simulator also allows the execution of applications in different times giving us the ability to test different arrival scenarios for the applications. Similar to [22], the simulator cannot consider contention effects on the many-core system.

The *turnaround time* of the proposed run-time manager is compared against the Divide & Conquer run-time mapping algorithm presented in [2] (with $MF = 0$ as presented in [2]). *Turnaround time* is defined as the total time taken between the arrival of a benchmark for execution and its completion. The configuration parameters for each scenario are: (i) The arrival interval; and (ii) The distribution of the benchmarks in each scenario. The arrival interval of an application that requests admission on the system can also be perceived as the interval between two consecutive incoming applications. It is a crucial parameter because it can create workload scenarios who are either too lightweight (when applications arrive slowly) or too stressful for the system (when an excessive amount of applications request admission and system resources are not enough to serve them). Examining a wide variety of different options for this parameter would result in an unmanageable design space. For that reason, we utilized the λ coefficient as presented in [24] in order to create twelve application arrival rate scenarios: (a) *Large interval*: Six scenarios in which applications arrive slowly ($\lambda = 48$); (b) *Small interval*: Six scenarios in which applications arrive close to one another ($\lambda = 16$). Regarding the distribution of the benchmarks, each scenario consists of multiple

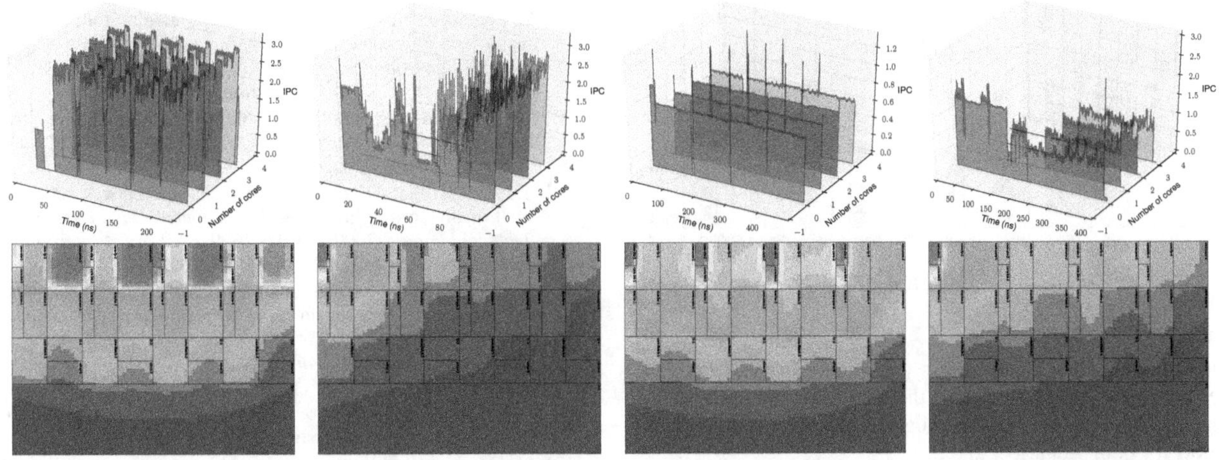

(a) *fmm* (Class A) (b) *cholesky* (Class B) (c) *barnes* (Class C) (d) *raytrace* (Class D)

Figure 6: IPC distribution and temperature profile of applications that belong to different classes

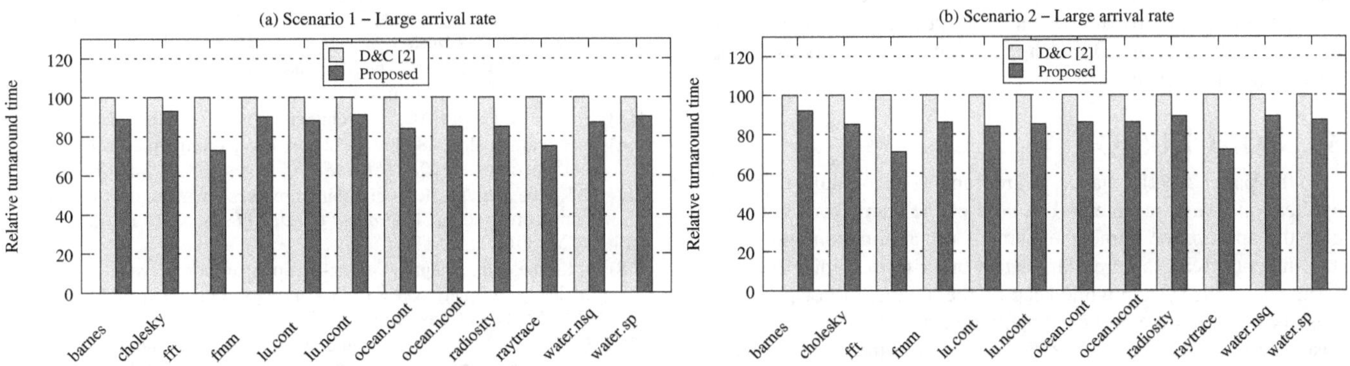

Figure 7: Scenarios 1 and 2 for large arrival rate

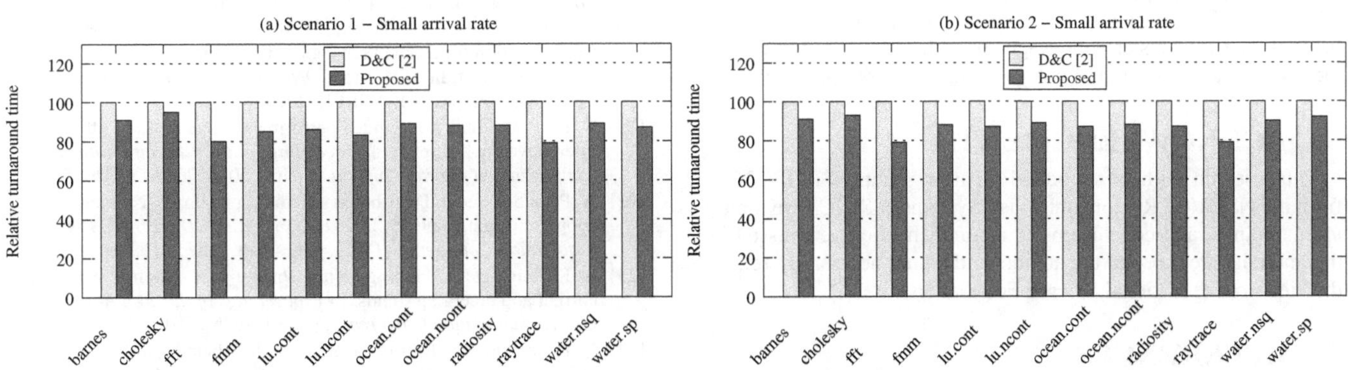

Figure 8: Scenarios 1 and 2 for small arrival rate

instances of the benchmarks. The number of the instances was selected based on the normal distribution.

Large interval: Figures 7(a)-(b) depict the results for the relative turnaround time for scenarios 1 and 2 respectively under large interval. In scenario 1, the proposed methodology achieves a total turnaround gain of 23% compared to the run-time mapping presented in [2], while having on average 17% gain per benchmark. In scenario 2, the proposed methodology achieves a total turnaround gain of 25% compared to [2] having on average 19% gain per benchmark. In both cases, the maximum temperature is the same, but the proposed methodology creates 26% and 34% less number of hotspots for scenario 1 and 2 respectively. As hotspots we define the number of points that have the maximum steady temperature. The gains that the proposed framework achieves are based on the fact that each class has a different behavior and the run-time thread-to-core manager takes advantage of the profile information and the current state of the cores.

Small interval: Figures 8(a)-(b) depict the results for the relative turnaround time for scenarios 1 and 2 respectively. In scenario 1, the proposed methodology achieves a total turnaround gain of 18% compared to [2], while having on average 14% gain per benchmark. In scenario 2, the proposed methodology achieves a total

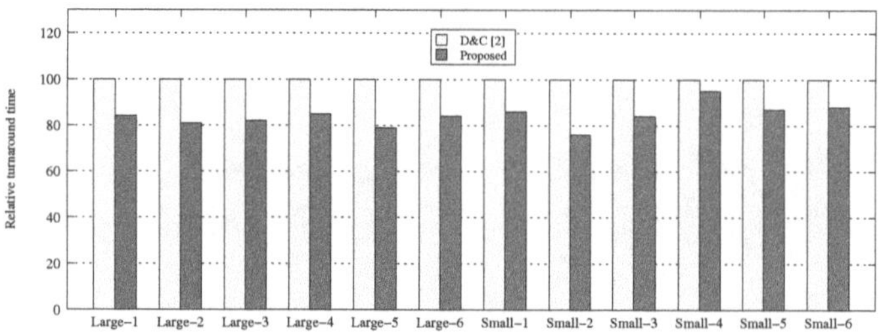

Figure 9: Relative turnaround time for all scenarios

turnaround gain of 28% compared to [2] having on average 24% gain per benchmark. In both cases, the maximum temperature is the same, but the proposed methodology creates 21% less number of hotspots for both scenario 1 and 2.

Last, Figure 9 presents the average performance gains for all twelve scenarios with large and small arrival rate. The proposed methodology, for large arrival rate, achieves on average a gain of 23% and each application completes its workload 18% faster on average. For small arrival rate, the presented scheme, achieves on average a gain of 18% and each application completes its workload 14% faster on average.

5. CONCLUSION

In this paper, a performance-aware framework for multi-threaded applications was presented. The goal of the framework is to decide the appropriate number of threads per application and apply an efficient thread to core mapping in order to maximize the performance of the system while keeping the number of hotspots low. Results show that the proposed mapping achieves: (i) for large arrival rate an average gain of 23% compared to the run-time mapping presented in [2] and each application completes its workload 18% faster on average; (ii) for high arrival rate an average gain of 18% compared to mapping in [2] and each application completes its workload 14% faster on average. In both cases, the system had the same steady temperature but less number of hot-spots.

6. ACKNOWLEDGMENT

This research has been supported in part by grants NSF IIP 1361847 from the NSF I/UCRC for Embedded Systems at SIUC. Any opinions, findings, and conclusions or recommendations expressed in this material are those of the authors and do not necessarily reflect the views of the National Science Foundation.

7. REFERENCES

[1] M. A. Al Faruque et al. Adam: run-time agent-based distributed application mapping for on-chip communication. In *Proc. of DAC*, pages 760–765. ACM, 2008.

[2] I. Anagnostopoulos et al. A divide and conquer based distributed run-time mapping methodology for many-core platforms. In *DATE, 2012*, pages 111–116. IEEE, 2012.

[3] I. Anagnostopoulos et al. Distributed run-time resource management for malleable applications on many-core platforms. In *Proceedings of the 50th Annual DAC*, page 168. ACM, 2013.

[4] E. Bauer and J. Carlos. Thermal management using pcm-based heatsinks. 2014.

[5] T. E. C. et al. An evaluation of high-level mechanistic core models. *ACM TACO*, 2014.

[6] E. Carvalho et al. Heuristics for dynamic task mapping in noc-based heterogeneous mpsocs. In *Rapid System Prototyping, 2007. RSP 2007. 18th IEEE/IFIP International Workshop on*, pages 34–40. IEEE, 2007.

[7] Z. Chen et al. Distributed reinforcement learning for power limited many-core system performance optimization. In *Proceedings of the 2015 Design, Automation & Test in Europe Conference & Exhibition*, pages 1521–1526. EDA Consortium, 2015.

[8] A. Coskun et al. A simulation methodology for reliability analysis in multi-core socs. In *Proceedings of the 16th ACM Great Lakes symposium on VLSI*, pages 95–99. ACM, 2006.

[9] T. Ebi et al. Tape: Thermal-aware agent-based power econom multi/many-core architectures. In *Computer-Aided Design-Digest of Technical Papers, 2009. ICCAD 2009. IEEE/ACM International Conference on*, pages 302–309. IEEE, 2009.

[10] T. Ebi et al. Economic learning for thermal-aware power budgeting in many-core architectures. In *Hardware/Software Codesign and System Synthesis (CODES+ ISSS), 2011 Proceedings of the 9th International Conference on*, pages 189–196. IEEE, 2011.

[11] M. Fattah et al. Smart hill climbing for agile dynamic mapping in many-core systems. In *Proceedings of the 50th Annual Design Automation Conference*, page 39. ACM, 2013.

[12] M. Fattah et al. Shifa: System-level hierarchy in run-time fault-aware management of many-core systems. In *Design Automation Conference (DAC), 2014 51st ACM/EDAC/IEEE*, pages 1–6. IEEE, 2014.

[13] Y. Ge et al. A multi-agent framework for thermal aware task migration in many-core systems. *Very Large Scale Integration (VLSI) Systems, IEEE Transactions on*, 20(10):1758–1771, 2012.

[14] Hewlett Packard Labs. The Machine: The future of technology, http://www.labs.hpe.com/research/themachine/.

[15] E. N. o. H. P. HiPEAC, E. Architecture, and Compilation.

[16] J. Howard et al. A 48-core ia-32 message-passing processor with dvfs in 45nm cmos. In *2010 IEEE ISSCC*, pages 108–109. IEEE, 2010.

[17] S. Kobbe et al. DistRM: distributed resource management for on-chip many-core systems. In *Proc. of CODES+ISSS*, pages 119–128. ACM, 2011.

[18] S. Kobbe et al. Adaptive on-the-fly application performance modeling for many cores. In *Proceedings of the 2015 DATE*, pages 730–735. EDA Consortium, 2015.

[19] S. Li et al. Mcpat: an integrated power, area, and timing modeling framework for multicore and manycore architectures. In *Proceedings of the 42nd Annual IEEE/ACM International Symposium on Microarchitecture*, pages 469–480. ACM, 2009.

[20] Z. Liu, X. Huang, S. X.-D. Tan, H. Wang, and H. Tang. Distributed task migration for thermal hot spot reduction in many-core microprocessors. In *ASIC (ASICON), 2013 IEEE 10th International Conference on*, pages 1–4. IEEE, 2013.

[21] D. Lo et al. Prediction-guided performance-energy trade-off for interactive applications. In *Proceedings of the 48th International Symposium on Microarchitecture*, pages 508–520. ACM, 2015.

[22] A. Pathania, , et al. Distributed scheduling for many-cores using cooperative game theory. In *2016 53nd ACM/EDAC/IEEE Design Automation Conference (DAC)*, pages 1–6, June 2016.

[23] A. K. Singh et al. Mapping on multi/many-core systems: survey of current and emerging trends. In *Proceedings of the 50th Annual Design Automation Conference*, page 1. ACM, 2013.

[24] V. Tsoutsouras et al. Job-arrival aware distributed run-time resource management on intel scc manycore platform. In *IEEE EUC*, pages 17–24. IEEE, 2015.

[25] S. C. Woo et al. The splash-2 programs: Characterization and methodological considerations. In *ACM SIGARCH computer architecture news*, volume 23, pages 24–36. ACM, 1995.

[26] B. Yang et al. Mapping multiple applications with unbounded and bounded number of cores on many-core networks-on-chip. *Microprocessors and Microsystems*, 37(4):460–471, 2013.

[27] R. Zhang, M. R. Stan, and K. Skadron. Hotspot 6.0: Validation, acceleration and extension. 2015.

[28] D. Zhu et al. Tapp: temperature-aware application mapping for noc-based many-core processors. In *Proceedings of the 2015 DATE*, pages 1241–1244. EDA Consortium, 2015.

Under-the-Cell Routing to Improve Manufacturability

Alex Vidal-Obiols
avidal@cs.upc.edu

Jordi Cortadella
jordi.cortadella@upc.edu

Jordi Petit
jpetit@cs.upc.edu

Department of Computer Science, Polytechnic University of Catalonia, 08034 Barcelona, Catalonia

ABSTRACT

The progressive miniaturization of technology and the unequal scalability of the BEOL and FEOL layers aggravate the routing congestion problem and have a negative impact on manufacturability. Standard cells are designed in a way that they can be treated as black boxes during physical design. However, this abstraction often prevents an efficient use of its internal free resources.

This paper proposes an effective approach for using internal routing resources without sacrificing modularity. By using cell generation tools for regular layouts, libraries are enriched with cell instances that have lateral pins and allow under-the-cell connections between adjacent cells, thus reducing pin count, via count and routing congestion.

An approach to generate cells with regular layouts and lateral pins is proposed. Additionally, algorithms to maximize the impact of under-the-cell routing are presented. The proposed techniques are integrated in an industrial design flow. Experimental results show a significant reduction of design rule check violations with negligible impact on timing.

1. INTRODUCTION

Routing is becoming an increasingly challenging task as on-chip component density grows [6]. Given the unequal scaling between BEOL and FEOL, pin accessibility in new technology nodes is a critical problem. The impact of routing congestion on metrics such as performance, area and yield poses a major obstacle that must be addressed.

Moreover, the chip design community is presented with the challenging task of finding new ways to improve manufacturability in the latest technology nodes. Some lithography processes have added coloring requirements for wires [5], and printed layout quality is becoming increasingly dependent on details such as line-end distribution [9]. The profusion of new and complex design rules has posed additional constraints to pin placement and accessibility, creating even more congested zones in the most pin-dense areas.

Such issues are already being addressed in a per-technology basis. One example is self-aligned double patterning (SADP), one of the technologies used for multi-patterning at 10nm nodes [5]. The concern for pin accessibility, ultimately resulting in routing congestion, can be seen in several proposals that consider constraints imposed by this fabrication process to the synthesis flow. The work presented in [7] considers the impact of SADP, as well as other technology constraints, to decide how to access I/O pins and offer maximized flexibility to the routing stage. Another interesting example is presented in [8], with a router which explicitly considers pin accessibility constraints induced by the SADP process. However, these methods are only valid for specific processes, and additional technology-independent solutions would be desirable.

Permission to make digital or hard copies of all or part of this work for personal or classroom use is granted without fee provided that copies are not made or distributed for profit or commercial advantage and that copies bear this notice and the full citation on the first page. Copyrights for components of this work owned by others than ACM must be honored. Abstracting with credit is permitted. To copy otherwise, or republish, to post on servers or to redistribute to lists, requires prior specific permission and/or a fee. Request permissions from permissions@acm.org.

GLSVLSI '17, May 10-12, 2017, Banff, AB, Canada

© 2017 ACM. ISBN 978-1-4503-4972-7/17/05...$15.00

DOI: http://dx.doi.org/10.1145/3060403.3060428

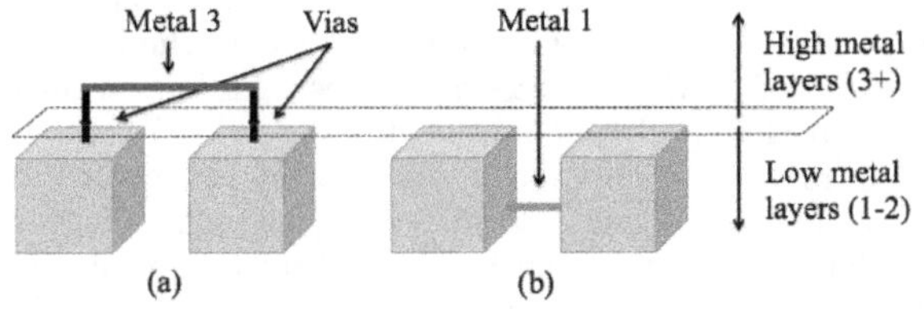

Figure 1: Symbolic cell interconnection: (a) over-the-cell and (b) under-the-cell routing.

The current paper proposes under-the-cell routing, that is, to systematically exploit the connection of adjacent circuit components using lateral connections in the internal routing metal layers. White space in those layers can be used for routing in current design flows, but to a fraction of the potential use that could be achieved by exploiting it systematically. Relying on the regularity imposed by technology constraints in modern nodes, standard cell libraries can incorporate several similar cell layouts for each logical cell. These layouts are enriched with lateral pins that can be abutted against neighboring cells for direct connection without the need of accessing the high level metal layers. Cell modularity allows the design tools to pick the most suitable cell layout after the placement stage.

This method decreases both pin count and congestion on the upper metal layers, resulting in a reduction of the number of design rule check violations with negligible impact on timing. The approach is technology independent and can be used in any fixed-height standard-cell technology node.

Challenges and contributions

Whereas standard cells in traditional synthesis flows only offer I/O pins on their top, the aim of our method is to take advantage of cells whose I/O pins can also be on their sides, reducing pin count and enabling better manufacturability.

Figure 1 conveys this idea by representing two pairs of adjacent standard cells that must be connected assuming that metals 1 and 2 are used for internal cell connections. The cells in Figure 1(a) show the traditional connection scheme: Higher metal layers (at least metal 3 and 4, depending on metal direction) must be used to connect the two pins of the cells. The cells in Figure 1(b) illustrate the new connection scheme: They can be connected directly using the lower level metal layers by abutting one cell to the other without reaching higher metal layers via I/O pins. We refer to a net that can be connected via lateral pins without accessing the high metal layers as a *buried net.*

More specifically, Figure 2 shows two views of a small circuit consisting of four NAND gates. The dotted wires in the schematic view represent connections that are routed using under-the-cell routing. The lower part shows the layout implementation of the circuit using gates with lateral pins: in particular, four different layouts for the NAND cell. Each routing presents a different lateral pin interface: C_1 has no pin, C_2 has an output lateral pin to the right, C_3 has an input lateral pin to the left and an output lateral pin to the right, and C_4 has an input lateral pin to the left. To simplify the design flow, the lateral pins are enforced to be in the same track, in this case track number 5, marked in red in the example. Moreover, each cell is allowed to have at most one input and one output lateral pin in its boundaries. The rationale for these decisions is discussed in Section 2.

In the example, the output of C_2 is routed to one of the inputs of C_3 by a straight metal-1 wire extension, and the same happens with the output of C_3 being connected with one of the inputs in C_4. The remaining connection between C_2 and C_1 is done via high-metal layers. This circuit would normally require five I/O pins for its internal connections, but given that we have routed two of the three nets using under-the-cell routing, only two I/O pins are needed. Notice that the connection between C_2 and C_3 does not allow us to also connect C_2 and C_1, given that each cell can have at most one output lateral pin. The process of mapping cells to layouts becomes an interesting optimization problem.

To fully take advantage of this novel technique, two major challenges appear:

- The library of standard cells must be extended with new layouts for each cell that has lateral pins. In particular, re-routing the cells is necessary to use their versions with lateral pins.
- Traditional EDA flows must be enhanced with a lateral pin-aware placement flow in order to take maximum advantage of the possibilities offered by under-the-cell routing. In particular, one wishes to maximize the number of laterally connected adjacent cells.

The collaboration of both cell library providers and EDA vendors is required for the proposed flow to be applied at industrial level. This paper proposes an approach to address the two previous challenges, along with experimental results to show the validity of the approach. The main contributions are:

1. The use of lateral connections to reduce the complexity of higher metal layer routing, improving circuit manufacturability.
2. A systematic approach that exploits regularity to generate standard cell layouts enriched with lateral pins.

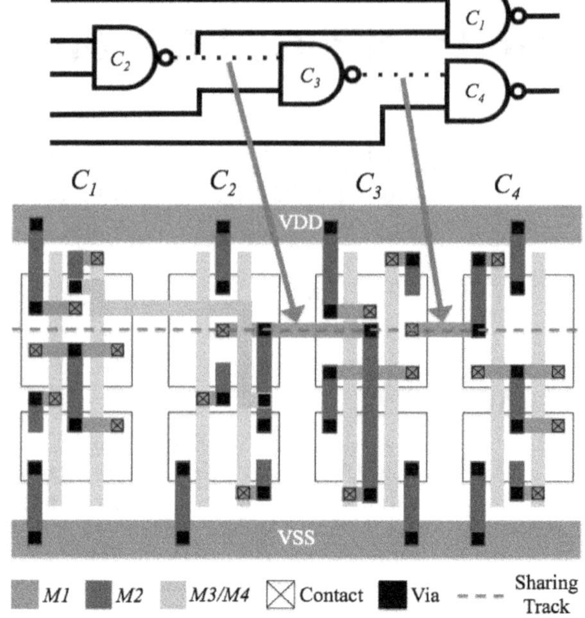

Figure 2: Small circuit consisting of four NAND gates

3. A dynamic programming and a graph-based algorithm to maximize the number of under-the-cell connections in a given circuit while preserving timing.
4. Experimental results showing a reduction in the number of design rule check violations, pins and vias with negligible timing degradation.

2. STANDARD CELLS WITH LATERAL PINS

Cell library providers must enrich their libraries incorporating cell layouts with lateral pins. Given an original standard cell library *Lib*, an extended version *eLib* is created. In *Lib* each logical cell is associated with a layout without lateral pins, whereas in *eLib*, each logical cell is mapped to the corresponding layout on *Lib* and to several other layouts with a set of lateral pins. The interface of these lateral pins is different in each one of the additional layouts, but all of them have the same area footprint.

As the number of cells in *eLib* is significantly larger than *Lib*, the first steps of the chip synthesis flow (e.g. technology mapping) will use only *Lib* to avoid an increase in algorithm complexity. The use of *eLib* is postponed until placement has been completed, at which point the final cell layout for each cell instance is determined.

Creating the extended library *eLib* requires some important decisions to be taken:

- Which pins must be provided as lateral connections?
- Are traditional pins needed in cells with lateral pins?
- At which cell tracks must the lateral pins be accessible?
- How to generate the cells with such features?

2.1 Defining the I/O interface

Potentially, any pin could be made accessible at any track if the routability of the cell would allow it. However, generating cell instances with all possibles subsets of pins accessible at any track would make the exploration of solutions unaffordable and the size of the library unmanageable. Based on empirical experimentation, a pragmatical approach has been taken by imposing the following two constraints:

One-Input/One-output sharing. Cells are only allowed to share (at most) one input and one output lateral pin, each one at a different side of the cell. The rationale behind this decision lies on the fact that most buried nets have 2 pins, thus requiring a balanced number of input and output pins. Moreover, most cells only have one output pin. In the case of sequential elements, the lateral pins are reserved for the `D` and `Q` (or $\bar{Q}$) pins.

Unique sharing track. One of the tracks is chosen to be the sharing track *for all cells*, thus unifying the position for lateral pins. This greatly simplifies routing as lateral pins are always connected via abutment, or with a straight metal segment if there is white space between the cells.

The fact that the final cell layout is decided for every cell after placement allows to synthesize cells without the full set of traditional I/O pins. In general, cell layouts with an input lateral pin can skip its corresponding traditional pin, given that they have a unique driver. However, cells with an output lateral pin might need to keep the corresponding traditional pin depending on whether they are driving only their neighbor cell or also other cells of the circuit. The top I/O pins removed from layouts with lateral pins are called *buried pins*.

Given the constraints mentioned above, three kinds of cells with lateral pins exist: cells with an input lateral pin, an output lateral pin, or both. For every cell in the last two groups we can have two versions, one keeping the I/O pin for the output and one without it. Since a large majority of cells have only one output, it is easy to see that the number of layouts in *eLib* will be about three times the number of input pins in *Lib*.

2.2 Generating the cells

When synthesizing different instances of the same standard cell, transistor placement can be kept identical in all the layouts. However, the internal routing of each cell instance must be recomputed to adjust it to its interface, as shown in Figure 2.

In order to automatically generate the routing for each extended cell, we advocate for the use of a Boolean rule-based approach such as the one described in [4]. This approach is efficient, technology-independent and parameterizable for different fabrics and design rules, including support for multiple-patterning lithography. Given the gridded transistor placement of a cell, such router generates a Boolean formula that encodes the routing problem and feeds it to a SAT solver. The returned model is translated into a valid routing.

The underlaying representation for a cell is a discrete 3D grid, whose edges correspond to potential metal segments; see Figure 3. For each edge in the grid, a set of Boolean variables describe whether certain nets of the cell use or not that edge and, therefore, ultimately define whether or not a segment of wire must be laid out on that edge. Using these variables, the routing problem is formulated through two kinds of clauses:

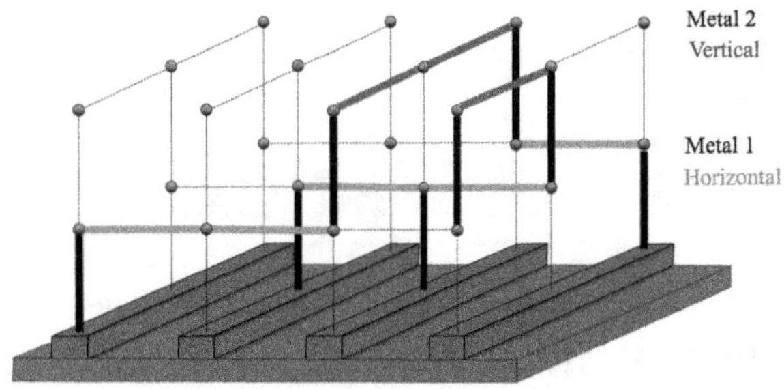

Figure 3: Grid representation for internal cell routing

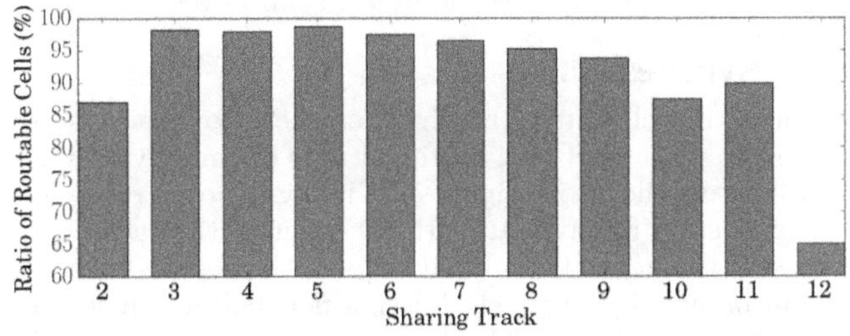

Figure 4: Routable cells per position of sharing track.

- Clauses that impose design-rule constraints.
- Clauses that represent routability constraints.

In particular, routability constraints guarantee that all pins of each net are connected. Such formulation can handle end-points whose position is either fixed at some grid point or selected from a specified set of grid points. In our context, lateral pins must be aligned with the sharing track at one side of the cell, whereas conventional pins can be located at any grid point of the top layer of the cell.

2.3 Selecting the sharing track

In order to find the sharing track that yielded more routable cells, we have undertaken the task of routing all cells in the Nangate 45nm cell library [2] using the routing approach discussed in Section 2.2 and honoring a commercial set of design rules (including rules for double patterning) on placements with minimal area. The template uses 13 tracks as shown in Figure 2: track 1 is reserved for VDD, track 13 for VSS, and tracks 2 to 12 for signal routing. Using the criteria for external pins described in the previous subsection, the extended library demands a total of 1576 layouts for the 125 cells.

The exploration began by obtaining routings with lateral pins on a reduced set of hard cells. The results of this exploration are shown in Figure 4. The vertical axis represents the percentage of cells that have been routed using the track indicated in the horizontal axis as sharing track. On the basis of this experiment, we have chosen track 5 (with a success ratio of 98.7%) to be the sharing track of the extended cell library. Then, using this sharing track, a valid routing was found for all cell instances except nine of them, leading to a routing ratio of 99.4% our *eLib*. In later experiments it was observed that virtually the 100% of the demanded layouts with lateral pins were among those successfully routed. Example of layouts obtained by the regular routing using these techniques are shown in Figure 2.

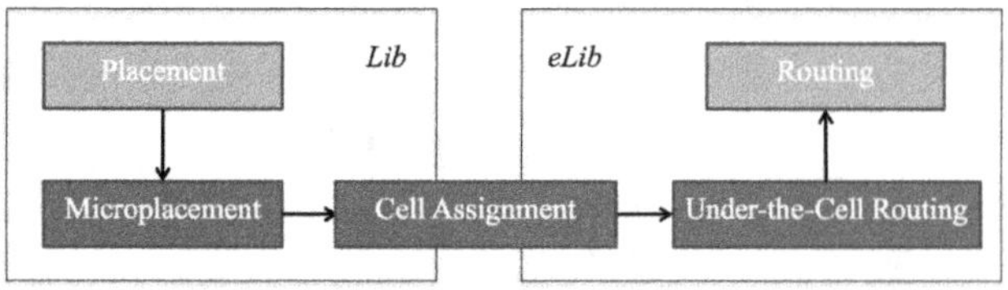

Figure 5: Proposed design flow modifications.

3. PLACEMENT AND ROUTING

The physical synthesis tools must be enhanced to take advantage of under-the-cell routing, in particular by mapping cells from *Lib* to *eLib* and modifying the placement to increase the opportunities for lateral connections.

3.1 Synthesis flow

Under-the-cell routing requires new steps to be added between the placement and routing stages of the physical design flow, as shown in Figure 5. The light boxes represent the usual steps in physical synthesis, whereas the dark boxes represent the newly introduced steps. The proposed process is transparent to the physical design flow before the cell assignment step, after which *eLib* is used.

The first new step is a *microplacement stage* which is performed after the tool has completed the placement. One of the conditions of lateral connections is that both cells to be connected must be placed side by side. Current placement tools optimize very complex functions that do not pay particular attention to having cells that need to be connected to be immediate neighbors: they try to place them close, but not necessarily adjacent. The microplacement stage presents the challenging problem of introducing small modifications to the original placement where opportunities to exploit adjacent connections are detected while preserving timing.

The second step is *cell assignment.* Each placed cell from *Lib* can be potentially substituted by one of the cell layouts in *eLib.* The enriched library provides several viable candidates, and the assignment of one cell to a layout with lateral pins affects the assignment of its neighboring cells. Cell assignment also impacts the amount of I/O pins that can be saved by using lateral pins. Finally, the *under-the-cell routing stage* adds horizontal wires for buried nets of cells which are not immediately adjacent, ie. are not connected by simple abutment.

3.2 Microplacement

The microplacement algorithm takes a valid placement and detects cells that could be connected using lateral pins. The entire flow is shown in Algorithm 1. The input is a placement P of cells from *Lib* generated by an generic placer, that is first partitioned into several regions r. Then, a greedy method is used to maximize the number of lateral connections. It generates relative placement constraints, which impose that some group of cells must be adjacent, for every region of the circuit. Finally, the generic tool performs an incremental placement on P with the newly added relative placement constraints, trying to improve the number of buried nets and pins.

Two mechanisms are applied to preserve the quality of the original placement.

Region partition: Lateral connections maximization is applied to exclusive regions of a fixed size, ensuring the global placement is preserved.

Algorithm 1 Microplacement Stage

```
Input: Placement P and slack tolerance ε
Output: Placement P'
RPC ← ∅
R ← partition_in_regions(P)
for each region r ∈ R do
    G ← build_graph(r)
    V' ← maximum_independent_set(G, ε)
    RPC ← RPC ∪ relative_place_constraints(V')
P' ← incremental_placement(P, RPC)
```

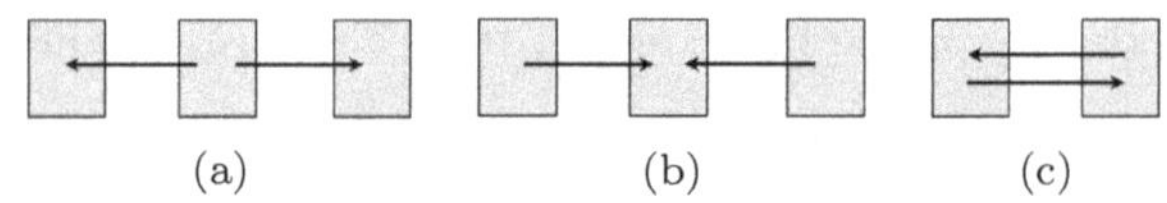

Figure 6: Microplacement incompatibilities

Slack control: Relative placement constraints are forbidden on cells with slack smaller than a tolerance ε to avoid significant timing alterations.

Maximizing lateral connections. Consider a set of placed cells $C = \{c_1, ..., c_n\}$. Each cell c_i has a set of input and output signals, $I(c_i)$ and $O(c_i)$, respectively. Each pair of cells, c_i and c_j defines a set of potential connections $S_{i,j} = \{s_{i,j,k} \mid k \in O(c_i) \cap I(c_j)\}$, where $s_{i,j,k}$ means that signal k is an output of c_i and an input of c_j. The union of all potential connections is

$$S = \bigcup_{\substack{1 \le i,j \le n \\ i \ne j}} S_{i,j}$$

Because of the restrictions explained in Section 2, not all potential lateral connections can coexist in the final placement. The method considers such restrictions only for every pair of potential lateral connections. Figure 6 shows the form of these incompatibilities for a given pair $s_{i,j,k}, s_{i',j',k'}$:

- The case $i = i'$ implies a cell with two output lateral pins (Figure 6a).
- The case $j = j'$ implies a cell with two input lateral pins (Figure 6b).
- The case $i = j' \wedge j = i'$ implies lateral connections in both directions between two cells (Figure 6c).

We can now define a graph $G = (S, E)$ as the graph where each vertex represents a potential connection and each edge an incompatibility:

$$E = \{(s_{i,j,k}, s_{i',j',k'}) \mid i = i' \vee j = j' \vee (i = j' \wedge j = i')\}.$$

By construction, the problem of maximizing the number of lateral connections of the cells C corresponds to finding a maximum independent set (MIS) of G, that is, the largest set of vertices such that no pair of them is adjacent. Each vertex can then be translated to a relative placement constraint that imposes both of the related cells to be placed one besides the other.

As the maximum independent set is a well-known NP-hard problem, a greedy approach is used as an approximation. A score is assigned to each potential lateral connection (represented by a node in our graph) and the algorithm iteratively picks the one with the highest score, incrementally propagating the incompatibilities on the graph. This score is obtained by performing a normal routing of the circuit and comparing the estimated wirelength and the final route of the nets, prioritizing nets that have taken a long detour in order to be routed.

3.3 Cell assignment

Cell assignment substitutes each cell in *Lib* by its version in *eLib* maximizing the amount of lateral connections and buried pins.

The entire cell assignment flow is shown in Algorithm 2. The input is a placement for all the cells and the output is an equivalent placement in which some of the cells from *Lib* have been substituted by one of their layouts with lateral pins in *eLib*. For each row, *lateral_connections* applies the dynamic programming technique explained below to obtain the set of lateral connections that maximizes the number of buried pins. For each lateral connection, the original cells in P and the proposed layouts with lateral pins are obtained via *original_cells* and *enhanced_cells*. The *substitution* finally changes them in the placement. As the mapping to lateral pins has already been decided, the routing stages that take place after cell assignment use *eLib*.

Algorithm 2 Cell Assignment Stage

Input: Placement P
Output: Placement P'
$P' \leftarrow P$
$R \leftarrow partition\_in\_rows(P)$
for each standard cell row $r \in R$ **do**
  $LC \leftarrow maximize\_lateral\_connections(R)$
  for each lateral connection $lc \in LC$ **do**
    $Lib\_cells \leftarrow original\_cells(lc)$
    $eLib\_cells \leftarrow enhanced\_cells(lc)$
    $substitution(P', Lib\_cells, eLib\_cells)$

A dynamic programming solution. The goal of the function *maximize_lateral_connections* is to determine the lateral connection to be used between each pair of cells of a row, $\{c_1, ..., c_n\}$, while maximizing the number of buried pins. The problem can be solved for each row independently, given that there are no incompatibilities among lateral connections between different rows. Interestingly, the problem for cells $\{c_1, ..., c_{i-1}\}$ is nested in the problem for $\{c_1, ..., c_i\}$, and thus solving the problem until c_{i-1} is helpful to solve it for c_i. We propose a dynamic programming approach exploiting the optimal substructure of the problem.

The following nomenclature is illustrated in Figure 7. Assume a set of the best solutions has been computed for the darker cells $\{c_1, ..., c_{i-1}\}$, and now these solutions must be extended up to c_i. Let k_i be the number of possible lateral connections between c_i and c_{i+1}. At each step between two cells, either one among k_i possible lateral connections is fixed, or none is. Given $i \in \{1..n\}$ and $j \in \{0..k_i\}$, let $buried\_pins(i, j)$ be the number of pins the local connection will bury. It takes value 0 for $j = 0$, representing that no lateral connection is taken, and either 1 or 2 for any other valid connection $1 \leq j \leq k_i$. Let $compatibles(i, j)$ be all the indices of connections from c_{i-i} to c_i such that they are compatible with connection j from c_i to c_{i+1}. The function f that counts the optimal number of buried pins from c_1 to c_i for a given connection from c_i to c_{i+1} (indexed for $1 \leq i \leq n$ and $0 \leq j \leq k_i$) is recursively defined by

$$f(i,j) = \begin{cases} buried(i,j) & \text{if } i = 1, \\ \max\{\ f(i-1,j') + buried(i,j) \mid \\ \qquad j' \in compatibles(i,j)\ \} & \text{otherwise.} \end{cases}$$

The case $i = 1$ represents the first cell, which has no lateral connection to its left side. In the general case, the optimal number of pins buried up to cell i using connection j depends on the pins j can bury at cell c_i and the best solutions of compatible lateral connections in the previous step. The value $f(n, 0)$ provides the optimal lateral connection assignment that maximizes the number of lateral pins for the whole row of standard cells.

Using a bottom-up approach, the algorithm sweeps the standard cell row from left to right and at each cell c_i the best solution for any lateral connection that can be taken to the right is kept. When the best solution for the final cell c_n is fixed, it suffices to trace back the cell row to fix the solution for each of the lateral connections. The complexity is $O(kn)$, where n is the number of cells and $k = \max\{k_i \mid i = 1..n\}$. As k is low, the algorithm is essentially linear in time and space with respect to the number of cells in the row.

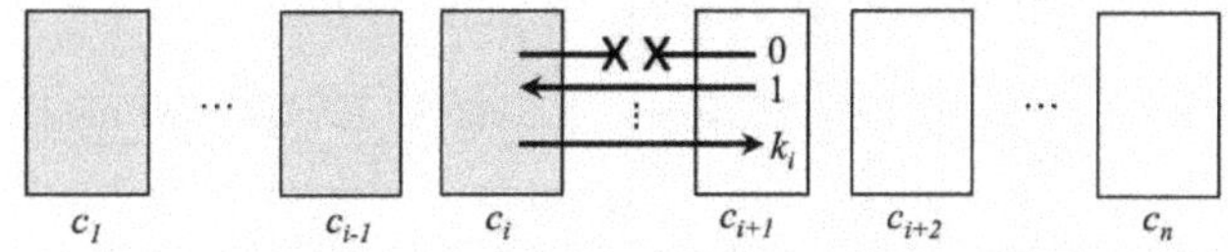

Figure 7: Dynamic programming nomenclature

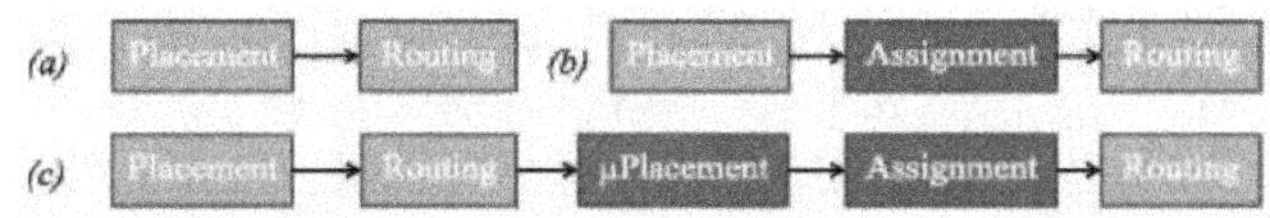

Figure 8: Synthesis flows analyzed in the experiments

4. EXPERIMENTAL RESULTS

We carried out the experiments using the 6 largest circuits of the itc99 benchmark [1], with a period of about 2ns. They were placed and routed with Synopsys IC Compiler [3] using the Nangate 45nm standard cell library [2]. The three synthesis flows that were used are depicted in Figure 8:

(*a*) **Original:** Placement and routing with DRC reduction. Gives the base number of DRC violations.

(*b*) **Assignment:** Placement, cell mapping into *eLib* and routing of the unburied nets with DRC reduction. This flow exploits lateral pins and shows the basic benefits of the approach.

(*c*) **μPlacement:** μPlacement is added before assignment to maximize the number of lateral connections.

The original Nangate library was used for physical synthesis (placement and routing) under the assumption that the *eLib* instances with lateral pins were available with identical timing characteristics. This assumption was made to avoid the complete timing characterization of *eLib*, which is an arduous task out of scope of the paper. We believe this is

Table 1: DRC violations and congestion

		DRC violations			ΔWNS	ΔVias	ΔPins
	Util.	65%	70%	75%		70%	
b17	Orig.	53	21	140			
M4	Assign.	26	10	37	-0.6%	-4.5%	-7.0%
18k	μPla.	4	0	50	+4.9%	-2.5%	-7.7%
b18	Orig.	105	53	184			
M5	Assign.	129	49	179	-1.1%	-4.9%	-7.2%
36k	μPla.	34	31	132	+2.1%	-4.9%	-10.3%
b19	Orig.	43	79	263			
M5	Assign.	19	53	180	-1.5%	-5.5%	-7.6%
79k	μPla.	12	59	245	-1.0%	-8.0%	-15.7%
b20	Orig.	0	42	147			
M4	Assign.	0	34	105	-0.7%	-6.4%	-8.7%
18k	μPla.	5	0	80	+1.2%	-8.1%	-11.9%
b21	Orig.	44	109	137			
M4	Assign.	5	15	47	-0.4%	-6.3%	-8.7%
20k	μPla.	2	0	23	+0.5%	-9.9%	-13.0%
b22	Orig.	58	107	82			
M4	Assign.	16	49	46	-3.5%	-5.3%	-8.1%
12k	μPla.	0	10	46	+0.1%	-5.6%	-10.4%

Table 2: Summary of results (Average)

Flow	# lat. wires	Buried 2-pin nets	ΔPins	ΔVias	ΔWL
Assignment	1x	18.1%	-7.7%	-5.4%	-1.1%
μPlacement	2.1x	33.1%	-11.5%	-6.7%	+0.3%

lat. wires reports the number of adjacent cells that can be connected using lateral pins. Buried 2-pin nets reports the percentage of 2-pin nets that are connected using lateral pins. ΔPins reports the percentage of cell I/O pins that are removed when using their lateral pin counterpart. ΔVias reports the reduction of vias when the circuit is routed with lateral pins. ΔWL represents the wirelength variation.

a conservative approach since timing with lateral pins could slightly improve, as routing of the I/O pins to the upper metal levels could be avoided in many cases.

Table 1 shows the reported number of DRC violations and variations on worst negative slack (in percentage of circuit period, positive means better WNS), vias and pins across the selected circuits obtained after using the three routing flows. The different area utilization and metal layers (indicated using M under the circuit name) are chosen to show the point at which a circuit begins to present DRC violations. Approximate cell count is also shown under the benchmark's name.

Applying the assignment synthesis flow obtains fewer DRC violations than the original flow in almost all circuits. The results show that the timing of the circuit can be preserved when using these techniques. Reduction for vias and pins is obtained in all cases. When comparing the two flows using lateral pins, μPlacement tends to perform better on close to all of the circuits in terms of DRC violations. Timing is improved except in one case (−1.0% in b19). Additionally, μPlacement achieves a better reduction on vias in almost all cases and performs specially well with I/O pins, achieving a reduction of up to a 15.7%.

Table 2 shows more statistics comparing lateral pin metrics between the assignment and μPlacement flows. One immediate result of the μPlacement stage is the increase on the number of lateral connections, which roughly doubles in all of the cases. However, the wirelength increases slightly after using the μPlacement flow, canceling part of its benefits and leading to examples in which the final DRC violation reduction is lower than when only assignment is used.

It is important to note that the experiments were obtained on a 45nm technology. The impact in buried pins would probably be more noticeable in modern technology nodes, where the different scaling between transistors and wires has increased the criticality of cell pins. At these nodes, the direct reduction on the number of pins would have a heavier impact on routing congestion and could overcome the placement degradation induced by the μPlacement stage.

5. CONCLUSIONS

This paper presents under-the-cell routing, a novel and effective way of exploiting internal routing resources and routing adjacent standard cells using lateral pins. The systematic extension of a standard cell library to support lateral pins is discussed in detail. Algorithms that apply and maximize the lateral connections are proposed and integrated in an industrial circuit design flow. The experiments show the viability of the approach and its potential to improve manufacturability by obtaining fewer design rule violations with negligible timing degradation. The presented techniques require the collaboration of cell library providers to enhance libraries with lateral pins and EDA companies to implement assignment and μPlacement in the circuit synthesis tools. Future lines of work include the refinement of μPlacement algorithms to maximize the number of lateral connections while preserving all quality metrics of the circuit.

6. ACKNOWLEDGMENTS

This work has been partially supported by funds from the Spanish Ministry for Economy and Competitiveness and the European Union (FEDER funds) under grants TIN2013-46181-C2-1-R and FPI 2015, and the Generalitat de Catalunya (2014 SGR 1034 and FI-DGR 2015).

7. REFERENCES

[1] itc99 Benchmark Homepage. www.cad.polito.it/downloads/tools/itc99.html.

[2] Nangate 45nm Open Cell Library. www.nangate.com/?page_id=2325.

[3] Synopsys IC Compiler Homepage. www.synopsys.com/Tools/Implementation/PhysicalImplementation/Pages/ICCompiler.aspx.

[4] J. Cortadella, J. Petit, S. Gómez, and F. Moll. A Boolean Rule-Based Approach for Manufacturability-Aware Cell Routing. *IEEE Transactions on Computer-Aided Design of Integrated Circuits and Systems*, 33(3):409–422, Mar. 2014.

[5] D. Pan, B. Yu, and J.-R. Gao. Design for Manufacturing With Emerging Nanolithography. *IEEE Transactions on Computer-Aided Design of Integrated Circuits and Systems*, 32(10):1453–1472, Oct. 2013.

[6] P. Saxena, R. S. Shelar, and S. S. Sapatnekar. *Routing Congestion in VLSI Circuits - Estimation and Optimization.* Series on Integrated Circuits and Systems. Springer, 2007.

[7] X. Xu, B. Cline, G. Yeric, B. Yu, and D. Pan. Self-Aligned Double Patterning Aware Pin Access and Standard Cell Layout Co-Optimization. *IEEE Transactions on Computer-Aided Design of Integrated Circuits and Systems*, 34(5):699–712, May 2015.

[8] X. Xu, B. Yu, J.-R. Gao, C.-L. Hsu, and D. Pan. PARR: Pin access planning and regular routing for self-aligned double patterning. In *2015 52nd ACM/EDAC/IEEE Design Automation Conference (DAC)*, pages 1–6, June 2015.

[9] H. Zhang, M. Wong, and K.-Y. Chao. On process-aware 1-D standard cell design. In *Design Automation Conference (ASP-DAC), 2010 15th Asia and South Pacific*, pages 838–842, Jan. 2010.

Improving Circuit Mapping Performance Through MIG-based Synthesis for Carry Chains

Zhufei Chu[1,2] Xifan Tang[2] Mathias Soeken[2] Ana Petkovska[2] Grace Zgheib[2]
Luca Amarù[3] Yinshui Xia[1] Paolo Ienne[2] Giovanni De Micheli[2] Pierre-Emmanuel Gaillardon[4]
[1]Faculty of Electrical Engineering & Computer Science, Ningbo University, Ningbo, China
[2]École Polytechnique Fédérale de Lausanne (EPFL), Lausanne, Switzerland
[3]Synopsys Inc., Sunnyvale CA, USA
[4]Electrical and Computer Engineering Department, University of Utah, Salt Lake City, UT, USA
Email: chuzhufei@nbu.edu.cn

ABSTRACT

Hard-wired carry chains in FPGAs are designed to improve efficiency of important arithmetic primitives. Although they are proven to be effective for arithmetic-rich functions, there are very few studies on the optimization opportunities of carry chains for general logic that is poor in arithmetic operations. Recently, *Majority-Inverter Graphs* (MIGs) were proposed for efficient Boolean logic optimization. MIGs open an opportunity for efficient mapping of critical paths onto hard carry chains, as the carry logic of a full adder is naturally a *majority* (MAJ) gate. In this paper, we propose an MIG-based synthesis method to exploit hard adders in FPGAs for the mapping of general logic. The proposed heuristic algorithm selects MAJ nodes to be mapped on the carry chains and the associated LUTs; then, the efficiency of carry chain mapping is examined theoretically for efficient LUT utilization. The experimental results show that, compared to traditional design flow *Verilog-to-Routing* (VTR 7.0), the proposed approach can improve delay by up to 25% with an average of 8%, while the channel width is reduced by up to 20% with an average of 6%.

Keywords

FPGA; majority-inverter graph; carry chain; technology mapping

1. INTRODUCTION

Many arithmetic intensive applications can be efficiently designed by FPGAs and display chains of additions mapped to *Logic Blocks* (LBs). When hard adder chains can be exploited, thus avoiding routing multiplexers, performance can improve up to 15% for arithmetic benchmarks [1]. Typically, the hard adders are technology mapped only when additions/subtractions are specified in *High-level Design Language* (HDL) descriptions. Although they have been shown to be very effective to implement arithmetic functions, these hard blocks have less flexibility compared to soft blocks due to their specificity. To further exploit the efficiency of hard adder chains, we concentrate on the problem of how to improve performance through mapping of general logic when the logic circuit contains a limited number of full adders.

Majority-Inverter Graph (MIG) [2, 3] is a new paradigm for logic optimization that receives renewed research attention due to the emergence of new computing devices as well as the increasing complexity of logic circuits. Regarding the carry chains, it is interesting that the carry function of a full adder is exactly the *majority* (MAJ) operator. This feature brings promising optimization possibilities in FPGA synthesis: a logic network represented as MIG corresponds directly to the physical implementation of the carry chains, i.e., chains of majority operations, even if no specific adder chains are found. This is a complex task when using other logic representations such as *And-Inverter Graphs* (AIGs) [4] or *Binary Decision Diagrams* (BDDs) [5]. In contrast, the MIG-based logic network gives us a great opportunity to improve mapping performance by taking advantage of carry chains.

In this paper, an MIG-based synthesis method for carry chains is proposed with the goal to improve mapping performance of general logic. Instead of exploiting arithmetic functions, we aim at automatic realization of logic that can be tightly implemented by both *Look-Up Tables* (LUTs) and specific carry chains for general logic functions. We present a heuristic algorithm that selects MAJ nodes from a given MIG to be mapped on carry chains and the associated LUTs. The efficiency of carry-chain mapping is examined theoretically for efficient LUT utilization. The experimental results show that the proposed approach improves delay by up to 25% with an average of 8%, while the channel width is reduced by up to 20% with an average of 6%.

This paper is organized as follows: Section 2 reviews the necessary background on FPGA architecture and MIG-based logic optimization. Section 3 presents a brief introduction of the state-of-the-art work. Afterwards, in Section 4, the proposed MIG-based synthesis for carry chains is described in detail. In Section 5, the experimental results are presented and discussed. Finally, Section 6 concludes this paper.

2. BACKGROUND

In this section, we review the necessary background about modern FPGA architectures and MIG logic optimizations.

2.1 Modern FPGA Architecture

Modern FPGA architectures consist of an array of tiles, as shown in Fig. 1, each of which contains a LB, *Connection Boxes* (CBs), *Switch Blocks* (SBs), and routing tracks [6]. CBs are used to connect the heterogenous blocks to routing tracks, while SBs interconnect the routing tracks. The functionalities of FPGAs are realized by the heterogenous logic

Permission to make digital or hard copies of all or part of this work for personal or classroom use is granted without fee provided that copies are not made or distributed for profit or commercial advantage and that copies bear this notice and the full citation on the first page. Copyrights for components of this work owned by others than ACM must be honored. Abstracting with credit is permitted. To copy otherwise, or republish, to post on servers or to redistribute to lists, requires prior specific permission and/or a fee. Request permissions from permissions@acm.org.

GLSVLSI '17, May 10–12, 2017, Banff, AB, Canada.

© 2017 ACM. ISBN 978-1-4503-4972-7/17/05...$15.00.

DOI: http://dx.doi.org/10.1145/3060403.3060432

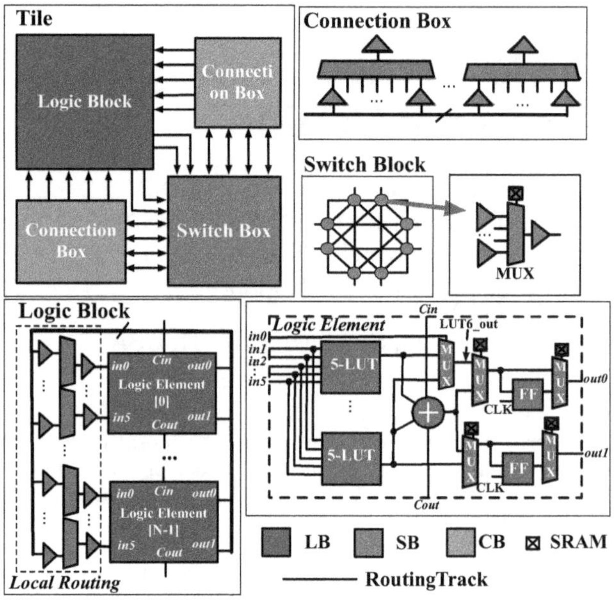

Figure 1: FPGA tile architecture and the considered LB.

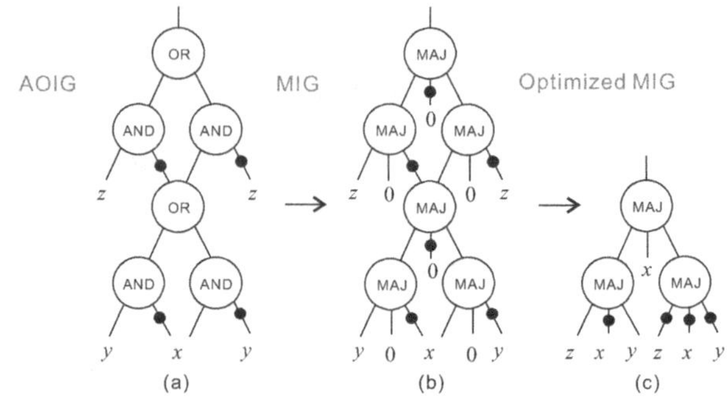

Figure 2: Example of transposing an optimal (a) AOIG representation into (b) an initial MIG representation and (c) an optimal MIG representation after using MIG algebraic transformation.

resources that consist of LBs, memory banks, and *Digital Signal Processing* (DSP) units. LBs comprise a number of *Logic Elements* (LEs) and a local routing architecture, which provides intra-block interconnections. Basically, there are at least a fracturable LUT [7], a *Flip-flop* (FF), and an output selector in every LE. To boost the functionality of logic resources, FPGA vendors embed additional elements, such as hard carry chains and shift registers, within the LBs. In this paper, we consider the LB resembling commercial FPGA architectures [8, 9]. As depicted in Fig. 1, a LB contains two 5-input LUTs, two FFs and a carry logic. The two LUTs, referred to as carry-chain LUTs in the rest of paper, can be either grouped to implement a 6-input LUT or realize two distinct 5-input LUTs with shared inputs. The output of carry logic can be connected to both fast carry output C_{out} and normal outputs of LEs, $out0$ and $out1$, which allow for early exits of carry signals. When only one or two inputs of carry logic are used (can happen in MIG), the 5-input LUTs can be efficiently utilized to map additional logic.

2.2 Majority-Inverter Graph

MIGs [2, 3] can efficiently represent Boolean functions due to the expressive power of the majority operator. Indeed, by means of fixing one input as constant binary value 0 or 1, the majority operator can be configured to behave as a traditional conjunction (AND) or disjunction (OR) operator, respectively. Consequently, traditional *And-Or-Inverter Graphs* (AOIGs) are a special case of MIGs. MIGs can be easily derived from AOIGs as shown in Fig. 2, in which the lines with bubbles indicate complemented edges require additional inverters.

MIG-based representations are extremely competitive at logic rewriting. The axiomatic system for the MIG Boolean algebra, referred to as Ω, is defined by five primitive transformation rules: commutativity ($\Omega.C$), majority ($\Omega.M$), associativity ($\Omega.A$), distributivity ($\Omega.D$), and inverter propagation ($\Omega.I$). The majority operation of three variables x, y, and z is denoted as $\langle xyz \rangle$ in Ω. A strong property of MIGs and their algebraic framework is reachability. It has been proven that, by using a sequence of transformations drawn from the primitive five rules, it is possible to traverse the entire MIG representation space [2]. This result is of paramount interest to logic synthesis because it guarantees that the best MIG under a given target metric can always be reached. However, deriving a sequence of Ω transformations is an intractable problem. As for traditional logic optimization, heuristic techniques can obtain fast solutions with reasonable quality [10]. From the perspective of logic optimization, it is practical to improve the FPGA performance by reducing the maximum number of logic levels (depth) with affordable area penalty, which leads to a better delay of the physical implementation of the circuit [14]. Thanks to the flexible MIG algebraic framework, it is possible to obtain a better MIG, both in depth and area, as shown in Fig. 2(c).

$$\Omega = \begin{cases} \textbf{Commutativity} - \boldsymbol{\Omega.C} \\ \langle xyz \rangle = \langle yxz \rangle = \langle zyx \rangle \\ \textbf{Majority} - \boldsymbol{\Omega.M} \\ \begin{cases} \langle xyz \rangle = x = y & if\ x = y \\ \langle xyz \rangle = z & if\ x = \bar{y} \end{cases} \\ \textbf{Associativity} - \boldsymbol{\Omega.A} \\ \langle xu \langle yuz \rangle \rangle = \langle zu \langle yux \rangle \rangle \\ \textbf{Distributivity} - \boldsymbol{\Omega.D} \\ \langle xy \langle uvz \rangle \rangle = \langle \langle xyu \rangle \langle xyv \rangle z \rangle \\ \textbf{Inverter Propagation} - \boldsymbol{\Omega.I} \\ \overline{\langle xyz \rangle} = \langle \bar{x}\bar{y}\bar{z} \rangle \end{cases}$$

3. RELATED WORK

Carry chains are widely studied since they were introduced by commercial FPGAs. Most of the existing papers focus on the carry-chain architectures and how to implement best the arithmetic operators. Most of the widely-used tools rely on users explicitly writing additions/subtractions using HDL primitives or using a predefined adder macro to recognize carry-chain logic. Frederick and Somanni [11] proposed a mapping algorithm that exploits carry chains for general circuits. The results proved that carry chains have the potential to improve the delay of general-purpose circuits. However, the technique proposed is only applicable to carry-select chains, which are no longer present in modern FPGAs. To target arbitrary carry-chain structures, Preußer and Spallek [12] proposed an approach to the automatic mapping that uses carry chains for general logic implementation. The algorithm searches the cuts that cover LUTs and the carry-chain node in the same logic block, which impose much tighter constraints than in our approach. The benefit of this approach is that it naturally utilizes the carry-chain LUTs, while the tight constraints may decrease the mapping possibilities. Petkovska et al. [13] propose to map logic

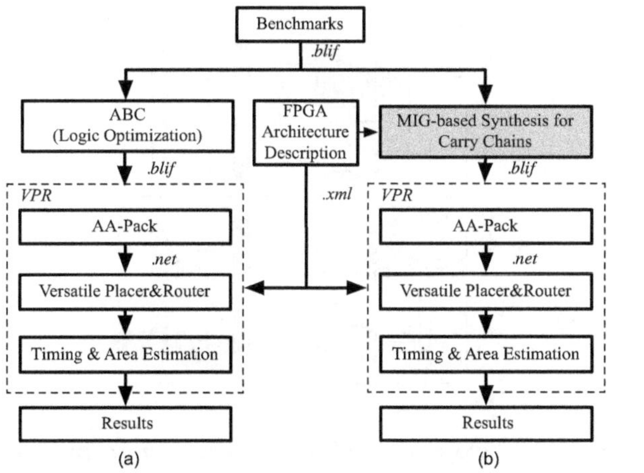

Figure 3: Comparison of (a) the state-of-the-art academic design flow and (b) the proposed design flow.

on the carry chains for circuits expressed using a gate-level descriptions. Moreover, the carry-chain LUTs are specified using a pre-mapping selection algorithm. The results show that they can identify more full adders than with the existing design flow, and that the area is improved by 6% on average, with no delay penalty. However, their method is effective only for circuits rich with adders.

In terms of MIG-based FPGA synthesis, Amarù et al. [14] proposed MIG optimization techniques targeting high-speed FPGA implementations, which aggressively reduce the logic depth and enable denser LUT mapping on FPGAs. They also gave insight on how to exploit the FPGA carry-chain logic during the logic optimization. However, their method targetted LUTs operating in normal mode instead of arithmetic mode, thus it misses out on some opportunities to improve the performance using carry chains.

4. MIG-BASED SYNTHESIS FOR CARRY CHAINS

In this section, we describe the proposed MIG-based synthesis for carry chains. First, we introduce proposed flow, before describing the details of the proposed algorithm.

4.1 Proposed Design Flow

We use the state-of-the-art FPGA design flow VTR 7.0 [15], shown in Fig. 3(a), as our baseline flow. The `BLIF` format circuit is first synthesized and technology mapped by ABC, the output of which serves as an input to VPR to pack, place, and route it for a given FPGA architecture description.

Instead of using ABC, which is based on AIGs, for logic synthesis and technology mapping, the proposed flow uses an MIG-based logic synthesis, as shown in Fig. 3(b). The algorithm consists of four main steps: critical path evaluation, inverter propagation, carry-chain candidate selection, and carry-chain LUT mapping. The extracted carry-chain logic are marked as *don't-touch* nodes and implemented on the FPGA's hard carry chains, while the rest is mapped onto LUTs as usual.

4.2 Critical Path Evaluation

Given an MIG, we enumerate all critical paths from primary inputs (PIs) to primary outputs (POs). For each critical path, a cost function is used to evaluate the carry-chain implementation benefits, including the gains of both nodes and edges after carry-chain extraction. The nodes gain N_{nodes}

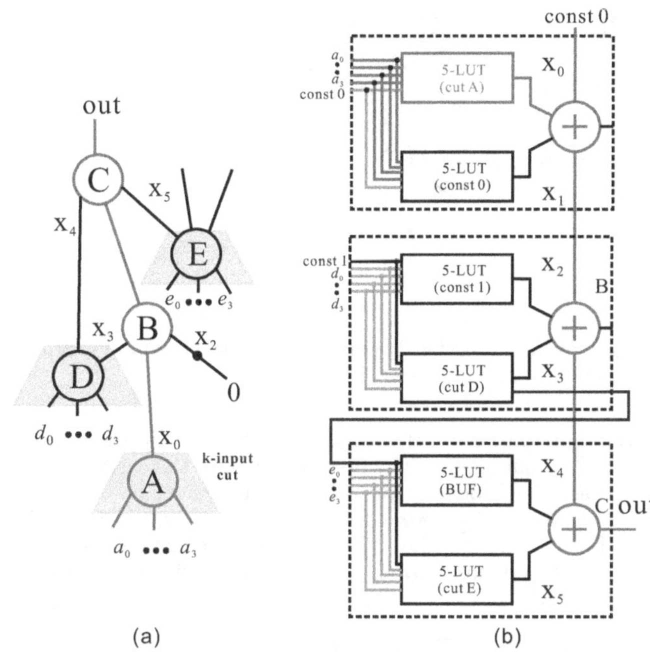

Figure 4: (a) A critical path in an MIG and (b) its LE carry-chain implementation.

consists of three parts: 1) the number of nodes in critical path, n_{path}; 2) the number of nodes that will be implemented by carry-chain LUTs, n_{fill}; 3) the number of nodes in 2) that will be duplicated due to its fanout to a node that does not belong to 1) and 2), n_{dup}. The nodes gain N_{nodes} is then defined as

$$N_{\text{nodes}} = n_{\text{path}} + n_{\text{fill}} - n_{\text{dup}} \tag{1}$$

The nodes in 1) and 2) are marked as blackbox nodes. The edges gain N_{edges} considers the number of internal edges to connect all blackbox nodes, n_{inter}, and the external nets that connect blackbox nodes to non-blackbox nodes, n_{exter}. Hence, edges gain N_{edges} is then defined as

$$N_{\text{edges}} = n_{\text{inter}} - n_{\text{exter}} \tag{2}$$

The cost function to evaluate a path is defined as

$$f = \alpha N_{\text{nodes}} + \beta N_{\text{edges}} \tag{3}$$

where α and β are weight factors used to provide similar weights to the two terms of the equation for combinational optimization:

$$\alpha + \beta = 1.0 \tag{4}$$

$$\alpha N^{\text{avg}}_{\text{nodes}} = \beta N^{\text{avg}}_{\text{edges}} \tag{5}$$

where $N^{\text{avg}}_{\text{nodes}}$ and $N^{\text{avg}}_{\text{edges}}$ are the average nodes and edges gain among all critical paths. The path with highest cost is selected as candidate for carry-chain implementation.

Figure 4(a) provides an example in which the nodes $\{A, B, C\}$ are on the candidate path, $n_{\text{path}} = 3$; supposing the nodes $\{D, E\}$ will be implemented by carry-chain LUTs, $n_{\text{fill}} = 2$; the blackbox nodes are then $\{A, B, C, D, E\}$, because node E has another fanout to a non-blackbox node, $n_{\text{dup}} = 1$. Therefore, $N_{\text{nodes}} = 3 + 2 - 1 = 4$. For edges gain, each MAJ node has 3 input edges and the number of blackbox nodes is 5, thus $n_{\text{inter}} = 15$. Node E has 2 external nets that connect non-blackbox nodes, thus $n_{\text{exter}} = 2$, and $N_{\text{edges}} = 15 - 2 = 13$. The carry-chain implementation of Fig. 4(a) is shown in Fig. 4(b), in which MAJ nodes $\{A, B, C\}$ on the critical path

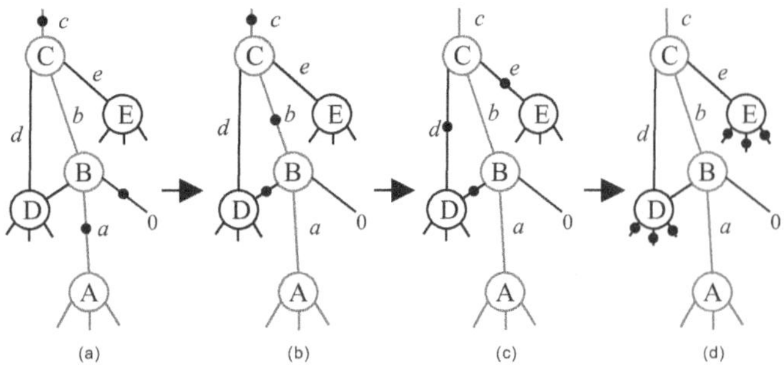

Figure 5: Inverter propagation in the carry-chain edges.

are mapped to carry chains, while nodes $\{D, E\}$ are mapped to carry-chain LUTs. The first full adder of the carry chain is used as a half adder because the first `Cin` must be connected to a constant 0 in order for A to be propagated from the LUTs to the `cout`. The details of how to determine the nodes to be implemented by carry-chain LUTs are described in Section 4.5.

4.3 Inverter Propagation

For most commercial products, the carry-chain architecture does not allow inverter operation along the carry-in/carry-out paths. Although inverters can be realized by the LUTs, it will bring in an additional delay and area overhead. To optimize the inverters used in carry chains, we used Boolean algebra inverter propagation ($\Omega.I$) rule. An approach by Testa et al. [17] shows that ($\Omega.I$) rule is efficient in complemented edges minimization for emerging nanotechnologies.

The $\Omega.I$ rule can be applied to all edges along the path recursively in a bottom-up or top-down manner. For example, Fig. 5(a) shows the original graph with inverters. The critical path $\{A, B, C\}$ is highlighted in red. In a bottom-up manner, we first find the output edge a of node A that is complemented, then we apply $\Omega.I$ to change complement states of all inputs/outputs of node B, as shown in Fig. 5(b). Next, after edges b and c are processed, as shown in Fig. 5(c), there are no inverters along the critical path. If the number of complemented edges in carry chains is even, then the complemented edges compensate each other and the final result is a carry chain with no inverters. Otherwise, at most one inverter exists at a primary input or output.

To make sure minimum number of inverters are used to feed the carry chains, the $\Omega.I$ can be also applied to carry-chain inputs by just one level. Figure 5 (c) shows an example. The output edges d and e, which are inputs to node D and E, respectively, are complemented. We apply $\Omega.I$ on node D and E to minimize inverter numbers in carry-chain inputs. Finally, the MIG after critical path inverter propagation is shown in Fig. 5(d).

4.4 Selection of Carry-Chain Candidates

Note that the carry-chain pattern (adder/MAJ + 5-input LUTs) is a better choice for technology mapping than a 6-input LUT only when the associated 5-input LUTs are efficiently utilized. After extracting a chain of MAJ nodes from a logic network, it is possible that two inputs of some MAJ nodes are primary inputs. Consequently, to accommodate such MAJ nodes, the two 5-input LUTs have to be configured as buffers, which we define as *loose carry-chain pattern.* In addition, there could be more than one loose carry-chain pattern in a chain. Figure 6 illustrates an example of two cascaded loose carry-chain patterns, where the number of

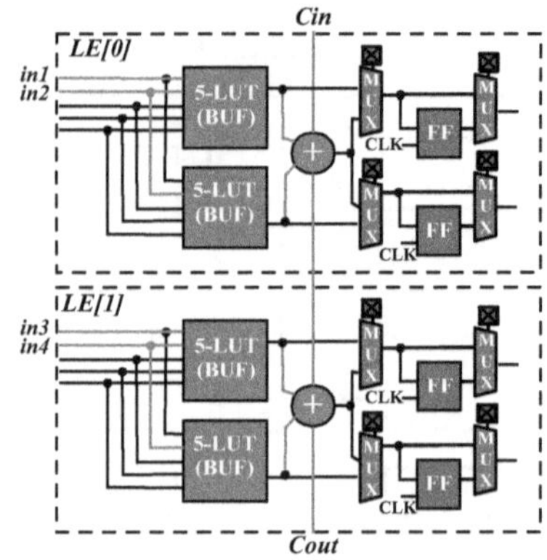

Figure 6: Two cascaded loose carry-chain patterns.

used inputs of the four 5-input LUTs is only four. Note that the two LEs in Fig. 6 have only five inputs (including `Cin`) in total. If only the carry-chain output `Cout` is used (the normal outputs `out0` and `out1` of LEs are not used), the two LEs could be alternatively implemented with a single 6-input LUT. Compared to a single 6-input LUT, the two LEs are less efficient in both area and delay. The pin-to-pin delays of two loose carry-chain patterns are

`Cin` to `Cout`: $2 \cdot t_{\text{adder}}$
`in1` to `Cout`: $t_{\text{lr}} + t_{\text{lut5}} + 2 \cdot t_{\text{adder}}$
`in2` to `Cout`: $t_{\text{lr}} + t_{\text{lut5}} + 2 \cdot t_{\text{adder}}$
`in3` to `Cout`: $t_{\text{lr}} + t_{\text{lut5}} + t_{\text{adder}}$
`in4` to `Cout`: $t_{\text{lr}} + t_{\text{lut5}} + t_{\text{adder}}$

Average: $t_{\text{lr}} + 0.8 \cdot t_{\text{lut5}} + 1.6 \cdot t_{\text{adder}}$

where t_{adder}, t_{lr} and t_{lut5} represent the delays of an adder, local routing and a 5-input LUT, respectively. The average pin-to-pin delay of a LE operating in the mode of a single 6-input LUT is $t_{\text{lr}} + t_{\text{lut6}} + t_{\text{mux}}$, where t_{lut6} and t_{mux} denotes the delay of a 6-input LUT and an output selector (a 2 : 1 multiplexer). When the pin-to-pin delay of two loose carry-chain patterns is larger than that of single 6-input LUT mode, two loose carry-chain patterns should be replaced by a 6-input LUT in terms of performance. Note this is only established on the fact that only `cout` is used, while other regular outputs are not used. Similar conclusion can be drawn for LE in fracturable 5-LUT mode.

Therefore, we restore some loose carry-chain patterns, which have less than four or five used inputs in total, to be processed by standard LUT technology mapping. Given a critical path extracted from an MIG (Section 4.2), the carry-chain nodes are selected based on the above described loose carry-chain patterns checking. Therefore, the original carry chain is decomposed into several parts. However, as the carry chains start with a half adder and exit through the `sumout`, small pieces of carry chains are also too expensive to be implemented. Considering this issue, we evaluate the loose pattern and carry-chain length simultaneously. For example, if two sub-carry-chains are separated by only one MIG node, we will connect them together to construct a rational chain implementation. From our experimental results, we found that MIG nodes that have relatively low logic-levels are prone to be removed from the carry chains. This is mainly because these low-level nodes generally are fed by primary inputs, which are loose pattern mapping.

4.5 Carry-Chain LUT Mapping

The MIG network will be partitioned into two parts after the critical path is extracted. As shown in Fig. 7, the first

Table 1: Experimental Results Compared to Traditional Design Flow

Benchmark	Traditional Design Flow						Improvement by the Proposed Flow (%)						#Adder
	#LUT	D	RA	TA	CW	WL	#LUT	D	RA	TA	CW	WL	
pm1	17	1.52	4.06	15.1	26	109	23.53	-1.24	2.68	0.00	7.69	7.34	3
f51m	23	2.30	3.36	22.6	24	95	13.04	-24.44	-18.68	-33.33	-16.67	-2.11	3
o64	35	2.40	21.5	30.2	34	808	11.43	-5.32	0.00	0.00	0.00	-15.84	7
C432	52	7.12	8.83	45.3	34	362	36.54	-7.79	16.69	16.67	5.88	9.39	11
i5	69	3.06	47.5	52.8	42	1294	11.59	-3.85	20.55	0.00	14.29	-1.78	5
m4	88	2.21	8.83	67.9	34	312	6.82	-1.87	-3.70	0.00	-11.76	-11.22	5
cavlc	122	2.79	13.9	98.1	30	395	14.75	-0.99	0.00	8.04	0.00	21.01	13
too_large	173	4.35	25.4	136	40	1327	3.47	-6.50	-15.04	0.00	-15.00	-4.67	5
dalu	234	5.20	31.9	181	50	1742	11.54	-9.11	8.08	12.71	-24.00	20.44	22
t481	290	4.85	35.2	219	40	2209	-1.72	-0.38	-16.58	-0.06	-20.00	-6.38	18
i8	307	3.42	57.2	234	48	3347	0.98	-8.31	-1.40	0.00	-4.17	5.71	8
in1	387	3.58	39.7	294	34	2640	3.88	-2.89	0.00	2.72	0.00	-8.71	10
C6288	433	11.18	46.6	332	40	3120	5.31	-25.60	-1.85	2.41	-5.00	-3.88	21
prom2	527	3.38	50.9	400	34	2553	-0.95	-11.85	-3.94	-2.00	-11.76	0.00	3
Avg.							10.01	-7.87	-0.94	0.51	-5.75	0.66	

#LUT: number of LUTs, D: delay (ns), RA: routing area, TA: total area (area unit: 10^4 number of minimum transistor size), CW: channel width, WL: wirelength, #Adder: number of adders

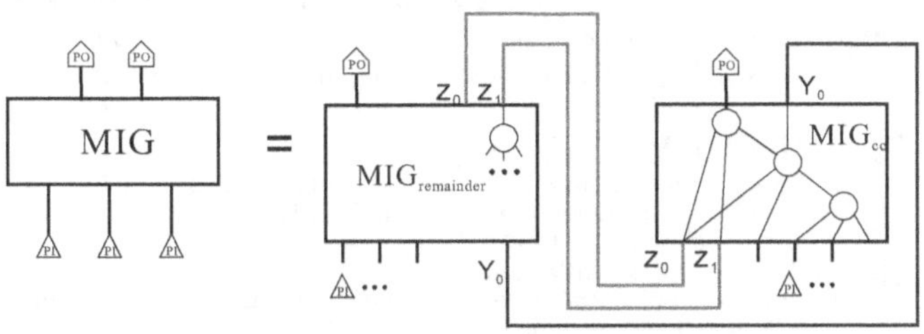

Figure 7: MIG network splitting.

part MIG_{cc} contains the carry-chain nodes and external edges, while the other part $MIG_{remainder}$ is the remainder MIG network without carry chains. For the inputs/outputs of carry-chain nodes, additional primary outputs/inputs are created to ensure correct circuit functionality.

Considering the utilization of carry-chain LUTs, we employ the CutMap algorithm [18] to find a pair of cuts, named cut_a and cut_b, in $MIG_{remainder}$ that will be implemented with the two carry-chain LUTs connected to an adder. Since there can be several options for each carry-chain LUTs, for each pair of LUTs, the two cuts with the highest cumulative gain are selected [13]. The gain of a cut is computed as the number of nodes covered by the cut that do not need to be duplicated. A node has to be duplicated if at least one of its fanout nodes is not covered by the cut.

To guarantee that the cuts are legally mapped to the LUTs, the maximum number of independent inputs among the two cuts should be less than or equal to K. Hence, for each cut pair, we make sure the cuts can be mapped by verifying that

$$nPI(cut_a) + nPI(cut_b) - nShared(cut_a, cut_b) \leq K \quad (6)$$

where K is the allowed maximum number of independent inputs, $nPI(cut_x)$ indicates the number of inputs of cut_x and $nShared(cut_a, cut_b)$ presents the shared number of inputs of cut_a and cut_b. In this paper, we consider $K = 5$ because the LB shown in Fig. 1 has at most five independent inputs.

For each input pair of carry-chain nodes in MIG_{cc}, we explore the corresponding primary outputs in $MIG_{remainder}$ to find two cuts. In Fig. 7, the Z0 node in $MIG_{reminder}$ drives two nodes in MIG_{cc} and therefore has a fanout of 2. Note that the LB in Fig. 1 supports at most two extra outputs among the two fracturable LUTs plus one carry output. To find the best cut size for all pairs, a heuristic algorithm is used to sort carry-chain inputs from bottom-up. The inputs of the pairs are marked as visited when they have extra output. Hence, if a input node is already visited, it means the other node in the pair can have a cut size of $K - 1$ because the visited node just occupy one independent input. An example can be found in Fig. 4(b) where the LUT to implement 'cut D' has an extra output.

5. EXPERIMENTAL RESULTS

In this section, we first introduce the experimental methodology used for the experiments. Then, the results of these experiments on several MCNC benchmarks are presented.

5.1 Methodology

The design flow used for our experiment is shown in Fig. 3. Instead of using ABC for logic optimization in the baseline flow, we implemented our MIG-based approach in C++ as a command called '`fpga`' on top of the CirKit framework.[1]. The benchmarks considered from MCNC are general combinational circuits that have limited number of full adders. The arbitrary circuit description is transformed into MIG using '`xmglut`' command in CitKit [19]. We use the proposed approach on top of FPGA physical design stage, as a preoptimization step, which produces an alternative but functional equivalent `BLIF` description to the flow. The '`cec`' command is used to check the equivalence. The script of ABC used for technology mapping is "`resyn; resyn2; if -K 6`" for all soft logics from $MIG_{remainder}$ that is mapped into 6-input LUTs.

In this paper, we consider the FPGA architecture shown in Fig. 1, where each LB consists of $I = 10$ LEs, and $N = 50$ inputs. A length-4 uni-directional routing architecture, featured by $F_s = 3$, $F_{c,in} = 0.15$ and $F_{c,out} = 0.10$ is employed. We add 30% slack to the minimum routing channel width to simulate the low stress routing.

5.2 Area and Delay

The results of evaluating the proposed approach are shown in Table 1. The left part indicates results for the traditional design flow, while the right part presents the improvement percentage by the proposed approach. The number of adders

[1]github.com/msoeken/cirkit

used for carry-chain implementation is also reported in the last column.

In total, the proposed flow reduces the delay by 8% on average. The delay is composed of the total amount of logic and net delay. The stacked bar plot of delay distribution is shown in Fig. 8. Generally, the net delay is reduced in most of the considered benchmarks. This is because we use hard-wired carry chains for delay-efficient connections. However, one can note that the carry-chain implementation does not guarantee the net delay reduction. As the cost of routing to the hard carry chain is high, the net delay for the routing purpose can be considerable. The logic delay is determined by the technology mapping, as presented in Section 4.5, several extra primary outputs should be created to feed the carry chains. Basically, the technology mapper use more LUTs to implement these extra connections. This is why the proposed flow consumes 10% more LUTs than the traditional approach. Without efficient carry-chain LUT utilization, the increased logic delay caused by additional LUTs is expected to compensate the decreased net delay. Consequently, it indicates that the impact of the hard adder logic on delay improvement of an application is highly dependent on how the rest of the application is implemented by the soft logic.

The channel width is reduced by 6%, while the routing and total used area is practically the same with only few percentages points of difference, on average. Finally, the benefits of carry-chain implementations, by absorbing more logic into carry-chain LUTs, result in channel width improvement. After loose pattern removal that are too expensive for carry-chain implementation, the number of used adders range from 3 to 22. The benchmark with the largest delay reduction is C6288, which used 21 adders to achieve a 25.6% performance improvement.

5.3 Discussion

The performance improvement for general logic using hard-wired FPGA carry chains is encouraging. However, as also discussed in [13], the VPR packer may fail to associate the carry-chain LUTs with their respective adders and ends up wasting the carry-chain LUTs as buffers while placing their targeted functions in other logic blocks. This leads to increased logic delay, number of logic blocks, and used area. Moreover, the current VPR tool does not allow the permutation of positions of carry chains during physical synthesis. These tight constraints limit the possibility of better physical results.

Moreover, the critical path in terms of logic levels, might not be a critical path in the circuit after packing, placement, and routing. The carry chains we extracted currently are based on only one critical path at logic level. Further improvement can be achieved by extracting more critical paths by iteratively extracting the carry chains, or refining the cost function to embody the physical significance.

6. CONCLUSIONS

Hard-wired carry chains are highly efficient for arithmetic primitives implementation. Although existing research demonstrated very effective results for arithmetic-rich applications, due to the inherent inflexible design, general applications can merely take advantage of it. The MIG-based logic synthesis opens opportunities for FPGA carry chains for general purpose circuits. Instead of identifying adder primitives in either high-level description or gate-level netlist, we find carry chains effortlessly by using MIGs since the carry signal of an adder is realized by a majority gate. The proposed synthesis method for carry chains first evaluates all critical paths to determine a path candidate for carry-chain implementation. Then, the nodes along the path are further analyzed to

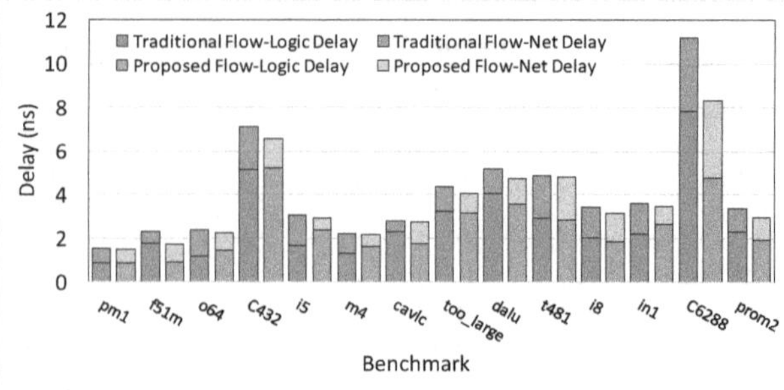

Figure 8: Comparisons of logic and net delay.

identify and remove inefficient carry-chain mapped blocks, called loose patterns. As a result, long critical paths are decomposed into several parts for efficient carry-chain implementation. By evaluating MCNC benchmarks, which have a limited number of adders by construction, the proposed method can improve performance by 8% and channel width by 6% on average, respectively.

Acknowledgments. This research was partly supported by H2020-ERC-2014-ADG 669354 CyberCare, by NSF China 61501268, by Zhejiang Provincial NSF LQ15F040001, and by Ningbo City NSF 2015A610112.

7. REFERENCES

[1] J. Luu, C. McCullough, S. Wang, S. Huda, B. Yan, C. Chiasson, K. B Kent, J. Anderson, J. Rose, and V. Betz. On hard adders and carry chains in FPGAs. In *FCCM*, pages 52–59. 2014.

[2] L. Amarù, P.-E. Gaillardon, and G. De Micheli. Majority-inverter graph: A novel data-structure and algorithms for efficient logic optimization. In *DAC*, pages 1–6. 2014.

[3] L. Amarù, P.-E. Gaillardon, and G. De Micheli. Majority-inverter graph: A new paradigm for logic optimization. *IEEE Trans on CAD*, 35(5):806–819, 2016.

[4] R. Brayton and A. Mishchenko. ABC: An academic industrial-strength verification tool. In *CAV*, pages 24–40. 2010.

[5] R. E Bryant. Graph-based algorithms for Boolean function manipulation. *IEEE Trans on Computers*, 100(8):677–691, 1986.

[6] V. Betz, J. Rose, and A. Marquardt. *Architecture and CAD for deep-submicron FPGAs*. Kluwer Academic Publishers, 1999.

[7] M. Hutton *et al.* Improving FPGA performance and area using an adaptive logic module. In *FPL*, pages 135–144, 2004.

[8] Altera. Stratix 10 advance information brief. *Altera Corporation*, July 2015.

[9] Xilinx. Virtex-7 user guide DS180 (v1.17). *Xilinx*, May 2015.

[10] G. De Micheli. *Synthesis and optimization of digital circuits*. McGraw-Hill Higher Education, 1994.

[11] M. T. Frederick and A. K. Somani. Beyond the arithmetic constraint: depth-optimal mapping of logic chains in LUT-based FPGAs. In *FPGA*, pages 37–46. 2008.

[12] T. B. Preußer and R. G. Spallek. Enhancing FPGA device capabilities by the automatic logic mapping to additive carry chains. In *FPL*, pages 318–325. 2010.

[13] A. Petkovska, G. Zgheib, D. Novo, M. Owaida, A. Mishchenko, and P. Ienne. Improved carry chain mapping for the VTR flow. In *ICFPT*, pages 80–87, 2015.

[14] L. Amarù, A. Petkovska, P.-E. Gaillardon, D. Novo, P. Ienne, and G. De Micheli. Majority-inverter graph for FPGA synthesis. In *SASIMI*, pages 165–170, 2015.

[15] J. Rose, J. Luu, C. W. Yu, O. Densmore, J. Goeders, A. Somerville, K. B Kent, P. Jamieson, and J. Anderson. The VTR project: Architecture and CAD for FPGAs from Verilog to routing. In *FPGA*, pages 77–86, 2012.

[16] Berkeley Logic Synthesis and Verification Group ABC: A system for sequential synthesis and verification, http://www.eecs.berkeley.edu/~alanmi/abc/.

[17] E. Testa, M. Soeken, O. Zografos, L. Amarù, P. Raghavan, R. Lauwereins, P.-E. Gaillardon, and G. De Micheli. Inversion optimization in majority-inverter graphs. In *NANOARCH*, 2016.

[18] J. Cong and Y.-Y. Hwang. Simultaneous depth and area minimization in LUT-based FPGA mapping In *FPGA*, 1995.

[19] W. Haaswijk, M. Soeken, L. Amarù, P.-E. Gaillardon, and G. De Micheli. A novel basis for logic rewriting. In *ASPDAC*, 2017.

Redundant Via Insertion with Cut Optimization for Self-Aligned Double Patterning

Youngsoo Song*†, Jinwook Jung*, and Youngsoo Shin*
*School of Electrical Engineering, KAIST, Daejeon 34141, Korea
†Samsung Electronics, Hwasung 18448, Korea
realyaps@kaist.ac.kr, jinwookjung@kaist.ac.kr, youngsoo@ee.kaist.ac.kr

ABSTRACT

Line-end cuts are employed to enable 1D gridded designs in self-aligned double patterning (SADP) process. Due to the minimum spacing constraints between adjacent cuts, cut optimization is important component. However, it brings a new challenge to redundant via (RV) insertion. As the cuts for RVs are not taken into account during line-end cut optimization, inserting some RVs may cause coloring conflicts or design rule violations. In this paper, we address integrated RV insertion and cut optimization problem. Given a via layout, the proposed approach optimizes the cuts in upper and lower metal layers, which are connected through a via, while RV candidate positions are considered. Only the RV candidates that do not incur coloring conflicts nor design rule violations are chosen. Our experiments indicate that only 55.3% of vias receive RVs when cut optimization and RV insertion are performed separately; corresponding number increases to 86.4% when our approach is applied.

1. INTRODUCTION

In sub-14nm technology, 1D-gridded layout is preferred over two dimensional one due to its regular patterning structure. SADP provides a smaller overlay error and finer metal track pitch, and has been considered as the most leading option for achieving the 1D layout [1–3]. In SADP, a set of uniform dense wires are first generated for a desired routing pattern. Each wire is then split into wire segments by line-end cuts. Some of them are used for actual routing wires, while the others, called dummy wires, remain floating.

To form the line-end cuts, conventional 193nm immersion lithography is still used [1]. There is a constraint on minimum spacing among the line-end cuts, and thus we use multiple cut masks for putting the cuts with closer spacing. However, using more masks comes with a cost; the number of masks to be used are limited, and so two or three masks are typically available for printing cuts. In this regard, many research efforts have been made on cut optimization, which study how we assign the line-end cuts for a given layout to

Permission to make digital or hard copies of all or part of this work for personal or classroom use is granted without fee provided that copies are not made or distributed for profit or commercial advantage and that copies bear this notice and the full citation on the first page. Copyrights for components of this work owned by others than ACM must be honored. Abstracting with credit is permitted. To copy otherwise, or republish, to post on servers or to redistribute to lists, requires prior specific permission and/or a fee. Request permissions from permissions@acm.org.

GLSVLSI '17, May 10–12, 2017, Banff, AB, Canada.
© 2017 ACM. ISBN 978-1-4503-4972-7/17/05...$15.00.
DOI: http://dx.doi.org/10.1145/3060403.3060440

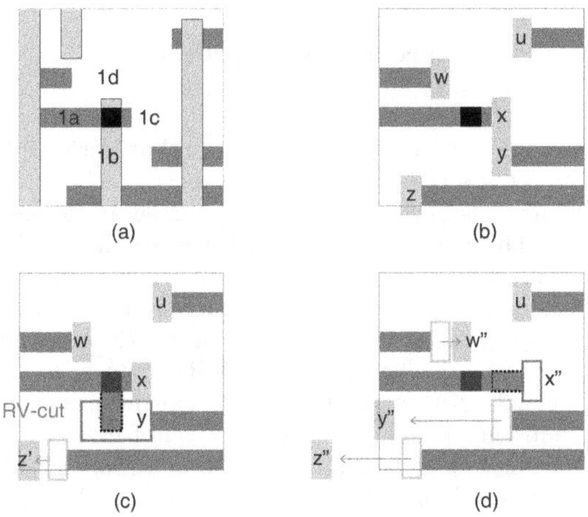

Figure 1: (a) An example layout, (b) M2 cut locations, (c) new M2 cut locations due to RV at 1b and its RV cut, and (d) another M2 cut locations when RV is inserted at 1c.

different cut masks, and how they are distributed within a cut mask [1, 4–6].

The cut optimization, however, brings a new challenge on RV insertion. As well as for line-end cutting, some dedicated cuts may be needed to generate RVs at certain positions in SADP. The cuts, which we call *RV cuts*, are also assigned to the same cut masks with line-end cuts. Conflicts may hence occur among RV cuts and line-end cuts. In addition, a wire needs to be extended when we insert an RV, which in turn makes the locations of line-end cuts become stale. Nonetheless, cut optimization do not take account of RVs since it is typically performed right after detailed routing, in which the locations of RVs are not determined yet. Once the cut optimization is completed, the location and mask assignment for each line-end cut are fixed; it makes the following RV insertion have only a limited number of candidate locations for RV due to coloring conflicts and minimum cut spacing rule violations (or cut conflicts for short).

1.1 Motivation and Contribution

Consider a layout shown in Figure 1(a), which consists of metal2 (M2) and metal3 (M3) layers, as well as a via layer between them (Via2). The layout includes one via whose candidate locations for RV insertion are $1a$, $1b$, $1c$, and $1d$. Figure 1(b) shows the M2 layer of the example layout, with

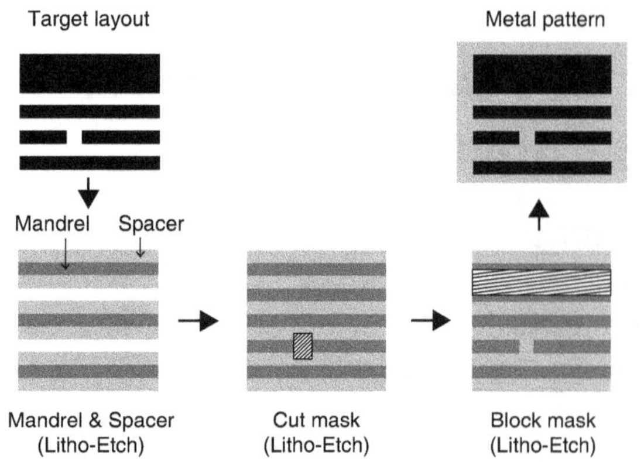

Figure 2: SADP process.

the line-end cuts u, w, x, y, and z. Note that, for simplicity, dummy wires are not illustrated in Figure 1.

Let us now assume that an RV is inserted at $1b$ (see Figure 1(c)). The wire associated with the RV has to be extended to its perpendicular direction in order to enclose the RV. It brings about an RV cut to be generated, as shown in Figure 1(c), which is three times larger than a line-end cut; the reason for the large size of RV cuts is described in Section 2.3. Although the RV cut can be merged with the line-end cuts x and y so that it does not cause conflicts with adjacent line-end cuts, minimum cut spacing rule violation of the RV cut with z cannot be resolved without a displacement of z. Therefore, the previous cut optimization becomes invalid. We should abandon the RV or redo cut optimization. Similarly, in Figure 1(d), when the RV is inserted at position $1c$, the line-end cut x has to be moved for via enclosure. The adjacent cuts w, y and z needs to be moved. Conflicts between cuts caused by RV insertion and adjacent cuts should be minimized so that the maximum number of RVs can be accommodated.

In this paper, we propose for the first time a cut mask optimization method which factors in the cuts generated for RV insertion in SADP process. Its primary goal is to reduce conflicts among cuts so that the RVs are maximally inserted. Given a via layer, our method optimizes the cuts in both the upper and lower metal layers considering the potential RV candidate positions. Only the RV candidates which do not cause cut conflicts are used for RV insertion afterward. We apply our proposed method on a set of test circuits, and demonstrate its effectiveness in improving RV insertion rate.

The remainder of this paper is organized as follows. Section 2 describes SADP process and how RVs are formed in SADP. RV insertion problem for SADP is defined in Section 3, and Section 4 presents the proposed method. Section 5 shows experimental results, and Section 6 gives some concluding remarks.

2. PRELIMINARIES

2.1 SADP Process

SADP is suitable for manufacturing uniform and regular patterns. Process variations caused by the limits of lithography or the loading effect of etch process can be mitigated in virtue of its fine alignment margin. Figure 2 depicts an SADP process, which consists of mandrel, cut, and block masks; this type of SADP is called a spacer-is-dielectric (SID) SADP. Given a desired routing pattern, denoted by target layout, parallel mandrels are uniformly patterned in the beginning. Spacer material is subsequently deposited and etched back without mask so that only the sidewall spacers remain. Then the line and space patterns with the half-pitch of mandrel are formed. The mandrels are segmented by cuts to generate actual routing wires. We can also use a block mask for creating wide or rectilinear patterns.

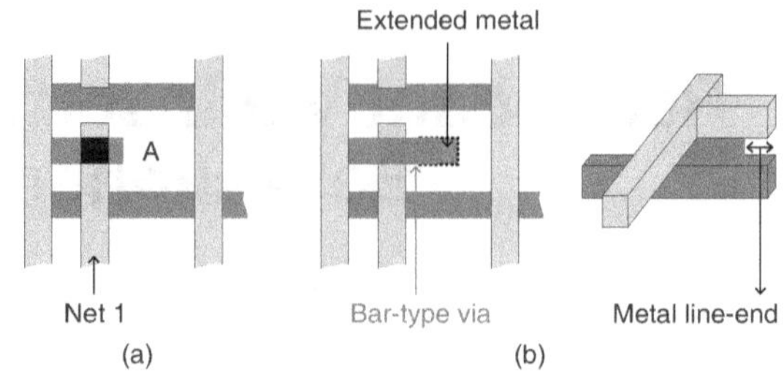

Figure 3: (a) Original layout without RV and (b) Combined via and RV as a bar-type via.

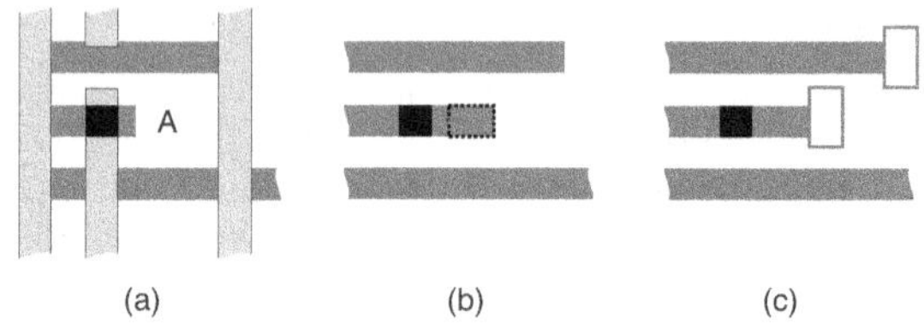

Figure 4: (a) Original layout without RV, (b) M2 extension due to RV insertion, and (c) corresponding line-end cut locations.

2.2 Bar-Type Via

Via enclosure rule specifies the minimum amount of margin with which a via must be covered by metal layer [7]. It is for reliable via formation during manufacturing process. However, it reduces the number of candidate position for RV insertion. Let us assume that we want to insert an RV at the position denoted by A in Figure 3(a). If we insert the RV, the M3 wire should be extended so that it satisfies the via enclosure rule, but it cannot be extended due to minimum line-end space rule. Therefore, we cannot insert an RV.

To this end, we assume that every pair of a single via and its RV is combined to form a bar-type via as shown in Figure 3(b). It helps reduce the area occupied by a via–RV pair, and thereby the total amount of metal extension caused by the RV insertion. The minimum line-end space rule violation between the two metals is now resolved, and so we are able to insert an RV for the example layout.

2.3 RV Formation in SADP

Because of the via enclosure rule, a metal wire must be extended as it covers a via with a margin. Its line-end cut is correspondingly re-distributed as it locates at the end of the extended wire. Assuming that an RV is inserted at the

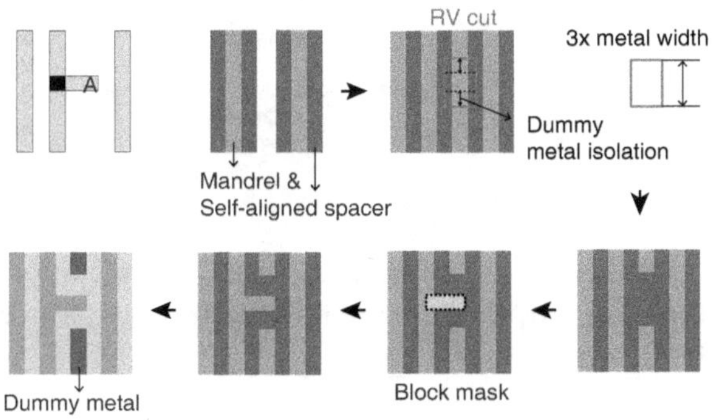

Figure 5: Extended M3 wire in its perpendicular direction for the example layout in Figure 3.

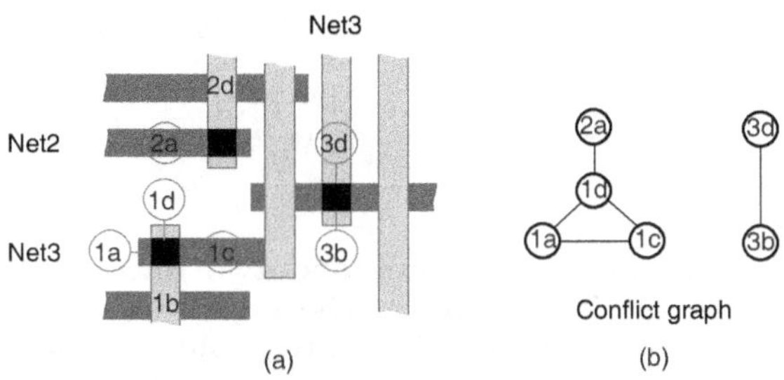

Figure 6: (a) Three vias (V1, V2, and V3) with their RV candidates, and (b) formulation of RV insertion as an MIS problem (a vertex corresponds to an RV candidate and an edge represents a conflict).

position A of Figure 4(a) , the M2 wire should be extended to the RV position. The amount of the wire extension is indicated in Figure 4(b) The corresponding line-end cut is relocated as shown in Figure 4(c).

The wire on the M3 layer should also be extended for inserting RV at A. However, the extension is toward its non-preferred direction, so it introduces a dedicated cut, named RV cut. The formation process of M3 wire for the extension to A is illustrated in Figure 5. To pattern for extended M3, the cut mask is assigned to be three times larger in size for isolation from the adjacent dummy metal. This can be merged with neighboring line-end cut; the merged cut can be patterned by a litho-etch-litho-etch (LELE) process with stitch. Then the extension of M3 wire is formed by using a block mask.

3. RV INSERTION FOR SADP

3.1 Conventional RV Insertion

RV insertion is usually performed in a post-routing stage with the goal of maximizing the number of RVs inserted [8–10]. It is reduced to a maximum independent set (MIS) problem through graph formulation. Figure 6(a) shows an example layout, where the candidate locations of RV insertion, which we call the RV candidates, for each via are identified. A via can have up to 4 RV candidates, but only those not incurring electrical or design rule violations are factored in as valid RV candidates. For example, the via of

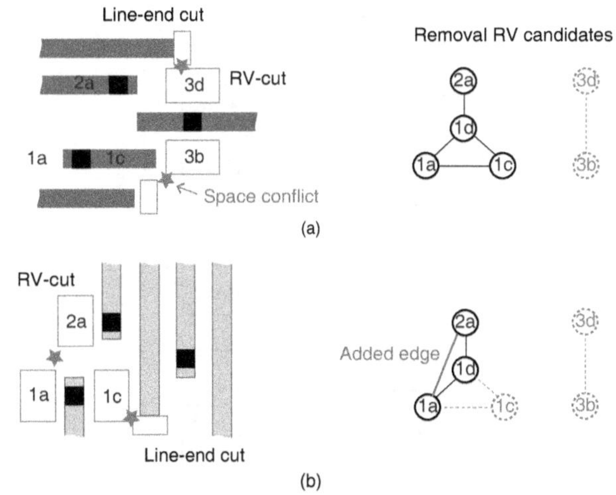

Figure 7: Reduced number of RV candidates in SADP process due to (a) M2 cut conflicts and (b) M3 cut conflicts.

Net1 has 4 RV candidates which are $1a$, $1b$, $1c$, and $1d$; $1b$ is not a valid candidate due to electrical short with the wire belonging to a different net. The RV candidate $2d$ is also excluded as it is within the minimum space from the via of Net2. Likewise, we identify the RV candidates for each via.

A conflict graph is then introduced with the identified RV candidates (Figure 6(b)). Each RV candidate becomes a vertex in the conflict graph. An edge is introduced between two vertices if they belong to the same via or they have conflict as in Figure 6(b). The RV insertion problem can now be reduced to an MIS problem on the conflict graph; the MIS corresponds to RV candidates of the maximum number without conflicts.

3.2 Problem Statement

In SADP process, every metal wire comes with line-end cuts as described in Section 2.1. A minimum spacing constraint among the cuts is imposed to ensure proper cut formation; the line-end cuts should be placed apart at least the minimum cut spacing or they must be assigned to different cut masks. In this regard, detailed routing is followed by a line-end cut mask optimization stage in a physical design flow for SADP process [1,5].

However, an RV candidate comes with an RV cut in SADP, so it may have a cut conflict with other pre-existing line-end cuts. This leads us to adjust the location of the line-end cuts or their mask assignment, or even to abandon the RV candidate for resolving the cut conflict. Cut conflicts may also occur among different RV cuts. Consider Figure 7(a) and Figure 7(b), where the individual metal layers of the example layout in Figure 6 are illustrated respectively. Assuming the locations and mask assignment for the line-end cuts are already determined, the RV candidates $3b$ and $3d$ cannot be inserted without metal2 cut conflicts with the line-end cuts (see Figure 7(a)); they have to be removed from the conflict graph formulation. In addition, if RV is inserted in $1c$, a metal3 RV cut is assigned and it is also removed as an RV candidates since small space conflict with below line-end cut is occurred. On the other hand, if RV-cuts are

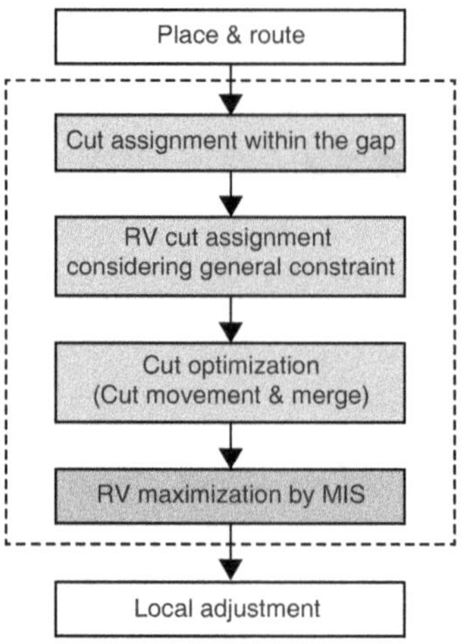

Figure 8: Overall flow of the proposed method.

assigned in 1a and 2a, they have a distance which can not be decomposable to different color, and then an edge is created. As a result, the conflict graph now has few vertex, and therefore we cannot insert many RV for the example layout.

To this end, RV insertion for SADP should be incorporated with line-end cut optimization in order to maximize the number of inserted RVs. We define the problem of RV insertion with cut optimization for SADP as follows: given a layout after detailed routing, determine the positions at which RVs are inserted as well as the mask assignments and locations of cuts, such that all the electrical and design rules are satisfied. The objective is to maximize the number of inserted RVs.

4. ALGORITHM

4.1 Overall Flow

Figure 8 outlines the proposed RV insertion method, which takes account of cut optimization for SADP. It optimizes line-end cuts in both metal layers so that the number of RVs inserted is maximized. The number of masks for patterning cuts is assumed to be 2 in this paper. The input of the proposed algorithm is a target via layer along with its upper and lower metal layers after detailed routing. Given the layers, line-end cuts of both metal layers are first assigned at the center of the gap between every two metal wires. The potential RV cuts are then generated wherever RVs can be inserted without any electrical and design rule violations. Cut mask optimization is performed in both metal layers with the line-end cuts and RV cuts through a conflict graph formulation. RVs are then inserted using a widely used MIS-based algorithm [7], considering only the RV candidates whose RV cuts do not cause cut conflicts. Finally, some line-end cuts are re-distributed to decrease the amount of wire extension.

4.2 Cut Assignment

Given a target via layer and both the upper and lower metal layers, two types of cuts are initially generated for cut optimization, namely line-end cuts and RV cuts.

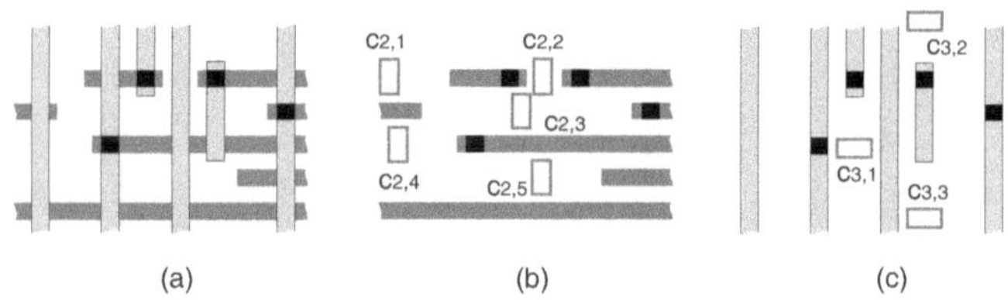

Figure 9: (a) An example layout of two metal layers, (b) line-end cut assignment in M2, and (c) line-end cut assignment in M3.

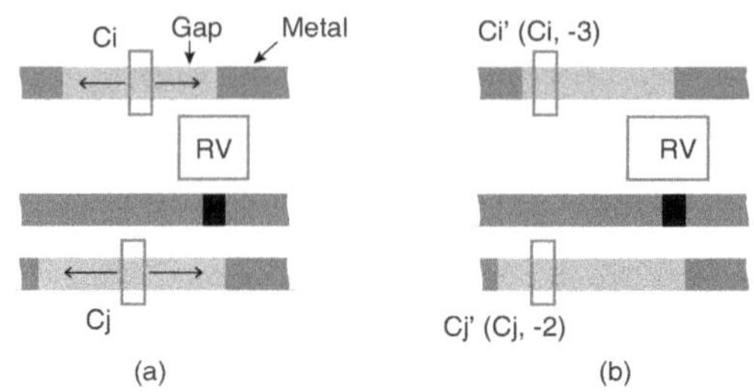

Figure 10: (a) An RV cut and two line-end cuts generated in the middle of the gaps, and (b) displacement of the line-end cuts to avoid cut conflict.

- **Line-end cuts:** Instead of assigning line-end cuts at both ends of each metal wire, cuts are initially generated in the middle of the space between every two metal wires, which we call the *gap*. It reduces the number of line-end cuts to be optimized; it also inherently distributes the cuts such that they are not likely to cause cut conflicts. For example, consider an example layout shown in Figure 9(a). Line-end cuts are assigned initially in the middle of the gaps as shown in Figures 9(b) and 9(c). If the *gap* is too wide, the cut assignment incur excessive wire extension. So, the line-end cut is generated at α grids apart from the corresponding line-end of the metal wire when the *gap* is wider than a certain threshold value (see the line-end cut $c_{2,5}$ in Figure 9(b)).
- **RV cuts:** We find every RV candidate position in the given layouts at which no electrical or design rule violations occur. The corresponding RV cuts are then assigned (see an example layout shown in Figure 10(a)).

4.3 Cut Optimization

Potential conflict graph construction. Given the initially assigned line-end cuts and RV cuts, we generate the potential conflict graph G_p for each metal layer. Each vertex in G_p represents a cut, and an edge is created between two vertices if potential coloring conflict exists between them. The potential coloring conflicts are identified using the feasible moving region of each cut. A line-end cut on a gap can move on the gap (see Figure 10(a)), while an RV cut has a fixed position. Potential conflict graph G_p is then decomposed into a set of independent sub-graphs by finding every connected component on G_p. Bridges and articulation points are also used for the decomposition of G_p [11]. Each subgraph of G_p is then independently optimized.

Move generation. We construct a conflict graph G for each decomposed subgraph of G_p. It has the same set of vertices as its corresponding subgraph of G_p, but includes only the conflict edges created using the initial cut locations. To optimize a conflict graph, we adopt the notion of "move" which is proposed in [5]. Let us take the example layout shown in Figure 10. Since the three cuts, c_i, c_j and the RV cut are placed within the minimum cut spacing each other, they construct a coloring conflict cycle in the conflict graph, which consists of an odd number of vertices. Considering the assumption that we are given only two masks for print cuts, these cuts cannot be patterned correctly. We can resolve the cyclic conflict by moving the line-end cut c_i or c_j to the left direction (see Figure 10(b)). Removing the RV cut is also an option for resolving the odd cycle.

To this end, we generate all the possible moves for each odd cycle that exists in a conflict graph. Then, a set of moves, denoted by M, that can resolve the odd cycle is generated using a similar method presented in [5]. Given an odd cycle, all the minimum displacements of each line-end that can remove the conflict associated with the cut is generated, and included in M. If an odd cycle includes an RV cut, removing the RV cut is also defined as a move and added in M.

Move selection. Once every possible move that can resolve odd cycles in a conflict graph is generated, only a subset of moves is selected to commit. Let us move be denoted by $m_i \in M$, its associated odd cycle be denoted by c_j, and a set of every odd cycle be denoted by C. The move selection is now formulated as integer linear programming (ILP) [5]:

$$\text{Minimize} \quad \sum_{\forall m_i \in M} w_i \cdot x_i, \tag{1}$$

$$\text{Subject to} \quad \sum_{\forall m_i \in M} e_{i,j} \cdot x_i \geq 1, \ \forall c_j \in C, \tag{2}$$

$$x_i + x_j \leq 1, \ \forall m_i \text{ incompatible with } m_j, \tag{3}$$

$$x_i, e_{i,j} \in \{0, 1\}, \tag{4}$$

where x_i is a selection variable for m_i. $e_{i,j}$ is 1 if m_i resolves a conflict in odd cycle c_j, and 0 otherwise. Each move m_i is associated with a weight w_i; if m_i removes an RV cut, it is assigned a large weight (10× larger value in this paper than the moves associated with line-end cuts). There may exist some incompatible moves that cannot be executed at the same time. For instance, two moves may try to displace a line-end cut toward opposite directions within a gap. Only one move has to be selected; Eq. (3) imposes such constraint.

Once selected moves are executed, we check whether each conflict graph still contains some coloring conflict cycles. If odd cycles are discovered, moves are re-generated and selected until no more odd cycles exist.

4.4 RV Insertion and Local Adjustment

After cut optimization, some RV cuts are removed to resolve cut conflicts. RV insertion is performed using the RV candidates that are associated with the surviving RV cuts. It is done by a standard MIS-based RV insertion method [7]; a conflict graph for RV insertion is created with those RV candidates. Then the RV insertion problem is reduced to an MIS problem. After solving MIS, RVs are inserted based on the MIS solution.

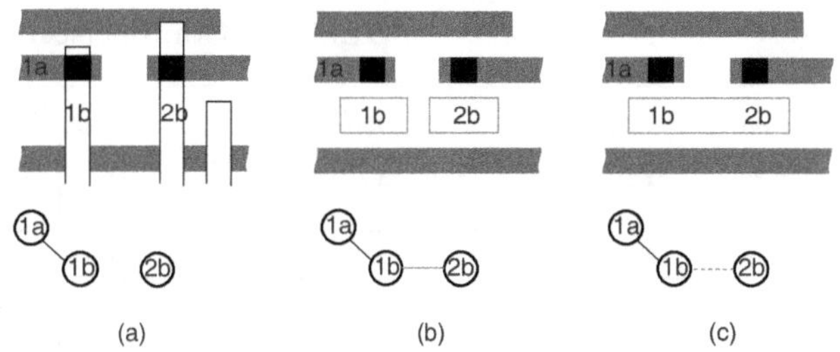

Figure 11: (a) RV candidates from general constraints, (b) conflict edge (1b, 2b) added due to cut conflict, and (c) conflict edge (1b, 2b) removed through RV cut merge.

During the RV insertion, it is necessary to consider cut conflicts among RV cuts. Let us assume an example layout shown in Figure 11(a) where $1a$, $1b$, and $2b$ are identified as RV candidates. The RV cuts for $1b$ and $2b$ are shown in Figure 11(b). They are located within the minimum cut spacing from each other, and hence a conflict edge has to be created between them. Yet, in some cases, the conflict edges due to RV cut conflicts can be eliminated by cut merge. Consider Figure 11(c). When the RV cuts are merged into a cut, the conflict edge can be removed.

Finally, the RV cuts that do not appear in the RV solutions are removed in the conflict graph G. This removes a large number of cut conflicts. Line-end cuts that do not have any incident edges in a conflict graph are then re-distributed to minimize wire extension. They are first separated to left and right cuts, and moved toward the line-end of corresponding wire segment. Then remaining line-end cuts are adjusted to minimize wire extension using a heuristic algorithm presented in [5].

5. EXPERIMENTS

We implemented the proposed algorithm with Python and C++, and adopted Gurobi [12] for ILP solution. A set of test circuits was taken from OpenCores [13], ITC'99 [14] and ISCAS'89 [15] benchmarks. They were synthesized with a 28-nm industrial library using a commercial logic synthesis tool. Placement and routing were performed assuming a 1D-gridded design rule. The proposed algorithm was used to insert RVs at Via2 layer. The layout of each circuit was appropriately shrunk to follow a 10-nm design rule that we assume in this paper. The number of vias and total wire length of M2/M3 layers are shown in columns 2–3 of Table 1. Metal track pitch is 50nm, and a via has a size of 25nm × 25nm. We assumed two masks are available for cut optimization. To solve MIS, the algorithm presented in [16] was employed.

Two other RV insertion methods were implemented for reference of comparison. The first method, named MIS in Table 1, simply applies MIS [8] to a basic conflict graph. Cut conflicts are not considered, so it causes large number of coloring conflicts and minimum cut spacing rule violations as shown in the fifth column, even though the percentage of RVs shown in column 4 is very high.

The second method, named as MIS-SADP in Table 1, takes account of line-end cuts. Specifically, line-end cut optimization [5] is performed after detailed routing. Vertices

Table 1: Comparison of three RV insertion methods

Circuit	#Vias	WL (*mm*)	MIS		MIS-SADP		Proposed	
			#RVs (%)	#Conflicts	#RVs (%)	ΔWL(%)	#RVs (%)	ΔWL(%)
s5378	3,467	6.4	96.8	3,158	59.4	1.2	89.8	3.2
des3_area	9,363	15.4	96.6	8,723	50.6	2.3	82.3	5.0
b15	20,284	33.4	95.9	18,614	53.9	1.6	85.6	4.4
s38417	27,048	52.0	97.3	24,664	58.8	1.1	90.2	2.9
b14_1	29,159	45.4	96.6	27,126	55.1	1.9	87.5	5.0
ac97_ctrl	31,926	57.5	97.4	29,817	59.2	1.3	91.2	3.1
usb_funct	38,625	68.6	97.0	35,729	55.7	1.4	87.0	3.7
aes_core	44,357	69.2	95.8	40,980	49.3	1.9	86.2	5.9
sd_card	46,046	86.0	97.9	41,823	58.4	1.2	90.3	2.9
b17	61,137	103.6	96.0	56,239	53.1	1.7	85.6	4.3
fpu	124,846	179.6	97.3	117,405	54.6	2.1	89.5	5.1
Average			96.8		55.3	1.7	86.4	4.3

in the initial conflict graph, which cause cut conflicts with line-end cuts, are removed; additional edges are added if two vertices are within minimum cut spacing. MIS is then applied to the updated conflict graph. The percentage of RVs substantially drops as reported in the sixth column, which motivates our work. Total wire extension is reported in column 7.

The results obtained using the proposed method is presented in the last two columns o Table 1. The RV percentage increases to 86.4% on average of test circuits, which is 31.1% more than that of MIS-SADP. This proves the importance of combined cut optimization and RV insertion. Metal extension slightly increases to 4.3%, but we believe it should be manageable. Note that minimizing wire extension is a goal of cut optimization in MIS-SADP, which however is not in cut optimization in the proposed approach.

6. CONCLUSION

We have addressed the combined RV insertion and cut optimization in SADP. The problem has been formulated as a conflict graph, in which potential cut conflicts are taken into account; applying MIS returns a solution. Given a via layout, the line-end cuts in both upper and lower metal layers are optimized in such a way that RVs can be inserted as much as possible. The proposed method has been demonstrated on a set of test circuits assuming 10*nm* technology. Experimental results indicate that our proposed algorithm achieves RV percentage of 86.4% on average of test circuits, while a standard approach of cut optimization followed by RV insertion achieves a corresponding figure of 55.3%.

We have assumed double patterning for cut formation in this paper. An extension of proposed algorithm for handling triple or quadruple patterning remains as a future work.

References

[1] K. Han *et al.*, "ILP-based co-optimization of cut mask layout, dummy fill, and timing for sub-14nm BEOL technology," in *Proc. SPIE Advanced Lithography*, Oct. 2015, pp. 96 350E1–96 350E14.

[2] M. Mirsaeedi, J. Torres, and M. Anis, "Self-aligned double patterning (SADP) layout decomposition," in *Proc. Int. Symp. Qual. Electron. Des.*, Mar. 2011, pp. 1–7.

[3] H. Zhang *et al.*, "Mask cost reduction with circuit performance consideration for self-aligned double patterning," in *Proc. Asia South Pacific Des. Autom. Conf.*, Jan. 2011, pp. 787–792.

[4] Z. Xiao *et al.*, "A polynomial time exact algorithm for overlay-resistant self-aligned double patterning (SADP) layout decomposition," *IEEE Trans. Comput.-Aided Des. Integr. Circuits Syst.*, vol. 32, no. 8, pp. 1228–1239, Aug. 2011.

[5] J. Kuang, E. F. Young, and B. Yu, "Incorporating cut redistribution with mask assignment to enable 1D gridded design," in *Proc. Int. Conf. Comput.-Aided Des.*, Nov. 2016, pp. 48–55.

[6] S. Owa *et al.*, "Immersion lithography extension to sub-10nm nodes with multiple patterning," in *Proc. SPIE Advanced Lithography*, Mar. 2014, pp. 90 520O1–90 520O9.

[7] K.-Y. Lee, T.-C. Wang, and K.-Y. Chao, "Post-routing redundant via insertion and line end extension with via density consideration," in *Proc. Int. Conf. Comput.-Aided Des.*, Nov. 2006, pp. 633–640.

[8] K.-Y. Lee and T.-C. Wang, "Post-routing redundant via insertion for yield/reliability improvement," in *Proc. Asia South Pacific Des. Autom. Conf.*, Jan. 2006, pp. 303–308.

[9] C.-K. Lei, P.-Y. Chiang, and Y.-M. Lee, "Post-routing redundant via insertion with wire spreading capability," in *Proc. Asia South Pacific Des. Autom. Conf.*, Jan. 2009, pp. 468–473.

[10] K.-Y. Lee *et al.*, "Fast and optimal redundant via insertion," *IEEE Trans. Comput.-Aided Des. Integr. Circuits Syst.*, vol. 27, no. 12, pp. 2197–2208, Dec. 2008.

[11] S.-Y. Fang, Y.-W. Chang, and W.-Y. Chen, "A novel layout decomposition algorithm for triple patterning lithography," *IEEE Trans. Comput.-Aided Des. Integr. Circuits Syst.*, vol. 33, no. 3, pp. 397–408, Feb. 2014.

[12] Gurobi optimizer reference manual. [Online]. Available: http://www.gurobi.com

[13] OpenCores. [Online]. Available: http://www.opencores.org

[14] ITC99. [Online]. Available: http://www.cerc.utexas.edu/itc99-benchmarks/bench.html

[15] "ISCAS89." [Online]. Available: http://www.cbl.ncsu.edu/benchmarks/ISCAS89/

[16] R. Boppana and M. M. Halldórsson, "Approximating maximum independent sets by excluding subgraphs," *BIT Numerical Mathematics*, vol. 32, no. 2, pp. 180–196, Jun. 1992.

Boolean Decomposition for AIG Optimization

Lucas Machado
Department of Computer Science
Universitat Politècnica de Catalunya
Barcelona, Spain
lmachado@cs.upc.edu

Jordi Cortadella
Department of Computer Science
Universitat Politècnica de Catalunya
Barcelona, Spain
jordi.cortadella@upc.edu

ABSTRACT

Restructuring techniques for And-Inverter Graphs (AIG), such as rewriting and refactoring, are powerful, scalable and fast, achieving highly optimized AIGs after few iterations. However, these techniques are biased by the original AIG structure and limited by single output optimizations. This paper investigates AIG optimization for area, exploring how far Boolean methods can reduce AIG nodes through local optimization. Boolean division is applied for multi-output functions using two-literal divisors and Boolean decomposition is introduced as a method for AIG optimization. Multi-output blocks are extracted from the AIG and optimized, achieving a further AIG node reduction of 7.76% on average for ITC99 and MCNC benchmarks.

Keywords

Boolean decomposition; AIG; KL-cuts; local optimization

1. INTRODUCTION

Logic synthesis is a key process in design automation, generating an optimized netlist of logic gates from an RTL representation, and it is often divided in two classes: technology independent and technology dependent [6]. Recently, technology independent algorithms using AIGs have been proposed, enabling efficient and scalable optimizations [10].

Restructuring methods such as refactoring [10], rewriting [13], and balancing [5] are powerful, obtaining highly optimized AIGs after few iterations. Still, these techniques are usually constrained by single output transformations, and iterations with technology mapping [7, 12] are often used to improve structurally biased results.

AIG rewriting and refactoring perform local transformations, extracting the local context with K-cuts [16], windows or maximum fanout-free cones (MFFCs). K-cuts can be considered a superior method to extract local context compared to windowing [7, 10], as it is possible to *control the support* of the Boolean functions to be optimized, while identifying a region of the circuit that *depends on this support.*

Permission to make digital or hard copies of all or part of this work for personal or classroom use is granted without fee provided that copies are not made or distributed for profit or commercial advantage and that copies bear this notice and the full citation on the first page. Copyrights for components of this work owned by others than ACM must be honored. Abstracting with credit is permitted. To copy otherwise, or republish, to post on servers or to redistribute to lists, requires prior specific permission and/or a fee. Request permissions from permissions@acm.org.

GLSVLSI '17, May 10-12, 2017, Banff, AB, Canada.
© 2017 ACM. ISBN 978-1-4503-4972-7/17/05...$15.00.
DOI: http://dx.doi.org/10.1145/3060403.3060420

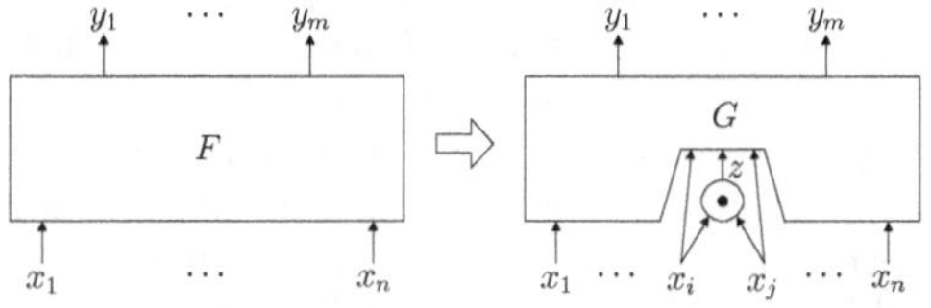

Figure 1: Decomposition using two-literal Boolean divisors.

Algorithms based on K-cut enumeration have been proposed, such as factor cuts [4] and priority cuts [14], reducing the search space and enabling cuts with more nodes and inputs. Also, *multi-output* blocks based on K-cuts were presented [8, 9], which extract the *complete local context.*

This paper studies technology-independent transformations that reduce the AIG size by exploring the use of Boolean decomposition. This is done by expanding the idea of two-literal divisors [15] to multi-output functions (see Fig. 1). The principle is as follows. A multi-output function

$$(y_1, \ldots, y_m) = F(x_1, \ldots, x_n)$$

can be decomposed into another multi-output function

$$(y_1, \ldots, y_m) = G(x_1, \ldots, x_n, z)$$

with z being a two-literal divisor ($z = x_i \odot x_j$) and $\odot$ being a Boolean operator (such as an AIG node). G is supposed to be a simpler function than F, which can be obtained by Boolean division. A multi-output Boolean function can be recursively decomposed using this paradigm, and the result can be represented as an AIG network.

The main purpose of this paper is to explore how far Boolean decomposition can go beyond the existing AIG rewriting methods. Unfortunately, scalability is an important issue when dealing with Boolean methods. Obviously, collapsing large networks into one-node functions and then decomposing is not computationally affordable.

This paper takes a significant leap forward regarding [15]:

- Boolean decomposition with two-literal divisors is generalized to be applicable to netlists with multiple outputs, instead of individual single-output functions.
- The selection of divisors is customized to increase the logic shared among multiple outputs.
- A set of filters to reduce the search space is presented.
- Scalability is addressed by iteratively applying Boolean decomposition to KL-cuts [9] of the AIG (see Fig. 2).

Note that a KL-cut represents a portion of the circuit that depends on the same set of variables. The *key idea* is to use this property of KL-cuts to identify divisors that are useful for several functions, sharing more logic and reducing area.

In [11], a resynthesis method that uses Boolean decomposition is performed on netlists of FPGA LUTs, by identifying and decomposing MFFCs. However, [11] does not perform

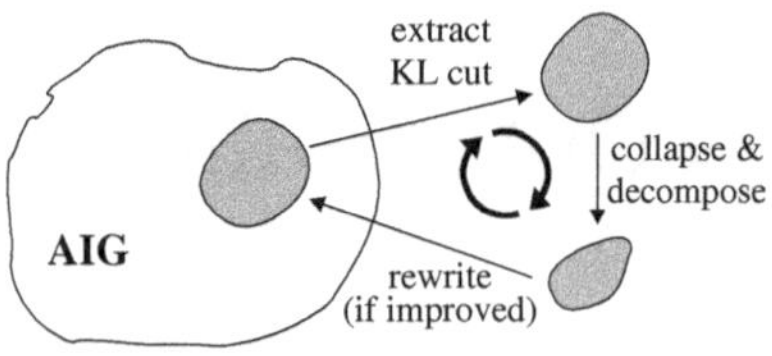

Figure 2: Iterative rewriting of AIG cuts.

a complete Boolean decomposition, as it is limited to a simplified version of Disjoint Support Decomposition. In [17], windows are enumerated and don't cares identified in the network are used to simplify these windows, while in [18] the algebraic decomposition method is improved by assigning previously calculated don't cares using a set of rules. In this work, there is neither search nor previous calculation of don't care conditions, as the optimization using don't cares occurs solely inside the KL-cut logic.

The results reported in the paper have been often obtained by applying computationally intensive methods (e.g., many divisors, many cuts). Bear in mind that our goal now is to establish the bounds potentially reachable by future work that could use smart *oracles* to drive the search. Some preliminary criteria are discussed in the paper. Still, the method proposed in this paper can be interesting for highly repetitive structures or area-critical components.

2. MULTI-OUTPUT DECOMPOSITION

Boolean decomposition is known to obtain good-quality results at the expense of a high computational cost. Finding good divisors is the most challenging task. Different approaches can be proposed to prune the search, e.g., use two-literal divisors [15], consider polarity information to ignore unpromising divisions, or reuse algebraic factored forms to select divisors. Considering all these simplifications, is it still possible to obtain good results?

To illustrate the method, consider the set of functions and its DC-set in (1). Any combination of two literals of F can be selected as a Boolean divisor. The number of literals is defined as the cost function, therefore the cost of F is 12.

$$F = \begin{cases} f_1 = b \cdot x + \bar{c} \cdot \bar{x} \\ f_2 = a \cdot x + d \cdot \bar{x} \\ f_3 = a \cdot x + b \cdot e \end{cases} \quad DC = \bar{a}\cdot b\cdot x + a\cdot \bar{b}\cdot x + a\cdot b\cdot \bar{x} \quad (1)$$

A reduction of 3 literals is achieved by performing a multi-output Boolean division using the divisor $y = a\cdot b$, generating the new set of functions and DC-set in (2). Note that this divisor is not easily extracted from the set of functions F: f_1 does not have the variable a and f_2 does not have the variable b. Still, all functions are reduced in 1 literal due to the effective use of the DC-set.

$$F_{new} = \begin{cases} f_1' = y + \bar{c} \cdot \bar{x} \\ f_2' = y + d \cdot \bar{x} \\ f_3' = y + b \cdot e \end{cases} \quad DC_{new} = DC + (y \oplus (a \cdot b)) \quad (2)$$

For further decomposition steps, it is possible to perform a DC-set projection, removing variables from the DC-set that are not in the support of F, and decreasing the computational effort of the Boolean division. By projecting DC_{new} to the support of F_{new}, $DC_{proj} = \bar{b} \cdot y$ is generated.

2.1 AIG optimization example

In order to demonstrate the potential benefits of the approach introduced in this paper, the circuit *b06* of ITC99 benchmarks suite [1] is used. The optimization flow and the results for the different solutions are depicted in Fig. 3.

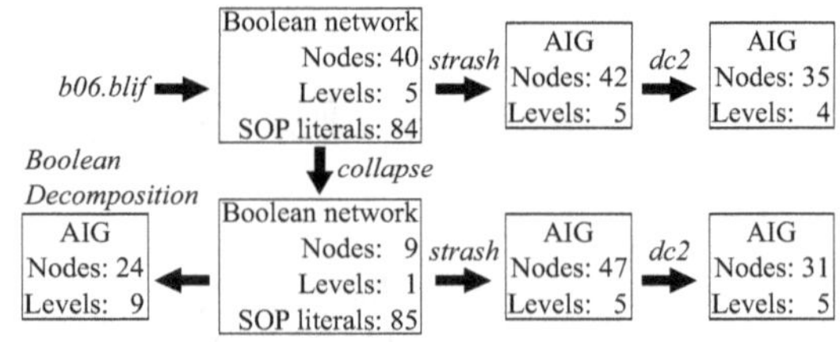

Figure 3: Optimization flow using different methods for *b06*.

The input circuit is a Boolean network represented in a BLIF file. An AIG with 42 nodes is obtained after decomposing the Boolean network with algebraic factorization and structural hashing (*strash* command in ABC [3]). After iteratively applying algebraic transformations using *dc2* command in ABC, the number of nodes is reduced to 35.

An alternative approach would start by collapsing the initial network, which results in a Boolean network with one node for each output. Decomposing these nodes results in a larger AIG with 47 nodes, but applying iterative algebraic transformations reduces it to 31 nodes.

The method proposed in this paper applies Boolean decomposition on top of the collapsed network using an approach inspired by [15]. In this work, multi-output decomposition is used by iteratively selecting the Boolean divisor that minimizes the literals of the functions factored forms [2]. This approach is able to achieve a better logic sharing, obtaining an AIG with only 24 nodes.

Also, a set of filters is applied to reduce the search space of divisors. By reducing the amount of two-level minimizations compared to [15], runtime is reduced 40 times on average, without sacrificing the quality of the results. Note that the results in this work cannot be directly compared with [15], which only presents the decomposition of single-output functions and it is not applied for circuit optimization.

3. BACKGROUND

3.1 Functions, unateness and containment

A completely specified Boolean function f is a mapping from an n-dimensional ($n \geq 0$) into a 1-dimensional Boolean space: $\{0,1\}^n \to \{0,1\}$. The positive (negative) *cofactor* $f|_{x=1}$ ($f|_{x=0}$) of f with respect to the variable x is a function obtained by assigning x to one (zero) in f.

A Boolean function f is positive (negative) unate in the variable x if $f|_{x=1} \supseteq f|_{x=0}$ ($f|_{x=0} \supseteq f|_{x=1}$), where $\supseteq$ is the set operation for inclusion. Otherwise, f is considered binate in x. This is the concept of *unateness* [6], intended for completely specified functions.

An incompletely specified function (ISF) g is a mapping from an n-dimensional ($n \geq 0$) into a 1-dimensional Boolean space: $\{0,1\}^n \to \{0,1,*\}$, where $*$ denotes a *don't care* value. The subdomains of g that evaluate to 1, 0 and $*$ are the ON-set, OFF-set and DC-set, and can be represented by the completely specified functions g_{on}, g_{off} and g_{dc}.

Containment [19] is a generalization of the concept of unateness for ISFs. The variable x in the positive polarity is *contained* in g if

$$(g_{dc}|_{x=1} \cup g_{on}|_{x=1}) \supseteq g_{on}|_{x=0}$$

and in the negative polarity if

$$(g_{dc}|_{x=0} \cup g_{on}|_{x=0}) \supseteq g_{on}|_{x=1},$$

where the operators $\cup$ and $\supseteq$ are the set operations of union and inclusion, respectively.

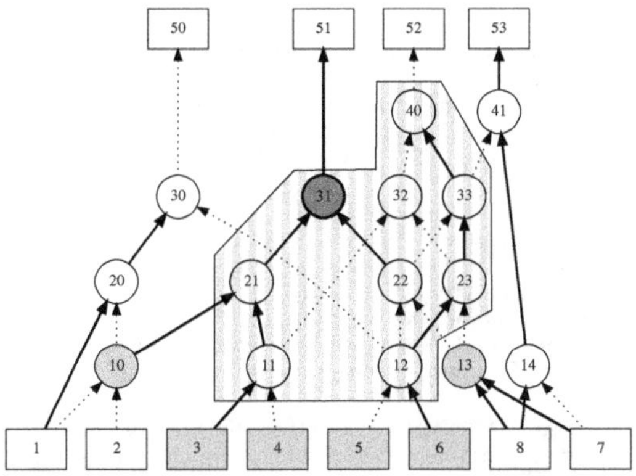

Figure 4: Example of KL-cut computation.

3.2 And-Inverter Graphs and K-cuts

An *And-Inverter Graph* is a directed acyclic graph where each node has either 0 incoming edges - the *primary inputs* (PI) - or 2 incoming edges - the AND nodes. Each edge can be negated or not. Some nodes are also *primary outputs* (PO). Sequential elements are considered as PI/PO pairs. An AIG example is depicted in Fig. 4. The dotted lines are negated edges, the circles are AND nodes, the rectangles at the bottom are PIs and at the top are POs.

A *cut* of a node n in a graph G is a set of nodes c such that every path between a PI and n contains a node in c. A cut is said to be irredundant if no subset of it is also a cut. A *K-cut* [16] of a graph G is an irredundant cut of K or fewer nodes. Consider the two sets of cuts A and B and the auxiliary set operation $\bowtie$ described in (3).

$$A \bowtie B \equiv \{a \cup b \mid a \in A, b \in B, \mid a \cup b \mid < K\} \quad (3)$$

The $\bowtie$ set operation removes the redundant cuts, and it is commutative, as the union set operation $\cup$ is also commutative. Let $\Phi_K(n)$ to be the set of K-cuts of $n \in G$ and, if n is an AND node, let n_1 and n_2 to be its inputs. Then, $\Phi_K(n)$ is defined recursively [4], as described in (4).

$$\Phi_K(n) = \begin{cases} \{\{n\}\}, & n \text{ is a PI} \\ \{\{n\}\} \cup \{\Phi_K(n_1) \bowtie \Phi_K(n_2)\}, & \text{otherwise} \end{cases} \quad (4)$$

3.3 KL-cuts

K-cuts can be an efficient way to represent a graph region regarding a single output. However, several K-cuts may be necessary to cover regions with multiple outputs, *duplicating logic*. A *KL-cut* [8,9] identifies a multi-output region in order to overcome this issue. A KL-cut is a sub-graph G_{KL} of a graph G with K inputs and L outputs. It is represented as two sets of nodes: the inputs G_K, and the outputs G_L.

If a node n belongs to a path between $n_K \in G_K$ and $n_L \in G_L$, being $n \notin G_K$, then n is contained in G_{KL}. Notice that all nodes in G_L are contained in G_{KL}, and G_{KL} does not contain any node of G_K. In this work, the number of outputs is not restricted in KL-cuts enumeration. Therefore, for every K-cut of a node n, there is a *unique* KL-cut G_{KL}.

The nodes that are part of G_{KL} are identified by traversing forward the graph G from G_K. A node n is part of G_{KL} if at least one of the K-cuts of n is a subset of or equal to G_K. A node of G_{KL} is contained in G_L if it is also a PO, or if it has a fanout to a node not contained in G_{KL}.

KL-cut enumeration example: Figure 4 depicts $G_K = \{3, 4, 5, 6, 10, 13\}$ with its nodes in light gray, which is one of the K-cuts at node 31, in dark gray. The KL-cut G_{KL} is obtained by traversing the AIG forward from G_K, identifying the sub-graph hatched in Fig. 4. Nodes 31 and 40 are also POs, and nodes 12 and 33 have fanout to nodes not contained in G_{KL}, therefore $G_L = \{12, 31, 33, 40\}$ is defined. Note that the logic of G_L nodes can be described as Boolean functions that depend on the same support: the G_K nodes.

Table 1: Results obtained through AIG transformations.

Name	Initial		(a) After *dc2*		(b) After collapse + *dc2*		Diff nodes (a) and (b)
	N	LV	N	LV	N	LV	
b04	546	24	487	21	871	16	78.85%
b05	830	54	459	23	4095	19	792.16%
b06	42	5	35	4	31	5	-11.43%
b07	365	27	331	22	566	22	71.00%
b08	155	20	131	15	119	9	-9.16%
b09	136	12	123	10	197	12	60.16%
b10	180	11	162	9	175	8	8.02%
b11	611	28	452	21	1085	18	140.04%
b12	1002	17	947	14	1399	13	47.73%
b13	261	12	220	11	224	10	1.82%
b14	6069	60	3924	100	-	-	-
b15	8432	65	7030	95	-	-	-
alu4	2654	14	1573	15	625	14	-60.27%
apex2	2960	17	991	17	142	14	-85.67%
bigkey	3081	10	2847	10	3302	10	15.98%
clma	11938	40	4842	38	527	16	-89.12%
diffeq	2575	40	2137	41	-	-	-
ex1010	7681	17	4664	15	2337	14	-49.89%
ex5p	1731	15	928	19	204	8	-78.02%
i10	3675	50	1637	36	-	-	-
misex3	2454	13	1267	15	754	14	-40.49%
pdc	7757	19	3219	19	1717	18	-46.66%
seq	2780	14	1373	13	1516	16	10.42%
spla	6660	19	2298	16	525	14	-77.15%
tseng	1927	47	1763	41	-	-	-
Mean I	1391.64	21.26	921.52	19.48	-	-	-
Ratio 1	1.00	1.00	0.65	0.92	-	-	-
Mean II	1090.95	17.03	698.38	14.93	550.87	12.78	-
Ratio 2	1.00	1.00	0.64	0.88	0.50	0.75	-
Ratio 3	-	-	1.00	1.00	0.79	0.86	-

3.4 Boolean division

Given the Boolean functions f and d, if it is possible to express f as $f = q \cdot d + r$, where $\cdot$ and $+$ represent the Boolean AND and OR operators respectively, then f can be divided by d, with q and r being the quotient and remainder of the division, respectively. This division operation can be performed by algebraic or Boolean methods.

A common approach to perform Boolean division is using two-level minimizers that accept don't care information [6]. A new variable x is added and the division is performed by adding the satisfiability don't care (SDC) expression $x \oplus d$ to the DC-set of f, where $\oplus$ represent the Boolean exclusive-OR operator, followed by a two-level minimization.

Example: Consider the function $f = \bar{a} \cdot b \cdot c + d \cdot (a + b)$ represented as a 6-literal factored form. It is possible to rewrite f as $f = \bar{a} \cdot b \cdot c + d \cdot x$ by performing algebraic division with the divisor $x = a + b$. Boolean division can be performed by incorporating $x \oplus (a + b)$ in the DC-set and doing a two-level minimization results in $f = \bar{a} \cdot c \cdot x + d \cdot x$, that can be represented as the 4-literal factored form $f = (\bar{a} \cdot c + d) \cdot x$.

4. AIG TRANSFORMATIONS RESULTS

This section presents the AIG size reduction achieved by AIG transformations for a set of ITC99 and MCNC benchmarks [1]. Each benchmark is read and tranformed into an AIG through algebraic factorization. Then structural hashing is performed, obtaining the number of AIG nodes (N) and levels (LV) shown in column "*Initial*" of Table 1.

```
1:  procedure BOOLEANDECOMPOSITIONAIG(AIG, cutParams)
    Input: An AIG network, and parameters to enumerate KL-cuts
2:      for each node N in AIG in topological order do
3:          for each kcut C of node N from kcut enumeration do
4:              obtain the klcut from C in AIG
5:              if the klcut is accepted based on cutParams then
6:                  F = set of klcut functions
7:                  DC = ∅ /* DC-set of F functions */
8:                  divisors = BOOLDECOMPOSE(F, DC)
9:                  if size of divisors < size of klcut then
10:                     new_klcut = AIG network of divisors
11:                     replace klcut by new_klcut in AIG
12:                     restart kcut enumeration
```

Figure 5: AIG optimization using Boolean decomposition.

In order to obtain a highly optimized AIG, the *dc2* command is executed iteratively until no changes are observed. This reduces the number of nodes for the majority of cases, as seen in column "*After dc2*". The number of levels is usually reduced, but not for all cases. Geometric mean I and the ratio 1 refer to the complete set of benchmarks.

An alternative experiment is performed by first collapsing the netlist, just after reading the input file. The collapsing operation cannot finish for all benchmarks due to its complexity. In the cases it can finish, the AIGs are obtained through algebraic factorization and structural hashing. Then, the *dc2* command is run iteratively until no changes are observed, generating the results shown in column "*After collapse + dc2*". Geometric mean II and the corresponding ratios 2 and 3 refer to the benchmarks in which collapsing could finish.

The final number of nodes varies from a 89% reduction (*clma*) to a 792% increase (*b05*). Collapsing the netlist may result in a larger AIG (see Sect. 2), and the AIG transformations may not obtain the same results as before collapsing, as these modifications are biased by the AIG structure. In the *b05* benchmark, the initial description has very good logic sharing between outputs, which is lost after collapsing. The shared logic is not recovered due to local optimization limitations, as some of the benchmark outputs depend in a large set of inputs. For other cases, collapsing enables significant AIG reduction by removing redundant logic.

5. AIG OPTIMIZATION APPROACH

This section introduces a new AIG optimization approach, based on Boolean decomposition with two-literal divisors [15]. Boolean methods are known to be inefficient and not scalable, but also to obtain better results when compared with algebraic methods. In this work, the Boolean decomposition method [15] is applied to multi-output functions and runtime is improved without losing quality of results. Still, the algorithm is not scalable for large circuits, and therefore applied via local optimization.

5.1 AIG local optimization using KL-cuts

A pseudo-code of the AIG optimization strategy is shown in Fig. 5. The procedure *booleanDecompositionAIG* receives the AIG and the parameters to enumerate the KL-cuts, which define the number of nodes and inputs, for example.

From the outputs to the inputs, each node is visited (line 2), and for each node all K-cuts enumerated based on the parameters are tried (line 3). In line 4, the KL-cut is obtained from the K-cut, and if accepted based on the parameters (line 5), the Boolean decomposition is performed on top of the KL-cut Boolean functions (line 8).

If the Boolean decomposition result is smaller than the number of nodes of the KL-cut, it replaces the logic in the AIG (line 11). Note that *boolDecompose* returns the set of divisors used to decompose the KL-cut functions, which can be easily translated to an AIG network. Also, since the AIG is changed when there is a KL-cut replacement, the previous K-cut enumeration has to be restarted (line 12).

```
1:  function BOOLDECOMPOSE(F, DC)
    Input: A set of functions F and their DC-set
    Return: A set of divisors that form an AIG
    /* Each recursive call generates one divisor */
2:      /* Step (I) - If all functions are decomposed, return */
3:      if all functions f ∈ F are trivial then return
4:
5:      /* Step (II) - Generate the candidate Boolean divisors */
6:      numLiterals = 0  /* Number of literals of all functions */
7:      D = ∅             /* Set of generated divisors */
8:      for each non-trivial f ∈ F do
9:          a = algebraic factored form of f
10:         numLiterals += number of literals in a
11:         D = D ∪ {two-literal leaves of a}
12:
13:     /* Step (III) - Perform Boolean division for each divisor */
14:     x = new variable  /* Variable of the new divisor */
15:     bestDivisor = ∅
16:     for each divisor d ∈ D do
17:         divLiterals = 0  /* Number of literals after division */
18:         for each non-trivial f ∈ F do
19:             /* DC(f) is the DC-set of f */
20:             DC_proj = DC(f) projection onto f and d support
21:             DC_div = DC_proj + (x ⊕ d)
22:             Flits, Rlits = number of literals in f factored form
23:             if d is accepted based on f vars polarities then
24:                 /* R(f) is the result of the division of f by d */
25:                 R(f) = twoLevelMinimization(f, DC_div)
26:                 Rlits = literals in R(f) factored form
27:             if Rlits > Flits then
28:                 /* If R(f) has more literals, or division was not
29:                    performed, select f as part of the solution */
30:                 R(f) = f; divLiterals += Flits
31:             else
32:                 divLiterals += Rlits
33:         /* If division reduced literals, update best result */
34:         if divLiterals < numLiterals then
35:             for each non-trivial f ∈ F do
36:                 bestR(f) = R(f)
37:             bestDivisor = d; numLiterals = divLiterals
38:
39:     /* Step (IV) - Set the functions for next recursive call */
40:     for each non-trivial f ∈ F do
41:         newF(f) = bestR(f)
42:         newDC(f) = DC(f) + (x ⊕ bestDivisor)
43:     /* Return the best divisor and make a new recursive call */
44:     return {bestDivisor} ∪ BOOLDECOMPOSE(newF, newDC)
```

Figure 6: Boolean decomposition procedure.

5.2 Boolean decomposition

The algorithm for *boolDecompose* is presented in Fig. 6, which recursively performs the Boolean decomposition on a set of functions F. The algorithm is divided into four steps: (I) detection of trivial cases, (II) generation of candidate Boolean divisors and definition of the cost function, (III) selection of the best divisor via Boolean division, and (IV) preparation of the next recursive call.

At line 3, detection of trivial cases (I) is performed, identifying when all functions in F are decomposed. The algorithm is executed recursively until this condition is satisfied.

Step (II) starts by obtaining the algebraic factored form for each function in F (line 9). The cost function to be minimized is defined as the sum of literals of all functions in factored form (*numLiterals*, line 10). Then, the two-literal leaves of the factored form trees are generated as candidate divisors for each function in F (see Fig. 7).

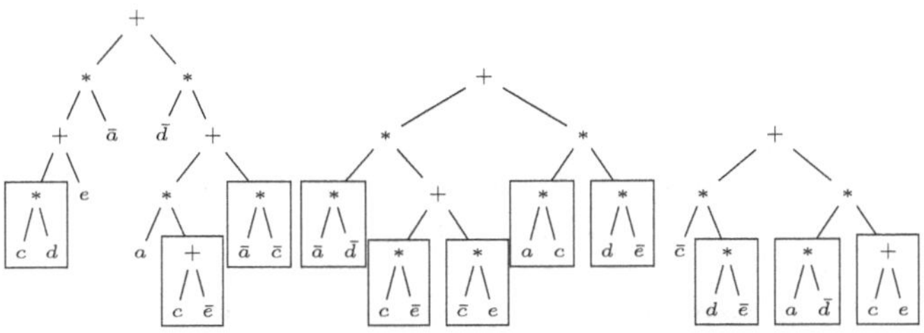

Figure 7: Factored form trees from *b06* benchmark.

Boolean division is performed for all functions in F using each divisor in D, in order to calculate the cost function for all divisors. The best divisor (III) is the one that achieves the largest reduction in number of literals.

As seen in Sect. 3.4, Boolean division is performed by adding the SDC of a divisor to the DC-set of a function and running two-level minimization. As the DC-set may contain variables not relevant to the division, a DC-set projection is performed to the support of the function f and divisor d (line 20). The projected DC-set is accumulated with the SDC generated by the evaluated divisor (line 21), generating the DC-set used in the two-level minimization (DC_{div}).

The division may be filtered due to the polarities of the variables (see Sect. 5.3). If the division is filtered or if the number of literals in the division result $R(f)$ is greater than in f (line 27), then f is used as part of the current solution (line 30). If the number of literals is reduced after a division (line 34), the best solution is updated: the division result (line 35), the divisor and the number of literals (line 37).

The next iteration is prepared at step (IV). The ON-set (line 41) and the DC-set (line 42) obtained by the best divisor are used in the next recursive call (line 44).

Note that the two-level minimization could be performed as a multi-output function. However, running single output two-level minimizations is preferred as it is more efficient, divisions can be filtered based on the variables polarities and the divisions that increase literals can be discarded for each output individually.

5.3 Filters to reduce runtime

Select divisors from factored forms. In comparison to [15], only pairs of literals obtained from the leaf nodes of the factored form trees are selected as potential divisors, instead of trying all possible pairs of variables and polarities. The divisors are selected from all output functions of the KL-cut. For the benchmarks analyzed with our method, the quality of results was not affected by applying this filter, while the optimization runtime was significantly improved.

To illustrate the divisor selection, factored form trees obtained from *b06* functions are depicted in Fig. 7. The two-literal leaves highlighted in Fig. 7 are the divisors selected. Notice that only one polarity is investigated, e.g., if the divisor $c + \bar{e}$ is chosen, its negated version $\bar{c} \cdot e$ is disregarded.
Use variable polarity information. This filter is used to avoid exploring divisions with unpromising polarities between the divisor and the divided function. Table 2 describes the divisors that are accepted based on its support and the polarities of the variables in the divided function. A total of 849 Boolean divisions are performed during the Boolean decomposition of *b06* when using this filter versus 943 without it (and 13829 divisions would be done without any filter).

The polarity of the variables can be obtained using the concept of unateness, which is defined for completely specified functions. Unateness can only be used in the first iteration of Boolean decomposition, when the DC-set is empty. After the first iteration, the DC-set contains the SDCs of the previously selected divisors, and the concept of containment [19] must be used (see Sect. 3.1).

Table 2: Divisors accepted based on the divided function f.

Divisor variables a and b w.r.t. f	Divisors accepted
$a \notin f$ support or $b \notin f$ support	None
a is binate or b is binate	$(a \cdot b)$, $(\bar{a} \cdot \bar{b})$, $(a \cdot \bar{b})$, $(\bar{a} \cdot b)$
a and b have the same polarity	$(a \cdot b)$, $(\bar{a} \cdot \bar{b})$
a and b have different polarities	$(a \cdot \bar{b})$, $(\bar{a} \cdot b)$

Table 3: AIG results of Boolean decomposition.

Name	Initial		(a) ABC smallest		(b) Boolean Decomp.		Runtime (s)	Diff. nodes (a) and (b)
	N	LV	N	LV	N	LV		
b04	546	24	487	21	442	21	222	-9.24%
b05	830	54	459	23	409	29	140	-10.89%
b06	42	5	31	5	23	9	0.55	-25.81%
b07	365	27	331	22	320	27	125	-3.32%
b08	155	20	119	9	113	10	2	-5.04%
b09	136	12	123	10	117	11	4	-4.88%
b10	180	11	162	9	156	10	14	-3.70%
b11	611	28	452	21	427	24	178	-5.53%
b12	1002	17	947	14	920	15	212	-2.85%
b13	261	12	220	11	207	12	3	-5.91%
b14	6069	60	3924	100	3810	120	14421	-2.91%
b15	8432	65	7030	95	6656	107	14592	-5.32%
alu4	2654	14	625	14	570	16	268	-8.80%
apex2	1960	17	142	14	128	15	5	-9.86%
bigkey	3081	10	2847	10	2396	15	2209	-15.84%
clma	11938	40	527	16	449	17	46	-14.80%
diffeq	2575	40	2137	41	2015	51	407	-5.71%
ex1010	7681	17	2337	14	2306	15	2004	-1.33%
ex5p	1731	15	204	8	197	8	127	-3.43%
i10	3675	50	1637	36	1530	37	882	-6.54%
misex3	2454	13	754	14	731	14	288	-3.05%
pdc	7757	19	1717	18	1543	18	1371	-10.13%
seq	2780	14	1373	13	1320	16	626	-3.86%
spla	6660	19	525	14	436	15	211	-16.95%
tseng	1927	47	1763	41	1696	42	445	-3.80%
Mean	1391.5	21.2	614.4	17.5	566.7	19.9	147.4	-7.76%
Ratio 1	1.000	1.000	0.442	0.826	0.407	0.939	-	-
Ratio 2	-	-	1.000	1.000	0.922	1.137	-	-

6. EXPERIMENTAL RESULTS

Table 3 shows the AIGs metrics (N: nodes, LV: levels) before and after Boolean Decomposition. Column *Initial* reports the metrics of the AIGs after input and structural hashing, and column *ABC smallest* reports the AIGs with least number of nodes from Table 1.

The AIG optimization via Boolean decomposition is applied on top of the AIGs of column *ABC smallest.* KL-cuts with K=8 and unbounded L are enumerated in order to obtain smaller parts of the AIG with complete local context. Also, the number of nodes of the KL-cuts is restricted to 30, therefore having a very limited scope of optimization. Boolean decomposition is performed on top of the KL-cut outputs functions, only replacing the KL-cut logic if the number of nodes is reduced. The experiments were run on an Intel Core i7 processor with 4GB of RAM. All AIGs passed formal verification using ABC command *cec.*

The column "*Boolean Decomp.*" reports the results obtained after performing two iterations of the Boolean decomposition method. By using Boolean decomposition, it was possible to reduce the number of AIG nodes further by 7.76% on average, with important results such as 25.81% (*b06*), 16.95% (*spla*), 15.84% (*bigkey*) and 14.8% (*clma*).

Our approach is able to identify a better logic sharing, therefore increasing the number of levels, which is not con-

Table 4: Technology mapping results.

Name	FPGA (LUT4)				Standard cell (μm^2, ns)			
	(a) ABC		(b) Bool. Dec.		(a) ABC		(b) Bool. Dec.	
	N	LV	N	LV	Area	Delay	Area	Delay
b04	183	7	177	8	14041	1879	12735	1833
b05	222	9	201	11	14350	2057	12687	2545
b06	17	2	17	2	1191.9	567	993	754
b07	145	8	146	8	9828	1949	9645	2205
b08	55	4	50	5	3659	873	3460	934
b09	55	4	53	5	3554	876	3716	1060
b10	73	5	75	5	5076	881	4893	957
b11	179	7	175	8	13215	1916	12551	2086
b12	452	6	455	6	28188	1322	27922	1409
b13	95	4	94	4	6890	975	6482	1046
b14	1608	33	1544	37	112586	8639	112277	10068
b15	3021	33	2922	33	204689	8110	195332	9398
alu4	293	7	277	7	18114	1308	16446	1450
apex2	65	6	61	6	4218	1300	3884	1398
bigkey	1254	3	921	4	81867	901	73250	1327
clma	277	6	249	6	15934	1446	13968	1512
diffeq	824	14	754	14	61892	3658	57616	4129
ex1010	1132	7	1118	7	66649	1314	65849	1415
ex5p	129	3	122	4	6356	784	6090	789
i10	724	14	688	14	47974	3222	45120.5	3187
misex3	363	6	363	6	21716	1222.7	21162.1	1218
pdc	904	7	821	7	50301	1585	45429	1592
seq	716	6	673	7	40718	1232	38957	1438
spla	262	5	222	6	15108	1218	12991	1303
tseng	758	13	741	13	50583	3598	49251	3561
Mean	284.35	6.84	268.64	7.39	18356	1607	17217	1859
Ratio	1.000	1.000	0.945	1.081	1.000	1.000	0.938	1.157

trolled by our method. Still, there is an increase of up to 1 level for 15 out of 25 benchmarks evaluated. Also, the average number of levels is still smaller than the *Initial* results.

Table 4 shows technology mapping performed for FPGAs and standard cells using the AIGs from Table 3. Area reduction was observed simply by changing the input with smaller AIGs. Mapping to LUT4s was performed with the ABC command "*if -K 4*", obtaining 5.5% area reduction on average. Mapping to standard cells was performed with the ABC command "*map*" using the library "*GSCLib_3.0.lib*" of [1], obtaining 6.2% area reduction on average.

7. CONCLUSIONS

This paper introduced an approach to explore the potential use of Boolean decomposition in the optimization of AIGs. The experiments show promising results, with an average reduction of 7.76% in AIG nodes. Scalability is one of the aspects that requires more investigation. We envision a synthesis system in which smart oracles could guide the search for divisors based on simple correlation metrics between functions and divisors.

As future work, there are some directions that could be explored. For example, different types of cuts and more combinations of divisors could be studied. Using other models of flexibility (Boolean relations) could also be considered. Delay is another important aspect that is not considered in this work, but could be incorporated, controlling the number of levels and reducing the resulting circuit delay.

8. ACKNOWLEDGMENTS

We thank Mayler Martins for helpful discussions. The present work was performed with the support of CNPq, Conselho Nacional de Desenvolvimento Científico e Tecnológico - Brasil. This work has been partially supported by funds from the Spanish Ministry for Economy and Competitiveness and the European Union (FEDER funds) under grant TIN2013-46181-C2-1-R, and the Generalitat de Catalunya (2014 SGR 1034).

9. REFERENCES

[1] C. Albrecht. IWLS 2005 benchmarks. http://iwls.org/iwls2005/benchmarks.html, 2005.

[2] R. Brayton and C. McMullen. The decomposition and factorization of Boolean expressions. In *Proc. of ISCAS*, pages 49–54, 1982.

[3] R. Brayton and A. Mishchenko. ABC: An academic industrial-strength verification tool. In *Computer Aided Verification*, pages 24–40. Springer, 2010.

[4] S. Chatterjee, A. Mishchenko, and R. Brayton. Factor cuts. In *Proc. of ICCAD*, pages 143–150. ACM, 2006.

[5] J. Cortadella. Timing-driven logic bi-decomposition. *IEEE TCAD*, 22(6):675–685, 2003.

[6] G. De Micheli. *Synthesis and optimization of digital circuits*. McGraw-Hill Higher Education, 1994.

[7] P. Fišer and J. Schmidt. Improving the iterative power of resynthesis. In *Proc. of DDECS*, pages 30–33. IEEE, 2012.

[8] L. Machado, M. G. A. Martins, V. Callegaro, R. P. Ribas, and A. I. Reis. KL-cut based digital circuit remapping. In *Proc. of NORCHIP*, pages 1–4. IEEE, 2012.

[9] O. Martinello Jr, F. S. Marques, R. P. Ribas, and A. I. Reis. KL-cuts: a new approach for logic synthesis targeting multiple output blocks. In *Proc. of DATE*, pages 777–782. EDAA, 2010.

[10] A. Mishchenko and R. Brayton. Scalable logic synthesis using a simple circuit structure. In *Proc. of IWLS*, pages 15–22, 2006.

[11] A. Mishchenko, R. Brayton, and S. Chatterjee. Boolean factoring and decomposition of logic networks. In *Proc. of ICCAD*, pages 38–44. IEEE, 2008.

[12] A. Mishchenko, R. Brayton, J. R. Jiang, and S. Jang. Scalable don't-care-based logic optimization and resynthesis. *ACM TRETS*, 4(4):34, 2011.

[13] A. Mishchenko, S. Chatterjee, and R. Brayton. DAG-aware AIG rewriting a fresh look at combinational logic synthesis. In *Proc. of DAC*, pages 532–535. ACM, 2006.

[14] A. Mishchenko, S. Cho, S. Chatterjee, and R. Brayton. Combinational and sequential mapping with priority cuts. In *Proc. of ICCAD*, pages 354–361. IEEE, 2007.

[15] N. Modi and J. Cortadella. Boolean decomposition using two-literal divisors. In *Proc. of VLSID*, pages 765–768. IEEE, 2004.

[16] P. Pan and C. Lin. A new retiming-based technology mapping algorithm for LUT-based FPGAs. In *Proc. of FPGA*, pages 35–42. ACM, 1998.

[17] H. Savoj and R. Brayton. The use of observability and external don't cares for the simplification of multi-level networks. In *Proc. of DAC*, pages 297–301. IEEE, 1990.

[18] C. Scholl. Multi-output functional decomposition with exploitation of don't cares. In *Proc. of DATE*, pages 743–748. IEEE, 1998.

[19] L. Wang and A. Almaini. Multilevel logic simplification based on a containment recursive paradigm. In *IEE Proceedings Computers and Digital Techniques*, volume 150, pages 218–226. IET, 2003.

Mixed-Cell-Height Standard Cell Placement Legalization

Chung-Yao Hung
National Tsing Hua University
Hsinchu, Taiwan
eruption@live.jp

Peng-Yi Chou
National Tsing Hua University
Hsinchu, Taiwan
super5516@gmail.com

Wai-Kei Mak
National Tsing Hua University
Hsinchu, Taiwan
wkmak@cs.nthu.edu.tw

ABSTRACT

A traditional standard cell library consists of various functional cells with the same height, which could speed up VLSI design flow since designers could align cells to placement sites in rows. However, in advanced nodes, cells are designed with different heights. With mixed cell heights, we can design simple cells (e.g. inverters) as single-row-height cells, and complex cells (e.g. flip-flops) as multiple-row-height cells. Nevertheless, placement legalization becomes more difficult with mixed-cell-height libraries. In this paper, we propose a parallel legalization method for mixed-cell-height standard cell libraries to minimize total displacement. Experimental results show that our method has a 19% improvement on average in displacement compared with the state-of-the-art work [9].

Keywords

Mixed-cell-height; Multiple-row-height; Legalization; Placement

1. INTRODUCTION

A traditional standard cell library consists of various functional cells with the same height[10], which could speed up VLSI design flow since designers could align cells to placement sites in rows. Thanks to the development of advanced technology node, we can achieve higher performance and smaller size with same functionality. As a result, the height of standard cell row has decreased steadily with reduced number of routing tracks. However, this can induce higher routing congestion within a cell[2], which makes it harder to fit complex circuits into such small height. Therefore, in order to increase layout efficiency, modern standard cell library adopts the concept of mixed-cell-height[5], i.e., a library containing not only single-row-height cells but also multiple-row-height cells. With mixed cell heights, we can design simple cells (e.g. inverters) as single-row-height cells, and complex cells (e.g. flip-flops) as multiple-row-height cells.

Permission to make digital or hard copies of all or part of this work for personal or classroom use is granted without fee provided that copies are not made or distributed for profit or commercial advantage and that copies bear this notice and the full citation on the first page. Copyrights for components of this work owned by others than ACM must be honored. Abstracting with credit is permitted. To copy otherwise, or republish, to post on servers or to redistribute to lists, requires prior specific permission and/or a fee. Request permissions from permissions@acm.org.

GLSVLSI '17, May 10-12, 2017, Banff, AB, Canada

© 2017 ACM. ISBN 978-1-4503-4972-7/17/05...$15.00

DOI: http://dx.doi.org/10.1145/3060403.3060473

Nevertheless, some VLSI design stage, namely the placement stage, will be influenced by using mixed-cell-height libraries. The placement stage could be divided into three steps: (i) global placement, (ii) legalization, (iii) detailed placement. During global placement, each cell will be placed to optimize some characteristics of the layout, e.g. minimize total wirelength, balance cell density. Because global placement allows cells to overlap with each other, we need to resolve cell-overlapping problems and to align every cells to placement sites by moving cells, that is what legalization does. Finally, detailed placement will further improve the quality of legalized solution by some techniques, such as shifting or swapping cells. As moving a multiple-row-height cell will have an impact on cells on multiple rows, it makes legalization and detailed placement more difficult to accomplish.

There are only a few previous works for mixed-cell-height standard cell design placement. Wu et al. [11] are the first to handle legalization and detailed placement with double-row-height cells. By cell pairing and cell expansion, they transform all single-row-height cells into double-row-height cells. Thus, a traditional detailed placer could still be adopted. However, they did not take power-rail alignment constraints into consideration, which make their result impractical. Besides, their method could only deal with cells up to double-row-height. Chow et al. [4] proposed the first placement legalization algorithm for multiple-row-height cell designs to minimize displacement. They greedily find a legalization solution with minimal displacement for each cell within the defined local region around its global placement position in a sequential manner. They also implemented an integer linear programming (ILP) based algorithm for comparison. Lin et al. [7] proposed a two-stage method composed of legalization stage and detailed placement stage for multiple-row-height cell designs. The chain move method they proposed will iteratively pick the largest unmoved cell at the time and try to place it in the defined local region, and handle the overlapped cells sequentially. Combining chain move with the legalization approach in [4], they could find an overlap-free solution in the legalization stage. Wang et al. [9] modified Abacus[8], a well-known legalization method for single-row-height cell designs, to handle multiple-row-height cell designs. For each cell, they will evaluate and find the best position by trying to place it in each row. Therefore, they could get a better solution than [4]. The above works [4], [7], and [9] have one thing in common that they do the legalization cell by cell, whereas we legalize multiple cells simultaneously.

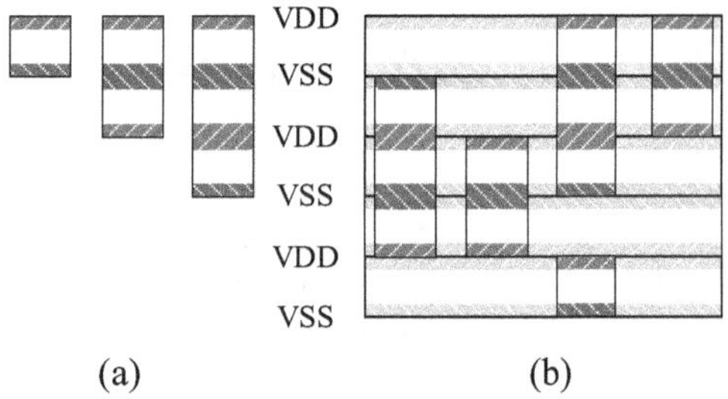

Figure 1: (a) Standard cells with multiple-row-height. (b) Some examples of power-rail alignment with multiple-row-height cells.

The rest of this paper is organized as follows. In Section 2, we introduce the difficulties faced in legalization using mixed-cell-height libraries, and give the problem formulation of this work. Section 3 describes the proposed method. Experimental results are shown in Section 4. Finally, Section 5 gives the conclusion.

2. PRELIMINARIES

2.1 Legalization

Traditionally, for a legal placement, it has to satisfy the following constraints:

- Cells must be aligned to placement sites.
- Cells are overlap-free.

However, as mentioned in Section 1, global placement will try to optimize some characteristics of the layout. Thus, during legalization, we will try not to move each cell far from its global placement position to preserve the characteristics. In other words, the cell displacement should be minimized.

2.2 Power-Rail Alignment Constraint

In reality, standard cells have to connect to VDD on the top or bottom side, and to VSS on the other side. Therefore, when it comes to multiple-row-height cells, legalization is not as simple as it used to be. For multiple-row-height cells with even row height, both sides of the cell are either connected to VDD or VSS, which means they could only be placed on rows with proper power-rail alignment. On the other hand, cells with odd row height could be placed at any row by vertically flipping them if necessary. Figure 1 shows some examples.

2.3 Problem Formulation

Given a global placement result containing multiple-row-height cells, the objective is to legalize the placement while minimizing total cell displacements. The total cell displacements is obtained through the following equation:

$$\sum_{i=1}^{n}(|x_i - x'_i| + |y_i - y'_i|)$$

where n denotes the total number of cells, x_i/y_i the x-/y-coordinate of the final position of cell i, x'_i/y'_i the x-/y-coordinate of the global placement position of cell i.

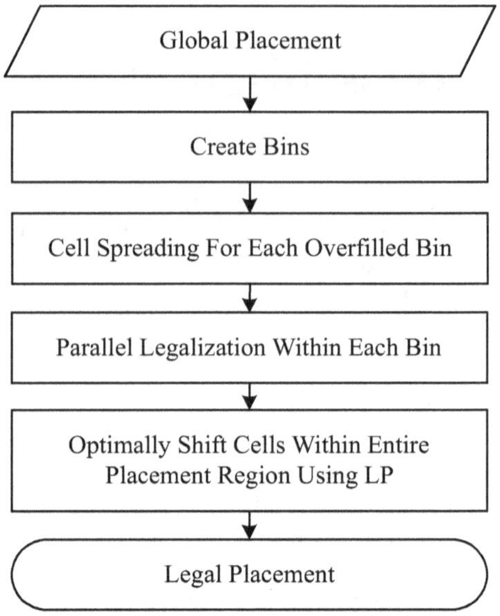

Figure 2: The overall flow of the proposed method.

3. PROPOSED ALGORITHM

3.1 Overall Flow

Figure 2 gives the overall flow of the proposed method. First, we partition the placement region to form uniform bins, and generate an initial cell-to-bin assignment according to the global placement solution. Then, we spread the cells from high density bins to neighboring and relatively low density bins. After that, a legalization solution is obtained through an integer linear programming based formulation. Finally, a linear programming based approach is performed to improve the solution quality by optimally shifting all the cells horizontally within the entire placement region. We will describe the first step here, and the rest of the steps will be detailed in the following sub-sections.

The purpose of creating bins is to speed up the ILP formulation in the following step. Although ILP formulation guarantees to obtain an optimal solution under the given objective and constraints, it is time consuming when the number of variables is large. Hence, we divide the entire layout into bins and solve them as sub-problems. However, the act of dividing will harm the optimality of the solution. Hence, we also propose some techniques (described in Section 3.3) to mitigate the effect.

After creating bins, we generate an initial cell-to-bin assignment that assigns cells to proper bins according to their global placement positions. As a result, bins in dense areas will be assigned too many cells and make them impossible to have a feasible placement solution. We call those bins overfilled bins. In order to find a feasible placement solution, we need to spread some cells in overfilled bins to neighboring bins that have enough space to accommodate them.

3.2 Cell Spreading

During cell spreading, we want to determine the cells we should move out from overfilled bins and the bins we should move them to. At the same time, we want to minimize

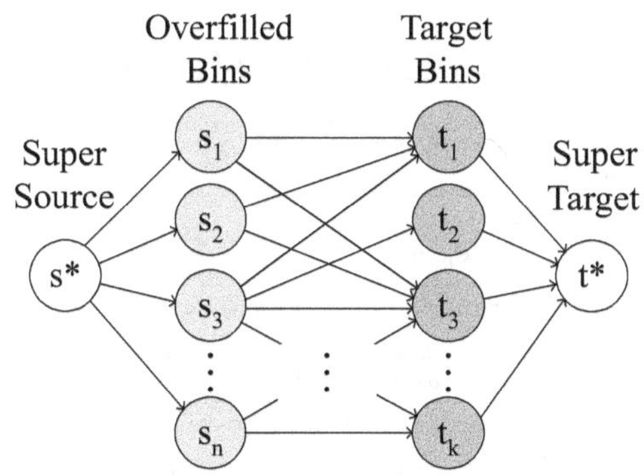

Figure 3: The structure of our network flow model.

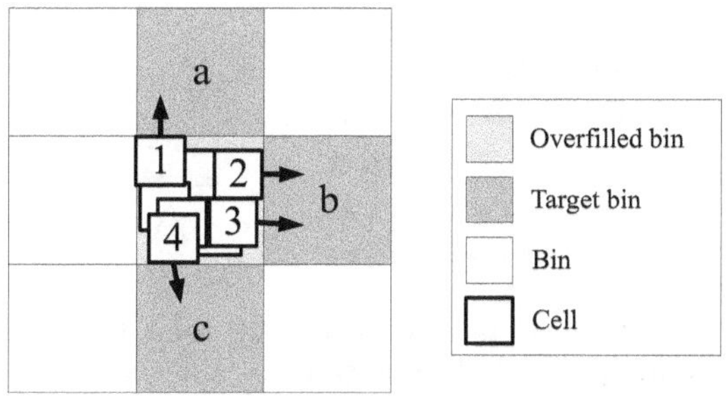

Figure 4: An example of *boundary cell moving*. Since cells that are nearer to the target bin will be moved with higher priority, cell 1 will be moved to bin a, cell 2 and 3 will be moved to bin b, and cell 4 will be moved to bin c.

the total displacement. Therefore, we define a cell's moving distance as follows:

Bin-wise displacement: The bin-wise displacement of a cell is the Manhattan distance between the bins to which the cell is assigned before and after movement.

And then we could formulate this problem as follows:

The Cell Spreading Problem: Given a cell-to-bin assignment solution, for each overfilled bin, determine the cells to move out and the target bins to which they should be moved to, while minimizing the total bin-wise displacement.

We further divide the cell spreading problem into two parts: (i) *budgeting* and (ii) *boundary cell moving*, and solve them sequentially. For *budgeting*, we use network flow model[1] to determine how much cell area should be moved out from overfilled bins to nearby bins that have extra spaces. We call those nearby bins target bins. For each overfilled bin s_i, we only assign a few nearby bins that are within a range of bin-wise distance as its target bins t_j. The structure of our network flow model is shown in Figure 3. There are four columns of nodes, super source, overfilled bins, target bins, and super target, respectively. Each overfilled bin node s_i has an edge from the super source node s^*, and each target bin node t_j has an edge to the super target node t^*. Each overfilled bin node s_i has an edge to target bin node t_j if that bin is a target bin of this overfilled bin. In addition, the capacity and cost of an edge between the first two columns are set to be the amount of area needed to be moved out from the overfilled bin and 0, respectively. The capacity and cost of an edge between the middle two columns are set to be infinity and the corresponding bin-wise displacement, respectively. The capacity and cost of an edge between the last two columns are set to be the amount of free space in the corresponding target bin and 0, respectively.

Since we know the budgeted amount of cell area to move from an overfilled bin s_i to a target bin t_j after *budgeting*, we then move cells in s_i that are nearest to t_j to the target bin t_j according to the budgeted amount, as shown in Figure 4. This completes the *boundary cell moving* part.

3.3 Parallel Legalization

In the previous subsection, we have determined which cell should be placed in which bin. Therefore, we still need to place each cell onto a proper placement site within each bin. To legalize the placement while minimizing total cell displacement, we first enumerate a number of valid candidate positions of each cell within the bin it belongs to. To be more specific, we enumerate candidate positions within a fixed range around each cell's global placement position. And then compute the cell placement inside each bin using an ILP formulation inspired by [6]. Note that for each cell that has been moved during cell spreading stage, we will enumerate candidate positions within a fixed range from the bin boundary nearest its global placement position.

A valid candidate position is a position that when cell is placed on it, there will be no power-rail alignment violation and overlapping with macros, as shown in Figure 5. Due to the power-rail alignment constraint of multiple-row-height cells, we allow them to be placed partially outside the top or bottom bin boundary. Therefore, for a multiple-row-height

Table 1: Notations of the ILP Formulation

C	Set of cells
R	Set of rows
Q	Set of columns
K_c	Set of candidate positions of cell c
S_{rq}	Set of candidate positions occupying site (r, q)
D_c^k	Displacement of k-th candidate position of cell c from c's global placement position
p_c^k	0/1 variable, $p_c^k = 1$ if k-th candidate position of cell c is chosen

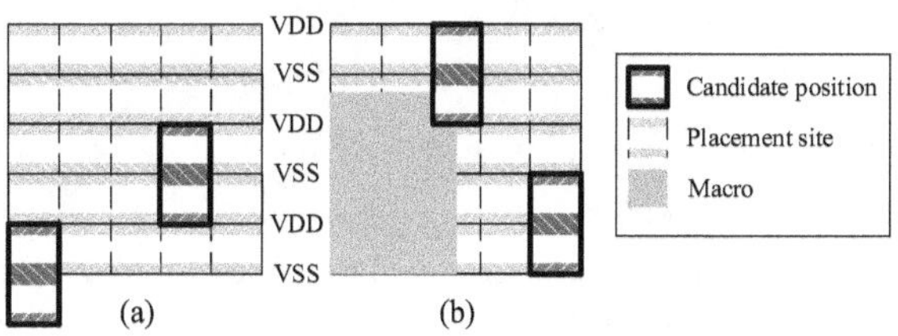

Figure 5: (a) Some examples of valid candidate positions that satisfy power-rail alignment and do not overlap with macros nor obstacles. (b) Some examples of invalid candidate positions that have power-rail alignment violation or overlap with macros/obstacles.

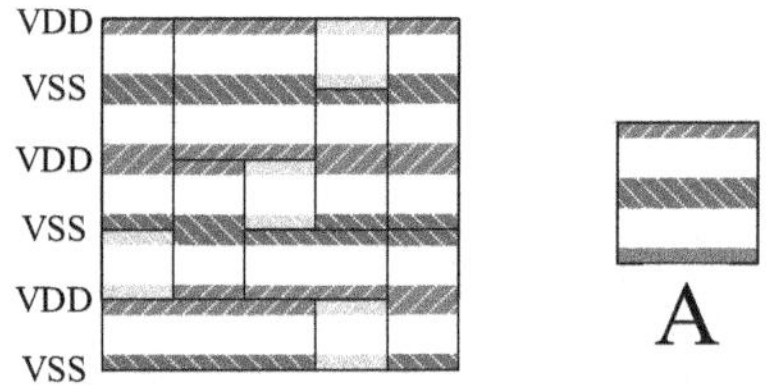

Figure 6: Cell A is left unplaced even though the total dead spaces is larger than A's area.

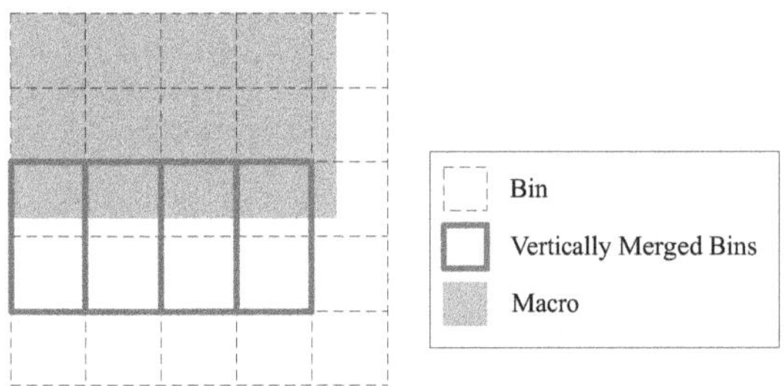

Figure 7: An example of vertically merging bins. After merging, bins with little free placement space could find solution more easily.

cell, we will generate a candidate position even if it crosses the top or bottom boundary of the bin that it has been assigned to, as long as it is a valid position for the cell. Note that we can solve the ILPs for all bins in the same row in parallel since their placement problems are independent, but since we allow a multiple-row-height cell to protrude to a vertically adjacent bin, we process the bins row by row from bottom to top. Thus, if any candidate position is chosen during the ILP process, the cell will be treated as an obstacle from other bin's viewpoint afterwards.

The notations used in our ILP formulation are listed in Table 1. Having the notations, the ILP formulation is given as follows:

minimize

$$\sum_{c \in C} \sum_{k \in K_c} D_c^k \cdot p_c^k$$

subject to

$$\sum_{k \in K_c} p_c^k = 1, \forall c \in C \tag{1}$$

$$\sum_{p_c^k \in S_{rq}} p_c^k \leq 1, \forall r \in R, q \in Q \tag{2}$$

In the formulation, constraint (1) ensures that every cell will be placed and that for each cell, only one candidate position will be chosen. Constraint (2) prevents cells from overlapping with each other.

However, even if the total area of cells assigned within the bin is less than the available bin area, we might not find a legal placement due to dead spaces as shown in Figure 6. Hence, after each run of ILP process, we will mark those bins that could not find feasible solution as *infeasible bins*, and merge them with a horizontal neighboring bin to form bin clusters. By doing so, every cell within a cluster will have

Table 2: Notations of the LP Formulation

C	Set of cells
C_r	Set of cells on row r with increasing order of x-coordinate
R	Set of rows
W_c	The width of cell c
X_c	The x-coordinate of the global placement position of cell c
x_c	The x-coordinate of the final position of cell c
x_{c+1}	The x-coordinate of the final position of cell $c+1$, which is to the right of cell c
d_{x_c}	Horizontal cell displacement of cell c from its global placement position

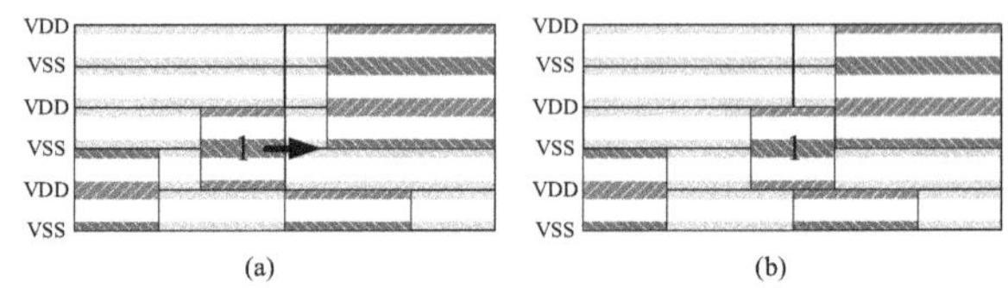

Figure 8: The quality of a legal placement solution may be further improved by shifting cells horizontally across bin boundary. If the global placement position of cell 1 is within the bin at right, we could horizontally shift it to reduce cell displacement.

more candidate positions, then the solution space could be enlarged.

Additionally, when there are large macros in the layout, we will inevitably have some bins that have much of their space occupied by macros. Chances are that these bins cannot find feasible solutions easily even after they are merged with their horizontal neighbors, since their neighbors also have little free placement space. Besides, the solution quality will be degraded because even if there is a feasible placement after merging a few consecutive horizontal bins, some cells may be moved far away and results in higher displacement. To prevent this from happening, we simply merge each bin partially occupied by macros with its vertical neighboring bin before candidate position enumeration, as shown in Figure 7.

3.4 LP-based Refinement

As mentioned before, bin boundaries will restrict solution space, as shown in Figure 8, so we want to further improve the solution quality by doing post-processing. After obtaining a legal placement solution, we optimally shift the cells horizontally within the same row while keeping their relative order. We use a linear programming (LP) formulation to accomplish this task. The notations used in our LP formulation are listed in Table 2. Having the notations, the LP formulation is given as follows:

minimize

$$\sum_{c \in C} d_{x_c}$$

subject to

$$x_c + W_c \leq x_{c+1}, \forall c \in C_r, \forall r \in R \tag{3}$$

Table 3: Experimental Results Compared with [9] and [4].

Benchmark	#S. cells	#D. cells	Density	Average Displacement(sites)				Runtime(s)			
				Ours	MLL[4]	ILP[4]	[9]	Ours	MLL[4]	ILP[4]	[9]
des_perf_1	103842	8802	0.91	1.44	3.32	2.13	3.46	1162	7.0	4099	18.0
des_perf_a	99775	8513	0.43	0.65	0.96	0.66	0.68	27	2.6	194	6.1
des_perf_b	103842	8802	0.5	0.62	0.85	0.62	0.64	23	2.4	251	6.2
edit_dist_a	121913	5500	0.46	0.44	0.47	0.45	0.47	76	1.9	206	7.8
fft_1	30297	1984	0.84	1.06	1.81	1.58	1.55	215	1.1	777	1.3
fft_2	30297	1984	0.5	0.63	0.86	0.66	0.64	12	0.4	73	0.8
fft_a	28718	1907	0.25	0.56	0.64	0.60	0.64	17	0.3	38	0.8
fft_b	28718	1907	0.28	0.62	0.80	0.73	0.62	17	0.4	62	1.0
matrix_mult_1	152427	2898	0.8	0.38	0.53	0.49	0.48	148	3.9	967	9.1
matrix_mult_2	152427	2898	0.79	0.36	0.49	0.45	0.44	132	4.0	825	8.9
matrix_mult_a	146837	2813	0.42	0.25	0.33	0.27	0.27	55	1.6	151	9.3
matrix_mult_b	143695	2740	0.31	0.23	0.30	0.25	0.25	49	1.3	128	8.9
matrix_mult_c	143695	2740	0.31	0.27	0.29	0.27	0.27	58	1.4	139	9.0
pci_bridge32_a	26268	3249	0.38	0.86	0.95	0.88	0.88	10	0.3	49	0.8
pci_bridge32_b	25734	3180	0.14	0.90	0.96	0.95	0.52	9	0.2	15	0.7
superblue11_a	861314	64302	0.43	1.85	1.96	1.85	1.86	1798	23.4	3074	80.2
superblue12	1172586	114362	0.45	1.33	1.63	1.45	1.63	1487	106.5	5079	91.1
superblue14	564769	47474	0.56	2.18	2.62	2.56	2.38	3436	17.1	3360	70.3
superblue16_a	625419	55031	0.48	1.61	1.73	1.61	1.68	965	21.7	2471	61.0
superblue19	478109	27988	0.52	1.48	1.60	1.52	1.68	929	10.9	1849	44.6
Norm.				1.00	1.30	1.13	1.19				

$$d_{x_c} \geq x_c - X_c, \forall c \in C \quad (4)$$

$$d_{x_c} \geq -(x_c - X_C), \forall c \in C \quad (5)$$

In the formulation, constraint (3) ensures the same cell ordering is kept and prevents cells from overlapping with each other. Since the final position of cell c may be to the right or to the left of c's global placement position, we use constraints (4) and (5) to get a tight lower bound on the magnitude of c's horizontal displacement d_{x_c}. Since d_{x_c} appears in the minimization objective of the LP, it will force d_{x_c} to be exactly equal to the horizontal displacement of c.

4. EXPERIMENTAL RESULTS

We implemented the proposed method using C++ programming language, and performed experiments on a Linux workstation with Intel Xeon 2.6GHz CPU with 28 threads and 64GB memory. Gurobi is selected as the LP and ILP solver. Benchmarks used in the experiments are from the authors of [4]. They modified the benchmarks from the 2015 ISPD Detailed-Routing-Driven Placement Contest[3] by randomly picking 10% of the cell to double their heights and half their widths. To strike a balance between better solution quality and faster runtime, we set the bin size as 160 placement sites wide and 9 rows high. In addition, for the ILP formulated for each bin, we would terminate early if no better solution can be found for a period of 15 seconds. During cell spreading stage, bins with density higher than 0.9 are treated as overfilled bins.

Table 3 shows the statistics of the benchmarks and the legalization results. "#S. cells" gives the total number of single-row-height cells, "#D. cells" the total number of double-row-height cells, "Density" the density of design, "Average Displacement(sites)" the average displacement measured in the number of the placement site width, "Runtime(s)" the running time in seconds. Finally, "Ours," "MLL[4]," "ILP[4]," and "[9]" give the results from our method, the fast greedy legalizer proposed in [4], the ILP implemented by the authors in [4], and the method proposed in [9], respectively[1].

We first compare our results with [4]. They proposed a fast greedy legalizer and implemented an ILP based algorithm for comparison. However, judging from their results, the only advantage of their greedy legalizer is the runtime. For fair comparison, we will focus on the effectiveness and efficiency of their ILP based algorithm. We could see from Table 3 that our method could achieve better average displacement with as much as 32% improvement on benchmark des_pref_1 and 13% improvement on average.

Next, we compare our results with the latest work on legalization for mixed-cell-height standard cells[9]. In addition to displacement, they also put efforts on minimizing the half perimeter wirelength (HPWL) and get better results than [4] did. But since our objective does not include HPWL, we only compare the results of displacement with them. We could see from Table 3 that we get better quality in all but one case with a 19% improvement on average.

5. CONCLUSION

For circuit designs in advanced technologies, mixed-cell-height standard cell libraries become popular. In this paper we proposed a parallel legalization method which uses ILP formulation to minimize total cell displacement. We can see from the experimental results that our method has a 19% improvement on average in displacement compared with the state-of-the-art work [9].

Acknowedgements

This work was supported in part by the Ministry of Science and Technology under grant MOST 104-2628-E-007-003-MY3.

[1]The results for [4] are directly taken from their paper and their platform was Intel Xeon 3.4GHz with 32GB memory, *lpsolve* was chosen as the ILP solver. The results for [9] are directly taken from their paper and their platform was Intel Xeon 2.93GHz with 48GB memory.

6. REFERENCES

[1] R. K. Ahuja, T. L. Magnanti, and J. B. Orlin. *Network Flows: Theory, Algorithms, and Applications.* Prentice-Hall, Inc., Upper Saddle River, NJ, USA, 1993.

[2] S.-H. Baek, H.-Y. Kim, Y.-K. Lee, D.-Y. Jin, S.-C. Park, and J.-D. Cho. Ultra-high density standard cell library using multi-height cell structure. In *Proc. SPIE*, volume 7268, pages 72680C–72680C–8, 2008.

[3] I. S. Bustany, D. Chinnery, J. R. Shinnerl, and V. Yutsis. Ispd 2015 benchmarks with fence regions and routing blockages for detailed-routing-driven placement. In *Proceedings of the 2015 Symposium on International Symposium on Physical Design*, ISPD '15, pages 157–164, 2015.

[4] W.-K. Chow, C.-W. Pui, and E. F. Y. Young. Legalization algorithm for multiple-row height standard cell design. In *Proceedings of the 53rd Annual Design Automation Conference*, DAC '16, pages 83:1–83:6, 2016.

[5] S. Dobre, A. B. Kahng, and J. Li. Mixed cell-height implementation for improved design quality in advanced nodes. In *Proceedings of the IEEE/ACM International Conference on Computer-Aided Design*, ICCAD '15, pages 854–860, 2015.

[6] S. Li and C.-K. Koh. Mixed integer programming models for detailed placement. In *Proceedings of the 2012 ACM International Symposium on International Symposium on Physical Design*, ISPD '12, pages 87–94, 2012.

[7] Y. Lin, B. Yu, X. Xu, J.-R. Gao, N. Viswanathan, W.-H. Liu, Z. Li, C. J. Alpert, and D. Z. Pan. Mrdp: Multiple-row detailed placement of heterogeneous-sized cells for advanced nodes. In *Proceedings of the 35th International Conference on Computer-Aided Design*, ICCAD '16, pages 7:1–7:8, 2016.

[8] P. Spindler, U. Schlichtmann, and F. M. Johannes. Abacus: Fast legalization of standard cell circuits with minimal movement. In *Proceedings of the 2008 International Symposium on Physical Design*, ISPD '08, pages 47–53, 2008.

[9] C.-H. Wang, Y.-Y. Wu, J. Chen, Y.-W. Chang, S.-Y. Kuo, W. Zhu, and G. Fan. An effective legalization algorithm for mixed-cell-height standard cells. In *Proceedings of the 22nd Asia and South Pacific Design Automation Conference*, ASP-DAC '17, 2017.

[10] J. Wang, A. K. Wong, and E. Y. Lam. Standard cell layout with regular contact placement. *IEEE Transactions on Semiconductor Manufacturing*, 17(3):375–383, Aug 2004.

[11] G. Wu and C. Chu. Detailed placement algorithm for vlsi design with double-row height standard cells. *IEEE Transactions on Computer-Aided Design of Integrated Circuits and Systems*, 35(9):1569–1573, Sept 2016.

Covert Timing Channels Exploiting Non-Uniform Memory Access based Architectures

Fan Yao, Guru Venkataramani and Miloš Doroslovački
Department of Electrical and Computer Engineering
The George Washington University, Washington, DC, USA
{albertyao, guruv, doroslov}@gwu.edu

ABSTRACT

Covert timing channels are a class of information leakage attacks where two processes, namely the *trojan* and *spy*, collude with intent to stealthily exfiltrate privileged information even when the underlying system security policy prohibits any direct communication between the two processes. In this paper, we present a new type of covert timing channel that exploits the access timing difference between various caches in Non-Uniform Memory Access (NUMA)-based architectures, especially multi-socket CPUs. We demonstrate a realistic covert timing channel implemented on a dual-socket Intel Xeon server. We then explore use of statistical analysis techniques to characterize and quantify the presence of covert timing channel activity. Our experimental results show that such quantification techniques could be a useful first step in formulating an effective defense against NUMA-based covert timing channels.

1. INTRODUCTION

Computer security attacks, especially those that leak sensitive data, are a fast growing concern in our everyday lives. Covert channels are a class of information leakage attacks where two colluding processes, namely the trojan and the spy, intentionally subvert the underlying system security policy to exfiltrate privileged information. Compared to side channels in which the activities of an unsuspecting victim process are monitored stealthily by a spy, covert channels operate through an *insider* trojan process that communicates the secrets to the spy even when the underlying system policy prohibits such interaction [5]. Covert channels are usually classified into two broad categories: storage-based (that hide secrets within legitimately communicated data) and timing-based (that simply manipulate the timing of access to certain hardware or software resources). Among these covert channel implementations, timing-based attacks are notoriously hard to detect since they do not leave any physical trace of an attack for inspection and forensic analysis [18].

Permission to make digital or hard copies of all or part of this work for personal or classroom use is granted without fee provided that copies are not made or distributed for profit or commercial advantage and that copies bear this notice and the full citation on the first page. Copyrights for components of this work owned by others than ACM must be honored. Abstracting with credit is permitted. To copy otherwise, or republish, to post on servers or to redistribute to lists, requires prior specific permission and/or a fee. Request permissions from permissions@acm.org.

GLSVLSI '17, May 10-12, 2017, Banff, AB, Canada
© 2017 ACM. ISBN 978-1-4503-4972-7/17/05...$15.00
DOI: http://dx.doi.org/10.1145/3060403.3060417

With rapid improvements in software confinement and isolation mechanisms, it is becoming increasingly difficult for covert timing channels to exploit software resources. Naturally, malicious attackers are turning to exploit hardware. The multi-core processors, that have multitude of shared hardware resources (e.g., caches, interconnect and functional units), offer rich space for such exploits. Note that these multi-core processors dominate the entire computing landscape today ranging from mobile phones to cloud computing. Therefore, it becomes critical to understand how malicious attackers exploit such shared resources, and devise strategies to neutralize such efforts by the adversary.

Recently, there have been a growing number of studies on hardware covert timing channel attacks that manipulate the access timing on caches [15, 23, 14], functional units such as integer multipliers [19], processor-memory bus [22] and branch predictors [7]. In all of these attacks, the trojan creates contention on a particular shared resource by creating a certain number of events, and lets the spy observe the altered access timing on that resource, and infer the transmitted bit.

In this paper, we investigate and present a new type of hardware vulnerability to covert timing channels exposed by the difference in access timing across multiple levels of the cache hierarchy in Non-Uniform Memory Access (NUMA)-based architectures. We implement a realistic covert timing channel based on this vulnerability, and demonstrate the attack on a dual-socket Intel Xeon server where the trojan modulates the cache access timing by locating itself on a socket different from the spy. We then explore statistical techniques to characterize and quantify the possible presence of covert timing channel activity. We utilize Degree of Sparseness [13] to quantify and analyze the pattern of time intervals for inter-socket cache data transfers when observed during covert channel activity and regular application execution (with no known covert information leakage channels). We note that developing such quantification techniques will be a useful first step in mounting successful defense against such timing channels.

The contributions of our paper are:

1. We present a new hardware-based covert timing channel implementation where the trojan, in order to communicate the secrets to the spy, exploits the timing differences in cache read accesses exposed by NUMA-based architectures.
2. We demonstrate the viability of our new covert timing channel on a real system testbed using Intel Xeon X5650 dual-socket processors.
3. We explore statistical methods to quantify NUMA-based

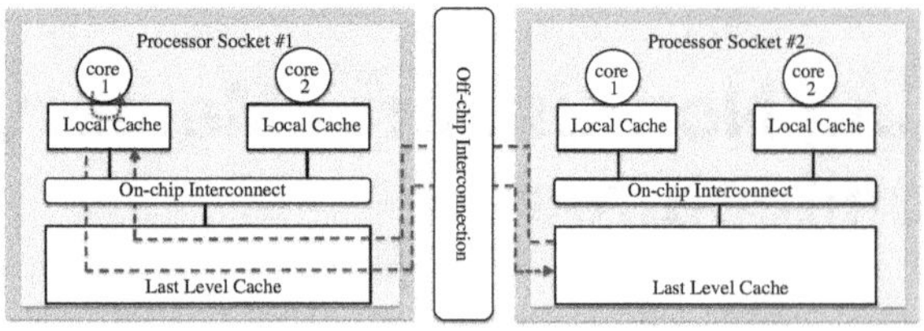

Figure 1: Local and remote cache accesses in NUMA system.

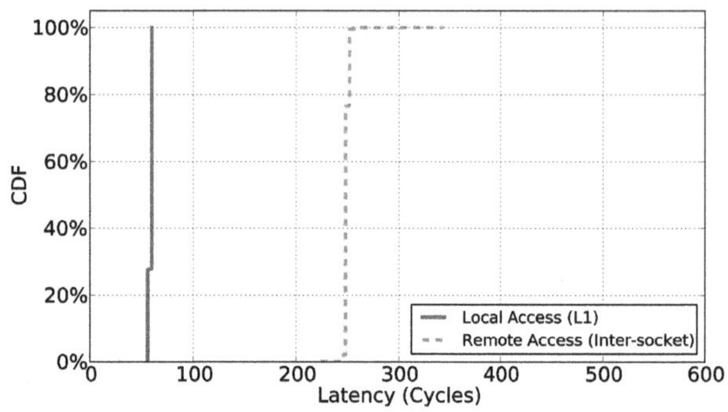

Figure 2: Cumulative Distribution Function for local (Level 1) and remote/cross-socket (Last Level) cache access latency

covert timing channel activity, that can eventually help guide defense strategies against such channels.

2. BACKGROUND

The memory hierarchy in recent processors includes several levels of caches and DRAM, some that are used privately by the individual cores and some that are shared between multiple cores. Also, with the use of multi-socket CPUs communicating via high speed interconnect (e.g., Quick Path Interconnect (QPI) in Intel architectures [2] and HyperTransport links in AMD architectures [6]), processor cores can now share cache contents across processors with coherence protocols running between them. Due to these hierarchical memory levels, there is usually a shorter latency period for read/write requests satisfied by a cache situated locally within the processor (local socket) when compared to memory requests that are satisfied by a cache belonging to a different processor (cross-socket or inter-socket). An unintended side-effect of these timing differences in NUMA-based machines is that, a malicious hacker can exploit such timing variations to force data to be placed in different caches, and ultimately implement covert timing channels. Figure 1 illustrates the difference between cache accesses that are satisfied locally within the same socket (local cache hit– shown using a dotted line) versus those that are satisfied by the remote cache (cache hit in another socket– shown using a dashed line).

2.1 NUMA Latency

To understand the access latency variations in NUMA, we perform experiments that read data from local and remote processor caches in a multi-socket processor. For this study, we use a dual-socket Intel Xeon X5650 server with 6 cores in each socket running at 2.67 GHz frequency. Each processor has a 32 KB private L1, 256 KB private L2 caches, 12 MB shared L3 cache within each socket. All of the caches are kept coherent in hardware. To model real system settings, applications such as browser, dropbox, code editors are run alongside our experiments.

We generate 1,000 memory read operations that target caches in the local socket (specifically, L1 cache) and remote socket (specifically, Last Level Cache or LLC in another socket). To target local caches for reads, our test profiler runs a tight loop with repeated reads that are satisfied by the local L1 cache. To target remote LLC for reads, our profiler issues periodic read requests. Meanwhile, a control program, that is pinned to a socket different from where the test profiler resides, explicitly issues a flush operation (using x86 ISA-supported instructions such as *clflush* that clears the block from all caches) and then loads the block into corresponding socket's cache hierarchy (that includes its LLC). When the test profiler issues its read access to the cache block, this block is guaranteed to be routed to the remote socket where the control program is located. All of the cache accesses and the associated instructions are timed using *rdtsc* instruction. Figure 2 shows the Cumulative Distribution Function (CDF) for cache access latencies from local and remote sockets. As we can see, the cache accesses to local and remote caches show distinct bands of latency distributions. This shows the viability for exploiting the latency difference between caches in different sockets.

3. THREAT MODEL

In our covert timing channel, we assume that the trojan and spy are running on the same machine that features two or more multi-core processors. The trojan intentionally modulates the cache access timing through issuing a flush operation, and later places a data block in its local cache so that the spy can infer the covertly transmitted information. We assume that a compromised trojan, that has sufficient privileges to access sensitive data, is able to run inside the target multi-socket CPU. Our attack model fits into *flush+reload* category of attacks [26], where the trojan clears its memory blocks and reloads them to alter the access times.

As confinement mechanisms continue to offer stronger isolation between software applications, hardware structures will become natural targets for covert timing channels. In this vein, we illustrate the vulnerabilities exposed by NUMA-based architectures (specifically, multi-socket CPU systems) that provide for timing difference in cache accesses depending on the caches that satisfy the memory requests.

4. NUMA-BASED TIMING CHANNELS

In this section, we demonstrate a covert timing channel implementation that exploits the cache access timing differences in NUMA. The trojan and the spy are two separate physical processes with the trojan having higher privileges than the spy in terms of access to sensitive secrets such as Operating System- or user-related data. In order to sufficiently modulate the timing of cache accesses, the trojan process is run in a socket different from the spy.

Figure 3 illustrates the communication protocol between the trojan and the spy for bit transmission. The spy issues the *load* or read instructions periodically to a memory address that is known (and accessible) to both the trojan and spy. Typically, this memory address points to a shared code region such as a library function shared between

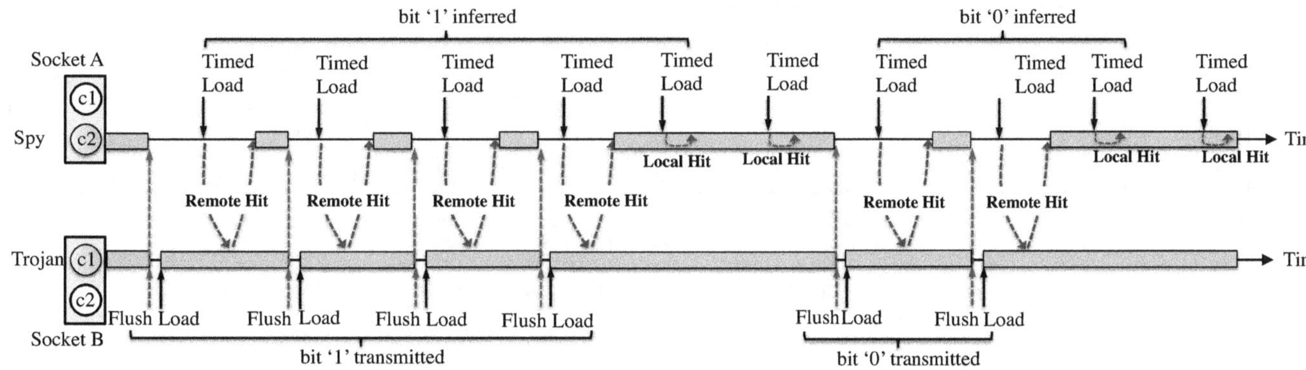

Figure 3: Illustration of the communication protocol between the spy and trojan showing a transmission of bit sequence '10'.

processes [26]. There are two possibilities in NUMA-based CPUs when load operations are issued by the spy: 1. the load hits in the local L1 cache or LLC of the spy's socket, 2. the load misses in the cache hierarchy of the spy's socket, and the requested memory address is resident in the remote socket or DRAM. Our experiments show two distinct bands of latencies for the above two possibilities (Figure 2). The spy *times* these loads to infer whether the loads resulted in a *local cache hit* or a *remote cache hit*. If the loads are satisfied by the DRAM (i.e., neither socket's cache can satisfy), the spy observes a longer latency compared to remote cache hit and ignores them.

The trojan manipulates the access timing to the shared memory address to communicate the bits covertly to the spy. Whenever the trojan wants to communicate a bit, it performs a *cache flush* operation using instructions such as *clflush*. This clears the target memory address from all of the caches that are kept coherent in the multi-socket CPU, including that of the spy located in another socket. The trojan, then immediately, performs a load from that memory location. This populates the shared memory address data in the cache hierarchy of the trojan's socket (i.e., the corresponding L1 cache and LLC). When the spy performs its periodic load from this memory address, the spy's cache cannot service this load since the corresponding contents have been previously flushed by the trojan. Effectively, this enables the spy to detect the timing difference in cache access compared to its local cache hit.

Now that, we have seen how the trojan manipulates the timing of cache access for the spy, it is important to understand how the transmission of '1' and '0' bits can be accomplished. In our current implementation, this is done through trojan performing a specific number of *consecutive* flush+reload operations to be observed by the spy. In our current design, for transmitting a '1', the trojan performs *four* consecutive flush+reload; and for transmitting a '0', the trojan performs *two* consecutive flush+reload operations. The spy infers the end of bit transmission when it observes its load operation result in a local cache hit (via timing the load), i.e., the trojan has not performed flush+reload on the memory block.

Finally, we note that our implementation does not have explicit synchronization between the trojan and the spy. Based on our experimental measurements, a flush+reload operation by the trojan took 350 cycles. To allow for sufficient time, the spy performs its periodic timed load accesses every 1,000 cycles. This minimizes the possibility of the spy missing the trojan's transmitted bit. We note that, in order to further improve the reliability of transmission while maximizing the effective bit rate of covert channel, the spy could reduce the time interval between its load requests, and the trojan could utilize one or more of the following features: 1. add parity bits, 2. packetize the transmission and include packet headers containing metadata, 3. synchronize using existing system features such as CPU clock.

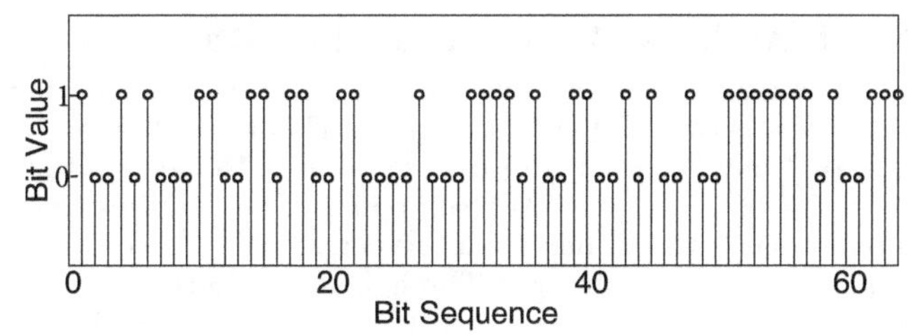

Figure 4: Bit pattern (64 bits) transmitted by the trojan.

5. TIMING CHANNEL DEMONSTRATION

Using the Linux system call *sched_setaffinity*, the spy and the trojan thread are pinned to two different sockets of Intel Xeon X5650 server. To create shared memory pages, we programmed the trojan and spy to load a shared page from the *libgcrypt library* [1], a widely used Linux cryptography library.

The spy runs a *while* loop with *timed* loads to a cache block in the shared libgcrypt library. Figure 4 shows a random 64 bits that are transmitted from the trojan. Correspondingly, Figure 5 shows the sequence of latencies measured using *timed load* by the spy. As we can see, there are several consecutive tall bars (corresponding to *remote cache hits*) fenced by consecutive short bars (corresponding to *local cache hits*). The spy deciphers the bit based on the number of consecutive tall bars (see Section 4). In our experiments, the spy observes 1-2 tall bars during '0' transmission, and 3-4 tall bars during '1' transmission. This small variance stems from tail latencies in remote cache latency distribution and the background noise from other processes. Despite this minor variation, the spy could still correctly distinguish between '1' and '0' with 100% accuracy. Overall, the transmission achieves an effective bit rate of 190 Kbit/sec. Note that it is possible to further improve the speed through ad-

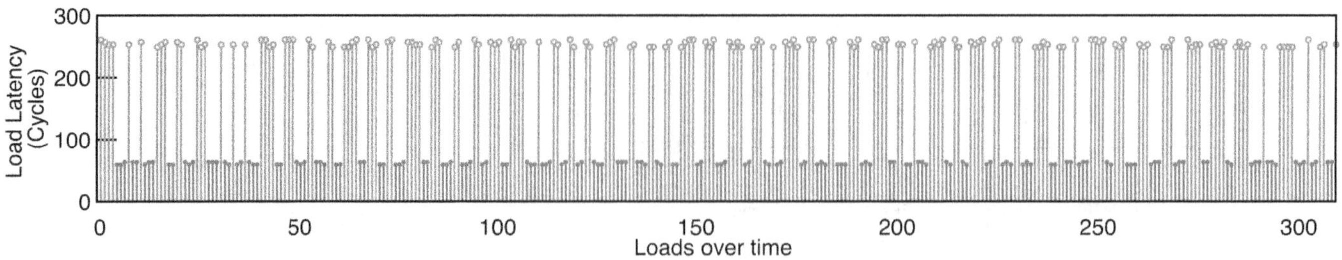

Figure 5: Latency sequence for load operations measured by the spy. The (taller) red bar and (shorter) purple bars correspond to remote cache and local cache hits respectively.

ditional optimizations to the trojan and spy described in Section 4.

6. TIMING CHANNEL ANALYSIS

To prepare for an effective defense, we first attempt to characterize the NUMA-based timing channels. We envision that any detection strategy would need to monitor the activities of multiple NUMA components, and capture the interactions between individual components (e.g., cache miss requests and data transfers). Through analyzing the activity of cache hierarchy during covert transmission, we made an important observation: *The time-interval between two consecutive remote cache accesses (i.e., time-interval between inter-socket cache data transfers) exhibits a concentrated distribution in the case of a covert channel attack compared to regular applications with legitimate communication.* The concentration is due to the fact that the spy relies on observing a consecutive number of remote load accesses in order to infer the transmitted bits. As such, the spy issues a number of load operations at a pre-determined sampling interval that can be observed over the interconnect. Our experiments show that covert channels have only a *few possible values for time-intervals between remote cache accesses* (see Section 6.1 for details). We note that it is conceivable for a spy to change the sampling interval at runtime to evade from being noticed. However, in asynchronous environments, the spy may begin to see a rapid rise in bit error rate due to lack of synchronization. On the contrary, for regular applications that do not intentionally manipulate the timing between inter-socket data transfers, a higher level of randomness is expected in time between inter-socket cache transfers, which is verified through our experiments.

6.1 Time-Intervals between Remote Accesses

Since real hardware does not support measuring the time-intervals between remote cache accesses, we setup *Gem5* [4], a cycle-accurate, full system simulator to perform our measurements. We configure Gem5 with eight x86 cores, and use a minimal Linux distribution with kernel version 2.6.32. We build Parsec-2.1 benchmarks [3] with 8 threads, where each thread is pinned to a separate core. We also configure the spy and trojan to run on Gem5, where we record the timestamps for inter-core cache data transfers. Since any core pair can be used in a covert channel attack, the monitor filters the timestamps associated with cache data transfers for each source-destination core pair. We generate histograms for time-intervals between inter-socket cache accesses.

As expected, our experiments in Figure 6 show that regular (Parsec-2.1) benchmarks exhibit higher randomness in time-intervals. We show results for a representative core in each benchmark. Also, we eliminate time-intervals greater than 5,000 cycles since they represent lengthy idle periods without inter-core cache transfers, and collectively constitute less than 0.5% of the population. We observe that, though some time interval bins are more favored than other bins (i.e., higher probability), the probability of any single bin does not exceed 25% and the expected probability in almost all of the bins are non-trivial. In contrast, for covert channel scenario (Figure 7), the time-interval distribution is highly concentrated and is non-zero only for a very few bins. Notably, the bins between 1,500 and 2,000 cycles correspond to *bit transmission phases* when more frequent remote cache accesses are observed, and the bins between 4,300 and 5,000 cycles correspond to *idle phases* when time interval between remote cache accesses are long. *We note that, though the absolute locations of the histogram bins corresponding to bit transmission and idle phases may change, the characteristic of concentration in certain bins over others would remain, as they are inherently needed to covertly communicate bits between the trojan and the spy.*

6.2 Quantifying NUMA Covert Channels

From Section 6.1, we see that the time-interval histograms for regular applications and covert channels are significantly different. Specifically, the time-interval distribution in covert channel is highly concentrated within a small number of bins to improve *bit inference accuracy* for the spy. In other words, the highly probable bins are *sparse* for covert channels compared to regular applications. Therefore, we use the metric *Degree of Sparseness* (S) [13] to capture this phenomenon. An S value of 1 denotes that the distribution is very sparse, and a value of 0 means that the distribution is not sparse (i.e., uniform). Given the probability vector for the histogram bins as P, Degree of Sparseness (S) is defined as:

$$S = \frac{M}{M - \sqrt{M}}\left(1 - \frac{\|P\|_1}{\sqrt{M} \times \|P\|_2}\right) \tag{1}$$

where M equals to the number of histogram bins, and $\|P\|_1$, $\|P\|_2$ are norm-1 and norm-2 for vector P respectively. It is worth noting that there are a number of histogram bins in regular applications which have *near-zero* probabilities. Since S depends on the absolute probability values, the histogram bins with near-zero probabilities may be outweighed. To account for such bins and amplify their influence during computation of S, we pre-process the probability values with the μ-law compression function [16] to get a new vector Q:

$$Q_i = \frac{\log(1 + \mu P_i)}{\log(1 + \mu)} \tag{2}$$

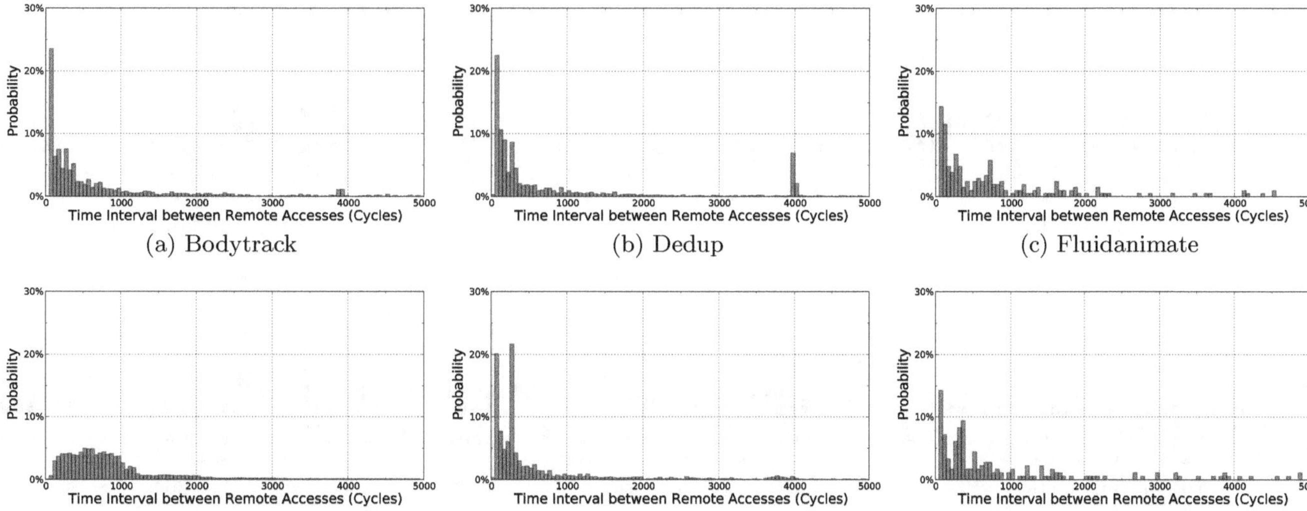

(a) Bodytrack (b) Dedup (c) Fluidanimate

(d) StreamCluster (e) Swaptions (f) x264

Figure 6: Histograms of time-intervals between remote cache accesses in Parsec-2.1 benchmarks for representative cores.

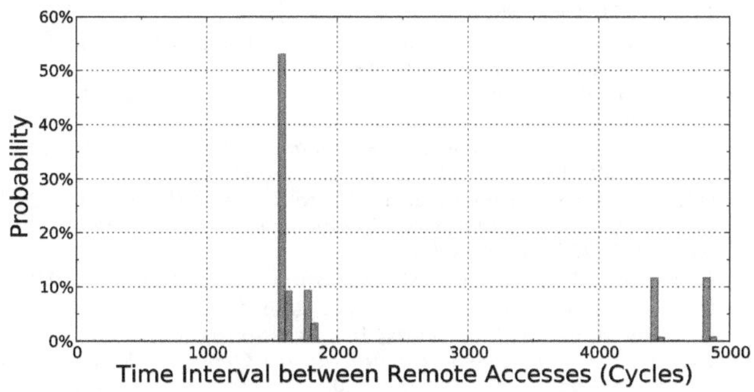

Figure 7: Histogram of time-intervals between remote cache accesses in the covert channel.

where μ is a tunable parameter that controls the degree of compression for large values while increasing the level of amplification for small values. We set $\mu = 500$ in our experiments.

We compute values of S on our histograms for time-intervals for remote cache accesses. Figure 8 shows the *Sparseness* measurement for each of the (source, destination) core pairs for six Parsec-2.1 benchmarks. We observe the S values to be less than 0.4 in all regular benchmarks. On the other hand, S value is very high, and around 0.8 for covert channels (which is at least 2× compared to regular applications). This proves that our quantification technique can indeed be applied as an effective indicator for the possible presence of NUMA-based covert timing channels.

7. RELATED WORK

Several prior works have studied hardware-based side- and covert channels [26, 23, 11, 24, 10]. Recently, Irazoqui et al. [9] demonstrate a side channel implementation that takes advantage of the cache access timing difference exposed by the high speed point-to-point interconnect between processors compared to DRAM accesses. This attack manipulates accesses to the remote cache and DRAM. Different from this attack, our paper demonstrates an attack that exploits local/remote cache access latency differences.

Architecture support for safeguarding computer systems from information leakage attacks have been widely studied [20, 25]. Venkataramani et al. [18] study how to detect contention-based covert timing channels through dynamically tracking conflict patterns on shared hardware resources. Liu et al. [12] propose a cache design that provides dynamic and randomized memory-to-cache mapping to mitigate contention based side channels. Gu et al. [8] have shown the potential of leveraging the merging 3D die-stacking techniques for secure system design. Hardware-based side channel resistant S-Box designs for the AES crypto-systems are studied in prior works [17, 21]. Such techniques can help detect and mitigate information leakage channels, and work synergistically with our detection mechanism to improve the overall system security.

8. CONCLUSIONS

In this paper, we presented a new type of covert timing channel that exploits the cache access timing difference in NUMA-based architectures. Unlike most prior timing channel attacks that exploit a single cache, the proposed attack manipulates different levels of caches across multiple sockets. We implemented a realistic covert timing channel on a dual-socket Intel Xeon CPU. We explored statistical analysis techniques to characterize and quantify the presence of covert timing channel activity using *Degree of Sparseness* for inter-socket cache data transfers. Our experimental results showed that such quantification techniques can sufficiently distinguish covert timing channel activity from regular applications, and ultimately help design defense mechanisms.

9. ACKNOWLEDGMENTS

This material is based on work supported by the US National Science Foundation under CAREER Award CCF-1149557 and CNS-1618786, and Semiconductor Research Corp. (SRC) contract 2016-TS-2684. Any opinions, findings, con-

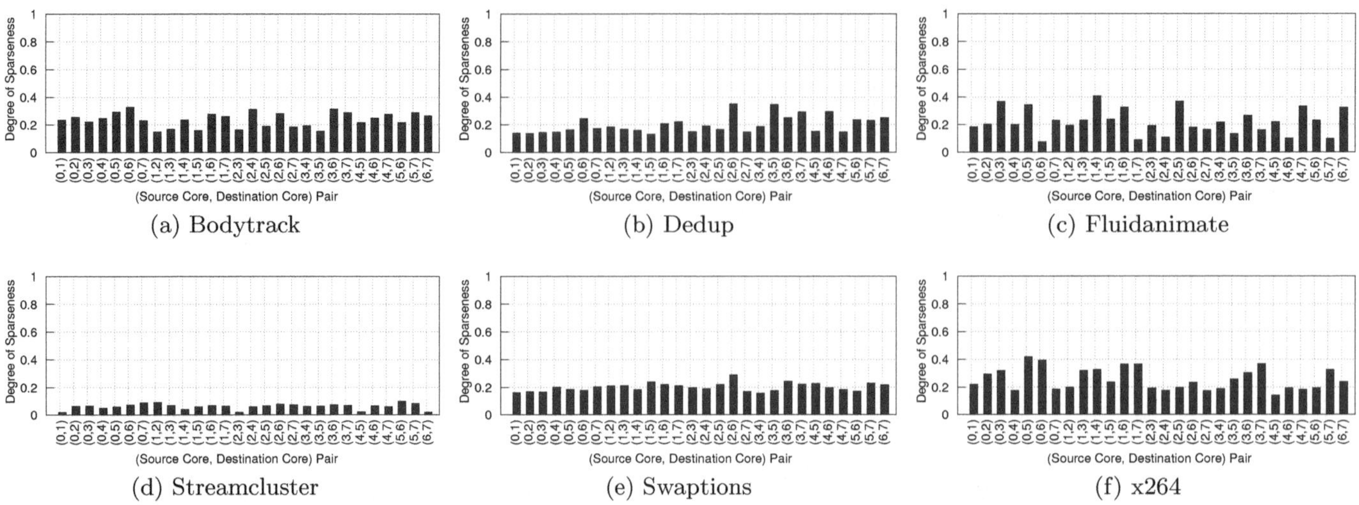

(a) Bodytrack (b) Dedup (c) Fluidanimate

(d) Streamcluster (e) Swaptions (f) x264

Figure 8: Degree of Sparseness for (Source, Destination) pairs for the Parsec-2.1 Benchmarks.

clusions, or recommendations expressed in this article are those of the authors, and do not necessarily reflect those of the NSF or SRC.

10. REFERENCES

[1] Libgcrypt project. https://www.gnu.org/software/libgcrypt/.

[2] Intel QuickPath Architecture, 2012. http://www.intel.com/pressroom/archive/reference/whitepaper_QuickPath.pdf.

[3] C. Bienia, S. Kumar, J. P. Singh, and K. Li. The PARSEC benchmark suite: Characterization and architectural implications. In *Proceedings of the 17th International Conference on Parallel Architectures and Compilation Techniques*, pages 72–81. ACM, 2008.

[4] N. Binkert, B. Beckmann, G. Black, S. K. Reinhardt, A. Saidi, A. Basu, J. Hestness, D. R. Hower, T. Krishna, S. Sardashti, et al. The gem5 simulator. *ACM SIGARCH Computer Architecture News*, 39(2):1–7, 2011.

[5] J. Chen and G. Venkataramani. Cc-hunter: Uncovering covert timing channels on shared processor hardware. In *47th Annual International Symposium on Microarchitecture (MICRO)*. IEEE, 2014.

[6] P. Conway, N. Kalyanasundharam, G. Donley, K. Lepak, and B. Hughes. Cache hierarchy and memory subsystem of the AMD Opteron processor. *IEEE micro*, 30(2):16–29, 2010.

[7] D. Evtyushkin, D. Ponomarev, and N. Abu-Ghazaleh. Understanding and mitigating covert channels through branch predictors. *ACM Transactions on Architecture and Code Optimization*, 13(1):10, 2016.

[8] P. Gu, S. Li, D. Stow, R. Barnes, L. Liu, Y. Xie, and E. Kursun. Leveraging 3D technologies for hardware security: Opportunities and challenges. In *Proceedings of the 26th edition of the Great Lakes Symposium on VLSI*, pages 347–352. ACM, 2016.

[9] G. Irazoqui, T. Eisenbarth, and B. Sunar. Cross processor cache attacks. In *Proceedings of the 11th Asia Conference on Computer and Communications Security*, pages 353–364. ACM, 2016.

[10] Z. H. Jiang, Y. Fei, and D. Kaeli. A complete key recovery timing attack on a GPU. In *Proceedings of the 22nd International Symposium on High Performance Computer Architecture*, pages 394–405. IEEE, 2016.

[11] J. Lee, M. Tehranipoor, C. Patel, and J. Plusquellic. Securing designs against scan-based side-channel attacks. *IEEE Transactions on Dependable and Secure Computing*, 4(4):325–336, 2007.

[12] F. Liu, H. Wu, K. Mai, and R. B. Lee. Newcache: Secure cache architecture thwarting cache side-channel attacks. *IEEE Micro*, 36(5):8–16, 2016.

[13] P. Loganathan, A. W. Khong, and P. A. Naylor. A class of sparseness-controlled algorithms for echo cancellation. *IEEE Transactions on Audio, Speech, and Language Processing*, 17(8):1591–1601, 2009.

[14] D. A. Osvik, A. Shamir, and E. Tromer. Cache attacks and countermeasures: the case of AES. In *Proceedings of the Cryptographers' Track at the RSA Conference*, pages 1–20. Springer, 2006.

[15] T. Ristenpart, E. Tromer, H. Shacham, and S. Savage. Hey, you, get off of my cloud: exploring information leakage in third-party compute clouds. In *Proceedings of the 16th Conference on Computer and Communications Security*, pages 199–212. ACM, 2009.

[16] K. Sayood. *Introduction to data compression*. Newnes, 2012.

[17] C. Teegarden, M. Bhargava, and K. Mai. Side-channel attack resistant rom-based aes s-box. In *Proceedings of the International Symposium on Hardware-Oriented Security and Trust*, pages 124–129. IEEE, 2010.

[18] G. Venkataramani, J. Chen, and M. Doroslovacki. Detecting hardware covert timing channels. *IEEE Micro*, 36(5):17–27, 2016.

[19] Z. Wang and R. B. Lee. Covert and side channels due to processor architecture. In *Proceedings of the 22nd Annual Computer Security Applications Conference*, pages 473–482. IEEE, 2006.

[20] Z. Wang and R. B. Lee. New cache designs for thwarting software cache-based side channel attacks. In *ACM SIGARCH Computer Architecture News*, volume 35, pages 494–505. ACM, 2007.

[21] J. Wu, Y.-B. Kim, and M. Choi. Low-power side-channel attack-resistant asynchronous s-box design for aes cryptosystems. In *Proceedings of the 20th edition of the Great Lakes Symposium on VLSI*, pages 459–464. ACM, 2010.

[22] Z. Wu, Z. Xu, and H. Wang. Whispers in the hyper-space: high-speed covert channel attacks in the cloud. In *USENIX Security 12*, 2012.

[23] Y. Xu, M. Bailey, F. Jahanian, K. Joshi, M. Hiltunen, and R. Schlichting. An exploration of l2 cache covert channels in virtualized environments. In *Proceedings of the 3rd Workshop on Cloud Computing Security Workshop*, pages 29–40. ACM, 2011.

[24] B. Yang, K. Wu, and R. Karri. Scan based side channel attack on dedicated hardware implementations of data encryption standard. In *Proceedings of the International Test Conference*. IEEE, 2004.

[25] F. Yao, J. Chen, and G. Venkataramani. Jop-alarm: Detecting jump-oriented programming-based anomalies in applications. In *Proceedings of the 31st International Conference on Computer Design*, pages 467–470. IEEE, 2013.

[26] Y. Yarom and K. Falkner. Flush+ reload: a high resolution, low noise, L3 cache side-channel attack. In *USENIX Security*, 2014.

A Low-Cost GPS Spoofing Detector Design for Internet of Things (IoT) Applications

Md Tanvir Arafin
ECE Department
University of Maryland
College Park, Maryland
marafin@umd.edu

Dhananjay Anand
National Institute of Standards and Technology
Gaithersburg, Maryland
dhananjay.anand@nist.gov

Gang Qu
ECE Department
University of Maryland
College Park, Maryland
gangqu@umd.edu

ABSTRACT

The civilian Global Positioning System (GPS) is widely used for precise positioning, timekeeping, and synchronization in embedded systems. As a result, emerging digital infrastructure such as the Internet of Things (IoT) are dependent on GPS to locate and synchronize *Things* in the network. From a security perspective, civilian GPS signals are vulnerable to malintent because they are not encrypted and can easily be spoofed. Several countermeasures have been proposed to detect GPS spoofing attacks, but most of them require extensive signal processing capabilities and additional electronic components to capture and analyze RF signals. These add-ons may not be available to IoT devices, and if present, they will affect the device's power budget significantly. Therefore, new techniques for spoofing detection and survival are required before integrating GPS receivers with IoT devices and other critical infrastructures where energy and computation power are limited. In this work, we propose a novel GPS spoofing detection scheme based on hardware oscillators. Our design depends on measuring the frequency drift and offset of a free-running crystal oscillator with respect to the GPS signals. In our secure GPS spoofing detector design the trust is intrinsic, *i.e.*, the receiver only trusts the on-board free running local oscillator. Intrinsic properties of these oscillators exhibit a strong correlation with the authentic GPS signals and any anomaly in this measurement will indicate potential attacks on the received GPS signals. This proposed design is cost-effective, secure, backward compatible with existing receivers, and does not require additional RF circuitry or network connection with other clocks for detecting attacks.

Keywords

GPS Spoofing, Hardware Oscillator, Anomaly Detection, Hardware-Oriented Security and Trust.

1. INTRODUCTION

The progress towards an Internet of Things (IoTs) is highly dependent on the secure and successful integration of a trusted and robust geospatial localization and clock synchronization mechanism for *Things* across a large distributed network.

ACM acknowledges that this contribution was authored or co-authored by an employee, or contractor of the national government. As such, the Government retains a nonexclusive, royalty-free right to publish or reproduce this article, or to allow others to do so, for Government purposes only. Permission to make digital or hard copies for personal or classroom use is granted. Copies must bear this notice and the full citation on the first page. Copyrights for components of this work owned by others than ACM must be honored. To copy otherwise, distribute, republish, or post, requires prior specific permission and/or a fee. Request permissions from permissions@acm.org.

GLSVLSI '17, May 10-12, 2017, Banff, AB, Canada

© 2017 ACM. ISBN 978-1-4503-4972-7/17/05. . . $15.00

DOI: http://dx.doi.org/10.1145/3060403.3060455

Currently, both these functions are predominantly provided by the Global Positioning System (GPS). As a result, in today's world, GPS receivers have become a ubiquitous component in embedded systems: from the smart-phones and smart devices to automated vehicles and Phasor Measurement Units (PMUs) in the electric grid. However, this pervasive nature of GPS receivers in current and next-generation smart *Things* necessitates a thorough study of their security vulnerabilities and corresponding countermeasures.

Recently, there have been several demonstrations of weaknesses and vulnerabilities of GPS signals and GPS receivers [2, 7, 8, 11, 15, 13]. It has been argued that the future of navigation is crucially dependent on defending spoofing attacks on global navigation satellite system (GNSS) signals such as GPS [13]. Moreover, the common trend in IoT application designs is to use the civilian GPS signals, these signals are broadcast without encryption and several practical demonstrations of spoofing mechanisms have been documented in the literature [2, 7, 8, 15]. Most of the analysis on GPS spoofing is directed towards the spoofing of position data, however, GPS system is also used for large area clock synchronization, and therefore, attacks on GPS signals can impact networked infrastructure where accurate time keeping is important. For example, Phasor Measurement Units (PMUs) used in the electrical power system synchronize themselves using GPS signals, and an attack on this synchronization can induce failures in the power system across a wide area [9].

Along with research on potential attacks, several authentication and anti-spoofing techniques for GNSS signals have been developed in recent years. These techniques can be broadly categorized as signal and data-level authentication. For signal authentication, received signal characteristics of the civilian signal may be verified against encrypted GPS transmissions, additionally, the plane-of-polarization and angle-of-arrival can be measured to validate the signal as well. Data-level techniques are based on authentication of the received data with reference to a-priori knowledge of position or authentication using corroborative localization and timing sources. These methods have been shown to be effective; however, they are not usually used in the commercial GPS receivers due to implementation cost[11]. Moreover, the accuracy, computational and power efficiency, security against complex attacks and real-time performance of these approaches are still areas of active research.

In this paper, we present a data-level GPS spoofing detection mechanism that relies on intrinsic hardware properties of a free-running crystal oscillator. Since the free-running oscillator is located on the device and not externally synchronized, it presents a minimal attack surface while exhibiting a strong correlation with authentic GPS signals. It is our proposition that '*anomalies*' in the correlation index may indicate potential attacks on the received GPS data. Our approach is simple, fast and can perform at near real-time. Additionally, the design is low cost and can act as an add-on to virtually any GPS receiver.

2. PRELIMINARIES

2.1 The GPS System

The GPS system consists of satellite transmitters and (usually) terrestrial receivers. Each transmitter satellite broadcasts at two frequencies: 1575.42 MHz (L1) and 1227.6 MHz (L2). The L1 carrier messages are available for civilian purposes. These messages are not encrypted but modulated with pseudo-random noise (PRN) codes to distinguish each satellite. The L2 carrier is modulated by encrypted codes and reserved for military purposes. Message from each GPS satellite contains information about the position of the satellite and the time of the on-board atomic clock[12].

To calculate true receiver-to-satellite distance, the receiver requires the range (r_{true}) of a satellite at a given time. This can be calculated by the multiplying the signal propagation time (from the transmitter to the receiver) with the speed of light (c). Then, for a receiver located in (x_r, y_r, z_r) and a transmitter at (x_t, y_t, z_t) position, the range is given as:

$$r_{true} = c\, t_{propagation} = \sqrt{(x_t - x_r)^2 + (y_t - y_r)^2 + (z_t - z_r)^2} \quad (1)$$

To solve equation 1 for (x_r, y_r, z_r), one requires ephemerides for three satellites. However, since the clock on the GPS transmitter (t_{GPS}) and the clock on the receiver (t_{local}) are not perfectly synchronized, there exists an offset t_r between these two time-scales. Therefore, the satellite-to-receiver distance that a receiver perceives is a pseudo-range (r_{pseudo}), where:

$$r_{pseudo} = r_{true} - ct_r \quad (2)$$

Therefore, a GPS receiver needs to solve for four unknowns (x_r, y_r, z_r, t_r) for precise location and perfect synchronization. At least four satellite data is required for solving this system of equations. Using this solution, a GPS receiver updates its position, and synchronizes its local clock frequently to t_{sync} for keeping perfect synchronization with the universal coordinated time (UTC) where:

$$t_{sync} = t_{local} + t_r \quad (3)$$

In practice, this method provides an accuracy in the order of 10 meters in position and nearly $0.1\mu s$ in time [3]. As a result, GPS signals can be used not only for positioning of the receivers but also for precise clock synchronization of receivers across the globe.

2.2 GPS SPOOFING

Attacks on the GPS signal are usually performed by an adversary by either jamming or spoofing one or both radio channels. For the jamming attack, an adversary transmits overwhelming radio interference over the L1 and/or L2 band. For spoofing attacks, the adversary mimics real GNSS transmissions to intentionally alter data received by a victim receiver. Since civilian GPS signals are not encrypted and the structure of the signal is well known, spoofing attacks are relatively straightforward to execute using a commercial signal generator and RF transmitter.

2.3 Existing Spoofing Detection Techniques

As discussed in Section 1, signal-level detection methods can take on several forms including (1) check/validate the received RF signal strength against a level threshold, (2) compare L1 and L2 carrier signals, (3) justify the directional characteristics and polarization of the received signal [11]. The strength of a received GPS signal is typically less than -150dBW and presence of substantially stronger signals for a single satellite or over the entire frequency band can be a sign of attack in progress. However, it is possible for a spoofing attacker to adjust power levels to evade detection limiting the usefulness of the threshold detection mechanism in practice[11]. Furthermore, most consumer grade receivers only support a single RF band, and therefore, comparing L1 and L2 carriers would require complete replacement of the internal RF-circuitry. Also, in a case of a replay attack, an attacker can delay both L1 and L2 signals to avoid detection. Finally, using directional characteristics of the receiver antenna to cross-validate received signals from each satellite requires specialized phase tracking hardware to detect directional variations. Similarly, signal polarization characteristics have been shown to be an effective authentication aid [7], however, specialized receiver front ends and signal processing are required to effectively implement the approach.

Data-level spoofing detection uses demodulated GPS data to detect spoofing. GPS data can be validated with known position data or otherwise obtained time to detect attacks[6]. For example, a stationary receiver can check its known position with the position-solution of the receiver. Since trilateration position error can be ± 10 meters, the position solution is a weak measure of credibility. It has been recently demonstrated by Jiang *et al.* [9] that attackers can use this uncertainty to induce a phase angle error of 52 degrees in a PMU receiver by using simple optimization based evasion algorithms. Monitoring jumps in the time reported by the GPS signals is another possible GPS spoofing countermeasure. One can deploy accurate clocks to measure time deviation between the reported GPS clock and the on-board clock. However, precise clocks (such as atomic clocks *etc.*) are expensive and not used in practice for commercial purposes. For IoT components, one can also compare the GPS time with networked time protocols such as NTP, however, the approach can suffer when the network is down. Moreover, the resolution of attack detection is limited by the accuracy of the networked clocks.

While it is likely that signal threshold based authentication will be integrated into commercial GPS receivers used for critical applications, the solutions discussed in this section are currently cost prohibitive for consumer grade GPS receivers in the nascent IoT infrastructure. Hence, we propose a low-cost, computation and power-budget friendly data-level GPS spoofing detection mechanism in Section 3.

3. PROPOSED APPROACH

The key idea of this work is to cross-validate GPS time signals with intrinsic properties of a hardware oscillator to detect spoofing attacks. The spoofing detector will calculate frequency states of this hardware clock using the received GPS signal as a reference. Any attacks on the received GPS data will create anomalies on the internal frequency states of this clock. Once an attack is detected, the design will attempt to generate an approximated version of the correct GPS time t_{GPS} to holdover the timing system during an attack. This design would require two additional resources in addition to the GPS receiver: (1) a single (or multiple) free running oscillator(s), (2) additional data processing capabilities. The architecture of the system is shown in Figure 1.

Our approach depends on the internal frequency states (*i.e.*, frequency drifts and skew) of a hardware oscillator for spoofing detection. Hence, we provide details on hardware clock models in the next section to elucidate this approach.

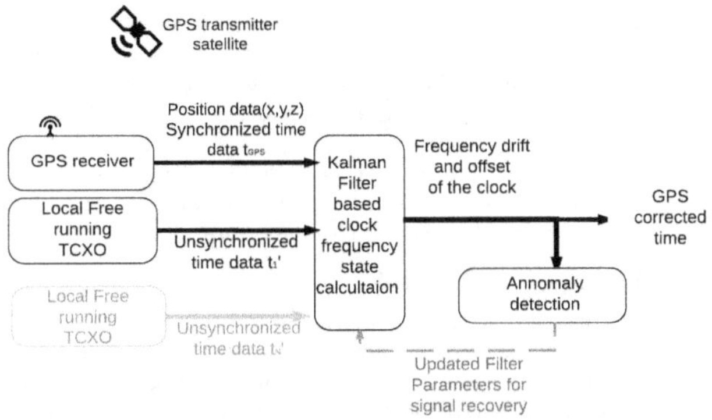

Figure 1: Design of the proposed secure GPS receiver with on-board spoofing detection. The receiver is equipped with a single (or multiple) free running temperature controlled oscillator(s). Kalman filter-based state estimation is used for calculating frequency states of this clock. In the case of multiple clocks, time from each free running oscillator can be used for generating a low noise stable virtual clock. Anomalies in the frequency drift and offset of this single clock (or the low noise virtual clock) calculated with respect to the GPS signal can reveal spoofing attacks on GPS signal. Updated filter parameters can help to reconstruct the approximated *true* time-offset during a spoofing attack.

3.1 Hardware Clocks

Clocks and oscillators in embedded systems are primarily used for time-keeping and synchronization purposes. In the majority of the embedded systems, crystal-based real-time clocks (RTCs) are used for precise time-keeping. These RTCs are far from perfect and they deviate from ideal time due to both systematic and random variations. These systematic variations arise from the imperfections in the physical realization of the clock and they are observed as time and frequency offsets and frequency drift. Therefore, at a given time t, the deviation of a clock from ideal time can be expressed as [1]:

$$x(t) = x_0 + y_0 t + \frac{1}{2}Dt^2 + \epsilon(t) \tag{4}$$

where x_0, y_0 and D represents the time offset, frequency offset (also known as skew) and frequency drift. $\epsilon(t)$ represents non-deterministic random deviations. The frequency offsets and drifts of an RTC arise from the microscopic variations in the crystal used in these oscillators. The frequency offsets and drifts also vary with the dissimilarity in design, power supply, and environmental factors. These properties have been found to be different for similar oscillators working in a same operating condition. Therefore, we have the following assumptions regarding the frequency states of hardware clocks:

- A1. Frequency drifts and skew of a clock with respect to a more precise reference are nearly constant and unique for a clock reference pair for a given duration.
- A2. The states of a known free-running local oscillator are predictable for a given reference, and one can detect unusual activity in the reference by looking at the properties of the local oscillator.
- A3. These properties vary uniquely for different clock pairs due to the random variations in their fabrication and are impossible to recreate without tampering the hardware of both the clocks.

Based on our assumption, the GPS induced internal states of a given free running oscillator are relatively constant, and therefore, can be used to detect spoofing attacks. This is the key concept for our approach. It should be noted that Khono *et al.* [10] first proposed the idea of remote device fingerprinting using the uniqueness of frequency offset of hardware clocks. Since the publication of Khono's work [10], there has been a significant development in this field of remote device fingerprinting using hardware oscillators. Our assumptions can be validated by Khono's work, the subsequent works in the literature and our experimental results and analysis presented in this work.

3.2 State-Space Model of Hardware Clocks

For precisely calculating hardware clock states, we use a stochastic model of the clocks where a clock-state is characterized by a column vector $x(t) = [x_1(t)\ y_1(t)\ D_1(t)]^T$. Here, $x_1(t), y_1(t)$ and $D_1(t)$ represents the time offset state, frequency offset state and frequency drift state respectively. The clock state follows the stochastic difference equations as given in [4]:

$$\frac{dx_1}{dt} = y_1 + w_1; \frac{dy_1}{dt} = D_1 + w_2; \frac{dD_1}{dt} = w_3; \tag{5}$$

where, $w_i(t)$ represents the associated zero mean white noise with spectral densities q_i. For an ensemble of q clocks the state vector can be written as $[x_1, y_1, D_1 \ldots x_q, y_q, D_q]^T$. Discrete-time equations for a system described by 5 can be written as [4]:

$$\mathbf{X_n} = \mathbf{F_n X_{n-1}} + \mathbf{W_n} \tag{6}$$

$$\xi_\mathbf{n} = \mathbf{H_n X_n} + \mathbf{V_n} \tag{7}$$

where, $n = 0, 1, 2, \ldots$ corresponds to discrete time t_n and measuring time interval $\Delta = t_n - t_{n-1}$.

For a single clock measurement, the $\mathbf{X_n} = [x_1, y_1, D_1]^T$ represents the state vector, and $\xi_\mathbf{n}$ denotes the observation vector. $\mathbf{F_n}$ is the state transition matrix which is calculated as:

$$\mathbf{F_n} = \begin{bmatrix} 1 & \Delta & \Delta^2/2 \\ 0 & 1 & \Delta \\ 0 & 0 & 1 \end{bmatrix} \tag{8}$$

The process noise $\mathbf{W_n}$ is considered to be zero mean additive white noise with covariance matrix $\mathbf{Q}$, where

$$\mathbf{Q} = \begin{bmatrix} q_1\Delta + q_2\frac{\Delta^3}{3} + q_3\frac{\Delta^5}{20} & q_2\frac{\Delta^2}{2} + q_3\frac{\Delta^4}{8} & q_3\frac{\Delta^3}{6} \\ q_2\frac{\Delta^2}{2} + q_3\frac{\Delta^4}{8} & q_2\Delta + q_3\frac{\Delta^3}{3} & q_3\frac{\Delta^2}{2} \\ q_3\frac{\Delta^3}{6} & q_3\frac{\Delta^2}{2} & q_3\Delta \end{bmatrix} \tag{9}$$

This state model for a clock ensemble is amenable to the design of optimal stochastic filters, which are broadly used for minimizing variance within a clock ensemble. In this work, we use this state space model for hardware oscillators and use an optimal filter (Kalman Formulation) to estimate these states for a single oscillator. It should be noted that if there are more than one on-board free running oscillators available, one could create a virtual time reference using an ensemble of clocks offering improved detection thresholds for spoofing attacks.

3.3 Kalman Filter Design for Spoofing Detection

We use discrete time state-model for developing a Kalman filter based spoofing detector. For our single clock experiment, we have the measurement matrix $\mathbf{H_n} = [1, 0, 0]$. $\mathbf{V_n}$

represents the zero mean measurement noise with covariance $\mathbf{R}$. For local measurements, we set $\mathbf{R} = \mathbf{0}$ to neglect the noise term. The algorithm for this linear Kalman filter [5] is given by the following equations:

Prediction Step:

$$\mathbf{m_{n|n-1}} = \mathbf{F_n m_{n-1|n-1}} \tag{10}$$

$$\mathbf{P_{n|n-1}} = \mathbf{F_n P_{n-1|n-1} F_n^T} + \mathbf{Q} \tag{11}$$

Update Step:

$$\mathbf{K_n} = \mathbf{P_{n|n-1} H_n^T (H_n P_{n|n-1} H_n^T + R)^{-1}} \tag{12}$$

$$\mathbf{m_{n|n}} = \mathbf{m_{n|n-1}} + \mathbf{K_n}(\xi_n - \mathbf{H_n m_{n|n-1}}) \tag{13}$$

$$\mathbf{P_{n|n}} = \mathbf{P_{n|n-1}} - \mathbf{K_n H_n P_{n|n-1}} \tag{14}$$

Here $\mathbf{m_{n|n}}$, $\mathbf{P_{n|n}}$ are the Gaussian posterior mean and covariance at n^{th} time-step, and $\mathbf{K_n}$ is the Kalman gain at that step. The clock states at n^{th} time-step is given by the components of $\mathbf{m_{n|n}}$, since $\mathbf{m_{n|n}}$ is the learned estimate of time offset, frequency offset and drift at that step. For our simulations, we assume the Gaussian posterior mean at the beginning is zero and the initial posterior covariance is $\mathbb{I}^{3\times 3}$.

3.4 Anomaly Detection

Spoofing attacks induce variations in the GPS reference signal ranging from discrete step changes to slowly evolving changes in the demodulated GPS data. Our anomaly detection strategy classifies changes in the time offset, frequency drift, and frequency offset measurements in the received GPS data in relation to the hardware oscillator as anomalous when $\mathbf{X_n}$ lies outside the confidence interval of its predicted value $\mathbf{m_{n|n-1}} \pm \mathbf{S_{n-1}}$, where,

$$\mathbf{S_{n-1}} = \mathbf{H_n P_{n|n-1} H_n^T} + \mathbf{R} \tag{15}$$

is the predicted variance of the offset. This approach can be used for detecting simpler attacks inducing a step change in the time offset. This technique depends only on a single data point and an estimate, and therefore, leads to a large number of false positives. Moreover, an *advanced* attacker will self-consistently change the offset to avoid such detection.

A better approach is to use a windowed strategy that takes account of a number of recent measurements and find out the likelihood of a new measurement and estimate. For this approach, we calculate

$$p(m_{i,n}|m_{i,n-1}, \dots m_{i,n-k}) = \frac{1}{\sqrt{2\pi\sigma_{i,n-1}^2}} e^{(-\frac{(m_{i,n}-\bar{m}_{i,n-1})^2}{\sigma_{i,n-1}^2})} \tag{16}$$

where, $i \in \mathbb{Z}^+$ for a 3×1 Gaussian posterior mean, k is the window size, $\sigma_{i,n-1}^2$ is the variance and $\bar{m}_{i,n-1}$ is the mean of the predicted values inside the window $(n-1)$ to $(n-k)$. By calculating a moving average of the log-likelihood z_n, we can detect an anomalous event when z_n crosses a predefined threshold. Here,

$$z_{i,n} = \alpha z_{i,n-1} + (1-\alpha)\ln(p(m_{i,n})) \tag{17}$$

with α as the smoothing factor.

4. EXPERIMENTAL SETUP AND RESULTS

For our experiments, we use a commercial GPS receiver and temperature-compensated crystal oscillators (TCXOs) to build an ensemble of free-running hardware oscillators. We use this design to validate the assumptions and formulation presented in Section 3. The measurement infrastructure is comprised of an ARM microprocessor-based data acquisition system with on-board data storage. Since this is a data-level spoofing detection technique, we inject attacks by altering the GPS time-offsets of the received GPS data and detect the attacks by using the free-running TCXO clock offsets measured with respect to this spoofed GPS data.

4.1 Adversary Model

The major goal of the adversary is to produce erroneous time or position measurements in the GPS receiver. We assume that the adversary has complete access to the RF channel during the attack, *i.e.,* he can replay, alter and/or replicate the RF carrier, spreading code and data bits of any or all of the visible satellites. We can divide the attackers in two categories: a *naive* and an *advanced* attacker. A *naive attacker* changes the time and/or the position bits in the GPS signal, which is reflected a sudden jump in the perceived time/location of the victim. An *advanced* attacker first induces the receiver to lock onto its spoofed signal by transmitting code, phase, and Doppler-matched signals with gradually increasing power, and then drags off the code and phase carrier in such a way that he avoids a discontinuous step change in time or the location estimates of the victim receiver. The adversary is time bound, *i.e.,* he has a limited time to spoof the receiver.

4.2 Attack Example and Spoofing Detection

To demonstrate the proposed spoofing detection approach, we consider an *advanced* attacker, who performs an attack on a GPS trained Phasor Measurement Unit (PMU) as shown in [14]. The attack involves the deployment of a simulated gradually increasing delay on GPS signals, which results in an anomalous exaggeration of signal transmission time, and in turn, induces an offset error in the GPS receiver. This attack described by the authors has been used by other experimental evaluations of fault detection algorithms and provides a well-documented baseline to study the effectiveness of our proposed approach. Figure 2(a) illustrates the evolution of the attack starting at 5130 seconds causing a gradual deviation of the GPS trained clock (solid line) against the true reference (dashed line).

To detect the attack, we modeled the TCXOs using the stochastic model presented in Section 3. Existing time offset based data level detection techniques can only detect spoofing if there is a discontinuous change in time, caused by a step change in the GPS reference. However, in this attack, the time is delayed slowly making the attack mostly undetectable. Since the process noise measurements of our TCXO were unknown, we used empirical values based on prior literature on clock jitter $q_1 = 10^{-3}, q_2 = 10^{-6}, q_3 = 10^{-9}$. We then design a state space model and use the Kalman filter formulation to detect anomalies in the received GPS signal.

From Figure 2, we can see that if we use the simultaneous negative values of averaged log-likelihood of frequency drift and offset as an indication of spoofing attack, the detector is able to detect the first anomaly at 5752s, (about 10 minutes after the start of the attack). Note that in this particular experiment the spoofing attack was detected when the cumulative error on the local clock was less than $4\mu s$. This is a relatively small error for some GPS-dependent systems.

5. ANALYSIS

Accuracy: The accuracy of the proposed detection technique depends on the noise margin and stability of the hardware clocks. For our experiments, we have used inexpensive temperature controlled crystal oscillators (TCXOs), which

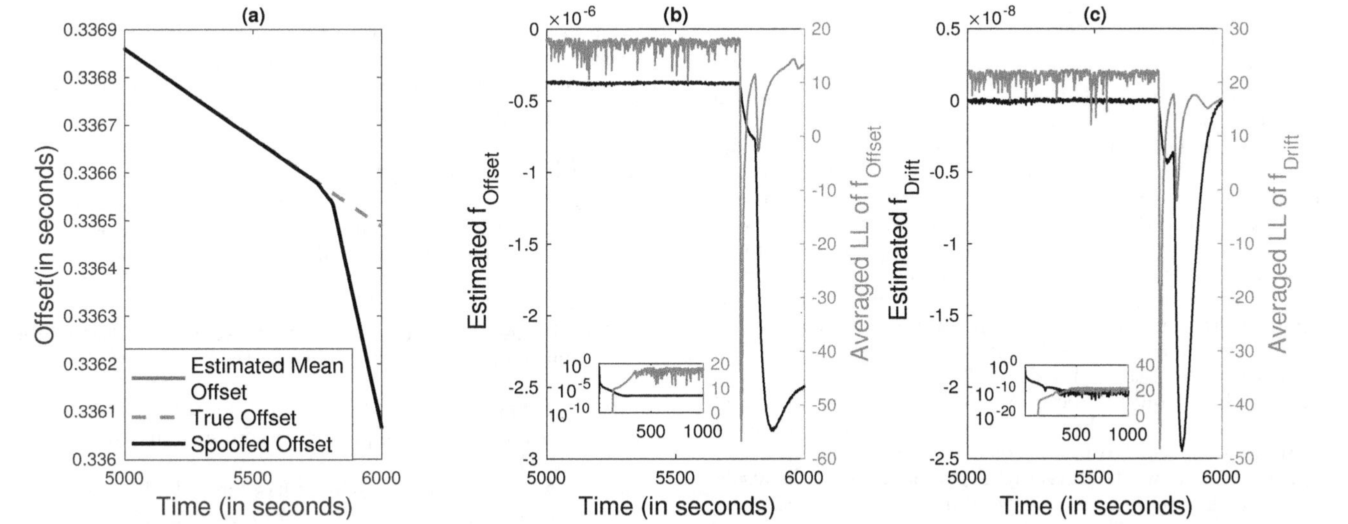

Figure 2: (a) Clock offset of a free running TCXO with respect to a GPS reference. A spoofing attack is initiated at 5130 seconds. The estimated time offset faithfully follows the spoofed signal as there is no sudden jump in the time offset;(b) Estimation of the frequency offset (black curve) and the averaged log-likelihood of the frequency offset(red curve) of the local clock with respect to the spoofed GPS signal during before and after the attack. The initial start-up and transition period for f_{offset} and the log-likelihood is shown in the inset. (c) Similar estimation of frequency drift (black curve) and the averaged log-likelihood of the frequency drift (red curve) of the local oscillator. The window size (k) for this computation is 128 data points.

provides a degree of immunity to temperature variations. One can use an ensemble of hardware oscillators to create a virtual clock using the system of equations as discussed in section 3.2 to reduce this noise. It should be noted that the accuracy and robustness of our detection mechanism requires a prior estimate of the measurement noise $\mathbf{Q}$. Without any prior estimate, for example, if we set the spectral densities q_1, q_2 and q_3 to 1, then this technique detects the attack at 5811 and 5813 seconds and reports a false positive at 3183 seconds.

Moreover, the detection mechanism is dependent on the window size (k) that provides a historical moving average. Larger windows provide better estimates; however, larger window size requires more memory and longer start-up time. For the experiment shown in Figure 2, $k = 8$ gives a false alarm rate of 66% which reduces to 20% for $k = 16$ and 0% for $k = 32\%$ and higher. Furthermore, there is a transient period during startup for the Kalman filter (as shown in the insets of Figure 2(b) and (c)) which requires a finite wait period before a consistent estimation of the log-likelihood. Therefore, the weakness of this proposed approach is the start-up period before effective detection is possible. For the example attack provided in this work, it takes about 600 seconds for system start-up.

Computation Cost: The cost of matrix-vector computations for a Kalman filter in the prediction and update step contains computation in the order of $O(\mathbf{D}^2)$, $O(\mathbf{MD})$, and $O(\mathbf{M}^3)$ complexity. The covariance matrices are symmetric, and therefore, Cholesky factorization can be used for maintaining $\mathbf{P}$ in a square-root form. Since the prediction and update step requires the knowledge of only current and previous steps, this construction has a very low memory complexity. The anomaly detection step has logarithmic complexity which can be simplified by approximating $p(m_{i,n}) \approx \mathbf{e}^{\left(-\frac{(m_{i,n}-\bar{m}_{i,n-1})^2}{\sigma^2_{i,n-1}}\right)}$. The averaging window has a fixed memory requirement which can be lowered by reducing the number of historical data points.

Hardware Overhead: GPS receivers already contain a hardware oscillator which is synchronized using the GPS signals. By turning off the synchronization it may be possible to convert this clock to a free running oscillator. The synchronization based timing corrections can be performed in software. Another approach is to add a hardware component with embedded free running oscillators to employ the proposed method without altering the GPS receiver design. The computation can be performed using on-board processors in IoT devices or by adding a low power microcontroller that takes GPS derived time as an input and provides the corrected time and spoofing detection capability to the system.

Power Constraints for IoT: It should be noted that using this spoofing detection technique for IoT devices may significantly increase the device's power consumption due to the need for continuous monitoring of the GPS signal. In order to save power by turning off monitoring periodically, the detector should compute the current frequency states as quickly as possible. Since there is a start-up time for this approach to detect spoofing, one can store the historic values for the Gaussian mean and variance along with the noise measurements to reduce the startup time. For low power GPS receivers, if the receiver is in sleep mode and starts with a spoofed GPS data from an attacker then this detection technique may be ineffective due to convergence transients during startup.

Signal Recovery: This detection technique has a-priori knowledge of the correct clock states, and one can calculate an approximated value of the true time offset using the historical clock states. For example, to recover from the example spoofing attack, once the attack is detected, the *approximately* correct value of the time offset can be calculated with the Gaussian posterior mean ($\mathbf{m_{n|n-1}}$) and the historical mean of the predicted values $\bar{\mathbf{m}}_{\mathbf{n,n-1}}$ using:

$$m_{1,n|n} = m_{1,n-1} + \Delta m_{2,n|n-1} + \frac{1}{2}\Delta^2 m_{3,n-1|n} \tag{18}$$

$$m_{2,n|n} = \bar{m}_{2,n-1} \quad (19)$$

$$m_{3,n|n} = \bar{m}_{3,n-1} \quad (20)$$

and then using $m_{1,n|n}$ as the *approximate* value of the true time offset at a time step n.

Hardware Intrinsic Security: Our approach does not depend on networked components for synchronization or attack detection. The hardware oscillator(s), as well as the computational and measurement components, are located on the receiver and algorithm updates may be introduced using existing firmware update infrastructure. Since dependency on other networked components can make the system vulnerable to network attacks, the proposed method provides better security and reliability.

Tamper Resistant Design: Tampering with the onboard clock(s) would detectably affect and change the clock frequency states. As the changes are hardware dependent and unique, the design is inherently tamper-resistant.

Comparison with Existing Approaches As discussed earlier in this paper, attack detection via comparison of time-offset between the GPS-clock and a local clock is not always reliable and self-consistent attacks can easily spoof such detection techniques. Furthermore, offset comparison requires time from a single local clock to be synchronized with a trusted clock periodically to keep the readings accurate. As a result, current spoofing detection solutions in the literature on comparing time with a known entity requires a notion of trust to a third party time provider. To avoid these shortcomings, our proposed design measures the clock states of a hardware oscillator with respect to the GPS-time to verify the authenticity of the GPS signal.

It should be noted that commercially available low-cost GPS receivers do not use any of the countermeasures described in the previous section [11]. Most of the measures are only implemented as prototypes in the lab environment where software-defined radio platforms are used in most of the tracking, analysis, and detection approaches. Implementation cost for practical deployment of these prototypes significantly limits their widespread use. The spoofing detection method presented in this paper does not require additional RF circuitry or antennas and uses low-cost TCXOs and data analysis to detect attacks. Furthermore, since our method is a data-level detection mechanism, no change to the receiver architecture is required to integrate our countermeasure as an add-on to existing systems.

6. CONCLUSIONS

In this work, we present a design for integrating data-level spoofing detection with an existing GPS-based timing system. The design uses single (or multiple) free running oscillators to detect anomalies in the GPS-derived frequency drift and the offset. We demonstrate that this approach is able to provide fast and accurate detection of GPS spoofing attacks published in the literature. Since GPS spoofing attacks pose a significant threat to IoT systems, there is value in including spoofing detection methods such as the method presented in this paper in future GPS receiver designs.

7. DISCLAIMER

Official contribution of the National Institute of Standards and Technology; not subject to copyright in the United States. Certain commercial equipment, instruments, or materials are identified in this paper in order to specify the experimental procedure adequately. Such identification is not intended to imply recommendation or endorsement by the National Institute of Standards and Technology, nor is it intended to imply that the materials or equipment identified are necessarily the best available for the purpose.

Parts of this paper may have been presented in technical seminars and included in government publications. Recorded versions of those seminars and copyright free versions of publications are available through the National Institute of Standards and Technology.

8. REFERENCES

[1] D. W. Allan. Time and frequency(time-domain) characterization, estimation, and prediction of precision clocks and oscillators. *IEEE Transactions on Ultrasonics, Ferroelectrics, and Frequency Control*, 34(6):647–654, 1987.

[2] C. Bonebrake and L. R. O'Neil. Attacks on GPS time reliability. *Security & Privacy, IEEE*, 12(3):82–84, 2014.

[3] P. H. Dana and B. M. Penrod. The role of GPS in precise time and frequency dissemination. *GPS World*, pages 38–43, 1990.

[4] C. A. Greenhall. A review of reduced Kalman filters for clock ensembles. *IEEE Transactions on Ultrasonics, Ferroelectrics and Frequency Control*, 59(3):491–496, 2012.

[5] S. S. Haykin. *Adaptive filter theory*. Pearson Education India, 2008.

[6] T. E. Humphreys. Detection strategy for cryptographic GNSS anti-spoofing. *IEEE Transactions on Aerospace and Electronic Systems*, 49(2):1073–1090, 2013.

[7] T. E. Humphreys, B. M. Ledvina, M. L. Psiaki, B. W. OHanlon, and P. M. Kintner Jr. Assessing the spoofing threat: Development of a portable GPS civilian spoofer.

[8] A. Jafarnia-Jahromi, A. Broumandan, J. Nielsen, and G. Lachapelle. GPS vulnerability to spoofing threats and a review of antispoofing techniques. *International Journal of Navigation and Observation*, 2012, 2012.

[9] X. Jiang, J. Zhang, B. J. Harding, J. J. Makela, and A. D. Dominguez-Garcia. Spoofing GPS receiver clock offset of Phasor measurement units. *IEEE Transactions on Power Systems*, 28(3):3253–3262, 2013.

[10] T. Kohno, A. Broido, and K. C. Claffy. Remote physical device fingerprinting. *IEEE Transactions on Dependable and Secure Computing*, 2(2):93–108, 2005.

[11] M. G. Kuhn. Signal authentication in trusted satellite navigation receivers. In *Towards Hardware-Intrinsic Security*, pages 331–348. Springer, 2010.

[12] P. Misra and P. Enge. *Global Positioning System: Signals, Measurements and Performance Second Edition*. Lincoln, MA: Ganga-Jamuna Press, 2006.

[13] M. L. Psiaki and T. E. Humphreys. Protecting GPS from spoofers is critical to the future of navigation. *IEEE Spectrum*, 2016.

[14] D. P. Shepard, T. E. Humphreys, and A. A. Fansler. Evaluation of the vulnerability of phasor measurement units to GPS spoofing attacks. *International Journal of Critical Infrastructure Protection*, 5(34):146 – 153, 2012.

[15] N. O. Tippenhauer, C. Pöpper, K. B. Rasmussen, and S. Capkun. On the requirements for successful GPS spoofing attacks. In *Proceedings of the 18th ACM Conference on Computer and Communications Security*, pages 75–86. ACM, 2011.

A Novel Side-Channel Timing Attack on GPUs

Zhen Hang Jiang, Yunsi Fei, David Kaeli
Electrical & Computer Engineering Department, Northeastern University
Boston, MA 02115, USA
zjiang@ece.neu.edu, yfei@ece.neu.edu, kaeli@ece.neu.edu

ABSTRACT

To avoid information leakage during program execution, modern software implementations of cryptographic algorithms target constant timing complexity, i.e., the number of instructions executed does not vary with different inputs. However, many times the underlying microarchitecture behaves differently when processing varying data inputs, which covertly leaks confidential information through the timing channel. In this paper, we exploit a novel fine-grained microarchitectural timing channel, stalls that occur due to bank conflicts in a GPU's shared memory. Using this attack surface, we develop a differential timing attack that can compromise table-based cryptographic algorithms. We implement our timing attack on an Nvidia Kepler K40 GPU, and successfully recover the complete 128-bit AES encryption key using 10 million samples. We also evaluate the scalability of our attack method by attacking a 8192-thread implementation of the AES encryption algorithm, recovering some key bytes using 1 million samples.

1. INTRODUCTION

Originally, GPU devices were solely designed to perform efficient graphic rendering. Since the birth of programmable shader cores and high-level programming language frameworks [2, 7], GPU devices have assumed a major role in a range of parallel computing environments. Cloud-based services, such as encryption/decryption of large data sets stored on disks, can effectively exploit the parallelism found on GPU devices to deliver high throughput. Earlier work by Jiang et al. [3] explored the vulnerability of running encryption algorithms on GPU devices to side-channel timing attacks, despite the fact that the encryption algorithm is mathematically proven to be secure. In this paper, we identify another timing side-channel that can be utilized to reveal sensitive information. Specifically, we develop a differential timing attack that exploits timing variability due to shared memory bank conflicts. We exploit this microarchitectural feature to recover all AES encryption key bytes.

Permission to make digital or hard copies of all or part of this work for personal or classroom use is granted without fee provided that copies are not made or distributed for profit or commercial advantage and that copies bear this notice and the full citation on the first page. Copyrights for components of this work owned by others than ACM must be honored. Abstracting with credit is permitted. To copy otherwise, or republish, to post on servers or to redistribute to lists, requires prior specific permission and/or a fee. Request permissions from permissions@acm.org.

GLSVLSI '17, May 10-12, 2017, Banff, AB, Canada

© 2017 ACM. ISBN 978-1-4503-4972-7/17/05. . . $15.00

DOI: http://dx.doi.org/10.1145/3060403.3060462

The GPU on-chip shared memory is an important hardware unit for alleviating memory traffic to off-chip device memory. It is designed to serve data that is shared and frequently accessed by many running threads. In order to optimize Single Instruction Multiple Thread (SIMT) execution on the GPU, the shared memory needs to provide high memory throughput. Thus, in modern GPUs a shared memory is divided into multiple memory banks, versus a monolithic bank. With multiple shared memory banks, multiple memory access requests for different memory banks can be served in parallel, therefore significantly improving overall memory throughput.

However, when multiple memory requests access the same bank, they are serviced in a serial fashion. As a result, the time to service multiple memory requests that reside in same bank is noticeably longer as compared to accesses that reside in different banks. This has been studied in terms of tuning memory performance, but has only recently been considered as a potential vulnerability. Yarom et al. investigate how the sensitive information can be leaked when a public cipher is running on CPUs with multi-bank caches [9]. A GPU presents a much more complex microarchitecture, especially when we consider the degree of parallelism on a GPU, as well the non-deterministic behavior of the hardware-based scheduler. In this paper, we carefully examine this timing channel in GPUs and develop an effective differential timing attack to retrieve the secret key.

The paper is organized as follows: In Section 2, we provide background on the Advanced Encryption Standard (AES) algorithm, as well as touch on the GPU memory hierarchy and execution model. In Section 3, we explore timing variations present due to shared memory bank conflicts, i.e., identifying the memory bank timing channel. In Section 4, we describe our differential timing attack targeting table lookup-based cryptographic algorithms, and attack AES encryption. In Section 5, we discuss feasible countermeasures to prevent the attack. Finally, we conclude the paper in Section 6.

2. BACKGROUND

In this section, we describe the AES implementation is evaluated on the targeted GPU platform, as well as the memory hierarchy and execution model of Nvidia's Kepler GPU architecture [7].

2.1 AES Encryption

In this paper, we evaluate the timing leakage vulnerability of a table-based cryptographic algorithm on a GPU. We use

128-bit ECB mode AES encryption as an example. The implementation was ported from the OpenSSL 0.9.7 library into CUDA code, which is similar to the implementation used in [3]. However, instead of storing lookup tables in the global memory, we store them in the shared memory to demonstrate the timing leakage in the shared memory. We transform the AES encryption procedure into a single GPU kernel, where each GPU thread can process one block encryption, independently. Each block consists of 16 bytes.

The AES algorithm is composed of nine rounds of SubByte, ShiftRows, MixColumn, and AddRoundKey operations, and the last round omitting the MixColumni operation. For faster processing, the first three operations are integrated into T-table lookups in the first nine rounds, and in the last round, a special T-table ($Te4$) lookup is performed, integrating the SubByte with the ShiftRow operation.

Each encryption round requires one 16-byte round key. Ten round keys are generated by the key scheduler using one 16-byte user-specified secret key during encryption. Knowing any round key, an attacker can compute the original 16-byte secret key. Our attack strategy targets the last-round key. A code snippet of the last round operations generating the first four bytes of ciphertext is shown in Listing 1.

Listing 1: AES Last Round Code Snippet

```
s0 = (Te4[(t0 >> 24)       ] & 0xff000000)^
     (Te4[(t1 >> 16) & 0xff] & 0x00ff0000)^
     (Te4[(t2 >>  8) & 0xff] & 0x0000ff00)^
     (Te4[(t3      ) & 0xff] & 0x000000ff)^
     k0;
```

Variable $s0$ is the first four bytes of the 16-byte ciphertext. Each of variables, t0, t1, ..., t3, contains 4 bytes of the input state for the last round. A selected byte of each variable is used to look up a T-table to obtain a four-byte output, of which only one byte contributes to the final ciphertext. k_0 is the first four bytes of the last round key. From the original algorithm, the last-round can be simplified as byte-wise operations shown below:

$$c_j = SBox[s_i^9] \oplus rk_j \tag{1}$$

where the input byte position (i), for the SBox operation, differs from the output ciphertext byte position (j), due to the ShiftRow operation. Each byte of the 9_{th}-round output state, s_i^9, can be calculated once the corresponding cipher and key byte are known by:

$$s_i^9 = SBox^{-1}[c_j \oplus rk_j] \tag{2}$$

2.2 Nvidia GPU Memory Hierarchy

Our testing platform is equipped with an Nvidia Tesla K40 GPU. There is an off-chip DRAM memory (device memory), and it is partitioned into global, texture, and constant memory regions. Data in those memories are shared among all threads running on all 15 Streaming Multiprocessors (SMXs). Each SMX (with 192 single-precision cores) also has L1, texture, and constant caches. Data in those caches are private to threads running in the SMX. In addition, there is a shared memory in each SMX, and only the block of threads that allocate the data in the shared memory can access them. Also, each GPU thread owns an exclusive set of 255 registers to store its current state.

The GPU shared memory and L1 cache reside in the same physical memory storage. On the K40 GPU, the total size is 64 KB. The individual size of the shared memory and L1 cache can be configured. In our case, we allocate 48 KBs of space as shared memory and 16 KB for the L1 cache. Note that the size configuration does not affect the results presented in this paper.

The shared memory is divided into 32 banks, and it has a configurable bank line size (annotated as *banksize* in the Nvidia documentation [7]): 4 bytes or 8 bytes. For evaluating the AES algorithm, we use a bank size of 8 bytes, enabling faster encryptions. The memory address breakdown for shared memory is shown in Figure. 1, where the three least-significant bits are used for the bank offset, and the next five bits (bit 3-7) are the bank index and are used for selecting a bank.

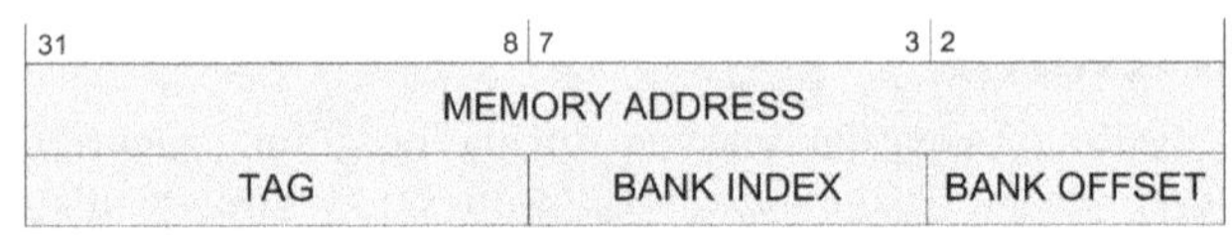

Figure 1: Memory address to shared memory bank mapping

When multiple memory requests address different shared memory banks (i.e., bits 3-7 are different), they can be serviced in a single GPU cycle, providing much higher memory bandwidth than that of a single bank design. On the other hand, when two memory requests (with the same bank index, but different tag values) are accessing the same bank, they will be handled in a serialized fashion, which we refer to as a *bank conflict*. Thus, there will be a noticeable timing difference between memory requests with and without bank conflicts.

2.3 Single Instruction Multiple Threads Execution Model

With the SIMT execution model, one GPU instruction is executed by at least a warp of 32 threads, and each thread has its own set of registers. However, each thread within a warp must be synced at an instruction boundary, which means that no thread in a warp can execute the next instruction until all threads complete the current instruction.

For a memory instruction, each thread will generate one memory request. A warp of threads will generate 32 memory requests for one memory instruction. Across the accesses, any duplicate memory requests will be merged and the distinct addresses are sent to the shared memory. Under the SIMT model, the execution time of this memory instruction will be determined by the memory bank that receives the highest number of bank conflicts (the largest number of requests resolving to the same bank). In other words, the execution time of a shared memory instruction becomes highly dependent on the memory address issued, and any resulting bank conflicts. We can use these differences to identify when the GPU is potentially leaking secret information.

3. CACHE BANK CONFLICTS

In this section, we conduct experiments to examine the impact of bank conflicts on the program execution time. We develop a kernel that uses a warp of threads to perform loads from the shared memory. Depending on the address of data that each thread accesses, a number of bank conflicts occur, resulting in different execution time of the load operation.

We deliberately create a specific number of bank conflicts by selecting the address that each thread is accessing. Using a high resolution time-stamping mechanism, we can study the impact of bank conflicts on kernel execution time. We have developed the micro-benchmark shown in Listing 2.

Listing 2: Micro-Benchmark 1

```
register uint32_t tmp,tmp2,offset = 64;
__shared__ uint32_t share_data[1024*4];
...
int tid=blockDim.x*blockIdx.x+threadIdx.x;
tmp = clock();
tmp2  = share_data[tid*stride+0*offset];
tmp2 += share_data[tid*stride+1*offset];
...
tmp2 += share_data[tid*stride+39*offset];
times[tid] = clock() - tmp;
in[tid] = tmp2;
```

The purpose of the microbenchmark is to measure the time for a sequence of memory accesses of each thread in a block. In Listing 2, the variable *share_data* points to a continuous 16KB memory space in shared memory. Each thread is accessing 40 memory locations in a sequence, with an offset of 64 words between two adjacent addresses. From Figure. 1, we know that two adjacent memory addresses have the same bank index and bank offset (64 words = 2^8 bytes), and therefore all the memory addresses requested by a single thread are on the same bank. Each thread accesses one memory region, and the offset between memory regions by different threads is one or multiple *strides*. By manipulating the value of *stride*, we can intentionally create bank conflicts among threads in a block. We run this kernel 10,000 times and collect 10,000 timing information for each stride value, ranging from 1 to 32 word. The timing distribution for 32 different stride values is shown in Figure. 2.

We observe that there are only 5 distinct timing distributions for the 32 stride values. Clearly, some stride values have the same timing behavior, and we suspect that those stride values result in the same number of bank conflicts. We next calculate the number of bank conflicts for each stride value. Recall that in our testing platform, shared memory is divided into 32 banks, the bank size is configured to be 8 bytes, and the memory address breakdown is shown in Figure 1. Given a word index for the *shared_data* array, we can calculate the bank index by dropping the first least-significant bit and then module 32, as described in the formula below:

$$idx_B = mod(idx_M >> 1, 32) \quad (3)$$

where idx_B is the bank index, and idx_M is the array index. The right shift operator, >>, drops the least-significant bit, and the *mod* is the modulus operation.

As an example, assuming a stride value 2, for a memory access instruction issued across a warp of 32 threads, we will generate the following 32 memory indices: {0, 2, 4, 6, 8, 10, 12, 14, 16, 18, 20, 22, 24, 26, 28, 30, 32, 34, 36, 38, 40, 42, 44, 46, 48, 50, 52, 54, 56, 58, 60, 62}. By using Equation (3), we have the following bank access indices for the warp: {0, 1, 2, 3, 4, 5, 6, 7, 8, 9, 10, 11, 12, 13, 14, 15, 16, 17, 18, 19, 20, 21, 22, 23, 24, 25, 26, 27, 28, 29, 30, 31}. Thus, there is no bank conflicts produced when the stride is 2. Similarly, we calculate the number of bank conflicts for each stride value in the range of 1 to 32 words, and they end up in five groups, as shown in Figure. 2. Each group corresponds to a different number of bank conflicts and average timing.

We also plot the average execution time for a group (for selected stride values) versus the number of shared memory bank conflicts in Figure. 2. We can easily identify a linear relationship. The slope of the linear line is 392, with an offset of 1002 GPU cycles. Since we are performing 40 sequential shared memory loads, the result implies that the average penalty per bank conflict is 9.8 GPU cycles, which is also the strength of the timing channel signal in the shared memory banks. Although the penalty for bank conflicts is not as large as the cache miss penalty (another well-studied cache side-channel), we will show the feasibility of exploiting this fine-grained timing channel for key retrieval through statistical methods.

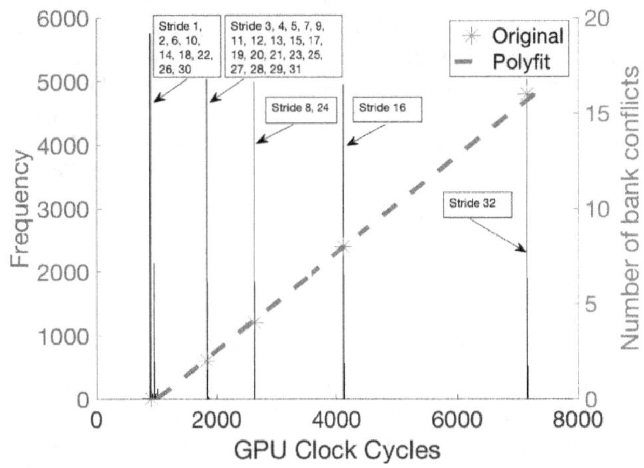

Figure 2: Number of bank conflicts vs timing for 32 stride values

4. DIFFERENTIAL TIMING ATTACK

In this section, we apply our differential timing analysis method to exploit the timing channel in shared memory banks. We start by attacking an AES algorithm, because its table lookup operations are key-dependent memory accesses.

In our AES implementation, the lookup table is word aligned, similar to the *shared_data* array used in Microbenchmark 1. Therefore we expect the execution time of one table lookup operation of a warp of threads to be linearly dependent on the number of bank conflicts generated by the threads. The execution time of an entire encryption is also dependent on the number of bank conflicts created by the table lookup operations.

Since the index for table lookup operations is related to the round key, with the correct key guess, we can predict the number of bank conflicts during one round of AES operation across a warp using Equation (3). By using many different blocks of plaintext, the correlation between the average encryption timing and the number of shared memory bank conflicts for the correct key guess should be high, and the correlation for incorrect key guesses tend to be low. This is the basic principle for differential timing attack, similar to the traditional differential power attack (DPA).

Next, we present the details of our attack methodology on AES. We specifically look at the mapping between the AES lookup tables and shared memory banks, as well as collect data and recover the last round AES encryption key.

4.1 Mapping Between the AES Lookup Tables and GPU Shared Memory Banks

As we describe in Section 2, the AES implementation we use contains 5 lookup tables, which are placed one after another and occupy a contiguous memory space in the shared memory. Since we are attacking the last round of AES encryption, we only need to examine the *Te4* lookup table in the shared memory. Note that attacking more rounds (more than three) becomes infeasible due to the algorithm-inherent statistical confusion and diffusion properties. There are 256 4-byte elements in the *Te4* lookup table. The same Equation (3) can be used to calculate the bank index, given a lookup table index.

4.2 Collecting Data

The data collection procedure is similar to the experiments that we performed in Section 3. Instead of 40 shared memory load instructions, each thread performs an actual AES encryption using a random input data block. We record both the encryption time and the ciphertext for a warp of 32 threads. Each data sample is composed of 32 16-byte ciphertexts and a timing sample, as shown in the following format:

$$[\{C^0, C^1, ..., C^{15}\}, t]$$

$$where\ each\ C^i\ is\ a\ 16-byte\ ciphertext\ produced\ by$$
$$thread\ i,\ consisting\ of\ 16\ bytes\ \{c_0^i, c_1^i, ..., c_{15}^i\},$$
$$and\ t\ is\ the\ encryption\ time\ for\ this\ warp$$

In this paper, we consider the encryption time measured both from the GPU and CPU. The encryption time measured from the GPU side provides more accurate measurements of the encryption, while measurements on the CPU side contain more noise sources because of the the non-deterministic data transfer times between the GPU and the CPU, as well as other required initialization procedures in the GPU device for running a kernel.

4.3 Calculating the Shared Memory Bank Index

For the last round AES operation, with the output ciphertext known, the input state byte can be calculated using Equation (2). For a warp of 32 threads, there are 32 such table lookups running concurrently, and therefore we have:

$$\{s_i^0, s_i^1, ..., s_i^{31}\} = SBox^{-1}[\{c_j^0, c_j^1, ..., c_j^{31}\} \oplus rk_j] \quad (4)$$

where c_j^0 is the cipher byte produced by thread 0, s_i^0 is the lookup table index for thread 0, and rk_j is the jth last round key byte, which is common to all the threads. These lookup table indices, $\{s_i^0, s_i^1, ..., s_i^{31}\}$, are exactly the shared memory indices. We use Equation (3) to calculate the bank indices used by all threads in a warp for this table lookup instruction, and can derive the number of bank conflicts.

4.4 Recovering Key Bytes

We can launch a correlation timing attack (CTA) using the collected data. As shown in Listing 1, the code snippet for the last round AES, each T-table lookup uses one state byte, and therefore, each round key byte can be attacked independently. For each data sample we collected, we calculate the number of bank conflicts for the table lookup instruction that is using the jth last round key byte. For each byte value guessed (ranging from 0 to 255), we can calculate the correlation between the average timing and the number of bank conflicts, and use the correlation value to differentiate the correct key byte from other incorrect key guesses. This is called CTA. For the data collected, the number of bank conflicts between the 32 threads falls in the range of [2, 4].

The power of CTA is determined by the linearity of the timing model, i.e., the total execution time should consist of a deterministic component, linearly dependent on the number of bank conflicts, and an independent Gaussian random variable contributed by the other nine rounds. During an actual AES execution, the timing distribution does not conform to the ideal model, and therefore CTA may not be more effective than differential timing attack (DTA), which only considers two points. We adopt a DTA approach, and calculate two average timing values, one for the bin of data samples that generate two bank conflicts, and the other for the bin of data samples that generate four bank conflicts. The difference-of-means (DoMs) between them should be about two times the penalty for one bank conflict, i.e., around 19 cycles. We first apply the attack method to the 15th key byte, and the result is shown in Figure. 3 (the upper plot).

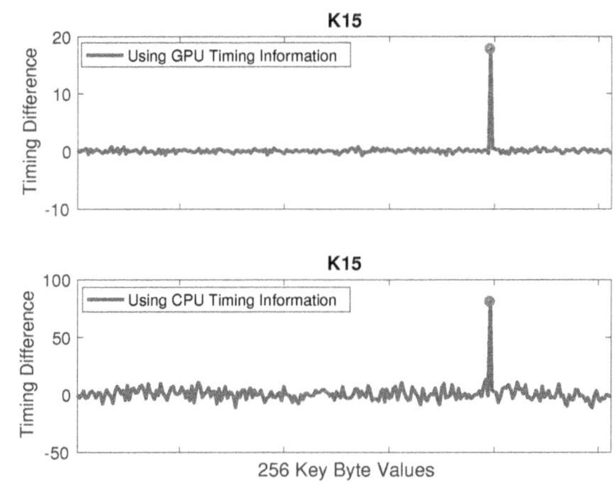

Figure 3: 15th key byte recovery using 10 million samples with both GPU and CPU timing information.

The correct key byte value (198) is highlighted in red. The timing difference for the true key value is 17.75 GPU cycles, which is about 2 GPU cycles less than the predicted signal, 19.6 GPU cycles, and the timing difference for other values is much smaller, between -2.3 to 2.3 GPU cycles. By increasing the sample size to 10 million, we found that the timing difference for the true value remains the same, while the timing differences for wrong values are reduced to a range between -0.8 and 0.8 GPU cycles.

We apply this attack methodology and recover other key bytes. The result is shown in Figure. 4. All 16 true key byte values clearly stand out in the plots, which means we have successfully recovered all key bytes. Although the same attack runs on all key bytes, some key bytes have much smaller peak timing differences, such as k_0 and k_1, as compared to other key bytes. We observe that the key bytes that are used closer to the end of encryption tend to have larger and distinct timing difference, e.g., k_{15}. The reduced signal in k_0 is probably caused by instruction-level parallelism. Although the architectural details of the Nvidia Kelper GPU are not public, we suspect that the Kepler GPU can continue issuing independent instruction(s) in each cycle until all resources are being used up, and therefore, it hides the latency due to shared memory bank conflicts by issuing and executing other independent instructions.

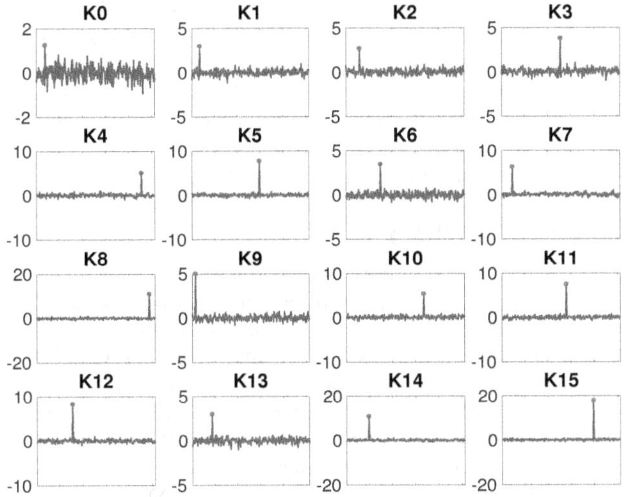

Figure 4: All 16 key bytes recovery using 10 million samples

To gain more insights into the GPU internals and resulting timings, we slightly modify Microbenchmark 1, as shown in Listing 3, to make each load instruction and the addition instruction independent from each other:

Listing 3: Micro-Benchmark 2

```
...
tmp2 = share_data[tid*stride+0*offset];
tmp3 = share_data[tid*stride+1*offset];
tmp4 = share_data[tid*stride+2*offset];
...
tmp41 = share_data[tid*stride+39*offset];
times[tid] = clock() - tmp;
in[tid] = tmp2+tmp3+tmp4+...+tmp41;
```

We run Micro-benchmark 2 10,000 times for each stride value in the range of [1, 32] and collect the timing information. We calculate the average timing for each stride value and the number of bank conflicts, and obtain similar linear relationship shown in Figure. 2. However, the slope and offset are 177 and 368 GPU cycles, respectively, and therefore the per-conflict penalty is reduced to 4.4 from 9.8 GPU cycles in Micro-benchmark 2.

In the modified kernel, each of 40 load instructions loads data into a different register, and at the very end, the addition is performed. The execution of Micro-benchmark 2 is similar to a non-blocking execution mode of Micro-benchmark 1, because all the loads are independent and therefore can be issued in an out-of-order manner. Listing 5 shows the SASS code for the modified benchmark, which is a sequence of independent loadings. While Micro-benchmark 1 introduces blocking, as shown in the original SASS code in Listing 4, where the loaded data is used by another operation that is 3 instructions away from the load operation. The read-after-write (RAW) data dependencies prevent later load instructions from being executed earlier.

Listing 4: Original SASS Code

```
LDS R4, [R3+0x1b00];
IADD R7, R8, R5;
LDS R6, [R3+0x1c00];
IADD R7, R7, R4;
```

Listing 5: Modified SASS Code

```
LDS R15, [R38+0x1b00];
LDS R14, [R38+0x1c00];
LDS R13, [R38+0x1d00];
```

For our AES algorithm implementation, each lookup operation in the last round (16 lookups in total) is independent from each other. Since k_0 is being used in the first lookup operation, its delay due to bank conflicts is diminished by executing other independent lookup operations. Thus, we see a weaker signal in the k_0. While k_{15} is the last one to be processed, and the delay due to its bank conflict is completely exposed in the execution time, i.e., k_{15} has the strongest signal.

4.5 More Threads and Noise Sources

In the previous section, we have been using timing information taken from the GPU side, which contains much less noise than the timing information measured from the CPU side. Also, we evaluated our attack method only on a 32-thread AES encryption. It is important to understand the scalability of the attack (i.e., how the number of traces needed grows as we increase the number of threads). In this section, we evaluate the effectiveness of the attack using the CPU timing information and on implementations with higher numbers of threads, which better reflect typical scenarios for GPU execution.

4.5.1 Using the CPU Timing Information

To collect timing data from the CPU side, we record the kernel execution time using an x86 instruction *rdtscp*. Since the CPU runs at a higher frequency than the GPU, it has a higher resolution (4.8 times higher). However, the CPU timing information is much more noisy than the GPU timing information. We perform the same differential timing attack against our 32-thread implementation, and we can still recover key bytes, but with a weaker signal, as shown in Figure. 3 (the lower plot).

Using the CPU timing information, the timing difference is around 80.75 CPU cycles (16.83 in GPU cycles) between the two bins for the correct key guess (which is slightly lower than using the GPU timing information). The standard deviation of the timing difference using CPU timing is larger than that using GPU timing (6.7 vs 1.1). This implies that CPU timing contains more noise than GPU timing, and more data samples would be needed to achieve the same attack result as using GPU timing.

4.5.2 Higher Number Threads Implementation

In this section, we evaluate the scalability of our attack by attacking an 8192-thread AES implementation using 16 blocks of 512 threads (each block contains 16 warps), which is several times more than the maximum number (2880) of threads that can run in parallel on the Kepler K40 GPU.

Note, in such a real attack scenario, the attackers cannot manipulate the kernel code running on GPUs (they cannot easily insert time stamps before and after the encryption). Instead, they would typically rely on the timing information measured from the CPU side. When a higher number of threads are running, the measured execution time of the kernel is dominated by the slowest SMX (and the corresponding blocks running on it). However, the details of the

GPU scheduler are not public, and we cannot know how blocks and warps are distributed and scheduled on the GPU SMXs.

We choose to select one warp to attack, and use the entire kernel execution time. We anticipate much high noise contained in this attack model, because the selected warp may not run on the slowest SMX, and also even if it does, there are other warps competing for the same SMX resources. Attributing the kernel execution time to this warp is not accurate. This non-deterministic process adds a larger amount of noise into our data samples. Other activities, such as saving threads register states, can also contribute to the noise.

We use exactly the same attack method described before. We collect 1 million samples (rather than 10 million due to its excessively slow execution) of the 8192-thread AES encryption, and we apply our differential timing attack to recover the 15th key byte. The result is shown in Figure. 5. The timing difference for the 15th true key value is 94.2 CPU cycles, but it has a standard deviation of 16.8, which indicates there is a high degree of noise in the data samples that we collected.

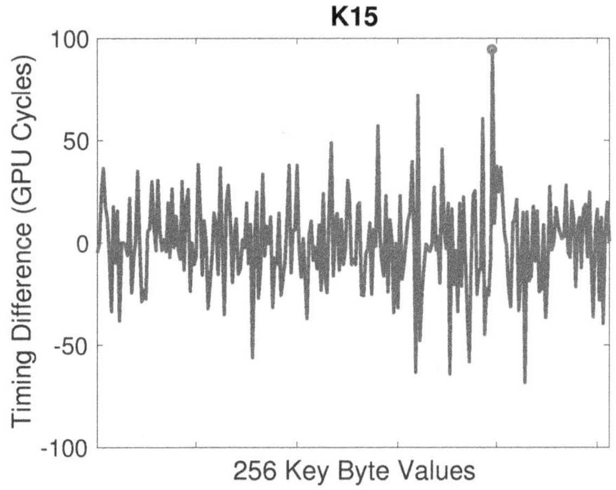

Figure 5: 15th key byte recovery using 1 million samples

5. DISCUSSION

Although the penalty for each bank conflict is small, we are still able to exploit this fine-grained timing channel to recover confidential information. We choose to attack the AES encryption algorithm to demonstrate the feasibility and scalability of our attack. The attack should be applicable to other table-based cryptographic algorithms or even public ciphers on GPUs, as long as there are sensitive data-dependent shared memory accesses in the cryptosystem.

Our attack exploits the timing difference due to shared memory bank conflicts. Avoiding using shared memory unit can prevent the attack, but would incur performance degradation for some applications. However, removing shared memory bank conflicts can improve an application's performance as well as mitigating a differential timing attack. This can be done by reducing the shared memory data usage, such that the size of our data is no larger than 256 bytes (bank size * number of banks, $8 * 32$). In this way, no bank conflict can happen. For the AES encryption algorithm, we can revert the AES implementation back to the SBox version. Such implementation uses only a 256-byte table, spanning 32 banks. There will be no bank conflicts for 32 threads. However, an SBox-based implementation may not be as efficient as a T-table based one.

Although there have been a large number of countermeasures proposed to prevent timing attacks on CPUs [5, 4, 1], to our knowledge, we have not found any of them that can be used to avoid our attack, since our attack exploits a different timing channel than the cache timing channel [8, 6]. As more research is carried out in the side-channel attack field, more timing channels will be found and exploited. Thus, we need new countermeasures against such newly found timing channels in order to prevent those unexpected attacks.

6. CONCLUSION

In this paper, we expose a new class of side-channel vulnerability in GPUs. We exploit the relationship between the AES execution time and the number of bank conflicts. We construct a differential timing attack on the GPU AES implementation to retrieve the key. Our attack is shown to effectively exploit this fine-grained timing channel. We also demonstrate that our attack can scale well. Future work includes developing countermeasures at multiple hardware and software levels.

Acknowledgment

This work was supported in part by National Science Foundation under grants STARSS-1618379 and MRI-1337854.

7. REFERENCES

[1] L. Domnitser, A. Jaleel, J. Loew, N. Abu-Ghazaleh, and D. Ponomarev. Non-monopolizable caches: Low-complexity mitigation of cache side channel attacks. *ACM Transactions on Architecture and Code Optimization (TACO)*, 8(4):35, 2012.

[2] B. Gaster, L. Howes, D. R. Kaeli, P. Mistry, and D. Schaa. *Heterogeneous Computing with OpenCL: Revised OpenCL 1*. Newnes, 2012.

[3] Z. H. Jiang, Y. Fei, and D. Kaeli. A complete key recovery timing attack on a gpu. In *IEEE Int. Symp. on High Performance Computer Architecture (HPCA)*, March 2016.

[4] J. Kong, O. Aciiçmez, J.-P. Seifert, and H. Zhou. Hardware-software integrated approaches to defend against software cache-based side channel attacks. In *IEEE Int. Symp. on High Performance Computer Architecture*, pages 393–404, 2009.

[5] F. Liu, Q. Ge, Y. Yarom, F. Mckeen, C. Rozas, G. Heiser, and R. B. Lee. Catalyst: Defeating last-level cache side channel attacks in cloud computing. In *IEEE Int. Symp. on High Performance Computer Architecture*, pages 406–418. IEEE, 2016.

[6] F. Liu, Y. Yarom, Q. Ge, G. Heiser, and R. B. Lee. Last-level cache side-channel attacks are practical. In *IEEE Symp. on Security & Privacy*, 2015.

[7] Nvidia. Nvidia cuda toolkit v7.0 documentation, 2015.

[8] Y. Yarom and K. Falkner. Flush+ reload: a high resolution, low noise, l3 cache side-channel attack. In *USENIX Security Symp.*, pages 719–732, 2014.

[9] Y. Yarom, D. Genkin, and N. Heninger. Cachebleed: A timing attack on OpenSSL constant time RSA, Aug. 2016.

Cyclic Obfuscation for Creating SAT-Unresolvable Circuits

Kaveh Shamsi[1], Meng Li[2], Travis Meade[1], Zheng Zhao[2], David Z. Pan[2], and Yier Jin[1]
[1]ECE Department, University of Central Florida, Orlando, FL, USA
[2]ECE Department, University of Texas at Austin, Austin, TX, USA
[1]{kaveh, travm12}@knights.ucf.edu, [2]{meng_li,zzhao,dpan}@utexas.edu,
[1]yier.jin@eecs.ucf.edu

ABSTRACT

Logic locking and IC camouflaging are proactive circuit obfuscation methods that if proven secure can thwart hardware attacks such as reverse engineering and IP theft. However, the security of both these schemes is called into question by recent SAT based attacks. While a number of methods have been proposed in literature that exponentially increase the running time of such attacks, they are vulnerable to "find-and-remove" attacks, and only slightly hide the circuit functionality. In this paper, we present a novel approach towards creating SAT attack resiliency based on creating densely cyclic obfuscated circuit topologies by adding dummy paths to the circuit. Our methodology is applicable to both IC camouflaging and logic locking. We demonstrate that cyclic logic locking creates SAT resilient circuits with 40% less area and 20% less delay compared to an insecure XOR/XNOR-obfuscation with the same key length. Furthermore, we show that cyclic IC camouflaging can be implemented at the layout level with no substrate area overhead and little delay and power overhead with respect to the original circuit.

1. INTRODUCTION

With the globalization of the IC supply chain and the advent of fabless design houses, several security concerns have been raised [22]. These include reverse engineering by end-users, and malicious modification or overproduction by foundries. VLSI design for trust (DfTr) [12] refers to design-time techniques for thwarting these threats. Among them, IC camouflaging [4] and logic locking/-encryption [14] are two promising directions. With these approaches the designer can hide design information from a malicious foundry or end-user. We therefore categorize both schemes as circuit obfuscation, since they rely on the concept of "security through obscurity". IC camouflaging is based upon creating indistinguishable silicon layout structures that hamper reverse engineering of the IC by the end-user. In logic locking the circuit is augmented with additional key inputs such that it operates incorrectly without the correct key values applied. Therefore logic locking can prevent reverse engineering, as well as cloning or theft of intellectual property (IP) by the foundry or any other party that does not posses the correct key. Table 1 lists the protection provided by these circuit obfuscation schemes.

Permission to make digital or hard copies of all or part of this work for personal or classroom use is granted without fee provided that copies are not made or distributed for profit or commercial advantage and that copies bear this notice and the full citation on the first page. Copyrights for components of this work owned by others than ACM must be honored. Abstracting with credit is permitted. To copy otherwise, or republish, to post on servers or to redistribute to lists, requires prior specific permission and/or a fee. Request permissions from permissions@acm.org.

GLSVLSI '17, May 10-12, 2017, Banff, AB, Canada
© 2017 ACM. ISBN 978-1-4503-4972-7/17/05...15.00
DOI: http://dx.doi.org/10.1145/3060403.3060458

Defense	Reverse engineering	Trojan Insertion	Overproduction
IC Camouflaging	by user only	no protection	no protection
Logic Locking	by user & foundry	by foundry	by foundry

Table 1: Protection provided by obfuscation schemes against a malicious end-user or foundry.

The security of these schemes has been the topic of research over the past several years through a competition of obfuscation defenses and deobfuscation attacks [11, 13, 5, 18]. Deobfuscation attacks are developed under various assumptions on the capabilities of the adversary. A prominent adversary-model in deobfuscation assumes the attacker has access to the inputs and outputs of a functional or unlocked chip. With such oracle-access to the chip the attacker can *query* the circuit for different inputs and use correct input-output pairs to find the correct key values or camouflaged functions. The most recent and strongest attack under this assumption is a disagreement based approach that queries the oracle circuit on input patterns that results in different outputs for different key values or camouflaged function hypotheses [5, 18]. These patterns are referred to as discriminating input patterns (DIP). Since the attack is formulated as a Boolean Satisfiability (SAT) problem and uses SAT-solvers, it is commonly referred to as the SAT attack. The SAT attack is successful in deobfuscating almost all known gate-level obfuscation solutions that have reasonable overhead [18].

To counter the SAT attack a number of defenses have been presented in literature [24, 26, 7, 23]. In these obfuscation schemes it is ensured that each DIP removes a limited number of key possibilities and therefore, the SAT attack will require an exponential number of queries to resolve the correct key. However, almost all these defenses rely on large low-activity blocks that can either be found and removed as was shown in [25], or are fundamentally capable of hiding only a few input patterns from the attacker due to their low corruptibility [17].

In this paper we present a novel SAT-resilient obfuscation scheme. This methodology is inspired by how configurable and cyclic interconnection networks allow modern programmable logic to implement a large set of Boolean functions with small logic components. The key idea is that if a logical loop is created in the circuit (which is typically avoided in prior work [16]), through adding dummy wires and gates, the adversary cannot launch the existing SAT attacks, since the circuit can no longer be represented as a directed acyclic graph (DAG). We show that from a graph theoretic perspective the number of possible ways for opening these loops can be made excessively large. In summary we make the following contributions:

- We present cyclic obfuscation as the first topological, wire-based approach to creating SAT attack resiliency;

- We discuss implementation details for ensuring the hardness of the attack, as well as silicon level techniques to implement the idea in both of IC camouflaging and logic locking flavors;
- We implement prototype cyclic logic locking and cyclic IC camouflaging schemes using the Nangate OpenCell 15nm technology library [1]. The results show both area and delay improvements for for cyclic logic locking compared to traditional schemes, and much smaller overheads for cyclic IC camouflaging.

The rest of the paper is organized as follows: Section 2 presents background information and prior work. Section 3 discusses SAT attack resiliency through topology obfuscation. Section 4 presents our cyclic obfuscation scheme and security and implementation aspects. Section 5 presents experimental results and section 6 concludes the paper.

2. BACKGROUND

2.1 Circuit Obfuscation

IC camouflaging. the goal in IC camouflaging is to prevent recovery of the netlist from layer-by-layer images of the IC. There exists an array of industrial fabrication technologies for creating indistinguishable layout structures [4, 20]. Some notable techniques include, using dummy vias, altering doping patterns, or using filler cells. Dummy vias are metal-to-metal or metal-to-diffusion contacts that appear to be connected from the top view while they are not in fact conducting. Modifying doping patterns allows altering the type of transistors or junctions while conventional IC imaging techniques cannot detect the difference [8]. Dummy cells can also be inserted in the empty areas of the chip and connected to active logic. With these techniques, camouflaging logic units can be built such that their overall Boolean function cannot be resolved to a specific function. Inserting these camouflaged units with different strategies creates obscurity during the reverse engineering process. This can be seen in Fig. 1a.

Logic Locking. Figure 1b shows a circuit obfuscated with logic locking. Logic locking was originally presented for hiding design details from the foundry and allowing for authenticated usage of the IC [14]. The first logic locking scheme was based on XOR/XNORing randomly selected wires in the circuit with key inputs [14]. Later proposals included more complex strategies for improving security. These techniques include inserting XOR/XNOR or MUX gates at locations that maximize properties such as output hamming-distance [9], or the size of cliques in the interference graph of key inputs [10]. Interconnect obfuscation schemes were also proposed such as shuffling wires in bus architectures [15], combinational logic [21, 3], or most recently, inserting dummy wires into the circuit through chip-level modification [16]. All of these schemes avoid creating logical cycles in the circuit.

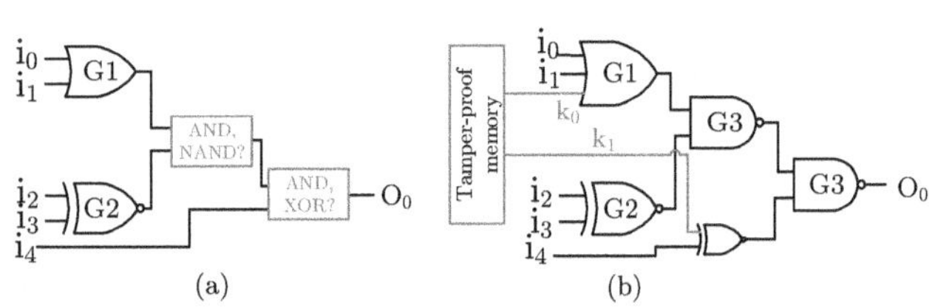

Figure 1: (a) IC camouflaging by replacing gates with camouflaged gates. (b) Logic locking with tamper-proof key inputs.

2.2 SAT Attacks

The SAT attack assumes the oracle-guided attack threat-model where the attacker has input-output access to an operational chip (as black-box) and a netlist of the obfuscated chip layout. The first step in the SAT attack is to model the obfuscated circuit with a Boolean function, C_{enc}, from input space I, and an obfuscation-secret (key)[1] space, K, to outputs ($C_{enc} : K \times I \rightarrow O$). For logic locking this is a direct transformation. Most camouflaging scheme can also be represented in such a form with polynomial overhead. For instance, a camouflaged gate can be modeled as a key-controlled MUX selecting among a set of possible functionalities of the camouflaged gate.

The attack begins by satisfying a mitter SAT problem, $C_{enc}(i, k_1) \neq C_{enc}(i, k_2)$ with some i, k_1, k_2. The solution input, i, is called a discriminating input pattern (DIP) since it differentiates k_1 and k_2. i is queried on the black-box C_o and the output y_i is obtained. The input-output relation, $(C_{enc}(i, k_1) = y_i) \wedge (C_{enc}(i, k_2) = y_i)$, is appended to the mitter SAT problem as a new constraint. The process continues until no more DIPs can be found. At this point satisfying the constraints will return a key, $k_* \in K_*$, which agrees with the black-box on all the input-output observations and cannot be differentiated by a query. El massed [5] showed that any key from K_* is necessarily a correct key ($\forall i \in I, C_{enc}(i, k_*) = C_o(i)$). The SAT attack is successful in deobfuscating almost all traditional logic locking schemes [18], and gate-level IC camouflaging schemes [5]. Furthermore, Shamsi et al. [17] extended the SAT attack to include approximation which allows the SAT attack to approximate the original circuit defeating the recently proposed SAT-resilient obfuscation schemes [24, 26, 7, 23].

3. SAT-RESILIENT OBFUSCATION

3.1 Security Criteria

Defining general and meaningful security criteria for circuit obfuscation is an elusive task. However, in the context of SAT attacks on combinational logic locking and camouflaging schemes the following criteria can be defined: 1) High query complexity: The query complexity measure, QC, of an obfuscated circuit, C_{enc}, with black-box access to the original circuit, C_o, is the minimum number of queries required to resolve the key. 2) High corruptibility: the corruptibility measure of the obfuscation, Cr, captures the effect of the key on the output. This can be defined as the disagreement probability: $\mathsf{Cr} = \mathsf{Pr}_{i \in I,\, k \in K}[C_{enc}(i, k) \neq C_o(i)]$. 3) As for approximation resiliency which is a stricter criteria there should not exist an algorithm that learns an ϵ-approximation of the original circuit with a success rate of $1 - \delta$ where ϵ and δ are small factors [17].

3.2 Existing Defenses Against SAT Attacks

A number of defenses against the SAT attack have been proposed in literature [24, 26, 7, 23]. These methods all rely on limiting the number of incorrect keys that each DIP can exclude. All these methods require tree structures that will output 1 for only a single input pattern and output 0 for all others. Therefore these schemes have a very low output corruptibility [23] and are hence all combined with high-corruptibility obfuscation schemes such as XOR/XNOR locking etc. The low-corruptibility schemes are generally vulnerable to "find-and-remove" style attacks that search the circuit structure or its function for the tree-like blocks and remove

[1]For most logic locking schemes the obfuscation secret or key is the physical key. For IC camouflaging the key is an abstract variable that decides the function of camouflaged logic. We will use key to refer to both.

them as was shown in [25]. Furthermore, with the approximate SAT attack the high-corruptibility schemes can be attacked independent of the low-corruptibility obfuscation [17].

3.3 Obfuscating Topology

It is easy to see that a fully programmable function is difficult to deobfuscate using the SAT attack. A function $\mathcal{X}_n : \{0,1\}^n \times K \rightarrow \{0,1\}$, which we define to be a function that implements all 2^{2^n} different Boolean functions from $\{0,1\}^n$ to $\{0,1\}$ by configuring $k \in K$, is secure against SAT attacks. Each query will reveal a single entry in the truth-table and hence $\mathsf{QC}(\mathcal{X}_n) = |I| = 2^n$. Furthermore, corruptibility is high since the probability of predicting the correct output given an incorrect key is no better than random guessing. Approximation resiliency is also high since the rate of discovering the truth-table is no faster than linear with respect to the queries.

It is well known that modern programmable logic such as FPGAs are practically fully programmable functions. An FPGA achieves this large expressiveness through combining small LUTs with 6 or less inputs and *programmable interconnects* as seen in Fig. 2a . With programmable interconnections, the small units can be arranged in different topologies to implement a large number of possible functionalities. A sea of AND/OR/NOT gates, plus a sea of configurable wires is capable of implementing a prohibitively large number of functionalities[2].

With respect to SAT attacks, one difficulty in deobfuscating programmable interconnects is to model the fabric with an acyclic Boolean circuit of keys and inputs. When reverse engineering a sea of programmable wires, any terminal on a logic unit can potentially be connected to any other logic unit. Therefore, in the graph model of such a circuit there are many edges and potentially many loops. However, existing SAT attacks require an directed acyclic graph (DAG) to begin the attack. It seems that at least additional abstract key-bits are required to represent the cyclic topology as a DAG. Cyclic obfuscation exploits this idea to create a highly complex circuit structure in ASICs without incurring the high overheads of fully programmable logic (30X area, 3X delay, and 10X power). Note that if such overhead is acceptable simply using programmable devices and using the configuration bitstream as the key is a secure defense against SAT based deobfuscation.

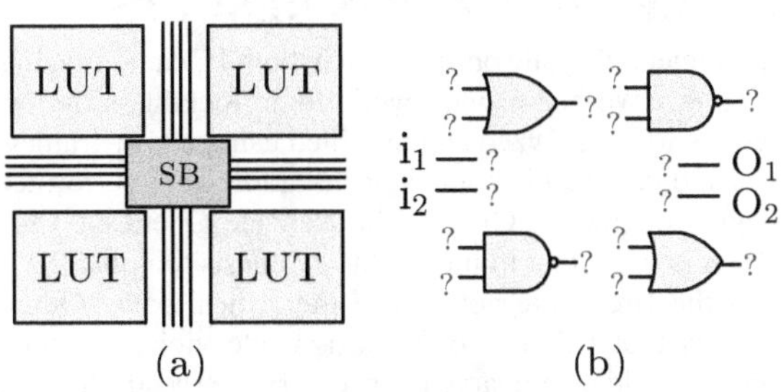

Figure 2: (a) FPGA programmable logic with configurable interconnects. (b) A circuit with known components but unknown interconnects is greatly unintelligible.

4. SECURE AND LIGHT-WEIGHT CYCLIC-OBFUSCATION

While it is possible to flood the circuit with dummy interconnections to achieve a highly complex and expressive cyclic structure, our light-weight cyclic obfuscation scheme relies on using the minimum number of dummy edges to create loops that are difficult to remove.

We will model circuits with a directed graph. Consider the original Boolean circuit C_o as seen in Fig. 3. In the graph representation of C_o, input wires are represented by nodes with no incoming edges. Similarly, output wires are represented by nodes with no outgoing edges. Each gate is represented by a node where the gate inputs are incoming edges and the gate output is represented by outward edges. The fanout cone of a node u includes every node v reachable from u, and the fanin cone of u includes every node v that can reach u.

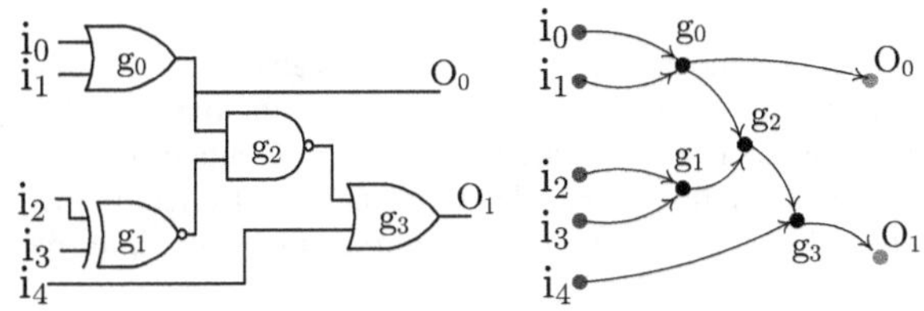

Figure 3: Directed graph model of Boolean circuit.

4.1 Creating Hard Loops

We can begin adding edges to the circuit DAG to create logical loops. In order for an edge to create a logical loop it has to connect a node in the fanout cone of u to a node in the fanin cone of u which will create a loop with u being on the loop. The goal of the defender is to first ensure that there are more than one ways to open the loop, all of which are feasible from the attacker perspective. Furthermore, the defender wants to maximize the number of possible ways to open this loop. These require two conditions that are discussed herein.

CONDITION 1. *Any created loop has to be non-reducible.*

Given a general cyclic graph the problem of finding edges in the graph to remove to obtain an acyclic graph is known as the *feedback arc set* problem [2] which is NP-complete. However, the NP-complete hardness of this problem may not necessarily be used to ensure the difficulty of recovering the original acyclic circuit in our case. The inputs and outputs of a circuit graph are known as sources and sinks to the attacker which help infer a general direction in the graph and potentially remove edges that oppose this direction. More precisely, a cyclic circuit graph is a *flow-graph* [6].

Flow-graphs and loops are studied in depth in the context of programs [6]. Loops in flow-graphs can be *reducible* or non-reducible. If a flow-graph has only reducible loops, the depth-first-search (DFS) traversal of this graph is unique. This unique DFS tree will allow all reducible loops to be opened by removing a unique set of edges which can be found efficiently. Since this would be greatly detrimental to the security of cyclic obfuscation any loop created during the obfuscation has to be non-reducible. A sufficient condition for a loop to be non-reducible is for it to have multiple entry points. An entry point in a loop is an edge arriving on one of the vertices in the loop from a vertex outside the loop.

Example: Consider graph in Fig. 4a. In this graph if we add edge e_3, the loop $\{e_1, e_2, e_3\}$ is reducible since it has a single entry through g_1 and in the DFS traversal of this graph e_3 will always be a backward edge. On the other hand in graph Fig. 4b, the loop $\{e_1, e_2, e_3\}$ is non-reducible since if we enter the loop from g_1, e_2 will be a backward edge, but if we enter the loop from g_2, a different edge, e_1, will be opposing the flow.

[2]Note that having g gates and infinite interconnect resources may not implement all 2^{2^n} Boolean functions but for sufficiently large values of g implements a prohibitively large number of functions for an attacker to prune.

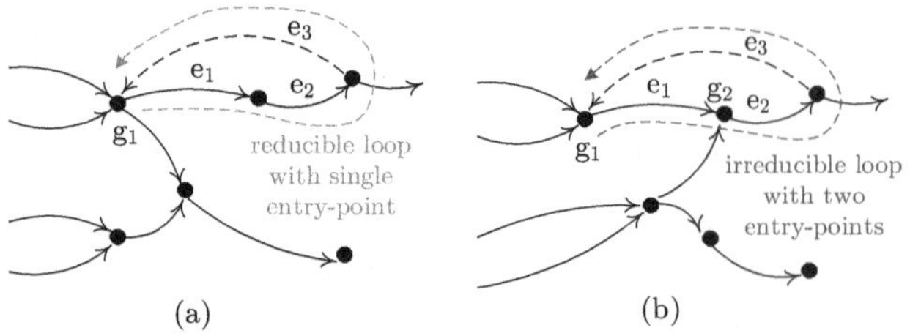

Figure 4: Reducible and non-reducible loops.

CONDITION 2. *At least $n \geq 2$ edges in a loop have to be "removable". This will result in a loop complexity of 2^n.*

An edge is removable if 1) the attacker is able to modify the key to remove that edge from the graph; 2) removing the edge through a key value, should not create gates with no inputs or no outputs. Otherwise, even though the edge removal is controlled by the key, its removal is not possible without introducing errors into the circuit.

Example: In the graph in Fig. 4b, if the removal of edge e_1 is controlled by a key-bit it would still not be a removable edge, since removing e_1 will leave the gate, g_1, with no outputs.

If an edge is removable, then it creates a dilemma for the attacker during reverse engineering. If a loop has n removable edges, there are $\binom{n}{m}$ ways to open it by removing m edges. Thus in total there are $\sum_{m=1}^{n} \binom{n}{m} = 2^n - 1$ ways to open a loop with n removable edges.

4.2 Dummy Logic as Extra Nodes

Thus far we only discussed adding edges (wires) to the design to create obscurity. However, dummy gates can also be added to the circuit as extra nodes and included in loops. This will have the following benefits: 1) inserting dummy gates in realistic designs can have a virtually zero area overhead, since they can be inserted in empty areas that would be otherwise filled with filler cells. Therefore, dummy gates can be easily used to increase the length of a given loop at no cost. 2) As was discussed, for an edge to be removable, its removal should not result in a gate with empty fanout or fanin. However, if the attacker is faced with the possibility of dummy cells, this condition can be relaxed, since if the gate is dummy it can have an empty fanout or fanin.

4.3 Light-Weight Implementation Algorithm

We will first discuss a logic locking implementation of the obfuscation scheme. For logic locking, from a graph level, we first need to identify a path (v_1, v_2) and make sure that at least one node between v_1 and v_2 has more than one incoming edges to ensure the non-reducibility of the loop. If this is the case then we can feed v_2 back into v_1. We then have to ensure that edges on this loop are removable.

To create removable feedback wires we can either use a gate to nullify the effect of a a wire on a gate as seen in Fig. 5a, or use a MUX gate to select between two wires as seen in Fig. 5b. To make edges along the path (v_1, v_2) removable, depending on the fanout count of the nodes on the path we can use one or two MUX gates to implement this as is discussed in the bellow example. a general algorithm for performing the above cyclic logic locking is presented in Algorithm 1.

Example: Per Fig. 6, we first feedback the wire w_3 into w_0 and then we need to make the edges on the path (w_1, w_3) removable. For wire w_1, the wire already connects to more than one location. Therefore, simply including the MUX gate, M_1, in this path will allow the key-bit k_1 to open this edge. When k_1 opens the loop, the

Algorithm 1 Obfuscate circuit C_o with N loops of length M (attack complexity is $(2^M)^N$).

```
function CYCLICOBFUSCATE(C_o, N, M)
    while loops found < N do
        repeat
            u ← random gate from C_o
            start DFS at u to find path of length M
        until path of length M found
        feed v back to u
        for each g on path (u, v) do
            if fanoutSize(g) = 1 then
                make g removable with two MUXs
            else
                make g removable with single MUX
            end if
        end for
    end while
end function
```

input of gate g_2 is fed from a randomly selected wire in the circuit r_0. For the wire w_2 however, since it is driving the gate g_2 only, two MUXs are used to make this edge removable. First, M_2 selects between w_2 and the random wire r_1. Second, M_3 is used to open a path from w_2 to a randomly selected location r_2. MUXs M_2 and M_3 are controlled by the same key-bit k_2 which will remove the edges from the loop and redirect them to other locations.

For IC camouflaging a similar procedure can be used, except that MUXs in IC camouflaging can be implemented with dummy vias with virtually zero gate area overhead as seen in Fig. 7. Even for the case of logic locking one-time-programmable contacts, such as anti-fuse vias, high R_{on}/R_{off} non-volatile memory devices, or other metal-to-metal programmable switches can be used to implement a light-weight and non-volatile MUX element for cyclic logic locking. We note that cyclic obfuscation heavily relied on the security of such silicon level techniques. We allow the attacker to tell the difference between true vias and potentially-true vias, however, the attacker should not be able to tell apart true and fake vias. For instance, doping based programmable/camouflaged connections can be revealed with selective etching, or capacitive imaging [19] and should not be used, whereas Mg/MgO connections [3] are more difficult to differentiate at least with current scanning electron microscopy techniques.

5. EXPERIMENTATION RESULTS

We implemented cyclic obfuscation in both IC camouflaging and logic locking. We begin with cyclic logic locking. The benchmark netlists were analyzed and modified using a C++ framework. Synthesis and delay and area characterization were performed using Design Compiler (DC) with the Nangate OpenCell 15nm library [1]. It is important to inform the synthesis tool that the loops created in the circuit are not part of the critical path. Otherwise the synthesis tool will try to fix design-rule violations for such paths which would create large unnecessary overheads. The results for cyclic logic locking on the c432 ISCAS benchmark circuit are shown in Table 3. Since c432 is the smallest benchmark, overhead trade-offs are more significant. Larger circuits will have negligible overheads.

We then applied the cyclic logic locking to a larger set of ISCAS and MCNC benchmarks as shown in Table 2, for $N = 6$ (loop count) and $M = 6$ (loop length). The same benchmark circuits were obfuscated with a traditional random XOR/XNOR obfuscation with the same number of key-bits (72). The area and delay results from synthesis in the 15nm OpenCell library are shown in Figs. 8 and 9 which shows the feasibility of a low overhead implementation of cyclic logic locking in comparison with traditional methods. Note that SAT resilient proposals [24, 26, 7, 23] are not

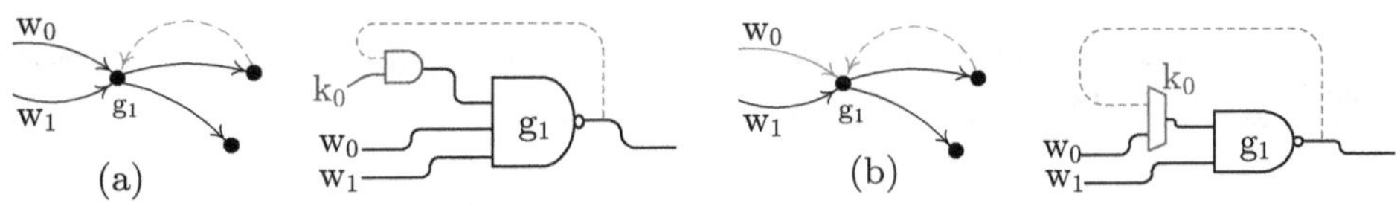

Figure 5: Add-edge operations: (a) Nullify with key-gate. (b) Choose with key-controlled MUX.

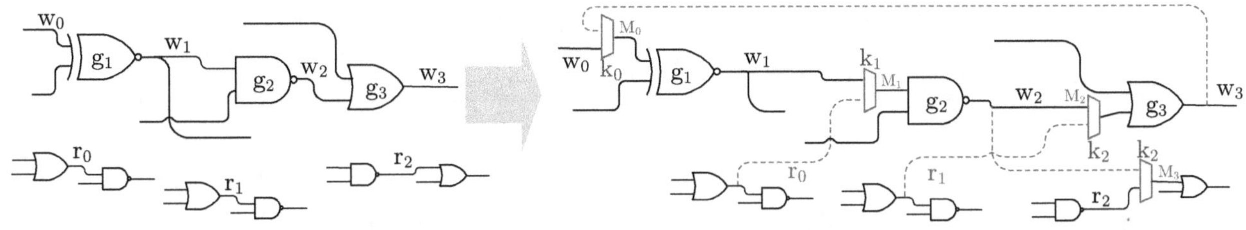

Figure 6: Cyclic logic locking example ensuring the removabillity of edges on path.

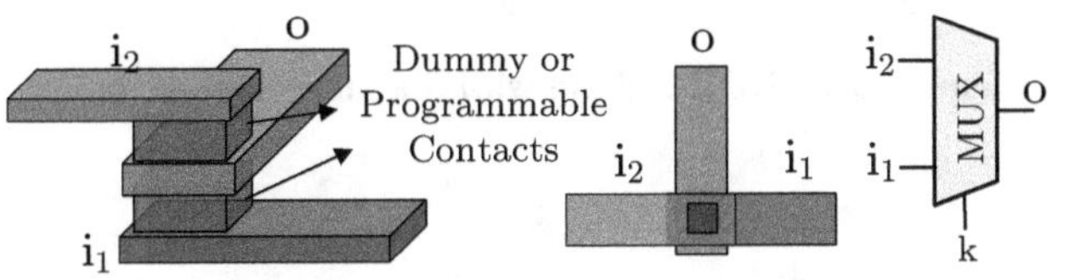

Figure 7: 2-to-1 MUX with dummy contacts or one-time-programmable vias.

ISCAS				MCNC			
circuit	#inputs	#outputs	#gates	circuit	#inputs	#outputs	#gates
c432	36	7	160	apex2	39	3	610
c499	41	32	202	ex5	8	63	1055
c880	60	26	383	i9	88	63	1315
c1355	41	32	546	i7	199	67	1581
c1908	33	25	880	k2	46	45	1815
c2670	157	64	1193	ex1010	10	10	5066
c3540	50	22	1669	des	256	245	6437
c5315	178	123	2307				
c7552	207	108	3512				

Table 2: Benchmark circuits adopted from [18]. Gate count is in terms of number primitive gates.

included in the comparison since they all utilize XOR/XNOR obfuscation internally to increase corruptibility.

As for cyclic IC camouflaging, we created a set of dummy vias and MUXs using Cadence Virtuoso and utilized them in Encounter as part of a physical-only library. As seen in Figure 10c the dummy vias are automatically placed and routed using Encounter. Our layout experiments with three benchmark circuits, c432, c1908 and c3540 showed that with a core utilization of 70%, the cyclic camouflaged circuit does not increase the core area and only contributes to additional congestion and wire-length. The maximum wire-length increase was for 8 cycles of 6 edges long inserted in the c1908 benchmark circuit with 32% wire-length overhead and all designs converged without design-rule violations. Accurate delay and power overhead analysis require capacitance details from the camouflaged vias, however, by assuming capacitance values of two crossing wires for the fake vias, delay overhead was a maximum of 6.2% and power overhead was a maximum of 5% for 8 cycles of length 8 across the benchmarks. Extensive layout implementation and characterization is a topic of our future work.

6. CONCLUSION

In this paper a novel approach towards thwarting SAT attacks was proposed based on creating interconnection cyclic obscurity. The method is applicable to both logic locking and IC camouflaging and as was demonstrated in this paper can be performed with very low performance and area overhead. While the current SAT attacks are incapable of reverse engineering cyclic circuits, investigating novel oracle-guided attacks that are able to model such circuits is essential to further evaluating the security of cyclic obfuscation. Extensive layout level characterization and implementation utilizing dummy gates is also a significant future direction.

7. REFERENCES

[1] Nangate freepdk15 open cell library. http://www.nangate.com/?page_id=2328.

[2] P. Charbit, S. Thomassé, and A. Yeo. The minimum feedback arc set problem is np-hard for tournaments. *Combinatorics, Probability and Computing*, 16(01):1–4, 2007.

[3] S. Chen, J. Chen, D. Forte, J. Di, M. Tehranipoor, and L. Wang. Chip-level anti-reverse engineering using transformable interconnects. In *Proc. IEEE Int. Symp. Defect and Fault Tolerance in VLSI and Nanotechnology Systems*, pages 109–114. IEEE, 2015.

[4] R. P. Cocchi, J. P. Baukus, L. W. Chow, and B. J. Wang. Circuit camouflage integration for hardware ip protection. In *Proc. Design Automation Conf.*, pages 1–5. IEEE, 2014.

[5] M. El Massad, S. Garg, and M. V. Tripunitara. Integrated circuit (ic) decamouflaging: Reverse engineering camouflaged ics within minutes. In *NDSS*, 2015.

[6] M. S. Hecht and J. D. Ullman. Characterizations of reducible flow graphs. *Journal of the ACM (JACM)*, 21(3):367–375, 1974.

[7] M. Li, K. Shamsi, T. Meade, Z. Zhao, B. Yu, Y. Jin, and D. Z. Pan. Provably secure camouflaging strategy for ic protection. In *Proc. Int. Conf. on Computer Aided Design*, page 28. ACM, 2016.

[8] S. E. Quadir, J. Chen, D. Forte, N. Asadizanjani, S. Shahbazmohamadi, L. Wang, J. Chandy, and M. Tehranipoor. A survey on chip to system reverse engineering. *ACM Journal on Emerging Technologies in Computing Systems (JETC)*, 13(1):6, 2016.

[9] J. Rajendran, Y. Pino, O. Sinanoglu, and R. Karri. Logic encryption: A fault analysis perspective. In *Proc. Design, Automation and Test in Eurpoe*, pages 953–958, 2012.

[10] J. Rajendran, Y. Pino, O. Sinanoglu, and R. Karri. Security analysis of logic obfuscation. In *DAC*, pages 83–89, 2012.

[11] J. Rajendran, O. Sinanoglu, and R. Karri. Vlsi testing based security metric for ic camouflaging. In *Proc. IEEE Int. Test Conf.*, pages 1–4. IEEE, 2013.

[12] J. Rajendran, O. Sinanoglu, and R. Karri. Regaining trust in vlsi design: Design-for-trust techniques. *Proceedings of the IEEE*, 102(8):1266–1282, 2014.

[13] J. Rajendran, H. Zhang, C. Zhang, G. S. Rose, Y. Pino, O. Sinanoglu, and R. Karri. Fault analysis-based logic encryption. *IEEE Trans. on Computers*, 64(2):410–424, 2015.

[14] J. A. Roy, F. Koushanfar, and I. L. Markov. Epic: Ending piracy of integrated circuits. In *Proc. Design, Automation and Test in Eurpoe*, DATE '08, pages 1069–1074, 2008.

Table 3: Loop count and length versus loop complexity (number of possible ways to open loops), and delay/area overhead% for the c432 circuit. loop complexity can be a measure of security.

cycle length	3			4			6			8			12		
cycle count	area	delay	comp	area	delay	comp	area	delay	comp	area	delay	comp	area	delay	comp
2	12.21	2.88	64	24.59	5.08	256	19.07	11.47	4096	18.12	11.95	10^4	29.74	13.19	10^7
3	17.93	6.07	512	17.74	7.64	4096	24.02	9.31	10^5	46.88	43.79	10^7	50.89	16.04	10^{10}
4	20.21	4.42	4096	23.64	7.41	10^4	28.02	18.34	10^7	46.50	16.07	10^9	52.41	14.22	10^{14}
6	23.45	8.02	10^5	34.31	-3.40	10^7	39.45	22.58	10^{10}	76.60	46.30	10^{14}	102.51	44.64	10^{21}
8	48.22	36.40	10^7	50.50	38.27	10^9	54.50	14.47	10^{14}	91.85	30.31	10^{19}	111.85	36.81	10^{28}

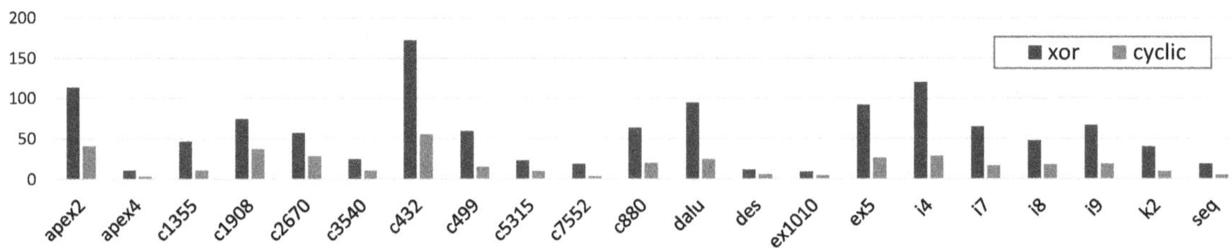

Figure 8: Area overhead of cyclic logic locking with 6 loops of length 6 versus XOR/XNOR locking with the same number of keybits(72).

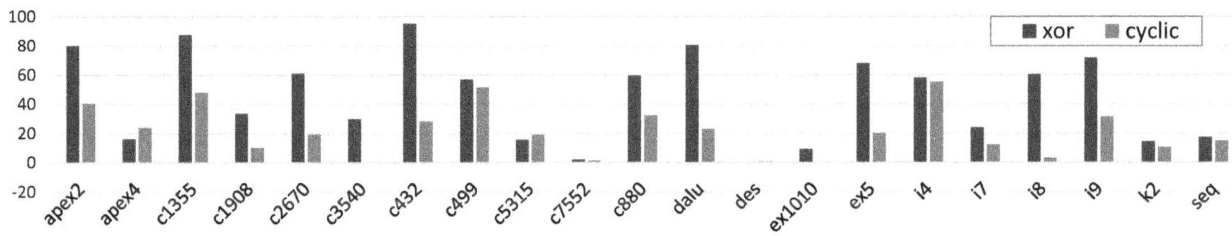

Figure 9: Delay overhead ($M = N = 6$).

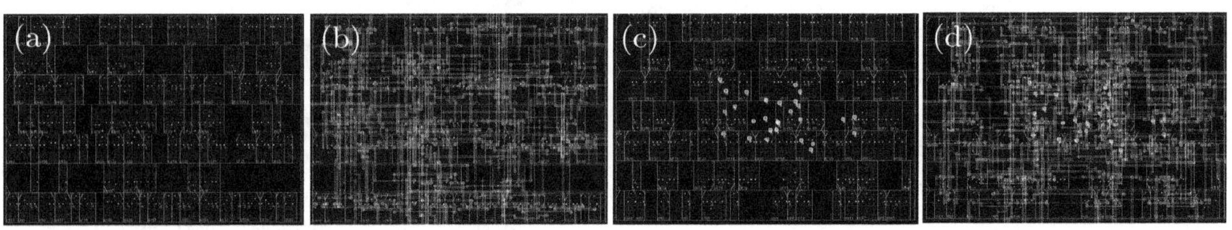

Figure 10: Layout-level cyclic camouflaging with 4 loops of length 4 on the small c432 circuit. Figure (a) shows the original circuit and Figure (b) shows the original routing. In Figure (c) the placement of the dummy vias are shown. As seen from Figure (d) the routed camouflaged circuit only contributes to wire overhead.

[15] J. A. Roy, F. Koushanfar, and I. L. Markov. Protecting bus-based hardware ip by secret sharing. In *Proceedings of the 45th annual Design Automation Conference*, pages 846–851. ACM, 2008.

[16] B. Shakya, N. Asadizanjani, D. Forte, and M. Tehranipoor. Chip editor: leveraging circuit edit for logic obfuscation and trusted fabrication. In *Proceedings of the 35th International Conference on Computer-Aided Design*, page 30. ACM, 2016.

[17] K. Shamsi, M. Li, T. Meade, Z. Zhao, Y. Jin, and D. Z. Pan. Appsat: Approximately deobfuscating integrated circuits. In *Proc. IEEE Symp. Hardware-Oriented Security and Trust*. IEEE, 2017.

[18] P. Subramanyan, S. Ray, and S. Malik. Evaluating the security of logic encryption algorithms. In *Proc. IEEE Symp. Hardware-Oriented Security and Trust*, pages 137–143. IEEE, 2015.

[19] T. Sugawara, D. Suzuki, R. Fujii, S. Tawa, R. Hori, M. Shiozaki, and T. Fujino. Reversing stealthy dopant-level circuits. In *Cryptographic Hardware and Embedded Systems*, pages 112–126. Springer, 2014.

[20] A. Vijayakumar, V. C. Patil, D. E. Holcomb, C. Paar, and S. Kundu. Physical design obfuscation of hardware: A comprehensive investigation of device and logic-level techniques. *IEEE Transactions on Information Forensics and Security*, 12(1):64–77, 2017.

[21] T. F. Wu, K. Ganesan, A. Hu, H.-S. P. Wong, S. Wong, and S. Mitra. Tpad: Hardware trojan prevention and detection for trusted integrated circuits, 2015.

[22] K. Xiao, D. Forte, Y. Jin, R. Karri, S. Bhunia, and M. Tehranipoor. Hardware trojans: Lessons learned after one decade of research. *ACM Transactions on Design Automation of Electronic Systems (TODAES)*, 22(1):6, 2016.

[23] Y. Xie and A. Srivastava. Mitigating sat attack on logic locking. http://eprint.iacr.org/2016/590.pdf.

[24] M. Yasin, B. Mazumdar, J. Rajendran, and O. Sinanoglu. Sarlock: Sat attack resistant logic locking. In *Proc. IEEE Symp. Hardware-Oriented Security and Trust*, pages 236–241, 2016.

[25] M. Yasin, B. Mazumdar, O. Sinanoglu, and J. Rajendran. Security analysis of anti-sat. https://eprint.iacr.org/2016/896.pdf.

[26] M. Yasin, B. Mazumdar, O. Sinanoglu, and J. Rajendran. Camoperturb: secure ic camouflaging for minterm protection. In *Proc. Int. Conf. on Computer Aided Design*, page 29. ACM, 2016.

Double DIP: Re-Evaluating Security of Logic Encryption Algorithms

Yuanqi Shen
Department of Electrical Engineering and Computer Science
Northwestern University
Evanston, IL 60208
yuanqishen2020@u.northwestern.edu

Hai Zhou
Department of Electrical Engineering and Computer Science
Northwestern University
Evanston, IL 60208
haizhou@eecs.northwestern.edu

ABSTRACT

Logic encryption is a hardware security technique that uses extra key inputs to lock a given combinational circuit. A recent study by Subramanyan et al. shows that all existing logic encryption techniques can be successfully attacked. As a countermeasure, SARLock was proposed to enhance the security of existing logic encryptions. In this paper, we re-evaluate the security of these approaches. A SAT-based attack called Double DIP is proposed and shown to successfully defeat SARLock-enhanced encryptions.

1. INTRODUCTION

The active participation of external entities in the design and manufacturing of ICs has produced numerous hardware security issues. Among all the hardware security problems, the counterfeiting, piracy, and unauthorized overproduction of electronic components have become a major challenge for government and industry [6, 14]. Most leading-edge design houses have outsourced their fabrication to the offshore foundries for the sake of lower labor and manufacturing cost. However, many offshore foundries are hard to be trusted since they may be in a country without consummate enforcement law for IP protection [13]. The economic impacts and security hazards of hardware piracy are not apt to be neglected compared to software, but is even more severe. The loss due to global hardware piracy has now reached the level of billions per month, with a major share in almost all electronic devices [1]. It was reported by the Alliance for Gray Market and Counterfeit Abatement that about 10% of the start-of-the-art technology products available on market are counterfeits [6].

Logic encryption is a technique proposed to thwart counterfeiting, piracy, and unauthorized overproduction of electronic components [3, 7–10]. It inserts extra gates called key gates into IC design to hide its original functionality. The key inputs are connected to a tamper-proof memory, and the IC only produces all correct input-output pairs if key inputs are correct key values. In that case, even though the foundry is able to access the netlist, and attackers can either steal the netlist from the foundry or reverse engineering the netlist from layout and mask information [12], they will not get functional circuit without loading the correct key value.

Various logic encryption techniques have been exploited. Rajendran et al. [9] propose a logic encryption algorithm that inserting XOR/XNOR gates and Multiplexers based on fault analysis. Dupuis et al. [4] propose a rare value based logic encryption technique and insert AND/OR gates to balance the probability of a signal between 0 and 1. Wendt et al. [15] use multiplexers to select paths in the netlist, and the signal of selection depends on the output of a PUF. The input of the PUF is counted as key inputs. Rajendran et al. [8] analyze the netlist and carefully insert the key gates by assigning weights to key gates. Alkabani et al. [2] replicate a few states of the finite state machine (FSM), and key values control the flow of state transitions.

It should be mentioned that after the procedure of logic encryption, the inserted key gates can be further obfuscated so that it is hard for untrusted foundry and attackers to directly remove them from the netlist [5].

However, almost all existing (combinational) logic encryptions techniques have been decrypted by a SAT-based attack proposed by Subramanyan et al. [11]. It utilizes advanced SAT solver to narrow down the scope of correct key values. Then a work by Yasin et al. called SARLock successfully thwarts SAT-based decryption algorithm by rendering the attack effort exponential in the number of bits in the secret key [17].

This paper develops a new SAT-based decryption technique called Double DIP, which can be used to attack SARLock technique. Contributions of this paper are as follows:

1. We present a new logic decryption algorithm called Double DIP. Double DIP excludes at least two wrong keys each iteration, ensuring wrong keys in the part of traditional logic encryption being excluded without taking exponential iterations.

2. We evaluate the correctness and efficiency of Double DIP comparing with SAT attack. Double DIP takes a small number of iterations to find key values K, and the encrypted circuit with K will behave the same as the correct one except for one or very limited numbers of inputs.

3. If traditional logic encryption key value K_1 is not unique, Double DIP may take similar number of iter-

Permission to make digital or hard copies of all or part of this work for personal or classroom use is granted without fee provided that copies are not made or distributed for profit or commercial advantage and that copies bear this notice and the full citation on the first page. Copyrights for components of this work owned by others than ACM must be honored. Abstracting with credit is permitted. To copy otherwise, or republish, to post on servers or to redistribute to lists, requires prior specific permission and/or a fee. Request permissions from permissions@acm.org.

GLSVLSI '17, May 10-12, 2017, Banff, AB, Canada.

© 2017 ACM. ISBN 978-1-4503-4972-7/17/05...$15.00.

DOI: http://dx.doi.org/10.1145/3060403.3060469

ations as SAT attack. However, we demonstrate that Double DIP can still efficiently thwart SARLock technique if K_1 and SARLock key K_2 can be separated.

The rest of the paper is organized as follows. Section 2 provides a brief overview of SAT attack and SARLock. Section 3 describes the mechanism of Double DIP and why Double DIP can be treated as a successful attack. Section 4 compares the efficiency of SAT attack and Double DIP to solve benchmarks encrypted by the combination of traditional logic encryption and SARLock technique. Section 5 discusses the influence if the key of traditional logic encryption is not unique, and Section 6 concludes the paper.

2. PRELIMINARIES

In this section, we will introduce SAT attack and SARlock techniques. SAT attack is a SAT-based technique to attack logic encryptions [11]. SARLock is a logic encryption enhancement against SAT attack [17], and the SAT attack needs an exponential number of iterations to exclude all wrong keys after the circuit is encrypted by SARLock.

2.1 SAT attack

As we already discussed in the previous section, an encryption of a circuit is to modify the circuit into another one with some extra key inputs such that the input-output relation is the same as the original one only when the correct key value is applied. Fig. 1 presents a simple logic encryption example. Fig. 1(a) is an original circuit with AND/OR/XOR gates. Fig. 1(b) inserts AND/OR key gates into netlist, and correct key inputs value is 01. Fig. 1(c) inserts XOR/XNOR key gates and correct key inputs value is 10.

The attack model assumes that the logic of modified circuit (denoted as *locked circuit*) is known, and the original circuit could be bought and accessed as a black-box. A recent work by Subramanyan et al. [11] has attracted lots of attention in hardware security. They proposed a SAT attack to (combinational) logic encryptions, and found that almost all of encrypted circuits of all existing logic encryption approaches [3, 4, 8–10] have been corrupted by their approach. The SAT attack works as Algorithm 1.

Algorithm 1 SAT Attack Algorithm

Input: C and $eval$.
Output: K_c.

```
i = 1
F_1 = C(X, K_1, Y_1) ∧ C(X, K_2, Y_2)
while sat[F_i ∧ (Y_1 ≠ Y_2)] do
    X_i = sat_assignment_X(F_i ∧ (Y_1 ≠ Y_2))
    Y_i = eval(X_i)
    F_{i+1} = F_i ∧ C(X_i, K_1, Y_i) ∧ C(X_i, K_2, Y_i)
    i = i + 1
end while
K_c = sat_assignment_{K1}(F_i)
```

It iteratively finds the assignment to the following CNF (Conjunctive Normal Form) until it is unsatisfiable:

$$C(X, K_1, Y_1) \wedge C(X, K_2, Y_2) \wedge (Y_1 \neq Y_2),$$

where $C(X, K, Y)$ is the CNF of the locked circuit with input X, key K, and output Y. Each time when X_i as an assignment of X is generated, its corresponding output Y_i from the original circuit is found, and they are used to further constrain K_1 and K_2 by adding

$$C(X_i, K_1, Y_i) \wedge C(X_i, K_2, Y_i)$$

to the existing CNF. The X_i generated in each iteration is called *DIP* (Differentiating Input Pattern), since it is the input that differentiates two possible keys under existing constraints. The iteration will stop when the CNF is no longer satisfiable, which means that there exists no input that can differentiate possible keys. Therefore, any key that satisfies the current constraints is the correct key, which can be computed by SAT on the constraints.

After the publication of the SAT attack on logic encryption, quickly there were many approaches being proposed to enhance logic encryption against the SAT attack. Ideas include either to increase the complexity of the locked circuit such that finding a DIP cannot be easily solved by SAT, or to increase the number of iterations in the process. There is no solid proposal in the first direction, since even though SAT is in general NP-hard, creating a hard instance is generally an unsolved problem.

One of the reasons that the SAT attack has been successful is that it needs to use only a small number of DIPs to exclude all wrong keys for a locked circuit. This means that some DIPs in the iterations exclude a substantial number of wrong keys. Therefore, in the second direction, one way to increase the number of necessary iterations in SAT attack is to make sure that there are substantially large number of wrong keys requesting similarly large number of DIPs to exclude.

2.2 SARLock

SARLock is a logic encryption enhancement against SAT attack proposed by Yasin et al. [17]. The idea of SARLock is to make sure that each wrong key can only be excluded by one DIP. Therefore, the SAT attack needs an exponential number of DIPs to exclude all wrong keys. The simplest design is to have the output flipped only when the key is equal to the input, unless the key is the correct one. As we can see, only the same input can exclude a given wrong key.

Of course the simple design might be easily broken by an attacker, for example, by just picking a random key and flipping the output when the input is the same as the key. To secure against this, they proposed to add the SARLock with a key K_2 on top of any traditional logic encryption with a key K_1. They also proposed to scramble K_1 and K_2 together (e.g., by XORing them) and then apply the simple SARLock on it. Fig. 2 shows the schematic of the combination of traditional logic encryption and SARLock. The circuit is initially encrypted by a traditional logic encryption with a key K_1. Then K_1 is scrambled with SARLock key inputs K_2, and the scrambled result is compared with inputs to generate a flip signal, which is used to flip the output of encrypted circuit when they are equal. This flip signal is 1 when inputs are equal to the scrambled result of K_1 and K_2, and this scrambled result is not equal to the scrambled result of correct K_1 and correct K_2. The mask guarantees when K_1 and K_2 are correct key values, the output of encrypted circuit will not be flipped.

As we can see, the SARLock part can ensure that the SAT attack needs to take exponential time while the traditional logic encryption part can ensure security against simple guess attacks.

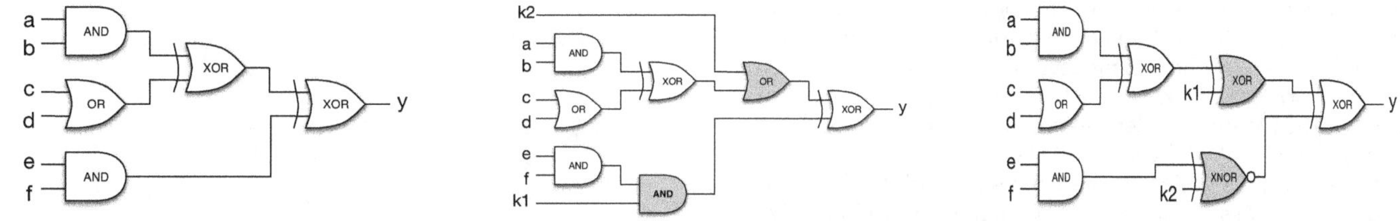

(a) Original Circuit with AND/OR/XOR gates.

(b) Encrypted circuit with AND/OR key gates. Correct key is 01.

(c) Encrypted circuit with XOR/XNOR key gates. Correct key is 10.

Figure 1: Logic encryption example.

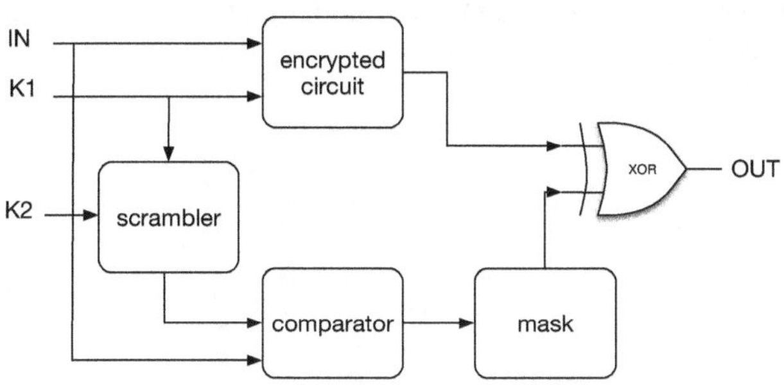

Figure 2: Traditional logic encryption + SARLock.

3. DOUBLE DIP: A NEW ATTACK

Can we then say that this combined SARLock is secure now? Hardly so, since we have developed a new attack approach nick-named *Double DIP* to corrupt the combined SARLock. The ideas can be described as follows. Double DIP is an extension of the SAT attack, whose main idea is to iteratively find DIPs (differentiating input pattern) to exclude more and more wrong keys. Instead of finding a DIP, Double DIP will find 2DIP (doubly differentiating input pattern) in each iteration by finding SAT assignment for the following CNF:

$$C(X, K_1, Y_1) \wedge C(X, K_2, Y_2) \wedge C(X, K_3, Y_1) \wedge$$
$$C(X, K_4, Y_2) \wedge (Y_1 \neq Y_2) \wedge (K_1 \neq K_3) \wedge (K_2 \neq K_4),$$

where $C(X, K, Y)$ is the locked circuit with input X, key K, and output Y.

If the CNF is satisfiable, the input assignment X_i will be used to find the corresponding Y_i in the original black-box circuit, and the following constraint will be added to the CNF:

$$C(X_i, K_1, Y_i) \wedge C(X_i, K_2, Y_i)$$
$$\wedge C(X_i, K_3, Y_i) \wedge C(X_i, K_4, Y_i).$$

The algorithm of Double DIP is shown in Algorithm 2. In the algorithm, a 2DIP can exclude at least two wrong keys, ensuring wrong keys in the traditional logic encryption part being excluded. When the iterations stop, meaning the constrained CNF is not satisfiable, we will find a key K that satisfies all the existing constraints $\forall_{i=1}^{n} C(X_i, K, Y_i)$.

It should be mentioned that Double DIP can be further extended to K DIP, which excludes k wrong keys in each iteration. However, the increasing of k leads to an increasing number of clauses in SAT solver, which takes SAT solver more execution time to find an assignment in each iteration.

Algorithm 2 Double DIP

Input: C and *eval*.
Output: K_c.

i = 1
$F_1 = C(X, K_1, Y_1) \wedge C(X, K_2, Y_2) \wedge C(X, K_3, Y_1) \wedge C(X, K_4, Y_2)$
while $sat[F_i \wedge (Y_1 \neq Y_2) \wedge (K_1 \neq K_3) \wedge (K_2 \neq K_4)]$ **do**
  $X_i = sat\_assignment_X(F_i \wedge (Y_1 \neq Y_2) \wedge (K_1 \neq K_3) \wedge (K_2 \neq K_4))$
  $Y_i = eval(X_i)$
  $F_{i+1} = F_i \wedge C(X_i, K_1, Y_i) \wedge C(X_i, K_2, Y_i) \wedge C(X_i, K_3, Y_i) \wedge C(X_i, K_4, Y_i)$
  $i = i + 1$
end while
$K_c = sat\_assignment_{K1}(F_i)$

Theorem 3.1. *When applied on the same encrypted circuit, there always exists a SAT configuration such that SAT attack has at least the same number of iterations as Double DIP. When the Double DIP terminates, the key of traditional logic encryption K_1 is guaranteed to be correct.*

Assume $(X_0, Y_0), (X_1, Y_1), ..., (X_i, Y_i)$ are input-output pairs that Double DIP finds from the beginning to the termination. Since Double DIP adds extra constraints into constraints of SAT attack, (X_0, Y_0), (X_1, Y_1), ..., (X_i, Y_i) are also input-output pairs that satisfy constraints of SAT attack. When Double DIP and SAT attack apply on the same encrypted circuit, they can have the same constraints of input-output pairs (X_0, Y_0), (X_1, Y_1), ..., (X_i, Y_i) after i+1 iterations. If DIP X that can exclude only one wrong key exists, SAT attack takes extra iterations to add (X, Y), which is a pair of X and the corresponding output Y in the original circuit, into constrained CNF until such X cannot be found. However, if such X does not exist, SAT attack and Double DIP take the same number of iterations. So when applied on the same encrypted circuit, there always exists a SAT configuration such that SAT attack has at least the same number of iterations as Double DIP.

Then we prove when the Double DIP terminates, the key of traditional logic encryption K_1 is guaranteed to be correct. Assume K_1 is extended to $K_1 \cdot K_2$ by the SARLock technique. Proving K_1 is correct when the Double DIP terminates is equivalent to prove that the Double DIP does not terminate when K_1 is not correct. Then we prove by contradiction. In traditional logic encryption, K_1^c is a correct key, and K_1^{inc} is one of the wrong keys. K_2^{incl} and K_2^{inc2} are two of the incorrect keys in SARlock. Assume the K_1 is not correct, but the Double DIP terminates. Then we have an assignment $K_1 = K_1^c \cdot K_2^{incl}$, $K_2 = K_1^{inc} \cdot K_2^{incl}$, $K_3 = K_1^c \cdot K_2^{inc2}$ and $K_4 = K_1^{inc} \cdot K_2^{inc2}$ to meet the satisfiability. Then the Double DIP does not terminate, which is contradict to our assumption.

It should be noted here that the key K found by the Double DIP cannot be guaranteed to be the correct one. This is because the existing constraints, when combined with the DIP CNF in the original SAT attack, may still be satisfiable. However, even in this case, since the 2DIP CNF, when combined with the existing constraints, is not satisfiable, the found key K can be wrong on at most one input.

Now we will argue that, if a key is wrong on at most one input or even a few inputs, it can be treated as a successful attack. Firstly, when an attacker plugs in this key in the locked circuit, the circuit will behave the same as the correct one except for one or very limited numbers of inputs. The chance to excite the error is exponentially small. Even the attacker sells this circuit to the market, the chance for the market to detect it is similarly small. Secondly, even if an error is discovered by luck, it can be easily corrected by hardwiring the correct output for that specific input. Since it is guaranteed to have only one or a few errors, such a correction is much better than finding a new key by adding the new input pattern.

The last, but not the least, justification comes from a solid theoretical foundation. Statistical techniques are commonly used in cryptography. In cryptography, the information is secure if there does not exist a polynomial time algorithm that can compute the same information with high probability. Based on this definition, we can see that our Double DIP attack has achieved the correctness since the key it finds will produce the correct results with very high probability.

4. EVALUATION

Now we evaluate the effectiveness of Double DIP. The benchmarks are from Subramanyan et al. [11], which are encrypted combinational circuits by a robust encryption technique proposed by Dupuis et al. [4], and these encrypted circuits are originally encrypted on circuits from the Microelectronics Center of North Carolina (MCNC). Dupuis et al. [4] is an algorithm that computes the probabilities of all signals and carefully inserts AND and OR gates so that rare values are minimized. We choose each benchmark with an area overhead of encryption in 5%, 10% and 25%. Then we further encrypt circuits with SARLock technique for the purpose of evaluation. Bits of SARLock keys K_2 are set to be equal with bits of inputs for the convenience of comparison.

The Figure 3-5 show the time to decrypt Dupuis et al. [4] + SARLock for both SAT attack and Double DIP. The comparison shows the Double DIP dramatically decreases the execution time since it avoids solving K_2 with exponential iterations. The execution time of Double DIP for most benchmarks is less than 10 seconds, however the SAT attack cannot solve most of benchmarks within our time limit, an hour.

The Table 1 illustrates how many DIPs are needed to solve the benchmark. For most cases, Double DIP takes less than 100 DIPs to finalize the key. However, the SAT attack needs to take exponential iterations. The SAT attack may handle

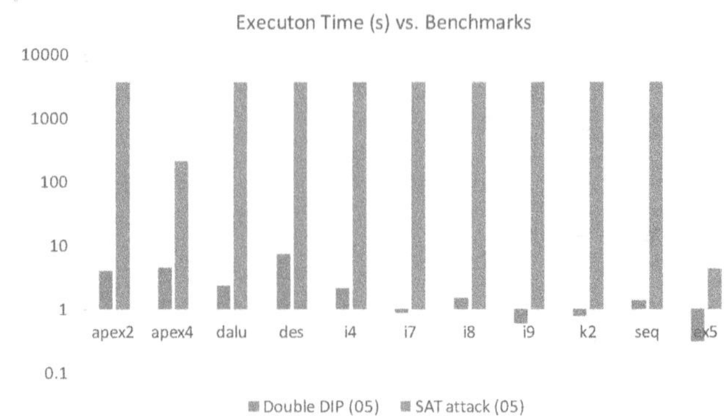

Figure 3: Evaluating Double DIP and SAT attack on benchmarks encrypted with Dupuis et al. [4] (5% area overhead) + SARLock.

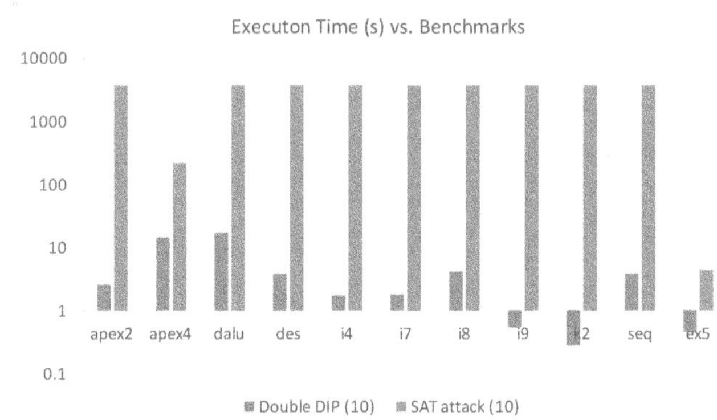

Figure 4: Evaluating Double DIP and SAT attack on benchmarks encrypted with Dupuis et al. [4] (10% area overhead) + SARLock.

the SARLock technique if the number of K_2 is relatively small, but with the increasing of bits of K_2, only Double DIP can solve K_1 efficiently.

The Figure 6-8 compare the execution time of Double DIP to decrypt Dupuis et al. [4] + SARLock and the execution time of SAT attack to decrypt Dupuis et al. [4]. Even though SARLock is further implemented, Double DIP can still efficiently decrypt most of benchmarks with slightly extra execution time.

5. DISCUSSION

During the experiment, surprisingly we found that for some combinations of benchmarks and logic encryption techniques, the Double DIP still took exponential iterations to stop. The reason is that for some logic encryption techniques, more than one correct K_1 is allowed. If correct K_1 is not unique and K_1^{c1} and K_1^{c2} are two of correct K_1 values, then for each iteration, the SAT solver can always find an assignment $K_1 = K_1^{c1} \cdot K_2^c$, $K_2 = K_1^{c1} \cdot K_2^{inc}$, $K_3 = K_1^{c2} \cdot K_2^c$ and $K_4 = K_1^{c2} \cdot K_2^{inc}$, and a DIP $(X_i,\ Y_i)$ may prune K_2 and K_4. In that case, only the combination of one correct K_1 and incorrect K_2 can be pruned, and necessary DIPs are exponential to the bits of K_2.

It leads to an interesting direction to match Double DIP with different logic encryption techniques with several cor-

Table 1: Bits of keys and required iterations for SAT attack and Double DIP.

circuits	# of K_2	5% overload			10% overload			25% overload		
		# of K_1	Double DIP	SAT	# of K_1	Double DIP	SAT	# of K_1	Double DIP	SAT
apex2	39	32	56	7106	65	50	8594	162	30	8966
apex4	10	269	44	1022	537	87	1022	1343	98	1022
dalu	75	119	20	4879	237	119	5453	593	1526	4829
des	256	336	12	3046	673	5	2982	1682	11	2795
i4	192	27	9	3601	53	17	7596	133	17	7286
i7	199	76	5	6071	151	12	5547	379	19	5189
i8	133	130	11	5294	260	33	5155	649	28	4874
i9	88	56	3	7552	112	3	6440	281	6	6074
k2	46	93	16	6960	186	2	6970	465	5	6510
seq	41	178	18	5314	356	35	5481	890	366	5149
ex5	8	53	14	254	106	18	254	266	254	254

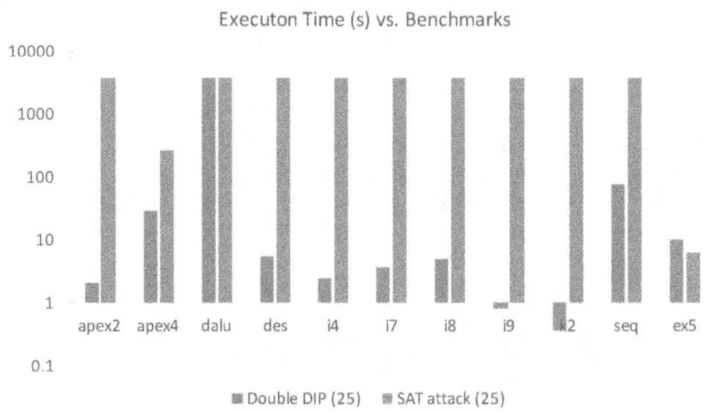

Figure 5: Evaluating Double DIP and SAT attack on benchmarks encrypted with Dupuis et al. [4] (25% area overhead) + SARLock.

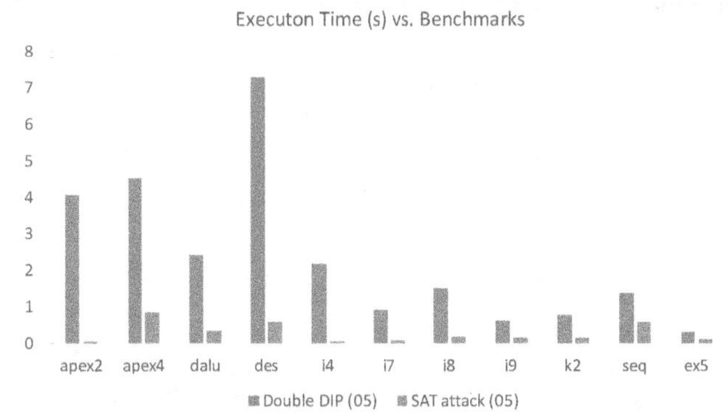

Figure 6: Evaluating Double DIP on benchmarks encrypted with Dupuis et al. [4] (5% area overhead) + SARLock and SAT Attack on benchmarks encrypted with Dupuis et al. [4] (5% area overhead).

rect K_1 values. One of possible solutions will use statistical techniques to separate K_1 and K_2, and set K_2 as a random fixed number. In that case, Double DIP still can find correct K_1 without exponential iterations. It should be mentioned that SAT attack cannot solve correct K_1 value by setting K_2 as a fixed number since the K_2 is most likely to be incorrect, and SAT attack guarantees the final key K is correct for all input-output pairs.

An experiment is performed on the benchmarks from Section 4. We choose Rajendran et al. [8] as traditional logic encryption technique. Each benchmark is encrypted with Rajendran et al. [8] and SARLock, and assume we could separate traditional logic encryption key K_1 and SARLock technique key K_2. We evaluate the Double DIP with and without setting K_2 as zero. The Figure 9-10 illustrate that with a fixed K_2, Double DIP could efficiently solve K_1 of most of benchmarks within 100 seconds. However, if K_2 is not fixed, K_1 of most of benchmarks cannot be solved within an hour.

6. CONCLUSION

In this paper, we propose Double DIP to evaluate the security of the combination of traditional logic encryption and SARLock. SARLock minimizes the efficiency of SAT attack by exponentially increasing the required number of distinguishing input patterns, and only one incorrect key can be pruned each iteration. To avoid exponential iterations, Double DIP only consider incorrect keys causing more than one incorrect input-output pairs, which disables the SARLock and gets the correct key for traditional logic encryption.

We argue that if a key is wrong on at most one input or even a few inputs, it can be treated as a successful attack. The evaluation demonstrates that Double DIP can efficiently thwart SARLock technique if traditional logic encryption key K_1 is unique. We also show that if K_1 is not unique and k_1 and K_2 can be separated, Double DIP can still solve correct K_1 quickly by setting K_2 as a random fixed number.

Our future work involves two aspects. First, proposing new logic decryption approach to attack a state-of-art logic encryption scheme called Anti-SAT [16] since Double DIP still takes exponential iterations to decipher the correct key of Anti-SAT [16]. Second, implementing Double DIP on logic encryption techniques which keys are not unique. Statistical analysis would be a good start to separate K_1 and K_2.

7. ACKNOWLEDGMENT

This work is partially supported by NSF under CNS-1651695 and CNS-1441695, and by SRC under 2014-TS-2559.

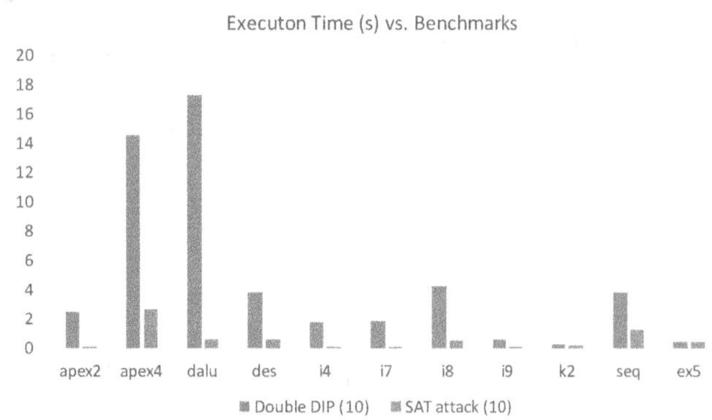

Figure 7: Evaluating Double DIP on benchmarks encrypted with Dupuis et al. [4] (10% area overhead) + SARLock and SAT Attack on benchmarks encrypted with Dupuis et al. [4] (10% area overhead).

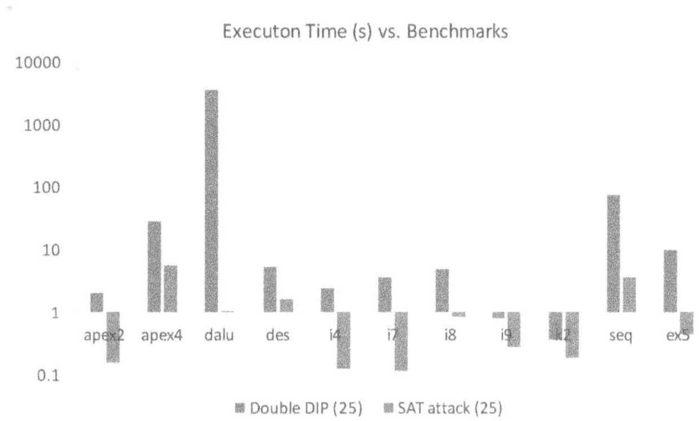

Figure 8: Evaluating Double DIP on benchmarks encrypted with Dupuis et al. [4] (25% area overhead) + SARLock and SAT Attack on benchmarks encrypted with Dupuis et al. [4] (25% area overhead).

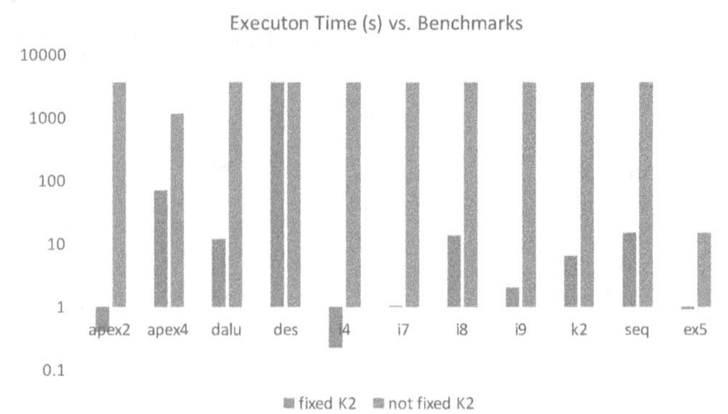

Figure 9: Evaluating Double DIP on benchmarks (Rajendran et al. [8] (5% area overhead) + SARLock) with and without fixed K2.

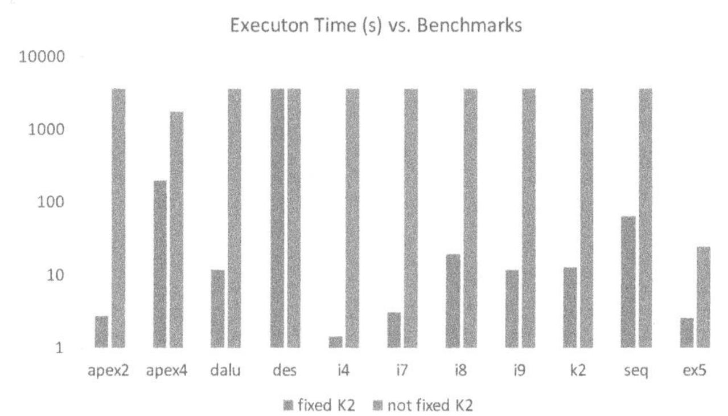

Figure 10: Evaluating Double DIP on benchmarks (Rajendran et al. [8] (10% area overhead) + SARLock) with and without fixed K2.

8. REFERENCES

[1] White paper: The value and management of intellectual assets. http://www.vsi.org.

[2] ALKABANI, Y., KOUSHANFAR, F., AND POTKONJAK, M. Remote activation of ics for piracy prevention and digital right management. In *Proceedings of the 2007 IEEE/ACM international conference on Computer-aided design* (2007), IEEE Press, pp. 674–677.

[3] BAUMGARTEN, A. C. Preventing integrated circuit piracy using reconfigurable logic barriers.

[4] DUPUIS, S., BA, P.-S., DI NATALE, G., FLOTTES, M.-L., AND ROUZEYRE, B. A novel hardware logic encryption technique for thwarting illegal overproduction and hardware trojans. In *2014 IEEE 20th International On-Line Testing Symposium (IOLTS)* (2014), IEEE, pp. 49–54.

[5] LI, L., AND ZHOU, H. Structural transformation for best-possible obfuscation of sequential circuits. In *Hardware-Oriented Security and Trust (HOST), 2013 IEEE International Symposium on* (2013), IEEE, pp. 55–60.

[6] PECHT, M., AND TIKU, S. Bogus: electronic manufacturing and consumers confront a rising tide of counterfeit electronics. *IEEE spectrum 43*, 5 (2006), 37–46.

[7] RAJENDRAN, J., PINO, Y., SINANOGLU, O., AND KARRI, R. Logic encryption: A fault analysis perspective. In *Proceedings of the Conference on Design, Automation and Test in Europe* (2012), EDA Consortium, pp. 953–958.

[8] RAJENDRAN, J., PINO, Y., SINANOGLU, O., AND KARRI, R. Security analysis of logic obfuscation. In *Proceedings of the 49th Annual Design Automation Conference* (2012), ACM, pp. 83–89.

[9] RAJENDRAN, J., ZHANG, H., ZHANG, C., ROSE, G. S., PINO, Y., SINANOGLU, O., AND KARRI, R. Fault analysis-based logic encryption. *IEEE Transactions on Computers 64*, 2 (2015), 410–424.

[10] ROY, J. A., KOUSHANFAR, F., AND MARKOV, I. L. Epic: Ending piracy of integrated circuits. In *Proceedings of the conference on Design, automation and test in Europe* (2008), ACM, pp. 1069–1074.

[11] SUBRAMANYAN, P., RAY, S., AND MALIK, S. Evaluating the security of logic encryption algorithms. In *Hardware Oriented Security and Trust (HOST), 2015 IEEE International Symposium on* (2015), IEEE, pp. 137–143.

[12] TORRANCE, R., AND JAMES, D. The state-of-the-art in ic reverse engineering. In *Cryptographic Hardware and Embedded Systems-CHES 2009*. Springer, 2009, pp. 363–381.

[13] TRIMBERGER, S. Trusted design in fpgas. In *Proceedings of the 44th annual Design Automation Conference* (2007), ACM, pp. 5–8.

[14] VILLASENOR, J., AND TEHRANIPOOR, M. Chop shop electronics. *IEEE Spectrum 50*, 10 (2013), 41–45.

[15] WENDT, J. B., AND POTKONJAK, M. Hardware obfuscation using puf-based logic. In *Proceedings of the 2014 IEEE/ACM International Conference on Computer-Aided Design* (2014), IEEE Press, pp. 270–277.

[16] XIE, Y., AND SRIVASTAVA, A. Mitigating sat attack on logic locking. In *International Conference on Cryptographic Hardware and Embedded Systems* (2016), Springer, pp. 127–146.

[17] YASIN, M., MAZUMDAR, B., RAJENDRAN, J. J., AND SINANOGLU, O. Sarlock: Sat attack resistant logic locking. In *Hardware Oriented Security and Trust (HOST), 2016 IEEE International Symposium on* (2016), IEEE, pp. 236–241.

Efficient Critical Path Selection Under a Probabilistic Delay Model *

Ahish Mysore Somashekar
Department of Electrical and Computer Engineering, Southern Illinois University
Carbondale, Illinois, USA 62901
msahish@siu.edu

Spyros Tragoudas
Department of Electrical and Computer Engineering, Southern Illinois University
Carbondale, Illinois, USA 62901
spyros@engr.siu.edu

ABSTRACT

In this paper, an approach to select critical paths using a probabilistic delay model is presented. Paths through each fault site are selected to effectively test a device for small delay defects that may occur due to random process shifts in different pockets of the physical layout. Experimental evaluation shows significant improvement in time performance and quality of selected paths over existing work.

Keywords

Path delay faults; Delay testing; Critical paths

1. INTRODUCTION

Delay testing targets the timing behavior of the manufactured Integrated Circuits (ICs) to guarantee that no timing defect would affect the performance of the circuit. The fault models used for delay testing include Gate Delay Fault (GDF), Transition Delay Fault (TDF) and Path Delay Fault (PDF) models. While the first two models target gross delay defects at individual gates, the path delay fault represents the cumulative effect of smaller delay defects on one or more gates along a path. The PDF model is considered to be very effective in detecting failures caused by undesirable variations in manufacturing processes. There can be an exponential number of PDFs in the circuit and there can very well be an exponential number of long paths. It is ideal to test all long paths in the circuit to guarantee that the device is defect free but this is prohibitive and therefore, only a subset of long paths called the critical paths are tested.

The authors in [4, 6, 9, 10] propose to select a longest testable path through each gate. In [8] the authors try to account for small delay variations and so, proposed to select longest paths that covered each gate up to k times, for a predetermined value of k. The algorithm for path selection in [8] is called k longest path generation (kLPG) and maintains a priority queue called path-store to enumerate all partial paths leading up to a node.

The authors in [2] analyze the optimality of path selection in [8]. They show that the path selection in [8] is optimal only if the path store has infinite capacity. They further propose an algorithm that has close to optimal performance when the path-store has memory constraints. All the above approaches employ a static timing model and propose to account for process variations through selection of k longest paths through each gate output, which may result in $O(G \cdot k)$ paths, where G is the number of gates in the circuit. These approaches do not consider the number of different instances in which each path is longest. Therefore, the paths selected may not achieve the highest coverage for process related defects.

In [5] the authors model the path delays as linear expressions of the process variations and try to gather the longest paths through every segment under different process conditions. The authors then use a path enumerative approach to prune the large number of non-critical and redundant paths at each fault site and this process is repeated for all fault sites. The approach does not use statistical delays, and the number of paths selected may be prohibitively large.

Authors in [13] and [11] select a small set of paths by considering path correlations. Both approaches are based on exhaustive Monte Carlo simulations and are more suitable towards selecting a small set of paths to detect defects arising from spatially correlated process shifts. The proposed approach, however, is focused on selecting paths to detect random process shifts.

The authors in [14] introduce a branch and bound search based methodology for selecting paths that collectively represent the timing behavior of the circuit. These paths are called critical. The statistical delay of a critical path has higher probability of violating the clock period when compared to other paths. They maintain a set of critical paths at all times. After every search for complete paths the set of critical paths is updated based on the path criticalities. This method performs an exhaustive search for all paths in the circuit. The authors in [14] employ a heuristic based on sub-path criticalities in order to prune the search space. They continue their search through the cone of an internal gate in the circuit only if any of the sub-paths to that gate can be a potential critical path. The heuristic used for search

*This research has been supported in part by grants NSF IIP 1432026, and NSF IIP 1361847 from the NSF I/UCRC for Embedded Systems at SIUC. Any opinions, findings, and conclusions or recommendations expressed in this material are those of the authors and do not necessarily reflect the views of the National Science Foundation

Permission to make digital or hard copies of all or part of this work for personal or classroom use is granted without fee provided that copies are not made or distributed for profit or commercial advantage and that copies bear this notice and the full citation on the first page. Copyrights for components of this work owned by others than the author(s) must be honored. Abstracting with credit is permitted. To copy otherwise, or republish, to post on servers or to redistribute to lists, requires prior specific permission and/or a fee. Request permissions from permissions@acm.org.

GLSVLSI '17, May 10 - 12, 2017, Banff, AB, Canada.

© 2017 Copyright held by the owner/author(s). Publication rights licensed to ACM.

ISBN 978-1-4503-4972-7/17/05. . . $15.00.

DOI: http://dx.doi.org/10.1145/3060403.3060468

space pruning and the path set criticality computation employs the non-linear stat-max operator which may lead to a skewed analysis and potentially misguide the process of critical path selection. [1] derives from [14] and employs a similar branch and bound methodology to search and update critical paths. The authors in [1] integrate path sensitization checking in the path selection process so as to avoid the iterative nature of path selection followed in [14]. In [1], the authors determine criticality of a path by comparing with a set of previously selected paths as against [14] where in paths are compared to the clock. A common drawback of both approaches is the use of SSTA and the intensive branch and bound search that may occur due to the presence of several long non-sensitizable paths.

This paper focuses on quickly selecting the top k critical paths through each gate to cover the various process instances for a predetermined value of k. Testing such a set of paths is crucial to detect devices in which small delay defects (SDDs) on several gates may lead to its failure during in-field operation. This is the equivalent problem formulation to the kLPG problem, in [8], in the presence of process variations. The SDDs are introduced by undesired shifts in process parameters, such as random dopant fluctuations, line edge roughness etc., that is localized in different parts of the device.

The rest of the paper is organized as follows: Section 2 outlines the approach. Section 3 presents a dynamic programming algorithm for critical path selection. Experimental evaluation and comparison to previous approaches is presented in Section 4. Finally, Section 5 concludes.

2. OVERVIEW OF THE APPROACH

The statistical timing quantity ($\mathcal{D}$) is commonly represented in a linear parameterized canonical form as:

$$\mathcal{D} = \mu + \sum_{i=1}^{n} a_i \Delta X_i \tag{1}$$

$$\sigma = \sqrt{\sum_{i=1}^{n} a_i^2} \tag{2}$$

where μ is the nominal or the mean value of the timing quantity. ΔX_i are normalized Gaussian random variables representing all correlated and uncorrelated process variations and a_i represents the sensitivity to corresponding process variations. The delays of gates, wires, paths and even the circuit delay is represented in this linear form. The results of operations, such as addition, subtraction, minimum and maximum, on such timing quantities are also represented in this linear form.

Consider a path x. If the delay of each gate g along x is given in the form of equation 1 then the delay of path x is derived as

$$\mathcal{D}(x) = \sum_{\forall g \in x} \mu_g + \sum_{i=1}^{n} \Big(\sum_{\forall g \in x} a_i(g) \Big) \Delta X_i$$

The critical probability of a path x w.r.t to a threshold τ is

$$\varphi_\tau(x) = Prob(x > \tau) \tag{3}$$

It is necessary to use a threshold based on the scale of small delays defect sizes that one is targeting. Selecting different thresholds may result in a different sets of critical paths. This is illustrated in Figure 1, where, for threshold τ_1 the critical probability of path A is insignificant and path B has a significant critical probability. However, for threshold $\tau_2 < \tau_1$, path A is more critical than path B. If one were to measure the critical probability of paths based on tightness probability (TP) [12], which is given as $Prob(A > B)$, then clearly critical probability of A is always greater than critical probability of B because this is calculated irrelevant of the test threshold.

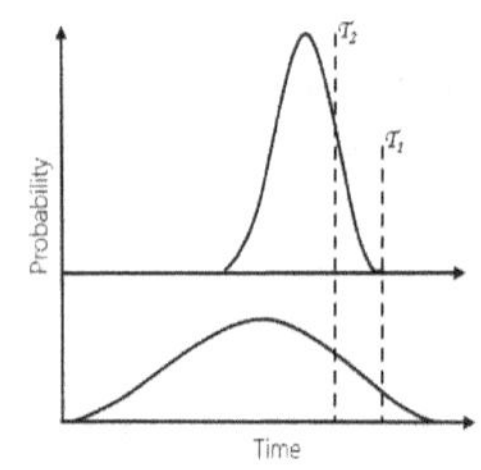

Figure 1: Identifying critical paths for a given threshold

The standard deviation σ gives the spread of the random variable and, therefore, is a determining factor in estimating the upper bound $(\mu + 3\sigma)$ and lower bounds $(\mu + 3\sigma)$ of delay represented using Normal/Gaussian probability distributions. As shown in Figure 1, the upper bound $(\mu + 3\sigma)$ can help determine if a given path is critical or not because if $\mu + 3\sigma < \tau$ then the critical probability, is 0 or insignificant. If $\mu + 3\sigma > \tau$ then the critical probability (φ_τ) is calculated as in Equation 3. The random variable (μ_c, σ_c) for the sum of two statistical quantities (μ_a, σ_a) and (μ_b, σ_b) is

$$\mu_c = \mu_a + \mu_b \;\; and \;\; \sigma_c = \sqrt{\sigma_a^2 + \sigma_b^2}$$

which implies, $\mu_c > \mu_a$ $\mu_c > \mu_b$ and $\sigma_c > \sigma_a$, $\sigma_c > \sigma_b$.

Consider two Gaussian random variables π_1 and π_2.

Assertion 1. It is assumed that when $\varphi_\tau(\pi_1) > \varphi_\tau(\pi_2)$ either $\mu_{\pi_1} > \mu_{\pi_2}$ or $\mu_{\pi_1} + 3\sigma_{\pi_1} > \mu_{\pi_2} + 3\sigma_{\pi_2}$.

Consider the following cases for two pdfs A and B. In some cases Assertion 1 is provably shown. For example, it holds true when $\mu_A > \mu_B$ and $\mu_A + 3\sigma_A > \mu_B + 3\sigma_B$ (see Case 1 in Figure 2(a))

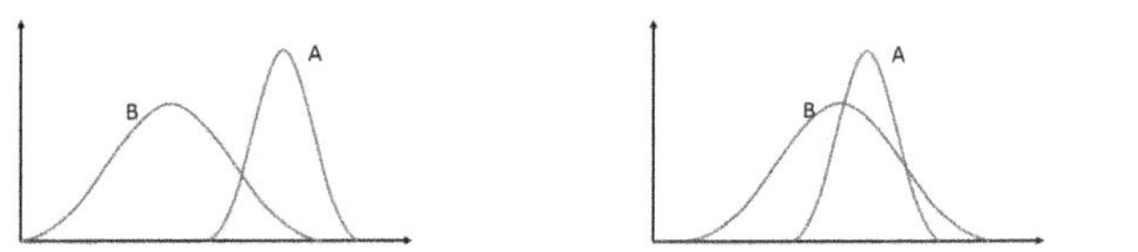

(a) Case 1. (b) Case 2.

Figure 2: Relation between pdf critical probabilities

Consider now the remaining cases of Assertion 1 which are modeled by $\mu_A > \mu_B$ but $\mu_A + 3\sigma_A < \mu_B + 3\sigma_B$(see also Case 2 in Figure 2(b)). In this case, it is not clear which pdf would dominate the criticality and the relation between $\varphi_\tau(A)$ and $\varphi_\tau(B)$ depends on the position of the threshold τ. This is better shown in Figure 1. In cases like this a longest path tracing algorithm, that works for a DAG with deterministic edge weights, fails to optimally select the longest (most critical) path on a DAG with weights given as statistical timing quantities.

In the following, we present a heuristic to select one input partial path at G which has the potential to exhibit the highest critical probability among all the input partial paths at G.

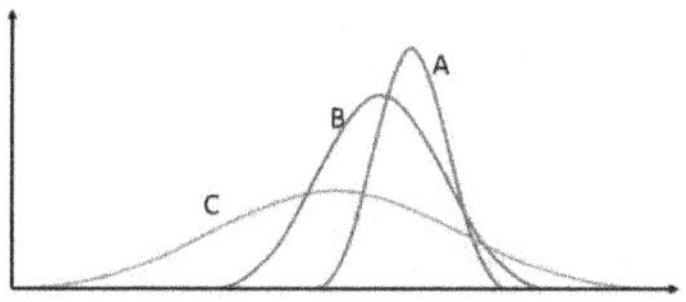

Figure 3: Pdfs where $\mu_A > \mu_B > \mu_C$ and $\mu_A + 3\sigma_A < \mu_B + 3\sigma_B < \mu_C + 3\sigma_C$

Consider a Normal pdf π and pdfs A and C. Let π_A and π_C represent the statistical sum of π with A and C, respectively. The heuristic assumes that $\mu_{\pi_A} > \mu_{\pi_C}$ and $\mu_{\pi_A} + 3\sigma_{\pi_A} < \mu_{\pi_C} + 3\sigma_{\pi_C}$.

This assumption holds in practice if the standard deviation (σ) is not very large as in the examined application where the variation in gate delays/path delays is expected to be less than $\pm 20\%$ of the mean.

As mentioned before, the critical probability of a path is computed w.r.t a given τ which is defined based on the global circuit delay. The challenge is to select one partial path that maximizes Equation 3. The critical probability of any pdf depends on the given τ and, in this regard, the proposed heuristic considers the pdf with the maximum μ and the pdf with the maximum $\mu + 3\sigma$. The pdf with the highest $\mu + 3\sigma$ enables a pdf to extend its spread beyond τ and the pdf with the highest μ enables the pdf to achieve a higher critical probability.

The heuristic traverses the circuit in a topological manner. While at gate G partial paths from the primary inputs (PIs) to gate G have been selected. At that point, it may be prohibitive to consider all possible augmentations by gate G. Due to re-convergences, we may have to prune some partial paths. We propose to identify two partial paths from the output of G to primary outputs (POs) such that one exhibits the maximal μ (see Type A pdf in Figure 3), and the other exhibits the maximal $\mu + 3\sigma$ (see Type C pdf in Figure 3). Such pdfs for maximal μ and maximal $\mu + 3\sigma$ are denoted as $\xi^\mu(G)$ and $\xi^\sigma(G)$, respectively. We call this set of pdfs as the bounding pdfs.

Note, it is possible that the same partial path may hold both properties of maximal μ and maximal $\mu + 3\sigma$. Each input partial path at G is extended by each of the bounding pdfs and its critical probability under both scenarios is calculated. The input partial path which exhibits the highest critical probability under both scenarios is selected. If the same input partial path is not the highest critical under the current set of bounding pdfs then a new set of bounding pdfs is selected so that the condition is satisfied. The bounding pdf under which the maximum critical probability is lower is eliminated by removing the corresponding the partial path from the output of G to the PO, and is replaced with a new pdf with similar properties. This is akin to locating the position of τ. The following illustrates.

Let $\{\pi_1, \pi_2 \dots \pi_m\}$ be a set of Normal pdfs corresponding to the input partial path of G. Let π^μ_{max} correspond to $\max_{i\in\{1\dots m\}}(\varphi_\tau(\pi_i + \xi^\mu(G)))$. Let π^σ_{max} correspond to $\max_{i\in\{1\dots m\}}(\varphi_\tau(\pi_i + \xi^\sigma(G)))$. The heuristic will identify the most critical input partial path at G such that $\varphi_\tau(\pi^\mu_{max} + \xi^\mu(G)) > \varphi_\tau(\pi^\sigma_{max} + \xi^\sigma(G))$ and $\pi^\mu_{max} = \pi^\sigma_{max}$. This condition helps to overcome the ambiguity presented by Case 2 in Figure 2(b).

Pdfs of type A and C act as bounding pdfs to identify the critical pdf among $\{\pi_1, \pi_2 \dots \pi_m\}$. The proposed approach identifies two such pdfs at the output of each gate in order to select the most critical partial path which will then be extended through the gate and made available at the inputs of the subsequent gates in the circuit. The process to identifying such bounding pdfs at the output of each gate and the eventual PI-PO critical path selection is detailed in the next section.

The proposed method makes local decisions at each gate to determine which among the input partial paths is the most critical w.r.t the given τ. Consider a gate g. Let ξ^μ_g and ξ^σ_g represent the sub-path with the largest μ and $\mu + 3\sigma$, respectively, from the output of g to any of the POs. If g has m inputs then the set of input sub-paths at g are $\{\pi_1, \pi_2 \dots \pi_m\}$. A statistical sum is performed for input partial path π_i with each of ξ^μ_g and ξ^σ_g to form a complete PI-PO path. The critical probability of each PI-PO path w.r.t τ is calculated using Equation 3. The input partial path corresponding to the highest φ_τ is chosen and is extended to the output of gate g.

For example, consider the circuit shown in Figure 4. Inside each gate is there is the gate label and below that is the statistical delay corresponding to the gate represented as (μ_d, σ_d). Figure 4 also shows the ξ^μ and ξ^σ values corresponding to each gate.

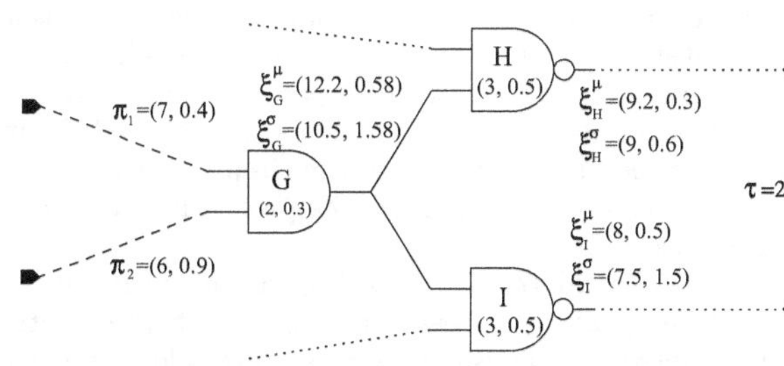

Figure 4: Identifying critical paths for a given threshold

In Figure 4, at gate G there are two input partial paths represented using π_1 and π_2 and their respective statistical delays. Gates H and I are the fan-out gates of gate G. $\xi^\sigma(G)$ for gate G is calculated as follows

$$\begin{aligned}\xi^\sigma(G) &= max_\sigma((\xi^\mu(H) + \mathcal{D}(H)), (\xi^\mu(I) + \mathcal{D}(I)))\\ &= max_\sigma((7.5, 1.5) + (3, 0.5), (9, 0.6) + (3, 0.5))\\ &= max_\sigma((10.5, 1.58), (12, 0.78))\\ &= (10.5, 1.58) \quad \because (10.5 + 3 * 1.58) > (12 + 3 * 0.78)\end{aligned}$$

Similarly, $\xi^\mu(G)$ for gate G is calculated to be $(12.2, 0.58)$, using the operator max_μ which identifies the pdf with the maximum μ.

For $\tau = 22$, the critical probabilities of the input partial paths at gate G, when extended by $\xi^\mu(G)$ and $\xi^\sigma(G)$, respectively, are calculated as follows

$$\begin{aligned}\varphi_\tau(\pi_1 + \xi^\mu(G)) &= Prob((\mathcal{D}(\pi_1) + \mathcal{D}(g) + \xi^\mu(G)) > 22)\\ &= 0.1488\\ \varphi_\tau(\pi_1 + \xi^\sigma(G)) &= Prob((\mathcal{D}(\pi_1) + \mathcal{D}(g) + \xi^\sigma(G)) > 22)\\ &= 0.065\\ \varphi_\tau(\pi_2 + \xi^\mu(G)) &= Prob((\mathcal{D}(\pi_2) + \mathcal{D}(g) + \xi^\mu(G)) > 22)\\ &= 0.052\\ \varphi_\tau(\pi_2 + \xi^\sigma(G)) &= Prob((\mathcal{D}(\pi_2) + \mathcal{D}(g) + \xi^\sigma(G)) > 22)\\ &= 0.028\end{aligned}$$

From the above critical probability computations one can observe that π_1 has the potential to exhibit the highest critical probability. Therefore, π_1 is selected and extended with gate G. It is now an input partial path for gates H and I.

3. CRITICAL PATH SELECTION

This section presents a dynamic programming (DP) based algorithm to extract PI-PO critical paths in the circuit. The proposed approach is applied on a sub-circuit of sensitizable paths derived from [7]. Sensitizable paths are kept compactly in a data-structure called the zero suppressed binary decision diagram (ZBDD) [7]. The ZBDD is a directed acyclic graph. Sensitizable paths are logical paths where each node along the path in a ZBDD represents the circuit gate w.r.t the rising or falling transition at the gate. For the sake of simplicity we assume equal rise and fall delays along paths but the approach can be easily extended to include delays specific to rising and falling transitions along circuit paths. Sensitizable paths can be identified using techniques in [7] [3], among many others. However, it is shown later that the presented method can be applied directly on the netlist which contains untestable paths, and once a critical path is identified then we can use established methods to determine if there exists a pair of patterns that propagate a transition along the path.

The proposed approach is carried out for several iterations with each iteration yielding one critical path. Each iteration of the proposed approach involves one backward traversal and one forward traversal. Critical path identified during previous iteration is removed from the circuit for subsequent iterations. The following explains the procedure carried out during one iteration.

First, a backward traversal starting at the primary outputs identifies ξ^μ and ξ^σ at each gate, as described in Section 2. Next, a forward traversal is performed to select one critical path from PI to PO w.r.t the given threshold τ. At each node one input partial path (π) with the largest $\varphi_\tau(\pi)$ is selected, as described in section 2, and extended with the current gate. It is then made available as the input partial path at the fan-out gates.

Finally, at each PO the complete PI-PO critical path is available. Among these PI-PO paths the path with the highest φ_τ is selected and added to the set Π. This path is later removed from the current circuit and a new sub-circuit (ζ_{sub}) is derived. This ends one iteration.

The following describes the procedures involved in the selection of the longest (most critical) paths in the circuit under a probabilistic delay model. The procedure `BoundingPdfs()` (Procedure 1) lists the process of identifying the bounding pdfs ξ^μ and ξ^σ at the output of each gate in the given circuit. The inputs to `BoundingPdfs()` is ζ, which is ZBDD containing sensitizable paths. The output of `BoundingPdfs()` are the vectors ξ^μ and ξ^σ which contain the respective bounding pdfs corresponding to each gate in the circuit. Lines 1 to 5 present a loop that iterates over a reversed list of topologically sorted nodes in ζ and identifies the bounding pdfs at the output of each gate using the process described earlier in this section.

The procedure `CriticalPartialPath()` (Procedure 2) lists the steps involved in selecting the longest partial path at the input of a gate. The inputs to procedure `CriticalPartialPath()` are a ZBDD ζ which implicitly holds all sensitizable paths in the given circuit, the gate g at which to select the most critical input partial path and the vectors ξ^μ and ξ^σ, which contain the respective bounding pdfs corresponding

Procedure 1: BoundingPdfs

Input: ζ
Output: ξ^μ, ξ^σ
1 **foreach** $g \in$ `ReverseTPsort(`ζ`)` **do**
2   **if** $g \neq PrimaryOutput$ **then**
3     $\mathcal{FO} \leftarrow$ `Fan-outs(`g`)`
4     $\xi^\mu(g) \leftarrow \max_\mu(\xi^\mu(f) + \mathcal{D}(f)\ \forall f \in \mathcal{FO})$
5     $\xi^\sigma(g) \leftarrow \max_\sigma(\xi^\sigma(f) + \mathcal{D}(f)\ \forall\ f \in \mathcal{FO})$
6 **return** ξ^μ, ξ^σ

to each gate in the circuit. The output of `CriticalPartialPath()` is the input partial path, denoted by π_{max} that must be extended through g in order to eventually identify a critical PI-PO path.

Line 1, in `CriticalPartialPath()`, identifies the fan-ins (in-edges) of gate g. The loop in lines 3 to 14 undertakes the process of identifying the appropriate pair of bounding pdfs such that the condition stated in the heuristic (see Section 2) is satisfied and, in this process, selects π_{max}. Line 4 identifies the input partial path that exhibits the maximum critical probability (φ_τ) when extended (stat-sum) by $\xi^\mu(g)$. We denote this partial path as π^μ_{max}. Similarly, line 5 identifies the partial path, denoted by π^σ_{max}, which exhibits the maximum critical probability (φ_τ) when extended (stat-sum) by $\xi^\sigma(g)$. Line 6 and 7 validate the condition, where ξ^μ corresponds to pdf of type A and ξ^σ corresponds to pdf of type C. If the condition does not hold, i.e. it is not the same partial path that exhibits the maximum critical probability when extended by ξ^μ and $\xi^\sigma(g)$, then the path corresponding to ξ^σ is removed and line 11 identifies a new $\xi^\sigma(g)$. If, however, the condition in line 6 was false then the path corresponding to $\xi^\mu(g)$ is removed and a new $\xi^\mu(g)$ is identified in line 14.

Procedure 2: CriticalPartialPath

Input: ζ, g, ξ^μ, ξ^σ
Output: π_{max}
1 $\mathcal{FI} \leftarrow$ `Fan-ins(`g`)`
2 $\pi_{max} \leftarrow \emptyset$
3 **while** $\pi_{max} = \emptyset$ **do**
4   $\pi^\mu_{max} \leftarrow \max_\pi(\varphi_\tau(\pi_f + \xi^\mu(g))\ \ \forall\ f \in \mathcal{FI})$
5   $\pi^\sigma_{max} \leftarrow \max_\pi(\varphi_\tau(\pi_f + \xi^\sigma(g))\ \ \forall\ f \in \mathcal{FI})$
6   **if** $\varphi_\tau(\pi^\mu_{max} + \xi^\mu(g)) > \varphi_\tau(\pi^\sigma_{max} + \xi^\sigma(g))$ **then**
7   **if** $\pi^\mu_{max} = \pi^\sigma_{max}$ **then**
8       $\pi_{max} \leftarrow \pi^\mu_{max}$
9   **else**
10       $\zeta \leftarrow$ `RemovePath(`$\zeta, \xi^\sigma(g)$`)`
11       $\xi^\sigma(g) \leftarrow$ `BoundingPdfs(`ζ`)`
12   **else**
13     $\zeta \leftarrow$ `RemovePath(`$\zeta, \xi^\mu(g)$`)`
14     $\xi^\mu(g) \leftarrow$ `BoundingPdfs(`ζ`)`
15 **return** π_{max}

Procedure `SelectTop`k`()` (Procedure 3) lists the process of identifying the k longest (most critical) PI-PO paths in the given circuit. The input to `SelectTop`k`()` is the ZBDD ζ which contains all sensitizable paths in the given circuit and the numeric value k which denotes the number of paths to select. The output is a set, denoted by Π, of the longest (most critical) PI-PO paths in the given circuit.

Procedure 3: SelectTop$k$

```
Input: ζ, k
Output: Π
1  while k > 0 do
2      ξ^μ, ξ^σ ← BoundingPdfs(ζ)
3      for g ← 0 to MaxNodeID(ζ) do
4          if g ≠ PrimaryInputs then
5              π_g ← CriticalPartialPath(ζ, g, ξ^μ, ξ^σ)
6              π_g ← π_g * g
7      PO ← PrimaryOutputs(ζ)
8      π_C ← max_π(φ_τ(π_po)) ∀ po ∈ PO)
9      Π ← Π ∪ π_C
10     ζ ← RemovePath(ζ, π_C)
11     k ← k − 1
12 return Π
```

In procedure SelectTop$k$(), k iterations are performed over lines 1-11 and one path is selected in each iteration. Line 2 identifies the initial bounding pdfs at each node in the circuit. In lines 3 to 6, the input partial path with highest critical probability is identified and extended through each gate in the circuit. Line 8 identifies the most critical path among all paths ending at a PO and this path is included in the set Π in line 9. Line 10 removes the newly selected path from ζ before continuing for the next iteration.

As mentioned before, procedure SelectTop$k$() (Procedure 3) selects the top k most critical paths in the given ζ. In order to cover local variations in processes and spot defects one should select the top k critical paths through each gate in the circuit, as described in [5] [2]. To achieve this, the Procedure SelectTop$k$() is called for each gate and ζ contains all paths through that gate. The union of the k most critical paths though each gate gives the final path set which contains all paths that must be tested in order to cover local process variations and spot defects.

The use of ZBDDs allows us to implicitly extract all sensitizable paths through a given gate. The presented procedures can also be applied on a circuit graph (netlist) and each time a path is selected its testability is determined using existing Automatic Test Pattern Generation (ATPG) techniques. Also, one can easily extend the proposed approach to integrate testability in the selection process just as in [2] [1].

The complexity of procedure SelectTop$k$() depends on three factors: (1) the number of paths to be selected, denoted by k; (2) the number of edges in the ZBDD/circuit graph, denoted by E; (3) the number of re-computations of the bounding pdfs at each node in order to select the appropriate input partial path, denoted by L. The factors (1) and (3) determine the total number circuit traversals that take place in order to select k paths, which is $O(k + \sum_{i=1}^{|V|} L_i)$, where V is the set of vertices in the ZBDD. The overall complexity of the approach is expressed as $O(E \times (k + \sum_{i=1}^{|V|} L_i))$. The values of k and E are known before the start of the path selection process. The value of L, however, can only be determined empirically and is demonstrated through our experimental results.

4. EXPERIMENTAL RESULTS

Experimental evaluation was performed on some of the largest circuits from ISCAS' 85, ISCAS' 89 and ITC' 99 benchmarks. Experiments were conducted on a Linux machine with Intel Xeon processor and 24 Gb memory. The procedures discussed in this article were implemented in C++. The nominal delay for each gate was obtained from a 45nm technology library. The wire delays are accumulated into the gate delays. In order to model the spatially correlated process variations we used a three level quad tree. This quad tree results in 21 grids each of which is associated with a random variable. With this model the gate delays can change up to 10% in the 3σ case. Due to space limitations the experimental analysis is restricted to a comparative study with existing approaches.

The proposed approach for path selection was compared against the opt-kLPG algorithm in [2]. The authors in opt-kLPG use a deterministic delay model and select up to k longest paths through each gate. We use the $\mu + 3\sigma$ of the pdf at each gate as the discrete delay value of the gate. As mentioned before, $\mu + 3\sigma$ represents an upper bound on the gate delay. So the paths were selected based on their longest delays under the deterministic delay model.

The authors in [14] use a statistical delay model in their approach, referred to as BnB-SPM, that selects the k statistically longest paths in the given circuit. The approach is not targeted for spot defects arising from local process variations. To address this, we adopt the framework in [14] to select k critical paths through each gate. The approach uses branch and bound search to select the first k paths, and then the path set is improved by updating the path set if better paths are found as it continues to explore the complete graph. This exhaustive search is required to guarantee that the highest critical path is included in the path set.

The following describes the metric, denoted by Ω, used to evaluate the quality of paths selected by each approach. As shown in Equation 4, the quality of paths selected is determined by summing the critical probabilities of the k paths selected through each gate and then obtaining the sum over all gates. This quantity is then normalized by the number of paths selected, which is k multiplied by the number of gates in the circuit. In Equation 4, g represents a gate and g_i represents a selected path through gate g. G is the set of all gates. φ_τ is the critical probability, as in Equation 3.

$$\Omega = \frac{\sum_{\forall g \in G} \sum_{i=1}^{k} \varphi_\tau(g_i)}{k \times |G|} \quad (4)$$

The proposed approach as well as opt-kLPG [2] and BnB-SPM [14] are evaluated using the metric given in Equation 4. We set the test clock τ to be 90% of the maximum circuit delay calculated using static timing analysis.

Table 1 presents a comparative study for the quality of paths selected and the time complexity, when 5 paths are selected per gate. In Table 1, Column 1 lists the circuit name. Columns 2 and 3 list the results for the proposed approach. In particular, Column 2 lists quality of the se-

Table 1: Comparative study for selecting 5 critical paths through each gate

Benchmark	Proposed		opt-kLPG [2]		BnB-SPM [14]	
	$\Omega(P)$	Time (s)	$\Omega([6])$	Time (s)	$\Omega([10])$	Time (s)
C5315	87.33	4.94	75.36	1.76	87.12	40.9
C7552	83.55	11.07	74.09	9.12	82.90	44.12
S38417	69.78	528.27	54.22	986.93	68.91	2322.34
S38584	68.57	398.65	56.81	603.17	68.49	2766.13
b05	90.84	3.85	78.99	75.54	90.60	212.45
b15	77.57	70.25	73.97	506.90	77.07	427.96
b17	85.93	910.77	76.25	3248.74	84.97	6546.22
b20	82.16	343.32	68.78	2578.99	81.51	3122.12
b21	83.30	354.85	71.47	2342.82	82.77	3755.36
b22	79.88	753.31	68.52	4116.44	79.45	5933.7
Ave	80.89	337.93	69.84	1591.65	80.37	2517.13

lected paths (see Eq 4) and Column 3 lists the CPU time. Columns 4 and 5 list the corresponding results for the approach in [2]. Observe that, for each circuit, the quality of path selected by the proposed approach is significantly better than those selected by opt-kLPG. Also, notice that the proposed approach is, on average, 4× faster than opt-kLPG.

Columns 6 and 7, in Table 1, list the corresponding results for BnB-SPM [14]. This approach uses a statistical delay model and selects paths that have the highest critical probabilities. For this reason the quality factor($\Omega([9])$) of BnB-SPM is similar to that of the proposed approach. However, BnB-SPM uses an exhaustive search strategy, as described earlier in this Section, for selecting the k paths through each gate. This is reflected in the time taken by this approach. Notice that the proposed approach is, on average, 7.4× faster than BnB-SPM.

5. CONCLUSION

In this paper, we proposed an effective path selection method which uses the probabilistic delay model to select paths capable of detecting defects occurring due to isolated local process variations. The proposed heuristic for statistical path tracing was shown to be considerably faster than the existing statistical critical path selection method.

6. REFERENCES

[1] J. Chung, J. Xiong, V. Zolotov, and J. Abraham. Testability-driven statistical path selection. *IEEE Transactions on Computer-Aided Design of Integrated Circuits and Systems*, 31(8):1275–1287, Aug 2012.

[2] J. Jiang, M. Sauer, A. Czutro, B. Becker, and I. Polian. On the optimality of k longest path generation algorithm under memory constraints. In *Design, Automation Test in Europe Conference Exhibition (DATE), 2012*, pages 418–423, March 2012.

[3] J. Kim, J. Whittemore, J. a. P. Marques-Silva, and K. Sakallah. On applying incremental satisfiability to delay fault testing. In *Proceedings of the Conference on Design, Automation and Test in Europe*, pages 380–384, 2000.

[4] W. N. Li, S. M. Reddy, and S. Sahni. On path selection in combinational logic circuits. *IEEE Transactions on Computer-Aided Design of Integrated Circuits and Systems*, 8(1):56–63, Jan 1989.

[5] X. Lu, Z. Li, W. Qiu, D. Walker, and W. Shi. Longest path selection for delay test under process variation. In *Asia and South Pacific Design Automation Conference*, pages 98–103, Jan 2004.

[6] A. Murakami, S. Kajihara, T. Sasao, I. Pomeranz, and S. M. Reddy. Selection of potentially testable path delay faults for test generation. In *Proceedings IEEE Internation Test Conference*, pages 376–384, 2000.

[7] S. Padmanaban and S. Tragoudas. Efficient identification of (critical) testable path delay faults using decision diagrams. *IEEE Transactions on Computer-Aided Design of Integrated Circuits and Systems*, 24(1):77–87, Jan 2005.

[8] W. Qiu and D. M. H. Walker. An efficient algorithm for finding the k longest testable paths through each gate in a combinational circuit. In *Proceedings of IEEE International Test Conference*, pages 592–601, Oct 2003.

[9] Y. Shao, S. M. Reddy, I. Pomeranz, and S. Kajihara. On selecting testable paths in scan designs. *Journal of Electronic Testing*, 19(4):447–456, 2003.

[10] M. Sharma and J. H. Patel. Finding a small set of longest testable paths that cover every gate. In *Proceedings of IEEE International Test Conference*, pages 974–982, Oct 2002.

[11] A. M. Somashekar, S. Tragoudas, R. Jayabharathi, and S. Gangadhar. Non-enumerative generation of path delay distributions and its application to critical path selection. *ACM Trans. Des. Autom. Electron. Syst.*, 22(1):17:1–17:21, Dec. 2016.

[12] C. Visweswariah, K. Ravindran, K. Kalafala, S. Walker, S. Narayan, D. Beece, J. Piaget, N. Venkateswaran, and J. Hemmett. First-order incremental block-based statistical timing analysis. *IEEE Transactions on Computer-Aided Design of Integrated Circuits and Systems*, 25(10):2170–2180, Oct 2006.

[13] L.-C. Wang, J.-J. Liou, and K.-T. Cheng. Critical path selection for delay fault testing based upon a statistical timing model. *IEEE Transactions on Computer-Aided Design of Integrated Circuits and Systems*, 23(11):1550–1565, Nov 2004.

[14] V. Zolotov, J. Xiong, H. Fatemi, and C. Visweswariah. Statistical path selection for at-speed test. *IEEE Transactions on Computer-Aided Design of Integrated Circuits and Systems*, 29(5):749–759, May 2010.

Combining Restorability and Error Detection Ability for Effective Trace Signal Selection

Binod Kumar
CADSL, IIT Bombay, India
binodkumar@ee.iitb.ac.in

Ankit Jindal
CADSL, IIT Bombay, India
ankitjindal@ee.iitb.ac.in

Masahiro Fujita
University of Tokyo, Japan
fujita@ee.t.u-tokyo.ac.jp

Virendra Singh
CADSL, IIT Bombay, India
viren@ee.iitb.ac.in

ABSTRACT

Persistent growth in design complexity has led to increased chances of bugs appearing during post-silicon validation. Debugging errors at this stage requires some arrangement for expanding the observability of internal signals of the design. Limited number of trace buffers help in increasing visibility of these internal states. However, appropriate trace signal selection is very difficult. Restorability of untraced states with the help of traced ones is a popular approach for signal selection although it fails to address the main issue of error detection. We propose a signal selection methodology which combines the restoration capability and error detection ability of these signals. Experimental evaluation of the proposed signal selection approach on benchmark circuits indicates improved error detection for various kind of design errors. Practical consideration like minimizing routing overhead has also been analyzed.

Keywords

Restoration; Trace signal selection; Error detection; Post-silicon validation; Trace buffers

1. INTRODUCTION

Surge in demand of miniature size and power efficient devices enabled with rich features has led to enormous design complexity of VLSI circuits in present era. This has increased the chances of functional as well as electrical errors escaping to the first released silicon. Owing to the complexity of designs, verification methods employed at pre-silicon stage such as design emulation, logic simulation and formal techniques are not sufficient to address issues that appear in actual silicon. This inefficiency of pre-silicon techniques has led to inevitability of post-silicon validation methods [9]. At the post-silicon stage, debugging and isolating the root cause of functional failures due to design bugs plays an important role in bringing down the number of re-spins required for a chip. However, the practice of debug and root-cause analysis of the first silicon lot becomes very challenging because of limited accessibility of internal signals of the design which is easily available at the pre-silicon stage.

To address the problem of restricted observability of internal states, one solution is placing limited number of trace buffers and capturing some signals for limited clock cycles[2]. Selecting these *important* signals (i.e., trace signals) in case of regular designs like microprocessors (instruction footprint recording as in [10]) can be performed systematically as compared to general VLSI designs. For these designs, various researchers have proposed and developed signal selection algorithms which are aimed at maximizing the observability enhancement. This is achieved through principles of state restoration of untraced signal values with the help of traced ones. This technique is useful as the observability of internal states is increased despite placing only limited number of trace buffers. However, these signal selection approaches fail to address the error detection ability of these signals which may result into the information obtained from trace buffers being less useful for validation/debugging.

This paper proposes a signal selection methodology which combines the best of both the features required for a quick debug and root-cause isolation process: restorability as well as error detection capability of trace signals. While selection from the viewpoint of restoration capability helps in achieving an enlarged view of internal states with the help of traced signals, selecting signals capable of error detection ensures that the information obtained from these on-chip buffers is important for the debug process. It is absolutely necessity to contain the congestion due to routing of these on-chip trace buffers. For this purpose, we analyze the routing overhead resulting from these trace signals and relate it with the other two parameters (restoration and error detection). The rest of the paper is organized as follows. Related work is briefly analyzed and motivation is explained in Section 2. The proposed signal selection methodology is explained in detail in Section 3 and Section 4. The evaluation criteria for the proposed signal selection methodology is explained in Section 5. The experimental results for various benchmark circuits are discussed in Section 6. Finally, the paper is concluded in Section 7 with some directions on future research.

Permission to make digital or hard copies of all or part of this work for personal or classroom use is granted without fee provided that copies are not made or distributed for profit or commercial advantage and that copies bear this notice and the full citation on the first page. Copyrights for components of this work owned by others than ACM must be honored. Abstracting with credit is permitted. To copy otherwise, or republish, to post on servers or to redistribute to lists, requires prior specific permission and/or a fee. Request permissions from permissions@acm.org.

GLSVLSI '17 May 10-12, 2017, Banff, AB, Canada
© 2017 ACM. ISBN 978-1-4503-4972-7/17/05...$15.00
DOI: http://dx.doi.org/10.1145/3060403.3060475

2. BACKGROUND AND MOTIVATION

2.1 Related work

Trace buffers assist in observability enhancement by storing certain signals for a fixed number of clock cycles. Owing to the area overhead constraint, very few signal states can be visualized with this technique. The concept of *state restoration*[7] can be applied to overcome this limitation of trace buffers. By applying forward propagation and backward justification, untraced signal states can be inferred from the traced ones. For the purpose of illustration of usage of the restoration technique at post-silicon validation/debugging stage, we consider Fig. 1 ([3, 11]) as a running example.

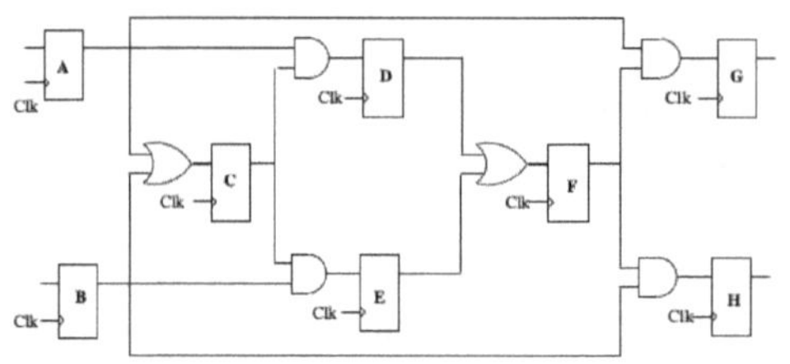

Figure 1: Circuit for illustration [3, 11]

Suppose, a logic bug is introduced into the above design. Table 1 reports the restored states when FFs C and F are traced (assuming buffer width as 2) for five clock cycles (c1-c5). As it is evident from Table 1, barring a few states (represented as X) all other states of the design are restored. If restoration technique is not applied, we know only 10 signal values out of total 40 signal values. However, by applying restoration approach, we can discover additional 20 signal values. Therefore, internal signals visibility expands from 10 to 30, which is quite significant.

Table 1: Restored States Illustration

FF	A	B	**C**	D	E	**F**	G	H
c1	X	X	**1**	0	0	**0**	X	X
c2	0	0	**1**	0	0	**0**	0	0
c3	0	0	**0**	0	0	**0**	0	0
c4	X	X	**0**	0	0	**0**	0	0
c5	X	X	**1**	X	X	**0**	0	0

By comparison with corresponding golden response, the error can be detected. Note that post-silicon errors do not reach the primary output (PO) in many cases or their manifestation at PO occurs after many clock cycles. If the error propagates to any/all of these internal signals, the error localization effort can be reduced with the help of state restoration as we can observe large number of internal signals. Signal selection techniques [11, 3, 8, 6] use "Restoration Ratio (RR)" as a metric to evaluate the efficacy of signal selection since it serves as a measure of extent of observability enhancement. It is defined as follows:

$$RR = \frac{no.\ of\ signals\ traced + no.\ of\ signals\ restored}{no.\ of\ signals\ traced} \tag{1}$$

As is evident from Table 1, traced states are 10 and restored states are 20, RR comes out to be 3 for this scenario. For maximizing observability of internal states (RR), heuristics based [11, 3], simulation based [6] or a mix of heuristics and simulation [8] has been employed. However, these methods do not consider the error detection ability of the trace signals resulting in an ineffective trace signal selection from the viewpoint of error detection/localization.

2.2 Motivation

For the example circuit (Fig. 1), we analyze the ability of each of the trace signals to detect design errors. Generally, no standard design error models are available like those of manufacturing testing [9]. However, for gate level design descriptions, some cases of design bugs include missing gate or inputs to gates, gate replacements, incorrectly placed input wires, extra inverters or extra wires [5, 1]. We introduce two kind of errors (four iterations for each error): random replacement of gate with another (rgr) and exchange of some of the wires of the circuit with one another (wex). The four iterations of these bugs are referred to as $rgr1$, $rgr2$, $rgr3$, $rgr4$, $wex1$, $wex2$, $wex3$ and $wex4$. In Table 2, we report whether the error is captured by the flip-flop (trace signal) or not by the FF (1-detected, 0-not detected).

Table 2: Error detection by trace signals

Error	A	B	C	D	E	F	G	H
$rgr1$	0	0	0	1	0	1	1	1
$rgr2$	0	0	1	1	1	1	1	1
$rgr3$	0	0	1	1	1	1	1	1
$rgr4$	0	0	0	0	0	0	0	1
$wex1$	0	0	1	1	0	1	1	1
$wex2$	0	0	0	0	0	1	1	1
$wex3$	0	0	0	0	1	1	1	1
$wex4$	0	0	1	0	1	0	1	0

For the example circuit (Fig. 1), if trace buffer width is 2, some trace signal selection (out of different possible combinations) as per RR maximization principle are: A and C[3] or C and F[7] or A and B[11]. It can be observed from Table 2 that these trace signals have different error detection ability from each other. However, the major drawback in deciding the trace signals based on error detection of certain kind of errors (selection approach presented by Vali et al. [13] for bit-flip errors) is that this restricts the efficacy of these signals to those errors/bugs. While debugging hard to find errors, the visibility of complete internal signals for some part of the circuit is required. For this purpose, scan chains have been used with appreciable success. However, in this scenario, circuit execution needs to be halted for felicitating read-out of internal values. This can be avoided by the usage of trace buffers.

During localization of difficult to find bugs, some states can be read-out from these buffers in a non-destructive fashion and a sizable portion of the remaining states can be known with the help of state restoration technique. Thus, we formulate our signal selection technique considering both parameters: error detection ability and restoration capability of the trace signals.

3. PROPOSED METHODOLOGY OF SIGNAL SELECTION

The proposed methodology focuses on the selection of trace signals from two groups of ranked signals: S_{res} (signals leading to high restoration) and S_{ed} (signals capable of maximum error detection). This can be described as follows:

$$Signals(S) = k * S_{res} + (1 - k) * S_{ed} \tag{2}$$

Here, k is a factor which depends on the number of trace signals to be selected. Typically, it may vary between 0 & 1, corresponding to extreme choices of the signal selection.

To capture the error at some/all of the traced FFs, the error must propagate to some/all of them. This in turn depends on the gates present along the combinational paths between flip-flops. To determine the error propagation, the controlling input values of these gates must be known. One method to obtain these values is through execution of the buggy circuit/design. However, the signal selection has to be done at the design stage itself. Another kind of approach is to obtain conditional probabilities of signal transition at the inputs of these gates [4]. However, for the purpose of ranking of the signals, the actual determination of these probabilities depend on simulating the design for some inputs making the ranking dependent on these inputs. We propose a different technique to account for the error detection ability of the trace signals in our methodology.

3.1 The proposed methodology

The proposed methodology selects signals such that error detection is maximized and the restoration of untraced states is also high. We first introduce the terminology for various parameters to be used in rest of the paper.

3.1.1 *Terminologies used*

Table 3: Terms and their meaning

Term	Meaning
RR(S_{res})	Restoration Ratio of S_{res} group
RR(S_{ed})	Restoration Ratio of S_{ed} group
N	Trace buffer width
k	partitioning factor
S	final group of N signals
n	number of partitions

3.1.2 *The methodology*

The methodology begins with the group of signals having high restoration ratio (S_{res}), creates the group of signals capable of error detection (S_{ed}) and performs final selection for N signals based on S_{res} and S_{ed}. Note that signals of S_{res} can be obtained by any of the reported restorability techniques [11, 3, 8, 6] or any other such methodology. The methodology takes 2 inputs: n and k depending on the level of granularity desired for selecting the final set of N signals. These parameters can vary from one circuit to another and need to be fixed at design stage.

S_{ed} is created using topological analysis of the design, accounting for error propagation to all the candidate trace signals (flip-flops). Apart from the number of connections a flip-flop has with other flip-flops, the nature of combinational logic along paths between two flip-flops is also important. For example- if a path contains a NOT gate while other path contains NOT/OR gate(s), then signal transmission (i.e., error propagation) is not identical in both cases. $S_{ed}build()$ part of the proposed signal selection methodology is based on this observation.

procedure *SelectSignal*(In:*Design*,S_{res},n,k; Out:S_{ed},S)
    $S_{ed}build()\{$
    for each flip-flop FF_i in *Design* **do**
        check all incoming paths to FF_i
        for each FF_j linked to FF_i by incoming path **do**
            count no. of inputs(*inps*) for each gate
            $pscore_{ed} \leftarrow \prod(1/inps)$ for gates along path
        end for
        $score_{ed} \leftarrow \Sigma\ pscore_{ed}$
    end for
    $S_{ed}^{temp} \leftarrow$ sort each FF by its $score_{ed}$
    $S_{ed} \leftarrow$ top N signals from S_{ed}^{temp}
    $\}$
    current partition(*cp*) = 1
    while $cp < n$ **do**
        $S_1 \leftarrow k{*}S_{res}$
        $S_2 \leftarrow (1\text{-}k){*}S_{ed}$
        $common \leftarrow S_1 \cap S_2$
        if $common$!= $\emptyset$ **then**
            remove *common* from S_2
            add next element(s) from S_{ed} to S_2
        end if
        $S' \leftarrow S_1 \cup S_2$
        Evaluate RR for S'
        $cp = cp + 1$
    end while
    $S \leftarrow S'$ for which RR is highest
end procedure

In the beginning, both the sets, S_{ed} and S_{res} have N elements (signals) each. Then, the procedure creates different partitions (by using partitioning factor, k) of the two groups ($score_{ed}$ and $score_{res}$) such that always N signals are selected and at each stage of partition, Restoration Ratio (RR) is evaluated. We illustrate the method of assigning $score_{ed}$ to different trace signals and the final trace signal selection by taking an example in the next subsection. The worst case time complexity of the above algorithm is $O(N_{path})$ where N_{path} is the number of paths in the circuit netlist.

The proposed methodology is scalable in the same manner as any of the restorability techniques [11, 3, 8, 6]. For a large design, the restorability calculation and error detection ability computation can be carried out independently for different sub-modules of the design and then the proposed signal selection methodology can be applied.

3.2 Illustration of methodology

For the gate level representation (Fig. 2) of a portion of an example design, instead of showing various partitions we exhaustively explore the possible options of trace signal selection given that trace buffer width is 2.

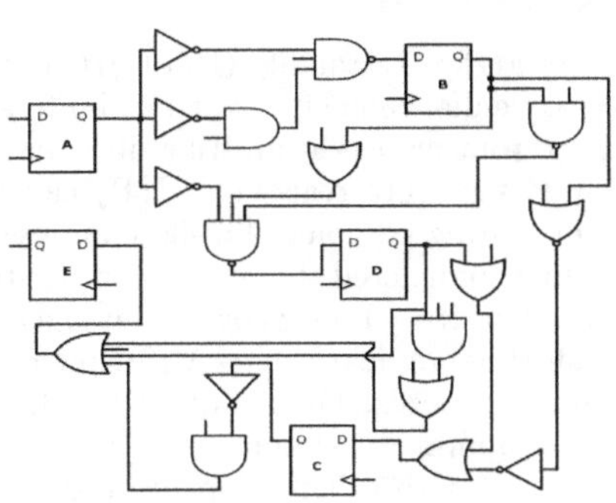

Figure 2: Circuit for illustrating methodology

Note that for brevity in illustrating the methodology, only some of the inputs of the gates are shown in the above diagram. Let's assume that these inputs are connected to PIs (primary inputs). By $S_{ed}build()$ portion of the procedure (*SelectSignal*) described in above sub-section, for the partial gate level netlist shown above, $score_{ed}$ of different candidate trace signals (flip-flops) are given as follows:

1. $score_{ed}$(A) = 0

Table 4: Illustration of possible TSC

TSC	*RR*	$score_{ed}(1)$	$score_{ed}(2)$	$\Sigma\ score_{ed}$
C,B	1.08	0.50	0.50	1.00
C,A	1.68	0.50	0	0.50
E,A	1.66	0.42	0	0.42
E,C	1.25	0.42	0.50	0.92
B,D	1.63	0.50	0.67	1.17
E,B	1.58	0.42	0.50	0.92
C,D	1.80	0.50	0.67	1.17
A,D	1.90	0	0.67	0.67
B,A	1.81	0.50	0	0.50
E,D	1.46	0.42	0.67	1.09

2. $score_{ed}$(B) = 1*1/2*1/3 + 1*1/3 = 0.50
3. $score_{ed}$(C) = 1*1/2*1/2 + 1/2*1/2 = 0.50
4. $score_{ed}$(D) = 1*1/3 + 1/2*1/3 + 1/2*1/3 = 0.67
5. $score_{ed}$(E) = 1*1/2*1/4 + 1/2*1/3*1/4 + 1/4 = 0.42

With the ranking of trace signals as per above $score_{ed}$, the ordering of the candidate trace signal in the set S_{ed} is given by {B,E,D,C,A}. Next, we check RR for each possible combination of trace signals for N=2. As we have total 5 signals, there are a total of 10 candidates for selection. Table 4 shows the different trace signal combinations (TSC), the corresponding RR obtained, the $score_{ed}$ of the two signals (i.e., $score_{ed}(1)$, $score_{ed}(2)$) and the sum of $score_{ed}$ of this combination of signals. The RR values are obtained with simulation with random inputs for 100 cycles. This parameter ($\Sigma\ score_{ed}$) is an indication of the error detection with the help of respective TSC.

As it is evident from the above Table, TSC with maximum RR does not have highest $\Sigma\ score_{ed}$, suggesting the need of a joint trace signal selection methodology. For the different combinations presented in this table, the choice of {C,D} (with the highest $\Sigma\ score_{ed}$) is profitable as its restoration ability (indicated by RR) is higher than the other signal combination with same $\Sigma\ score_{ed}$ (i.e., {B,D}).

4. PRACTICAL CONSIDERATION FOR SIGNAL SELECTION

Similar to Design-for-Testability (DfT) structures, Design-for-Debug (DfD) enhancements like trace buffers introduce on-chip area and routing overhead. To reduce area overhead, a multiple input signature register (MISR) can be used so that instead of storing complete flip-flop values for certain clock cycles, time compacted signatures can be stored. This reduces the depth of trace buffer however at the cost of drastically diminished debug features as MISR introduces aliasing in response signatures. On the other hand, the routing overhead can be minimized simply by a layout aware trace signal selection [12] with a little impact on debug features. We analyze the impact of layout aware signal selection on the proposed signal selection methodology, *SelectSignal* which optimizes two key parameters (*RR* and *Error detection*). The key goal here is to select those signals which are near to trace buffer (thereby reducing the *wire-length* and hence routing congestion) while keeping a balance between restoration and error detection ability of these signals.

As a representative of routing congestion, *wire-length* is used. For calculating *wire-length*, euclidean distance is employed in place of manhattan distance (utilized in [12]). Assuming (x_{tb}, y_{tb}) are the coordinates of trace buffer and (x_i, y_i) are coordinates of ith traced flip-flop (signal), total euclidean distance for N signals is computed by Eqn-4 (which utilizes Eqn-3).

$$dist_i = \sqrt{(x_{tb} - x_i)^2 + (y_{tb} - y_i)^2} \tag{3}$$

$$dist(N) = \sum_{i=1}^{N} dist_i \tag{4}$$

Analysis of trade-off between restoration, error detection and *dist(N)* helps in selecting most profitable set of signals suitable for a practical implementation as they would incur minimum routing congestion.

5. EVALUATION CRITERION

Given the requirement that N trace signals are to be selected by the proposed methodology, N_1 signals are chosen from S_{res} and N_2 signals are chosen from S_{ed}. This is represented by Eqn-5. Note that if N_2=0, N=N_1=N_{res} and if N_1=0, N=N_2=N_{ed}.

$$N = N_1 + N_2 \tag{5}$$

- To measure the change (mainly degradation is expected) with the proposed set of trace signals as compared to a signal set capable of high restorability, we define the following metric:

$$\Delta(RR) = RR(N) - RR(N_{res}) \tag{6}$$

- Similar to the above metric, as a measure of routing congestion, the euclidean-distance for the proposed set of trace signals with respect to signal set capable of having high restoration ratio (RR), the following metric is defined:

$$dist\_factor = \frac{dist(N)}{dist(N_{res})} \tag{7}$$

- From the view-point of debugging, a measure of the efficacy of the signal selection can be defined as the number of erroneous responses (i.e., states) observed at the traced flip-flops. The reasoning behind it lies in the fact that if the responses (i.e., states) captured at the traced flip-flops matches exactly with the golden responses (i.e., states), we don't get many clues regarding the location of the bug.

$$det_{err} = \frac{erroneous\ responses}{total\ number\ of\ responses} \tag{8}$$

6. EXPERIMENTAL RESULTS AND DISCUSSION

For illustrating the proposed methodology, we show the derivation of final N trace signals with n=5 and k=10% of N. As is the general practice with signal selection methodologies [11, 3, 8, 6], we chose N=32 here.

To evaluate the efficacy of the proposed signal selection, we have performed experiments with different kind of design bugs for ISCAS'89 benchmark circuits. For the selected trace signal set, RR (restoration ratio) and error detection needs to be compared with a methodology which only caters to achieving high restorability with the trace signals (we consider the restoration technique presented in [8]).

6.1 Restorability(RR) variation

Table 5 shows the different partitions of candidate trace signals from the two sets S_{res} and S_{ed} to obtain final N signals as per the proposed methodology. It is clear that as N_1 increases, $\Delta(RR)$ reduces implying that restoration obtained from selected set of signals is getting closer to that of RR obtained from signals selected as per technique proposed in [8]. Note that beyond a certain partition, either decrease in $\Delta(RR)$ becomes minuscule or it even increases slightly. The choice of the final set of N_1 and N_2 is to be done accordingly. Also, increasing N_1 reduces N_2 which is undesirable as signals in N_2 are more capable of error detection as compared to N_1. Hence, for s13207 circuit, the final N signals include N_1=15, N_2=17 whereas for s15850 circuit, the corresponding set includes N_1=9, N_2=23. Note the difference in the two case. The contribution of N_1 and N_2 towards final set of N signals is reported in Table 6 and Table 7 for all the benchmark circuits.

Interestingly, the negative values of $\Delta(RR)$ (which means RR of signal set by proposed methodology is less than that of [8]) are not observed for some circuits. Instead, positive values are observed due to the reason that restoration depends (to some extent) on factors like inputs applied for performing the restorability simulation and number of cycles for which the restoration is carried out. Within our simulation set-up, the proposed signal set outperformed the signals of [8] for s38584 circuit by large margin. The variation of RR with the increase in N_1 is shown in Fig-3. Note that tracing 32 flip-flops out of hundreds of total flip-flops (indicated in $FFtotal$ column) of the design does not introduce significant area overhead.

Table 5: Variation in Euclidean distance and Restoration Ratio for different trace signal selection

Circuit	*FFtotal*	N	N_1	N_2	$\Delta(RR)$	$dist(N)$
			3	29	-5.62	3237275
			6	26	-4.12	3319320
s13207	638	32	9	23	-4.18	3206742
			12	20	-3.73	3078070
			15	17	-2.5	2931768
			3	29	-11.14	4039295
			6	26	-11.09	4097012
s15850	534	32	9	23	-0.96	4225186
			12	20	-1.02	4261473
			15	17	-1.02	4279689
			3	29	-19.65	5328104
			6	26	-19.75	5286150
s35932	1728	32	9	23	0.62	5154906
			12	20	0.54	5286643
			15	17	0.46	5507580
			3	29	-5.62	6998971
			6	26	-4.12	6975643
s38417	1636	32	9	23	-4.18	6954786
			12	20	-3.73	6876532
			15	17	-2.5	6786534
			3	29	9.44	7927297
			6	26	10.06	8054481
s38584	1426	32	9	23	10.39	8244191
			12	20	10.53	8509850
			15	17	9.98	8656889

In the above Table, last column represents the sum of euclidean distance for selected N signals as per different partitions. There is considerable variation in the euclidean-distance sum suggesting an optimized selection is capable of diminishing the routing congestion. A plot of variation in *dist_factor* v/s N_1 is shown in Fig. 4. If the metric, *dist_factor* has a value smaller than unity, the proposed signal set (i.e., signals after partitions) has less routing congestion than those of [8]. For the cases, where this metric has a value higher than unity, the proposed signal set has degraded the situation. Therefore, $dist(N)$ parameters must be an essential constituent of the signal selection process.

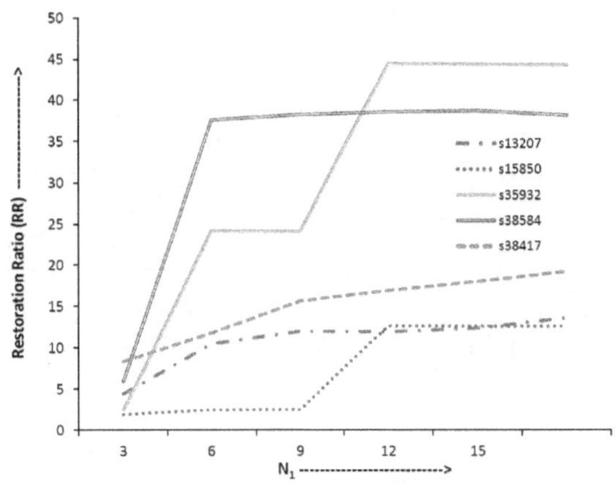

Figure 3: Variation in RR with N_1

The variation of RR with N_1 (shown in Fig-3) supports our hypothesis of the need of selection from two set of signals (i.e., a combined selection) instead of a selection based on a single parameter. The improvement in error detection (a major advantage with our selection) is explained next.

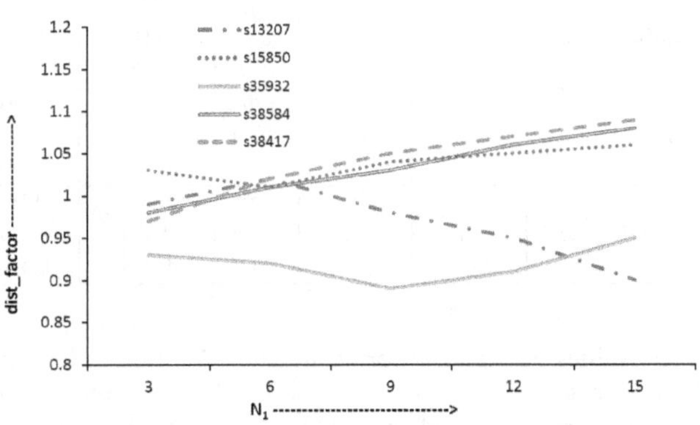

Figure 4: Variation in $dist\_factor$ with N_1

6.2 Improvement in error detection

We performed experiments by two different methods to assess the error detection with the proposed signal selection and that of [8].

- We injected random gate replacements into the design description for 1000 times. The detection with the set of signals was noted after each iteration.
- In each iteration, we inject a different bug into the design description- rgr (random gate replacement), wex (wire exchange) and exi (extra inverter insertion).

The results for the above two methods of error injection are reported in Table 6 and Table 7 respectively. The signals selected by the proposed methodology capture more erroneous responses as compared to [8] (implied by high values of det_{err} over $det_{err}[8]$). Note that the values reported in Table 6 are averaged over 1000 times to avoid any bias towards a particular bug injection. We report the restoration ratio values also in this table. As mentioned in previous subsection, RR values with the proposed methodology are quite close to that of [8]. Therefore, there is minuscule RR degradation for selected signals. Note that for s38584 circuit, the trace signal set from the proposed technique achieves quite higher RR than that of [8].

Table 6: Comparison with only-restorability technique: 1000 iterations of rgr bug

Circuit	N_1	N_2	$det_{err}[8]$	det_{err}	$RR[8]$	RR
s13207	15	17	0.78	0.92	16.10	13.60
s15850	9	23	0.97	0.99	13.59	12.63
s35932	9	23	0.22	0.51	43.84	44.46
s38584	12	20	0.95	1.00	28.15	38.68
s38417	15	17	0.45	0.77	20.95	19.21

Table 7: Comparison with only-restorability technique: 3 different bugs

Circuit	N	$N_1(\%)$	$N_2(\%)$	*bug*	$det_{err}[8]$	det_{err}
s13207	32	47	53	*rgr*	0.69	0.93
				wex	0.99	1.00
				exi	0.97	0.99
s15850	32	28	72	*rgr*	1.00	1.00
				wex	0.97	1.00
				exi	0.97	1.00
s35932	32	28	72	*rgr*	0.11	0.42
				wex	0.99	1.00
				exi	0.26	0.26
s38584	32	38	62	*rgr*	0.89	0.96
				wex	0.99	1.00
				exi	0.99	0.99
s38417	32	47	53	*rgr*	0.96	0.99
				wex	1.00	1.00
				exi	0.93	0.97

The values of det_{err} reported in Table 7 show wide variability for some bugs. However, with the proposed signal set, det_{err} values are either equal or greater than that of [8] in all the cases, suggesting that the proposed selection is profitable for these kind of bugs.

7. CONCLUSION

During post-silicon validation, a large number of inputs can be applied to explore a wide portion of the state space of design. In spite of this advantage, debugging becomes very difficult due to highly restricted visibility at this stage. Trace buffers help to overcome this obstacle by tracing few signals. This paper presented a methodology for signal selection such that the visibility of internal signals is expanded and the signals are capable of error detection as well. The methodology needs to be refined considering the routing congestion and area overhead constraints for a highly effective trace signal selection. We intend to evaluate the impact of the restored states on bug detection and relate error localization/detection with the restoration of the untraced states in an explicit manner.

8. REFERENCES

[1] E. J. Aas, K. Klingsheim, and T. Steen. Quantifying design quality: a model and design experiments. In *Euro ASIC '92, Proceedings.*, pages 172–177, Jun 1992.

[2] M. Abramovici, P. Bradley, K. Dwarakanath, P. Levin, G. Memmi, and D. Miller. A reconfigurable design-for-debug infrastructure for socs. In *2006 43rd ACM/IEEE Design Automation Conference*, pages 7–12, 2006.

[3] K. Basu and P. Mishra. Rats: Restoration-aware trace signal selection for post-silicon validation. *IEEE Transactions on Very Large Scale Integration (VLSI) Systems*, 21(4):605–613, April 2013.

[4] K. Basu, P. Mishra, P. Patra, A. Nahir, and A. Adir. Dynamic selection of trace signals for post-silicon debug. In *14th International Workshop on Microprocessor Test and Verification*, pages 62–67, Dec 2013.

[5] D. V. Campenhout, T. Mudge, and J. P. Hayes. Collection and analysis of microprocessor design errors. *IEEE Design Test of Computers*, 17(4):51–60, Oct 2000.

[6] D. Chatterjee, C. McCarter, and V. Bertacco. Simulation-based signal selection for state restoration in silicon debug. In *2011 IEEE/ACM International Conference on Computer-Aided Design (ICCAD)*, pages 595–601, Nov 2011.

[7] H. F. Ko and N. Nicolici. Algorithms for state restoration and trace-signal selection for data acquisition in silicon debug. *IEEE Transactions on Computer-Aided Design of Integrated Circuits and Systems*, 28(2):285–297, Feb 2009.

[8] M. Li and A. Davoodi. A hybrid approach for fast and accurate trace signal selection for post-silicon debug. In *Design, Automation Test in Europe Conference Exhibition (DATE), 2013*, pages 485–490, March 2013.

[9] S. Mitra, S. A. Seshia, and N. Nicolici. Post-silicon validation opportunities, challenges and recent advances. In *Design Automation Conference (DAC), 2010 47th ACM/IEEE*, pages 12–17, June 2010.

[10] S. B. Park and S. Mitra. Ifra: Instruction footprint recording and analysis for post-silicon bug localization in processors. In *Design Automation Conference, 2008. DAC 2008. 45th ACM/IEEE*, pages 373–378, June 2008.

[11] K. Rahmani, P. Mishra, and S. Ray. Efficient trace signal selection using augmentation and ilp techniques. In *Fifteenth International Symposium on Quality Electronic Design*, pages 148–155, March 2014.

[12] P. Thakyal and P. Mishra. Layout-aware selection of trace signals for post-silicon debug. In *2014 IEEE Computer Society Annual Symposium on VLSI*, pages 326–331, July 2014.

[13] A. Vali and N. Nicolici. Bit-flip detection-driven selection of trace signals. In *2016 21th IEEE European Test Symposium (ETS)*, pages 1–6, May 2016.

Radiation-Hardened Designs for Soft-Error-Rate Reduction by Delay-Adjustable D-Flip-Flops

Yuwen (Dave) Lin
Department of Electrical and Computer Engineering,
National Chiao Tung Univ.,
Hsinchu, Taiwan 300
linyeuwen0112.eed04g@g2.nctu.edu.tw

Charles H.-P. Wen
Department of Electrical and Computer Engineering,
National Chiao Tung Univ.,
Hsinchu, Taiwan 300
opwen@g2.nctu.edu.tw

Herming Chiueh
Department of Electrical and Computer Engineering,
National Chiao Tung Univ.,
Hsinchu, Taiwan 300
chiueh@soclab.org

ABSTRACT

For reducing soft error rate (SER) in system-level failures, this paper proposes a radiation-hardened design by **D**elay-**A**djustable **D** **F**lip-**F**lop (**DAD-FF**), which can be generally applied to sequential circuits such as shift registers. DAD-FF, modified from the Built-In Soft-Error Resilience (BISER) latch, can be easily integrated in the CAD flow and its delay can be adjusted to reject particle strikes with the maximum energy level. As a result, at the device level, DAD-FF eliminates 99.999997%[1] soft errors by heavy ions on a satellite orbiting at a height of 720 km, and shows greater reduction on SER (e.g. 1.3×10^{10}X in the best case) than the standard DFF (STD-FF) through TCAD and SPICE simulation. Moreover, a real chip was also fabricated in a CMOS 90nm technology and performed the experiment of radiation exposure in UCL, Belgium. The laboratory measurement indicates that at the system level, the radiation-hardened design by DAD-FFs achieves 15.69X and 2.62X improvements on the overall SER, compared with those by STD-FFs and DICEs, respectively.

Keywords

soft error, single-event transient (SET), radiation hardening, modified cad flow, heavy ion, tcad simulation, radiation exposure measurement.

1. INTRODUCTION

The continued scaling of technology nodes brings about many technical benefits such as faster clock frequency and less area overhead. However, such advance also makes electronic devices more vulnerable and reliability becomes one of the most important issues in VLSI designs. Soft error induced by radiation is one key factor of system-level reliability and stems from single-event transients (SETs) and single-event upsets (SEUs) [1, 4, 5]. Once a SET/SEU is latched by a memory element, a system failure occurs and makes the design out of work. Moreover, in the nanometer era, the smaller transistor size as well as the faster clock frequency results in higher latching probability for SETs/SEUs and thus worsens the problem of system failures [2, 11].

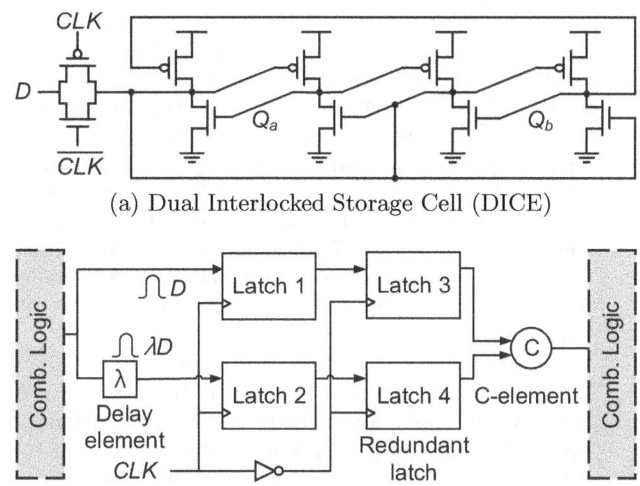

(a) Dual Interlocked Storage Cell (DICE)

(b) Built-In Soft-Error Resilience (BISER)

Figure 1: Important types of radiation-hardened designs

As a consequence, a series of radiation-hardening techniques [6, 10] are proposed to deal with soft errors, including Dual Interlocked Storage Cell (DICE) and Built-In Soft-Error Resilience (BISER). As shown in Figure 1(a), in a DICE, the feedback storage node is an important feature where a SET/SEU can be eliminated rapidly. However, the input node of DICE is unprotected and thus becomes its fatal weakness. Once a SET/SEU occurs at the input node, such fault will stay in the internal storage and can never be detected. Although the variants of DICE like [8] continue to improve the performance on SER, the problem of input vulnerability remains unsolved.

BISER [10] is another important type of the radiation-hardened flip-flop designs and utilizes the notion of **delayed latching** to mitigate SETs. Figure 1(b) illustrates the architecture of a BISER flip-flop; latch 1 and latch 3 form the first data path for the original signal at node D whereas the delay element and redundant latches (i.e. latch 2 and latch 4) form the second data path for the delayed signal at node λD. At the end, C-element checks output signals from latch 3 and latch 4 for error detection. Compared with DICE, BISER has an advantage of simultaneously protecting every node (including the input node) and thus is extended by many later works [12].

[1]Statistical data from http://creme.isde.vanderbilt.edu/

Permission to make digital or hard copies of all or part of this work for personal or classroom use is granted without fee provided that copies are not made or distributed for profit or commercial advantage and that copies bear this notice and the full citation on the first page. Copyrights for components of this work owned by others than the author(s) must be honored. Abstracting with credit is permitted. To copy otherwise, or republish, to post on servers or to redistribute to lists, requires prior specific permission and/or a fee. Request permissions from permissions@acm.org.

GLSVLSI '17, May 10 - 12, 2017, Banff, AB, Canada

© 2017 Copyright held by the owner/author(s). Publication rights licensed to ACM.
ISBN 978-1-4503-4972-7/17/05. . . $15.00

DOI: http://dx.doi.org/10.1145/3060403.3060442

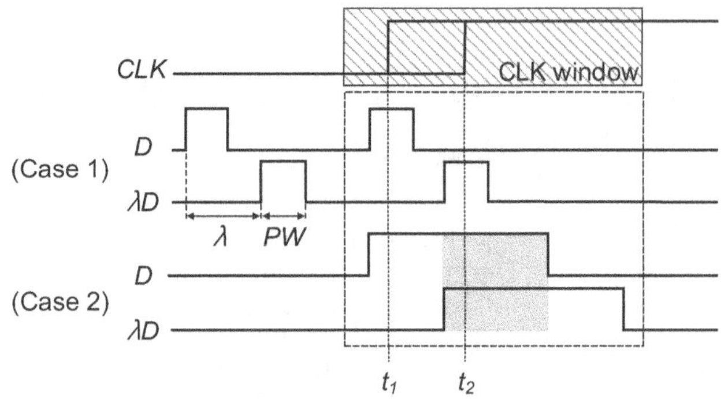

Figure 2: BISER under two different delayed time λs and pulse width PWs

In general, the effectiveness of BISER flip-flops depends upon two factors: (1) the delayed time λ and (2) the pulse width PW of the incoming transient. As shown in Figure 2, the corresponding analysis can be divided into two cases:

- (**case 1**) If the delayed time is larger than the pulse width of the transient (i.e. $\lambda > PW$), the two transients arriving at node D and node λD will become separated completely. Then, whenever the clock signal triggers, the C-element can always detect the conflict of signals coming from two nodes and then sends out the **recompute** message.
- (**case 2**) If the delayed time is smaller than or equal to the pulse width of the transient (i.e. $\lambda \leq PW$), partial overlapping of the two transients will occur, as illustrated by the gray area in Figure 2. Then, if the clock signal triggers outside the gray area (e.g. at t_1), the C-element can successfully detect the conflict of signals as in case 1. But if the clock signal triggers inside the gray area (e.g. at t_2), the C-element will fail to detect the conflict of signals and a soft error occurs.

Hence, according to the above two cases, we understand that the delayed time in BISER is critical not only to the overall performance in timing but also to the resistability to soft errors. It is even better if the delayed time can be determined automatically and the corresponding design overhead can be estimated correctly. Therefore, on the basis of BISER, a **D**elay-**A**djustable **D** **F**lip-**F**lop design named **DAD-FF** is proposed in this work. Moreover, its delayed time can be easily determined in the modified CAD flow according to the maximum energy level of particle strikes in radiation.

Our experimental results indicate that under three different maximum energy levels (i.e. 20, 32, and 69 LETs) of particle strikes in radiation, DAD-FF achieves the 7.9×10^4X, 1.7×10^8X, and 1.3×10^{10}X improvement over the standard flip-flop (STD-FF) on SER, respectively, through SPICE simulation.

Moreover, as to the above three energy levels, DAD-FF statistically rejects 99.76%, 99.999912%, and 99.999997% soft errors on a satellite orbiting at a height of 720 km. In particular, a real chip of 500-stage shift registers implemented with STD-FFs, DAD-FFs and DICEs was fabricated and later tested under the experiment of radiation exposure in UCL[2], Belgium. The laboratory measurement shows that the design by DAD-FFs achieves 15.69X and 2.62X improvements on overall SER than the designs by the STD-FFs and DICEs, respectively. In summary, DAD-FF's resisitability

[2]http://www.uclouvain.be/index.html

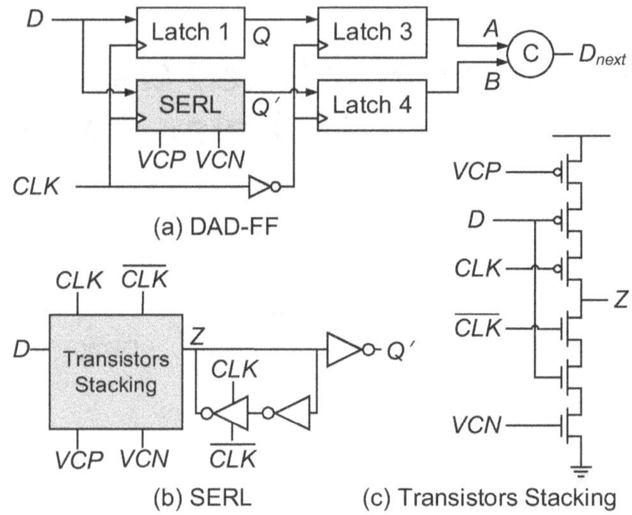

Figure 3: Design structure of DAD-FF and its components

to soft errors is verified under three different maximum energy levels of particle strikes in radiation. Furthermore, the radiation-exposure measurement on the fabricated chip also validates the superiority of the design with DAD-FFs over the designs with STD-FFs and DICEs.

The rest of the paper is organized as follows. Section 2 details the proposed DAD-FF design and the modification on the CAD flow. Section 3 shows the experimental results from the mixed (TACD and SPICE) simulation and the radiation-exposure measurement on the fabricated chip. Finally, Section 4 draws the conclusion.

2. PROPOSED DESIGN AND CAD FLOW

This work not only proposes a delay-adjustable D-Flip-Flop (called DAD-FF) design for radiation hardening but also modifies the CAD flow for integration. To demonstrate the advantages of the modified CAD flow, the design structure of DAD-FF and its related properties will be introduced first. Second, to embody the concept of delay latching, the waveform behavior in DAD-FF is analyzed. Third, instead of using the conventional double-exponential current-source model, a new characterized current-source model derived from technology computer aided design (TCAD) simulation is applied to DAD-FFs for estimating SER correctly. Last, we elaborate the modification on the CAD flow with DAD-FFs and the related design decision (e.g. the delayed time of DAD-FF).

2.1 Design Structure of DAD-FF

As mentioned in Section 1, the delayed time of a DAD-FF determines its resistability to soft errors. Our objective is to apply DAD-FFs to the original design with the modified CAD flow where the corresponding delayed time can be automatically determined. To enable flexibility of the delayed time, DAD-FF merges the delay element into a special type of latches (termed **Soft Error Resilient Latch (SERL)**), as shown in Figure 3(a), where VCP and VCN jointly control the latency of the input signal. Figure 3(b) illustrates the schematic of SERL, which mainly consists of **transistors stacking** and a **signal keeper** (i.e. the three inverters). Transistors stacking as shown in Figure 3(c) is built upon a tri-state buffer and further added with two transis-

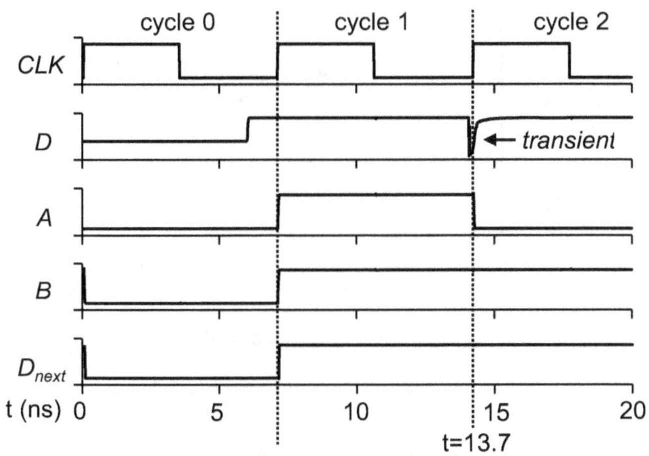

(a) Particle strikes D at 13.7ns

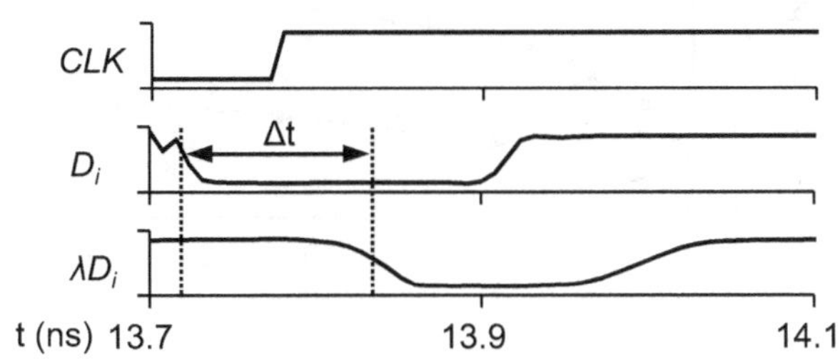

(b) Contribution of delay element

Figure 4: Waveform behavior in DAD-FF

tors controlled by *VCP* and *VCN*, respectively, to determine the latency of the signal from D to Z. Meanwhile, SERL features higher capacitance stacking than BISER and thus induces a single-event transient (SET) with smaller pulse width under the same amount of collected charge. After passing through transistors stacking to node Z, the latched signal is then stored in the signal keeper, which provides signal Q' for latch 4 in the slave stage.

Later, a C-element connects two output nodes (i.e. node A and node B) of latch 3 and latch 4, respectively, as shown in Figure 3(a). Such C-element (initially proposed in BISER [10]) is used for detecting occurrence of soft errors. If two signals at A and B are the same, either no soft error occurs or the soft error cannot be detected as described by **case 2** in Figure 2(b). If two signals at A and B are different, the C-element senses a soft error, excludes the influence of the transient, and keeps the stored value unchanged. Additionally, the C-element will send out a **recompute** signal once detecting a soft error. The recompute technique[3] is frequently used for handling system errors in the computer architecture area.

2.2 Waveform Behavior in DAD-FF

In this section, we would like to further observe the behavior of DAD-FF by waveform as illustrated in Figure 4. D is the input node to DAD-FF; A is the output node of the original data path (i.e. Latch1+Latch3) whereas B is the output node of the delayed data path (i.e. SERL+Latch 4) as mentioned in Figure 3(c). D_{next} is the output node of the entire DAD-FF.

At clock cycle 1, the data of input node D is 1 and therefore A and B are 1. Supposing that a particle strikes node D at t=13.7ns, a voltage transient is induced as the rising edge of the clock triggers from cycle 1 to cycle 2. However, this voltage transient is latched, making node A become 0 instead of 1. Protected by the delay element, node B remains 1 without being affected by the voltage transient. Detecting different values on node A and node B, C-element will send a **recompute** signal and keep the output value unchanged.

More specifically, the contribution of the delay element is elaborated. Figure 4(b) is zoomed into t=13.7ns to t=14.1ns. D_i is the observation node inside latch 1 along the original data path, whereas λD_i is another observation node inside SERL along the delayed data path. It is clear that the delay element results in a time shift by Δt and successfully separates signals at D_i and λD_i. Later, value 0 at node D_i is latched at the rising edge of the clock and makes node A become 0. Meanwhile, influenced by the delay element, node B instead receives value 1 from node λD_i. Such phenomenon explains how DAD-FF eliminates a soft error.

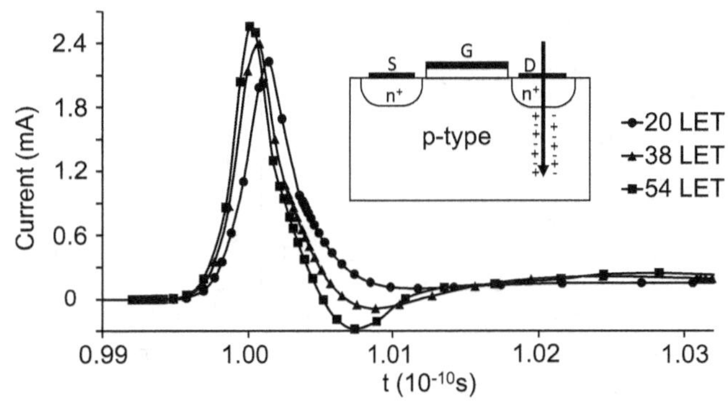

Figure 5: Modelling heavy ion by TCAD simulation

2.3 Transient Modelling for DAD-FF

To precisely understand a transient induced by a particle strike (as shown in Figure 4(a)), a current-source model will be used to describe its behavior. Conventionally, double-exponential current-source model in [9] have been widely utilized for modelling a SET over the decades. However, this model is too simplified so that the nature of the manufacturing process cannot be reflected, especially in the nanometer era [7]. As a result, TCAD is used straight to derive an exact waveform of transient current induced by heavy ions in our solution. Figure 5 shows the result from the TCAD simulation with heavy ions, where its x-axis and y-axis denote time and current, respectively. The waveforms represent the current pulses on the drain of nMOS struck by heavy ions subject to different energy levels (i.e. 20 LET, 38 LET, and 54 LET). Obviously, those waveforms do not match a double-exponential model.

After deriving data points in the current pulse from the TCAD simulation, a look-up table is pre-characterized for a device. Although the TCAD simulation takes long time (e.g. one hour) for a current pulse, the current waveform of a SET can be re-built rapidly (e.g. less than one second) by looking up the pre-characterized table. In other words, the TCAD simulation is a one-time cost. Once the pre-characterized tables are built, transient modelling can be done precisely and efficiently.

2.4 Modified CAD Flow with DAD-FF

To apply DAD-FF to a VLSI design, the conventional CAD flow needs modification which consists of two parts, as

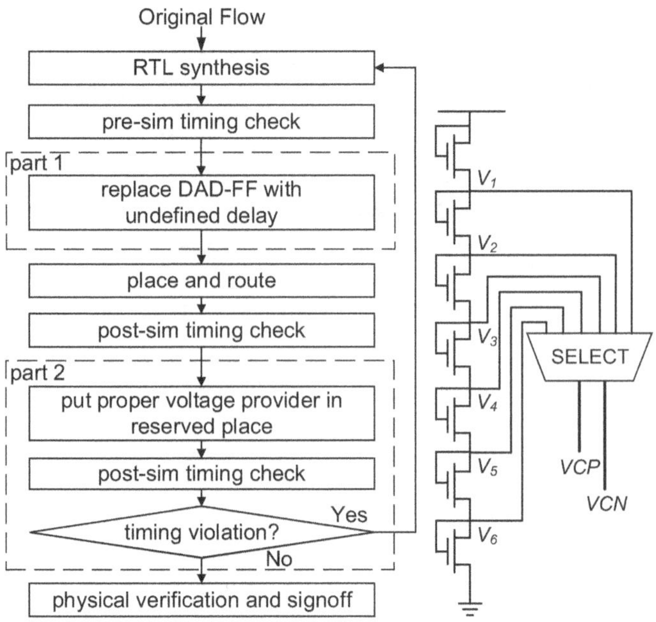

(a) Modified CAD flow (b) RVG

Figure 6: Modified CAD flow and design of reference voltage generator (RVG)

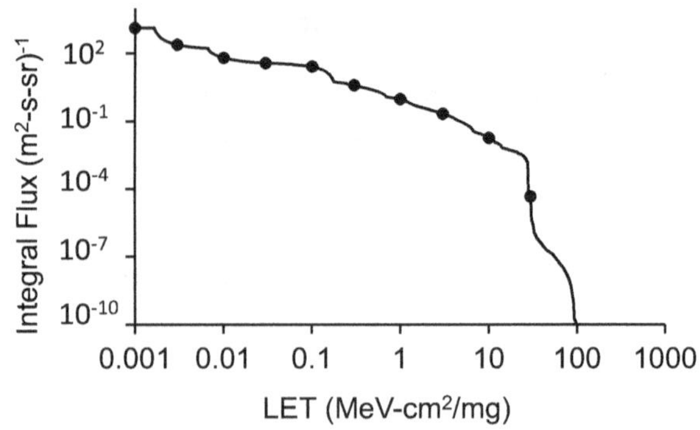

Figure 7: Integral flux of heavy ion at height of 720 km

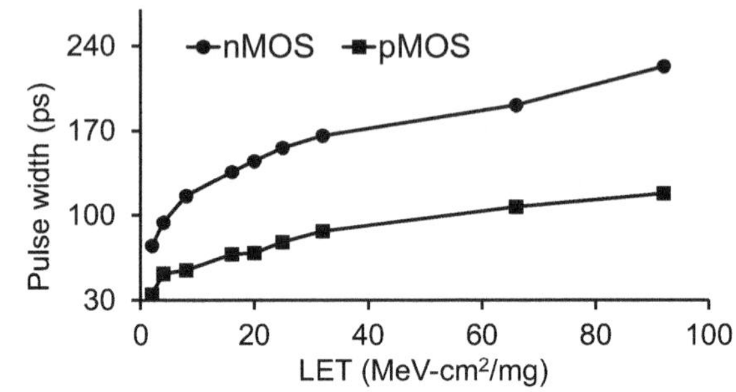

Figure 8: Relation between pulse width of SET and energy level of heavy ion

indicated in Figure 6(a). After the RTL synthesis and timing check by pre-layout simulation, the flow comes to part 1. Part 1 is to replace target STD-FFs with DAD-FFs, in which all delayed times are not specified yet, and to reserve a place for reference voltage generator (RVG). After the place-and-route stage and post-layout simulation, timing analysis must be done for not only checking setup-/hold-time violation, but also finding the maximum delay margin. Once the maximum delay margin is derived, part 2 begins to compute the number and size of transistors in RVG. RVG, as shown in Figure 6(b), is used for providing *proper* reference voltages that *VCP* and *VCN* request. After part 2, timing check by post-layout simulation should be performed again to ensure timing safety on all critical paths. Such modification successfully integrates the proposed radiation-hardened design (i.e. DAD-FF) with adjustable delay into the conventional CAD flow and thus provides a low-cost solution for SER optimization.

In the modified CAD flow with DAD-FF, a *proper* reference voltage is the key to success and provided by RVG. One simple realization of RVG can be implemented with transistors. A series of nMOSs are connected as shown in Figure 6(b), and work as resistors to divide the voltage into multiple levels. By choosing voltages of different levels from RVG, *VCP* and *VCN* jointly determine the latency of the delayed signal in SERL. Such latency depends on a variable named ***controlling*** voltage V_C, which relation with *VCP* and *VCN* can be defined as $V_C = VCP/VCN$. Given the maximum energy level of particle strikes in radiation as a target, the corresponding delayed time can be derived automatically. Meanwhile, its controlling voltage V_C can also be computed by *VCP* and *VCN*. As a result, the modified CAD flow can automatically synthesize the required RVG for SER reduction.

Compared with BISER, DAD-FF provides a more flexible way for adjusting the delayed time λ with the modified CAD flow. For example, once the design implemented with BISER intends to change with λ for different resistibility to soft errors, design cost (including size change on buffers and routing effort) cannot be avoided and must be paid accordingly. Moreover, the radiation-hardened designs by DAD-FF can save more area from sharing RVGs between DAD-FFs whereas each BISER requires its own buffers. To sum up, hardening designs with DAD-FF is economical and can be easily done by the modified CAD flow.

3. EXPERIMENTAL RESULTS

Experimental results are mainly divided into two parts. In part 1, mixed simulation of TCAD and SPICE is conducted to compare SERs of STD-FF and DAD-FF with different V_C's. Each V_C results in corresponding delayed time on DAD-FF and can be further deduce its **critical energy level** (i.e. the maximum energy level of a particle strike that DAD-FF can reject), which reflects its resistibility to soft errors. Sensitivity analysis under process variation is also discussed in detail. In part 2, a real chip designed for 500-stage shift registers was fabricaetd and implemented with three different types of flip-flips (i.e. STD-FF, DICE and DAD-FF) using a 90nm CMOS technology. Laboratory report from the radiation exposure experiments conducted in UCL, Belgium is also provided. All above experimental data are normalized with integral flux of heavy ion, as shown in Figure 7, for mimicking the real environment of the satellite orbiting at a height of 720 km.

3.1 Mixed Simulation of TCAD and SPICE

The first experiment aims at SER comparison between STD-FF and DAD-FF. It starts with the TCAD simulation for building the current-source model of a SET after particle strikes with different energy levels. Later, the current-source

Table 1: DAD-FFs with different controlling voltage V_C under 0%, 2%, and 5% process variations

Type of D Flip-Flop	Process Variation (%)	Delayed Time λ (ps)	Critical Energy Level (LET)	Soft Error Rate (FIT)	SER Improvement (X)
STD-FF	0	–	0	3.7×10^{-4}	–
DAD-FF$_1$ V_C=0.790	0	142	20	4.7×10^{-9}	7.9×10^4
	2	140	16	6.3×10^{-9}	5.9×10^4
	5	138	16	8.8×10^{-9}	4.2×10^4
DAD-FF$_2$ V_C=1.000	0	172	32	2.2×10^{-12}	1.7×10^8
	2	169	32	2.4×10^{-12}	1.6×10^8
	5	166	25	4.9×10^{-12}	7.6×10^7
DAD-FF$_3$ V_C=1.325	0	215	69	2.8×10^{-14}	1.3×10^{10}
	2	210	69	4.8×10^{-14}	7.7×10^9
	5	205	64	1.2×10^{-13}	3.0×10^9

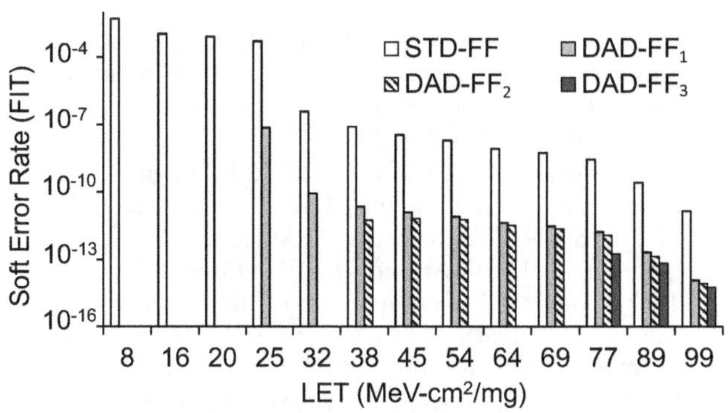

Figure 9: SER distribution for STD-FF, DAD-FF$_1$, DAD-FF$_2$ and DAD-FF$_3$

model is applied to the circuit during SPICE simulation for SER estimation. Both TCAD and SPICE simulation are performed on a Linux machine with dual E5-2650 v3 processors and 256G ECC Ram using the 45nm NanGate Open Cell Library.

Figure 8 first illustrates the pulse width PW of the SET on nMOS and pMOS, respectively, struck by heavy ions with different energy levels by the TCAD simulation. The x-axis denotes the energy level of heavy ion whereas the y-axis denotes the pulse width PW of the SET. As one can see, drifting-diffusion current on nMOS is stronger than that on pMOS. Therefore, nMOS induces a larger PW than pMOS does when struck by a heavy ion with the same energy level. Moreover, once the **critical energy level** (i.e. the maximum energy level of a particle strike that DAD-FF can reject) is determined, the corresponding delayed time of DAD-FF can be derived, accordingly.

After the TCAD simulation, SPICE simulation iterates for 100,000 times to estimate SER. Table 1 shows the experimental results where three types of DAD-FFs with different V_C's are used under 0%, 2%, and 5% process variations. As a result, DAD-FF$_3$ reduces 1.3×10^{10}X SER when compared with STD-FF and has the strongest resistibility (i.e. 2.8×10^{-14} in FIT) to soft errors.

Moreover, according to Table 1, the critical energy level of DAD-FF$_3$ with 0% process variation is 69 LET, indicating that 99.999997% heavy ions are rejected for the satellite on the 720-km orbit in Figure 7. However, to protect the circuit from the critical energy level of 69 LET, the delayed time λ needs to be set as 215 ps. Figure 9 details the SER distributions of STD-FF, DAD-FF$_1$, DAD-FF$_2$, and DAD-FF$_3$ under particle strikes with respective energy levels. To take DAD-FF$_3$ with 0% process variation for example, since its critical energy level is 69 LET, soft errors start to appear from 77 LET.

We further conduct delay-sensitivity analysis of DAD-FF under different process variations. In general, 2% and 5% process variations on DAD-FF lead to different **degradation** on the resistibility to soft errors, as shown in Table 1. For example, the critical energy level of the DAD-FF$_1$ without process variation is 20 LET, but decreases to 16 LET under both 2% and 5% process variations. For DAD-FF$_2$ and DAD-FF$_3$ under both 0% and 2% process variations, their critical energy levels are 32 LET and 69 LET, respectively. However, as process variation increases to 5%, the critical energy levels of DAD-FF$_2$ and DAD-FF$_3$ decreases to 25 LET and 64 LET, respectively.

3.2 Radiation Exposure of Fabricated Chip

For validation, in part 2 of our experiments, a chip was fabricated in a CMOS 90nm technology with DAD-FF, DICE, and STD-FF and designed for a satellite orbiting at a height of 720 km with inclination of 98.27 degree. In the fabricated chip, the layout of DAD-FF is shown in Figure 10. We further performed the radiation exposure measurement in UCL, Belgium. To speed up radiation exposure, high-flux heavy ion beams with 10 different energy levels were injected to provide the same doze as that for 2 years at the space.

The measurement results are shown in Figure 11. The x-axis denotes the energy level of heavy ion whereas the y-axis denotes the corresponding ***bit error rate***. Note that bit error rate (BER) is defined as

$$BER = \frac{\text{error bits}}{\text{received data bits}}$$

where error bits are collected from scanned-out shift registers. Note that in Figure 11, without any protection, STD-FF starts to receive errors at energy level 1 and its BER is at least one-order worse than those for DICE and DAD-FF at any energy level. As one can see, DAD-FF and DICE reject all particle strikes below 10 LET, corresponding to 98.95% radiation. Moreover, DAD-FF outperforms DICE in BER after 32 LET. To sum up, DAD-FF reduces 15.69X and 2.62X BER of STD-FF and DICE, respectively. Not only with better resistiblity to soft errors, DAD-FF takes less power consumption (only 1.83mW) while DICE takes 2.10mW and STD-FF takes 1.05mW.

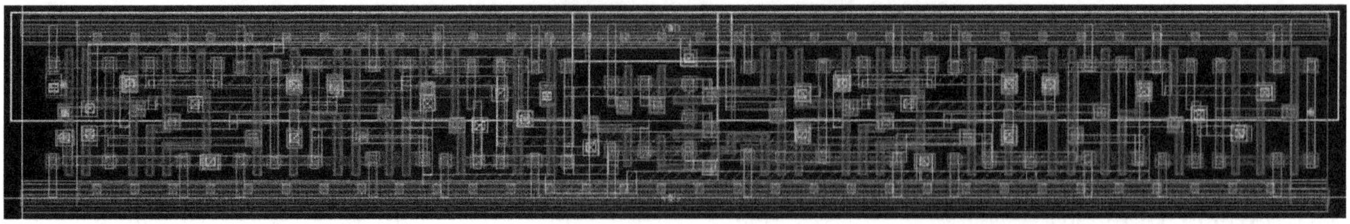

Figure 10: Layout of DAD-FF with area 2.52×19.32 um^2

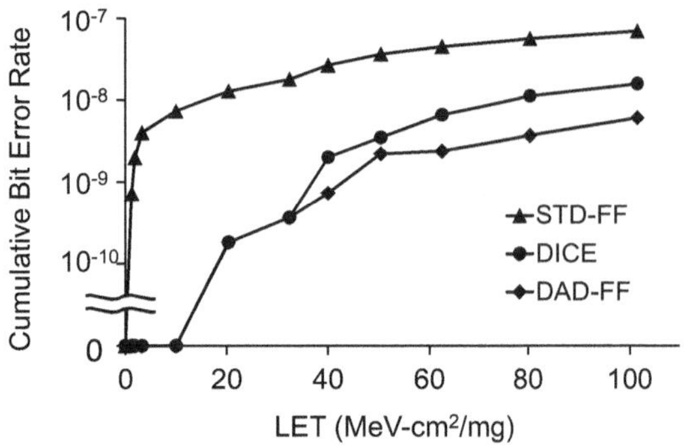

Figure 11: BER comparison of 500-stage shift registers in radiation exposure measurement

4. CONCLUSION

For reducing soft error rate (SER) in system-level failures, a **D**elay-**A**djustable **D** **F**lip-**F**lop design named **DAD-FF** is proposed in this work and can be easily integrated in the current CAD flow with proper modification. Given the maximum energy level of particle strikes in radiation, its delayed time λ can be determined automatically. Simulation shows that at the device level, DAD-FF eliminates 99.999997% soft errors induced by heavy ions on a satellite orbiting at a height of 720 km. Under three different maximum energy levels (i.e. 20, 32, and 69 LETs) of particle strikes in radiation, DAD-FF achieves the 7.9×10^4X, 1.7×10^8X, and 1.3×10^{10}X SER improvement, respectively, over STD-FF. Moreover, the radiation exposure measurement on a real chip fabricated with three types of flip-flops (i.e. DAD-FF, DICE, and STD-FF) indicates that the design by DAD-FF reduces 15.69X and 2.62X BER of those by STD-FF and DICE, respectively, and meanwhile consumes less power at the system level. In summary, DAD-FF's resisitability to soft errors is validated by mixed simulation and measurement on a fabricated chip, inferring the effectiveness of the modified CAD flow to SER reduction.

5. ACKNOWLEDGMENTS

This work was partially supported by Ministry of Science and Technology, Taiwan, R.O.C. under grant no. MOST104-2628-E-009-009-MY3.

6. REFERENCES

[1] R. C. Baumann. Radiation-induced soft errors in advanced semiconductor technologies. *IEEE Transactions on Device and Materials Reliability*, 5(3):305–316, Sept 2005.

[2] A. Dixit and A. Wood. The impact of new technology on soft error rates. In *2011 International Reliability Physics Symposium*, pages 5B.4.1–5B.4.7, April 2011.

[3] D. Ernst, N. S. Kim, S. Das, S. Pant, R. Rao, T. Pham, C. Ziesler, D. Blaauw, T. Austin, K. Flautner, and T. Mudge. Razor: a low-power pipeline based on circuit-level timing speculation. In *Proceedings. 36th Annual IEEE/ACM International Symposium on Microarchitecture, 2003. MICRO-36.*, pages 7–18, Dec 2003.

[4] V. Ferlet-Cavrois, L. W. Massengill, and P. Gouker. Single event transients in digital cmos - a review. *IEEE Transactions on Nuclear Science*, 60(3):1767–1790, June 2013.

[5] N. J. Gaspard, S. Jagannathan, Z. J. Diggins, M. P. King, S. J. Wen, R. Wong, T. D. Loveless, K. Lilja, M. Bounasser, T. Reece, A. F. Witulski, W. T. Holman, B. L. Bhuva, and L. W. Massengill. Technology scaling comparison of flip-flop heavy-ion single-event upset cross sections. *IEEE Transactions on Nuclear Science*, 60(6):4368–4373, Dec 2013.

[6] P. Hazucha, T. Karnik, S. Walstra, B. A. Bloechel, J. W. Tschanz, J. Maiz, K. Soumyanath, G. E. Dermer, S. Narendra, V. De, and S. Borkar. Measurements and analysis of ser-tolerant latch in a 90-nm dual-vt cmos process. *IEEE Journal of Solid-State Circuits*, 39(9):1536–1543, Sept 2004.

[7] H. M. Huang, Y. Lin, and C. H. P. Wen. Fast-yet-accurate variation-aware current and voltage modelling of radiation-induced transient fault. In *2016 Design, Automation Test in Europe Conference Exhibition (DATE)*, pages 211–216, March 2016.

[8] J. E. Knudsen and L. T. Clark. An area and power efficient radiation hardened by design flip-flop. *IEEE Transactions on Nuclear Science*, 53(6):3392–3399, Dec 2006.

[9] G. C. Messenger. Collection of charge on junction nodes from ion tracks. *IEEE Transactions on Nuclear Science*, 29(6):2024–2031, Dec 1982.

[10] S. Mitra, M. Zhang, N. Seifert, T. Mak, and K. S. Kim. Built-in soft error resilience for robust system design. In *2007 IEEE International Conference on Integrated Circuit Design and Technology*, pages 1–6, May 2007.

[11] N. Seifert, X. Zhu, D. Moyer, R. Mueller, R. Hokinson, N. Leland, M. Shade, and L. Massengill. Frequency dependence of soft error rates for sub-micron cmos technologies. In *International Electron Devices Meeting. Technical Digest (Cat. No.01CH37224)*, pages 14.4.1–14.4.4, Dec 2001.

[12] M. Zhang, S. Mitra, T. M. Mak, N. Seifert, N. J. Wang, Q. Shi, K. S. Kim, N. R. Shanbhag, and S. J. Patel. Sequential element design with built-in soft error resilience. *IEEE Transactions on Very Large Scale Integration (VLSI) Systems*, 14(12):1368–1378, Dec 2006.

Effective Mitigation of Radiation-induced Single Event Transient on Flash-based FPGAs

Luca Sterpone, Sarah Azimi
Boyang Du
Dipartimento di Automatica e Informatica
Politecnico di Torino
Torino, Italy
{luca.sterpone, sarah.azimi, boyang.du}@polito.it

David Merodio Codinachs
European Space Agency
ESTEC
Noordwijk, The Netherlands
david.merodio.codinachs@esa.int

Raoul Grimoldi
CGS SpA
Milano, Italy
r.grimoldi@cgspace.it

ABSTRACT

Due to the decreasing feature sizes of VLSI circuits, radiation induced Single Event Transients (SETs) are increasingly dominating the event ratio on modern VLSI devices. In particular, Flash-based FPGAs are characterized by the main concern of radiation-induced voltage glitches or SETs in the combinational logic. Transient pulses can be sampled by a storage element and can propagate through the circuit up to the outputs and leading to an error. In this paper, we propose a complete implementation flow including sensitivity analysis, fault tolerant mapping and fault tolerance-oriented place and route for the effective design of SET tolerant circuits on Flash-based FPGAs. In details, the proposed method allows accurate measurement of the transient pulse source induced by radiation particles and estimation of the SET error rate on the overall circuit. Besides the developed method provides a netlist mapping and place and route tool for the selective mitigation of SET effects. The proposed method has been applied to an industrial design oriented to the Euclid European Space Agency mission including more than ten different modules. The obtained results show an improvement of the total filtering capability of around 43 times with respect to the original netlist without affecting the timing constraints of the circuit.

Keywords

Reconfiguration, Design Flow, Placement, Routing, Reliability, Fault Tolerance, Flash-based FPGA.

1. INTRODUCTION

The Single Event Transient (SET) effects occur in nanoscale devices are mostly caused by radiation-induced phenomena [1]. When a highly charged particle crosses the silicon junction, the produced free mobile carriers are concentrated within the depletion region of a p-n junction, generating a transient pulse due to the transitory current traversing the junction [2].

Different from permanent errors such as Single Event Latch-ups (SELs) where threshold voltage shifts and destroys the semiconductor area by burnouts [3], transient error can cause electrical pulse with narrow length (e.g., below 1.2 ns) which is transitory, thus does not electrically damage the silicon device.

Permission to make digital or hard copies of all or part of this work for personal or classroom use is granted without fee provided that copies are not made or distributed for profit or commercial advantage and that copies bear this notice and the full citation on the first page. To copy otherwise, or republish, to post on servers or to redistribute to lists, requires prior specific permission and/or a fee. Request permissions from Permissions@acm.org
GLSVLSI'17, May 10-12, 2017, Banff, AB, Canada.
©2017 ACM. ISBN 978-1-4503-4972-7/17/05...$15.00
DOI: http://dx.doi.org/10.1145/3060403.3060454

Transient errors may cause two major issues. In case a storage element junction is affected, it may create a Single Event Upset (SEU), which consists in the flip original logic value of the storage element. On the other hand, if it hits a transistor as part of combinational logic generating a Single Event Transient (SET), the pulse can propagate through routing and logic resources in the circuit until it is captured by a sequential element, typically a Flip-Flop (FF), becoming a bit error thus propagating its effect during the circuit execution [4]. The first issue is addressed by designing hardware redundant storage element using a Triple Modular Redundant (TMR) scheme; meanwhile the second issue requires the adoption of ad-hoc solutions in order to achieve an effective protection [5].

Considering reprogrammable devices such as Flash-based FPGAs, transient error affecting the combinational logic is nowadays the primary design concern for safety-critical applications since the devices are immune from configuration memory bit upsets [6]. Three are the reasons: (1) the increased design complexity results in a wider radiation sensitive area; (2) the device shrinking technology process is decreasing the electrical charge representing the logic information, which makes them more prone to be affected by a radiation particle; (3) the probability of sampling an SET is increasing due to the faster clock frequency used.

The SET propagation phenomena have been addressed by different research activities in the last 5 years. Most of the available works focus on the physical and electrical modeling where physical simulation allows to characterize and validate the propagation of SET pulse shapes [7][8]. Though effective, these approaches require a time consuming modeling activity that cannot be applied directly in an industrial design flow.

Mitigation solutions based on gate filtering have been proposed and applied mainly on benchmark circuits without considering timing and resource overhead constraints [9]. Other solutions are based on analytical tools that have been recently developed and validated on radiation-test experimental analysis identifying a possible alternative to time-consuming physical design simulation [11].

In this work, we present a novel SET-aware design flow to implement SET-tolerant circuits on Flash-based FPGAs. This approach takes into account not only the mitigation of the SET occurrences within sequential element but in particular the filtering of the propagation of SETs affecting the combinational logic. Besides, the SET analysis process includes a pre-characterization of the Flash-based standard cells providing an effective correlation between the radiation particle energy and location, amplitude and duration of the SET pulse.

The main innovation of this work is the capability of controlling and managing the transient propagation through the Flash-based FPGA heterogeneous resources. When the SET analysis phase is considered, the method permits the effective pulse generation related to the type and energy of the radiation; and the effective resistive and capacitive loads are taken in account for the propagation through gates and routing since each traversed resource is analyzed considering a pre-characterized Propagation Induced Pulse Broadening (PIPB) effect. Furthermore, the approach has the capability to include the SET filtering optimization during the implementation phase. The main difference with respect to already available solutions is that the SET filtering is not achieved anymore using the traditional and resource demanding guard gate scheme inserted in front of the considered Flip-Flop. Instead, a specific design macro provides the SET filtering when being inserted in ad-hoc position within the circuit netlist.

Finally, the place and route layout process includes a SET filtering-driven constraint during its execution achieving target circuit performance without weakening the SET filtering capability implemented in the previous phase. The paper has the following structure: Section II provides an overview of the already developed works; Section III presents the whole mitigation flow with the functional description of all the phases. Section IV describes the experimental results, finally Section V draws some conclusions and discusses future works.

2. RELAED WORK

Many researches have been dedicated to the Single Event Transient effects in digital circuits. Among various approaches, several works have been dedicated to the SET effects on Flash-based FPGAs. During the beginning of the last decades, most of the works proposed the characterization of SETs on Flash-based FPGAs. The main goal has been the identification of the type of SET generated within the silicon structure of Flash-based FPGA considering different types of radiation sources. Considering this purpose, different works such as [6]-[12] developed a SET detection circuitry, mapped on the FPGA, used to monitor the SET during the radiation beam tests. Thanks to these tests, it has been possible to individuate the sensitive points of the Flash-based FPGA functional structure and to determine the correlation between the radiation Linear Energy Transfer (LET) and the shape (e.g., amplitude and duration) of the SETs.

Further studies investigated the SET influence on the logic and routing structure of the FPGA [13]. The main achieved result has been the relation between the layout geometrical characteristics of the main logic block (e.g., Versatile) in the Flash-based FPGA and the SET basic mechanism demonstrating that SET mitigation by electrical filtering is a possible solution. More recently, researches proposed internal electrical injection approaches to evaluate and characterize the SET phenomena [15] and more relevant effective test strategies such as internal Built-In-Self-Test (BIST) and on-line checker were introduced to improve the SET testing capabilities and to identify the correlation of radiation effects versus permanent faults [16].

Latest research results in the field identify the relevant influence of the routing and logic propagation demonstrating that generation of SET pulse shape is dependent on several factors. The first type of factors is related to the layout and it is general with respect to the used device and the technology. This includes the shape and width of physical structure where the radiation particle hits, the ratio of the NMOS and PMOS layout sections affecting falling and rising time, the kind of logic gates on the path of the traversing SET. The second type of factors is specific to the Flash-based FPGA technology and it includes the type of routing segment and the Versatile configuration [17].

Finally, before this work, a full implementation flow is still not available by far that is able to integrate the characterization results obtained with previous researches into effective mitigation techniques of large size circuits on Flash-based FPGAs.

3. THE DEVELOPED SET MITIGATION INTEGRATED FLOW

The developed Integrated Design Flow (IDF) includes three groups of tools: a SET analyzer, a netlist modifier and a design physical implementation tool. As illustrated in Figure 1, the developed IDF is linked with the classical design tool chain consisting of the synthesis, mapping and place and route tools.

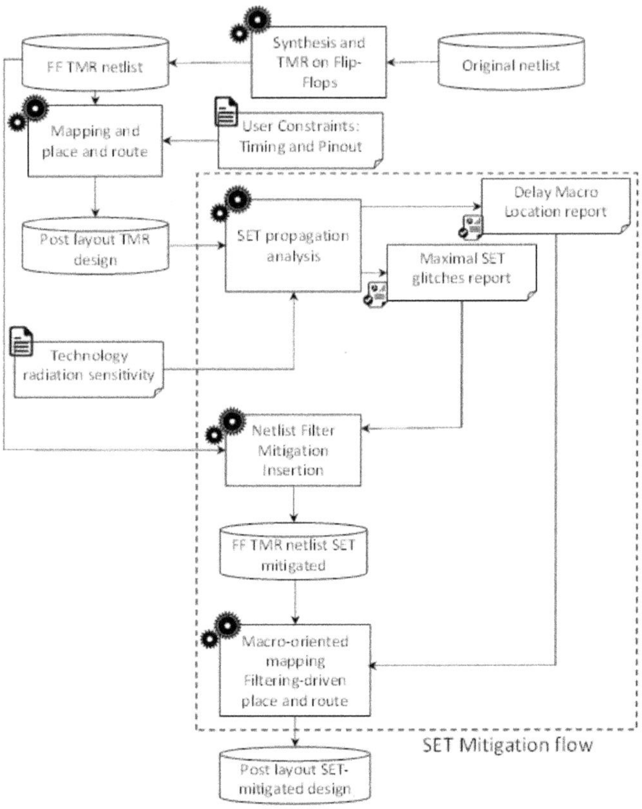

Figure 1. The overview of the SET-aware mitigation flow including the SET propagation analysis, the Netlist Filter Mitigation insertion and the macro-oriented mapping and filtering-driven place and route.

The IDF starts the elaboration using the post-layout design and adopting a technology radiation sensitivity data provided by the FPGA manufacturer or generated by preliminary radiation-test characterization, including elementary radiation sensitivity information per each type of logic functions or routing segment implemented by the FPGA [13].

The SET mitigation flow executes the mitigation in three phases:

1. SET analysis: the implemented circuit is analyzed generating two reports: a list of maximal glitches observed at the input of each Flip-Flop; a report including the location of the Flip-Flop cells and their logic path delays.

2. Netlist Filter Mitigation insertion: the synthesized netlist is modified by inserting filtering circuitry to improve the SET

mitigation. The elaboration is executed on the post-synthesis Verilog description of the design. In details, the tool modifies the paths indicated by the maximal glitches report generated in the previous phase. As a result, it generates a new Verilog netlist.

3. Physical Implementation: it implements the modified netlist executing the mapper and the place and route tool. The mapper elaborates the netlist optimizing the SET filtering capability by creating proper design macro. Finally, the place and route algorithm defines the logic versatile locations and the routing segments that optimize the SET filtering of the design without penalize the circuit performances.

3.1 SET Propagation Analysis

The SET analysis we developed is based on a layout-oriented SET injection directly applied to the Flash-based FPGA logic core cells and propagated using the logic and routing model.

The layout-oriented SET injection adopts the Graphic Database Systems-II (GDS-II) file describing the FPGA logic block where three-dimensional data structure is adopted for modeling internal gates, switches and input/output logic points. As an example, in Figure 2, we illustrated the basic scheme: we modeled the radiation particle energy spectrum affecting the Versatile block; as a result an SET pulse with a specific amplitude and width is generated. For the purpose of our analysis, the incidental radiation particle projection is vertical affecting a random position of the implemented circuit with two different Linear Energy Transfer (LET) values.

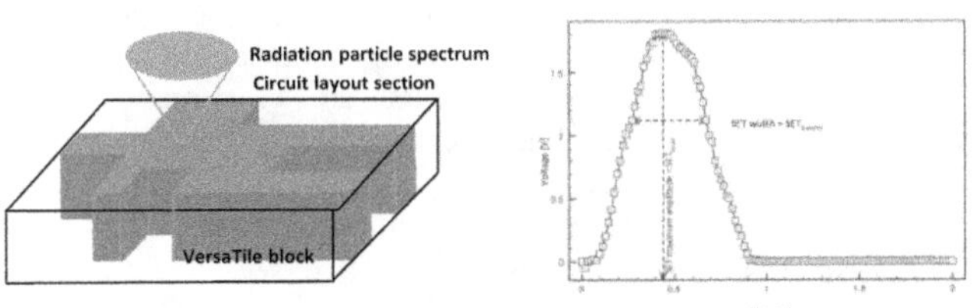

Figure. 2. The SET propagation basic mechanism overview developed by the proposed Single Event Transient analyzer.

To implement the cell GDS description, we used the information of the configuration layout provided by Microsemi and synthesized the main cell description using Synopsys Design Compiler. Then, we created the final GDS-II description with our place and route tool. Finally, a tool implemented in C-language is used to extract the position of each gate and configuration switches and to apply the selected radiation energy in terms of Linear Energy Transfer (LET).

Once the SET source shape is generated, it is propagated adopting the Propagation Induced Pulse Broadening (PIPB) model to elaborate the transformation of the pulse shape along traversed path up to a Flip-Flop or other storage element for each logic cone.

The propagation tool calculates the new SET shape at each propagation node of the circuit (e.g., each logic gate traversed) considering the PIPB coefficient of the mentioned node. Please note that the PIPB coefficient is obtained based on the number and type of logic gates spanning from the SET sensitive nodes to the drain Flip-Flop and logic input node Fan-in. In the example illustrated in Figure 3, the PIPB coefficient of the propagation node is calculated considering the gate chain composed of G2 and G4 while the Fan-in composed of the gate G3.

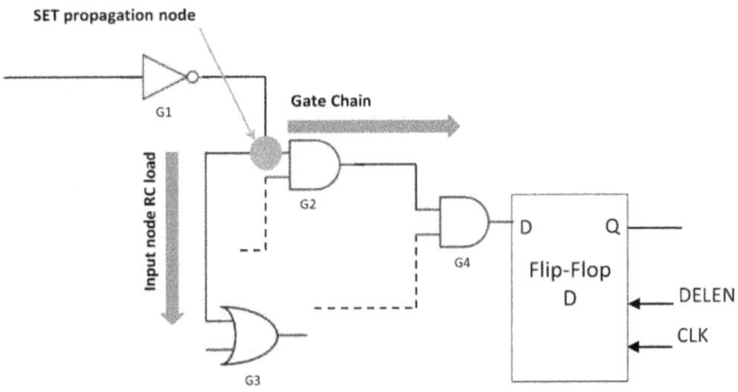

Figure. 3. The SET propagation method including the PIPB computation on the propagation node.

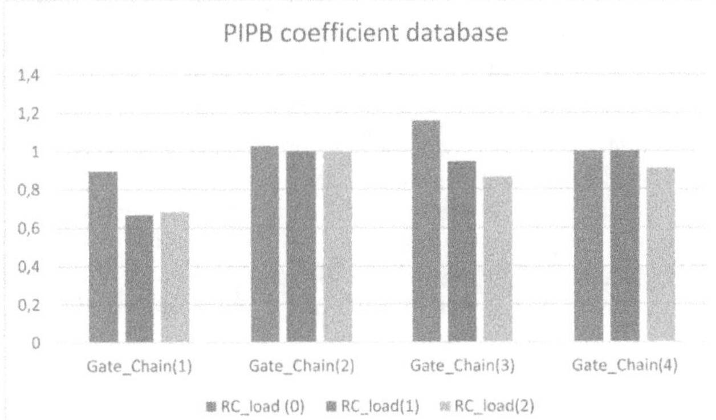

Figure. 4. An example of the PIPB calculation. By the interpolation of the number of gate on the chain (Gate_Chain) and the number of gate on the Fan-in (RC_load) it is possible to achieve the correspondent PIPB value. Please note that a positive PIPB is related to a broadening of the SET pulse.

3.2 Netlist Filter Mitigation Insertion

State-of-the-art SET mitigation methods for Flash-based FPGAs use Guard Gate (GG) logic gate structure [12] applied at the input of each addressed Flip-Flops, as illustrated in Figure 5, in order to improve the SET mitigation. In this case, any SET reaching the input of the GG and having SET width lower than the filtering delay is nullified. This solution has two main drawbacks. The former is related to the need of inserting a filtering scheme at the input of all the selected Flip-Flops (FFs) thus introduces a drastic increase of area overhead. The latter is related to the performance degradation, since the guard gate scheme requires at least 6 gates for each Flip-Flop, as illustrated in Figure 5.a.

The algorithm we developed inserts the SET-filtering scheme illustrated in Figure 5.b for all logic gates shared between logic cones. The algorithm identifies the points in the netlist where to insert the mitigation structure and calculates the effective SET filtering delay.

In details, the algorithm executes in two phases. At first, it calculates the broadening coefficient for each used resource according to the maximal SET glitches report. The broadening coefficient is computed for each logic gate as ΔBGi with i representing the gate index and for each routing net as ΔBRj with j representing a specific routing segment.

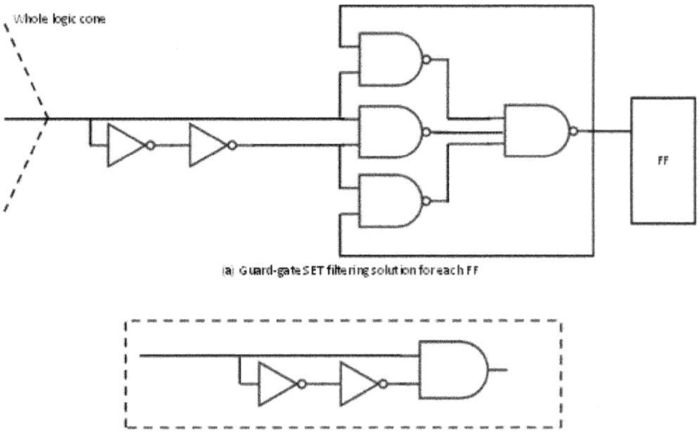

Figure. 5. Traditional Flip-Flop based guard-gate and SET-filtering solution (a) compared to the SET-filtering scheme inserted by the netlist insertion mapper on logic gates shared by logic cones (b).

A positive value of the coefficient corresponds to a broadening effect, while a negative value to the filtering of the SET. The computation provides further information related to the entire broadening contribution of each logic path, represented by ΣB. The broadening contribution is calculated for each Flip-Flop element and for all the gates shared between two or more logical paths.

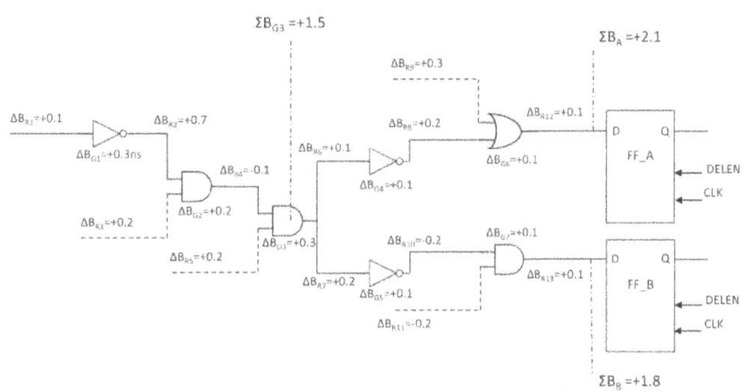

Figure. 6. An example of the netlist mitigation algorithm's first phase on a circuit portion: the calculation of the broadening coefficients in nanoseconds.

Figure 6 shows the application of this execution to a portion of circuit. In real case, the progressive maximal SET broadening width contribution (ΔB) and the total SET broadening contribution (ΣB) are computed for each logic gate and routing segment in the target design. Please note that without any filtering scheme the maximal SET width at the input of the Flip-Flop A and B is 2.1ns and 1.8ns respectively.

The second phase of the algorithm executes the insertion of the gates represented in Figure 5.b. In details, the algorithm calculates the number of inverters depending on the required filtering. As illustrated in Figure 7, the mitigation algorithm inserts a filtering scheme able to filter pulses having a maximal width of 1.6 ns by inserting the filtering logic gates group after the shared gate G3. The filtering scheme nullifies any type of SET coming from the top part of the logic cones. At the same time, the SET broadening contributions at the Flip-Flop A and B are reduced to 0.6ns and 0.3ns, then the FF input driver is able to filter these SET pulses.

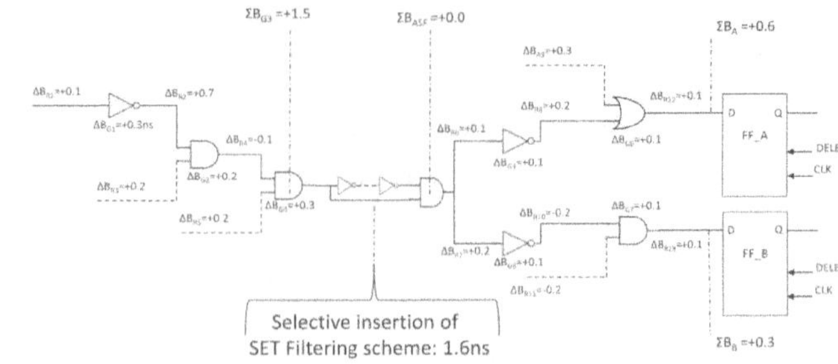

Figure. 7. Application of the netlist mitigation algorithm second phase to a circuit portion: the insertion of the filtering scheme on the shared logic path.

3.3 Physical Implementation

The physical implementation is performed by a macro-oriented placement and routing algorithm. Since the Flash-based FPGA architecture is based on the classical island-style FPGA architecture, we developed a global placement algorithm for macro-blocks dedicated to the SET filtering. The global placement is executed prior to floor-planning and it is mandatory to guarantee the effective locality of the filtering scheme inserted during the netlist modification phase. Besides, we developed a filtering-based place and route algorithm to generate the final design for producing the configuration memory file.

The global placement algorithm we developed generates a floor-planning solution through a set of constraints. At first, the algorithm creates a set of macro-blocks to be placed in the FPGA area corresponding to the gates used by the netlist insertion algorithm. Thus, considering MB0, MB1, …, MBn the set of macro-blocks generated during the netlist modification phase, where each MBi has an associated dimension (height and width), the global placement algorithm tries to find a placement rectangular area R for each of the macro-block such that:

1. The resources of the area Ai used by the macro-block has the sufficient resources

2. Two MBs do not overlap

3. The resources within the MBs respect the timing delay defined during the netlist insertion phase.

In details, our algorithm considers all the macro-blocks simultaneously and the placement is forced to fix the position of the filtering gates. To allow the full implementation of the fixed filtering logic resources, a hierarchical isolation approach has been applied using a weighted clustering algorithm where the weight is correlated to the number of inverters used by the filtering structure.

```
initialization of design macro-blocks (MB)
clustering (MB)
for TBP to total MB
   while Dimension(TBP)>1
       select (MBi,MBj) for maximizing Fk
       add MB to Area Cluster (AC)
       update AC available regions
   end while
end for
```

Algorithm 1. The global placement implementation algorithm.

As illustrated in Algorithm 1, the execution starts from the initialization of the design macro-blocks. The list of macro-blocks is provided by the SET analysis and the netlist insertion algorithm back annotates it. In the second phase, the various MBs are clustered by number of inverters (e.g., filtering delay), a set of block

To Be Placed (TBP) is created. The third phase consists on the allocation of the clustered MBs. In details, a MB is added to the Area Cluster (AC) only if it is able to maximize its filtering capability considering also the positions of the other placed MBs.

4. EXPERIMENTAL RESULTS

The experimental evaluation of the proposed method has been performed on a complete SoC design from the EUCLID space mission for monitoring the dark space and has been implemented on a Microsemi ProASIC3 A3P3000L PQ208 Flash-based FPGA device. In general, 12 functional modules characterize the Euclid design with four different clock domains, while the nominal duration of the mission is 6.25 years. The Euclid space environment has been also characterized considering SET events and determining that longest SET are of maximum 1.0 ns. We therefore tune (when applied) the filtering capability up to 1.0 ns. The design has been implemented with five different implementation flows, whose characteristics are described in Table I:

1. Plain Design: native version of the circuit without any mitigation.

2. Selective Filter 1.0ns: implementation including selective filter up to 1.0 ns established using the static analysis of SET developed in [15].

3. TMR FF: implementation applying Triple Modular Redundancy (TMR) on all the user Flip-Flops using Synopsys Synplify Pro.

4. TMR FF Filter 1.0ns: implementation applying TMR as in (3) with the addiction of selective filter up to 1.0 ns. It represents the state-of-the-art mitigation solution.

5. Our Approach: implementation using TMR on all the Flip-Flops and our filtering method.

Table 1. Euclid designs used resources

Euclid Design	Sequential [#]	Logic gates [#]
Plain Design	5,907	27,826
Selective Filter 1ns	5,907	38,430
TMR FF	17,719	31,782
TMR FF Filer 1ns	17,719	56,408
Our Approach	17,719	48,625

As it is possible to notice, the TMR FF Filter 1.0ns has the largest overhead of area due to the extra filtering logic and the TMR voting circuitry applied to each Flip-Flop. Our version has a reduction of logic gates of around 15% with respect to the state-of-the-art.

We compared the performances of the five designs checking the working frequencies of four different clock domains and the result is reported in Table II. As it is possible to notice, our approach satisfies the entire frequency requirements. It is interesting to notice that our approach is not affecting high frequency domains that remain almost identical to the plain (original) implementation. Meanwhile, solutions including traditional filtering have a degradation of more than 25%.

In order to perform the SET analysis of the implemented designs, we performed several fault simulation campaigns injecting seven types of SET pulses, ranging from 0.32 ns up to 0.96 ns. We injected 70,000 SETs in random positions for each design gate level model, 10,000 injections per SET type. As for design workload, we considered a test program able to reach a fault coverage of 96%.

Table 2. Euclid design working frequencies

Euclid Design	CLK-60 [MHz]	CLK-30 [MHz]	CLK-70 [MHz]	CLK-20 [MHz]
Plain	81.4	35.4	79.4	39.4
Sel. Filter 1ns	68.1	30.8	71.4	31.7
TMR FF	81.8	31.8	79.6	38.6
TMR Filter 1ns	66.4	30.3	71.5	34.8
Our Approach	81.9	30.3	78.8	33.4

The results we achieved are depicted in Figure 8 reporting the percentage of SET fully filtered among the various mitigation solutions. We compared the filtering capabilities considering the SET pulses reaching the input of sequential element, without taking in account SETs that are logically masked by the circuit logic. As it is possible to notice, very narrow SETs are always filtered by the technology, therefore even the plain design will intrinsically filter those pulses. On the other hand, broader SETs are critical for all the mitigation solutions except for our approach, which is able to filter almost all the possible pulses shorter than 1ns.

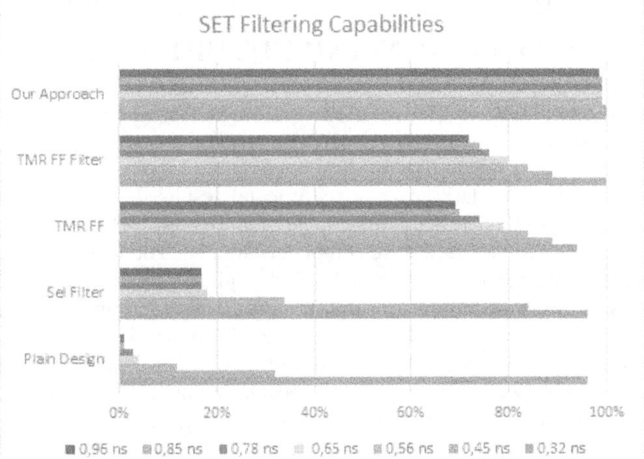

Figure. 8. SET filtering capabilities between various mitigation solutions on narrow SET (shorter than 1 ns). The results have been obtained by means of SET fault injection on the gate level model of each design.

Besides, we used the CRÈME96 and SETA tools to evaluate the overall SET error cross-section sensitivity for the two most resilient versions: our approach and the previous state-of-the-art solution with TMR and SET filtering. In details, we analyzed the integral fluency expected for the nominal duration of the mission, which is 6.25 years. In order to perform the SET error estimation, we normalized the CRÈME96 data for each single ProASIC3 Versatile and routing segment. The SET normalized cross-section coefficients have been elaborated with the SETA tool applied to the topological architecture of the place and routed circuits [14]. For the unmitigated version, we obtained a normalized transient error cross-section of 1.77E-4.

We show in Table III the overall results of the SET cross-section per module comparing the two EUCLID designs. The experimental analysis shows that the Control Block module is the most sensitive one though it is not the module with the most number of sequential or combinational element. The explanation of this result is related to the wider routing complexity that significantly contributes to the final transient cross-section count. The design mitigated with the proposed approach results in three order of magnitude less sensitive to SET. Please note that the data reported in Table 3 refers to the entire space mission LET spectrum.

TABLE 3. SET Cross-section comparison

Module	TMR + Filtering SET sensitivity [Cross-section]	Our Approach SET sensitivity [Cross-section]
SPW_CTRL_1	2.84E-5	1.12E-8
SPW_CTRL_0	2.66E-5	1.35E-8
UART_TMTC	1.57E-5	6.49E-9
DMA_B_0	1.85E-5	6.54E-9
SIDECAR_D	1.62E-5	5.66E-9
SD_CTRL	1.10E-5	1.22E-9
PROCES_B_0	6.07E-6	2.23E-9
SIDECAR_B	7.67E-6	2.35E-9
CONTROL_B	3.70E-5	1.01E-8
AHB_0	2.99E-6	8.15E-10
APB_0	4.64E-6	9.32E-10
CLOCK_H	2.20E-6	8.32E-10

5. CONCLUSION AND FUTURE WORKS

In this paper, we presented an integrated design flow for the implementation of SET tolerant circuits on Flash-based FPGAs. The developed environment has been evaluated on a realistic space-oriented SoC design within the ESA EUCLID space mission for monitoring the dark space. Experimental results demonstrated a reduction of three order of magnitude of the overall SET sensitivity, while all narrow SETs were completely filtered. The methodology requires a limited area overhead of 20% with respect to the original design implementation. Besides, the proposed environment has a negligible working frequency penalty. As for future works, we plan to extend our characterization with extensive LET analysis considering various incident angle, besides we are investigating the applicability of the methodology to ASIC or regular fabric circuits.

6. REFERENCES

[1] R. Baumann, "Radiation-induced soft errors in advanced semiconductor technologies", IEEE Transactions on Device and Materials Reliability, Vol. 5, Issue 3, 2005, pp. 305 – 316

[2] T. Karnik, P. Hazucha, J. Patel, "Characterization of Soft-Errors caused by Single Event Upsets in CMOS processes", IEEE Transactions on Dependable and Secure Computing, Vol. 1, Issue 2, 2004, pp. 128 – 143

[3] A. Dixit, A. Wood, "The impact of new technology on soft error rates", IEEE International Reliability Physics Symposiym, 2011, pp. 5B.4.1 – 5B.4.7

[4] M. J. Gadlage, P. J. Eaton, J. M. Benedetto, M. Carts, V. Zhu, T. L. Turflinger, "Digital device error rate trends in advanced CMOS technologies", IEEE Transactions on Nuclear Sciencem, Vol. 53, Issue 6, 2006, pp. 3466 – 3471

[5] D. Mavis, P. Eaton, "Single Event Upsets and Single Event Transient modeling and mitigaion in deep submicron technologies", 45th Annual IEEE International Reliability physics symposium, 2007, pp. 293 – 305

[6] S. Rezgui, J. McCollum, R. Won, "Design and Layout Effects on SET Propagation in 90-nm ASIC and FPGA Test Structures", IEEE Transactions on Nuclear Science, Vol. 57, Issue 7, 2010, pp. 3716 – 3724

[7] M. Arevalo-Garbayo, M. Portela-Garcia, M. Garcia-Valderas, C. Lopez-Ongil, L. Entrena, "C-Element model for SET fault emulation", 14th Radiation and Its Effects on Components and Systems (RADECS), 2013, pp. 1 – 4

[8] W. Mansour, R. Velazco, R. Ayoubi, H. Ziade, W. El Falou, "A method and an automated tool to perform SET fault-injection on HDL-based design", 25th International Conference on Microelectronics (ICM), 2013, pp. 1 – 4

[9] Y. Lien, L. He, "Device and architecture concurrent optimization for FPGA transient soft error rate", IEEE/ACM International Conference on Computer-Aided Design, 2007, pp. 194 – 198

[10] L. Sterpone, B. Du, "SET-PAR: Place and Route Tools for the Mitigation of Single Event Transients on Flash-based FPGAs", International Sympisuym on Applied Reconigurable Computing, 2015

[11] C. H. Chen, S. Song, Z. Zhang, "An FPGA-based Transient Error Simulator for Resilient Circuit and System Design and Evaluation", IEEE Transactions on Cinrcuits and Systems II: Express Briefs, Vol.62, Issue 5, 2015, pp. 471 – 475

[12] S. Rezgui, J.J. Wang, E. Chan Tung, B. Cronquist, J. McCollum, "New Methodologies for SET Characterization and Mitigation in Flash-based FPGAs", IEEE Transactions on Nuclear Science, Vol. 54, Issue 6, 2007, pp. 2512 – 2524

[13] S. Rezgui, J. J. Wang, Y. Sun, B. Cronquist, J. McCollum, "Configuration and Routing Effects on the SET Propagation in Flash-based FPGAs", IEEE Transactions on Nuclear Science, Vol. 55, Issue 6, 2008, pp. 3328 – 3335

[14] L. Sterpone, D. Boyang, "Analysis and mitigation of Single Event Effects on Flash-based FPGAs", IEEE European Test Symposiym, 2014.

[15] A. Evans, D. Alexandrescu, V. Ferlet-Cavrois, M. Nicolaidis, "New Techniques for SET Sensitivity and Propagation Measurement in Flash-based FPGAs", IEEE Transactions on Nuclear Science, Vol. 61, Issue 6, 2014, pp. 3171 – 3177.

[16] N. Rezzak, J. J. Wang, "Single Event Latch-Up Hardening Using TCAD Simulations in 130 nm and 65 nm Embedded SRAM in Flash-based FPGAs", IEEE Transactions on Nuclear Science, Vol. 62, Issue 4, pp. 1599 - 1608

[17] Y. Lien, L. He, "Device and architecture concurrent optimization for FPGA transient soft error rate", IEEE/ACM International Conference on Computer-Aided Design, 2007, pp. 194 – 198

Energy Efficient Adaptive Approach for Dependable Performance in the presence of Timing Interference

Nikolaos Zompakis
ECE, MicroLab-NTUA
Athens, Greece

Michail Noltsis
ECE, MicroLab-NTUA
Athens, Greece

Dimitrios Rodopoulos
IMEC
Leuven, Belgium

Francky Catthoor
IMEC
Leuven, Belgium

Dimitrios Soudris
ECE, MicroLab-NTUA
Athens, Greece

ABSTRACT

Silicon design miniaturization has dramatically improved the integration scale in one chip, highlighting in the same time reliability issues. Error-correction mechanisms deal with these issues ensuring the operation Reliability, Availability and Serviceability (RAS), paying a price in performance. The current study deploys a run-time mechanism that mitigates the correction overhead, guaranteeing the performance dependability. In this direction, a closed-loop controller absorbs the RAS-induced delay by triggering Dynamic Voltage and Frequency Scaling (DVFS) schemes. The novelty is the run-time adjustment of the DVFS responses to the identified performance variability norms. To achieve this, we exploit an adaptive scenario scheduler that reorganizes the scenario hierarchy at run-time. Compared against an approach utilizing a 30% operation frequency guardband, the proposed configuration achieves an 83.9% exploitation of the nominal improvement margins that corresponds to an energy gain up to 15%.

Keywords

Dependable Performance, Dynamic Voltage and Frequency Scaling (DVFS), Reliability, Availability and Serviceability (RAS), System Scenarios

1. INTRODUCTION

Chip design miniaturization brings about reliability issues, highlighting the need for ensuring the Integrated Circuit (IC) functionality in a least-intrusive way. Functional errors can be induced by stochastic factors like random manufacturing defects, aging and gate oxide break down effects or temporary particle interference. The unpredictable nature of such events leads to the deployment of Reliability, Availability and Serviceability (RAS) mechanisms that automatically correct the potential errors, ensuring the system's error-free operation. For the first time, IBM introduces the acronym RAS as a term to describe the robustness of a system in maintaining its availability and data integrity [13]. Considering that the shrinking of device dimensions has rendered the threat of failure manifestation an essential design aspect of a system, several approaches have proposed different RAS mechanisms, targeting either processor or memory failures. In this direction, the exploration of Error Correction Codes (ECC) [9] is widely acceptable as an approach for recovering memory errors. Additionally, memory sparing and mirroring [8] techniques are also popular solutions that exploit hardware redundancy to ensure reliability. Respectively, transient errors on the processor pipeline can be easily mitigated by restarting the CPU, activating an instruction rollback technique as mentioned in [11]. Each RAS instantiation has a timing impact due to the required cycles needed to detect and recover the functionality errors which depends on the failure type as well as the RAS mechanism itself. Related work [6] has quantified this temporal overhead, introducing the term of Performance Vulnerability Factor (PVF).

Permission to make digital or hard copies of all or part of this work for personal or classroom use is granted without fee provided that copies are not made or distributed for profit or commercial advantage and that copies bear this notice and the full citation on the first page. Copyrights for components of this work owned by others than ACM must be honored. Abstracting with credit is permitted. To copy otherwise, or republish, to post on servers or to redistribute to lists, requires prior specific permission and/or a fee. Request permissions from permissions@acm.org.

GLSVLSI '17, May 10-12, 2017, Banff, AB, Canada.
© 2017 ACM. ISBN 978-1-4503-4972-7/17/05...$15.00
DOI: http://dx.doi.org/10.1145/3060403.3060449

Applications' deadline restrictions demand the elimination of the PVF effects apart from correcting functional errors. The definition of a frequency operation guardband that absorbs the timing overhead of extra cycles due to such events is a straight-forward solution that significantly increases energy demands. Though recent approaches [14] have improved the guardband margins, such solutions remain ineffective, especially for resource-restricted devices. Hence, flexible approaches that detect the RAS interventions and take reactions to mitigate the performance degradation, should be studied. In this direction, the exploitation of a Dynamic Voltage and Frequency Scaling (DVFS) technique to ensure performance seems to be promising. Existing work [15], has developed a DVFS energy-aware reliability technique investigating static and dynamic management schemes, applying an earliest-deadline-first (EDF) scheduling. In addition, studies exist focusing on both thread-mapping methodologies and DVFS algorithms that evaluate the use of the latter in real workload scenarios, targeting mostly low-power concerns [7]. Other studies [3], combine DVFS and task mapping to provide trade-offs between performance and reliability. In the domain of mixed criticality systems, task migration is a popular technique [12] to develop fault-tolerant systems that react based on the time criticality of the running task.

The majority of performance and resource-aware reliability approaches in literature can be included in one of the previous indicative solutions, including the guardband technique. The current study attempts to exploit the system scenario concept and solve performance dependability issues. In addition, we present an adaptive approach that imports innovative scheduling schemes, new to the system scenario domain. *The novelty in our implementation lies on identifying norms of RAS performance interference based on the running application situations (RTSs), enabling a partly-proactive mitigation approach.*

In a more elaborate comparison, we can distinguish some common characteristics between the aforementioned approaches that are differentiated from our implementations, which provides improved design perspectives. The existing approaches 1) activate system reactions in a task-level granularity, unable to exploit energy and performance margins in the intra-task level, 2) utilize heuristics to dynamically manage system slack and 3) provide mostly reactive rather than proactive capabilities, expect from study [3] that incorporates soft-error tolerance exploiting a genetic algorithm. Respectively, the current study: 1) schedules intra-task scenario-based [5] reactions, relying on run-time system variability and thus exploiting resource trade-offs in a more efficient manner, 2) instead of having heavy computational heuristics to restrain system slack, a design time analysis in RTS-level permits a more accurate and cost-efficient identification of the operation variability, and 3) incorporates proactive characteristics via the adjustment to the estimated norms of the performance fluctuations, instead of relying on heuristic algorithms (as in [3]). Lastly, compared to existing work in the system scenario scheduling [5], we add the dependability context through substantial extensions, as outlined in Sections 3, 4.

2. FOUNDATIONS

A system scenario approach utilizes a PID controller with the mission to mitigate performance degradation effects by applying suitable DVFS schemes. The controller traces the time delay due to the RAS interventions, exploiting a scenario detector. The latter provides the expected execution cycles for each run time situation (RTS) of the application namely, the cycle budgets ($\hat{R}[n]$). An excess of a cycle budget is identified as a RAS intervention. The application RTSs have been analyzed at design time and have been clustered in a number of scenario cycle budgets as later explained. During the application's execution, the scenario detector identifies the current RTS, monitoring specific application RTS-related variables [5]. The PID controller recognizes the deviation from the scenario budget as a RAS intervention and triggers a respective DVFS scheme that equalizes the produced time slack. The slack for an RTS ($s[n]$) with a given cycle budget is the time deviation between a reference frequency (m_{ref}) operation and the current operating frequency (m_n). Figure 1 depicts the functionality of the proposed PID controller which is thoroughly discussed in previous work [10] and although exploits cycle budgets, does not include the scenario concept. Table 1 explains the involved variables. The aim of the PID controller in each identified scenario is to eliminate either the negative slack (due to RAS intervention) or the positive slack (due to frequency over-boosting).

The accurate identification of the running slack is critical to achieve optimal PID responses and is directly correlated

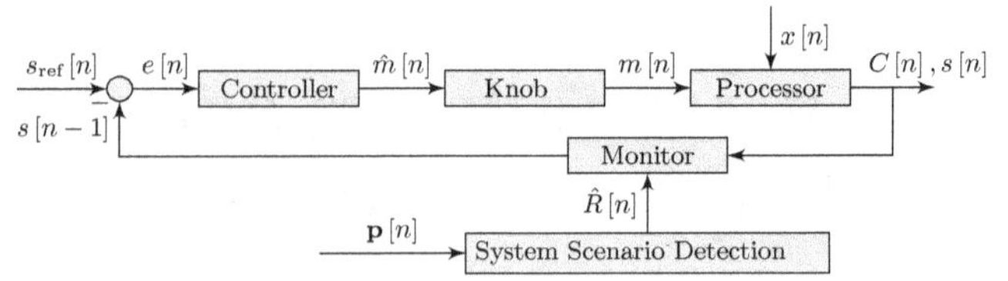

Figure 1: Block diagram of the PID controller [10]

Table 1: Variables of the proposed controller [10]

$s_{ref}[n]$	Target slack specification (0 unless else specified)	$x[n]$	Timing noise interfering with RTS
$s[n-1]$	Slack at the end of the previous RTS	$C[n]$	Actual budget of current RTS
$e[n]$	Error signal $s_{ref}[n-1] - s[n-1]$	$s[n]$	Slack at the end of the current RTS
$\hat{m}[n]$	Proposed frequency multiplier	$\hat{R}[n]$	Default timing budget for current RTS

to the scenario definition. In this point, it is important to examine in more details the meaning of the RTS and the system scenarios. A RTS is a deterministic piece of an application code with constant cost dimensions that can be used as an execution unit [5]. The wealth of RTSs in a real application is produced by any source of variation such as conditional branches and workload fluctuations. In our work, each RTS respects a timing deadline, as indicted by a default cycle budget and the applicable reference frequency (m_{ref}). Each application function corresponds to a sequence of RTSs. In fact, we can easily expand our definition so that a sequence rather than one RTS respects a timing deadline. However, this is outside the scope of our implementation since we focus on working on RTS-level. Nevertheless, the surplus of RTSs in real applications, renders their exploitation as cycle budget references prohibitive. The system scenario approach [5], overcomes this issue by replacing the RTSs with representative cases called system scenarios, paying a price in accuracy. Assuming a workload of A different RTSs, each with cycle budget N_i, where $i = 0, 1, \ldots, A$, the goal of the methodology is to narrow down to B scenarios, each with cycle budget estimators $\hat{N}_j$, where $j = 0, 1, \ldots, B$ and $A >> B$. The detection of the cycle budgets can be implemented with a cost efficient way in hardware or in software, replacing RTSs with scenarios.

The key point in the definition of the scenarios is the efficient clustering of the RTSs into groups based on their cost similarity. Considering that each RTS has a constant cycle budget, several DVFS schemes provide different cost trade-offs. Given a number of DVFS points on a processor, we can draw an energy vs delay line for each RTS. A depicture of the RTS on a Pareto space creates a hierarchy of RTSs based on their position in the cost space, as shown in Figure 2. RTSs closer to the start of the axes have more restricted cycle budgets. The system scenarios cluster the metric space into scenario areas, hiding the details of the individual RTSs. Each RTS in a scenario is represented by the minimum RTS cycle budget (see Figure 2, RTS3) to ensure the most restricted deadline in the scenario. This is important considering that scenarios are used to estimate the reference slack (s_{ref}) in the PID controller. Moreover, this approach creates an overestimated impression of negative slack for the other RTSs in the scenario (RTS1 and RTS2) that leads to over-boosting frequencies with inefficient energy results. Characterizing RTSs under the most restricted budget (MRB) of the scenario inevitably introduces a clustering overhead (light gray and brown area, see

Figure 2). As clustering overhead ($Cl_{RTS[i]}$) for each RTS is defined the cost distances (D_1 and D_2) between the original position ($OP_{RTS[i]}$) of the involved RTSs (RTS1 and RTS2) from MRB (RTS3). Equation 1 formulates the problem. This overhead manifests every time the RTS occurs at run-time. Thus, the total clustering overhead ($Cl\_ov_{RTS[i]}$) will be proportional to the frequency of the RTS appearance (Equation 2). $Cl\_ov_{RTS[i]}$ represents the deviation between the reference and the actual cycle budget and it is always negative since clustering tends to provide more restricted deadlines compared to the optimal case where every RTS is treated fully individually. The distance of each RTS pareto curve expressed as clustering overhead, defines the scenario accuracy and represents the first clustering criterion of RTSs into scenarios.

$$Cl_{RTS[i]} = \sum_{i=0}^{n} MRB_{RTS[i]} - OP_{RTS[i]} \quad (1)$$

$$Cl\_ov_{RTS[i]} = \sum_{i=0}^{n} Fr_{RTS[i]} * Cl_{RTS[i]} \quad (2)$$

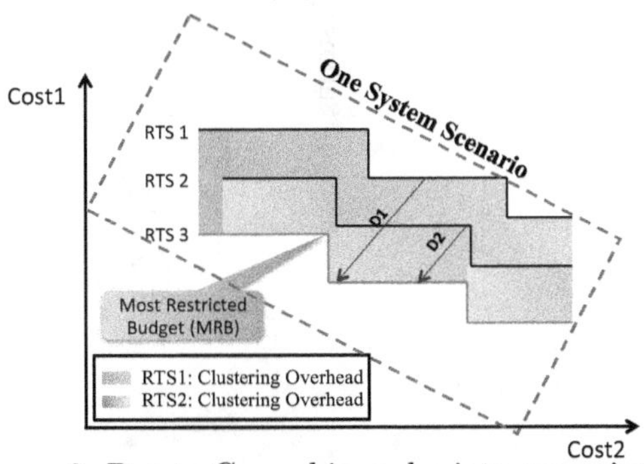

Figure 2: Pareto Curve hierarchy into scenarios [4]

The second criterion is the scenario switching. We prefer stable scenarios due to the transition cost between the scenarios. This cost will normally depend heavily on the initial and final state. Considering the average transition frequency ($Fr_{Sen[i\rightarrow j]}$) from scenario j to the next scenario j+1 and the respecting switching cost ($Swit_{Sen[j\rightarrow j+1]}$), the mathematical formulation of the total switching overhead ($Swit\_ov_{RTS[i]}$) is given by the following equation:

$$Swit\_ov_{RTS[i]} = \sum_{i=0}^{n} Fr_{Sen[j\rightarrow j+1]} * Swit_{Sen[j\rightarrow j+1]} \quad (3)$$

Optimization approaches of the aforementioned overheads tend to be competitive in respect to the targeted objectives. A decrease of the clustering overhead increases the switching overhead and vice versa. A balance between them can be achieved [4] by applying a suitable initial distribution of the RTSs into scenarios at design time.

Therefore, the exploitation of the scenario detector allows to the PID controller to react at the presence of negative slack, enabling respective DVFS schemes. However, the time to absorb the extra cycles can create transition effects with temporary delays that can effect the stability of the application performance. The next section examines how this instability can be avoided applying revisions of the scenario sets at run-time.

3. SCENARIO ADAPTATION

On the condition that RTS positions in the scenarios can be updated at run-time, the scenario detector can modify the RTS hierarchy by re-clustering the existing scenario distribution. This process provides a run-time adjustment of the RTS cycle budget estimations. If a RTS often appears with a specific cycle noise, this RTS fits to a new scenario by removing cycles from its budget equal to the noise. This new fit forces the PID controller to absorb the time delay before its presence. Figure 3 presents the two trends. The RAS interventions shift the RTS position far from the start of the axes. The re-clustering creates a positive slack (see Figure 3) that works as an offset of the expected negative slack equalizing the time loss. The scope is to keep the RTS's original position stable. The RTS slack history is recorded and updated on fixed time windows, available to be exploited at run-time. The re-clustering is applied with priority in RTSs with the most intense cycle noise instances. This leads the PID controller to act partially proactive, considering that RAS events are gradually becoming a norm on the target processor. For each RTS re-positioning, an individual re-clustering decision aims to equalize performance degradation as described in the following section. Considering the re-clustering decisions, the key point is to distinguish transient from (quasi-) permanent cycle noise interference events. For example, a very brief cycle noise burst that is never reoccurring should not be triggering a re-clustering process. The hardware degradation effects that occur during operation lifetime cannot be predicted in advance. Thus, an updated history trace of the slack per RTS is needed to consider the error fluctuation during execution time. The current slack ($RTS\_Slack[i]$) for a moving average window of K_w RTS executions is given by Equation 4. After identifying a new trend in cycle noise manifestation, a re-clustering of the RTSs into system scenarios follows.

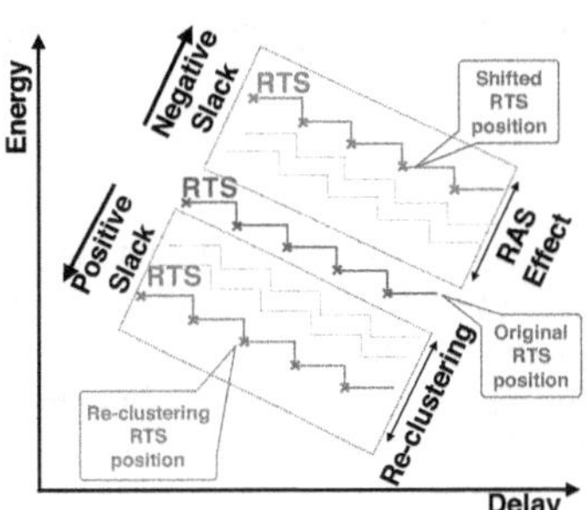

Figure 3: Slack Impact

$$Slack_{RTS[i]} = \frac{\sum_{i=0}^{N} (RTS\_Slack[N - k_w + i])}{k_w} \quad (4)$$

Algorithm 1 provides a brief description of the re-clustering process. For each RTS execution, its original scenario cycle budget (sc_{rts}) and cycle noise (sl_{rts}) are recorded while the traced RTS slack is registered to a list ($rts\_list(rts)$). If the RTS already exists in the list, its record is updated ($update\_rts\_slack$). A re-clustering is triggered for a specific time window ($check\_slack\_status(rts)$) if the status of the involved RTS shows a stable behavior. Also, information about the distance from the neighboring scenarios ($Find\_scenario(Np)$) is exploited to recognize the optimal re-clustering decision, updating only the scenario data that have changed. Each re-clustering ($Merge(rts, Sc\_fit)$) is based on the new RTS position ($new\_rts\_pos(rts, sl\_rts)$) in the metric space after reviewing the noise updated data, ensuring that the RTS deadlines in the new scenario will be respected with the minimum clustering overhead. The re-clustering is a parallel process that does not interrupt the operation of the PID controller. In any case, the re-clustering time can easily remain as fraction of the RTS operation time,

Algorithm 1 Re-clustering Algorithm

```
sc_rts=detect_scenario(rts) {scenario identification}
sl_rts = pid_controller(sc_rts) {slack identification}
if sl_rts > 0 then
    if rts_list(rts) then
        update_rts_slack(rts, sl_rts) {update rts slack history}
        if check_slack_status(rts) then
            Np=new_rts_pos(rts, sl_rts) {new rts position}
            Sc_fit=Find_scenario(Np) {best fitting to scenario}
            Merge (rts, Sc_fit) {merge rts to the new scenario}
        end if
    else
        store_rts_list(rts, sl) {new rts slack registration}
    end if
end if
```

due to the simplicity of the RTS-reordering algorithm (Section 4). At the end of each re-clustering, the PID controller triggers the suitable DVFS scheme, eliminating slack with the minimum energy cost. A trade-off between slack and energy exists that will be explored in Section 5 with simulation results.

4. RE-CLUSTERING DECISIONS

The re-clustering process changes the RTS hierarchy into scenarios by removing from the default RTS reference budgets the cycle noise (Equation 4), artificially creating positive slack by shifting the position of the RTSs into the scenarios (see Figure 3). This creates the impression of an extra delay to the PID controller proportional to the removed cycles, triggering more aggressive DVFS schemes that absolve the negative slack. Examining the re-clustering decisions that have to be considered at run-time, we outline the following cases:

- In the first case, the scenario budget is restricted enough and no slack exists, hence there is no need for scenario change (see Figure 4a). The added noise (red shifted Pareto curve) activates a revision of the RTS budget (green Pareto curve) that does not exceed the distance between the RTS and the scenario (Sc_2), exploiting the clustering overhead as an offset. Thus, clustering overhead can be utilized as a proxy of cycle noise tolerance. A high clustering overhead permits wide RTS shifts, absorbing slack and paying the cost of overestimated DVFS schemes. The next four cases cover situations where the slack cannot be avoided.
- In the second case (see Figure 4b), in order to equalize the noise delay (red Pareto curve), the revised RTS (green Pareto curve) is located just under the scenario budget SC_1. Thus, Scenario #1 represents a new more restricted case due to the RTS shifting that modifies the existing scenario budget.
- In the third case (see Figure 4c), a new distinct scenario budget is created. Two reasons lead to such a decision: 1) none of the existing scenario cycle budgets cover the new RTS shift or 2) the creation of an individual scenario is more cost-effective than merging with an existing scenario.
- In the fourth case (see Figure 4d), the shifted RTS (green Pareto curve) is closer to a neighboring scenario (SC_2) than to the original (SC_1). Thus, the RTS is merged into the new scenario (SC_2) achieving a more optimal fit, considering the distance.
- The fifth case (see Figure 4e) is a combination of the second and the third aforementioned cases. A neighboring scenario merges the revised RTS. However, the position of the RTS in the new scenario is located just under the scenario budget, changing the new scenario cycle budget as the most restricted case.

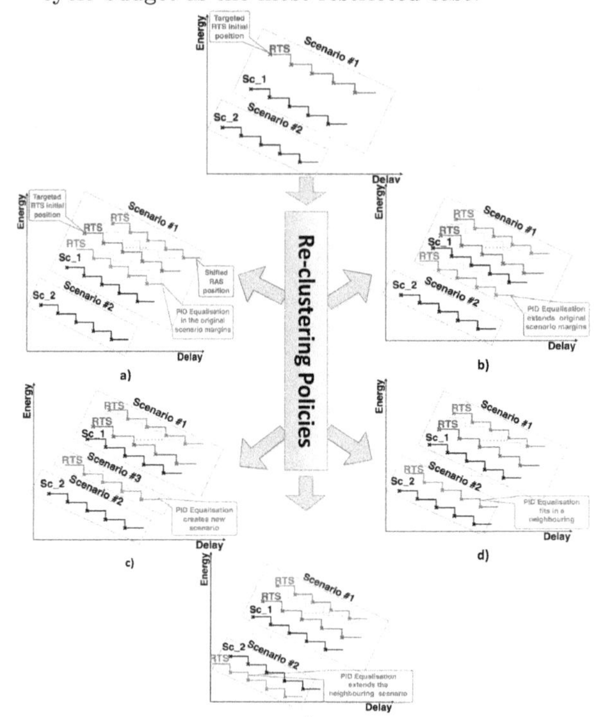

Figure 4: Reclustering policies

5. SIMULATION RESULTS

The application under study is commercially used for spectrum sensing and band allocation purposes [2], and constitutes an exploration space of about 800 RTSs, clustered in 30 scenarios that achieve an efficient initial balance between scenario overheads [4]. We submit this workload to a simulator that has been presented in previous work [10], to study our proposed mitigation scheme. We will focus on an implementation based on the system scenario approach with no re-clustering mechanisms and also on an implementation that incorporates the scenario adjustment concept and examine the efficiency of both configurations. For the sake of completeness, we repeat the basic functionality of the simulator here. The PID controller operates at RTS-granularity thus, the scenario unit instantiates also the cycle budget estimator $\hat{N}_n$ in the same basis.

Additionally, cycle noise is injected based on the values of Λ and M that represent respectively the rate and amplitude of RAS events in terms of clock cycles. We assume that cycle noise follows a bivariate Gaussian distribution with mean Λ and M values (λ and μ) and σ ($\sigma\{\Lambda\}$, $\sigma\{M\}$). The timing and power models of the simulator create traces from which DVF (Deadline Vulnerability Factor) and total energy can be deduced. Given the definition of cycle budget estimators in Table 1 and their derivation, DVF expresses the per unit increase in execution time required for an instruction stream, following the temporal overhead of invoked

RAS mechanisms. Respectively, PVF (Performance Vulnerability Factor) expresses the per unit increase in number of clock cycles required for a specific workload, as a result of RAS technique invocation. It is noteworthy that all overheads of DVFS actuations are included in both the timing and power models. Finally, at the end of each RTS, the PID controller selects the frequency multiplier of the next iteration, as detailed in Figure 1.

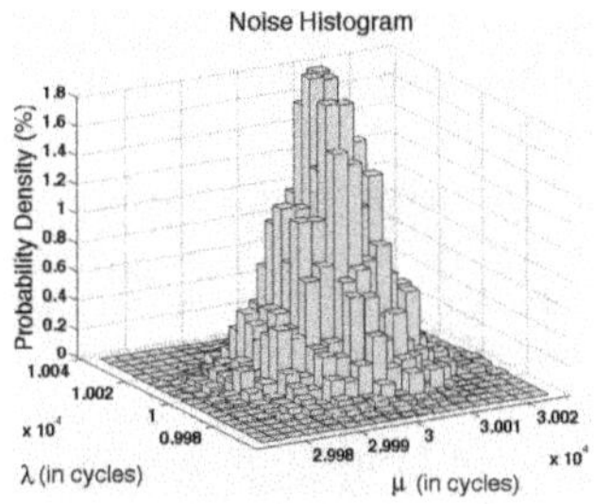

(a) Cycle Noise

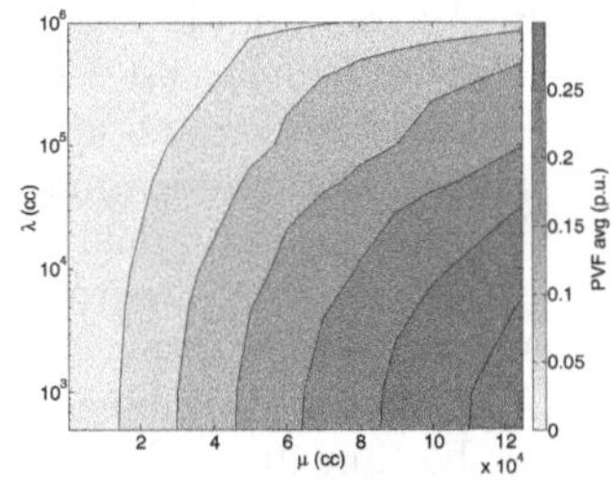

(b) PVF

Figure 5: a) Cycle Noise for one RTS stream b) Average PVF values for 100 iterations

The simulation results presented herein correspond to a set of random streams of the target application RTS. The simulated workload assumes equally probable RTSs. Cycle noise is injected by sweeping μ and λ values while $\sigma\{M\}$,$\sigma\{\Lambda\}$ are kept constant. The noise histogram for one stream of RTSs is shown in Figure 5a. In fact, each measurement corresponds to a stream of RTSs and PID controller gains are set following the tuning Zieger Nichols method [1]. For each combination of μ and λ, we present the average over 100 random measurements to provide insight into the statistical variability of our simulation results. To highlight the benefits of the scenario concept we will examine three test-cases: 1) a 30% frequency guardband utilized to alleviate cycle noise, 2) a system scenario scheduling without re-clustering capabilities and 3) an adaptive scenario implementation that realizes the aforementioned re-clustering schemes. A first conclusion of our experiments is that apart from extreme noise cases (high μ and low λ values), the PID controller manages to enable dependable performance, especially considering the increment in PVF (see Figure 5b) which is the result of cycle noise injection.

5.1 Dependability Results

From Figure 6, we clearly distinguish the effectiveness of the adaptive scenario configuration over the system scenario one. While in the system scenario implementation, DVF seems to balance to a fixed value close to zero, in the adaptive scenarios implementation, DVF adjusts more accurately. The reader should keep in mind that since DVF describes the increase in execution time due to cycle noise, a DVF equal to zero implies that our configuration has successfully absorbed all temporal overhead with no time penalty. In fact, the timing performance gain of the adaptive scenario approach is 5% higher than that achieved by the system scenario while it is less effective than the guardband approach only for limited and extreme noise cases. For a transition period (0-2000 ms), the number of the adaptive scenarios is fluctuating to reach to a stable state, as shown in Figure 7. During this time, the re-clustering process generates new scenarios, increasing gradually their number up to 38 (1000 ms) and after this point some of the existing scenarios are merged to finally reach the number of 33 (2000 ms). Thus, the adaptation process creates and merges scenarios by applying the aforementioned re-clustering decisions (Section 4) to find the optimum scenario hierarchy. When this is achieved (after 2000 ms), the scenarios remain stable and the DVF comes close to zero.

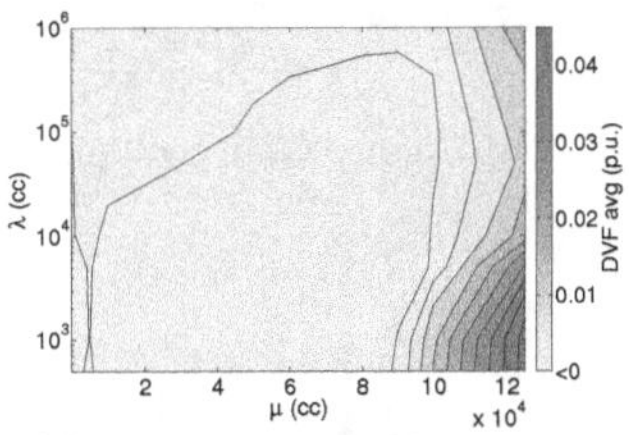

(a) DVF Adaptive Scenarios

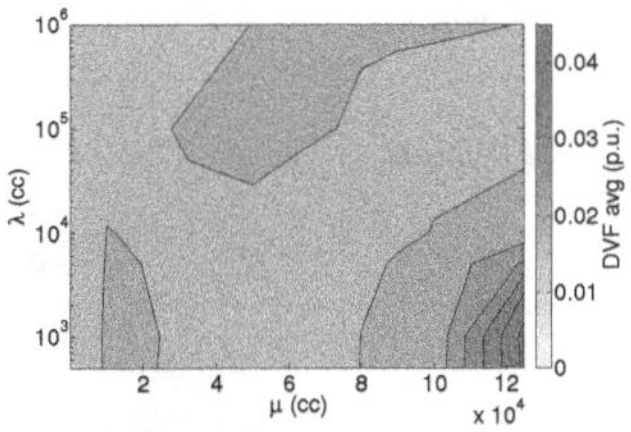

(b) DVF System Scenarios

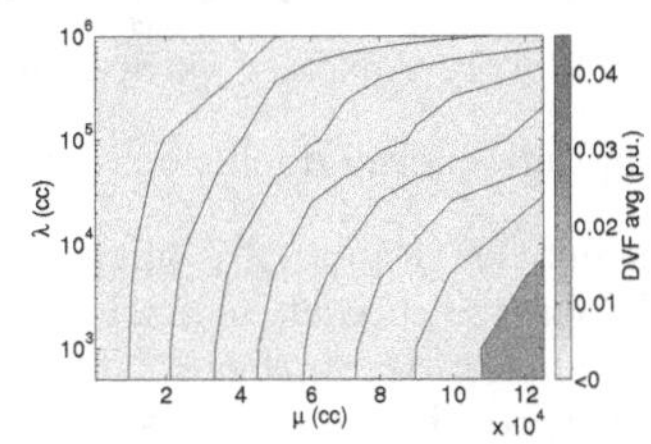

(c) DVF Guardband

Figure 6: Average DVF values for 100 iterations

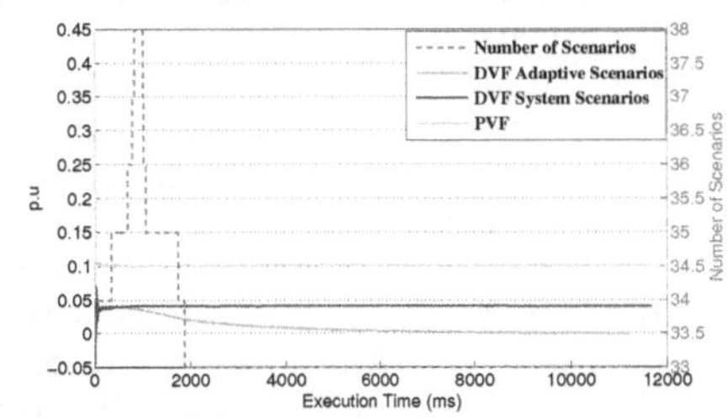

Figure 7: Performance adjustability instance

5.2 Energy Results

The energy gain comparing (see Fig. 8a, 8b) the two scenario approaches with the frequency guardband test-case is clearly beneficial and reaches up to 15%. The gain is decreasing as the injected cycle noise profile becomes more aggressive (high μ and low λ). This result is not unexpected, due to fact that the scenarios are stabilized to a state similar to the guardband's for extreme noise cases. Hence, without applying an over-boosting frequency policy with unnecessary energy consumption results, both scenario approaches seem to ensure performance dependability. In fact, considering the notional energy gain margins as highlighted by the energy deviation between the guardband frequency as worst-case and the reference frequency as basis, adaptive scenarios achieve an average exploitation of 83.9%, ensuring performance dependability.

The energy consumption deviation between the system and adaptive scenario is minor and does not exceed the 3% (see Figure 8c). This occurs due to the fact that the extra energy consumption from frequency boosting on the adaptive scenarios is partially equalized by the less number of DVFS switches due to the adjustment. Nevertheless, a fundamental trade-off exists between the achieved performance as expressed by the DVF and the energy impact that will be examined in the next subsection.

5.3 Design Trade-offs

The key issue in the achievement of several trade-offs is the increase of the reference cycle budgets both in system and adaptive scenarios. This is implemented by applying homogeneously a percentage relaxation factor F_{rel} to the

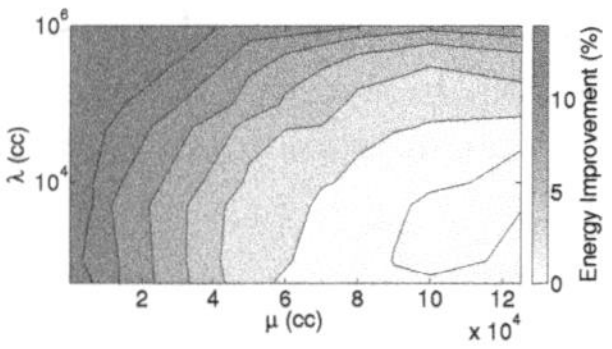

(a) Energy Gain Adaptive

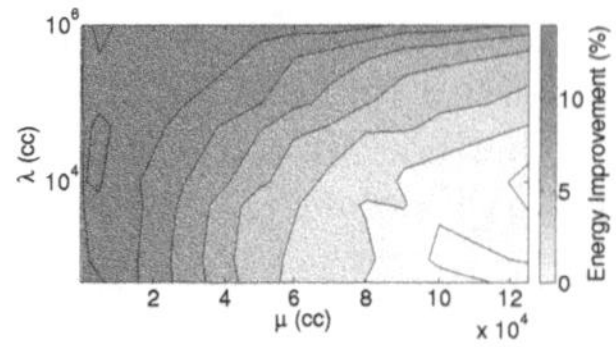

(b) Energy Gain System

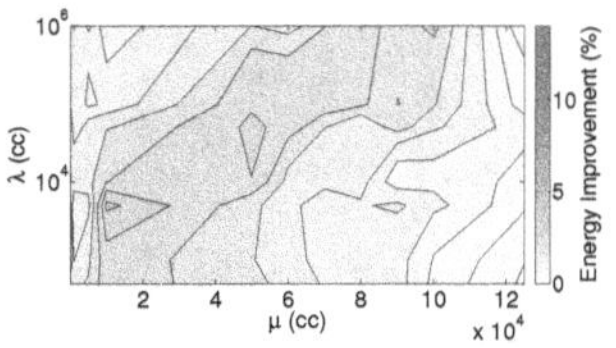

(c) Energy Adaptive vs System Scenarios

Figure 8: Percentage energy deviations for 100 iterations

MRB of each scenario (Figure 2), having an equal clustering overhead increase in each scenario. Equation 5 formulates the new clustering overhead. This approach provides better energy results due to less accurate slack estimations in the PID controller and worst performance due to the increase of the clustering overhead. Figure 9 presents the trade-offs between system and adaptive scenarios for several relaxation factors (0-10%) and two noise instantiations. The Pareto curves of the two approaches (adaptive vs system scenarios) seem to be very close, presenting similar cost trade-offs (delay-energy) for a specific constraint area ($0.04 < DVF < 0.08$). The adaptive scenario appears just a little worse trend (longer distance from the start of the metric axes) due to the extra implementation cost that they require. We can observe that the adaptive scenario approach is of high value when strict dependability constraints are demanded. In fact, it is clear that the system scenario approach is unable to meet such demands. However, when timing constraints relax ($DVF > 0.04$), the system scenario approach appears to be Pareto-optimal.

$$Cl'_{RTS[i]} = \sum_{i=0}^{n} (1 + F_{rel}) \times MRB_{RTS[i]} - OP_{RTS[i]} \quad (5)$$

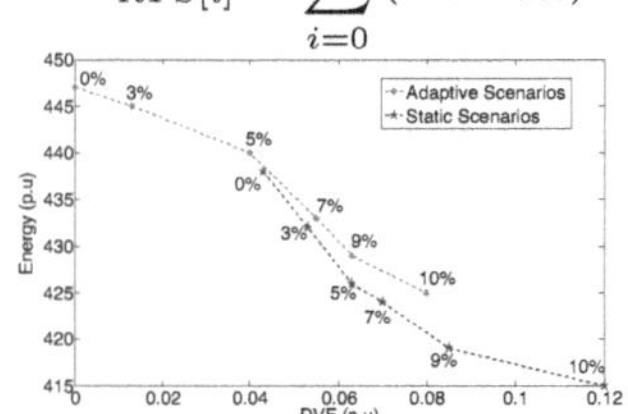

(a) Noise #1 (μ=1×10^4, λ=5×10^3)

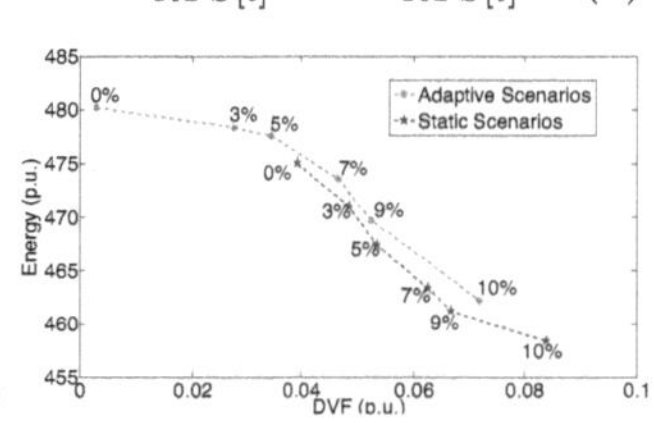

(b) Noise #2 (μ=5×10^4, λ=5×10^3)

Figure 9: Performance (DVF) Vs Energy trade-offs

6. CONCLUSION

In the context of the current study, we deployed both a system scenario-based PID mechanism and a partially proactive scenario configuration that adjust the reactions of the controller at the presence of RAS interventions ensuring performance dependability. The key point in the adaptive approach is the re-clustering of the existing system scenarios with a flexible way, absorbing the cycle noise that is gradually becoming a norm during the observed application operation. The simulation results prove the efficiency of this approach, ensuring the system dependability constraints while achieving an energy gain up to 15% compared to a guardbanding implementation and exploiting in average 83.9% of the notional energy gain margins. Future work consists of implementing a fully proactive mechanism that will further increase performance dependability.

7. ACKNOWLEDGMENTS

Current work is partially supported by the FP7-612069-HARPA EU project.

8. REFERENCES

[1] K. Astrom and T. Hagglund. *PID Controllers: Theory, Design and Tuning*. International Society of Automation, second edition, 1995.

[2] Thales. Communication and Security. Spectrum monitoring and homeland security. https://www.thalesgroup.com/en/worldwide/security/spectrum-monitoring-and-homeland-security.

[3] A. Das et al. Combined dvfs and mapping exploration for lifetime and soft-error susceptibility improvement in mpsocs. In *2014 Design, Automation & Test in Europe Conference & Exhibition (DATE)*, pages 1–6. IEEE, 2014.

[4] N. Z. et al. Enabling efficient system configurations for dynamic wireless applications using system scenarios. *International journal of wireless information networks*, 20(2):140–156, 2013.

[5] S. V. Gheorghita et al. System-scenario-based design of dynamic embedded systems. *ACM Transactions on Design Automation of Electronic Systems (TODAES)*, 14(1):3, 2009.

[6] D. Hardy et al. The performance vulnerability of architectural and non-architectural arrays to permanent faults. In *2012 45th Annual IEEE/ACM International Symposium on Microarchitecture*, pages 48–59. IEEE, 2012.

[7] S. Herbert et al. Analysis of dynamic voltage/frequency scaling in chip-multiprocessors. In *Int. Symp. on Low Power Electronics and Design (ISLPED) ACM/IEEE*, pages 38–43. IEEE, 2007.

[8] C. S. Mugunda et al. Improving fault tolerance. Dell Power Solutions, August 2005.

[9] G. Neuberger et al. A multiple bit upset tolerant sram memory. *ACM Transactions on Design Automation of Electronic Systems (TODAES)*, 8(4):577–590, 2003.

[10] D. Rodopoulos et al. Tackling performance variability due to ras mechanisms with pid-controlled dvfs. *IEEE Comput. Archit. Lett.*, 14(2):156–159, 2015.

[11] T. Sakata et al. A cost-effective dependable microcontroller architecture with instruction-level rollback for soft error recovery. In *37th Annual IEEE/IFIP Inter. Conf. on Dependable Systems and Networks (DSN'07)*, pages 256–265. IEEE, 2007.

[12] P. K. Saraswat et al. Task migration for fault-tolerance in mixed-criticality embedded systems. *ACM SIGBED Review*, 6(3):6, 2009.

[13] D. Siewiorek and R. Swarz. *Reliable Computer Systems (3rd Ed.): Design and Evaluation.* A. K. Peters, Ltd., Natick, MA, USA, 1998.

[14] V. M. van Santen et al. Designing guardbands for instantaneous aging effects. In *Proc. of the 53rd Ann. Design Automation Conf.*, pages 69–75. ACM, 2016.

[15] D. Zhu and H. Aydin. Reliability-aware energy management for periodic real-time tasks. *IEEE Trans. Comput.*, 58(10):1382–1397, 2009.

Design Automation for Paper Microfluidics with Passive Flow Substrates

Joshua Potter[1], William Grover[2], Philip Brisk[1]
[1]Department of Computer Science and Engineering, [2] Department of Bioengineering
University of California, Riverside

ABSTRACT

This paper introduces a novel software framework to support automated development of paper-based microfluidic devices. Compared to existing lab-on-a-chip technologies, paper-based microfluidics differs in terms of substrate technologies and point-of-care usage across a wide variety environmental conditions. This paper addresses the contexts in which the software can address these challenges and presents several initial case studies that demonstrate the capabilities of the framework to produce workable and usable paper microfluidic devices.

CCS Concepts

•**Applied computing** → *Computer-aided design; Health care information systems;*

Keywords

Paper Microfluidics; Design Automation; Capillary; Passive Flow; Assay

1. INTRODUCTION

Each year, approximately 5 million people worldwide die from AIDS and tuberculosis, another 4.3 million die from respiratory infections, around 2.9 million die from enteric infections, and about 1 million die from malaria. Virtually all of these deaths occur in developing countries [5]. Diagnostics suitable for use in resource-limited settings have the potential to save millions of lives each year and improve the quality of life worldwide. Even in first-world countries, a lack of adequate diagnostics makes healthcare less efficient and a financial burden to society. Better point-of-care diagnostics can play a crucial role in health care by providing doctors with rapid diagnoses, enabling treatment to begin while the patient is still at the hospital. This reduces the number of hospital visits and helps patients recover faster; however, developing diagnostics for successful use in resource-limited and point-of-care settings is a formidable challenge.

Permission to make digital or hard copies of all or part of this work for personal or classroom use is granted without fee provided that copies are not made or distributed for profit or commercial advantage and that copies bear this notice and the full citation on the first page. Copyrights for components of this work owned by others than ACM must be honored. Abstracting with credit is permitted. To copy otherwise, or republish, to post on servers or to redistribute to lists, requires prior specific permission and/or a fee. Request permissions from permissions@acm.org.

GLSVLSI '17, May 10-12, 2017, Banff, AB, Canada

© 2017 ACM. ISBN 978-1-4503-4972-7/17/05...$15.00

DOI: http://dx.doi.org/10.1145/3060403.3060476

1.1 Motivation

The *World Health Organization (WHO)* recently defined the *ASSURED* criteria, a set of characteristics that are essential for diagnostics in both resource-limited and point-of-care applications [5]. *ASSURED* diagnostics must be:

A: Affordable by those at risk of infection
S: Sensitive (few false-negatives)
S: Specific (few false-positives)
U: User-friendly (requiring minimal training)
R: Rapid (treatment at first visit) and robust (no refrigerated storage)
E: Equipment-free (no additional equipment needed for use)
D: Delivered to those who need it (small and portable)

Paper microfluidic diagnostic devices satisfy all seven of the *ASSURED* criteria [7]. In contrast to expensive conventional laboratory-scale instruments or integrated laboratories-on-a-chip, paper microfluidic devices are made from inexpensive materials, are easily mass-produced, and exhibit the high sensitivity and specificity that are hallmarks of more complicated microfluidic technologies. Meanwhile their simple operation is user-friendly and easy to use (consider the simplicity of the home pregnancy test strip).

By operating on extremely small sample volumes (nanoliters to microliters), paper microfluidic diagnostics can be very rapid. Using dehydrated reagents immobilized in the paper eliminates the need for refrigeration and making them more robust than laboratories-on-a-chip or laboratory-scale instruments. Paper microfluidics often integrate the readout into the paper itself (e.g., as a color change), eliminating the need for equipment like microscopes or sensors and makes paper microfluidics essentially equipment-free; in fact, recent work has shown that cellular phone cameras can provide effective readout capabilities for paper microfluidics. Being small and disposable, paper microfluidic devices can easily be delivered to doctors in the field and stocked at the point-of-care. As such, these devices are poised to proliferate as healthcare diagnostic solutions throughout the world.

1.2 Current Paper Microfluidic Design Practices

Despite the aforementioned advantages, designing, testing, and validating paper microfluidic diagnostics remains a significant hurdle, as the task is presently done by hand using software such as AutoCAD® or Adobe Illustrator®. Each design is essentially a "hard-coded" ASPMD (application-specific paper microfluidic device; analogous to an ASIC).

Although paper microfluidic devices are one-time use and disposable, during the development phase, researchers must create multiple variations to compare design performance and accuracy, and possibly to adapt the device for use in varying environmental conditions. Under the current design paradigm, the researcher would need to hand-design each variation, which is time-consuming, labor-intensive and prone to inaccuracy. These issues also limit the potential complexity of the biochemical assays (step-by-step chemical reactions) that a paper microfluidic device can realistically be designed to perform.

1.3 Traditional Circuits vs. Passive Flow Devices

Although there are many parallels between traditional circuit design and the proposed passive-flow technologies, the fundamental difficulties stem from the differences between electricity and fluids. When working with electricity, our design concerns stem from resistance, voltage, amperage, and heat. As long as we complete a circuit, the electrons will get there eventually.

When dealing with fluids, we have similar concerns when it comes to resistance to flow, capacity of flow and rate of flow. However additional concerns related to fluid dynamics include gravitational effects, fluid surface tension alongside substrate resistance, and finally, a limited amount of fluid to perform the process under test. Further complicating placement and routing, locations and distances are not necessarily discrete as successful device and layout generation may need fractional modification, therefore we have a continuous range of viable locations.

1.4 Contribution

This paper presents a software framework created by the authors intended to assist developers to design new paper microfluidic devices. Developers can use the framework to prototype and test new designs, which includes varying the underlying substrates and experimenting with passive flow networks. The framework also provides the capability to reliably reproduce devices streamlined for in-situ fabrication and to provide tools for testing and analysis of the designs; this, in turn, informs the alteration and rapid prototyping of design variations, helping to account for test results, environmental conditions, impact on physical substrates and fluids, and accuracy under test.

2. DESIGN AUTOMATION FRAMEWORK

Fig.1 provides an overview of the framework. It includes a library of paper microfluidic components, which can be rapidly assembled into netlists which form new devices. Once the netlist is assembled, the framework renders the device using established file formats (*PDF*, *DXF*, *SVG*). We now introduce the framework's operation from the bottom-up.

2.1 Technical Details

The framework has been developed using C++ 11 in the Ubuntu v14.0.4 Linux distribution. Code is compiled using GCC v5.1 compiler via a *makefile* utilizing multi-threading, `-Wall` and `-Werror` flags. The programs and libraries are constructed to be platform-independent as much as possible, performing file I/O and other platform-specific tasks in individual libraries. As of this publication, the application is command-line only.

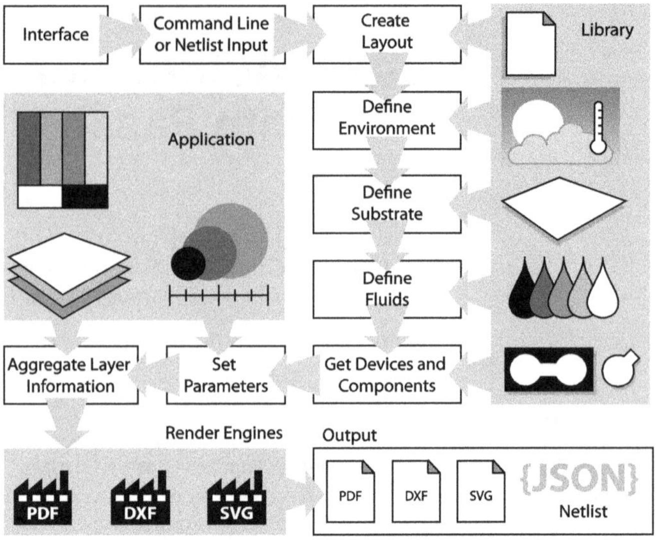

Figure 1: Framework overview

2.2 Segments, Paths, and Primitives

Segments, *paths*, and *primitives* refer to the elemental geometric shapes that can be printed onto a paper substrate. A segment is a Bezier curve, featuring source and sink coordinates that indicate a direction of drawing when rendered by the framework. The source and sink have handle coordinates that define the curve. If the handle coordinates are the same as the source and sink coordinates, then the curve degenerates to a line segment (Fig.2(a)) otherwise, they form a curve (Fig.2(b)).

Paths are constructed by concatenating multiple segments (Fig.2(c)). Primitives are closed paths, representing geometric shapes such as quadrilaterals, circles, ellipses, and polygons (Fig.2(d)). Union and intersection operations applied to Primitives can form complex shapes and Primitives with negative space (Fig.2(e)). The *Zero-sum Winding Rule* [2] can identify overlapping and negative spaces to determine the underlying paths that characterize the final shape.

2.3 Components and Devices

A *component* is a dynamically generated, re-usable object whose geometry is defined by one or more primitives, coupled with its functionality in terms of fluidic actions and abstract dynamics, such as mixing, transport, timing, etc.

A *device* consists of at least one or more components that encapsulate the desired actions and parameters needed to characterize biochemical behavior as described in the assay protocols. Individual components may be scaled or rotated

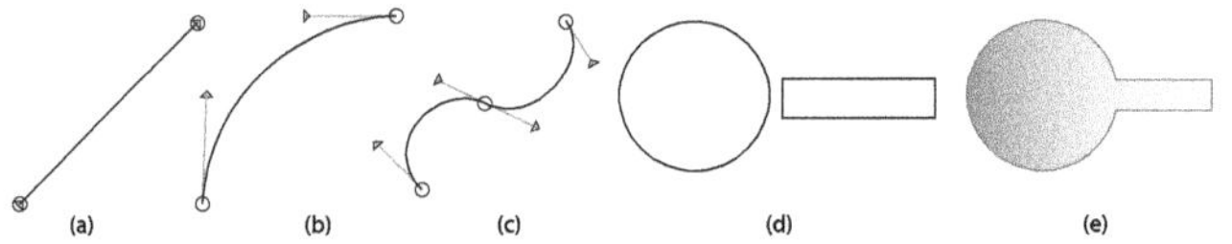

Figure 2: a) line segment, b) curve segment; c) a path constructed from two curve segments; d) a circle and a polygon primitive constructed from curve and straight segments; e) a component formed from multiple primitives.

as needed. Large devices may be specified hierarchically in terms of smaller devices, facilitating composition of multiple assays, either in sequence or in parallel.

2.4 Parameterization

The framework supports *parameterized components and devices*; for example, a straight fluid transport channel can be characterized in terms of its length and width. The device designer can then iterate over multiple versions, for example, to assess behavior of an assay under various loads, conditions, configurations, etc. This can be automated via dynamic drawing based on user-specified parameters. As the designer varies parameter values, the software adjusts and re-renders the component or device as needed.

2.5 Substrates and Substances

It is necessary to understand the properties of both the physical materials that the fluids that are expected to flow through it. The *substrate* abstracts the production of the output to individual pages (for printing) or other options (e.g., computer controlled-paper cutters). It encapsulates physical properties of materials, such as dimensions, margins, output area, expected flow rate, and fluid capacities. Attributes such as base flow rate for a given substrate can be used to calculate flow and dispersion times which can then determine expected execution time, timing variability, fluid consumption, and the probability of successful assay completion. Paper dimensions can be specified including margin size, along with mean flow rate for a fluid to travel within the substrate.

The *substance* encapsulates the physical characteristics of the various fluids, reagents, solutes, flow rates given a particular environment, etc., which are used to evaluate assay feasibility and accuracy, given a substrate.

2.6 Registries

Each device or component has a *registry*, which tracks and resolves the substrates onto which it will be printed. When two components or devices are merged, their registries are merged and reconciled to determine if the substrates and layers are compatible; if not, the device cannot be fabricated. If the device is feasible, a *layer registry* is built to determine which primitives, components, and devices will be printed on each layer. When appropriate, duplicates may be eliminated and components may be transferred from one layer to another, if needed. This reconciliation process produces a distilled list of substrates which the user can then verify for correctness.

2.7 Layouts

Paper dimensions can be specified including margin size, along with mean flow rate for a fluid to travel within the substrate. The *layout* represents the context in which a paper-based biochemical assay operate, including environmental information, substances and substrates, and the base units of measurement. The layout contains the netlist representation of each device, as well as its layer registry.

2.8 Scale and Color

Scale and *color* are application-level attributes that speak to the accuracy of components and may define the basic operating modes of a device. Scale refers to units of measurement (e.g., *mm*-scale devices), including conversion between

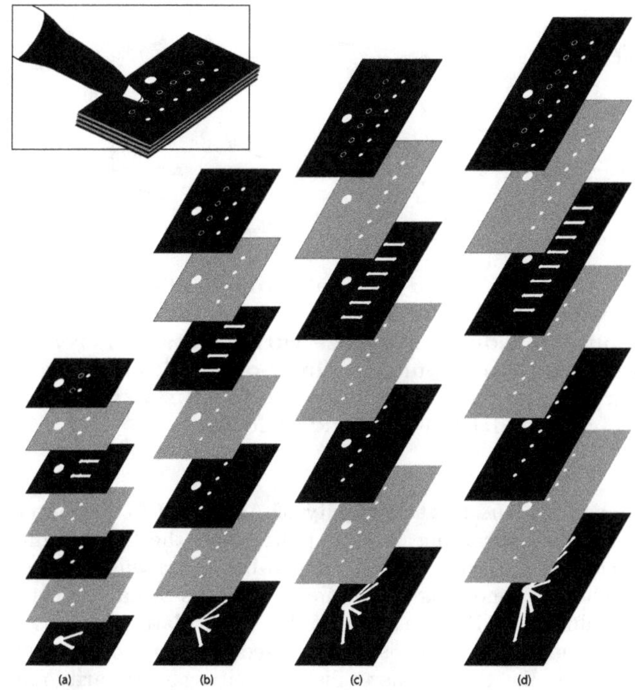

Figure 3: Parameterized fMux designs with a) two channels; b) four channels; c) six channels; and d) eight channels

units. The default internal unit of measurement is millimeters. Storing and maintaining a metric standard minimizes rounding error accumulation and reduces measurement error that can occur when multiple conversions between non-metric measurements cascade. The notion of color includes standard four to six color inks as well as non-ink materials such as wax or metallic ink for printing.

2.9 Environment

The *environment* provides measurements that may influence assay performance and accuracy, such as temperature, barometric pressure, and humidity; this allows designers to characterize the environmental conditions under which a device will properly operate. For example, should a warm temperature prolong flow rates, then various channels and other components should be shortened to maintain the expected runtime; in a humid environment, runtime may increase or cause incorrect mixing. Thus, it may be necessary to produce a general family of devices that are capable of executing one assay under different environmental conditions.

2.10 Rendering Engines

The framework's initial rendering engine outputs the PDF format, which is ubiquitous, and supports vector graphics with high resolution output; in practice, the print or output device, not the PDF format, will limit the achievable resolution of our framework. PDF is platform independent, which simplifies distribution of device designs and enhances reproducibility.

The second rendering engine targets AutoCAD's DXF file format, which has been a stable of computer-aided design (CAD) for decades. The DXF is a platform-agnostic drawing technology that can produce highly accurate vector

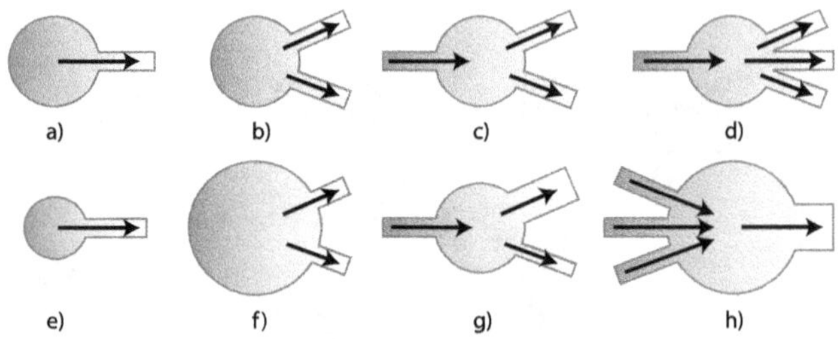

Figure 4: Well and channel components in 8 configurations: a) 1-out; b) 2-out; c) 1-in, 2-out; d) 1-in, 3-out; e) reduced well size with 1-out; f) increased well size with 2-out; g) 1-in, 2-out with channels of varying width; and h) increased well size with 3-in (narrow width), 1-out (wide width).

drawings. Due to the ubiquity of AutoCAD in computer-controlled machining (CNC) applications, the DXF format is compatible with cutting and pen-based drawing devices.

The last rendering engine targets W3C's Scalable Vector Graphics (SVG) format, an XML-based platform-agnostic file format. As SVG is widely used for web content, we expect to use this engine to distribute images primarily rendered for visual display and scientific dissemination.

3. CASE STUDIES

We briefly summarize a set of successful case studies which demonstrate that our framework can be used to print a variety of useful parameterizable components and devices. These case studies validate the practical usability of the framework, along with its basic capabilities.

3.1 Fluidic Multiplexers

We used the framework to reproduce a *fluidic multiplexer (fMux)* [6] (Fig.3), which is constructed from multiple layers of paper and tape. The user "programs" the fMux by squeezing the layers together at pre-specified locations (buttons) on the top layer, connecting two passive flow substrates; the tape layer ensures that each button remains pressed (i.e., the two passive flow substrates remain in contact) after compression.

The user can program a K:1 fMux so that any subset of K input fluids will merge and mix (by passive diffusion) at the fMux output. Parameterization allows the design to generate fMuxes with any desired number of inputs; the user may also adjust the fMux dimensions, channel length, and well size. The framework then draws the fMux channels algorithmically using the rendering engine.

3.2 Channel and Well Components

Channels and wells (Fig.4) can be parameterized to change dimensions, capacities, orientations, and signal counts.

A *channel* is specified by its source and sink coordinates, along with its width; it may also be specified as a vector with a source coordinate, angle, length, and width. The framework can assess the impact of channel design parameters on issues such as assay execution time, reagent consumption, etc.

A *well* is a circular region that contains one or more fluids; the primary parameter of interest is its radius. Using the framework, we produced two calibration devices that capture performance data across varying environmental conditions. These devices can enhance reproducibility of scientific findings across a variety of external conditions which are often beyond the control of the practitioners.

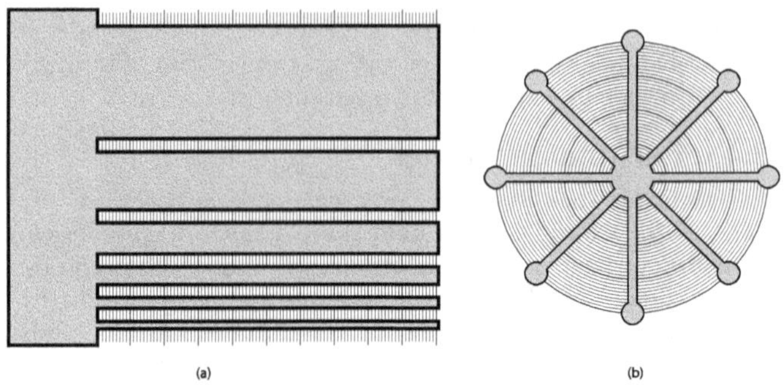

Figure 5: a) Raceway Calibration Device; b) Bullseye Calibration Device.

3.3 Calibration Devices

The Raceway Calibration Device (Fig.5(a)) comprises a varying number of fixed-length lanes (channel segments) with varying width. The Raceway allows a researcher to compare fluid transport velocities over time, enabling characterization of dispersion rates. Running multiple "races" using a median benchmark fluid under fixed environmental conditions will enable a researcher to characterize the +/- margin of the substrate with a high degree of confidence.

The Bullseye Calibration Device (Fig.5(b)) allows for lanes to be specified at various angles in a radial distribution around a central source or sink. It includes a measurement scale that expands out from the central point in concentric marks giving appearance of a bullseye target. Paper substrates may exhibit a flow orientation as a result of manufacturing processes; unlike the Raceway, the Bullseye device allows for the calibration process to take the flow orientation into account, as it may influence accuracy and performance.

Once the calibration profiles are obtained, they may be incorporated into the layout of a device, especially when tuning the device for specific environmental conditions. We anticipate that this will increase accuracy, reproducibility, and efficiency in terms of time and material utilization, both in laboratory and point-of-care settings.

4. EXPERIMENTAL RESULTS

This section summarizes the experimental setup, preliminary tests performed, observed difficulties, and solutions and processes that were develoepd to mitigate those difficulties. The reported experiments 1) determined a reliable width of the printed barrier walls to contain fluid transfer; and 2) assessed the reliability and replicability of experiments performed with devices produced by the software.

4.1 Experimental Setup

Microfluidic layouts generated by the framework for testing were printed using a Xerox ColorQube 8570DN wax-based ink printer connected via USB cable directly to a PC used for development. The printer driver's output resolution was set to 1200 dots-per-inch (dpi) with zero-scaling during output to maintain accurate rendering of files to substrates.

The wax printer delivers color solid wax "inks" to paper by

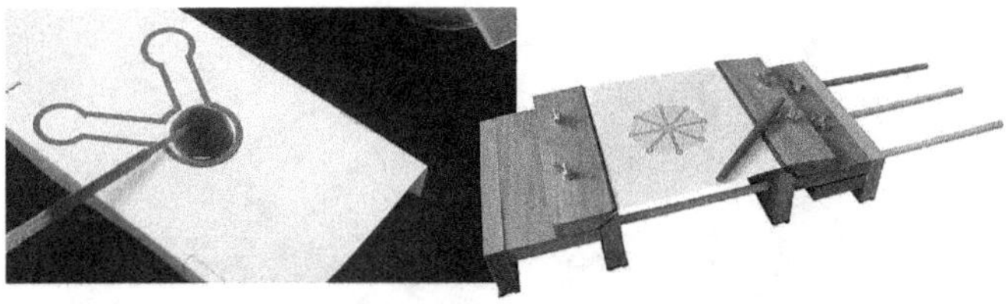

Figure 6: On the left, the first tests when creating wax-based channels for fluid flow. On the right, the test rig isolates the material and fluids from contact while under test.

activating an internal heating element, which melts the wax to a fluid state before depositing it on the surface material, where it rapidly cools before being ejected from the printer. Although the wax ink is hydrophobic, it resides on top of the paper, so fluids delivered to the substrate at this stage would penetrate beneath the ink, bypassing the desired barried on the surface. Passing the printed page over a heating element re-melts the wax, which then flows into the substrate to create the desired hydrophobic barrier.

A $100 - 1000\mu$L-range pipette was used for measurement and delivery of a solution of filtered water colored with a standard food colorant. LabNerd® filter paper cut to $7.875'' \times 4.875''$ served as the substrate.

4.2 Test Rig

In our initial tests, the ends of the paper were folded over to create a rigid support (Fig.6, Left), which elevated the test area, but did not create a taut and level surface; consequently, when liquid was applied to the substrate, undesired flow would occur. Even with a 2 mm border to contain liquid flow to the desired regions, the uneven surface caused warping and uncontrolled and transport (Figure 7). Our solution was to design and construct a test rig which isolates the substrates from other surfaces and maintains a level flow surface such to ensure that fluid is not under the influence of gravity while under test (Fig.6, Right). Results for subsequent experiments are reported using the test rig.

4.3 Fluid Containment

The goal of this experiment was to determine a border width for reliable fluid containment for channels and wells under test. We ran several passes on the Raceway and Bullseye calibration devices using fluid volumes of 1000μL, 500μL, 300μL, and 250μL. For the Raceway device, 500μL of fluid caused a failure in the reservoir section, while 300μL reliably filled a Bullseye device with a $40mm$ radius. Subsequent experiments to test fluid containment were performed on the Bullseye device using 300μL of fluid with border widths of $0.5mm$, $1.0mm$, $1.5mm$, and $2.0mm$.

As shown in Figure 8, border widths of $0.5mm$ and $1.0mm$ failed to contain the fluid delivered to the source location in the center with fluid seeping through the channel barriers. The $1.5mm$ width performed better, but exhibited a failure at the $30mm$ mark (as indicated by the arrow in Figure 8), but otherwise contained most of the fluid. The $2mm$ width reliably contained the 300μL fluid, which was delivered to the source and then flowed to each of the eight sinks. In principle, this will allow us to test flow rates over varying device sizes; additional testing will attempt to determine the relationship (if any) of fluid volume to barrier size.

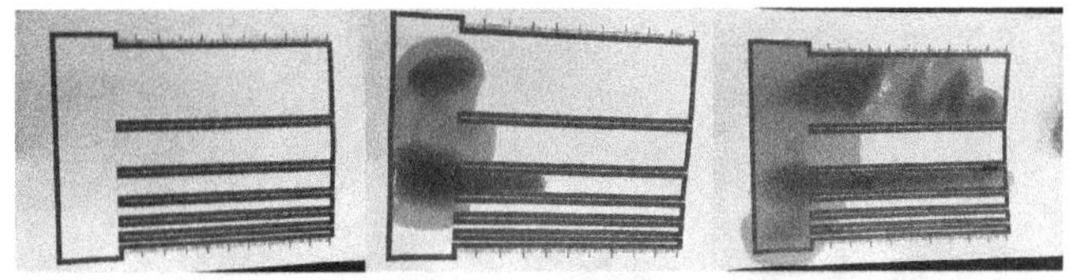

Figure 7: Simple experiment to test the Raceway Calibration device's containment efficacy. From left, @t=0 min, prior to dispensing fluid, @t=1 min, fluid contained by $2mm$ borders, @t=2 min, fluid flows beyond borders due to improper handling of substrate.

4.4 Flow Characterization and Replicability

We fabricated thirty $40mm$-radius Bullseye devices, two per sheet, and pipetted 200 μL of fluid to the source. For each device, we measured the fastest and slowest times at which fluid reached one of the eight $40mm$ sinks. The results (Table 1) suggest exceptionally high variability: fluid transport time ranged from $144-560$ s, with a median of 427 s and a standard deviation of 76.54 s. The primary cause for the variability turned out to be inconsistent pipetting, which, in turn, led to inconsistent fluid transport. Taken in its proper context, this variability is likely to manifest itself in real-world use cases, where the user of a paper-based diagnostic is a layperson, not a trained healthcare professional. Thus, there is likely to be similar high variability between different users of otherwise identical devices. Thus, experiments such as this can provide, at a bare minimum, upper and lower bounds on the time required to execute a biological assay on a paper microfluidic device; this type of information can and should be included in experimental protocols to ensure that the user has a realistic estimate of how long to wait before trying to interpret the results.

Table 1: Maximum and minimum fluid transport times recorded using the Bullseye device with eight $3mm$ sinks and $40mm$ long channels, having a $2mm$ border width, with 200μL fluid delivered to the source.

Trial	MIN	MAX	Trial	MIN	MAX
1	488 s	560 s	16	392 s	440 s
2	468 s	480 s	17	396 s	428 s
3	432 s	462 s	18	354 s	414 s
4	416 s	446 s	19	144 s	157 s
5	374 s	456 s	20	157 s	384 s
6	374 s	432 s	21	334 s	468 s
7	450 s	504 s	22	426 s	468 s
8	458 s	488 s	23	368 s	440 s
9	372 s	372 s	24	438 s	438 s
10	358 s	358 s	25	360 s	398 s
11	392 s	432 s	26	338 s	376 s
12	406 s	406 s	27	438 s	476 s
13	376 s	480 s	28	442 s	462 s
14	408 s	482 s	29	328 s	446 s
15	452 s	452 s	30	314 s	422 s

5. RELATED WORK

To the best of our knowledge, there has been no prior work on design automation for paper microfluidic devices

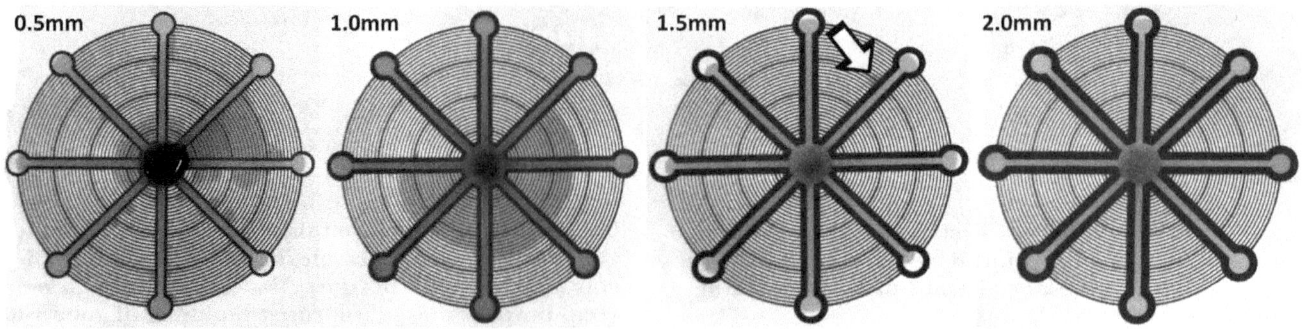

Figure 8: Fluid containment experiment to determine reliable border thickness for fluid containment. Note: photos had contrast adjusted to more clearly show fluid location)

based on passive flow substrates; many individual devices, designed manually, have been reported [4, 5]. There has been some prior work on physical design and droplet routing [9], control pin optimization [8] and test [10] for paper-based electrowetting devices patterned using conductive ink [1, 3]; these devices transport liquid through the application of high-voltage electrostatic forces, as opposed to passive capillary flow. In principle, our framework could be used to print the conductive ink patterns on the paper. In the future, we may try to use our framework to build paper devices that integrate electrowetting circuitry with passive flow substrates.

6. CONCLUSION AND FUTURE WORK

Paper-based microfluidics provide portable laboratory tests without expensive actuation equipment. Paper microfluidics replaces externally-actuated pumps and high-voltage-driven electrodes with low-cost wicking materials, thereby reducing the cost of fabricating new devices and performing diagnostic tests; however, this does not automatically imply a reduction in complexity of the design process.

To address these concerns, we have introduced a software framework that can simplify and automate the design process. Although we do not expect to attain end-to-end push-button automation any time soon, we do believe that this software can help device designers deal with many of the most pressing challenges.

Future work will focus on integrating design automation algorithms such as placement and routing of paper microfluidic components and fluid channels as well as conduct further exploration of the physical characteristics of both substrates and fluids used in biological assays to create profiles which will inform those algorithms to help determine both successful placement of components and viability of routing solutions of layouts.

We have highlighted challenges associated with paper substrate heterogeneity and variations in environmental conditions: as paper microfluidic devices are expected to yield consumer-facing products, they are unlikely to be used in high controlled laboratory settings.

ACKNOWLEDGMENTS

This work was supported in part by NSF Award #1423414.

7. REFERENCES

[1] A. Abadian and S. Jafarabadi-Ashtiani. Paper-based digital microfluidics. *Microfluidics and Nanofluidics*, 16(5):989–995, 2014.

[2] A. Jacobson, L. Kavan, and O. Sorkine-Hornung. Robust inside-outside segmentation using generalized winding numbers. *ACM Transactions on Graphics (TOG)*, 32(4):33, 2013.

[3] H. Ko, J. Lee, Y. Kim, B. Lee, C.-H. Jung, J.-H. Choi, O.-S. Kwon, and K. Shin. Active digital microfluidic paper chips with inkjet-printed patterned electrodes. *Advanced Materials*, 26(15):2335–2340, 2014.

[4] A. M. López-Marzo and A. Merkoçi. Paper-based sensors and assays: a success of the engineering design and the convergence of knowledge areas. *Lab-on-a-Chip*, 16(17):3150–3176, 2016.

[5] D. Mabey, R. W. Peeling, A. Ustianowski, and M. D. Perkins. Tropical infectious diseases: diagnostics for the developing world. *Nature Reviews Microbiology*, 2(3):231–240, 2004.

[6] A. W. Martinez, S. T. Phillips, Z. Nie, C.-M. Cheng, E. Carrilho, B. J. Wiley, and G. M. Whitesides. Programmable diagnostic devices made from paper and tape. *Lab-on-a-Chip*, 10(19):2499–2504, 2010.

[7] A. W. Martinez, S. T. Phillips, G. M. Whitesides, and E. Carrilho. Diagnostics for the developing world: Microfluidic paper-based analytical devices. *Analytical Chemistry*, 82(1):3–10, 2010. PMID: 20000334.

[8] Q. Wang, Z. Li, H. Cheong, O.-S. Kwon, H. Yao, T.-Y. Ho, K. Shin, B. Li, U. Schlichtmann, and Y. Cai. Control-fluidic codesign for paper-based digital microfluidic biochips. In *Proceedings of the 35th International Conference on Computer-Aided Design*, pages 103:1–103:8, 2016.

[9] S.-J. Wang, K. S.-M. Li, and T.-Y. Ho. Congestion-and timing-driven droplet routing for pin-constrained paper-based microfluidic biochips. In *Proceedings of the 21st Asia and South Pacific Design Automation Conference*, pages 593–598, 2016.

[10] S.-J. Wang, K. S.-M. Li, and T.-Y. Ho. Test and diagnosis of paper-based microfluidic biochips. In *Proceedings of the 4th IEEE VLSI Test Symposium*, pages 1–6, 2016.

Neuromorphic 3D Integrated Circuit: A Hybrid, Reliable and Energy Efficient Approach for Next Generation Computing

Md Amimul Ehsan[1], Zhen Zhou[2], and Yang Yi[1]
[1]Department of Electrical Engineering and Computer Science, University of Kansas, Lawrence, KS 66045
[2]Intel Corporation, 3600 Juliette Ln, Santa Clara, CA 95054, USA
[1]amimul_e@ku.edu, [2]zhen1.zhou@intel.com, [1]yyi@ku.edu

ABSTRACT

In this paper, we proposed to use 3D integration technology to create a neuromorphic hardware system that is compatible with current technology, provides high system speed, high density, massively parallel processing, low power consumption, and small footprint. The Through Silicon Vias (TSVs) used in the 3D neuromorphic structure provide high density integration and energy efficient links for transferring information through multiple neuron layers. This work details how a 3D neuromorphic system is benefited from the redundant TSV with substantial design-area reduction. We discussed the yield and reliability issues and explained the impact in neuromorphic 3D system design. A spiking neuron model is developed for the proposed 3D system. Furthermore, a new methodology have been proposed by introducing oxide around the bump that could significantly enhance the TSV capacitance in 3D Neuromorphic Computing (NC) system.

Keywords

Neuromorphic computing; 3D integration; TSV; Yield; Reliability; Spiking neuron.

1. INTRODUCTION

With the increasing demand of high performance computing system, neuromorphic computing gains significant momentum and spurs the brain-inspired computing hardware development. Such systems could offer biological perception and process cognitive information efficiently within a very compact platform without being constrained by the scaling issues of conventional Complementary metal–oxide–semiconductor (CMOS) technologies [1]. Neuromorphic computing system containing 100 million "neurons" with 1 trillion "synaptic connections" have been projected within the near future [2]. Such systems will require high complexity, high connectivity, and massively parallel processing to accomplish increasingly demanding computational tasks [2]. Traditional two-dimensional (2D) integration will be incapable of meeting these requirements. Hence, three-dimensional (3D) integrated circuit (ICs) is very advantageous for neuromorphic computing which offer a promising near-term solution for pushing beyond Moore's Law [3].

Permission to make digital or hard copies of all or part of this work for personal or classroom use is granted without fee provided that copies are not made or distributed for profit or commercial advantage and that copies bear this notice and the full citation on the first page. Copyrights for components of this work owned by others than ACM must be honored. Abstracting with credit is permitted. To copy otherwise, or republish, to post on servers or to redistribute to lists, requires prior specific permission and/or a fee. Request permissions from Permissions@acm.org.
GLSVLSI '17, May 10–12, 2017, Banff, AB, Canada.
© 2017 ACM. ISBN 978-1-4503-4972-7/17/05…$15.00
DOI: http://dx.doi.org/10.1145/3060403.3060470

Having excellent scalability, and compatibility with current technology, 3D IC successfully overcome the limitation of 2D neuromorphic IC [4]. Applying 3D integration to neuromorphic computing will offer the following benefits:

- ❑ Provide high complexity, connectivity, and massively parallel processing circuital system for highly demanding computational task.
- ❑ Bandwidth limitation, higher routing cost, larger occupied area by 2D circuits [5] can be resolved by incorporating 3D IC technology with the neuromorphic hardwire system.
- ❑ 3D interconnections offer very fast and energy efficient links [6] that make excellent distribution and communication among the neuron layers.

In neuromorphic computing, high density membrane capacitor plays a key role in the synaptic signaling process, especially in a spike firing analog implementation of neurons. Membrane capacitance generally occupies a significant portion of the design area of neuromorphic chips. Since redundant and dummy TSVs constitute a significant fraction of the total TSVs, we can make them more "useful" by configuring them to serve as membrane capacitors. However, the complicated process technology and fabrication methodology of TSV based 3D IC introduces significant yield and reliability challenges. Due to the fault occurs during the manufacturing process and failures during the execution-time, these issues appear and significantly affects the performance of the system. The yield of a 3D IC mainly depends on the process variation, defects, and changing the physical structures of TSV/dies and their bonding. Whereas, the reliability comes from the associated thermal issues and fabrication process. Therefore, it is very important to study the yield and reliability assessment demonstration in neuromorphic 3D IC.

This work details how a 3D neuromorphic system can be implemented with a virtual neuronal membrane that included TSV interconnects. In this paper, we propose a novel 3D neuromorphic computing architecture by exploring TSV configurations to adapt them for use as capacitors. We discussed how our proposed methodology does not degrade yield and reliability, but gets benefit from the overall system architecture. Besides, we come up with a new method to enhance the TSV capacitance to serve as necessary membrane capacitance.

2. 3D NEUROMORPHIC COMPUTING SYSTEM

In this section, the necessity of 3D integration in neuromorphic computing, proposed 3D neuromorphic structure, TSVs as membrane capacitance in 3D NC IC, yield and reliability issues of neuromorphic 3D structure are illustrated.

2.1 Necessity of 3D Integration in NC

In order to realize the true potential of neuromorphic computing in VLSI technology, the application of analog, digital, and mixed-signal IC based neural chips has been explored and fabricated. To reproduce the biophysical process, there are some potential neural chips like TrueNorth chip: IBM, Neurogrid chip: Stanford University, and BrainScales project by EU FET HBP has been developed [7]. Table 1 describes the total number of neurocores, neurons, and synapses of these neuromorphic chips.

Table 1. Large scale neuromorphic chip implementation

Neuromorphic Chip	**BrainScales**	**NeuroGrid**	**TrueNorth**
Neurons	200K/wafer	1 million	1 million
Synapses	5300/wafer	>1 billion	256 million
Neurocores	-	16	4096

However, all of these neuromorphic chips are fabricated using 2D technology while some insurmountable obstacles are introduced by 2D planar circuitry like bandwidth problem, with larger area etc. Figure 1 shows the die photo and layout of a neuron in TrueNorth chip. The scalability and higher routing cost are the paramount factors in these 2D chips and very challenging to overcome.

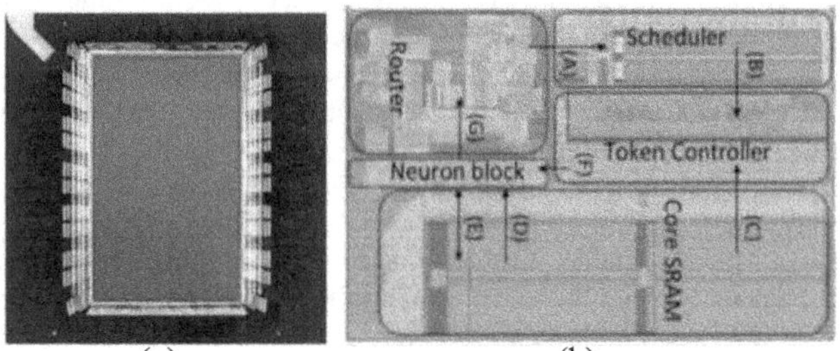

(a) (b)

Figure 1. TrueNorth Chip (a) Die Photo (b) Physical layout of single core [8]

Applying 3D interconnection in neuromorphic system, all the issues can be resolved and it becomes possible to get excellent distribution and communication among the neuron layers. The massive parallelism provides main contribution to estimate the performance of human brain. Therefore, the fast massively parallel processing in biological neural systems can be utilized for the high speed computation with low energy cost. In neuromorphic 3D IC, synaptic crossbars are being used that provides high density interconnection with greater reduction in parasitic. In particular, these are regarded as promising solution for modeling key features of biological synapses due to their nano scale dimensions, capacity to store multiple bits of information per element and low energy requirement to write distinct states. Physically well connected synapses can enhance the performance of neural network which naturally makes the necessity of 3D integration technology in neuromorphic computing.

2.2 Novel Neuromorphic 3D IC Structure

3D neuromorphic device is mounted on a semiconductor substrate and each chip in the 3D structure represents a functional unit. In a neuromorphic device, neurons are represented by CMOS substrate, while axons and dendrites are implemented by nanowires, and synapses denotes the junctions of crossing wires. As illustrated in Figure 2, the 3D neuromorphic structure contains different cell layers that include High speed buses, CMOL Crossnet, CMOS substrate, membrane capacitance, nano devices, and bipolar spin neurons. This neuromorphic electronic architecture of brain and retina can be fabricated by using CMOS IC that contains a great number of microcircuit and TSV interconnects. TSVs offer a great deal of benefits in a neuromorphic 3D IC as it adds all the features of vertical stacking of conventional 3D IC.

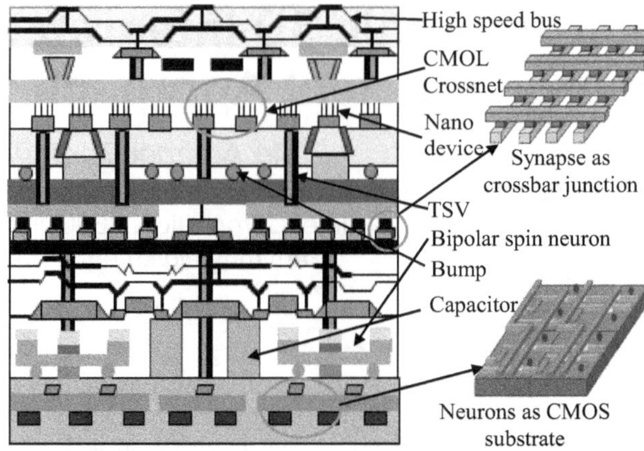

Figure 2. Proposed TSV based 3D neuromorphic IC

2.3 TSV in 3D NC IC

Neuromorphic system introduces huge capacitance for the storage of internal information. In general, neuron capacitance occupies a significant portion of the design area of neuromorphic chips. Figure 3 (a) and 3 (b) represents the layout of a single neuron using 90nm and 130nm CMOS technology respectively where in both cases the capacitor consumes a large portion of the neuron's design area.

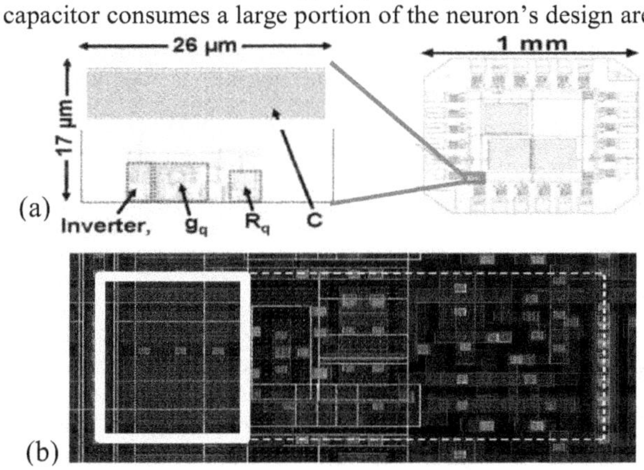

Figure 3. Capacitor (yellow) in neuron chip (a) 90nm CMOS [9] (b) Layout, 130nm CMOS [10]

In the current state-of-the-art of neuromorphic IC design, it has been found that, most of the analog and mixed signal neuron design requires larger capacitors which occupies a notable area of the chip. In these design methodology, the capacitors occupy from 25% to 75% of the total design area while their values vary from 40 fF to 1.1 pF [11-13]. According to the International Technology Roadmap for Semiconductors (ITRS), the current CMOS technology of capacitance 5-7 fF/um^2 need to be increased up to 13 fF/um^2 by next 5 years. This slow increase presents a huge density-scaling challenge for conventional MOS capacitors. Hence, the unused TSVs in 3D neuromorphic chip are promising candidate that could provide the alternative route to achieve high density capacitance.

Among different capacitances of neuromorphic chip, membrane capacitance plays a key role for the implementation of spiking neuron. It is the stored charge of ions across either side of cell that results from the membrane composition of bilayer phospholipids. The cell membrane serves as an insulating dielectric between the intracellular and extracellular fluid with opposite polarity ions at either side. This disequilibrium ionic charge on each side of the membrane generates potential difference which forms the membrane capacitance and these are illustrated in Figure 4.

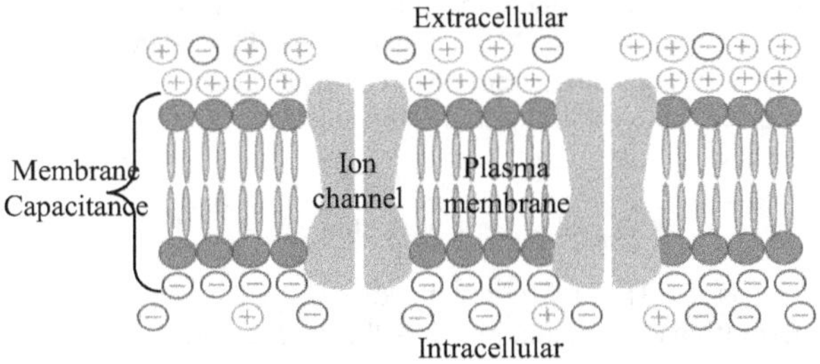

Figure 4. Structure of the cell membrane of a neuron

This capacitance often used as a measure of the changes to membrane surface area and therefore, the total membrane capacitance is directly proportional to surface area and the dielectric properties of membrane. However, TSVs in 3DIC is composed of metal conductor lined with insulator dielectric and buried in silicon substrate and similar to the MOS structure shown in Figure 5(a). Depending on the substrate doping and voltage condition, a capacitance is formed between the metal and substrate in different regions like accumulation, depletion, and inversion.

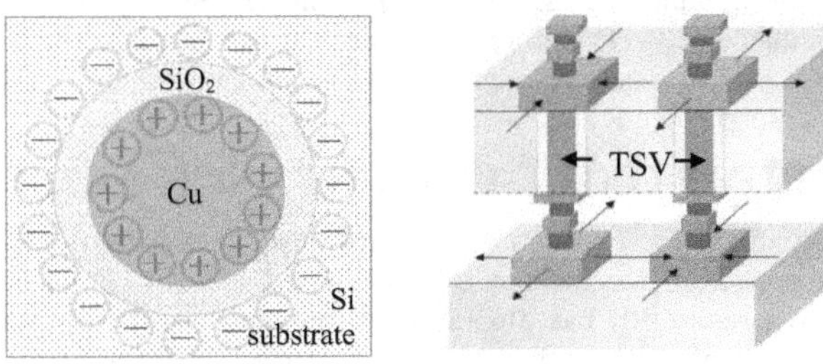

(a) (b)

Figure 5. TSVs as capacitance (a) Cross-section top view (b) Neuromorphic structure [5]

This TSV capacitance can be used as membrane capacitance and all the unused TSVs can be perfectly utilized by producing capacitance in an energy efficient hardware analog neuron design. The architecture of utilizing the unused TSVs as membrane capacitance is shown in Fig. 5(b) where the active TSVs can also be used as interconnects to transmit signals. It has been found that a single TSV with 38.5 um^2 footprint can offer capacitance of 550fF which is equal to 91.7 um^2 conventional MOS capacitors [14].
Joulbert *et al* [5] provides some example of neuron connectivity where it has been found that the TSV can vertically connect neuron blocks and can be used as capacitive elements.

2.4 Yield Issue in the Proposed Design

The yield in 3D neuromorphic IC depends on die yield, TSV Yield, and the bonding yield and this is illustrated in Figure 6. These yields are mainly affected by the process variation and changing the physical structure of dies/TSVs. The process variation and optimization are the key issues that causes Cu extrusion and hence the TSV parasitic characteristics are changed. Besides this, misalignment and random open defects can happen in TSV bonding and fabrication process respectively which severely impact the TSV yield.
However, the foundries impose a minimum TSV density rule to maintain the planarity of the wafer during chemical and mechanical polishing (CMP). This rule results in many dummy TSVs, for example, the 3D-MAPS processor contains 2,240 dummy TSVs [15]. Due to the requirement of high density interconnect in neuromorphic 3D IC, theses dummy TSVs are very helpful.

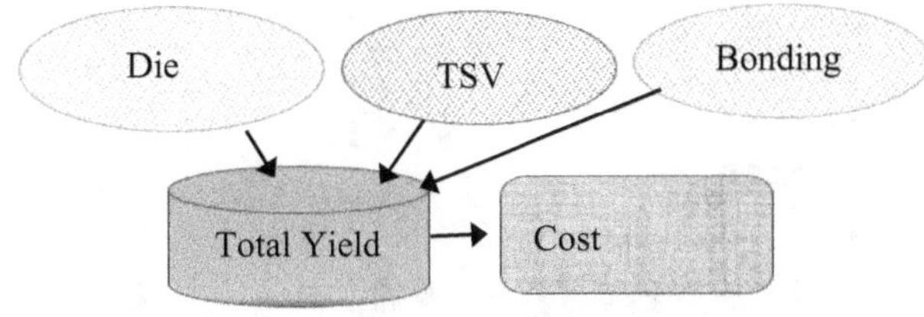

Figure 6. Total Yield in 3D neuromorphic IC

It has been reported that 15%–25% of all redundant TSVs in 3D chips are truly necessary [16] for the enhancement of chip yield. Therefore, the design rule naturally enhance the yield in 3D neuromorphic chip and huge amount of dummy TSVs remains left. Figure 7 shows the grouping of regular and redundant TSVs for the improvement of yield in 3D IC.

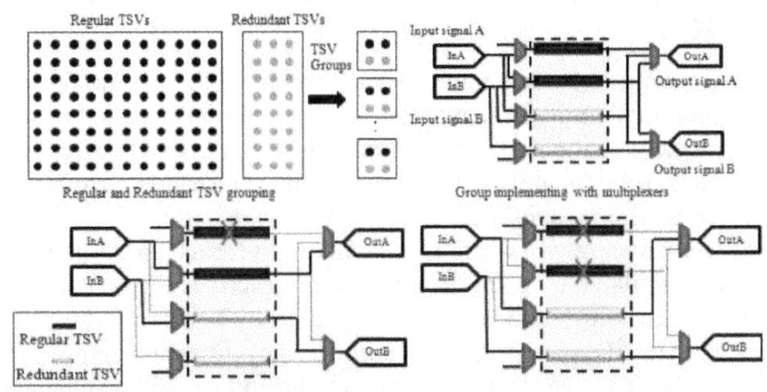

Figure 7. Grouping technique of regular and redundant TSVs [17]

By inserting new spare/ground TSVs and sharing the redundant TSVs across the neighboring die could change the yield. However, in our study we don't change the signal to ground ratio or the number of the TSVs or their physical sizes. We only need to utilize the remaining dummy TSVs which will not affect in the physical structure. Also, our introduced methodology for capacitance enhancement does not require any process change and we don't deal with these factors that affect TSV/die/bonding yield. Hence, the proposed technique in this work will not change the TSV assignment or TSV array physical structure and the yield will not be impacted negatively by this work.

2.5 Reliability in Neuromorphic 3D IC

Reliability is considered as one of the major concerns in designing 3D ICs and need to be quantified and evaluated perfectly before the real production application. Due to the imperfect fabrication process and thermal issues, the critical reliability problem occurs. Having higher density integration in traditional 3D IC, the thermal dissipation is inefficient and causes the reliability challenges. The higher thermal density accelerates the electromagnetic effect in the ultra-fine electrical path and introduced thermal induced crack in TSV and silicon substrate. These issues can be resolved by making ensure the low temperature bonding and TSV process which can reduce the thermal stress and improve the reliability. Figure 8 shows the fabricated stacked wafer with multiple TSVs where the pumping stress is reduced by lowering the TSV process temperature and the reliability is enhanced.
However, the computation in 3D neuromorphic system is inherently parallel and this massive parallelism characteristic helps to implement the lower operating clock frequency in the circuital system without any compromise with the output. This low clock

frequency in neural system requires lower power density which is directly related to thermal issues.

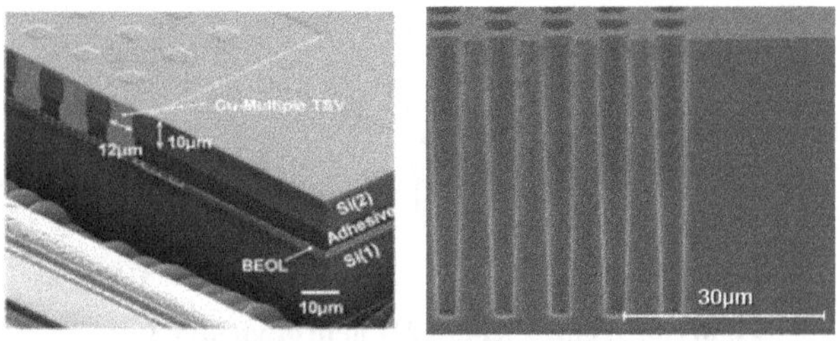

Figure 8. SEM image of fabricated stacked wafers and multiple TSVs [18, 19]

Therefore, compared with traditional high frequency 3D IC, neuromorphic 3D system has the ability to reduce the thermal stress and the reliability is greatly improved.

3. SPIKING NEURON MODEL IN 3D NC IC

The spiking neuron model has become an essential key computational unit for neuronal action potential across the cell membrane. For the integration of electrical inputs of a neuron, it is necessary to estimate the membrane capacitance that determines the neuronal time constant.

The leaky integrate-and-fire (LIF) model is a formal spiking neural model stimulated by external current and describes the neuron as a passive capacitor connected by a linear leaky resistor. Using LIF model in a 3D system will change the key features of neurons membrane. Therefore, neuronal membrane voltage will be changed accordingly. From the TSV property serving as membrane capacitor in this work, we modified the LIF model and the circuit model of neuron membrane using TSV is shown in Figure 9.

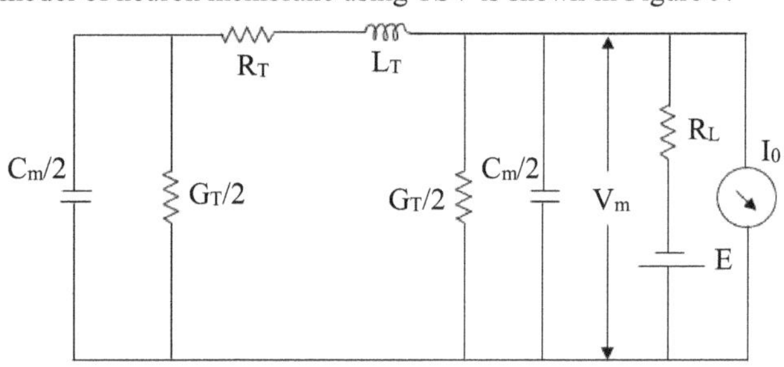

Figure 9. Circuit Model of LIF neuron in 3D IC

The membrane capacitance model basically describes the electrical activity of neuron corresponding to the ionic charge diffusion through the membrane. The current flow through the leak channels of the neurons membrane is given by,

$$I_c = G_L(V_m - E) \tag{1}$$

where G_L is the leaky conductance, V_m is the membrane potential, and E is the equilibrium potential.

Change in membrane potential due to the current flow depends on membrane capacitance as the charges accumulate. The rate of change of the total charge in a membrane capacitance gives the current through it as,

$$I_c(t) = -\frac{\partial Q(t)}{\partial t} \tag{2}$$

Therefore, the RC behavior of the membrane model is expressed as below,

$$C_m \frac{\partial V_m}{\partial t} = -G_L(V_m - E) + I_0 \tag{3}$$

where C_m is the membrane capacitance, and I_0 is the applied steady current.

For the TSV as membrane capacitance C_m, the space charge and surface potential of the MIS structure of TSV determine its capacitance-voltage characteristics. The total charge on the TSV can be calculated by integrating the electric filed through the surface as,

$$Q_m = -2\pi \times r_{ox} \times L \times \varepsilon_{Si} \times \frac{\partial \varphi}{\partial r}|_{r=r_{ox}} \tag{4}$$

where, r_{ox} is the TSV oxide outer radius, L is the length of TSV, ε_{Si} is permittivity of silicon, and φ is the charge potential.

Now, the TSV capacitance which will serve as membrane capacitance can be obtained from the total charge and TSV potential as below,

$$C_m = \frac{Q_m}{V_m} \tag{5}$$

where, V_m is the TSV surface potential.

The total TSV capacitance is parallel to the leakage resistor as demonstrated in Figure 9.

While the typical membrane capacitance values of 0.5 – 1 pF corresponds to 50 – 200 um^2 capacitors [5], a signal TSV with multiple ground TSVs (up to 8) estimates 90 – 130 fF of capacitance [20]. Therefore, it is necessary to increase the TSV capacitance to meet the requirement of membrane capacitance in 3D neuromorphic IC.

4. BUMP OXIDE CAPACITANCE MODEL

To conduct an excellent reliability test, the importance of interconnection mechanism of TSV based 3D IC using solder bumps (Figure 10) has already been proven [21]. The physical dimension of the bump is significantly larger compared to the dimension of TSV as demonstrated in [22]. Hence, adding an additional layer of oxide around the bump increases its capacitance appreciably and consequently increases the overall TSV capacitance.

A new TSV structure is proposed in 3D chips as demonstrated in Figure 11. In this structure, the isolation silicon dioxide outside the bump contact area is introduced, which will contribute an additional parasitic capacitance due to the higher dielectric constant of SiO_2 compared to the small air gap surrounding the bump. This capacitance will be formed between the lateral side of the bump and the conductive silicon substrate which would be accounted to calculate the total TSV parasitic capacitances [23 - 24].

When, TSV is buried in Si substrate, the TSV capacitance will be the capacitance of two wire transmission line with dielectric loss layer. It is given by the equation below,

$$C_{TSV} = \frac{\pi\varepsilon_0\varepsilon_{Si}[1 - j(tan\delta_d + 1/\omega\varepsilon_0\varepsilon_{Si}\rho_{Si})]}{ln\left[\left(\frac{d_{TSV}}{2r_{ox}}\right) + \sqrt{\left(\frac{d_{TSV}}{2r_{ox}}\right)^2 - 1}\right]} \tag{6}$$

where, d_{TSV} is the pitch between the TSV, ε_0 is the permittivity of vacuum, ρ_{Si} is the resistivity of substrate material, and $tan\delta_d$ is the polarization loss of Si.

The per unit length capacitance for oxide layer of conventional TSV structure can be found by using the formula of coaxial capacitance. The cylindrical capacitance with the TSV conductor radius of r_{TSV} and oxide outer radius of r_{ox} is given by,

$$C_{ox} = \frac{\pi\varepsilon_0\varepsilon_{ox}}{ln\left(\frac{r_{ox}}{r_{TSV}}\right)} \tag{7}$$

where, ε_{0x} is the permittivity of the dielectric silicon-di-oxide.

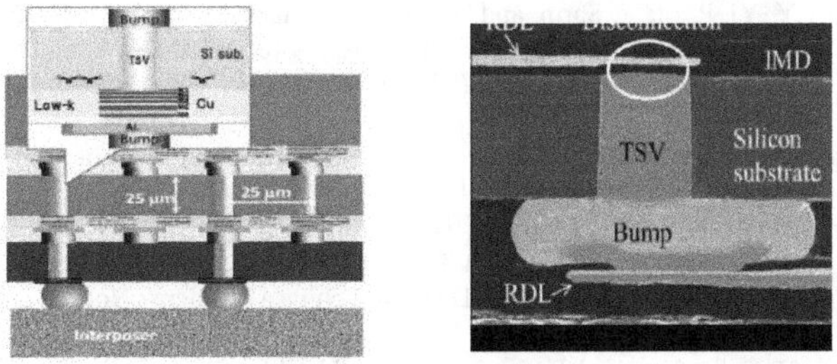

Figure 10. TSV bump (a) In 3D IC [21] (b) Cross-sectional SEM image [22]

Once, oxide is introduced to the lateral side of bump, the coaxial capacitance is formed and it is expressed by the following equation,

$$C_{Bump\_ox} = \frac{\pi\varepsilon_0\varepsilon_{0x}}{ln\left(\frac{r_{Bump}+t_{ox}}{r_{Bump}}\right)} \quad (8)$$

where, t_{ox} is the thickness of oxide at bump, and r_{Bump} is the radius of bump.

For the estimation of total capacitance of the proposed TSV structure, we need to sum up the capacitance of conventional two TSV with bump and the capacitance induced by introducing bump oxide. The proposed TSV capacitance will be,

$$C_{TSV\_total} = \frac{(C_{ox}+C_{Bump\_ox})C_{TSV}}{C_{ox}+C_{Bump\_ox}+C_{TSV}} \quad (9)$$

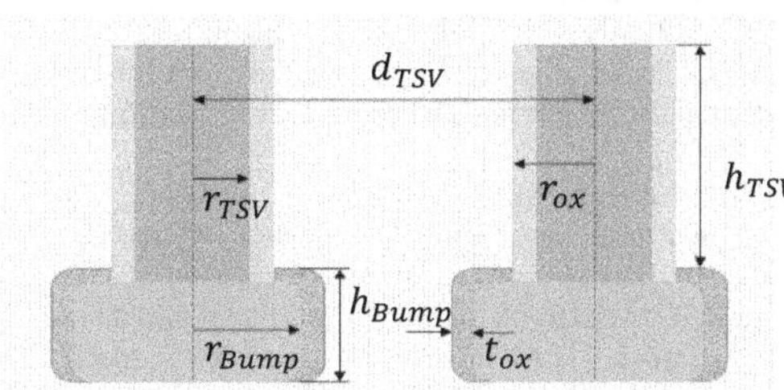

Figure 11. Proposed TSV structure with oxides around the bumps

In our proposed methodology, silicon-di-oxide and air are the dielectric between the bump of the TSV. Hence we get the relationship below,

$$C_{Bump\_proposed} = C_{Bump\_ox} + C_{Bump\_air} \quad (10)$$

Now, it can be found from the equation above that, our proposed method could significantly increase the bump capacitance as well as total TSV capacitance. Also, the TSV-Si substrate-TSV capacitance can be presented as parallel plate capacitance. Therefore, the total TSV capacitance will be enhanced which is required to store the internal membrane voltage.

By using the above mentioned method, the TSV capacitance could be enhanced significantly which will greatly improve the implementation of 3D neural system by serving as membrane capacitance. The simulation results are discussed in the next section.

5. RESULTS AND ANALYSIS

To evaluate the effectiveness of the proposed structure and method, the capacitance, the voltage, and the current in a 3D NM IC are simulated and compared to the ones using the conventional method. To conduct the simulation, a simple LIF neuron model is employed.

5.1 Capacitance Enhancement

The capacitance of TSVs including one pair of signal and ground using oxide around the bump are plotted in Tables 2-3 for wafer level, and chip level respectively. The simulated capacitances using the conventional and the proposed TSV structures show significant differences for both the bonding types of TSVs. It can be seen that more than 15% capacitance is increased through the addition of bump oxide.

Table 2. TSV capacitance using conventional and proposed method (wafer level TSV)

Freq (MHz)	**10**	**20**	**30**	**40**	**50**
Conventional Cap (fF)	204	203	201	199	197
Proposed Model (fF)	250	248.8	246	242.4	238
% Improved	22.5	22.4	22.3	21.8	20.8
Freq (MHz)	**60**	**70**	**80**	**90**	**100**
Conventional Cap (fF)	194.6	191.2	188	184	180
Proposed Model (fF)	234	229	222.4	216	208
% Improved	20.2	19.7	18.3	17.4	15.6

Table 3. TSV capacitance using conventional and proposed method (chip level TSV)

Freq (MHz)	**10**	**20**	**30**	**40**	**50**
Conventional Cap (fF)	624	622	618	614	610
Proposed Model (fF)	766	760	754	748	740
% Improved	22.7	22.1	22.0	21.8	21.8
Freq (MHz)	**60**	**70**	**80**	**90**	**100**
Conventional Cap (fF)	604	596	586	574	560
Proposed Model (fF)	730	718	704	684	664
% Improved	20.8	20.4	20.1	19.2	18.6

For wafer level TSV, the capacitance is improved from 15.6% - 22.5% and for chip level TSV, it is improved from 18.6% - 22.7%. This is a significant improvement of capacitance using a pair of signal and ground TSV. Besides, the frequency dependent simulation result shows that, the TSV capacitance is decreasing while frequency is increasing. This is because of the electrical field becoming less confined in SiO_2 layer and penetrates in Si region.

5.2 Membrane Spike Response

To demonstrate the effectiveness of a neuron, the membrane capacitance implemented by employing TSVs, a 3D model of neuron is constructed and its performance is simulated in SPICE. The simulation results are compared to the ones using LIF model. The comparisons are illustrated in Figure 12 to Figure 13. It is clear that the voltage and current of the TSV based 3D neuron proposed in this work are comparable to the LIF model based neuron. It is observed that the spike frequency for both the voltage and current is also increased when the TSV based neuron is used, and which could ensure a higher volume of information. The threshold potentials are the same for both models despite the different in spike length and reset voltage which may potentially result from the difference in their capacitance values. A similar behavior is also observed for the neuronal current in both models.

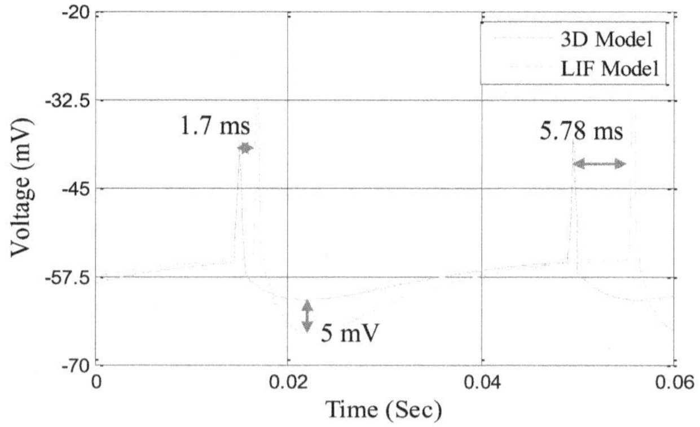

Figure 12. Spike response (voltage) of 3D model and LIF model of neuron

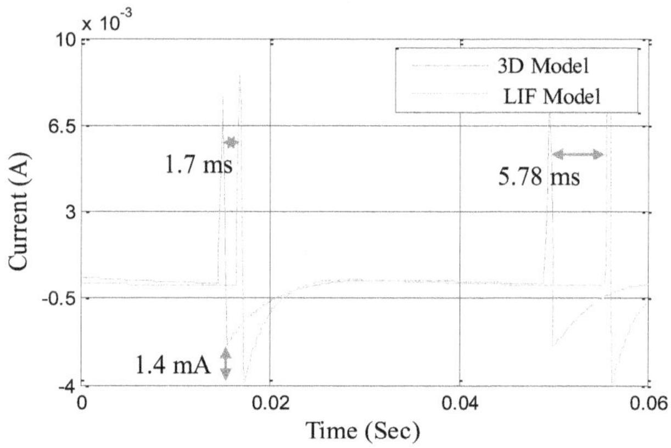

Figure 13. Spike response (Current) of 3D model and LIF model of neuron

Due to the enhanced capacitance in the proposed design, it can achieve long time constant and this is necessary for communacating with the external world in real time.

6. CONCLUSION

With the trend of energy efficiency in modern system, TSV based 3D neuromorphic chip could exhibit higher performance which are very competitive for the next generation potential technology in neuromorphic hardware system. In this work, we investigated the TSV properties that can be used as membrane capacitance and significantly benefits the system. Also, a new technique has been proposed that could significantly enhance the TSV capacitance in 3D neuromorphic system. This increasing capacitance is necessary to deal with the neuronal membrane potential which performs the key activity in 3D neural systems.

7. REFERENCES

[1] P. Camilleri, M. Giulioni, V. Dante, D. Badoni, G. Indiveri, B. Michaelis, et al., "A neuromorphic aVLSI network chip with configurable plastic synapses," *in Proc. Int. Conf. HIS*, Sep. 2007, pp. 296–301.

[2] T. J. Koickal, A. Hamilton, S. L. Tan, J. A. Covington, J.W. Gardner, T.C. Pearce, "Analog VLSI Circuit Implementation of an Adaptive Neuromorphic Olfaction Chip," *IEEE Trans. Circuits Syst.* 54, 1(Jan. 2007), 60-73.

[3] Y. Yi, P. Li, V. Sarin, and W. Shi, "Impedance extraction for 3-D structures with multiple dielectrics using preconditioned boundary element method," in *proc. IEEE/ACM Int. Conf. Computer-Aided Design*, 2007, pp. 7-10.

[4] Y. Yi and Y. Zhou, "A novel circuit model for multiple Through Silicon Vias (TSVs) in 3D IC," in *proc IEEE Int. 3D Systems Integration Conf. (3DIC)*, 2013, pp. 1-4.

[5] A. Joubert, M. Duranton, B. Belhadj, O. Temam, and R. Heliot, "Capacitance of TSVs in 3D stacked chips a problem? Not for neuromorphic systems," *in Proc. DAC'12,* 2012, pp. 1260–1261.

[6] B. Belhadj *et al.*, "The improbable but highly appropriate marriage of 3D stacking and neuromorphic accelerators," in *Proc. CASES'14*, pp. 1-9

[7] G. Indiveri, and S. C. Liu, "Memory and Information Processing in Neuromorphic Systems," in *Proc. of the IEEE*, vol. 103, no. 8, pp. 1379-1397, Aug. 2015.

[8] F. Akopyan *et al.*, "TrueNorth: Design and Tool Flow of a 65 mW 1 Million Neuron Programmable Neurosynaptic Chip," *IEEE Trans. Computer-Aided Design of Integrated Circuits and Syst.*, vol. 34, no. 10, pp. 1537-1557, Oct. 2015.

[9] J. M. Cruz-Albrecht, M. W. Yung, and N. Srinivasa, "Energy-efficient neuron, synapse and STDP integrated circuits," *IEEE trans. biomedical circuits and systems,* vol. 6, no. 3, pp. 246-256, 2012.

[10] R. Wang, C. S. Thakur, T. J. Hamilton, J. Tapson, and A. van Schaik, "A compact aVLSI conductance-based silicon neuron." pp. 1-4.

[11] J. H. Wijekoon, and P. Dudek, "Compact silicon neuron circuit with spiking and bursting behaviour," *Neural Networks,* vol. 21, no. 2, pp. 524-534, 2008.

[12] C. Zhao, B. T. Wysocki, Y. Liu, C. D. Thiem, N. R. McDonald, and Y. Yi, "Spike-time-dependent encoding for neuromorphic processors," *ACM Journal Emerging Tech. Comp. Syst,* vol. 12, no. 3, pp. 23, 2015.

[13] J. M. Cruz-Albrecht, M. W. Yung, and N. Srinivasa, "Energy-efficient neuron, synapse and STDP integrated circuits," *IEEE trans. biomedical circuits and systems,*6(3):246-256, 2012.

[14] C. Hwang, B. Achkir, and J. Fan, "Capacitance-Enhanced Through-Silicon Via for Power Distribution Networks in 3D ICs," *in IEEE Electron Device Letters*, 37,(4):478-481, April 2016.

[15] D. Fick et al., "Centip3De: A Cluster-Based NTC Architecture With 64 ARM Cortex-M3 Cores in 3D Stacked 130 nm CMOS," *IEEE Journal of Solid-State Circuits*, 48,(1), pp.104–117, 2013

[16] J. H. Lau, "TSV Manufacturing Yield and Hidden Costs for 3D IC Integration," in *Proc. Of Electronic Components and Technology Conference (ECTC)*, pp. 1031-1042, 2010.

[17] Y. Zhao, S. Khursheed and B. M. Al-Hashimi, "Cost-Effective TSV Grouping for Yield Improvement of 3D-ICs," in Proc. *Asian Test Symp.*, 2011, pp. 201-206.

[18] C-T. Ko, and K-N. Chen, "Reliability of key technologies in 3D integration," *Microelect. Reliability*, vol. 53, no. 1, pp. 7-16, 2013

[19] http://electroiq.com/blog/2010/08/process-equipment/

[20] R. Weerasekera *et al.*, "An Analytical Capacitance Model for Through-Silicon Vias in Floating Silicon Substrate," *IEEE Trans. Electron Devices*, vol. 63, no. 3, pp. 1182-1188, March 2016.

[21] K. W. Paik, Y. Choi and J. Shin, "3D-TSV vertical interconnection method using Cu/SnAg double bumps," in *Proc. IEEE Int. Workshop Low Temp. Bonding 3D Integr., 2012*, pp. 215-215.

[22] D. H. Jung *et al.*, "Frequency and time domain measurement of through-silicon via (TSV) failure," in *Proc. IEEE Conf.Elect. Perform. Electronic Packag. Syst.*, 2012, pp. 331-334.

[23] M. A. Ehsan, Z. Zhou, L. Liu and Y. Yi, "An Analytical Through Silicon Via (TSV) Surface Roughness Model Applied to a Millimeter Wave 3-D IC," *IEEE Trans. Electromag. Compat.*, vol. 57, no. 4, pp. 815-826, Aug. 2015.

[24] Y. Yi and Y. Zhou, "A novel circuit model for multiple Through Silicon Vias (TSVs) in 3D IC, in *Proc. IEEE Int. 3D Systems Integr. Conf.,* 2013, pp. 1-4.

A Method for Phase Noise Analysis of RF Circuits

Dimo Martev
Institute for Electronic Design Automation
Technical University of Munich
80333 Munich, Germany
dimo.martev@tum.de

Sven Hampel
Intel Germany
47259 Duisburg, Germany
sven.hampel@intel.com

Ulf Schlichtmann
Institute for Electronic Design Automation
Technical University of Munich
80333 Munich, Germany
ulf.schlichtmann@tum.de

ABSTRACT

In this paper we present a method for analysis of phase noise in logic circuits. This method allows the design and verification of phase noise critical circuits using a digital toolchain, significantly reducing the design time and effort compared to the traditional approach using analog tools such as SPICE simulation. It is based on a set of pre-characterized standard cells and the generated phase noise is estimated using a lookup table approach. Comparison of the estimation results with back-annotated analog simulations in 28 nm CMOS technology show that the error of the estimation is within 7.2 % of the actual phase noise, and the runtime is reduced by three orders of magnitude.

Keywords

Phase noise; phase noise analysis; RF circuits

1. INTRODUCTION

Modern radio-frequency (RF) transceivers feature a complex clock generation and distribution system in order to provide all the frequencies needed for the various supported bands and modes of operation. In full-duplex systems there are always at least one transceiver frequency synthesizer and a transmitter synthesizer operating in parallel. Due to crosstalk between their digitally controlled oscillators (DCO) an effect called injection pulling can occur, where the oscillator shifts towards the interfering frequency [1]. To reduce this effect the DCOs should operate at frequencies with distant spread. Therefore, the DCOs are operated at integer multiples of the required frequency and the output is then divided to achieve the necessary frequency.

DCOs for RF applications are usually based on LC resonators whose tuning range is limited, hence there are often multiple DCOs in the frequency synthesizer to generate the wide range of required output frequencies. The output of the active DCO is then multiplexed to the downstream modules. Furthermore, advanced transceivers offer carrier aggregation to achieve high data rates, necessitating multiple transmitter and receiver chains in a single chip. This increases the distance over which the clock signal needs to be distributed and requires re-powering of the clock signal by logic gates. Additionally, clock gating logic is required for blocking the clock propagation towards inactive system blocks in order to save power.

The circuitry required to achieve the above mentioned functionality – programmable clock dividers, multiplexers, clock gating, buffers – adds noise to the clock signal. This noise leads to random fluctuations in the phase of the signal, referred to as *phase noise*, and has negative effects on RF systems. Phase noise in the local oscillator signal affects both the transmitter and receiver subsystems. In receivers, it causes downconversion of interferers from adjacent channels into the signal band, an effect known as reciprocal mixing. In transmitters phase noise leads to degradation of the error vector magnitude performance and out-of-band emissions.

A typical design process of a submodule in the RF clock system includes the creation of a schematic and simulation of the block in an analog toolchain. The circuit is drawn in a schematic editor, and after the functionality is guaranteed, the layout is created and the sizing of the logic gates should be selected to meet the required phase noise performance. This is usually an iterative process, involving multiple people for design and layout, and an analog simulator to estimate the phase noise. Analog simulation offers very accurate noise estimation, but is a time consuming process [2].

In this work we present a new method for phase noise performance estimation of CMOS circuits. This method offers a substantial speed-up of the analysis and allows phase noise sensitive circuits to be designed and layouted using a digital toolchain. It operates with a set of pre-designed and pre-characterized cells and uses lookup tables to estimate the generated phase noise, hence analog simulation is not needed. This reduces the design effort and decreases the design time of building blocks with phase noise requirements.

Contributions of this paper:
The main contribution of this paper is the development of an automated method for phase noise analysis in logic circuits. The work encompasses fast and accurate estimation of the phase noise in logic gates using in-house characterized cells, a technique of tracking the clock distribution and the accumulated noise within a netlist, and interfacing with commercial analog and digital design toolchains.

The rest of the paper is structured as follows: Section 2 discusses the origins of phase noise in logic circuits. Section 3

Permission to make digital or hard copies of all or part of this work for personal or classroom use is granted without fee provided that copies are not made or distributed for profit or commercial advantage and that copies bear this notice and the full citation on the first page. Copyrights for components of this work owned by others than the author(s) must be honored. Abstracting with credit is permitted. To copy otherwise, or republish, to post on servers or to redistribute to lists, requires prior specific permission and/or a fee. Request permissions from permissions@acm.org.

GLSVLSI '17, May 10 - 12, 2017, Banff, AB, Canada

© 2017 Copyright held by the owner/author(s). Publication rights licensed to ACM.

ISBN 978-1-4503-4972-7/17/05. . . $15.00

DOI: http://dx.doi.org/10.1145/3060403.3060430

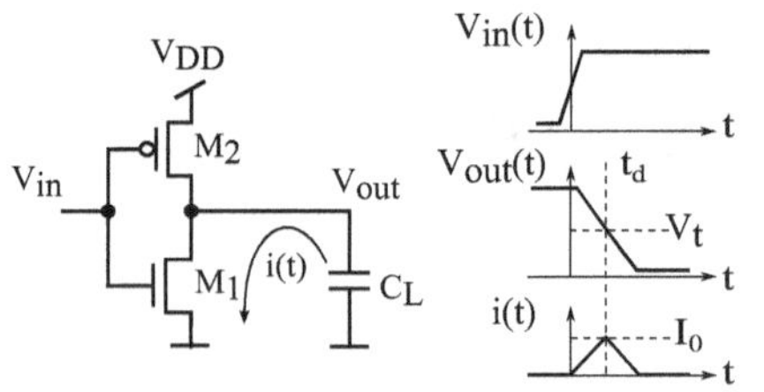

Figure 1: A CMOS inverter and its transient response

presents the proposed method for phase noise analysis and its basic principles. The workflow for using the proposed method is presented in Section 4. Experimental results are presented in Section 5 and Section 6 concludes the paper.

2. PHASE NOISE AND JITTER

CMOS logic gates are thresholding circuits, hence they are only sensitive to noise around the point where the input crosses the switching threshold; noise present at other times is ignored. Therefore only the noise at the threshold crossing moment needs to be considered when analyzing phase noise.

A large periodic signal present at the input of the logic causes a periodic operating point for the logic gate and modulates the existing noise. The noise is folded around dc by the fundamental frequency of the modulating signal [3].

Phase noise in inverters

The most basic logic element in CMOS circuits is the inverter. It is therefore beneficial to analyze the noise in inverters to understand the mechanisms of noise generation. The presented analysis holds for all other more complex logic gates.

Each transistor produces noise in its channel during operation; the main noise contributors are the thermal and flicker noise. A low to high transition at the input turns off the PMOS transistor and turns on the NMOS transistor, creating a falling transition at the output (Fig. 1). During the transition, discharge current flows from the load capacitor C_L through the NMOS transistor and noise in the transistor channel at that time will integrate on the load capacitor, creating noise voltage v_n. This in turn modulates the threshold crossing time and causes time displacement known as jitter. The slew rate $SR = dv_{out}/dt$ of the inverter gives the relation between the noise voltage and jitter. The jitter power spectral density (PSD) is expressed in (1) and it is folded around dc due to the sampling nature of the threshold crossing caused by the modulating frequency f_0.

$$S_\sigma(f) = S_{v_n}(f)/SR^2 \tag{1}$$

A time shift of ΔT in one of the edges of a square wave produces a phase change of $\Delta\phi = \pi f_0 \Delta T$ [4], and the power spectral density (PSD) of the resulting phase noise is

$$S_\phi(f) = \pi^2 f_0^2 S_\sigma(f) = \frac{\pi^2 f_0^2}{SR^2} S_{v_n}(f) \tag{2}$$

Phase noise and jitter in logic circuits

When N logic gates operate in series, each of the gates generates noise. The noise arising in every MOSFET is uncorrelated [5], thus the PSDs of the corresponding jitter sum as $S_\sigma(f) = \sum_{i=1}^{N} S_{\sigma,i}(f)$, where $S_{\sigma,i}$ is the jitter generated by stage i. The phase noise PSDs also sum up accordingly.

Furthermore, interconnect resistance causes degradation of the noise performance. Hence, the interconnect impedance should be decreased by keeping the distance between gates short, and using the low-ohmic global interconnect layers for routing over large distances.

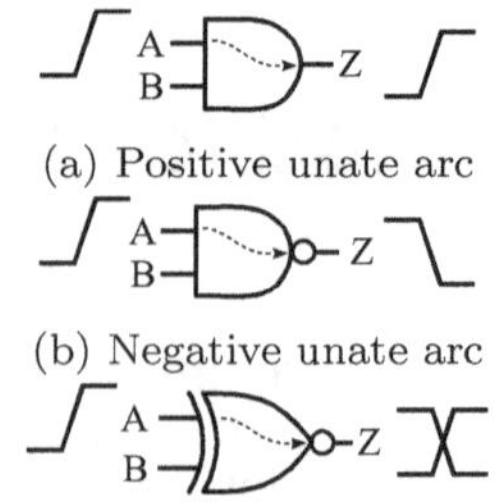

(a) Positive unate arc

(b) Negative unate arc

(c) Non-unate arc

Figure 2: Unateness of arcs

3. STATIC PHASE NOISE ANALYSIS

This chapter presents the proposed method for phase noise estimation that we call static phase noise analysis (SPNA). The name was selected to allude to static timing analysis (STA), on which principles SPNA is based. The basic concepts of SPNA are derived from STA and are described below.

3.1 Concepts of SPNA

Standard cell: A standard cell is a pre-designed logic gate with fixed functionality and layout. Each standard cell has known noise performance and output transition times under a given range of operating conditions (output load and input signal transition time). The set of standard cells available to the designer is called standard cell library.

Arc: An arc is a path from input to output pin of a standard cell. Each arc contains information about the phase noise and transition times of the output signal under given conditions. It also defines the condition under which an arc can be traversed, depending on the function of the cell. If the arc does not exist, then there is no path between the pins or the path cannot be traversed.

Unateness of arcs: An arc can be positive unate, negative unate or non-unate. An arc is *posivite unate* if a transition on the input pin causes a transition with the same polarity, or no change, on the output pin.. If the output transition is in reversed polarity with regard to the input, the arc is *negative unate.* If the polarity of the output transition depends not only on the input pin, but also the state of other inputs, then the arc is *non-unate* [6]. Deciding if a non-unate arc is positive or negative unate based on the states of gate inputs is called *resolving* the unateness. The unateness is important for the analysis as it indicates the polarity of the signal that propagates through a cell. Figure 2 shows examples for the different unateness of arcs.

Static signals: A signal is static, if it does not change during the operation of the circuit. In SPNA, all data (control) signals are considered static. At points where data and clock signal merge (clock inversion, clock enabling etc.) the data signal should be in a defined static value for the tool to be able to predict the behavior, the noise performance of the gate and to resolve the unateness. This is not a limitation, as in general data signals are used to configure the clock distribution path during power-up and are rarely switched during operation.

3.2 Operation

SPNA operates on a netlist, the parasitics description, and the standard cell library. The design constraints, i.e. the environment of the analyzed circuit should also be defined; this includes the clock source position, transition times, and driver strength and static values for the data primary inputs. Fig. 3 presents an exemplary netlist, including most of the structures that can be found in clock distribution networks, including division, clock gating, clock inversion and multiplexing.

The circuit is modeled as a directed graph, with the vertices representing gates and primary inputs and outputs, and the edges representing the nets. Each gate object has properties such as a name, pointer to a corresponding cell type, and pins. Each net has a name, fanin and fanout lists, corresponding capacitance value, transition time and accumulated jitter.

After the netlist is loaded into the data structure, the static values of the control signals, defined in the design constraints, are propagated through the circuit by traversing the graph in a breadth first manner. Each net or primary input with a defined static signal is put into a queue. The static values of the corresponding nets are then set and the gates in the transitive fanout are pushed into the queue. Based on the functionality of each gate, SPNA decides if the static value propagates further or not. Then the static value of the output nets are set and the cycle repeats until the queue is empty. In the example from Fig. 3, CLK_INV, CLK_EN and CLK_SEL should have a defined static value so that the clock path is defined. As an illustration, a static '0' on the primary input CLK_EN will force a '0' on net 'n7', which in turn will push n3 to '1', and the gate I3 won't be able to propagate the clock signal coming from net n2. Similarly, a static '0' on port CLK_INV will force a '1' at net n6, and this will be used to resolve the unateness of I2 and later to estimate the proper transition and noise values.

The propagation of the clock signal is executed in a similar manner, starting from the defined clock input port. For each gate in the transitive fanout, the noise and output transition time are estimated by using its input transition, output load, and the cell description, as outlined in Section 3.3. The output load of a gate is the sum of the capacitances of the gates in the fanout plus the wiring capacitance. The clock stops propagating at primary outputs or when a net with a static value is reached. In this example, for $CLK\_EN = 1$ and $CLK\_SEL = 1$, the clock will propagate through gates I1 to I6 and will reach the primary output OUT1.

The jitter is independent of the frequency of the signal (see Section 2), and can be accumulated regardless of frequency changes within the circuit. This allows SPNA to operate without knowledge of the functionality of the circuits or necessity for the user to define clock domains within the design. Under the premise of independent noise sources, the jitter generated by each cell on the signal path can be summed, using equation (1). The resulting output phase noise is then calculated, using (2).

3.3 Cell characterization

The backbone of the above mentioned method is the phase-noise/jitter information of each cell under various operating conditions. Each cell from the library is characterized for output jitter and transition times using large signal noise analysis within an analog circuit simulator. The testbench

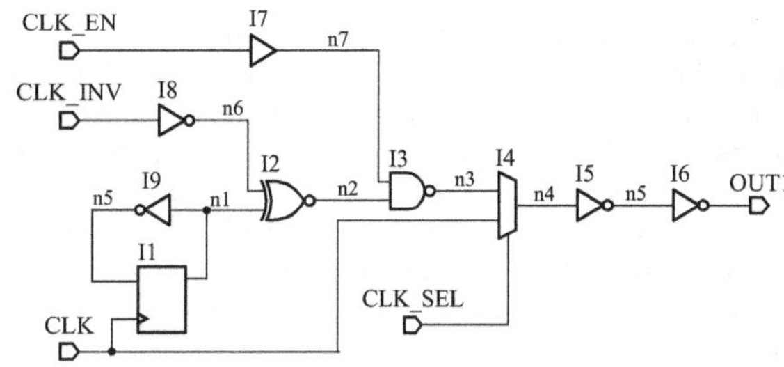

Figure 3: Exemplary netlist

consists of a driver cell, a back annotated view of the device under analysis (DUA), and power supply. A non-ideal driver cell is required to model a real world waveform and the driver impedance. The simulations are performed in the most critical process corner for noise, which varies with the technology node. However, the proposed method is not limited to a single PVT set.

The cell is simulated with different combinations of loads C_L, and input transitions t_{in} (rising or falling). The distinct input transitions are produced by varying the capacitance C_{TR} (Fig. 4). The simulations run on a fixed input frequency f_{in} and thanks to the low complexity of the simulated schematic, they execute very fast. Due to the noise folding, all the noise power is folded into the frequency range $[-f_{in}/2; f_{in}/2]$. The noise power due to flicker and white sources on an arbitrary offset frequency f_a within this range are then evaluated. The white noise is uniformly distributed and its mean-square value is

$$\langle v_n^2 \rangle = \int_{-f_{in}/2}^{f_{in}/2} S_v(f)df = S_v^{wh}(f_a).f_{in} \tag{3}$$

RF circuits operate on frequencies f_{in} higher than the corner frequency of the flicker noise, hence the flicker noise does not undergo folding and its power at 1 Hz is estimated as

$$S_v^{fl}(1) = S_v^{fl}(f_a) \cdot f_a \tag{4}$$

The dependencies of $\langle v_n^2 \rangle$ and $S_v^{fl}(1)$ on the load and input transition time are then organized in two-dimensional tables. In between the existing data points, a linear interpolation algorithm computes the missing values. Note that both values are independent of f_{in}.

Static signals and logic gates:
The arcs within a multi-input logic gate usually depend on the state of the other inputs, thus during the characterization of a gate the state of each input should be considered. For example, in a two input XNOR gate (Fig. 2c), the unateness, the noise performance and transition times of the arc $A \rightarrow Z$ are dependent on the state of B. Therefore, this arc should be characterized twice, once for each valid logic level ('1' or '0') of the input B.

Flip-flops:

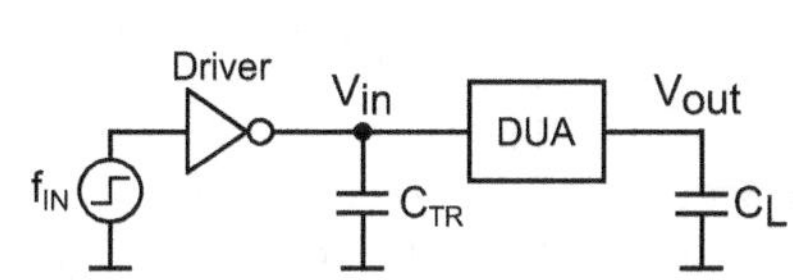

Figure 4: Cell characterization testbench

In STA, flip-flops (FF) require special handling, because of their synchronization character. However, in SPNA the only relevant information about a FF is the CLK-to-Q arc and its unateness. A FF with a non-static D-pin value is assumed to toggle and therefore propagates the clock signal, so a rising edge on the CLK pin (for positively clocked device) causes both rising and falling transitions on the output. The rate of change, i.e. the output frequency is not relevant, as discussed in Section 3.2.

3.4 Limitations

There are certain limitations when using SPNA. This method can only work with a set of already characterized cells. However, if a new cell is introduced to the flow, it can be easily and quickly characterized following the approach outlined in section 3.3 and added to the cell library. It is a one-time effort and the cell can then be used for all circuit analyses in the future.

Furthermore, SPNA does not take the impedance of the interconnects into account. To keep the inaccuracy caused by this simplification low, the impedance of the interconnects should be small compared to the channel resistance of the driving transistors. Increased interconnect impedance also degrades the transition time of the signal and leads to an increase in the generated phase noise. Therefore, usually precautions are taken to reduce the interconnect impedance in circuits with critical phase noise performance: keeping interacting logic gates close to each other, using global interconnect layers when the signal should be propagated across a longer distance, and using extra wide wires. Analog simulations of typical representative phase noise critical circuits have shown that for designs following these rules, the error caused by ignoring interconnect resistance is below 5 %.

4. WORKFLOW

This section presents the workflow for phase noise analysis using the SPNA method. The description follows the chart in Fig. 5.

A netlist description of the circuit and information about its parasitics are necessary for the operation of the SPNA. The *design exchange format* (DEF) was selected as the format for netlist representation, because it is an open EDA file format that can be produced by most commercial tools. The *standard parasitic exchange format* (SPEF) was chosen for transferring the parasitics information, due to its simplicity and wide acceptance in industry. The SPEF file contains the extracted parasitics for every net in the layout in ASCII format. Together the DEF and SPEF files contain all the necessary data to fully describe the design.

The starting point for the analysis is a phase noise critical placed and routed design derived from rtl2gds activities in the digital toolchain. (I) First, the netlist of the schematic and its parasitics are written in the DEF and SPEF files, accordingly. Alternatively, the SPNA can also operate on a schematic with explicit parasitic components from an analog toolchain. In this case explicit capacitances need to be placed in the schematic to model the layout parasitics. (II) Additionally, the description of each cell is loaded, containing its function, transition times and noise performance, as discussed in Section 3.3. (III) Thereafter, the design constraints describing the clock and static signals are imported. (IV) Then, the noise estimation takes place, following the procedure described in Section 3.2.

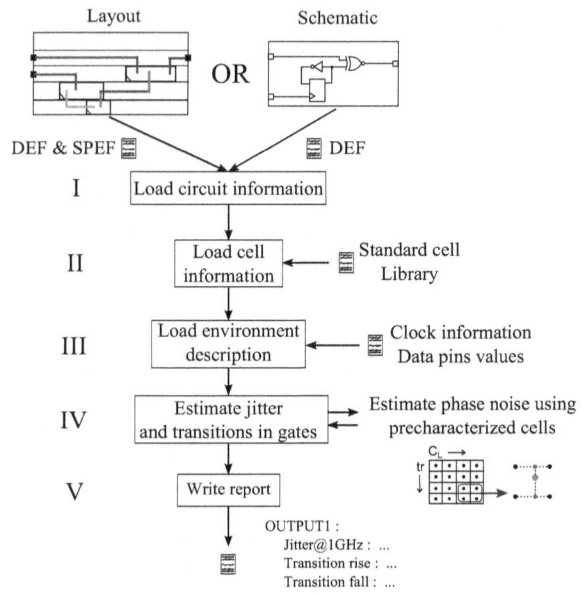

Figure 5: Workflow

(V) After the SPNA completes the noise estimation, the output is stored in a report file. All the primary output ports, to which the clock signal propagates under the given conditions, are listed with their corresponding jitter. The phase noise produced by the circuits is then calculated using the provided output frequency and equation (2).

SPNA interfaces with commercial EDA tools using automated routines, written in the scripting language used by the respective tool.

5. EXPERIMENTAL RESULTS

The SPNA code was written in C++ and runs on an Intel(R) Xeon(R) CPU E5-2670, operating at 2.60 GHz. A standard cell library in a 28 nm CMOS process containing 30 cells is used. The cells have various logic functions and driver strengths from 1X to 8X. The smallest driver (1X) has $W_p = 0.35\,\mu m$, $W_n = 0.27\,\mu m$ and the sizes of the others scale accordingly. The simulations were performed using slow process corner, 0.99 V supply voltage, and temperature of 125° C.

To validate the SPNA method, four industrial reference designs implemented in an analog toolchain were considered. The results are summarized in Table 1. The circuits that were selected represent typical building blocks for clock distribution systems. Test case 1 contains clock gating and multiplexing logic, with 6 gates in the critical path. Test 2 features a clock divider with enabling function (5 gates). Test 3 is a clock buffer circuit with 10 buffers in a chain,

Table 1: Noise estimation on industrial test cases in analog environment

No	Phase noise (rad^2/Hz)		Runtime (sec)		Error	Speed-
	SPNA	SPICE	SPNA	SPICE	(%)	up
1	1.68e-15	1.60e-15	0.03	1220	5.13	38437
2	8.13e-16	7.99e-16	0.035	1010	1.73	28857
3	9.69e-16	9.59e-16	0.04	950	1.03	22500
4	1.19e-16	1.11e-16	0.042	900	7.13	21428

Table 2: Noise estimation on test cases in digital toolchain

No	Phase noise (rad^2/Hz)		Runtime (sec)		Error	Speed-
	SPNA	SPICE	SPNA	SPICE	(%)	up
1	8.65e-16	8.33e-16	0.029	255	3.87	8793
2	1.73e-15	1.71e-15	0.035	310	1.17	9393
3	4.44e-16	4.26e-16	0.027	130	4.13	4814
4	1.43e-15	1.48e-15	0.042	460	-3.46	11219

and Test 4 is a derivative of Test 3, without the parasitics capacitances of the interconnects. The circuits operate at input frequency of 3.5 GHz, under a square wave stimulus.

The SPNA analysis and the reference analog simulation (SPICE) used explicit parasitic capacitances for the simulation. The error in all four cases is lower than 7.2 % and the SPNA runtime is significantly shorter than analog simulation. The two-dimensional lookup tables describing the phase noise of the standard cells are predominantly concave, therefore the interpolation tends to overestimate the noise value, causing the observed error. The load-noise characteristic is very steep close to the origin (load below 2 fF), making the interpolation error larger for smaller loads. The result of this effect is visible in Test 4 in the table.

To verify the operability of the SPNA method in conjunction with a digital tool chain, a second set of test cases was created (Table 2). These generic test cases were selected to feature typical functional blocks in a clock distribution network. Test 1-3 contain clock dividers, enabling and gating logic with 4 to 6 gates on the critical path. Test 4 is a clock buffering network, spanning 1.2 mm. Here, the SPNA estimation is based on the capacitive parasitic extraction from the digital toolchain, whereas the analog simulator uses extracted RC view. Additionally to the error from linear interpolation, the error caused by neglecting the interconnect resistance is affecting the accuracy, especially noticeable in test 4. Another source of error is the misalignment between the extraction engines of the digital and analog toolchains. The accuracy of prediction is again very good, and the runtime is thousandfold faster.

The proposed method provides phase noise analysis of logic circuits in digital toolchains, a functionality that was previously not available. This, combined with the automated place and route capabilities of the digital flow eliminates the need of setting up and performing analog simulations and handing over the task of layout generation to a layout designer. This allows for much faster design iterations in the hands of a single designer, profoundly reducing the total design time. Furthermore, usually gate sizing optimizers are applied iteratively until convergence, thus a potential circuit optimizer based on the proposed method could highly benefit from the offered analysis speed-up.

6. CONCLUSION

We presented a new method for phase noise analysis, based on pre-characterized standard cells that can be used for both schematic and layout based projects in digital and analog toolchains. The reported phase noise values in 28 nm CMOS technology are within 7.2 % of analog simulation, and the runtime is reduced drastically. This method adds phase noise analysis as a new functionality to place and route tools. This enables the implementation of circuits with phase noise requirements in a digital toolchain, significantly reducing the design and layout efforts.

7. REFERENCES

[1] B. Razavi, *RF Microelectronics*. Upper Saddle River, NJ, USA: Prentice-Hall, Inc., 1998.

[2] L. C. Severo, F. N. Kepler, and A. G. Girardi, "Automatic Synthesis of Analog Integrated Circuits Including Efficient Yield Optimization," in *Computational Intelligence in Analog and Mixed-Signal (AMS) and Radio-Frequency (RF) Circuit Design*, Springer Publishing Company, Inc., 1st ed., 2015.

[3] J. Phillips and K. Kundert, "Noise in mixers, oscillators, samplers, and logic an introduction to cyclostationary noise," in *Custom Integrated Circuits Conference, 2000. CICC. Proc. of the IEEE*, pp. 431–438, 2000.

[4] A. Homayoun and B. Razavi, "Analysis of Phase Noise in Phase/Frequency Detectors," *IEEE Trans. Circuits Syst. I, Reg. Papers*, vol. 60, pp. 529–539, March 2013.

[5] A. A. Abidi, "Phase Noise and Jitter in CMOS Ring Oscillators," *IEEE J. Solid-State Circuits*, vol. 41, pp. 1803–1816, Aug 2006.

[6] J. Bhasker and R. Chadha, *Static Timing Analysis for Nanometer Designs: A Practical Approach*. Springer Publishing Company, Incorporated, 1st ed., 2009.

Revealing On-chip Proprietary Security Functions with Scan Side Channel Based Reverse Engineering

Leonid Azriel, Ran Ginosar and Avi Mendelson
Viterbi Faculty of Electrical Engineering
Technion – Israel Institute of Technology, Haifa 32000 ISRAEL
leonida@tx.technion.ac.il, ran@ee.technion.ac.il, avi.mendelson@technion.ac.il

ABSTRACT

Proprietary cryptographic algorithms or protection schemes often constitute part of the security solution in electronic devices. Hence, these devices are prone to reverse engineering attacks that may reveal the details of these algorithms. We propose a novel non-invasive method of reverse engineering of digital integrated circuits that exploits the scan chains originally inserted into the device for production test automation. The scan chains unfold the sequential logic of the device to form a combinational function. The device's functionality is then exposed by examining this function. The resulting function is too large for direct learning, so we developed heuristic learning algorithms that exploit common properties of digital circuits, in particular limited transitive fan-in of combinational logic and sub-circuit sharing properties. With these algorithms we show fast reconstruction of an AES cryptographic accelerator. The algorithm used for the AES is scalable, making it applicable to much larger circuits.

Keywords

Hardware reverse engineering, Side-channel analysis and countermeasures, Embedded Systems Security

1. INTRODUCTION

Reverse engineering of an integrated circuit is a complex task that traditionally requires tedious work and expensive equipment. Its ultimate goal is to discover the underlying algorithm of a given physical device: the device's behavioral definition. We can represent the discovery task as a two-stage process: (1) Extracting of the circuit from the physical device and (2) extracting of the behavioral model from the circuit. The boundary between the two stages may be blurred; nevertheless, these are usually two distinct tasks. The first stage, as a rule, involves invasive techniques, such as removing the package, performing cross-section, delayering, and nanoscale imaging [19]. The second stage is usually algorithmic [13, 15]. This paper addresses the first stage, circuit extraction, but proposes to do it non-invasively by exploiting the internal scan chains. This approach provides notable accuracy with simple and inexpensive equipment.

Permission to make digital or hard copies of all or part of this work for personal or classroom use is granted without fee provided that copies are not made or distributed for profit or commercial advantage and that copies bear this notice and the full citation on the first page. Copyrights for components of this work owned by others than ACM must be honored. Abstracting with credit is permitted. To copy otherwise, or republish, to post on servers or to redistribute to lists, requires prior specific permission and/or a fee. Request permissions from permissions@acm.org.

GLSVLSI '17, May 10-12, 2017, Banff, AB, Canada
© 2017 ACM. ISBN 978-1-4503-4972-7/17/05...$15.00
DOI: http://dx.doi.org/10.1145/3060403.3060464

Scan insertion is a widely used DFT (Design-For-Test) technique that allows for the automatic generation of test vectors for production test of an integrated circuit. Thanks to its efficiency, it has become a de facto standard for testing digital circuits. Recent research shows that scan insertion may turn into an easy target for the attacker [6, 10]. Previous work primarily focuses on the vulnerability of the registers that participate in the scan chain. Easy access to these registers may reveal confidential information, such as cryptographic keys. This paper presents a different attack that reveals the functionality of the design itself. This security breach broadens the scope of possible exploits of the scan mode to any device that may contain trade secrets or proprietary cryptographic algorithms or protection schemes. The proposed reverse engineering method can also serve positive purposes, such as competitive analysis, IP theft detection [1], or discovery of malicious hardware implanted by a third party during physical design.

The scan introduces a new *shift mode*, which arranges the internal registers in one or more shift registers, called scan chains (see Figure 1). The production tester may switch the chip to the shift mode and use the scan chains to place the chip in the desired state (*ShiftIn*) and to sample its current state (*ShiftOut*). The *ShiftIn* and *ShiftOut* operations can be combined with a single functional (*Capture*) cycle to learn (*Probe*) the output of the combinational function F for a given input. An exhaustive search over all possible states of the device's registers and input pins then reveals a truth table that fully describes the function F.

The exhaustive search, due to its exponential complexity, is practical only for very small devices, containing no more

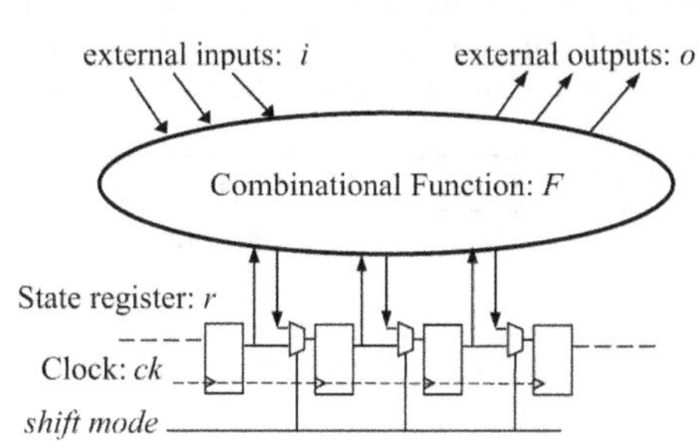

Figure 1: Scan Design.

than a few dozen registers. For the general case of learning an n-input Boolean function, the number of possible functions is 2^{2^n}. However, not every Boolean function can be realized by a physically constrained integrated circuit. In fact, most of the functions are not realizable. In other words, the search space in the case of integrated circuits is much smaller than in a general case. This is a direct corollary from the Shannon Effect [14]. Whether it is possible to devise an upper bound for the number of n-input Boolean functions with limited complexity is an open question. If such a bound exists, it may define the search space for our problem. Until this question is answered, we take a heuristic approach based on function properties. Our work correlates with the field of Computational Learning theory, which studies learning algorithms for functions with certain properties, such as linear functions, decision trees, DNF and junta functions [16]. We use some of the algorithms developed in this field, in particular algorithms that learn juntas.

We assume that the scan test interface is present and accessible in the target device. Vendors of secure integrated circuits often protect their scan interface with authentication, obfuscation or other mechanisms. The scan-based reverse engineering method may overcome some protection mechanisms, especially when combined with other methods, as detailed in Section 4. We refer the reader to [2] for more details and discussion.

2. ALGORITHMS FOR LEARNING A BOOLEAN FUNCTION WITH PROBES

The scan based attack turns the problem of reverse engineering into the problem of learning a stateless Boolean function. Here we describe the algorithms that learn the circuit's combinational function F exposed by the scan. We start with a formal definition of the circuit (see Figure 1).

Definition 1. *Let S be a digital circuit comprising a vector of inputs $i = (i_1, \ldots, i_a) \in \{0,1\}^a$, a vector of outputs $o = (o_1, \ldots, o_b) \in \{0,1\}^b$, a state register $r = (r_1, \ldots, r_n) \in \{0,1\}^n$, a clock input $ck \in \{0,1\}$ and a collection of combinational gates that implement the next state and output function $F = (F_0, \ldots, F_{n+b})$ s.t. $(r \parallel o)_{next\_ck\_cycle} = F(r \parallel i)$, when $|r \parallel i| = N = n + a$.*

The scan insertion arranges the bits of the state register r in c scan chains For brevity, we omit the description of the scan control, and assume immediate access to the state register r. However, for computing the time complexity, we keep in mind that the *Probe* operation lasts $2n/c{+}1$ clock cycles, one cycle for *Capture* and n cycles for each of the *ShiftIn* and *ShiftOut* operations. The parameter c depends on the number of pins, and we assume $c \ll n$. A probe operation $Probe(S, v)$ over circuit S is defined in Algorithm 1.

Algorithm 1 Probe(Circuit S, vector v)

1: $r \parallel i := v$	▷ Set registers and inputs state to v
2: $o_{t-1} := o$	▷ Sample outputs of S
3: Capture	
4: **return** $r \| o_{t-1}$	▷ New register values and outputs

A truth table of F can be obtained by running *Probe* operations on circuit S with all possible input vectors. This is an exhaustive search over a truth table algorithm (*ESoTT*)

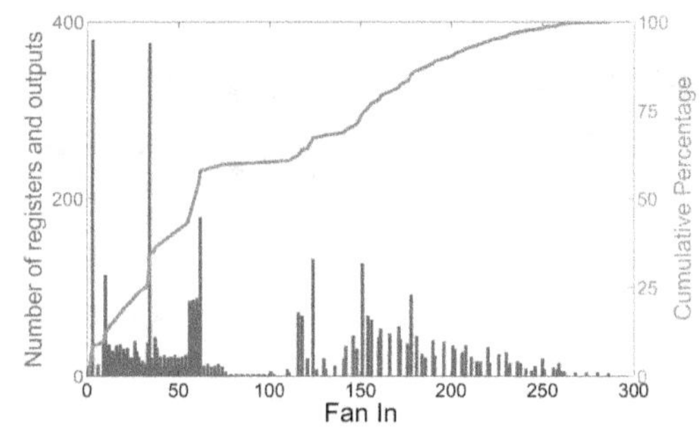

Figure 2: Transitive fan-in histogram for flip-flop inputs and primary outputs in the ITC'99 benchmark circuits.

that grows exponentially and is not practical. Later in this section, we present algorithms that leverage the limited transitive fan-in property of the circuit S to reduce the learning complexity. Transitive fan-in reflects the number of inputs of a combinational logic cone; for a typical combinational logic cone, it is much smaller than N. Figure 2 shows a histogram of transitive fan-ins of the logic cones from the circuits in the ITC'99 benchmark [4] set. More than half of the cones have a transitive fan-in of 64 or smaller. This observation allows the use of heuristic based algorithms.

2.1 Algorithm CSoTT (Compact K-Search over Truth Table)

In the Boolean function domain, the transitive fan-in is represented by the support size of the function. Strictly speaking, the transitive fan-in of a logic cone is greater or equal to the support size of the corresponding function. The learner may assume some limit K_{max} on the transitive fan-in of the combinational logic cones in the circuit of interest based on prior knowledge or statistics. Choosing $K_{max} \ll N$ reduces the search space significantly.

Every output bit y_i depends on some subset G_i of all the function variables. Hence, it is sufficient to examine the function F with a set of input vectors that cover all value combinations of all subgroups G s.t. $|G| \leq K_{max}$. As a trivial example, when $K_{max} = 1$, the function can be learned using the 0 vector and all input vectors, in which only one bit is set. More generally, to reconstruct the function F, it is sufficient to test it with a group of vectors with Hamming weight (HW) of up to K_{max}. *CSoTT* (Algorithm 2) implements this method by iterative probing of the function F with vectors v, starting with vectors with HW=0 and going up to K_{max}. If bit i of the probe result is equal to 1, i's entry of the *Onset* table is updated with a new implicant candidate, unless a cover of the corresponding term already exists in the table. If the bit is 0, but the *Onset* table includes an implicant candidate t, which is a cover of v, then t is removed from the table. Instead, *Onset* is updated with all the terms covered by t, all literals of which match bits in v equal to 1, excluding v itself.

For intuition, suppose that for some output bit i, the function F_i is positive unate, namely, all the literals in its DNF form are positive. Recording only positive literals is then sufficient to represent F_i. Moreover, only primary implicants can be stored. Now suppose there is a term t with a single negative and l positive literals. After l Hamming

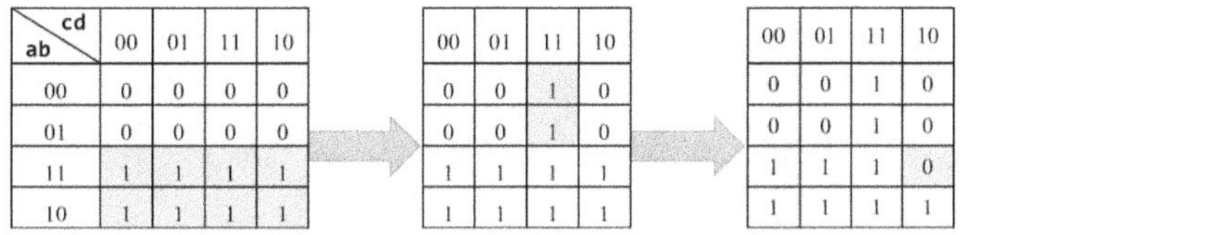

Figure 3: *CSoTT* algorithm stages with their respective Karnaugh maps.

weight iterations, the algorithm's table will contain a vector that includes all the positive literals in t. At the iteration $l+1$, the probe operation on the vector with all the variables from the term t set to 1 will return 0. As a result, the algorithm will add the required negative literal to the stored vector. This approach can be extended to any number of negative literals.

Algorithm 2 CSoTT

```
F0 := Probe(S,0)
Onset[i] = ∅ for all i from 1 to n+b
for K from 1 to K_max do
    for all v ∈ {0,1}^N s.t. HW(v)=K do
        P := Probe(S,v)⊕F0
        T := ∧T_j s.t. v_j=1                    ▷ compose term
        for i from 1 to n+b do
            if P[i]=1 & cover(T)∉Onset[i] then
                add(Onset[i],T)
            else if P[i] = 0 then
                call updateOnset(T,i)
            end if
        end for
    end for
end for
procedure UPDATEONSET(T,i)
    for all t ∈Onset[i]=cover(T) do
        for all t̂=cover(v) s.t. t=cover(t̂) do
            t_inv := ∧¬t_n for n s.t. t_n=1 AND t_n ∉ t̂
            t̂ := t̂ || t_inv
            add(Onset[i],t̂)
        end for
    end for
    remove(Onset[i],t)
end procedure
```

The algorithm's iterative operation can also be demonstrated using Karnaugh maps. Figure 3 shows the algorithm stages for an example single-bit function $F(a,b,c,d) = (a \wedge \neg(b \wedge c)) \vee c \wedge d$. At stage 1 ($HW = 1$), the only recorded implicant candidate is a. At stage 2 ($HW = 2$) the implicant $c \wedge d$ is added. At stage 3 ($HW = 3$), the implicant candidate a is found incomplete, since the probe operation on a vector $\{a,b,c,d\} = 1110$ yields a result of 0. Thus, it is replaced with higher order terms as shown in the corresponding Karnaugh map in the figure. At the end of the algorithm's execution, the Onset table contains a DNF representation of the function F.

CSoTT Time and Space Complexity The number of probes in *CSoTT* equals the number of elements in $\{0,1\}^N$ with Hamming weight of K_{max} or smaller, that is $\sum_{i=0}^{K_{max}} \binom{N}{i} \leq 1 + N^{K_{max}}$. Hence, the time complexity of the algorithm can be written as:

$$T_{CSoTT} = O[(2n/c+1) \cdot (1+N^{K_{max}})] \qquad (1)$$

The space required for *CSoTT* is bounded by the worst-case size of a DNF representation of a function with K_{max} variables. In practice, the memory space for *CSoTT* is roughly the size of the minimal DNF representation of F.

$$S_{CSoTT} = O[N_o \cdot K_{max} \cdot 2^{K_{max}-1}] \qquad (2)$$

Clearly, due to exponential growth, K_{max} of a typical circuit is too high for the algorithm to be practical. A lower K can be selected for partial reconstruction of the function F. For example, in approximately half of the cases from the ITC'99 statistics, the transitive fan-in is smaller than 50, and for 25% of them it is below 32. This partial information may provide an adversary with sufficient information to carry out the attack.

2.2 Algorithm ISoTT (Incremental CSoTT)

Algorithm 3 ISoTT

```
Pick K_init, K_step
K := K_init
Run CSoTT(K_max=K) on S
do
    for all m ∈Onset s.t. HW(m)=K_init do
        for all j s.t. m_j ∈ m: set v_j to constant 1;
        Run CSoTT(K_max=K) on remaining bits of v
    end for
    K := K_max + K_step
while there is a change in Onset
```

ISoTT is a speculative algorithm that invokes *CSoTT* a number of times. After the first invocation of *CSoTT* with a computationally reasonable K_{max}, the *Onset* table will contain a set of implicants $\{T\}$, each comprising a set of variables $\{G_T\}$. We speculate that if the function F contains higher order terms, many of them are a superset of some set in $\{G_T\}$. This is supported by the observation that the same sub-circuit may belong to several logical cones. One example of this phenomenon is the carry propagation logic in arithmetic circuits. The *ISoTT* algorithm thus adds incremental phases, in which for each of the terms recorded in the *Onset* table, *CSoTT* runs over a subset of vectors, where each of the vectors is an extension of the vector represented by this term. The parameter K_{step} controls the magnitude of the extension. The algorithm runs as long as there is a change in the *Onset* table.

ISoTT implements a greedy best-first search method. At every step of the algorithm, *CSoTT* is called as many times as the number of implicants with the maximum Hamming weight in the table at the beginning of running this step. Thus, the time complexity of a single algorithm is:

$$T_{ISoTT} \leq O[S_{ISoTT(step-1)} \cdot T_{CSoTT}(K_{max} = K_{step})] \quad (3)$$

From (3), $ISoTT$'s performance depends on the structure of the circuit and on the size of its minimal DNF representation. $ISoTT$ is based on speculation, therefore it does not guarantee correctness. However, for some examples, such as the arithmetic circuits, $ISoTT$ achieves full reconstruction.

2.3 Algorithm JSoTT (Junta based Search over Truth Table)

$JSoTT$ is a randomized algorithm that also exploits the limited transitive fan-in property. A function f: $\{0,1\}^n \rightarrow \{0,1\}$ is called a *k-junta* for $k \in x$ if it depends on at most k of its input coordinates; i.e., $f(x) = g(x_{i_1}, \cdots, x_{i_k})$ for some g: $\{0,1\}^n \rightarrow \{0,1\}$ and $i_1, \cdots, i_k \in [n]$ [16]. Hence, algorithms that learn junta functions from queries can be used to reconstruct combinational logic cones with a limited transitive fan-in. We take the adaptive algorithm from [7]. The algorithm runs for every output bit and comprises two phases: finding dependencies and function discovery. At the first phase, a set of probes with random input vectors is prepared. The results of the probes are used to find input bits affecting the output (relevant variables or RV).

Algorithm 4 JSoTT

```
Phase 1: Find relevant variables
F0 := Probe(S,0)
RV[i] = ∅ for all i from 1 to n+b
loop K_max · 2^K_max times
    v := random(1,...,2^N − 1)
    P := Probe(S,v)⊕F0
    add(Probes, ⟨v,P⟩)
end loop
for i from 1 to n+b do        ▷ Each output bit separately
    for all ⟨v, P⟩ in Probes do
        v̂ := {v̂_1, ..., v̂_N} = v
        For all j from 1 to N: v̂_j = 0 if (v_j ∉RV[i])
        P̂ := Probe(S,v̂)⊕F0
        if P_i ≠ P̂_i then
            find next RV by binary search on v keeping all v_j ∈ RV[i] fixed[1]
            add(RV[i], RV)
        end if
    end for
end for
Phase 2: Discover logical functions
for i from 1 to n+b do
    Call CSoTT[2] for output bit i with input composed from bits in RV[i] and K_max = |RV[i]|
end for
```

The algorithm finds variables that result in different probe results between vectors. Consider two input vectors v and u from the random vector set, such that $Probe(S, v) \neq Probe(S, u)$. The vectors v and u differ in the number of bits. If we start swapping the discriminating bits in v one by one (moving towards u), there will be a step at which the probe result will change. The variable that caused this change is a relevant variable. This operation is repeated for all the vectors in the set in order to find additional relevant variables, while the variables already known to be relevant will not be swapped. Finally, for faster search, rather than going one by one, the variables can be swapped in groups using the binary search principle. After the relevant variables are found for each output bit, a logical function is discovered by checking all the value combinations of the variables relevant to this output bit. This is the second phase.

JSoTT Time and Space Complexity. From [7]:

$$T_{JSoTT} \leq O[K_{max} \cdot 2^{K_{max}} \cdot logN_o + N_o \cdot (logN_o + 2^{K_{max}})] \quad (4)$$

$JSoTT$ scales well with the circuit size. Hence, it is better than $ISoTT$ for large circuits. However, thanks to its heuristic nature, $ISoTT$ overperforms for certain circuits.

3. EXPERIMENTAL RESULTS

We evaluated the algorithms from Section 2 on a set of synthetic benchmarks and one real application benchmark. For this, we built a software simulator that models digital circuits with a $Probe$ operation: an operation that represents the circuit's next state function F according to Definition 1. The simulator also implements the algorithms defined in Section 2. The output of the algorithm, the circuit hypothesis function f, is further matched against the original circuit function F. The simulator performs the matching by comparing the outputs of the functions F and f using a statistical method with a sufficiently large sample set of randomly selected inputs. $ESoTT$ serves as a baseline. For $ISoTT$, we perform a series of runs with different K_{init} and K_{step} parameters, and then select the best results.

3.1 Validation of Concept

We first checked the correctness of the scan based implementation of $Probe$, with the Validation of Concept experiment. For this experiment, we used a simple incrementor circuit S. The circuit description was written in Verilog and synthesized, including scan insertion, using Synopsys tools. On the netlist with scan we ran $ESoTT$ using the Verilog behavioral simulator. Note that the algorithm execution was preceded by learning the length of the scan chain from shifting in a pattern to the scan input and counting the number of cycles until the pattern was observed at the scan output. The reconstructed circuit S' (Figure 4) comprises (1) a register R comprising all n flip-flops in the scan chain, and (2) a combinational function (represented by a truth table) obtained by $ESoTT$. After obtaining the reconstructed circuit S', we confirmed its equivalence to the original circuit S with a formal logic equivalence tool. The remainder of this section presents results from the software simulator, which uses the $Probe$ abstraction assuming correctness of its underlying scan-based implementation.

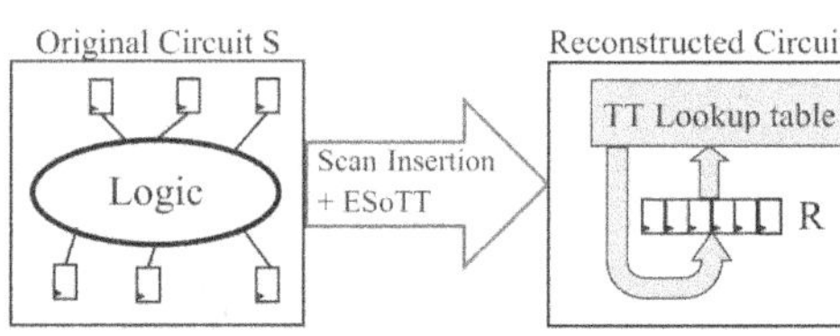

Figure 4: Validation of Concept Circuit Diagram.

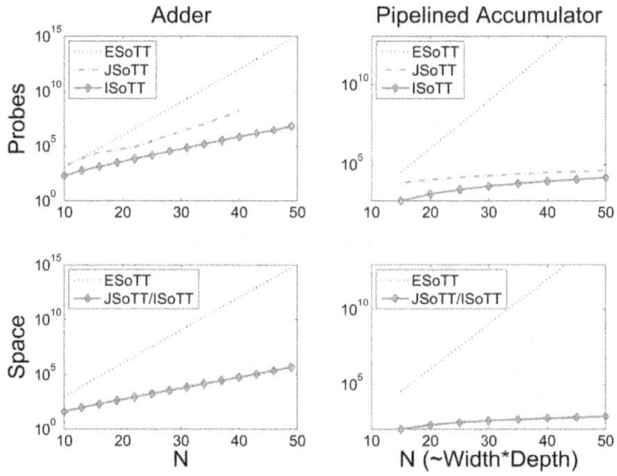

Figure 5: Algorithm results with arithmetic circuits. Runtime (in number of probes) and space requirements for a single adder and a pipelined accumulator with different sizes.

3.2 Arithmetic and Data Path Elements

We first evaluate the algorithms when applied to common building blocks of the digital circuits. We start with arithmetic circuits and measure the runtime and space required for a full reconstruction of the adder circuit. Although arithmetic circuits are characterized by tight dependency, which makes the limited fan-in optimization inefficient, their regular and recursive structure is useful for the incremental $ISoTT$ algorithm. Indeed, as shown in Figure 5, $ISoTT$ is the most efficient for the adder.

The adder implements a single function, where the limited fan-in approach has little advantage; thus, all the algorithms still run in exponential time. We expect to see the speedup with structures having loose dependencies between their sub-structures. As an example, we took a pipelined accumulator circuit built of pipeline stages; each merely adds the result of the previous stage to the input vector. When unfolded to a combinational structure, it turns to a set of adders in a parallel construction. Here, K_{max} is derived from the size of the single adder and does not depend on the number of pipeline stages. Therefore, we observe polynomial growth of space and time in Figure 5.

Next, we evaluate our algorithms with a multiplexer, a typical element of a data path. For example, unfolding a register file with scan results in a multiplexer. The size of the input vector to the multiplexer with bus width W and rank (number of input busses) R is $N{=}R{\cdot}W$. However, every output bit depends on only $R{+}log_2R$ bits; namely, K_{max} does not depend on the bus width. This makes the algorithms, which leverage the limited fan-in, particularly efficient for wide data path structures. Interestingly, $ISoTT$ performs better for all the arithmetic circuits, despite $JSoTT$'s lower theoretical complexity. A partial explanation is that while for $JSoTT$ K_{max} represents the maximum transitive fan-in of combinational circuits, for $ISoTT$ the maximum implicant size can be used as K_{max}. In this sense, $ISoTT$ can be regarded as a DNF learning algorithm [3].

3.3 AES Accelerator

$ISoTT$ is superior with regular and structured circuits: the more structure (or less entropy) is present in the circuit, the better $ISoTT$ can exploit it. $JSoTT$, however, is better suited to high entropy circuits characterized by the avalanche effect, which facilitates exploration of dependencies. We took the tiny AES core from the Open Cores repository [11] as an ultimate example of a high-entropy circuit. This is a highly pipelined implementation of the AES encryption/decryption, which contains 6848 internal registers. The maximum transitive fan-in of the circuit is 8. Nevertheless, thanks to the avalanche effect, K_{max} as low as 4 suffices for detecting all the dependencies. Hence, $JSoTT$ learns the AES circuit precisely and with little effort, despite its formidable size; see Table 1. The accuracy indicates the number of correctly reconstructed flip-flops. Because the algorithm is random, results differ slightly between invocations.

Table 1: AES Circuit Reconstruction

Selected K_{max}	Accuracy	Number of probes
2	44%	389109
3	93%	1251169
4	100%	1594819

Note that cryptographic functions, considered complex, are actually an easy target for our reverse engineering attack. Additionally, thanks to the scalability of $JSoTT$, the size of the circuit is less important than its structure. For example, a deeper pipeline increases the chance of successful reverse engineering thanks to the finer partitioning of the logic.

4. RELATED WORK

Several papers discuss non-invasive methods for reverse engineering. Kash et al. [12] propose an optical method for monitoring switching activity of different locations in the circuit. This method requires prior knowledge of the circuit and access to test patterns. The Side Channel Analysis for Reverse Engineering (SCARE) [20] employs power analysis to obtain design information. This information is coarse due to the natural limitations of the power analysis. [13] and [15] present various techniques addressing phase two of the reverse engineering process, behavioral model extraction. Our work focuses on the first phase, netlist extraction.

Saab et al. [17] first proposed using the scan to extract the functionality of an integrated circuit. They present a randomized algorithm that finds dependencies between registers and evaluate it with small benchmarks and an AES function. We add the discovery phase and provide a systematic learning method along with a discussion of the algorithms' complexity and scalability metrics. We also propose a heuristic algorithm tuned for certain types of (e.g. arithmetic) circuits. In [8], scan based techniques are combined with invasive methods to discover camouflaged cells. The authors use SAT solvers to discover the function of the camouflaged cells, achieving notable efficiency. Our non-invasive scan based attack assumes the entire logic cone as a black box.

Other papers propose countermeasures against the scan based side-channel attack. Da Rolt et al. [5] present their comprehensive classification, which we use to show that some of the countermeasures are ineffective against the scan based reverse engineering attack. For example, Da Rolt shows that the Advanced DFT Structure is insecure against the scan side channel attack in general. The BIST structure resists any scan based attack by disabling external access to the scan chains, assuming no bypass modes. This complicates debug and field failure diagnostics. In addition, fault coverage of BIST is insufficient. Hence, pure BIST solutions are rarely selected by vendors. The scrambling and modified scan chain types present an additional countermeasure, but they are inefficient against the reverse engineering attack. The attack is still possible in the presence of the aforementioned structures, but the output of the reverse engineering will include both the functional and the protection circuits. The adversary can then distinguish between the two. Finally, the Secret-free Test solution prevents volatile data from being exposed but does not prevent reverse engineering of the design data. Solutions of the types Access Restriction and Secure Wrapper prevent unauthorized access to scan chains. Thus, while they are also efficient against reverse engineering, combined attacks are possible that first target the authorization mechanism, for example using DPA [18].

Previous work relies on the circuit's ability to switch between mission and scan modes. One of the popular countermeasures against the scan-based attacks is thus to enforce reset when switching between the modes [9]. Because the reverse engineering attack retrieves static design information from the scan chains, it is immune to this countermeasure.

5. CONCLUSIONS AND FUTURE WORK

The reverse engineering attack is a threat for devices that rely on the secrecy of their proprietary algorithms and protection mechanisms. In this paper, we demonstrated a new attack that allows for the non-invasive reverse engineering of an entire device at the logical netlist level. We introduced new methods that exploit the limited transitive fan-in property for efficient learning. Using an algorithm that employs junta learning, we successfully reconstructed a hardware implementation of the AES cryptographic function. Hence, our experimental results show that exploitation of the scan side channel for reverse engineering is a real threat. It can give the adversary full or partial information about the circuit contents. Even partial information may reveal sufficient data to serve malicious purposes. The presented attack is also immune to some popular countermeasures.

Our future work will focus on examining algorithms that are more efficient or are tuned for specific circuit types. *JSoTT*'s scalability makes the presented method potentially applicable also to large scale SoC devices. Combining *JSoTT* with algorithms that exploit additional heuristics (such as *ISoTT*) can target complex logic within large devices. Of special interest is when some part of the circuit is known a priori. Here, the reverse engineering technique may help in detecting hardware Trojans.

6. ACKNOWLEDGMENTS

This research was partially supported by the Hasso Plattner Institute (HPI).

7. REFERENCES

[1] L. Azriel, R. Ginosar, S. Gueron, and A. Mendelson. Using Scan Side Channel for Detecting IP Theft. In *HASP 2016*, pages 1–8, NY, USA, 2016. ACM Press.

[2] L. Azriel, R. Ginosar, and A. Mendelson. Exploiting the Scan Side Channel for Reverse Engineering of a VLSI Device. Technical Report CCIT Report 897, Technion, Israel Institute of Technology, 2016.

[3] N. Bshouty, J. Jackson, and C. Tamon. More efficient PAC-learning of DNF with membership queries under the uniform distribution. *Journal of Computer and System Sciences*, 68(1):205–234, Feb 2004.

[4] F. Corno, M. S. Reorda, and G. Squillero. RT-level ITC'99 benchmarks and first ATPG results. *IEEE Design & Test of Computers*, 17(3):44–53, 2000.

[5] J. Da Rolt, A. Das, G. Di Natale, M.-L. Flottes, B. Rouzeyre, and I. Verbauwhede. Test Versus Security: Past and Present. *IEEE Transactions on Emerging Topics in Computing*, 2(1):50–62, Mar 2014.

[6] J. Da Rolt, G. Di Natale, M.-L. Flottes, and B. Rouzeyre. New security threats against chips containing scan chain structures. *IEEE HOST 2011*, pages 110–110, Jun 2011.

[7] P. Damaschke. Adaptive Versus Nonadaptive Attribute-Efficient Learning. *Machine Learning*, 41(2):197–215, 2000.

[8] M. El Massad, S. Garg, and M. V. Tripunitara. Integrated Circuit (IC) Decamouflaging: Reverse Engineering Camouflaged ICs within Minutes. In *NDSS*, 2015.

[9] D. Hely, F. Bancel, M. Flottes, and B. Rouzeyre. Test Control for Secure Scan Designs. *European Test Symposium (ETS'05)*, pages 190–195, 2005.

[10] D. Hely, K. Rosenfeld, and R. Karri. Security challenges during VLSI test. In *IEEE 9th International New Circuits and systems conference*, pages 486–489. Ieee, Jun 2011.

[11] H. Hsing. tiny_aes IP project, 2012.

[12] J. Kash, J. Tsang, and D. Knebel. Method and apparatus for reverse engineering integrated circuits by monitoring optical emission, Dec 2002.

[13] W. Li, Z. Wasson, and S. A. Seshia. Reverse Engineering Circuits Using Behavioral Pattern Mining. In *IEEE HOST*, pages 83–88, 2012.

[14] O. B. Lupanov. On circuits of functional elements with delay. *Probl. Kibern*, (23):43–81, 1970.

[15] K. S. McElvain. Methods and apparatuses for automatic extraction of finite state machines, 2001.

[16] R. O'Donnell. *Analysis of Boolean Functions*. Cambridge University Press, 2014.

[17] D. G. Saab, V. Nagubadi, F. Kocan, and J. Abraham. Extraction based verification method for off the shelf integrated circuits. In *1st Asia Symp. on Quality Electronic Design*, pages 396–400. IEEE, Jul 2009.

[18] S. Skorobogatov and C. Woods. Breakthrough silicon scanning discovers backdoor in military chip. In E. Prouff and P. Schaumont, editors, *CHES 2012*, volume 7428, pages 23–40. Springer, Sep 2012.

[19] R. Torrance and D. James. The State-of-the-Art in IC Reverse Engineering. In C. Clavier and K. Gaj, editors, *CHES 2009*, volume 5747, pages 363–381. Springer Berlin Heidelberg, Aug 2009.

[20] X. Wang, S. Narasimhan, A. Krishna, and S. Bhunia. SCARE: Side-Channel Analysis Based Reverse Engineering for Post-Silicon Validation. In *25th Intl. Conf. VLSI Design*, pages 304–309. IEEE, Jan 2012.

Analysis of SEU Propagation in Combinational Circuits at RTL Based on Satisfiability Modulo Theories

Ghaith Kazma
Concordia University
Montreal, Quebec, Canada
g_kazma@encs.concordia.ca

Ghaith Bany Hamad
Polytechnique Montréal
Montreal, Quebec, Canada
ghaith.bany-hamad@polymtl.ca

Otmane Ait Mohamed
Concordia University
Montreal, Quebec, Canada
ait@ece.concordia.ca

Yvon Savaria
Polytechnique Montréal
Montreal, Quebec, Canada
yvon.savaria@polymtl.ca

ABSTRACT

The vulnerability of VLSI designs to soft errors grows with technology scaling. In order to allow a cost-effective reliability aware design process, it is critical to assess soft error reliability parameters in early design stages. This paper presents a new methodology to estimate digital circuit vulnerability to soft errors of circuits described at Register Transfer Level (RTL). Single Event Upsets (SEUs) propagation through RTL bit-vector operations is modeled and analyzed based on Satisfiability Modulo Theories (SMT). For instance, the bit-vector reduction operators and arithmetic operators were modeled using SMT to include their fault propagation properties. In order to illustrate the practical utilization of our work, we have analyzed different RTL combinational circuits. Experimental results demonstrate that the proposed framework is on average about 4 times faster than other comparable contemporary techniques. Moreover, it provides more accurate and detailed results of the circuit vulnerability allowing a more efficient applicability of fault tolerance techniques.

Keywords

Satisfiability Modulo Theories (SMT); Single Event Upset (SEU); Soft Error Rate (SER); Register Transfer Level (RTL)

1. INTRODUCTION

Soft errors induced by Single Event Upsets (SEUs) have become one of the most challenging issues that impact the reliability of modern electronic systems. Exponential growth in the number of transistors per chip has brought tremendous progress in the performance of semiconductor devices; however it has increased their vulnerability to soft errors. Therefore, there is a growing need to analyze and estimate the impact of soft errors at an earlier stage in the design cycle. Several techniques have been proposed to analyze soft errors propagation at gate level, such as [1] and [2]. At Register Transfer Level (RTL), SEUs propagation is analyzed using fault simulation [3], [4] and formal verification methods [5], [6], [7], [8]. Simulation based techniques have serious shortcomings as they are very time consuming for large circuits with many primary inputs. Furthermore, these techniques have their drawbacks in terms of accuracy. This is mainly because their accuracy is determined by the ratio of the simulated sample size over the total vector space size. Formal verification based techniques are resource hungry and require the use of reduction techniques to handle moderate size designs such as in [5] and [6].

Permission to make digital or hard copies of all or part of this work for personal or classroom use is granted without fee provided that copies are not made or distributed for profit or commercial advantage and that copies bear this notice and the full citation on the first page. Copyrights for components of this work owned by others than ACM must be honored. Abstracting with credit is permitted. To copy otherwise, or republish, to post on servers or to redistribute to lists, requires prior specific permission and/or a fee. Request permissions from permissions@acm.org.

GLSVLSI '17, May 10-12, 2017, Banff, AB, Canada

© 2017 ACM. ISBN 978-1-4503-4972-7/17/05...$15.00

DOI: http://dx.doi.org/10.1145/3060403.3060438

In this paper, we introduce a methodology to evaluate the vulnerability of digital circuits to soft errors due to SEUs at RTL. A new modeling of SEUs propagation as a Satisfiability problem using Satisfiability Modulo Theories (SMT) is proposed. The behavior of the basic RTL operations (such as logical, reduction, arithmetic, and case statement) in the presence of SEUs is modeled. Thereafter, we adapted the data type reduction technique presented in [6] to our SMT model and investigated its impact on our results. The proposed methodology allows the analysis of SEUs propagation from each vulnerable node to the output. This is done by evaluating the generated SMT model of the RTL design against a set of assertions.

Our results demonstrate that our technique is more efficient than existing formal based techniques that use pure Boolean representation to model SEU propagation [7]. Moreover, the results demonstrate that using a data type reduction technique such as the one proposed in [6] results in a loss of accuracy.

The rest of this paper is organized as follows. Section 2 reviews the relevant contemporary techniques. Section 3 gives an overview of Satisfiability Modulo Theories and SMT model counters. The data type reduction technique we are adapting in this paper is discussed in Section 3.2. Section 4 explains our proposed modeling and analysis of SEUs propagation at RTL. In Section 5, we explain our experiments and results. Section 6 concludes this work.

2. RELATED WORK

Several techniques have been proposed to analyze the growing vulnerability of digital circuits to soft errors due to SEUs at RTL. In [5], [6], the behavior of the RTL circuits due to SEUs is formally modeled as finite Discrete Time Markov Chains (DTMCs). For each SEU injection scenario, specified properties are verified against the constructed model using the PRISM model checker. Data type reduction and partitioning techniques were applied in [6] and [5] respectively to overcome the state explosion problem. However those techniques result in loss in accuracy and the verification time still grows exponentially with the size of the circuit.

In [7], the problem of SEUs propagation at RTL is modeled as a Boolean Satisfiability problem. The modeling of the circuit includes a fault-free model, a faulty model, and a comparator at the top level. This model is converted into a Boolean Conjunctive Normal Form (CNF) formula which is sent to a SAT-solver. However, this technique has a high complexity when dealing with basic RTL arithmetic operations. This is mainly because the proposed modeling is limited to Boolean representation, i.e. all RTL constructs have to be modeled at the bit level.

3. BACKGROUND

3.1 SMT and SMTApproxMC

The advent of Satisfiability Modulo Theories (SMT) [9] solved the problem of being restricted to a pure Boolean representation, which is not efficient and sometimes inadequate when representing several classes of systems. SMT is an extension of the SAT decision problem, where the formulas are expressed in first-order logic, with associated background theories. SMT have been used to model and solve software and hardware engineering problems. In this paper, we show how linear arithmetic and bit-vector theories can be used to model SEUs propagation.

If the constructed SMT model satisfies the set of assertions being verified, the SMT solver generates a satisfiability assignment. In this assignment, each variable is assigned a valid value such that the SMT model satisfies the verified assertions. However, when dealing with a large number of variables, model counting (#SAT) i.e., counting the number of satisfying assignments of a first order logic formula, is a problem of significant theoretical and practical complexity. Different methods to reduce the complexity of this problem and to eliminate the need for exact model counting were proposed. One of the main approaches in this area is *approximate model counting*. This is used in tools such as ApproxCount [10], SearchTreeSampler [11], SE [12], SampleSearch [13]. Recently, a new technique that is based on approximate model counting was proposed. This technique was successfully implemented in a tool called SMTApproxMC [14]. The accuracy and the scalability of this tool were demonstrated through different experiments. Results show that SMTApproxMC scales to formulas with tens of thousands of variables. Moreover, based on the desired level of confidence, SMTApproxMC can provide bounds that are close to the exact model count.

3.2 Data Type Reduction

Existing formal analysis methods can be combined with different reduction techniques to improve their scalability. SEUs propagation at RTL can be reduced as follows:

1. For a bit-vector signal, if one bit is faulty, then the whole vector is considered faulty. In other words, a multi-bit signal is considered as one Boolean variable. Moreover, the SEUs propagation through register transfer operations such as addition and multiplication is modeled to transparently propagate from inputs to outputs.
2. For a *case* statement or a block of *if* statements, represented as multiplexers, if the selection signal is faulty, then the output is considered to be faulty as well.

The main issue with the utilization of such a reduction technique is that we lose track of the exact error location. For example, consider the 2-bit multiplexer in Fig. 1. If the select signal *sel* is faulty, then the output y is considered to be faulty. However, in this example, a faulty *sel* signal can cause at most 2 bits of y to be faulty. The propagation of the fault is conditional on having an active path from the *sel* signal to the output i.e., the fault is not logically masked. However, this level of detail is fully abstracted when using data type reduction techniques. Therefore, this causes the computed vulnerability of the circuit to be inaccurate.

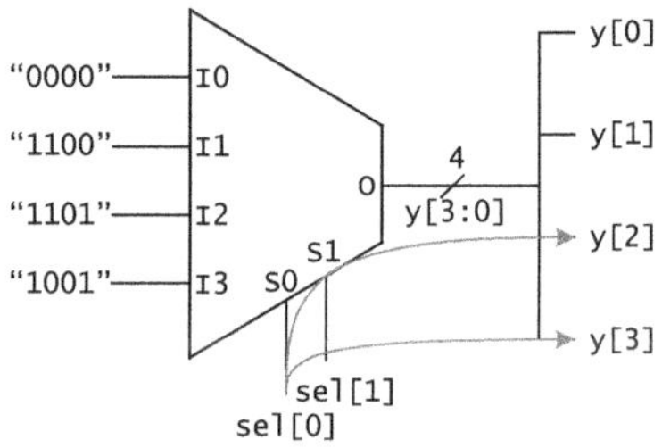

Figure 1: Fault Propagation Example in 2-bit Multiplexer.

4. THE PROPOSED METHODOLOGY

In this section, the proposed SMT modeling and analysis of SEUs propagation at RTL are explained.

4.1 Modeling of RTL Constructs

In this section, the modeling of SEUs propagation through basic RTL constructs is explained in details. In this paper, we use capital symbols (e.g., A) to represent bit-vector variables. Reduction operators will be represented using single symbols (e.g., & for reduction AND and | for reduction OR).

4.1.1 Bit-Vector Signals

In order to keep track of the exact bits that are affected by an SEU, RTL bit-vectors are modeled using a data-type consisting of two bit-vectors in SMT format. The first vector represents the logic state of the bits (e.g., A_l) and the second vector represents the fault state of the bits (e.g., A_f). For example, in Fig. 2, A_l = "0100" and A_f = "0011" indicates that the error free logic state of bit-vector A is "0100" and there are two bit flips at positions 0 and 1, i.e., the faulty value of A is "0111".

4.1.2 Logical Operators

Logical operators are encoded as bit-vector operations over the logic and fault states of the input bit-vectors. For an AND gate with inputs A, B and output C, the logic state of C is given by:

$$C_l = A_l \wedge B_l$$

The bits of C_f are "1" (i.e., faulty) under any of the following two conditions. The first condition is if the corresponding bits of either input is faulty and the other is of non-controlling logic. The second condition is if the corresponding bits of both inputs are faulty and of equal logic value. The second condition is needed to consider re-convergent faults. Therefore, the fault state of C is given by:

$$C_f = (A_f \wedge B_l \wedge \overline{B_f})|(B_f \wedge A_l \wedge \overline{A_f})|(A_f \wedge B_f) \wedge (\overline{A_l \oplus B_l})$$

In the example in Fig. 2, C_l = "0100", which is the result of the logical AND operation over bit-vectors A_l and B_l. The fault state C_f = "0001" indicates that only the LSB of C_l is faulty, since the fault at $A_l[1]$ was logically masked due to the controlling logic value of B (i.e., $B_l[1]$ = "0").

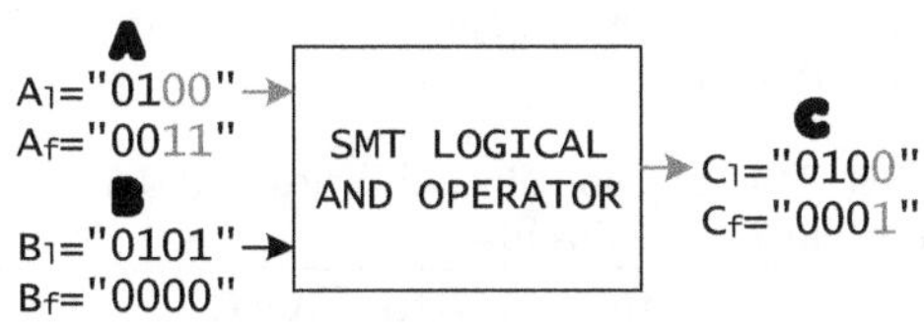

Figure 2: SMT Logical And Operator.

4.1.3 Reduction Operators

These operators are unary i.e., they perform a bit-wise operation on one operand and produce a 1-bit output. In our model, the output of a reduction operator is faulty if at least one bit of the input vector is faulty, all the non-faulty bits are of non-controlling logic and the logic states of all the faulty bits are equal. For example, for a reduction AND with input A and output B, the logic state of B is the reduced AND operation over the logic state of A as follows:

$$B_l = \&A_l$$

For B to be faulty (B_f = "1") the following two conditions must be satisfied. First, at least one bit of A is faulty which is determined by performing a reduced OR operation over A_f. Second, all the non-faulty bits have a "1" logic value and the logic state of all the faulty bits is equal. Therefore, the fault state of B is given by:

$$(|A_f = 1) \wedge (\&(A_l \oplus A_f) \vee \&A_l)$$

4.1.4 Arithmetic Operators

The SMT theory of bit-vectors allows arithmetic operations to be performed on bit-vectors. It is therefore possible to perform the multiplication, division, addition, and subtraction operations (i.e. *, /, +, -) on both the faulty and non-faulty values of the signals to keep track of the faulty bits. To obtain the faulty value of signal A, we simply perform a logical XOR operation with its fault state:

$$A_l \oplus A_f$$

In the case of an addition $C = A+B$, the non-faulty result is evaluated using:

$$C_l = A_l + B_l$$

The faulty result is evaluated using $(A_l \oplus A_f) + (B_l \oplus B_f)$. From this, the fault state of C is computed by performing a logical XOR operation over the two vectors:

$$C_f = (A_l + B_l) \oplus ((A_l \oplus A_f) + (B_l \oplus B_f))$$

4.1.5 Case Statements

These are modeled using Boolean implication operators (i.e., =>) or using if-then-else (i.e., *ite*) operators. In order to keep track of the faulty bits in the output, if the select signal is faulty, both the faulty and non-faulty outputs are compared to compute the fault state vector.

4.1.6 Concatenation, Extraction, and Extension

For concatenation operations, i.e., $A :: B$, the logic states and the fault states are concatenated using the SMT concatenation operator as follows:

$$A_l :: B_l$$
$$A_f :: B_f$$

For bit extraction, the bits are simply extracted along with their corresponding fault bits using the SMT extract operator. For signed and unsigned extension, an SMT sign-extend and unsigned-extend operation is applied on both the logic and fault states of the bit-vectors respectively. For example, given:

$$A_l = \text{"1011"}$$
$$A_f = \text{"1000"}$$

If we apply a 4-bit sign extension, the result is:

$$A_l = \text{"11111011"}$$
$$A_f = \text{"11111000"}$$

4.2 Analysis of SEUs Propagation and SER

The first step in our methodology, shown in Fig. 3, is to convert the RTL behavioral Verilog description into a Python SMT model using our basic RTL function libraries. Those libraries were developed using the Microsoft Z3 [15] Python API. Then, SEU is injected at one bit by setting its corresponding fault state bit to "1". The next step is to convert the design into the SMT2 format, which is then fed to the SMTApproxMC tool [14] to perform the following tasks: 1) verify SEUs propagation to the output using the Boolector SMT solver; 2) estimate the number of input vectors that allow the SEU injected at node i to reach output j, which is equal to the number of satisfiability assignments (i.e., $Num\_Assignments_{i \longrightarrow j}$). Thereafter, the probability that an injected SEU at input i propagates to an output j is computed as follows:

$$P(SEU_{i \longrightarrow j}) = \frac{Num\_Assignments_{i \longrightarrow j}}{N} \tag{1}$$

where $Num\_Assignments_{i \longrightarrow j}$ is the number of satisfiable SMT assignments for the current injection scenario and N is the total number of input vectors. This analysis is performed for all possible inputs and outputs combinations. Therefore, the vulnerability of an output j for a circuit which has m vulnerable nodes, is calculated as follows:

$$Vuln(j) = \sum_{i=1}^{m} P(SEU_{i \longrightarrow j}) \tag{2}$$

Finally, the Soft Error Rate (SER) of a circuit, which has n outputs, is calculated as follows:

$$SER = \sum_{j=1}^{n} Vuln(j) \tag{3}$$

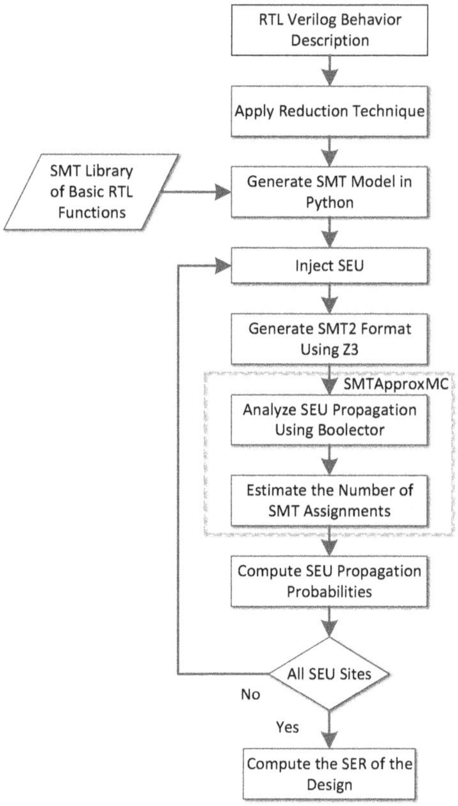

Figure 3: Main Steps of the Proposed Modeling and Analysis of SEU Propagation at RTL.

4.3 Example

As an example, the proposed methodology was implemented on the 4-bit magnitude comparator circuit shown in Figure 4 to illustrate its main steps and investigate the results. This circuit implements a magnitude comparator by a carry function with an inverted input. In this circuit, common elements of the three comparator functions, i.e., $A < B$, $A > B$ and $A = B$ are combined.

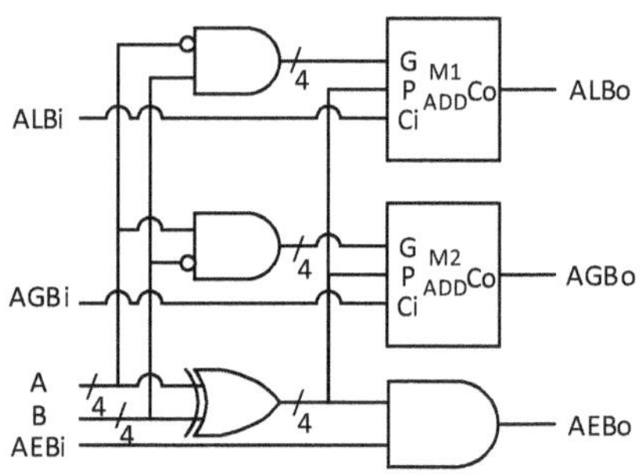

Figure 4: RTL structure of the 74L85 benchmark that is a 4-bit Magnitude Comparator.

A high level description of the circuit in Verilog was converted into an SMT equivalent formula using the developed libraries. The propagation probabilities from every input to every output were evaluated. These probabilities are shown in Table 1. Using the probabilities obtained from this analysis, it is then possible to identify the most critical bits (i.e, input and output flip-flops) for SEU propagation. In other words, we can identify the inputs from which SEUs have the highest probabilities to propagate to a given output. Using these results, it is also possible to identify not only the most vulnerable bits, but the propagation paths as well. For example, SEUs injection at inputs $A[3]$ and $B[3]$ have the highest probability to propagate to $ALBo$ and $AGBo$. Such results can be very useful for any SEU tolerant technique to selectively harden the most vulnerable bits in order to achieve the desired SER with minimum area overhead.

The probability of SEU propagation from each input bit to each output is computed based on equation 1. Using equation 2, the vulnerability of each output is computed and the results are reported in the last row of Table 1. Thereafter, the SER of the circuit is evaluated to be equal to 4.4375 based on equation 3. Note that vulnerabilities are sums of probabilities that are not disjoint and they can add up to values larger than 1.

Table 1: SEU Propagation Probabilities and derived vulnerabilities for the 74L85 Circuit

	ALBo	**AGBo**	**AEBo**	**Vulnerability**
A[3]	0.5	0.5	0.0625	1.0625
A[2]	0.25	0.25	0.0625	0.5625
A[1]	0.125	0.125	0.0625	0.3125
A[0]	0.0625	0.0625	0.0625	0.1875
B[3]	0.5	0.5	0.0625	1.0625
B[2]	0.25	0.25	0.0625	0.5625
B[1]	0.125	0.125	0.0625	0.3125
B[0]	0.0625	0.0625	0.0625	0.1875
ALBi	0.0625	0	0	0.0625
AGBi	0	0.0625	0	0.0625
AEBi	0	0	0.0625	0.0625
Vulnerability	1.9375	1.9375	0.5625	4.4375

5. EXPERIMENTAL RESULTS

In this section, we report results from experiments performed to validate the proposed methodology and its efficiency. The proposed modeling and analysis is fully automated using the Z3 SMT solver [15], the SMTApproxMC tool [14], and Python scripts. Our experiments were performed on a workstation with an Intel Core i7 6820HQ running at 3.0 GHz and 16 GB RAM.

Typically, SEU analysis is done using two versions of a circuit, a fault-free version and a faulty version. A fault is injected by flipping a single bit in the faulty version of the circuit. The outputs of the two versions are then compared to check if the SEU reached the output. The accuracy of the two-versions modeling approach was proven in [7]. In order to validate the accuracy of our technique, we implemented the two-versions based modeling using SMT to compare the results with the modeling proposed in Section 4. Moreover, we applied the data type reduction described in Section 3.2 on our model in order to evaluate the loss in accuracy due to this reduction technique. It is assumed that the inputs of the circuits are latched, i.e., the data comes from registers, where the SEUs will be injected.

5.1 Performance Analysis

The first detailed analysis consisted of investigating the applicability and the performance of our methodology. Different behavioral descriptions of the ISCAS85 benchmarks

[16] and MSI components in the 74xxx series were analyzed. The results are reported in Table 2. The computation times are compared with the results presented in [7] (shown in the second column) which are based on pure Boolean SAT. Moreover, we compare the computation time of the modeling proposed in Section 4 with the computation time of the two-versions modeling that was implemented using SMT as well. As expected, it can be observed that the proposed SMT modeling and analysis provides a better solution to analyze SEUs at RTL in comparison with the pure Boolean SAT implementation. It is observed that our methodology is on average about 4 times faster.

Table 2: Comparison of the CPU Time Between the Proposed Methodology, the Technique Proposed in [7] and the Two-Versions Technique

circuit	Technique in [7] Time (s)	Two-Versions Time (s)	Proposed Methodology Time (s)
74283	0.27	0.25	0.13
74182	0.22	0.15	0.11
74181	9.36	7.01	1.29
74L85	8.68	6.45	1.22
c432	266.80	245.22	114.22
c499	46.80	42.11	22.92
c1908	-	432.64	345.78
c2670	-	733.43	548.54
c3540	-	335.11	245.98

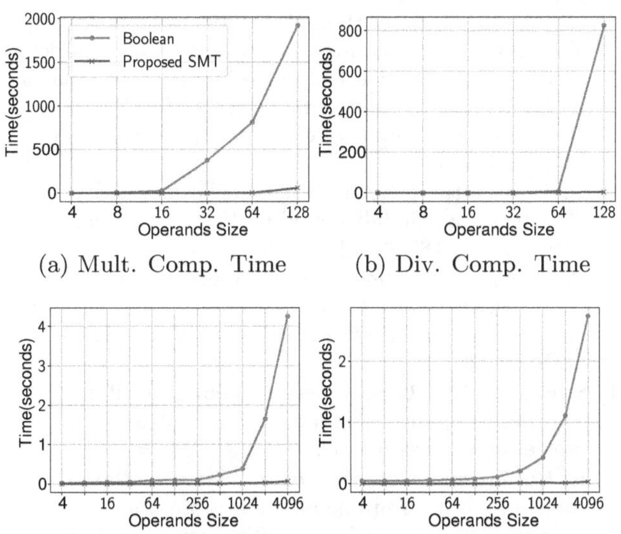

(a) Mult. Comp. Time (b) Div. Comp. Time

(c) Add. Comp. Time (d) Sub. Comp. Time

Figure 5: Comparisons of the Computation Time Between the Boolean Based Modeling and the Proposed SMT Modeling for Different Sizes of Arithmetic Operations.

On the other hand, analyzing the fault propagation of SEUs using a fault-free and faulty versions of the RTL circuit implicitly doubles the number of inputs and operations in the resulting model. Therefore, this technique results in significant modeling redundancy. Using our proposed modeling, instead of two-versions modeling significantly reduced the computation time.

Another analysis was conducted to compare our technique with the technique proposed in [7] for larger designs. In this analysis, we implemented the modeling proposed in [7] using the SAT formulation and our proposed modeling using the SMT formulation. Results demonstrate that with SAT based modeling, the computation time grows exponentially with the design size. Fig. 5 shows the time required to analyze the propagation of an SEU injected at the input of arithmetic circuits using the modeling proposed in [7] (called Boolean in Fig. 5(a)) and our proposed modeling for various circuit sizes. For example, analyzing SEUs propagation for a 128-bit multiplication using the technique in [7] can take up to 1920.0 seconds, whereas analyzing the same size operation using our technique takes only 57.6 seconds.

5.2 Accuracy Analysis

The accuracy of our method was compared with the technique proposed in [6], which employs a data type reduction technique. We also validate our results by comparing the SERs computed with our methodology with those computed with the two-versions technique. In Table 3, the results in the first column represent the SER values computed when using the data type reduction technique [6] discussed in Section 3.2. The two-versions modeling and the modeling proposed in Section 4 do not use any reduction. Therefore, comparing the results of column 1 to those of columns 2 and 3, we can observe a large inaccuracy in the computed SER when using the data reduction technique.

Table 3: Comparison of the Computed Soft Error Rate (SER) Between the Proposed Methodology, the Technique Proposed in [6] and the Two-Versions SMT Modeling

circuit	Technique in [6] SER	Two-Versions SER	Proposed Methodology SER
74283	22.5	16.1	16.1
74182	20.75	5.72	5.72
74181	28.0	18.31	18.31
74L85	13.5	4.44	4.44
c432	25.56	13.89	13.50
c499	32.01	31.23	32.22
c1908	95.65	78.88	81.53
c2670	157.65	127.54	130.00
c3540	96.81	41.59	44.70

We illustrate the reason behind the loss in accuracy when using the data type reduction technique by analyzing the Program Counter (PC) address datapath of the MIPS architecture shown in Fig. 6. The main issue when using data type reduction is that it assumes all the bits in an input register have equal propagation probabilities. Based on the technique proposed in [6], it is estimated that all SEUs injected at PC propagate through this datapath with probability 1. Our analysis shows that these results provide an over approximation of the actual SEU propagation probabilities in this circuit. Given equal probability of R-type, jump, and branch instructions, our results show that an SEU at the 2 LSBs will only propagate given R-type or branch instructions (i.e., probability of 2/3). An error occurring at bits [27 : 2] has a propagation probability slightly above 2/3 since these bits are always used for regular and branch type instructions. SEUs that occur when the current instruction is a jump instruction have a small propagation probability through the addition. In Pseudo-Direct Addressing for a jump instruction, the current PC is incremented by 4, then the four most significant bits are concatenated with the 26 least significant bits of the jump instruction, shifted by 2 to the left i.e., $PC \leftarrow PC[31:28] :: IR[25:0] :: 00$. In this case, an SEU occurring at bits [27 : 2] of the current PC address will be masked if the current instruction is a jump and the error does not propagate through the carries to reach the four MSBs. An SEU occurring on the four MSBs of the PC address, will always propagate to the computed effective address, because these 4 bits are always used to compute the next PC address. This analysis illustrates the accuracy of our technique that provides detailed vulnerabilities of the specific register bits.

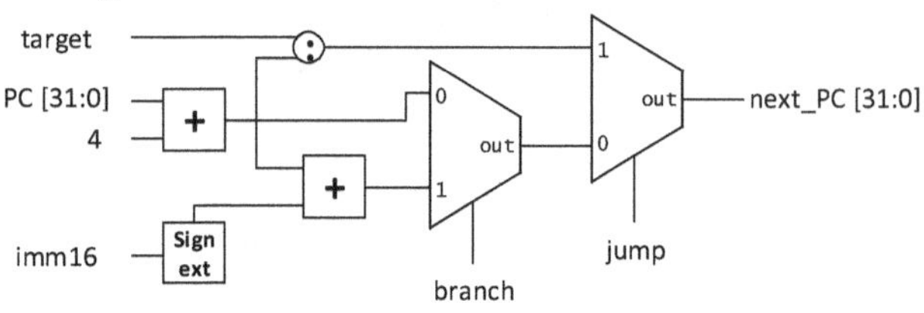

Figure 6: Program Counter Datapath.

Columns 2 and 3 of table 3 represent the SERs computed using the two-versions technique and the modeling proposed in Section 4. The small difference in computed SER values can be justified by the model count estimation technique used in the SMTApproxMC tool, and not by the modeling accuracy. For small circuits where the SMTApproxMC tool is able to generate all solutions, then the SER generated using the proposed methodology is exactly equal to the SERs of the two-versions models. However, for large circuits, the SMTApproxMC tool randomly partitions the solution space of a given formula into smaller cells of roughly the same size using word-level hash functions. This causes small variations in the computed probabilities of two equivalent formulas.

6. CONCLUSION

In this paper, we proposed a new methodology to investigate the vulnerability of combinational circuits to SEUs at RTL. SMT libraries of RTL constructs (e.g., arithmetic operations and case statements) are built to model SEU propagation. The proposed modeling significantly reduces the complexity of the analysis compared to other techniques while improving the accuracy. For instance, the CPU time required to compute the SER of ISCAS85 RTL benchmarks is on average about 4 times faster than with other techniques that use pure Boolean SAT to model SEU propagation. Moreover, this speed-up increases exponentially with larger circuits such as multipliers. The proposed technique improves the accuracy by providing detailed vulnerability information for specific bits in comparison with techniques that apply data type reduction.

7. ACKNOWLEDGMENTS

The authors would like to thank the Natural Sciences and Engineering Research Council of Canada (NSERC) and the Microsystems Strategic Alliance of Quebec (ReSMiQ) for their partial financial support of this research.

8. REFERENCES

[1] G. Bany Hamad, S. R. Hasan, O. Ait Mohamed, and Y. Savaria. Characterizing, modeling, and analyzing soft error propagation in asynchronous and synchronous digital circuits. *Microelectronics Reliability*, 55(1):238–250, 2015.

[2] G. Bany Hamad, G. Kazma, O. Ait Mohamed, and Y. Savaria. Efficient and accurate analysis of single event transients propagation using smt-based techniques. In *Proceedings of the 35th International Conference on Computer-Aided Design*, page 54. ACM, 2016.

[3] J.C. Baraza, J. Gracia, S. Blanc, D. Gil, and P.J. Gil. Enhancement of fault injection techniques based on the modification of vhdl code. *IEEE Transactions on Very Large Scale Integration (VLSI) Systems*, 16(6):693–706, 2008.

[4] X. Li, S.V. Adve, P. Bose, and J.A. Rivers. Softarch: an architecture-level tool for modeling and analyzing soft errors. In *Dependable Systems and Networks, 2005. DSN 2005. Proceedings. International Conference on*, pages 496–505. IEEE, 2005.

[5] J.A. Kumar. Statistical guarantees of performance for rtl designs. 2012.

[6] L. Chen, M. Ebrahimi, and M.B. Tahoori. Formal quantification of the register vulnerabilities to soft error in rtl control paths. *Journal of Electronic Testing*, 31(2):193–206, 2015.

[7] S.Z. Shazli and M.B. Tahoori. Using boolean satisfiability for computing soft error rates in early design stages. *Microelectronics Reliability*, 50(1):149–159, 2010.

[8] G. Kazma, G. Bany Hamad, O. Ait Mohamed, and Y. Savaria. Investigating the efficiency and accuracy of a data type reduction technique for soft error analysis. In *Electronics, Circuits and Systems (ICECS), 2016 IEEE International Conference on*, pages 273–276. IEEE, 2016.

[9] C.W. Barrett, R. Sebastiani, S.A. Seshia, and C. Tinelli. Satisfiability modulo theories. *Handbook of satisfiability*, 185:825–885, 2009.

[10] W. Wei and B. Selman. A new approach to model counting. In *International Conference on Theory and Applications of Satisfiability Testing*, pages 324–339. Springer, 2005.

[11] S. Ermon, C.P. Gomes, and B. Selman. Uniform solution sampling using a constraint solver as an oracle. *arXiv preprint arXiv:1210.4861*, 2012.

[12] R. Rubinstein. Stochastic enumeration method for counting np-hard problems. *Methodology and Computing in Applied Probability*, pages 1–43, 2013.

[13] V. Gogate and R. Dechter. Samplesearch: Importance sampling in presence of determinism. *Artificial Intelligence*, 175(2):694–729, 2011.

[14] S. Chakraborty, K.S. Meel, R. Mistry, and M.Y. Vardi. Approximate probabilistic inference via word-level counting. *arXiv preprint arXiv:1511.07663*, 2015.

[15] L. De Moura and N. Bjørner. Z3: An efficient smt solver. In *International conference on Tools and Algorithms for the Construction and Analysis of Systems*, pages 337–340. Springer, 2008.

[16] M.C. Hansen, H. Yalcin, and J.P. Hayes. Unveiling the iscas-85 benchmarks: A case study in reverse engineering. *IEEE Design & Test of Computers*, 16(3):72–80, 1999.

Fine-Grain Program Snippets Generator for Mobile Core Design

Shuang Song, Raj Desikan*, Mohamad Barakat*, Sridhar Sundaram*,
Andreas Gerstlauer and Lizy K. John
The University of Texas at Austin, Austin, TX, USA
*Samsung Austin R&D Center, Austin, TX, USA
songshuang1990@utexas.edu,{gerstl,ljohn}@ece.utexas.edu,
{r.desikan,m.barakat,s.sundaram}@samsung.com

ABSTRACT

As mobile devices have come to dominate modern computing systems, improving mobile processors' performance and energy consumption has become an important topic for both industry and academia. Similar to desktop and server CPUs, the design of mobile processors relies on a combination of high-level micro-architectural and low-level RTL simulations for design exploration and optimization. Shrinking simulation times remains a critical design issue, as it directly impacts turnaround time and time-to-market. Many prior works have been proposed to generate smaller program snippets (simulation points) aimed at reducing the simulation times for the micro-architecture design process. However, as emerging mobile applications are divergent from traditional desktop/server workloads in terms of functionality, code length, and code composition, prior strategies may no longer be satisfactory. In this paper, we propose a novel approach to generate fine-grain application snippets of mobile benchmarks that can accurately represent the full application performance for both high-level micro-architectural and low-level RTL simulations. Compared to prior work, snippets produced by our generator reduce performance estimation error by 5.6% while saving 76% simulation time on average.

1. INTRODUCTION

In the era of mobile computing, processor design still plays an essential role, as it can significantly impact device performance, energy consumption, and user satisfaction [8]. Therefore, improving mobile CPU performance and energy efficiency is considered as a primary goal [8][14][15][11] for industry and academia. Similar to conventional CPU design, design of mobile CPU design relies on high-level micro-architecture and low-level RTL simulations for design space exploration and implementation. Hence, reducing simulation time becomes extremely important to keep design time manageable. At the same time, mobile applications differ from desktop and server applications in terms of service functionality, software length, and code composition. This causes significant differences in micro-architectural behavior, such as instruction cache misses/stall cycles and branch mis-predictions [7].

Permission to make digital or hard copies of all or part of this work for personal or classroom use is granted without fee provided that copies are not made or distributed for profit or commercial advantage and that copies bear this notice and the full citation on the first page. Copyrights for components of this work owned by others than ACM must be honored. Abstracting with credit is permitted. To copy otherwise, or republish, to post on servers or to redistribute to lists, requires prior specific permission and/or a fee. Request permissions from permissions@acm.org.

GLSVLSI '17, May 10-12, 2017, Banff, AB, Canada
© 2017 ACM. ISBN 978-1-4503-4972-7/17/05...$15.00
DOI: http://dx.doi.org/10.1145/3060403.3060439

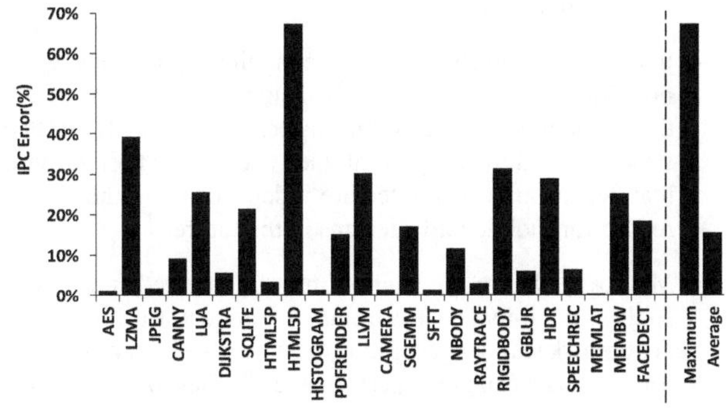

Figure 1: Errors in IPC for 24 emerging mobile applications with prior approach [13].

Many prior work [10] [13] [6] have proposed sampling-based methodologies to represent full benchmark by using sampled program snippets. Although such work can significantly reduce snippet length, they still require simulating hundreds of millions of instructions. This limits the number of micro-architecture explorations that can be performed even with fast micro-architectural simulators. Furthermore, this also makes RTL-based explorations practically infeasible. RTL simulations are slow. In practice, they have to finish over night, where only smaller segments of sampled snippets generated by prior work or completely different micro-benchmarks with affordable instruction lengths are used by industry. However, this can lead to mismatches between high-level micro-architectural and low-level RTL simulations. Such correlations are necessary to help diagnose potential implementation bugs and reveal performance/energy issues.

To make use of the existing sampling-based approach [13] for both micro-architecture and RTL simulations, the granularity of snippets needs to be reduced from the 100M to the 100K instructions level. However, as shown in Figure 1, program snippets generated by prior work [13] at a granularity of 100K instructions (with 100K-instruction warmup) cause unsatisfactory performance estimation errors for emerging mobile applications. The maximum instructions per cycle (IPC) error is around 67% and the average error reaches 15.4%. The inaccuracy of performance estimation can result in misleading design decisions.

In this paper, we present a novel approach for automatic generation of fine-grained snippets of mobile applications to speed up the simulation time of mobile CPU designs. Compared to prior works, our approach does not solely rely on code structures (basic blocks) to characterize program phases. Therefore, even when the basic block distribution becomes sparse at fine-granularity, we can still achieve better clustering. In addition, to achieve comprehensive program characterization with better accuracy, we add more micro-architecture independent features that are specific to emerging mobile applications. The specific contributions of this paper are as follows:

- We propose a novel generator that leverages principal component and clustering analysis to capture representative program snippets of mobile applications at fine-granularity, and use them to substitute the full trace in the simulation process. These finer-grained snippets can be applied for both high-level micro-architecture and low-level RTL simulations, which help hardware designers correlate the micro-architecture simulation to the RTL one. Compared to prior work, the snippets provided by our generator can reduce the average performance estimation error from 15.4% to 9.8% while saving 76% simulation time.
- In order to precisely characterize mobile applications, we define domain-specific features to capture unique characteristics of mobile workloads, such as percentage of CRYPTO instructions and memory misaligned accesses. Those provided features are micro-architecture independent, so they can be reused for mobile CPU designs in the future.
- Moreover, due to the length limit of generated snippets, we analyze the impacts of warmup and preload for fine-grained benchmark snippet generation on state-of-the-art mobile CPUs. This analysis can guide performance studies to generate fine-grain snippets from other applications for modern mobile CPU designs.

2. RELATED WORK

In this section, we want to review several prior works that are relevant to this paper. Simpoint [13] method makes the use of basic block distribution to find small portions of the application to simulate that can represent the full program's behavior. This approach is heavily based upon the program's code structure. Each simpoint/snippet is collected at the granularity of 100 million instructions for SPEC95 and SPEC2000 benchmarks. However, if the snippet granularity is reduced by 1000 times, the basic block distribution will become very sparse, which is really difficult to cluster. Our approach does not solely depend on the code structures (basic blocks), so it achieves better accuracy for mobile applications at fine-granularity.

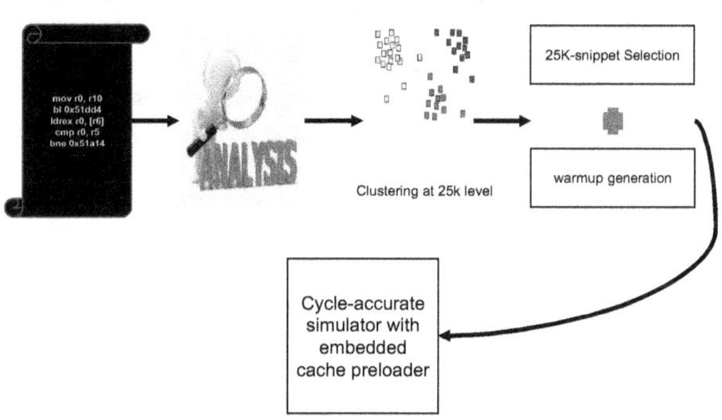

Figure 2: The flow overview of the proposed generator.

Eeckhout et al. [6] define 47 micro-architecture independent features based on instruction mix, working set sizes, etc., to characterize the conventional CPU applications (from SPECint2000 and SPECfp2000) at the level of 100 million instructions per interval. We extend, provide, and use more mobile application specific features, as we target on these emerging applications for mobile processor designs. Different from Simpoint work, Eeckhout et al. study the similarities among all applications, and select the snippets to represent the entire benchmark suite instead of an individual benchmark. These chosen snippets are used to perform design space exploration, which requires a huge number of executions to cover various micro-architectural configurations. Since the program length and simulation time of these conventional benchmarks are much longer than the modern mobile applications', we do not necessarily have to perform this further reduction among all applications. Additionally, most mobile application suites score processor's performance based on the execution speed of each application, like [1]. Therefore, it is necessary for the hardware designers to monitor the performance of each workload, when optimization is applied on the design.

Other than these two prior works, Gutierrez et al. [7] discover the differences between SPEC CPU2006 benchmarks and smartphone applications, and reflect the poor performance of instruction cache, instruction TLB, and branch predictor. Lau et al. [10] study the applications to identify the program phases at the variable length. Since we target at 25K-instruction granularity, snippets from a giant repeated loop will all be collected. Dhodapkar and Smith [5] found a relationship between phases and instruction working sets, as phase changes occur when the working set changes. We include multiple instruction working set sizes as micro-architecture independent features in our generator. SMARTS [16] employs full functional warmup during the entire non-sampling units in-between sampling units, which provides nearly perfect warmup effects. However, it significantly limits the time reduction due to the long warmup, which occupies more than 99% of the entire simulation time. Conte [4] deploys the adaptive functional warmup. Compared to them, our generator provides a just-right warmup trace and only preloads for the necessary components. Jiang and Yu [9] target on the optimization of warmup for multi-thread simulations, such as PARSEC benchmarks [2], which is different from our emphasis.

3. METHODOLOGY

In this section, we first give an overview of proposed generator's flow, then describe the details of deployed micro-architectural independent features, snippet selection, and warmup/preload trace generation.

3.1 Generator Flow

The input of our generator is the program trace. As shown in Figure 2, we split the trace into 25K-instruction snippets, then apply predefined micro-architectural independent features to characterize these snippets. Snippets with similar features will be clustered in one group, and the snippet located in the center of the cluster will be selected to represent the cluster. Corresponding warmup and preload traces are generated for each selected snippet.

3.2 Program Features

Eeckhout et al. proposed 47 micro-architecture independent features to characterize the conventional CPU applications, such as SPEC CPU benchmarks. In our work, we make use of these characteristics and extend them with more mobile-specific features. These added features are categorized in several groups, such as instruction mix, instruction level parallelism (ILP) for load and store instructions, and misaligned accesses. All the features used in our methodology, including the previous and our new ones, are summarized in Table 1 for integrity.

Table 1: List of micro-architectural independent fingerprinting parameters used to characterize mobile workloads.

Category	Fingerprints	Explanation
Instruction mix	Load, store, control, arithmetic	% load, store, control, arithmetic instructions
	Float, SIMD, CRYPTO	% floating-point, single instruction multiple data, crypto instructions
Instruction level parallelism (ILP) for load&store	LLP_W-32, 64, 128, 256	ILP counts for load&store instruction in 32, 64, 128, 256 instructions window
Instruction level parallelism (ILP)	ILP_W-32, 64, 128, 256	ILP counts in 32, 64, 128, 256 instructions window
Register traffic	RegNOp	average number of operands
	RegTc_1	% of instructions with 1 target register
	RegTc_2	% of instructions with 1< target register
	RegUse	average degree of freedom
	RegD_1, 4, 8, 16, 32, 64	pro register dependency = 1, <= 2, <= 4, <= 8, <= 16, <= 32, <= 64
Working set	D-WS_32, 64, 128, 4096	number of data stream within 32, 64, 128, 4096B block level
	I-WS_32, 64, 128, 4096	number of instruction stream within 32, 64, 128, 4096B block level
Data stream stride	IcLdS_0, 8, 16, 32, 64, 512, 4096	pro local load stride = 0, <= 8, <= 16, <= 32, <= 64, <= 512, <= 4096
	lcStS_0, 8, 16, 32, 64, 512, 4096	pro local store stride = 0, <= 8, <= 16, <= 32, <= 64, <= 512, <= 4096
	glLdS_0, 8, 16, 32, 64, 512, 4096	pro global load stride = 0, <= 8, <= 16, <= 32, <= 64, <= 512, <= 4096
	glStS_0, 8, 16, 32, 64, 512, 4096	pro global store stride = 0, <= 8, <= 16, <= 32, <= 64, <= 512, <= 4096
Branch predictability	GAg	PPM predictor global history, global predictor
	GAs	PPM predictor global history, local predictor
	PAg	PPM predictor local history, global predictor
	PAs	PPM predictor local history, local predictor
Misaligned access	ld-ma-8, 16, 32, 64, 4096	Pro load 8B, 16B, 32B, 64B, 4096B miss aligned
	st-ma-8, 16, 32, 64, 4096	Pro store 8B, 16B, 32B, 64B, 4096B miss aligned

3.2.1 Instruction mix

We include the percentage of load, store, control, arithmetic, floating point, SIMD, and CRYPTO operations in this category to fully analyze the instruction mix of mobile workloads. Compared to the prior work, SIMD and CRYPTO are the new metrics we added. For mobile workloads leveraging vector instructions, such as SGEMM and SFFT, SIMD operation is heavily used in major program phases. CRYPTO instruction is largely deployed in AES workload, which is not widely used in traditional SPEC benchmarks.

3.2.2 ILP for load&store instructions

Load and store instructions become more important for the mobile devices, as the sizes of caches and memory subsystem are limited but highly related to the performance/user experience. Therefore, we dedicate four fingerprinting features to quantify the amount of ILP for only load & store instructions. We assume an idealized out-of-order mobile processor model, where all components are idealized and all resources are unlimited except for the instruction window. These added features measure the number of independent load & store instructions located in the instruction window, which has four different sizes (32, 64, 128, and 256).

3.2.3 Misaligned access

Misalignment happens when read or write operations try to read N bytes of data starting from an address that is not evenly divisible by N. Different architectures attempt to perform the misaligned memory accesses in different manner. For example, some processors raise exceptions when unaligned access is detected, and some are able to perform them transparently. However, none of them can avoid the performance degradation for such memory access. For mobile processors, these existing misalignments in the mobile applications can easily impact the application's execution speed. Therefore, we consider misalignment as one of important performance factors. In our application characterization, we separate load & store instructions, and categorize these accesses by the size of data they are attempting to touch. As the capacity of mobile processor's caches and memory grows, our feature set contains the misalignment of 8B, 16B, 32B, 64B, and 4096B for both load and store instructions.

3.2.4 Other features

Similar to Section 3.2.2, window size is the only tunable parameter of ILP metrics. Different from Section 3.2.2, ILP metrics quantify the amount of ILP for all types of instructions (not only load & store). All the register traffic, working set, and data stream strides are included in the prior work. Register traffic characteristics are used to capture the number of input operands, the average number of times a register is consumed, and register dependency distance. Working set features count the number of unique blocks (32B, 64B, 128B, 4096B) in each interval. Data stream analyzes both local and global data strides. The branch behavior is also an important characteristic we want to capture. Same as prior work, we want to measure how predictable the branches are for a given execution interval. To accomplish this, we deploy the Prediction by Partial Matching (PPM) predictor [3], which is built on the notion of a Markov predictor. 'G' stands for global branch history, and 'g' means one global predictor table. 'P' stands for local branch history, and 's' means an individual table for each branch. PPM is a theoretical basis for predicting branch prediction, therefore, these features still hold the characteristic of being micro-architectural independent.

3.3 Snippet Selection

To select the most representative snippets for each benchmark, we need to study the similarity of split snippets in order to avoid choosing repeated ones. We leverage two statistical methods, which are the Principal Component Analysis (PCA) and K-means Clustering. Both of them are widely used in the performance evaluation and benchmark analysis domain [12].

3.3.1 Principal Component Analysis

After characterizing all snippets using predefined program features, we have to group the snippets in multiple clusters and select the representative one from each cluster. Due to the size of the deployed program feature set, the number of dimensions for clustering becomes too high to produce a limited number of compact clusters. Therefore, we leverage the PCA method to remove the correlation among these features. Since we are not studying similarities across benchmarks, the snippets of each trace may end up having different sets of important features after the PCA process. For example, SFFT application with a high percentage of floating point (fp) instructions has the percentage of fp instructions as one of principal components, where the integer applications will not consider it as an important characteristic. For all mobile applications in this work, the generator selects the reduced set of principal components to cover more than 90% of the program variances. Other than the 90% minimal bound requirement, we add one more constraint in the generator. We define the component with more than 1% program variance coverage as an important feature to include. Therefore, some applications end up having more principal components than necessary to cover 90% variance, as we want to incorporate all the important features. On average, each application has 14 private principal components.

3.3.2 *Clustering Analysis*

After we identify the principal components, we can move on to the clustering phase in the generator. We use the K-means clustering algorithm, as we can directly control the number of clusters by setting the k value. Of course, other clustering algorithms with the same functionality can substitute the K-means algorithm. In this phase, the issue we are facing is how to choose the minimal number of clusters that can provide good clustering quality. We deploy a metric called 'cubic clustering criterion' (CCC) to quantify the clustering quality. The CCC value is proportional to the clustering quality, as higher CCC means better quality. To achieve better quality, increasing the number of clusters is the most effective way. However, as the number of clusters (k value) can directly determine the number of snippets to be selected for simulation. This is considered as a tradeoff problem. Therefore, we provide two knobs in the clustering phase of the proposed generator, which are the qualified CCC value and maximum k value (the maximum number of clusters). From our experience, most of the applications reach robust CCC value (> 800) with less than 10 clusters. Thereafter, we set the maximum number of clusters for each workload to be ten.

3.4 Warmup/Preload Trace Generation

Due to the length limitation, most generated snippets suffer from the impact of cold misses in multiple hardware components, such as multi-level caches. Prior work does not face this issue, as their snippets are long enough that negative influences due to the lack of warmup cannot affect the performance significantly. However, for fine-grained snippets, warmup can cause severe performance impact, which will be demonstrated in section 4. To avoid this problem, our generator can automatically extract the warmup trace for each snippet. The warmup trace is defined as the section of instructions located prior to the target snippet. For example, after the snippet A is selected from its cluster, the generator uses its beginning instruction to trace back certain number of instructions and extract those instructions to form the corresponding warmup trace. For our snippets, the length of warmup trace is set to be 100K-instruction (same as the baseline we are comparing to).

Even though the warmup trace can indeed help reflect the true performance of snippets, it has a non-negligible disadvantage, as it still requires to be executed on the simulator, which can be expensive if the length is long. However, after we diagnose the state-of-the-art mobile processor designs, we recognize that the multi-layer cache system is a critical component that needs a long warmup trace. Therefore, we deploy the preloading technique and implement the preloader on top of our in-house micro-architectural simulator to generate the trace for preloading. Similar to warmup trace capturing, we extract a section of code prior to the snippet and feed them to our preloader. The preloader will execute the trace and dump the image of multi-layer caches into a yaml file. This cache image file can be preloaded back to both micro-architectural simulator and RTL simulator before executing the warmup trace and representative snippet. Since we only need to generate this preloading file once and it can be reused, the overhead can be ignored.

4. EXPERIMENTS AND RESULTS

In this section, we would like to review the experiment infrastructure and selected mobile applications, discuss the insightful observations, and analyze the experimental results.

4.1 Experiment Infrastructure

To demonstrate the accuracy and effectiveness of our generator, we evaluate it with 24 emerging mobile applications. These 24 benchmarks are categorized into four groups, which are cryptography workloads, integer workloads, floating-point workloads, and memory workloads. The information about each application's type can be found in Table 2. Each of them is deployed as a single-core application. All of them are implemented in C++ and compiled by Clang compiler. The performance data is collected on the in-house micro-architecture simulator, which simulates the Samsung Exynos M1 mobile processor. The preloader is embedded in the simulator to snapshot the cache status image at any given moment. In addition, the simulator can take the cache image as an input and reside the status in the multi-layer caches before executing the snippet. The baseline (named as Prior_work in the figures) we are comparing to is the 100K-instruction program snippets generated from Simpoint method [13] associated with 100K-instruction warmup.

Table 2: 24 Emerging mobile workloads classification [1].

Type	Applications
Cryptography workloads	AES
Integer workloads	LZMA compression, JPEG compression, Canny, Dijkstra, SQLite, LLVM, HTML 5 Parse, HTML 5 DOM, PDF rendering, Lua, Camera
Floating point workloads	SGEMM, SFFT, Gaussian blur, Ray trace, N-Body physics, Rigid body physics, HDR, Histogram equalization, Face detection, Speech recognition
Memory workloads	Memory bandwidth, Memory latency

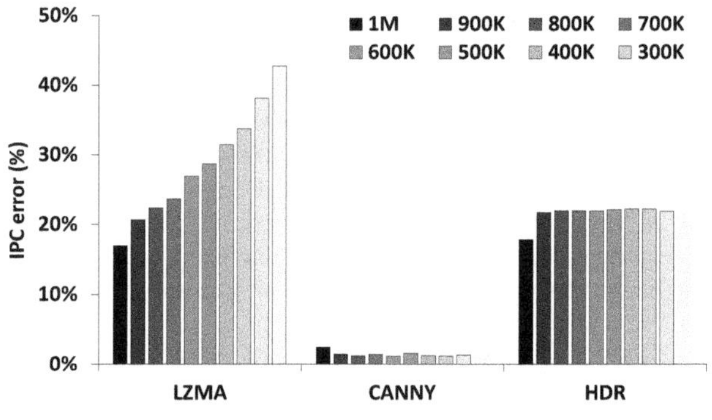

Figure 3: Warmup sensitivity study for LZMA, CANNY, and HDR.

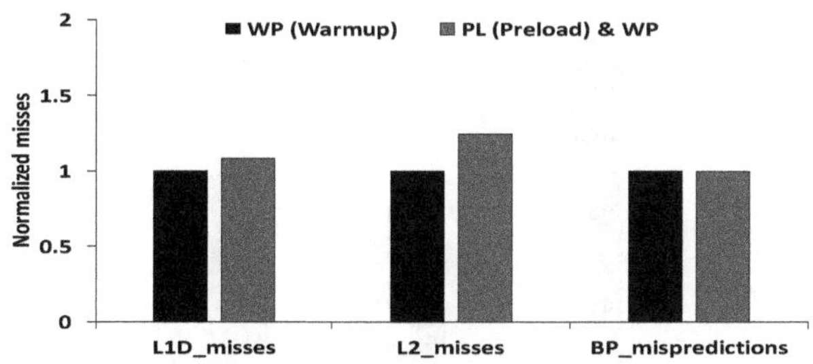

Figure 4: Component-level performance comparison between solely using warmup trace and using combination of preloading and warmup tarce.

4.2 Mobile Applications

Cryptography workloads: The Advanced Encryption Standard (AES) is the only cryptography workload, which defines a symmetric block encryption algorithm. It is widely used to secure communication channels and information. This workload encrypts a 32MB string using AES running in CTR mode with a 256-bit key.

Integer workloads: LZMA is lossless compression algorithm, while JPEG is a lossy image compression. LZMA compresses and decompresses a 450KB HTML ebook using SDK as the implementation of core algorithm. Compared to traditional bzip2 benchmark in SPEC, LZMA features a high compression ratio. JPEG works by encoding an image in 8 * 8 blocks, and each block is transformed using a discrete cosine transform (DCT). Canny is a typical sophisticated technique in image processing and computer vision, which contains four components, such as noise removal (Gaussian Blur), gradient calculation, minimum maximum threshold pass, and edge following (BFS). The Dijkstra workload computes driving direction between destinations. The data for this workload is captured from Open Street Map data for the Waterloo region, which includes 79392 nodes and 162644 edges with integer weights. SQLite is a self-contained SQL database engine that executes queries against an in-memory database. This SQLite benchmark is created to stress the underlying engine using a variety of SQL features and query keywords, such as SELECT, COUNT, SUM, etc. The LLVM workload processes an LLVM IR file through its optimizer and code-generation routines. The IR file is generated from a 3,900 line C file using Clang. HTML 5 Parse and DOM constructs a parse tree from a HTML5 document using Gumbo, and creates a HTML5 Document Object Model (DOM), respectively. Both of them stress the multi-layer cache system in the mobile CPU. PDF rendering parses and renders a 29-page PDF document, which contains mostly text with a few small images. Lua executes a Lua script using standard Lua interpreter to parse data from a JSON file, and uses Mustache to combine data to produce an HTML file. Camera replicates a photo sharing application like Instagram that merges several functions into one, such as AES, Lua parsing, JPEG, and SQLite. All these functions are executed on the CPU without GPU support.

Floating point workloads: The SGEMM (general matrix multiplication) workload computes the result of C = AB + C, where A, B, and C are matrices with 512 * 512 single precision. GEMM is implemented using vector instructions, such as AVX, SSE2, SSE3, and ARMv8 NEON. SFFT executes an FFT algorithm on an 32MB input in 16KB chunks. Similar to SGEMM, it also deploys vector instructions. Face detection and HDR are from the computer vision domain. The Face detection includes scale, pose, occlusion, expression, makeup, and illumination operations. Gaussian blur benchmark blurs an image using Gaussian spatial filter with a fixed sigma of 1.0f. This sigma translates into a filter diameter of 9 pixels. Histogram equalization workload is designed to improves the contrast in an image by implying mapping one distribution to another. It contains four steps, which are image loading, image converting, equalizing histogram, and displaying equalized image.

Memory workloads: The Memory Latency benchmark measures the latency of system memory by traversing a circular linked-list. The nodes in the linked-list are arranged to reduce the TLB misses to the level of 1 miss per page. The Memory Bandwidth captures the sustained memory bandwidth by using vector instructions, such as AVX and ARMv7 NEON.

4.3 Warmup Sensitivity Study

In this experiment, we attempt to quantify application's sensitivity to the length of warmup trace. Since our snippets are 25K-instruction each, we perform this study only with the warmup trace ranging from 1M-instruction to 100K-instruction. As shown in Figure 3, a different application has different reactions to the warmup length. LZMA snippets can be concluded that they are extremely sensitive to its warmup traces, as the application is doing compression work that needs to exercise the L1 and L2 caches heavily. Therefore, with 1M warmup instructions, LZMA snippets achieve the minimal IPC estimation error. However, compared to LZMA, CANNY and HDR are much less sensitive. CANNY snippets' performance is very stable with various warmup lengths, and HDR snippets lose 4% accuracy by decreasing 1M warmup instructions to 100K instructions.

4.4 Warmup vs. Preload

To reduce the long warmup trace for applications that are sensitive, such as LZMA, we deep dive into the performance analysis of LZMA. As we mentioned above, LZMA is a compression application that stresses the multi-level memory subsystems during execution. Therefore, we deploy the preloading technique to resolve this issue. Our preloader can snapshot the cache system at any given time and preload it back. As shown in Figure 4, we can see that using a 900K preload image with 100K warmup trace results in similar number of misses in the L1 data cache and L2 cache. Moreover, we observe another interesting behavior, as the 100K warmup can approximately reach the same level of performance for the branch predictor, which has some storage components like branch history tables. Similar behaviors are also captured in other applications so that we can claim using 100K warmup should be able to provide enough exercise to the major core components. Caches need to preload the status image in order to reduce the negative impacts of modeling the performance of modern mobile processor.

4.5 Performance Estimation and Simulation Time Reduction

The maximum error generated by prior work appears in the HTML 5 DOM application. The reason behind it is HTML 5 DOM needs a long time to warmup the 'cold' cache hierarchies. As we discussed above, long warmup trace is too expensive for simulations. Our implemented preloader indeed helps solve this problem. Figure 5a shows that we reduce the max error from 67.2% to 1.0%. We evaluate our generator across all 24 applications. As shown in Figure 5b, our generator with 1 million instructions warmup can significantly decrease the average performance estimation error by half (around 7.6%), however, 1 million instructions are too costly in terms of simulation time. Using a low overhead preloading technique for 900K instructions with 100K warmup can provide an average error of 9.8%. Compared to the prior work, our snippets are extremely fine-grained, so the number of instructions for the simulation has been saved by 76%, as Figure 6 illustrates. The number of instructions to be simulated is strongly proportional to the simulation time.

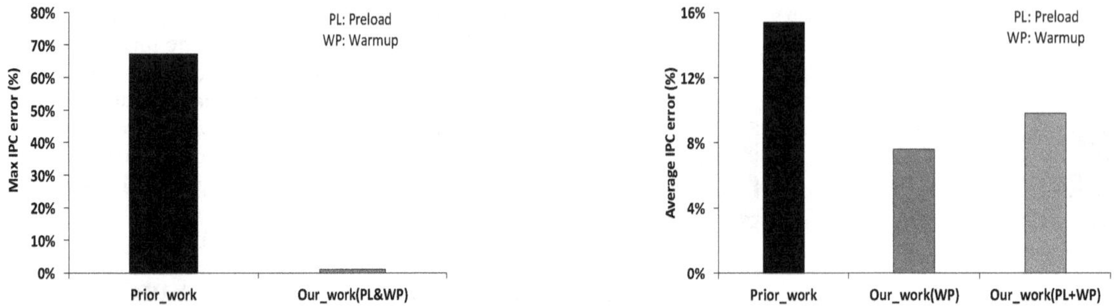

(a) Maximum IPC error reduction on HTML5DOM workload.

(b) The comparison of average errors in IPC between prior work and our work.

Figure 5: Comparing the IPC estimation errors of our proposed work to the errors caused by Simpoint for 24 emerging mobile workloads.

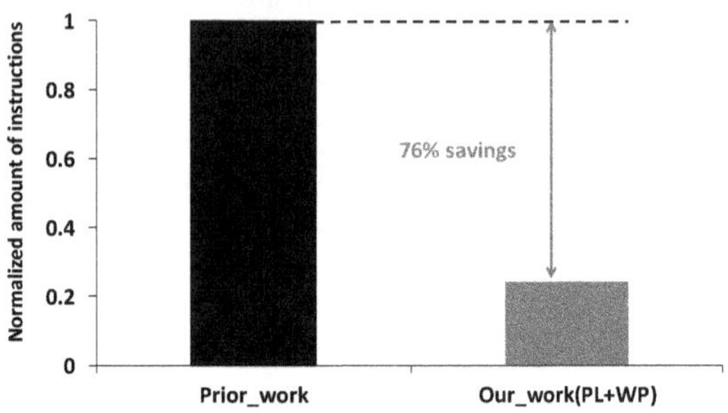

Figure 6: Comparison of the number of simulated instruction needed for Simpoint and our work.

Hence, we expect that our snippets can reduce the simulation time significantly as well.

5. CONCLUSIONS

In this paper, we propose a novel snippet generator that can produce representative program snippets for emerging mobile applications at fine-granularity. Our generated snippets are short enough to fit in both RTL and microarchitecture simulators. Compared to prior work, snippets provided by our generator reduce the average performance estimation error from 15.4% to 9.8% across 24 emerging mobile workloads. Meanwhile, these snippets shrink the total simulation time by up to 76%, which benefits the mobile processor's time to market. Furthermore, we define mobile-specific program characteristics that can be leveraged to analyze the mobile applications for other embedded research areas. Lastly, we study and quantify the mobile applications' sensitivity to the warmup length and propose the use of cache preloading technique to replace the long warmup trace.

6. ACKNOWLEDGMENTS

This work was supported in part by Samsung GRO grant, and National Science Foundation grant CCF-1337393. Any opinions, findings, conclusions, or recommendations are those of the authors and do not necessarily reflect the views of these funding agencies.

7. REFERENCES

[1] Geekbench 4 CPU Workloads. Technical report, Primate Labs, 08 2016.

[2] C. Bienia, S. Kumar, et al. The parsec benchmark suite: Characterization and architectural implications. In *PACT*, 2008.

[3] I.-C. K. Chen, J. T. Coffey, et al. Analysis of branch prediction via data compression. In *ASPLOS VII*, New York, NY, USA, 1996. ACM.

[4] T. M. Conte, M. A. Hirsch, et al. Reducing state loss for effective trace sampling of superscalar processors. In *ICCD '96*. IEEE Computer Society, 1996.

[5] A. S. Dhodapkar and J. E. Smith. Managing multi-configuration hardware via dynamic working set analysis. In *ISCA '02*. IEEE Computer Society, 2002.

[6] L. Eeckhout, J. Sampson, et al. Exploiting program microarchitecture independent characteristics and phase behavior for reduced benchmark suite simulation. In *IISWC*, 2005.

[7] A. Gutierrez, R. G. Dreslinski, et al. Full-system analysis and characterization of interactive smartphone applications. In *IISWC*, 2011.

[8] M. Halpern, Y. Zhu, et al. Mobile cpu's rise to power: Quantifying the impact of generational mobile cpu design trends on performance, energy, and user satisfaction. In *HPCA*, 2016.

[9] C. Jiang, Z. Yu, et al. Shorter on-line warmup for sampled simulation of multi-threaded applications. In *ICPP '15*. IEEE Computer Society, 2015.

[10] J. Lau, E. Perelman, et al. Motivation for variable length intervals and hierarchical phase behavior. In *ISPASS '05*, Washington, DC, USA, 2005. IEEE Computer Society.

[11] X. Li, G. Yan, et al. Smartcap: User experience-oriented power adaptation for smartphone's application processor. In *DATE '13*, San Jose, CA, USA, 2013. EDA Consortium.

[12] A. Phansalkar, A. Joshi, et al. Analysis of redundancy and application balance in the spec cpu2006 benchmark suite. In *ISCA '07*. ACM, 2007.

[13] T. Sherwood, E. Perelman, et al. Basic block distribution analysis to find periodic behavior and simulation points in applications. In *PACT '01*, Washington, DC, USA, 2001. IEEE Computer Society.

[14] Y. Shin, H. J. Lee, et al. 28nm high-k metal gate heterogeneous quad-core cpus for high-performance and energy-efficient mobile application processor. In *ISOCC*, 2013.

[15] S. Swanson and M. B. Taylor. Greendroid: Exploring the next evolution in smartphone application processors. *IEEE Communications Magazine*, 2011.

[16] R. E. Wunderlich, T. F. Wenisch, et al. Smarts: Accelerating microarchitecture simulation via rigorous statistical sampling. In *ISCA '03*. ACM, 2003.

Coupling-Aware Functional Timing Analysis for Tighter Bounds: How Much Margin Can We Relax?

Jack S.-Y. Lin
Dept. Electrical & Computer Engineering, National Chiao Tung University, Taiwan 300
sjack1017@gmail.com

Louis Y.-Z. Lin
Dept. Electrical & Computer Engineering, National Chiao Tung University, Taiwan 300
louislin9432@gmail.com

Ryan H.-M. Huang
Dept. Electrical & Computer Engineering, National Chiao Tung University, Taiwan 300
cksckb@gmail.com

Charles H.-P. Wen
Dept. Electrical & Computer Engineering, National Chiao Tung University, Taiwan 300
opwen@g2.nctu.edu.tw

ABSTRACT

As the manufacturing technology keeps scaling, crosstalk noise induces a greater impact on timing. Although many previous works proposed techniques like timing correlation, functional correlation and path refinement to consider crosstalk noise during static timing analysis, they often suffered from descendant problems including overly-pessimistic timing bound, bad aggressor selection and false paths. Therefore, in this paper, a coupling-aware functional timing analysis tool named CA-FTA is proposed to tame the three problems stated above and to derive a tighter timing bound for the true longest path. Experimental results show that CA-FTA averagely reduces timing bounds of those obtained from crosstalk STA (with path refinement) by 7.26% on several ISCAS'85 and ISPD-2012 benchmark circuits (in particular, by 34.6% for b19). As a result, CA-FTA successfully solves the aggressor-selection problem as well as the false-path problem and relaxes more margins when considering crosstalk noise.

Keywords

crosstalk noise; coupling wire; functional timing analysis (FTA); static timing analysis (STA).

1. INTRODUCTION

For traditional VLSI designs, signal transition between two coupling wires often introduces interference and may induce extra delay on the wire. Typically, the wire of interest is referred as the victim whereas the coupling wires are referred as aggressors. When a victim and a aggressor have transitions (near-)simultaneously, the charge and discharge behavior of coupling capacitances further cause delay noise depending on the switching directions of signals on both wires (i.e. speed up under the same direction and slow down under the opposite directions). However, with continuous scaling of process technologies, capacitive coupling between adjacent wires has significantly increased and dominated total wire capacitances [1]. Such delay (as known as *crosstalk*) may cause timing violation. Therefore, coupling-aware timing analysis becomes more important in the nano-scaled era.

Permission to make digital or hard copies of all or part of this work for personal or classroom use is granted without fee provided that copies are not made or distributed for profit or commercial advantage and that copies bear this notice and the full citation on the first page. Copyrights for components of this work owned by others than the author(s) must be honored. Abstracting with credit is permitted. To copy otherwise, or republish, to post on servers or to redistribute to lists, requires prior specific permission and/or a fee. Request permissions from permissions@acm.org.

GLSVLSI '17, May 10 - 12, 2017, Banff, AB, Canada

© 2017 Copyright held by the owner/author(s). Publication rights licensed to ACM.

ISBN 978-1-4503-4972-7/17/05...$15.00

DOI: http://dx.doi.org/10.1145/3060403.3060443

Since crosstalk is a mutually-influenced problem (i.e. victim delay depends on aggressor's timing window which in turn depends on victim arrival time and slews), several works proposed iterative STA approaches [3, 4, 5, 6]. Zhou[4] established a theoretical foundation for static timing analysis with coupling. Xiao et al.[5] used an effective skew window to consider coupling effect and proposed a method to estimate maximum-stage delay under multiple aggressors during crosstalk STA. In general, these works focus on timing correlation for coupling wires during timing analysis. Despite efficiency, these works run into two problems: (1) STA does not take into account functional correlation between the victim and aggressors. Even with all input patterns, the victim and aggressor may not have signals with opposite transitions to slow down signal propagation. (2) STA is a net-based approach [8], which calculates the crosstalk-induced delay using worst-delay from all paths passing through the victim net. Although the analysis provides a *conservative* upper bound on timing, the resulting path delay is often overly pessimistic.

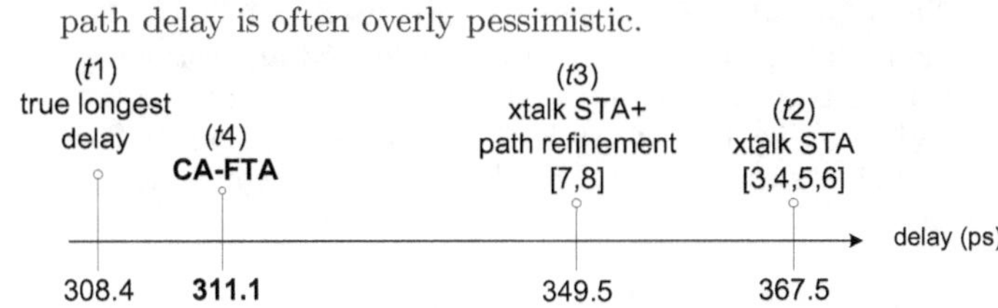

Figure 1: Applying various coupling-aware timers on a 8-to-3 decoder

To overcome the stated problems, later works considering path-based analysis proposed to refine paths, such as [7, 8]. Nevertheless, these path-refinement works results in time-consuming path enumeration, and may suffer from the false-path problem. Some other works consider functional correlation for coupling wires during timing analysis. Arunachalam et al.[9] proposed an automatic test pattern generation (ATPG) approach with multi-valued algebra to identify invalid coupling interactions. Das et al.[1] derived equations for the aggressor and victim state combinations and used a SAT engine to determine if certain combinations are possible. Ran et al.[10] proposed a SAT-based formulation for checking feasibility of particular switching patterns. In short, these works explored functional correlation with formal engines (e.g. ATPG or SAT) [1, 10], but applies heuristics to select partial (like top k) aggressors to perform functional checking or functional formulation. As a result, not all aggressors can be taken into account and victims need to be checked one by one.

To consider timing correlation between signal transitions and functional correlation between all victim-aggressor pairs simultaneously, we use *transition-aware functional timing analysis* (TA-FTA)[11] as the basic engine and further incorporate the crosstalk effect into *coupling-aware function timing analysis (CA-FTA)* to search the path with true longest delay automatically. As a result, *path enumeration* can be avoided and path refinement is only applied on the true longest path found by CA-FTA. Meanwhile, *functional correlation* is also considered during path search and invalid signal combinations will not occur.

A 8-to-3 decoder is used as a motivational example to compare results between CA-FTA with previous works. Since a 8-to-3 decoder consists of only 10 PIs, 5 POs, and 34 gates, we are allowed to enumerate all paths to extract the true longest delay. Figure 1 shows the result comparison where $t1$ represents the true longest delay of the 8-to-3 decoder from exhaustive simulation, $t2$ represents the timing bound derived from crosstalk STA which considers timing-window overlapping, $t3$ refers to the maximum timing bound after path refinement on critical paths, and $t4$ is the timing bound derived by CA-FTA. As you can see, $t4$ relaxes more timing margins and is closer to the true longest delay $t1$ than $t3$ and $t4$. More experimental result shows that CA-FTA can reduce the timing bound ranging from 0.8% to 34.6% on ISCAS'85 and ISPD-2012 benchmark circuits.

In overall, the contributions of the *coupling-aware function timing analysis (CA-FTA)* can be summarized as:

1. consider **all victim-aggressor pairs** simultaneously;
2. avoid **exhaustive enumeration** during path search;
3. preserve **strictly upper bound** after path refinement.

The remainder of this paper is organized as follows. The background of the coupling-delay model and an overview of the TA-FTA engine is provided in Section 2. Later, the proposed CA-FTA framework is elaborated in Section 3. Section 4 shows experimental result. Finally, we conclude this paper in Section 5.

2. BACKGROUND

In this section, the coupling model is briefly reviewed and used to calculate the crosstalk-induced delay between coupled pairs of nets and the background of TA-FTA in Sections 2.1 and 2.2, respectively.

2.1 Coupling-Delay Model

We use the waveform-based accurate coupling model proposed in [2] as the core crosstalk-induced delay engine during STA and path refinement. As shown in Figure 2, the model

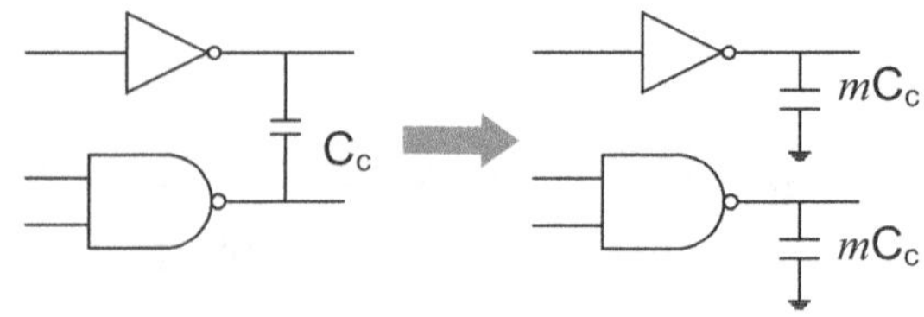

Figure 2: Coupling-delay model

computes a switching factor m through output-waveform information, and decouples the coupling capacitor to ground. Moreover, the coupling capacitance is multiplied by a switching factor m.

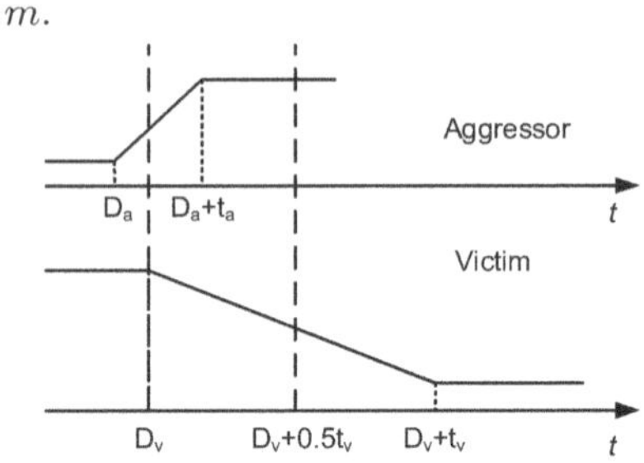

Figure 3: Coupling-factor computation

To compute the switching factor, Das et al.[2] defined a ratio k to capture the overlapping condition of victim and aggressor waveform using slew t and arrival time D as shown in Figure 3. The formulation of k can be expressed as:

$$k = \begin{cases} 1 & D_a \geq D_v,\ D_a + t_a < D_v + 0.5t_v \\ \frac{D_a + t_a - D_v}{t_a} & D_a < D_v,\ D_a + t_a < D_v + 0.5t_v \\ \frac{D_v + 0.5t_v - D_a}{t_a} & D_a \geq D_v,\ D_a + t_a \geq D_v + 0.5t_v \\ \frac{0.5t_v}{t_a} & D_a < D_v,\ D_a + t_a \geq D_v + 0.5t_v \\ 0 & No\ overlap\ condition \end{cases} \quad (1)$$

where D_a and t_a represents the aggressor's arrival time and slew and D_v and t_v is the victim's arrival time and slew.

Note that k ranges between 0 and 1. When k is calculated using Eq.(1), the switching factor m can be further obtained by $(1-2k)$ or $(1+2k)$ depending on the switching direction. That is, the coupling delay model ensures that the switching factor to speed up varies from -1 to 1 while the switching factor for slow down varies from 1 to 3. Although the model uses an exact waveform to calculate coupling factor, it also provides a technique to choose a specific timing point from arrival time and slew window. As a result, such solution can induce the worst and best coupling factors for rise and fall delay computation in crosstalk STA, respectively. More details about the technique can be referred to [2]. Since the model is quite efficient and easy to implement, it is used in our delay engine of our framework. Note that our framework can be further extended to a SPICE-like crosstalk delay model, but details of the extension are beyond the scope of this paper.

2.2 Transition-Aware Functional Timing Analysis (TA-FTA)

Transition-aware functional timing analysis is proposed in [11] and formulates the problem of delay computation subject to functional and temporal constraints with a novel four-valued encoding to consider the signal-transition effect. Unlike the Boolean encoding, the four-valued encoding uses two-timeframe approach to encode signal values as either falling, rising, stable 1 or stable 0. For instance, a rising signal initializes a 0 of the first timeframe and causes a $0 \rightarrow 1$ transition at the second timeframe. Functional constraints represents the logic behavior of the circuit and can be extracted from *circuit consistency function* while temporal constraints capture the circuit's temporal behavior using *timed characteristic function* (TCF). Given a target timing, the corresponding circuit information including function and timing are transformed into CNF formula to check whether there exists a input vector that can activate a path with such timing. By shrinking target timing iteratively, TA-FTA is expected to derive the maximum delay for the design as well as its propagation paths. The following sections briefly describe the four-valued functional and temporal constraints, respectively.

2.2.1 Four-valued functional constraints

Given a gate with n-input pins, x_1, x_2,...,x_n, one output pin y, and logic function $f(x_1, x_2, ..., x_n)$, the circuit consistency function can be derived from $f(x_1, x_2, ..., x_n) \odot y$ where $\odot$ denotes the XNOR operation. Due to the four-valued encoding, the output has four transition cases and each has its own controlling cube. Figure 4 lists all controlling cubes of each case for the output of a NAND gate.

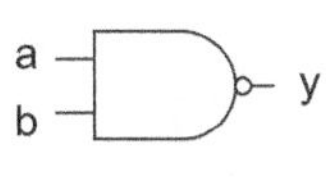

y_f	y_r	y_0	y_1
$a_r b_r$ $a_r b_1$ $a_1 b_r$	$a_f \neg b_0$ $b_f \neg a_0$	$a_1 b_1$	a_0 b_0

Figure 4: Controlling cubes of a NAND gate

For example, the corresponding CNF clauses for y_f can be transformed from *circuit consistency function* (CCF) and expressed as:

$$\begin{aligned} &y \odot (a_r b_r \vee a_r b_1 \vee a_1 b_r) \equiv \\ &(a_r \vee a_1 \vee \neg y_f) \wedge (b_r \vee b_1 \vee \neg y_f) \wedge (a_r \vee b_r \vee \neg y_f) \end{aligned} \quad (2)$$

2.2.2 Four-valued temporal constraints

As mentioned earlier, the circuit's temporal behavior can be translated into a *timed characteristic function* (TCF), which can be further augmented into CNF formula for checking satisfiability. To take the signal-transition effect into account, Chang et al. [11] modified the original TCF formula with a four-valued encoding, which is shown as follows:

$$\begin{aligned} \chi^{y_f,t} &= y_f \wedge \bigwedge_{c \in C_f} \bigvee_{lit(g) \in c} (\chi^{g_r, t-d_{pin}} \vee \neg lit(g)) \\ \chi^{y_r,t} &= y_r \wedge \bigwedge_{c \in C_r} \bigvee_{lit(g) \in c} (\chi^{g_f, t-d_{pin}} \vee \neg lit(g)) \end{aligned} \quad (3)$$

where y and g represents a gate's output and input, respectively, and d_{pin} is the pin-to-pin delay. If $\chi^{y_f,t}$ is satisfied, it indicates that a falling transition occurs on y after time t. That is, for every cube c in C_f, either at least one controlling literal for y_f must be evaluated to true not earlier than time $t - d_{pin}$, or such cube is not satisfied.

To take the falling transition y_f on NAND gate as an example (Figure 4), with the controlling cubes $C_f = \{a_r b_r, a_r b_1, a_1 b_r\}$ and $g = \{a_r, b_r\}, \{a_r, b_1\}, \{a_1, b_r\}$, the corresponding TCF can be written as follows:

$$\chi^{y_f,t} = y_f \wedge (\chi^{a_r, t-d_{pin(a)})} \vee \neg a_r \vee \chi^{b_r, t-d_{pin(b)})} \neg b_r) \quad (4)$$

Moreover, Eq.(3) can be transform into CNF clauses by replacing the equality sign with the implication sign ($p \rightarrow q \equiv \neg p \vee q$) and then becomes

$$(\neg \chi^{y_f,t} \vee y_f) \wedge \bigwedge_{c \in C_f} (\neg \chi^{y_f,t} \vee \bigvee_{lit(g) \in c} (\chi^{g_r, t-d_{pin}} \vee \neg lit(g)) \quad (5)$$

3. COUPLING-AWARE FUNCTIONAL TIMING ANALYSIS (CA-FTA)

In this section, we describe the proposed CA-FTA in detail. The flow of our CA-FTA starts from the crosstalk STA to obtain the worst-case pin-to-pin delay and interconnect delay. Then TCF and crosstalk formulation is built under target timing t for extracting long paths in sequence. We perform path refinement on the longest path first and update its delay value. If the timing of the second longest path (before path refinement) is smaller than the refined timing of the first longest path, we stop and the maximum delay is found. Figure 5 shows the overall flowchart which consists of three steps: (1) crosstalk static-timing analysis (2) crosstalk formulation and (3) path refinement. The following sections provided the details of each step.

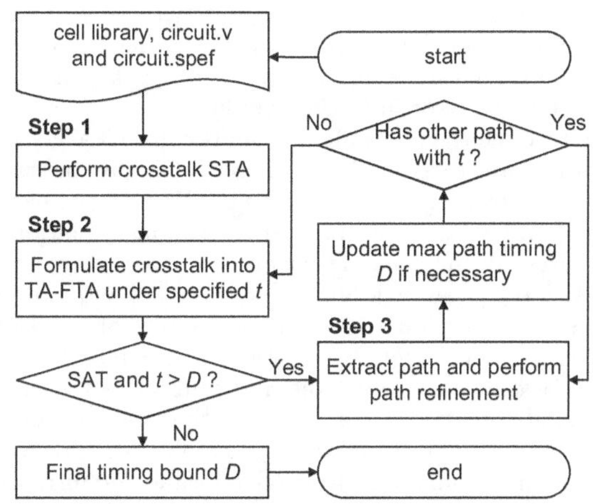

Figure 5: Overall flowchart of CA-FTA

3.1 Crosstalk Static-Timing Analysis

In the first step, crosstalk STA is performed to obtain the timing and slew window on each gate and further reduce the pessimism. Given input arrival times and starting with initial crosstalk-induced delays, the information of timing windows on all interconnects are iteratively updated during crosstalk STA. However, to exclude the timing effect from the ineffective aggressors (i.e. such aggressor can never switch simultaneously with the victim), all aggressors are assumed to introduce maximum delays on corresponding victims initially. In other words, in the first iteration of crosstalk STA, the switching factor of all aggressors are set to 3 for maximum timing analysis and -1 for minimum timing analysis. By doing so, the ultimately best and worst delay can be derived after the first run. Therefore, if a aggressor's timing window can never overlap with the victims', such aggressor cannot introduce any delay on the victim and then the corresponding coupling capacitance can be connected to ground for removal. Such removal helps reduce the number of CNF clauses during crosstalk formulation and avoids ineffective aggressors. Similar to [2], the iteration continues until all timing windows converge.

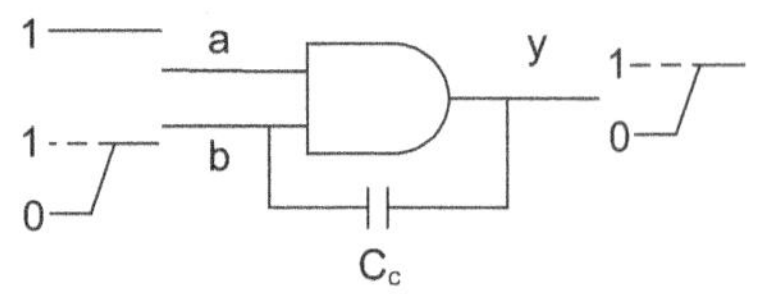

Figure 6: Example for false coupling

3.2 Formulating Crosstalk into TA-FTA

As mentioned earlier, the original TA-FTA does not take the temporal and functional correlation between victims and aggressors into account. To take Figure 6 for example, if a is the non-controlling value 1, it refers that the signal value on b and y are the same due to the gate function (i.e. b is rising signal and y is rising signal). In other words, the coupling capacitance C_c can only cause speedup noise on each other, since the requirement of the slowdown noise is that victim and aggressor's transition occurs with opposite directions (e.g. b is rising signal and y is falling signal). Therefore, after crosstalk STA, original TA-FTA will obtain the pessimistic delay activated by path $b \rightarrow y$ instead of the true longest delay path $a \rightarrow y$. Considering such case, crosstalk formulation is applied to capture relation between victim and aggressor in CNF formula.

To introduce the crosstalk formulation into TA-FTA, it is straightforward to expand the original TCF with aggressors' condition. However, if we look into the NAND gate example in Fig. 4 and assume that input a has coupling relation with other wires, all the clauses that involve a need to expand as well. As a result, we will obtain more clauses and more variables, not to mention when multiple inputs of a gate have coupling relation. Therefore, instead of expanding the TCF formula of the gate, we use the interconnect as the medium to formulate crosstalk. Traditionally, the interconnect delay is assumed to be absorbed into gate's pin-to-pin delays because the interconnect delay is a fixed value and formulating the interconnect explicitly introduce useless TCF variable. Figure 7 illustrates expanding crosstalk formulation on the interconnect. As you can see, the coupling wire a is regarded as a buffer to introduce the correlation between aggressors and itself. By doing so, we can split the formulation of the interconnect and the gate. The total number of the clauses for gates remains the same as before.

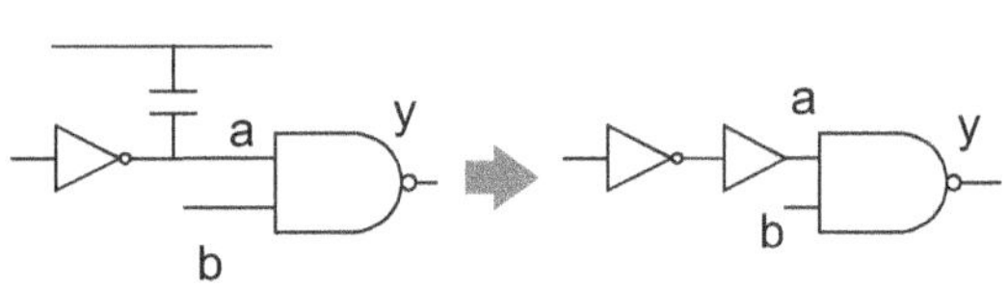

Figure 7: Modeling crosstalk as a delayed buffer

The nominal gate delay of the buffer is the nominal interconnect delay and the crosstalk effect will reflect on the change of the gate delay. The original formula for a buffer with a falling transition can be expressed as follows (in terms of input a and output y):

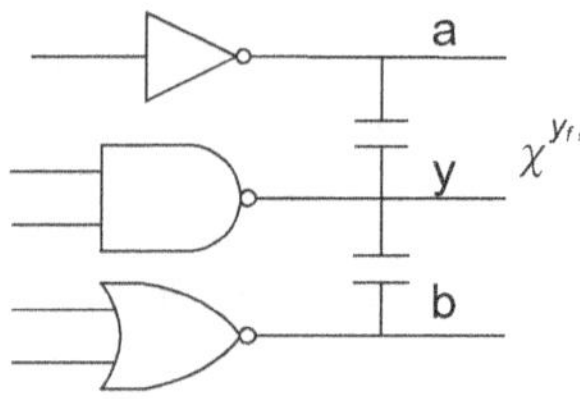

Figure 8: Example for crosstalk formulation

$$(\neg\chi^{y_f,t} \vee y_f) \wedge (\neg\chi^{y_f,t} \vee \chi^{a_f,t-d} \vee \neg a_f) \tag{6}$$

where d is the pin-to-pin delay. In order to consider the aggressors' transition, we add the functional constraint of the aggressor into the controlling cube as the crosstalk formulation. That is, each controlling cube represents a combination of victim and aggressors' transitions and may cause different gate delays.

Figure 8 shows an example for the complete crosstalk formulation. In Figure 8, the victim output y is coupled with aggressors a and b. Hence, the controlling cube of a falling transition on y (i.e. $\chi^{y_f,t}$) can be defined as $C_f = \{a_r b_r, a_r b_f, a_r b_n, a_f b_r, a_f b_f, a_f b_n, a_n b_r, a_n b_f, a_n b_n\}$ where the subscript n denotes the stable 1 or the stable 0 (neither rising nor falling) on the interconnect. The complete crosstalk formulation for $\chi^{y_f,t}$ can be unfolded as follows:

$$\begin{aligned}
&(\neg\chi^{y_f,t} \vee y_f)\wedge \\
&(\neg\chi^{y_f,t} \vee \chi^{y_f,t-d_1} \vee \neg y_f \vee \neg a_r \vee \neg b_r) \\
&(\neg\chi^{y_f,t} \vee \chi^{y_f,t-d_2} \vee \neg y_f \vee \neg a_r \vee \neg b_f) \\
&(\neg\chi^{y_f,t} \vee \chi^{y_f,t-d_3} \vee \neg y_f \vee \neg a_r \vee b_r \vee b_f) \\
&(\neg\chi^{y_f,t} \vee \chi^{y_f,t-d_4} \vee \neg y_f \vee \neg a_f \vee \neg b_r) \\
&(\neg\chi^{y_f,t} \vee \chi^{y_f,t-d_5} \vee \neg y_f \vee \neg a_f \vee \neg b_f) \\
&(\neg\chi^{y_f,t} \vee \chi^{y_f,t-d_6} \vee \neg y_f \vee \neg a_f \vee b_r \vee b_f) \\
&(\neg\chi^{y_f,t} \vee \chi^{y_f,t-d_7} \vee \neg y_f \vee a_r \vee a_f \vee \neg b_r) \\
&(\neg\chi^{y_f,t} \vee \chi^{y_f,t-d_8} \vee \neg y_f \vee a_r \vee a_f \vee \neg b_f) \\
&(\neg\chi^{y_f,t} \vee \chi^{y_f,t-d_9} \vee \neg y_f \vee a_r \vee a_f \vee b_r \vee b_f)
\end{aligned} \tag{7}$$

where $d_1, d_2, ..., d_9$ represent different gate delays calculated by the coupling delay model under various combination of victim and aggressors' signal transition for the buffer. The complete formulation can capture all possible conditions of the aggressors. Through the stepping strategy and SAT solving, we can exactly find the true condition that causes the max delay and filter the false coupling automatically.

However, the complete formulation may cause enormous but unavoidable clauses. Therefore, we relax the condition to reduce the number of clauses. The whole condition can be easily classified into three groups: slowdown (e.g. $y_f a_r b_r$), nominal (e.g. $y_f a_n b_n$), and the speedup (e.g. $y_f a_f b_f$). However, the speedup group is not our target and thus combined to the nominal case. To further relax conditions, we combine the slowdown group into one as the worst case. Once an aggressor has a slowdown noise on the victim, the SAT solver uses the worst condition (i.e. the gate delay of the buffer is the worst-case delay) only to ensure conservativeness. To sum up, we classify the conditions into the worst condition and the nominal condition for reducing clauses. The newly relaxed crosstalk formulation is shown as:

$$\begin{aligned} &(\neg\chi^{y_f,t} \vee y_f)\wedge \\ &(\neg\chi^{y_f,t} \vee \chi^{y_f,t-d_{worst}} \vee \neg y_f \vee \neg a_r) \\ &(\neg\chi^{y_f,t} \vee \chi^{y_f,t-d_{worst}} \vee \neg y_f \vee \neg b_r) \\ &(\neg\chi^{y_f,t} \vee \chi^{y_f,t-d_{nominal}} \vee \neg y_f \vee a_r \vee a_f \vee b_r \vee b_f) \end{aligned} \quad (8)$$

By expanding crosstalk formulation, TA-FTA is capable of finding true longest paths spontaneously and avoids false coupling in our CA-FTA.

3.3 Path Refinement

The timing bound of the extracted critical paths can be further reduced by performing path refinement. Since crosstalk STA uses the worst case to propagate timing event towards output, it can reduce timing bound if we perform timing analysis on one target path. Figure 9 illustrates the concept of reducing pessimism by path refinement. Original timing window W_y obtained from crosstalk STA overlaps aggressor's timing window W_x and thus x induces a delay noise on y. However, if after performing path refinement on path $a \rightarrow y$, updated timing window $W_y^{'}$ does not overlap W_x any more. As a result, the pessimism in crosstalk STA can be reduced, accordingly. Moreover, the delay impact of the aggressors originally not overlapped with the victim on the target path can also be removed after path refinement.

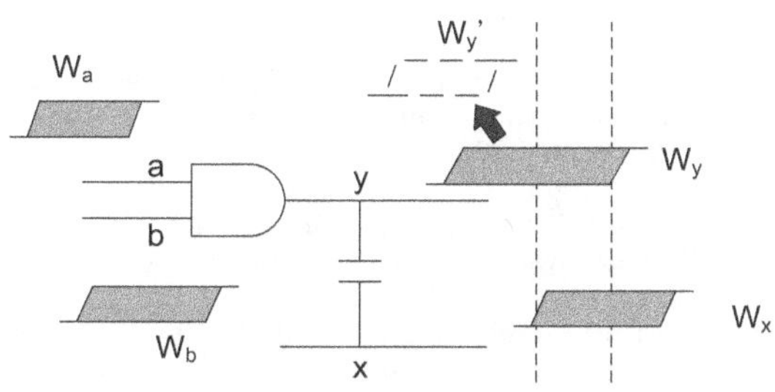

Figure 9: Example for path refinement

To further improve runtime, two more techniques are incorporated into our CA-FTA. One is cone separation as proposed in [11]. By splitting the circuits into individual fan-in cones, the size of SAT clauses for each sub-circuit can be greatly reduced compared to that of the entire circuit. Note that we still maintain constraints of the corresponding cones (i.e. the cone that has coupling relation to the current processing cone) into the formulation to consider all the relations of aggressors. The second one is to preset a lower bound to eliminate the unnecessary calculation during TA-FTA. Different from finding the worst-case delay in each end node of the cone, our CA-FTA aims at searching the worst-case timing among the entire circuit. Therefore, if we find that the maximum delay of the cone is smaller than the lower bound that we set, we can ignore the cone and continue to perform the next one. With two such techniques, our CA-FTA can efficiently eliminate redundant SAT clauses and avoid unnecessary calculation.

4. EXPERIMENTAL RESULT

Our CA-FTA is implemented in C++. All experiments are conducted on a Linux machine with Intel Xeon core 4 2.33GHz CPU and 16GB RAM. We perform experiments on several ISCAS'85 and ISPD-2012 [13] benchmark circuits, with 45nm Nangate Open Cell Library [12]. A commercial tool is used to perform placement and routing and extracts coupling information between interconnects from the SPEF output file. More implementation details help improve efficiency of our CA-FTA and are shown through the following experiments. In the first experiment, runtime and final delay (with and without the relaxation of crosstalk formulation) are compared. Later, the effect of setting lower bounds for reducing runtime is shown in the second experiment. At last, we compare the timing bound computed by CA-FTA and crosstalk STA among all benchmark circuits.

circuit	runtime(sec)		delay (ns)	
	complete	relaxed	complete	relaxed
c1908	356	654	0.86	0.89
DMA	> 1 day	566	-	7.74
pci_bridge32	54	453	4.96	4.98
des_perf	> 1 day	5070	-	10.73
vga_lcd	> 1 day	3155	-	11.33
b19	> 1 day	10457	-	18.47

Table 1: Comparison of runtime and delay between complete and relaxed formulation

4.1 Complete v.s. Relaxed Formulations

Table 1 shows runtimes and final delays with and without relaxing crosstalk formula on several benchmark circuits. With the complete formulation, the result is slightly better and has smaller runtime in some cases. Since the complete formulation enumerates all possible cases in SAT clauses, it has the exact timing information on all paths and thus uses fewer iterations of path checking after refinement. Moreover, since the speed up case is combined with the nominal case, in the relaxed formulation, delay from exact timing of the complete formulation will be smaller than that from the relaxed formulation. However, when a larger design consists of more coupling capacitances, path enumeration becomes infeasible and leads to enormous SAT clauses which are difficult to solve, like DMA, des_perf, vga_lcd, and b19 in Table 1. Hence, the relaxed crosstalk formulation instead of the complete one is used in our CA-FTA due to practicality.

4.2 Preset Lower Bound for Efficiency

The second experiment demonstrates the effectiveness of using a preset lower bound on path checking for speedup. Table 2 shows runtime between setting and not setting a lower bound for path checking. With preset lower bounds, all benchmark circuits converge faster. In particular, two-time speedup can be achieved on benchmark circuit b19 be-

circuit	original (sec)	w/ lower bound (sec)	speedup (x)
c1908	654	616	1.06
DMA	566	505	1.12
pci_bridge32	652	581	1.12
des_perf	5070	3543	1.43
vga_lcd	3155	2261	1.40
b19	10457	5176	2.02
		average	**1.36**

Table 2: Comparison between original and with-lower-bound runtime

circuit	#gate	#clauses	(a) xtalk STA (ns)	(b) xtalk STA +PR (ns)	(c) our framework (ns)	(a-c)/a (%)	(b-c)/b (%)
c432	394	139,499	0.62	0.62	0.61	1.09	0.22
c880	411	29,397	0.75	0.73	0.67	10.57	8.33
c1355	609	1,948,602	1.39	1.37	1.37	1.72	0.00
c1908	478	707,211	0.96	0.94	0.89	7.43	5.77
c3540	1240	4,468,992	1.14	1.14	1.01	11.79	11.52
c5315	2045	4,073,186	3.68	3.60	3.29	10.48	8.44
c7552	2475	790,926	6.31	6.17	4.96	21.36	19.61
usb_phy	626	1,033	0.90	0.89	0.89	1.75	0.82
DMA	25983	336,068	8.05	7.78	7.74	3.83	0.49
pci_bridge32	33362	12,315	5.08	5.03	4.98	1.97	1.00
des_perf	111462	407,528	10.82	10.73	10.73	0.83	0.01
vga_lcd	164975	518,187	12.09	11.93	11.33	6.33	5.08
b19	219289	4,082,390	28.24	27.63	18.47	34.58	33.14
average						**8.75**	**7.26**

Table 3: Timing-bound comparison for crosstalk STA, crosstalk STA with path refinement and CA-FTA

cause a lot of path delays (after refinement) are still smaller than the preset lower bound. Hence, setting a lower bound in advance helps reduce redundant path checking in CA-FTA.

4.3 Timing-Bound Comparison

Table 3 shows the result of comparing the maximum crosstalk-induced delay obtained by crosstalk STA (denoted by xtalk STA as the fourth column), and crosstalk STA with path refinement (denoted by xtalk STA + PR as the fifth column) with CA-FTA (sixth column). The seventh column calculates the reduction ratio of CA-FTA with crosstalk STA whereas the eighth column represents the reduction ratio between ours and crosstalk STA with path refinement. We can observe that CA-FTA reduces the overall delay by $0.8\% \sim 34.6\%$ compared to crosstalk STA among all benchmark circuits. Moreover, the reduction ratio between crosstalk STA with path refinement and CA-FTA is 7.26% on average. In particular, for benchmark circuit b19, the reduction ratio is as high as 34.6%. It is because a lot of false paths in b19 are not worth path refinement. With TA-FTA, delay due to these false paths can be completely removed and thus results in tighter bounds.

5. CONCLUSION

As the technology scales down, the crosstalk-induced delay effect due to capacitive coupling is becoming more important in timing analysis. In this paper, we propose a CA-FTA that can explore the worst-case delay and critical path under the consideration of all aggressors. Through the incorporation of *crosstalk STA*, *path refinement*, and *TA-FTA*, we can reduce pessimism from temporal and functional perspectives. Crosstalk formulation is also proposed to encode information between victims and aggressors into CNF. Experimental result shows that our CA-FTA provides tighter bounds on crosstalk delay for all benchmark circuits (in particular, by 34.6% for b19). Moreover, the relaxed crosstalk formulation can incorporate the coupling relation between victims and aggressors while remaining conservativeness of the final delay. A speedup technique (i.e. preset lower bound) is also used to help reduce runtime and improves efficiency by 36% in average.

6. ACKNOWLEDGMENTS

This work was partially supported by Ministry of Science and Technology, Taiwan, R.O.C. under grant no. MOST104-2628-E-009-009-MY3.

7. REFERENCES

[1] D. Das, K. Killpack, C.V. Kashyap, A. Jas, and H. Zhou, "Pessimism reduction in coupling-aware static timing analysis using Timing and Logic Filtering," in Proc. Asian South Pacific Design Autom. Conf., 2008, pp. 486-491.

[2] D. Das, A. Shebaita, H. Zhou, Y. Ismail, and K. Killpack, "FA-STAC: A framework for fast and accurate static timing analysis with coupling," in Proc. Int. Conf. Comput. Design, 2007, pp. 43-49.

[3] R. Arunachalam, K. Rajagopal, and L. T. Pilleggi, "Taco: Timing analysis with coupling," in Proc. Design Autom. Conf., 2000, pp. 266-269.

[4] H. Zhou, "Timing analysis with crosstalk is a fixpoint on a complete lattice," IEEE Trans. Comput.-Aided Design Integr. Circuits Syst., vol. 22, no. 9, pp. 1261-1269, Sep. 2003.

[5] T. Xiao and M. Marek-Sadowska, "Worst delay estimation in crosstalk aware static timing analysis," in Proc. Int. Conf. on Computer Design, 2000, pp. 115-120.

[6] Franzini, B., Forzan, C. Pandini, D., Scandolara, P., Dal Fabbro, A., "Crosstalk aware static timing analysis: a two step approach", in Proc. Int. Symposium on Quality Electronic Design, 2000, pp. 499-503.

[7] Y. Li, R. Murgai, T. Miyoshi, A.Verma, "XTalkDelay: A Crosstalk-aware Timing analysis Tool for Chip-level Designs," in Proc. Int. Conf. on Computer Design, 2004, pp. 208-215.

[8] M. R. Becer, V. Zolotov, R. Panda, A. Grinshpon, I. Algor, R. Levy, and C. Oh, "Pessimism reduction in crosstalk noise aware STA." in Proc. Int. Conf. Computer-Aided Design, 2005, pp. 954-961.

[9] R. Arunachalam, R. D. Blanton, and L. T. Pileggi, "False coupling interactions in static timing analysis," in Proc. Design Automation Conf., 2001, pp. 726-731.

[10] Y. Ran, A. Kondratyev, K. H. Tseng, Y. Watanabe, and M. Marek-Sadowska, "Eliminating false positives in crosstalk noise analysis," IEEE Trans. Comput.-Aided Des. Integr. Circuits Syst., vol. 24, no. 9, pp. 1406-1419, Sep. 2005.

[11] Jasper C. C. Chang, Ryan H.-M. Huang, Louis Y.-Z. Lin, and Charles H.-P. Wen, "TA-FTA: Transition-aware functional timing analysis with a four-valued encoding," in Proc. Design Autom. Conf., 2015, pp. 1-6.

[12] Nangate 45nm Open Library, Nangate Inc., http://www.nangate.com/, 2009.

[13] M. M. Ozdal, C. Amin, A. Ayupov, S. Burns, G. Wilke, C. Zhuo, "The ISPD -2012 Discrete Cell Sizing Contest and Benchmark Suite", Proc. ACM International Symposium on Physical Design, pp. 161-164, 2012.

A Thermal-Balanced Variable-Sized-Bin-Packing Approach for Energy Efficient Multi-Core Real-Time Scheduling

Shi Sha*, Wujie Wen†, Shaolei Ren‡, Gang Quan§
Department of Electrical and Computer Engineering
*†§Florida International University, Miami, Florida, 33174
‡University of California-Riverside, Riverside, California, 92521
*ssha001, †wwen, §gang.quan@fiu.edu, ‡sren@ece.ucr.edu

ABSTRACT

In this paper, we study the problem of how to schedule real-time tasks on multi-core platforms to maximize the energy efficiency under a peak temperature constraint. Different from the traditional load-balancing approach, we propose energy saving solutions under the "thermal balancing" heuristic, which can effectively avoid hotspots and maximize the throughput. We first establish and formally prove a lower bound of energy when scheduling a periodic task set on a multi-core platform using the thermal-balancing approach. Considering the NP-nature of this problem, we formulate the problem as a variable-sized-bin-packing (VSBP) problem and develop a partitioning heuristic. We further introduce an enhanced algorithm to improve the quality of the solution. The experimental results show up to 256.4% improvement of the energy efficiency and an average 9.95% higher feasibility than the traditional load balancing approach.

Keywords

Energy minimization; temperature control; real-time systems; power; multi-core platform; real-time scheduling.

1. INTRODUCTION

As chip power dissipation keeps increasing, the escalated energy consumption becomes a prominent issue. Energy-efficient computing is widely used, ranging from mobile devices to data centers, for reducing electricity bills, extending/shrinking battery life/size, relieving environmental pressures, etc. Moreover, high power dissipation also leads to rising operating temperatures, which negatively impacts circuit delay, reliability, and increases the leakage power consumption [11]. How to improve the thermal profile and eliminate hotspots should be considered in both design and runtime for computing system design. To this end, thermal-constrained energy-aware scheduling is considered as an effective approach either smooth the thermal gradient by *dynamic voltage frequency scaling* (DVFS), or shut down the unused cores by *dynamic power management* (DPM).

Permission to make digital or hard copies of all or part of this work for personal or classroom use is granted without fee provided that copies are not made or distributed for profit or commercial advantage and that copies bear this notice and the full citation on the first page. Copyrights for components of this work owned by others than ACM must be honored. Abstracting with credit is permitted. To copy otherwise, or republish, to post on servers or to redistribute to lists, requires prior specific permission and/or a fee. Request permissions from permissions@acm.org.
GLSVLSI '17, May 10-12, 2017, Banff, AB, Canada
© 2017 ACM. ISBN 978-1-4503-4972-7/17/05... $15.00
DOI: http://dx.doi.org/10.1145/3060403.3060444

There have been extensive research efforts on improving the multi-core energy efficiency, but many of them, e.g. [2, 7], did not take temperature constraints into consideration. For energy reduction under a pre-defined temperature threshold, a genetic approach, essentially a meta-heuristic search algorithm, has been proposed in [10] and a linear programming method (ILP) was developed in [5]. However, both [10] and [5] can be computationally expensive as the design space becomes larger. To avoid rapid increases of the searching time, some simple energy-saving heuristic, e.g. *workload-balancing* approach was developed, to spread workload evenly to lower the processing speeds [12, 6]. However, these strategies become less useful as the high chip temperature impacts become more substantial. Considering the energy efficiency and heat dissipation tradeoffs among different cores, Zhou et al. [14] first minimized the dynamic energy by balancing the dynamic power; then, it reduced the leakage energy by slack assignment. For homogeneous multi-core platforms, this approach is simply reduced to the traditional workload-balancing approach.

In this paper, we study the problem of how to improve the energy efficiency when scheduling a hard periodic real-time task set on a multi-core platform under a given peak temperature constraint. Instead of the traditional load-balancing approach, we adopt a "*thermal-balancing*" approach to solve this problem with following contributions:

1. First, we establish and formally prove a lower bound of the energy consumption by a thermal-balancing approach for accomplishing a given task set.
2. We transform the temperature-constrained energy efficient task partitioning on the multi-core platform as a variable-sized-bin-packing (VSBP) problem and proposed a polynomial time algorithm;
3. We further enhance the VSBP algorithm with a better feasibility and energy reduction result.

The rest of this paper is organized as follows. Section II introduces the problem models, followed by a motivation example in Section III. Our proposed energy efficient algorithm is discussed in Section IV. Experimental results are shown in Section V, and Section VI concludes the paper.

2. PRELIMINARIES

We present the system model and formulate our research problem formally. The **bold characters** represent the vectors and matrices; the regular fonts are used for ordinary variables and coefficients.

2.1 System / Task Model

We consider a multi-core platform $\mathfrak{N}$ with N cores, $\mathfrak{N} = \{core_i | i = 1, \cdots, N\}$. Each core can set different running speeds/modes independently, which are characterized by the corresponding supply voltage v and working frequency f. Since $v \propto f$, we use a normalized v ($0 \le v \le 1$) to denote the processing speed for ease of presentation. By applying the power gating techniques, the idle cores (denoted by $\mathfrak{N}_{dark}$) without any task assignment can be shut down to avoid leakage power consumptions. Other active cores with task assignments belong to $\mathfrak{N}_{active}$, as $\mathfrak{N}_{active} = \mathfrak{N} \setminus \mathfrak{N}_{dark}$.

We assume a periodic task set with M tasks, $\mathbf{\Gamma} = \{\tau_k | k = 1, \cdots, M\}$. Each task is defined by its inter-arrival time *(Period)* and the worst-case-execution-time (ET) at the maximum speed, i.e. $\tau_k = \{Period_k, ET_k\}$. Each task's deadline equals its period. For simplicity, we assume all tasks are scheduled by *earliest deadline first* (EDF) policy, and our approach can be extended to use other scheduling policies.

2.2 Power/Thermal Model

The total power consumption (P) consists of dynamic power and leakage power [11]. Dynamic power is proportional to the cubic of supply voltage and leakage power depends linearly on the instantaneous temperature T, i.e. $P_{leak} = \alpha(v) + \beta T(t)$. The total power of the i-th core is

$$\begin{cases} P_i(t) = \alpha(v_i) + \beta \cdot T_i(t) + \gamma(v_i) \cdot v_i^3, & \text{if } core_i \in \mathfrak{N}_{active}; \\ P_i(t) = 0, & \text{if } core_i \in \mathfrak{N}_{dark}, \end{cases} \tag{1}$$

where α and γ are positive constants within the interval that $core_i$ runs at supply voltage v_i. β is a constant.

For each **state interval** (i.e. the interval in which each core runs only in one unique mode), the supply voltage in (1) is a constant. The thermal dynamic within one interval can be built upon the duality between heat transfer and electrical phenomena as [11]

$$\frac{d\mathbf{T}(t)}{dt} = \mathbf{A}\mathbf{T}(t) + \mathbf{C}^{-1}(\mathbf{\Psi}(\mathbf{v}) + \boldsymbol{\eta}), \tag{2}$$

where $\mathbf{T}(t)$ represents an $N \times 1$ temperature vector at time t. Coefficient matrix $\mathbf{A}$ is an $N \times N$ architecture-related constant matrix. $\mathbf{C} = diag\{C_i\}_{N \times N}$ consists by thermal capacitances on its diagonal; $\mathbf{\Psi}(\mathbf{v}) = [\alpha(v_i) + \gamma(v_i)v_i^3]_{N\times 1}$; $\boldsymbol{\eta} = [\frac{T_{amb}}{R_{ii}}]_{N\times 1}$ are constants, and R_{ii} is the thermal resistance of $core_i$ to itself.

2.3 Energy Model

The energy consumption vector of the q-th state-interval $\mathbb{I}_q = [t_{q-1}, t_q]$, which starts at t_{q-1} and ends at t_q, can be formulated as [3]

$$\begin{aligned} \mathbf{E}(t_{q-1}, t_q) = (\mathbf{I} - \mathbf{\Phi}\mathbf{A}^{-1}\mathbf{C}^{-1}) l_q \mathbf{\Psi}_q - l_q \mathbf{\Phi}\mathbf{A}^{-1}\mathbf{C}^{-1}\boldsymbol{\eta} \\ + \mathbf{\Phi}\mathbf{A}^{-1}[\mathbf{T}(t_q) - \mathbf{T}(t_{q-1})], \end{aligned} \tag{3}$$

where $l_q = t_q - t_{q-1}$; $\mathbf{\Phi} = diag\{\beta\}_{N\times N}$; $\mathbf{\Psi}_q$ is the power-related factor of the q-th interval; $\mathbf{I}$ is an identity matrix. For interval $\mathbb{I}_q$, the total energy is $E_{total}(\mathbb{I}_q) = \sum E_i(t_{q-1}, t_q)$, in which $E_i(t_{q-1}, t_q)$ is the i-th entry of $\mathbf{E}(t_{q-1}, t_q)$.

To evaluate the energy efficiency of a periodic schedule, we adopt the concept of *"workload-per-Joule"* (WPJ) [5], which is defined as the ratio of the total completed workload and the total amount of energy consumed in one period. Specifically, for a schedule that contains z state intervals with period t_p, the energy efficiency is $WPJ = W/E_{total}(t_0, t_p)$, where in one period, t_0 is the starting time, W denotes the total workload as $W = \sum_{q=1}^{z} \sum_{i=1}^{N} v_i l_q$; $E_{total}(t_0, t_p)$ denotes the total energy consumption. A larger WPJ value indicates that more workload can be completed with each unit of energy consumption, which means a better energy efficiency.

2.4 Problem Formulation

With the models introduced above, our problem can be formulated as follows.

PROBLEM 1. *Given a periodic hard real-time task set* $\mathbf{\Gamma} = \{\tau_k | k = 1, \cdots, M\}$ *scheduled on a multi-core platform* $\mathfrak{N} = \{core_i | i = 1, \cdots, N\}$ *with maximum allowed temperature* (T_{max})*, find the task-to-core assignment matrix* ($\mathbf{\Theta}_{N\times M}$) *and the speed for each task* ($\mathbf{S}_{M\times 1}$)*, to maximize the overall energy efficiency (WPJ) in the thermal stable status.*

$$\begin{aligned} Max: \quad & WPJ\,; \\ St: \quad & \sum_{k=1}^{M} \Theta_{i,k} = 1\,; \\ & \mathbf{0} \le \mathbf{S}_{M\times 1} \le \mathbf{1}\,; \\ & T_{peak} \le T_{max}\,; \\ & \text{Utilization}_{corei} \le 1\,, \end{aligned} \tag{4}$$

where $\Theta_{i,k} = 1$, if task τ_k assigned to the $corei$; otherwise $\Theta_{i,k} = 0$; $\mathbf{S}_{M\times 1}$ is the speed vector for all the tasks; $Utilization_{corei}$ represent $corei$'s utilization.

3. MOTIVATION EXAMPLE

Before presenting our approach, we first use a simple example to motivate our research. Partitioning a task set optimally is a well-known NP-hard problem [2]. Using mixed integer programming methods, e.g. [5], results in a rapid increase of the computational cost. Thus, it is necessary to develop more computationally efficient solutions.

Given five tasks, as the first column of Table 1, to be allocated on a 3-core platform arranged in a row, with six speed levels as $[0, 0.2, 0.4, 0.6, 0.8, 1]V$. The ambient temperature and temperature threshold are 35°C and 44°C, respectively. The second column in Table 1 shows the task partitioning results based on the workload-balancing strategy as cores' utilization be 50%, 40% and 30%. Note that, due to the heat transfer from both core 1 and core 3, the temperature of core 2 is significantly higher than the case when it runs the same workload when core 1 and core 3 are idle. The peak temperature of "workload balance" is 44.27°C, which exceeds the temperature constraints, as shown in Figure 1.

Alternatively, the thermal-balancing approach intends to balance the temperature of different cores. We can allocate the tasks, as shown in the third column of Table 1, to make their temperatures keep close to each other. Note that, when using the thermal-balancing heuristic, core 1 and core 3 take 60% of the cores' utilization, while no tasks are assigned to core 2. The peak temperature of "thermal balance" is 43.94°C and its energy efficiency (WPJ) is 0.0230, which is higher than the result of "workload-balance" as 0.0199.

The above example clearly shows that workload balancing is no longer effective when the leakage power becomes significant. The thermal-balancing approach is promising to achieve a high throughput and energy efficiency. The problem, however, is how to partition tasks to cores at different locations and also how to set core speeds accordingly

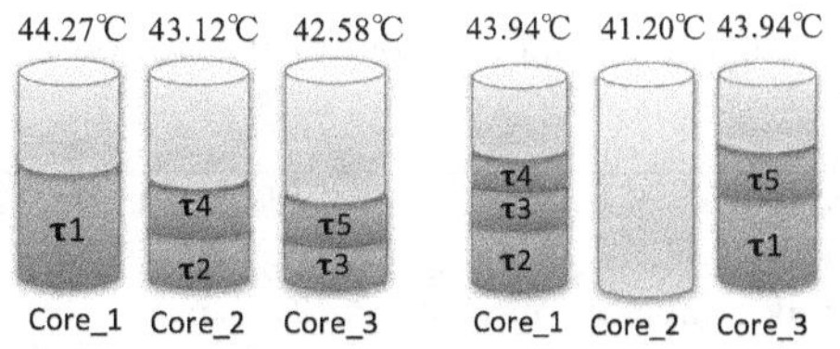

(a) Workload balance (b) Thermal balance

Figure 1: Peak temperature example of "thermal balance" and "workload balance" on a 3-core platform

Table 1: Task assignments under "workload balance" (WB) and "thermal balance" (TB)

Task Set	WB	TB
τ_1={10, 5, 1}	{10, 8.33, 0.6, 1}	{10, 8.33, 0.6, 1}
τ_2={10, 3, 1}	{10, 7.50, 0.4, 2}	{10, 5.00, 0.6, 3}
τ_3={10, 2, 1}	{10, 5.00, 0.4, 3}	{10, 3.33, 0.6, 3}
τ_4={10, 1, 1}	{10, 2.50, 0.4, 2}	{10, 1.67, 0.6, 3}
τ_5={10, 1, 1}	{10, 2.50, 0.4, 3}	{10, 1.67, 0.6, 1}

* $\tau_k = \{Period_k,\ ET_k,\ S_k,\ task\text{-}to\text{-}core\ assignment\}$.

to achieve a thermal balanced situation while satisfying the temperature and real-time constraints. In what follows, we present our algorithm for the energy efficient scheduling on multi-core platforms under the thermal constraint.

4. ENERGY EFFICIENT APPROACHES

Our motivation example indicates that a thermal-balancing approach can potentially optimize the throughput on active cores [9, 11], and achieve a better energy efficiency. For ease of our discussions, we first introduce the definition of *thermal-balancing state* on multi-core platform as follows.

DEFINITION 1. *Given a multi-core platform with n active cores, the multi-core platform achieves the thermal-balancing state at T_m, if all active cores maintain the same constant temperature T_m.*

Based on [9], we can easily prove the following theorem.

THEOREM 1. *Given a multi-core platform (n active cores) and the maximal allowed temperature of T_{max}, the overall throughput of the platform is maximized, if the multi-core platform achieves the thermal-balancing state at $T_m = T_{max}$.*

In what follows, we first introduce the lower bound of energy consumption when accomplishing a given task set on a multi-core platform under the thermal-balancing strategy.

4.1 The Lower Bound of Thermal-Balanced Energy Consumption

Given a task set $\mathbf{\Gamma} = \{\tau_k |\ k = 1, \cdots, M\}$ and an N-core platform $\mathfrak{N}$ with a T_{max} constraint, our goal is to find the most energy efficient way to complete all tasks in $\mathbf{\Gamma}$ within their deadlines using the thermal-balancing strategy. Then, for each $core_i \in \mathfrak{N}_{active}$ we have $v_i > 0$, and $T_i = T_m$. In the meantime, for $core_i \in \mathfrak{N}_{dark}$, we have $v_i = 0$. Note that, with given T_m and $\mathfrak{N}_{active}$ (and thus $\mathfrak{N}_{dark}$), the supply voltage v_i for each $core_i \in \mathfrak{N}_{active}$ and T_j for each $core_j \in \mathfrak{N}_{dark}$ are uniquely defined, which is formulated as follows.

Without loss of generality, assume the first h cores are turned off and the rest n cores are activated, where $n + h = N$. We have $\mathbf{T} = [\mathbf{T}_h, \mathbf{T}_n]_{N\times 1}$ and $\mathbf{\Psi} = [\mathbf{\Psi}_h, \mathbf{\Psi}_n]_{N\times 1}$, in which $\mathbf{T}_h = [T_1, \cdots, T_h]_{h\times 1}$; $\mathbf{T}_n = [T_m, \cdots, T_m]_{n\times 1}$; $\mathbf{\Psi}_h = [\alpha_0, \cdots, \alpha_0]_{h\times 1}$; $\mathbf{\Psi}_n = [\Psi_{h+1}, \cdots, \Psi_N]_{n\times 1}$. Since $\Psi_i = \alpha(v_i) + \gamma(v_i)v_i^3$, when $v_i = 0$, the power-related factor becomes a constant as $\Psi_i = \alpha(0) = \alpha_0$. Let $\mathbf{U} = -\mathbf{A}^{-1}\mathbf{C}^{-1}$ and $\mathbf{\Omega} = \mathbf{\Psi} + \boldsymbol{\eta}$. Then, according to Equation (2), we have

$$\begin{bmatrix}\mathbf{T}_h\\ \mathbf{T}_n\end{bmatrix} = \begin{bmatrix}\mathbf{U}_0 & \mathbf{U}_1\\ \mathbf{U}_2 & \mathbf{U}_3\end{bmatrix}\begin{bmatrix}\mathbf{\Omega}_h\\ \mathbf{\Omega}_n\end{bmatrix} \quad \text{and} \quad \begin{bmatrix}\mathbf{\Omega}_h\\ \mathbf{\Omega}_n\end{bmatrix} = \begin{bmatrix}\mathbf{\Psi}_h + \boldsymbol{\eta}_h\\ \mathbf{\Psi}_n + \boldsymbol{\eta}_n\end{bmatrix} \tag{5}$$

where $\boldsymbol{\eta}_h = [\eta_i]_{h\times 1}$ and $i = 1, \cdots, h$; $\boldsymbol{\eta}_n = [\eta_i]_{n\times 1}$ and $i = h+1, \cdots, N$. In Equation (5), the dimensions for $\mathbf{U}_0$, $\mathbf{U}_1$, $\mathbf{U}_2$ and $\mathbf{U}_3$ are $h\times h$, $h\times n$, $n\times h$ and $n\times n$, respectively. Note that, matrices/vectors $\mathbf{T}_n$, $\mathbf{U}_0$ to $\mathbf{U}_3$, $\mathbf{\Psi}_h$, $\boldsymbol{\eta}_h$ and $\boldsymbol{\eta}_n$ are determined once the power and thermal characteristics of the multi-core platform are given. Accordingly, $\mathbf{T}_h$ and $\mathbf{\Psi}_n$ can be solved as follows.

$$\begin{cases}\mathbf{T}_h = \mathbf{U}_0\mathbf{\Omega}_h + \mathbf{U}_1\mathbf{\Omega}_n\\ \mathbf{T}_n = \mathbf{U}_2\mathbf{\Omega}_h + \mathbf{U}_3\mathbf{\Omega}_n\end{cases} \Rightarrow \begin{cases}\mathbf{T}_h = \mathbf{U}_0\mathbf{\Omega}_h + \mathbf{U}_1\mathbf{\Omega}_n\\ \mathbf{U}_3\mathbf{\Omega}_n = \mathbf{T}_n - \mathbf{U}_2\mathbf{\Omega}_h\end{cases}$$
$$\Rightarrow \begin{bmatrix}\mathbf{I} & \mathbf{0}\\ \mathbf{0} & \mathbf{U}_3\end{bmatrix}\begin{bmatrix}\mathbf{T}_h\\ \mathbf{\Omega}_n\end{bmatrix} = \begin{bmatrix}\mathbf{0} & \mathbf{U}_1\\ \mathbf{0} & \mathbf{0}\end{bmatrix}\begin{bmatrix}\mathbf{T}_h\\ \mathbf{\Omega}_n\end{bmatrix} + \begin{bmatrix}\mathbf{U}_0\mathbf{\Omega}_h\\ \mathbf{T}_n - \mathbf{U}_2\mathbf{\Omega}_h\end{bmatrix}$$
$$\Rightarrow \begin{bmatrix}\mathbf{T}_h\\ \mathbf{\Omega}_n\end{bmatrix} = \begin{bmatrix}\mathbf{I} & -\mathbf{U}_1\\ \mathbf{0} & \mathbf{U}_3\end{bmatrix}^{-1}\begin{bmatrix}\mathbf{U}_0\mathbf{\Omega}_h\\ \mathbf{T}_n - \mathbf{U}_2\mathbf{\Omega}_h\end{bmatrix} \tag{6}$$

As a result, with the solvable $\mathbf{\Omega}_n$ and $\mathbf{\Psi}_n$, we can readily obtain the supply voltage (v_i) for each active core, so that they can maintain their temperatures at T_m. In the meantime, to ensure all tasks meet their deadlines, the total capacity of active cores must be no smaller than the total utilization of all the tasks, as

$$\sum_{task\_k \in \mathbf{\Gamma}} \frac{ET_k}{Period_k} \leq \sum_{core\_i \in \mathfrak{N}_{active}} v_i. \tag{7}$$

The highest WPJ can thus be found by exhaustively searching different configurations (with different numbers of active cores, different active core combinations, and different thermal balance temperatures) that satisfy equation (7). The detailed algorithm is shown in Algorithm 1.

Algorithm 1 Lower bound of thermal balancing approach (**LB**)

```
Input: Multi-core platform 𝔑 = {core_i | i = 1···N};
    Peak temperature constraint T_max;
    Total utilization Σ_Γ ET_k/Period_k, task k ∈ Γ;
Output: Active core subset 𝔑_active, speeds S_active;
    Overall energy-efficiency criteria WPJ;

for each possible 𝔑_active with 1 ≤ number(𝔑_active) ≤ N do
    Solve Equation (5) and (6);
    Binary search the lowest T_m ∈ [T_amb, T_max] that satisfy
  Equation (7);
end for
Output the highest WPJ solutions;
```

Algorithm 1 searches the platform configurations with the highest WPJ by exploring all possible active core subset choices (i.e. 2^N). For each active core subset, Algorithm 1 employs the binary search method to find the lowest thermal-balancing temperature (T_m) that can make the given task set feasible. The complexity of Algorithm 1 is $2^N ln(T_{max} -$

T_{amb}). Algorithm 1 provides an effective lower bound of the energy efficiency when scheduling a given task set to a multi-core platform, which is formally formulated in Theorem 2.

THEOREM 2. *Given a task set* $\mathbf{\Gamma} = \{\tau_k | k = 1, \cdots, M\}$ *and an* N*-core platform* $\mathfrak{N}$ *with its peak temperature constraint* T_{max}*, the energy efficiency for any feasible partition of* $\mathbf{\Gamma}$ *to the multi-core platform based on the thermal-balancing strategy is no higher than the output from Algorithm 1.*

4.2 Task Partitioning via Variable Sized Bin Packing

Algorithm 1 determines a theoretical lower bound for the thermal-constrained energy consumption when scheduling a periodic real-time task set on a multi-core platform under the thermal-balancing heuristic. There are two issues for Algorithm 1: First, its complexity is high; Second, it does not provide feasible task-to-core assignments for Problem 1. Consider the NP-nature of multi-core task partitioning problems, one common approach is to translate the partitioning to the traditional bin-packing problem. Specifically, given a list of objects (tasks) and their weights (utilizations), and a collection of bins (cores), the multi-core task partitioning problem is to pack objects to bins while optimizing the different design objectives. For example, some existing works (e.g. [2, 14]) assume all cores' capacities are identical. Then, they pack tasks and check the real-time and thermal feasibility iteratively until all the tasks have been assigned.

Note that, considering the topologies of different cores, their maximum supply voltages under the thermal constraint are different, which can be translated to each core having different "capacities," i.e. the maximum total task utilizations that can be accommodated in that core. To this end, we transform Problem 1 into the following variable-sized-bin-packing problem (VSBP).

PROBLEM 2. *Given a set of objects* $\mathbf{\Gamma} = \{\tau_k | k = 1, \cdots, M\}$ *with each item size be* $size(\tau_k)$*, and a set of bins* $\mathfrak{N} = \{core_i | i = 1, \cdots, N\}$ *of capacities* $\{c_i | i = 1, \cdots, N\}$*, pack* $\mathbf{\Gamma}$ *into* $\mathfrak{N}$ *such that the least number of bins are used.*

The optimization goal of Problem 2 is to minimize the total number of active cores. The rationale behind the assumption is to maximally use less cores to shut down as many cores as possible to save the leakage power consumption. It is not difficult to prove the following theorem.

THEOREM 3. *A feasible solution for Problem 2 is a feasible solution for Problem 1.*

Problem 2 can be solved using some traditional bin-packing approaches, such as those with equal-sized bins via first-fit or best-fit heuristic. Existing work [4] shows a worst-case approximation ratio (i.e. the ratio between the quality of an approximate solution to that of an optimal solution) of 3/2 for a linear time approximation algorithm.

In our approach, we develop an iterative algorithm built upon the general principle of Algorithm A1 in [13], which has a proven approximation ratio of 3/2. Specifically, it clusters items into four size ranges as $(0, \frac{1}{3})$, $(\frac{1}{3}, \frac{1.5}{3})$, $(\frac{1.5}{3}, \frac{2}{3})$, $(\frac{2}{3}, 1)$; then, by matching different objects from different clusters, Algorithm A1 in [13] ensures that each allocated bin is at least 2/3 full or there must be a matching bin in the optimal solution using less capacity. More details for this approach can be found in [13], and the detailed solution is shown in Algorithm 2.

Algorithm 2 Varialbe-sized-bin-packing **(VSBP)** method

1: **Input:** Multi-core platform $\mathfrak{N} = \{core_i | i = 1 \cdots N\}$;
2: Peak temperature constraint T_{max};
3: Task set $\mathbf{\Gamma} = \{\tau_k | k = 1 \cdots M\}$, $\tau_k = \{\text{Period}_k, \text{ET}_k\}$;
4: **Output**: Task allocation matrix $\mathbf{\Theta}$;
5: Task speeds vector $\mathbf{S}$;
6: Overall energy-efficiency WPJ;

7: $\mathfrak{N}_{active} = \mathfrak{N}$, $\mathbf{\Theta} = \emptyset$, $WPJ = 0$, $n = N$ and $h = 0$ in (5);
8: **while** succeed **do**
9: Determine core capacities by (5);
10: Cluster and order core types decreasingly by capacities ;
11: **for** each core type in $\mathfrak{N}_{active}$ **do**
12: N_μ = The number of available cores in the μ-th type;
13: Packing tasks according to Algorithm A1 [13] assuming there is unlimited number of cores in this type;
14: **if** succeed **then**
15: Save workload assignment of first N_μ cores to $\mathbf{\Theta}$;
16: **else**
17: Return (Task set is not schedulable!);
18: **end if**
19: $\mathbf{\Gamma}'$ = workload in first N_μ cores of current type;
20: $\mathbf{\Gamma} = \mathbf{\Gamma} - \mathbf{\Gamma}'$;
21: **end for**
22: **if** exists any core in $\mathfrak{N}_{active}$ with no task assignment **then**
23: Update $\mathfrak{N}_{active}$; n and h in (5);
24: **else**
25: Return $\mathbf{\Theta}$ and WPJ;
26: **end if**
27: **end while**

In Algorithm 2, we first compute core capacities (line 9). The cores are then categorized to different types based on their capacities and sorted in a decreasing order (line 10). Then, we pack tasks to each core type using Algorithm A1 [13] by assuming an unlimited number of cores available in this type. This ensures that, except for the last core, each core is filled at least 2/3 full. Then, we save the task assignment for the first N_μ cores (line 15), due to the limitation of available cores of that type. We then modify the available task set and try the next core type until all tasks are assigned. At the end, if any core is idle, we modify the active core set and repeat the procedure again. It is not difficult to prove that Algorithm 2 has the following property.

THEOREM 4. *The worst case absolute approximation ratio of Algorithm 2 is 3/2, and the bound is tight.*

Note that Algorithm A1 [13] ensures that there is at most one bin with capacity filled less than 2/3. The bound is tight since the bin-packing problem with identical bins, with a proven absolute approximation ratio of 3/2, is a special case of Problem 2.

4.3 The Enhanced Bin-Packing Method

There are two significant limitations in Algorithm 2. First, initializing all cores as active limits the largest utilization of a real-time task in a task set. For example, on a 3-core platform with $T_{max} = 50°$C, the maximum supply voltage for each core is $[0.64, 0.51, 0.64]V$. Assume there is a task set including a task $\tau = \{Period = 10ms, ET = 7.5ms\}$ with utilization of 0.75. Item size 0.75 is larger than all the bin sizes, so Algorithm 2 cannot partition the task set no matter how small the total utilization of this task set can be. On the other hand, if we turn off both core 2 and core

3, the maximum voltage of core 1 becomes 0.81, and thus this task can be feasibly scheduled without violating the given thermal constraint. Second, for task sets with light utilization, the needed core capacity by Algorithm 2 may result in a peak temperature lower than T_m, which presents the opportunity to reduce the core capacity (proportional to core power) and therefore improve the energy efficiency.

Considering these limitations, we develop an Enhanced VSBP (En-VSBP) solution in Algorithm 3.

Algorithm 3 Enhanced varialbe-sized-bin-packing **(En-VSBP)** method

1: **Input**: $\mathfrak{N}$, $\mathbf{\Gamma}$, T_{max};
2: **Output**: $\mathbf{\Theta}$, $\mathbf{S}$, WPJ;
3: $\mathbf{\Theta} = \emptyset$;
4: $T_{peak} = T_{max}$, $T'_{peak} = T_{amb}$;
5: **while** $T'_{peak} < T_{peak}$ **do**
6: $\quad \mathfrak{N}_{active} = \mathfrak{N}, \mathbf{\Theta}' = \emptyset$;
7: $\quad$ Calculate and decreasingly sort core capacities;
8: $\quad$ Order tasks decreasingly by their utilizations;
9: $\quad$ **for** each unpacked τ_k **do**
10: $\quad\quad$ Assign τ_k to $\mathfrak{N}_{active}$;
11: $\quad\quad$ **if** failed **then**
12: $\quad\quad\quad$ Pack heavy task τ_k;
13: $\quad\quad\quad$ **if** failed **then**
14: $\quad\quad\quad\quad$ Return current best solution;
15: $\quad\quad\quad$ **end if**
16: $\quad\quad$ **end if**
17: $\quad$ **end for**
18: $\quad$ Calculate the lowest core speed for each core;
19: $\quad$ Save the current best solution;
20: $\quad$ Update T'_{peak} by current task partitioning results;
21: **end while**

One major difference between En-VSBP (Algorithm 3) and VSBP (Algorithm 2) is how to schedule *heavy task*, i.e. the task with utilization higher than any available utilization in any type. For VSBP, if a heavy task cannot fit in any type, it simply claims failure for the task partitioning. For En-VSBP, if a task cannot fit in any available type of core, we check if there is any idle core (with no task assignment) in the available active core set. If such a core does exist, we can turn other cores off (to be an inactive core), which potentially leads to a higher capacity for this core to accommodate the *heavy task*. Otherwise, there is no way we can assign the task without violating the peak temperature constraint (line 12). In addition, Algorithm 3 iteratively improves the task partitioning results. At the end of each iteration, the lowest speed that can ensure the timing constraints for the tasks allocated to that core and the peak temperature based on the task partitioning results are calculated. If the peak temperature is lower than the previous one, we can further improve the task partitioning results using the new peak temperature for the outer-most while loop (line 5-21).

The computational complexity of Algorithm 2 depends on how many iterations the algorithm needs to go through, which can be controlled using a threshold to limit the difference of peak temperatures for two consecutive iterations. Within each iteration, the complexity to compute core capacity is $O(N^3)$, sorting tasks (line 8) has a complexity of $O(MlogM)$, the bin packing (line 9-17) has a complexity of $O(MN)$, and temperature calculation has a complexity of

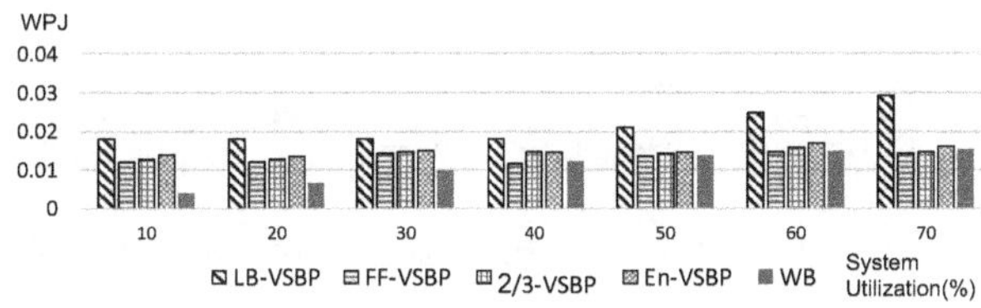

Figure 2: Energy efficiency (WPJ) on different system utilization

$O(N^3 * M)$. Therefore the overall computational complexity is $O(N^3 * M)$.

5. EXPERIMENTAL RESULTS

In this section, we compare the energy efficiency, feasibility ratio and computational cost by simulations.

The thermal and parameters are abstracted from HotSpot 5.02 and McPAT simulator [8]. There are three multi-core configurations: 3×2, 3×3 and 4×4 corresponds to 6, 9,16 cores, respectively. Each core has 6 speed modes with supply voltages $[0, 0.2, 0.4, 0.6, 0.8, 1.0]V$; the core size is $4 \times 4mm^2$ and the ambient temperature is $T_{amb} = 35°$C. The maximal allowed temperature T_{max} ranges from $55 - 70°$C (absolutely values) with a 5°C step size. The random task sets are generated by UUniFast Algorithm [1] with a uniform distribution of the periods and utilization.

Our experiments compare five approaches: (1) **LB-VSBP** identifies a lower bound of energy for thermal-balancing approach as depicted in Algorithm 1; (2) **FF-VSBP** represents Algorithm 2 with the first-fit heuristic in line 13; (3) **2/3-VSBP** represents Algorithm 2 with the 2/3 approximation heuristic in line 13; (4) **En-VSBP** is the Enhanced VSBP algorithm, as illustrated in Algorithm 3; (5) **WB** is the workload-balancing approach, as shown in [14].

5.1 Energy Efficiency (WPJ) Comparison

To compare the energy efficiency, we randomly generate 100 test cases with tasks' periods no more than $10ms$. The system utilization is defined as the sum of the utilization of all tasks divided by the total number of cores. The energy data is collected only from the task set which is feasible for all the approaches. Figure 2 shows the **LB-VSBP** method has the best result because it ideally assumes all the tasks can be perfectly split to fit the core capacity when seeking the least system resources; however, its applicability is limited. Generally, the energy efficiency of **En-VSBP** is higher than **FF-VSBP** and **2/3-VSBP**, because Algorithm 3 further reduces the leakage energy by lower down the chip temperature constraint. It is also worth noting that as the system utilization increases, the improvement between **En-VSBP** and **WB** becomes smaller, e.g. as the system utilization increases from 10% to 70%, the average improvement gradually decreases from 231.6% to 4.7% . The reason is that as the utilization increases, the leakage energy saving of the **En-VSBP** approach becomes smaller as more cores are activated; however, the total energy consumption increases dramatically. Thus, the percentage of the energy saving decreases as the total system utilization increases.

5.2 Feasibility Comparison

The feasibility ratio for each approach is defined as the

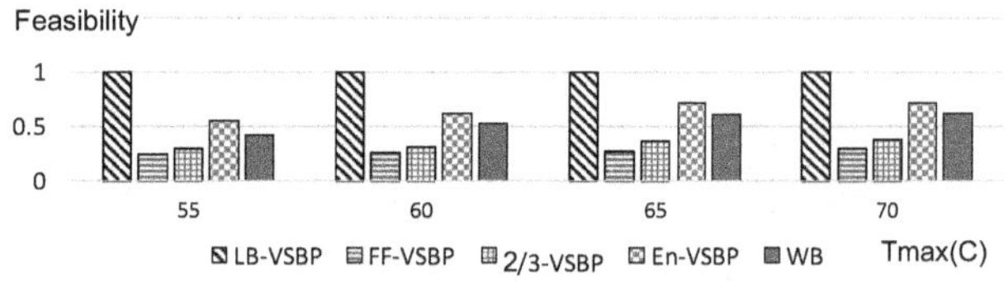

Figure 3: Feasibility comparisons on different T_{max}

Table 2: Computation time comparison (Seconds)

	6 core			9 core			16 core		
Num. Tasks	1×	2×	3×	1×	2×	3×	1×	2×	3×
LB-VSBP		0.47			3.59			378	
FF-VSBP	0.16	0.42	0.63	0.30	0.77	1.45	0.79	2.02	4.01
2/3-VSBP	0.35	0.87	1.19	0.62	1.73	2.61	2.01	5.67	11.1
En-VSBP	2.25	2.42	2.55	6.32	6.59	6.91	34.0	35.9	37.4
WB	0.17	0.39	0.67	0.32	0.73	1.29	0.90	2.17	4.12

total number of the feasible solutions divided by total randomly generated test cases. The results are normalized to **LB-VSBP**. In Figure 3, the feasibilities of all methods are non-decreasing with the increase of the maximal allowed temperature. The feasibilities of **FF-VSBP** and **2/3-VSBP** methods are extremely low, because some *heavy tasks* cannot fit into any core, especially when core capacity is small, e.g. when T_{max} is low, or when the number of active cores are large. The proposed **EN-VSBP** outperforms **WB** because the **En-VSBP** approach has a more rigorous temperature constrained policy than **WB** by limiting the different maximal allowed core utilization to satisfy T_{max}. For example, when $T_{max} = 55°\text{C}$, the proposed **En-VSBP** exceeds **WB** by 13.51%.

5.3 Computation Time Comparison

In Table 2, we listed the computational cost by different numbers of tasks selected as 1×, 2× and 3× of number of cores and each setting runs with 100 test cases. Since the **LB-VSBP** method is independent of the number of tasks, the **LB-VSBP**'s computational cost is only studied by a different number of cores.

Table 2 shows that the computational time increases as the number of cores/tasks. Although **FF-VSBP** and **2/3-VSBP** increase slower than **En-VSBP** as the design space becomes larger, **FF-VSBP** and **2/3-VSBP**'s feasibility ratio is low. The proposed **En-VSBP** shows an affordable overhead for an offline approach. **WB** method has the lowest computational time, but its energy efficiency and feasibility are pessimistic.

6. CONCLUSION

As the IC industry enters a multi-core and many-core era, the energy-efficiency becomes a more prominent criterion in design of real-time schedules. In this paper, we present a novel technique to schedule a real-time task set with maximized energy-efficiency under a given peak temperature constraint. Our techniques are built upon the *thermal-balancing* heuristic and use the *variable-sized-bin-packing* method to maximally utilize system resources under a peak temperature constraint for energy minimization purpose. Our results show an average of 37.15%, and up to 256.4% improvement of energy efficiency in comparison with the most recent existing approach.

7. ACKNOWLEDGMENTS

This work is supported in part by NSF under project CNS-1423137, CNS-1551661, CNS-1565474 and ECCS-1610471.

8. REFERENCES

[1] E. Bini and G. C. Buttazzo. Measuring the performance of schedulability tests. *Real-Time Systems*, 30(1):129–154, 2005.

[2] J. J. Chen and L. Thiele. Task partitioning and platform synthesis for energy efficiency. In *RTCSA*, pages 393–402, 2009.

[3] M. Fan, V. Chaturvedi, S. Sha, and G. Quan. An analytical solution for multi-core energy calculation with consideration of leakage and temperature dependency. In *ISLPED*, pages 353–358, 2013.

[4] D. K. Friesen and M. A. Langston. Variable sized bin packing. *SIAM J. Comput.*, 15(1):222–230, Feb. 1986.

[5] V. Hanumaiah and S. Vrudhula. Energy-efficient operation of multicore processors by dvfs, task migration, and active cooling. *IEEE Transactions on Computers*, 63(2):349–360, 2014.

[6] H. Izakian, A. Abraham, and V. Snasel. Comparison of heuristics for scheduling independent tasks on heterogeneous distributed environments. In *CSO*, volume 1, pages 8–12, April 2009.

[7] D. Li and J. Wu. Minimizing energy consumption for frame-based tasks on heterogeneous multiprocessor platforms. *IEEE Transactions on Parallel and Distributed Systems*, 26(3):810–823, March 2015.

[8] S. Li, J. H. Ahn, R. D. Strong, J. B. Brockman, D. M. Tullsen, and N. P. Jouppi. Mcpat: An integrated power, area, and timing modeling framework for multicore and manycore architectures. In *MICRO*, pages 469–480, 2009.

[9] R. Rao and S. Vrudhula. Efficient online computation of core speeds to maximize the throughput of thermally constrained multi-core processors. In *ICCAD*, pages 537–542, 2008.

[10] S. Saha, Y. Lu, and J. S. Deogun. Thermal-constrained energy-aware partitioning for heterogeneous multi-core multiprocessor real-time systems. In *RTCSA*, pages 41–50, 2012.

[11] S. Sha, W. Wen, M. Fan, S. Ren, and G. Quan. Performance maximization via frequency oscillation on temperature constrained multi-core processors. In *ICPP*, pages 526–535, 2016.

[12] W. Sun and T. Sugawara. Heuristics and evaluations of energy-aware task mapping on heterogeneous multiprocessors. In *IPDPSW*, pages 599–607, 2011.

[13] A. N. Zehmakan. Bin packing problem: Two approximation algorithms. *International Journal in Foundations of Computer Science and Technology*, 5(4):1–11, 2015.

[14] J. Zhou, T. Wei, M. Chen, J. Yan, S. Hu, and Y. Ma. Thermal-aware task scheduling for energy minimization in heterogeneous real-time mpsoc systems. *IEEE Transactions on Computer-Aided Design of Integrated Circuits and Systems*, PP(99):1–1, 2015.

Quantitative Modeling of Thermo-Optic Effects in Optical Networks-on-Chip

Weichen Liu*
Chongqing University
Chongqing, China

Peng Wang
Chongqing University
Chongqing, China

Mengquan Li
Chongqing University
Chongqing, China

Yiyuan Xie
Southwest University
Chongqing, China

Nan Guan
Hong Kong Polytechnic University
Hong Kong

ABSTRACT

Optical networks-on-chip (ONoCs) is a new promising communication paradigm that upgrades the traditional on-chip networks (NoCs) with the ultra-high communication bandwidth and low latency. Silicon microring resonators (MRRs), as a critical component of ONoCs used to implement the selection and redirection of optical signals, are inherently sensitive to the environmental temperature. The applicability of the ONoCs is essentially restricted by the performance of these optical devices that relies on the thermal conditions of the chip. In this paper, we study the thermo-optic effects of the MRRs quantitatively, build and verify the models of the MRRs based on the finite-difference time-domain (FDTD) method. We present formal relationship models between the temperature of a MRR and its optical losses and resonance wavelength. For the first time, the variation between the two types of MRRs, the parallel microring resonators (PMRs) and the crossing microring resonators (CMRs), are systematically addressed, which greatly improves the accuracy and applicability of the models. The results presented in this paper are systematically verified using professional optics methodology, and can be widely applied for accurate and efficient analysis of the thermo-optic effects in different domains of the ONoC community.

Keywords

Silicon microring resonator; Thermo-optic effects; Optical network-on-chip

1. INTRODUCTION

Dark silicon problems have become one of the biggest restrictions on the development of traditional on-chip networks (NoCs) [1]. Optical networks-on-chip (ONoCs), as a promising update to NoCs, also faces the threat of temperature and sometimes even worse. To reduce or eliminate the thermo-optic effects on ONoCs has been one of the most significant works on the progress of ONoCs. The optical devices, whose performances are influenced by the temperature deeply, are essential to generate/transmit/convert the optical signal in optical networks. The VCSEL (Vertical Cavity Surface Emitting Laser) is one of the most widely used laser emitters for generating the optical signal in optical networks with a small volume and low energy consumption. The temperature can affect the resonance wavelength of cavity in the VCSEL in an exponential order [2, 3]. The basic function of the optical router is transmitting the optical signal to its destination. The router takes extra power to eliminate the effects of the temperature and other factors [4]. The photodetector can convert the detected optical signal into electrical signal. The dark current of the photodetector at 85 °C is 10 times that at 10 °C [5, 6].

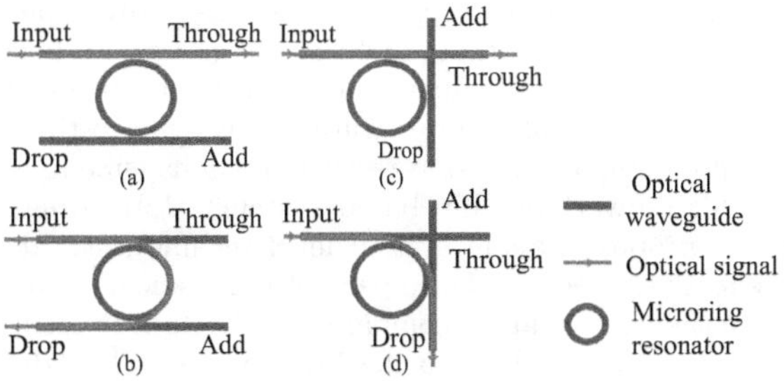

Figure 1: The microring resonators. (a) the PMR in the OFF state; (b) the PMR in the ON state; (c) the CMR in the OFF state; (d) the CMR in the ON state.

Silicon microring resonators (MRRs), the basic components of the optical devices, are crucial for the performance of the devices and ONoCs. Studying the thermo-optic effects on the MRRs is very important for studying those on the devices and ONoCs. There are two types of MRRs. One is the parallel microring resonators (PMRs), and the other is the crossing microring resonators (CMRs). As shown in Figure 1, a PMR has two parallel waveguides and an optical waveguide which is looped back on itself. A CMR consists of two vertical waveguides and a looped waveguide. When

*Corresponding author: Weichen Liu.
Email: {mengquan,pengw,wliu}@cqu.edu.cn.

Permission to make digital or hard copies of all or part of this work for personal or classroom use is granted without fee provided that copies are not made or distributed for profit or commercial advantage and that copies bear this notice and the full citation on the first page. Copyrights for components of this work owned by others than ACM must be honored. Abstracting with credit is permitted. To copy otherwise, or republish, to post on servers or to redistribute to lists, requires prior specific permission and/or a fee. Request permissions from permissions@acm.org.

GLSVLSI '17, May 10 - 12, 2017, Banff, AB, Canada.
© 2017 ACM. ISBN 978-1-4503-4972-7/17/05...$15.00.
DOI: http://dx.doi.org/10.1145/3060403.3060457

the resonance of MRRs occurs, the incident signal light from the input-port is delivered into the drop-port, corresponding to the state of ON. On the contrary, it is directly delivered through the through-port, corresponding to the state of OFF.

The thermo-optic effects are the well-known physical phenomena in the photonics. These phenomena existing in the MRRs have a great impact on the performances of optical devices. The temperature shift changes the refractive index of silicon, and then alters the resonance wavelength and optical losses of the MRRs. If the temperature rises, the resonance wavelength will increase. Conversely, if the temperature drops, the resonance wavelength will decrease.

In this paper, we analyze the basic thermal theories in ONoCs through studying the thermo-optic effects of MRRs quantitatively, build and verify the models of MRRs based on the finite-difference time-domain (FDTD) method.

The contributions of this paper are listed below: firstly, our work is *fundamental and essential* for the later researches on optimizing the optical devices and ONoCs. The theories and models in this paper are very important for the initial designs and optimization in ONoCs. Secondly, it is the first time to quantitatively analyze the variation between the PMRs and CMRs under different temperatures, which is one of the foremost concern of ONoCs designers.

The rest of this paper is structured as follow: the related work is discussed in Section 2; Section 3 introduces an overview of the thermo-optic effects; Section 4 presents the model between the resonance wavelength of MRRs and temperature; Section 5 shows the model between the optical losses of the PMR and temperature; Section 6 presents the variation between the optical losses of the PMR and those of the CMR. And the optical losses model of the CMR is also presented; Experiments and analysis are given in Section 7; we draw the conclusions in Section 8.

2. RELATED WORK

Dark silicon refers to a phenomenon that only a part of a many-core chip is working and the others have to become "dark" or "dim" at the same time, in order to ensure that the system is in a safe temperature range. Due to the dark silicon problem, thermal-aware system management is essential for network-on-chip based systems. Liu, Yang and li *et al.* proposed many system level techniques that not only effectively reduce the impact of dark silicon, but also improve the performances compared to the traditional structure, such as a folded torus-like NoC, a thermal model for the chip peak temperature prediction and so on [1, 7, 8, 9, 10]. In ONoCs, the impact of thermal effects in the MRRs are also very important to the performances of devices and whole system.

The thermo-optic effects in the MRRs derive from the thermal reaction of the silicon. Investigations of the thermal sensitivities of silicon show that the silicon has significant thermo-optic effects and its refractive index is almost linear growth with the temperature. The thermo-optic coefficient(dn/dT) of silicon is on the order of $10^{-4}/K$ [11, 12]. The variation of silicon refractive index can directly influence the resonance wavelength of MRRs through the couple mode theory, when the perimeter and the series of waveform of MRR are fixed [13].

As the MRRs have played an important role in the success of silicon optical devices, the performance of MRRs was gained much attention of many researchers. Chan *et al.* presented a methodology for characterizing and modeling the fundamental elements of optical devices and analyzed the optical losses of the PMR and CMR [14]. Xie *et al.* discussed the crosstalk noise and the optical losses in the PMR and CMR [15]. However, they didn't consider the effects of temperature on the optical losses. The studies indicated that the losses and resonance wavelength of PMR have a corresponding relationship [16, 17]. They presented an analytical model to quantify the optical losses of PMR in the resonators and bends. In order to calculate the losses, the model needed to obtain the resonance wavelength of PMR. And after analyzing the relationship between the resonance wavelength and temperature, there was a new thermo-optic effects model to quantify the optical losses. But they didn't discuss the thermo-optic effects of the CMR.

3. OVERVIEW OF THE THERMO-OPTIC EFFECTS

The refractive index of silicon MRRs is affected by the temperature significantly and the variation of it results in the thermo-optic effects. The resonance wavelength and the optical losses are directly or indirectly affected by the change of refractive index. There are progressive physical relationships between these three properties of MRRs and the temperature. First of all, the ambient temperature affects the refractive index of silicon, causing it to be increased or decreased with the increasing/decreasing temperature, respectively. Then, the resonance wavelength of MRRs is influenced by the variation of refractive index and remains monotonicity with the same tendency. Finally, the shift of resonance wavelength creates a mismatch between the wavelength of the incident light and the resonance wavelength of MRRs, which causes that a part of the light can not couple into the ring cavity. A change of the optical losses occurs.

Our quantitative analysis of the thermo-optic effects is fundamental and essential for the study of optical devices and ONoCs. The thermo-optic effects instinctually exist in the optical devices and ONoCs. They can affect the performances of them and make a great difference between the design situation and the actual situation. The models in the subsequent sections can be considered as the estimation and verification methods of the thermo-optic effects. The variation model is a new method to calculate the optical losses of the CMR. It has greatly positive effects on the future optimization designs of ONoCs.

In the subsequent sections, we mainly discuss the relationships between the ambient temperature and the resonance wavelength and optical losses of a MRR. According to the different application requirements, we build the thermo-optic effects models to describe the relations. After that, we propose a variation model between the optical losses of a PMR and those of a CMR under different temperatures for the first time, in order to increase the accuracy and applicability of the models.

4. EFFECTS ON THE RESONANCE WAVELENGTH

In general, a MRR consists of a looped optical waveguide and a coupling mechanism to access the loop. It is one of the most valuable working principles that the MRR can precisely couple the light whose wavelength is accordant with the resonant wavelength(λ_{res}) of the MRR, and discard the other light. While the wavelength of the light fits a whole number of times inside the optical length of the ring, the waves interfere constructively and the cavity is in resonance. The resonance condition is drawn as:

$$\lambda_{res} \cdot m = L \cdot n_{eff} \quad (1)$$

where L is the perimeter of the ring cavity, m is a positive integer denoted the mode number of the ring resonator and n_{eff} is the effective index of the waveguide.

According to Equation 1, the λ_{res} has a linear relationship with the n_{eff}. And the n_{eff} varies with the temperature and wavelength [13].

$$\Delta_{n_{eff}} = \frac{\partial_{n_{eff}}}{\partial_\beta} \cdot \frac{\partial_\beta}{\partial_T} \cdot \Delta T + \frac{\partial_{n_{eff}}}{\partial_\lambda} \cdot \Delta\lambda \quad (2)$$

$$n_{group} = n_{eff} - \lambda \frac{\partial_{n_{eff}}}{\partial_\lambda} \quad (3)$$

where $\Delta_{n_{eff}}$, ΔT and $\Delta\lambda$ are represented the the variation of the n_{eff}, temperature and wavelength, respectively. β is the relative dielectric constant. And the n_{group} is the group refractive index of the waveguide.

Combining the three formulas above, we can gain the variation coefficient (α) of the resonance wavelength under different temperatures, when $\lambda = \lambda_{res_0}$:

$$\alpha = \frac{\Delta_{n_{eff}}}{m} L = \frac{\lambda_{res_0}}{n_{group}} \cdot \frac{d_{n_{eff}}}{d_T} \quad (4)$$

where λ_{res_0} is the initial resonance wavelength of a MRR. $d_{n_{eff}}/d_T = \frac{\partial_{n_{eff}}}{\partial_\beta} \cdot \frac{\partial_\beta}{\partial_T} \cdot \Delta T$ is the thermo-optic effects coefficient of the effective refractive index, which is slower than the refractive index of silicon($(d_n/d_T) = (1.86 \pm 0.08) \times 10^{-4}/K$) [18]. The n_{group} is about 4.63 at $1.55\mu m$.

Therefore, a linear relationship between λ_{res} and ambient temperature T can be draw as:

$$\lambda_{res} = \lambda_{ref} + \alpha \cdot (T - T_{ref}) \quad (5)$$

where λ_{ref} and T_{ref} are the reference resonance wavelength and the corresponding reference temperature.

An one-to-one linear relationship can be obtained. One of the variables, λ_{res} or T in Equation 5, can be calculated if the other one is measured. This model is applicable to both the PMRs and the CMRs.

5. EFFECTS ON THE OPTICAL LOSSES

The losses of a MRR can be separated into two different parts: waveguide propagation losses and the losses in the coupling section. There is an extra losses due to the mismatch between the light wavelength and λ_{res}, considering the influence of ambient temperature. As shown in Figure 1(a) and 1(b), there are four power values can be detected in the four ports, respectively. The P_{in} as the input optical power, is injected by the input-port. The $P_{through}$ is the transmitted optical power delivered from the through-port. The filtered or detected optical power from the drop-port is P_{drop}, whose optical losses are what we concern. And the feedback optical power detected from the add-port is P_{add}. Without considering the P_{add}, the relation among them is $P_{drop} = P_{in} - P_{through}$, by the energy conservation.

We use the k^2 to represent the fraction of optical power that the input waveguide couple into the ring cavity and the fraction of optical power that the output waveguide couple out of the ring cavity on the symmetrically coupled MRRs. The power transmission of a PMR is [19]:

$$\frac{P_{drop}}{P_{in}} = \frac{4(k^2)^2 \cdot a}{(\lambda_{in} - \lambda_{res})^2 + (2k^2 + k_p^2)^2 \cdot a}, \quad a = (\frac{\lambda_{ref}^2}{2\pi c})^2 \quad (6)$$

where k_p^2 is the fraction of intrinsic optical losses per round-trip in the MRRs, which can be caused by the bending and the roughness of the waveguide. λ_{in} is the incident light wavelength from the input-port. c is the speed of the light in the vacuum.

We assume that γ_t is the optical power transmission from the through-port, while the state of the PMR is ON. FSR is the free spectral range and $FWHM$ is the full width at half maximum of the resonance spectrum for the PMR. When $\lambda_{in} = \lambda res$, we can gain the $k_p^2 = \frac{2\pi \times FWHM \cdot \sqrt{\gamma_t}}{FSR}$ and $k^2 = \frac{\pi \times FWHM \cdot (1-\sqrt{\gamma_t})}{FSR}$ [17]:

Substituting the λ_{res} from Equation 5 into Equation 6, the relationship between the optical losses of a PMR (L_p) and the temperature can be acted as:

$$L_p = 10log10(\frac{(\lambda_{in} - \lambda_{ref} - \alpha \cdot (T - T_{ref}))^2 + b}{c}) \quad (7)$$

In Equation 7, the $b = (2k^2 + k_p^2)^2 \cdot a$ and $c = 4(k^2)^2 \cdot a$ can be considered as constants, because the k^2 and k_p^2 are calculated by FSR, γ_t and $FWHM$, which are nearly invariable with the temperature variation. So, there is only one unknown variable of T on the right. Finally, we obtain the relation model between the optical losses and the temperature of a PMR.

However, this model considers only the case of the PMR. In order to obtain the optical losses of a CMR, we analyze the variation of the optical losses between a CMR and a PMR, and propose a quantifiable model for their variation. In the subsequent section, we will discuss the variation and the corresponding model.

6. THE VARIATION OF THE OPTICAL LOSSES

Because the optical losses of a CMR (L_c) can not be simply calculated by Equation 7, we research the variation of the optical losses between the PMR and CMR. A large number of experiments and theories show that the optical losses of a PMR and those of a CMR are affected by temperature differently [15]. The cross of two straight waveguides in the CMR will add the additional crosstalk noise comparing to the PMR, as shown in Figure 2. The crosstalk noise makes differences between the optical losses of a CMR and those of a PMR under the different temperatures. We experimentally study their differences and propose a variation model to quantify it. The relationship between the losses of the CMR and temperature is further derived.

First of all, we assume a relation coefficient $\eta = L_p/L_c$, and the $\eta = f(T)$ is varied with the ambient temperature to show the differences between the optical losses of a CMR and those of a PMR. As shown in Figure 3, the η is segmented as the temperature changes. When the variation of the temperature is small, most of the light couples into the

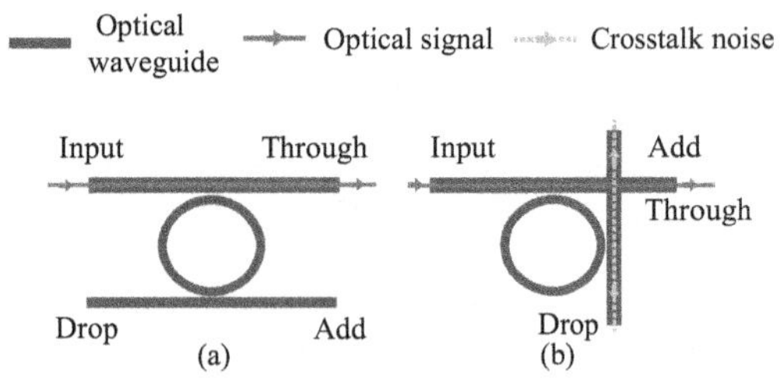

Figure 2: The crosstalk noise

ring cavity and is delivered to the drop-port both in a CMR and a PMR. The impact of the crosstalk noise is small to the optical losses, due to the magnitude of the optical losses is very bigger than that of the crosstalk noise. But, when the temperature variation reaches a certain critical value, most of the light is delivered to the through-port. Ignoring the crosstalk noise that occurs between the ring cavity and straight waveguide both in a CMR and a PMR, the impact of the crosstalk noise occurring in the cross will be correspondingly increased a lot with the reduction of the optical losses. And then the optical losses of a CMR will be smaller than those of a PMR.

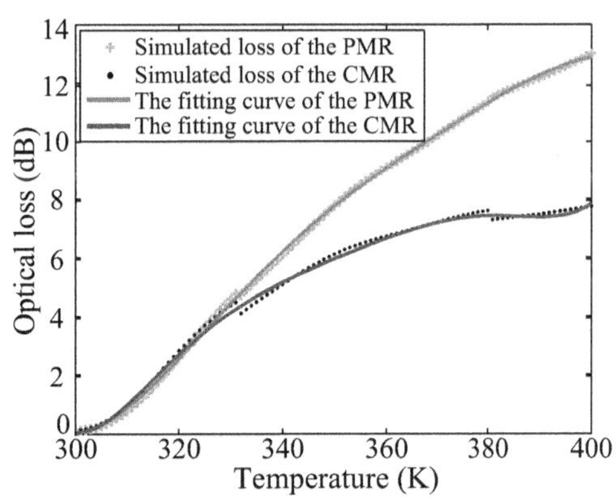

Figure 3: The variation between the optical losses of a PMR and those of a CMR

In the different segments, there are good linear relationships between the η and the temperature, with the correlation coefficients of $\sim$ 0.9962 in the first segment and ~ -0.9938 in the second segment. So, we present a linear and segmented relation model as:

$$\eta = \begin{cases} a_1 * T + b_1 & T_{ref} <= T < T_{cri}, \\ a_2 * T + b_2 & T_{cri} <= T <= T_{lim}. \end{cases} \quad (8)$$

An then, we can also build a new relation model between L_c and temperature through the model in Equation 7 of the PMR.

$$L_c = \frac{10log10(\frac{(\lambda_{in} - \lambda_{ref} - \alpha \cdot (T - T_{ref}))^2 + b}{c})}{\eta} \quad (9)$$

where the relationship between L_c and T can be one temperature corresponding to one value of the optical losses, as same as Equation 7.

7. EXPERIMENTS

In this section, we use the FDTD method to vary the thermo-optic effects models discussed in the previous sections. The FDTD method is a numerical analysis technique used for the simulation and computation in the electrodynamics. It has a wide range of material types, accurate simulation results and a high degree of recognition in the optics area. We compare the theoretical modeling values with the simulation values to vary the accuracy of the thermo-optic effects models. In Section 7.1 and 7.2, we verify the thermo-optic effects models in Section 4, 5 and 6. We further validate the correctness of the variation model of the PMR and CMR with the extracted coefficients from the simulation results in Section 7.3.

We construct a PMR and a CMR with the typical and identical parameters and simulate them via the FDTD method. The parameters of the subsequent parts are as following: the gap between the ring cavity and the straight is 100 nm; the radius of the ring cavity is 4 μm; and the cross section of the waveguide is 180×400 nm. The refractive indexes of the silicon are set as varying with the temperature, which is in the range from 300 K to 400 K.

7.1 The resonance wavelength V.S. temperature

To study the performance of the resonance wavelength and temperature model, we compare the simulation and modeling values of the resonance wavelengths under different temperatures. As we can seen in Figure 4, the relationships between the resonance wavelength and temperature are one-to-one linear relationships corresponding to Equation 5, both in the PMR and CMR. The figure shows the model can have a good description to the relationships between the temperature and resonance wavelength. The average errors between the simulation values and modeling values are 0.14 nm and 0.12 nm of the PMR and the CMR, respectively. This indicates that the resonance wavelength and temperature model are applicable for both the PMR and the CMR, and can accurately calculate the values of the resonance wavelength at the corresponding temperature.

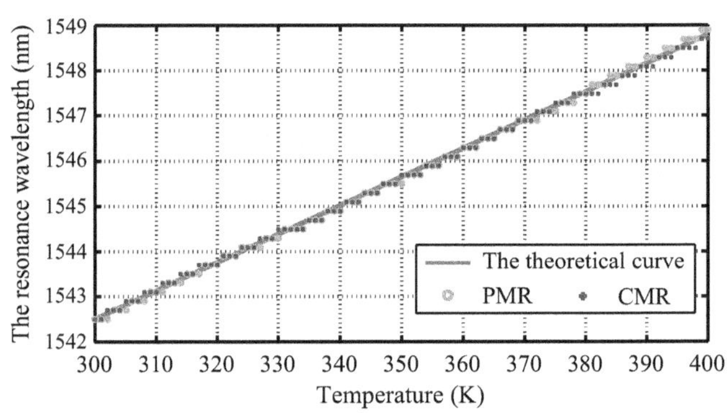

Figure 4: The resonant wavelengthes under different temperatures of a PMR and a CMR

In ONoCs, the model may be used to assist the adjustments of the resonance wavelength in order to improve the information transmission rates which are influenced by the temperature. Next, this model may be used to estimate and verify the accuracy in the design of optical devices or ONoCs and assist to avoid that the effect of temperature on the resonance wavelength leads to a large differences between the actual results and the design values.

7.2 The optical losses V.S. temperature

In this section, we select the incident light, whose wavelength is the resonance wavelength of MRRs about 1543 nm, at the reference temperature of 300 K. As shown in Equation 7, the relationship between the optical losses and temperature is a quadratic corresponding relation. There will be two temperatures under the same optical losses. However according to Equation 5, the λ_{res} will shift 6 nm in the concerned temperature range of $[300k - 400k]$. The FSR in our experiments is ~ 23 nm, which shows that there is a monotonic interval in the wavelength region of ~ 11.5 nm. So, if we select a suitable wavelength of the incident light and a reasonable reference temperature as choosen above, we can get a one-to-one corresponding relationship in the concerned temperature region as shown in Figure 5.

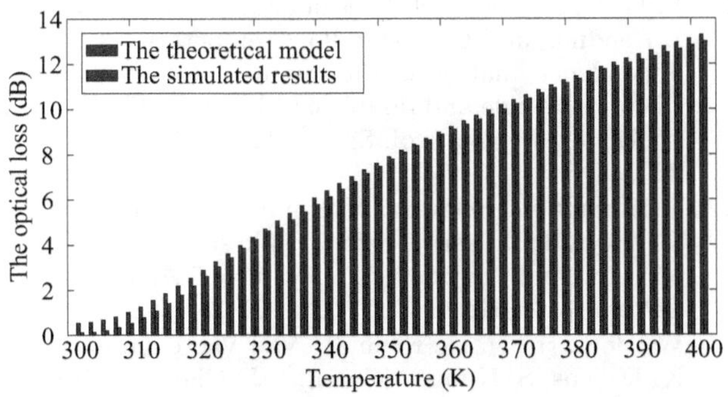

(a) The relation between the optical losses of a PMR and temperature

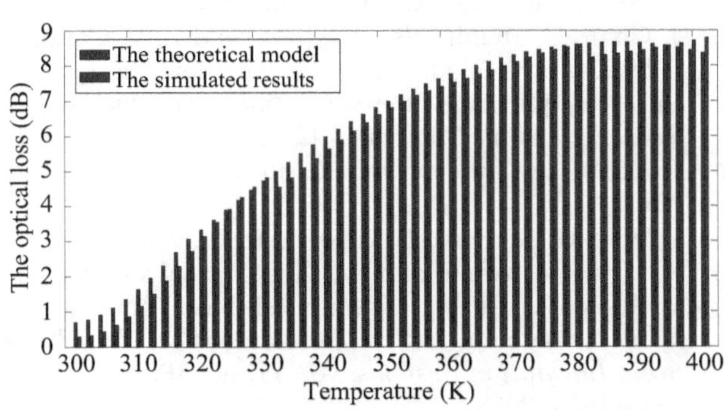

(b) The relation between the optical losses of a CMR and temperature

Figure 5: The optical losses under different temperatures of a PMR and a CMR

In Figure 5(a), we can obtain that the optical losses of a PMR increases monotonically with temperatures in $[300\ K - 400\ K]$, which is one of the concerned temperature regions in ONoCs. The average error between the simulation values and modeling values is ~ 0.23 dB. Combining the figure and the average error, it is shown that this model can be considered as a good expression of the relationship between the optical losses of a PMR and the temperature. The result indicates that the model can work better in the high temperature region, which is more concerned by ONoCs than the low temperature region.

In Figure 5(b), the average error between the simulation values and modeling values is ~ 0.84 dB. It explains that the model of temperature and optical losses of a CMR can precisely calculate the optical losses of CMR. Compared with the model of PMR, the overall error of CMR model is bigger. But, they each have their own intervals in which the performance of the model is better than the other one, separately.

In ONoCs, the models may be used to assist to compensate the optical losses of light power influenced by the temperature. The designer can calculate the compensation amount through the models. Besides, the models may also used to help to design the routing algorithm. The designer can calculate the optical losses of routing pathes and select the path whose optical losses are the minimum.

7.3 The optical losses variation

In order to accurately gain the optical losses of CMR under different temperatures, we analyze the variation relationship between the optical losses of CMR and PMR and assume a relationship coefficient η to show the relationship. As shown in Figure 6, the relationship is segmented in two segments. Through the analysis of the correlation coefficients between η and the temperature, we find that the two segments have the good linear relationships with temperature. In the first segment, the correlation coefficient is ~ 0.9962, and it is ~ -0.9938 in the second segment. This explains that the η and temperature have a strong linear relationship in the two segments.

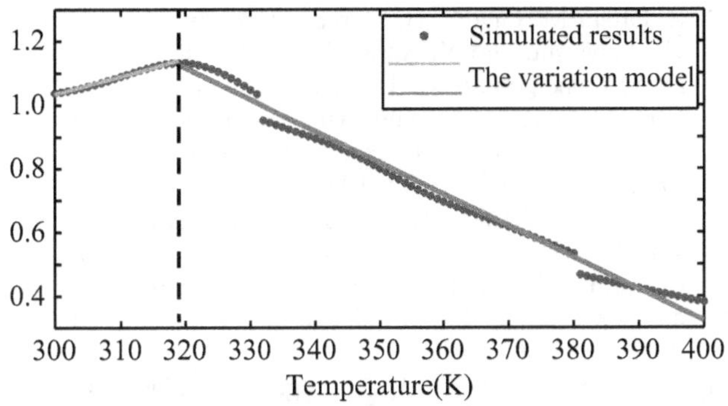

Figure 6: The coefficient η and fitting values under different temperatures

So, we fit the $\eta = L_p/L_c$ in two steps. The first step is to fit the η in $[300\ K - 320\ K]$ in order to obtain the parameters a_1 and b_1 in the Equation 8. The determination coefficient of the fitting curve is ~ 0.9923 and the standard deviation is ~ 0.0030. In the second step, we fit the η in $[320\ K - 400\ K]$ to get the parameters a_2 and b_2 with a determination coefficient ~ 0.9876 and a standard deviation ~ 0.026. This shows that the two fitting results are good.

And then, we calculate the η under different temperatures through the fitting coefficients, respectively. Substituting the η into Equation 9, we gain the modeling values of the CMR under different temperatures and compare them with the simulation values in the Figure 5(b).

In ONoCs, this model may be used to gain the optical losses of a CMR, when we only have the optical losses of a PMR under the same ambient temperature. While we design the optical devices or ONoCs, it may be used to assist to calculate the single or total optical losses, on the condition of that we only need to detect the optical losses of the PMRs under the same circumstances.

8. CONCLUSIONS

In this paper, we quantitatively studied the thermo-optic effects in ONoCs. Formulas are presented to describe the relationships between the temperature of a MRR and its resonance wavelength and optical losses. In addition, we analyzed the variation between the behavior of the thermo-optic effects in the PMRs and that in the CMRs for the first time. With the help of variation model, the relationship between the optical losses of the CMR and the temperature is well described. The findings in this paper will lay a foundation for the future research in ONoCs and may be applied to improve the performances of ONoCs.

Acknowledgments

This work is partially supported by NSFC No. 61402060, National 863 Program 2015AA015304, and Chongqing High-Tech Research Program cstc2015jcyjA40042, China.

9. REFERENCES

[1] L. Yang, W. Liu, W. Jiang, C. Chen, M. Li, P. Chen, and H. Edwin, "Hardware-software collaboration for dark silicon heterogeneous many-core systems," *Future Generation Computer Systems*, vol. 68, pp. 234–247, 2017.

[2] S. Chen, M. Okano, B. Zhang, M. Yoshita, H. Akiyama, and Y. Kanemitsu, "Blue 6-ps short-pulse generation in gain-switched ingan vertical-cavity surface-emitting lasers via impulsive optical pumping," *Applied Physics Letters*, vol. 101, no. 19, pp. 191 108 – 191 108–3, 2012.

[3] J. Wu, W. Xiao, and Y.-M. Lu, "Temperature and wavelength dependence of gain and threshold current detuning with cavity resonance in vertical-cavity surface-emitting lasers," *IET Optoelectronics*, vol. 5, no. 1, pp. 206–210, 2007.

[4] Y. Ye, X. Wu, J. Xu, W. Zhang, M. Nikdast, and X. Wang, "Holistic comparison of optical routers for chip multiprocessors," in *Anti-Counterfeiting, Security and Identification (ASID), 2012 International Conference on.* IEEE, 2012, pp. 1–5.

[5] Z. Sheng, L. Liu, J. Brouckaert, S. He, and D. Van Thourhout, "Ingaas pin photodetectors integrated on silicon-on-insulator waveguides," *Optics express*, vol. 18, no. 2, pp. 1756–1761, 2010.

[6] S. Koester, L. Schares, C. L. Schow, G. Dehlinger, and R. John, "Temperature-dependent analysis of ge-on-soi photodetectors and receivers," in *Group IV Photonics, 2006. 3rd IEEE International Conference on.* IEEE, 2006, pp. 179–181.

[7] L. Yang, W. Liu, N. Guan, M. Li, P. Chen, and H. Edwin, "Dark silicon-aware hardware-software collaborated design for heterogeneous many-core systems," in *Design Automation Conference (ASP-DAC), 2017 22nd Asia and South Pacific.* IEEE, 2017, pp. 494–499.

[8] L. Yang, W. Liu, W. Jiang, M. Li, J. Yi, and E. H.-M. Sha, "Fotonoc: A hierarchical management strategy based on folded lorus-like network-on-chip for dark silicon many-core systems," in *Design Automation Conference (ASP-DAC), 2016 21st Asia and South Pacific.* IEEE, 2016, pp. 725–730.

[9] L. Yang, W. Liu, W. Jiang, M. Li, P. Chen, and E. Sha, "Fotonoc: A folded torus-like network-on-chip based many-core systems-on-chip in the dark silicon era," *IEEE Transactions on Parallel and Distributed Systems*, 2016.

[10] M. Li, J. Yi, W. Liu, W. Zhang, L. Yang, and E. H.-M. Sha, "An efficient technique for chip temperature optimization of multiprocessor systems in the dark silicon era," in *High Performance Computing and Communications (HPCC), 2015 IEEE 7th International Symposium on Cyberspace Safety and Security (CSS), 2015 IEEE 12th International Conferen on Embedded Software and Systems (ICESS), 2015 IEEE 17th International Conference on.* IEEE, 2015, pp. 688–693.

[11] F. G. Della Corte, M. E. Montefusco, L. Moretti, I. Rendina, and G. Cocorullo, "Temperature dependence analysis of the thermo-optic effect in silicon by single and double oscillator models," *Journal of Applied Physics*, vol. 88, no. 12, pp. 7115–7119, 2000.

[12] J. Komma, C. Schwarz, G. Hofmann, D. Heinert, and R. Nawrodt, "Thermo-optic coefficient of silicon at 1550 nm and cryogenic temperatures," *Applied Physics Letters*, vol. 101, no. 4, p. 1905, 2012.

[13] W. Bogaerts, P. De Heyn, T. Van Vaerenbergh, K. De Vos, S. Kumar Selvaraja, T. Claes, P. Dumon, P. Bienstman, D. Van Thourhout, and R. Baets, "Silicon microring resonators," *Laser & Photonics Reviews*, vol. 6, no. 1, pp. 47–73, 2012.

[14] J. Chan, G. Hendry, K. Bergman, and L. P. Carloni, "Physical-layer modeling and system-level design of chip-scale photonic interconnection networks," *IEEE Transactions on Computer-Aided Design of Integrated Circuits and Systems*, vol. 30, no. 10, pp. 1507–1520, 2011.

[15] Y. Xie, M. Nikdast, J. Xu, X. Wu, W. Zhang, Y. Ye, X. Wang, Z. Wang, and W. Liu, "Formal worst-case analysis of crosstalk noise in mesh-based optical networks-on-chip," *IEEE Transactions on Very Large Scale Integration Systems*, vol. 21, no. 10, pp. 1823–1836, 2013.

[16] Y. Vlasov and S. McNab, "Losses in single-mode silicon-on-insulator strip waveguides and bends," *Optics express*, vol. 12, no. 8, pp. 1622–1631, 2004.

[17] S. Xiao, M. H. Khan, H. Shen, and M. Qi, "Modeling and measurement of losses in silicon-on-insulator resonators and bends," *Optics Express*, vol. 15, no. 17, pp. 10 553–10 561, 2007.

[18] R. Amatya, C. W. Holzwarth, M. A. Popovic, and F. Gan, "Low power thermal tuning of second-order microring resonators," in *Conference on Lasers and Electro-Optics*, 2007, pp. 1–2.

[19] B. E. Little, S. T. Chu, H. A. Haus, J. Foresi, and J.-P. Laine, "Microring resonator channel dropping filters," *Journal of lightwave technology*, vol. 15, no. 6, pp. 998–1005, 1997.

A Reconfigurable Replica Bitline to Determine Optimum SRAM Sense Amplifier Set Time

Samira Ataei and James E. Stine
Department of Electrical and Computer Engineering
VLSI Computer Architecture Research Group
Oklahoma State University
Stillwater, OK 74078, USA
{ataei, james.stine}@okstate.edu

ABSTRACT

Process variation in deep nanometer technologies causes read, write and retention failures in SRAM and results in yield loss. Although using larger transistors and higher supply voltages helps to mitigate these failures and improve the yield, they come at the cost of more power consumption, more area overhead and performance degradation. Reconfigurable control-signal circuits in SRAM not only help to reduce the failure rates, but also allow calibration after fabrication to improve the yield, reduce the power consumption and upgrade the performance. In this paper, a reconfigurable replica bitline scheme for sense amplifier set time is proposed to reduce the read failures and provide a wide operating-voltage range for SRAM. The proposed reconfigurable replica bitline also allows recalibration when SRAM performance deteriorates due to device aging degradation. Monte Carlo simulation results for a 64 kb SRAM array show that the proposed technique can reduce the access time by 20% compared to conventional replica bitline design in IBM/Global Foundries (GF) cmos32soi 32nm technology at 0.9 V with no area overhead.

Keywords

SRAM, Random process variation, Sense amplifier timing, Reconfigurable replica bitline

1. INTRODUCTION

Sensing failures which are related to the performance variation of SRAM and improper setup time of amplifiers (SAs) can be reduced by using a variable control-signal generator to restrain the optimum sense amplifier enable (SAE) signal. The sense amplifier allows the read access to speed up the SRAM and reduce its access time by amplifying a small swing on heavily-loaded bitlines. An accurate enable time for the sense amplifier is critical, because if the SA enables early when the developed swing on the bitlines is smaller than the input offset voltage of the SA, a read failure may occur. Conversely, if the SA enables late, power consumption and the access time of SRAM will increase.

With the pronounced effects of random process variations within deep nanometer technologies, defining the optimum SAE time becomes more desirable. Conventional replica bitline (RBL) delay techniques [1], although less sensitive to variations in process, voltage and temperature (PVT) compared to an inverter delay chain, are fixed at design time and do not allow a dynamic power-yield management. Besides, increased local threshold voltage variation in scaled process nodes make conventional RBLs less accurate in finding the optimum SAE time.

Several circuit techniques have been proposed to improve the accuracy of SAE time; multi stage RBL [2] [3], digitized RBL [4] and configurable RBL [5]. These schemes reduce the effect of process variations in SAE by averaging the signal. Although these techniques are more effective to generate less sensitive SAE signals and improve SRAM access times compared to conventional RBLs, they are still all fixed at design time and cannot be adjusted later (e.g., post-production silicon). And most importantly, these designs cannot be easily ported from one operating voltage to another. On the other hand, statistical methods to generate SA timing, such as methodologies in [6] and [7], are based on the worst-case delay generation that results in extra power consumption and performance degradation.

In [8], a built-in self-test timing-tracking scheme is presented to automatically define the control code for optimum variable delay element. In this technique the output of RBL is connected to an inverter chain and several transmission gates. Transmission gates are controlled by predefined control codes and add delay to the SAE signal, when needed. This technique only generates SAE timings that have equal or bigger delay compare to conventional RBL circuitry and does not produce faster SAE signal with smaller delay. Besides, by using transmission and inverter gates, variation on the SAE signal increase which eventually results in larger access times. In another technique, a programmable delay element [9] provides a variable delay for the SAE signal. Again, this technique does not generate faster SAE signal and increases the timing deviation (σ) of the generated SAE signal (considering a normal distribution for SAE timing with μ_{SAE} (mean) and σ_{SAE} (deviation)).

In this paper, a reconfigurable replica bitline is proposed to find the optimum timing with minimum deviation for the set time of SA. This technique is suitable for SRAMs that support a wide range of different applications in dif-

Permission to make digital or hard copies of all or part of this work for personal or classroom use is granted without fee provided that copies are not made or distributed for profit or commercial advantage and that copies bear this notice and the full citation on the first page. Copyrights for components of this work owned by others than ACM must be honored. Abstracting with credit is permitted. To copy otherwise, or republish, to post on servers or to redistribute to lists, requires prior specific permission and/or a fee. Request permissions from permissions@acm.org.

GLSVLSI '17, May 10-12, 2017, Banff, AB, Canada.
© 2017 ACM. ISBN 978-1-4503-4972-7/17/05... $15.00.
DOI: http://dx.doi.org/10.1145/3060403.3060463

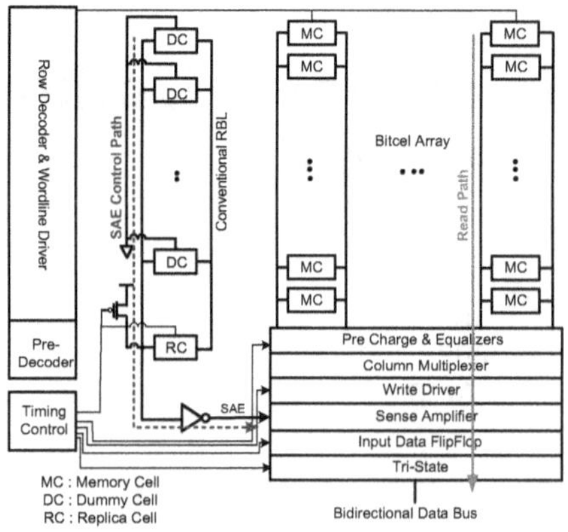

Figure 1: SRAM array with conventional replica bitline delay technique (solid red line : Read path, dashed blue line: Sense amplifier enable path).

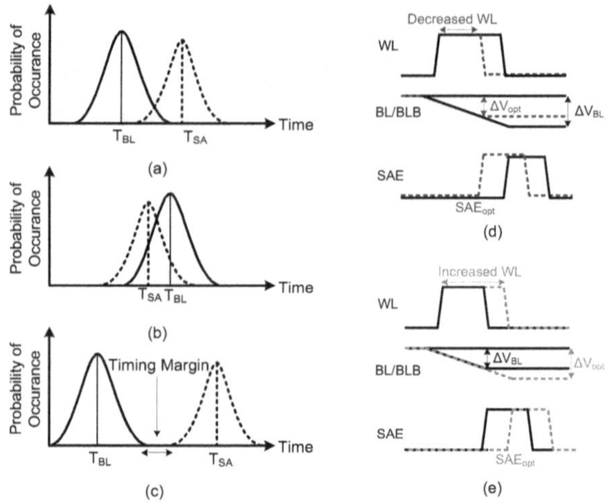

Figure 2: (a) A correct read operation when $T_{SA} > T_{BL}$, (b) An incorrect read operation when $T_{SA} < T_{BL}$, (C) Timing margin between T_{BL} and T_{SA} due to random process variation effect, (d) A decreased SAE and wordline pulse width to improve the access time and (e) An increased SAE and wordline pulse width to reduce the failure rate.

ferent operating voltages. The proposed technique can be used more safely compared to conventional RBL techniques and achieves the best timing tracking for SAE under PVT variations. This technique not only finds the optimum SAE signal to improve the power, performance and yield, but it also allows calibration after fabrication and recalibration due to device aging degradation. Due to constant stress on silicon devices due to device-aging degradation, SRAM cells become weak over time and cannot perform at their designed performance.

The proposed technique generates faster and slower SAE based on specific characteristics of chip and environmental parameters through a digital control code. This reconfigurable replica bitline technique allows calibration for PVT and time-dependent variations and brings the SAE signal to its optimum value, when needed. Therefore, with the proposed scheme there is no need to design the SRAM for its worst-case scenario.

Section 2 explains operation and structure of conventional RBL technique and its limitations at deep nanometer technologies. Section 3 introduces the reconfigurable replica bitline and explains how this technique is effective in generating optimum SA timing under random variations and in different voltages. Section 4 shows the Monte Carlo (MC) simulation results and Section 5 concludes the paper.

2. BACKGROUND

Figure 1 shows the conventional replica bitline delay (RBL) technique [1]. In this design, both data path (i.e., solid red line) and the SAE control path (i.e., dashed blue line) are driven by SRAM bitcells. Consequently, the effect of global PVT variations is same for both paths. Before any read operation, the bitlines and replica bitlines are precharged to V_{DD}. Thus, during read mode, selected memory cells discharge the bitlines based on their stored value and develop a differential swing that can be sensed and amplified by the SA. At the same time, The RBL is discharged by a replica cell (a memory cell that is hard-wired to always store zero) to generate the SAE signal. Other memory cells on the RBL are used as dummy cells to mimic the same parasitic loads of the main bitline. The height of RBL is a fraction of main bitline (normally 10% at nominal voltage) therefore, the RBL is discharged faster than main bitline and generates its SAE signal when bitlines are discharged by a small amount. The differential swing that is developed on the main bitlines must be bigger than SA input offset voltage to be sensed and amplified. And, the size of the RBL and number of replica cells (RC) determine the activation time of the SA and is determined through circuit simulations at design time. While the RBL is able to track the global variation, it cannot handle the effect of local variations between cells on the SRAM and replica bitlines and may result in a non-optimum setup time for the SA.

Figure 2(a), (b) and (c) show the statistical distribution of T_{SA} (the time that the SA enables) and T_{BL} (the time that sufficient voltage is developed on the bitline) considering the effect of variations. Specifically, Figure 2(a) shows an example of a correct read operation when the SA enables after sufficient swing is developed on bitlines ($T_{SA} > T_{BL}$). On the other hand, Figure 2(b) displays a possible read failure due to insufficient swing on bitlines when the SA is enabled ($T_{SA} < T_{BL}$). Finally, Figure 2(c) demonstrates the necessary time margin between T_{BL} and T_{SA} as distributions become wider using deep nanometer nodes. Therefore, finding the optimum SAE timing is challenging and difficult considering the following parameters:

1. Threshold voltage variations due to dopant fluctuation in transistor channel results in different bitcell read current and different discharge rate for bitlines.

2. Different input offset voltage due to process variation or aging degradation makes the SA and memory cell asymmetric and results in incorrect sensing. Accurate and symmetric layout helps to minimized the SA input offset voltage but still local threshold voltage variation results in mismatch. This mismatch can make the SA metastable and cause a slow sensing operation when

the differential developed swing on bitlines is equal to threshold voltage of SA.

3. Leakage current of unselected SRAM bitcells on the active bitline is dependent on stored data pattern. The worst-case leakage occurs when all unselected cells have the opposite data value from selected cell. Leakage current and data pattern change the set time of SA.

4. When stress is applied on the device continuously, it results in aging degradation. The main reason of device aging degradation is bias temperature instability (BTI) which leads to a shift in threshold voltage for devices that are at strong inversion for a long time [10]. Negative BTI happens for PMOS when $V_D = V_S = V_{DD}$ and $V_G = 0$ and positive BTI occurs for NMOS when $V_D = V_S = 0$ and $V_G = V_{DD}$ ($V_{DS} \approx 0$, $V_{GS} \neq 0$). BTI can be applied asymmetrically to a SRAM cell that stores a fixed value for a long time and results in weakening one side of a cell. This effect makes the SRAM cell asymmetric and weak in reading a specific value which results in higher read failure probability.

5. Temperature, voltage, resistance and capacitance variations increase failure probability as well.

By considering the above-mentioned effects, in case of using the conventional RBL, the time margin between T_{SA} and T_{BL} should be increased for proper functionality in scaled technologies. Unfortunately, increasing the time margin by considering the worst case scenario to reduce the SRAM failure rate, deteriorates the performance and increases the SRAM power consumption. Therefore, it is necessary to design new timing control circuitries that allow SAE timing calibration after silicon fabrication to reduce the access time of SRAM based on the characteristics of specific chip. Post silicon calibration allows the ability to dynamically improve SRAM yield and power consumption and recalibrate the SRAM when parameters changes from their nominal values by aging degradation.

Read operations are normally the slowest operation in SRAM and define its operating frequency. Therefore, having an accurate SAE signal generator is critical to minimize the access time and provide the highest frequency for the SRAM. Figure 2(d) shows how a variable timing controller can decrease the SAE delay to not only resolve the data correctly but also reduce the wordline pulse width in order to reduce the swing on bitlines and save energy. Figure 2(e) demonstrates how an incorrect read operation due to insufficient swing can be avoided by delaying the SAE, increasing the wordline pulse width and developing more swing on bitlines that can be sensed by the SA to generate the correct digital output.

3. RECONFIGURABLE REPLICA BITLINE

Figure 3 presents the proposed reconfigurable replica bitline as the control circuitry for the SAE. This design generates variable delay based on input control code Aji and Bj (i is the number of replica cell in each column and j is the number of RBL column).

If local variation in memory cells on the main bitline or RBL causes an early-generated SAE signal when sufficient swing is not developed on the bitlines, it is possible to increase the SAE delay using a reconfigurable replica bitline.

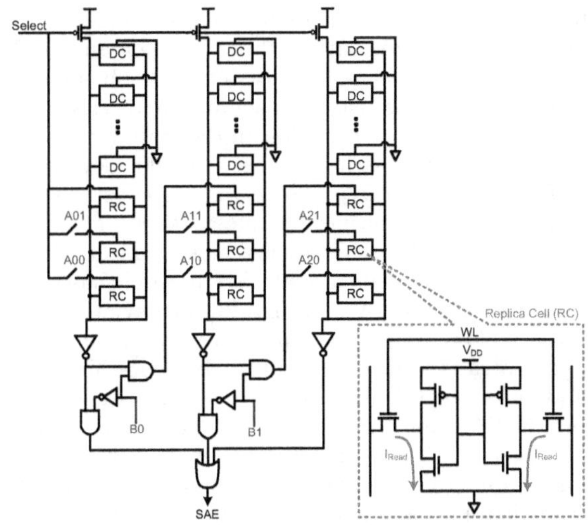

Figure 3: Proposed Reconfigurable Replica Bitline delay scheme (A_{ji} and B_j are control code bits).

This extra delay allows SRAM to develop bigger differential swings to overcome the input offset voltage of SA. Conversely, if the SAE signal enables late, the reconfigurable replica bitline can decrease the SAE delay to avoid extra discharge on bitline and eliminate the excessive power dissipation and access time.

Figure 3 shows how the control code changes the SAE delay. When all bit of digital code are zero (Aji =0 and Bj = 0), reconfigurable replica bitline acts like conventional RBL. In cases that less SAE delay is needed, control bits in the first replica column (A0i) are set to high one by one to increase the number of activated replica cells (increase the discharge current) and reduce the SAE delay.

Equation 1 demonstrates how increasing the discharge current, reduces the SAE delay and its deviation.

$$\begin{aligned} \mu_{SAE} + \sigma_{SAE} &= \frac{C_{BL} \cdot V_{DD}}{I + \Delta I} \\ &= \frac{C_{BL} \cdot V_{DD}}{I \cdot (1 + \frac{\Delta I}{I})} \\ &\approx \frac{C_{BL} \cdot V_{DD}}{I} \cdot \left(1 - \frac{\Delta I}{I}\right) \\ &\approx \frac{C_{BL} \cdot V_{DD}}{I} - \frac{C_{BL} \cdot V_{DD} \cdot \Delta I}{I^2} \end{aligned} \quad (1)$$

In this equation μ_{SAE} and σ_{SAE} are the mean and deviation of SAE signal. C_{BL} is the capacitance load on the replica column, I in the discharge current by one replica cell and ΔI shows the effect of variation on the discharge current and it is assumed that $\Delta I \ll I$. Increasing the number of activated replica cells (K replica cell instead of one) in first replica column leads to more discharge current ($K \cdot I$, $\sigma^2 = K \cdot \Delta I^2$ or $\sigma = \sqrt{K} \cdot \Delta I$). According to Equation 1 using K replica cells divides the mean value by K and deviation by $K \cdot \sqrt{K}$. Therefore, the reconfigurable replica bitline generates the SAE signal with less delay and smaller variation by increasing the value by K.

Another difference between a reconfigurable RBL and conventional RBL is that a reconfigurable RBL uses both bitlines in its discharge path while conventional RBL uses only one bitline. The structure of replica cell is changed in order to provide two discharge path as shown in the Figure 3. This replica cell has the same size transistors as the memory cell, so it adds the same parasitic capacitance and resistance on the RBL as the memory cell adds on the main bitline. And, having two discharge path provides a smaller deviation for the SAE timing with the proposed technique through averaging [2]. Using both bitlines doubles both the capacitance load ($2 \times C_{BL}$) and discharge current ($2 \times I$) of RBL column, therefore, based on Equation 1 it would not change the mean value of the SAE but divides the deviation by $\sqrt{2}$.

In case a slower SAE compared to what a conventional RBL generates is needed, control bit Bj, goes high one by one and adds extra delay to the SAE signal. It is possible to tune the SAE delay by both coarse tuning bits (Bj) and fine tuning bits (Aji) to get the optimum value for SAE. The mean value of the SAE signal changes when reconfigurable replica bitline adds extra delay (e.g., when B0B1= 10, μ_{SAE} equals $2 \cdot C_{BL} \cdot V_{DD}/I$). Therefore, having two RBL column with one replica cell multiplies the mean and deviation by 2 and $\sqrt{2}$, respectively, based on Equation 1. However, because the deviation on each RBL is divided by $1/\sqrt{2}$ by using both bitlines, there would be no increase in deviation and the proposed design results in the same amount of deviation as conventional RBL. It is worth mentioning that techniques in [8] and [9] increase the deviation by using inverter gate delays and eventually result in more unnecessarily access time. In addition, using fine tuning bits in the second RBL column allows the ability to determine the optimum SAE **and** also reduce the deviation. Reconfigurable replica bitline can be extended to more RBL columns and replica cells in each column for better tuning in smaller supply voltage, near threshold and sub-threshold regions, where conventional RBL and techniques in [8] and [9] are not effective.

The flowchart in Figure 4 shows how the control code for reconfigurable replica bitline can be defined based on specific parameters, process and environment variations. The height of each RBL column, number of replica cells in each column and number of RBL columns can be defined by simulation at typical, fast and slow process corners, respectively. And the digital control code can be defined based on desired yield for SRAM through few iterations, as shown in Figure 4.

A reconfigurable replica bitline allows the optimum SAE to be found for each chip based on its specific characters. The proposed technique not only allows the ability to dynamically manage the power-yield tradeoff based on an application, but also provides a wide supply voltage for a SRAM array. By using reconfigurable replica bitline the setup time for the SA can be increased or reduced for lower or higher supply voltages compared to a nominal one. This feature allows the SRAM array to be used in different applications and a wide-voltage ranges.

4. SIMULATION RESULTS

The reconfigurable RBL is simulated with a 64 kb (256 × 256 bits) SRAM array and is compared with a conventional RBL at different supply voltages, temperatures and input offset voltages of SA. The number of RBL columns and replica cells are 3 and 3 based on simulations results in slow and fast process corners and the height of RBL is 26 cells that is defined by simulation in typical corner. To define the number of RCs, RBLs and RBL height (SAE delay), nominal supply voltage for 32 nm (0.9 V) and a 99.9% yield (0.1% read failure) are considered in all simulations. To evaluate the effectiveness of proposed design thousands of Monte Carlo (MC) simulation in IBM/GF cmos32soi 32nm technology are done. Monte Carlo transistor models for cmos32soi technology are supported by the manufacturing vendor. In transient MC simulations, 3σ random dopant variation and device geometric mismatch are included to model the most complete representation of statistical variation during chip manufacturing. Before a read/write operation, the bitlines are precharged to V_{DD} in the first half of the cycle and read/write is done in the second half. Table 1 displays how the mean and deviation of SAE signal changes based on the proposed digital control code. When all control bits are at zero, the reconfigurable RBL acts like a conventional RBL and no extra delay is added or subtracted from the SAE signal. When B_{0-1} are at zero and A_{00-01} goes high, the reconfigurable RBL generates SAE signals with less delay and deviation compared to conventional RBL. As shown in Table 1 by setting A_{00} and A_{01} to 1, the SAE delay decreases by 41 and 60 ps, and deviation decreases by 7 and 10 psec, respectively. By activating B_0 and B_1 switches, the mean value of the SAE signal increases while its deviation decreases or stays almost the same as a conventional design. The generated SAE signal for different control bits of the

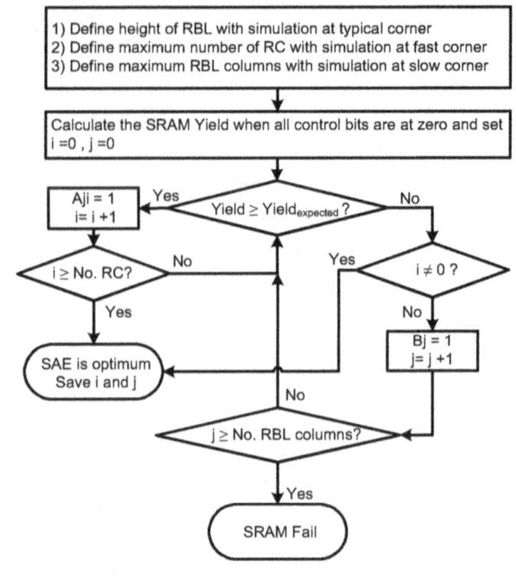

Figure 4: Optimum SAE timing generation Flow.

Table 1: 1,000 point MC Simulation for $\Delta\mu_{SAE}$ & $\Delta\sigma_{SAE}$ based on digital control code (Δ : Reconfigurable RBL - Conventional RBL).

Control Code (A_{ji} B_j)	$\Delta\mu_{SAE}$ [pSec]	$\Delta\sigma_{SAE}$ [pSec]	Variation (6σ) improvement
000000 00	0	0.00	0.000%
100000 00	-41	-7.00	35.554%
110000 00	-60	-10.00	48.500%
000000 10	81	-0.90	4.785%
001000 10	55	-5.20	23.745%
001100 10	39	-7.10	35.605%
000000 11	140	0.75	-3.525%
000010 11	107	-0.50	2.425%
000011 11	92	-5.20	23.745%

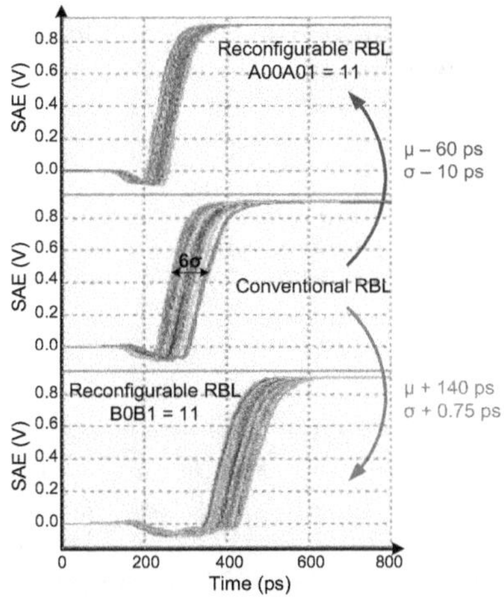

Figure 5: Decrease in μ_{SAE} and σ_{SAE} by setting A_{00} and A_{01} bits and increase in μ_{SAE} with no degradation in deviation by setting B_0 and B_1 bits of control code in reconfigurable RBL.

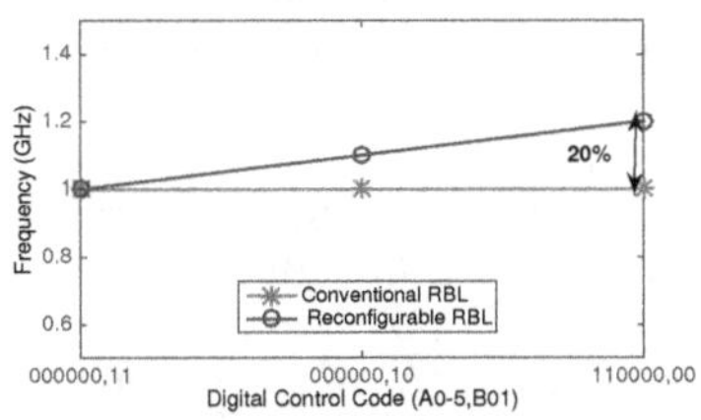

Figure 6: Operation frequency of a 64 kb SRAM array at 0.9 V voltage based on digital control code (Operating frequency of conventional RBL is fixed at design time for worst case).

reconfigurable RBL and comparison with conventional RBL are shown in Figure 5.

Figure 6 shows how operation frequency of SRAM changes based on the fastest and slowest SAE timing in proposed design, compared to conventional RBL. As shown in this figure operation frequency of an SRAM can increase by 20% using reconfigurable RBL compared to an conventional RBL that is designed for worst case scenario.

We consider a maximum of 0.15 V as input offset voltage of the SA, because of its small layout size (i.e., SA layout must be pitch match with 6T layout). Figure 7(a) shows how the TSAE increase with an increase in input offset voltage of the SA using reconfigurable RBL while it is fixed in conventional RBL design because the conventional RBL is designed for the worst case input offset voltage (0.15 V). Figure 7(b) demonstrates how a design for the worst input offset voltage results in 20% bigger access time for conventional RBL. On the other hand, Figure 8(a) shows the case when the conventional RBL is designed considering zero input offset voltage for SA. Figure 8(b) shows how the yield decreases with an increase in the SA offset voltage for a conventional RBL and the reconfigurable RBL is able to tune the delay of SAE in order to keep the SRAM yield (150 mV is considered as the maximum input offset voltage for a small size sense amplifier [11]).

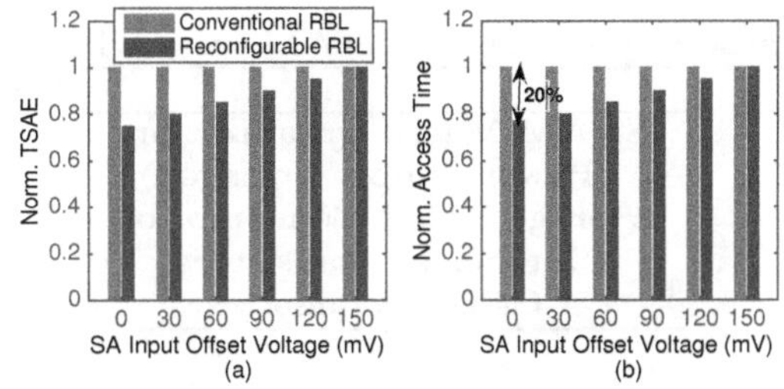

Figure 7: (a) SAE enable time and (b) Access-time comparison when conventional RBL is designed with 150 mV input offset voltage for SA.

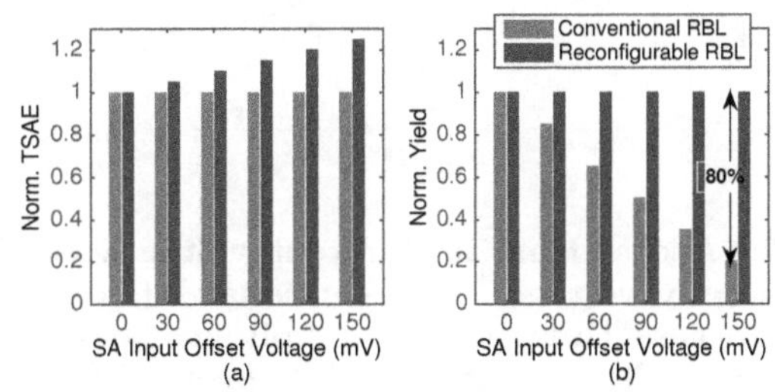

Figure 8: (a) SAE enable time and (b) Yield comparison when conventional RBL is designed with zero input offset voltage for SA.

Figure 9 presents how the reconfigurable RBL generates sufficient SAE delay for different supply voltages. In lower voltages the effect of variation is more and therefore a bigger time margin between T_{BL} and T_{SA} is needed (more access time). This larger time margin allows more swing on the bitlines at the time of the SA activation and results in less failure. Based on the transient MC simulation for 64 kb array sufficient swing on bitline for a 99.9% yield at 1.1 and 0.7 V are 100 mV ($\approx$ 10% V_{DD}) and 320 mv ($\approx$ 50% V_{DD}), respectively. As shown in Figure 9 reconfigurable replica bitline can generate the delay to meet this yield, while conventional RBL with fixed number of replica and dummy cells fails at lower voltages (when extra SAE delay is needed).

Figure 10 presents how the SAE timing of the proposed design changes with temperature variation. Higher temperature leads to more subthreshold leakage current and it takes more time for SRAM to develop the sufficient differential swing on the bitlines. Therefore, as temperature rises more SAE delay is needed to maintain the yield. Proposed design provides more delay by adjusting the control code while conventional RBL results in extra delay at lower temperature if it is designed for worst case temperature. Again, proposed design results in less access time and less power consumption compared to traditional RBL scheme for temperature variation. Proposed design does not have any dependency on SRAM configuration and can easily be applied to SRAM compilers such as OpenRAM [12]. Table 2 summarizes and compares the specifications of SRAM arrays with conventional and proposed reconfigurable RBL. As shown in this table, SRAM array with reconfigurable RBL can set the performance (clock frequency) based on supply voltage using the digital control code in order to have the minimum access-time/power consumption. On contrary, the performance of

Table 2: Characteristics of 64 kb SRAM array with Conventional and Reconfigurable RBL at 32nm technology.

	Conventional RBL	Reconfigurable RBL
SRAM Macro Organization	256×256 bit	256×256 bit
Power Supply Voltage	0.9 V	0.9 V $\pm 25\%$
Average Power Consumption	4.06 mW	$3.10 - 4.45$ mW
Number of Transistors	402,939	403,327
Clock Frequency	1 GHz	1 GHz $\pm 20\%$

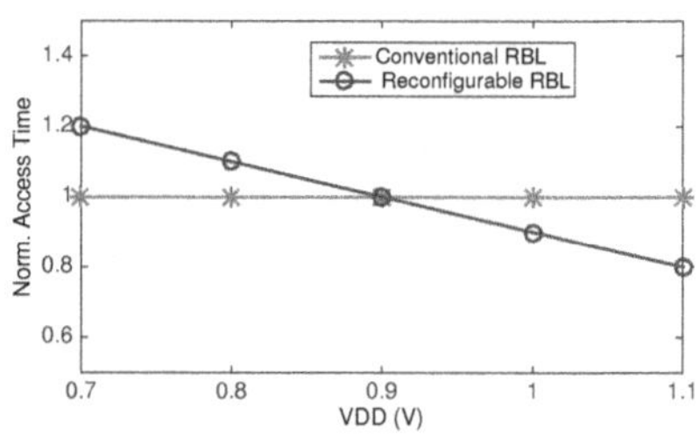

Figure 9: Access time in different voltages (variation in supply voltage). Conventional RBL results in extra access time in higher voltages and more read failure in lower voltages while proposed reconfigurable RBL sets the optimum SAE time.

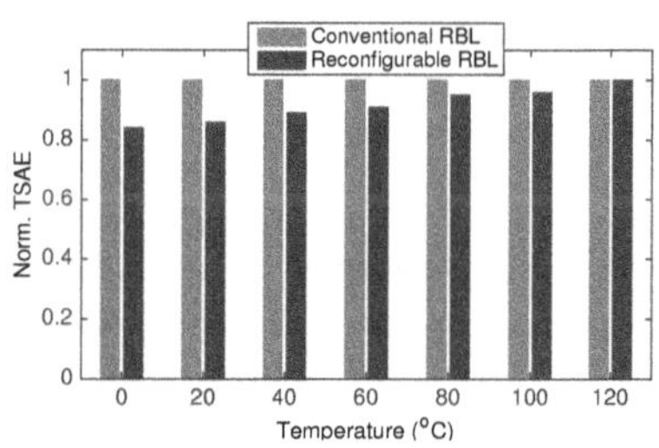

Figure 10: Reconfigurable RBL can generate optimum TSAE with temperature variation.

the SRAM array with conventional RBL is fixed for a specific supply voltage at design time and any PVT or time dependent variation may result in performance degradation or yield loss for this array.

5. CONCLUSION

A reconfigurable replica bitline technique to determine the optimum set time of SRAM sense amplifier under PVT and time-dependent variations is presented. The timing of the sense amplifier directly affects the performance and power consumption of SRAM. A reconfigurable replica bitline sets the sense amplifier activation time to the minimum required value for reliable operation based on a desired yield. The proposed design allows SRAM to be used for different applications with different voltages. A 64 kb SRAM array with a reconfigurable RBL technique is simulated in IBM/GF cmos32soi 32nm technology at 0.9 V and produces a 20 % smaller access time compared to the same size array with a conventional RBL technique.

6. REFERENCES

[1] B. Amrutur and M. Horowitz, "A replica technique for wordline and sense control in low-power SRAM's," *IEEE Journal of Solid-State Circuits*, vol. 33, pp. 1208–1219, Aug. 1998.

[2] S. Ataei and J. E. Stine, "Multi replica bitline delay technique for variation tolerant timing of SRAM sense amplifiers," in *25th edition on Great Lakes Symposium on VLSI (GLSVLSI)*, pp. 173–178, May 2015.

[3] S. Komatsu, M. Yamaoka, M. Morimoto, N. Maeda, Y. Shimazaki, and K. Osada, "A 40-nm low-power SRAM with multi-stage replica-bitline technique for reducing timing variation," in *IEEE Custom Integrated Circuits Conference (CICC)*, pp. 701–704, Sep. 2009.

[4] Y. Niki *et al.*, "A digitized replica bitline delay technique for random-variation-tolerant timing generation of SRAM sense amplifiers," *IEEE Journal of Solid-State Circuits*, vol. 46, pp. 2545–2551, Nov. 2011.

[5] U. Arslan *et al.*, "Variation-tolerant SRAM sense-amplifier timing using configurable replica bitlines," in *IEEE Custom Integrated Circuits Conference (CICC)*, pp. 415–418, Sep. 2008.

[6] A. Kawasumi *et al.*, "A 47% access time reduction with a worst-case timing-generation scheme utilizing a statistical method for ultra low voltage SRAMs," in *IEEE Symposium on VLSI Circuits*, Jun. 2012.

[7] M. H. Abu-Rahma *et al.*, "A methodology for statistical estimation of read access yield in SRAMs," in *45th ACM/IEEE Design Automation Conference (DAC)*, Jun. 2008.

[8] Y.-C. Lai and S.-Y. Huang, "Robust SRAM design via bist-assisted timing-tracking (BATT)," *IEEE Journal of Solid-State Circuits*, vol. 44, pp. 642–649, Feb. 2009.

[9] A. Neale and M. Sachdev, "Digitally programmable SRAM timing for nano-scale technologies," in *IEEE International Symposium on Quality Electronic Design (ISQED)*, May 2011.

[10] S. V. Kumar, C. H. Kim, and S. S. Sapatnekar, "An analytical model for negative bias temperature instability," in *25th IEEE/ACM international conference on Computer-aided design*, pp. 493–496, Nov. 2006.

[11] M. E. Sinangil and A. P. Chandrakasan, "Application-specific SRAM design using output prediction to reduce bit-line switching activity and statistically gated sense amplifiers for up to 1.9 lower energy/access," *IEEE Journal of Solid-State Circuits*, vol. 49, pp. 107–117, Jan. 2014.

[12] M. R. Guthaus *et al.*, "OpenRAM: An open-source memory compiler," in *35th IEEE/ACM International Conference On Computer Aided Design (ICCAD)*, Nov. 2016.

Building a Fast and Power Efficient Inductive Charge Pump System for 3D Stacked Phase Change Memories

Lei Jiang
Indiana University
Bloomington
jiang60@iu.edu

Sparsh Mittal
Indian Institute of Technology
Hyderabad
sparsh@iith.ac.in

Wujie Wen
Florida International University
wwen@fiu.edu

ABSTRACT

Phase change memory emerges as one of the most promising alternatives to traditional DRAM in terabyte main memory constructions. 3D stacking technology further enhances the scalability and capacity of PCM. However, write bandwidth of emerging 3D stacked PCMs is seriously limited by capacitive change pump widely adopted in 2D PCM chips. In this paper, we propose an inductive charge pump system design for 3D stacked PCMs. We further present a novel ICP aware page management technique to reduce average charging latency and improve memory bandwidth in a 3D stacked PCM-based main memory. Compared to a capacitive charge pump system, our inductive charge pump and page management technique improve the CPU performance by 54% and reduce the system energy by 29%.

1. INTRODUCTION

The explosion of emerging cloud services and intelligent devices connected to the internet is accelerating the production of big data. To process massive amounts of data fast and efficiently, an increasing number of cores have been integrated into a single chip. Therefore, more threads can be enabled to run concurrently in a processor. For instance, Intel Xeon Phi [10] has already supported up to 72 cores and 288 threads on a chip. To maintain scalable performance, a future processor requires a low power, scalable and large capacity main memory system to accommodate working sets of all simultaneously executing threads.

In the deep sub-micron era, traditional DRAM suffers from large power consumption, critical timing parameter degradation and poor scalability. Large capacity DRAM requires frequent refresh operations [25] to maintain its data integrity. Due to process variation, future DRAM has to prolong its timing parameters, e.g., write recovery time (t_{WR}) [36], to tolerate low quality cells. Moreover, DRAM stops scaling [12] and has to stay with $7F^2$ cell size [6] beyond $20nm$. For instance, the DRAM cell size is not further reduced at $10nm$ [3].

Recent studies [27, 5] show that phase change memory (PCM) emerges as one of the most promising alternatives to DRAM by designing and evaluating a hybrid main memory system incorporating both DRAM and PCM. PCM enjoys zero cell leakage, read latency comparable to DRAM's and better scalability, i.e., $4F^2$ [6] cell size at $20nm$. To reduce cost-per-bit, a PCM cell is able to store more than 1 bit [16], because of the large resistance difference between ON and OFF states. Furthermore, PCM can take advantage of 3D stacking technology to enlarge its capacity [21]. Intel and Micron have released their 3D stacked PCM-like memory technology, 3D XPoint [7, 32, 8], for server market.

However, the write bandwidth of PCM is seriously limited by on-chip capacitive charge pumps (CPs) [17, 15]. Phase change material requires higher than V_{dd} voltages [27] to enable resistance transition. To achieve the theoretical minimal cell size ($4F^2$), PCM has to adopt vertical diodes to access cells in memory arrays. The vertical diode [6] has higher threshold voltages, which further elevate read and write voltages in highly dense PCM arrays. Therefore, 2D PCM chips usually use on-chip CPs to boost voltages and supply current for reads and writes [6]. Capacitive CPs (CCPs) consisting of only capacitors and transistors are CMOS-compatible [17] and can be easily fabricated with PCM arrays on a chip. Unfortunately, due to wide transistors and large capacitors, on-chip CCPs undergo long charging latency ($> 100ns$) [17, 15], huge hardware overhead ($> 10\%$ chip area) [6] and low power conversion efficiency ($< 30\%$) [22]. As a result, on-chip CCPs suppress PCM write bandwidth below 15% [9] of the maximum bandwidth on a DDR3 1066MHz DIMM.

For a 3D stacked PCM substrate, naively stacking multiple CCPs cannot improve the limited write bandwidth. In this paper, we propose a fast and power efficient inductive CP (ICP) system to boost the bandwidth of the 3D stacked PCM-based main memory. With the same input power, our ICP increases write throughput of 3D stacked PCMs by supplying larger currents. Our contributions can be summarized as:

- We architect an ICP system with small charging latency, low hardware overhead and high power conversion efficiency, into our 3D stacked PCM baseline.
- We study the impact of through-silicon-vias (TSVs) and 2D wires connecting the ICP to PCM arrays on ICP charging latencies. TSVs and wires on the ICP charging paths introduce significant RC delays. We also perform a design space exploration on positions of ICP interposer in the 3D stacked PCM-based main memory.
- We propose a novel ICP aware page management technique to move access intensive memory pages to PCM banks with shorter ICP charging latencies.
- We evaluate our ICP design with proposed techniques, and compare them against the state-of-the-art. The experimental results show that our ICP system improves CPU performance

Permission to make digital or hard copies of all or part of this work for personal or classroom use is granted without fee provided that copies are not made or distributed for profit or commercial advantage and that copies bear this notice and the full citation on the first page. Copyrights for components of this work owned by others than ACM must be honored. Abstracting with credit is permitted. To copy otherwise, or republish, to post on servers or to redistribute to lists, requires prior specific permission and/or a fee. Request permissions from permissions@acm.org.

GLSVLSI '17, May 10-12, 2017, Banff, AB, Canada

© 2017 ACM. ISBN 978-1-4503-4972-7/17/05...$15.00

DOI: http://dx.doi.org/10.1145/3060403.3060412

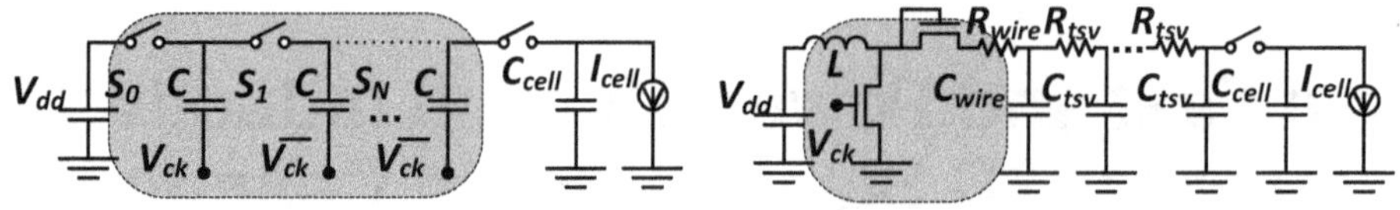

(a) Capacitive CP (b) Inductive CP

Figure 1: Charge pump

by 54% and reduces system energy by 29%, compared to the same system configuration with CCPs.

In the rest of paper, Section 2 describes 3D stacked PCMs, CPs and related work. Our design motivation is presented in Section 3. Section 4 elaborates the details of our 3D stacked ICP and ICP aware page management technique. Section 5 summarizes the experiment methodology. We report and analyze the experimental results in Section 6. At last, Section 7 concludes this paper.

2. BACKGROUND AND RELATED WORK

2.1 Phase Change Memory

PCM uses phase change material (GST) to record data [27]. The GST has two resistance states: the highly resistive amorphous state indicates "0", and the low resistance crystalline state represents "1". A PCM cell is shown in Figure 2. In the middle of the cell, there is a thin layer of GST connected to the top electrode and the joule heater. By applying electrical pluses with higher than V_{dd} voltages, the joule heater switches the cell between crystalline and amorphous states.

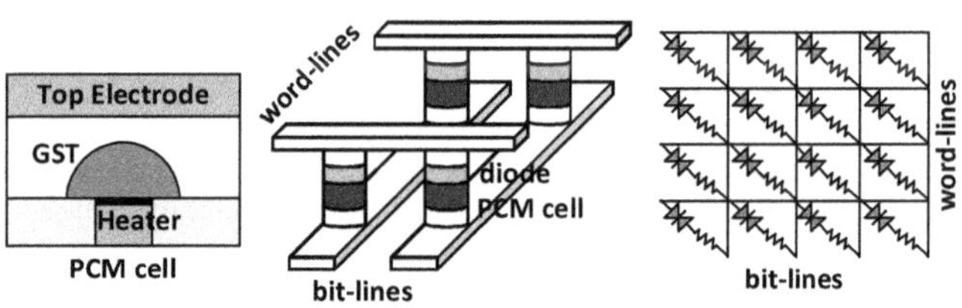

Figure 2: A PCM cell and a PCM array

Figure 2 also shows a PCM array consisting of word-lines, bit-lines and cells. To achieve the theoretical minimal $4F^2$ cell size, the latest PCM chip demonstration [6] adopts vertical diode as cell access device. However, since vertical diodes have higher threshold voltage [22], read and write voltages are also elevated above V_{dd} in PCM arrays.

2.2 3D Stacked PCM

To further improve memory density and reduce cost-per-bit, recently both DRAM [29] and NAND Flash [14] have adopted 3D stacking technologies. PCM is also proved to be 3D stackable [21]. Intel and Micron unveil their 3D stacked PCM-like memory product, 3D XPoint, for the memory hungry server market [7, 32, 8]. As Figure 3 shows, our 3D stacked PCM substrate baseline includes multiple PCM array dies and a logic die, where there are PCM PHY and inter-connections. All dies in the 3D stacked structure are connected by TSVs.

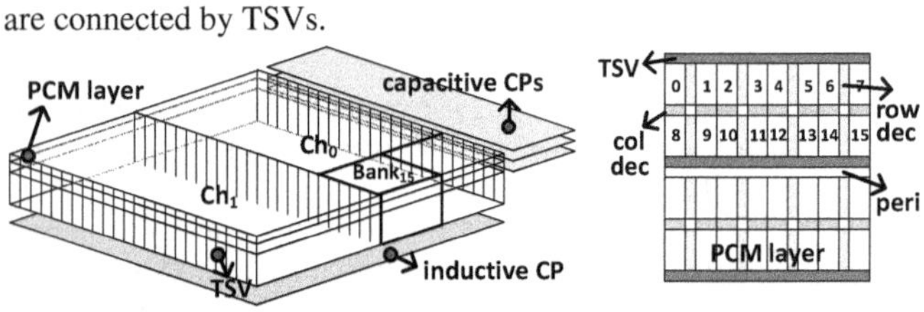

Figure 3: 3D stacked PCM

Our baseline memory architecture: Since PCM is too slow to match the HMC interface, we modeled our 3D stacked PCM baseline by following 3D stacked DDR3 DRAM design [19] to balance the tradeoff between memory density and bandwidth. In our baseline, there are 2 channels, each of which has 16 banks. We used eight 2GB PCM dies connected by TSVs to build our main memory. Each die is separated into two individual channels by peripheral circuits and TSVs, as shown in Figure 3. A die costs $104mm^2$ at $20nm$ [6]. One bank consists of eight sub-arrays, each of which is on one die. We modeled PCM banks based on the latest $20nm$ 2D chip demonstration [6]. By following the 3D stacked design [19], we modeled $\sim$ 400 TSVs including 128 signal TSVs, 128 power TSVs and other redundant TSVs. Each bank has 64 signal TSVs and 4 power TSVs.

2.3 Charge Pumps

To supply higher than V_{dd} voltages, 2D PCM chips [6, 22, 18] deploy on-chip CCPs, as shown in Figure 1(a). CCPs consist of only capacitors and transistors, so they are CMOS-compatible and can be easily fabricated with PCM arrays [17]. However, a CCP suffers from slow charging operations, since it has multiple stages, each of which elevates the output voltage a little. A CCP charging operation usually adds $> 200ns$ on read and write operations [22]. The hardware overhead of a CCP is also significant, e.g., $> 10\%$ of a PCM chip area [6]. The most significant disadvantage of an on-chip CCP is the low power conversion efficiency, which is typically around 30% [22]. In other words, 70% of the total input power with V_{dd} voltage from power source is wasted during the voltage boosting process of a CCP in the form of leakage power and parasitic power [22]. As a result, the write bandwidth of a PCM chip is severely limited by the CCP. For example, with a 800Mb/s/pin LPDDR2 IO interface, the latest PCM chip demonstration [6] only supports 40MB/s write bandwidth.

CCP modeling in our baseline: We modeled the CCP for each PCM die by following the CP designs in [6, 22] and the CCP model in [17]. Like [6], we also allocated $\sim 14\%$ of die area to the on-chip CCP on each die, which can support 128 parallel RESETs in one bank. We fed V_{dd}, read/SET/RESET voltages and currents [6] into the CCP model [17]. We further tuned constant parameters in the model by charging latency and power conversion efficiency in [22]. All other CCP parameters including SET/RESET/READ charging energy are calculated by the CCP model. We list all CCP parameters in Table 1.

There is another type of CP called ICP, as shown in Figure 1(b). It comprises only an inductor and transistors. Because of its simple structure, an ICP can be built with small hardware overhead [11]. An ICP boosts the output voltage by an inductor, which resists current changes by creating and destroying a magnetic field [30]. Since the magnetic field polarity switching occurs fast, an ICP can increase voltage to the target level in a short time with small energy consumption. And thus, the power conversion efficiency of ICPs is usually high (> 85%) [11]. Compared to a CCP, an ICP is able to supply more output power with the target voltage and support larger write throughput with the same input power. However, it is difficult to fabricate large inductors and conventional CMOS transistors on the same die [11, 30, 23], since on-chip inductors suffer from low inductance density and high parasitic resistance [34]. ICPs have been successfully integrated into a NAND Flash chip package [30] or stacked at the bottom of multiple NAND Flash chips [11].

2.4 Related Work

Previous works [35, 13] investigate the feasibility of 3D stacking technology on PCMs and attack the PCM reliability problems, e.g., short endurance and resistance drift, in a 3D stacked PCM substrate. Various write scheduling techniques [17, 15] are proposed to enlarge the write concurrency under power constraints imposed by on-chip CCPs in a 2D PCM-based main memory system. Integrating highly efficient ICPs into the package of 2D Flash chips improves write bandwidth, but it also increases packaging costs [30]. In this paper, the 3D stacking technology is a key to overcome the on-chip fabrication difficulties of inductors and enable ICPs on 3D stacked PCMs. To the best of our knowledge, this work is the first to improve 3D stacked PCM bandwidth by ICPs.

To reduce the hardware cost of peripheral circuits and TSVs, recent studies [31, 29] present frugal 3D stacked designs that seriously suffer from IR drop problem, where only few banks can be accessed concurrently. To build a reliable 3D stacked PCM system, our baseline has enough power TSVs and C4 bumps by following the reliable 3D stacking design rules in [35, 13, 14, 19] to guarantee that all banks can be accessed simultaneously.

3. MOTIVATION

A 3D stacked PCM can still use the same on-chip CCPs as those of 2D PCM chips [6, 17]. As Figure 3 exhibits, each PCM die can have its own CCP in the 3D stacked structure. However, the CCPs seriously limit the write bandwidth of the 3D stacked PCM. Figure 4 shows the performance degradation due to the CCPs. Our experimental methodology can be viewed in Section 5. The results in Figure 4 are normalized to an *ideal CCP*, which always has enough high voltage power to do writes but has to wait for CCP charging latencies. Therefore, for the ideal CCP, writes cannot be blocked by the shortage of write power. On average, power inefficient and realistic *CCP*s reduce CPU performance by 19.2%. Because of the inadequacy of power, writes have to be serialized, even when their target banks are idle. Naïvely integrating $2\times CCPs$ on each die brings down the performance loss to 4.4%, but $2\times CCPs$ occupy $\sim$ 28% of the die area [6]. Since our baseline has 8 PCM dies, totally $2\times CCPs$ may consume more than 2-die area. We will show our ICP design achieves even better performance but costs much less hardware resource.

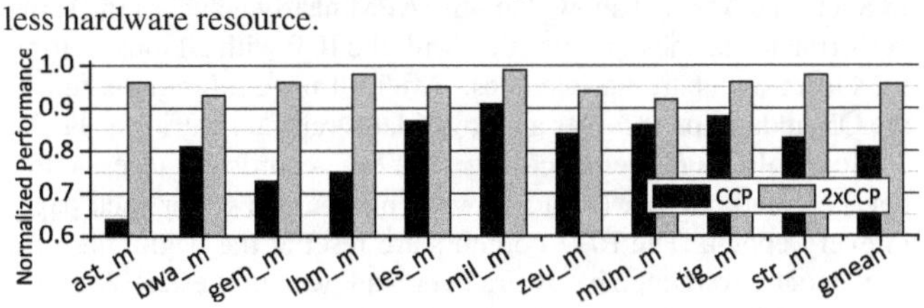

Figure 4: CCP performance (normalized to *ideal CCP*).

4. PROPOSED TECHNIQUES

In this section, we first present our 3D stacked ICP design significantly improving write power conversion efficiency and write throughput. Then, we show that banks in the 3D stacked substrate may have different ICP charging latencies, because TSVs and wires on their charging paths introduce different amounts of RC delays. At last, we propose an ICP aware page management technique to prioritize access intensive memory pages by moving them into banks with shorter charging latencies.

4.1 3D Stacked Inductive Charge Pumps

Figure 5(a) describes the design of our ICP interposer. Integrating inductors on-chip in a standard CMOS technology leads to low inductance density and high parasitic series resistance [34], because the line width is narrow and the metal is thin. A wider metal line can reduce parasitic series resistance, but it also enlarges parasitic capacitance. The CMOS technology is heavily optimized for digital circuits that do not require native passive components. In our design, the inductors and the ICP controller are fabricated on two different dies respectively. Both dies are integrated and mounted on an interposer stacked in our 3D stacked PCM baseline.

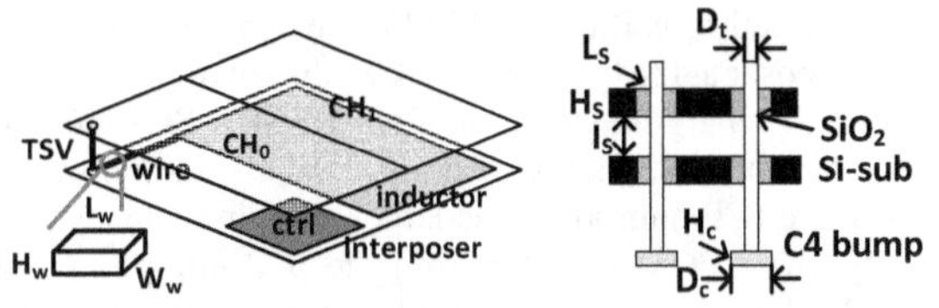

(a) Inductive CP (b) TSV

Figure 5: ICP interposer

ICP modeling: We configured the inductor in our ICPs as a 7-turn square coil. The inductance of the inductor is $1328nH$, and the parasitic series resistance of the inductor is 0.68Ω. The detailed design parameters of our ICPs can be found in *ICP* columns in Table 1. We simulated our ICP design by HSPICE and Cadence Virtuoso ($20nm$). We synthesized the ICP controller with the BSIM-CMG version of predictive technology model [1]. The read/write voltages, load currents and load capacitance are adopted from [17]. The details of CCP modeling can be viewed in Section 2.3. From Table 1, we can see that the power conversion efficiency of our ICPs is around $78\%\sim92\%$, which is similar to that in [11]. Our ICPs improve the power conversion efficiency by $180\%\sim261\%$ over CCPs with the same 1.8V V_{dd}. Moreover, compared to CCPs, our ICPs also halve the charging latency and energy. Unlike CCPs, our ICPs for 8 PCM dies only occupy 62% of one die area.

Table 1: CP comparison.

Freq. 13.3MHz	CCP			ICP		
Type	RESET	SET	READ	RESET	SET	READ
V_{output} (V)	5	3	3	5	3	3
I_{load} (mA)	112	56	34	390	151	34
C_{load} (nF)	1	1	1	1	1	1
$Efficiency$ $(\%)$	21.6	30.9	30.9	78	87	92
$Lat_{charging}$ (ns)	159	132	132	69	51	43
$E_{charging}$ (nJ)	18.78	2.76	1.67	8.21	0.97	0.65
$Area$ (mm^2)	118			64.5		

TSV and 2D wire modeling: PCM dies and the ICP interposer are connected by TSVs, which is shown in Figure 5(b). A TSV passing through each PCM die provides a vertical connection of all PCM dies. The C4 bump at the end of a TSV can be connected to V_{dd} or ground. As Figure 5(a) shows, since the ICPs cannot cover all the area of the interposer, 2D horizontal wires are required to connect to the TSVs. We adopted the TSV model from [20], C4 bump model from [33] and the power wire model from [24]. The design parameters of power TSV, C4 bump and 2D wire are shown in Table 2.

Table 2: TSV, C4 bump and wire parameters.

Device	Parameters
Wire	$W_w = 380\mu m$, $L_w = 2.8mm$, $H_w = 35\mu m$, $\rho = 0.0171\Omega * mm^2/m$
TSV	$L_s = 0.1\mu m$, $D_t = 5\mu m$, $H_s = 50\mu m$, $I_s = 50\mu m$, $R_t = 44.9m\Omega/50\mu m$, $C_t = 14.8fF/50\mu m$, 128 TSVs
C4 bump	$D_c = 50\mu m$, $H_c = 4\mu m$, $R_c = 5m\Omega$, $C_c = 2.3fF$, 128 bumps

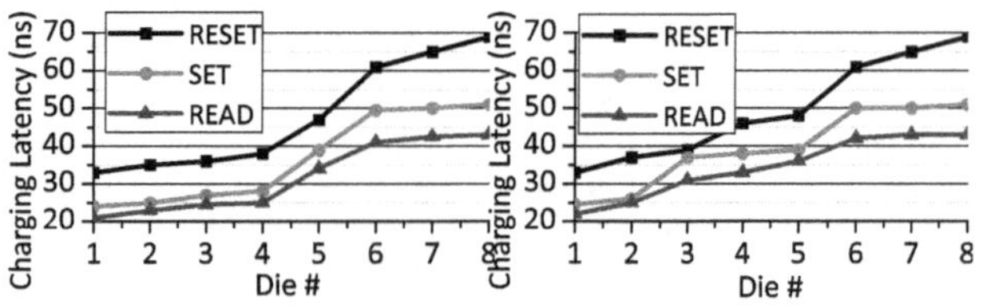

(a) Without wire. (b) With wire.

Figure 6: ICP charging latencies with varying die #.

Both horizontal wires and vertical TSVs have nontrivial parasitic resistances and capacitances introducing extra RC delays on ICP charging paths, as illustrated in Figure 1(b). We first stacked the ICP interposer at the bottom of 8 PCM dies in our baseline. Figure 6 shows the charging latencies of our RESET, SET and READ ICPs for different dies. As Figure 6(a) shows, the farther one PCM die is from the ICP interposer, the larger charging latency this die has to pay. The PCM dies far from the ICP interposer require longer TSVs having larger parasitic resistances and capacitances to connect to the ICP. Compared to the closest die (die 1) to the ICP interposer, the die (die 8) farthest from the ICP has to wait for 104%∼112% longer charging latencies, because of the TSV RC delays. A PCM die contains two channels: a right channel and a left channel. We deployed our ICP underneath the right one. Since our ICP holds only more than half of the interposer area, it needs long wires to connect to the TSVs of banks in the left channel. The additional charging latencies due to wires are shown in Figure 6(b). The wires prolong charging latencies substantially on the PCM dies closer to the ICP interposer, e.g., dies $1-4$. Compared to banks in the right channel without long wires, charging latencies are increased by up to 35.7% for banks in the left channel on dies $1-4$. On the contrary, long wires add trivial RC delays on charging latencies of the PCM dies far from the ICP interposer, e.g., dies $5-8$, since the resistance and capacitance of long TSVs of these dies have already been large enough to dominate charging latencies.

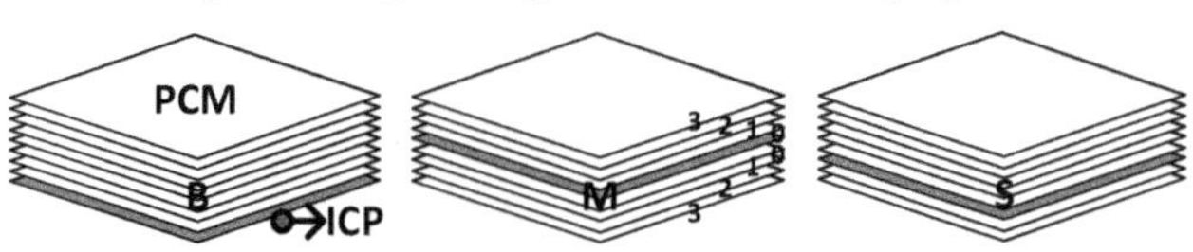

Figure 7: ICP interposer positions in a 3D stacked PCM.

Instead of the bottom of the 3D stacked PCM, we also investigate other possible positions to stack the ICP interposer in our baseline to avoid the worst case charging latency. As shown in Figure 7, besides the bottom position (B), we show two other integration positions for the ICP interposer: M and S. Scheme M puts the ICP interposer at the 5th layer in the 3D structure, so that the distance between the ICP and the worst case die is reduced by 50%, compared to Scheme B. We can also place the ICP interposer two-die away from the bottom position in Scheme S. Figure 8 shows the system performance with different ICP integration positions. *ICP_W* indicates the performance with a ICP with CCP charging latencies. *ICP-X* represents the performance with a ICP with the integration position X. In the figure, we can see that, even with the same charging latencies, our ICP (*ICP_W*) improves the system performance by 4.2% averagely, since our ICP provides more write power and supports larger write concurrency. The benchmarks with a large number of bit flips in each write, such as *gemsFDTD*, *leslie3d*, *zeusmp* and *mummer*, benefit a lot from our ICP. Among three ICP integration positions, Scheme M obtains the best performance, since it avoids the worst case ICP charging latency and minimizes the average ICP charging latency. With shorter read and write charging latencies, on average, our ICP with Scheme M improves the CPU performance by 44.1% over the realistic CCP design and by 16.4% over the ideal CCP.

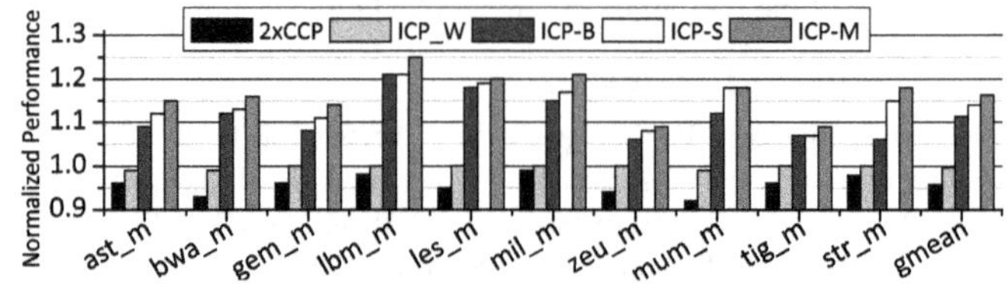

Figure 8: Performance improvement with different ICP interposer integration positions (normalized to *ideal CCP*).

4.2 ICP Aware Page Management

Due to the extra RC delays caused by TSVs and wires on ICP charging paths, our 3D stacked PCM-based main memory has become a NUMA (non-uniform memory access) system. Since one bank consists of eight sub-arrays, each of which is on one die, there are sub-arrays with shorter ICP charging latencies (aka. faster charging sub-arrays) and sub-arrays with longer ICP charging latencies (aka. slower charging sub-arrays) in a bank. We present an ICP aware page management (IAPM) scheme to (1) promote performance critical and access intensive memory pages into faster charging sub-arrays and (2) demote non-critical and rarely accessed pages into slower charging sub-arrays for each bank. The rationale behind IAPM is that typically only a very small set of memory pages directly influence the performance of an application [4]. The task of IAPM is to identify the critical pages and move them to faster charging sub-arrays. Furthermore, the set of these critical pages and the importance of a single page may change over time. Therefore, IAPM needs to adapt the behavior and phase changes of a workload.

Our IAPM relies on both memory controller (MC) and operating system (OS), since neither the MC nor the OS has a complete picture on the criticality of pages of a workload. IAPM requires the MC to monitor the misses in the DRAM last level caches (LLCs) and write-backs from LLCs to each memory page. By analyzing these information, IAPM dynamically identifies "hot" pages to promote and "cold" pages to demote in each epoch. At the end of each epoch, the MC initializes page migrations to move hot pages to faster charging sub-arrays and cold pages to slower charging sub-arrays within each bank. The page migration activity is limited in only each bank, since page swapping overhead between two sub-arrays within a bank is smaller than that between two banks [28]. In Section 6, we will show that our IAPM nearly achieves the same performance as the configuration with the ICP with all dies sharing the closet die charging latencies. After all page migrations finish, the OS updates page tables and invalidates relevant entries in TLBs.

Hot / cold page identification: The MC records the access number, i.e., read number (*R#*) and write number (*W#*) for each page, in every epoch. The R/W counters are reset at the beginning of a new epoch. To reduce hardware overhead, we put these R/W counters into DRAM LLCs and created a SRAM cache in the MC to reduce accesses to DRAM LLCs. We calculated the page access number as $(R\# + \alpha \cdot W\#)$, where α is the write weight value. In each epoch, pages having access number larger than the Hot Page Promotion Threshold (*HPPT*) are candidates for moving to faster charging sub-arrays. Any page whose access number in an epoch is smaller than the Cold Page Demotion Threshold (*CPDT*) can be potentially moved to slower charging sub-arrays. Different sub-arrays may have different values of *HPPT* and *CPDT*, which are initialized to 2000 and 200.

Page migration: At the end of each epoch, the MC performs all page migrations and does not respond to cores for P cycles, where

P is the page migration overhead, which is similar to the DRAM refresh penalty. The number of pages moved into a sub-array has to be equal to the number of pages moved out of that sub-array. The *HPPT* and *CPDT* for each sub-array are dynamically revised such that all page migrations in that sub-array can be finished within P cycles. If page migrations cannot be accommodated within P cycles, *HPPT* adds 200 and *CPDT* is decreased by 100. On the contrary, if page migrations needs less cycles than P, *HPPT* reduces 200 and *CPDT* is increased by 100. *HPPT* must be larger than *CPDT*. Since we adopt *ICP-M*, as Figure 8 shows, eight dies are separated into 4-die top and bottom groups. In each group, hot pages are promoted from the sub-array on *die-X* to the sub-array on *die-(X-1)%4*, while cold pages are demoted from the sub-array on *die-X* to the sub-array on *die-(X+1)%4*. We adopt a similar data movement technique to [28] to conduct page migrations. Data are read to global sense amplifiers from a sub-array, and then written to another sub-array on another die in the same bank.

Migration overhead: We set the length of an execution epoch as 20.48M cycles. And the page migration overhead P after each epoch is 819.2K cycles (an overhead of 4%). The DRAM refresh overhead can reach 8% [25] of the execution time of a workload. A 4KB page contains 64 64B memory lines. And the copy operation for a 64B memory line takes 250ns, which is 800 CPU cycles. One single PCM page migration costs 51.2K cycles, and thus 16 pages can be moved for a bank. And 32 page migrations happen concurrently in 32 banks.

Lifetime guarantee: Always moving written intensive pages to faster charging sub-arrays hurts the lifetime of those sub-arrays. We emphasized read intensive pages in hot page selections by setting the write weight (α) in the page access number equation as 0.2, so that the concentration of write intensive pages in faster charging sub-arrays can be prevented. From our experiments, α=0.2 only introduces $\sim$13% more write traffic to faster charging sub-arrays. Compared to reads, writes influence the CPU performance less, since they are not on the critical path in most cases. Moreover, by setting α to 0, we can ignore written intensive pages during hot page selections to remove the negative impact of our IAPM on PCM endurance.

4.3 Hardware Overhead

As Table 1 shows, our ICP costs 64.5 mm^2 at 20nm. Compared to a CCP, it reduces the area overhead by 45.3%. In IAPM, the MC tracks the access number for each page. We have 2 channels, each of which has 16GB capacity. A set of read and write (R/W) counters for a 4KB page needs 2-byte. The total storage of R/W counters for 2 channels is 16MB. We stored these counters in DRAM LLCs (32MB/core$\times$8 cores) and built a 16KB 8-way SRAM cache on the MC to reduce accesses to DRAM LLCs. We estimated cache power consumption and hardware overhead by CACTI [26]. The cache dissipates $13.4mW$ leakage power and occupies $0.22mm^2$ at 32nm on the logic die in the 3D stacked PCM substrate.

5. EXPERIMENTAL METHODOLOGY

Baseline modeling: Table 3 summarizes the core and cache configuration that we simulated in this paper. MESI snoopy protocol is deployed to maintain the cache coherence.

MC, CP and main memory configuration: The MC always prioritizes reads, while writes are issued only when there is no read. When the write queue is full, the MC packs and issues a burst with all writes blocking the pending reads [9, 15]. A request can only be scheduled when there is enough power supply from CP. The detailed configuration of CPs can be viewed in Table 1. When there is no request, the CP is shut down immediately to reduce power consumption and prolong its time-dependent gate oxide breakdown lifetime [17]. The CP cannot be turned off in the middle of a request burst. We adopted the SLC PCM cell model from the 20nm chip [6]. A 64B read requires $3V$ voltage, $8.4\mu A$ current, $5.6nJ$ energy and $100ns$ latency. 1 bit SET needs $3V$, $50\mu A$, $22.5pJ$ and $150ns$, while 1 bit RESET costs $5V$, $100\mu A$, $29.7pJ$ and $50ns$. Flip-N-Write [5] is also adopted in our baseline.

Table 3: Baseline configuration.

CPU	eight 3.2GHz, X86 out-of-order cores, 4-wide issue, 8MSHRs/core, 64-entry instruction window
L1 I/D	private, 32KB&32KB/core, 4-way, LRU, 2-cycle hit
L2 Cache	private, 2MB/core, 8-way, LRU, 64B line, write back, 2-cycle tag, 5-cycle data hit, 8-cycle CPU to L2
DRAM L3	private, off-chip, 32MB/core, 16-way, LRU, write back, 64B line, 50ns (200-cycle hit), 16-cycle CPU to L3
Main Mem.	32GB, 64-entry R/W queues in MC, MC to bank, 16-cycle, 2 channels, 8 dies and 16 banks/channel

Simulator and benchmarks: We evaluated our proposed schemes using PIN-based simulator Sniper [2]. We modified the simulator to model all memory hierarchies including caches and PCM-based main memory. We selected various workloads from SPEC-CPU2006 (astar [ast_m], bwaves, gemsFDTD, lbm, leslie3d, milc, and zeusmp), STREAM (stream) and BioBench (mummer and tigr) suites to study memory accesses in the 3D stacked PCM-based main memory. Each core runs one copy of a workload. We simulated 5 billion instructions for performance results. For our results, we define speedup as: $Speedup = \frac{IPC_{tech}}{IPC_{base}}$ [27], where IPC_{tech} and IPC_{base} are the instruction-per-cycle of the setting with scheme $tech$ and our baseline, respectively.

6. RESULTS AND ANALYSIS

We compared four schemes as follows.

- `ideal CCP` indicates our baseline with unlimited power output and CCP charging latencies.
- `ICP-M` represents ICP with Scheme M position.
- `ICP-M+IAPM` denotes ICP-M plus IAPM technique.
- `ICP-M+Oracle` means ICP-M with all dies sharing the closet die charging latencies.

IAPM Performance Improvement: Figure 9 describes the performance improvement achieved by our IAPM. Compared to *ICP-M*, IAPM increases the CPU performance by 6.3% averagely. For applications, like *bwaves* and *leslie3d*, IAPM boosts the performance by >10%, since most accesses of these applications happen on only a small number of pages. However, our scheme helps workloads, such as *stream* and *tigr*, little, because they have less spatial locality. Compared to *ICP-M+Oracle*, IAPM degrades the system performance by only 1.2%.

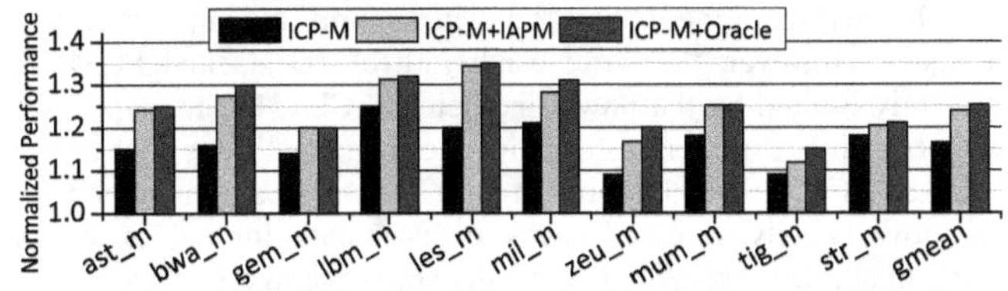

Figure 9: IAPM performance improvement (normalized to *ideal CCP*).

Design space exploration: Figure 9 exhibits the sensitivity study on the IAPM parameters including cache size, write weight α and page migration overhead P. For the R/W counter 8-way *cache*, 8KB is too small to cover the frequently accessed page footprint. Compared to 16KB, 32KB does not significantly improve the IPC, since 16KB covering 32K pages reduces enough number of accesses to DRAM LLCs. For α, 0.2 is large enough to identify heavily written pages. And α=1 does not obviously increase the IPC, since the latency asymmetry between reads and writes becomes less significant at $20nm$, i.e., the SET latency is only 1.5$\times$ the read latency. α=0 improves the performance by 2.1% over *ICP-M*. P defines the hotness and coldness of pages by adjusting *HPPT*s and *CPDT*s. 409.6K-cycle is not long enough for our IAMP to prompt hot pages and demote cold pages. And 1638.4K-cycle makes IAMP move some "not-so-hot" pages unlikely accessed in the next epoch to faster charging sub-arrays. For workloads, e.g., *milc* and *tigr*, the page migration overhead of 1638.4K even outweighs the benefit of IAMP and slightly degrades the CPU performance. Therefore, we set P=819.2K.

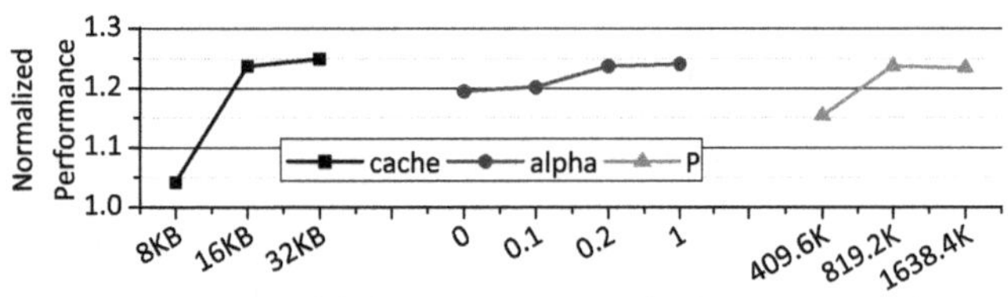

Figure 10: Sensitivity study (normalized to *ideal CCP*).

Power and Energy Results: Recent works [27, 17] find that the 32GB PCM-based main memory typically dissipates 25% of the total power in an 8-core system. We summarize the total power, total energy, performance and energy delay squared product (ED^2) for the entire system consisting of cores and all memory hierarchy in Figure 11. Our *ICP-M+IAPM* increases the CP power conversion efficiency and thus write throughput, but does not reduce the total power consumption. *ICP-M+IAPM* reduces total energy by 29% over *CCP*. Most energy reduction comes from the core part, because our schemes reduce the total execution time and the CPU dominates the total system power consumption. Compared to *CCP*, *ICP-M+IAPM* improves the system performance by 53.5% and the ED^2 by 70%.

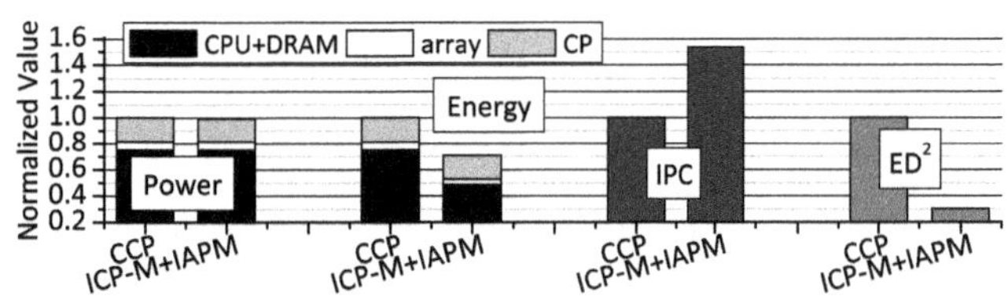

Figure 11: Power, Energy, Performance, and ED^2 (normalized to *CCP*).

7. CONCLUSION

The booming cloud services necessitate large capacity 3D stacked PCM-based main memory systems in memory hungry server machines. However, the write bandwidth of 3D stacked PCMs is severely limited by the power inefficient CCPs. In this paper, we propose an ICP system to improve the memory throughput of 3D stacked PCMs. We also present an ICP aware page management to move heavily accessed pages to faster charging sub-arrays in each bank. Our experimental results show averagely our schemes achieve 54% CPU performance improvement and 29% system energy reduction over a CCP design.

8. REFERENCES

[1] Y. K. Cao, "What is Predictive Technology Model (PTM)?" *SIGDA News letter*, 39(3):1–1, March 2009.

[2] T. E. Carlson, *et al.*, "Sniper: Exploring the level of abstraction for scalable and accurate parallel multi-core simulation," in *SC*, 2011.

[3] K. Chae, *et al.*, "A 690mV 4.4Gbps/pin all-digital LPDDR4 PHY in 10nm FinFET technology," in *ESSCIRC*, Sept 2016.

[4] S. Chhabra and Y. Solihin, "i-NVMM: A Secure Non-volatile Main Memory System with Incremental Encryption," in *ISCA*, 2011.

[5] S. Cho and H. Lee, "Flip-N-Write: A Simple Deterministic Technique to Improve PRAM Write Performance, Energy and Endurance," in *MICRO*, 2009.

[6] Y. Choi, *et al.*, "A 20nm 1.8V 8Gb PRAM with 40MB/s program bandwidth," in *ISSCC*, 2012.

[7] D. Eggleston, "3D XP: What the Hell?!!" in *Flash Memory Summit*, conference concepts, inc, 2015, http://goo.gl/ulGWOz.

[8] J. Handy, "3D XPoint Today: Any Change?" in *Flash Memory Summit*, conference concepts, inc, 2016, http://goo.gl/3apJgi.

[9] A. Hay, *et al.*, "Preventing PCM Banks from Seizing Too Much Power," in *MICRO*, 2011.

[10] Intel, "Xeon Phi Processor 7290," http://ark.intel.com/products/95830/Intel-Xeon-Phi-Processor-7290-16GB-1_50-GHz-72-core.

[11] K. Ishida, *et al.*, "A 1.8 V 30nJ adaptive program-voltage (20V) generator for 3D-integrated NAND flash SSD," in *ISSCC*, 2009.

[12] ITRS, "The International Technology Roadmap for Semiconductors Report," , 2009, http://www.itrs.net/.

[13] M. Jalili, *et al.*, "A Reliable 3D MLC PCM Architecture with Resistance Drift Predictor," in *DSN*, 2014.

[14] W. Jeong, *et al.*, "A 128 Gb 3b/cell V-NAND Flash Memory With 1 Gb/s I/O Rate," *JSSC*, 51(1):204–212, Jan 2016.

[15] L. Jiang, *et al.*, "FPB: Fine-grained Power Budgeting to Improve Write Throughput of Multi-level Cell Phase Change Memory," in *MICRO*, 2012.

[16] L. Jiang, *et al.*, "Improving Write Operations in MLC Phase Change Memory," in *HPCA*, 2012.

[17] L. Jiang, *et al.*, "A low power and reliable charge pump design for Phase Change Memories," in *ISCA*, 2014.

[18] S. Kang, *et al.*, "A 0.1-um 1.8-V 256-Mb Phase-Change Random Access Memory (PRAM) With 66-MHz Synchronous Burst-Read Operation," *JSSC*, 2007.

[19] U. Kang, *et al.*, "8Gb 3D DDR3 DRAM using through-silicon-via technology," in *ISSCC*, 2009.

[20] G. Katti, *et al.*, "Electrical Modeling and Characterization of Through Silicon via for Three-Dimensional ICs," *IEEE Transactions on Electron Devices*, 57(1):256–262, Jan 2010.

[21] D. Kau, *et al.*, "A stackable cross point Phase Change Memory," in *IEDM*, 2009.

[22] K. Lee, *et al.*, "A 90 nm 1.8 v 512 mb diode-switch pram with 266 mb/s read throughput," *JSSC*, 2008.

[23] P. Li, *et al.*, "Digitally assisted discontinuous conduction mode 5V/100MHz and 10V/45MHz DC-DC boost converters with integrated Schottky diodes in standard 0.13 um CMOS," in *ISSCC*, 2010.

[24] D. Liu and C. Svensson, "Power consumption estimation in CMOS VLSI chips," *JSSC*, 29(6):663–670, Jun 1994.

[25] J. Liu, *et al.*, "RAIDR: Retention-Aware Intelligent DRAM Refresh," in *ISCA*, 2012.

[26] N. Muralimanohar, *et al.*, "CACTI 6.0: A Tool to Understand Large Caches," *HP TECH REPORT*, 2013.

[27] M. K. Qureshi, *et al.*, "Scalable High Performance Main Memory System Using Phase-Change Memory Technology," in *ISCA*, 2009.

[28] V. Seshadri, *et al.*, "RowClone: Fast and Energy-efficient in-DRAM Bulk Data Copy and Initialization," in *MICRO*, 2013.

[29] M. Shevgoor, *et al.*, "Quantifying the Relationship Between the Power Delivery Network and Architectural Policies in a 3D-stacked Memory Device," in *MICRO*, 2013.

[30] R. Sundaram, *et al.*, "A 128 Mb NOR flash memory with 3 MB/s program time and low-power write performance by using in-package inductor charge-pump," in *ISSCC*, 2005.

[31] Y. Wang, *et al.*, "PSI Conscious Write Scheduling: Architectural Support for Reliable Power Delivery in 3-D Die-Stacked PCM," *TVLSI*, 24(5):1613–1625, May 2016.

[32] M. Webb, "3D XPoint Status and Forecast," in *Flash Memory Summit*, conference concepts, inc, 2016, http://goo.gl/9Dh8ff.

[33] S. L. Wright, *et al.*, "Characterization of micro-bump C4 interconnects for Si-carrier SOP applications," in *Electronic Components and Technology Conference*, 2006.

[34] C. P. Yue and S. S. Wong, "On-chip spiral inductors with patterned ground shields for Si-based RF ICs," *JSSC*, 33(5):743–752, 1998.

[35] W. Zhang and T. Li, "Exploring Phase Change Memory and 3D Die-Stacking for Power/Thermal Friendly, Fast and Durable Memory Architectures," in *PACT*, 2009.

[36] X. Zhang, *et al.*, "Restore truncation for performance improvement in future DRAM systems," in *HPCA*, 2016.

Design Space Exploration of TAGE Branch Predictor with Ultra-Small RAM

Chaobing Zhou, Libo Huang*, Zhisheng Li, Tan Zhang, Qiang Dou
School of computer, National University of Defense Technology
Changsha 410073, China
{zhouchaobing15, libohuang, lzs123, zhangtan15, douq}@nudt.edu.cn

ABSTRACT

In embedded processors, the RAM resources required by branch predictor compared to desktop or server processors are far from being reached. Utilizing the limited resources to design superior performance branch predictor has become urgent challenge. In this paper, we exploit the performance of complex TAGE implemented in ultra-small RAM processor. We first define design space exploration problem of the TAGE under the constraints of given RAM size and maximum global history register length. Then, based on the trace-driven simulation, the improved Particle Swarm Optimization algorithm is used to efficiently explore the specific parameters, rewarding design parameters with high prediction accuracy under RAM ranging from 0.125KB to 4KB. We found that, for the traces of this paper, the parameters under the 1.5KB RAM explored by our algorithm can achieve adequate accuracy. The performance loss is considerably small if we reduce the RAM resources from 8KB to 1.5KB. In addition, the misprediction rate of 1.5KB TAGE are reduced by 63.41% compared to 1.5KB Bi-mode. And, 0.25KB TAGE has almost the same accuracy with 4KB GShare.

Keywords

branch prediction; TAGE; design space exploration; particle swarm optimization

1. INTRODUCTION

Modern microprocessors rely on deep-pipelined to boost instruction-level parallelism [14]. Predictor is designed to reduce pipeline stalls imposed by branch instruction. However, if the prediction fails, the instructions cleared by misprediction recovery have done useless work, wasted processor power and reduced the throughput of the processor, what's worse, may bring secondary effects, such as I-Cache misses [12]. Therefore, the microprocessors need a branch predictor with particularly high accuracy.

*corresponding author

Permission to make digital or hard copies of all or part of this work for personal or classroom use is granted without fee provided that copies are not made or distributed for profit or commercial advantage and that copies bear this notice and the full citation on the first page. Copyrights for components of this work owned by others than ACM must be honored. Abstracting with credit is permitted. To copy otherwise, or republish, to post on servers or to redistribute to lists, requires prior specific permission and/or a fee. Request permissions from permissions@acm.org.

GLSVLSI '17, May 10-12, 2017, Banff, AB, Canada

© 2017 ACM. ISBN 978-1-4503-4972-7/17/05...$15.00

DOI: http://dx.doi.org/10.1145/3060403.3060423

In hardware implementation, in order to obtain higher prediction accuracy, allocating more RAM resources to the branch predictor is necessary. However, for embedded processors, the resources that can be allocated to predictor are rather limited, usually below 4KB, or even 1KB. Designers need to make trade-offs between RAM resources allocation and performance improvement. Championship Branch Prediction (CBP) provides contestants a fixed storage budget to implement their best predictors on a common framework. Most of the best branch predictors in previous CBP are based on TAGE [8]. TAGE-SC-L won CBP-4 [6] and TAGE-SC-L again won CBP-5 [7].

This paper seeks to find a way of using the excellent TAGE branch predictor configuration suitable for ultra-small RAM processor. The resource occupancy of the TAGE branch predictor is mainly due to the RAM storing the branch information of a plurality of prediction components and the global history register (GHR). We choose the number of subpredictors (N), the number of entries of the base predictor T0 ($logb$), and the number of entries, tag width, GHR length of each tagged subpredictors (T1$\sim$Tn) as the parameters to be explored. Based on the trace-driven simulation method, the improved Particle Swarm Optimization (PSO) algorithm is used to automatically explore the specific design parameters of the TAGE branch predictor with RAM ranging from 0.125KB to 4KB.

In the exploration, we found that, for our traces used in CBP-4, the parameters under the 1.5KB RAM our algorithm explored can achieve adequate accuracy, more RAM result in a linear decrease in misprediction. The performance loss is considerably small if we reduce the RAM resources from 8KB to 1.5KB. In addition, occupied the same ultra-small RAM resources, the misprediction rate of 1.5KB TAGE are reduced by 63.41% compared to 1.5KB Bi-mode [4], while 2KB TAGE achieve 61.43% misprediction rate decrease to 2KB GShare [13]. A meaningful finding is that 0.25KB TAGE has almost the same accuracy with 4KB GShare. TAGE effectively utilize the limited storage resources and obtain high prediction accuracy.

The remainder of this paper is organized as follows. Section 2 provides background on TAGE, and the motivation for design space exploration (DSE). In Section 3, the DSE problem of TAGE is defined. Section 4 presents the improved PSO algorithm. Section 5 describes the evaluation methodology and results. Section 6 introduces the related work. And, Section 7 gives conclusions.

2. BACKGROUND

Branch predictor design of embedded processors in the past takes into account the constraints of die-area and power consumption, often using ultra-low power static branch prediction or static and dynamic hybrid approach [2, 3]. As the available resources increase, the performance of branch predictor receives more attention. The predictor of ARM A15 processor is similar to the Bi-mode branch predictor [1] The motivation of this paper is to study the performance of TAGE implemented in the embedded processors with limited RAM resources.

2.1 TAGE

As shown in Figure 1, TAGE predictor consists of a base predictor T0 and n (T1,T2,···,Tn) tagged predictor components. T0 providing a basic prediction is the 2-bit counter bimodal table indexed by the PC. Ti (i>0) is indexed by a hashed result of PC and length $L(i)$ branch history. $L(i)$ is a sequence that satisfies the geometric progression, i.e $L(i) = (int)(\alpha^{i-1} * L(1) + 0.5), (i > 1)$.

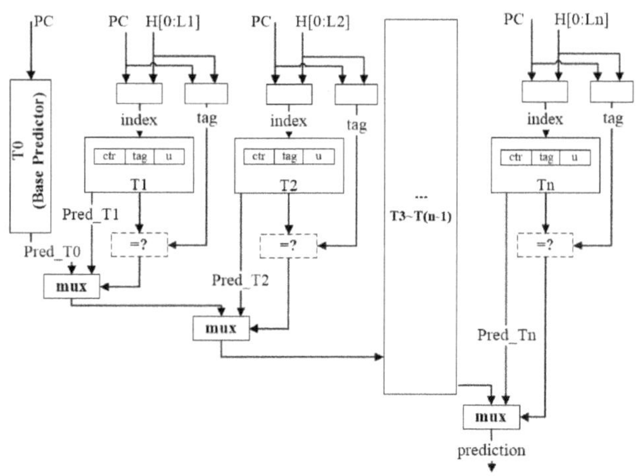

Figure 1: The TAGE predictor

Each tagged component contains a number of configurable entries. Each entry is composed of *ctr*, *tag* and *u*. *ctr* (pred, 3 or 2bit) is a saturation counter, used to indicate the direction of a branch (if $|2 * ctr + 1| \geq ([1 \ll ctrwidth] - 1)$, the prediction is strong, else the prediction is weak). *tag* is used to confirm that this entry is matches the branch, and the tag width of each component can be different. *u* (useful, 2 or 1 bit) indicates whether the entry is valid, also is an age counter. There are two definitions:

provider: the matching component with the longest history.

alternator: the matching component with the history length only shorter than the longest. If there is no matching component, alternator is T0.

2.1.1 prediction computing

If no matching is found in the tagged components, the prediction result of the base branch predictor T0 is used. In general, the final prediction direction is the prediction result of provider, if the tags of the tagged component matched. However, some of the tests found that, the predictions generated by alternator are sometimes better than the prediction from a newly allocated entry in provider. This situation is global to the application. The use of a 4-bit USE_ALT_ON_NA counter can be a good dynamic monitor of the occurrence of such a situation. One of the following conditions occurs using predict value from provider, otherwise alternator's predict value is adopted.

1) USE_ALT_ON_NA is negative.
2) The provider's prediction is strong.

2.1.2 predictor updating

ctr: First determine whether there is a tagged component hit. If no, only update T0. Otherwise, the *ctr* of provider will be updated. The *ctr* of alternator is only updated if the provider prediction fails. When predict correctly, *ctr* self-increments, otherwise *ctr* self-decrements.

u: The u of provider increments when TAGE prediction is correct while alternator prediction fails. TICK, a periodic reset flag of u is introduced. In the process of allocating new entry, if the corresponding u of the candidate Tk is already reaching the maximum value (in the case, the mandatory allocation is required), TICK will be incremented, otherwise it will be decrement. When TICK reached the threshold, u is reset and TICK is change to 0.

allocation: If provider is Ti giving misprediction, and Ti is not Tn, a new entry will be allocated. The allocation position is Tk ($i < k \leq n$) whose u is 0, and the higher probability of allocation is given to the component closer to Ti. The *ctr* of new allocated entry is set to weak mode and its u is set to 0.

USE_ALT_ON_NA: It will be updated when the prediction of provider is weak and provider's prediction is different from that of alternator. If alternator has done a correct prediction, USE_ALT_ON_NA will self-increments, otherwise self-decrements.

2.1.3 Why TAGE is state-of-the-art

TAGE implements a hybrid branch predictor that uses geometric lengths of historical information for different branch instructions. **First**, TAGE partially tags its entries, so that TAGE determine which instruction an entry corresponds to in context with high certainly, well avoiding the aliasing between multiple branches. **Second**, TAGE uses entries with geometric history length for different branch situation for the same branch instruction. For easily predictable branch instruction, it can be accurately predicted by the entries trained in a short time. This allows TAGE to make a good trade-off between historical length selection and the warm-up time.

2.2 The motivation for DSE

In TAGE, many parameters can be configured, such as the number of sub-predictors. TAGE performance may vary considerably with different parameter configurations. We randomly generate several sets of parameters under the constraints of 26Kbits RAM (to express precisely, Kbits is used for RAM size in latter part) and 360bits GHR to roughly find the gain room of parameter exploration. The statistical results of running SHORT-MM-4 in CBP-4 are shown in Figure 2. For each group, the average misprediction per kiloinstruction (misp/KI) decrease in the minimum value compared to the maximum is 4.47%. While The global minimum compared to the global maximum, there is a 5.64% misp/KI decrease.

With RAM constraints, only by changing the parameter

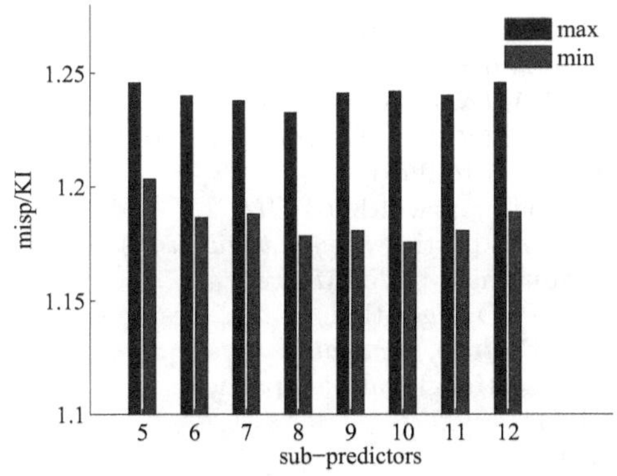

Figure 2: Performance of random parameters

design can get such huge misp/KI decrease, indicating that the design space exploration is necessary. Using an efficient exploration algorithm, it's possible to find better design parameters obtaining higher prediction accuracy for embedded processors which may allocate only a few Kbits RAM to branch predictor.

3. DSE OF TAGE

3.1 Problem definition

TAGE design mainly involves the control module (part 2.1, including prediction computing and updating) and the data storage module which is the main point of this paper. Figure 3 show the bank structure of each sub-predictor. The number of entries of the basic predictor T0 is *N0*, and each entry is a counter of width CWIDTH. To save storage space, several counters share the hysteresis bit. Ti ($0 < i \leq n$) has *Ni* entries, and each entry is composed of *ctr*, *tag* and u.

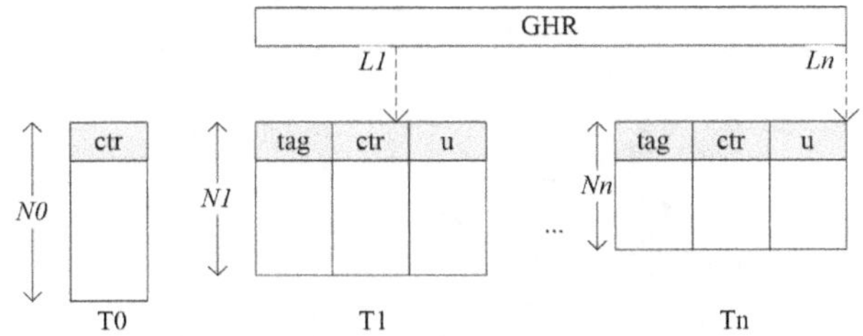

Figure 3: Bank structure of TAGE

We define DSE problem as follow.

Problem input: M (the RAM TAGE used must be less than M) and *GHR_MAX* (the maximum length of GHR)

Exploration (output) parameters: N (the total number of sub-predictors, and the number of tagged predictors is $nhist(N-1)$), $logb$ (the number of T0's entries), $logg$[N] (the array of Ti's entry number), tag[N] (the tag width array of Ti), ghr[N] (GHR length of the Ti using), CWIDTH (the width of ctr), UWIDTH (the width of u).

Objective function: seeking the parameters of TAGE that gain the minimum misp/KI running the corresponding traces.

$$min\{MISPKI(N, logb, logg[], tag[], ghr[])\} \quad (1)$$

where, for ultra-small RAM, we set CWIDTH = 2 and UWIDTH = 1.

Restrictions:

a) RAM storage limitation

$$2^{logb} + 2^{logb-HYST} + \sum_{i=1}^{n} 2^{logg[i]} * (3 + tag[i]) \leq M \quad (2)$$

where, the hysteresis bit $HYST$ for the limited size predictor usually is 2.

b) The range of each parameter

$N \in [N\_MIN, N\_MAX]$, the minimum of N_MIN is 1, that TAGE only has T0, becoming bimodal.

$logb \in [LOGB\_MIN, LOGB\_MAX]$, if the number of T0's entries is small, serious branch aliasing problem will occur On the contrary, the resources allocated to tagged predictors will be too few.

$logg[i] \in [Logg\_MIN, Logg\_MAX]$.

$tag[i] \in [Tag\_MIN, Tag\_MAX]$, Tag[] is a non-descending sequence ($Tag[i] \leq Tag[i+1], 0 \leq i < N$).

c) About $ghr[]$

The ghr array can be calculated from $L1$ and N when GHR_MAX is given (assume the last sub-predictor uses the historical information with length GHR_MAX).

$$\alpha = \sqrt[N-2]{(GHR\_MAX - 0.5)/L1} \quad (3)$$

then, $ghr[i]$ can be solved by $int(\alpha^{i-1} * L1 + 0.5)$. So, for $ghr[]$, we just explore L1 ranging from 4 to 9.

3.2 Design space analysis

This section attempts to analyze the design space size. Since the RAM TAGE really used in 32Kbits TAGE-SC-L of CBP-4 is 26Kbits [6], we suppose 26Kbits RAM is available. The range of parameters selected is shown in Table 1.

Table 1: Parameters candidate

Para	*N*	*LOGB*	*tag[i]*	*logg[i]*	*L1*
MIN	5	9	7	7	4
MAX	14	14	14	13	9
candidate	10	6	8	7	6

As equation (4), the total number of candidate parameter combinations is $1.09 * 10^{26}$.

$$\sum_{k=N\_MIN}^{N\_MAX} R(logb) * (R(tag))^k * (R(logg))^k * R(L1) \quad (4)$$

where $R()$ function means the range of, which is $MAX - MIN + 1$. Assuming the probability of the parameter sets satisfying the storage constraint are only 0.01%. As part 2.2, the performance testing time of a set of parameters is 10 seconds. In a single-threaded environment, it takes about many years to run 10^{22} parameter sets. Even with multi-core, multi-threaded parallel acceleration, the time-consuming of iterative search is unacceptable. So we have to find a efficient algorithm to explore the proper parameters with acceptable time cost.

4. USING PSO

4.1 Particle Swarm Optimization

PSO is a computational method that optimizes a problem by iteratively trying to improve a candidate solution with regard to a given measure of quality [11]. Each set of parameters is called a particle which is a potential solution to the problem, and particle population consists of several particles. Each particle adjusts their position according to its local best position and the best position in the search-space updated by all particles. Finally, the entire population is aggregated toward one location. Let $Xi = (X_{i1}, X_{i2}, \cdots, X_{im})$ be the position of particle i. Let $Vi = (V_{i1}, V_{i2}, \cdots, V_{im})$ be the velocity of particle i. and $pbest_i = (P_{i1}, P_{i2}, \cdots, P_{im})$ is the best position of particle i. $gbest = (g_1, g_2, \cdots, g_m)$ is the best known position of the entire swarm. The iteration equation of velocity and position are shown below:

$$V_i(k+1) = wV_i(k) + c_1r_1(pbest_i - X_i(k)) + c_2r_2(gbest - X_i(k)) \quad (5)$$

$$X_i(k+1) = X_i(k) + V_i(k+1) \quad (6)$$

where i is the particle number, k is the number of iterations, and r_1,r_2 are the random numbers used to maintain the population diversity. w is the inertia factor, which reflects the influence of the current velocity of the particle on the velocity afterwards, balancing the global search and local search. c_1 and c_2 are positive constants, as a learning factors, making the particles achieve the ability of self-summary and learning from the best individual.

Algorithm 1 Particle Swarm Optimization

Input: *particles. Max_Iteration*
Output: *particles*

```
initialize the particle population
iterator=0
while iterator<Max_Iteration do
    calculate individual fitness
    update the population optimal individual and the best
    individual of particle
    adjust the speed and position of individual particles
    iterator++
end while
```

4.2 Design Space Exploration Based on PSO

The number of parameters of this DSE problem varies depending on the number of tagged predictor. The method proposed in this paper is that for the number of sub-predictors (N) and the entries number of T0 ($logb$), the exhaustive method is used. And evolutionary algorithm is introduced to explore tag width array, tagged predictors entry number array. Algorithm 2 describes the DSE framework in detail. The outer loop traverses N and $logb$, respectively. $L1$ traverses the range from 4 to 9. Combining $L1$ and GHR_MAX, the ghr array can be solved, which includes the optimal Li the Ti needs. Within the loop, the length of tag array and $logg$ array is fixed (N), and the dimension of the particle is determined. Then, PSO is introduced to seek the local optimal under this N and $logb$. The global optimal is updated when local optimal is found.

4.3 Improving algorithm framework

In the implementation of Algorithm 2, we found that the other parameters have less influence on the performance when N and $logb$ are given. We propose the improved framework that, first, PSO evolve less times, recording N and $logb$, which their average performance is the best. Then, the other parameters will be deep explored under this N and $logb$. The improvement is shown in Figure 4.

Algorithm 2 Design Space Exploration

Input: *RAMsize. GHR_MAX*
Output: *parameters*

```
for N = N_MIN to N_MAX do
    for logb = LOGB_MIN to LOGB_MAX do
        for L1 = 4 to 9 do
            compute ghrwidth(L1,GHR_MAX)
            random particles(logg[],tagwidth[]) meeting the
            requirement of RAMsize
            run PSO algorithm to find best particle under
            this [N, logb, ghrwidth]
            update the global best particle;
        end for
    end for
end for
return parameters of the global best particle
```

When RAM is large, the global optimum is not in the parameters set which N is small. As Figure 4 shown, the improved version (V2) reduces some useless search cost, and only makes a deep exploration on the sets which the global optimum may exists. If algorithm 2 (V1) performs 20 iterations over 20 individuals in each set of N and $logb$, for 26 Kbits RAM, parameters as Table 1, V1 need to run the trace 144000 times (10*9*6*20*20), while the improved version V2 only run 22000 times (10*9*6*3*20+20*20).

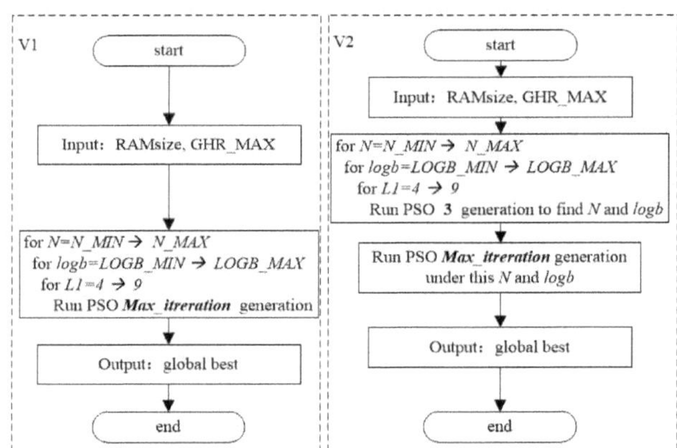

Figure 4: Algorithm 2 (V1) and improved (V2)

5. EVALUATION

5.1 Methodology

After several tests, we set the population size to 20, and *Max_Iteration* to 20, which could get both better timing efficiency and exploration results. When calculating individual fitness, the evaluation framework of CBP-4 is used [9]. For traces, the combination containing SHORT-FP-4, SHORT-INT-4, SHORT-MM-4 and SHORT-SERV-4 is selected. These 4 traces include SPEC floating-point and integer applications, multimedia and servers applications. For the application with different characteristics, it's only need to replace the corresponding trace set. The evaluation metric (individual fitness) is the average misp/KI of the trace

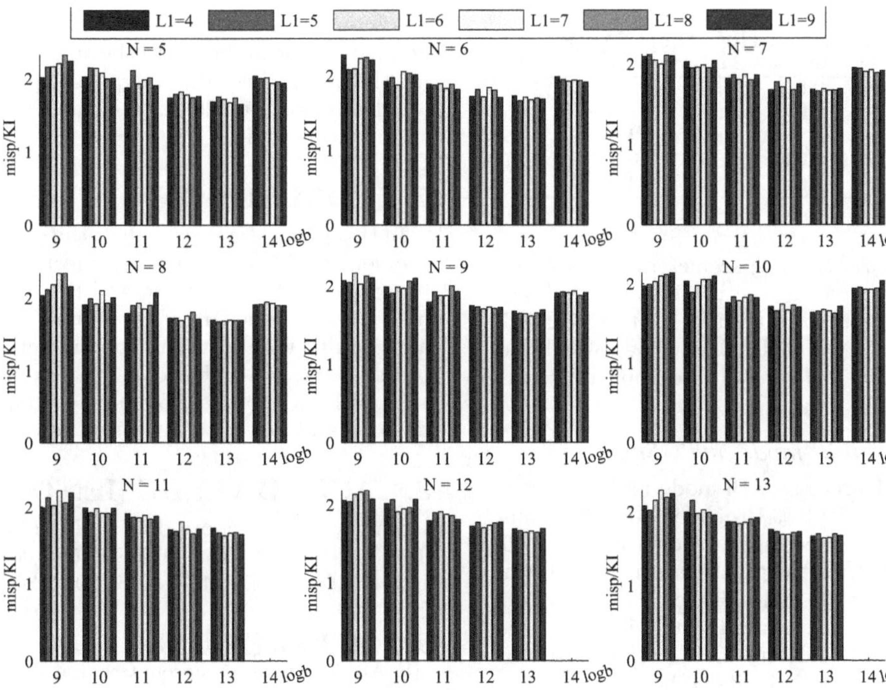

Figure 5: Running record of V1 with 26 Kbits RAM, 360 bits GHR inputs.

set. In the CBP environment, we have implemented a configure TAGE class. When calculating the performance of one parameters set, first initialize the TAGE using the parameter set, and re-initialize the TAGE after one trace simulated, ready to simulate another trace. When simulating a single trace, an instruction record is fetched from the trace file. If the instruction is a conditional branch, it is predicted by TAGE. TAGE is updated with the predicted value and the actual branch taken value immediately after the prediction finished.

5.2 Results and discussion

5.2.1 Run 26 Kbits

We record the average performance of each parameter set (N, *logb*, $L1$) under the 26 Kbits RAM, 360 bits GHR constraint. The running record is shown in Figure 5.

1) Under 26K RAM limit, misp/KI appears to U-type with the *logb* increasing in each N. When *logb* is small, the number of T0's entries is insufficient, resulting in a severe alias for the base predictor. When *logb* reached 14, fewer resources are allocated to the tagged component, and the prediction entry that can be stored is limited. The best *logb* is 12 or 13.

2) When N and *logb* is given, $L1$ (from 4 to 9) has little effect on accuracy. Each set of N and *logb* has certain ceiling value which can't be change by other parameters. This provides the basis for V2, the improvement of the DSE algorithm.

3) The best parameters performance in $N = 12$ (1.6406) has only 0.08% improved compared with best parameters in $N = 5$ (1.64192). In embedded processors, less N means less RAM port, and die-area. TAGE implemented in little tagged components (4 or 5) can also get outstanding performance.

5.2.2 Run ranging from 1 Kbits to 32 Kbits

For comparison and verification, we run our Algorithm 2 (V1) and its improved version V2 with RAM ranging from 1 Kbits to 32 Kbits. The results are shown in Table 2. The RAM and GHR are input parameters. For each set of inputs,

Table 2: Results of RAM inputs ranging from 1 Kbits to 32 Kbits

RAM (Kbits)	GHR (bits)	V1 (misp/KI)	V1*para* (N, *logb*)	V2 (misp/KI)	V2*para* (N, *logb*)
1	80	6.8120	(5,8)	6.6483	(5,7)
2	80	5.1806	(5,9)	5.1207	(5,9)
3	80	4.2658	(5,10)	4.2101	(5,10)
4	80	3.7489	(5,11)	3.716	(5,11)
5	80	3.3243	(5,11)	3.3373	(5,11)
8	80	2.7473	(6,11)	2.7483	(6,11)
10	100	2.4704	(6,12)	2.4595	(5,12)
12	160	2.2980	(7,12)	2.2770	(7,12)
16	240	2.0659	(6,12)	2.0330	(6,12)
20	300	1.8684	(7,13)	1.8337	(6,13)
24	360	1.7046	(9,13)	1.6656	(8,13)
28	400	1.5859	(9,13)	1.5364	(10,13)
32	480	1.4882	(11,13)	1.4408	(7,13)

V1 and V2 have similar results. Under 12Kbits RAM, TAGE designed by parameters our algorithm explored can achieve adequate accuracy, more RAM result in a linear increase in accuracy.

To compare the performance gap between our explored results and the other TAGE, we list the accuracy of 64 Kbits TAGE implemented with 5 components (5C-TAGE) and 8 components (8C-TAGE) in [8], 32 Kbits TAGE-SC-L in [6], 12 Kbits and 32 Kbits TAGE we explored (DSE-TAGE). From the Table 3, our exploration has excellent results. The performance loss is considerably small if we reduce the RAM resources from 64Kbits to 12Kbits. Comparing with

Table 3: Performance of the other TAGE

model(Kbits)	FP-4	INT-4	MM-4	SERV-4	MEAN
8C-TAGE(64)	0.092	0.818	1.319	2.629	1.2145
5C-TAGE(64)	0.091	0.954	1.280	2.679	1.2510
TAGE-SC-L(32)	0.018	0.992	1.020	3.812	1.4605
DSE-TAGE(12)	0.092	1.634	1.310	6.072	2.2770
DSE-TAGE(32)	0.017	1.048	1.182	3.516	1.4408

64 Kbits 5C-TAGE, our 32Kbits parameters performance loss is only 15.17%. Our algorithm with 32Kbits RAM input has almost the same performance with 32 Kbits TAGE-SC-L. However, TAGE-SC-L, the CBP 2016 winner, which has integrated loop predictor, is difficult to be implemented in hardware.

5.2.3 Comparing with Bi-mode and GShare

For ultra-small RAM processor, Bi-mode and GShare is easy to be implemented. We test Bi-mode and GShare under the same RAM for comparing.As shown in Figure 6, TAGE with ultra-small RAM has great performance advantage comparing with Bi-mode and GShare. The misprediction rate of 12Kbits TAGE are reduced by 63.41% compared to 12Kbits Bi-mode, while 16Kbits TAGE achieve 61.43% misprediction rate decrease to 16Kbits GShare.

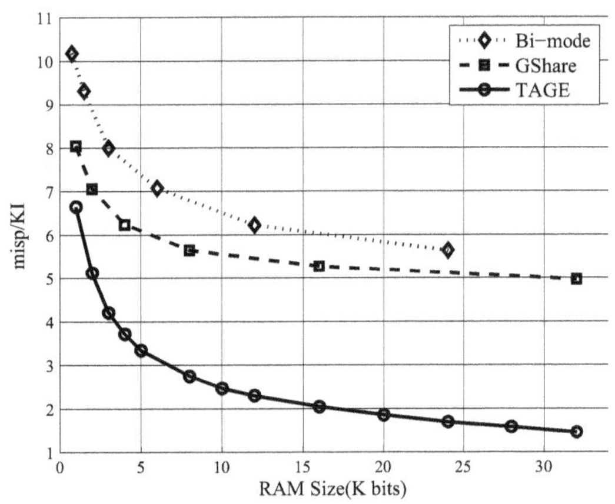

Figure 6: Performance of TAGE, Bi-mode, GShare with ultra-little RAM

2Kbits TAGE has almost the same accuracy with 32Kbits GShare. This finding is very meaningful. Less RAM can lead to small die-area, at the same time, there may be potential benefits in power consumption.

6. RELATED WORK

Today's best branch predictors fall into two broad categories: neural-inspired and TAGE-based [9]. In the TAGE research, the existing papers are mainly to add various small predictors to increase the prediction accuracy. Such as, IT-TAGE for the indirect branch prediction, COTTAGE combining TAGE and ITTAGE [8], TAGE-SC-L integrating the loop predictor and statistics corrector [6]. For design space exploration of branch predictor, Sherwood *et al.* proposed automated design of finite state machine predictors for customized processors [10]. Matthew Bielby *et al.* has done ultra-low power design space exploration of the hybrid branch predictor which combined the BTFN and GShare [2]. Stephen *et al.* dynamically allocate the size of the TAGE table during the benchmarks running [5]. No prior works are done on the design space exploration of the TAGE under ultra-small storage constraints.

7. CONCLUSION

In this paper, we first analyze the design space exploration problem of TAGE. Then, an effective exploration method based on PSO is proposed, and the design parameters with high prediction accuracy are found. We believe our method and results will be useful for predictor designers. In the future work, we will add more real hardware information such as RAM port, adopt more evaluation metrics such as die-area and power consumption to the exploration.

8. ACKNOWLEDGMENTS

This work is supported by NSFC (No. 61472435 and No. 61433019), CHB (No. 2015ZX01028-001-001), HPNSF (No. 12JJ4070), and DFMEC (No. 20114307120010).

9. REFERENCES

[1] ARM. Cortex-a15 mpcore technical reference manual, revision:r3p3. In *http://infocenter.arm.com/help/index.jsp.*

[2] M. Bielby, M. Gould, and N. Topham. Design space exploration of hybrid ultra low power branch predictors. In *International Conference on Architecture of Computing Systems*, pages 184–199. Springer, 2012.

[3] M. Hicks, C. Egan, B. Christianson, and P. Quick. Towards an energy efficient branch prediction scheme using profiling, adaptive bias measurement and delay region scheduling. In *Design and Technology of Integrated Systems in Nanoscale Era*, pages 19–24. IEEE, 2007.

[4] C.-C. Lee, I.-C. K. Chen, and T. N. Mudge. The bi-mode branch predictor. In *Proceedings of the 30th annual ACM/IEEE international symposium on Microarchitecture*, pages 4–13. IEEE Computer Society, 1997.

[5] S. Pruett, S. Zangeneh, A. Fakhrzadehgan, B. Lin, , and Y. N. Pat. Dynamically sizing the tage branch predictor. In *CBP 5*, 2016.

[6] A. Seznec. Tage-sc-l branch predictors. In *4th JILP-Championship Branch Prediction (CBP-4)*, 2014.

[7] A. Seznec. Tage-sc-l branch predictors again. In *5th JILP-Championship Branch Prediction (CBP-5)*, 2016.

[8] A. Seznec and P. Michaud. A case for (partially) tagged geometric history length branch prediction. *Journal of Instruction-Level Parallelism*, 8, 2006.

[9] A. Seznec, J. S. Miguel, and J. Albericio. The inner most loop iteration counter: a new dimension in branch history. In *Proceedings of the 48th International Symposium on Microarchitecture*, pages 347–357. ACM, 2015.

[10] T. Sherwood and B. Calder. Automated design of finite state machine predictors for customized processors. In *ACM SIGARCH Computer Architecture News*, volume 29, pages 86–97. ACM, 2001.

[11] Y. Shi and R. C. Eberhart. Parameter selection in particle swarm optimization. In *International Conference on Evolutionary Programming*, pages 591–600. Springer, 1998.

[12] K. Skadron, P. S. Ahuja, M. Martonosi, and D. W. Clark. Branch prediction, instruction-window size, and cache size: Performance trade-offs and simulation techniques. *IEEE Transactions on Computers*, 48(11):1260–1281, 1999.

[13] J. E. Smith. A study of branch prediction strategies. In *Proceedings of the 8th annual symposium on Computer Architecture*, pages 135–148. IEEE Computer Society Press, 1981.

[14] E. Sprangle and D. Carmean. Increasing processor performance by implementing deeper pipelines. In *ACM SIGARCH Computer Architecture News*, volume 30, pages 25–34. IEEE Computer Society, 2002.

A Power Efficient Architecture with Optimized Parallel Memory Accessing for Feature Generation

Peng Ouyang
Institute of micro-electronics
Tsinghua University
Beijing,China

Shouyi Yin*
Institute of micro-electronics
Tsinghua University
Beijing,China

Chunxiao Xing
Research Institute of Information Technology
Tsinghua University
Beijing,China

Leibo Liu
Institute of micro-electronics
Tsinghua University
Beijing,China

Shaojun Wei
Institute of micro-electronics
Tsinghua University
Beijing,China

ABSTRACT

Visual feature detection has been widely used in many computer vision applications. In comparison with popular feature detection algorithms, AFFINE-SIFT (ASIFT) achieves the strongest robustness on image illumination, image rotation and image scale transformation, etc., however, since feature vectors of different feature points need to be computed, feature generation of ASIFT exhibits high computing complexity. Meanwhile, it also shows low efficiency on parallel memory accessing since multiple computing processes of feature points need to access the same memory concurrently, which causes memory accessing conflicts and incurs high power consumption. In this work, we improve the feature generation based on a rotation invariant block binary pattern(RIBBP) to reduce computation and design a parallel processing architecture. Meanwhile, a spatial relevance based memory accessing(SRBMA) optimization is performed to improve data reuse and enhance parallel memory accessing. Evaluations using TSMC 65 nm 1P9M LP process show that this work improves the processing speed and energy efficiency of feature generation by 17% and 37.9%, respectively, when compared with state-of-the art work.

1. INTRODUCTION

Feature detection plays a significant role in many computer vision applications, e.g., object detection, object recognition and object tracking[7, 13], which require high computing efficiency and strong detection robustness. Traditional feature detection algorithms like SIFT, KAZE[1, 4], etc., achieve strong robustness on rotation, illumination and scale, but show weakness in viewpoint variation. The ASIFT [6] exhibits stronger robustness on all the aspects including viewpoint, than current feature algorithms, regarding performing SIFT feature detection in affine space to simulate viewpoint variations, at the cost of high computation complexity.

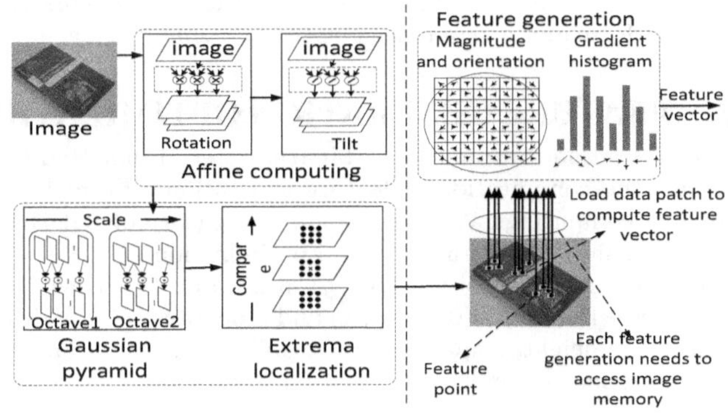

Figure 1: The computation flow of ASIFT

As Fig. 1 shows, ASIFT mainly includes affine computing, Gaussian pyramid, extrema localization and feature generation. Affine computing simulates image to different viewpoints independently by means of image rotation and image tilt, which contributes to the robustness on viewpoint variations. Gaussian pyramid generates Gaussian space on the simulated images by Gaussian filtering. The Gaussian pyramid contains multiple octaves and each octave contains multiple filtered Gaussian layers. Extrema localization seeks extremas on the difference of Gaussian space by means of comparing the pixel value among its neighboring pixel values. Feature generation weights the gradient of pixels around extrema to compute descriptors. The feature generation is independent for each extrema, and exhibits high computation complexity since many extremas in an image need to be processed. The number of extremas is determined by the image content. The characteristics of feature generation exhibits that multiple processes of feature generation for extremas can work in parallel. Meanwhile the problem of concurrent memory accessing for different feature extremas exists, and incurs memory conflicts and causes low data reuse. Testings on Grafftic dataset[5] using

*Email:yinsy@tsinghua.edu.cn.

Permission to make digital or hard copies of all or part of this work for personal or classroom use is granted without fee provided that copies are not made or distributed for profit or commercial advantage and that copies bear this notice and the full citation on the first page. Copyrights for components of this work owned by others than ACM must be honored. Abstracting with credit is permitted. To copy otherwise, or republish, to post on servers or to redistribute to lists, requires prior specific permission and/or a fee. Request permissions from permissions@acm.org.

GLSVLSI '17, May 10-12, 2017, Banff, AB, Canada

© 2017 ACM. ISBN 978-1-4503-4972-7/17/05...$15.00

DOI: http://dx.doi.org/10.1145/3060403.3060436

CPU platform (E7200@2.53GHz) show that, feature generation takes up 40% of total time cost, which makes it become the main performance bottleneck in ASIFT algorithm. Currently, there are many works based on hardware to construct specific design for feature generation[2, 3, 8]. These works focus on the optimized feature detection algorithms, like SIFT and SURF. However, as we have explained, these optimized algorithms have limited robustness regarding illumination, rotation, scale, and especially the viewpoint variation. Yin [12] focuses on ASIFT and performs optimization on feature generation. However, the parallelization for feature generation is not well exploited and the redundant magnitude memory that causes extra memory consumption exists. Meanwhile, the conflicts of multiple feature generations when accessing the same memory are not resolved. Park [9] considers load balance for different feature generation process, but ignors the data reuse when different feature generations access the same memory. In this work, in order to improve the computing efficiency of feature generation in ASIFT, we first improve feature generation based on a rotation invariant block binary pattern, to exploit the parallelism and reduce computation. Then design a parallel processing architecture for feature generation. Meanwhile, a spatial relevance based memory accessing based optimization is proposed to improve data reuse and enhance parallel memory accessing. Evaluations show that this work achieves high performance on computing speed and energy efficiency.

2. FEATURE GENERATION OPTIMIZATION

The rotation invariant block binary pattern is adopted to reduce the computation of feature generation and achieve parallel computing. We first explain the theory of RIBBP, and then show the detailed design optimization.

Define image intensity as $I(x,y)$ in location (x,y), where $x \in [0, w-1]$ and $y \in [0, h-1]$. w and h denote image width and image height, respectively. Thus illumination variation in affine space is modeled in equation (1):

$$I'(x,y) = \alpha(\sum_{i=1}^{k} w_i I(x + d_x^i, y + d_y^i)) + \beta \quad (1)$$

where w_i, α and β represent the weighting factor, scaling factor and shifting factor respectively. d_x^i and d_y^i denote the location shift in x orientation and y orientation. k equals to the number of pixels in original image to attend transformation for computing the pixel in $I'(x,y)$. $I'(x,y)$ denotes the affine transformed image. Since Gaussian pyramid technique and affine simulation technique are adopted in ASIFT to achieve affine and scaling invariant, the image pair, which is approximately same, is achieved after affine computing. Thus original equation (1) is rewritten as equation (2):

$$I'(x,y) \approx \alpha I(x + d_x, y + d_y) + \beta \quad (2)$$

As have mentioned in works[10, 11], binary pattern mode can achieve strong robustness on illumination. Thus given the pixels $I'(x,y)$ and $I'(x+1, y+1)$, assume $I'(x,y) > I'(x+1,y+1)$, we have $\alpha I(x + d_x, y + d_y) + \beta > \alpha I(x + 1 + d_x, y + 1 + d_y) + \beta$. Then we construct the binary pattern mode to denote the relationship of intensity value. The relationship shown in equation (3), is achieved by means of binary pattern mode transformation $\psi(para1, para2)$ mentioned in [10, 11].

$$\psi(I'(x,y), I'(x+1,y+1)) = \psi(I(x + d_x, y + d_y), I(x + 1 + d_x, y + 1 + d_y)) \quad (3)$$

In equation (3), $\psi(para1, para2)$ denotes 1 if $para1 > para2$, and denotes 0 if $para1 < para2$. According to equation (3), the illumination disturbance on the pixels is well handled. According to equation (2), the relationships are approximately equivalent. Hence, in order to reduce approximation error, we perform intensity accumulation to construct block based binrary pattern in equation (4), where $i' = i + d_x$, $j' = j + d_y$ and $\beta_s = \sum_{-1 \le i,j \le 1} \beta$.

$$\sum_{-1 \le i,j \le 1} I'(x+i, y+j) \approx \sum_{-1 \le i,j \le 1} \alpha I(x + i', y + j') + \beta_s \quad (4)$$

Then we construct the block binary pattern image based on the original image block to enhance the illumination robustness according to equation (5),

$$\psi(BP'_a, BP'_b) = \psi(BP_a, BP_b) \quad (5)$$

where

$$BP'_a = \sum_{-1 \le i,j \le 1} I'(x+i, y+j),$$
$$BP'_b = \sum_{-1 \le i,j \le 1} I'(x + i + b_{width}, y + j + b_{height}),$$
$$BP_a = \sum_{-1 \le i,j \le 1} I(x + d_x + i, y + d_y + j),$$
$$BP_b = \sum_{-1 \le i,j \le 1} I(x + d_x + i + b_{width}, y + d_y + j + b_{height})$$

in which b_{width} and b_{height} represent the width and height of the image block, respectively. We rotate the binary pattern around the center pixel to the minimal value to achieve a stable descriptor. The corresponding commuting method is shown in equation (6), where the binary vector constructed by $(\psi_1(\cdot), \psi_2(\cdot), ...\psi_8(\cdot))$, circularly shifts to a minimal value $(\psi_z(\cdot), ...\psi_8(\cdot), ...)_{min}$. Based on this method, the rotation invariant block bingray pattern representation for the center pixel is achived. Each pixel in original image is computed according to this way to geneate RIBBP image. The computation complexity of this process is low since it mainly involves 2 kinds of operation: addition and comparison.

$$(\psi_1(\cdot), \psi_2(\cdot), ...\psi_8(\cdot)) \overset{Shift}{\longrightarrow} (\psi_z(\cdot), ...\psi_8(\cdot), ...)_{min} \quad (6)$$

Further, RIBBP based circular histogram is designed based on RIBBP image to generate final feature vector. Denote $R(R1, R2)$ as the region between $R1$ and $R2$ in the circular region, where $R1$ denotes outer radius and $R2$ denotes inner radius. Denote θ as the angle occupied by each ring section, and Bin as the number of statistical classification in histogram. After acquiring main orientation and extrema location, this method constructs ring section based on main orientation and binary pattern value to generate histogram in region of $R(R1, R2)$. The center of initial ring section is located in the region of main orientation, and multiple ring sections construct the joint circular histograms. The number of ring section is $N = [(2 * PI)/\theta]$. We compute feature vector: $Fea = \{F_0, F_1, ...F_{N-1}\}$, where $F_j = \{c_1, c_2.....c_{bin}\}$, and F_j is the statistics of rotation invariant binary patterns, and $c_1, c_2.....c_{bin}$ denote the statistics of RIBBP in different histogram regions. Given the main orientations O_1 and O_2, the feature vectors for the matched feature points in two images are computed as shown in equation (7) and (8).

$$Fea1 = \{F_{([\frac{O_1 \times N}{2 \times PI}])\%N}, ..F_{([\frac{O_1 \times N}{2 \times PI}]+N-1)\%N}\} \quad (7)$$

$$Fea2 = \{F_{([\frac{O_2 \times N}{2 \times PI}])\%N}, ..F_{([\frac{O_2 \times N}{2 \times PI}]+N-1)\%N}\} \quad (8)$$

Though the main orientations of feature pair are different, RIBBP histograms in circle region achieve high rotation invariant. The relationship of $Fea1$ and $Fea2$ is $|Fea1 - Fea2| \leq \tau$, where τ is a small threshold value for comparison. Smaller τ denotes high discriminative for the feature algorithm. Hence, as shown in equation (9), the goal is to minimize τ to achieve strong robustness.

$$\begin{aligned} & Min(\tau) \\ & s.t.\ |Fea1 - Fea2| \leq \tau \\ & \phi(R1, R2, Bin, \theta) < T_{max} \end{aligned} \quad (9)$$

$|Fea1 - Fea2| \leq \tau$ denotes the constraint for robust detection. The parameters $R1$, $R2$, Bin and θ, are related to the amounts of informative pixels and computation operations. They affect the discrimination performance and computing time. $\phi(R1, R2, Bin, \theta)$ denotes the computing time. T_{max} is maximal computing time constraint. According to equation (4), (5) and (6), RIBBP is first computed based on the binary patterns of image blocks, the corresponding illustration is shown in Fig. 2. Further, as shown in Fig. 2, according to equation (7) or equation (8), the ring sections are constructed based on RIBBP image according to the main orientation and extrema location to generate feature vectors between $R1$ and $R2$. This computing is independent of orientation, thus main orientation computing and RIBBP histograms based feature vector generation are processed in parallel rather then the serial processing in origianl feature geneartion. Meanwhile the feature vector can be rotated to main orientation by indexing RIBBP histograms.

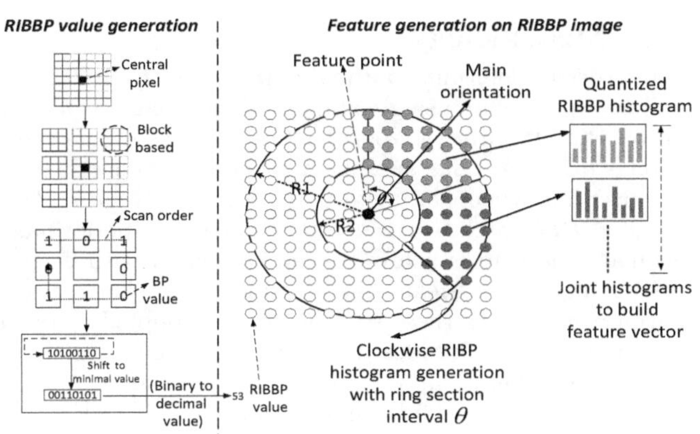

Figure 2: Improved feature generation

3. PARALLEL HARDWARE ARCHITECTURE

As shown in Fig. 3, according to the algorithm optimization explained above, we design the parallel feature generation architecture (FG). The RIBBP value and orientation value of each pixel are loaded into architecture to attend computation. RIBBP value is used to compute the feature vector, and the orientation value is used to compute the main orientation. The RIBBP histogram is generated through the operations of comparisons and counting for different histogram regions, and the generated histogram vectors are stored into vector buffers. In this work, the number of vector buffers equals to the value of $2 \times PI/\theta$. Each vector buffer stores Bin data of RIBBP histogram. Meanwhile, the discretized orientation value of the pixels are used to implement the operations of comparison and counting that statistically record the number of pixels belonging to different orientation regions. This process computes main orientation that represents the orientation of most pixels. Guided by the main orientation, the vector buffers are jointed and loaded from vector buffers. The output order of feature vectors is beginning from the main orientation. In this way, the main orientation and vector generation are computed in parallel, the main operations are the comparison and counting rather than large amounts of multiplications in traditional implementation, it greatly improves the computing speed.

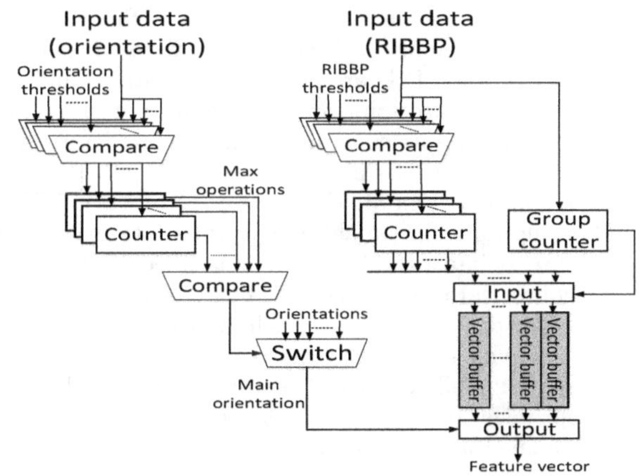

Figure 3: The architecture design of FG

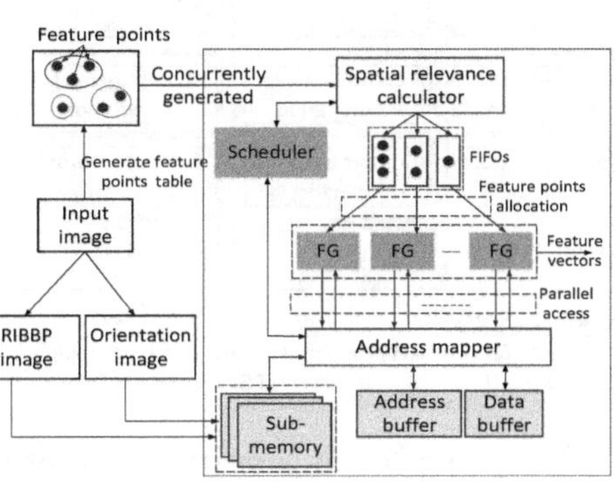

Figure 4: Multiple FGs work concurrently to achieve feature generation for multiple extremas

Further, as shown in Fig. 4, we present the working case for multiple FGs. In this architecture, multiple FGs that are processed in parallel can largely enhance the throughput of feature vector computing. However, as the algorithm explained above, these FG units need to access memory to fetch needed data of orientation and $RIBBP$. Since the data bandwidth of memory is fixed, the conflicts of memory accessing occur when FGs are processed in parallel and the requests of memory accessing are concurrently sent. The locations of feature points generated in image are determined by image contents, meanwhile each feature point needs its neighboring data to compute the feature vector. The overlap of neighboring data for adjacent feature points mean that these feature points exhibit spatial relevance that can be used to achieve data reuse when loading data. By means of data reuse, the processing time to achieve feature generation for all the extremas can be largely reduced. Meanwhile the memory accessing efficiency will be improved. The detailed memory optimization to schedule FGs for feature generation will be explained in next section.

4. MEMORY ACCESSING OPTIMIZATION

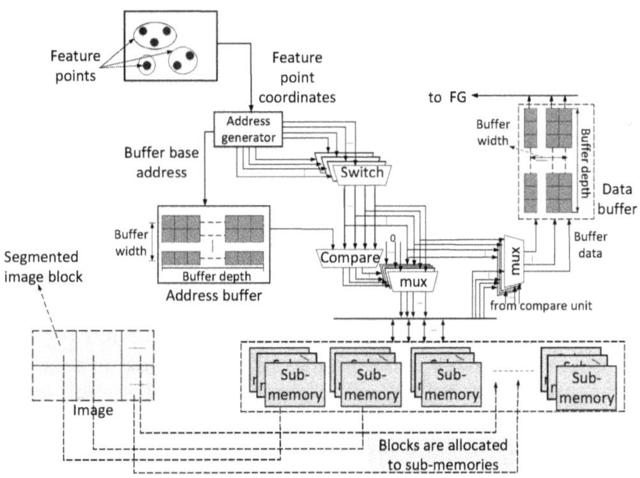

Figure 5: The architecture of scheduling

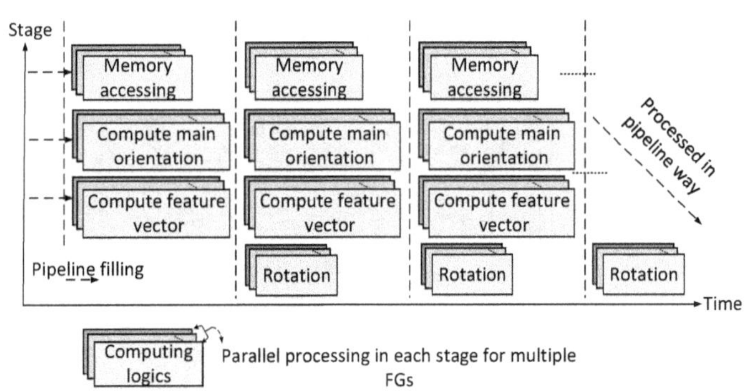

Figure 6: FG performs feature generation in a pipeline way and multiple FGs work in parallel

As shown in Fig. 5, the feature points exhibit spatial relevance, and share parts of data in data patch, thus they can be grouped together to enhance data reuse with the metric of space distance. We could exploit data reuse for the features points in the same group to reduce the conflicts of memory accessing. In practical execution, for different feature points, we calculate the spatial relevance feature point groups by means of clustering method with the metric of the euclidean distance. The image is segmented into several image blocks, and the spatial relevance is calculated on each image block that can reduce the time of spatial relevance computing. Then different feature point groups are allocated to different FGs. Meanwhile, as shown in Fig. 5, the memory that is designed to store orientation and $RIBBP$ values are partitioned into sub-memory arrays according to the segmented image block to enhance data bandwidth. When each FG loads data from sub-memories, the loaded data are firstly buffered into data buffers. Meanwhile the base addresses of the feature point that denote central locations of each ring section around the feature point, are buffered into address buffers. When computing the next feature point in the same group, the base address of the next feature point is compared with the buffered base addresses to check whether the data has been buffered. When the base addresses are hit, it denotes that the needed data are buffered, thus they are loaded from data buffer directly so that these data are reused for these adjacent feature points. When the base addresses are not hit, it means that the needed data for these adjacent feature points cannot be completely reused, it loads data from the sub-memories to refill data buffer. In our improved feature generation algorithm, the needed data for computing feature vector of each feature point are order insensitive, hence, they can be filled into data buffer in an arbitrary order. And without complex data management, the address generator loads them into data buffer directly for those missed data. Based on these memory mechanism, as shown in Fig. 6, multiple FGs compute feature vectors in parallel. Meanwhile the computing stages of each FG, including memory accessing, main orientation computing, feature vector computing, and rotation, are executed in a pipeline way. Note that, the data preparation achieves data filling process for data buffers, and the stages of computing main orientation and feature vector are processed in parallel.

5. EXPERIMENTS

5.1 Methodology

In order to determine optimal parameters of $R1$, $R2$, Bin and θ, experiments using commonly-used image set INRIA [5] on PC platform (E7200@2.53GHz, 4G DDR3 memory, 32bit win7 operations system) are performed. Evaluations show that when parameters are set at ($R1 = 7, R2 = 2$), $\theta = PI/3$ and $Bin = 8$, the comparable performance on matching rate is achived when compared with original ASIFT algorithm. Meanwhile, it achieves the shortest computing time. Thus these parameters are adopted to define the architecture. Besides, in order to evaluate our design on feature generation, we propose a verification architecture that achieves a full implementation for ASIFT. The corresponding verification architecture is shown in Fig. 7. Meanwhile, TSMC 65 nm 1P9M LP process is adopted on post-synthesis to evaluate hardware performance. The corresponding performance are shown in Table 1 and the layout of design is shown in Fig. 8. In order to evaluate memory accessing optimization, the reference work [12], which performs round robin method, is adopted for comparison in Table 2. In Table 3, the comparisons with reference works [3, 8, 12] are presented for full feature detection.

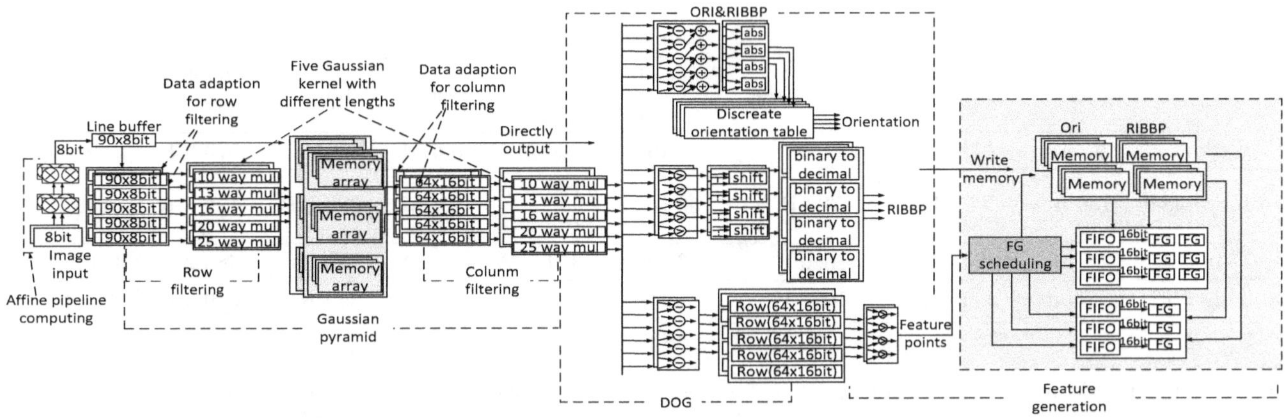

Figure 7: Verification architecture

5.2 Verification Architecture

As shown in Fig. 7, the baseline architecture includes affine unit, Gaussian pyramid unit, DOG unit and Feature generation unit. The whole computations for these units are processed in a pipelined way. In this pipeline processing, the image (64×64 in size, which is segmented from image of larger size by means of image scanning with 64×64 window.) is firstly input into dual buffers to enhance data throughput of interface. In affine computing, the widths of affine images are different due to image rotation and tilt (the largest width is 90 in this work). Then the affine computed image data are output to Gaussian pyramid unit. Two groups of RAM arrays in Gaussian pyramid unit work in a ping-pong way to support stream processing of row and column filtering. The design of RAM array, row filter and column filter support the full parallel processing in Gaussian filtering. Before feature generation, DOG (Difference of Gaussian to locate Extrema) unit and ORI&RIBBP unit (in charge of computing orientation and RIBBP) work in parallel to geneate feature points, and orientation image and RIBBP image. To match the data throughput between FGs (feature vector generation) and DOG, nine FGs work in parallel to compute feature vectors. These FGs need to fetch the data from the memory of *RIBBP* ram and *Ori* ram concurrentlys. The FG scheduling unit performes scheduling policy to allocate extremas to FGs and load data from memory for FGs.

5.3 Hardware Performance

As shown in Table 1, for the whole implementation, the processing speed of 97fps@1080p with 300 mW power consumption when processing 1000 feature points, is achieved with the technology process of TSMC 65 nm 1P9M LP. The layout size is 4.0 ×4.0 mm^2, in which FGs cosume computing resource of 0.4 million gates, with a maximal throughput of 21 (Gb/s) and power consumption of 32 mW.

As shown in Table 2, our method of FG scheduling contributes higher processing speed and lower power consumption to the whole system when compared with the baseline method. With a small cost (3%) of extra hardware resources on registers and control logics, our method largely exploits the data reuse among the generations of feature vectors for extremas, and also reduces redundant memory accessing for the adjacent feature extremas. Improving data reuse and reducing memory conflicts to make FGs work in parallel, play a very important role in reducing the power consumption and improving computing speed. Meanwhile, due to our algorithm optimization, the redundant memory on storing magnitude are removed which saves 14.3% memory and contributes to reduction of power consumption. According to Table 2, the processing speed for the feature vector generation is improved by 16.8%, with a 15.3% reduction on power consumption.

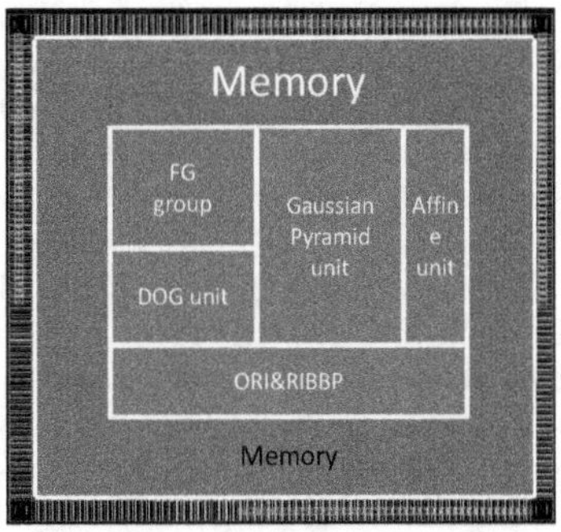

Figure 8: Layout of verification design

Table 1: Implementation results

Process	TSMC 65nm 1P9M GP+
Area	4.0×4.0 mm^2
Voltage	3.3 V I/O, 1 V Core
Gates/Memory	2.9 M/240KB
Power	300 mW@200MHz
Processing Speed	97 fps@1080P 1000 feature points

Table 2: Performance of different scheduling schemes on 1080P image with 200MHz)

Scheduling scheme	Gates	Memory	Processing speed	Power
RoundRobin[12]	2.8 M	280 KB	83 fps	354 mW
SRBMA	2.9 M	240 KB	97 fps	300 mW

Table 3: Performance Comparison

Works	Process	Frequency	Resolution	Processing speed	Power	Gates	Memory	Pixels/s @1mW	Pixels/s @1MHz
Leibo [3]	65 nm	200 MHz	1080 P	57 fps	220 mW	0.6 M	409.6 KB	573.2 K	591 K
Jinwook[8]	130 nm	200 MHz	720 P	30 fps	160 mW (65 nm)	2.4 M	382 KB	172.8 K	138 K
Yin [12]	65 nm	200 MHz	1080 P	83 fps	354 mW	2.8 M	280 KB	486.2 K	860.5 K
This work	65 nm	200 MHz	1080 P	97 fps	300 mW	2.9 M	240 KB	670.5 K	1005.6 K

Further, in comparison with other works, as shown in Table 3, the power results of the others works are scaled to 65nm technology to achieve a fair comparison. Meanwhile the computing efficiency is normalized to pixels per second with same frequency and the energy efficiency is normalized to pixels per second with same power. In comparison with the state-of-the-art works, this architecture achieves the fastest processing speed of 97fps@1080p with 300 mW power consumption. In terms of computing efficiency, this work is 70.2% and 6.29 times higher if compared with the ASIC works [3][8]. In terms of energy efficiency, this work is 17% and 2.88 times higher if compared with the ASIC works [3][8]. In comparison with [12], which uses the same baseline verification architecture, due to our optimization on parallel scheduling when multiple FGs access same memory, and improvement on the parallel computing architecture for feature generation, the computing efficiency is improved by 16.8% and the energy efficiency is improved by 37.9%.

6. CONCLUSION

In order to improve the computing efficiency of ASIFT, a rotation invariant block binary pattern technique is used, thus a high efficient pipelined and parallel hardware architecture is designed that improves computing speed. Meanwhile, a spatial relevance based memory accessing for multiple feature generations is proposed to optimize parallel memory accessing to improve data reuse. Evaluation shows that higher computing speed with low power consumption is achieved, which is promising for many vision applications.

7. ACKNOWLEDGMENTS

This work was supported in part by the China National High Technologies Research Program (No.2015AA016601),the China Major ST Project (No.2013ZX01033001-001-003) and the China Postdoctoral Science Foundation(043206002).

8. REFERENCES

[1] P. F. Alcantarilla, A. Bartoli, and A. J. Davison. Kaze features. In *Computer Vision–ECCV 2012*, pages 214–227. Springer, 2012.

[2] J.-Y. Kim, M. Kim, S. Lee, J. Oh, K. Kim, and H.-J. Yoo. A 201.4 gops 496 mw real-time multi-object recognition processor with bio-inspired neural perception engine. *Solid-State Circuits, IEEE Journal of*, 45(1):32–45, 2010.

[3] L. Liu, W. Zhang, C. Deng, S. Yin, S. Cai, and S. Wei. Surfex: A 57fps 1080p resolution 220mw silicon implementation for simplified speeded-up robust feature with 65nm process. In *Custom Integrated Circuits Conference (CICC), 2013 IEEE*, pages 1–4. IEEE, 2013.

[4] D. G. Lowe. Object recognition from local scale-invariant features. In *Computer vision, 1999. The proceedings of the seventh IEEE international conference on*, volume 2, pages 1150–1157. Ieee, 1999.

[5] K. Mikolajczyk, T. Tuytelaars, C. Schmid, et al. Affine covariant features. *Collaborative work between: the Visual Geometry Group, Katholieke Universiteit Leuven, Inria Rhone-Alpes and the Center for Machine Perception*, 2004.

[6] J.-M. Morel and G. Yu. Asift: A new framework for fully affine invariant image comparison. *SIAM Journal on Imaging Sciences*, 2(2):438–469, 2009.

[7] T. N. Nizar, N. Anbarsanti, and A. S. Prihatmanto. Multi-object tracking and detection system based on feature detection of the intelligent transportation system. In *System Engineering and Technology (ICSET), 2014 IEEE 4th International Conference on*, volume 4, pages 1–6. IEEE, 2014.

[8] J. Oh, G. Kim, J. Park, I. Hong, S. Lee, J.-Y. Kim, J.-H. Woo, and H.-J. Yoo. A 320 mw 342 gops real-time dynamic object recognition processor for hd 720p video streams. *Solid-State Circuits, IEEE Journal of*, 48(1):33–45, 2013.

[9] J. Park, I. Hong, G. Kim, B.-G. Nam, and H.-J. Yoo. Intelligent network-on-chip with online reinforcement learning for portable hd object recognition processor. *IEEE Transactions on Circuits and Systems I: Regular Papers*, 61(2):476–484, 2014.

[10] X. Tan and B. Triggs. Enhanced local texture feature sets for face recognition under difficult lighting conditions. *Image Processing, IEEE Transactions on*, 19(6):1635–1650, 2010.

[11] X. Wang, T. X. Han, and S. Yan. An hog-lbp human detector with partial occlusion handling. In *Computer Vision, 2009 IEEE 12th International Conference on*, pages 32–39. IEEE, 2009.

[12] S. Yin, P. Ouyang, L. Liu, and S. Wei. A 83fps 1080p resolution 354 mw silicon implementation for computing the improved robust feature in affine space. In *Custom Integrated Circuits Conference (CICC), 2015 IEEE*, pages 1–4. IEEE, 2015.

[13] L. Zhenjun, H. Nisar, and A. S. Malik. A framework for real time indoor robot navigation using monte carlo localization and orb feature detection. In *Consumer Electronics (ISCE 2014), The 18th IEEE International Symposium on*, pages 1–2. IEEE, 2014.

Design of Approximate High-Radix Dividers by Inexact Binary Signed-Digit Addition

Linbin Chen
Fabrizio Lombardi
ECE Department
Northeastern University
lombardi@ece.neu.edu

Paolo Montuschi
ECE Department
Polytechnic University of Turin, Italy
paolo.montuschi@polito.it

Jie Han
ECE Department
University of Alberta
Edmonton, AB, Canada
jhan8@ualberta.ca

Weiqiang Liu
College of EIE.
Nanjing University of Aero & Astro., China
liuweiqiang@nuaa.edu.cn

ABSTRACT
Approximate high radix dividers (HR-AXDs) are proposed and investigated in this paper. High-radix division is reviewed and inexact computing is introduced at different levels. Design parameters such as number of bits (N) and radix (r) are considered in the analysis; the replacement schemes with inexact cells and truncation schemes of exact cells in the binary signed-digit adder array is introduced. Circuit-level performance and the error characteristics of the inexact high radix dividers are analyzed for the proposed designs. The combined assessment of the normal error distance, power dissipation and delay is investigated and applications of approximate high-radix dividers are treated in detail. The simulation results show that the proposed approximate dividers offer extensive saving in terms of power dissipation, circuit complexity and delay, while only incurring in a small degradation in accuracy thus making them possibly suitable and interesting to some applications and domains such as low power/mobile computing.

CCS Concepts
• Hardware~Integrated circuits • Hardware~Arithmetic and datapath circuits • Hardware~Combinational circuits

Keywords
Approximate Divider; High-radix; Normalized Error Distance; Power Dissipation

1. INTRODUCTION
Most computer arithmetic applications are implemented using digital logic circuits, thus operating with a high degree of precision. However, many applications such as multimedia and image processing can tolerate errors and imprecision in computation and still produce results that can be useful in which human senses (such as vision) are involved. Approximate (or inexact) computing relies on using this property to design simplified, yet approximate circuits operating at higher performance and/or lower power consumption compared with precise (exact) logic circuits.

There are increasing demands for high-speed dividers in today's floating point units (FPU) and digital signal processors. Reductions in delay and power consumption have been studied for the division operation; different algorithms for division can be found in the technical literature [1]. Digit-by-digit (digit recurrence) methods are widely used in hardware design; implementations can be either sequential, combinational, or a combination of both. Based on these findings, the combinational implementations of a divider based on restoring, non-restoring [2] and SRT algorithms [3] are treated in more detail as they employ highly modularized structure for inexact designs.

In the previous work by the same authors [4], the designs of approximate unsigned non-restoring and restoring dividers (denoted as AXDnr and AXDr) have been proposed. New approximate AXDnr cells (denoted as AXDCnr) have been investigated and approximate computing has been applied to division by considering different schemes by which exact cells are replaced/truncated in the array divider circuit.

[5] has presented an algorithm for high-radix exact division; this algorithm is based on a prescaling technique of division by digit recurrence. In this manuscript we revisit, generalize and extend the results of [5] and present a novel architecture for approximate division. The approximate design concept of [4] is explored in more detail for a high-radix array divider (such as proposed in [5]). At circuit level, the signed-digit adder cell is simplified; replacement or truncation is utilized in the divider. The contribution of this manuscript extends also to an algorithmic domain as different numbers of bits *(N),* radix number (*r*) and the replacement/truncation depth *(d)* are also considered. Circuit-level performance and the error characteristics of these inexact high radix dividers are analyzed, inclusive of error analysis for image processing applications.

2. REVIEW OF DESIGN BASIS
In a high-radix division circuit design, Redundant Binary Representation (RBR) is used to represent the quotient digits when they are selected at each stage. For example, in the radix-4 divider discussed later, the intermediate quotient $q_j \in [-3,+3]$ is represented in signed-magnitude form; a Binary Signed-Digit (BSD) numbering system (as a subcategory of a RBR system [6]) with a digit set of {-1,0,1} is used to represent the partial remainder at each stage. RBR allows addition without propagating a carry. When compared to a non-redundant representation, RBR makes digit-wise logic operations slower, however arithmetic operations are faster when a large bit width is used [3].

2.1 High-radix Division Algorithm
There are two approaches for division by digit recurrence [3]. The first approach is based on selection tables; the second approach is based on prescaling. In the first approach, the digits of the quotient are obtained by inspecting the dividend and the partial remainder; as per the number of value combinations (as stored in digit selection tables), the quotient digit is obtained at each iteration [7]. However, for higher radix the size of these tables increases, yielding large implementations. Among the techniques for addressing this negative design feature, prescaling technique

Permission to make digital or hard copies of all or part of this work for personal or classroom use is granted without fee provided that copies are not made or distributed for profit or commercial advantage and that copies bear this notice and the full citation on the first page. Copyrights for components of this work owned by others than ACM must be honored. Abstracting with credit is permitted. To copy otherwise, or republish, to post on servers or to redistribute to lists, requires prior specific permission and/or a fee. Request permissions from Permissions@acm.org.
GLSVLSI '17, May 10-12, 2017, Banff, AB, Canada
© 2017 ACM. ISBN 978-1-4503-4972-7/17/05…$15.00.
DOI: http://dx.doi.org/10.1145/3060403.3060404

(as proposed in [8, 9]) is widely employed. An efficient and unified implementation of high-radix array dividers with no lookup table for quotient digit selection using prescaling has been presented in [5]. In this algorithm, by doing additional prescaling and converting the number representation, the quotient digit is directly obtained from the most significant (integer) part of the partial remainder at every iteration; this makes possible the construction of fully combinational high-radix dividers exhibiting a lower latency compared to a radix-2 divider.

Let the dividend and divisor be denoted by X and D respectively (normalized as $1/2 \leq X < D < 1$); A standard SRT division algorithm with n-bit precision is given by the recursive equations:

$$R^{(0)} = X$$
$$R^{(j+1)} = rR^{(j)} - q_{j+1}D, \quad (1)$$

where $(j = 0,1,2,\dots,n-1)$, r is the radix value (usually $r = 2^m (m = 1,2,3,\dots)$, j is the iteration step, $R^{(j)}$ is the partial remainder at step j, and q_j is the jth quotient digit selected from {-(r-1), … -1, 0, 1, …, r-1}. The quotient Q and the final remainder R are given by

$$Q = \sum_{j=1}^{n} r^{-j} \cdot q_j, \quad (2)$$
$$R = r^{-n} \cdot R^{(n)}. \quad (3)$$

The number of iterations in the division process can be reduced by increasing the radix r, i.e. by selecting $r = 2^m$; this allows the generation of m quotient bits at each step, such that the number of steps is reduced to $\lceil n/m \rceil$.

Normally, (1) as a recursive equation is calculated using Signed-Digit (carry-free) adders based on a redundant BSD representation. The shifted partial remainder $rR^{(j)}$ is bounded as

$$0 \leq |rR^{(j)}| < rD < r = 2^m. \quad (4)$$

So, $rR^{(j)}$ can be represented by using a BSD numbering system (denoted as SD2) as

$$rR^{(j)} = [a_{m-1} \dots a_1 a_0 . a_{-1} a_{-2} \dots a_{-k}]_{SD2}$$
$$= \sum_{i=-k}^{m-1} 2^i a_i, \quad (5)$$

where $a_i \in \{-1,0,1\}$.

The high-radix division algorithm of [5] is based on a SRT digit-by-digit division; additionally, it requires the following two steps (or conditions) to be performed (or satisfied): (A) The divisor D and the dividend X must be prescaled transforming the divisor range from [1/2,1) to [D_{min}, 1) as described later (operand scaling does not affect the result of division, because $X/D = MX/MD$, where M denotes the scale factor. Note that it is well known to affect the value of the final partial remainder, if necessary, because its value is multiplied by M. (B) Convert the t most significant digits $a_{-1}a_{-2} \dots a_{-t}$ of the fractional part of $rR^{(j)}$ to a non-redundant form, containing only digits from the set {-1, 0} or {0, 1}. After the second step, (5) is given by

$$rR^{(j)} = [c_{m-1} \dots c_1 c_0 . b_{-1} \dots b_{-t} a_{-t-1} \dots a_{-k}]_{SD2},$$

where $b_i \in \{-1,0\}$ or $\{0,1\}$, $a_i, c_i \in \{-1,0,1\}$. Then, the $(j+1)^{th}$ quotient digit q_{j+1} can be obtained directly from the integer part of $rR^{(j)}$, i.e.

$$q_{j+1} = [c_{m-1} \dots c_1 c_0]_{SD2} = \sum_{i=-k}^{m-1} 2^i c_i, \quad (6)$$

where $c_i \in \{-1,0,1\}$ and $q_{j+1} \in \{-(r-1),\dots,0,\dots,r-1\}$.

The proof of the algorithm in [5] as well as the derivation of the scaling range [D_{min},1) are as follows. Since, $rR^{(j)}$ can be represented as

$$rR^{(j)} = q_{j+1} + \epsilon \quad (7)$$

where ϵ denotes explicit value of the fractional part digits and it is given by

$$\epsilon = [0.b_{-1} \dots b_{-t} a_{-t-1} \dots a_{-k}]_{SD2}$$
$$= \sum_{i=1}^{t} 2^{-i} b_{-i} + \sum_{i=t+1}^{k} 2^{-i} a_{-i}$$

The fractional part ϵ is a function of t and is bounded in the following rages:

$$\text{If } b_i \in \{-1,0\}, \text{ then } -1 < \epsilon < 2^{-t} \quad (8)$$
$$\text{If } b_i \in \{0,1\}, \text{ then } -2^{-t} < \epsilon < 1 \quad (9)$$

In SRT division using the maximally redundant digit set $\{-(r-1),\dots,r-1\}$, $q_{i+1} (\in \{-(r-1),\dots,r-1\})$ is obtained if q_{i+1} satisfies the following conditions:

$$rR^{(j)} \leq (q_{i+1}+1)D \;\; (q_{i+1} \in \{-(r-1),\dots,r-2\}) \quad (10)$$
$$(q_{i+1}+1)D \leq rR^{(j)} \;\; (q_{i+1} \in \{-(r-2),\dots,r-1\}) \quad (11)$$

By substituting (7) in (10) and (11), then

$$q_{i+1} + \epsilon \leq (q_{i+1}+1)D \;\; (q_{i+1} \in \{-(r-1),\dots,r-2\}) \quad (12)$$
$$(q_{i+1}-1)D \leq q_{i+1} + \epsilon \;\; (q_{i+1} \in \{-(r-1),\dots,r-2\}) \quad (13)$$

Using (12) and (13) and considering the bound of ϵ given by (8) or (9), the possible scaling range of D must be satisfied for selecting q_{j+1} (as the explicit value of the integer part of $rR^{(j)}$) is derived as in (14). Finally, the process to select q_{j+1} is summarized as following:

- Prescale the operands X and D to satisfy

$$D_{min} = \frac{r-2+2^{-t}}{r-1} \leq D \leq 1, \quad (14)$$

where D_{min} is the lower bound of the scaled D.

- Convert the t most significant digits $a_{-1}a_{-2} \dots a_{-t}$ ($a_i \in \{-1,0,1\}$) of the fractional part of every partial remainder $rR^{(j)}$ into its non-redundant representation $b_{-1}b_{-2} \dots b_{-t}$ as

$$b_{-1}b_{-2} \dots b_{-t} \in \{-1,0\} \text{ for } rR^{(j)} > 0 \quad (15)$$
$$b_{-1}b_{-2} \dots b_{-t} \in \{0,1\} \text{ for } rR^{(j)} < 0 \quad (16)$$

2.2 Exact High-radix Divider (HR-EXD)

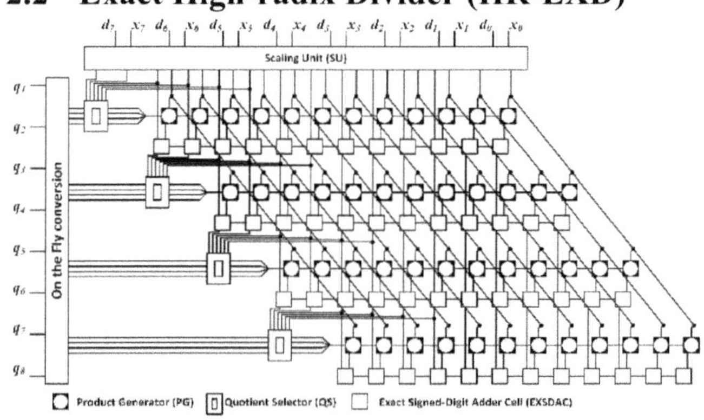

Figure 1. Example of HR-EXD for 8-bit radix-4 [5]

The implementation of the HR-EXD for the algorithm reviewed previously is presented in [5]. The structure of an 8-bit radix-4 divider with r=4, t=2 is shown in Figure 1; it consists of the following modules as basic blocks.

Scaling Unit (SU): as input operands, the divisor D and the dividend X must be prescaled prior to starting the division iterations. For example, in a divider with r=4 and t=2, the divisor and the dividend must be prescaled to transform the divisor range from $[\frac{1}{2}, 1)$ to $[\frac{3}{4}, 1)$; prescaling can be done using different scale factors for 3 different ranges of D (D>=3/4, 5/8<=D<3/4, 1/2<D<=5/8). All these constant-scale multiplications can be achieved by shift-and-add operations; Figure 2(a) shows the operand scaling unit using shifters and carry propagation adders (CPA). In general, as the radix r increases and the number of digit t increases, a higher complexity is required for operand scaling and the multiplication at each iteration. Therefore, the values of r and t must be selected to meet the requirements of performance and complexity. In this paper, the parameter $t=m$ *(where* $r=2^m$) has been selected so the same configuration as in [5], as it does not lead to a loss of generality of the proposed method. For radix-8 and a higher radix, the structure of the scaling unit is also the same and it can be extended based on the radix-4 case (Figure 2(a)).

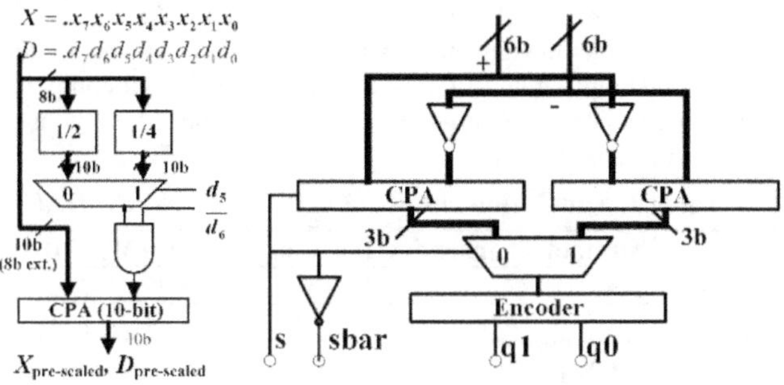

(a) (b)

Figure 2. (a) SU module for r=4, t=2 (b) QS module for radix 4 (s: sign, q_1q_0: magnitude) [5]

Quotient Digit Selector (QS): According to the algorithm in [5], the real binary value of the integer part of $rR^{(j)}$ is selected as the $(j+1)^{th}$ quotient digit q_{j+1}. Implementation of this quotient selection rule does not need a digit selection table; it needs only a high-speed signed-digit carry propagation adder (SDCPA) for a limited number of bits (Figure 2(b)). The word length of SDCPA is $2m+t$ bits, because the integer part of $rR^{(j)}$ must also be converted into a non-redundant form to obtain the explicit value of q_{i+1}. This conversion is performed by adding the positive digits and the two's complement of the negative digits of $rR^{(j)}$ for $rR^{(j)} >= 0$, and by adding the negative digits and the two's complement of the positive digits of $rR^{(j)}$ for $rR^{(j)} <= 0$. The obtained quotient digit q_{j+1} is in a sign-magnitude redundant form; it is then finally transformed into a non-redundant 2's complementary representation using the on-the-fly scheme of [10]. For a higher radix, the design of the QS can be extended based on the radix-4 case (Figure 2(b)).

On-the-Fly Conversion: The quotient must be converted from a signed-digit representation to a two's complement representation. This is accomplished by an addition after the quotient is completely computed; however, this addition increases the overall execution time. So to avoid this step, the on-the-fly algorithm of [10] is used to perform the conversion in a digit-serial fashion to generate the digits of the quotient.

Product Generator (PG): The high-radix division algorithm employs a BSD number representation for partial remainders and quotient digits, because this representation exploits the hardware simplicity of a radix-2 scheme; a drawback of high-radix algorithms is that they require the generation of multiples of the divisor qD ($q \in \{-(r-1), \ldots, r+1\}$). In the radix-4 divider, this problem is addressed by designing a qD product generator (PG). PG represents all multiples of D $(-3D, \ldots, 3D)$ as pair of multiples that are generated by shift operations. The circuit diagram of a PG is shown in Figure 3(a); to transfer the output directly to the binary signed digit adder, PG must have the additional function of complementing the outputs. The PG module for radix-8 and higher, can be extended from the radix-4 case.

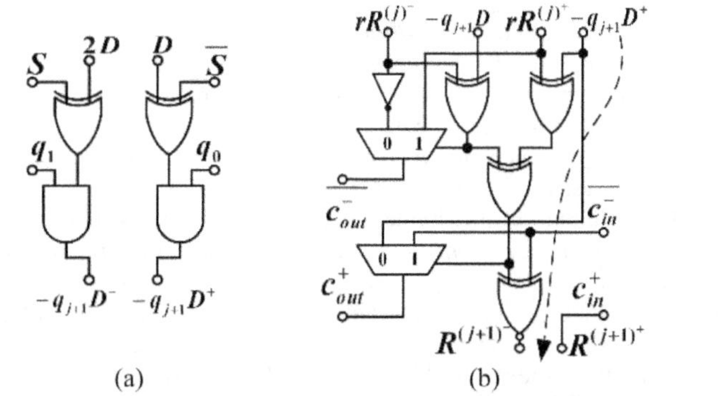

(a) (b)

Figure 3. (a) PG module for radix-4 case (b) EXSDAC module [5]

Exact Signed Digit Adder Cell (EXSDAC): Figure 3(b) shows the Exact Signed Digit Adder Cell (EXSDAC); it consists of XOR/XNOR gates and 2-1 MUXs (each designed by modifying 4-2 compressors). The EXSDACs implement (1); the adder inputs $rR^{(j)}$, $-q_{j+1}D$ and output $R^{(j+1)}$ are represented in binary signed digit form $(rR^{(j)^+}, rR^{(j)^-})$, $(-q_{j+1}D^+, -q_{j+1}D^-)$ and $(R^{(j+1)^+}, R^{(j+1)^-})$ respectively. The EXSDAC remains the same for all HR-EXD at different bit width and radix. The approximate designs shown next are based on the approximation of EXSDAC; thus, the proposed approximate design methodology is suitable for HR-EXD with different bit width and radix.

3. PROPOSED APPROXIMATE DESIGNS

3.1 Approximate Signed-Digit Adder Cell (AXSDAC)

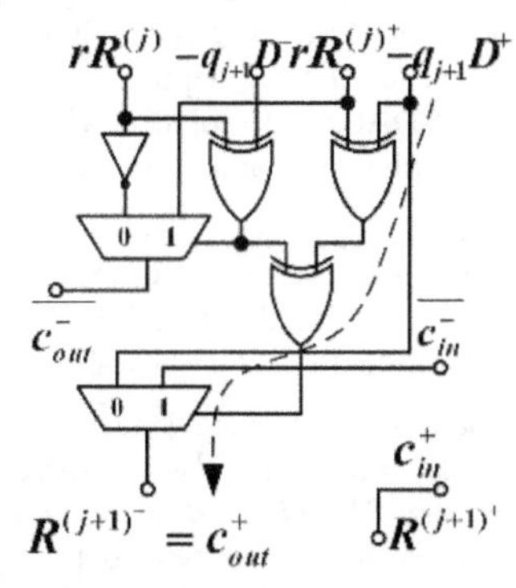

Figure 4. Approximate design of EXSDAC (AXSDAC)

The EXSDAC computes the subtraction or addition according to the quotient selection output. As $R^{(j+1)^+} = C_{in}^+$, so the input and output functions of these two signals can be ignored. The critical path of this design has a delay of 3Δ, where Δ is the unitary delay through any gate (Figure 4(b)). By observing the truth table of EXSDAC, the C_{out}^+ has the same value as the input $R^{(j+1)^-}$ in 24 out of 32 state combinations; therefore, an approximate design must consider this feature. The approximate design of EXSDAC (denoted as AXSDAC) is shown in Figure 4. $R^{(j+1)^-}$ is simplified to be equal to C_{out}^+ by changing the 8 outputs value of C_{out}^+. This design has therefore 8 incorrect outputs out of 32 outputs, so in theory its error rate is 25% (assuming that all combinations are equally probable). In terms of circuit implementation, pass-transistor logic design of [4] is utilized to further decrease the circuit complexity, the delay and the power consumption.

3.2 Approximate High Radix Divider (HR-AXD)

3.2.1 Replacement Scheme

When designing the approximate divider, EXSDACs are selectively replaced by AXSDACs; hence, approximation is the process by which an exact cell is replaced by an approximate cell. The extent by which this replacement process is performed in a divider, is quantified by the depth *d*, i.e. the number of rows (and/or columns) in the divider with approximate cells. For an *N* bit width of a radix $2^m (m = 1, 2, 3 \ldots)$ divider, the number of EXSDACs is given as $(N + 2m) * (N/m)$; *m* EXSDACs are combined together into a replacement element (RE). For example, in the 8-bit radix-4 divider, two EXSDACs are treated together as a single RE (shown in Figure 5 by the dotted rectangles of EXSDACs). The replacement configurations and corresponding depth *d* for an 8-bit radix-4 array divider are shown in Figure 5. Four types of replacement are used for approximation:

Vertical Replacement (VR): The least significant REs in each row of the divider are replaced. So, both the remainder and the quotient show a small error distance, while taking advantage of the power-saving characteristics of the AXSDACs. The depth of the vertical replacement can be increased to further decrease the power, while tolerating more errors at output. Hence, $m\left(\frac{N}{m}\right)d = Nd$. An example for *m*=2, *d*=2 is shown in Figure 5(a).

Horizontal Replacement (HR): In a divider, the value of the quotient is mostly related to the carry signal of each cell in a single row. For example, consider the last row corresponding to the LSB of Q; if the final value of reminder R is not of significant concern, then all EXSDACs in the last row can be replaced with AXSDACs at no significant loss of accuracy in Q. If an error can be tolerated in Q, then an increase in the depth of the horizontal replacement up to the *d*th LSB of Q is possible. An example of a horizontal replacement divider of depth *d*=2 is shown in Figure 5(b). $(N + 2m)d$ EXSDACs are replaced with AXSDACs in an approximate divider with a horizontal replacement of depth *d*.

Square Replacement (SR): the so-called square configuration is generated by combining the vertical and horizontal replacements. So, md^2 EXSDACs are replaced with AXSDACs; an example of a square replacement of depth *d=2* is shown in Figure 5(c).

Triangle Replacement (TR): Consider the integer pair (x,y) as coordinates of each individual RE in a divider. For the replacement of an exact RE *(i,j)* (*i*<*d* or *j*<*d*) with an inexact RE in a triangle approximation divider with depth *d* (*d*≥1), $md(d + 1)/2$ EXSDACs are replaced with AXSDACs. An example of a triangle replacement divider with *d=2* is shown in Figure 5(d).

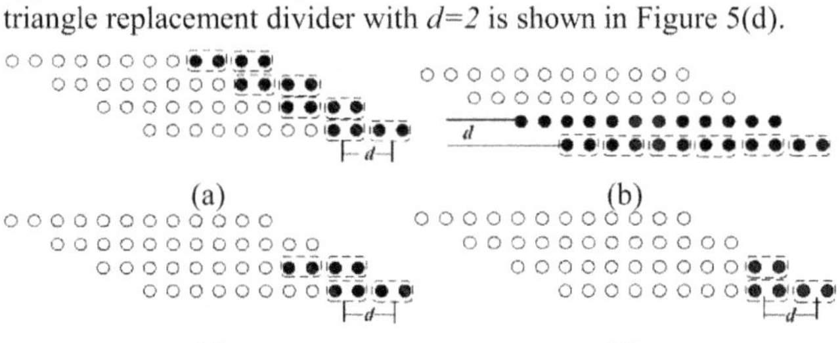

Figure 5. Different approximate configurations and replacement depths for 8-bit radix-4 divider (a) VR *d*=2 (b) HR *d*=2 (c) SR *d*=2 (d) TR *d*=2

3.2.2 Truncation Scheme

Truncation is different from replacement, because the EXSDACs are not changed to AXSDACs, instead, are completely eliminated. Same as replacement, four types of truncation are used as approximation in the divider design: Vertical Truncation (VT), Horizontal Truncation (HT), Squared Truncation (ST) and Triangle Truncation (TT).

4. SIMULATION RESULTS

4.1 AXSDAC

Predictive technology models at 45nm feature size are utilized in the HSPICE simulation. AXSDAC and EXSDAC are simulated at a 1GHz frequency; a fan-out of 4 is utilized in all simulations. The simulation results for the delay, power consumption and the power-delay product (PDP) are given in Table 1. As expected, the proposed inexact design shows significant improvements in delay, power consumption and PDP. As a measure of circuit complexity; the approximate designs incur in a reduction of 18% in the number of transistors.

Table 1. Simulation results of EXSDAC and AXSDAC

Design	Num. of Transistors	Delay (ps)	Power (μW)	PDP (aJ)
EXSDAC	22	6.36	2.98	18
AXSDAC	18	4.35	1.14	5

4.2 HR-AXD

4.2.1 NED

The Normalized Error distance (NED) is defined as the Mean Error Distance (MED) normalized by the maximum ED [11]. The maximum value of the ED is 1, so in this case the NED is equal to the MED. Only the 8-bit radix-2 and radix-4, 12-bit radix-2, radix -4 and radix 8 divider are evaluated (the trend and conclusions for these dividers are applicable also to a higher radix divider). The NED simulation results are shown in Figure 6 and Figure 7 for different bit width, radix, and approximation configurations.

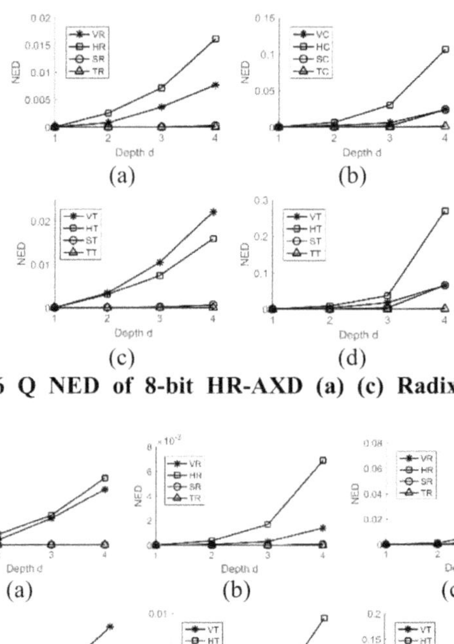

Figure 6 Q NED of 8-bit HR-AXD (a) (c) Radix-2 (b) (d) Radix-4

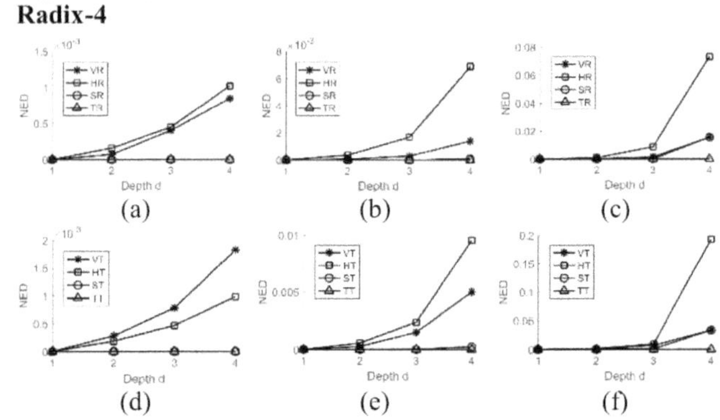

Figure 7. Q NED of 12-bit HR-AXD with (a)(d) Radix-2 (b)(e) Radix-4 (c)(f) Radix-8

As expected, the divider with a higher depth *d* has a larger NED. The horizontal configurations have the worst NED among all different bit width, radix and schemes, while the triangle configurations are the best. All dividers employing truncation have the worst NED compared to the other two inexact schemes. So a truncation scheme has a higher NED than a replacement scheme; Compare the 8-bit Radix-4 divider and the 12-bit Radix-4 divider. A larger bit width provides a higher precision for the divider; hence, the NED decreases as the bit width increases. When considering the three different radix schemes of a 12-bit divider, it is observed that a higher radix results in a higher NED; this occurs because a higher radix makes the quotient digit q_j (as generated at each iteration of the divider) to a larger weight for generating the final Q result. Therefore, the error introduced at each iteration by these approximated configuration has a larger weight and is reflected in the NED of the output Q.

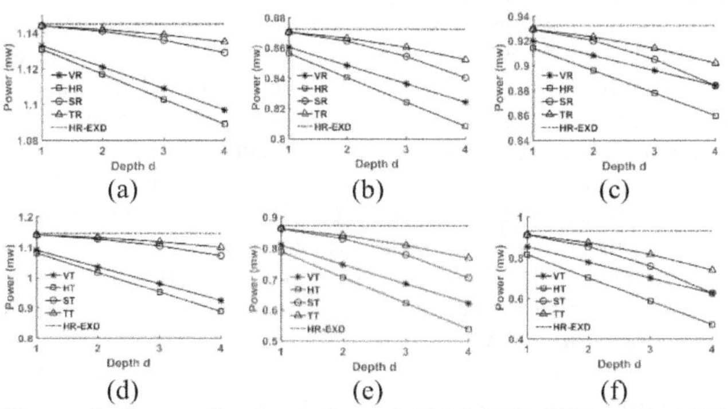

Figure 8. Power Consumption of 12-bit HR-AXD with (a)(d) Radix-2 (b)(e) Radix-4 (c)(f) Radix-8

4.2.2 Power

One of the primary goals of an approximate design is to decrease the power consumption by tolerating a computational error. The power simulation results are shown as Figure 8.

As expected, the divider with a higher depth *d* has the smaller power consumption. By increasing *d*, the power consumption for a horizontal configuration decreases faster than for the other types of configuration, so the square and triangle configurations decrease their power consumption at a lower rate than the horizontal and vertical configurations. All truncated dividers save more power than the replacement scheme counterpart. When comparing the 8-bit radix-4 and the 12-bit radix-4 divider, a larger bit width divider consumes more power as expected; when the three 12-bit dividers (at different radix) are compared, the radix-4 and radix-8 dividers consume a lower power than the radix-2 divider, because a high radix divider can reduce the number of iterations in the division process, thus significantly decreasing the circuit complexity of the sign-digit adder array. Moreover, the radix-8 divider consumes more power than radix-4 divider, because, as the radix increases, the implementation of the SU module, the PG module and the On-the-Fly conversion module are more complex, so becoming dominated in the whole divider.

4.2.3 Delay

The delays of the SU and QS are proportional to the bit width and the radix. The delay of the PG for each stage is not related to the bit width, but it is proportional to the radix. Each binary signed digit adder row has a constant delay. The critical path of the whole divider starts from the SU through each stage of the PG and the row of the signed digit adder; it finally passes through the QS and On-the-fly conversion module.

For a divider with an approximate configuration, (either replacement or truncation), the approximation takes place at the adder array, so the delay of the inexact divider is almost the same as the exact counterpart; the only exception is the horizontal configuration. For the horizontal configuration, the replacement scheme has a smaller delay because a number of stages (equal to the value of the replacement depth) are designed using AXSDACs, that have a smaller delay than EXSDACs. A truncation scheme has even a lower delay than the replacement scheme, because cells are removed. The average delays of the different approximate schemes versus bit width and radix are plotted in Figure 9; as the radix increases, the delay decreases, because a high radix divider requires a fewer number of add-subtract iterations, hence the critical path delay is also shorter. However, the delay of the radix-8 divider is higher than for radix-4; as the radix increases, the SU, QS and PG are more complex and the delay is dominated by QS and PG at each iteration stage. The advantage of fewer number of iteration stages is therefore not of a significant impact. A pipelined version of the high-radix divider can be realized by inserting flip-flops at the output of each adder stage to increase the overall computation throughput.

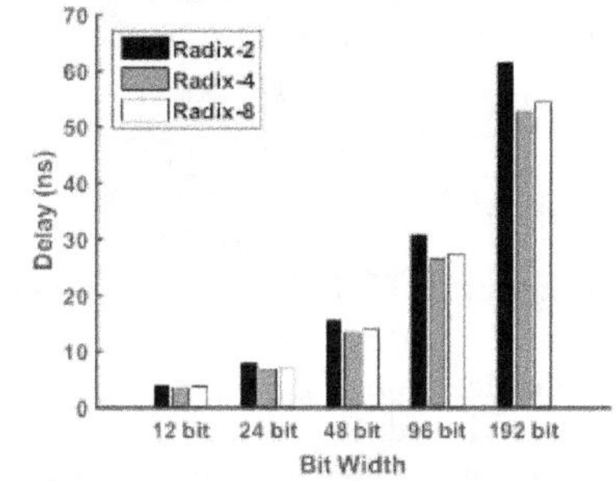

Figure 9. Average Delay with different radix

4.2.4 Trade-off between NED and Power

An approximate arithmetic design always must balance accuracy and energy dissipation. As shown previously as the depth changes, the power dissipation increases while the NED decreases. To further evaluate this trade-off, the MED Power Product (MPP) has been introduced in [4]. In this paper the NPP (NED power product) is used as more relevant than the MPP. Figure 10 show the NPP of the 12-bit radix-2, radix-4 and radix-8 dividers using different approximation schemes; the replacement scheme has the lowest NPP compared to the other two schemes.

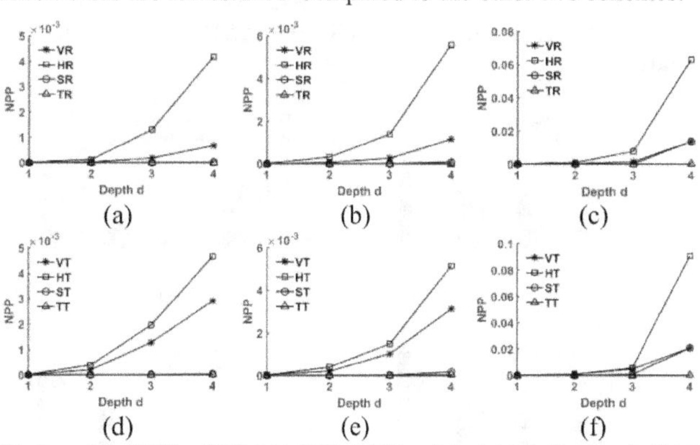

Figure 10. NPP of 12-bit HR-AXD with (a)(d) Radix-2 (b)(e) Radix-4 (c)(f) Radix-8

5. APPLICATIONS

In this section, the approximate schemes for high radix division are evaluated using different applications involving image analysis (on a pixel basis). The proposed high-radix dividers are assessed for pixel division applications. For image analysis, the input gray scale images are normalized in the range [1/2, 1). 12-bit approximate dividers with different configurations are utilized;

the approximations used in these applications are shown in Table 2; these configurations are chosen such that the power dissipation of these dividers is nearly the same.

Table 2. Approximation depth d configurations of 12-bit HR-AXD Used for Application Analysis

	VR/VT	HR/HT	SR/ST	TR/TT
Radix-2	2	2	5	7
Radix-4	3	2	4	5
Radix-8	4	2	4	3

Change detection: The fractional change or ratio between two frames of a sequence of images is used for change detection. If there is no movement in the scene, then the output image mostly consists of one value pixels. However, when there is a movement, then the pixels in the regions of the image in which the intensity spatially changes, exhibit significant differences between the two frames. After calculating the pixel division, the resulting pixels are scaled up and rounded to the integer range [0,255] to display the resulting images. Figure 11 shows an example of the results for change detection of a sequence of two frames X and Y.

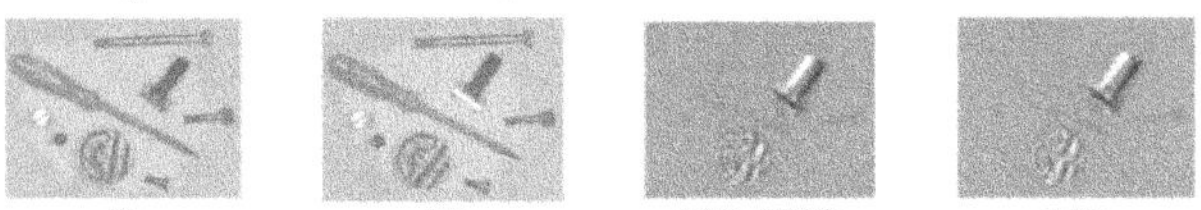

X Y HR-EXD TR

Figure 11. An example of TR HR-AXD for change detection

Background removal: In this case, background variations in illumination are divided from a scene, such that the foreground objects can be better viewed. For example, the image X in Figure 12 shows some text that has been badly illuminated during capture (i.e. there is a strong illumination gradient across the image). If a blank page Y is divided from the poorly illuminated image X, the output has a relatively constant illumination. Following this operation, a simple step for the threshold can be used to produce a high-contrast text image. Figure 12 shows an example of the results.

X Y HR-EXD TR

Figure 12. An example of TR HR-AXD for background removal

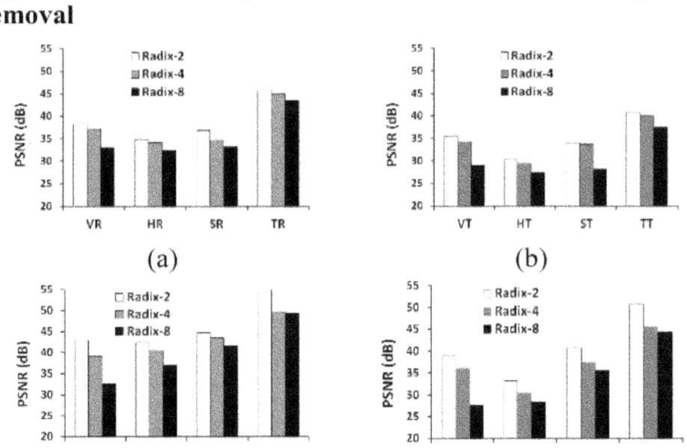

Figure 13. PSNR of 12-bit HR-AXD for image application Change detection with replacement (a) and truncation (b); Background removal with replacement (c) and truncation (d)

Figure 13 shows the Peak Signal-to-Noise Ratio (PSNR) for change detection and background removal. In both cases, the triangle approximations have the best PSNRs; moreover, the PSNR is lower for higher radix dividers. A truncated scheme has a lower PSNR than the corresponding replacement scheme.

6. CONCLUSION

This paper has presented a detailed analysis, design and evaluation of high radix parallel dividers that utilize approximate criteria in their operation. The following conclusions can be drawn: A larger value for d provides a larger NED; among all schemes, the triangle replacement divider has the best NED among the replacement schemes. A truncated scheme introduces more error. The power consumption reduces rapidly as the depth increases, i.e. the higher the depth is, more pronounced is the power reduction. A truncation scheme provides a significant power reduction compared to a replacement scheme. The approximation schemes have only a small impact on the delay of the divider; the delay is reduced for higher radix dividers, because it takes only N/m stages to complete the division. This advantage is reduced when the radix is higher than 8. Compared to radix-2 division, a high radix approximate divider is faster; its power dissipation is lower for radix-4 and radix-8, although it increases for radix values greater than 8. In conclusion, when designing an approximate array divider, metrics (and related design parameters) have to be considered and met as per the application. This paper has shown that a triangle-based replacement scheme at a moderate radix value (not higher than 8) is the best approximate divider scheme to achieve low power consumption, high speed and a small error for an application such as image division.

REFERENCES

[1] S. F. Oberman and M. Flynn, "Division algorithms and implementations," *Computers, IEEE Transactions on,* vol. 46, pp. 833-854, 1997.

[2] B. Parhami, *Computer Arithmetic: Algorithms and Hardware Designs*: Oxford University Press, 2000.

[3] M. D. Ercegovac and T. Lang, *Digital Arithmetic*: Morgan Kaufmann, 2004.

[4] L. Chen, J. Han, W. Liu, and F. Lombardi, "On the Design of Approximate Restoring Dividers for Error-Tolerant Applications," *Computers, IEEE Transactions on,* vol. PP, pp. 1-1, 2015.

[5] T. Aoki, K. Nakazawa, and T. Higuchi, "High-radix parallel VLSI dividers without using quotient digit selection tables," in *Proc. 30th IEEE International Symposium on Multiple-Valued Logic*, 2000, pp. 345-352.

[6] A. Avizienis, "Signed-Digit Number Representations for Fast Parallel Arithmetic," *IRE Transactions on Electronic Computers,* vol. EC-10, pp. 389-400, 1961.

[7] S. F. Oberman and M. Flynn, "Division algorithms and implementations," *IEEE Trans. Comput.,* vol. 46, pp. 833-854, 1997.

[8] M. D. Ercegovac, T. Lang, and P. Montuschi, "Very-high radix division with prescaling and selection by rounding," *IEEE Trans. Comput.,* vol. 43, pp. 909-918, 1994.

[9] P. Montuschi and T. Lang, "Boosting very-high radix division with prescaling and selection by rounding," *IEEE Trans. Comput.,* vol. 50, pp. 13-27, 2001.

[10] M. D. Ercegovac and T. Lang, "On-the-Fly Conversion of Redundant into Conventional Representations," *IEEE Trans. Comput.,* vol. C-36, pp. 895-897, 1987.

[11] L. Jinghang, H. Jie, and F. Lombardi, "New Metrics for the Reliability of Approximate and Probabilistic Adders," *IEEE Trans. Comput.,* vol. 62, pp. 1760-1771, 2013.

Advanced Low Power Spintronic Memories beyond STT-MRAM

Wang Kang, Zhaohao Wang, He Zhang, Sai Li, Youguang Zhang, and Weisheng Zhao
Fert Beijing Institute, BDBC and School of Electronic and Information Engineering
Beihang University, Beijing 100191, China
{wang.kang, zhaohao.wang, zhanghe, saili, zyg, weisheng.zhao}@buaa.edu.cn

ABSTRACT
Until now, spin transfer torque magnetic random access memory (STT-MRAM) has drawn considerable R&D interest worldwide. A number of companies and universities are currently involved in this promising technology. In 2016, Everspin released the first 256M STT-MRAM chip, indicating the commercialization and application of STT-MRAM. Nevertheless, STT-MRAM still has some intrinsic limitations, such as dynamic write power and speed, compared with CMOS-based memory technologies. Following the technical evolution process from toggle-MRAM to STT-MRAM, the continuous pursuit of high performance, high density, low power and scalability, drives the intensive R&D of new memory technologies. In this paper, we will show the recent progress in advanced spintronic memories beyond STT-MRAM, such as the spin Hall effect (SHE)-driven and voltage-driven MRAMs. These advanced MRAM technologies do have some unique advantages compared with STT-MRAM, but they also suffer from new design and fabrication challenges. In addition, we will present the latest research in emerging spintronic devices, e.g., magnetic skyrmions, which are potential as information carriers in future spintronic memories, e.g., racetrack memory. [1]

CCS CONCEPTS
• **Hardware → Integrated circuits → Semiconductor memory →** Non-volatile memory**; Hardware → Emerging technologies →** Spintronics and magnetic technologies**.**

Keywords: Spintronic memory; STT-MRAM; SHE-MRAM; voltage-driven MRAM; magnetic skyrmions; racetrack memory

1 INTRODUCTION
Energy consumption, in particular, the static energy consumption caused by leakage currents, has become one of the key technical problems in conventional semiconductor-based memories [1, 2]. Emerging nonvolatile memories, such as resistive random access memory (ReRAM), phase change memory (PCM) and magnetic random access memory (MRAM) etc. [3-5], provide us inspiring alternatives for solving this problem, because of the zero stand-by power dissipation during the system idle state. Among them, spin transfer torque (STT)-driven MRAM (STT-MRAM) is considered as one of the most promising candidates in the next-generation computer architectures, thanks to the high integration density, low energy consumption, high speed, good scalability and tremendous endurance [5-7]. Until now, STT-MRAM has drawn considerable interest worldwide after the commercialization of toggle-MRAM in 2006. Since 2009, a number of semiconductor companies and universities have been involved in the R&D of this promising nonvolatile memory technology. In 2012, Everspin released the first 64Mb STT-MRAM chip [8], and then, in 2016, the 256Mb STT-MRAM chip [9], indicating the practical commercialization and application of STT-MRAM.

Nevertheless, based on our investigations, there is still a big performance gap (about 1-2 orders of magnitude larger) in terms of dynamic write energy and access delay between STT-MRAM and conventional CMOS-based memories (e.g., SRAM) [5]. The dynamic write energy and delay of STT-MRAM depend on its inherent data storage and write mechanisms. In STT-MRAM, the basic storage element is called magnetic tunnel junction (MTJ) and the associated data write mechanism relies on the STT effect flowing through the MTJ device, as shown in the inset of Fig. 1. For writing data into MTJ device, the drivability of the STT effect is positively correlated to the magnetization vector product of the free and reference layers of the MTJ. Unfortunately, before data write operation, the magnetization of the free and reference layers of the MTJ is almost collinear (parallel or anti-parallel depending on the initial data bit stored in the MTJ device) except for a little misalignment owing to thermal fluctuations. Thus, at the initial stage of a data write operation, the STT drivability is rather weak, and then it gets enhanced with the process of magnetization reversal of the free layer. During the magnetization reversal of the free layer, the magnetization of the reference layer of the MTJ is generally pinned, thus the magnetization vector angle between the free and reference layers of the MTJ increases gradually. Finally, the magnetization of the free layer will be switched if the STT effect is strong enough to overcome the energy barrier, resulting a successful data write operation. Fig. 1 shows the magnetization dynamics of the free layer of an MTJ device under the STT effect. As can be seen, the initial incubation delay significantly limits the data write speed and energy efficiency.

Permission to make digital or hard copies of all or part of this work for personal or classroom use is granted without fee provided that copies are not made or distributed for profit or commercial advantage and that copies bear this notice and the full citation on the first page. Copyrights for components of this work owned by others than ACM must be honored. Abstracting with credit is permitted. To copy otherwise, or republish, to post on servers or to redistribute to lists, requires prior specific permission and/or a fee. Request permissions from Permissions@acm.org.
GLSVLSI '17, May 10-12, 2017, Banff, AB, Canada
© 2017 ACM. ISBN 978-1-4503-4972-7/17/05…$15.00
DOI: http://dx.doi.org/10.1145/3060403.3060589

1

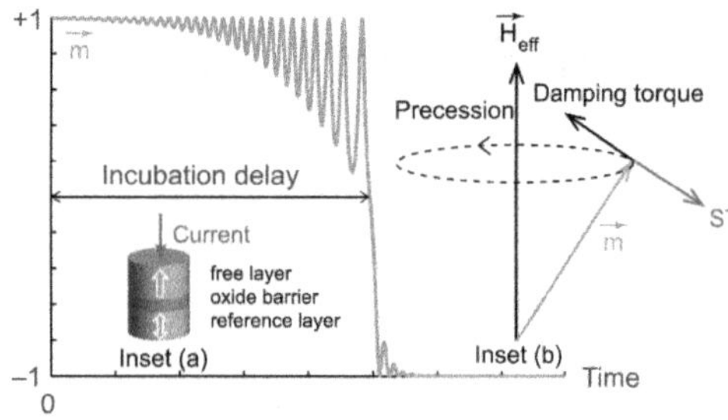

Figure 1: Time-resolved magnetization dynamics of the free layer of an MTJ under the STT effect. Insets (a) is the STT-MTJ device schematic and inset (b) illustrates the STT-driven MTJ magnetization switching mechanism.

Following the technical evolution process from toggle-MRAM to STT-MRAM, the continuous pursuit of high performance, high density, low power and scalability, drives the intensive R&D of new spintronic memory technologies. Recently, spin Hall effect (SHE) driven MRAM (SHE-MRAM) [10-13] and voltage-driven MRAM (VC-MRAM) [14-16], which have the potential to narrow the energy and delay performance gap to the CMOS technology owing to their different data write mechanisms, have received wide attention beyond STT-MRAM. In addition, some emerging spintronic objects, e.g., magnetic skyrmion, which are particle-like topologically stable nanoscale spin configurations, have been considered as potential information carriers in future spintronic memories, e.g., racetrack memory [17-20]. In this paper, we will present the recent progress in these advanced spintronic memories, and analyze their perspectives and challenges.

The rest of this paper is organized as follows. Section 2 and Section 3 introduce the technical evolution from STT-MRAM to SHE-MRAM and VC-MRAM respectively. Section 4 presents the advancement of SHE-MRAM and VC-MRAM compared to STT-MRAM. Section 5 shows the latest research in emerging magnetic skyrmions and its potential applications in racetrack memory. Finally, Section 6 concludes this paper.

2 FROM STT-MRAM TO SHE-MRAM

As discussed above, the STT-driven MTJ magnetization switching needs an undesirable incubation delay, which induces high power consumption and delay. In order to reduce the incubation delay, a relatively large write current is required, which adds the risk of the oxide barrier breakdown of the MTJ device. To overcome the above challenge, spin Hall effect (SHE) was recently investigated to provide an alternative write approach [10-12]. Fig. 2 shows the three-terminal device structure of the SHE-driven MTJ, in which a heavy metal strip is attached in direct to the free layer of the MTJ. In such a device, an in-plane charge current flowing through the heavy metal can generate spin orbit torque (SOT) to switch or assist to switch the magnetization of the free layer of the MTJ, as shown in Fig. 2(a) [21, 22]. It is worthy noting that for in-plane-anisotropy MTJ (i-MTJ) devices, the charge current passing the heavy metal strip can produce the anti-damping SOT to switch the magnetization orientation of free layer (see Fig. 2(b)), whereas for the perpendicular-anisotropy MTJ (p-MTJ), an additional in-plane magnetic field is generally required to achieve fully deterministic magnetization switching of the free layer (see Fig. 2(c)), which adds the device complexity and limits the scalability. In practice, as p-

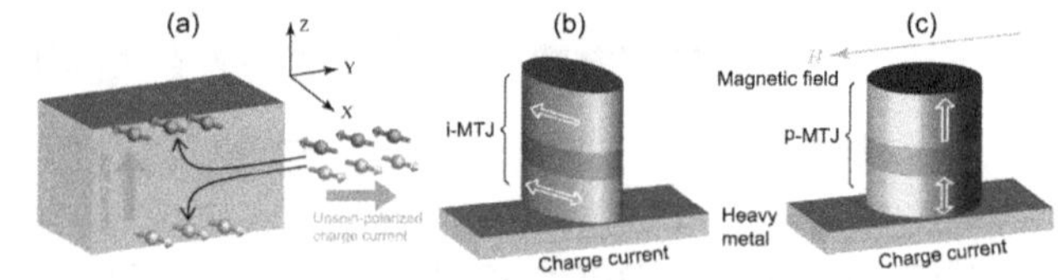

Figure 2: Illustration of the (a) SHE mechanism, (b) i-MTJ and (c) p-MTJ device schematics respectively [21, 22].

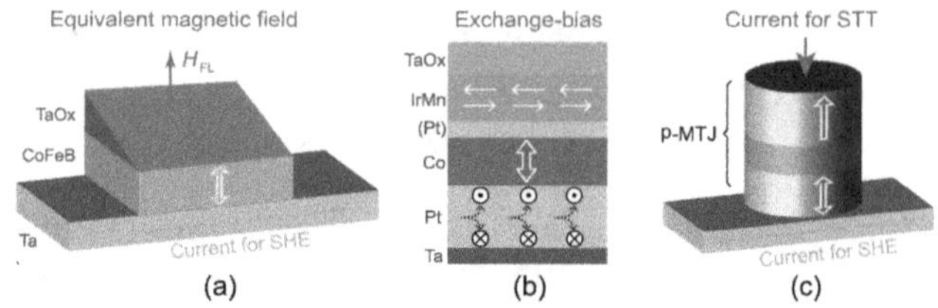

Figure 3: Illustration of the device structures for eliminating the magnetic field by introducing (a) lateral asymmetry [26, 27], (b) exchange bias [28, 29], and (c) STT assistance [12, 21].

MTJ offers better scalability and thermal stability than those of i-MTJ, thus is much prepared in MRAM design [21-25], but the required magnetic field for SHE-driven switching puts the device into a dilemma for SHE-MRAM application.

To solve this dilemma, recent studies have reported that the in-plane magnetic field can be eliminated by introducing a lateral asymmetry-breaking structure [26, 27], as shown in Fig. 3(a), which induces an equivalent magnetic field along the z-axis, or by introducing an exchange bias from an antiferromagnetic layer [28, 29], as shown in Fig. 3(b). Another solution is to replace the role of the magnetic field with an STT write current [12, 21], as shown in Fig. 3(c), in which the SHE current is used to assist the STT current for magnetization switching, named SHE-assisted STT. All the device designs have been experimentally proved, but their practical applications in SHE-MRAM are still a question, taking into consideration the fabrication complexity and performance. In our study, we will choose the SHE-assisted STT based p-MTJ for MRAM design due to its device simplicity and technical maturity.

Fig. 4 shows the memory array (1-by-3) of SHE-MRAM. Due to the separated write/read current paths of the SHE-MTJ device, two access transistors with their gates being controlled by a write-word-line (WWL) and a read-word-line (RWL) respectively are required per bit-cell to control the separated write/read operations. Obviously, such a bit-cell structure adds area overhead compared with that of STT-MRAM. Therefore, the potential application of SHE-MRAM is high-speed and low-power working memory, e.g., on-chip cache, rather than high-density storage. Nevertheless, the area overhead can be reduced via layout optimization techniques, e.g., shared BL/SL structures. By using the SHE-assisted STT based p-MTJ device (with our developed electrical model [21]) and a CMOS design-kit, we designed a SHE-MRAM circuit and performed hybrid MTJ/CMOS simulations. Fig. 5 illustrates the comparison of the magnetization dynamics of the free layer of the STT-based p-MTJ and SHE-assisted STT based p-MTJ devices, respectively. As can be seen, the SHE current greatly reduces the incubation delay, which can also be clearly proved by comparing the magnetization trajectories between the STT-based p-MTJ and SHE-assisted STT based p-MTJ devices, as shown in Fig. 6. It is worth noting that the SHE current does not always assist STT for magnetization

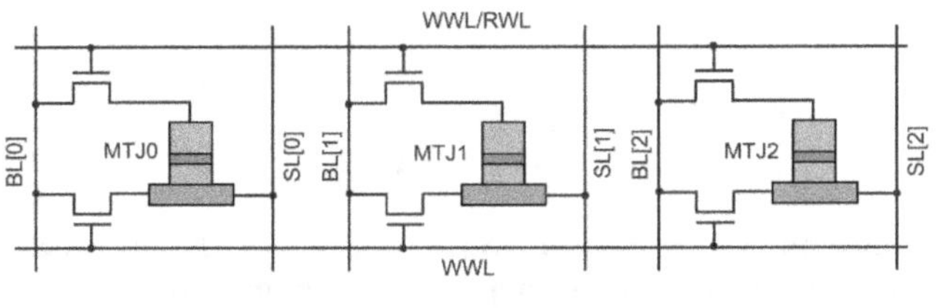

Figure 4: Schematic of the SHE-MRAM memory array.

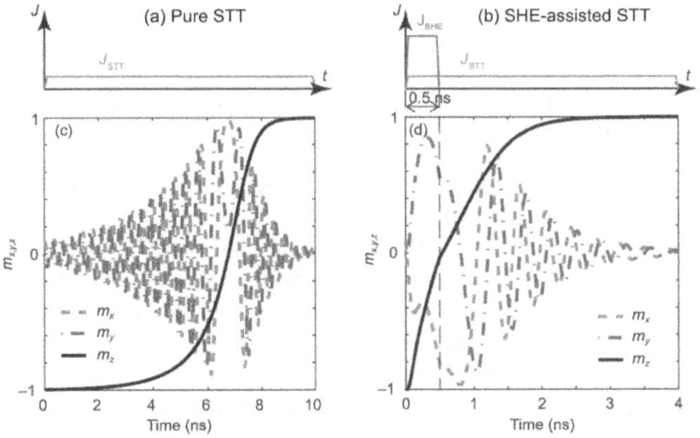

Figure 5: Time-resolved magnetization dynamics of the free layer of the p-MTJ device under (a) pure STT effect, and (b) SHE-assisted STT effect, respectively [22, 25].

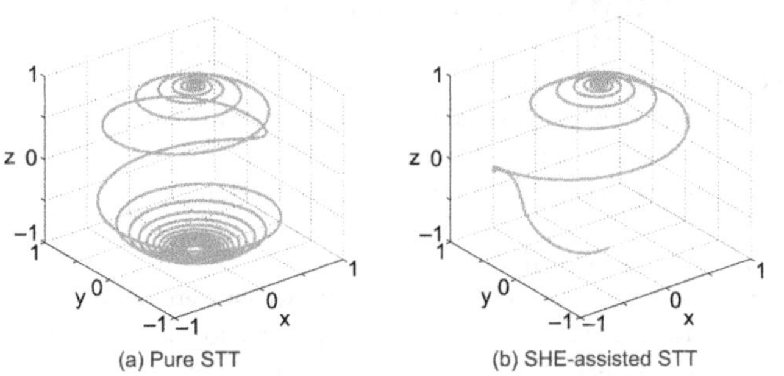

Figure 6: Trajectories of the magnetization of the free layer of the p-MTJ device under (a) pure STT effect, and (b) SHE-assisted STT effect, respectively [22, 25].

switching but depends on the pulse duration [21, 22]. Thus it should be removed at an appropriate time.

3 FROM SHE-MRAM TO VC-MRAM

Following the lessons learnt from the bipolar junction transistors to CMOS evolution, replacing current-driven mechanisms (either STT or SHE) by voltage-driven effects would result in significant energy reduction [14-16]. Recently, voltage-controlled magnetic anisotropy (VCMA) effect enables us a new possibility to utilize voltage (or electric field) for efficiently switching a p-MTJ device and thus has gained intensive investigation [14-16, 30-34]. The use of a voltage allows for much lower power dissipation since in principle no or little charge flow is required, thereby significantly reducing or even eliminating Ohmic losses and Joule heating. In addition, the voltage-driven mechanism brings other advantages, e.g., high density, as the size of the access transistors can be reduced owing to the decrease of the drivability of the transistors. One of the current challenges is to improve the VCMA coefficient so as to reduce the voltage amplitude for data write operations. The device schematic of a VCMA-MTJ (see Fig. 7(a)) is similar to that of a STT-MTJ,

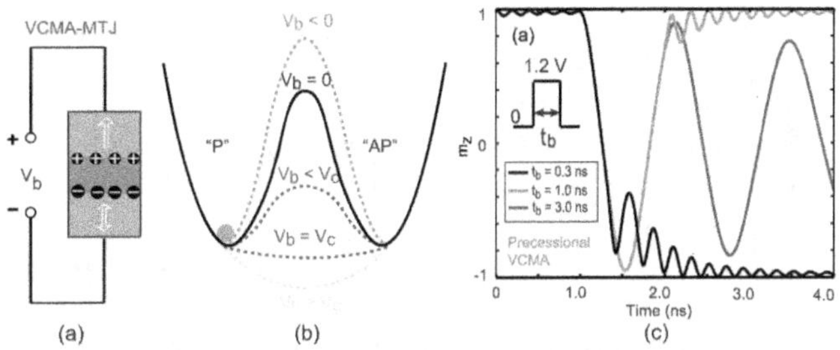

Figure 7: Illustration of (a) VCMA-MTJ device schematic, (b) energy barrier of the p-MTJ device under a voltage, and (c) the magnetization dynamics of the free layer under a voltage with different pulse durations [32].

except that the oxide barrier in a VCMA-MTJ is far thicker than that in a STT-MTJ. In such a device, the oxide barrier acts as a capacitor and the application of a voltage on the MTJ device will result in an electric field through the oxide barrier, and in an accumulation of charges near the interface between the oxide barrier and the free layer. The accumulated charges induces change of occupancy of atomic orbitals at the interface, which, in conjunction with the spin-orbit interaction, results in a change of the interfacial magnetic anisotropy (IMA) or energy barrier of the MTJ device (see Fig. 7(b)) [16]. In specific, regarding the mainstream CoFeB|MgO-based p-MTJ devices, a positive voltage reduces the IMA, whereas a negative voltage increases the IMA [32]. If a positive voltage (with amplitude larger than a threshold) is applied on the MTJ, the magnetization of the free layer will precessionally oscillates around the effective field and the final state depends on the duration of the voltage pulse (see Fig. 7(c)). This behavior, unfortunately, adds potential challenges in the VC-MRAM robust design, as the precise control of the voltage pulse duration for each memory bit-cell is rather difficult in practice for a huge memory bit-array, taking into consideration the process and thermal variations.

To solve this problem, recent studies have reported that the final magnetization state of the free layer in a VCMA-MTJ device can be determined by a STT current rather than by controlling the pulse duration [32-34], named VCMA-assisted STT. In such a device, two voltage pulses with different amplitudes and durations are employed to write data into the MTJ, as shown in Fig. 8(a). In specific, a relatively large voltage pulse (say V_H, for generating VCMA effect) with a short duration (T_H) is first employed in order to induce precessional magnetization oscillation of the free layer, then followed by a small voltage pulse (V_{STT} for generating STT effect) with a long duration (T_{STT}) to stabilize the final magnetization orientation of the free layer of the MTJ [32]. The behind physical explanation of this phenomenon can be described as the completion between STT and VCMA effects [33]. Fig. 8(b) demonstrates the magnetization dynamics of the free layer of the VCMA-assisted STT based p-MTJ device. In this study, we will choose the precessional VCMA and VCMA-assisted STT based p-MTJ devices for our VC-MRAM designs. The memory bit-cell and array structures of VC-MRAM are similar to those of STT-MRAM except for the write driver. By using the precessional VCMA-based and the VCMA-assisted STT based p-MTJ devices (with our developed electrical models [32]) and a CMOS design-kit, we designed a VC-MRAM circuit and performed hybrid MTJ/CMOS simulations.

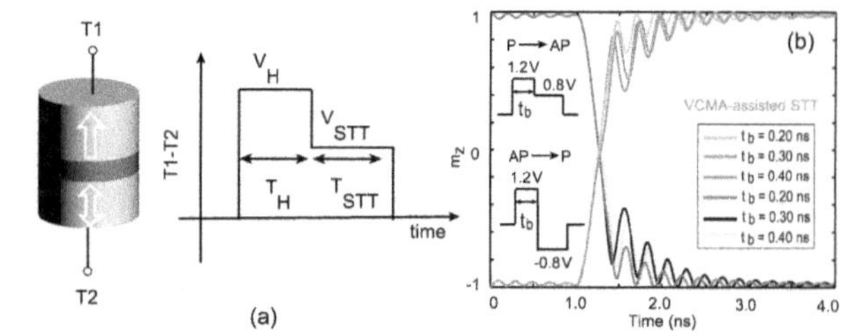

Figure 8: Illustration of the (a) VCMA-assisted STT based p-MTJ and its related write voltage pulse sequence, (b) the corresponding magnetization dynamics of the free layer [22].

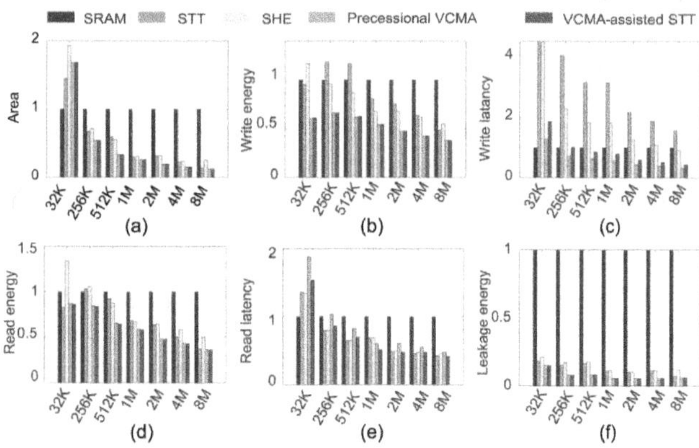

Figure 9: Performance comparison among all the MRAMs in terms of area, write energy, write latency, read energy, read latency, and leakage energy, normalized to SRAM

4 PERFORMANCE COMPARISON AMONG STT-MRAM, SHE-MRAM AND VC-MRAM FOR CACHE APPLICATIONS

In this section, we compare the key performance (e.g., power and latency) among STT-MRAM, SHE-MRAM and VC-MRAM from circuit and system design perspectives. First, we performed hybrid MTJ/CMOS simulations to obtain the bit-cell performance. Here all the MRAM designs utilize the same peripheral circuits, such as row/column decoders and read circuits. Since the main difference among these MRAM designs is the data write mechanism, the read principle and the related circuit are similar, thus are omitted here, please refer to [35, 36] for more details. Then by using the NVSim [37], a cache memory simulator, we simulate various cache configurations for exploring the design space for these memories. We performed an iso-capacity replacement of baseline SRAM for the L2 cache with STT-MRAM, SHE-MRAM, and VC-MRAM respectively. Fig. 9 compares the area, write energy, write latency, read energy, read latency, and leakage energy for various cache capacities, in which all the values were normalized to the base-line SRAM [38]. As can be seen, all these MRAMs outperform SRAM in leakage energy, thanks to the nonvolatility of the MTJ devices. Furthermore, as the cache capacity increases (e.g., >256K bytes), MRAMs outperform SRAM in terms of area, energy and latency. In particular, VC-MRAMs exhibit the best performance, due to the unique voltage-driven mechanism. These results indicate that SHE-MRAM and VC-MRAM have the better potential to be used for cache memory beyond STT-MRAM. Further system-level studies

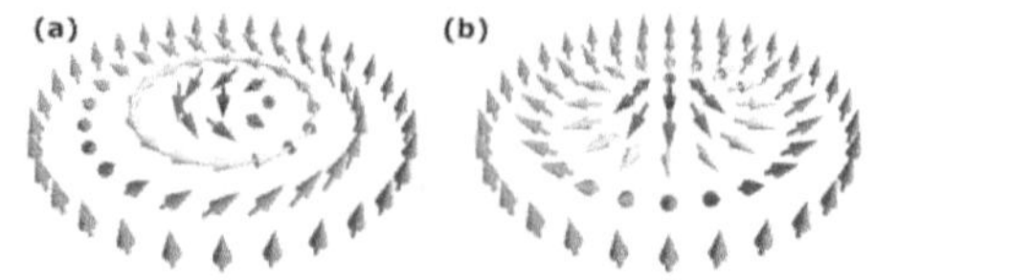

Figure 10: Magnetization configurations of the (a) Bloch-type and (b) Neel-type magnetic skyrmions, respectively [19].

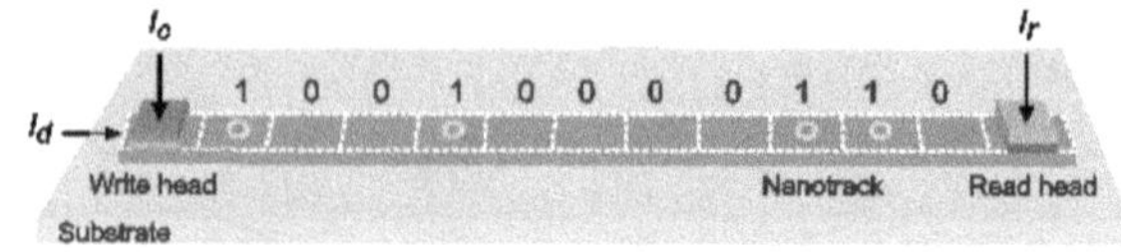

Figure 11: Schematic of a typical SK-RM with skyrmions as the information carriers [19].

have revealed that both SHE-MRAM and VC-MRAM are able to fulfill the instruction-per-cycle (IPC) performance requirements of the L2 cache and bring benefits in reduction of cache area and energy consumption. Moreover, VC-MRAM has even the potential to be utilized in the L1 cache [38]. Nevertheless, more efforts are expected to bring SHE-MRAM and VC-MRAM into real products in the near future.

5 EMERGING MAGNETIC SKYRMIONS AS INFORMATION CARRIERS

Beyond MRAM technology, some emerging spintronic objects or devices, e.g., magnetic skyrmions, exhibit promising potential in future spintronic memory and logic applications [17-20, 39-45]. In this section, we present the latest research of utilizing magnetic skyrmions as information carriers in racetrack memory.

5.1 Magnetic Skyrmions

Magnetic skyrmions, as shown in Fig 10, which were discovered in bulk ferromagnets, and magnetic thin films, are topologically stable nanoscale magnetization configurations with particle-like properties [17-20]. They mostly originate from the competitions among ferromagnetic exchange coupling, magnetic anisotropy and Dzyaloshinskii-Moriya interaction (DMI, either interfacial or bulk) in magnetic systems lacking inversion symmetry [17-19]. Depending on the material properties, two types of skyrmions can be stabilized [18, 19]. In specific, bulk DMI supports Bloch-type chiral skyrmions as shown in Fig. 10(a), whereas interfacial DMI supports Neel-type hedgehog skyrmions as shown in Fig. 10(b). Although firstly discovered in bulk ferromagnets [39], skyrmions have recently been more investigated in magnetic thin films or multilayer systems because of the improved thermal stability, size and manipulability [40-42]. Owing to the promising merits, such as topological stability, small size and low driving current density, tremendous research has been made for exploring skyrmions in future spintronic memories and logics [20, 43-45]. Nevertheless, many challenges should be addressed before this technology can be employed in practical applications. One of the key challenges of skyrmions is to search a proper material system which supports stable skyrmions with high thermal stability at room temperature.

Most recently, asymmetric multilayer structure has been reported as one of the candidates, in which stable sub-100 nm skyrmions have been experimentally obtained at room temperature [41, 42].

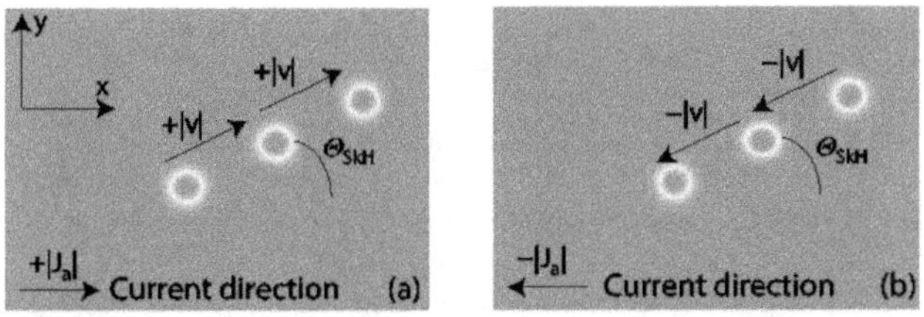

Figure 12: Observation of the skyrmion Hall effect [50].

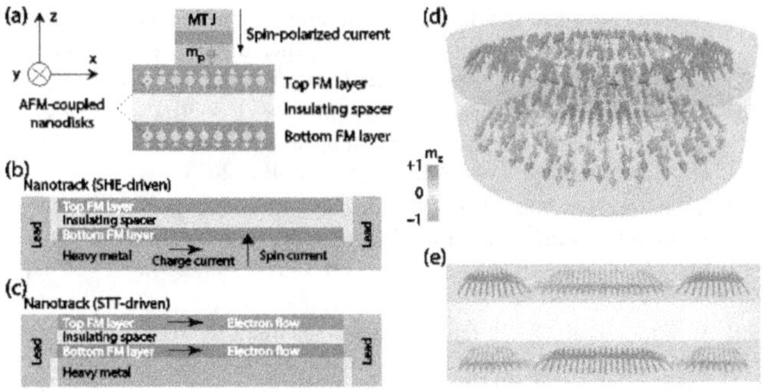

Figure 13: Schematic of (a) the antiferromagnetically (AFM) exchange-coupled ferromagnetic (FM) bilayer nanodisk; (b)-(c) AFM-coupled bilayer nanotracks with the SHE- and STT-driven mechanisms receptively; (d) Illustration of the bilayer-coupled skyrmion and (e) the corresponding side view [51].

Meanwhile, robust and efficient skyrmion manipulation methods are required for employing skyrmions in device construction.

5.2 Skyrmion-Based Racetrack Memory

One of the most potential applications of skyrmions is to build racetrack memory instead of utilizing domain walls (DWs) [46]. Fig. 11 shows the typical schematic of a skyrmion-based racetrack memory (SK-RM) [43-45], in which binary data information is encoded in the form of magnetic skyrmions rather than in the form of DWs. In comparison with DW-based racetrack memory (DW-RM), SK-RM has the potential to achieve higher package density, lower energy, and more robust data stability, since the information carriers (i.e., skyrmions) in SK-RM provides smaller size, lower driving current density and higher robustness against defects than DWs [17-19]. Similar to that of DW-RM [46], SK-RM is composed of four main parts: a write head for skyrmion creation, a nanotrack for skyrmion motion, a read head for skyrmion detection and some peripheral CMOS circuits for generating the skyrmion creation current (I_c), driving current (I_d) and perpendicular read current (I_r). The write head can use either an MTJ or spin-valve device to inject a local spin-polarized current for generating skyrmions [19, 40, 43]. One of the current challenges is how to energy-efficiently generate skyrmions with high speed. The read head can also employ an MTJ device to detect skyrmions via the magneto-resistance effect [47, 48]. As we discussed above, one of the key advantages of skyrmions is the potential for ultrahigh package density, owing to its small size, which, however, makes it difficult to be readout reliably with a high signal-to-noise ratio. Possible solutions include exploring novel material systems, device structures, generation/detection approaches, are strongly required for SK-RM implementation. Skyrmion motion along the nanotrack can be achieved by an electrical current through either the STT or SHE mechanism [40, 45]. However, particular attention should be paid to the skyrmion Hall effect, which denotes the phenomenon that skyrmion does not move parallel to the direction of the applied current, as shown in Fig. 12, owing to the Magnus force [49, 50]. The skyrmion Hall effect poses a severe challenge for realistic SK-RM applications, as it may result in destruction of a moving skyrmion at the edge of a device. Fortunately, recent studies have reported that using antiferromagnetically exchange-coupled ferromagnetic bilayer as the skyrmion motion nanotrack instead of ferromagnetic layer can eliminate skyrmion Hall effect [51, 52]. As shown in Fig. 13, the bilayer-coupled skyrmion is composed of two topological objects with opposite topological charge. In this configuration, Magnus force acts in opposite directions for two objects and the strong coupling between the sublattices yields perfect cancellation of the two opposing Magnus forces. Antiferromagnetic materials enable an alternative option for skyrmion study and have attracted wide attention in the community. Beyond in memory, skyrmions can also be exploited in logics, please refer to [19, 20] for more details.

Amazing advances have been made in skyrmion research in the past few years. Meanwhile, a rich variety of skyrmion-based device concepts have been proposed, indicating the considerable potential of skyrmions for future spintronic applications. However, lots of challenges are existing and should be addressed before this technology can be translated into a real product. At present, the primary challenges are related to the exploration of novel material systems and device structures that can stabilize small skyrmions at room temperature and that can support all-electric manipulation.

6 CONCLUSIONS

In summary, we have presented a review on the recent progress of advanced spintronic memory beyond STT-MRAM. We showed two new MRAM technologies based on SHE- and voltage-driven mechanisms as well as studied their potential application in cache memories. Afterwards, we introduced magnetic skyrmion, which is an emerging spintronic object, as potential information carriers in racetrack memory design. We discussed the perspectives and challenges of these advanced spintronic memories. We expect that this paper can provide the society a clear overview of the current research of spintronic memory and could attract more efforts into this field to translate these technologies into real products.

ACKNOWLEDGMENTS

This work was supported in part by the National Natural Science Foundation of China (Grant 61501013 and 61571023).

REFERENCES

[1] N. S. Kim, T. Austin, D. Baauw, et al., "Leakage current: Moore's law meets static power," *Computer*, vol. 36, no. 12, pp. 68-75, 2003.

[2] M. M. Waldrop, "The chips are down for Moore's law," *Nat. News*, vol. 530, no. 7589, pp. 144, 2016.

[3] W. Kang, et al., "Spintronics: Emerging Ultra-low Power Circuits and Systems Beyond MOS Technology," *ACM JETC*, vol. 12, no. 16, pp. 1-42, Aug. 2015.

[4] B. C. Lee, E. Ipek, O. Mutlu, et al., "Architecting Phase Change Memory as A Scalable Dram Alternative," *ACM SIGARCH Computer Architect. News*, vol. 37, no. 3, pp. 2-13, Jun. 2009.

[5] D. E. Nikonov and I. A. Young, "Overview of beyond-CMOS devices and a uniform methodology for their benchmarking," *Proc. IEEE*, vol. 101, pp. 2498-2533, 2013.

[6] W. Kang, et al., "Reconfigurable Codesign of STT-MRAM under Process Variations in Deeply Scaled Technology," *IEEE Trans. Electron Devices*, vol. 62, no. 6, pp. 1769-1777, Jun. 2015.

[7] C. Chappert, et al., "The emergence of spin electronics in data storage," *Nature Mater.*, vol. 6, no. 11, pp. 813–823, 2007.

[8] J. M. Slaughter, et al., "High density ST-MRAM technology (Invited)", in *IEEE IEDM.*, California, USA. Dec. 2012, pp. 1-4.

[9] J. M. Slaughter, et al., "Technology for reliable spin-torque MRAM products," in *IEEE IEDM.,* California, USA. Dec. 2016, pp. 21-5.

[10] I. M. Miron, K. Garello, G. Gaudin, et al., "Perpendicular switching of a single ferromagnetic layer induced by in-plane current injection," *Nature*, vol. 476, no. 7359, pp. 189, 2011.

[11] L. Liu, et al., "Spin-torque switching with the giant Spin Hall effect of Tantalum." *Science*, vol. 336, no 6081, pp. 555–558, 2012.

[12] A. van den Brink et al., "Spin-hall-assisted magnetic random access memory," *Appl. Phys. Lett.*, vol. 104, no. 1, pp. 1-3, 2014

[13] W. Kang, W. Lv, Y. Zhang et al., "Low store power high-speed high-density nonvolatile SRAM design with spin Hall effect-driven magnetic tunnel junctions," *IEEE Trans. Nanotechnol.*, vol. 16, no. 1, pp. 148-154, Jan. 2017.

[14] P. K. Amiri, et al., "Electric-field-controlled magnetoelectric RAM: progress, challenges, and scaling," *IEEE Trans. Magn.*, vol. 51, no. 11, pp. 1-7, 2015.

[15] K. L. Wang, et al., "Magnetoelectric random access memory-based circuit design by using voltage-controlled magnetic anisotropy in magnetic tunnel junctions," *IEEE Trans. Nanotechnol*, vol. 14, no. 6, pp. 992-997, 2015.

[16] J. G. Alzate, "Voltage-controlled magnetic dynamics in nanoscale magnetic tunnel junctions," *Ph.D. dissertation, Dept. Elect. Eng. UCLA*, 2014.

[17] A. Fert, V. Cros, and J. Sampaio, "Skyrmions on the track," *Nat. Nanotechnol.*, vol. 8, no. 3, pp. 152-156, 2013.

[18] R. Wiesendanger, "Nanoscale magnetic skyrmions in metallic films and multilayers: a new twist for spintronics," *Nat. Rev. Mater.*, p. 16044, 2016.

[19] W. Kang, et al., "Skyrmion-Electronics: An Overview and Outlook," *Proc. IEEE*, vol. 104, no, 10. pp. 2040-2061, 2016.

[20] Y. Huang, W. Kang, X. Zhang, et al., "Magnetic skyrmion-based synaptic devices," *Nanotechnol.* vol. 28, no. 8, pp. 08LT02, 2016.

[21] Z. Wang, W. Zhao, E. Deng, et al., "Perpendicular-anisotropy magnetic tunnel junction switched by spin-Hall-assisted spin-transfer torque." *J. Phys. D: Appl. Phys.*, vol. 48, no. 6, pp. 065001, 2015.

[22] Z. Wang, "Compact modeling and circuit design based on ferroelectric tunnel junction and spin-Hall-assisted spin-transfer torque," *Ph.D. Dissertation, Dept. Phys., Université Paris-Sud,* 2015.

[23] L. Chang, Z. Wang, Y. Gao, et al., "Evaluation of spin-Hall-assisted STT-MRAM for cache replacement," in *IEEE/ACM NANOARCH,* Beijing, China, July. 2016, pp. 73-78.

[24] W. Kang, Z. Wang, Y. Zhang, et al., "Spintronic Logic Design Methodology Based on Spin Hall Effect–Driven Magnetic Tunnel Junctions," *J. Phys. D: Appl. Phys.*, vol. 49, no. 6, pp. 1-2, Feb. 2016.

[25] W. Zhao, et al., "Recent progresses in spin transfer torque-based magnetoresistive random access memory (STT-MRAM)," *SCI. SINICA Phys., Mech. & Astron.*, vol. 46, no. 10, pp. 107306, 2016.

[26] G. Yu, P. Upadhyaya, Fan Y, et al. "Switching of perpendicular magnetization by spin-orbit torques in the absence of external magnetic fields," *Nature Nanotech*, vol. 9, pp. 548–554, 2016.

[27] M. Akyol, et al., "Current-induced spin-orbit torque switching of perpendicularly magnetized Hf|CoFeB|MgO and Hf|CoFeB|TaOx structures," *Appl. Phys. Lett.*, vol. 106, pp. 162409, 2015.

[28] S. Fukami, C. Zhang, S. Duttagupta, et al., "Magnetization switching by spin-orbit torque in an antiferromagnet-ferromagnet bilayer system," *Nature Mater*, vol. 15, pp. 535–541, 2015.

[29] A. V. Brink, et al. "Field-free magnetization reversal by Spin-Hall effect and exchange bias." *Nature Commun.*, vol. 7, pp. 10854, 2016.

[30] W. G. Wang, et al., "Electric-field-assisted switching in magnetic tunnel junctions," *Nature Mater.*, vol. 11, no. 1, pp. 64-68, 2012.

[31] S. Wang, et al., "Comparative Evaluation of Spin-Transfer-Torque and Magnetoelectric Random Access Memory," *IEEE J. Emerg. Select. Top. Circ. Syst.*, vol. 6, no. 2, pp. 134-145, Apr. 2016.

[32] W. Kang, et al., "Modeling and exploration of the voltage controlled magnetic anisotropy effect for the next generation low-power and high-speed MRAM applications," *IEEE Trans. Nanotechnol.*, 2017.

[33] S. Kanai, et al., "Magnetization switching in a CoFeB/MgO magnetic tunnel junction by combining spin-transfer torque and electric field-effect," *Appl. Phys. Lett.*, vol. 104, pp. 212406, 2014.

[34] S. Sharmin, A. Jaiswal, K. Roy, "Modeling and Design Space Exploration for Bit-Cells Based on Voltage-Assisted Switching of Magnetic Tunnel Junctions." *IEEE Trans. Electron Devices*, vol. 63, no. 9, pp. 3493-3500, 2016.

[35] W. Kang, et al., "High reliability sensing circuit for deep submicron spin transfer torque magnetic random access memory," *Electron. Lett.*, vol. 49, no. 20, pp. 1283-1285, Sep. 2013.

[36] W. Kang, Z. Li, J. Klein, et al., "Variation-tolerant and disturbance-free sensing circuit for deep nanometer STT-MRAM," *IEEE Trans. Nanotechnol.*, vol. 13, no. 6, pp. 1088-1092, Nov. 2014.

[37] X. Dong, et al., "NVSim: A circuit-level performance, energy, and area model for emerging nonvolatile memory," *IEEE Trans. Comput. Aid. Design Integr. Circ. Syst.*, vol. 31, no. 7, pp. 994-1007, 2012.

[38] W. Kang, et al., "Voltage-Controlled MRAM for Working Memory: Perspectives and Challenges" in *IEEE DATE.*, 2017.

[39] S. Mühlbauer, B. Binz, F. Jonietz, et al., "Skyrmion lattice in a chiral magnet," *Science*, vol. 323, no. 5916, pp. 915–919, 2009.

[40] J. Sampaio, et al., "Nucleation, stability and current-induced motion of isolated magnetic skyrmions in nanostructures.," *Nature Nanotechnol.*, vol. 8, no. 11, pp. 839–44, 2013.

[41] C. Moreau-Luchaire, et al., "Additive interfacial chiral interaction in multilayers for stabilization of small individual skyrmions at room temperature," *Nat. Nanotechnol.,* vol. 11, no. 5, pp. 444-448, 2016.

[42] O. Boulle, J. Vogel, H. Yang, et al., "Room temperature chiral magnetic skyrmion in ultrathin magnetic nanostructures," *Nature Nanotechnol.*, vol. 11, no. 5, pp. 449–454, 2016.

[43] W. Kang, et al., "Voltage controlled magnetic skyrmion motion for racetrack memory," *Sci. Rep.*, vol. 6, pp. 23164, Feb. 2016.

[44] W. Kang, et al., "Complementary skyrmion racetrack memory with voltage manipulation," *IEEE Electron Devices Lett.,* vol. 37, no. 7, pp. 924-927, 2016.

[45] R. Tomasello, et al., "A strategy for the design of skyrmion racetrack memories," *Sci. Rep.*, vol. 4, p. 6784, 2014.

[46] S. S. P. Parkin, et al., "Magnetic domain-wall racetrack memory," *Science*, vol. 320, no. 5873, pp. 190-194, Apr. 2008.

[47] D. M. Crum, et al., "Perpendicular reading of single confined magnetic skyrmions," *Natrue Commun.*, vol. 6, p. 8541, 2015.

[48] C. Hanneken, F. Otte, A. Kubetzka, et al., "Electrical detection of magnetic skyrmions by tunnelling non-collinear magnetoresistance," *Nature Nanotechnol.*, vol. 10, pp. 1039-1042, 2015.

[49] W. Jiang, X. Zhang, G. Yu, et al., "Direct observation of the skyrmion Hall effect". *Nature Phys.*, vol. 13, pp. 162-169, 2016.

[50] X. Zhang, et al., "Magnetic bilayer-skyrmions without skyrmion Hall effect," *Nature Commun.*, vol. 7, p. 10293, 2016.

[51] K. Litzius, et al., "Skyrmion Hall effect revealed by direct time-resolved X-ray microscopy," vol. 13, pp. 170-175, 2016.

[52] J. Barker, and O. A. Tretiakov, "Static and dynamical properties of antiferromagnetic skyrmions in the presence of applied current and temperature," *Phys. Rev. Lett.*, vol. 116, no. 14, pp. 147203, 2016.

Exploiting Non-Volatility for Information Processing

Robert Perricone
Department of Computer Science and Engineering
University of Notre Dame
Notre Dame, Indiana 46556
rperrico@nd.edu

Li Tang
Department of Computer Science and Engineering
University of Notre Dame
Notre Dame, Indiana 46556
ltang@nd.edu

Michael Niemier
Department of Computer Science and Engineering
University of Notre Dame
Notre Dame, Indiana 46556
mniemier@nd.edu

X. Sharon Hu
Department of Computer Science and Engineering
University of Notre Dame
Notre Dame, Indiana 46556
shu@nd.edu

ABSTRACT

The emergence of non-volatile (NV) technologies provides an opportunity to overcome limitations of CMOS (e.g., the growth of leakage power), while simultaneously providing a degree of non-volatility to the processor. Spintronic NV technologies are of particular interest due to their high integration density, low device count, radiation hardness, and non-volatility when compared to CMOS. Quantifying the impact of spintronic NV technologies at the architecture and application levels introduces a unique challenge as the granularity of technology integration can vary significantly (i.e., from heterogeneous architectures with NV cache and CMOS-based logic, to completely NV architectures). In this work, we explore three classes of NV processors (NVPs) and define metrics for quantifying their respective energy savings. As case studies, we evaluate the impact of NV technologies for both an energy harvesting non-pipelined processor and a general purpose processor executing scientific applications under varying degrees of parallelism.

CCS Concepts

•**Hardware → Spintronics and magnetic technologies;** *Power estimation and optimization;* Emerging architectures;

Keywords

Non-volatility; Spintronics; Energy Harvesting; C-States

1. INTRODUCTION

Many beyond-CMOS devices are being investigated in the hope of replacing or augmenting CMOS based processing engines. However, benchmarking results for both Boolean logic-based computing units as well as multi-core processors show that it is rather difficult for these devices to significantly outperform their CMOS counterparts [16, 19]. Nonetheless, many of beyond-CMOS devices exhibit some unique properties that may offer alternative ways for them to greatly surpass CMOS in certain aspects. One such unique property is non-volatility, where devices can maintain their internal device indefinitely without power supply.

This paper investigates energy benefits that can be offered by devices with inherent non-volatility. Specifically, we study processors based on two spintronic non-volatile (NV) devices: All Spin Logic (ASL) and CoMET. Studies of existing spintronic logic based processors (e.g., [7, 22, 5]) have mainly focused on performance and dynamic energy associated with continuous processing, where it seems challenging for spintronic logic to compete with CMOS. However, in such continuous processing scenarios, the NV property is typically not leveraged.

In this paper, we consider two intermittent processing scenarios where NV processors (NVPs) can help save significant amounts of energy. The first scenario is from applications powered by harvested energy sources, which are frequently unreliable. In a processor built with NV devices, the need for backup/recovery to/from NV memory, as well as the energy and delays associated with the backup and recovery operations can be eliminated. The second scenario is from applications with long idle intervals due to long stall cycles. Such scenarios can benefit from extremely low sleep-state overheads offered by NV processors. The question then becomes how *much* energy saving can be achieved under these two scenarios.

The rest of the paper is organized as follows. First, in Sec. 2, we provide an overview our target spintronic devices and summarize related NVP work. Next, in Sec. 3, we explain three classifications of NVPs and discuss their tradeoffs. Then, in Secs. 4 and 5 we provide our metrics and results for energy harvesting NVPs and general purpose processors (GPPs), respectively.

Permission to make digital or hard copies of all or part of this work for personal or classroom use is granted without fee provided that copies are not made or distributed for profit or commercial advantage and that copies bear this notice and the full citation on the first page. Copyrights for components of this work owned by others than ACM must be honored. Abstracting with credit is permitted. To copy otherwise, or republish, to post on servers or to redistribute to lists, requires prior specific permission and/or a fee. Request permissions from permissions@acm.org.

GLSVLSI '17 May 10–12, 2017, Banf, AB, Canada
© 2017 ACM. ISBN 978-1-4503-4972-7/17/05...$15.00
DOI: http://dx.doi.org/10.1145/3060403.3066872

2. BACKGROUND

In this section, we provide a brief overview of our target spintronic devices and summarize related work on NVPs.

2.1 Overview of Select Spintronic Devices

We have selected four spintronic devices – STT-RAM,

SHE-RAM, ASL, and CoMET – for our evaluation work as they represent near-term, mid-term, and long-term developments in the research spectrum of spintronic devices. Below, we discuss the basic operating principles of these spintronic devices.

STT-RAM: A Spin Transfer Torque RAM (STT-RAM) bit-cell consists of an access transistor and a Magnetic Tunnel Junction (MTJ) as shown in [7]. The write operation is accomplished by applying a write current in one of two directions. The direction of the write current through the access transistor changes the state (which indicates a '1' or '0') of the MTJ device. The state of the MTJ is changed as this charge current becomes spin polarized based on the pinned layer magnetization and exerts a torque on the free layer. The read operation is performed using a small read current through the access transistor to sense the resistance of the MTJ. STT-RAM chips with sufficient capacities have been experimentally demonstrated (e.g., [21, 17]).

SHE-RAM: Spin Hall Effect RAM (SHE-RAM) consists of two access transistors, an MTJ, and a spin Hall metal (SHM) structure as shown in [7]. The write operation is performed with a bidirectional current through the SHM. Here, the charge current becomes spin polarized, traversing along the direction of charge current. The charge current is along the x-axis and the spin current is polarized along the y-axis. The spin current along the z-axis exerts a torque on the MTJ free layer sitting on top of the SHM. SHE can switch an in-plane MTJ naturally, but requires an external in-plane field to switch an MTJ with perpendicular anisotropy. The read operation is performed using the MTJ access transistor which is identical to the STT-RAM read operation. Spin Hall effect has been predicted to be more efficient at switching the MTJ than the spin transfer torque mechanism [13, 10, 8]. Spin-torque switching by SHE has been experimentally demonstrated (e.g., [9, 23]).

ASL: An elementary All-Spin Logic (ASL) [2] gate consists of input and output magnets that have two stable magnetization states and are connected through a channel as shown in [7]. A non-zero voltage pulse applied to the input terminal and induces a spin current that passes through the input magnet, which results in spin-polarized electrons in the channel. The accumulated spins produce the channel spin current, which transfers angular momentum to the output magnet. If the channel spin current exceeds a certain threshold on the output magnet, the magnetization state of the output magnet is toggled. Depending on the polarity of the input voltage, a *COPY* or *INVERT* operation is accomplished. Majority gates can be readily realized with ASL. A key factor here is that the spin current propagation distance is limited by the length and material of the channel. This material property is known as the "spin diffusion length" and it is an important consideration for processor design as it necessitates the placement of interconnect buffers.

CoMET: Composite input MagnetoElectric-based logic Technology (CoMET) [15] is a fast, low-energy spintronics-based logic device concept. A voltage applied on an input ferroelectric (FE) capacitor nucleates a domain wall (DW) through the magnetoelectric (ME) effect [4]. A composite ferromagnet (FM) structure with an in-plane magnetic anisotropy (IMA) layer is placed above the perpendicular magnetic anisotropy (PMA)–FM channel to enable fast, energy-efficient nucleation in the PMA–FM at the input end. The DW is propagated to the output end of the FM channel, using a charge current applied to a layer of spin-Hall material placed under the PMA channel. The inverse–ME (IME) effect induces a voltage at the output, and a dual-rail inverter structure efficiently transmits this voltage to the input of the next gate. The device maps easily to a majority logic structure, as shown in [15], where DWs from the three inputs compete to create the majority magnetization under the output. As before, a voltage is induced at the output node using the IME, and is transmitted to the next stage through the dual-rail inverter.

2.2 Related Work on NVPs

In general, existing NVP works evaluate a specific NV device for a target architecture. For example, the use of spintronic memory devices (e.g., STT-RAM) in microprocessors has been previously studied for various purposes such as leveraging their zero leakage energy [5, 20] and implementing hybrid CMOS+NV memory checkpointing architectures [12, 6, 11]. Zero leakage energy and their inherent non-volatility make NV technologies an ideal candidate for energy harvesting architectures.

A recent work by Ma et al. [12] studied a non-pipelined processor (NPP) comprised of STT-RAM caches and memory for energy harvesting applications. Their NPP runs at 8 kHz since it assumes a weak WiFi power source. The instruction memory and instruction cache are assumed to be ROM and a NV memory, respectively. The data memory and data cache are also implemented by NV memories with the data cache assuming a write-back policy that preserves dirty data on power outages. As the processor is non-pipelined, a single instruction characterizes the entire state of the processor. On power outages, architectural state is preserved by writing the program counter (PC) and register file (RegFile) to a NV memory. They evaluate their design by comparing the energy per instruction for various checkpointing/restore policies and intervals between power outages.

Converse to energy harvesting architectures, there have not been many works that explore the use of spintronic NV technologies for general purpose processing (GPP). Given their expensive read/write operations and inferior performance to CMOS, spintronic NV technologies appear ill-suited for GPP. A recent work by Kim et al. [7] leveraged a drop-in approach to evaluate an ASL-based Intel Core i7 processor. The drop-in approach replaces all CMOS-based pipeline logic and flip-flops by their equivalent ASL-based logic gates and storage elements (note that the cache is not considered). They show how ASL gates can be cascaded to form pipelined logic, how edge-triggered ASL flip-flops can be formed, and how the clock signal can be manipulated to achieve equivalent functionality to their CMOS counterparts. They explain how transistor device counts can be utilized to estimate the number of equivalent ASL devices and interconnect buffers, which ultimately provides a methodology for comparing CMOS vs. ASL-based processors. Their results demonstrate that an ASL-based processor requires more than one order of magnitude power versus a CMOS-based processor. However, the authors note that it is possible to reduce the ASL power by tuning parameters such as magnetic retention time.

3. CLASSIFYING NVPS

As discussed in [18], NVPs can be classified into three

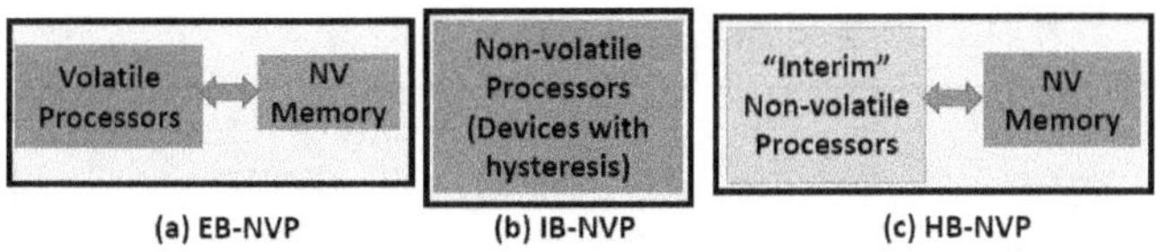

Figure 1: Three types of NVPs: (a) NVP with explicit backup, (b) NVP with implicit backup, and (c) NVP with hybrid backup [18].

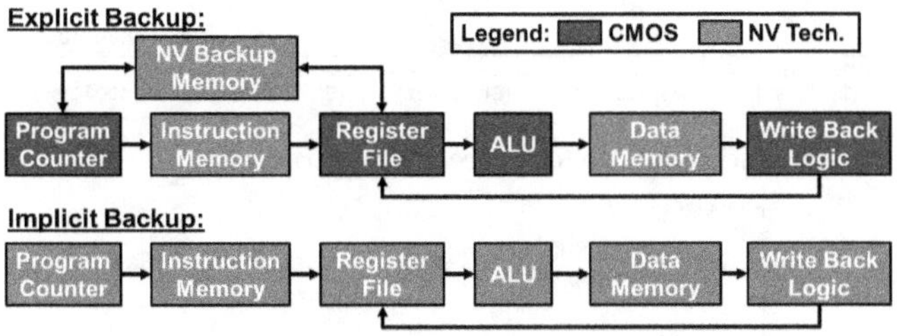

Figure 2: Explicit vs. implicit backup processor

types: NVP with explicit backup (EB-NVP), NVP with implicit backup (IB-NVP), and NVP with hybrid backup (HB-NVP) (see Fig. 1). In EB-NVPs, processor states must be explicitly backed up to and restored from NV memory. As an example, we illustrate an EB-NVP in the upper part of Fig. 2. The figure illustrates that the program counter and register file must be backed up to a NVM to preserve architectural state. Most existing NVPs belong to this category.

IB-NVPs use NV devices to realize all the storage elements (i.e., all the flip-flops and latches) while the combinational circuits in the processor may or may not be implemented in NV devices. The bottom of Fig. 2 illustrates an IB-NVP. Here, there is no longer a need for a separate backup NVM as the entire processor consists of NV technology.

For HB-NVPs, the retention time of the storage elements in the "interim" NVP cannot be treated as "infinitely" long as for IB-NVPs. Thus, NV memory is still needed. However, if the power outage time is shorter than the retention time of the "interim" NVP, no backup/recovery is needed. For many NV devices, reducing retention time could significantly reduce operating energy. Therefore, HB-NVP can provide an effective way to trade off operating energy with backup/recovery overhead.

4. NVPS FOR ENERGY HARVESTING APPLICATIONS

In this section, we summarize our framework for benchmarking NVPs (Sec. 4.1) and results (Sec. 4.2) from our previous work [18].

4.1 Summary of Benchmarking Framework

To implement an NVP based on a von Neumann architecture and to exploit the spintronic devices discussed in Sec. 2.1, a straightforward approach is to do a drop-in replacement, i.e., replacing basic CMOS circuit/logic elements with spintronic elements. The STT-RAM and SHE-RAM can be readily used as the memory elements for cache or main memory, while ASL and CoMET devices can readily implement combinational logic and flip-flops. With the drop-in replacement approach, many of the existing high-level design tools as well as architectural level techniques can be leveraged, which should significantly reduce development effort.

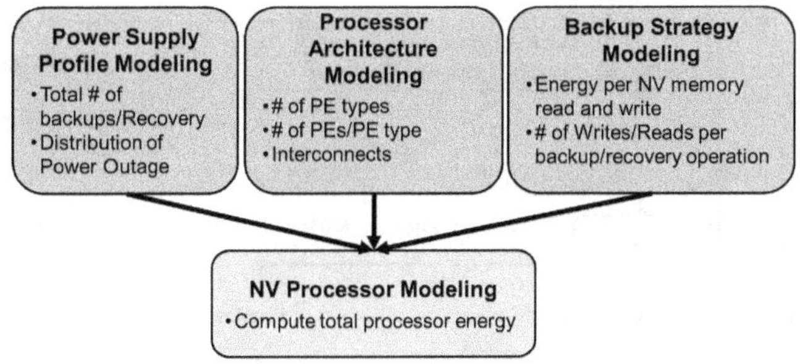

Figure 3: NVP benchmarking framework [18]

Our NVP benchmarking framework, referred to as `EvaNVP`, is illustrated in Fig. 3. `EvaNVP`builds on the drop-in replacement approach from Kim et al. [7] and estimates the total computation and backup/recovery energy of the NVP. The main idea behind `EvaNVP`is to integrate (i) the power supply patterns, (ii) the backup/recovery policies, and (iii) the processor performance/energy models to account for their collective impacts on the overall system energy. As seen in Fig. 3, `EvaNVP`consists of four separate modules. A more detailed discussion of module content appears in [18].

4.2 Energy Harvesting NVP Results

In this subsection, we present a case study that illustrates the use of `EvaNVP`. Our target architecture is the 32 bit MIPS NPP from [12]. This processor runs at 8 kHz and is comprised of CMOS (computation) and STT-RAM (backup) technology. In our study, we compare three different NV technologies to the baseline CMOS+STT-RAM architecture: (i) ASL, (ii) CoMET, and (iii) SHE-RAM. For brevity, we discuss the important device parameters as necessary in the text below and point the reader to the individual device references for additional parameters.

In our previous work, we discussed how we leveraged the Beyond-CMOS Benchmarking (BCB) methodology [16] and the data from the 2011 ITRS report [1] to scale the 45 nm CMOS+STT-RAM data used in [12] to the 15 nm technology node. However, the selected 15 nm CMOS data point used in our scaling represents a high performance CMOS (HP CMOS) device. Given that our target NPP runs at 8 kHz, we have scaled our previously computed 15 nm HP CMOS to a low voltage CMOS (LV CMOS) data point from BCB[1]. This update is reflected in the results presented in Fig. 4 for the CMOS-based computational energy per instruction.

We now apply `EvaNVP`to examine the impact of ASL and CoMET based NV NPP. The first step in `EvaNVP`is *Power Supply Profile Modeling.* For both the ASL and CoMET technologies, their retention times are selected to be 10 years; therefore, they perform implicit backups (i.e., IB-NVP) for three selected BIs (i.e., 1, 10, and 1000 instructions) associated with the weak WiFi power source. Similarly, for *Backup Strategy Modeling*, we do not specify any inputs as both ASL and CoMET lead to IB-NVPs.

The next step in our framework is *Processor Architecture*

[1]The HP CMOS and LV CMOS devices have supply voltages of 0.73 V and 0.3 V, respectively.

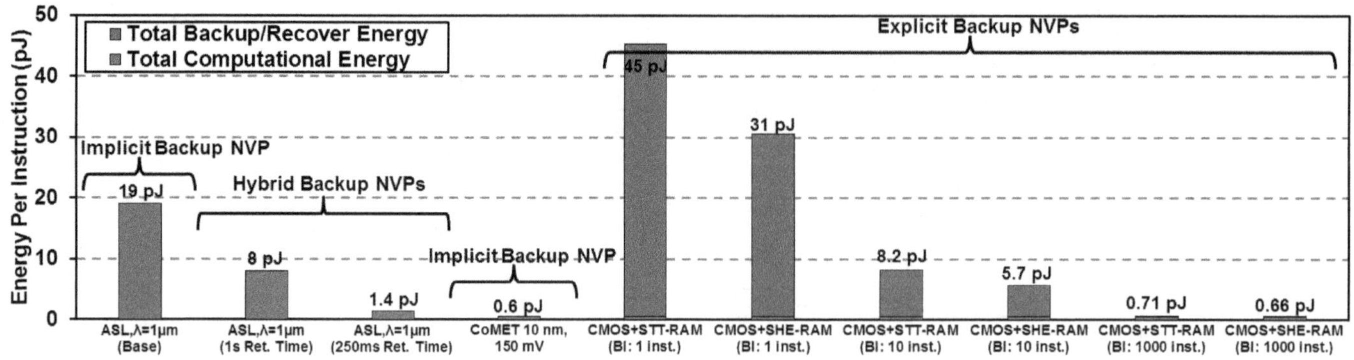

Figure 4: Benchmarking results comparing implicit, explicit, and hybrid backup/recovery strategies.

Modeling. As both the ASL and CoMET processor implementations are comprised completely of one technology, we have only one processing element (PE) type. Next, we select the logic gate level for our PEs, which is consistent with the drop-in replacement approach used in this study. Based on the logic area of the NPP reported by Ma et al. [12], we estimate a total of 7000 CMOS transistors. According to Kim et al. [7], we can determine that approximately 3500 ASL/CoMET devices would be necessary to completely implement the logic of the NPP. The final step in *Processor Architecture Modeling* is to determine the number of buffer interconnects. Using the probability distribution function summarized in [7], we found that a processor of this size would not require any interconnect buffers. CoMET also does not require interconnect buffers as data is propagated through wires connecting CMOS devices.

For the ASL-based NVP, we examined 3 different retention times as indicated by the 3 leftmost bars in Fig. 4[2]. Our results illustrate that the base ASL (IB-NVP) is more energy efficient than CMOS+STT-RAM for a BI of 1. To further lower the energy, we consider a HB-NVP by reducing the retention time to be closer to the clock cycle time of $125\mu s$. By reducing the retention time to 1 s, the ASL energy was reduced by 2.4×.

We further explored the design space of ASL under different retention time requirements by targeting a 250 ms retention time. This time is selected based on the clock cycle time of $125\mu s$ and instruction BI of 1000. By reducing the retention time to 250 ms, the computational energy is reduced by 13.6× and 5.7× versus the 10 year and 1 s retention times, respectively (third bar from the left in Fig. 4). However, compared to to CMOS+STT-RAM for BI of 1000, this HB-NVP utilizes 2× more energy.

To benchmark CoMET, we use the parameters given in [14] where the switching energy of a 3-input majority gate comprised of CoMET technology is computed for the 10 nm technology node with 10 year retention time. Our result, the 4th bar in Fig. 4, shows that a CoMET based NVP is about 2.3× more energy efficient than the best ASL data point (250 ms retention time) and between 75× and 1.2× more energy efficient than the CMOS+STT-RAM for BIs between 1 and 1000, respectively.

Our final analysis involves STT-RAM vs. SHE-RAM. Here, we have replaced the STT-RAM for backup storage in the NPP by SHE-RAM. The parameters for SHE-RAM are obtained from LLG simulation and are as follows: write current is $320\mu A$, write time is 0.84 ns and the technology node is 14 nm. For a similar technology node, STT-RAM has a write current of $150\mu A$ and a write time of 2.7 ns. Given that the switching energy is the product of the supply voltage, write current, and write time, we can estimate that the SHE-RAM is 1.5× more energy efficient than the STT-RAM (assuming equal supply voltage). The total energy per instruction for the SHE-RAM based NVP is represented by the 1st, 3rd and 5th bar from the right in Fig. 4 for BI of 1000, 10, and 1, respectively.

[2]The ASL parameters are taken from [7] and represent a 5 nm technology node with $\lambda_{ch} = 1\mu m$ from [7].

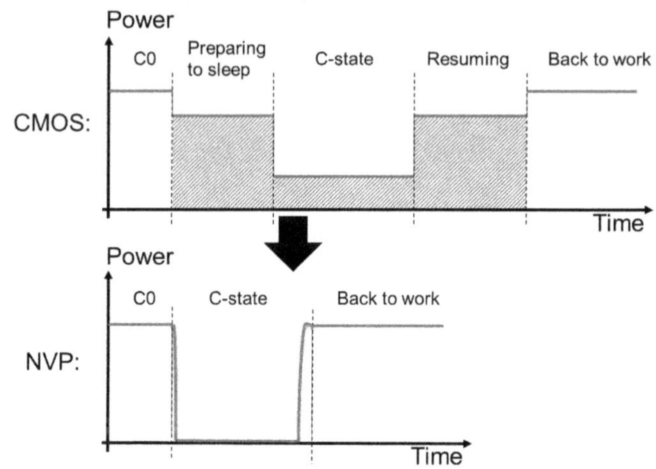

Figure 5: C-state transition for CMOS-based CPU and NVP

5. NVPS FOR GENERAL-PURPOSE APPLICATIONS

Modern multi-core processors conserve power by selectively turning off components to unused cores. Idle cores enter increasing levels of "C-states" depending on the core's idle time. For example, C0 represents normal operation, C1 turns the clock off, and C6 involves flushing the cache and power gating the core. This process generates some additional operations, which are not required in NVPs due to their non-volatility. Fig. 5 shows a typical C-state transition procedure in both a CPU and a NVP. In the CPU, a C-state transition needs to store and restore cache data and core states before and after the C-state residency, respectively. However, NVPs require approximately 100 ns for the NVP to resume work due to the charging of power rails [20]. We assume that the C-state storing and restoring transitions have the same power.

To quantify the potential energy savings of NV technologies at the processor level, we propose the energy benefit (EB) metric in Eq. 5 below.

$$EB = \frac{(1-D)E_s + 2AE_t}{E_{total}} \tag{1}$$

Here, D represents the average duty cycle that represents the fraction of time that a processing element is busy. A represents the average activity rate that represents the frequency of active/inactive alternations. E_s, E_t, and E_{total} are the sleep energy, transition energy, and total computational energy, respectively. The EB metric yields the fraction of a processing element's total computational energy that is spent transitioning to and residing in an inactive state. As NV technologies do not consume energy when inactive (i.e., turned off) or during transition periods, the EB provides a means for predicting energy savings from trading a volatile to NV technology for a given processing element.

5.1 Experimental Methodology

To begin to assess the energy benefit of using NVPs, we have measured both the C-state transition and residency energy usage on a CPU. Specially, we have conducted two sets of experiments by running three scientific applications (i.e., OpenMP versions of BFS, HeartWall and HotSpot3D) from the Rodinia benchmark suite [3] on an Intel i5 5675C (14 nm, 4 cores, 3.1 GHz) with Ubuntu Linux 16.04 OS. The two sets of experiments study how the application parallelism and the number of unused cores impact the C-state energy benefits of using NVPs. We use Intel PCM and Linux cpupower to obtain the parameter values and input them to Eq. 5 to quantify the energy benefit for a NVP.

5.2 C-State Data and Analysis

In the first set of experiments, for each application, we have three tests that launch one, two and four threads for the same dataset, respectively. For each test, we measure the total execution time and energy and collect the parameter values required by Eq. 5. Fig. 6 shows the per C-state energy benefit percentages (bars) and the associated execution time (line). First, it can be seen from the data that the majority of C-state energy is the C6 residency energy which takes 28%, 28.5% and 26.8% of the total energy for single-threaded BFS, HeartWall and HotSpot3D. This is due to only one core being used for most of the execution time while the three unused cores are in the C6 state. Second, we can observe that the C6 residency energy percentage decreases to 1.0% quickly when launching four threads for HeartWall. However, this trend is not observed for BFS and HotSpot3D. This is due to HeartWall achieving much higher parallelism than BFS and HotSpot3D. If we look at the speedup ratios of launching four threads to one thread, we can observe that HeartWall has 3.7× speedup, while BFS and HotSpot3D only have 1.1× and 1.3× speedups, respectively. Therefore, NVPs can bring more energy benefits for applications with less available parallelism.

In the second set of experiments, we run the three applications in serial on different core configurations of our Intel processor. Specially, we turn off cores in BIOS and make three core configuration, which are single-core, dual-core and quad-core. Fig. 7 shows the C-state transition and residency energy percentages for each configuration. First, we can observe that the C6 residency energy is still the major part of C-state energy for the dual-core and quad-core configurations. It takes 18.7% 18.4% 15.8% of the total energy for BFS, HeartWall and HotSpot3D on the dual-core configuration. Second, it can be seen that the C6 residency energy percentages increase with the number of unused cores regardless of applications. Moreover, processors with higher core counts may observe larger energy benefits from use of NV technologies for serial applications.

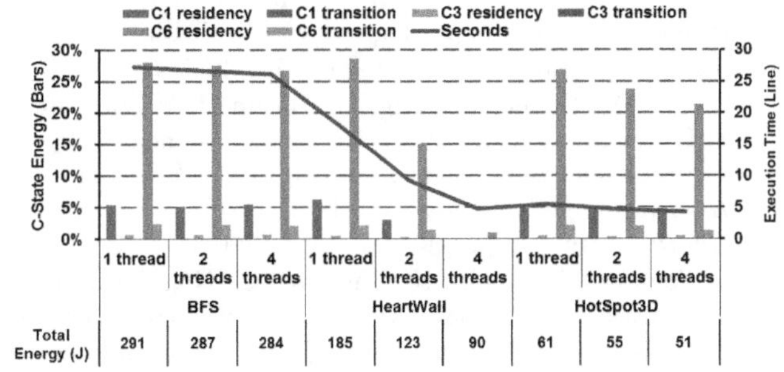

Figure 6: Impact of parallelism on C-state transition and residency energy

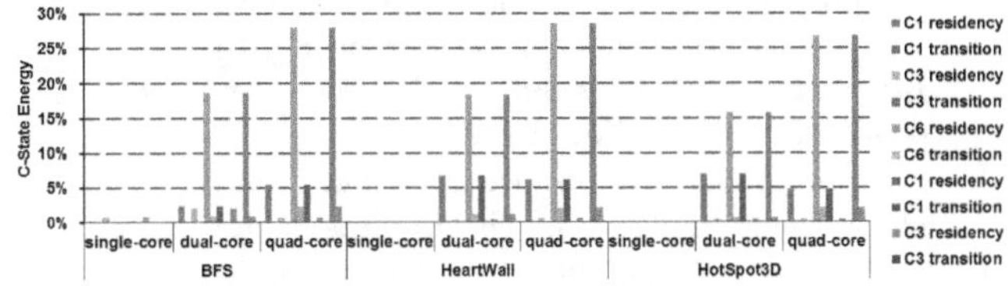

Figure 7: Impact of power gating cores on C-state transition and residency energy

6. CONCLUSION

As research on fundamental theories of spintronic devices is advancing steadily, it is imperative to understand the potential of spintronic devices used as memory and/or logic elements in the context of different application domains. In this paper, we introduce a high-level framework that aims to estimate overall energy savings for NVPs based on NV devices including spintronic devices. Employing this framework, we conducted preliminary studies of representative advanced spintronic memory (SHE-RAM) and logic (ASL and CoMET) elements as building blocks of both EB-NVPs and HB-NVPs. Furthermore, we evaluated potential energy benefit of NV GPPs based on application C-state behavior. As future work, we plan to develop more robust simulation models, collect additional energy data for different applications, and extend energy benefit analysis to specialized hardware based on NV technologies.

Acknowledgment

This work was supported in part by C-SPIN, one of six centers of STARnet, a Semiconductor Research Corporation program, sponsored by MARCO and DARPA.

7. REFERENCES

[1] International technology roadmap for semiconductors, 2011 report.

[2] B. Behin-Aein, D. Datta, S. Salahuddin, and S. Datta. Proposal for an all-spin logic device with built-in memory. *Nature nanotechnology*, 5(4):266–270, 2010.

[3] S. Che, M. Boyer, J. Meng, D. Tarjan, J. W. Sheaffer, S. H. Lee, and K. Skadron. Rodinia: A benchmark suite for heterogeneous computing. In *IEEE International Symposium on Workload Characterization*, pages 44–54, Oct 2009.

[4] S. Fukami, T. Suzuki, N. Ohshima, K. Nagahara, and N. Ishiwata. Micromagnetic analysis of current driven domain wall motion in nanostrips with perpendicular magnetic anisotropy. *Journal of Applied Physics*, 103(7):07E718, 2008.

[5] X. Guo, E. Ipek, and T. Soyata. Resistive computation: Avoiding the power wall with low-leakage, stt-mram based computing. In *International Symposium on Computer Architecture*, pages 371–382. ACM, 2010.

[6] S. Kannan, A. Gavrilovska, K. Schwan, and D. Milojicic. Optimizing checkpoints using nvm as virtual memory. In *International Symposium on Parallel and Distributed Processing*, pages 29–40, May 2013.

[7] J. Kim, A. Paul, P. A. Crowell, S. J. Koester, S. S. Sapatnekar, J. P. Wang, and C. H. Kim. Spin-based computing: Device concepts, current status, and a case study on a high-performance microprocessor. *Proceedings of the IEEE*, 103(1):106–130, Jan 2015.

[8] L. Liu, O. J. Lee, T. J. Gudmundsen, D. C. Ralph, and R. A. Buhrman. Current-induced switching of perpendicularly magnetized magnetic layers using spin torque from the spin hall effect. *Phys. Rev. Lett.*, 109:096602, Aug 2012.

[9] L. Liu, C.-F. Pai, Y. Li, H. Tseng, D. Ralph, and R. Buhrman. Spin-torque switching with the giant spin hall effect of tantalum. *Science*, 336(6081):555–558, 2012.

[10] L. Liu, C.-F. Pai, Y. Li, H. W. Tseng, D. C. Ralph, and R. A. Buhrman. Spin-torque switching with the giant spin hall effect of tantalum. *Science*, 336(6081):555–558, 2012.

[11] Y. Liu, Z. Wang, A. Lee, F. Su, C. P. Lo, Z. Yuan, C. C. Lin, Q. Wei, Y. Wang, Y. C. King, C. J. Lin, P. Khalili, K. L. Wang, M. F. Chang, and H. Yang. A 65nm reram-enabled nonvolatile processor with 6x reduction in restore time and 4x higher clock frequency using adaptive data retention and self-write-termination nonvolatile logic. In *IEEE International Solid-State Circuits Conference*, pages 84–86, Jan 2016.

[12] K. Ma, Y. Zheng, S. Li, K. Swaminathan, X. Li, Y. Liu, J. Sampson, Y. Xie, and V. Narayanan. Architecture exploration for ambient energy harvesting nonvolatile processors. In *International Symposium on High Performance Computer Architecture*, pages 526–537, Feb 2015.

[13] S. Manipatruni, D. E. Nikonov, and I. A. Young. Energy-delay performance of giant spin hall effect switching for dense magnetic memory. *Applied Physics Express*, 7(10):103001, 2014.

[14] M. G. Mankalale, Z. Liang, A. K. Smith, D. C. Mahendra, J. Wang, and S. S. Sapatnekar. A fast magnetoelectric device based on current–driven domain wall propagation. In *IEEE Device Research Conference*, June 2016.

[15] M. G. Mankalale, Z. Liang, Z. Zhao, C. H. Kim, J. Wang, and S. S. Sapatnekar. CoMET: Composite input magnetoelectric based logic technology. 2016. https://arxiv.org/abs/1611.09714.

[16] D. Nikonov and I. Young. Benchmarking of beyond-cmos exploratory devices for logic integrated circuits. *IEEE J. on Exploratory Solid-State Computational Devices and Circuits*, 1:3–11, Dec. 2015.

[17] T. Ohsawa, H. Koike, S. Miura, H. Honjo, K. Kinoshita, S. Ikeda, T. Hanyu, H. Ohno, and T. Endoh. A 1 mb nonvolatile embedded memory using 4t2mtj cell with 32 b fine-grained power gating scheme. *IEEE Journal of Solid-State Circuits*, 48(6):1511–1520, 2013.

[18] R. Perricone, I. Ahmed, Z. Liang, M. Mankalale, X. S. Hu, C. Kim, M. Niemier, S. Sapatnekar, and J. Wang. Advanced spintronic memory and logic for non-volatile processors. In *Design, Automation Test in Europe Conference Exhibition*, March 2017.

[19] R. Perricone, X. S. Hu, J. Nahas, and M. Niemier. Can beyond-cmos devices illuminate dark silicon? In *Design, Automation Test in Europe Conference Exhibition*, pages 13–18, March 2016.

[20] N. Sakimura, Y. Tsuji, R. Nebashi, H. Honjo, A. Morioka, K. Ishihara, K. Kinoshita, S. Fukami, S. Miura, N. Kasai, T. Endoh, H. Ohno, T. Hanyu, and T. Sugibayashi. A 90nm 20mhz fully nonvolatile microcontroller for standby-power-critical applications. In *IEEE International Solid-State Circuits Conference*, pages 184–185, Feb 2014.

[21] R. Takemura, T. Kawahara, K. Miura, H. Yamamoto, J. Hayakawa, N. Matsuzaki, K. Ono, M. Yamanouchi, K. Ito, H. Takahashi, S. Ikeda, H. Hasegawa, H. Matsuoka, and H. Ohno. A 32-mb spram with 2t1r memory cell, localized bi-directional write driver and '1'/'0' dual-array equalized reference scheme. *IEEE J. of Solid-State Cir.*, 45(4):869–879, 2010.

[22] Y. Wang, Y. Liu, S. Li, D. Zhang, B. Zhao, M. F. Chiang, Y. Yan, B. Sai, and H. Yang. A 3us wake-up time nonvolatile processor based on ferroelectric flip-flops. In *ESSCIRC*, pages 149–152, Sept 2012.

[23] Z. Zhao, M. Jamali, A. K. Smith, and J.-P. Wang. Spin hall switching of the magnetization in ta/tbfeco structures with bulk perpendicular anisotropy. *Applied Physics Letters*, 106(13):132404, 2015.

Neuromorphic Computing Based on Resistive RAM

Zixuan Chen
Institute of Microelectronics, Tsinghua University
czx14@mails.tsinghua.edu.cn

Huaqiang Wu
Institute of Microelectronics, Tsinghua University
wuhq@tsinghua.edu.cn

Bin Gao
Institute of Microelectronics, Tsinghua University
gaob1@tsinghua.edu.cn

Peng Yao
Institute of Microelectronics, Tsinghua University
yaop14@mails.tsinghua.edu.cn

Xinyi Li
Institute of Microelectronics, Tsinghua University

He Qian
Institute of Microelectronics, Tsinghua University
qianh@tsinghua.edu.cn

ABSTRACT
Resistive random access memory (RRAM) has gained significant attentions because of its excellent characteristics which are suitable for next-generation non-volatile memory applications. It is also very attractive to build neuromorphic computing chip based on RRAM cells due to non-volatile and analog properties. Neuromorphic computing hardware technologies using analog weight storage allow the scaling-up of the system size to complete cognitive tasks such as face classification much faster while consuming much lower energy. In this paper, RRAM technology development from material selection to device structure, from small array to full chip will be discussed in detail. Neuromorphic computing using RRAM devices is demonstrated, and speed & energy consumption are compared with Xeon Phi processor.

CCS Concepts
• Hardware → Emerging technologies • Computing methodologies → Machine learning approaches.

Keywords
Resistive RAM; Neuromorphic Computing; Array; Full Chip.

1. INTRODUCTION
Recently neuromorphic computing has gained great attention due to its application in many intelligent tasks such as real-time big data analytics [1], visual recognition [2] and driverless vehicle [3]. Currently, these demonstrations use conventional central processing units (CPU) and graphics processing units (GPU) with off-chip memories to implement large scale neural networks [4] that are trained offline and require kilowatts of power consumption. Custom designed neuromorphic chips greatly reduce the energy consumption [5]. However, the customized chips usually use static random access memory (SRAM) as on chip weight storage and is thus limited in memory capacity since SRAM is area inefficient [6]. And off-chip weight storage uses dynamic random access memory (DRAM) which incurs more than 100 times larger power consumption than on-chip memory [7]. Integrating non-volatile, analog weight storage on-chip, in close proximity to the neuron circuits is essential for future, large-scale energy-efficient neural networks that are trained online to respond to changing input data instantly like the human brain.

Permission to make digital or hard copies of all or part of this work for personal or classroom use is granted without fee provided that copies are not made or distributed for profit or commercial advantage and that copies bear this notice and the full citation on the first page. Copyrights for components of this work owned by others than ACM must be honored. Abstracting with credit is permitted. To copy otherwise, or republish, to post on servers or to redistribute to lists, requires prior specific permission and/or a fee. Request permissions from Permissions@acm.org.
GLSVLSI '17, May 10-12, 2017, Banff, AB, Canada
© 2017 ACM. ISBN 978-1-4503-4972-7/17/05…$15.00
DOI: http://dx.doi.org/10.1145/3060403.3066873

In this paper, Resistive Random Access Memory (RRAM) based neuromorphic computing has been discussed. With new material stack, RRAM shows good analog behavior as an electronic synapse [8-11] to store the information of network weight. Meanwhile RRAM can be integrated in chips with large scale as well as low power consumption. All these characteristics make RRAM a promising candidate for the synapse. The RRAM device performance is showed to demonstrate its feasibility in neuromorphic work with the combination of storage and computing. The RRAM array is employed to be trained as a neural network to recognize and classify grey-scale face images. Then a full chip with larger RRAM arrays is designed to classify numbers from MNIST database.

2. ANALOG BEHAVIORS OF RRAM
RRAM is firstly designed as a new memory device to store '0' and '1' by controlling its conductance with SET (high conductance state to low conductance state transition) and the RESET (low conductance state to high conductance state transition) operation. Figure. 1 shows our RRAM material stack including Top Electrode (TE), Oxygen Ion Reservoir (OIR), Switching Layer and Bottom Electrode (BE). The mechanism of the resistive switching is due to the oxygen migration and forms conductive filaments in the Switching Layer which makes the device conductive, and the reverse process can cut down the filaments to make the device back to high resistance [12].

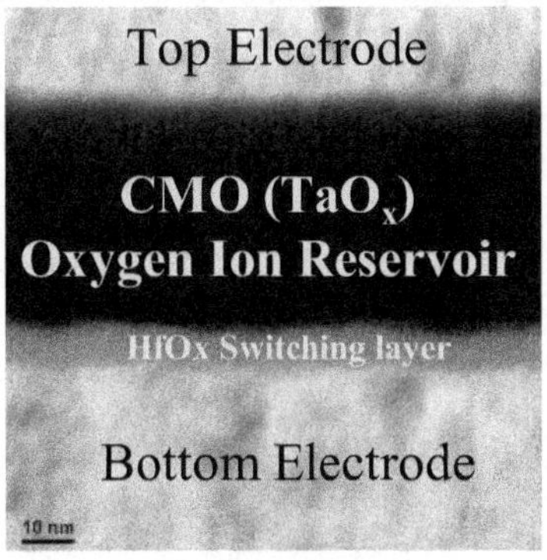

Figure 1. Insert caption to place caption below figure.

However, abrupt resistive switching [13] behaviors were generally observed in all kinds of RRAM cells as Figure. 2(a) shows. This figure shows a typical I-V curve of the RRAM device. An abrupt current increase is observed when voltage is applied to the device and reached the SET voltage threshold. When a neural network is training, the values of synaptic weights are considered to be modulated gradually. So it is expected that no abrupt resistive switching occurs on RRAM cells. Besides, traditional RRAM cells used in neural network have disadvantages of lacking uniformity between cells and repeated cycles.

We figure out two ways to solve these problems: (a) we insert an AlO barrier layer between TaOx Switching Layer and TE [14], (b) HfAlyOx is applied to the stack of Switching Layer to control the generation of oxygen vacancies, and thus abrupt resistive switching is controlled. A gradual current changing phenomenon (Figure. 2b) is observed after insert AlO barrier. Both SET and RESET process show good analog performance compared with Figure. 2(a).

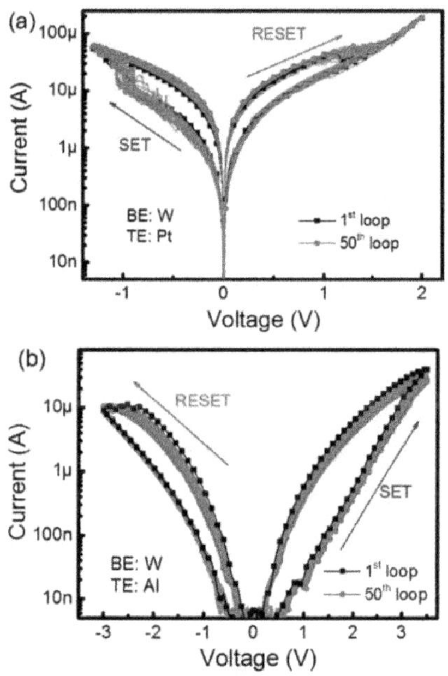

Figure 2. DC sweep I-V curves of RRAM devices: (a) traditional structure and material; (b) new structure and material.

RRAM device is a kind of bidirectional device. So single device in an array can pass the current from both directions which is unlike the one-way synapse. Since all these RRAM processes are compatible with CMOS fabrication process [15-17], 1T1R structure, as shown in Figure. 3, is used to build the network. TE of RRAM is connected to bit line (BL) of the array and BE is connected to drain of transistor. The transistor gate is connected to word line (WL) in the array and the source of transistor is connected to source line (SL) of the array. Transistor acts as a switch to control RRAM and eliminates the sneak path accordingly, so the array can be scaling up persistently. This structure further improves analog switching performance and uniformity of RRAM by controlling the transistor's gate voltage. The current through RRAM cell will be controlled precisely, and the controllability of continuous weight tuning will be improved.

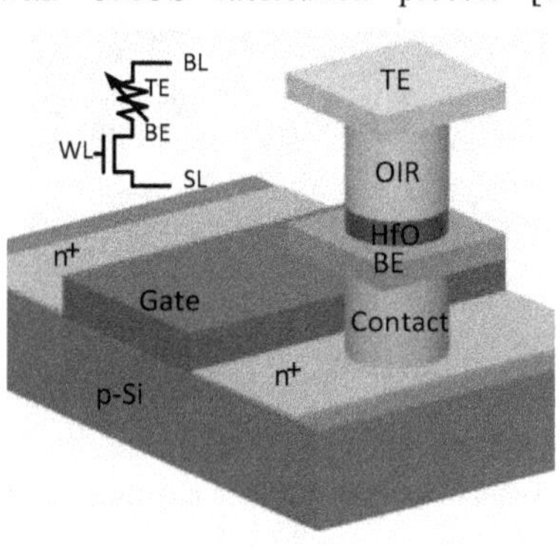

Figure 3. 1T1R architecture and material stack of RRAM cell.

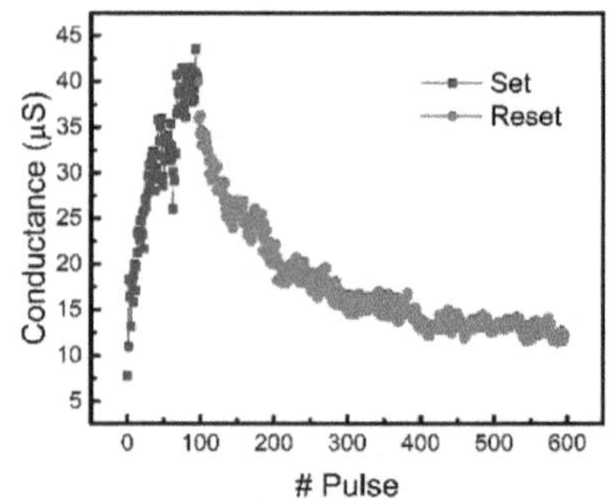

Figure 4. Continuous conductance tuning of Set and Reset.

The elimination of abrupt resistive switching at both SET and RESET process and transistor gate control strategy enable RRAM continuous conductance change for weight update in the neural network. Figure. 4 shows the relationship of conductance of RRAM device and programming pulses. The pulse used in Set and Reset share the same voltage value and period and apparent analog behavior can be seen from Figure. 4. In such way the RRAM realizes the weight storage of the synapse.

3. RRAM ARRAY FOR NEURAL NETWORK

Schematic of 1T1R array is shown in Figure. 5. WL connects transistor gates and SL connects transistor source in horizontal way while BL connects TE of resistive memories in vertical direction. The array is a perfect matching to the one-layer perceptron neural network structure.

It can be seen from the figure that pre-neuron layer, which is the input of the network, defines the input from BLs and post-neuron

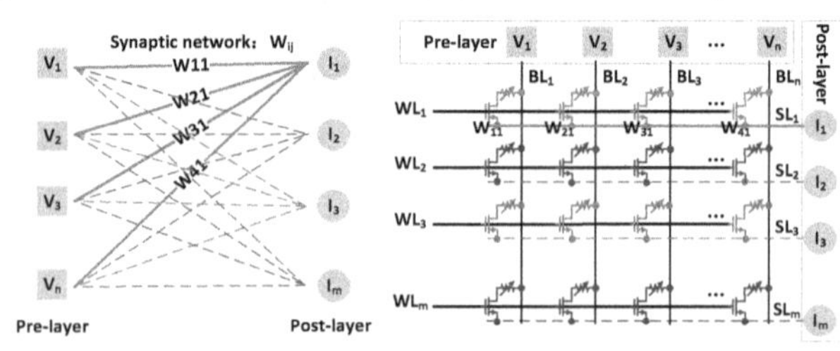

Figure 5. Mapping of a one-layer neural network on the 1T1R array.

layer is in accordance with output of SLs. The synaptic weight consists of conductance of RRAM device and transistor. The input of BL is set to be a sequence of identical voltage pulses and the output through SL is current. The final output current of this network will be accumulated by the following equation:

$$I_j(n) = \sum_{i=1}^{m} W_{ij} V_i(n) \tag{1}$$

Here the Wij is the conductance of RRAM on the line j, column i.

To testify the feasibility of 1T1R array in neuromorphic computing, we use a 1Kb RRAM array chip, consists of 1024 1T1R cells with 128 rows and 8 columns as shown in Figure. 6, to be trained as a neural network to recognize and classify grey-scale face images.

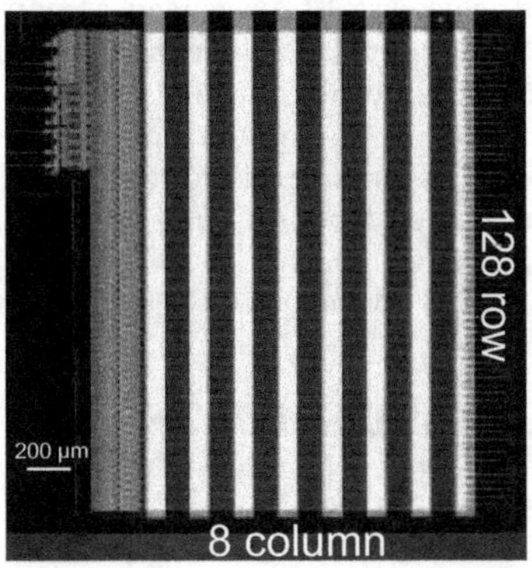

Figure 6. The micrograph of a fabricated 1024-cell-1T1R array using fully CMOS compatible fabrication process.

Before the array can distinguish different face expression images (3 classes including smile, anger and sadness as Figure. 7(a) shows) the array should be trained. And the training process include two steps: inference and update.

During the inference process, 27 training images firstly would be translated into binary numbers. Each image has 169 pixels. The pixel ranges from 1 to 5, representing different color depth. The

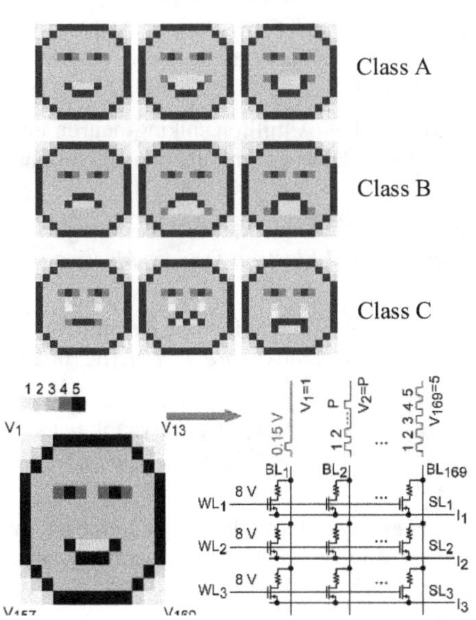

Figure 7. (a) Training image samples. (b) Schematic of parallel input and how a pattern is mapped to the BLs.

value 5 means the pixel is the darkest. All these pixels will be transmitted into a sequence of pulses applied on the BL. For example, if a pixel has color depth 5 then the input will be 5 identical voltage pulses. The 169 pixels are input in parallel [18] (Figure. 7(b)). The output currents are measured by semiconductor parameter analyzer and applied to the activation function (tanh function) to get 3 output values.

The weight updating process begins after loading entire 27 training patterns [19]. Each pattern has its respective label. By comparing the neuron outputs, an image will be classified to the class according to the largest output value. The calculated error between the output value and the target value [20] determines the programming direction. During programming, each RRAM device experiences either a Set pulse or a Reset pulse, following the Manhattan rule [21].

4. FULL CHIP FOR NEUROMORPHIC COMPUTING

A full chip with RRAM arrays was designed to classify the numbers from MNIST database. In this chip, the neural network was designed to be a two-layer perceptron neural network structure with two 1T1R arrays.

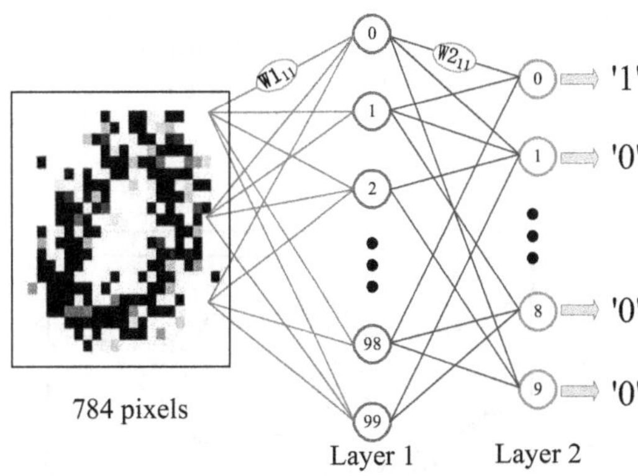

Figure 8. Two-layer perceptron neural network structure to classify numbers from MNIST database.

As Figure. 8 shows, each image in MNIST database consists of 28x28 pixels. To classify these pictures, a two-layer network is designed with two synapse matrix, 784x100 and 100x10, in totally about 80k synapses. The hidden layer has 100 neurons, and the output layer has 10 neurons. 784 pixels were simplified into with pure black-white format. So one pixel can be simplified to be a binary code. Meanwhile in these 1T1R arrays, each synapse employ 2 differential 1T1R cells to indicate the positive and negative values of the weights. So in this chip there are 160k 1T1R cells in total.

This full chip (Figure. 9) includes all the peripheral circuits such as logic control circuits, ADC and DAC circuits, and counters. The input of this chip is voltage pulses in sequence. Each pulse represents a pixel. Output currents from each neuron are integrated by integrator circuits and then the currents are converted into voltage pulses. So the output of layer 1 transmits to layer 2, and the output of layer 2 transmits outside the chip. Meanwhile the weight update process can also be realized in this chip. By comparing the chip's output and target output, the switching direction of each RRAM cell will be calculated on chip.

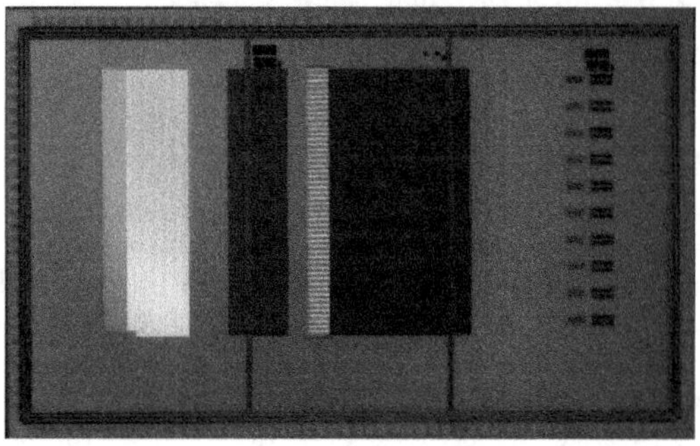

Figure 9. The micrograph of two-layer neural network chip.

5. DISCUSSION

The system recognizes all the training patterns correctly after 76 iterations. Figure. 10 shows how the output changes during training process of Class 1. Then the performance of face image classification on 1Kb array is evaluated. In the test, a set of 5400 images are used. These images are constructed by adding noise pixels randomly to the training images. Figure. 11 implies how noise pixel percentage affects recognition rate and the average test accuracy is 89.1%.

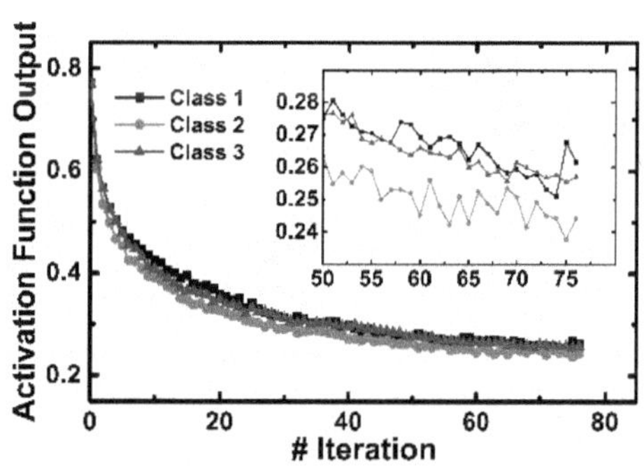

Figure 10. Measured evolution of activation function output of the 1st class as a function of iteration number during the training process.

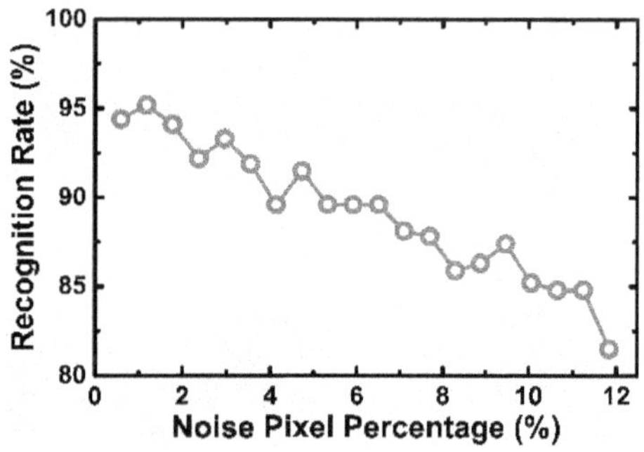

Figure 11. Recognition rate changes with noise pixel percentage increases.

The energy consumption of the same network is compared between this hardware system and conventional computing platforms [22]. This system realizes significantly energy saving.

6. CONCLUSIONS

In this paper, RRAM is demonstrated to be a promising candidate for neuromorphic computing. By insert an AlO_x barrier layer between TaOx and the TE or applying $HfAl_yO_x$ Switching Layer, the abrupt resistive switching is eliminated. The analog behavior is observed and proved RRAM to be suitable for synapse. RRAM is also compatible with CMOS fabrication process, which makes RRAM to be designed on chip and even can be scaled down remarkably to reach density as high as 10^{11} synapses per cm2. That is a good information for the future large scale neural network.

The 1Kb analog 1T1R array is realized to be trained as a one-layer perceptron neural network to recognize and classify grey-scale face images and achieved 89.1% accuracy. Meanwhile, the analog RRAM array realizes remarkable energy consumption saving compared with conventional computing platform. Based on the good performance of 1T1R array, a full chip consisting of 110 neurons, 80 Kb synapses consisted of 160 Kb RRAM and peripheral circuits is designed to realize a two-layer perceptron neural network, aiming at classifying images in MNIST database. And on-chip RRAM synapse array weight updating is also integrated on this chip.

7. ACKNOWLEDGMENTS

This work was supported in part by NSFC (61674089, 61404006), National Hi-tech (R&D) project of China (2014AA032901), China key research and development program (2016YFA0201800), and 863 program (2015AA016501).

8. REFERENCES

[1] Najafabadi, M. M. et al. Deep learning applications and challenges in big data analytics. J. *BIG DATA* 2, 1-21 (2015).

[2] Le, Q. V. in Acoustics, Speech and Signal Processing (ICASSP), *2013 IEEE International Conference on.* 8595-8598 (IEEE).

[3] X. Huang, et al., Optimization of TiN/TaOx/HfO2/TiN RRAM Arrays for Improved Switching and Data Retention, *IEEE IMW*, pp. 30-33, May 2015.

[4] Rosenblatt, F. The perceptron: a probabilistic model for information storage and organization in the brain. *Psychol. Rev.* 65, 386 (1958)..

[5] Merolla, P. A. et al. A million spiking-neuron integrated circuit with a scalable communication network and interface. *Science.* 345, 668-673 (2014).

[6] Eryilmaz, S. B., Kuzum, D., Yu, S. & Wong, H. S. P. in 2015 *IEEE International Electron Devices Meeting (IEDM).* 4.1.1-4.1.4.

[7] Han, S. et al. Eie: Efficient inference engine on compressed deep neural network. *arXiv preprint arXiv*:1602.01528 (2016).

[8] Kuzum, D., Yu, S. & Wong, H. P. Synaptic electronics: materials, devices and applications. *Nanotechnology.* 24, 382001 (2013).

[9] Ohno, T. et al. Short-term plasticity and long-term potentiation mimicked in single inorganic synapses. *Nat. Mater.* 10, 591-595 (2011).

[10] Alibart, F., Zamanidoost, E. & Strukov, D. B. Pattern classification by memristive crossbar circuits using ex situ and in situ training. *Nat. Commun.* 4 (2013).

[11] Yu, S. et al. A low energy oxide-based electronic synaptic device for neuromorphic visual systems with tolerance to device variation. *Adv. Mater.* 25, 1774-1779 (2013).

[12] Wong, H.-S. P. et al. Metal–oxide RRAM. *Proc. IEEE.* 100, 1951-1970 (2012).

[13] Burr, G. W. et al. Experimental demonstration and tolerancing of a large-scale neural network (165 000 Synapses) using phase-change memory as the synaptic weight element. *IEEE Trans. Electron Devices.* 62, 3498-3507 (2015).

[14] Li, X., Wu, H., Gao, B., et al. Electrode-induced digital-to-analog resistive switching in TaOx-based RRAM devices. *Nanotechnology.* 30, 305201 (2016).

[15] Kim, K.-H. et al. A functional hybrid memristor crossbar-array/CMOS system for data storage and neuromorphic applications. *Nano Lett.* 12, 389-395 (2011).

[16] Indiveri, G., Linares-Barranco, B., Legenstein, R., Deligeorgis, G. & Prodromakis, T. Integration of nanoscale memristor synapses in neuromorphic computing architectures. *Nanotechnology.* 24, 384010 (2013).

[17] Fackenthal, R. et al. in *Solid-State Circuits Conference Digest of Technical Papers (ISSCC)*, 2014 IEEE International. 338-339 (IEEE).

[18] Yao, P., Wu, H., Gao, B., et al. Online Training on RRAM based Neuromorphic Network: Experimental Demonstration and Operation Scheme Optimization. *ETDM (2017).*

[19] LeCun, Y. A., Bottou, L., Orr, G. B. & Müller, K.-R. in Neural networks: Tricks of the trade. 9-48 (Springer, 2012).

[20] Gao, L., Chen, P.-Y. & Yu, S. Programming protocol optimization for analog weight tuning in resistive memories. *IEEE Electron Device Lett.* 36, 1157-1159 (2015).

[21] Hertz, J., Krogh, A. & Palmer, R. G. Introduction to the theory of neural computation. Vol. 1 (Basic Books, 1991).

[22] Yao, P. et al. Face classification using electronic synapses. *Nat. Commun.* 8, 15199 doi: 10.1038/ncomms15199 (2017).

Implications of the Use of Magnetic Tunnel Junctions as Synapses in Neuromorphic Systems

Adrien F. Vincent, Nicolas Locatelli, Qifan Wu and Damien Querlioz
C2N, CNRS, Univ Paris-Sud, Université Paris-Saclay
91405 Orsay, France
damien.querlioz@u-psud.fr

ABSTRACT

Spin transfer torque magnetic random access memory (STT-MRAM) is a major breakthrough for embedded and standalone memory applications. Its basic cell, the magnetic tunnel junction, can also be used in a low-energy stochastic regime and implement a "synaptic" function. It can then be the basic element for learning-capable neuromorphic chips that do not separate logic and memory and exploit the magnetic tunnel junctions with an optimum energy efficiency. Implementing this vision, however, raises challenges at the circuit level. Proper addressing of the junctions can perturb their synaptic function. In this work, we investigate several architectures for a system based on stochastic synapses, and compare them in terms of reliability and energy efficiency. These results show the high potential of this technology, and pinpoint some main design challenges and tradeoff.

KEYWORDS

MRAM; magnetic tunnel junction; neuromorphic computing

1 INTRODUCTION

Spin transfer torque magnetic random access memory (STT-MRAM) is a current major breakthrough for embedded and standalone memory applications. Based on a nanodevice, the magnetic tunnel junction (MTJ), it provides a fast, low-energy, compact and fully compatible CMOS resistive memory. One of its biggest challenge, however, is the presence of intrinsic write errors, due to the basic physics of the nanodevice [1, 14]. These errors need to be mitigated through increased write programming time [15], or advanced programming techniques [6]. Both approaches cause an overhead in programming energy.

An alternative and unconventional approach, which has been proposed recently, is to reinterpret this stochastic behavior of MTJs. By using MTJs as synapses in brain-inspired or "neuromorphic" systems, the stochastic behavior of the MTJs can be harnessed as a feature of the device. This approach also allows using the devices with optimum programming energy, and is tolerant to their imperfections [13].

Implementing this idea, however, raises some challenges. In this work, we discuss some of these challenges and in particular, from a circuit and system perspective, discuss the best approach to connect the synapses. First, we remind the basic ideas underlying the use of MTJs as stochastic synapses. Second, we compare the advantages and drawbacks of two connection schemes for the MTJs. This allows us to conclude on the most relevant approach and some major tradeoffs.

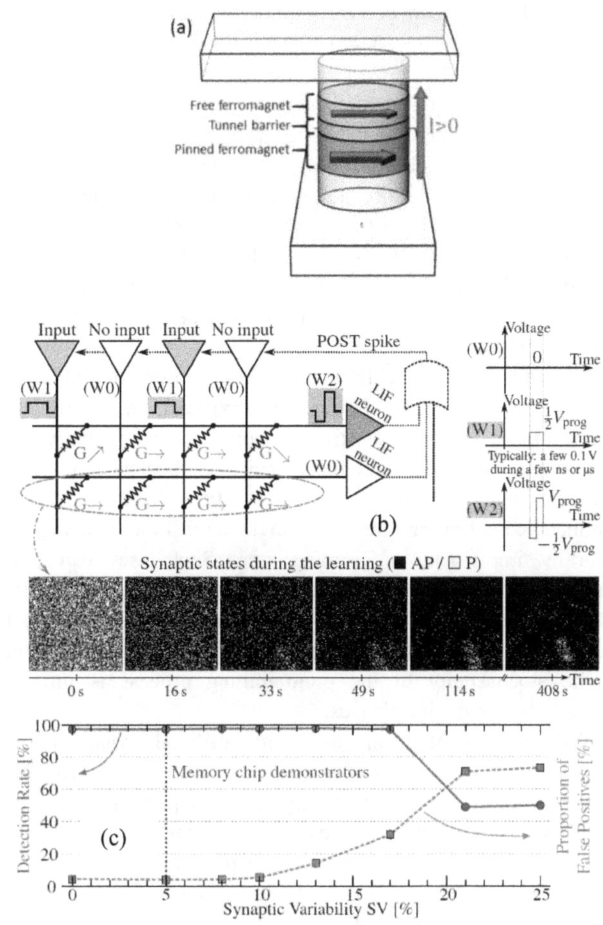

Figure 1: (a) Schematic representation of a Magnetic Tunnel Junction (MTJ). (b) Simplified architecture exploiting MTJs as stochastic synapses. Details about the architecture are presented in [13]. (c) Simulated performance of this architecture on a task of car counting (data reproduced from [13]), as a function of device variability. In MTJ industrial process, device variation is typically 5%.

Permission to make digital or hard copies of all or part of this work for personal or classroom use is granted without fee provided that copies are not made or distributed for profit or commercial advantage and that copies bear this notice and the full citation on the first page. Copyrights for components of this work owned by others than ACM must be honored. Abstracting with credit is permitted. To copy otherwise, or republish, to post on servers or to redistribute to lists, requires prior specific permission and/or a fee. Request permissions from Permissions@acm.org.
GLSVLSI '17, May 10-12, 2017, Banff, AB, Canada
© 2017 ACM.
ISBN 978-1-4503-4972-7/17/05…$15.00
DOI: http://dx.doi.org/10.1145/3060403.3060587

2 MAGNETIC TUNNEL JUNCTIONS AS STOCHASTIC SYNAPSES

Magnetic tunnel junctions are nanodevices composed of two nanomagnets separated by an oxide layer (Fig. 1(a)). The magnetization of the bottom nanomagnet is fixed, while the orientation of the top nanomagnet can be parallel (P) or antiparallel (AP) to the one of the bottom nanomagnet. Both P and AP states are stable, and therefore constitute the two states of the memory device. The electrical resistance of the device is differs between the P and AP state. This difference is quantified by the tunnel magnetoresistance $TMR=(R_{AP}-R_{P})/R_{P}$ and typically ranges between 100% and 300%.

Due to a physical phenomenon known as spin transfer torque, the state of the MTJ can be changed by applying current or voltage pulses to it: positive pulses can program a MTJ from the AP to the P state, while negative pulses can program it from the P to the AP state. This operation can be repeated extensively: their cyclability is one the major advantage of MTJs with regards to other resistive memories. A specificity of MTJs, however, is the random nature of the write operations: a programming pulse has only a probability to switch the state of the MTJs, which increases with pulse current (or voltage) and duration [1, 2, 14, 15]. Unlike most memory devices with random programming effects, this stochasticity is not due to defects or atomic effects. It is intrinsic to magnetism physics and has been modeled extensively [11, 14]. It is therefore possible to design programming pulses for a specific programming probability [13]. Using this techniques, MTJs have been used as true random number generators, whose quality has been validated using standardized statistical tests [3]. Unfortunately, switching probability is prone to device variations. For use as a true random number generators, a "whitening" process is required.

An alternative idea is to use MTJs programmed in an intentionally stochastic fashion as artificial synapses in a neuromorphic system. Resistive memories have frequently been proposed as synaptic analogues, device conductance being the analogue of a synaptic weight [4, 9, 10]. Conventionally, the conductance is programmed in an analogue fashion, in a way that naturally implements a learning rule. Such uses can allow designing circuits with a built in learning capability [5, 8]. It is also possible to rely on binary synapses, but those need to be programmed in a stochastic fashion [12]. MTJs are ideal for this, as the stochasticity of the programming process is provided naturally by the device physics.

The concept of using MTJs as artificial synapses in a neuromorphic system has been studied extensively in [13]. This works shows a simple system with such synapses organized in a "crossbar" architecture could learn complex tasks such as vehicle counting in a video (Fig 1(b)) using a process of "unsupervised learning". The use of the MTJs would be highly energy efficient: only 180 nW are required for programming the MTJs when learning the vehicle counting tasks. Such a system would also be extremely robust to MTJs' device variations. Fig 1(c), based on Monte Carlo simulation shows that the vehicle counting tasks can tolerate variations in the MTJs significantly higher to the variations seen in typical MRAM demonstrator such as [15]. Although the switching probabilities of the MTJs are prone to device variations, the neuromorphic system is naturally resilient to these imperfections.

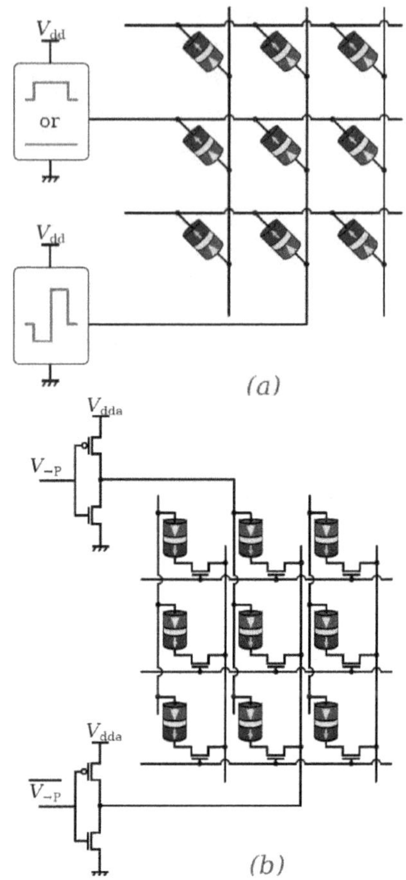

Figure 2: Two connection schemes for MTJs used as artificial synapses. (a) 1R and (b) 1T1R.

3 CIRCUIT LEVEL CHALLENGES

Neural networks operate in a highly parallel fashion, and an architecture based on artificial synapses can read and write the memory devices in parallel. An often-remarked benefit of this parallelism is that crossbar architectures where devices are used as synapses are less prone to the sneak path issue than crossbar architectures used for conventional memories. For this reason, for neuromorphic application, it can be possible to connect the memory devices without access transistor [8, 10], in what is called a "1R" structure (Fig. 2(a)). This allows organizing the memory devices in a particularly compact fashion: theoretically, a density of $4F^2$/device is possible. The 1R structure is also compatible with a backend-of-line integration of the memory devices.

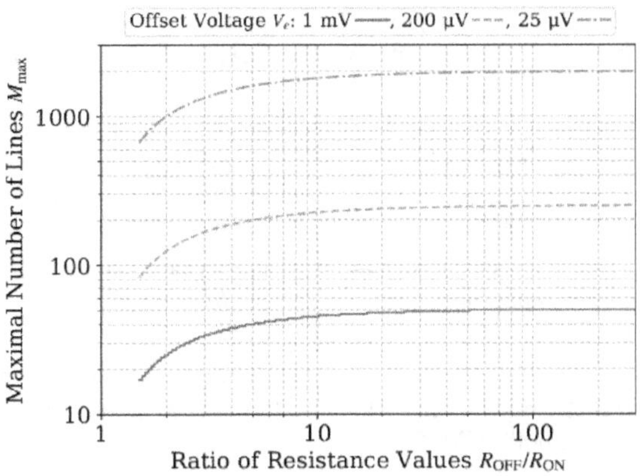

Figure 3: Maximum number of lines as a function of ratio of resistance between the OFF (or AP) and ON (or P) state, for different offset V_ε due to read circuitry, for a 1R crossbar.

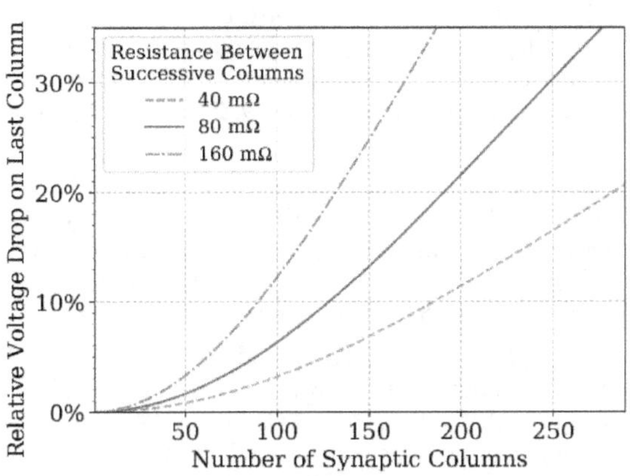

Figure 4: Maximum voltage drop due to wire resistance, in the worst case situation, as a function of number of columns, for a 1R crossbar.

However, even in a neuromorphic context, the 1R architecture still comes with challenges that we assess here in the case of MTJs.

In a 1R structure, when an input is applied, the output needs to read the electrical current through the devices, while maintaining a fixed voltage. This can be achieved by circuits such as current conveyers [7]. Such circuits are imperfect and possess offsets. Such offsets cause current in devices that should not be read. When the crossbar is too large, this current can perturb read operations. Fig. 3, based on circuit analysis, shows the maximum size of a crossbar as a function of ratio of resistance between the OFF (AP for MTJs) and ON (P for MTJs) state, for different values of read offset. Many resistive memories have R_{OFF}/R_{ON} value higher than 100 [10]. For MTJs, this ratio typically ranges 2 to 4. Fig. 3 therefore suggests that the maximum number of lines of the crossbar is more limited in the case of MTJs than other resistive memory.

Another issue of the 1R architecture is the voltage drop due to crossbar wire resistance during write operations. Fig. 4 shows, in the worst case situation, and again based on circuit analysis, the maximum voltage drop on a MTJ due to this parasitic resistance. We see that the voltage drop can rapidly become significant when the crossbar scales. Voltage drop affects very significantly the probability to switch a nanodevice [14].

Finally, performing the write operations is also a challenge in a 1R architecture. It is not possible to strictly select a cell in a 1R structure, which wastes considerable energy for a conventional memory structure. The neuromorphic structure of [13] supports parallel write operation and in principle largely mitigates this issue. However, a parallel write may require considerable current draw. With a naïve layout of the crossbar such as Fig. 2(a), in a worst case situation, the circuit would have to produce 400mA during a ns-duration. This is not realistic, and means that the 1R crossbar should be split into several pieces.

These considerations can be contrasted with the choice of a 1T1R architecture (Fig. 2(b)), conventional for memory applications. In this case, provided no two inputs are presented at the same time (which is the case in the application studied in [13]), read operations can be performed by compact and simple sense amplified circuits such as [16]. These circuits are considerably more compact and lower energy than current conveyors. Also, in a 1T1R architecture, offset and wire resistance effects are considerably reduced, and based on circuit analysis would have no effect, even in the full application of [13]. Finally, write operations can be performed sequentially. This is much slower than parallel write, but neuromorphic operation are usually slow enough that they are not affected by this programming time. Full system-level analysis of the task of [13] showed that parallel and sequential programming are equivalent in terms of application (detection rate and number of false positives).

4 CONCLUSIONS

Using magnetic tunnel junctions as artificial synapses in a neuromorphic system is a highly attractive vision. This could allow fabricating non-volatile learning-capable systems that use a minimal energy for programming memory cells. An apparent benefit is also the possibility to lay out the memory cells in a 1R structure, possibly even in the backend of the circuit. However, we saw in this paper that this vision raises considerable challenges. The area benefit can be suppressed by the need of complex read circuitry, and the necessity to cut a large crossbar into smaller ones so that read and write operations are manageable. The conventional 1T1R structure might therefore be much better suited for benefitting from MTJs' stochastic synapses capabilities.

These results also highlight that when dealing with emerging devices, devices, circuits and systems questions should be considered simultaneously.

ACKNOWLEDGMENTS

This work was supported by the ANR COGNISPIN (ANR-13-JS03-0004-01) and by a public grant overseen by the French National Research Agency (ANR) as part of the "Investissements d'Avenir" program (Labex NanoSaclay, reference: ANR-10-LABX-0035).

REFERENCES

[1] Devolder, T., Hayakawa, J., Ito, K., Takahashi, H., Ikeda, S., Crozat, P., Zerounian, N., Kim, J.-V., Chappert, C. and Ohno, H. 2008. Single-Shot Time-Resolved Measurements of Nanosecond-Scale Spin-Transfer Induced Switching: Stochastic Versus Deterministic Aspects. *Phys. Rev. Lett.* 100, 5 (Février 2008), 057206.

[2] Diao, Z., Li, Z., Wang, S., Ding, Y., Panchula, A., Chen, E., Wang, L.-C. and Huai, Y. 2007. Spin-transfer torque switching in magnetic tunnel junctions and spin-transfer torque random access memory. *Journal of Physics: Condensed Matter.* 19, 16 (Apr. 2007), 165209.

[3] Fukushima, A., Seki, T., Yakushiji, K., Kubota, H., Imamura, H., Yuasa, S. and Ando, K. 2014. Spin dice: A scalable truly random number generator based on spintronics. *Applied Physics Express.* 7, 8 (Aug. 2014), 083001.

[4] Jo, S.H., Chang, T., Ebong, I., Bhadviya, B.B., Mazumder, P. and Lu, W. 2010. Nanoscale Memristor Device as Synapse in Neuromorphic Systems. *Nano Lett.* 10, 4 (Avril 2010), 1297–1301.

[5] Kim, S., Ishii, M., Lewis, S., Perri, T., BrightSky, M., Kim, W., Jordan, R., Burr, G.W., Sosa, N., Ray, A., Han, J.P., Miller, C., Hosokawa, K. and Lam, C. 2015. NVM neuromorphic core with 64k-cell (256-by-256) phase change memory synaptic array with on-chip neuron circuits for continuous in-situ learning. *2015 IEEE International Electron Devices Meeting (IEDM)* (Dec. 2015), 17.1.1–17.1.4.

[6] Lakys, Y., Zhao, W.S., Devolder, T., Zhang, Y., Klein, J.-O., Ravelosona, D. and Chappert, C. 2012. Self-Enabled "Error-Free" Switching Circuit for Spin Transfer Torque MRAM and Logic. *IEEE Trans. Magn.* 48, 9 (2012), 2403–2406.

[7] Lecerf, G., Tomas, J., Boyn, S., Girod, S., Mangalore, A., Grollier, J. and Saighi, S. 2014. Silicon neuron dedicated to memristive spiking neural networks. *2014 IEEE International Symposium on Circuits and Systems (ISCAS)* (Jun. 2014), 1568–1571.

[8] Prezioso, M., Merrikh-Bayat, F., Hoskins, B.D., Adam, G.C., Likharev, K.K. and Strukov, D.B. 2015. Training and operation of an integrated neuromorphic network based on metal-oxide memristors. *Nature.* 521, 7550 (May 2015), 61–64.

[9] Querlioz, D., Bichler, O., Vincent, A.F. and Gamrat, C. 2015. Bioinspired Programming of Memory Devices for Implementing an Inference Engine. *Proceedings of the IEEE.* 103, 8 (Aug. 2015), 1398–1416.

[10] Saïghi, S. et al. 2015. Plasticity in memristive devices for spiking neural networks. *Neuromorphic Engineering.* 9, (2015), 51.

[11] Sun, J.Z. 2000. Spin-current interaction with a monodomain magnetic body: A model study. *Physical Review B.* 62, 1 (juillet 2000), 570–578.

[12] Suri, M., Querlioz, D., Bichler, O., Palma, G., Vianello, E., Vuillaume, D., Gamrat, C. and DeSalvo, B. 2013. Bio-Inspired Stochastic Computing Using Binary CBRAM Synapses. *IEEE Transactions on Electron Devices.* 60, 7 (2013), 2402–2409.

[13] Vincent, A.F., Larroque, J., Locatelli, N., Ben Romdhane, N., Bichler, O., Gamrat, C., Zhao, W.S., Klein, J.-O., Galdin-Retailleau, S. and Querlioz, D. 2015. Spin-Transfer Torque Magnetic Memory as a Stochastic Memristive Synapse for Neuromorphic Systems. *IEEE Transactions on Biomedical Circuits and Systems.* 9, 2 (Apr. 2015), 166–174.

[14] Vincent, A.F., Locatelli, N., Klein, J.-O., Zhao, W.S., Galdin-Retailleau, S. and Querlioz, D. 2015. Analytical Macrospin Modeling of the Stochastic Switching Time of Spin-Transfer Torque Devices. *IEEE Transactions on Electron Devices.* 62, 1 (Jan. 2015), 164–170.

[15] Worledge, D.C., Hu, G., Trouilloud, P.L., Abraham, D.W., Brown, S., Gaidis, M.C., Nowak, J., O'Sullivan, E.J., Robertazzi, R.P., Sun, J.Z. and Gallagher, W.J. 2010. Switching distributions and write reliability of perpendicular spin torque MRAM. *Electron Devices Meeting (IEDM), 2010 IEEE International* (Dec. 2010), 12.5.1–12.5.4.

[16] Zhao, W., Chappert, C., Javerliac, V. and Noziere, J.P. 2009. High Speed, High Stability and Low Power Sensing Amplifier for MTJ/CMOS Hybrid Logic Circuits. *IEEE Transactions on Magnetics.* 45, 10 (Oct. 2009), 3784–3787.

Security Threats and Countermeasures in Three-Dimensional Integrated Circuits

Jaya Dofe[1], Peng Gu[2], Dylan Stow,[2] Qiaoyan Yu[1], Eren Kursun[3], Yuan Xie[2]

[1]Department of Electrical and Computer Engineering
University of New Hampshire
qiaoyan.yu@unh.edu

[2]Department of Electrical and Computer Engineering
University of California
yuanxie@ece.ucsb.edu

[3]Department of Computer Science
Columbia University
ek2925@columbia.edu

ABSTRACT

Existing works on Three-dimensional (3D) hardware security focus on leveraging the unique 3D characteristics to address the supply chain attacks that exist in 2D design. However, 3D ICs introduce specific and unexplored challenges as well as new opportunities for managing hardware security. In this paper, we analyze new security threats unique to 3D ICs. The corresponding attack models are summarized for future research. Furthermore, existing representative countermeasures, including split manufacturing, camouflaging, transistor locking, techniques against thermal signal based side-channel attacks, and network-on-chip based shielding plane (NoCSIP) for different hardware threats are reviewed and categorized. Moreover, preliminary countermeasures are proposed to thwart TSV-based hardware Trojan insertion attacks.

1. INTRODUCTION

Three-dimensional (3D) integration is an emerging technology to ensure the growth in transistor density and performance that is expected for future integrated circuits (ICs) [1, 2]. It has been demonstrated that 3D techniques can be leveraged to reduce package size and power consumption while significantly improving bandwidth. However, 3D integration technology is a double-edged sword, as it introduces unique and unexplored challenges on managing related security issues.

1.1 History and Benefits of 3D IC

The growth of the semiconductor industry has long relied on the continual trend of increasing integration. As interconnect and transistor scaling both decelerate, the industry must look for alternate growth opportunities. 3D integration and similar forms of die-level integration provide novel design methodologies to increase transistor density, reduce interconnect distances, and integrate additional system components. 3D integration covers a range of different technologies, from interposer-based 2.5D methodology to monolithic sequential integration, but 3D stacked die-level integration, based on microbumps and Through-Silicon Vias (TSV), is widely seen as one of the most promising technologies for meeting future needs [3]. In this methodology, separate dies are fabricated using standard lithography, TSVs are added (during or after lithography), individual dies or wafers are thinned, and 3D stacks are formed through alignment and bonding. Over the last two decades, many improvements have been made in the process technology, design automation, and system architecture for these 3D circuits [4, 5]. Die-die interconnects with pitches from 1-40 μm [6, 7] provide high-bandwidth, minimal latency connections and can reduce total wirelength. With assembly yields consistently demonstrated to be >99% [8], partitioning of large designs into multiple small dies will improve yield, and employment of Known Good Die (KGD) testing before bonding can reduce the total manufacturing cost [9]. Further, heterogeneous process technologies, like DRAM or emerging Non-Volatile Memories, can be tightly integrated with the CMOS logic to greatly improve system performance and efficiency. 3D ICs have come to market over the last several years in a number of products, including CMOS image sensors, stacked High Bandwidth Memory for GPUs, and multi-die high-capacity FPGAs. Although most CMOS logic is still 2D, foundries anticipate that mainstream systems will begin employing 3D integration within the next several years due to demand for footprint, capacity, and efficiency improvement [10]. Further down the road, monolithic 3D integration may provide even higher integration between layers to further improve efficiency and performance [11]. The trend in 3D packaging technologies is shown in Fig. 1.

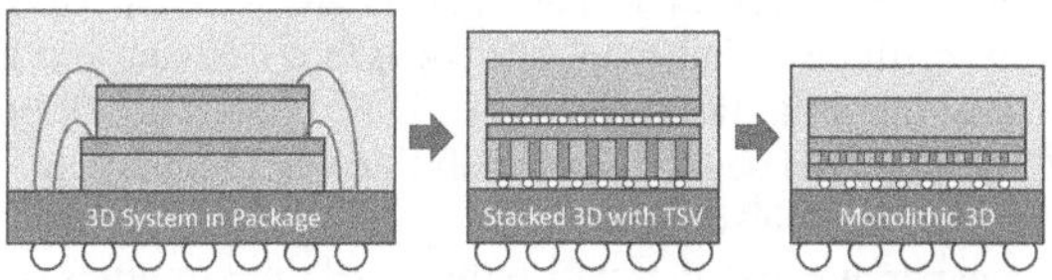

Figure 1: 3D packaging technology is expected to transition from current wire bond SiP to high-bandwidth TSV-based die stacking, and eventually to full monolithic integration.

1.2 General Challenges in 3D IC Design, Fabrication, and Deployment

Although 3D integration offers a range of promising benefits, like all new technologies, it also brings new challenges. Since 3D integration increases the number of transistors per area, it leads to an increase in power density that translates to more difficult thermal management and power delivery. High-performance systems may not be cost-effective in 3D when extra thermal management is considered [12]. However, design automation methods have been developed for thermal-aware 3D floorplanning and 3D power delivery to mitigate these problems [13]. From a process perspective, extra fabrication steps are needed to add TSVs and to perform thinning and bonding, thus incurring additional cost and complex-

Permission to make digital or hard copies of all or part of this work for personal or classroom use is granted without fee provided that copies are not made or distributed for profit or commercial advantage and that copies bear this notice and the full citation on the first page. Copyrights for components of this work owned by others than ACM must be honored. Abstracting with credit is permitted. To copy otherwise, or republish, to post on servers or to redistribute to lists, requires prior specific permission and/or a fee. Request permissions from Permissions@acm.org.

GLSVLSI '17, May 10 - 12, 2017, Banff, AB, Canada

© 2017 Copyright held by the owner/author(s). Publication rights licensed to ACM.

ISBN 978-1-4503-4972-7/17/05. . . 5.00

DOI: http://dx.doi.org/10.1145/3060403.3060500

ity. If cost-efficient scaling is desired, these overheads must be less than any yield improvements from fabricating smaller dies. Adding TSVs and multiple layers also requires adjustments to placement and routing tools, and partitioning across dies complicates testing methodology [14]. Finally, the extra complexity of multiple dies and new process steps have so far resulted in a lack of standardization and more complicated supply chains. However, the benefits of 3D integration have attracted significant industry demand and development, and most of these challenges will be resolved as tools and processes mature.

1.3 Contribution of this Work

Previous surveys on utilizing 3D integration for security purposes have addressed the advantages of die-stacking structures in secure split manufacturing [15], enhancing the protection against reverse-engineering [16], and side-channel attacks [17]. However, a majority of the existing work has focused on circuit and architecture level opportunities enabled by 3D IC but has not fully considered the potential security vulnerabilities and technology challenges in secure 3D IC designs.

In this paper, we first summarize the novel opportunities offered by 3D integration for security mechanism in Section 2. Then we list potential security vulnerabilities in 3D ICs in Section 3. To further analyze these security challenges, we formulate new attack models based on our observations in Section 4. We envision that TSVs introduce the vulnerabilities that can be utilized by adversaries to insert hardware Trojans. We also analyze a manufacturing scenario neglected by previous works, in which the full design details of the 3D chip are exposed to the untrusted foundries. Since limited 3D testing techniques are available to detect malicious circuits, we predict that a new form of threat, cross-tier hardware Trojans, is likely to occur. In Section 5, we summarize the state-of-the-art countermeasures against existing security threats in 3D designs and further propose new countermeasures. This work is concluded in Section 6.

2. UNIQUE OPPORTUNITIES THAT 3D STRUCTURE OFFERS FOR SECURITY MECHANISMS

Several existing works have comprehensive summaries on the advantages of 3D IC for security enhancement [15–17]. We classify these unique opportunities according to their applications in different stages of the semiconductor supply chain [18].

2.1 Synthesis and Verification Stage

In this stage, designers can utilize the unique die-stacking architecture of 3D ICs to implement new security features, enhance existing security metrics, or reduce the overhead of security applications.

- In order to incorporate new security features, designers are provided with a wide spectrum of CMOS and non-CMOS technologies thanks to the heterogeneous integration capabilities enabled by die-stacking architecture. For example, CMOS technologies in different process nodes can be integrated, and Physical Unclonable Function (PUF) implemented with non-CMOS technologies can be integrated with CMOS processors.
- To enhance existing security metrics, designers could optionally add a trusted control plane on top of the untrusted compute plane to monitor its behaviors. Since the die-stacking structure allows high-bandwidth communications between these planes, trusted computation can be guaranteed with negligible overhead.
- To reduce the overhead of security applications, die-stacking structures could enable high performance Process-In-Memory encryption to reduce the memory security overhead.

2.2 Fabrication Stage

In this stage, designers can employ the modularity features of the 3D IC for split manufacturing. Split manufacturing is proposed to hinder malicious foundry's efforts to overbuild the IC or insert hardware Trojans. In order to take advantage of the advanced manufacturing capability of the untrusted foundries, the original design is split, and performance-critical parts are fabricated by untrusted foundries and security-critical parts are fabricated by trusted foundries. 3D IC split manufacturing is more suitable compared with conventional 2D Back-End-of-Line (BEOL) and Front-End-of-Line (FEOL) based split manufacturing [19], since 2D design imposes stricter fabrication compatibility among foundries and provides limited design flexibilities. Designers can also utilize Intellectual property (IP)-reuse strategies for cost reduction during split manufacturing, since the secure die containing active components provided by trusted foundries could be reused across a wide range of designs.

2.3 Production Stage

After product shipping, designers can use the 3D IC stacking structures to protect against side-channel leakage and reverse-engineering attacks.

- To defend against side-channel attacks, novel components could be designed to reduce side channel leakage vulnerabilities [17]. For example, the cache could be designed to reduce timing side channel risks and noise generators could be added to reduce thermal side channel leakage.
- To protect against reverse engineering, circuit obfuscation techniques could be utilized to implement 3D IC [16]. For example, a Network-on-Chip (NoC) based shielding plane can be inserted between two commercial dies to thwart reverse engineering attacks on the vertical dimension. Also, Monolithic three-dimensional (M3D) integration can ensure that the layouts of different logic gates show indistinguishable patterns inside a standard cell [17].

3. UNIQUE SECURITY CHALLENGES IN 3D ICS

Although vertical integration brings new opportunities for defenders to address some of the security issues in 2D ICs, it also leaves more space for attackers to compromise 3D chips from various stages in the 3D IC supply chain. A previous work [16] summarizes the hardware security threats in 3D integrated circuits: (1) vertical communication trustworthiness, (2) hardware Trojan mechanisms, and (3) emerging side channel attacks as new security threats with immediate impact in 3D ICs.

Furthermore, existing testing techniques for 3D ICs have own limitations on malicious circuit detection such as: (1) the probe size and the probe pitch distance for mid-bond testing are not small enough for advanced 3D dies [20], (2) test probes may damage the TSVs after testing, causing reliability degradation, and (3) individual die performance and the integrity of vertical interconnects may reduce after final bonding. Due to these testing challenges, malicious components detection through 3D functional testing is not optimistic [15]. Moreover, large process, voltage, and temperature variations within 3D ICs may lead to a high false positive rate for traditional methods that rely on side-channel analysis based hardware Trojan detection.

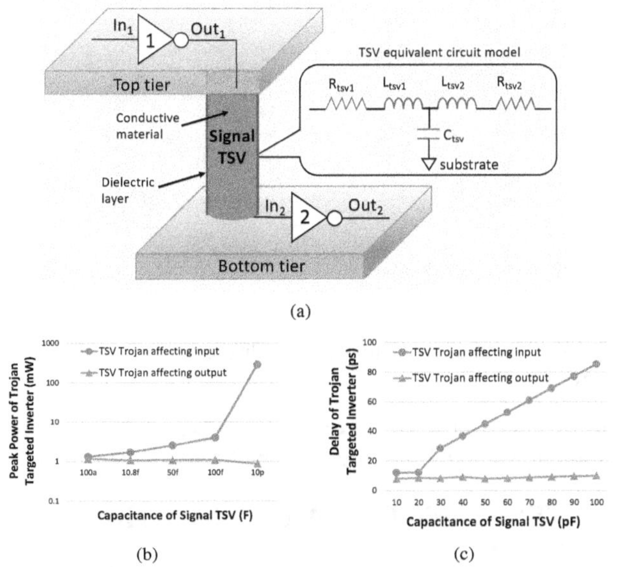

Figure 2: Signal-TSV based parametric hardware Trojan (a) simulation setup, (b) impact of Trojan on peak power, and (c) impact of Trojan on gate delay. Experiments conducted here are based on a 45nm NCSU FreePDK.

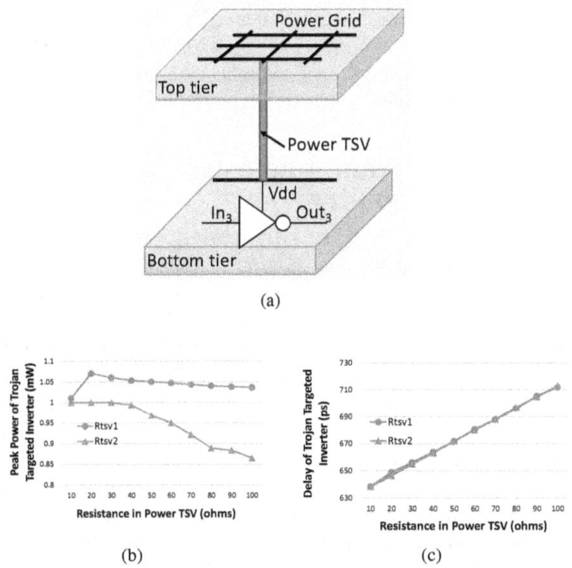

Figure 3: Power-TSV based parametric hardware Trojan (a) simulation setup, (b) impact of Trojan on peak power, and (c) impact on gate delay. Note, R_{tsv1} and R_{tsv2} are the equivalent resistance in the TSV model.

3D integration provides significant advantages in split manufacturing compared with 2D design in terms of fabrication compatibility and flexibility as discussed in Section 2. However, previous research mainly explored how to utilize 3D passive interposers [21] to hide wires and 2.5D passive interposers to hide connection cuts [22]. The circuit is split into trusted tiers which contain lifted metal wires [21] or connections between two outsourced dies [22], and untrusted tiers which contain transistors and the rest of the metal connections. Since only metal wires or connection cuts can be hidden in the passive interposer, to achieve certain degree of security enhancement, considerable amount of metal wires are needed to route through trusted tiers, creating large cut size (thus large micro-bump area). The security of the passive interposer is a serious concern, since reverse engineering can easily reveal the connections of the wires (these wires manufactured by less advanced foundries could easily be figured out). Even worse, the passive interposer can only be fitted to one design, making the cost of the passive interposer expensive and split manufacturing process hard.

4. ATTACK MODELS FOR 3D ICS

In this section, we analyze the security vulnerabilities of 3D ICs induced by the untrusted foundries. We specially target the hardware Trojan insertions scenarios which are unique to 3D chips.

4.1 Attacks from Untrusted Vertical Interconnect Foundry

A stacked 3D IC integrates all the dies with vertical interconnects (e.g. TSVs). In 3D SoCs with diverse dies, each die can be designed and fabricated by trusted vendors. A 3D foundry with TSV manufacturing capability processes and bonds these dies using TSVs. The untrusted manufacturer for vertical interconnect fabrication could introduce hardware Trojans to the TSVs, thus sabotaging the integrity and reliability of the 3D ICs. Due to limited testing coverage achieved by the post-bond testing in 3D ICs, TSV-based Trojans may not be detected during the functional verification. We conducted the basic experiment on signal TSVs and power TSVs to demonstrate the consequence of hardware tampering attacks. We envision that TSVs might be exploited as a parametric hardware Trojan. This means, the untrusted foundry can modify the fabrication process parameters for the TSV fabrication to change the TSV height and dielectric thickness. To model a TSV-based Trojan, we adopt the TSV model as in [23], in which a TSV is equivalent to a RLC network as shown in Fig. 2(a).

Signal-TSV based Hardware Trojan

In TSV-based 3D integration, via-last TSVs are fabricated after the Back-End-of-Line (BEOL). This type of TSV passes through the silicon substrate and the metalization layers, leaving a large exploitation space for hardware Trojan insertion. The triggered Trojan can alter the signal that the Trojan is targeted at. The impact of a Trojan inserted in a signal TSV on the peak power and gate delay is noticeable and varies with the Trojan location, as shown in Fig. 2(b). We swept C_{tsv} and measured the peak power of Inverter 1 and Inverter 2. If the malicious TSV is inserted before the input node of the target (Inverter 2), the peak power of Inverter 2 can increase by more than two orders of magnitudes with the increase of C_{tsv}. However, if the malicious signal TSV is considered as a load for the target (Inverter 1), the peak power of Inverter 1 slightly changes during the course of sweeping C_{tsv}.Therefore, a *signal-TSV based Trojan has more impact as a driver circuit than as a load circuit*. The impact of malicious signal TSVs on the delay of the targeted gate has a similar trend with the peak power, as shown in Fig. 2(c).

Power-TSV based Hardware Trojan

Via-first TSVs are fabricated during the Front-End-of-Line (FEOL). This type of TSV connects the bottom metal layer of the top tier, taking Fig. 3(a) as an example, with the top metal layer of the bottom tier. Via-first TSV is useful for power grid connection. If a power TSV is compromised by a hardware Trojan, the equivalent resistance of the TSV plays a significant role on the peak power and gate delay of the targeted logic gate. We assume that a malicious power TSV provides a Vdd for the inverter in the bottom tier as shown in Fig. 3(a). As we sweep the equivalent resistance of the

TSV, the inverter peak power is reduced by 15% and inverter delay is increased by 11%, as shown in Figs. 3(b) and (c). The changes on power are not negligible for those who take power measurements as side-channel signals.

4.2 Attacks from Untrusted Split Manufacturing Foundry

The split manufacturing foundry fabricates only untrusted tiers. The trusted tiers and the final assembly is carried out in the trusted foundries. Two different assumptions about the adversaries have been proposed by previous work [21, 22]. The first work [21] assumes that a malicious observer exists in the design stage to provide information to a malicious attacker in the foundry. The malicious observer has full knowledge of the circuit but cannot effect any changes. The malicious attacker in the foundry can modify the circuit layout before the chip is fabricated. The second work [22] assumes a weaker attacker who only knows the partial design layout and knows nothing about the complete design. The goal of the attacker is to acquire the whole design to overbuild ICs for profits or insert hardware Trojans to compromise the security of the system at certain time. If only wires are hidden from the untrusted foundries, as assumed by 2D BEOL/FEOL designs and 3D passive interposer-based designs, the attackers can utilize some placement and routing heuristics to guess the hidden connections, such as proximity attacks [22]. If the attacker can acquire the product after shipping, the passive interposer containing only metal wires are vulnerable to physical reverse engineering as well as logic profiling attack since only wires can be hidden.

4.3 Attacks from Untrusted Unified Foundry

The unified foundry fabricates both dies for multiple tiers and the vertical interconnect between tiers. Since the untrusted unified foundry has the full design details of the 3D chip, security benefits from split manufacturing are not achievable in this scenario neither. Reverse engineering, hardware IP piracy, and hardware tampering attacks will be more prevalent in this case. For TSV-based 3D ICs, the die and interconnect manufacturing steps are executed consecutively in the same foundry. To bypass the pre-bond, mid-bond, and post-bond testing, the untrusted unified foundry can collaboratively tamper the existing die design and TSVs in a way that the malicious component will not be active either in the die testing or TSV testing. Due to the limitation of 3D testing techniques, it will be more difficult to detect the untrusted unified foundry's malicious circuit in a 3D IC than in a 2D IC. We predict a new kind of hardware Trojan in this scenario: the cross-tier hardware Trojan, which is a more general Trojan in 3D ICs than the TSV-based hardware Trojan.

In the proposed cross-tier Trojan: (1) *Trojan trigger and payload circuits are not in the same tier*. The cross-tier hardware Trojan #1 in Fig. 4 depicts the conceptual idea. If the trigger circuit is located in another tier, side-channel analysis based Trojan detection methods cannot detect the presence of hardware Trojan during the pre-bond testing on each single die. As a 3D chip integrates a much larger number of transistors, the overhead induced by the Trojan circuit is relatively smaller in 3D ICs than that in 2D ICs. Thus, the separated Trojan trigger and payload circuits will increase the difficulty of Trojan detection. (2) *The Trojan is triggered by multiple trigger circuits, which are distributed in multiple tiers.* As shown in the cross-tier hardware Trojan #2 in Fig. 4, the signals from the top tier, bottom tier, and the vertical interconnect between the top and middle tiers collaboratively drive the trigger circuit for the hardware Trojan in the middle tier. Compared to hardware Trojans in 2D ICs, this type of cross-tier hardware Trojan may have significantly lower Trojan triggering probability.

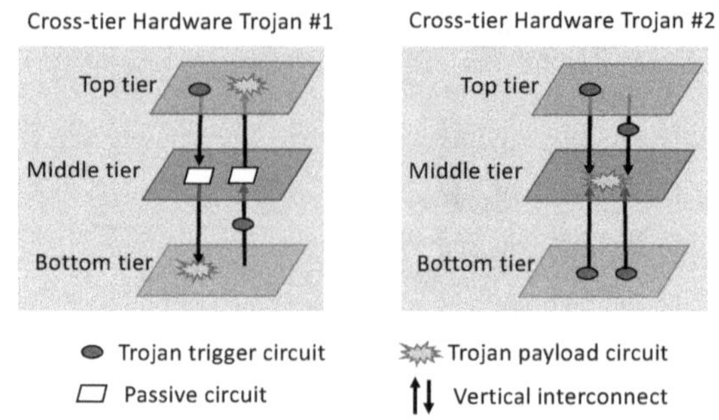

Figure 4: Examples of cross-tier hardware Trojans in TSV-based 3D ICs.

5. STATE-OF-THE-ART METHOD REVIEW

In this section, we review the existing countermeasures against the different threats in 3D integration. Further, we propose possible hardware Trojan detection and mitigation methods.

5.1 Split Manufacturing

The threats considered in this countermeasure are Reverse Engineering at untrusted foundry. As indicated by leading 3D manufacturing foundries [24], 3D ICs facilitate *split manufacturing* where the entire IC is distributed throughout multiple dies/planes. Due to the incompleteness of each layer, it is difficult for the attackers to reverse engineer the entire design from one die.

Existing 3D split manufacturing approaches fall into two primary categories. In the first category, as investigated in [25–27], the entire design is separated into two tiers: one plane is dedicated as the primary computation plane whereas the second plane is an optional control plane that should be provided by a trusted foundry. This control plane is used to monitor possible malicious behavior within the computation plane and overwrites the malicious signals, if necessary.

The second category, as studied by Imeson *et al.* [21], relies on interconnects of a trusted tier to obfuscate the entire 3D circuit. Thus, the circuit within the untrusted tier cannot be reverse engineered since interconnectivity is unknown. Similar studies have been performed that investigate methods to further enhance the obfuscation level achieved by split manufacturing [22, 28–30]. Some examples include layout-level techniques [28], heuristic attack [29], cell placement [30], circuit size cut algorithm and secure interposer layout [22]. These existing works prevent reverse engineering from retrieving the original circuit.

5.2 Camouflaging in Monolithic 3D ICs

The security threats target in this countermeasures are IP piracy and reverse engineering. The concept of camouflaging gates in monolithic three-dimensional (M3D) is presented in [17]. The main goal of this approach is to make M3D IC secure with smaller overhead. The camouflage IC can be classified into two categories. The first category addresses intra-standard cell camouflage where standard cells are redesigned to look identical by inserting dummy vias. The identical gates provide different functionalities. The other category addresses inter-standard cell camouflage where dummy circuits are filled in the empty spaces among standard cells [10, 12] such that the attackers cannot figure out standard cell parts. Authors suggested improvements in M3D IC context to minimize the overhead. The overhead of intra-camouflaged standard cells, is mainly due to extra wiring inside of the standard cell. This drawback could be alleviated using fine-grained inter-layer vias. For inter-standard cell camouflage, the authors proposed four different partition options for filling up the dummy cells to escalate the reverse engineering efforts of attackers.

5.3 Transistor Locking in Monolithic 3D ICs

Alternatively, IP piracy and reverse engineering attacks can be addressed by logic locking techniques. The work in [31] investigates a novel transistor-level logic locking method to address the security challenges in monolithic three-dimensional (M3D) ICs. This method locks logic gates by independently inserting parallel or serial locking transistors and camouflaged contacts in multiple tiers. The locking keys are only available to authorized users. The application of a wrong key to the locked functional block either leads to a logic malfunctions by opening or shorting pull-up or pull-down network or it significantly changes the power profile. Furthermore, the contact camouflaging is exploited to thwart image-analysis based reverse engineering attacks.

5.4 Techniques against Thermal Signal based Side-Channel Attacks

Thermal Side-channel (TSC) attacks [17] have been shown to disclose the activities of key functional blocks and even encryption keys by built-in thermal sensors, external attached thermal sensors, or high resolution thermal imaging. A previous work [32] proposes to protect ICs from thermal side-channel attacks by utilizing intrinsic characteristics of 3D chip integration, as well as proactively using dynamic shielding patterns to conceal critical activities on chip. The design includes a micro-controller unit that dynamically generates complementary activity patterns to prevent side-channel data leakage. Thermal patterns are generated in a randomized, non-repeating manner such that side-channel attackers cannot extract meaningful information by observing any pattern sequence. The proposed architecture covers all thermal sensor placement options such that noise injected by security layers will decrement the side-channel leakage of any critical areas.

5.5 Network-on-Chip based Shielding Plane (NoCSIP)

A novel network-on-chip based 3D obfuscation method is proposed in [16] to thwart reverse engineering attacks in TSV-based 3D ICs. The authors proposed to use a Network-on-Chip based shielding plane (NoCSIP) for cross-plane communication (i.e. vertical communication channel). The essence of NoCSIP is to provide an obfuscated communication channel between two planes that host commercial dies and block the direct communication between two commercial dies in a 3D structure. This NocSIP method makes it significantly more challenging to reverse engineer the 3D system. If the proposed shielding layer is sufficiently strong, the 3D system has more flexibility to use low end dies without sacrificing the overall system's security assurance.

5.6 Possible 3D Trojan Detection and Mitigation Methods

One low-cost countermeasure against the potential hardware Trojans inserted by the untrusted vertical interconnect foundry discussed in 4.1 is shown in Fig. 5(a). Each single die needs extra work to swap connections between the top metal layer and the TSVs. For instance, the single die is fabricated in trusted foundry and the 3D integration foundry intends to implement a parametric hardware Trojan for instance, on a clock TSV. A clock-TSV is the inter-die

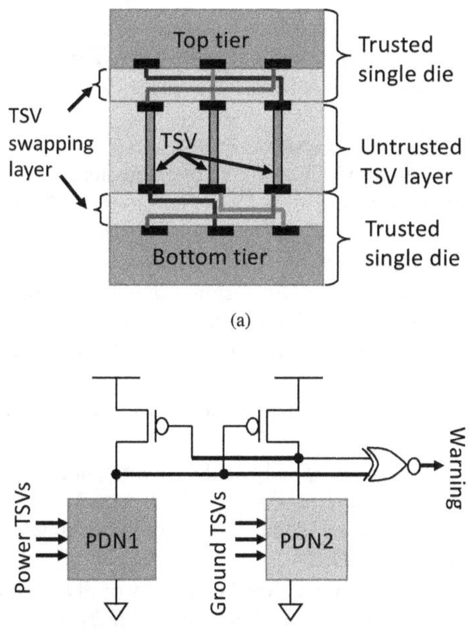

Figure 5: Possible countermeasures for 3D hardware Trojans. (a) TSV swapping, and (b) DCVSL-based abnormal power and ground grid detection.

connection between the clock networks on vertically adjacent tiers. By swapping the metal-to-TSV connection, the designed parametric Trojan could be placed to a signal TSV instead. Thanks to logic masking and inherent noise filtering of digital circuits, that parametric Trojan is very likely to be muted. The parametric hardware Trojans on the TSV will not cause a catastrophic effect on the clock network.

Differential Cascade Voltage Switch Logic (DCVSL) gates takes complementary inputs and generate complementary outputs. We can exploit the complementary characteristic to detect the abnormal power and ground voltages induced by malicious power and ground TSVs, as shown in Fig. 5(b). Once the multiple power/ground lines do not reach to the standard voltage, the outputs of the DCVSL gate are not complementary and thus the warning signal goes to high. This warning signal can be further used to alert the 3D chip user.

If 3D NoC is adopted in the 3D chip, we can also exploit obfuscated routing algorithms for the 3D switches to eliminate the explicit vertical communication between tiers.

6. CONCLUSION

Due to limited testing techniques, 3D ICs are expected to have new security threats than those existed in 2D ICs. Previous studies on 3D IC security mainly focus on the methods that leverage 3D structures to address the security concerns on 2D ICs, rather than understanding the security vulnerabilities inherently existed in 3D ICs. In this work, we first summarized the novel opportunities offered by 3D integration for security mechanism and then enlist the potential security vulnerabilities in 3D ICs. TSV-based 3D hardware Trojans and cross-tier hardware Trojans , which are unique to 3D chips, are discussed. Further, we reviewed several countermeasures against existing security threats and propose potential 3D Trojan detection and mitigation methods.

The countermeasures for new security threats on 3D ICs should be investigated by hardware security community. In future work, we will implement the possible countermeasures and assess the countermeasure's resistance against hardware Trojan and reverse engineering attacks from untrusted foundries.

7. REFERENCES

[1] L. Labrak and I. O'Connor, "Heterogeneous System Design Platform and Perspectives for 3D Integration," *Proc. of the IEEE International Conference on Microelectronics*, pp. 161–164, December 2009.

[2] L. Xue, *et al.*, "Three-Dimensional Integration: Technology, Use, and Issues for Mixed-Signal Applications," *IEEE Transactions on Electron Devices*, Vol. 50, No. 3, pp. 601–609, March 2003.

[3] Y. Xie and J. Zhao, *Die-stacking Architecture*. Morgan & Claypool Publishers, 2015.

[4] Y. Xie, J. Cong, and S. Sapatnekar, *Three-Dimensional Integrated Circuit Design: EDA, Design and Microarchitectures*, 1st ed. Springer Publishing Company, Incorporated, 2009.

[5] J. Zhao, Q. Zou, and Y. Xie, "Overview of 3D Architecture Design Opportunities and Techniques," *IEEE Design Test*, Vol. PP, No. 99, pp. 1-1, 2015.

[6] K. W. Lee, *et al.*, "Novel reconfigured wafer-to-wafer (W2W) hybrid bonding technology using ultra-high density nano-Cu filaments for exascale 2.5D/3D integration," *2015 IEEE International Electron Devices Meeting (IEDM)*, pp. 8.2.1-8.2.4, Dec 2015.

[7] P. Vivet, *et al.*, "3D advanced integration technology for heterogeneous systems," *2015 International 3D Systems Integration Conference (3DIC)*, pp. FS6.1-FS6.3, Aug 2015.

[8] C. C. Lee, *et al.*, "An Overview of the Development of a GPU with Integrated HBM on Silicon Interposer," *2016 IEEE 66th Electronic Components and Technology Conference (ECTC)*, pp. 1439-1444, May 2016.

[9] D. Stow, *et al.*, "Cost analysis and cost-driven IP reuse methodology for SoC design based on 2.5D/3D integration," *2016 IEEE/ACM International Conference on Computer-Aided Design (ICCAD)*, pp. 1-6, Nov 2016.

[10] S. Hou, "Interposer Technology: Past, Now, and Future," 2016, semicon Taiwan.

[11] J. Shi, *et al.*, "A 14nm FinFET transistor-level 3D partitioning design to enable high-performance and low-cost monolithic 3D IC," *2016 IEEE International Electron Devices Meeting (IEDM)*, Dec 2016.

[12] D. Stow, *et al.*, "Cost and Thermal Analysis of High-Performance 2.5D and 3D Integrated Circuit Design Space," *2016 IEEE Computer Society Annual Symposium on VLSI (ISVLSI)*, pp. 637-642, July 2016.

[13] W. L. Hung, *et al.*, "Interconnect and thermal-aware floorplanning for 3D microprocessors," *Proc. of ISQED'06)*, pp. 6 pp.-104, March 2006.

[14] Y. Chen, D. Niu, Y. Xie, and K. Chakrabarty, "Cost-effective integration of three-dimensional (3D) ICs emphasizing testing cost analysis," *2010 IEEE/ACM International Conference on Computer-Aided Design (ICCAD)*, pp. 471-476, Nov 2010.

[15] Y. Xie, *et al.*, "Security and Vulnerability Implications of 3D ICs," *IEEE Transactions on Multi-Scale Computing Systems*, Vol. 2, No. 2, pp. 108-122, April 2016.

[16] J. Dofe, Q. Yu, H. Wang, and E. Salman, "Hardware Security Threats and Potential Countermeasures in Emerging 3D ICs," *Proc. of GLSVLSI '16*, pp. 69–74, 2016.

[17] P. Gu, *et al.*, "Leveraging 3D Technologies for Hardware Security: Opportunities and Challenges," *Proc. GLSVLSI '16*, pp. 347–352, 2016.

[18] M. Rostami, F. Koushanfar, and R. Karri, "A primer on hardware security: Models, methods, and metrics," *Proceedings of the IEEE*, Vol. 102, No. 8, pp. 1283–1295, 2014.

[19] Y. Xie, C. Bao, and A. Srivastava, "3D/2.5 D IC-Based Obfuscation," *Hardware Protection through Obfuscation*. Springer, 2017, pp. 291–314.

[20] E. J. Marinissen, "Challenges and emerging solutions in testing TSV-based 2 1 over 2D- and 3D-stacked ICs," *Proc. of DATE '12*, pp. 1277-1282, March 2012.

[21] F. Imeson, A. Emtenan, S. Garg, and M. V. Tripunitara, "Securing Computer Hardware Using 3D Integrated Circuit (IC) Technology and Split Manufacturing for Obfuscation." *USENIX Security*, Vol. 13, 2013.

[22] Y. Xie, C. Bao, and A. Srivastava, "Security-Aware Design Flow for 2.5 D IC Technology," *Proc.of TrustED '15*, pp. 31–38, 2015.

[23] R. S. Jagtap, "A Methodology for Early Exploration of TSV Interconnects in 3D Stacked ICs," Master's thesis, Delft University of Technology, Netherlands, 2011.

[24] S. Bansal, "3D IC Design," *EETimes (Nov 14, 2011), http://www.eetimes.com/document.asp?doc_id=1279081*, 2011.

[25] M. Bilzor, "3D execution monitor (3D-EM): Using 3D circuits to detect hardware malicious inclusions in general purpose processors," *Proc. of the 6th International Conference on Information Warfare and Security*, p. 288. Academic Conferences Limited, 2011.

[26] J. Valamehr, *et al.*, "A 3-D Split Manufacturing Approach to Trustworthy System Development," *Computer-Aided Design of Integrated Circuits and Systems, IEEE Transactions on*, Vol. 32, No. 4, pp. 611–615, 2013.

[27] T. Huffmire, *et al.*, "Hardware trust implications of 3-D integration," *Proc. of the 5th Workshop on Embedded Systems Security*, p. 1. ACM, 2010.

[28] K. Xiao, D. Forte, and M. M. Tehranipoor, "Efficient and secure split manufacturing via obfuscated built-in self-authentication," *Hardware Oriented Security and Trust (HOST), 2015 IEEE International Symposium on*, pp. 14–19. IEEE, 2015.

[29] J. Rajendran, O. Sinanoglu, and R. Karri, "Is split manufacturing secure?" *Design, Automation & Test in Europe Conference & Exhibition (DATE), 2013*, pp. 1259–1264. IEEE, 2013.

[30] M. Jagasivamani, *et al.*, "Split-fabrication obfuscation: Metrics and techniques," *Hardware-Oriented Security and Trust (HOST), 2014 IEEE International Symposium on*, pp. 7–12. IEEE, 2014.

[31] J. Dofe, *et al.*, "Transistor-level camouflaged logic locking method for monolithic 3D IC security," *2016 IEEE Asian Hardware-Oriented Security and Trust (AsianHOST)*, pp. 1-6, Dec 2016.

[32] P. Gu, *et al.*, "Thermal-aware 3D design for side-channel information leakage," *2016 IEEE 34th International Conference on Computer Design (ICCD)*, pp. 520-527, Oct 2016.

Impact of Power Distribution Network on Power Analysis Attacks in Three-Dimensional Integrated Circuits

Jaya Dofe, Zhiming Zhang, Qiaoyan Yu
Department of Electrical and Computer Engineering
University of New Hampshire, USA
qiaoyan.yu@unh.edu

Chen Yan and Emre Salman
Department of Electrical and Computer Engineering
Stony Brook University, USA
emre.salman@stonybrook.edu

ABSTRACT

Correlation power analysis (CPA) attacks on the hardware implementation of cryptographic algorithms can retrieve the cipher key by analyzing the correlation between hypothesized keys and the power measurement of that crypto hardware. The existing CPA attacks and the countermeasures are mainly for two-dimensional (2D) integrated circuits (ICs). There is a lack of study on CPA in the context of three-dimensional (3D) ICs. To fill in this gap, this work investigates the impact of a 3D power distribution network (PDN) on the efficiency of CPA mounted on a cryptographic module, which is in one of the 3D planes. The Pearson correlation coefficient is used as a metric to assess the impact of different PDN types, circuit loads, and switching activities of the neighboring planes on the CPA efficiency.

1. INTRODUCTION

Three-dimensional (3D) integrated circuits (ICs) have become increasingly attractive due to higher density and better global interconnect performance. Researchers have also leveraged the 3D technology to address the security threats on 2D chips. Techniques, such as split manufacturing and placing a cryptographic module in the middle layer of 3D chips, are developed to achieve higher resistance against reverse engineering and side-channel analysis attacks. The expected improvement on attack resistance mainly relies on the shielding capacity from the multiple planes in 3D chips. Unfortunately, the noise and thermal issues in 3D ICs may also hinder the applied security mechanisms from fully achieving the expected attack resistance. Security opportunities and challenges on 3D ICs have been identified in recent literature [1–5].

The secret key adopted in a cryptographic algorithm can be retrieved by correlation power analysis (CPA) attacks [6] mounted on hardware implementation, through the analysis on the correlation between hypothesized keys and the power measurement of that crypto hardware. To thwart side-channel attacks, existing works propose randomized countermeasures [7], intermediate data duplication [8], Boolean masking [9], dynamic and differential logic [10], and noise addition [11]. Alternatively, [12] and [13] have proposed to revise the traditional voltage regulators to alter the power measurement of the crypto hardware, thus improving the resistance against power analysis attacks. Since an accurate power measurement is vital for the success of CPA, we investigate the impact of power distribution networks on the efficiency of CPA, with special emphasis on the encryption engine within a 3D design environment.

The remainder of this work is organized as follows. Preliminaries of this work are introduced in Section 2. The related work and our main contributions are summarized in Section 3. The experimental setup for our study is presented in Section 4. Various dependent factors for CPA in 3D ICs are examined in Section 5. We conclude this work and discuss some future work in Section 6.

2. PRELIMINARIES

2.1 Power Distribution for 2D and 3D ICs

A modern power distribution network (PDN) consists of a global grid and multiple virtual grids that are connected to the global grid through sleep transistors and/or voltage regulators. Nominal power supply voltage is provided to the global grid through controlled collapse chip connection (C4) bumps, which connect the global grid with the flip-chip substrate. The virtual grids form voltage islands/domains that can be independently power gated. The grids are typically modeled with equivalent parasitic resistance and inductance per unit length, determined from the physical characteristics of the meta layers such as thickness, width, and spacing. On-chip decoupling capacitors are also used within these grids to provide instantaneous charge to switching load circuits, thereby reducing the transient power supply noise.

Power gating is a common method to significantly reduce subthreshold leakage current in nanoscale technologies [14]. For 3D systems, power gating is critical due to higher and heterogeneous integration where the amount of nonswitching circuits can be significantly high [15]. Thus, 3D ICs are expected to be heavily power gated to sufficiently reduce leakage power, as shown in Fig. 1. In this figure, the global grids of multiple planes are connected by via-last TSVs, which pass through the metal layers and connect the topmost metal layer in each plane.

Similar to 2D planar technologies, sleep transistors with high threshold voltage are utilized to achieve power gating in 3D ICs. These sleep transistors are distributed throughout

Permission to make digital or hard copies of all or part of this work for personal or classroom use is granted without fee provided that copies are not made or distributed for profit or commercial advantage and that copies bear this notice and the full citation on the first page. Copyrights for components of this work owned by others than ACM must be honored. Abstracting with credit is permitted. To copy otherwise, or republish, to post on servers or to redistribute to lists, requires prior specific permission and/or a fee. Request permissions from Permissions@acm.org.

GLSVLSI '17, May 10 - 12, 2017, Banff, AB, Canada

© 2017 Copyright held by the owner/author(s). Publication rights licensed to ACM.

ISBN 978-1-4503-4972-7/17/05...$15.00

DOI: http://dx.doi.org/10.1145/3060403.3060501

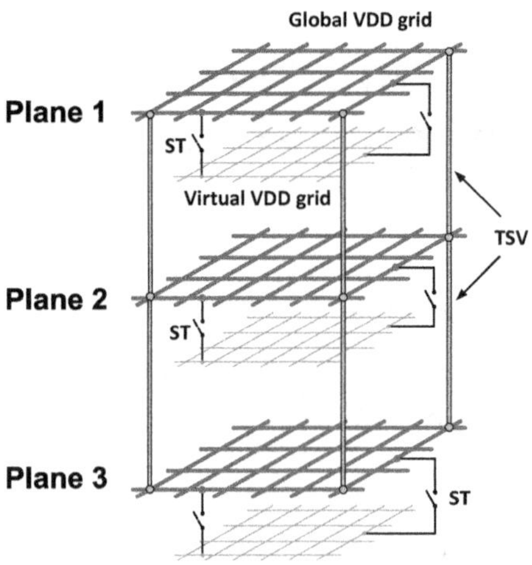

Figure 1: Power distribution network for a three-plane 3D IC with power gating, illustrating the global and virtual power grids, sleep transistors, and TSVs.

the entire 3D stack. In practice, a large number of sleep transistors is placed around the intended area to be power gated, forming a ring structure.

2.2 Power Supply Noise

A critical design challenge for TSV based 3D ICs is the reliable distribution of the power supply voltage to devices that are distributed throughout multiple planes [16]. The parasitic impedance of these additional planes, TSVs, and larger overall load current drawn from the power supply exacerbate the issue of power distribution by increasing both the peak and average power supply noise.

Furthermore, when a circuit block or an entire plane within a 3D IC transitions from sleep state to active state, a relatively large in-rush current is drawn to charge the capacitors in that block or plane, producing power noise at the semi-global or global power network. This noise affects the reliability of other active blocks and planes, and is referred to as *power gating noise* or *in-rush current noise*. Both power supply noise and power gating noise should be controlled to ensure that the functionality, timing performance, and reliability of the 3D system are satisfied. This paper studies whether power supply noise poses a challenge or offer an opportunity for power analysis attacks in 3D ICs.

2.3 Power Analysis Attacks

In cryptography, side-channel attacks (SCA) exploit the side-channel signals (e.g. timing, electromagnetic leak, thermal image, and power consumption) obtained from the hardware implementation of cryptographic algorithms to retrieve the confidential key applied in the cryptographic module. SCA techniques are more practical and time efficient than the brute force search. Among SCA techniques, power-based SCA (i.e. power analysis attack [6]) has been widely studied. Power analysis attacks are categorized in simple power analysis (SPA) [17], differential power analysis (DPA) [17], and correlation power analysis (CPA) [18].

In CPA, the attacker conducts theoretical predictions of the power consumption for the hardware implementation of the cryptographic algorithm. During the prediction, for a hypothesized key, the attacker can use the Hamming weight model or Hamming distance model to predict the number of bit transitions happened in the crypto state registers and thus estimate the associated power change between two consecutive clock cycles. Next, the theoretical estimation is compared with the real measurements. The Pearson correlation coefficient has been identified as an effective metric to assess how close a hypothesized key is to the true cipher key. The detailed CPA procedure is described in [6].

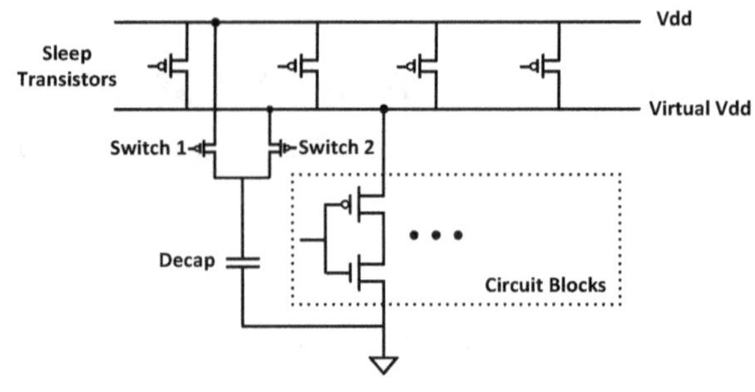

Figure 2: Conceptual representation of the reconfigurable decoupling capacitor topology with power gating.

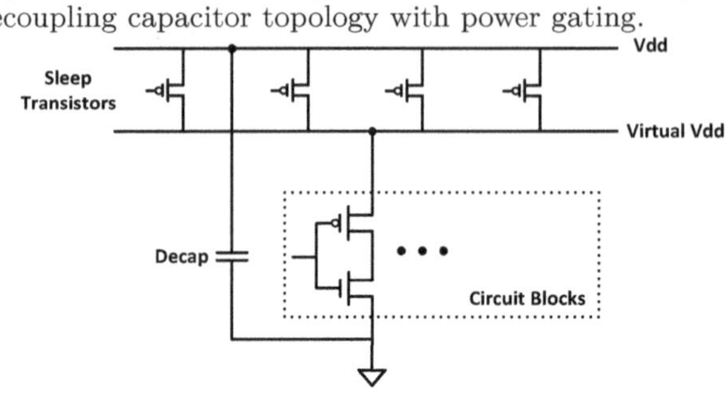

Figure 3: Conceptual representation of the always-on decoupling capacitor topology with power gating.

3. RELATED WORK

3.1 3D Power Noise Management

In traditional power networks, decoupling capacitors are typically connected to the virtual grids since a shorter physical distance between the capacitor and load circuit enhances the efficacy of the capacitor. In power gated 3D ICs, however, significant decoupling capacitance is lost when a block or plane is power gated. Thus, power gating in 3D ICs degrades the efficiency of decoupling capacitors in traditional power networks, thereby increasing the power supply noise. As demonstrated in previous research, decoupling capacitors placed in a plane can be highly effective for other planes in 3D ICs due to relatively low impedance TSVs [19]. Thus, unlike 2D ICs, decoupling capacitors in 3D ICs have a larger effective range. To leverage this characteristic, reconfigurable decoupling capacitors have been proposed for power gated 3D ICs [20]. In this method, as illustrated in Fig. 2, a decoupling capacitor is connected to the virtual grid through switch 2 when the load circuit (or the plane) is on. This configuration ensures that the impedance between the capacitor and the circuit is sufficiently low. Alternatively, when the plane is power gated, the decoupling capacitor is connected to the global grid through switch 1. Thus, even though the plane is gated, the decoupling capacitors within that plane can still be effective in reducing power supply noise of the other planes through low impedance TSVs. As a reference and comparison, an always-on topology has also been proposed where the decoupling capacitors are always connected to the global grid, as depicted in Fig. 3. Reconfigurable decoupling capacitor topology can achieve up to 50% and 87% reduction in, respectively, rms power supply and power gating noise at the expense of a moderate increase in physical area and power consumption [19]. The effect of these different 3D decoupling capacitor topologies on power analysis attacks is investigated in this paper.

3.2 Countermeasures for Power Analysis Attacks

A current flattening circuit based countermeasure is proposed in [21] to thwart DPA attacks in smart cards. This approach uses an analog control loop to maintain overall current consumption of the system to a predefined value. A dynamic voltage and frequency switching approach is presented in [22] to randomize the power traces and prevent the attacker from performing time correlation between different power traces. Double width single core (DWSC) method in [23] is another power balancing technique. The main idea of that work is to introduce complementary signal transitions along with the original ones to balance the power variations due to different input patterns, hence obscuring the correlation between internal computations and device power consumption. An internally generated random mask based digitally controlled ring oscillators is used to dynamically change the power consumption and thus thwart first order DPA attacks [24]. Other random masking based countermeasures are discussed in [25,26]. On-chip noise generation, clock randomization, and memory scrambling techniques are exploited in [11] to obscure the power profile.

3.3 Countermeasures for Other Side-channel Attacks in 3D ICs

Countermeasures for other side-channel attacks in 3D ICs have also attracted significant attention. In [27], a crypto co-processor is located in one of the 3D planes. To mitigate the side-channel attack on the access-driven cache in the co-processor, a dedicated memory is proposed to store cryptographic state and secret keys during the operations [27]. A 3D architecture is proposed to shield the thermal side-channel information in [2], where a micro-controller is applied to produce the dynamic random complementary activity patterns to hinder the side channel leakage. To defeat the cache-timing side-channel attacks in 3D ICs, a random eviction cache was introduced, which was designed to decorrelate timing information and key-dependent data [5].

3.4 Contributions of This Work

The main contributions of this work are as follows:

- To the best of our knowledge, this is the first work that studies the impact of the power supply noise induced by PDNs on the power analysis attacks in the context of 3D ICs.
- This work compares the power traces of a Sbox for the Advanced Encryption Standard (AES) measured with an ideal PDN, a nonideal 2D PDN, and a nonideal 3D PDN. We used a case study to quantitatively show the impact of different power supply noise on the correlation coefficient between the predicted and measured power consumption of the Sbox.
- We also examine the impact of different PDN topologies and the circuit switching activities in neighboring planes on the CPA efficiency.

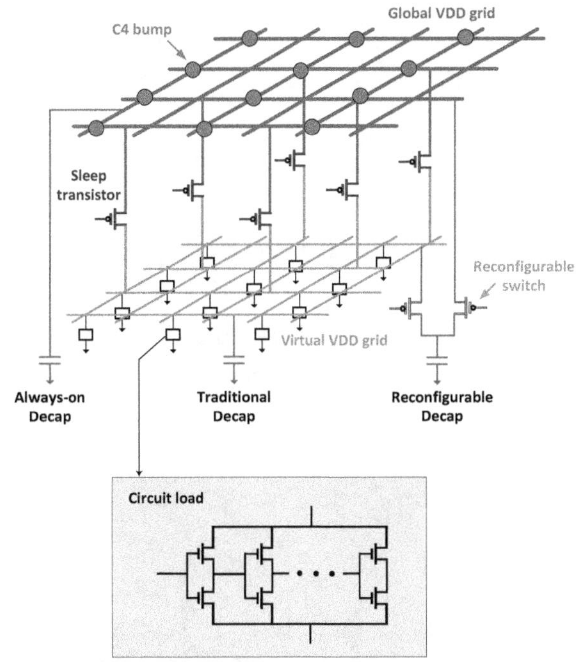

Figure 4: Plane-level power network illustrating distributed sleep transistors, decoupling capacitors (traditional and proposed topologies), switching load, and the C4 bumps.

4. EXPERIMENTAL SETUP

A power distribution network for a three-plane 3D IC with via-last TSVs is generated in 45 nm technology with 10 available metal layers in each plane. A portion of the power network with an area of 1 mm by 1 mm is analyzed. Each plane consists of a global power network, virtual power network, distributed sleep transistors [28], distributed decoupling capacitance, and distributed switching load circuit consisting of inverter gates and Sbox, as depicted in Fig. 4. Details of the power network characteristics can be found in [19].

We conducted power analysis attacks on a Sbox module for the iterative gate-level implementation of AES-128. We synthesized the Sbox Verilog HDL description in the Synopsys Design Compiler with a NCSU FreePDK at the 45nm technology node. The synthesized Sbox netlist was imported into the Cadence Virtuoso to perform transistor-level simulation. Pseudo-random inputs were provided as the stimulus for the Sbox. We used 10GHz frequency to sample the instantaneous power of the Sbox and formed 1000 power traces from our simulation. The Sbox module is placed in the middle plane of the 3D chip. The load circuits for the PDN are inverters with different sizes to mimic different load circuits in practical 3D ICs [19]. The analyses in Section 5 are based on the experimental setup mentioned here.

5. IMPACT OF POWER SUPPLY NOISE ON POWER ANALYSIS ATTACKS IN 3D ICS

5.1 Impact of Power Noise on Sbox Power Consumption

As the first step, we quantitatively compare the Sbox power trace extracted from an ideal Sbox power measure-

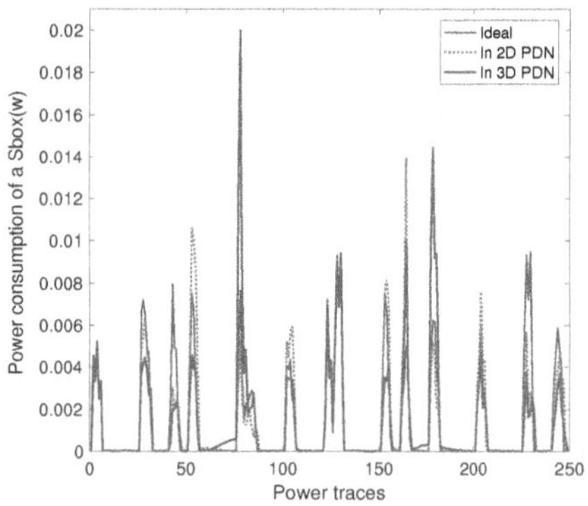

(a)

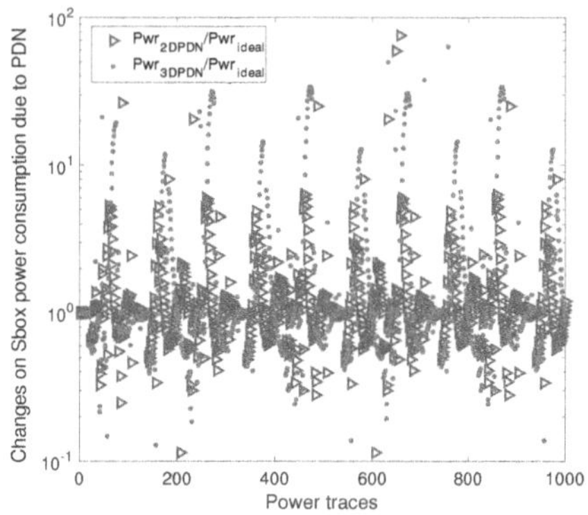

(b)

Figure 5: Impact of power distribution network on the Sbox power consumption. (a) Cropped 250 power traces, and (b) Changes on Sbox power consumption over ideal Sbox power.

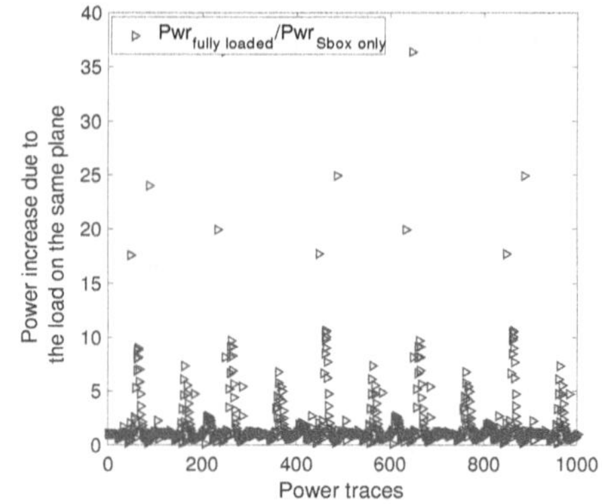

(a)

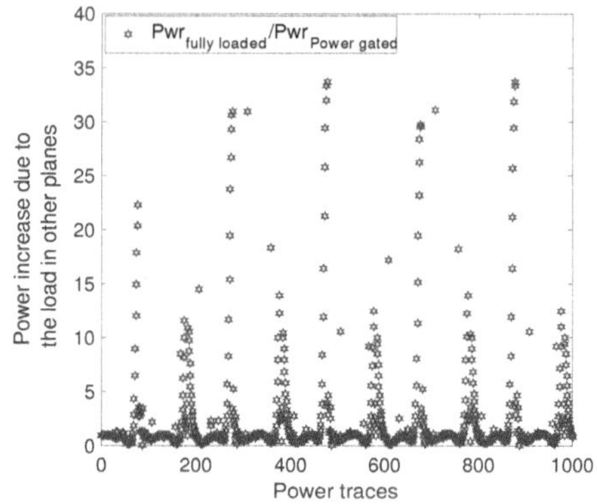

(b)

Figure 6: Impact of other circuit switching activities from (a) the same plane and (b) the other 3D planes on the Sbox power consumption.

ment (i.e. DC voltage supply for Vdd), with a 2D and 3D PDN. As shown in Fig. 5(a), the presence of 2D and 3D PDNs causes the peak power of the Sbox to shift, earlier or later, due to the power supply noise. Compared to the 2D PDN, the 3D PDN introduces larger noise and a more noticeable skew on power profile. Figure 5(b) indicates that the instantaneous power change caused by PDN is in the range of 0.1× and 100× over the ideal Sbox case. The average instantaneous power increase due to the 2D PDN is 172.22%, and the corresponding standard deviation is 4.6442. If the Sbox is connected to the 3D PDN, the average instantaneous power increase is 368.72% with a standard deviation of 7.5938. As a result, the 3D PDN can almost double the average change on the Sbox instantaneous power as compared to the 2D PDN.

5.2 Impact of Co-existing Load Circuits on Sbox Power Consumption

There are two load circuits (other than the Sbox module) within the 3D chip, those from the Sbox plane (denoted as same plane hereafter) and those from the neighboring planes (denoted as planes 1&3 hereafter). To study the impact of the co-existing load from the same plane on the Sbox power, we examined two cases: (1) Only one Sbox module is added to the middle plane (considered as Sbox only), and (2) one Sbox and many inverters (considered as fully loaded). As shown in Fig. 6(a), the other load circuits within the same PDN indeed affect the power trace of the Sbox, due to the power supply noise. If the planes 1 and 3 are fully loaded with inverters, the cross-plane current and voltage noise passed through the 3D PDN produces a more significant effect on the Sbox power as compared to 2D PDN. This is shown in Fig. 6(b). The circuit load in the neighboring planes causes 72.21% more power change than the load on the same plane with the Sbox. In addition, the standard deviation of power change due to the load on other planes is 1.72× larger as compared to the same plane load.

5.3 Variation of Power Noise Effects due to Different PDN Topologies

In this subsection, the impact of different PDN topologies on the Sbox power is examined. As shown in Fig. 7(a), if the middle plane has only Sbox as the load circuit and the other two planes (1 and 3) are power gated, the type of PDN adopted in the 3D design has negligible impact on the Sbox power. The measured instantaneous power in different PDNs is almost identical. In Fig. 7(b), the middle plane has other load circuit in addition to Sbox. In this case, when the planes 1 and 3 are power gated, all PDNs start to introduce random noise and thus change the Sbox power profile. Traditional PDN cannot reduce power noise as much, thus contributing more to the Sbox power change than the always-on and reconfigurable PDNs. As shown in Figs. 7(c)

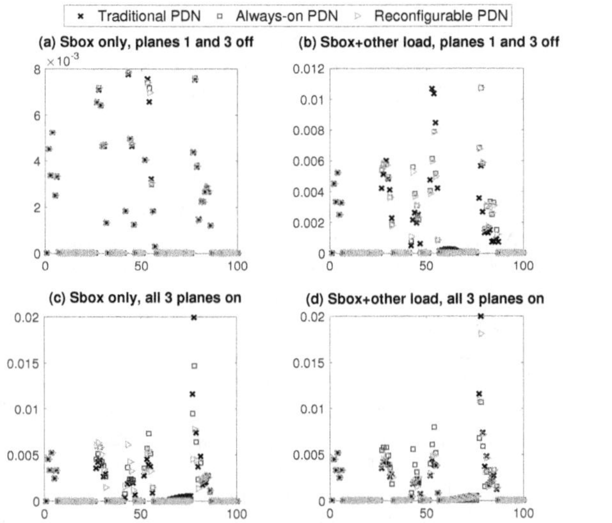

Figure 7: Impact of PDN types on the Sbox power consumption. (a) Only Sbox in plane 2, planes 1&3 off (b), Sbox and other load in plane 2, planes 1&3 off, (c) only Sbox in plane 2, all planes on, and (d) Sbox and other load in plane 2, all planes on. Note, in all subfigures above, X-axis and Y-axis are power traces and Sbox power consumption, respectively.

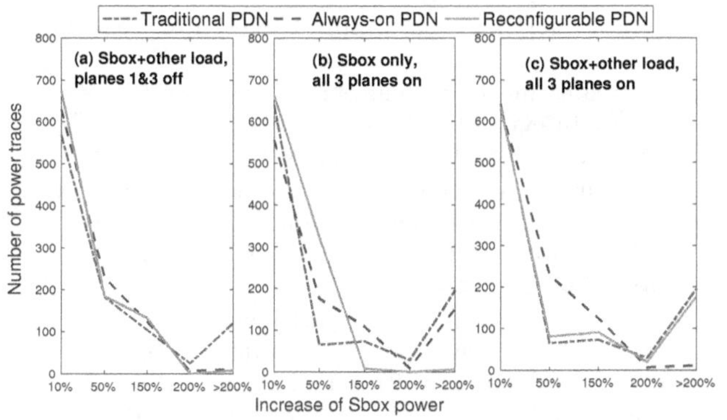

Figure 8: The percentage of Sbox power increase due to different PDNs and the load circuits in the 3D planes.

and (d), once all three planes are turned on, the effect of different PDNs on the Sbox power is noticeable. As compared to Fig. 8(a), the number of power traces that results in power increase by less than 50% is reduced, as indicated in Figs. 8(b) and (c). The reconfigurable PDN is capable to address the power grid noise even though the PDN in other planes is power gated, thus affecting the Sbox power the least (if the Sbox module occupies the entire plane). However, when the plane having the Sbox module includes other load circuits, the always-on PDN adds less noise than the traditional and reconfigurable PDNs. As a result, the Sbox power is less affected by the always-on PDN than the other two types of PDNs.

5.4 Power Correlation Modification due to PDN

As discussed in the previous subsections, the power distribution network changes the power profile of the cryptographic module of interest. The effect of the noise induced

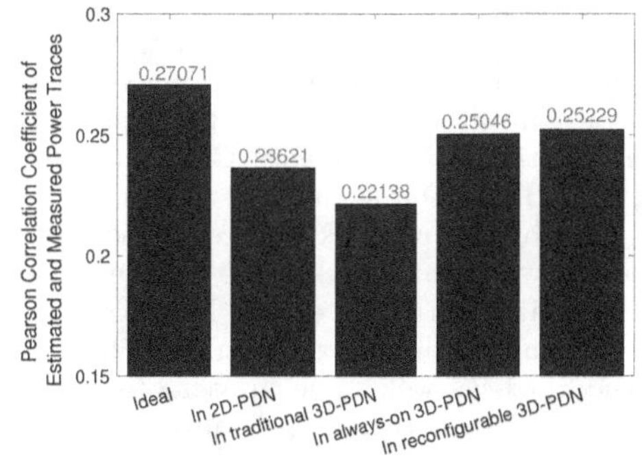

(a)

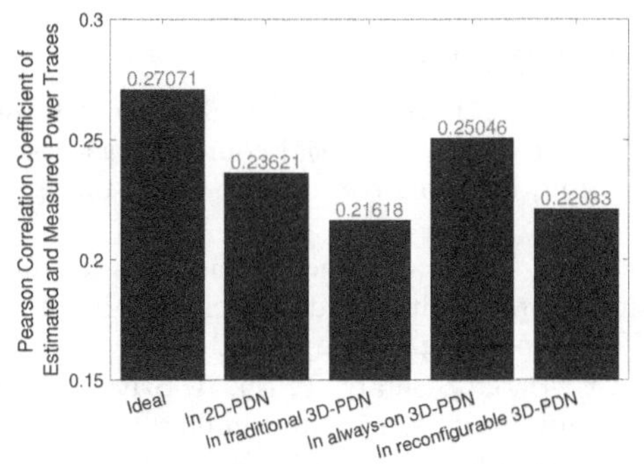

(b)

Figure 9: Pearson correlation coefficient between the measured and estimated Sbox power. (a) Sbox plane on and other planes off, (b) all planes on.

by the power grid on the correlation between the predicted and measured power of the Sbox is investigated in this section. We used Pearson correlation coefficient [6] as the evaluation metric. Each PDN is fully loaded with inverters, other than the Sbox module.

First, the planes 1 and 3 are power gated and only the Sbox plane is active. As shown in Fig. 9(a), the correlation coefficient for the other scenarios is less than that for the ideal Sbox power measurement case. This indicates that the power grid noise indeed can obscure the Sbox power profile. However, the degree of power profile alteration due to PDN varies with the PDN topology and the noise management mechanism applied in the PDN. The traditional 3D-PDN leads to the worst power grid noise, resulting in the lowest power correlation coefficient than other cases. Always-on and reconfigurable 3D-PDNs have different kind of noise management mechanisms, and hence the corresponding correlation coefficient goes up by 0.03 over the traditional 3D-PDN. When we turn on all three planes, the power correlation coefficient of the reconfigurable PDN case decreases. This is because the reconfigurable 3D-PDN offers similar performance on power grid noise to the traditional 3D-PDN when all planes are on.

6. CONCLUSION AND FUTURE WORK

Power analysis attacks have been demonstrated as a powerful mean to retrieve the secret key from the hardware implementation of a cryptographic algorithm. Generally, it is expected that the use of power analysis attacks on a cryptographic module embedded in a 3D chip is more difficult than a 2D IC due to the shielding effect among the 3D layers. There is a lack of detailed investigation on how the 3D structure affects the efficiency of power analysis attacks. In this work, we study the impact of power distribution networks on correlation power analysis (CPA) mounted on the non-linear unit, Sbox. Our simulation results show that the 3D power distribution network induces noise to the Sbox power measurement, which makes the CPA more challenging. The switching activities of the load circuits located in the same plane as the Sbox module change the power profile of the Sbox, as well. The impact of different types of decoupling capacitors (traditional, always-on, and reconfigurable) on the power traces for Sbox is examined. Our experiments indicate that the PDN with noise management modules makes the CPA easier.

7. REFERENCES

[1] J. Dofe, Q. Yu, H. Wang, and E. Salman, "Hardware security threats and potential countermeasures in emerging 3d ics," in *Proc. of GLSVLSI '16*, pp. 69–74, 2016.

[2] P. Gu *et al.*, "Leveraging 3d technologies for hardware security: Opportunities and challenges," in *Proc. of GLSVLSI '16*, pp. 347–352, 2016.

[3] Y. Xie, C. Bao, C. Serafy, T. Lu, A. Srivastava, and M. Tehranipoor, "Security and vulnerability implications of 3d ics," *IEEE Trans.on Multi-Scale Computing Systems*, vol. 2, pp. 108–122, April 2016.

[4] J. Dofe, C. Yan, S. Kontak, E. Salman, and Q. Yu, "Transistor-level camouflaged logic locking method for monolithic 3d ic security," in *Proc. of AsianHOST'16*, pp. 1–6, Dec 2016.

[5] C. Bao and A. Srivastava, "3d integration: New opportunities in defense against cache-timing side-channel attacks," in *Proc. of ICCD*, pp. 273–280, Oct 2015.

[6] O. X. Standaert, E. Peeters, G. Rouvroy, and J. J. Quisquater, "An overview of power analysis attacks against field programmable gate arrays," *Proceedings of the IEEE*, vol. 94, pp. 383–394, Feb 2006.

[7] E. Oswald and M. Aigner, "Randomized addition-subtraction chains as a countermeasure against power attacks," in *Proc. of CHES'01*, pp. 39–50, 2001.

[8] L. Goubin and J. Patarin, "Des and differential power analysis (the "duplication" method)," in *Proc.of CHES'99*, pp. 158–172, 1999.

[9] M.-L. Akkar and C. Giraud, "An implementation of des and aes, secure against some attacks," in *Proc. of CHES'01*, pp. 309–318, 2001.

[10] K. Tiri, M. Akmal, and I. Verbauwhede, "A dynamic and differential cmos logic with signal independent power consumption to withstand differential power analysis on smart cards," in *Proc. of ESSCIRC'02*, pp. 403–406, Sept 2002.

[11] G. Tim and M. Amir, "Generic side-channel countermeasures for reconfigurable devices," in *Proc. of CHES'11*, pp. 33–48, 2011.

[12] M. Kar *et al.*, "Exploiting fully integrated inductive voltage regulators to improve side channel resistance of encryption engines," in *Proc. of ISLPED '16*, pp. 130–135, 2016.

[13] W. Yu and S. Kose, "A voltage regulator-assisted lightweight aes implementation against dpa attacks," *IEEE Transactions on Circuits and Systems I: Regular Papers*, vol. 63, pp. 1152–1163, Aug 2016.

[14] H. Jiang, M. Marek-Sadowska, and S. Nassif, "Benefits and Costs of Power-gating Technique," in *Proceedings of IEEE International Conference on Computer Design*, pp. 559 – 566, October 2005.

[15] H. Wang and E. Salman, "Resource Allocation Methodology for Through Silicon Vias and Sleep Transistors In 3D ICs," in *Proc. IEEE ISQED*, pp. 528–532, March 2015.

[16] S. M. Satheesh and E. Salman, "Power Distribution in TSV-Based 3-D Processor-Memory Stacks," *IEEE Journal on Emerging and Selected Topics in Circuits and Systems*, vol. 2, pp. 692–703, December 2012.

[17] P. Kocher, J. Jaffe, B. Jun, and P. Rohatgi, "Introduction to differential power analysis," *Journal of Cryptographic Engineering*, vol. 1, no. 1, pp. 5–27, 2011.

[18] B. Eric, C. Christophe, and O. Francis, "Correlation power analysis with a leakage model," in *Proc. of CHES'04*, pp. 16–29, 2004.

[19] H. Wang and E. Salman, "Decoupling Capacitor Topologies for TSV-Based 3-D ICs With Power Gating," *IEEE Trans. on Very Large Scale Integration (VLSI) Systems*, vol. 23, pp. 2983–2991, December 2015.

[20] H. Wang and E. Salman, "Enhancing System-wide Power Integrity In 3D ICs With Power Gating," in *Proc. IEEE ISQED*, pp. 322–326, March 2015.

[21] R. Muresan and S. Gregori, "Protection circuit against differential power analysis attacks for smart cards," *IEEE Trans. on Computers*, vol. 57, no. 11, pp. 1540–1549, 2008.

[22] S. Yang, W. Wolf, N. Vijaykrishnan, D. N. Serpanos, and Y. Xie, "Power attack resistant cryptosystem design: a dynamic voltage and frequency switching approach," in *Proc. of DATE'05*, pp. 64–69 Vol. 3, March 2005.

[23] A. Arora, J. A. Ambrose, J. Peddersen, and S. Parameswaran, "A double-width algorithmic balancing to prevent power analysis side channel attacks in aes," in *Proc. of ISVLSI*, pp. 76–83, Aug 2013.

[24] P. C. Liu, H. C. Chang, and C. Y. Lee, "A low overhead dpa countermeasure circuit based on ring oscillators," *IEEE Transactions on Circuits and Systems II: Express Briefs*, vol. 57, pp. 546–550, July 2010.

[25] E. Prouff and M. Rivain, "Masking against side-channel attacks: A formal security proof," in *Proc. of EUROCRYPT'13*, pp. 142–159, 2013.

[26] C. Claude *et al.*, "Higher-Order Masking Schemes for S-Boxes," in *Proc. of FSE'12*, pp. 366–384, 2012.

[27] J. Valamehr *et al.*, "Cryptography and security," ch. A Qualitative Security Analysis of a New Class of 3-d Integrated Crypto Co-processors, pp. 364–382, 2012.

[28] H. Wang and E. Salman, "Power Gating Methodologies in TSV Based 3D Integrated Circuits," in *Proc. of the ACM/IEEE GLSVLSI*, pp. 327–328, May 2013.

The Need for Declarative Properties in Digital IC Security

Mohamed El Massad[†]
me1361@nyu.edu

Siddharth Garg[†]
sg175@nyu.edu

[†]Electrical and Computer Engineering
New York University, USA

Frank Imeson[§]
fcimeson@uwaterloo.ca

Mahesh Tripunitara[§]
tripunit@uwaterloo.ca

[§]Electrical and Computer Engineering
University of Waterloo, Canada

ABSTRACT

We emphasize the need to articulate precise, declarative properties in the context of securing Digital ICs. We do this by discussing two pieces of our work on securing Digital ICs. In one, we discuss a seemingly compelling approach to protecting Intellectual Property — IC camouflaging. We demonstrate that an adversary can carry out a decamouflaging attack, in practice, much more efficiently than previously thought. Underlying our attack is strong foundations: an identification of the computational-complexity of the problems an attacker faces, and how they can be addressed using off-the-shelf constraint solvers. We identify the lack of a precise characterization of 'security' in this context as an issue. In the other piece of work, we present an example of the articulation of such a security property for 3D IC technology, in the context of securing a supply-chain. The property is articulated declaratively, with explicit assumptions that underlie the threat model.

Keywords

Declarative properties, Computational complexity

1. INTRODUCTION

The security of digital ICs is recognized as an important topic in research and practice. There is considerable work both on threat and attack models and on mechanisms, or countermeasures, to achieve security. Our work addresses what we see as an important gap that often seems to exist in research on the security of digital ICs. The gap is a clear articulation of the security-objective that a defence-mechanism seeks to meet. We point out that such a security-objective must certainly reconcile the underlying threat and attack models that are adopted. In addition, once a property is articulated clearly in a given context, one must then convincingly establish that a mechanism achieves the property. It all is rooted, however, in the property. We argue that a *declarative* articulation of the property is important for clarity. What we mean by declarative, is an assertion with which one is able to associate a truth-value, i.e., 'true,' or 'false.'

Permission to make digital or hard copies of all or part of this work for personal or classroom use is granted without fee provided that copies are not made or distributed for profit or commercial advantage and that copies bear this notice and the full citation on the first page. Copyrights for components of this work owned by others than the author(s) must be honored. Abstracting with credit is permitted. To copy otherwise, or republish, to post on servers or to redistribute to lists, requires prior specific permission and/or a fee. Request permissions from permissions@acm.org.

GLSVLSI '17, May 10 - 12, 2017, Banff, AB, Canada

© 2017 Copyright held by the owner/author(s). Publication rights licensed to ACM.

ISBN 978-1-4503-4972-7/17/05...$15.00

DOI: http://dx.doi.org/10.1145/3060403.3066870

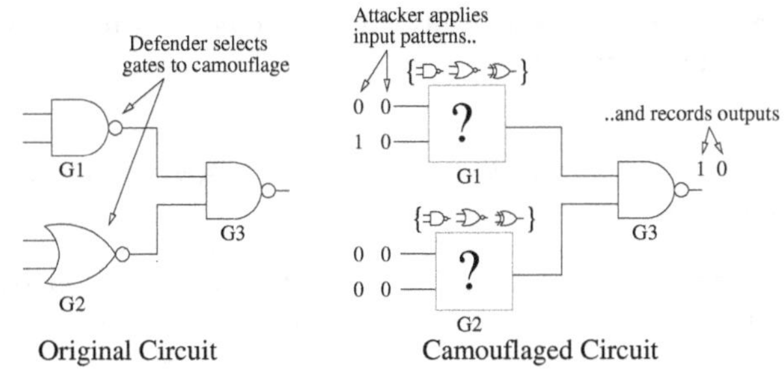

Figure 1: Overview of IC camouflaging via an example from prior work [Rajendran et al. 2013]. The defender (the IC designer) selects gates to camouflage. The attacker does not know the identity of the camouflaged gates, but can apply inputs and record outputs to decamouflage the circuit.

In this paper, we consider two pieces of our work with an emphasis on the points we make above. We first consider a seemingly compelling security-mechanism that has been proposed to protect Intellectual Property (IP) that is contained in a digital IC, which can be susceptible to compromise from a class of attacks called reverse-engineering. The mechanism is called IC camouflaging [Rajendran et al. 2013], and it works as follows. In Figure 1, we show an example of a circuit, the manner in which it would be camouflaged.

With the ability to camouflage individual gates, and the underlying assumption that an attacker can do no better than "brute-force" such a camouflaged gate to discover as what gate it behaves in operation, a question arises as to which gates in an IC one must camouflage to protect the IC. Underlying the question is a natural trade-off: every gate that is camouflaged introduces an increased area- and power-overhead on the functionining of the IC. Consequently, the defender seeks to camouflage as few gates as possible, yet achieve sufficient security. This trade-off, then, emphasizes the need for us to articulate a clear notion of the security we gain from camouflaging a particular set of gates in an IC.

As we discuss in Section 2, a lack of such a clear notion has enabled us to undermine an approach to choosing gates to camouflage in a rather devastating way. Whereas prior work asserts that it would take an attacker "thousands of

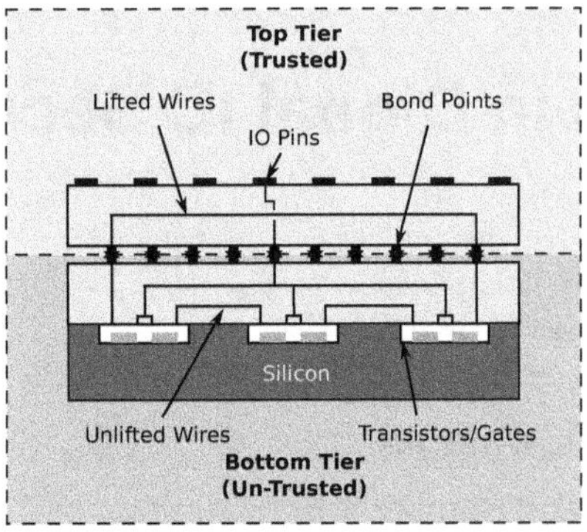

Figure 2: A two tier 3D IC. In this instance, the top tier is an interposer, i.e., it only implements metal wires, while the bottom tier has both transistors/gates and wires.

years" to break security for benchmark ICs, we demonstrate that it can be done in minutes.

The second piece of work we discuss regards a particular mechanism, called 3D IC technology, with which one can vertically stack two or more ICs [Davis et al. 2005]. In Figure 2, we show a two-tier 3D IC. 3D IC technology was originally conceived for properties other than security; for example, to achieve tighter packing of logic gates [Banerjee et al. 2001]. Prior to our work, its potential use for security was recognized, for example, by Tezarron [TZ0 2008]. However, it was unclear to what threat scenario the security pertained, and exactly what security was achieved.

Our work resolves these issues [Imeson et al. 2013]. We first clarify a threat model, under which an attacker inserts malicious circuitry in to an IC at a foundry. This threat is exacerbated by the outsourcing of IC fabrication to potentially untrusted parties, which is increasingly the norm. Under this threat model, we propose a precise, quantitative notion of security. Our notion is unconditional — if, in a particular setting, we say that we provide security of k, where k is an integer, an attacker is able to reconstruct the circuit with probability at most $1/k$. Thus, with the premise that an attacker must reconstruct the circuit to successfully attack it (insert malicious circuitry as she intends), we get clarity on what exactly the security that is provided is.

Layout The remainder of the paper is organized as follows. In the next section, we discuss our work on decamouflaging camouflaged ICs. In Section 3, we discuss our work on a notion of security for 3D IC technology. We conclude with Section 4 with discussions of the previous two sections as they relate to the theme of this paper: the need to articulate precise, declarative security properties that a mechanism seeks to achieve.

2. IC DECAMOUFLAGING

With increasing IC design costs, intellectual property (IP) infringement — ranging from counterfeiting to theft of core technologies and trade secrets — has become a significant concern for semiconductor design companies. One of the major threats arises from reverse engineering an IC, or a targeted module in the IC [Chipworks 2014, Degate 2014] — fully identifying its functionality by stripping it layer-by-layer (delayering) and extracting the underlying gate-level netlist.

To protect against the threat of reverse engineering, a technique called IC camouflaging has recently been proposed and developed [Rajendran et al. 2013, SypherMedia 2014]. The idea behind camouflaging is the following. In any IC, each logic gate is one of a set of gate-types, for example, XOR, NAND or NOR. A camouflaged gate is one whose gate-type cannot be determined by reverse engineering. That is, from the standpoint of an attacker that carries out reverse engineering, the gate may be any one of the possible gate-types. When inputs are applied, however, a camouflaged gate still performs the function as intended by the designer, for example, XOR, to produce the correct output. Rajendran et al. [Rajendran et al. 2013] provide an excellent description as to how a gate can be camouflaged in practice. IC camouflaging technology has been adopted commercially [AG 2014].

Figure 1 shows an example from prior work [Rajendran et al. 2013] of a net-list with three logic gates, two of which are camouflaged. An attacker who wishes to decamouflage a circuit, i.e., determine the Boolean functionality (or identity) of the camouflaged gates, does so by applying input patterns and generating the corresponding output pattern. An input pattern is a bit-string that assigns a boolean value to each input pin of a circuit. The attacker then analyzes these pairs of input-output patterns to determine the identities of camouflaged gates.

Under the premise that such camouflaging provides security, a defender camouflages as many gates as she can. However, camouflaged gates use more area, consume more power and are slower than gates that are not camouflaged. That is, camouflaging comes at a cost to the defender. This sets up a cost-security trade-off from the perspective of the defender, i.e., the defender can obtain greater security at the expense of increased circuit area, delay and power.

One of the main contributions of prior work [Rajendran et al. 2013] is that this cost-security trade-off can be made to heavily favor the defender by choosing the gates to be camouflaged judiciously. For instance, given an attacker that can exercise a billion inputs a second and a benchmark circuit of more than 2400 gates, there exists a set of only 63 gates (only 2.6% of the gates in the circuit) that if camouflaged, would take the attacker "several thousands of years" to identify [Rajendran et al. 2013]. The work proposes a technique, that they call "largest clique," to discover such small sets of gates so the cost of camouflaging is low, but the difficulty for the attacker is exponential in the number of camouflaged gates.

In our work, we re-examine the assertions of prior work [Rajendran et al. 2013, SypherMedia 2014] for realistic benchmark circuits. For those circuits, such work suggests that by camouflaging only a small, appropriately selected, set of gates, "...the attacker is forced to do brute force," which, as we mention above, for an attacker that is able to exercise the circuit with a billion input patterns a second, translates to "several thousands of years" [Rajendran et al. 2013].

Counter to such results, we have discovered that with the same number of gates chosen in the same manner as that work proposes for camouflaging, an attacker can find a correct completion (i.e., decamouflage the circuit) in only a few minutes, and not thousands of years. We have devised and implemented a new attack procedure for this, which we dis-

Table 1: Benchmark characteristics, and the number of camouflaged gates per circuit used to compare our attack against the brute force attack from prior work [Rajendran et al. 2013].

B'mark	Inputs	Outputs	Gates	Camouflaged
c5315	178	123	2406	63
c7552	207	108	3512	65
s5378	35	49	2779	56
s9234	19	22	5597	79
s38584	38	304	19234	128

cuss under "IC Decamouflaging: our attack," below.

2.1 Results

We first present some of our results. We have implemented our decamouflaging algorithm using C++ in ≈ 1400 lines of code, and use MiniSAT [Eén and Sörensson 2004] as the back-end SAT solver. All experiments were executed on a dual-core 2.8 GHz laptop with 6 GB of RAM and 750 GB disk space. We leave the resource limits of MiniSAT at their default values (68 years for the CPU time limit and ≈ 2147 TB for the memory usage limit). The camouflaged gates that we use, like the ones commercially available from Syphermedia [SypherMedia 2014], implement one of the three Boolean functions, {XOR, NAND, and NOR}. We have assessed the strength of our attack against two techniques for selecting gates for camouflaging: (1) the largest clique technique [Rajendran et al. 2013], and, (2) random selection, in which the camouflaged gates are picked uniformly at random. As benchmarks, we use circuits from the widely-used ISCAS'85 [Brglez 1985] and ISCAS'89 [Brglez et al. 1989] combinational and sequential benchmark suites for which canonical gate-level level netlists are publicly available. Our focus here is on larger benchmarks (c5315, c7552, s5378, s9234, s38584) — s38584 is the largest benchmark circuit across the two benchmark suites — with between 2400-19000 gates and a wide range of functionalities. c7552 for example contains a 34-bit adder, a 34-bit magnitude comparator using another 34-bit adder, and a parity checker. s9235 and s38584 are sequential circuits derived from industrial test-chips.

Table 1 provides details of the benchmark circuits, and shows the number of camouflaged gates per circuit.

Our Attack Vs. Brute Force Attack Our first goal is to demonstrate that our attack procedure effectively decamouflages circuits that are camouflaged using the largest clique technique. In this experiment, we camouflaged the same number of gates as in prior work. These numbers are shown in the last column of Table 1. We chose the gates to be camouflaged using both largest clique and randomly.

Figure 3 shows the time taken to decamouflage the five large benchmark circuits using our attack and the estimates of how long a brute force attack would take as reported in prior work [Rajendran et al. 2013]. Our attack is always able to successfully decamouflage circuits regardless of whether largest clique or random camouflaging is used. In all instances, our attack succeeded in less than about 40 minutes. This is in stark contrast to the estimates for a brute force attack, which range from 10^{10} to 10^{41} years. In addition, the largest clique camouflaging technique seems to offer no

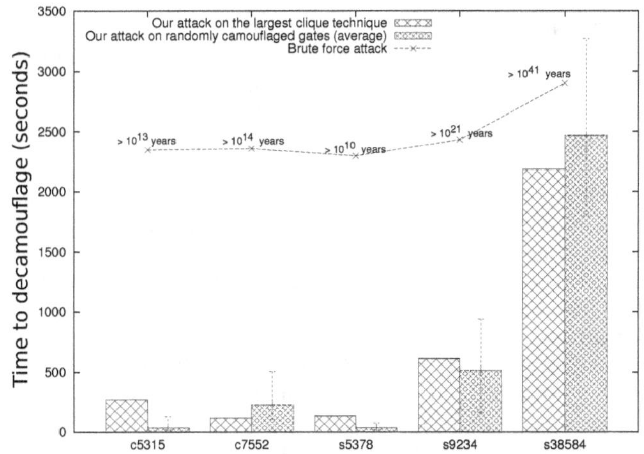

Figure 3: Time to decamouflage (in seconds) using our attack on large benchmark circuits camouflaged using (a) the largest-clique technique, and (b) random selection of camouflaged gates (average, max, min). Also shown is the estimated time it would take (in years) for a brute force attack to succeed when largest-clique camouflaging is used.

more security than random camouflaging from the standpoint of our attack. For two of the five benchmarks (c7552 and c38584), the average time to decamouflage randomly camouflaged circuits is greater than the time taken when largest clique camouflaging is used.

2.2 IC Decamouflaging: our attack

How have we been able to realize such a powerful attack? The answer to this question relates exactly to the theme of this paper. We ask, precisely, from a complexity-theoretic standpoint, what the difficulty for an attacker is to decamouflage a circuit. The answer to this question, in turn, suggests the attack procedure that we have designed and implemented. We examine problems that underlie two basic questions: (1) Is a given set of input patterns, I, a discriminating set for a camouflaged circuit C? (2) If the set I is indeed discriminating, what is a correct assignment of boolean functionalities (or identities) for each camouflaged gate in C? By iteratively calling a solver for the problem that corresponds to (1), we are able to obtain a discriminating input set. We then call a solver for the problem that corresponds to (2) to decamouflage C.

Our solvers for the two problems (1) and (2) above are based on the observation that the decision version of problem (1) is in co-**NP**, and that of problem (2) is in **NP**. **NP** is the class of decision problems that can be solved efficiently using a non-deterministic Turing machine; a decision problem is in co-**NP** if its complement is in **NP** [Arora and Barak 2009]. Thus, there exist efficient reductions from the complement of problem (1) and from problem (2) to CNF-SAT, the problem of determining whether a boolean formula in conjunctive normal form is satisfiable. Via the reductions, we can leverage off-the-shelf SAT solvers [Massad et al. 2015].

3. 3D IC TECHNOLOGY FOR SECURITY

The security of digital ICs can be compromised by covertly inserted malicious circuits. The threat from such maliciously inserted hardware is of increasing concern to government and military agencies [Adee 2008] and commercial semiconductor vendors. Skorobogatov et al. [Skorobogatov and Woods 2012], for example, has demonstrated the presence of a backdoor in a military grade FPGA manufactured by Actel that enabled access to configuration data on the chip.

The threat of maliciously inserted hardware arises from two factors. First, owing to their complexity, digital ICs are designed at sites across the world. In addition, parts of the design are often outsourced or purchased from external vendors. Second, a majority of semiconductor design companies are fabless, i.e., they outsource IC manufacturing to a potentially untrusted external fabrication facility (or foundry). Both factors make it easier for a malicious attacker in a design team or a malicious foundry (or a collusion between the two) to insert covert circuitry in a digital IC.

Three-dimensional (3D) integration, an emerging IC manufacturing technology, has been touted as a promising technique to enhance the security of computer hardware. A 3D IC consists of two or more independently manufactured ICs that are vertically stacked on top of each other — each IC in the stack is referred to as a *tier*. Interconnections between the tiers are accomplished using vertical metal pillars referred to as Through-Silicon Vias (TSV).

Tezarron, a leading commercial provider of 3D stacking capabilities, has alluded to the enhanced security offered by 3D integration in a white paper [TZ0 2008]. The white paper notes that "A multi-layer circuit may be divided among the layers in such a way that the function of each layer becomes obscure. Assuming that the TSV connections are extremely fine and abundant, elements can be scattered among the layers in apparently random fashion." However, the paper does not provide any formal notion of security for split manufacturing, nor does it propose techniques to quantify security or achieve a certain security level. These are the open challenges that we address in this paper.

Our threat model assumes a malicious attacker in an IC foundry who wants to modify the functionality of a digital IC in a specific, targeted manner. Examples of such attacks are those proposed by King et al. [King et al. 2008], and a fault-injection attack on DES [Boneh et al. 1997].

To effect a targeted attack, an attacker must first identify specific logic gates or wires in the circuit that implement the functionality that he wants to monitor and/or modify; for example, the gate or wire that corresponds to the privilege bit for the privilege escalation attack proposed in [King et al. 2008]. A malicious foundry can identify the functionality of every gate and wire in the circuit if it gets to fabricate the entire chip, i.e., if a conventional planar, 2D fabrication process is used. On the other hand, as we show in this paper, 3D integration significantly reduces the ability of an attacker in a malicious foundry to correctly identify gates or wires in the circuit that he wants to attack.

3.1 Security Property: k-security

Towards formulating our quantitative notion of security, which we call k-security, we first formulate the circuit obfuscation problem as a problem in the context of directed graphs. We explain via an example of a full adder that we show in Figure 4.

In the most powerful attack model we consider [Imeson et al. 2013], an attacker is in possession of two pieces of information: the originally designed (complete) circuit netlist,

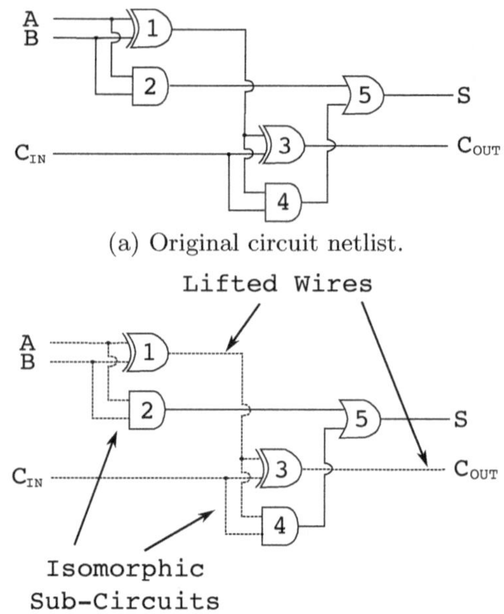

(b) Unlifted netlist.

Figure 4: Original and unlifted netlists corresponding to a full adder circuit. Grey wires in the unlifted netlist are lifted and are not observed by the attacker.

and the layout of the circuit that is sent to the foundry for fabrication, which we call the unlifted netlist. The latter results from the defender lifting wires from the former. Assume that the defender chooses to lift the wires $A \to \{1, 2\}$, $B \to \{1, 2\}$, $\mathsf{C_{IN}} \to \{3, 4\}$, $1 \to \{3, 4\}$ and $3 \to \mathsf{C_{OUT}}$.

Note that gates in the unlifted netlist in Figure 4(b) are labeled differently from those in the original circuit in Figure 4(a). This reflects the fact that the attacker obtains the original circuit netlist and the unlifted netlist in completely different formats. The original netlist is a set of gates and wires in HDL format. On the other hand, the unlifted netlist is reconstructed from the circuit layout, which is a set of shapes and their locations on the surface of the chip. The labeling and ordering of objects in the circuit layout file is unrelated to that in the netlist of the original circuit. Although not required, the defender can perform an additional random re-labeling and re-ordering step before the layout of H is sent to the foundry.

Given these two pieces of information, the attacker now seeks a bijective mapping of gates in the unlifted netlist to gates in the complete circuit netlist. If the attacker is successful in obtaining the correct mapping, he can carry out a targeted attack on any gate (or gates) of his choosing. The security obtained from lifting wires in the context of this example can be explained as follows. From the attacker's perspective, either Gate u or Gate w in the unlifted netlist could correspond to Gate 1 in the original netlist. Thus the attacker's ability to carry out a targeted attack on Gate 1 is hindered. The same can be said for the attacker's ability to carry out a targeted attack on Gate 2, 3 or 4. However, note that the attacker can determine the identity of Gate 5 with certainty — it must correspond to Gate y since this is the only OR gate in the netlist. Thus, in this example, the lifting does not provide any security for Gate 5.

Informally, our notion of security is based on the existence of multiple isomorphisms (mappings) between gates in the unlifted netlist and the original netlist. In our example, there exist 4 distinct bijective mappings between the gates in the unlifted and original netlists. However, this notion of security may be seen as too permissive. It can be argued that given the fact that across all mappings, gate 5 is mapped uniquely, we have no security at all (i.e., security of 1). A more restrictive notion of security, one that we adopt, requires that for *each* gate in the original netlist, there exist at least k different gates in the unlifted netlist that map to it over all isomorphisms. This is intended to capture the intuition that the attacker is unable to uniquely identify even a single gate.

Circuit obfuscation as a graph problem We now formulate our problem as a graph problem. A circuit can be perceived as a directed graph — gates are vertices, and wires are edges. The direction of an edge into or out of a vertex indicates whether it is an input or output wire to the gate that corresponds to the vertex. If G is a graph, we denote its set of vertices as $V[G]$, and its set of edges as $E[G]$. Each vertex in the graph is associated with a color that is used to distinguish types of gates (e.g, AND and OR) from one another. Consequently, a graph G is a 3-tuple, $\langle V, E, c\rangle$, where V is the set of vertices, E the set of edges and the function $c\colon V \to \mathbb{N}$ maps each vertex to a natural number that denotes its color. For example, the circuit in Figure 4 and its unlifted portion can be represented by the graphs in Figure 5.

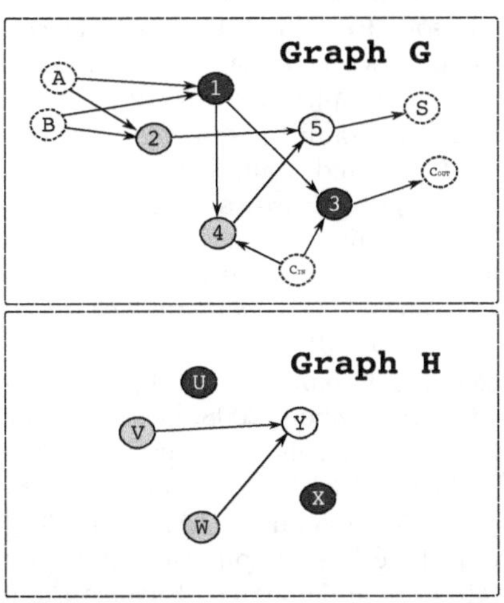

Figure 5: Full adder graphs: G is the full graph representation of the full adder circuit, H is the remaining graph after wires have been lifted.

A main challenge for the defender is to lift wires in a way that provides security. Our notion of security corresponds to a certain kind of subgraph isomorphism — given two graphs, G_1, G_2, where there exists a subgraph of G_1 that is isomorphic to G_2, i.e., has a bijective mapping between vertices under which the edges are preserved [Gary and Johnson 1979]. For example, in Figure 5, a subgraph isomorphism, ϕ, is $\phi(1) = U, \phi(2) = V, \phi(3) = X, \phi(4) = W, \phi(5) = Y$.

Intuition Let G be the graph that represents the original circuit with all wires, and H the graph of the circuit after wires have been lifted. Then, the attacker knows that G is subgraph isomorphic to H. What he seeks is the correct mapping of vertices in G to H (or vice versa). This is equivalent to him having reconstructed the circuit, and now, he can effect his malicious modifications to the circuit that corresponds to H.

From the defender's standpoint, therefore, what we seek intuitively is that there be several subgraph isomorphisms between G and H. This then gives a kind of security — the attacker cannot be sure which of the mappings is the correct one, and the number of possible mappings that are indistinguishable from one another is a measure of security.

k-security We now specify our notion of security. We do this in three stages. (1) We first define a problem that captures our intuition of a gate being indistinguishable from another gate. We do this by requiring the existence of a particular kind of subisomorphic mapping between graphs that represent circuits. (2) We then define the notion of a k-secure gate. Such a gate is indistinguishable from at least $k-1$ other gates in the circuit. (3) Finally, we define the notion of k-security, which is security across all gates in the circuit. This definition requires simply that every gate in the circuit is k-secure.

In the following definition, we characterize the problem GATE-SUBISO, which captures (1) above — a notion of what it means for a gate to be indistinguishable from another.

DEFINITION 1 (GATE-SUBISO). *Given as input $\langle G, E', u, v\rangle$, where G is a Directed Acyclic Graph (DAG), $E' \subseteq E[G]$, and two distinct vertices $u, v \in V[G]$, let H be the graph we get by removing the edges that are in E' from G. Then, GATE-SUBISO is the problem of determining whether there exists a mapping $\phi\colon V[G] \to V[H]$ that is a subgraph isomorphism from G to H such that $\phi(u) = v$.*

The above definition is a special case of the well-known subgraph isomorphism problem [Gary and Johnson 1979]. The intuition behind GATE-SUBISO is the following. G is the graph that corresponds to the original circuit, and H is the graph that corresponds to the circuit after wires are lifted. The above definition for GATE-SUBISO asks whether there exists a mapping under which the vertex u in the original circuit is indistinguishable from v in the unlifted circuit. That is, given that $u \neq v$, an attacker does not know whether u in G corresponds to u or v in H.

DEFINITION 2 (k-SECURE GATE). *Given a DAG, G, a vertex $u \in V[G]$, and a subgraph H of G constructed from G by removing some edges, $E' \subseteq E[G]$ only. We say that u is k-secure if there exist k distinct vertices $v_1, \ldots, v_k$ in G (and therefore in H), and mappings $\phi_1, \ldots, \phi_k$ from $V[G]$ to $V[H]$ such that every ϕ_i is a subgraph isomorphism from G to H, and for all $i \in [1, k]$, $\phi_i(u) = v_i$.*

The above definition expresses that u is indistinguishable from each of the v_i's. Of course, one of the v_i's may be u itself. Therefore, every gate is 1-secure, and if a gate is not 2-secure, then that gate is uniquely identifiable, for this particular choice of E'. The maximum that k can be is $|V[G]|$, the number of a vertices in G.

DEFINITION 3 (k-SECURITY). *Given a DAG G, and a DAG H that we get from G by removing the edges from a set $E' \subseteq E[G]$. We say that $\langle G, E'\rangle$ is k-secure if every vertex in G is k-secure.*

The above definition is a natural extension of the notion of a k-secure gate, to every gate in the circuit. What it requires for k-security is that every vertex in the corresponding graph is indistinguishable from at least k vertices. We point out that some gates may be more than k-secure; k-security is a minimum across all gates. A graph can be, at best, $|V[G]|$-secure. Every graph is 1-secure. In Figure 5, for example, we know that k is 1, because the node 5 can be mapped to itself only. The nodes 1, 2, 3 and 4, however, are 2-secure gates. The reason is that each can be mapped either to itself, or to another node.

The work of Imeson et al. [Imeson et al. 2013] expands on the work we discuss in this section in several ways. For example, it proposes an algorithm for identifying the wires that should be lifted to achieve a certain level of security. It studies also the application of that algorithm to a benchmark circuit. The work also discusses how a DES circuit can be protected from the kind of fault-injection attacks we discuss earlier in this section.

4. CONCLUSION

Our paper is a call for precise security properties in the context of digital ICs. We propose that such properties be articulated declaratively. Towards this, in Section 2, we have discussed a successful attack against a seemingly compelling security mechanism, IC camouflaging. We point out that a fundamental issue there is that no precise security property was associated with camouflaging. What is worse, given our attack, it is unclear that any meaningful notion of 'secure' exists for camouflaging, notwithstanding the fact that the technique appears to be compelling. Futher work along these lines can be seen as viable future work.

In Section 3, we show an example of articulating such a property: we propose a precise, quantitative, unconditional notion of 'secure' that we gain by judiciously using 3D IC technology. The specific approach on which we focus is to lift wires to a metal-only tier, which is fabricated at a trusted facility. For such an approach, we are able to clearly articulate a security property that we call k-security, where the integer k indicates, the strength of security we achieve. As future work, we point out that other mechanisms, such as logic locking [Roy et al. 2010], remain wanting of such precise, declarative security properties.

5. REFERENCES

[TZ0 2008] 2008. *3D-ICs and Integrated Circuit Security.* Technical Report. Tezzarron Semiconductors.

[Adee 2008] S. Adee. 2008. The Hunt For The Kill Switch. *IEEE Spectrum* 45, 5 (may 2008), 34 –39.

[AG 2014] Infineon Technologies AG. 2014. Semiconductor & System Solutions - Infineon Technologies. (August 2014). http://www.infineon.com/

[Arora and Barak 2009] S. Arora and B. Barak. 2009. *Computational Complexity: A Modern Approach.* Cambridge University Press.

[Banerjee et al. 2001] Kaustav Banerjee, Shukri J Souri, Pawan Kapur, and Krishna C Saraswat. 2001. 3-D ICs: A novel chip design for improving deep-submicrometer interconnect performance and systems-on-chip integration. *Proc. IEEE* 89, 5 (2001), 602–633.

[Boneh et al. 1997] Dan Boneh, Richard DeMillo, and Richard Lipton. 1997. On the importance of checking cryptographic protocols for faults. In *Advances in Cryptology - EUROCRYPT.* Springer, 37–51.

[Brglez 1985] F. Brglez. 1985. Neutral netlist of ten combinational benchmark circuits and a target translator in FORTRAN. In *Proc. IEEE Intl. Symp. Circuits and Systems, June 1985.* 663–698.

[Brglez et al. 1989] Franc Brglez, David Bryan, and Krzysztof Kozminski. 1989. Combinational profiles of sequential benchmark circuits. In *Proc. IEEE Intl. Symp. Circuits and Systems, 1989.* 1929–1934.

[Chipworks 2014] Chipworks. 2014. Reverse Engineering Software. http://www.chipworks.com/en/technical-competitive-analysis/resources/reerse-engineering-software. (2014). May 2014.

[Davis et al. 2005] W Rhett Davis, John Wilson, Stephen Mick, Jian Xu, Hao Hua, Christopher Mineo, Ambarish M Sule, Michael Steer, and Paul D Franzon. 2005. Demystifying 3D ICs: the pros and cons of going vertical. *Design & Test of Computers, IEEE* 22, 6 (2005), 498–510.

[Degate 2014] Degate. 2014. Reverse engineering integrated circuits. http://www.degate.org/documentation/. (2014). May 2014.

[Eén and Sörensson 2004] Niklas Eén and Niklas Sörensson. 2004. An Extensible SAT-solver. In *Theory and Applications of Satisfiability Testing*, Enrico Giunchiglia and Armando Tacchella (Eds.). Lecture Notes in Computer Science, Vol. 2919. Springer Berlin Heidelberg, 502–518. DOI: http://dx.doi.org/10.1007/978-3-540-24605-3_37

[Gary and Johnson 1979] M.R. Gary and D.S. Johnson. 1979. Computers and Intractability: A Guide to the Theory of NP-completeness. (1979).

[Imeson et al. 2013] Frank Imeson, Ariq Emtenan, Siddharth Garg, and Mahesh V. Tripunitara. 2013. Securing Computer Hardware Using 3D Integrated Circuit (IC) Technology and Split Manufacturing for Obfuscation. In *Proceedings of the 22th USENIX Security Symposium, Washington, DC, USA, August 14-16, 2013.* 495–510.

[King et al. 2008] S.T. King, J. Tucek, A. Cozzie, C. Grier, W. Jiang, and Y. Zhou. 2008. Designing and implementing malicious hardware. In *Proceedings of USENIX LEET.* USENIX Association, 1–8.

[Massad et al. 2015] Mohamed El Massad, Siddharth Garg, and Mahesh V. Tripunitara. 2015. Integrated Circuit (IC) Decamouflaging: Reverse Engineering Camouflaged ICs within Minutes. In *22nd NDSS 2015.*

[Rajendran et al. 2013] Jeyavijayan Rajendran, Michael Sam, Ozgur Sinanoglu, and Ramesh Karri. 2013. Security Analysis of Integrated Circuit Camouflaging. In *Proceedings of ACM CCS.* 709–720.

[Roy et al. 2010] Jarrod A. Roy, Farinaz Koushanfar, and Igor L. Markov. 2010. Ending Piracy of Integrated Circuits. *IEEE Computer* 43, 10 (2010), 30–38. DOI: http://dx.doi.org/10.1109/MC.2010.284

[Skorobogatov and Woods 2012] S. Skorobogatov and C. Woods. 2012. Breakthrough silicon scanning discovers backdoor in military chip. *CHES* (2012), 23–40.

[SypherMedia 2014] SypherMedia. 2014. Syphermedia library circuit camouflage technology. http://www.smi.tv/solutions.htm. (2014).

Securing Split Manufactured ICs with Wire Lifting Obfuscated Built-In Self-Authentication*

Qihang Shi[1], Kan Xiao[2], Domenic Forte[3], Mark M. Tehranipoor[3]
[1]ECE Department, University of Connecticut, Storrs, Connecticut
[2]Intel Corporation, Santa Clara, California
[3]ECE Department, University of Florida, Gainesville, Florida
qihang.shi@engr.uconn.edu, kan.xiao@intel.com, {dforte, tehranipoor}@ece.ufl.edu

ABSTRACT

Hardware Trojan insertion and intellectual property (IP) theft are two major concerns when dealing with untrusted foundries. Most existing mitigation techniques are limited in protecting against both vulnerabilities. Split manufacturing is designed to stop IP piracy and IC cloning, but it fails at preventing untargeted hardware Trojan insertion and incurs significant overheads when high level of security is demanded. Built-in self-authentication (BISA) is a low cost technique for preventing and detecting hardware Trojan insertion, but is vulnerable to IP piracy, IC cloning or redesign attacks, especially on original circuitry. In this paper, we propose an obfuscated built-in self-authentication (OBISA) technique that combines and optimizes both technique so that they complement and improve security against both vulnerabilities. Performance of the proposed OBISA technique is presented with experimental implementation on same benchmark circuits as used in the existing wire lifting technique. The security performance is evaluated with the most popular split manufacturing security metrics.

1. INTRODUCTION

Changing economic trends have resulted in a globalized IC supply chain. It is no longer economically feasible for most IC producers to own foundries and fabricate ICs in-house. For the great majority of the industry, fabrication is now being performed by contracted foundries and outside the direct control of original intellectual property (IP) owners. IP owners enjoy reduced cost and state-of-art fabrication technologies in off-shore fabrication, at the cost of reduced control and therefore reduced trust on the manufacturing process. This has raised serious concerns about whether trust between an IP owner and such fabs can be established [4]. An untrusted foundry could conduct a number of attacks including IP piracy [12], IC cloning and overproduction [3,5],

** This work is part of a Cisco funded research project *An Integrative Approach to Secure IC Design through Obfuscation and Authentication.*

Permission to make digital or hard copies of all or part of this work for personal or classroom use is granted without fee provided that copies are not made or distributed for profit or commercial advantage and that copies bear this notice and the full citation on the first page. Copyrights for components of this work owned by others than ACM must be honored. Abstracting with credit is permitted. To copy otherwise, or republish, to post on servers or to redistribute to lists, requires prior specific permission and/or a fee. Request permissions from permissions@acm.org.

GLSVLSI May 10-12, 2017 Banff, AB, Canada
© 2017 ACM. ISBN 978-1-4503-4972-7/17/05...$15.00
DOI: http://dx.dli.org/10.1145/3060403.3060588

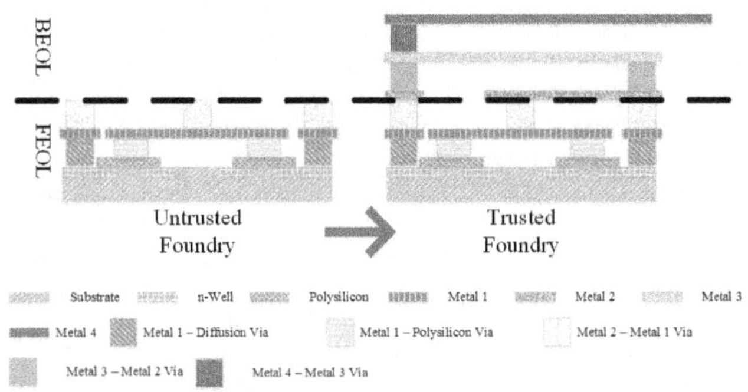

Figure 1: Typical split manufacturing arrangement (shown arrangement assumes split made between Metal-2 and Metal-1 layers).

and hardware Trojan insertion [13]. For off-shore fabrication to stay secure, capability of the IP owner to prevent such attacks must be thoroughly proven.

Split manufacturing has been proposed [1] to address the threat of IP piracy, cloning, and overproduction. This technique proposes that an untrusted foundry manufactures the front-end-of-line (FEOL) part of the IC, and then ships it to a trusted foundry to deposit back-end-of-line (BEOL) part onto it (see example in Figure 1). By this arrangement, the untrusted foundry is denied complete information of the layout, and therefore prevented from stealing IP information, or committing attacks that require knowledge of the complete design.

This leaves hardware Trojan insertion to address. Techniques against hardware Trojan insertion exist in two categories characterized by how they address the issue: The first category focus on detecting Trojans, either by functional verification, side-channel signal analysis, or by new front-end design techniques such as design-for-trust [2, 8, 10]. Techniques in this category detect existence of hardware Trojans by generating a signature of the circuit under test (CUT), then classifying the CUT with this signature. To perform classification, they require a golden model, i.e. signature of a copy of the same circuit that is known to be free from hardware Trojans. Unfortunately, it remains doubtful whether golden models can be acquired for real world applications. In addition, process variations introduce errors in classification, especially for small, hard-to-detect Trojans. On the other hand, techniques focused on preventing hardware Trojans from being inserted do not have this requirement. Built-in self-authentication (BISA) is the first proposed technique to prevent hardware Trojan insertion in circuit layout and mask [14, 16]. By occupying all available spaces for Trojan insertion and detecting malicious removal through built-in self test, BISA is able to deter hardware Trojan insertion without the requirement of golden models and free from classification errors introduced by process variation.

Both split manufacturing and BISA are effective techniques in addressing the threat they are designed to counter. However, problems remain with both techniques. Techniques against IP piracy do not usually consider the threat of hardware Trojan insertion, and neither do techniques against hardware Trojan insertion (such as BISA) consider IP theft, despite both attacks sharing the same adversary.

In this paper, we propose a new approach to an earlier proposed [15] technique called Obfuscated Built-In Self-Authentication (OBISA) that combines both techniques.The proposed technique not only prevents weakness from either kind of attacks, but also improves security performance of either of its predecessors. Compared to the earlier technique, this alternative OBISA technique described here focuses on obtaining a reasonably high level of security defined under an objective metric.

Rest of the paper is organized as follows: Section 2 provides a brief introduction of BISA, a survey of existing research related to split manufacturing security and BISA, elaborates on weaknesses of known techniques and proposes ways to address these weaknesses using OBISA, before providing a detailed list of contributions claimed by the OBISA technique; Section 3 presents the proposed OBISA technique in terms of its application flow, how it integrates with existing back-end design flow, and how each claimed contribution is realized; Section 4 presents experimental evaluation of the proposed OBISA technique using benchmark circuits used by prior research to demonstrate its capability to meet all other published security metrics for split manufacturing in addition to the security metric it chooses to optimize; and finally, Section 5 concludes this paper.

2. BACKGROUND

2.1 Built-In Self-Authentication (BISA)

Built-In Self-Authentication (BISA) prevents hardware Trojan insertion by exhausting one resource essential to it: *white spaces*. Normally, during the placement step of the back-end design of the circuit, gates in the circuit are placed at optimized locations based on density and routability [17]. This leaves spaces in the layout that are not filled by standard cells. White spaces have to exist, because meeting power dissipation, cross-talk, as well as routing objectives demands it. For design purposes other than security against hardware Trojan insertion, these white spaces can be filled with *filler cells* to serve as decoupling capacitors and/or extension of power tracks. However, unsupervised filler cells are not monitored by any logic, and therefore prone to malicious removal by Trojan inserters in order to make room for hardware Trojans. If white spaces or decoupling filler cells are replaced by Trojan gates, it would likely incur a mild level of performance loss, nothing more, and certainly not raising suspicion of Trojan presence.

BISA prevents hardware Trojan insertion by occupying white spaces with testable standard cells instead. Then, all inserted BISA cells are connected into tree-like structures to form a built-in self test (BIST) circuitry, so that they could be tested to verify no BISA cell has been removed. The main advantage of BISA over other techniques with similar objectives is that it has no golden chip requirement. Most detection approaches need golden chips either fabricated by a trusted foundry or verified to be Trojan-free through reverse engineering, both of which are prohibitively expensive, if not impossible in many scenarios. Since BISA relies on logic testing, process variation is not a factor either, as compared to Trojan detection techniques based on side-channel analysis. As an additional advantage, impact of BISA on the original design in terms of area and power is also negligible.

2.2 Split Manufacturing Security and Limitations

2.2.1 *Prior works on split manufacturing security*

Most cited studies in the field [6, 7, 9] are motivated by one objective: to establish a sound metric of security for designs fabricated using various split manufacturing methods. Most researchers attack the problem from a layout point of view. Publications in this category often examine irregularities in the layout (also known as "hints" or "clues") and theorize how they can be used by a hypothetical attacker. Authors in [9] pioneered the idea of *proximity attack*, which simulates an attacker who makes educated guesses on BEOL connections of open input/output pins in FEOL. Another study [7] also uses layout information, but instead of performing hypothetical attacks, it seeks to define objective measures of the layout that might become useful to exploit. In contrast, another research [6] evaluates split manufacturing security based on graph connectivity of FEOL layout and seeks to define difficulty by solving for the dimensions of the solution space from which the attacker must pick one correct solution. The proposed metric operates on Directional Acyclic Graphs (DAG) abstracted from both the complete layout (G) and FEOL layout (H) (see Figure 2 for an example). In the resulting DAG, gates are abstracted into vertices (represented with colored circles in Figure 2, whose color represents models of each gate), and nets are abstracted into sets of directional edges, each of which corresponds to a driving gate/vertex and driven gate/vertex pair (represented with arrows in Figure 2). Then it computes the number of legal mappings that maps each gate u_i

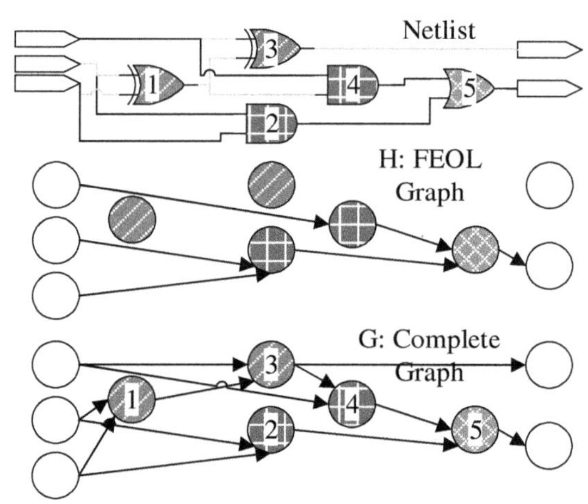

Figure 2: Principle of k-security applied on a full adder circuit as an example.

in complete layout graph G to a distinct gate v_j in FEOL layout graph H. This number k is defined as the security of that gate, and the security of the complete layout is defined as the lowest k of all gates. In the example shown in Figure 2, XOR gates have a security $k = 2$ but all other gates have $k = 1$, therefore the overall security of the circuit remains at $k = 1$. This security metric is often referred to using its letter of choice k as *k-security*. A greedy algorithm is then presented to find a minimal subset of wires in the layout to uplift to BEOL while satisfying minimum security k, an optimization of split manufacturing security also known as *wire lifting*. Compared to layout based approaches, k-security has the advantage of being based on matching layout gates to netlist gates itself, which makes it harder to circumvent; The definition of k-security is also mathematically sound, making it immune to invalidation or circumvention due to human error or change in design practice invalidating fundamental assumptions, for example possible unforeseen exploit and changed placement/routing optimizer rulesets.

Split manufacturing techniques prevent all attacks that require complete knowledge of the whole layout, which also include attacks against BISA such as identification of BISA cells. However, not all attacks require complete knowledge of the whole layout. One example is the untargeted Trojan insertion [15], a threat discussed in details in [11]. Untargeted hardware Trojans do not target specific functions of the original circuitry, and therefore cannot commit attacks that require knowledge of such functions. Nevertheless, untargeted hardware Trojans are still capable of degrading the performance and/or reliability of manufactured ICs, or trigger a denial-of-service (DoS) in critical control systems. This constitutes a threat that still needs to be addressed.

2.3 Motivation and Contributions

In light of respective limitations of BISA and split manufacturing techniques, it makes sense to combine them so that benefits of both techniques can be reaped. We henceforth term the combined technique obfuscated BISA (OBISA). The most apparent advantage of the resulting technique is the security against untargeted hardware Trojan insertion, as well as security against IP piracy and IC cloning, both of which are primary strengths of BISA and split manufacturing. Combining with split manufacturing can also make the resulting OBISA technique secure against redesign attack, since the attacker must first identify which existing cells are connected together before designing a functionally equivalent circuit to replace these existing cells. The obfuscation effect from split manufacturing can further enhance OBISA beyond protecting it against redesign attack. Combining with split manufacturing makes the threat of redesign attack by untrusted foundries much less of a problem due to security of BEOL information, and therefore reduces necessity of using detection based anti-Trojan techniques. Split manufacturing security in OBISA could also benefit from BISA insertion, owing to improved k-security by additional cells and FEOL interconnects BISA insertion introduces to the layout. Further, proximity attack based on FEOL-observable distribution of gates as well as distribution of white spaces could also be foiled by occupying white spaces and compensating spatial distribution of gate types with BISA cells. To summarize, a combined OBISA technique could derive advantages from both split manufacturing and BISA, as well as synergy of both techniques.

In a previous published work [15], an approach which assumes minimum computational cost is dedicated to split manufacturing (i.e., assume split manufacturing is simply implemented by separating FEOL from BEOL at a certain layer) was investigated. In this previous implementation of OBISA, obfuscation connections were added between OBISA circuits and functional circuits, and between OBISA tree-like structures, while optimization on wire lifting was kept to a minimum; In this paper, we propose to investigate the opposite scenario, where level of security is desired (i.e., wire lifting is optimized using k-security definition). In this implementation we dedicate as much computational cost as possible on improving split manufacturing security, so long as it remains applicable to industrial level of integration.

3. OBFUSCATED BISA VIA WIRE LIFTING

The proposed approach to implement OBISA is characterized by a major departure from its predecessor: it uses *wire lifting* as its principal strategy to ensure split manufacturing security. A naive implementation of this doctrine is to simply insert BISA cells, and then solve for the optimal wire lifting solution of the resulting netlist. Such an arrangement would allow most benefits we have theorized combining both techniques would ensue. However, it is not necessarily efficient, since it is also possible to modify BISA insertion to improve achievable security level of wire lifting. This is illustrated in an example using the same full adder circuit as was shown in Figure 2.

Consider the full adder as shown in Figure 2, and graph for its FEOL layout. It is apparently impossible to distinguish the two XOR gates (represented by vertices shaded in red slash) in FEOL layout. XOR gates in this full adder have a $k = 2$ security. If the same can be said for all other gate models, the FEOL layout would have $k = 2$ security. Unfortunately as we can see from the figure, it is impossible for the full adder to reach $k = 2$ no matter the lifting solution simply because it has only one OR gate. For this full adder, any further optimization of wire lifting solution will not improve its security.

An OBISA technique that performs wire lifting does not have to submit to this restriction, because the number of instances of rare gate models can be compensated by inserting OBISA cells. An example of this advantage is shown in Figure 3. In this example, OBISA cells and interconnects are added, shown in dashed lines. We can see from the example how the bottleneck in previous example - the single OR gate - is compensated with OBISA cells. In the shown wire lifting example, $k = 2$ security is reached; If we consider a more extreme solution, for example lifting all wires to BEOL, at maximum the layout could reach $k = 4$ security rating. OBISA insertion does not impact timing, because they are not connected electrically to the functional circuit. It does not impact dynamic power because it is not going to be active during the design's functional mode. This allows it to improve the wire lifting technique it uses.

3.1 Implementation Flow

The implementation flow of the proposed OBISA technique with regard to conventional layout design procedures is shown in Figure 4 and Figure 5. Boxes shaded with blue slashes represent procedures already present in BISA flow, while boxes shaded with red crosses represent new procedures in this approach. In order to manage the amount of computation needed for wire lifting, designs are first partitioned into hard macros (Figure 4). In this proposed tech-

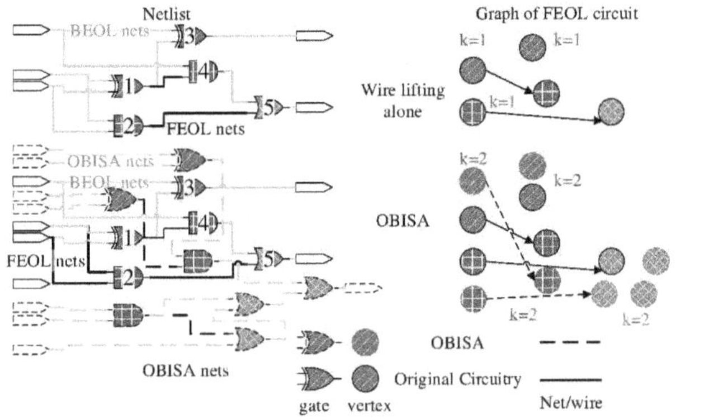

Figure 3: Example: Due to OBISA insertion, wire lifting optimization on the same full adder can achieve higher k-security rating..

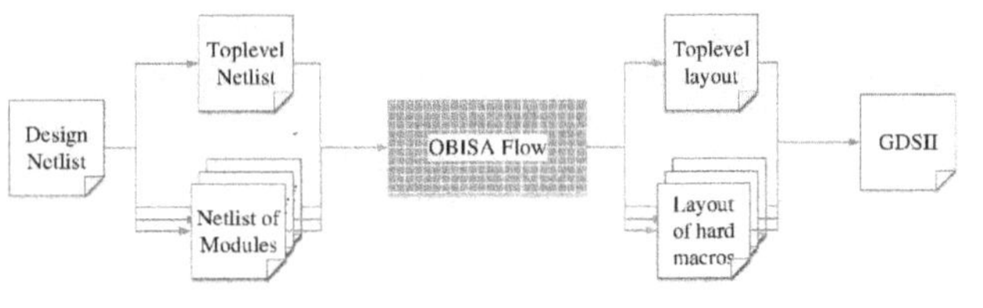

Figure 4: Dividing design into partitions, apply OBISA flow to each, then integrate into final GDSII.

nique, logic submodules are simply used as partitions; if recurring circuit subgraphs are discovered, this partition can be performed for each discovered subgraph. Steps taken to process each partition as well as the toplevel netlist is shown in Figure 5. The technique share steps with classic BISA but departs at BISA cell insertion: instead of performing optimized BISA cell placement using dynamic programming for lower resource consumption, our need for security requires cell model compensation as well as random placement for maximal obfuscation. Cells of the rare gate models are placed before others to compensate gate model distribution. The locations of these gates are chosen randomly to diminish possible leakage of information in FEOL layout; for the same purpose, remaining white spaces are filled with BISA cells with random gate models. This can be done with filler cell insertion function provided by the layout editor. This step uses all allowable standard cell models from the library to minimize entropy in standard cell model distribution and simplify BISA routing for the next stage. After that, classic BISA cell routing is performed. Before signal routing, an optimized wire lifting solution is found for the complete layout. This can be done by writing problem description files using information from the layout editor, then calling external solver tools to find the solution.

Actual wire lifting (i.e., placing lifted wires in BEOL and kept wires in FEOL) can then be performed with the help of layout-editor. In this proposed approach, we elevate all segments of chosen wires to BEOL to eliminate the opportunity to guess direction of dangling wire segments in FEOL, leaving only vias in the FEOL. In addition to hiding direction of dangling wires by eliminating dangling wires, this approach also allows insertion of dummy vias to pins in FEOL, which will effectively hide real BEOL wires among dummy vias to further obfuscate the FEOL layout against proximity and

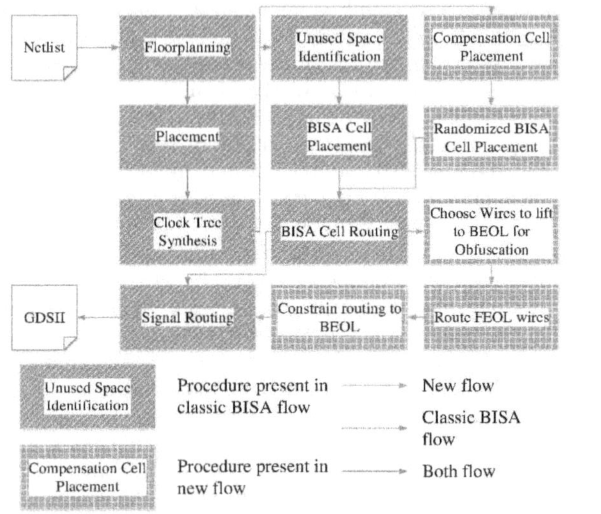

Figure 5: OBISA flow of each partition.

redesign attacks. This step is done by first routing chosen wires to be kept in FEOL by restricting routing layers to FEOL layers, then routing all other wires after restricting routing layers to BEOL layers. Dummy vias can then be added randomly.

4. EXPERIMENTAL EVALUATION

In this section we present experimental evaluation on the proposed technique. Results presented are collected using two benchmark circuits: Circuit432 from ISCAS'85 circuits, and DES core from www.opencores.org. Circuit432 is used to evaluate security performance and design overheads. The small size of this benchmark circuit poses a particular challenge to OBISA insertion, which is not enough white spaces are left when normal floorplanning density is used, forcing a trade-off between area overhead and restriction on number of standard cell models. To study this limitation, two netlists of Circuit432 benchmark circuits are synthesized: one where only three standard cell models are allowed, and one without such restriction [1]. DES core is used in demonstration of application on designs of large scale. For each synthesized netlist, three layout are created: *Ctrl* is the control group where neither OBISA insertion nor wire lifting is performed; *OBISA-Only* has OBISA cell occupying white spaces, but routed normally; *OBISA-Lifted* underwent both OBISA cell insertion and wire lifting. The presented results are collected using Synopsys IC Compiler and/or Design Compiler environment for the script. MiniSat, as was used in [6], is used as the boolean satisfiability problem (SAT) solver to determine existence of legal mapping between FEOL and complete graph used in greedy wire lifting algorithm.

4.1 Security Evaluation with Known Layout-based Metrics

In this sub-section we present evaluations of proposed method in terms of existing layout-based security metrics for split manufacturing techniques. We are presenting results taken with the following metrics: (i) Security against *proximity attack* is evaluated by a percentage of correct guess

[1]For Circuit432, not restricting standard cell models lead to 12 standard cells being used.

Table 1: Success rate of proximity attack on Circuit432.

Circuit432, 3 std-cells	Ctrl	OBISA	
		Only	Lifted
OBISA insertion	No	Yes	Yes
Lifted	No	No	Yes
Success	5.38%	1.99%	7.29%
#Cell	220	293	293
#OBISA cell	0	73	73
Open pins	93	184	686
Hit pairs	5	3	32
Circuit432, 12 std-cells	Ctrl	OBISA	
		Only	Lifted
OBISA insertion	No	Yes	Yes
Lifted	No	No	Yes
Success	0.00%	0.54%	0.00%
#Cell	115	309	309
#OBISA cell	0	194	194
Open pins	102	952	1320
Hit pairs	0	1	0
key_sel, DES core	Ctrl	OBISA	
		Only	Lifted
OBISA insertion	No	Yes	Yes
Lifted	No	No	Yes
Success	0.24%	0.04%	0.04%
#Cell	1608	3801	3801
#OBISA cell	0	2193	2193
Open pins	5461	13069	13069
Hit pairs	9	4	4

based on geometric proximity, as well as neighborhood connectedness ratio $C(R)$; (ii) Security against identification of functionality through *standard cell composition bias* is computed as defined in [7].

Security against proximity attack is studied by simulating a proximity attack on sample layouts and calculating percentage of correct guesses. Further, neighborhood connectedness ratio is plotted for a number of neighborhood radii. Layouts at various stages of implementation in the proposed OBISA flow were created to evaluate impact of each measure on success rate of proximity attack. In addition to Circuit432, *key_sel* module of DES core (to be elaborated in Section 4.2) is also shown as an example of effect on larger benchmarks. The results are shown in Table 1. A first impression from the results as shown in Table 1 is that the number of successful guesses for each layout can be rather stochastic. However, the number of open pins in FEOL does indeed become greatly improved by OBISA cell insertion as well as wire lifting. This is probably made more significant as larger k is requested - the lifted layout for 3-standard-cell-netlist is 46, much higher than $k = 10$ for the lifted layout of the 12-standard-cell-netlist. This is corroborated by the neighborhood connectedness ($C(R)$) plot shown in Figure 6. As can be seen from the figure, all $C(R)$ curves saturates as radii increases, but both OBISA insertion and wire lifting reduces the eventual saturated $C(R)$. As have been pointed out in [7], the lower the measure, the more "spread out" the circuit is, and less functional information is leaked, resulting in a more secure FEOL layout.

To evaluate *standard cell composition bias*, *key_sel* module and toplevel module of DES core are examined for its particular design characteristic. Being a control module, functional cells in both modules consists only of flip-flop and multiplexers. Thus, either unsecured module will be very weak in terms of Standard cell composition bias. This is compensated by inserting OBISA cells that are common in other modules of the same DES core. As shown in Table 2, standard cell composition bias of both modules decreased more than 50% after OBISA insertion.

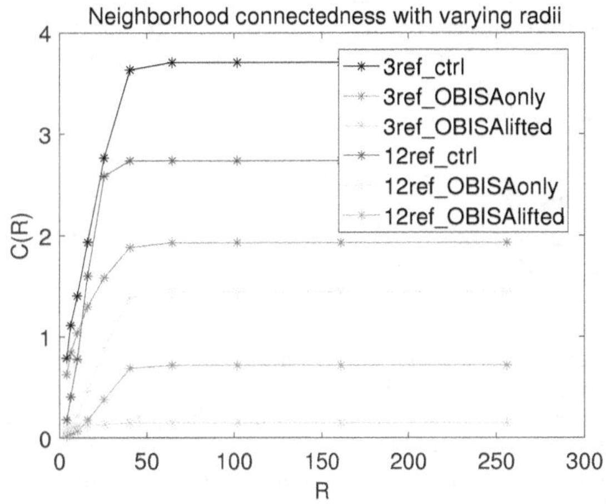

Figure 6: Neighborhood connectedness ($C(R)$) curve as radii (R) increases, on Circuit432 layouts.

Table 2: Standard cell composition bias of *key_sel* and DES toplevel.

	key_sel		DES	
	Ctrl	OBISA	Ctrl	OBISA
Flip-Flops	840	840	1144	1144
Muxes	768	768	0	984
XORs/XNORs	0	0	562	2324
#Cells	1608	3800	1761	29276
bias	6.67E-01	2.82E-01	6.53E-01	5.74E-02

4.2 Designs Overhead

In this implementation we chose a security level $k = 46$ for the wire lifted layout of Circuit432 netlist. One layout without any optimization (the *Ctrl* column) and one layout with only OBISA cells inserted but no wire lifted (the *Only* column) are provided as comparison. Implementation overheads in terms of power, timing delay, and area of each module are summarized in Table 3. The table provide two sets of comparisons:

In terms of total wire length, number of OBISA cells inserted as compared to that of functional cells, as well as num-

Table 3: Power, timing, and area overheads of wire-lifted Circuit432 layouts.

Module		Circuit432		
Layout		Ctrl	OBISA	
			Only	Lifted
Power	Internal	9.7769E-05	2.2107E-04	2.2110E-04
	Switching	7.6213E-05	1.1465E-04	1.1430E-04
	Leakage	3.2635E-06	1.3825E-05	1.3825E-05
	Total	1.7725E-04	3.4955E-04	3.4923E-04
Path Delays	Min	1.7	1.44	1.44
	Median	1.72	1.48	1.48
	Max	1.77	1.60	1.59
Total wire length		4.1651E+03	6.3281E+03	6.7440E+03
Area		1.2055E+03	2.5068E+03	2.5068E+03
#Std-cell		12	3	3
#Cell		115	282	282
#OBISA cell		0	73	73
Security Level k		1	1	46

ber of standard cell models instantiated, results are provided to illustrate impact upon OBISA due to specific functional module design. For example, close total wire length results between OBISA-inserted layout with (*Lifted* column) and without (*Only* column) wire lifting help to explain why little power and path delay difference were observed between these two types of layouts. In addition, difference in number of cells between netlist with and without restrictions on number of standard cell models, as well as resulting area and power differences help illustrate how much impact this restriction has on design overhead.

In terms of area, power, and path delays, OBISA-reinforced layout that underwent wire lifting (*Lifted* column under *OBISA*) column) is compared against similarly OBISA-reinforced layout without wire lifting (*Only* column under *OBISA* column) as well as layout of same module without any security enhancement (*Ctrl* column). The OBISA insertion incurred large area and power overhead primarily due to the small size of the Circuit432 design, and therefore having to restrict the number of standard cell models, which leads to doubled number of functional cells. Apart from that, the impact from OBISA insertion and wire lifting are both quite small. Path delays in the *Lifted* column, the *Only* column and the *Ctrl* column are small enough to be attributed to error in router optimization. Therefore, we are confident to conclude the proposed wire lifting based OBISA technique introduces no significant performance overhead to the original circuitry.

5. CONCLUSION

In this paper, we have presented a novel implementation approach of Obfuscated Built-In Self-Authentication (OBISA) technique that combines hardware Trojan deterrence through Built-In Self-Authentication (BISA) circuit insertion as well as optimized split manufacturing through wire lifting. The resulting technique is shown to be efficient, secure, and introduces very low performance overhead to the functional design that it is fit for industrial level of integration. Compared to its predecessors, the proposed approach removes the vulnerability to Hardware Trojan insertion of split manufacturing technique, the vulnerability to IP theft by untrusted foundries of BISA technique, and is more secure in terms of split manufacturing security metrics, secured against specific attacks to BISA such as redesign attacks due to the combination of both techniques. Above claims are substantiated with experimental implementation on Circuit432 benchmark circuit and DES core. The presented implmentation flow is tailored to work with all mainstream EDA tools, making it easy to integrate into any existing back-end design flow.

6. REFERENCES

[1] IARPA Trusted Integrated Circuits (TIC) program announcement. http://www.fbo.gov.

[2] R. S. Chakraborty and S. Bhunia. Security against hardware trojan through a novel application of design obfuscation. In *Proceedings of the 2009 International Conference on Computer-Aided Design*, pages 113–116. ACM, 2009.

[3] U. Guin. Establishment of trust and integrity in modern supply chain from design to resign. 2016.

[4] U. Guin, D. Forte, and M. Tehranipoor. Anti-counterfeit techniques: from design to resign. In *2013 14th International Workshop on Microprocessor Test and Verification*, pages 89–94. IEEE, 2013.

[5] U. Guin, Q. Shi, D. Forte, and M. M. Tehranipoor. Fortis: A comprehensive solution for establishing forward trust for protecting ips and ics. *ACM Transactions on Design Automation of Electronic Systems (TODAES)*, 21(4):63, 2016.

[6] F. Imeson, A. Emtenan, S. Garg, and M. Tripunitara. Securing computer hardware using 3d integrated circuit (ic) technology and split manufacturing for obfuscation. In *Presented as part of the 22nd USENIX Security Symposium (USENIX Security 13)*, pages 495–510, 2013.

[7] M. Jagasivamani, P. Gadfort, M. Sika, M. Bajura, and M. Fritze. Split-fabrication obfuscation: Metrics and techniques. In *Hardware-Oriented Security and Trust (HOST), 2014 IEEE International Symposium on*, pages 7–12. IEEE, 2014.

[8] Y. Jin, N. Kupp, and Y. Makris. Dftt: Design for trojan test. In *Electronics, Circuits, and Systems (ICECS), 2010 17th IEEE International Conference on*, pages 1168–1171. IEEE, 2010.

[9] J. J. Rajendran, O. Sinanoglu, and R. Karri. Is split manufacturing secure? In *Proceedings of the Conference on Design, Automation and Test in Europe*, pages 1259–1264. EDA Consortium, 2013.

[10] H. Salmani, M. Tehranipoor, and J. Plusquellic. A novel technique for improving hardware trojan detection and reducing trojan activation time. *IEEE Transactions on Very Large Scale Integration (VLSI) Systems*, 20(1):112–125, 2012.

[11] Q. Shi, K. Xiao, D. Forte, and M. M. Tehranipoor. Obfuscated built-in self-authentication. In *Hardware Protection through Obfuscation*, chapter 11, pages 263–289. Springer International Publishing, 2017.

[12] M. M. Tehranipoor, U. Guin, and D. Forte. Counterfeit integrated circuits. In *Counterfeit Integrated Circuits*, pages 15–36. Springer, 2015.

[13] K. Xiao. Techniques for improving security and trustworthiness of integrated circuits. 2015.

[14] K. Xiao, D. Forte, and M. Tehranipoor. A novel built-in self-authentication technique to prevent inserting hardware trojans. *IEEE Transactions on Computer-Aided Design of Integrated Circuits and Systems*, 33(12):1778–1791, 2014.

[15] K. Xiao, D. Forte, and M. M. Tehranipoor. Efficient and secure split manufacturing via obfuscated built-in self-authentication. In *Hardware Oriented Security and Trust (HOST), 2015 IEEE International Symposium on*, pages 14–19. IEEE, 2015.

[16] K. Xiao and M. Tehranipoor. Bisa: Built-in self-authentication for preventing hardware trojan insertion. In *Hardware-Oriented Security and Trust (HOST), 2013 IEEE International Symposium on*, pages 45–50. IEEE, 2013.

[17] X. Yang, B.-K. Choi, and M. Sarrafzadeh. Routability-driven white space allocation for fixed-die standard-cell placement. *IEEE Transactions on Computer-Aided Design of Integrated Circuits and Systems*, 22(4):410–419, Apr 2003.

An Empirical Study on Gate Camouflaging Methods Against Circuit Partition Attack

Xueyan Wang, Qiang Zhou, Yici Cai
Tsinghua National Laboratory for Information Science and Technology
CST Dept., Tsinghua University, Beijing, China
wangxueyan13@mails.tsinghua.edu.cn,
{zhouqiang, caiyc}@tsinghua.edu.cn

Gang Qu
ECE Department, University of Maryland
College Park, MD, USA
gangqu@umd.edu

ABSTRACT

Gate camouflaging has emerged as a leading proactive countermeasure for reverse engineering (RE) attacks. However, a recently proposed circuit partition attack (CPA) can significantly reduce the complexity of revealing the original design from a camouflaged circuit. In this paper, we first conduct an empirical study on how CPA can facilitate the state-of-the-art de-camouflaging methods to perform more efficient attacks. We then study how an equivalent class guided camouflaging approach may thwart these de-camouflaging attempts and re-establish the defense against RE. Experimental results demonstrate that (1) CPA is an effective pre-processing technique to boost de-camouflaging methods, and (2) Equivalent class guided camouflaging technique is resilient against the union of CPA and existing de-camouflaging methods.

1. INTRODUCTION

With the continually increasing design complexity and design cost of integrated circuits (IC), intellectual property (IP) infringement has become one significant concern in semiconductor industry. It has resulted in both security vulnerabilities in critical commercial and military systems, and economic loss of billions of dollars annually [1–5]. A significant portion of IP infringement involves reverse engineering (RE) which reveals detailed IC design information by depackaging, delayering and image-processing techniques. Attackers can utilize many advanced RE tools developed for circuit analysis and debugging to steal valuable design data [6, 7].

Although one cannot prevent RE based attacks from happening, ICs carefully designed and fabricated with security in consideration can increase the complexity and cost of reverse engineering. Gate camouflaging is one such proactive countermeasure for RE. In this approach, certain logic gates are deliberately selected and replaced by specially designed logic cells. These special logic cells can be configured to perform different functionalities while maintaining an identical look to RE attackers [8–12]. During RE based attacks, the attacker will not be able to directly observe the functionalities of the camouflaged gates. They have to pay additional efforts to reveal these unknown camouflaged gates. As a result, IC testing-based [9], SAT-based [13–15], and brute force de-camouflaging attacks [9] are proposed. Meanwhile, more sophisticated camouflaging methods are introduced to defeat these de-camouflaging attempts. The current state-of-the-art includes clique-based gate selection method [9], multiplexer-based camouflaging [11], CamoPerturb [16], and And-tree camouflaging [10]. We believe that it is such alternate 'attack and defense' process that makes gate camouflaging technique more practical, more secure and closer to being adopted commercially [17].

Permission to make digital or hard copies of all or part of this work for personal or classroom use is granted without fee provided that copies are not made or distributed for profit or commercial advantage and that copies bear this notice and the full citation on the first page. Copyrights for components of this work owned by others than ACM must be honored. Abstracting with credit is permitted. To copy otherwise, or republish, to post on servers or to redistribute to lists, requires prior specific permission and/or a fee. Request permissions from permissions@acm.org.

GLSVLSI '17, May 10-12, 2017, Banff, AB, Canada
© 2017 ACM. ISBN 978-1-4503-4972-7/17/05... $15.00
DOI: http://dx.doi.org/10.1145/3060403.3060493

One of the latest development in this arms race is our recently proposed circuit partition attack (CPA), where we apply the divide and conquer methodology to partition camouflaged gates into multiple sub-circuits and de-camouflage them separately [18–20].

Interestingly, we realize that CPA can be used as a pre-processing step before other de-camouflaging methods to dramatically reduce the complexity of these methods. This motivates us to conduct an empirical study on evaluating the integration of CPA into the de-camouflage flow. More specifically, we select three representative types of attacks: brute force attack, IC testing based-attack and SAT-based attack for our study. In this paper, we report our discovery when applying these to standard benchmark suites and the OpenSparc T1 microprocessor to answer the following questions :

- How CPA can facilitate other de-camouflaging methods to perform stronger attacks?
- Whether the equivalent class guided camouflaging can effectively thwart these new combined attacks?

The rest of this paper is organized as follows: Section 2 provides some preliminaries of the paper. Section 3 illustrates how circuit partition can be utilized to facilitate existing de-camouflaging methods. Circuit partition attack mitigation scheme is studied in Section 4. Section 5 concludes the paper.

2. PRELIMINARY

In this section, basics in gate camouflaging and current de-camouflaging attacks will be reviewed.

2.1 Basics in Gate Camouflaging

2.1.1 *What is Gate Camouflaging*

Gate camouflaging is a layout-level technique to thwart RE. In gate camouflaging, special logic cells are designed, which can be configured to perform different functionalities while maintaining an identical look to RE attackers. Then some conventional logic gates in the circuit are intentionally selected to be replaced with the special logic cells. Each special logic cell is configured to perform the same functionality as the replaced conventional logic gate.

Therefore, when an attacker performs top-down RE, he will not be able to directly observe the functionalities of the camouflaged gates. The attacker can of course guess or try all the possible configurations for the camouflaged gates, however, the complexity for RE will increase, and he may get a deceived netlist if not guessing out all correct configurations.

2.1.2 *Necessary Assumptions*

In the gate camouflaging research community, the following assumptions have been widely adopted.

1. For an unpackaged functional IC bought from the market, the attacker only has access to the IC's primary inputs (PIs) and primary outputs (POs).
2. The attacker is able to extract a camouflaged netlist with regular gates and camouflaged gates by the state-of-the-art RE tools and techniques.
3. The attacker seeks to identify the functionality of each camouflaged gate to reverse engineer the camouflaged IC.

Our discussions in this paper will also be based on the above assumptions.

2.2 Existing De-Camouflaging Attacks

An attacker can get a camouflaged netlist containing regular and camouflaged gates with existing RE techniques and tools. The process of resolving the functionalities of camouflaged gates to reveal the camouflaged circuit design is called *de-camouflaging attack*. In this part, several popular de-camouflaging attacks in the state-of-the-art will be briefly introduced.

2.2.1 *IC Testing-based Attack (ITA)*

ITA resolves the functionality of a camouflaged gate by managing to get the input-output pairs of the camouflaged gate. Having only access to the PIs and POs of a functional IC, this is achieved by controlling the gate's inputs to certain values from PIs, then sensitizing the gate's corresponding output to one PO [9]. Camouflaged gates that can be resolved by ITA are called *resolvable*. Otherwise, they are known as *unresolvable*. Interested readers can refer to [9] for more detailed elaboration.

2.2.2 *Brute Force Attack (BFA)*

Different with ITA to resolve one camouflaged gate each time, BFA directly brute force searches all the possible functionality combinations for camouflaged gates. Then for each possible combination, the attacker will simulate to get the corresponding outputs and compare them with those from a functional IC. If they are the same, the attacker has found out the correct combination and these camouflaged gates are resolved [9]. Otherwise, the attacker will try out the next possible combination and repeat the process.

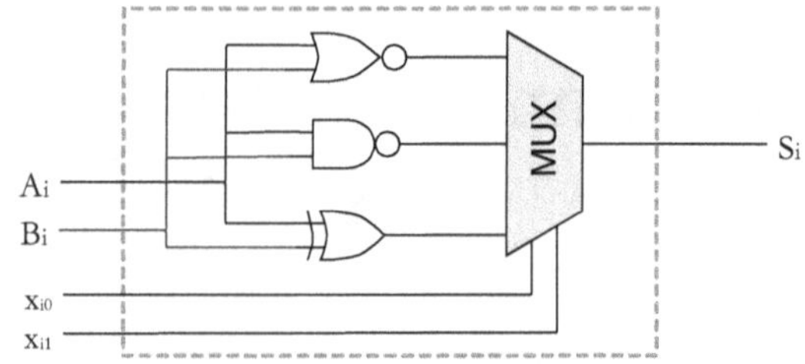

Figure 1: Model {NAND, NOR, XOR} camouflaged cell with LUT-structure [14].

2.2.3 *SAT-based Attack (SATA)*

Unlike BFA to directly search for the correct functionality combination (*assignment*), SATA iteratively prunes incorrect assignments from an initial possible assignment set [13–15].

SATA models camouflaged gates with LUT structures [14, 15]. Take the {XOR, NAND, NOR} camouflaging cell in [9] for example, as shown in Fig. 1, assignment "00", "01", and "10" to x_{i0}, x_{i1} corresponds to configuring the cell as XOR, NAND, and NOR, respectively.

Then the de-camouflaging problem is transformed to SAT problem. SATA starts with a possible assignment set for all camouflaged gates (When N gates camouflaged, and each camouflaged gate can perform M possible functionalities, there will be M^N possible assignments). Each time the SAT solver will compute a discriminating input[1] to prune at least one incorrect assignment. By iteratively applying SAT solver [21] to find DIs, the attacker gradually prunes all incorrect assignments, successfully bypassing the exponential complexity of brute force.

3. CIRCUIT PARTITION FACILITATED DE-CAMOUFLAGING

3.1 Circuit Partition Attack

Circuit partition attack reduces RE efforts by dividing camouflaged gates into multiple $MFIC$, then target each $MFIC$ individually, where $MFIC$ is defined as follows [18]:

The **M**aximum **F**an**I**n-**C**one rooted at a primary output PO, $MFIC_{PO}$, is the set of gates whose outputs will directly or indirectly feed into PO. Formally, $MFIC_{PO} = \{Gi|\exists path, Gi \to PO\}$[2]. For example, in Fig. 2(a),
$MFIC_{O1} = \{G1, C1, G2, G3, C2, G5, C3\}$, and
$MFIC_{O2} = \{C1, G2, G3, G4, C2, G5, G6\}$.

According to the definition, the function of $MFIC$ can be directly observed/tested from a functional IC. Therefore, when an attacker applies de-camouflaging attacks to resolve

[1]A discriminating input is an input pattern that when applied in a camouflaged netlist, produces incorrect output for at least one incorrect assignment.

[2]In this paper, we refer to $MFIC$ for simplification as maximum fanin-cone that rooted at a PO, and we will also refer to $MFIC$ as the corresponding sub-circuit, which can be easily differentiated according to contexts.

the camouflaged gates, he can start with the $MFIC$ that has the fewest number of camouflaged gates, then target another $MFIC$, until all camouflaged gates resolved.

We define the largest number of camouflaged gates in the same $MFIC$ that need to be resolved simultaneously as ***effective camouflaged gate number, marked by*** n_{max}. Therefore, when applied CPA before a de-camouflaging attack, the de-camouflaging complexity will be limited by n_{max}. Next, we will study how this feature can exponentially reduce the de-camouflaging complexities.

3.2 Facilitate IC Testing-based Attack

Intuitively, CPA can facilitate ITA from two aspects: reduce related PI and PO numbers to simplify ITA, and enable originally unresolvable camouflaged gates become resolvable. We use an illustrative example to validate the observations.

In Fig. 2(a), initially, none of gates C1, C2 and C3 can be resolved with ITA: C1's output cannot be observed from any of the POs without resolving C2 and C3 first; C3's inputs cannot be controlled before C1 and C2 are resolved; both the controllability of C2's inputs and the observability of its output rely on the functionalities of C1 and C3. There are 5 PIs and 2 POs involved in the analysis.

However, by applying CPA first, C1 and C2 can be resolved in $MFIC_{O2}$. As shown in Fig. 2(b), when applying (0,1,0,1) to (I2,I3,I4,I5), if we observe signal 0 at output O2, we know that gate G4 must produce a signal 1. Because I5=1, G4 must have received 0 from C1. From this, we know that C1 must be XOR. Similarly, if we observe signal 1 at O2, C1 must be either NAND or NOR, which we can find out by applying (0,1,1,1). After C1 resolved, C2 and C3 can be resolved with ease, one at a time. There are only 4 PIs and 1 PO involved in each round of ITA analysis.

3.3 Facilitate Brute Force Attack

We start with a motivational example in Fig. 2(a), without CPA, the attacker needs to brute force search 3^3 possible functionality combinations for C1, C2 and C3. By performing CPA before BFA, the attacker can first brute force search the 3^2 combinations for C1 and C2 in $MFIC_{O2}$, then resolve C3, either by ITA or BFA. In this case, CPA reduces BFA complexity from 3^3 to 3^2.

We then demonstrate the power of CPA in reducing BFA complexity on larger circuits. Fig. 3 shows one attack example to camouflaged Store Buffer Unit of OpenSparc T1 microprocessor controller [18]. It was claimed that the attacker had to brute force 3^{68} possible functionality combinations [9]. However, as shown in Fig. 3(a), the 68 camouflaged gates distribute in 84 $MFIC$, in which the numbers of camouflaged gates range from 1 to 17. By greedily selecting the $MFIC$ with the minimum camouflaged gates to attack in, we can see that $n_{max} = 6$ (see Fig. 3(b)), which means the brute force complexity is reduced from 3^{68} to 3^6. Then CPA is applied on all camouflaged circuits in [9]. Fig. 4 demonstrates a comparison between N and n_{max}. In all camouflaged circuits, the maximum n_{max} is only 10, which is too low to defense against RE attacks [18].

Conclusions can be made from the experimental results: first, CPA can significantly reduce the brute force complexity, from M^N to $M^{n_{max}}$, where M is the number of possible functionalities each camouflaged gate can perform, and N is the total camouflaged gate number; second, CPA is scalable

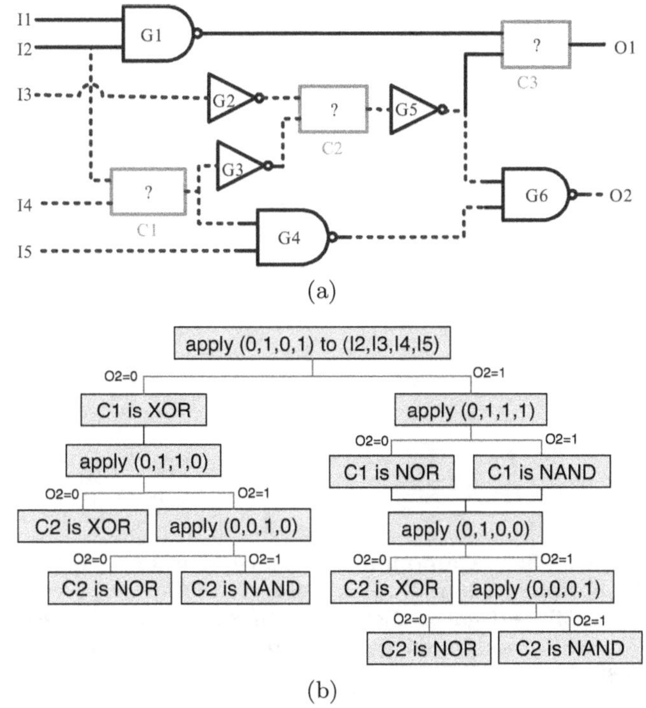

Figure 2: (a) Gate camouflaging example in [9, 18]. C1, C2 and C3 are camouflaged by {XOR, NAND, NOR} camouflaging cells. C1, C2 and C3 are *unresolvable*. (b) Resolve the functionalities of C1 and C2 by ITA in the sub-circuit marked with dotted lines.

for larger circuits for n_{max} does not increase with circuit size grows.

3.4 Facilitate SAT-based Attack

Similar with BFA, in Fig. 2(a), without CPA integrated to SATA, the attacker has to start with 3^3 possible assignments for C1, C2, and C3, then iteratively prunes the incorrect assignments. With circuit partition however, the attacker may start with 3^2 possible assignments for C1 and C2 in $MFIC_{O2}$, then resolve $C3$. The reductions to the initial possible assignment numbers can be referred to the experimental results in Fig. 3 and Fig. 4, in Section 3.3. Not only that, the complexity for SAT solver to find DIs is also reduced, for example in Fig 2(a), roughly speaking, the scale of the SAT problem reduces from 11 (5 PIs + 3x2 keys) variables to 8 (4 PIs + 2x2 keys) variables, which will make a difference to the NP-complete SAT problem in large circuits.

4. RESCUE GATE CAMOUFLAGING FROM CIRCUIT PARTITION ATTACK

4.1 Equivalent Class Guided Gate Selection

As demonstrated in Section 3, CPA has significantly threatened the effectiveness of gate camouflaging techniques. To thwart CPA, one needs to keep the camouflaged gates together such that the attacker cannot partition them into multiple $MFIC$ to attack separately. For this purpose, an

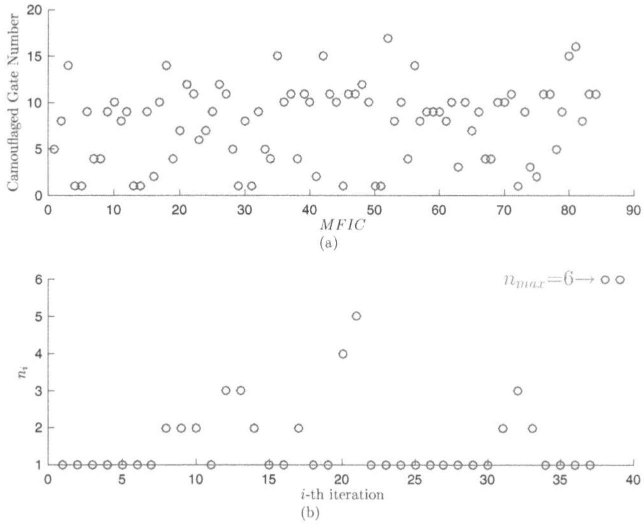

Figure 3: Camouflaged Store Buffer Unit of OpenSparc T1 microprocessor controller [9]. (a) 68 camouflaged gates distribute in 84 $MFIC$. (b) Resolved camouflaged gates number in each iteration [18].

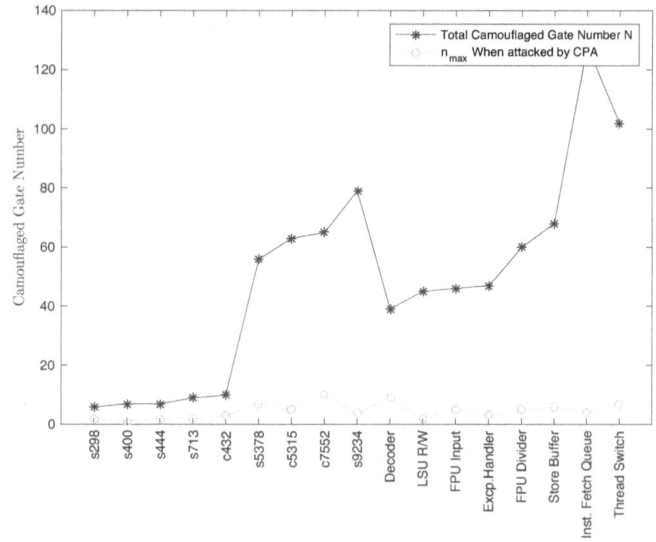

Figure 4: Attack camouflaged circuits in [9] with CPA. Comparisons between the camouflaged gate numbers and n_{max} when attacked by CPA [18].

equivalent class guided method has been proposed to select to-be-camouflaged gates.

We know that one logic gate can belong to several $MFIC$, in other words, each logic gate belongs to a certain set of $MFIC$. In [20], gates that belong to exactly the same set of $MFIC$ are partitioned to the same equivalent class. For example, in Fig. 2(a), $\{G1, C3\}$, $\{C1, G2, G3, G4, C2, G5\}$, and $\{G4, G6\}$ belong to three equivalent classes, corresponding $MFIC$ sets are $\{MFIC_{O1}\}$, $\{MFIC_{O1}, MFIC_{O2}\}$, and $\{MFIC_{O2}\}$, respectively.

As RE attackers has only access to the PIs and POs of a functional IC, $MFIC$ will be the minimum unit of subcircuit to attack separately. Therefore, if to-be-camouflaged gates are selected from the same equivalent class, for any $MFIC$ that the attacker can attack in, either all camouflaged gates belong to it, or none of the camouflaged gates belong to it. As a result, CPA will be thwarted.

4.2 Multiplexer-Based Camouflaging

Following the equivalent class guided method to select to-be-camouflaged gates, a multiplexer-based camouflaging method is proposed in [20]. Specifically, they adopt multiplexers (MUXs) that can be configured to perform 16 possible functionalities as camouflaging cells, and select to-be-camouflaged gates from one certain equivalent class, in addition, they also camouflage the gates that directly feed the POs of the $MFIC$ set (marked as $gate_{PO}$, for example in Fig. 2(a), $gate_{O2} = G6$).

In this paper, we implement this multiplexer-based camouflaging approach, and empirically study how the approach may rescue gate camouflaging from the union of CPA and existing de-camouflaging attacks. In detail, programs are written in JAVA to do gate classification and identify candidate gates to camouflage with MUXs, and experiments are performed on ISCAS, MCNC benchmark suites and OpenSparc T1 microprocessor. The resilience to SATA is evaluated by the published SAT-based de-camouflaging attack tool in [15] which achieved 5x speedup in execution time than [14]. The programs are executed on a 24-core 2.30 GHz, with 48GB RAM Linux server.

It's worth mentioning that in our implementation, to protect the camouflaged $gate_{PO}$ from being resolved by ITA, we additionally camouflage their at least one input gate (marked as $input_{gate_{PO}}$), with constraint that its $MFIC$ set is a subset of the class gates' $MFIC$ set (we can always find one such gate, which can be strictly proven, not included here due to space limitation).

Table 1 shows the benchmark circuit information including the number of PIs, POs, gates, nets, and logic levels. Columns 7-8 show the selected equivalent class information including the size of $MFIC$ set and total gate number. Columns 9-12 show a decomposition of the camouflaged gates. The '0's in the $input_{gate_{PO}}$ column correspond to the cases that the selected $input_{gate_{PO}}$ happen to belong to the equivalent class, which will be counted in $gate_C$ column.

4.3 Defend Against CPA & ITA

As analyzed in Section 4.1, equivalent class guided gate selection can thwart the partitioning of camouflaged gates into multiple $MFIC$. Therefore, to defend against CPA & ITA, we just need to ensure that the camouflaged gates cannot be resolved by ITA. Namely for each camouflaged gate, either its inputs cannot be controlled from PIs, or its output cannot be sensitized to POs.

In our implemented multiplexer-based camouflaging, for each MUX that camouflages one gate that belong to the equivalent class (marked as $gate_C$), its output cannot be sensitized to any PO, because all related $gate_{PO}$ are camouflaged. For each MUX that camouflages $input_{gate_{PO}}$, we ensure that its $MFIC$ set is a subset of $MFIC$ set of $gate_C$, thus its output cannot be sensitized to any PO as well. Finally, for each MUX that camouflages $gate_{PO}$, its inputs cannot be controlled from PIs because the MUX's at least one input gate ($input_{gate_{PO}}$) is camouflaged. Therefore, the multiplexer-based camouflaging is resilient to the union of CPA & ITA.

Table 1: Camouflaged Gates Decomposition.

Bench	PI	PO	Gate	Net	Logic Level	Selected Class C		Camouflaged Gates			
						$MFIC$	$Gates$	$Total$	$gate_C$	$gate_{PO}$	$input_{gate_{PO}}$
s713	54	42	142	290	16	1	19	7	6	1	0
c432	36	7	180	363	23	1	17	9	8	1	0
i2	201	1	222	460	10	1	222	11	10	1	0
s1196	32	32	397	897	17	6	22	19	7	6	6
s1238	32	32	444	999	18	1	25	22	21	1	0
too_large	38	3	519	1125	25	1	84	25	24	1	0
c2670	233	140	645	1324	18	2	121	36	34	2	0
c3540	50	22	861	1967	31	5	51	43	35	5	3
t481	16	1	1098	2596	15	1	1098	54	53	1	0
s5378	199	213	1151	2423	14	2	84	57	55	2	0
s9234	247	250	1505	3105	23	1	87	75	74	1	0
c7552	207	108	1611	3372	28	3	86	80	74	3	3
i10	257	224	1904	4145	36	10	121	95	76	10	9
c6288	32	32	2267	5220	89	16	142	113	82	16	15
s13207	700	790	2480	4741	26	19	137	124	86	19	19

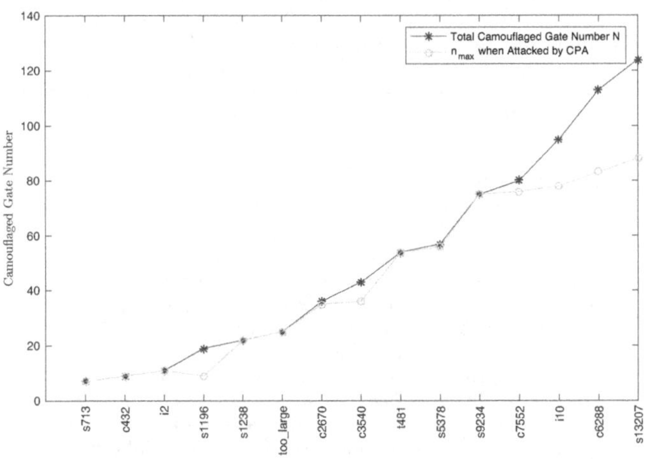

Figure 5: Perform CPA on circuits that camouflaged by equivalent class-based method. Comparisons between N and n_{max}.

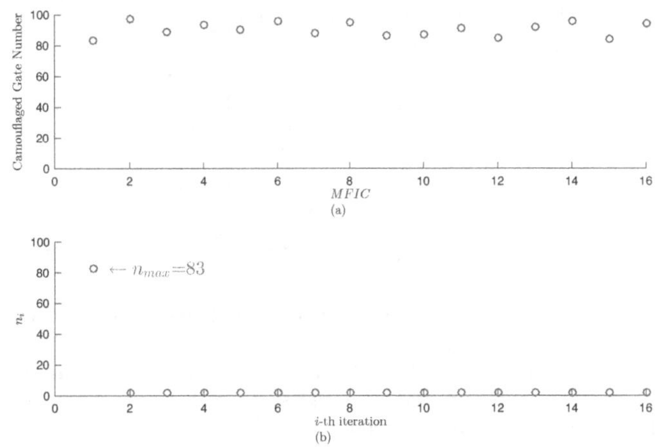

Figure 6: Perform CPA on camouflaged c6288. (a) Number of camouflaged gates in each $MFIC$. (b) Number of camouflaged gates resolved in each iteration.

4.4 Defend Against CPA & BFA

Fig. 5 shows comparisons between the total camouflaged gate number N and effective camouflaged gate number n_{max} when attacked by CPA. As demonstrated, n_{max} is very close to N, which means the BFA complexities are not reduced much by CPA. The gaps between them are caused by the gates that camouflaged to ensure resilience to ITA (consist of camouflaged $gate_{PO}$ and $input_{gate_{PO}}$).

Fig. 6 explains the results in Fig. 5 with c6288 circuit. As shown in Fig. 6(a), the camouflaged gates distribute in 16 $MFIC$, with camouflaged gates in each $MFIC$ ranging from 83 to 97. As demonstrated in Fig. 6(b), no matter which $MFIC$ the attacker selects to attack in, at least 83 gates must be resolved together. The BFA complexity will be $16^{83} = 2^{332}$.

Therefore, the multiplexer-based camouflaging is well resilient to CPA & BFA.

4.5 Defend Against CPA & SATA

We evaluate the resilience to CPA & SATA by comparing with three other gate selection methods: (1) Random Selection (RS) in which gates are selected to camouflage in a random manner; (2) Clique-Based Selection (CBS) where *interfered* gates are selected [9]; (3) $MFIC$-Based Selection (MBS) where gates are selected from one Maximum Fan-In Cone. The multiplexer-based camouflaging is called Equivalent Class-Based Selection (EBS) because gates are selected from the same equivalent class. In this part, we perform experiments on the same benchmark circuits with [9] for a fair comparison with their work.

As shown in Fig. 7, RS and CBS pose the weakest resilience to SATA. MBS needs more de-camouflaging time than RS and CBS, probably because gates that belong to the same $MFIC$ are less scattered. EBS incurs much longer de-camouflaging time, which is on average 10x the time needed by RS, with the largest one being 67x in FPU Input Unit.

Moreover, as shown in Table 2, when 40 gates are camouflaged, all circuits camouflaged by RS, CBS, and MBS are de-camouflaged within less than 15 seconds. However, by EBS, the de-camouflaging process does not terminate in 12 hours for c7552 and Store Buffer Unit, and needs 1.5×10^4 seconds for Exception Handler Unit. Table 2 has shown the very promising prospect of the EBS in thwarting SATA.

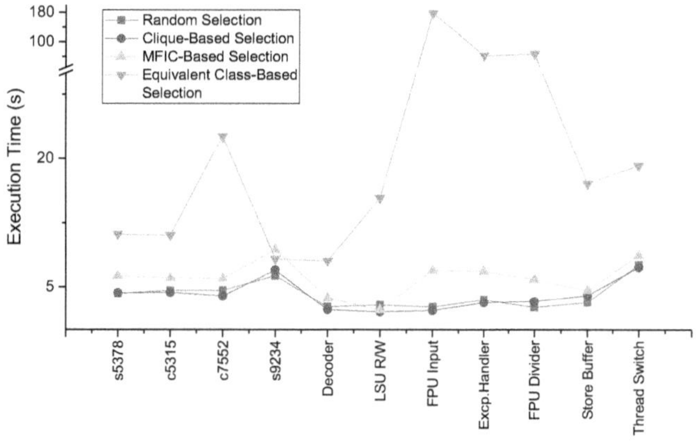

Figure 7: SATA de-camouflaging time (s) comparisons when camouflaging 20 gates.

Table 2: SATA de-camouflaging time (s) comparisons when camouflaging 40 gates.

Bench	RS	CBS	MBS	EBS
s5378	8.54596	8.55709	29.9581	37.8072
c5315	7.1328	8.20039	11.5577	633.566
c7552	9.36139	10.5082	19.455	>12 hours
s9234	12.2429	11.8097	12.4931	322.067
Excp.Handler	6.46539	6.56794	15.2583	15040.1
Store Buffer	6.72159	6.48989	15.4281	>12 hours
Thread Switch	12.2617	12.4722	15.0108	320.526

This is reasonable, when to-be-camouflaged gates are selected from the same equivalent class, they must be resolved simultaneously by SAT tool. As a result, the initial possible assignment number, and the scale of SAT problem to find DIs are both maximized, validating the analysis in Section 3.4.

5. CONCLUSIONS

Gate camouflaging is very promising to thwart reverse engineering attacks. A new circuit partition attack has been proposed in the literature to divide and conquer the de-camouflaging problem. In this paper, we have performed empirical studies on the facilitations of circuit partition attack to existing de-camouflaging methods, and the effectiveness of a equivalent class guided multiplexer-based camouflaging approach in rescuing gate camouflaging from these unions. Hopefully by this paper, researchers can get better aware of the challenges and potential countermeasures for circuit partition attack.

Acknowledgment

This work is supported by the National Natural Science Foundation of China under grant number 61176035. Gang Qu is supported in part by AFOSR MURI under award number FA9550-14-1-0351.

References

[1] Gang Qu and Miodrag Potkonjak. *Intellectual property protection in VLSI designs: theory and practice.* Springer Science & Business Media, 2007.

[2] Masoud Rostami, Farinaz Koushanfar, and Ramesh Karri.

[2] Masoud Rostami, Farinaz Koushanfar, and Ramesh Karri.
A primer on hardware security: Models, methods, and metrics. *Proceedings of the IEEE*, 102(8):1283–1295, 2014.

[3] Reverse engineering for war, May 2008.

[4] SEMI. Innovation is at risk as semiconductor equipment and materials industry loses up to $4 billion annually due to ip infringement, April 2008.

[5] Domenic Forte, Swarup Bhunia, and Mark M Tehranipoor. Hardware protection through obfuscation, 2017.

[6] Randy Torrance and Dick James. The state-of-the-art in semiconductor reverse engineering. In *Proc. ACM/IEEE Design Automation Conference (DAC)*, pages 333–338, 2011.

[7] Shahed E. Quadir, Junlin Chen, Domenic Forte, Navid Asadizanjani, Sina Shahbazmohamadi, Lei Wang, John Chandy, and Mark Tehranipoor. A survey on chip to system reverse engineering. *JETC*, 13(1):6:1–6:34, 2016.

[8] Lap Wai Chow, James P Baukus, Bryan J Wang, and Ronald P Cocchi. Camouflaging a standard cell based integrated circuit, April 3 2012. US Patent 8,151,235.

[9] Jeyavijayan Rajendran, Michael Sam, Ozgur Sinanoglu, and Ramesh Karri. Security analysis of integrated circuit camouflaging. In *Proc. ACM Conference on Computer and Communications Security (CCS)*, pages 709–720, 2013.

[10] Meng Li, Kaveh Shamsi, Travis Meade, Zheng Zhao, Bei Yu, Yier Jin, and David Z. Pan. Provably secure camouflaging strategy for IC protection. In *Proceedings of International Conference on Computer-Aided Design (ICCAD)*, page 28, 2016.

[11] Bao Liu and Brandon Wang. Embedded reconfigurable logic for ASIC design obfuscation against supply chain attacks. In *Proc. IEEE Design, Automation and Test in Europe (DATE)*, pages 1–6, 2014.

[12] Ronald P. Cocchi, James P. Baukus, Lap Wai Chow, and Bryan J. Wang. Circuit camouflage integration for hardware IP protection. In *Proceedings of Design Automation Conference (DAC)*, pages 153:1–153:5, 2014.

[13] Pramod Subramanyan, Sayak Ray, and Sharad Malik. Evaluating the security of logic encryption algorithms. In *Hardware Oriented Security and Trust (HOST), IEEE International Symposium on*, pages 137–143. IEEE, 2015.

[14] Mohamed El Massad, Siddharth Garg, and Mahesh V Tripunitara. Integrated circuit (ic) decamouflaging: Reverse engineering camouflaged ics within minutes. In *NDSS*, 2015.

[15] Duo Liu, Cunxi Yu, Xiangyu Zhang, and Daniel Holcomb. Oracle-guided incremental sat solving to reverse engineer camouflaged logic circuits. In *Design, Automation & Test in Europe Conference & Exhibition (DATE)*, pages 433–438. IEEE, 2016.

[16] Muhammad Yasin, Bodhisatwa Mazumdar, Ozgur Sinanoglu, and Jeyavijayan Rajendran. Camoperturb: secure IC camouflaging for minterm protection. In *Proceedings of International Conference on Computer-Aided Design (ICCAD)*, page 29, 2016.

[17] Semiconductor and system solutions - infineon technologies.

[18] Xueyan Wang, Qiang Zhou, Yici Cai, and Gang Qu. Is the secure ic camouflaging really secure? In *IEEE International Symposium on Circuits and Systems (ISCAS)*, pages 1710–1713. IEEE, 2016.

[19] Xueyan Wang, Mingze Gao, Qiang Zhou, Yici Cai, and Gang Qu. Gate camouflaging-based obfuscation. In *Hardware Protection through Obfuscation*, pages 89–102. Springer, 2017.

[20] Xueyan Wang, Xiaotao Jia, Qiang Zhou, Yici Cai, Jianlei Yang, Mingze Gao, and Gang Qu. Secure and low-overhead circuit obfuscation technique with multiplexers. In *Proceedings of the 26th edition on Great Lakes Symposium on VLSI*, pages 133–136. ACM, 2016.

[21] Niklas Eén and Niklas Sörensson. An extensible sat-solver. In *Theory and Applications of Satisfiability Testing, International Conference (SAT)*, pages 502–518, 2003.

What to Lock? Functional and Parametric Locking

Muhammad Yasin, Abhrajit Sengupta
Electrical and Computer Engineering
New York University
{yasin,as9397}@nyu.edu

Benjamin Carrion Schafer,
Yiorgos Makris
Electrical and Computer Engineering
The University of Texas at Dallas
{schaferb,yiorgos.makris}@utdallas.edu

Ozgur Sinanoglu
Electrical and Computer Engineering
New York University Abu Dhabi
ozgursin@nyu.edu

Jeyavijayan (JV) Rajendran
Electrical and Computer Engineering
The University of Texas at Dallas
jv.ee@utdallas.edu

ABSTRACT

Logic locking is an intellectual property (IP) protection technique that prevents IP piracy, reverse engineering and overbuilding attacks by the untrusted foundry or end-users. Existing logic locking techniques are all based on locking the functionality; the design/chip is nonfunctional unless the secret key has been loaded. Existing techniques are vulnerable to various attacks, such as sensitization, key-pruning, and signal skew analysis enabled removal attacks. In this paper, we propose a tenacious and traceless logic locking technique, TTlock, that locks functionality and provably withstands all known attacks, such as SAT-based, sensitization, removal, etc. TTLock protects a secret input pattern; the output of a logic cone is flipped for that pattern, where this flip is restored only when the correct key is applied. Experimental results confirm our theoretical expectations that the computational complexity of attacks launched on TTLock grows exponentially with increasing key-size, while the area, power, and delay overhead increases only linearly. In this paper, we also coin "parametric locking," where the design/chip behaves as per its specifications (performance, power, reliability, etc.) only with the secret key in place, and an incorrect key downgrades its parametric characteristics. We discuss objectives and challenges in parametric locking.

1. INTRODUCTION

Today's integrated circuits (ICs) are designed and fabricated in a globalized, multi-vendor environment due to the high cost of building and maintaining a foundry [1]. Further, to meet strict time-to-market constraints, a design company may purchase intellectual property (IP) cores from third-party IP vendors. A globalized IC supply chain allows for the crucial assets to be handled by untrustworthy agents and creates opportunities for IP/IC piracy, reverse engineering, counterfeiting, and malicious modifications to the IC in the form of hardware Trojans [2, 3].

Permission to make digital or hard copies of part or all of this work for personal or classroom use is granted without fee provided that copies are not made or distributed for profit or commercial advantage and that copies bear this notice and the full citation on the first page. Copyrights for third-party components of this work must be honored. For all other uses, contact the Owner/Author(s). Copyright is held by the owner/author(s).
GLSVLSI '17, May 10-12, 2017, Banff, AB, Canada
© 2017 ACM. 978-1-4503-4972-7/17/05 ...$15.00
DOI: http://dx.doi.org/10.1145/3060403.3060492.

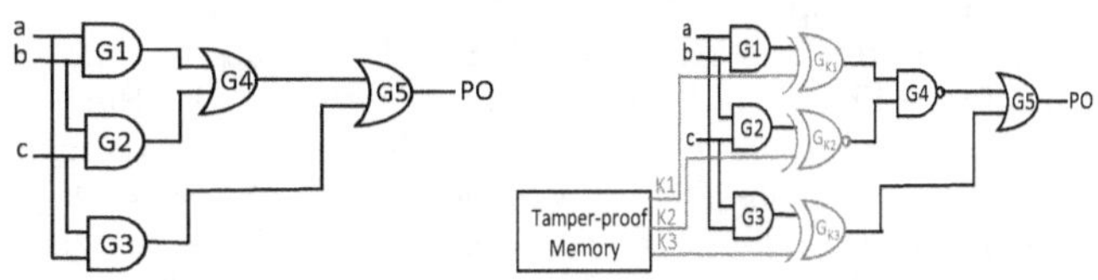

(a) Example circuit [12].

(b) Circuit locked using XOR/XNOR key gates. The correct key $\{K1, K2, K3\}$ value is 100.

Figure 1: Functional logic locking using XOR/XNOR gates [6].

To thwart such attacks, countermeasures such as IC camouflaging [4] and split manufacturing [5] have been developed. IC camouflaging and split manufacturing protect only against the untrusted user and untrusted foundry, respectively. *Logic locking* is a technique that thwarts IP piracy, overbuilding, and reverse engineering attacks by locking a chip with a secret key [6–11]. To enable chip-locking features, additional logic, e.g., XOR/XNORs gates referred to as *key-gates*, is added to the original netlist to obtain a *locked netlist.* Logic locking protects against both untrusted foundry and user. The secret key needs to be loaded for the design/chip to become functional; otherwise, the chip produces incorrect outputs. Logic locking techniques lock the functionality of the design/chip.

Figure 1(a) shows an example design netlist of a circuit, and Figure 1(b) shows its functionally locked version through two XOR and one XNOR key-gates. One of the inputs of each key-gate is driven by a wire in the original design, while the other input, referred to as the *key-input,* is driven by a key-bit stored in a tamper-proof memory. Logic locking aims to deliver the following protection: (i) Without the knowledge of the secret key, exact design details cannot be retrieved, and (ii) A locked IC (or a locked netlist) will not generate correct output unless it is activated, i.e., the secret key is loaded onto the chip's memory.

1.1 Prior work

Previous logic locking techniques have inserted key-gates based on strategies, such as random logic locking (RLL) [6] and fault analysis-based logic locking (FLL) [7]. **Sensitization attack** sensitizes the key-bits to the outputs by applying judiciously crafted patterns, which, when applied on a working chip, reveals the key-bit values. This attack breaks RLL and FLL [9]. Strong logic locking (SLL) inserts key-gates such that they interfere with each other, making it difficult to sensitize the individual key-bits to outputs [9].

A key-pruning attack that breaks all existing combinational logic-locking techniques has been proposed in [12]. The attack uses Boolean satisfiability (SAT) based algorithms, and we refer to it as the **SAT attack**. The SAT attack uses modern SAT solvers to compute *discriminating input patterns (DIPs)* [12] on the locked netlist (e.g., obtained by reverse-engineering). A working chip with the secret key loaded in its memory is then used as an *oracle* to obtain the responses to these DIPs. A DIP X_d is an input value for which at least two different key values, $k1$ and $k2$, produce differing outputs, $o1$ and $o2$, respectively. Since $o1$ and $o2$ are different, one of the key values or both of them are incorrect. It is possible for a single DIP to rule out multiple incorrect key values. In each iteration, a DIP is generated and applied to the chip. Based on the output observed, a set of keys is eliminated. The process repeats until no DIP can be found, and thus, eliminating all the incorrect keys. Thus, any key in the remaining search space is a valid key. The worst-case scenario for the SAT attack arises when the attack can discriminate at most one incorrect key value with each DIP. In this case, $2^k - 1$ DIPs are required for k key bits. The attack complexity can be represented in terms of the number of DIPs generated by the SAT attack to break a logic-locked circuit.

To thwart the SAT attack, two logic-locking techniques—SARLock [13] and Anti-SAT [14] (see Figure 2)—have been recently proposed. SARLock leaves the logic cone implementation, the IP-to-be-protected, as is, and corrupts the output of the logic cone for all keys but the correct one. The correct key values are hardcoded in logic gates to *mask* the output corruption for the correct key [13]. Anti-SAT inserts key-gates at the inputs of two complementary logic blocks that converge at an AND gate. The output of the AND gate is always 0 only for the correct key; otherwise, it may be 1 for some input values, corrupting an internal node in the original design to produce occasionally incorrect outputs.

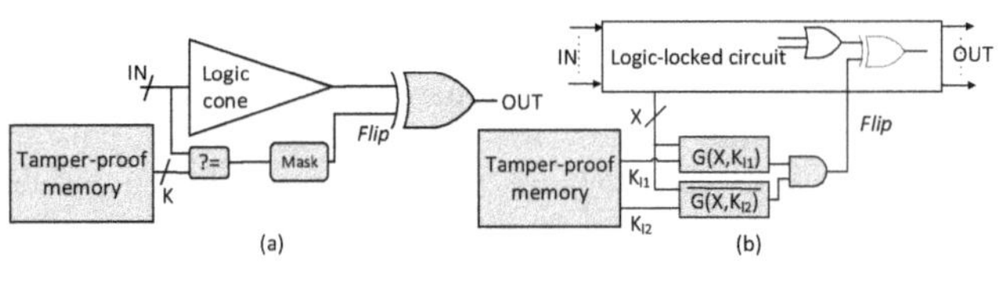

Figure 2: (a) SARLock: The *flip* signal goes low for all input values only on applying the correct key [13]. This technique is vulnerable to removal attack: (b) Anti-SAT: The *flip* signal goes low for all input values only on applying the correct key [14]. This technique is vulnerable to signal skew analysis (SSA) attack [15].

Limitations of existing work. All combinational logic-locking techniques except for SARLock [13] and Anti-SAT [14] are vulnerable to SAT attacks. Yet SARLock [13] and Anti-SAT [14] exhibit security vulnerabilities themselves. SARLock is vulnerable to **removal attack**: given a protected netlist, one can identify the comparator/mask blocks and the XOR gate that directly feeds the output by tracing the transitive-fanout of key-inputs, and remove these blocks, leaving only the unprotected logic cone. Thus, the proprietary IP is recovered. Anti-SAT is vulnerable to **signal skew analysis (SSA) attack** [15]: given a protected netlist, an attacker can identify the output gate of the Anti-SAT block; it is the node whose inputs have the maximal difference in signal probabilities. The attacker can then re-synthesize the design with a constant 0 (1) on the output of Anti-SAT, retrieving the original design.

1.2 Contributions

All existing logic-locking techniques are vulnerable. Thus, there is no provably-secure logic locking. Hence, in this paper, we first propose a provably-secure logic-locking technique:

1. We propose a novel logic-locking technique that we refer to as *TTLock*, which provably resists all known attacks, i.e., SAT [12], sensitization [16], and signal skew analysis attacks [15].

2. TTLock modifies the original logic cone by inverting the response to one protected input pattern, while an additional inversion introduced by TTLock restores the correct functionality only for the correct key.

3. Even though the TTLock logic can be identified via a signal-tracing attack, its removal will still leave the remaining logic different than the original one, thwarting removal attacks.

Furthermore, we introduce a novel locking approach, which we coin as *parametric locking*. As opposed to functional (logic) locking where keys are associated with design functionality, parametric locking ensures that the design/chip behaves as per its specifications (performance, power, etc.) only with the secret key in place; an incorrect key downgrades its parametric characteristics, leading to a reduced speed, increased power consumption, or degraded reliability. We elaborate on the objectives and challenges in parametric locking.

2. TTLOCK: CONSTRUCTION AND PROOF OF SECURITY

TTLock *modifies the design logic cone* to invert its output for a selected (protected) input pattern. The modification can be effected via logic gate insertions/replacements. The desired impact is an inverted output for only one input pattern corresponding to the correct key. The *restore unit* of TTLock then inverts the inverted output only for the correct key, thereby restoring the correct output. For any incorrect key, TTLock produces an inverted output for the protected input pattern. Both the key and the protected input pattern are the designer's secrets.

TTLock has the following properties:

- The modification applied to the logic cone is minimal to deliver maximal SAT attack resilience; the discriminating

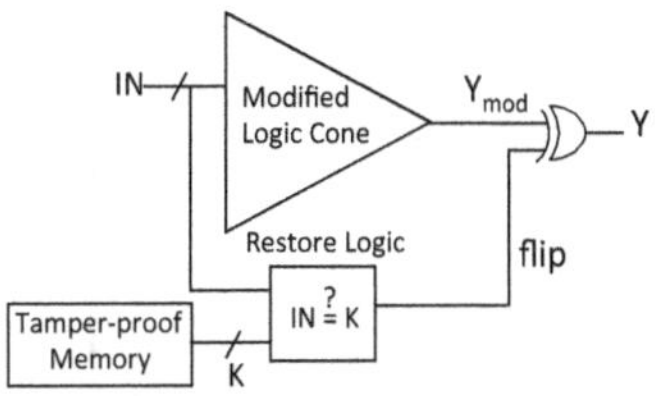

Ymod	IN	k0	k1	k2	k3	k4	k5	k6	k7
✔	0	✖	✔	✔	✔	✔	✔	✔	✔
✔	1	✔	✖	✔	✔	✔	✔	✔	✔
✔	2	✔	✔	✖	✔	✔	✔	✔	✔
✔	3	✔	✔	✔	✖	✔	✔	✔	✔
✔	4	✔	✔	✔	✔	✖	✔	✔	✔
✔	5	✔	✔	✔	✔	✔	✖	✔	✔
✖	6	✖	✖	✖	✖	✖	✖	✔	✖
✔	7	✔	✔	✔	✔	✔	✔	✔	✖

Figure 3: Proposed TTLock architecture. The logic cone is minimally modified by inverting the response of one input combination w.r.t. original logic cone. The restore logic fixes this inversion for the correct key for the intended input combination and introduces a second inversion for all incorrect keys. The secret key is k_6.

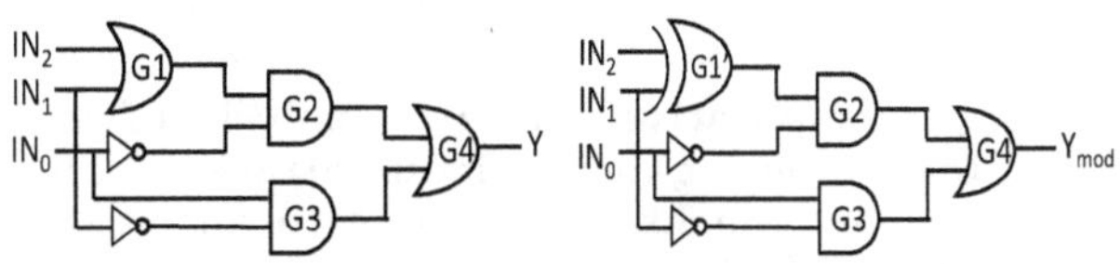

(a) (b)

Figure 4: a) Logic cone in the original circuit. b) Modified logic cone in TTLock. $G1$ in logic cone is replaced with $G1'$ in the modified logic cone that inverts the output Y_{mod} for IN=6.

ability of each input pattern is limited to a single incorrect key (See Section 2.2).

- Any reverse-engineering attack on the original logic cone recovers the modified, and thus, the incorrect functionality. The secret key should be known to understand the modification in the logic cone, protecting against removal attacks (See Section 2.2).

2.1 Construction of TTLock

Figure 3 depicts the generic architecture of the proposed TTLock using a simple example that assumes a three-input logic cone protected by a three-bit TTLock key. We consider the logic cone shown in Figure 4(a). Without loss of generality, we make a simplifying assumption that the logic cone input size n equals the key-size; in this example, n=3. TTLock includes a restore logic and an XOR gate. The restore logic consists of a comparator, whose output is 1 iff the input matches the key. The table in the same figure illustrates the inverted outputs. Y_{mod} column shows the inversion for the protected input pattern; this inversion is fixed only for the correct key k_6. Every incorrect key introduces the second inversion for a distinct input pattern.

The modified logic cone (MLC) implementing the inversion in Figure 3 is shown in Figure 4(b). The MLC produces an inverted output for input pattern 6. When the correct key K_{corr}=k_6 is applied, the restore logic asserts its output for input pattern 6, thereby canceling the inversion injected into the logic cone for that pattern and producing the correct/desired output. When an incorrect key, say k_2, is applied and for the input pattern 6, the restore logic output is 0. Consequently, the inverted output of the MLC is retained, thereby producing the wrong output. With k_2 applied, and for the input pattern 2, the restore logic output is 1. Consequently, the correct output of the MLC is inverted, thereby producing the wrong output again.

2.2 Security analysis of TTLock

Threat model: Consistent with all the logic-locking techniques proposed so far, the attacker is assumed to have access to (1) reverse-engineered (locked) netlist and (2) a working chip, i.e., oracle, that has the key loaded in its memory.
SAT attack resilience: TTLock achieves resilience against SAT attack by always ensuring that the SAT attack encounters its worst-case scenario: In each iteration, a DIP can eliminate at most only one incorrect key. For example, as shown in Figure 3, each input pattern eliminates only one incorrect key, thus, requiring 7=2^3-1 iterations. SAT attack can also perform random restarts. For instance, consider the circuit in Figure 3. If it randomly chooses IN=6 (the protected input pattern), it can eliminate all incorrect keys at once. However, an attacker/SAT attack does not know the protected input pattern. Thus, it can only choose the DIP uniformly at random. Thus, the probability of SAT attack choosing the protected input pattern is $\frac{1}{2^n}$. For a design with a large number of inputs, say 80, this probability becomes negligible (i.e., 2^{-80}), ensuring the security of TTLock.
Removal attack resilience. In removal attack, an attacker identifies and removes the protection logic. Since the *flip* signal (the output of the protection circuit) is highly skewed towards 0, it can be identified by the SSA attack. However, the input pattern(s) for which the design produces corrupted outputs are unknown to the attacker as is the secret key. Any removal attack would recover the MLC and not the original design.
Sensitization attack resilience. In TTLock, all the bits of the key converge on the *flip* signal. Therefore, sensitizing any given key-bit through the *flip* signal to Y requires setting all the other key-bits to known values. As all the key-bits are unknown, all the key-gates in TTLock are pairwise secure. Thus, the sensitization attack cannot be launched on TTLock.

2.3 Frequently Asked Questions

Question 1. Would minor modification(s) to the original SAT-based attack algorithm make the proposed scheme vulnerable to other SAT-based attacks? For example, can an attacker can introduce an additional constraint of IN=KEY in the SAT attack algorithm in order to eliminate all incorrect keys in just one iteration?
Answer. It would be feasible to add the suggested modifications/constraints only if the locked netlist had structural/functional traces that an attacker could exploit to identify the protected pattern. From the analysis of the locked netlist alone, the attacker cannot extract the protected input pattern; one has to exercise the oracle to determine whether a particular pattern is the protected one. The probability of an attacker determining the protected input pattern is $\frac{1}{2^n}$.
Question 2. The proposed TTLock scheme requires modification of the original logic cone. Assuming the logic cone has $n = 64$ inputs, such modification requires the construction of a truth table with 2^{64} inputs. Is it feasible to work with such large truth tables?
Answer. The original logic can be modified for the protected input pattern (minterm) by first introducing additional logic that modifies the output of the function for this minterm, and then by resynthesizing the entire design. The resynthesis process blends the added logic with the original design, eliminating its traces, due to various optimiza-

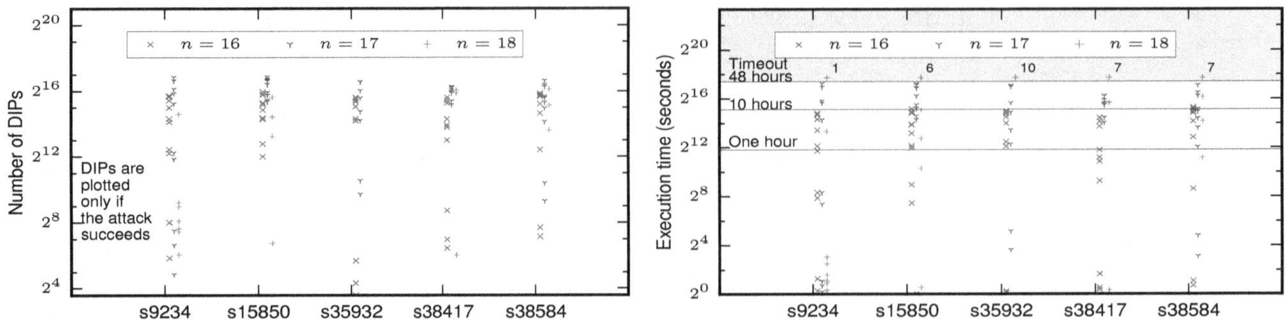

Figure 5: a) Number of DIPs required for the SAT attack [12], and b) execution time (seconds) for TTLock; $n=\{16, 17, 18\}$. The timeout is 48 hours. Timeout occurs only for $n=18$. The number of timeout instances (out of 10) for each circuit is shown above the timeout line.

tion and transformation steps. Conventional logic synthesis tools have traditionally been handling designs with input size greater than 64, and they are re-purposed for our objectives.

Question 3. Is the amount of entropy introduced minimal as TTLock only targets one output port of the original design?

Answer. There exists a trade-off between the SAT attack resilience and the output entropy, which is measured in terms of Hamming distance between the output for the correct key and the output for incorrect keys. For maximum SAT attack resilience, the entropy must be minimized. To achieve higher entropy while retaining maximal SAT attack resilience, TTLock may be used in conjunction with high entropy logic-locking techniques such as RLL or FLL.

3. RESULTS

3.1 Experimental setup

In this section, we present experimental results to confirm the security expectations and assess the implementation overhead for the proposed TTLock technique. We run our experiments on the largest ISCAS'89 benchmark circuits. Each experiment is repeated ten times in order to improve the statistical significance. The area, power, and delay overhead is obtained using Cadence RTL Compiler. FreePDK 45nm library is used [17].

3.2 Security analysis

The resilience of TTLock is dictated by the key-size n. The number of DIPs required for the SAT attack to succeed, and the corresponding execution time values are presented in Figure 5 for $n=\{16, 17, 18\}$.

Impact of key-size n. The expected number of DIPs required to break TTLock is 2^{n-1}. As shown in Figure 5(a), most of the blue entries ($n=17$) appear closer to 2^{16}, and most of the green entries ($n=16$) appear closer to 2^{15}. With the exception of a few cases where the attack may be fortuitously successful, TTLock thwarts the SAT attack by forcing the number of DIPs to be exponential in n. The SAT attack does not terminate for larger values of the key-size ($n \geq 18$); the probability of fortuitous attack success becomes exponentially smaller for larger values of n.

Execution time. As shown in Figure 5(b), the execution time of the SAT attack is proportional to the number of DIPs, although there is a slight variation of 3× to 4× across the benchmark circuits; the execution time grows exponentially in n. As noted earlier, most of the experiments with $n=18$ were aborted after 48 hours of execution.

Table 1: Comparative security analysis of logic-locking techniques against existing attacks. Vulnerability of a logic-locking technique to an attack is denoted by X. TTLock is secure against all attacks.

Attack	RLL [6]	FLL [7]	SLL [9]	Anti-SAT [14]	SARLock [13]	TTLock
Sensitization	X	X	✓	✓	✓	✓
SAT	X	X	X	✓	✓	✓
Removal	✓	✓	✓	X	X	✓

Table 2: APD overhead for TTLock.

Benchmark	s35932			s38417			s38584		
n	16	32	64	16	32	64	16	32	64
Area (%)	1.0	1.8	4.0	2.0	2.8	2.9	1.2	1.2	2.1
Power (%)	1.7	3.4	6.0	1.8	2.9	3.1	1.7	1.8	3.2
Delay (%)	1.2	1.2	1.4	0.2	0.2	0.1	0.8	0.6	0.5

3.3 Area, power, and delay (APD) overhead

Impact of key size n. While the security level increases exponentially in n for TTLock, the APD overhead must be accounted for in choosing n. As shown in Table 2, the APD overhead of TTLock is quite small. The average area, power, and delay overhead for $n=64$ is 3.0%, 4.1%, and 0.6%, respectively. TTLock comprises a single n-bit comparator, and the overhead increases linearly with n.

These APD results bode well for large-sized industrial circuits where the percentage overhead results are expected to be much smaller than those reported herein.

4. PARAMETRIC LOCKING APPLICATION: PERFORMANCE LOCKING

Till now, we have used logic locking to produce incorrect outputs on applying an incorrect key. We now leverage the logic locking technique to modify/protect the parametric behavior—power, delay, reliability, etc.—of the circuit. This is called parametric locking. Only on applying the correct key, the design exhibits a superior parametric behavior—for instance, high performance, low power, low-energy, highly reliable operations. On applying the incorrect key, the design exhibits a relatively poor parametric behavior. In this paper, we introduce an instance of parametric locking, namely, performance locking at the register-transfer (RT) level. Unlike functional locking, on applying an incor-

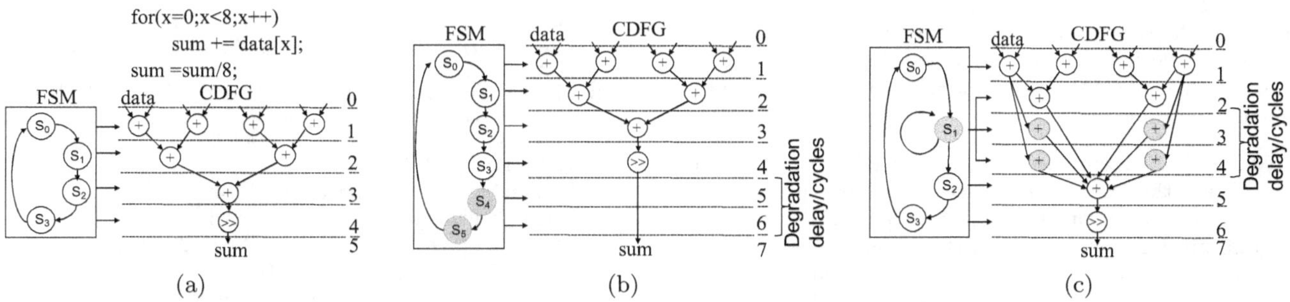

Figure 6: Performance locking. a) High-performance design with correct key. b) Performance locking using two wait states. c) Performance locking using two dummy computations.

rect key, parametric locking does not necessarily produce incorrect outputs but rather degrades the performance.

The section is organized as follows. We introduce the notion of performance locking with a motivating example. We then explain the business model, where performance locking will be useful, and the associated threat model. Security properties of performance locking are detailed next. Finally, outstanding challenges that need to be addressed to make performance locking feasible and effective are elaborated.

4.1 Performance locking at the RT-level

With an incorrect key applied, the design computes the final result by consuming an additional number of clock cycles. The application of the correct key provides a superior performance, i.e., a shorter execution time. In this work, we explain how this behavior can be implemented during high-level synthesis.

Motivational example: Consider the example of a design computing the average of the last eight numbers. The control data flow graph (CDFG) for this design with the correct key is shown in Fig. 6(a). The design requires four clock cycles. In the first three clock cycles, four, two and one addition operations are performed, respectively. At the final clock cycle, a three-bit right shift operation is applied on the data to get the average of eight numbers. Thus, we get the output at the start of fifth clock cycle, resulting in a latency of four clock cycles. We consider this CDFG as the representation of the high-performance design.

Consider the same design where the performance is degraded on applying an incorrect key. This can be performed in two ways, which are depicted in Fig. 6(b) and Fig. 6(c). In the first method shown in Fig. 6(b), two additional wait cycles are introduced to slow down the design. It can be observed that this has the effect of adding two redundant or null states (shown as shaded) in the finite state machine (FSM). Now, the latency of the design is increased from four to six clock cycles. In the second method depicted in Fig. 6(c), the same latency of six clock cycles is achieved. However, the final addition operation is performed during the fifth clock cycle, as opposed to the third clock cycle in the first method. During the third and fourth clock cycles, dummy computations (shown as shaded) are performed with the objective of adding further obscurity for the attacker; he/she faces the additional challenge of distinguishing the real computations from the dummy ones. Only one extra state is added; the FSM loops through this dummy state in the third and fourth clock cycles.

4.2 Business and threat models

Consider a company that intends to design and manufacture the same IC but has two sets of users. The first set of users can pay more than the second set and would naturally expect better IC performance. Currently, this type of business model is supported by speed binning, which is necessitated by unintended process variations. Parametric (performance) locking enables the companies to provide a similar feature intentionally, with security guarantees.

Threat model. The attacker is at the untrusted foundry or can be the end-user. He/she has black-box physical access to the IC with the superior performance. The objective of the attacker is to obtain the key to boost the performance of the ICs. To this end, he/she can buy an IC with high performance from the market, reverse engineer it, and obtain its netlist. Further, he/she can apply chosen inputs to another IC obtained from the market and collect the correct outputs.

4.3 Properties of performance locking

1. **Performance degradation ratio:** The effectiveness of performance locking is dictated by the performance ratio of the high-performance to low-performance design. Consider the same example, where the moving average of eight numbers is computed. The latency for the high-performance design, whose CDFG is shown in Figure 6(a), is four clock cycles. The latency for the low-performance designs, depicted in Figure 6(b) and Figure 6(c), is six clock cycles. Thus, the performance ratio is 1.5. To achieve higher degradation, one can introduce a larger number of wait cycles or insert a higher number of dummy computations, degrading the performance even further.

2. **Overhead:** The hardware added to perform performance locking must incur minimal overhead over the baseline high-performance design. The example presented above demonstrates that performance locking can be achieved at a minimal overhead. In the first method, only extra wait states are inserted, incurring a 31.67%, 35.21% and 1.1% overhead for the area, power, and timing respectively. In the second method, dummy computations are performed by reusing parts of the original design, thereby incurring an overhead of 147%, 150% and 27% in area, power, and timing, respectively. Here, the additional dummy operations lead to a higher power consumption. Here, for comparison the baseline design is the original design without any extra key logic. Thus, performance locking with added key logic leads to an overhead

presented above. However, since the considered example is small, the overhead is high. But, it will amortize for large-scale designs, as the number of flip-flops added to store the keys and the performance locking logic almost remain the same.

3. **Resilience against resynthesis attacks:** An attacker can obtain the high-performance CDFG by applying inputs and observing outputs of a functional IC. He/she can also obtain information about the resources used (number of adders, shift operations, etc.) and their connectivity using reverse engineering methods. He/she can then perform a performance-constrained synthesis for the obtained CDFG and the resource information; the performance constraint can be chosen as the number of clock cycles by which the CDFG has to complete its computation. In the previous example, it is four clock cycles. To this end, an attacker can use well-known resource-constrained synthesis algorithms [18]. Even though the worst-case complexity of those algorithms is NP-Hard, the algorithms obtain solutions much faster in reality. On obtaining the solution to the performance-constrained synthesis problem, an adversary resynthesizes the netlist to obtain the high-performance design. Currently, no defense techniques exist against such a resynthesis attack. This is the major impediment to developing provably-secure performance locking schemes.

5. CONCLUSION

In this paper, we attempt to widen the notion of logic locking. First, we follow the traditional path and propose a logic locking technique, TTLock, that is provably secure against all attacks such as sensitization, SAT, and removal attacks; all the previous logic locking techniques are susceptible to one or more of these attacks. TTLock modifies a logic cone by inverting the output for a protected input pattern and restores this inversion to recover the correct functionality for only the correct key. TTLock ensures provably-secure protection against SAT attacks, while the modification of the logic cone constitutes a strong defense against removal attacks.

Then, we introduce the notion of parametric locking, where the design specifications such as power, performance, and/or reliability may be locked, as opposed to the functionality. In parametric locking, an incorrect key still produces correct results but downgrades the power, performance, and/or reliability of the chip. We present the threat model and properties for parametric locking, and in particular, performance locking. The challenge for performance locking is to achieve increased performance degradation for incorrect keys and offer resilience against resynthesis attacks, without incurring a high overhead.

Acknowledgement. This work was supported by the New York University/New York University Abu Dhabi (NYU/NYUAD) Center for Cyber Security (CCS).

6. REFERENCES

[1] "Defense Science Board (DSB) study on High Performance Microchip Supply," 2005, [March 16, 2015]. [Online]. Available: www.acq.osd.mil/dsb/reports/ADA435563.pdf

[2] R. S. Chakraborty and S. Bhunia, "Security against Hardware Trojan through a Novel Application of Design Obfuscation," *IEEE/ACM International Conference on Computer-Aided Design*, pp. 113–116, 2009.

[3] M. Rostami, F. Koushanfar, and R. Karri, "A Primer on Hardware Security: Models, Methods, and Metrics," *Proceedings of the IEEE*, vol. 102, no. 8, pp. 1283–1295, 2014.

[4] SypherMedia, "Syphermedia library," http://www.smi.tv/syphermedia_library_circuit_camouflage_technology.html, [April 22, 2016].

[5] R. W. Jarvis and M. G. McIntyre, "Split Manufacturing Method for Advanced Semiconductor Circuits," *US Patent 7,195,931*, 2007.

[6] J. A. Roy, F. Koushanfar, and I. L. Markov, "Ending Piracy of Integrated Circuits," *IEEE Computer*, vol. 43, no. 10, pp. 30–38, 2010.

[7] J. Rajendran, H. Zhang, C. Zhang, G. Rose, Y. Pino, O. Sinanoglu, and R. Karri, "Fault Analysis-Based Logic Encryption," *IEEE Transactions on Computers*, vol. 64, no. 2, pp. 410–424, 2015.

[8] R. S. Chakraborty and S. Bhunia, "HARPOON: An Obfuscation-Based SoC Design Methodology for Hardware Protection," *IEEE Transactions on Computer-Aided Design of Integrated Circuits and Systems*, vol. 28, no. 10, pp. 1493–1502, 2009.

[9] M. Yasin, J. Rajendran, O. Sinanoglu, and R. Karri, "On Improving the Security of Logic Locking," *IEEE Transactions on Computer-Aided Design of Integrated Circuits and Systems*, vol. 35, no. 9, pp. 1411–1424, 2016.

[10] A. Baumgarten, A. Tyagi, and J. Zambreno, "Preventing IC Piracy Using Reconfigurable Logic Barriers," *IEEE Design & Test of Computers*, vol. 27, no. 1, pp. 66–75, 2010.

[11] S. M. Plaza and I. L. Markov, "Solving the Third-Shift Problem in IC Piracy With Test-Aware Logic Locking," *IEEE Transactions on Computer-Aided Design of Integrated Circuits and Systems*, vol. 34, no. 6, pp. 961–971, 2015.

[12] P. Subramanyan, S. Ray, and S. Malik, "Evaluating the Security of Logic Encryption Algorithms," *IEEE International Symposium on Hardware Oriented Security and Trust*, pp. 137–143, 2015.

[13] M. Yasin, B. Mazumdar, J. J. Rajendran, and O. Sinanoglu, "SARlock: SAT Attack Resistant Logic Locking," *IEEE International Symposium on Hardware Oriented Security and Trust*, pp. 236–241, 2016.

[14] Y. Xie and A. Srivastava, "Mitigating SAT Attack on Logic Locking," *International Conference on Cryptographic Hardware and Embedded Systems*, pp. 127–146, 2016.

[15] M. Yasin, B. Mazumdar, O. Sinanoglu, and J. Rajendran, "Security Analysis of Anti-SAT," *IEEE Asia and South Pacific Design Automation Conference*, pp. 342–347, 2016.

[16] J. Rajendran, Y. Pino, O. Sinanoglu, and R. Karri, "Security Analysis of Logic Obfuscation," *IEEE/ACM Design Automation Conference*, pp. 83–89, 2012.

[17] J. E. Stine, I. Castellanos, M. Wood, J. Henson, F. Love, W. R. Davis, P. D. Franzon, M. Bucher, S. Basavarajaiah, J. Oh *et al.*, "FreePDK: An Open-Source Variation-Aware Design Kit," *IEEE International Conference on Microelectronic Systems Education*, pp. 173–174, 2007.

[18] D. D. Gajski, N. D. Dutt, A. C.-H. Wu, and S. Y.-L. Lin, *High-level Synthesis: Introduction to Chip and System Design*. Norwell, MA, USA: Kluwer Academic Publishers, 1992.

Circuit Obfuscation and Oracle-guided Attacks: Who can Prevail?

Kaveh Shamsi[1], Meng Li[2], Travis Meade[1], Zheng Zhao[2], David Z. Pan[2], and Yier Jin[1]
[1]ECE Department, University of Central Florida, Orlando, FL, USA
[2]ECE Department, University of Texas at Austin, Austin, TX, USA
[1]{kaveh, travm12}@knights.ucf.edu, [2]{meng_li, zzhao, dpan}@utexas.edu,
[1]yier.jin@eecs.ucf.edu

ABSTRACT

This paper provides a systematization of knowledge in the domain of integrated circuit protection through obfuscation with a focus on the recent Boolean satisfiability (SAT) attacks. The study systematically combines real-world IC reverse engineering reports, experimental results using the most recent oracle-guided attacks, and concepts in machine-learning and cryptography to draw a map of the state-of-the-art of IC obfuscation and future challenges and opportunities.

1. INTRODUCTION

Two of the major security and privacy concerns in today's integrated circuit (IC) supply chain are 1) The threat of integrated circuit reverse engineering (RE), 2) the threat of malicious hardware modifications known as hardware Trojans. IC reverse engineering technologies have been constantly improving over the past decades resulting in a near fully automated process for extracting various kinds of information from modern ICs fabricated with nanometer scale features [39, 25, 1]. The trend of globalization of IC manufacturing has also continued, leaving designers in US with few competitive trusted fabrication facilities. Fabless design houses carry out high-profit design and intellectual property development tasks while the complex and costly manufacturing services are outsourced to off-shored foundries [33].

Over the past couple of decades, various design-time techniques have been proposed for thwarting the above threats [29]. The most prominent of this techniques include: 1) IC camouflaging: based on creating indistinguishable layout structures to hinder reverse engineering by end-users; 2) Logic locking: to lock down a circuit with active key bits that are programmed post-manufacturing hiding away details from the foundry as well as the end-user; 3) Split-manufacturing: manufacturing only part of the IC (e.g. Front End Of Line layers) in the untrusted fab. The focus of this paper is on the first two techniques and their security. Both of IC camouflaging and logic locking can be classified as circuit "obfuscation" schemes as they modify the design to obscure information away from the attacker while maintaining its functionality.

The two most important question regarding circuit obfuscation is whether they are secure and whether they can be implemented with low overhead. In 2015 a Boolean Satisfiability (SAT) based attack [17, 38] was proposed that was shown to be able to deobfuscate a significant portion of existing low-overhead IC camouflaging and logic locking schemes. Since then the problem of logic obfuscation/deobfuscation has reemerged. In this paper we will take a systematic look at some of the most prominent circuit obfuscation schemes discussed in literature with respect to the SAT attack and beyond the SAT attack. The main contribution of the paper is that it summarizes a broad range of adversary-models, recent attacks, most resilient low-overhead obfuscation schemes, and the silicon level technologies that enable them. This can help researchers identify the open problems in the domain.

The paper is organized as follows. We begin by first surveying IC camouflaging and logic locking algorithms and their nanodevice primitives presented in prior work in Section 2. We then discuss the various threats posed by end-users and the foundry and the emergence of SAT attacks in Section 3. We evaluate the security of select circuit obfuscation schemes under these threats in Section 4. Future directions are discussed in Section 5. Section 6 concludes the paper.

Permission to make digital or hard copies of all or part of this work for personal or classroom use is granted without fee provided that copies are not made or distributed for profit or commercial advantage and that copies bear this notice and the full citation on the first page. Copyrights for components of this work owned by others than ACM must be honored. Abstracting with credit is permitted. To copy otherwise, or republish, to post on servers or to redistribute to lists, requires prior specific permission and/or a fee. Request permissions from permissions@acm.org.

GLSVLSI '17, May 10-12, 2017, Banff, AB, Canada

© 2017 ACM. ISBN 978-1-4503-4972-7/17/05...5.00

DOI: http://dx.doi.org/10.1145/3060403.3060494

2. BACKGROUND

2.1 Integrated Circuit Supply Chain

The modern semiconductor industry operates on a global scale with a distributed design, verification and fabrication network [33]. The fabless design model has shown to be productive for several industries and it is predicted that it will continue to grow [33]. In this model, the design and the verification are performed in the design house. Then the design layout in form of a GDSII file is sent to the foundry. Fabrication, and possibly testing and packaging is performed at the foundry and the devices are shipped back to the designer for retail. The foundry has a special position in the IC supply chain. It has possession of the layout of the device, therefore, all hard silicon features are known to the foundry and it has the ability to maliciously modify the design.

Once the ICs arrive at the end-user's disposal, the threat of physical reverse engineering begins. There are standard techniques and automatic tools for an end-user to remove the IC package, scan the IC layer by layer, image each layer and then use image-recognition techniques to reconstruct the layout and subsequently the netlist of the chip [40]. Furthermore, micro-probing technology allows the attacker to read values stored in Flash or other active memories by probing specific wires that carry the information [25].

2.2 IC Camouflaging

IC camouflaging is the idea of fabricating integrated circuits with layout structures that are difficult to resolve to a certain functionality. The building blocks of IC camouflaging are silicon structures for which their functionality is difficult to determine through reverse engineering with microscopy, or chemical and mechanical processes [15]. Hence, designing these building blocks is a nano-device fabrication problem. There is an array of such technologies available [4, 11, 14, 10, 5] most of which are compatible with the CMOS process. Since our paper's focus is on the Boolean function level we broadly classify all camouflaging devices into the following categories of primitives:

- **Connectors**: these include metal-to-metal [10], or metal-to-diffusion [12] connectors that are either connected that appear unconnected, or unconnected that appear connected.
- **Fixed Transistors**: which are transistors that are always-on or always-off regardless of the gate-terminal voltage [5, 6, 4].

There are various nano-device structures that are used to implement each of the above primitives. A few that are important for the purpose of this paper include: 1) Doping-based camouflaging where two transistors with similar gate and contact structures but different doping types behave differently creating fixed transistors or connector diodes [36, 36]; 2) Metal-to-metal vias with a middle-gap [10]; 3) Mg/MgO metal-to-metal vias [9]; 4) Metal-to-diffusion connectors with a thin insulating layer between the drain and the contact arriving on top of it [12]; 5) Light-density-doping (LDD) can also be used to render always-on or always-off transistors [4].

Larger camouflaged functional units can be built using these primitives: 1) camouflaged gates that implement different functionalities using camouflaged connectors [28], 2) a single camouflaged bit using a voltage divider with two camouflaged contacts or a fixed transistor, 3) gates with dummy inputs using fixed transistors [21], 4) dummy paths using a wire and two fake metal-to-metal vias at the end-points can be built. These unites can then be dispersed throughout the netlist with different strategies [28] which are discussed further in Section 4.

2.3 Logic Locking

While the above camouflaging technologies make it difficult for an end-user to reverse engineer the correct netlist from the layout, the true functionality of the camouflaging units, such as which vias are fake or true is still disclosed to the foundry. In order to prevent the foundry from learning design secrets the secret should not be part of the layout.

Logic locking is an obfuscation scheme that relies on active key-inputs that are programmed on the chip after the chip returns from fabrication effectively hiding them from the foundry [31]. The goal is to have the circuit produce incorrect outputs for incorrect key values. At the silicon level, logic locking can be implemented either with a dedicated tamper-proof memory feeding key values, or with programmable primitives dispersed throughout the netlist. Some possible programmable primitives are oxide-breakdown-based anti-fuse devices, emerging non-volatile memory devices such as RRAMs [43] and other non-volatile programmable devices whose state is difficult to determine from microscopy.

At the functional level there are various strategies for logic locking. We can broadly categorize them into sequential logic locking and combinational logic locking. Combinational logic locking schemes corrupt the output of a directed-acyclic-graph (DAG) circuit using key-inputs. Notable schemes include adding key-controlled XOR/XNOR or MUX gates in randomly selected [31] or judiciously selected [30, 27] locations in the circuit; replacing gates with look-up-tables [7, 42] that store key-values; shuffling wires with key-controlled switch-boxes [32, 43]; and a few other gate insertion/replacement schemes [16].

Sequential logic locking schemes [8, 18] focus on adding dummy states to the state-transition-graph (STG) of a sequential circuit. We will focus on combinational obfuscation schemes in this paper as they assume a stronger threat-model which is that the attacker has access to all registers through the scan-chain. Furthermore, if a secure combinational obfuscation scheme exists, simply obfuscating the state-generation function of a sequential circuit with that scheme will result in a secure sequential obfuscation.

Logic-locking can be extended to prevent overproduction by including a physical unclonable function (PUF) onto the chip applying a device-unique mapping to the key. With the PUF every fabricated chip will have a different key value.

2.4 Circuit Diversification

Assume a circuit is implemented with a Boolean function c_o there is a large set of Boolean circuits that implement the same function, $c_o \in C$. Circuit diversification schemes [26, 24] try to replace c_o with another circuit $c_d \in C$ such that it is difficult for an attacker to find the structures in c_o given c_d. For instance, by replacing pieces of logic with another randomly selected equivalent circuit can potentially disguise an attacker-known structure in the circuit preventing graph-isomorphism based component matching in the netlist. Note that by itself this does not hinder recovery of the netlist of c_d which is functionally equivalent to c_o.

3. ADVERSARIAL MODELS

We will describe a classification of threats accounting for realistic reverse engineering reports such as [25]. The supply chain in view of this categorization is depicted in Figure 1.

3.1 High-level Recognition

Typically the first step in IC reverse engineering is optically imaging the chip. With optical images although transistor details in advanced technologies are not visible, the boundaries of memory arrays, digital logic or analog blocks are recognizable. This allows the attacker to establish a high-level knowledge of the position of different components. Next the attacker can proceed with scanning electron microscopy (SEM) and imaging to get down to nanometer scale features of the chip.

In addition, the attacker can utilize micro-probing technologies to probe accessible portions of the circuit. In order to probe the circuit the adversary has to find the particular wires that she is interested in such as the bus that carries the decrypted values from Flash memory to the processor. It is intuitive that with some knowledge of the high-level functionality and knowledge of the location of important wires the attacker can probe accessible wires or attach hardware Trojans to them for the case of a foundry adversary. Therefore, it is safer to assume that an obfuscation scheme will prevent hardware Trojan insertion only if it prevents high-level recognition which as we discuss later can be rather difficult to prevent using low-overhead obfuscation.

3.2 Netlist Recovery

A more difficult task for the adversary is to extract an unambiguous circuit netlist from the IC. In this case if the circuit is camouflaged or locked the attacker will recover an obfuscated netlist as seen in Figure 1. This obfuscated netlist can have camouflaged components that can implement a set of possible functions, or the netlist has a set of active key inputs that are unknown. Both cases can be modeled as Boolean function $c_e : I \times K \to O$ where I and K are input and key space respectively, and there exists a correct key k_* such that $\forall i \in I,\ c_e(i, k) = c_o(i)$ where c_o is the unobfuscated circuit. In terms of deobfuscation accuracy there are two cases:

- **Exact Attack**: the attacker wants to exactly find the original netlist or a functional equivalent of it.
- **Approximate Attack**: the attacker can allow for some inaccuracy in the attack.

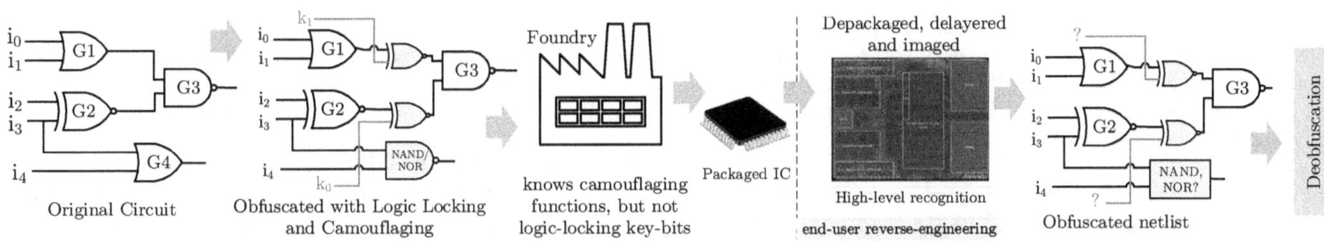

Figure 1: Integrated circuit life-cycle through obfuscation and deobfuscation (The chip image is from [1]).

Most recent and strong deobfuscation attacks assume that the attacker also has access to an "oracle", an unlocked or functional circuit that returns correct outputs for chosen inputs. In this dimension the attacks can be categorized as:

- **oracle-guided**: the attacker can query the oracle circuit with i and receive the output $c_o(i)$.
- **obfuscated-oracle-guided**: the attacker can query the oracle with i and will receive $\gamma(c_o(\alpha(i)))$ where α and γ are potentially obfuscated functions.
- **oracle-less**: the attacker does not have access to an oracle.

Another significant aspects in evaluating the resiliency of logic obfuscation schemes is assumptions on the physical reverse engineering capabilities of the attacker. Attacks can be categorized in this dimension by considering which of the following capabilities the attacker has:

- the attacker can differentiate between doping types;
- attacker sees all connections as potentially-fake;
- attacker can differentiate between potentially-fake and true connections;
- attacker can differentiate between fake and true connections.

Based on the abstract camouflaging primitive categorization in Section 2.2 the above questions should cover the entire space of attacker physical reverse engineering capabilities. To stress the importance of these assumptions, we note that with the last assumption none of existing camouflaging schemes would be secure, and with the second assumption the simplest camouflaging schemes would be extremely difficult to deobfuscate. Currently we know that doping types are easily visible. There is no extensive documented efforts on breaking non-doping camouflaged connectors.

3.3 Evolution of Oracle-guided Attacks

The first works on logic locking proved the security of their schemes by assuming that in order for the adversary to recover the key the attacker has to solve the following equivalence equation $c_e(i, k) = c_o(i)$ which is NP-complete due to alternating quantifies and hence difficult to solve for k. However, the reasoning is not accurate because the Boolean equation for c_o is not available to the attacker. The oracle-guided threat model then arrived in the work of Rajendran et al. [28] where they proposed that by sensitizing the output of the circuit to a particular key-bit that key-bit can be revealed through querying.

The SAT attack [17, 37, 34] which is the most recent and strongest oracle-guided attack queries the circuit on input patterns that result in disagreements for different key values. A novel aspect of the SAT attack is that the circuit is modeled as a SAT formula and the input-output observations are also stored as Boolean conjunctive clauses in the SAT formula. This allows an efficient SAT solver to wrestle with the NP-complete problem to both find disagreeing queries and find a key value that satisfies all of the observed queries with high performance. The SAT attack shows great capability against most known logic locking schemes and camouflaging schemes that replace a portion of gates in the design with camouflaged gates.

3.4 A General Model for Oracle-guided Deobfuscation

It is possible to construct a set of general security criteria for resiliency against deobfuscation. As was pointed out in [21, 34] oracle-guided attacks against circuit obfuscation are equivalent to learning a function with samples. The attacker begins with a set of possible functionalities in a function space C. This set C essentially denotes all the information that the attacker begins with including the obfuscated netlist (without the obfuscated netlist itself as a hint, C will be the set of all possible circuits). Then the attacker can query the oracle and use the observed information to further prune C to get to the target function c_o.

Given this model, an obfuscation scheme is computationally secure if there is no algorithm that will find c_o in time polynomial in the circuit size. An obfuscation is information-theoretically secure if there is no algorithm that finds c_o any better than random guessing given infinite amount of time. In machine learning terms approximation can also be modeled using the probably-approximately-correct (PAC)-learning scheme [2, 20]. In PAC-learning terms, an obfuscation is computationally approximation resilient if there exists no polynomial time randomized algorithm A that can learn an ϵ-approximation of the function c_o with success rate of $1 - \delta$ where δ and ϵ are arbitrarily small.

4. CASE STUDY DEFENSES

4.1 Programmable Logic Blocks

Using programmable logic blocks have been suggested in literature as an obfuscation strategy [22, 42]. Various forms of programmable logic such as SRAM-LUT based FPGAs, Anti-fuse FPGA, One-time Programmable PLAs, LUTs with doping based camouflaged configuration bits [36], LUTs with dummy via camouflaging, etc. can be used as an obfuscated circuit wherein the configuration bits are the secret key. If the attacker cannot observe the configuration bits the device appears to implement a large number of possible functionalities. Against high-level recognition, the layout of programmable device fabrics has a repetitive structure so that unlike an ASIC the optical images do not reveal logic boundaries. Essentially the circuit functionality is programmed electrically rather than physically as in ASICs.

It is easy to show that programmable logic based obfuscation is secure against key recovery if the input size is large. A programmable logic fabric that has g gates and reconfigurable interconnects, will implement all possible functions that can be implemented by rearranging l gates if $l \ll g$. Due to the high expressiveness of the programmable logic each query will reveal the output of the logic for only that particular input. Against oracle-guided approximation, the rate at which any algorithm learns the truth-table of the programmable block is linear in the size of the truth-table and thus for a large enough input size this rate can be slow.

The size of the programmable logic plays an important role. This is the main reason why replacing small gates with small LUTs [42] does not provide exponential security against SAT attacks. We obfuscated the c432 ISCAS benchmark circuit by replacing gates with LUTs of various sizes and attacked it using our C++ SAT attack framework[1]. As can be seen from Table 4.1 the number of necessary queries and running time in seconds do not increase exponentially with the number of small LUTs.

#LUT-inputs	2		3		5		6	
#LUTs	time	#iter	time	#iter	time	#iter	time	#iter
4	0.02	8	0.04	24	0.18	68	0.72	171
8	0.03	20	0.12	62	0.53	132	2.2	234
16	0.15	41	0.39	95	1.53	183	3.12	282
20	0.18	46	1.03	156	1.97	205	3.37	276
32	0.58	81	1.82	152	2.06	205	2.58	257

Table 1: LUT insertion resiliency with respect to the number of inputs to the LUT and the number of LUTs inserted.

While programmable units can provide possibly the maximum level of security available from an obfuscation scheme, they come at high area, power and delay costs. Averaged across different functions, FPGAs can cost 30X more area, 3-4X more delay, and 10X more power consumption [19]. Therefore, Liu et al. [23] proposed replacing only critical modules in the design such as the instruction decoder, in the case of a SPARC processor with FPGA fabric which can reduce the overall overhead costs.

4.2 Point-function based Logic Locking and IC Camouflaging

Since the advent of the SAT attacks several works have targeted defeating the attack by utilizing special key functions that are hard to break given oracle samples [21, 44, 45, 47]. A point-function $P(i, k)$ will return 0 for all $i \neq k$ and 1 otherwise. This function can be implemented by XORing bits in the k and i vectors and then feeding the resulting bits into an AND-tree. For IC camouflaging, small BUF/INV camouflaging gates can be used at the input of the AND-tree and for logic locking programmable switches can be used. It is easy to see that for this function querying i values will not reveal k unless $i = k$ which has a low probability if the bit-length of i and k is large.

This idea of low activity key functions is the basis of all of the proposed point-function schemes. Since the output corruptibility of such schemes is low they have to be combined with other high-corruptibility schemes such as random XOR/XNOR logic locking or gate-replacement IC camouflaging.

While it is easy to see that all these schemes provide computational security against exact SAT attacks for large input sizes, they fail to resist an approximation attack. This was exploited in the work of Shamsi et al. [34] where an approximate SAT attack was developed that stops the querying process early and justifies the entire key vector. The returned key will have effectively solved the high-corruptibility portions of the obfuscation. Thus only the low-corruptibility obfuscation would remain which due to the fact that it is corrupting the output for only a single input pattern, the attacker has obtained a very good approximation of the original circuit in polynomial queries. Hence point-function obfuscation schemes lack resiliency against approximate oracle-guided attacks.

In addition, some of the point-function schemes are vulnerable to structural and functional analysis [46]. In such attacks the attacker performs a structural search in the circuit to find the point-function block, and since most these schemes insert the point-function into the circuit at a single-point removing it from the obfuscated circuit will return the original circuit.

Against high-level recognition, as stand-alone solutions these schemes provide no security, since they have one point of entry in the circuit so only a single wire is affected by the obfuscation and the structure of the original circuit is largely preserved.

4.3 Layout Flooding

Since the SAT attack was proposed most researchers in academia have shifted towards developing new obfuscation schemes that can withstand the attack. For IC camouflaging the documented attacks [17] were against gate-level IC camouflaging where randomly selected or clique selected gates in the circuit are replaced with camouflaged gates that implement a possible set of three or four functionalities.

A particular camouflaging scheme that was not analyzed under the SAT attacks is present in a series of industrial patents and is currently part of commercialized circuit camouflaging technologies [13]. This scheme is based on flooding the layout of the circuit with dummy gates and dummy wires and then connecting them to active logic as seen in Figure 2.

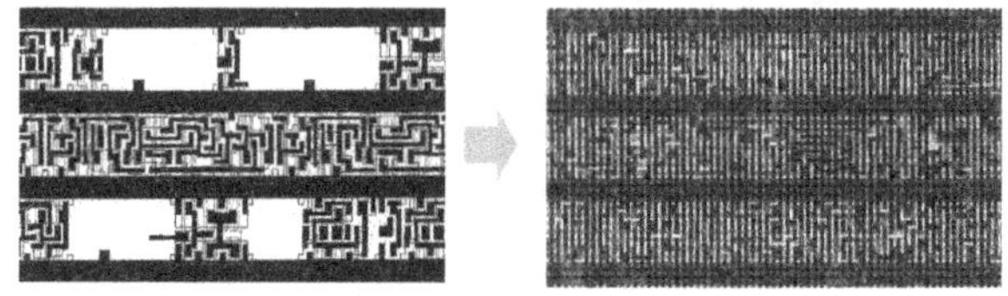

Figure 2: Layout flooding from [13].

While adding a large number of dummy elements to the design and filling empty areas of the chip with dummy logic can provide difficulties during layout image recognition, the specific insertion and connection algorithm determines SAT attack resiliency. The algorithms discussed in [13] insert filler cells into the empty areas of the layout and then connect them to active logic. However, the connections are passive with respect to the original circuit, meaning that the output of filler cells is not disrupting the functionality of the original circuit. Therefore, other than hindering cell recognition during layer-by-layer image analysis the defense does not affect the SAT attack complexity.

Acyclic wire-flooding obfuscation scheme experiment. Along the direction of layout flooding, we designed a dummy wire flooding obfuscation scheme. In this scheme for a certain percentage of the wires in the circuit we connect them to a number of randomly selected location using a MUX effectively creating dummy paths with the condition that no logical loops are created. We applied this scheme to a set of randomly synthesized circuits of input-size 8 with a few 100 gates and report the results in Table 4.3. As can be seen once the circuit is flooded with dummy paths the deobfuscation process becomes difficult. Around 50% coverage with more than 8-input MUXs the attack becomes ineffective. However, the overhead of adding all these dummy paths to 50% of the wires in the circuit can be high.

%wires	10%		20%		30%		50%	
MUX-size	time	#iter	time	#iter	time	#iter	time	#iter
2	0.06	10	0.29	17	0.54	28	2.22	38
4	0.29	19	1.02	22	2.89	41	27.3	68
6	0.48	20	1.91	25	10.1	47	1286	84
8	0.61	17	5.26	37	56	56	TO	TO

Table 2: LUT insertion resiliency with respect to the number of inputs to the LUT and the number of LUTs inserted.

Cyclic wire-flooding obfuscation. Shamsi et al. [35] recently proposed a topological obfuscation scheme that uses camouflaged/program

[1]All tests in this paper were run on a quad-core Intel Xeon E3 processor with a 3.4GHz CPU, and 16GB memory.

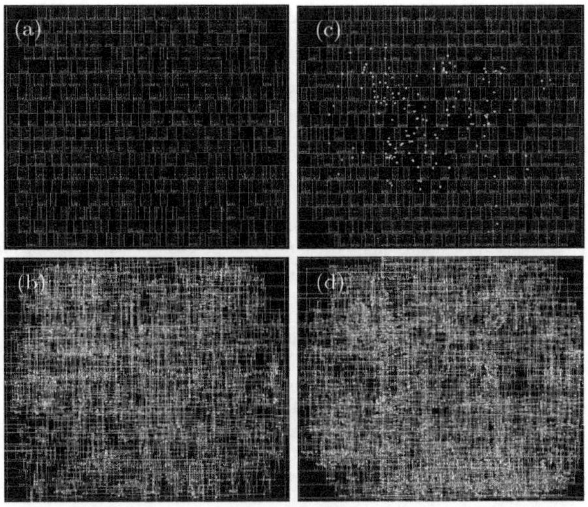

Figure 3: Cyclic camouflaging on the c1908 ISCAS benchmark where (a) and (b) are the original circuit, (c) shows the dispersed camouflaging vias and (d) is the routed obfuscated circuit. In Layout flooding schemes only wire overhead is incurred.

connectors to insert minimum number of dummy wires into the logic to create "unresolvable loops". If logical loops are created in the circuit the SAT attack will not be able to proceed since the obfuscated circuit can no longer be represented as a DAG. Hence combining this idea with layout flooding schemes, such that not only are all empty areas filled with dummy structures, but that many unresolvable loops are also created can result in a low overhead highly resilient obfuscation for ASICs. The looped structure of the circuit graph adds an additional dimension to the complexity of the SAT attack and therefore should result in higher attack complexities than acyclic flooding of the same size.

As for high-level recognition layout flooding schemes can potentially create security. The dummy connections can make it difficult for the attacker to find and trace specific wires or perform microsurgery to reach and probe arbitrary signals. Note that none of the obfuscation schemes discussed thus far are resilient against arbitrary probing. A layout implementation of the cyclic obfuscation scheme on the c1908 ISCAS benchmark can be seen in Figure 3.

4.4 Using Cryptographic Functions

Almost all IC camouflaging and logic locking schemes would break if the attacker can observe a significant number of internal signals. One of the most intriguing questions in cryptography over the last few decades has been to see whether there exists a general algorithm for obfuscating a function that remains secure even if all internal variables are public [3]. Although it is still an open problem, certain cryptographic primitives can be used to obfuscated specific functions providing security against probing. One such example which can be useful in authentication is the hashed password checking function. In this scheme a cryptographic hash of a secret key is stored on the device and then a comparison with this key is performed by taking the hash of the input and comparing it to the stored value. In such a circuit reading internal values will not reveal the password in plain-text.

It seems intuitive to utilize the numerous cryptographic blocks in obfuscation schemes. For instance the hash password checker can be used to raise a wire to signal the circuit to begin operation. Yasin et al. [48] also proposed inserting an AES block in the path of the secret key before feeding the key bits to key gates in logic locking. The security of the AES cipher against chosen plain-text attacks would imply the security of such an obfuscation against oracle-guided key-recovery. However, the main disadvantage of using cryptographic blocks in this way is that they can be vulnerable to structural/functional search attacks. For instance, the single wire that enables the circuit operation can be found and excluded from the circuit returning the original circuit. The AES block can also be found and simply removed from the circuit. Hiding these large blocks within the circuit with strong security guarantees would be very difficult and costly if not impossible.

5. FUTURE DIRECTIONS

5.1 Machine-learning Approaches

The existing SAT attacks are essentially machine-learning algorithms that learn the original functionality of the obfuscated circuit given input-output samples. However, machine-learning approaches can be applied to attack other aspects of obfuscation schemes. The obfuscation algorithm is public to the attacker and the synthesis and place & route tools that are used are a source of statistical signatures that can be detected through machine-learning. Generally, a machine-learning problem can be formed where the obfuscation algorithm, f was applied to the circuit and given samples of f the attacker wants to learn f^{-1} to reverse the obfuscation. Furthermore, machine-learning schemes can be used for searching structure or functionality of the circuit for finding obfuscation blocks such as point-functions and remove them from the circuit.

The reason for any machine-learning scheme to prevail in deobfuscation is that there exists small statistical variations in any obfuscation scheme that are dependant on the original circuit functionality. Unlike cryptography where these small variations are studied in depth and exploited in attacks, for circuit obfuscation this task has lacked motivation since few such attack have been documented. This direction also motivates designing algorithms that will destroy such secret-dependant variations. Circuit diversification schemes may be useful for this purpose.

5.2 Side-channel Attacks

The obfuscated circuit is physically implemented on a device. Therefore, they are vulnerable to power, timing, and electromagnetic side-channel attacks. Side-channels can reveal small statistical variations that are dependant on the key value. Thus far, most proposals have simply suggested that side-channel attacks will not be possible since the camouflaging elements that are used do not have secret-dependant power consumption profiles. However, there are various power models and higher order attacks that can be used. Therefore, designing such attacks and then preventing them with circuit and algorithmic solutions is a critical to the overall security.

5.3 Physical Aspects

The security of obfuscation schemes is significantly affected by the resiliency of the camouflaging primitives. For instance, if camouflaging metal-to-metal via can be made for which the attacker cannot differentiate between real and potentially-fake vias, it would be extremely difficult to attack layout flooding and cyclic interconnection camouflaging schemes. The ability of the attacker to tell apart real silicon constructs from potentially camouflaged ones allows the attacker to localize the uncertainty in the netlist to a fraction of the entire design. This is key to the success of SAT attacks on large circuits. This was also suggested in [41] where authors assert that resilient camouflaging primitives that can become ubiquitous in the netlist will create great attack complexity. Note that for logic locking it is more difficult to use ubiquitous programmable elements, due to the fact that each secret bit has to be programmed requiring programming circuitry that will help the attacker identify protected regions as well as creating additional overhead.

Another instance that stresses the importance of physical aspects of obfuscation is doping-based camouflaging. Various works [36] were published under the assumption that doping patterns cannot be detected with microscopy, however, there exists several microscopy and chemical processes to detect doping types. Unfortunately developing and securing camouflaging primitives is a nanofabrication research problem and is outside the scope of the EDA community, however, it has a significant impact on the security analysis at the functional level.

6. CONCLUSION

In this paper the state-of-the-art in IC protection through obfuscation was evaluated. In summary it was demonstrated that the ubiquitous flooding of the circuit layout with camouflaging or programmable components and the utilization of cyclic circuit structures will substantially increase the complexity of reverse engineering attacks with low overhead. Further research into the design and resiliency testing of camouflaging nano-structures is essential to the the security of circuit obfuscation.

7. REFERENCES

[1] Chipwork. http://ww.chipworks.com/.

[2] J. L. Balcázar, J. Castro, D. Guijarro, J. Köbler, and W. Lindner. A general dimension for query learning. *Journal of Computer and System Sciences*, 73(6):924–940, 2007.

[3] B. Barak, O. Goldreich, R. Impagliazzo, S. Rudich, A. Sahai, S. Vadhan, and K. Yang. On the (im) possibility of obfuscating programs. In *Annual International Cryptology Conference*, pages 1–18. Springer, 2001.

[4] J. Baukus, L. Chow, and W. Clark. Permanently on transistor implemented using a double polysilicon layer cmos process with buried contact, May 25 2004. US Patent 6,740,942.

[5] J. Baukus, L. Chow, and W. Clark. Programmable connector/isolator and double polysilicon layer cmos process with buried contact using the same, May 17 2005. US Patent 6,893,916.

[6] J. P. Baukus, W. M. Clark Jr, L.-W. Chow, and A. R. Kramer. Integrated circuit security system and method with implanted interconnections, Feb. 2 1999. US Patent 5,866,933.

[7] A. C. Baumgarten. Preventing integrated circuit piracy using reconfigurable logic barriers. 2009.

[8] R. Chakraborty and S. Bhunia. HARPOON: An obfuscation-based soc design methodology for hardware protection. *IEEE J. Technol. Comput. Aided Design*, 28(10):1493–1502, 2009.

[9] S. Chen, J. Chen, D. Forte, J. Di, M. Tehranipoor, and L. Wang. Chip-level anti-reverse engineering using transformable interconnects. In *Proc. IEEE Int. Symp. Defect and Fault Tolerance in VLSI and Nanotechnology Systems*, pages 109–114. IEEE, 2015.

[10] L. Chow, J. Baukus, and W. Clark. Integrated circuits protected against reverse engineering and method for fabricating the same using vias without metal terminations, Sept. 14 2004. US Patent 6,791,191.

[11] L. Chow, J. Baukus, and W. Clark. Integrated circuits protected against reverse engineering and method for fabricating the same using an apparent metal contact line terminating on field oxide, Nov. 13 2007. US Patent 7,294,935.

[12] L.-W. Chow, J. P. Baukus, and W. M. Clark Jr. Integrated circuits protected against reverse engineering and method for fabricating the same using an apparent metal contact line terminating on field oxide, Nov. 13 2007. US Patent 7,294,935.

[13] L. W. Chow, J. P. Baukus, B. J. Wang, and R. P. Cocchi. Camouflaging a standard cell based integrated circuit, Apr. 3 2012. US Patent 8,151,235.

[14] L.-W. Chow, W. M. Clark Jr, and J. P. Baukus. Covert transformation of transistor properties as a circuit protection method. US Patent 7,217,977.

[15] R. P. Cocchi, J. P. Baukus, L. W. Chow, and B. J. Wang. Circuit camouflage integration for hardware ip protection. In *Proc. Design Automation Conf.*, pages 1–5. IEEE, 2014.

[16] S. Dupuis, P.-S. Ba, G. Di Natale, M.-L. Flottes, and B. Rouzeyre. A novel hardware logic encryption technique for thwarting illegal overproduction and hardware trojans. In *Proc. IEEE Int. On-Line Testing Symposium*, pages 49–54. IEEE, 2014.

[17] M. El Massad, S. Garg, and M. V. Tripunitara. Integrated circuit (ic) decamouflaging: Reverse engineering camouflaged ics within minutes. In *NDSS*, 2016.

[18] F. Koushanfar. Provably secure active ic metering techniques for piracy avoidance and digital rights management. *IEEE Trans. on Information Forensics and Security*, 7(1):51–63, 2012.

[19] I. Kuon and J. Rose. Measuring the gap between fpgas and asics. 26(2):203–215, 2007.

[20] D. D. Lewis and J. Catlett. Heterogeneous uncertainty sampling for supervised learning. In *Proc. Int. Conf. on Machine Learning*, pages 148–156, 1994.

[21] M. Li, K. Shamsi, T. Meade, Z. Zhao, B. Yu, Y. Jin, and D. Z. Pan. Provably secure camouflaging strategy for ic protection. In *ICCAD*, page 28. ACM, 2016.

[22] B. Liu and B. Wang. Embedded reconfigurable logic for asic design obfuscation against supply chain attacks. In *Proc. Design, Automation and Test in Eurpoe*, pages 1–6, 2014.

[23] B. Liu and B. Wang. Reconfiguration-based vlsi design for security. 5(1):98–108, 2015.

[24] J. T. McDonald, Y. Kim, and D. Koranek. Deterministic circuit variation for anti-tamper applications. In *Proceedings of the Seventh Annual Workshop on Cyber Security and Information Intelligence Research*, page 68. ACM, 2011.

[25] T. Olivier and N. Dmitry. On the impact of automating the ic analysis process. In *Blackhat USA*, 2015.

[26] J. Parham, Y. Kim, et al. Hiding circuit components using boundary blurring techniques. In *Proc. of IEEE Annual Symposium on VLSI*, pages 5–7, 2010.

[27] J. Rajendran, Y. Pino, O. Sinanoglu, and R. Karri. Security analysis of logic obfuscation. In *DAC*, pages 83–89, 2012.

[28] J. Rajendran, M. Sam, O. Sinanoglu, and R. Karri. Security analysis of integrated circuit camouflaging. In *Proceedings of the 2013 ACM SIGSAC conference on Computer & communications security*, pages 709–720. ACM, 2013.

[29] J. Rajendran, O. Sinanoglu, and R. Karri. Regaining trust in vlsi design: Design-for-trust techniques. *Proceedings of the IEEE*, 102(8):1266–1282, 2014.

[30] J. Rajendran, H. Zhang, C. Zhang, G. S. Rose, Y. Pino, O. Sinanoglu, and R. Karri. Fault analysis-based logic encryption. *IEEE Trans. on Computers*, 64(2):410–424, 2015.

[31] J. A. Roy, F. Koushanfar, and I. L. Markov. Epic: Ending piracy of integrated circuits. In *Proc. Design, Automation and Test in Eurpoe*, DATE '08, pages 1069–1074, 2008.

[32] J. A. Roy, F. Koushanfar, and I. L. Markov. Protecting bus-based hardware ip by secret sharing. In *Proceedings of the 45th annual Design Automation Conference*, pages 846–851. ACM, 2008.

[33] S. K. Saha. Emerging business trends in the microelectronics industry. *Open Journal of Business and Management*, 4(01):105, 2015.

[34] K. Shamsi, M. Li, T. Meade, Z. Zhao, Y. Jin, and D. Z. Pan. Appsat: Approximately deobfuscating integrated circuits. In *Proc. IEEE Symp. Hardware-Oriented Security and Trust*. IEEE, 2017.

[35] K. Shamsi, M. Li, T. Meade, Z. Zhao, Y. Jin, and D. Z. Pan. Cyclic obfuscation for creating sat-unresolvable circuits. In *Proc. Great Lake Symp. on VLSI*. IEEE, 2017.

[36] M. Shiozaki, R. Hori, and T. Fujino. Diffusion programmable device: The device to prevent reverse engineering. *IACR Cryptology ePrint Archive*, 2014:109, 2014.

[37] P. Subramanyan, S. Ray, and S. Malik. Evaluating the security of logic encryption algorithms. In *Proc. IEEE Symp. Hardware-Oriented Security and Trust*, pages 137–143. IEEE, 2015.

[38] P. Subramanyan, N. Tsiskaridze, W. Li, A. Gascon, W. Y. Tan, A. Tiwari, N. Shankar, S. Seshia, and S. Malik. Reverse engineering digital circuits using structural and functional analyses. *IEEE Trans. on Emerging Topics in Computing*, 2(1):63–80, 2014.

[39] R. Torrance and D. James. The state-of-the-art in ic reverse engineering. In *Cryptographic Hardware and Embedded Systems*, pages 363–381. Springer, 2009.

[40] R. Torrance and D. James. The state-of-the-art in semiconductor reverse engineering. In *Proc. Design Automation Conf.* ACM, 2011.

[41] A. Vijayakumar, V. C. Patil, D. E. Holcomb, C. Paar, and S. Kundu. Physical design obfuscation of hardware: A comprehensive investigation of device and logic-level techniques. *IEEE Transactions on Information Forensics and Security*, 12(1):64–77, 2017.

[42] T. Winograd, H. Salmani, H. Mahmoodi, K. Gaj, and H. Homayoun. Hybrid stt-cmos designs for reverse-engineering prevention. In *Proc. Design Automation Conf.*, page 88. ACM, 2016.

[43] T. F. Wu, K. Ganesan, A. Hu, H.-S. P. Wong, S. Wong, and S. Mitra. Tpad: Hardware trojan prevention and detection for trusted integrated circuits, 2015.

[44] Y. Xie and A. Srivastava. Mitigating sat attack on logic locking. http://eprint.iacr.org/2016/590.pdf.

[45] M. Yasin, B. Mazumdar, J. Rajendran, and O. Sinanoglu. Sarlock: Sat attack resistant logic locking. In *Proc. IEEE Symp. Hardware-Oriented Security and Trust*, pages 236–241, 2016.

[46] M. Yasin, B. Mazumdar, O. Sinanoglu, and J. Rajendran. Security analysis of anti-sat. https://eprint.iacr.org/2016/896.pdf.

[47] M. Yasin, B. Mazumdar, O. Sinanoglu, and J. Rajendran. Camoperturb: secure ic camouflaging for minterm protection. In *Proc. Int. Conf. on Computer Aided Design*, page 29. ACM, 2016.

[48] M. Yasin, J. J. Rajendran, O. Sinanoglu, and R. Karri. On improving the security of logic locking. *IEEE Transactions on Computer-Aided Design of Integrated Circuits and Systems*, 35(9):1411–1424, 2016.

Comparative Analysis of Hardware Obfuscation for IP Protection

Sarah Amir
sarah.amir@ufl.edu

Bicky Shakya
bshakya@ufl.edu

Domenic Forte
dforte@ece.ufl.edu

Mark Tehranipoor
tehranipoor@ece.ufl.edu

Swarup Bhunia
swarup@ece.ufl.edu

Department of Electrical and Computer Engineering
University of Florida
Gainesville, FL 32611-6200

ABSTRACT

In the era of globalized Integrated Circuit (IC) design and manufacturing flow, a rising issue to the silicon industry is various attacks on hardware intellectual property (IP). As a measure to ensure security along the supply chain against IP piracy, tampering and reverse engineering, hardware obfuscation is considered a reliable defense mechanism. Sequential and combinational obfuscations are the primary classes of obfuscation, and multiple methods have been proposed in each type in recent years. This paper presents an overview of obfuscation techniques and a qualitative comparison of the two major types.

CCS Concepts

•Security and privacy → Hardware security implementation; Hardware-based security protocols;

Keywords

Hardware IP Protection; sequential obfuscation; combinational obfuscation

1. INTRODUCTION

In the era of Internet-of-Things (IoT) devices, every device around ourselves are getting connected, and the more they do so, the more vulnerable they become to cyber attacks. Hardware is the base of any system. If the hardware is compromised, no amount of software protection can secure the system. Among many hardware security features, hardware obfuscation is an important tool to ensure the integrity of the ICs. Encryption is a strong tool to ensure the security, but it can not protect the IP in all stages of it's life cycle. Hardware design must be transparent to the manufacturer and testing facility, but still needs to be obscure enough for anyone to understand or modify. Hardware obfuscation can conceal the design, protect it from attacks and allow the manufacturing and testing be performed securely.

In this paper we explore the requirement of hardware obfuscation in present day supply chain in Section 2; explain hardware obfuscation in Section 3 and present the taxonomy in Section 4 along with examples of state-of-art methodologies of the classifications. In Section 5, we present a comparative analysis of the two major class of obfuscation. Then we mention in Section 6 the key management issues and conclude in Section 7.

Permission to make digital or hard copies of all or part of this work for personal or classroom use is granted without fee provided that copies are not made or distributed for profit or commercial advantage and that copies bear this notice and the full citation on the first page. Copyrights for components of this work owned by others than ACM must be honored. Abstracting with credit is permitted. To copy otherwise, or republish, to post on servers or to redistribute to lists, requires prior specific permission and/or a fee. Request permissions from permissions@acm.org.

GLSVLSI '17, May 10-12, 2017, Banff, AB, Canada.

© 2017 ACM. ISBN 978-1-4503-4972-7/17/05...$15.00.

DOI: http://dx.doi.org/10.1145/3060403.3060495

2. IP THREATS IN SUPPLY CHAIN

The semiconductor industry used to follow a vertical business model. Having all the facilities in the same organization helped to secure IPs. But now with the adoption of horizontal business model, the scenario in changing. A key point in this model is that modern System-on-chip (SoC) designs rely predominantly on third party IP (3PIP) because of the benefit in reduction of cost in manufacturing and time-to-market. The system integrator purchases IP from third party vendors. These IP vendors and the manufacturing or testing facilities are distributed throughout the globe. As an inevitable by-product, trust becomes an issue in each step of the supply chain. Ensuring IP trust among entities distributed globally becomes a complex problem given that the IP protection laws are different among countries. The main categories [25] of these vulnerabilities and threats, can be analyzed as:

1. IP Piracy: This threat occurs when an entity, other than the IP owner, sells the IP to a third party, either as original IP or as renamed. This deprive the designer or the owner of their share on revenue.

2. IP Overuse: This threat relate to the scenario when an entity uses the IP in more instances than the ones they paid for or got licensed from the original owner.

3. IP Modification: There is always the risk that a malicious SoC designer or untrusted foundry may modify the IP to insert *backdoor* or Hardware Trojan, *e.g.* a kill switch. This affects the trusted operation of the IC and harms the goodwill of original IP vendor and makes them liable for the damages.

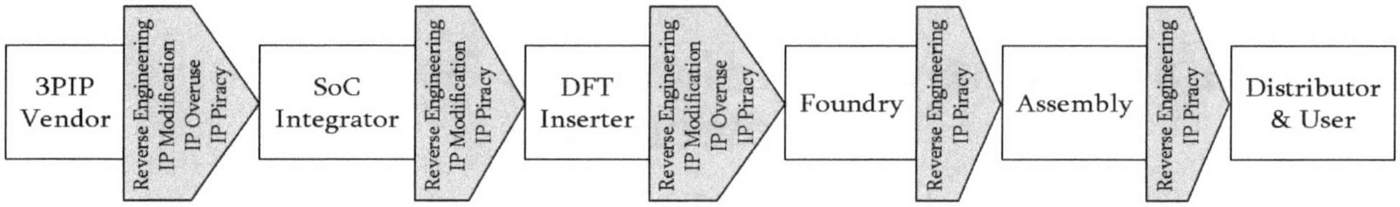

Figure 1: IP threats in supply chain.

4. Reverse Engineering(RE): This can be used with malicious intentions to get the higher level design of an IP and expose it to other threats explained above.

Figure 1 shows the threats in supply chain. The challenge to protect IP from all these threats is a diversified and complex problem. Depending on the type of an IP, the threats and challenges are different and so are the countermeasures. The IP vendors provides their IP in any of the three forms:

1. Soft IP: The IP is in behavioral or *Register Transfer Level* (RTL) format, written with Hardware Description Language (HDL). This is the most used format for 3PIP.
2. Firm IP: The IP is in structural or gate-level netlist format. The circuit is represented as list of gates and their interconnections.
3. Hard IP: The IP is in technology dependent layout format. This the physical design that can be used to manufacture the IC without further synthesis or optimization.

In a soft IP, the design is open and understandable to the receiver. It is vulnerable to IP piracy, overuse, and modification. A common practice to protect this soft IP is use of Encryption. An EDA tool provides a designer with an option to encrypt the whole or part of the IP with the tool's public key. In this way, the malicious integrator is restrained from directly observing the design in soft form. But a drawback of this is, in some cases, after the synthesis, the gate level netlist is no longer encrypted. This gate level design then becomes vulnerable to the threats nonetheless.

Unencrypted Firm IPs are vulnerable to IP piracy, overuse, modification, and it can be reverse engineered to retrieve the HDL design. But it is often necessary for the integrator to have the unencrypted netlist to do fuctional simulation and verification, or to insert scan chains. Because of that, solutions other than encryptions becomes necessary.

The hard IP is the design that usually is sent to offshore foundries to manufacture the IC and poses the threats of modification and reverse engineering to retrieve higher level design.

3. HARDWARE OBFUSCATION

To protect IP in all forms from retrieval and modification attacks, obfuscation is a vital tool. The software obfuscation has been there for sometimes now to protect software against piracy. The structure of this obfuscation is to have a functionally equivalent but structurally different design. As the designs are functionally equivalent, the input output association remains the same. But because the presentation gets altered, the interpretation becomes difficult. The hardware obfuscation to protect hardware IP is significantly different than the software obfuscation. In case of hardware, along with the structural design, the functionality is needed to be hidden to protect it from malicious modification and other attacks. That renders the need for a mechanism to control functional equivalence by the IP owner. Keeping with these requirements, the hardware obfuscation has two major aspects

1. Functional locking, and
2. Structural modification of the design.

The design is modified in a way that it implements different logic functions and it is not possible to retrieve the correct logic equation by reverse engineering. A locking mechanism has to be incorporated which ensures the design becomes functionally equivalent upon correct *unlocking* process.

4. TAXONOMY OF OBFUSCATION

Based on the locking mechanism and design modification methods, hardware obfuscation techniques can be divided into two major classes:

1. Sequential Obfuscation: The design modification is performed by state machine modification. There is no additional input ports for key.
2. Combinational Obfuscation: The design modification is purely on the combinational logic and the locking key is taken from additional input ports or memory.

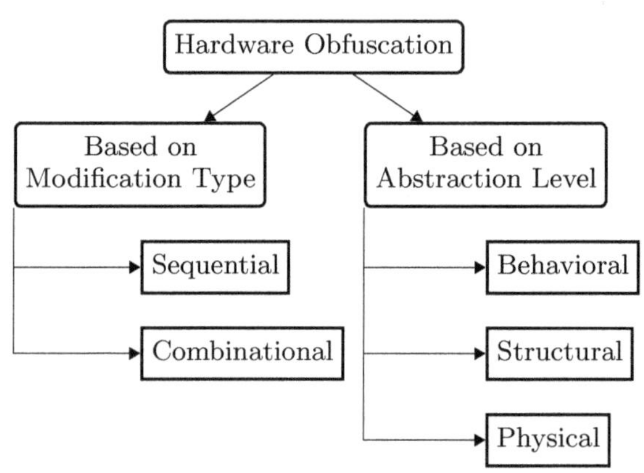

Figure 2: Hardware obfuscation taxonomy.

Based on the design level on which the obfuscation is done, as shown in Figure 3, the state-of-art hardware obfuscation methods can be classified into three categories:

1. Behavioral obfuscation: Some sequential obfuscation method works on this level of design. These are explained in details in Section 4.1.2.

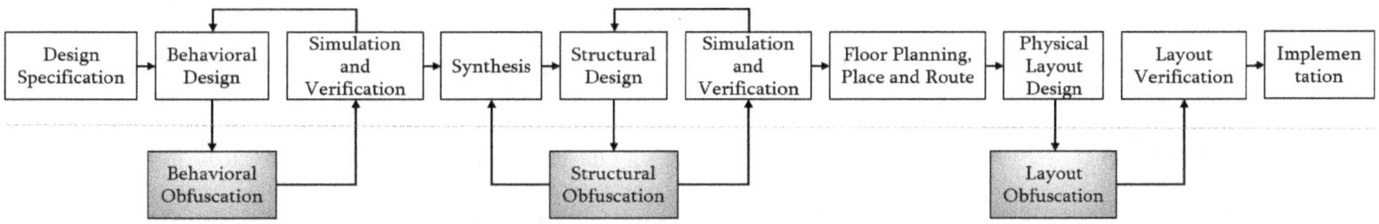

Figure 3: Integration of hardware obfuscation in standard design flow.

2. Structural obfuscation: Most of the sequential obfuscation and almost all of the combinational obfuscation is performed on structural level designs.
3. Physical obfuscation: Multiple techniques have been proposed for physical obfuscation, which include *Monolithic Integration* [21], *2.5D/3D IC* split manufacturing [11], *Camouflaging* [20], and *CircuitEdit* [24].

4.1 Sequential Obfuscation

The sequential obfuscation is based on judicious modification of the finite state machine (FSM) in the design. Researchers offered numerous methods to modify the state transition graphs to control the locking key or to perform structural variations. An example of sequential obfuscation is presented in Figure 4. State-of-art methods can be put into two categories based on whether the obfuscation is done in structural design or in behavioral design.

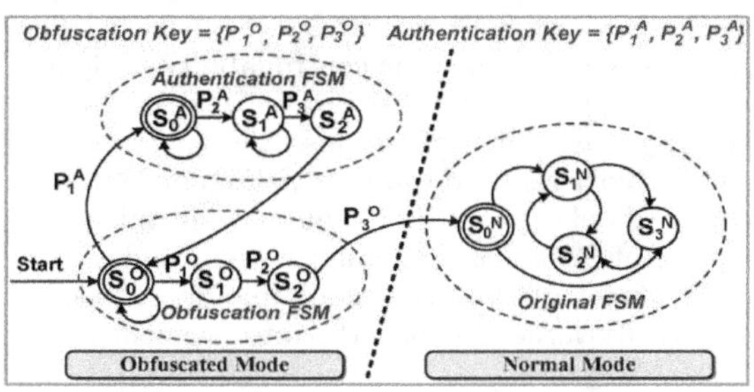

Figure 4: Example of sequential obfuscation [4].

4.1.1 *Sequential Obfuscation on structural design:*

A modified FSM was proposed in [1] by Alkabani and Koushanfar and termed as boosted finite state machine (BFSM). The existing FSM is modified to have additional states, the number of which are significantly higher than the number of original states. This ensures the probability of power-up state to be in original states be negligible. This additional states, along with original states, are called as Boosted FSM. In addition to the BFSM, a random unique block (RUB), which utilized unique identification circuitry, is used to put the BFSM into additional states at power up. The security is based on the assumption that only the designer would know the design of the BFSM, and can provide the sequence to put the circuit into working mode. The sequence is the unique unlocking key for each IC. Also, the authors suggested to design '*blackhole*' states to remotely disable the IC upon any evidence of tempering.

In [3], Chakraborty and Bhunia proposed *ObfusFlow*, in which a simple FSM is integrated in the sequential circuit for controlling the locking-unlocking mechanism. The output of the FSM is XORed with few internal nodes. This technique can be considered as *sequentially controlled combinational obfuscation.*

The authors improved the method in their follow-up paper [4], initiating the idea of obfuscation in gate level files to protect it from supply chain threats. They defined a methodology, *HARPOON*, for ensuring security in SoC designing. The method offers both obfuscation and authentication in designing and manufacturing steps by modifying both the state transition function and the internal logic structures of the design. In state transition modification part, they implemented an additional FSM for initialization. Upon successful input sequence this FSM drives the circuit to working mode. For structural obfuscation, modification cells are proposed, which takes input from the state elements and performs Boolean operation on selected circuit nodes. This cell XORs the original node in some specific scenario which are controlled by both the sequential and combinational logic. The nodes to insert these cells or to take input from are selected based on fan-out and fan-in size of the nodes. Along with the design process, the paper gives a detailed analysis of securing design flow with the help of obfuscation. The authors, on a separate paper [6], extended the applicability of the obfuscation to soft IPs by decompiling the obfuscated firm IP.

Along with IP protection, the role of sequential obfuscation in protecting against hardware Trojan attack was studied in [5]. In this paper, authors proposed the process to modify *State Transition Graph* (STG) to integrate obfuscation in the structural design.

Li and Zhou offered an obfuscation based on 'stuttering' [13]. The obfuscated circuit is not functionally different from the original one, but slower. The slow-down is expected to be polynomial-time to degrade the design. The state machine controls two modes of the IC, *normal* and *slow mode.* Until the IC reaches the end of supply chain, state elements are loaded with wrong sequence for the IC to be in *slow mode.* It is hypothesized that the throughput difference is large enough for the obfuscation to have any effect and small enough for any attacker to realize that.

4.1.2 *Sequential Obfuscation on behavioral design:*

Though soft IP or RTL level design obfuscation was mentioned before [6], but it was still performed on gate-level netlist, and then a de-compilation stage regenerated the RTL design. An actual RTL level obfuscation was introduced in [7]. In this paper, the authors extracts *Control Flow Graph* (CFG) from the high level description and modifies the graph to have extra decision nodes. The modified or obfuscated CFG is then converted to obfuscated RTL design. The additional control decisions are based on boolean operation on state elements of the obfuscation FSM.

Another technique that performs the obfuscation on RTL design is proposed in [9] where the authors considered multiple inputs together as *code-words* for driving the obfuscated FSM. The key aspect of the design is that, even with wrong *code-word*, the state of FSM goes from initial *entry mode* to *functional mode*, but in that case, the behavior of the *functional mode* is different. The authors additionally claimed that the *entry mode* FSM is inseparable from the *functional mode* FSM.

4.2 Combinational Obfuscation

The combinational obfuscation is the hardware obfuscation where the design modification and locking mechanism is purely combinational. Usually this obfuscation is performed on structural level design and the locking key is taken from outside as primary input or read from tamper-proof non volatile memories on chip. If the key is taken as inputs, the number of modified nodes or inserted locks are proportional to the increment in primary inputs. In most cases, the key exchange is performed through external secure encryption protocol. Figure 5 shows a example of combinational obfuscation technique. The state-of-art combinational obfuscation methods can be analyzed into different group based on the similarity in concepts.

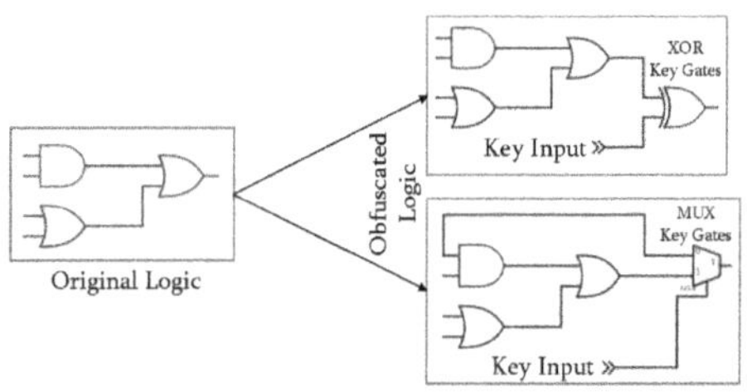

Figure 5: Example of combinational obfuscation.

4.2.1 Datapath obfuscation

Roy et. al. suggested the idea to scramble the bus connecting the components in the IC [23]. The scrambling on the output and de-scrambling on the input of each component is done with key-based Benes network. Each network has butterfly and reverse-butterfly models coupled, which offers scrambling flexibility, but at a higher cost. Authors also suggested Diffie-Hellman key exchange protocol for unlocking the chip. No analysis on overhead has been done, but structural modification with Benes network in this volume hints to large overhead.

A deeper insight in industrial designs gave rise to attacks based on scan chain [29, 16]. In these papers, respective authors used the vulnerability of *scan-enable* mode of IC to leak secrets. For protection against attacks on scan chain, methods have been developed to break scan chain into parts and the reconnection is done through a key-based scrambler block. [8, 17, 18]. In manufacturing and assembly testing, upon application of wrong key, the scan chains are scrambled but the designer knows about how the scrambling is done. As a result, though the scan chain based testing result would be different than un-obfuscated IC, the designer can still evaluate whether the IC is working as expected or not. This concept can be viewed as *Combinational obfuscation on sequential circuits.*

4.2.2 Logic obfuscation

The first proposition of combinational obfuscation was made by Roy et. al [22]. They introduced purely combinational locking mechanism of placing key-controlled XOR-XNOR gates randomly in the design. Along with the algorithm of obfuscation, they provided the model to implement chip activation and secure communication based on public key cryptography and true random number generator.

Rajendran et. al. published an improvement of the randomly insertion of locking gates in circuit by offering a heuristically selected insertion based on fault analysis [19]. They introduced a *fault impact* metric which indicates how much impact a locking gate would have in a particular position . In key gate type, the authors offered an alternate to XOR based design by proposing MUX gates to scramble the internal wire connections upon wrong key input. In order to decrease masking of locking effect, it is advised to minimize the correlation between those by avoiding placing new locks in the logic cone of previously inserted one. But later, the authors reverted this idea in follow-up paper and proposed a new heuristic to place locks with higher correlation, ranamed later as *Secure Logic Locking(SLL)* [32]. The design is based on the correlation type between locking gates. Though the SLL shows resiliency against *key-sensitizing attack* [32], the algorithm presented has polynomial complexity and not scalable for industrial size designs. The interconnection of these locking networks was improved by connecting them with MUX gates [12].

Dupuis et. al. explained an obfuscation technique that can also be used against hardware trojan attacks [10]. They designed a way to improve the controllability of signals with lowest controllabilities, termed as *Rare nodes*, which can be used as triggering signal of trojans. The heuristic to insert obfuscation block selected the *Rare node* signals that are not in the critical delay paths. The limitation of this method is, the number of *Rare nodes* among the total nodes in a practical IC is very high, and the small amount of modification with practical overhead makes the improvement negligible.

4.2.3 Reconfigurable logic based obfuscation

A proposal of using reconfigurable logic as an combinational obfuscation tool was presented by Baumgarten et. al. [2]. They explained about a hypothetical *slice* in the IC design through which all the data paths from input to output crosses and that is almost equidistant from the inputs and outputs in terms of observability and controllability. The authors suggested to replace the logic gates on the hypothetical *slice* with reconfigurable logic blocks, like look-up-table(LUT)s. A limitation of this model is, the size of the *slice* can be exponentially large for industrial design, hence insertion of large number of lock would have monstrous overhead. The protection lies in the concept that- as long the LUTs are not loaded with correct logic function, the design is essentially obfuscated and not possible to reverse engineer. For the same security concept, reconfigurable logic based obfuscation was suggested to obfuscate instruction decoder unit (IDU) to secure it from code injection Trojan [14].

Wendt and Potkonjak proposed methods of cascading Physically Unclonable Function (PUF) and reconfigurable logic to replace a block of combinational logic to render the entire circuit design to be hidden [27]. They also offered a method of datapath obfuscation with the reconfigurable logic.

Table 1: Comparison between sequential and combinational obfuscation techniques.

Comparison basis	Sequential obfuscation	Combinational obfuscation
Implementation method	The modification and addition are sequential logic based. In most scenarios, state machines are modified and utilized to lock the design .	The modification and addition are based on purely combinational logic. The logic can either be simple logic gates, look-up-tables (LUTs) or block of combinational logic.
Applicability	Applicable to designs that has sequential elements, i.e. registers. Most practical circuits have sequential components and state machines.	The authors of combinational obfuscation methods experimented their methods only on purely combinational benchmarks. In case of industrial IP, purely combinational designs are rare.
Scalability	Unless the graphs in [5, 7] of industrial design becomes too large to work on, scalability is not an issue. Also, cascading separate FSM [1, 4] would not be a an issue for scalability.	Some of the methods are easily incorporable to large scale designing [22], but there are few methods that are impractical for real world circuitry [32].
Overhead	Some methods have low overheads [1, 3, 5], but others have moderate [9, 13, 7].	Techniques of [14, 27] have low overheads, but [19, 2, 23] have fairly high overheads.
Design Flow	Most of the methods work on behavioral or structural design.	Almost all the models are based on structural design modification.
Security against RE attack	The security is built on the concept that it is not possible to reverse engineer the state machines efficiently.	Reverse engineering can easily detect the gates connected to key inputs. Whether it will then be removable depends on specific method.
Security against SAT attack [26]	No obfuscated sequential circuit was broken with SAT attack. The tools authors used to attack can only work with a file type that cannot handle memory component.	SAT attack is shown to find the key inputs unless a dedicated resiliency block [28, 30] is accompanied.
Security against KSA [32]	The attack takes the advantage of the direct dependency of output bits to key values. Whether memory delays or sequential key input successfully thwarts the attack is yet to be proven.	Keys can be deduced if those are not securely correlated with other key gates. If the original circuit itself has high correlation in gates, like a multiplier, the attack efficiency is lessened.

5. COMPARISON OF SEQUENTIAL AND COMBINATIONAL OBFUSCATION

While the decision whether the obfuscation of any particular IP should be sequential or combinational or both depends on the characteristic of the IP and the choice of the designer, a comparative analysis can be drawn between these two types on various properties. Table 1 presents such a qualitative comparison.

6. LOCKING AND KEY MANAGEMENT

The locking mechanism of hardware obfuscation can both be key-less and keyed. In keyless obfuscation, there is no necessity of a secret key. The physical obfuscations- *Monolithic Integration* [21], *2.5D/3D IC* split manufacturing [11], *Camouflaging* [20], and *CircuitEdit* [24] are examples of keyless obfuscation.

In case of keyed obfuscation, one or more secret key is required to 'lock' and 'unlock' the functionality of the circuit [22, 19, 32, 1, 4]. In a combinational obfuscated circuit, all the key bits are applied at once, while in sequential obfuscated IC, the key bits are applied sequentially. These keys need to be stored within the IC in a tamper-proof memory, or be generated by a PUF. Also, to provide safe communication of the key between the designer and the IC, often there arise the requirement to have strong encryption hardware like AES or RSA inside the chip.

There had been a number of attacks proposed to retrieve the key from the IC. Among those, two prominent attack are key-sensitizing attack (KSA) and Boolean satisfiability (SAT) attack. In KSA [32], the keys are propagated to primary output by specific input pattern utilizing automatic test pattern generation tool. In SAT attack, the Boolean satisfiability algorithm is utilized to rule out wrong keys for distinguishing input patterns (DIPs) [26] using conventional SAT solvers. This attack can efficiently break obfuscation and extract key in negligible amount of iterations.

It is worth mentioning here that, both these attacks have been proposed on purely combinational circuits. How efficient these will be against sequential obfuscation is still an open question.

Methods to resist these attacks has been published. In [30, 28], respective authors proposed comparing key inputs and only selectively obfuscating the circuit for certain key patterns, to increase the number of DIPs in boolean satisfiability attack. But recently, it was pointed out that protecting from SAT attack, the SAT resilient circuit blocks makes the obfuscation vulnerable to emerging attacks like *signal probability skew (SPS)* attack [31]. That renders the combinational logic locking with major challenges.

7. CONCLUSIONS

Hardware obfuscation is an emerging field in hardware security. New attacks are surfacing and countermeasures that are feasible, scalable, and practical are desired. Emerging concepts like using polymorphic gates in logic level obfuscation [15] and using focused ion beam (FIB) to modify chip post-fabrication [24] are promising. Further, various sequential obfuscation techniques appear to be very powerful for protecting all forms of IP. As we are entering an all-connected device era, we have to be prepared with a strong and secure hardware platform to accommodate high level of security. And for that, hardware obfuscation, along with other hardware security features, are becoming increasingly significant.

8. ACKNOWLEDGMENTS

This work is supported in part by Cisco Systems and National Science Foundation.

9. REFERENCES

[1] Y. Alkabani and F. Koushanfar. Active hardware metering for intellectual property protection and security. In *Proceedings of the 16th USENIX Security Symposium, Boston, MA, USA, 2007*, 2007.

[2] A. Baumgarten, A. Tyagi, and J. Zambreno. Preventing IC piracy using reconfigurable logic barriers. *IEEE Design & Test of Computers*, 27(1):66–75, 2010.

[3] R. S. Chakraborty and S. Bhunia. Hardware protection and authentication through netlist level obfuscation. In *ICCAD 2008, San Jose, CA, USA, 2008*, pages 674–677, 2008.

[4] R. S. Chakraborty and S. Bhunia. HARPOON: an obfuscation-based soc design methodology for hardware protection. *IEEE Trans. on CAD of Integrated Circuits and Systems*, 28(10):1493–1502, 2009.

[5] R. S. Chakraborty and S. Bhunia. Security against hardware trojan through a novel application of design obfuscation. In *ICCAD 2009, San Jose, CA, USA, 2009*, pages 113–116, 2009.

[6] R. S. Chakraborty and S. Bhunia. Security through obscurity: An approach for protecting register transfer level hardware IP. In *IEEE Intl. Workshop on HOST 2009, San Francisco, CA, USA, 2009. Proceedings*, pages 96–99, 2009.

[7] R. S. Chakraborty and S. Bhunia. RTL hardware IP protection using key-based control and data flow obfuscation. In *VLSI Design 2010: 23rd Intl.Conf. on VLSI Design, 9th ICES, Bangalore, India, 2010*, pages 405–410, 2010.

[8] G. K. Contreras, M. T. Rahman, and M. Tehranipoor. Secure split-test for preventing IC piracy by untrusted foundry and assembly. In *IEEE Intl. Symposium on DFTS 2013, New York City, NY, USA, 2013*, pages 196–203, 2013.

[9] A. R. Desai, M. S. Hsiao, C. Wang, L. Nazhandali, and S. Hall. Interlocking obfuscation for anti-tamper hardware. In *CSIIRW '13, Oak Ridge, TN, USA, 2013*, page 8, 2013.

[10] S. Dupuis, P. Ba, G. D. Natale, M. Flottes, and B. Rouzeyre. A novel hardware logic encryption technique for thwarting illegal overproduction and hardware trojans. In *IEEE 20th IOLTS 2014, Platja d'Aro, Girona, Spain, 2014*, pages 49–54, 2014.

[11] F. Imeson, A. Emtenan, S. Garg, and M. V. Tripunitara. Securing computer hardware using 3d integrated circuit (IC) technology and split manufacturing for obfuscation. In *Proceedings of the 22th USENIX Security Symposium, Washington, DC, USA, 2013*, pages 495–510, 2013.

[12] Y. Lee and N. A. Touba. Improving logic obfuscation via logic cone analysis. In *16th LATS 2015, Puerto Vallarta, Mexico, 2015*, pages 1–6, 2015.

[13] L. Li and H. Zhou. Structural transformation for best-possible obfuscation of sequential circuits. In *IEEE Intl. Symposium on HOST 2013, Austin, TX, USA, 2013*, pages 55–60, 2013.

[14] B. Liu and B. Wang. Embedded reconfigurable logic for ASIC design obfuscation against supply chain attacks. In *DATE 2014, Dresden, Germany, 2014*, pages 1–6, 2014.

[15] J. T. McDonald, Y. C. Kim, T. R. Andel, M. A. Forbes, and J. McVicar. Functional polymorphism for intellectual property protection. In *IEEE Intl. Symposium on HOST 2016, McLean, VA, USA, 2016*, pages 61–66, 2016.

[16] A. Nahiyan, K. Xiao, K. Yang, Y. Jin, D. Forte, and M. Tehranipoor. AVFSM: a framework for identifying and mitigating vulnerabilities in fsms. In *Proceedings of the 53rd Annual DAC 2016, Austin, TX, USA, 2016*, pages 89:1–89:6, 2016.

[17] M. T. Rahman, D. Forte, Q. Shi, G. K. Contreras, and M. Tehranipoor. CSST: an efficient secure split-test for preventing IC piracy. In *IEEE 23rd NATW 2014, Johnson City, NY, USA, 2014*, pages 43–47, 2014.

[18] M. T. Rahman, D. Forte, Q. Shi, G. K. Contreras, and M. M. Tehranipoor. CSST: preventing distribution of unlicensed and rejected ics by untrusted foundry and assembly. In *IEEE Intl. Symposium on DFT 2014, Amsterdam, The Netherlands, 2014*, pages 46–51, 2014.

[19] J. Rajendran, Y. Pino, O. Sinanoglu, and R. Karri. Logic encryption: A fault analysis perspective. In *DATE 2012, Dresden, Germany, 2012*, pages 953–958, 2012.

[20] J. Rajendran, M. Sam, O. Sinanoglu, and R. Karri. Security analysis of integrated circuit camouflaging. In *ACM SIGSAC Conference on CCS'13, Berlin, Germany, 2013*, pages 709–720, 2013.

[21] J. Rajendran, O. Sinanoglu, and R. Karri. Is split manufacturing secure? In *DATE 13, Grenoble, France, 2013*, pages 1259–1264, 2013.

[22] J. A. Roy, F. Koushanfar, and I. L. Markov. EPIC: ending piracy of integrated circuits. In *DATE 2008, Munich, Germany, 2008*, pages 1069–1074, 2008.

[23] J. A. Roy, F. Koushanfar, and I. L. Markov. Protecting bus-based hardware IP by secret sharing. In *Proceedings of the 45th DAC 2008, Anaheim, CA, USA, 2008*, pages 846–851, 2008.

[24] B. Shakya, N. Asadizanjani, D. Forte, and M. M. Tehranipoor. Chip editor: leveraging circuit edit for logic obfuscation and trusted fabrication. In *Proceedings of the 35th ICCAD 2016, Austin, TX, USA, 2016*, page 30, 2016.

[25] B. Shakya, M. Tehranipoor, S. Bhunia, and D. Forte. *Introduction to Hardware Obfuscation: Motivation, Methods and Evaluation. Hardware Protection through Obfuscation*, chapter 1, pages 3–32. Springer, 2017.

[26] P. Subramanyan, S. Ray, and S. Malik. Evaluating the security of logic encryption algorithms. In *IEEE Intl. Symposium on HOST 2015, Washington, DC, USA, 2015*, pages 137–143, 2015.

[27] J. B. Wendt and M. Potkonjak. Hardware obfuscation using puf-based logic. In *The IEEE/ACM ICCAD 2014, San Jose, CA, USA, 2014*, pages 270–277, 2014.

[28] Y. Xie and A. Srivastava. Mitigating SAT attack on logic locking. In *Proceedings of 18th Intl.Conf. on CHES 2016, Santa Barbara, CA, USA, 2016*, pages 127–146, 2016.

[29] B. Yang, K. Wu, and R. Karri. Scan based side channel attack on dedicated hardware implementations of data encryption standard. In *Proceedings (ITC 2004), 2004, Charlotte, NC, USA*, pages 339–344, 2004.

[30] M. Yasin, B. Mazumdar, J. J. V. Rajendran, and O. Sinanoglu. Sarlock: SAT attack resistant logic locking. In *IEEE Intl. Symposium on HOST 2016, McLean, VA, USA, 2016*, pages 236–241, 2016.

[31] M. Yasin, B. Mazumdar, O. Sinanoglu, and J. Rajendran. Security analysis of anti-sat. In *22nd ASP-DAC 2017, Chiba, Japan, 2017*, pages 342–347, 2017.

[32] M. Yasin, J. J. V. Rajendran, O. Sinanoglu, and R. Karri. On improving the security of logic locking. *IEEE Trans. on CAD of Integrated Circuits and Systems*, 35(9):1411–1424, 2016.

Efficient and Secure On-Chip Reconfigurable Voltage Regulation for IoT Devices

Selçuk Köse
Electrical Engineering
University of South Florida
Tampa, Florida
kose@usf.edu

ABSTRACT

The emergence of internet of things (IoT) devices is challenging the conventional design targets for integrated systems such as performance, power efficiency, and cost. With the proliferation of IoT devices, ensuring safe operating margins will become more crucial due to the limited power budget and physical constraints. Additionally, IoT devices are vulnerable to hardware attacks as they may be easily accessible to an attacker. The limitations when combined with the cost constraints make the design of security measures for the IoT devices quite challenging. In this perspective paper, reconfigurable voltage regulators are investigated to simultaneously improve the overall power efficiency of the system and provide enhanced security against certain side-channel attacks. A brief survey of randomized reconfiguration of voltage regulators to scramble to power consumption profile is proposed. The randomized reconfiguration makes the the synchronization of the attack more difficult for the attacker, boosting the security benefits of conventional voltage regulators with negligible power and area overhead.

CCS Concepts

•**Hardware** → **Chip-level power issues;**

Keywords

Voltage regulation, power efficiency, hardware security, IoT

1. INTRODUCTION

With the advancement in the semiconductor technology in the last couple of years, the number of devices connected to the internet has increased significantly. It is projected that more than 50 billion internet of things (IoT) devices will be connected to the internet by the end of 2020, marking one of the fastest growing segment in the semiconductor industry [30]. The stringent design constraints for these IoT devices are challenging and changing the conventional design paradigms of power efficiency, area requirement, noise constraint, high performance, reliability, and security. Out of these design constraints, power management and security can be identified as the two primary challenges [30, 27].

Power management becomes challenging due to multiple factors stemming primarily from the limited available area, cost, power budget, and intermittent operation. In a system such as automotive, enterprise, and cloud services, several IoT devices are integrated, putting a significant constraint on the size and cost of these devices. The limited cost and size necessitate novel techniques for both battery technologies to increase the amount of charge that can be stored in unit area, circuit and architectural techniques to convert, regulate, and deliver the stored charge to the load circuits efficiently, and power management techniques and circuit architectures to increase performance per watt. The innovations in the battery technology to increase the amount of charge stored in unit area have been slower than the continuous demand for higher power consumption over the past decade. There is considerable amount of research on developing power management techniques to increase the performance per watt for IoT devices [30, 27]. In this paper, we will focus on circuit techniques that would potentially increase the power conversion efficiency from the battery to the load circuits as there is significant opportunity to increase the overall power efficiency of the system using a tailored power delivery system.

Security has also become a more important design constraint for IoT devices as these devices are highly accessible to malicious attacks (*i.e.,* side channel attacks) as compared to general purpose computing devices [30]. IoT devices should therefore provide sufficient level of security without significant area and performance overhead. To enhance security with negligible overhead, the existing components of a device can be designed and implemented in a security-aware fashion. As each active IoT device should house a voltage regulator/converter to either up/down convert/regulate the harvested energy or regulate the battery voltage to the load circuits, the leveraging of voltage regulators as a security primitive has been recently proposed [49]. We will investigate several voltage regulator topologies and summarize their propriety as a security primitive against certain side-channel attacks for IoT devices.

The rest of the paper is organized as follows. Background regarding on-chip voltage regulation and potential side-channel attacks is provided in Section 2. The most widely used three voltage regulator types are investigated in terms of their security and power efficiency characteristics for IoT devices in Section 3. The unique advantages and potential drawbacks

Permission to make digital or hard copies of all or part of this work for personal or classroom use is granted without fee provided that copies are not made or distributed for profit or commercial advantage and that copies bear this notice and the full citation on the first page. Copyrights for components of this work owned by others than ACM must be honored. Abstracting with credit is permitted. To copy otherwise, or republish, to post on servers or to redistribute to lists, requires prior specific permission and/or a fee. Request permissions from permissions@acm.org.

GLSVLSI '17, May 10–12, 2017, Banff, AB, Canada.

© 2017 ACM. ISBN 978-1-4503-4972-7/17/05...$15.00.

DOI: http://dx.doi.org/10.1145/3060403.3060496

of reconfigurable voltage regulators for IoT devices are explored in Section 4. Conclusions are offered in Section 6.

2. BACKGROUND

Ensuring a robust communication between several *things* is a key design constraint for IoT devices. Equally important is the efficient analysis, computation, storage of the data that are obtained from the environment or from other connected devices. To maintain a robust communication and efficient computation while also reducing the cost of the packaging, on-chip voltage regulation is more of a necessity than luxury for IoT devices [30].

2.1 On-chip voltage regulation

Over the past decade, fortunately, there is significant amount of research focusing on the development of fully integrated on-chip voltage regulators to down-convert and regulate the voltage at the point-of-load for general purpose computing devices [41, 21, 31, 39, 15, 4, 1, 16, 19]. There are several advantages of on-chip voltage regulation. First, the number of dedicated pins for power/ground can be reduced as the power is delivered at a higher voltage and lower current level, liberating some of the pins which can be used for signaling and other purposes. Second, the response time to transient changes in the load is improved as the voltage regulator is physically closer to the load circuits, reducing the parasitic impedance in between. Additionally, the control loop of a voltage regulator is faster due to the lower parasitic impedances, improving the response time. Third, power management techniques such as dynamic voltage scaling can be performed faster (*i.e.,*fine granular), potentially paving the way for significantly improving power efficiency for devices that perform intermittent computation. Fourth, more number of voltage levels can be generated that are tailored for different heterogeneous techniques that can be housed in a single IoT device. This will potentially reduce the cost of multiple voltage regulators integrated at the package, each of which generates a different voltage level that is delivered through dedicated pins [18, 5].

The number of on-chip voltage regulators on a single die also increases significantly owing to the high power densities that can be achieved by leveraging advanced capacitance technologies such as the trench capacitors that are available for DRAM cells in certain processes. For example, IBM's high end server processor Power8 houses hundreds of digital low dropout regulators that are sprinkled throughout the die [9]. Intel also utilizes multi-phase buck converters that have output stages distributed across the die [5] in the Haswell processor. The number of voltage regulators in IoT devices has also increased recently as ARM [26], Intel [6, 25], and Samsung [24] have fabricated prototype IoT devices with multiple integrated voltage regulators.

There is considerable amount of recent research on voltage regulators with reconfigurable topologies [29, 8, 43, 23, 22, 37, 5]. The primary objectives of reconfigurable voltage regulators are to maintain a high power conversion efficiency for a wider range of output currents and enable multiple voltage conversion ratios with the same circuitry that can generate different supply voltage levels [37, 8]. More than half of the voltage regulator designs presented in ISSCC'16 have reconfigurable features [8, 43, 7, 20]. The reconfigurable voltage regulators either change some of the connections at runtime to change the voltage conversion ratio Vout=Vin [29, 8, 43] or turn-on and turn-off certain regulator stages to save power during low power modes of operation [23, 22, 37, 5].

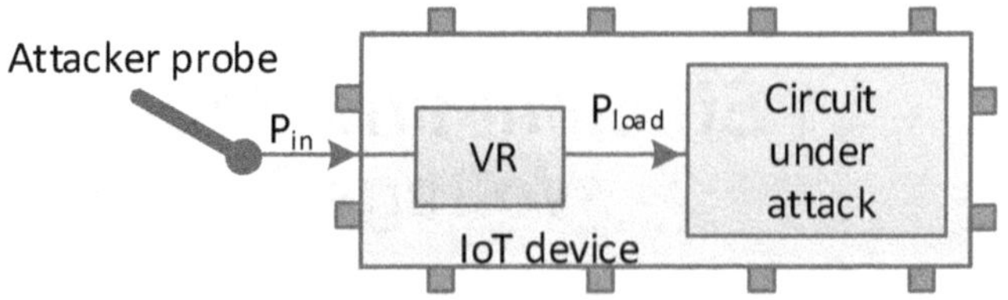

Figure 1: On-chip voltage regulators can disrupt the correlation between the leakage power consumption P_{out} and the monitored power consumption P_{in} by a malicious attacker.

2.2 Side-channel attacks

Non-invasive side-channel attacks are performed to extract information from an integrated circuit (IC) or a smart card by monitoring different physical leakage sources such as power consumption, timing information, temperature, electromagnetic (EM) emanations, and acoustic waves while loading/executing/storing information. The side-channel leakage of a circuit depends on and contains information about i) the data that the circuit is processing and ii) the operations that the circuit is performing while processing data. Due to the low cost and non-invasive nature, side-channel attacks pose a serious threat to the security of personal, commercial, and military information. Unfortunately, IoT devices are inherently more vulnerable to side-channel attacks as compared to general purpose devices as IoT devices are typically more accessible to an attacker.

Power analysis attacks are a widely used side-channel attack that exploits the data dependence of the power consumption profile due to the asymmetric power consumption of the ($0 \rightarrow 1$) and ($1 \rightarrow 0$) transition in CMOS circuits. The power delivery network of an IC has a significant impact on the side-channel power leakage profile [44, 11, 33]. Thus, the design of power delivery network has a significant impact on the side-channel power leakage profile. A security-aware power delivery network therefore greatly enhances the trustworthiness of critical systems. Several countermeasures have been proposed against power analysis attacks which typically either significantly increase the power consumption [36] or cause considerable area overhead [10]. The role of the on-chip power delivery network against power analysis attacks has been investigated in [44].

3. ON-CHIP VOLTAGE REGULATORS FOR SECURITY AND EFFICIENCY

Recently, on-chip voltage voltage regulators have attracted significant attention as a countermeasure against power analysis attacks [35, 11, 33, 14, 34, 12, 13]. While conventional voltage regulators provide a certain level of security against power analysis attacks, reconfigurable voltage regulators have been investigated as a countermeasure to further enhance security [45, 46, 48, 47]. The reason why on-chip voltage regulators naturally increase security against power analysis attacks is that they serve as a circuit block that can modify the media communication channel between the attacker and the circuit under attack, as shown in Fig. 1. IoT devices typically house at least one voltage regulator. When these existing voltage regulators are designed in a security-aware fashion as a countermeasure against side-channel attacks, the power, performance, area, and design time overheads can be significantly reduced while ensuring a higher level of security.

Three types of voltage regulators are widely used in modern ICs to down-convert the voltage; namely low dropout (LDO) regulator, switched capacitor voltage converters, and buck converters. The related tradeoffs of these voltage regulator topologies are explained in the following subsections.

3.1 Leveraging low dropout regulators

LDO regulators are linear voltage regulators with a quite low dropout voltage (*i.e.,* voltage difference between input voltage V_{in} and output voltage V_{out} of the regulator). Although the power efficiency of LDO regulators is limited to V_{out}/V_{in}, when the dropout voltage is small, these regulators can achieve over 90% efficiency. Recently, digital LDO (D-LDO) regulators have attracted significant attention from the industry [9].

LDO regulators can effectively be utilized as a countermeasure against power analysis, as shown in [33, 34, 14] where the authors model the transfer function of the LDO regulator both in frequency and time domains. Although LDO regulators can increase the immunity against side-channel attacks, LDO regulators may still leak information regarding the operating frequency of the circuit-under-attack [48].

3.2 Leveraging buck converters

Buck converters utilize a second order inductor-capacitor (LC) filter to remove the high frequency components of the input switching signal and generate a DC output voltage with a certain amount of ripple voltage. The input switching signal is typically generated by a pulse width modulator (PWM) [40] to adaptively control the duty cycle of the switching signal to regulate the output voltage level. Buck converters can provide quite high power conversion efficiency even when the voltage conversion ratio (*i.e.*, V_{out}/V_{in}) is low. The primary problem with buck converters for on-chip integration is the inductor which requires a large chip area with a reduced quality-factor [42]. The inductors can be implemented at the package right above the IC, as performed recently by Intel [5].

Buck converters have also been explored as a potential side-channel attack countermeasure [11, 12, 13]. The delay loop and the compensator pole-zero locations are controlled to increase the security of the buck converter, however, with some power conversion efficiency degradation. The required number of measurements to disclose (MTD) the correct key from an AES encryption engine has increased over 400 times with a security-aware design of buck converter [12]. Although the buck converters can increase the security against power analysis attacks, certain level of information related to the supply voltage of the circuit-under-attack can still leak to the attacker if the attacker analyzes the slope of the inductor current [48].

3.3 Leveraging switched capacitor voltage converters

SC voltage converters utilize a flying capacitor network and several switches that control the charge transfer from the input node to the flying capacitor and from the flying capacitor to the output node. When the charging of the flying capacitor from the input node and the discharging to the output node occur at a considerably high frequency, a steady voltage with certain amount of ripple can be generated at the output node. Similar to buck converters, the power efficiency of SC converters can be quite high even when the voltage conversion ratio V_{out}/V_{in} is low. With the recent advancements in capacitor density improvements, high power density SC converters can be integrated on-chip without significant area overhead [2, 32].

SC converters can also provide increased security against power analysis attacks similar to LDO and buck converters [37, 49, 45, 46, 47]. The main advantage of SC converters over LDO and buck converters is that SC converters neither leak the supply voltage nor the clock frequency of the circuit-under-attack. This advantage is important when a type of voltage/frequency scaling (VFS) scheme is employed as a countermeasure against power analysis attacks where the leakage if either supply voltage level or the frequency can nullify the VFS based countermeasures [48].

4. RECONFIGURABLE VOLTAGE REGULATION FOR IOT DEVICES

IoT devices may perform different functionalities such as image capturing and processing, computation, monitoring the environment with different sensors, and communication. Performing these diverse functions within a single IoT device may necessitate a heterogeneous integration of different technologies in a single die using 3-D or 2.5-D integration. Each technology can operate optimally at a specific supply voltage level. Delivering various levels of supply voltage to diverse technologies can be facilitated by reconfigurable voltage regulators. Reconfigurable voltage regulation is particularly beneficial for IoT devices (as compared to general purpose computing devices) due to their intermittent operation. The voltage regulator can provide supply voltage at a specific level to a circuit block during its intermittent operation and can change voltage conversion ratio at runtime to generate a different voltage level to power another circuit block.

We investigate reconfigurable voltage regulators for IoT devices in terms of power efficiency, cost, and security implications in the following subsections.

4.1 Power efficiency benefits of reconfigurable regulators

The primary benefit of reconfigurable voltage regulation is the increased power conversion efficiency under a wide range of load power consumption from idle to high-power modes of operation. One technique to realize a reconfigurable voltage regulator is to turn-on and turn-off certain stages of a multi-phase switched capacitor or buck converter [5] or activate and deactivate a certain number of stages of parallel connected LDO regulators [17, 38]. One of the challenges in IoT devices is to generate a stable supply voltage from a battery which delivers a variety of voltage levels based on the amount of charge stored [8, 43]. A high power conversion efficiency and robust supply voltage can be easily generated with a reconfigurable voltage regulator without sacrificing the speed of the transient load response[8].

Another objective of reconfigurable voltage regulators is to improve the transient response speed by reconfiguring the regulator during the transients. When the load current demand increases abruptly, the voltage regulator can configure itself with a higher voltage conversion ratio during the transients and reconfigure to the actual conversion ratio immediately after the transient [37]. Another reason for the load voltage drop is an abrupt change in the input voltage level. Accordingly, an SC reconfigurable voltage regulator is proposed in [3] that adaptively changes the voltage conversion ratio to mitigate the output voltage drop during input voltage changes. Since IoT devices may encounter instant changes both in the input voltage of the regulator and in the load current demand, reconfigurable voltage regulators would potentially enhance the robustness of IoT devices.

4.2 Cost benefits of reconfigurable regulators

The output voltage of a battery and the power generated by energy harvesting circuitry vary significantly over time depending, respectively, on the remaining charge of the battery and the input power to the energy harvesting circuitry. To generate a stable voltage level to be delivered to the active circuits, specialized interface circuitry is typically utilized [28, 6]. With reconfigurable voltage regulators, the design specifications can be considerably relaxed for the output of the battery voltage. Accordingly, the specialized circuits that up- or down-convert the voltage level, which the voltage regulator can handle, may no longer be needed for a robust operation.

4.3 Security benefits of reconfigurable regulators

Although reconfigurable voltage regulators have been proposed to enhance the power conversion efficiency and increase the response speed, a major side-benefit of reconfiguring a voltage regulator is the increased security against side-channel attacks. Noteworthy is that an attacker exploits the dependence of the power consumption of the circuit on the processed secret key. The reconfiguration of the voltage regulator topology at runtime disrupts the correlation between the input and output power of the regulator. Reconfiguring the voltage regulator therefore adds a non-trivial time-dependent parameter to the power consumption signature, significantly increasing the number of measurements that is required by an attacker to determine the secret key [37, 49].

Converter-gating (CoGa) technique based on a multi-phase SC based reconfigurable voltage regulator is proposed as a countermeasure against power analysis attacks in [37]. The number of active SC stages is determined that maximizes the power conversion efficiency based on the workload requirement. Given the number of active stages that maximizes the power efficiency, a pseudo random number generator (PRNG) then decides which stages need to be active. Since each regulator stage is driven by a different phase of the input clock signal, the signature of input power profile of the regulator has spikes with delay uncertainty. Although a delay uncertainty of $\sim$20 ns is added to the input power signature in [37], this delay uncertainty can be increased by modifying the switching frequency of the SC voltage regulator.

One of the drawbacks of CoGa technique is that if the attacker performs an attack while keeping the power consumption of the circuit too low to trigger any change in the number of required voltage regulator stages, CoGa technique can be bypassed. Converter-reshuffling (CoRe) technique is proposed in [49] to overcome this drawback by periodically shuffling the active and inactive stages while keeping the number of active stages the same. When there is a considerable change in the power consumption, the number of active stages is increased and shuffling operation continues. A time delayed CoRe technique is proposed by adding another PRNG in [45] to make the synchronization with the regulator frequency more difficult for the attacker, increasing the security against machine learning based side-channel attacks. In a conventional multi-phase SC regulator, all of the flying capacitors are discharged to the output node after every switching cycle. A charge withheld CoRe technique is proposed in [46] to charge a higher number of flying capacitors than needed and randomize the discharging of those flying capacitors to the output node by discharging them a couple of cycles later.

5. DISCUSSION

The reconfigurable voltage regulators increase the power trace entropy (PTE) value of the voltage regulator 40 to 60% as compared to conventional voltage regulators. Additionally, there is a risk of bypassing and nullifying the security benefits of the voltage regulators if the attacker knows the impedance characteristics of the voltage regulator. Although the impedance characteristics strongly depend on the workload information and loosely on the environmental conditions, a simple voltage regulator model can be used. In such a case, the attacker can post-process the monitored power signature data based on the voltage regulator characteristics and increase the correlation between the input and output power profiles of the voltage regulator (*i.e.*, reduce the PTE). Although the process, temperature, and environmental (PTE) variations affect the impedance characteristics of the voltage regulators, their impact on the attacker might be quite limited.

Reconfigurable voltage regulators, however, do not depend on the PTE variations or on the changes in the workload to alter the regulator characteristics, but depend strongly on the reconfiguration of the topology that changes the impedance characteristics at runtime. As explained in Section 4.3, randomness can also be inserted during the reconfiguration process without sacrificing the power efficiency. Since reconfigurable voltage regulation simultaneously improves the power conversion efficiency and security, unlike most of the countermeasures, the power overhead of the reconfigurable voltage regulation is negligible.

6. CONCLUSION

Maintaining high power efficiency while enhancing security is the primary design challenge that IoT devices face. On-chip voltage regulators can be leveraged as a countermeasure against power analysis attacks with negligible area and power overhead. Different voltage regulator topologies are investigated based on their power efficiency and security. The power efficiency and security benefits of the voltage regulators can be significantly enhanced with reconfigurable voltage regulation. Various techniques that utilized reconfigurable voltage regulators for both power efficiency and security are investigated. The reconfiguration can be performed in a randomized fashion to provide increased security while conserving the power efficiency benefits.

7. ACKNOWLEDGMENTS

The author would like to thank Dr. Weize Yu for his help. This work is supported in part by the National Science Foundation CAREER award under Grant CCF-1350451, by the USF Presidential Fellowship, by a Cisco Research Award, and by a seed grant from Florida Center for Cybersecurity (FC^2).

8. REFERENCES

[1] E. Alon and M. Horowitz. Integrated regulation for energy-efficient digital circuits. *IEEE Journal of Solid-State Circuits*, 43(8):1795–1807, August 2008.

[2] T. M. Andersen et al. A 4.6 w/mm^2 power density 86% efficiency on-chip switched capacitor dc-dc converter in 32 nm soi cmos. In *Proceedings of the IEEE International Applied Power Electronics Conference and Exposition*, pages 692–699, March 2013.

[3] T. M. Andersen et al. A feedforward controlled on-chip switched-capacitor voltage regulator delivering 10w in 32nm soi cmos. In *International Solid-State Circuits Conference*, pages 1–3, February 2015.

[4] L. Benini, A. Bogliolo, and G. De Micheli. A survey of design techniques for system-level dynamic power management. *IEEE Transactions on Very Large Scale Integration (VLSI) Systems*, 8(3):299–316, March 2000.

[5] E. A. Burton et al. Fivr - fully integrated voltage regulators on 4th generation intel core socs. In *Proceedings of the IEEE International Applied Power Electronics Conference and Exposition*, pages 432–439, March 2014.

[6] S. Carreon-Bautista, L. Huang, and E. Sanchez-Sinencio. An autonomous energy harvesting power management unit with digital regulation for iot applications. *IEEE Journal of Solid-State Circuits*, 51(6):1457–1475, June 2016.

[7] P. R. D. Lutz and B. Wicht. A 10mw fully integrated 2-to-13v-input buck-boost sc converter with 81.5% peak efficiency. In *International Solid-State Circuits Conference*, pages 224–225, February 2016.

[8] W. J. et al. A 60%-efficiency 20nw-500μw tri-output fully integrated power management unit with environmental adaptation and load-proportional biasing for iot systems. In *International Solid-State Circuits Conference*, pages 154–155, February 2016.

[9] E. Fluhr et al. The 12-core power8 processor with 7.6 tb/s io bandwidth, integrated voltage regulation, and resonant clocking. *IEEE Journal of Solid-State Circuits*, 50(1):10–23, January 2015.

[10] D. Hwang, K. Tiri, A. Hodjat, B.-C. Lai, S. Yang, P. Schaumont, and I. Verbauwhede. Aes-based security coprocessor ic in 0.18-um cmos with resistance to differential power analysis side-channel attacks. *IEEE Journal of Solid-State Circuits*, 41(4):781–792, April 2006.

[11] M. Kar, D. Lie, M. Wolf, V. De, and S. Mukhopadhyay. Impact of inductive integrated voltage regulator on the power attack vulnerability of encryption engines: A simulation study. In *Proceedings of the IEEE Custom Integrated Circuits Conference*, pages 1–4, September 2014.

[12] M. Kar, A. Singh, S. Mathew, A. Rajan, V. De, and S. Mukhopadhyay. Exploiting fully integrated inductive voltage regulators to improve side channel resistance of encryption engines. In *Proceedings of the IEEE/ACM International Symposium on Low Power Electronics and Design*, pages 130–135, August 2016.

[13] M. Kar, A. Singh, S. Mathew, A. Rajan, V. De, and S. Mukhopadhyay. Improved power-side-channel-attack resistance of an aes-128 core via a security-aware integrated buck voltage regulator. In *International Solid-State Circuits Conference*, February 2017.

[14] M. Kar, A. Singh, A. Rajan, V. De, and S. Mukhopadhyay. What does ultra low power requirements mean for side-channel secure cryptography? In *Proceedings of the IEEE International Conference on Computer Design*, pages 686–689, October 2016.

[15] W. Kim, D. Brooks, and G.-Y. Wei. A fully-integrated 3-level dc-dc converter for nanosecond-scale dvfs. *IEEE Journal of Solid-State Circuits*, 47(1):206–219, January 2012.

[16] W. Kim, M. S. Gupta, G.-Y. Wei, and D. Brooks. System level analysis of fast, per-core dvfs using on-chip switching regulators. In *Proceedings of the IEEE International Symposium on High Performance Computer Architecture*, pages 123–134, February 2008.

[17] S. Kose. Regulator-gating: Adaptive management of on-chip voltage regulators. In *Proceedings of the ACM/IEEE Great Lakes Symposium on VLSI*, pages 105–110, May 2014.

[18] S. Kose and E. G. Friedman. Distributed on-chip power delivery. *IEEE Journal on Emerging and Selected Topics in Circuits and Systems*, 2(4):704–713, December 2012.

[19] S. Kose, S. Tam, S. Pinzon, B. McDermott, and E. G. Friedman. Active Filter Based Hybrid On-Chip DC-DC Converters for Point-of-Load Voltage Regulation. *IEEE Transactions on Very Large Scale Integration (VLSI) Systems*, 21(4):680–691, April 2013.

[20] J. G. L. L. G. Salem and P. P. Mercier. A flying-domain dc-dc converter powering a cortex-m0 processor with 90.8% efficiency. In *International Solid-State Circuits Conference*, pages 234–235, February 2016.

[21] C. F. Lee and P. K. Mok. A Monolithic Current-Mode CMOS DC-DC Converter with On-Chip Current-Sensing Technique. *IEEE Journal of Solid-State Circuits*, 39(1):3–14, January 2004.

[22] W. Lee, Y. Wang, and M. Pedram. Optimizing a reconfigurable power distribution network in a multicore platform. *IEEE Transactions on Computer-Aided Design of Integrated Circuits and Systems*, 34(7):110–1123, July 2015.

[23] W. Lee et al. Power conversion efficiency characterization and optimization for smartphones. In *Proceedings of the IEEE/ACM International Symposium on Low Power Electronics and Design*, pages 103–108, July-August 2012.

[24] Y. J. Lee et al. A 200ma digital low-drop-out regulator with coarse-fine dual loop in mobile

application processors. In *Proceedings of the IEEE International Solid-State Circuits Conference*, pages 150–151, February 2016.

[25] X. Liu, L. Huang, K. Ravichandran, and E. Sánchez-Sinencio. A highly efficient reconfigurable charge pump energy harvester with wide harvesting range and two-dimensional mppt for internet of things. *IEEE Journal of Solid-State Circuits*, 51(5):1302–1312, May 2016.

[26] J. Myers et al. A subthreshold arm cortex-m0+ subsystem in 65 nm cmos for wsn applications with 14 power domains, 10t sram, and integrated voltage regulator. *IEEE Journal of Solid-State Circuits*, 51(1):31–44, January 2016.

[27] A. M. Nia and N. K. Jha. A comprehensive study of security of internet-of-things. *IEEE Transactions on Emerging Topics in Computing*, 2017.

[28] Y. K. Ramadass and A. P. Chandrakasan. A battery-less thermoelectric energy harvesting interface circuit with 35 mv startup voltage. *IEEE Journal of Solid-State Circuits*, 46(1):333–341, January 2011.

[29] Y. K. Ramadass, A. A. Fayed, and A. P. Chandrakasan. A fully-integrated switched-capacitor step-down dc-dc converter with digital capacitance modulation in 45 nm cmos. *IEEE Journal of Solid-State Circuits*, 45(12):2557–2565, December 2010.

[30] S. Ray, Y. Jin, and A. Raychowdhury. The changing computing paradigm with internet of things: A tutorial introduction. *IEEE Design and Test of Computers*, 33(2):76–96, February 2016.

[31] S. Rusu et al. A 65-nm Dual-Core Multithreaded Xeon® Processor with 16-MB L3 Cache. *IEEE Journal of Solid-State Circuits*, 42(1):17–25, January 2007.

[32] S. R. Sanders, E. Alon, H.-P. Le, M. D. Seeman, M. John, and V. W. Ng. The road to fully integrated dc-dc conversion via the switched-capacitor approach. *IEEE Transactions on Power Electronics*, 28(9):4146–4155, September 2013.

[33] A. Singh, M. Kar, J. H. Ko, and S. Mukhopadhyay. Exploring power attack protection of resource constrained encryption engines using integrated low-dropout regulators. In *Proceedings of the IEEE/ACM International Symposium on Low Power Electronics and Design*, pages 134–139, July 2015.

[34] A. Singh, M. Kar, A. Rajan, V. De, and S. Mukhopadhyay. Integrated all-digital low-dropout regulator as a countermeasure to power attack in encryption engines. In *Proceedings of IEEE International Symposium on Hardware-Oriented Security and Trust*, pages 145–148, May 2016.

[35] V. Telandro, E. Kussener, A. Malherbe, and H. Barthelemy. On-chip voltage regulator protecting against power analysis attacks. In *Proceedings of the IEEE International Midwest Symposium on Symposium on Circuits and Systems*, pages 507–511, August 2006.

[36] C. Tokunaga and D. Blaauw. Securing encryption systems with a switched capacitor current equalizer. *IEEE Journal of Solid-State Circuits*, 45(1):23–31, January 2010.

[37] O. A. Uzun and S. Kose. Converter-gating: A power efficient and secure on-chip power delivery system. *IEEE Journal on Emerging and Selected Topics in Circuits and Systems*, 4(7):169–179, June 2014.

[38] O. A. Uzun and S. Kose. Regulator-gating methodology with distributed switched capacitor voltage converters. In *Proceedings of the IEEE Computer Society Annual Symposium on VLSI*, pages 13–18, July 2014.

[39] V. Pinon, B. Allard, and C. Garnier. High Frequency Monolithic DC/DC Converter for System-on-Chip Power Management. In *Proceedings of the IEEE International Symposium on Power Semiconductor Devices and ICs*, pages 1–4, June 2006.

[40] I. Vaisband, M. Azhar, S. Kose, and E. G. Friedman. Digitally controlled pulse width modulator for on-chip power management. *IEEE Transactions on Very Large Scale Integration (VLSI) Systems*, 22(12):2527–2534, December 2014.

[41] I. Vaisband, R. Jakushokas, M. Popovich, A. V. Mezhiba, S. Köse, and E. G. Friedman. *On-Chip Power Delivery and Management, Fourth Edition.* Springer, 2016.

[42] G. Villar-Pique, H. J. Bergveld, and E. Alarcon. Survey and benchmark of fully integrated switching power converters: Switched-capacitor versus inductive approach. *IEEE Transactions on Power Electronics*, 28(9):4156–4167, September 2013.

[43] D. S. W. Jung and D. Blaauw. A rational-conversion-ratio switched-capacitor dc-dc converter using negative-output feedback. In *International Solid-State Circuits Conference*, pages 218–219, February 2016.

[44] X. Wang, W. Vueh, D. B. Roy, S. Narasimhan, and Y. Zheng. Role of power grid in side channel attack and power-grid-aware secure design. In *Proceedings of the IEEE/ACM Design Automation Conference*, pages 1–9, May 2013.

[45] W. Yu and S. Kose. Time-delayed converter-reshuffling: An efficient and secure power delivery architecture. *IEEE Embedded Systems Letters*, 7(3):73–76, September 2015.

[46] W. Yu and S. Kose. Charge-withheld converter-reshuffling (core): A countermeasure against power analysis attacks. *IEEE Transactions on Circuits and Systems II: Express Briefs*, 63(5):438–442, May 2016.

[47] W. Yu and S. Kose. A voltage regulator-assisted lightweight aes implementation against dpa attacks. *IEEE Transactions on Circuits and Systems I: Regular Papers*, 63(8):1152–1163, August 2016.

[48] W. Yu and S. Kose. Exploiting voltage regulators to enhance various power attack countermeasures. *IEEE Transactions on Emerging Topics in Computing*, March 2017.

[49] W. Yu, O. A. Uzun, and S. Kose. Leveraging on-chip voltage regulators as a countermeasure against side-channel attacks. In *Proceedings of the IEEE/ACM Design Automation Conference*, pages 1–6, June 2015.

Design Space Modeling and Simulation for Physically Constrained 3D CPUs

Caleb Serafy
Oracle Corporation
Santa Clara, CA, USA
caleb.serafy@oracle.com

Zhiyuan Yang and Ankur Srivastava
University of Maryland
College Park, MD, USA
{zyyang, ankurs}@umd.edu

ABSTRACT

Design space exploration (DSE) is becoming increasingly complex and 3D integration compounds the problem by imposing a more complex design space. Moreover, 3D design is a new frontier of CPU design, expected to rely more heavily on statistical modeling than designer intuition. Past work has used regression modeling with random sampling of the design space. In this paper we propose a directed simulation technique where intermediate predictions more efficiently direct simulation resources. Our results show over 98% model accuracy while simulating less than 5% of the design space and reducing simulation time more than 4.5x compared to random sampling.

1. INTRODUCTION

Design space exploration (DSE) involves the evaluation of a multitude of design choices prior to detailed implementation. Such a technique is necessary to identify regions of interest in the design space and perform educated trade-off analysis of conflicting objectives. In its simplest form, DSE can be performed by exhaustively simulating the entire design space. However as CPU designs become ever more complex in the pursuit of Moore's law performance scaling, the DSE problem has become increasingly intractable as the design space grows combinatorially in the number of design parameters. Exhaustive simulation across such large design spaces is inefficient and potentially infeasible or unaffordable in terms of run-time.

Past work has attempted to overcome the computational infeasibility of exhaustive simulation in two ways. One is to reduce simulation time by orders of magnitude using techniques such as host-compiled simulation [2] or statistical simulation [3]. Although these approaches can make exhaustive simulation possible, the accuracy of such fast simulation techniques is reduced, and the applicability of the techniques is limited in scope. Another approach to the DSE problem is to simulate only a small subset of the the full design space and use modeling techniques to predict the properties of un-simulated designs. Modeling approaches [8, 7, 11, 9] have shown promising results on large architectural design spaces.

Vertical integration of circuits (3D ICs) is an up-and-coming technology that shows great potential towards improving circuit power and performance as well as facilitating new CPU architecture paradigms such as stacked memory and highly connected on-chip networks [18]. However 3D ICs also bring new challenges, chief among them thermal management [15, 19], and moves the architectural design problem into uncharted territory where traditional domain knowledge and designer intuition may no longer apply. Moreover, past work [18, 19] has shown that significant portions of the 3D CPU design space can be infeasible due to physical constraint violations. 3D integration significantly complicates the DSE problem as follows:

- 3D integration brings many new architectural opportunities that compound the intractability of exhaustive simulation.
- The effects of these new architectures on the design trade-off space are currently not well understood.
- 3D ICs are more thermally sensitive to architectural changes than equivalent 2D chips due to their physical structure.
- 3D ICs can eliminate communication bottlenecks that are inherent in 2D ICs, making performance and power more sensitive to architectural changes.
- *Ad hoc* fixes late in the design cycle due to poor architectural design choices can be more costly in 3D ICs because of resource conflicts between transistors and TSVs.

Physically aware DSE is becoming more important, especially in the context of 3D ICs. Past work [13, 19] has examined the effect of physical constraints on a CPU design space, but has only done so with exhaustive simulation over a small design space. On the other hand, the literature on design space modeling [8, 7, 11, 9] has only attempted to model optimization variables such as performance or energy efficiency with no consideration of physical constraints.

In this paper we introduce a modeling and simulation technique for 3D CPUs. The proposed technique models physical properties (*e.g.*, power, area and temperature) and traditional optimization metrics (*e.g.*, instructions per second or energy-delay-product) and uses these models to direct simulation effort towards user-defined regions of interest in the design space for the purpose of identifying interesting trends such as the Pareto optimal trade-off curve. Our models accurately predict the performance and temperature of a diverse 3D CPU design space and identify the optimal feasible design point (Pareto optimal design set) with 100% (98%) accuracy while simulating less than 2% (5%) of the design space.

In the rest of this paper we discus the related work in the literature, describe our power-performance-temperature simulation methodology and design space modeling technique, and demonstrate its effectiveness and accuracy using two case studies.

1.1 Previous Work

Methodologies to facilitate large scale DSE have taken two orthogonal approaches: drastically reduce simulation time or predict the properties of un-simulated design points through design space modeling. Towards the former, techniques such as statistical simulation [3] and host-compiled simulation [2] have been pursued. Both techniques massively reduce simulation time, but at the cost of reduced accuracy and limited applicability.

Design space modeling likewise trades off accuracy for decreased simulation time by predicting rather than actually simulating significant portions of the design space. Historically, design space modeling techniques [8, 7, 11, 9] have used uniform random sampling to build models of the entire design space. Early work by Joseph *et al.* [9] used linear regression to model instructions per cycle (IPC) across a 23-variable CPU design space. However only two factors of each variable were considered which is not sufficient to evaluate the accuracy of the technique. Two similar works were published the same year by Lee and Brooks [11] and İpek *et al.* [7]. These applied spline regression and artificial neural network

Permission to make digital or hard copies of all or part of this work for personal or classroom use is granted without fee provided that copies are not made or distributed for profit or commercial advantage and that copies bear this notice and the full citation on the first page. Copyrights for components of this work owned by others than ACM must be honored. Abstracting with credit is permitted. To copy otherwise, or republish, to post on servers or to redistribute to lists, requires prior specific permission and/or a fee. Request permissions from permissions@acm.org.

GLSVLSI '17, May 10-12, 2017, Banff, AB, Canada

© 2017a ACM. ISBN 978-1-4503-4972-7/17/05... $15.00

DOI: http://dx.doi.org/10.1145/3060403.3060499

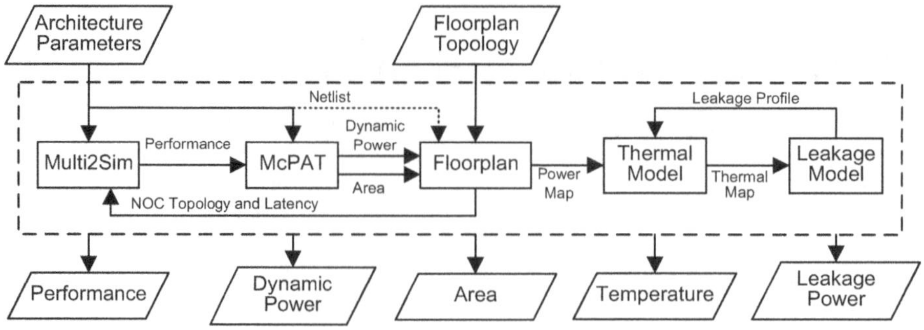

Figure 1: 3D CPU simulation flow

models to accommodate multi-factor non-linear design space properties. They yielded average errors less than 10% and maximum error around 50%. More recent work by Jia *et al.* [8] applied spline regression to GPUs. This technique reduced maximum error to around 15% and had average error in the single-digit range. However, a limitation of the current state of the literature is a lack of focus on application of the proposed modeling techniques to efficiently solve DSE problems.

Moreover, in the aforementioned prior art there is a missed opportunity. A significant potential advantage of modeling approaches is the ability to control the accuracy of the model in different regions of the design space, which we refer to as directed simulation. This is important because it is often the case that accuracy of the simulations is only important in a small subset of the design space, such as the Pareto front for the design objectives at hand, or the region of physically feasible design points. Directed simulation can improve the efficiency of design space modeling by optimizing the amount of useful information in each simulation.

1.2 Contributions

This paper makes the following contributions:

- We propose a directed simulation technique that builds regression models to identify the region of the design space that is of interest to the designer and predict optimization metrics and physical properties within that region while only simulating a small subset of the design space.
- To the best of our knowledge our work is the first to apply design space modeling techniques to 3D CPUs. 3D CPU design is expected to rely more on design space modeling than traditional CPU architectures due to a lack of designer experience and intuition regarding this emerging technology and architectural paradigm.
- To the best of our knowledge our work is the first to apply design space modeling to physical properties such as temperature to predict the feasibility region of a design space. This is extremely important for designing 3D CPUs which are known to be heavily thermally constrained.

2. 3D CPU SIMULATION FLOW

The simulation flow used to evaluate power, performance, area and temperature of a specific 3D CPU architectural design point is shown in Figure 1. The details of each component of the simulation flow are explained in the following subsections.

2.1 Performance Simulation

Performance simulation is performed by Multi2Sim (M2S) [22], a cycle accurate CPU simulator. Architectural definitions are passed to the simulator that describe parameters such as: number of cores, pipeline width, buffer/queue/register size, cache size/associativity/latency, network-on-chip (NOC) topology/latency *etc.* Cache and register latencies are determined using CACTI [21] to provide realistic architectural setups to the simulator. DRAM latency is calculated using the model proposed in [18] and NOC topology/latency is calculated as explained in Section 2.4. M2S simulates the execution of an x86 binary file on the described CPU. The simulator outputs a list of performance statistics such as IPC, memory reads, writes, hits and misses, branch prediction rate *etc.* The specific architectural configurations and software workloads simulated for this study are discussed in Section 4.

2.2 Power and Area Estimation

Power and area estimation is performed by McPAT [12], a multicore power, area and timing estimation tool. Based on the provided architectural parameters, the area and energy per access and leakage power density of each CPU component is estimated for a selected technology node. Using the performance statistics generated by M2S, the dynamic power dissipation of each CPU component can be estimated. The leakage power density is estimated for a nominal temperature, but is thermally scaled during thermal simulation (Section 2.5).

2.3 Floorplan

Each core is partitioned into a set of components (*e.g.*, data cache, register alias table (RAT), branch predictor, instruction queue and execution unit) which are interconnected by an abstract netlist. Detailed descriptions of each component can be found in [12]. A general core floorplan (FP) topology was generated offline which minimizes the wirelength between connected components.

2.4 Core Tiling and NOC Design

The core floorplan is replicated on an $i \times j \times k$ grid such that $i \cdot j \cdot k = n$ where n is the total number of cores. The values i, j and k are chosen such that:

- Total footprint area $i \cdot width_{core} \cdot j \cdot height_{core} < A_{max}$.
- Total number of layers is minimized.
- Layer aspect ratio $({}^{i \cdot width_{core}}/_{j \cdot height_{core}})$ is relatively square.

NOC topology is defined as an $i \times j \times k$ 3D mesh [18] and NOC latency is defined as the wire delay of length $\max(width_{core}, height_{core})$, calculated using the wire delay model from [16] with technology parameters extracted from McPAT source code. NOC topology and latency are fed back into the performance simulator to get accurate inter-core communication simulations.

2.5 Thermal Model

Once the chip floorplan has been constructed and component power estimation is complete, we have a power density map for each tier of the 3D stack. Power density maps are converted into thermal maps using our compact thermal model [20]. A 3D grid is constructed representing the physical structure of the 3D IC. Likewise the power map is discretized into a 3D grid and the total power of each power grid is assigned to the respective physical grid.

2.6 Leakage Model

McPAT reports a base leakage value for each CPU component which is estimated at a fixed temperature T_0. To obtain more accurate leakage power estimates we iteratively solve our thermal model and then scale leakage estimates at each grid based on the estimated temperature of that grid after the previous iteration.

3. DSE MODELING TECHNIQUE

In this section we introduce our modeling and simulation technique for 3D CPU DSE subject to physical constraints. We use the

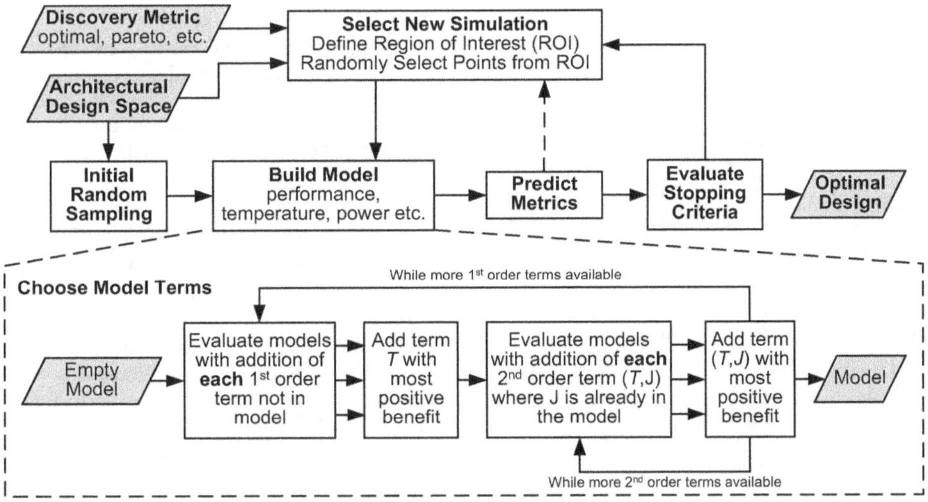

Figure 2: Modeling and simulation technique

smoothing spline analysis of variance (SS-ANOVA) [5] modeling technique to build models for each design parameters of interest (*e.g.*, performance, temperature and power). Models are composed from cubic spline functions evaluated on combinations of design variables (*i.e.* model terms). First we give some background on SS-ANOVA modeling and then describe our proposed modeling and directed simulation technique. Figure 2 illustrates the overall flow of our modeling and simulation technique, and details are given in the subsections below. The basic flow is an iterative back-and-forth between model building and choosing new simulation points based off the intermediate model predictions.

3.1 SS-ANOVA Modeling

A spline is a piecewise polynomial function [5]. Splines are both differentiable and continuous at the piecewise boundaries [5]. The smoothing spline is a regression technique to smooth noisy data by fitting a spline function to the data. Analysis of variance (ANOVA) is a statistical technique for analyzing the underlying source of variations in a population [5]. Multi-factor ANOVA can be used to generate models of a data set as a function of descriptive properties of each observation. An observation f can be modeled as a function of the variables $\mathbf{x} = x_1, x_2, \ldots, x_n$ as shown in Equation (1) [5]. SS-ANOVA limits the set of functions $\{f_1, \ldots, f_{1,2,\ldots,n}\}$ to be spline functions which operate on some subset of the variables in $\mathbf{x}$. Each unique subset of input variables is called a term, and the order of a term is the size of the subset.

$$f(\mathbf{x}) = c + \Sigma_{j=1}^{n} f_j(x_j) + \Sigma_{j=1}^{n} \Sigma_{k=j+1}^{n} f_{j,k}(x_j, x_k) + \cdots + f_{1,2,\ldots,n}(x_1, x_2, \ldots, x_n) \quad (1)$$

In this work we use the `gss` [4] package for the statistical computing environment `R` [17] to generate a unique smoothing spline model for each design property of interest. To generate each model, `gss` requires a set of simulation data and a set of model terms. However, choosing the appropriate simulation points and model terms are nontrivial problems. The choice of model terms and simulations points strongly affects the quality of the model and suboptimal choices have a high cost in terms of total simulation time and model complexity. Our iterative technique for model term and simulation point selection and is explained in detail in the following subsections.

3.2 Choosing Model Terms

The maximum number of terms associated with n variables is 2^n. However as a rule of thumb a model is unreliable when the number of terms is greater than $s/20$ [6] where s is the number of simulated points. If too many model terms are used, the model can suffer from over-fitting, making it very accurate with respect to the observed data, but a poor predictor of the un-simulated data we wish to predict. Thus the number of model terms must be kept relatively small in order to maintain model accuracy when the number of simulations is small. The intended goal of the modeling and simulation approach is to build accurate models while requiring only a small number of simulations, so avoidance of the over-fitting problem is of critical importance.

The coefficient of determination (R^2) is a commonly used metric to evaluate model quality. However, by construction R^2 monotonically increases as new terms are added to a model [8]. Thus optimization of R^2 itself would inevitably lead to inclusion of all model terms, unnecessarily complicating the model and potentially causing over-fitting. Adjusted R^2 ($\bar{R}^2$) (Equation (2)) scales R^2 relative to the number of model terms, m, and the number of data points, s, allowing the significant terms to be identified.

$$\bar{R}^2 = 1 - (1 - R^2) \cdot \frac{s-1}{s-m-1} \quad (2)$$

We use a forward selection $\bar{R}^2$ based technique to select the terms in the model. The model building technique is shown in the bottom half of Figure 2. Starting with an empty model we consider each model consisting of one first order term. We evaluate the $\bar{R}^2$ metric for each model and accept the one with the largest value. We then consider adding each remaining first order term (in decreasing order of improvement) and accept the terms that increase the quality of the model by at least θ.

Every time a new first order term is added to the model, we consider all second order interaction terms created by combining the new term with any other terms already in the model. Amongst all new second order terms generated this way we add (in decreasing order of improvement) any that cause the model quality to improve by at least θ. The model is complete once all first order terms have been added to the model, or when adding any new first order terms causes model quality to improve less than θ.

3.3 Adding Simulation Points

The designer defines a discovery metric, which defines the point(s) in the design space they are interested in identifying. Some examples of potential discovery metrics are the optimal design point subject to a set of constraints (*e.g.*, design space optimization), or the set of Pareto optimal designs (*e.g.*, trade-off analysis). The optimality metric (*e.g.*, performance or energy efficiency), constraints (*e.g.*, temperature, power, area or timing) and Pareto metrics are defined by the designer. The goal of our proposed modeling and simulation technique is to identify these points by iteratively predicting them and concentrating simulator effort around the predicted point(s) to improve the accuracy of the prediction.

Initial models are built using a random sampling of η simulation points. Using model predictions, the predicted design point(s) of interest are identified. Due to model error, the identified point(s) are not necessarily the true points of interest. However, the true points

Table 1: Architectural design space (baseline values shown in bold).

Variable	Value(s)
Technology Node	32 nm
Number of cores (*core*)	{**8**, 16, 32}
Memory controllers	$core \cdot \{1/2, 1/4, 1/8\}$
Clock frequency	{**2.4**, 3.0} GHz
NOC width	128 bits
L2 cache size (per core)	{**256**, 512, 1024} kB
L2 cache associativity	{**4**, 8, 16}
L1 cache size (per core)	{**16**, 32, 64} kB
L1 cache associativity	1
Pipeline width	{**2**, 4, 6}
Branch predictor	Tournament
Local history table	1024 8-bit entries
Global predictor	4096 2-bit entries
BTB size	32 kB
BTB associativity	1
Reorder buffer length (*rob*)	{**96**, 128, 160}
Issue queue length	$0.4 \cdot rob$
Load-store queue length	$0.5 \cdot rob$
Fetch queue length	64
Int architectural registers	$0.67 \cdot rob$
FP architectural registers	$0.33 \cdot rob$
RAT size	*rob* 8-bit entries
DRAM size	4 GB
Cache line size	64 B
DRAM bus width	64 B

of interest are likely to be close to the predicted points of interest. Thus a region of interest (ROI) is defined which contains the design points which are close to the predicted point(s) of interest, and additional simulation effort is concentrated towards this ROI to improve model fidelity in that region.

Each iteration of the flow identifies χ new design points from the predicted ROI and queues them for simulation. Once the simulations are performed, the model is rebuilt and the process repeats. If the initial model mispredicts the ROI, additional simulation effort in the mispredicted region will reduce model residuals in that region and improve ROI prediction on the next iteration.

3.4 Stopping Criteria

Stopping criteria could involve reaching a maximum number of simulations, or a sustained convergence in predictions of ROI and/or point(s) of interest across multiple iterations. In order to evaluate the behavior of our algorithm we simply set the stopping criteria to terminate when the total number of simulations reaches ζ. We investigate the trade-off between number of simulations and optimality of our selected design space in Section 5, and the point at which prediction convergence is achieved is observed *post hoc*.

4. EXPERIMENTAL SETUP

In this section we describe the experimental setup to evaluate the proposed modeling and simulation technique (Section 3). In the following subsections we introduce the 3D CPU design space, the discovery metrics and associated ROI definitions considered in our case studies and the metrics we use to measure the effectiveness of our approach. Results are presented and discussed in Section 5.

4.1 Architectural Design Space

Our study searches the architectural design space given in Table 1 which contains 4374 unique design points. We consider 3D CPUs with stacked DRAM which is considered to be one of the primary advantages of 3D CPUs [10, 14]. By integrating the DRAM on chip using through silicon vias (TSVs), the core-memory bandwidth can be increased drastically due to increased memory bus width, more memory controllers and faster bus speed [15, 18].

Each architectural design point is evaluated using a set of software workloads from the SPLASH-2 [23] and PARSEC [1] benchmark suites. The performance of each workload is normalized to the baseline architecture (Table 1) to allow unbiased averaging across workloads. Maximum temperature for a design point is the maximum across all workloads.

4.2 Discovery Metrics

The goal of our DSE study is to identify the design point(s) of interest as defined by the discovery metric chosen by the designer. Two discovery metrics are considered as case studies in this paper, but our proposed methodology is applicable to any arbitrary discovery metric. In this study the modeled design parameters are performance and temperature and the discovery metrics are:

- **"Optimal"**: design point with highest normalized performance subject to thermal constraint $temp_p < T_{violation}$.
- **"Pareto"**: Pareto optimal set of design points in thermal-performance space.

Each discovery metric defines an accompanying ROI of radius $\phi = (\phi_{perf}, \phi_{temp})$. The ROI for the "Optimal" and "Pareto" discovery metrics are given in Equations (3) and (4)* respectively, where $perf_i$ and $temp_i$ are the performance and temperature of design point i and Ω is the design space. Design point p is the predicted optimal feasible point for the discovery metric "Optimal". The defined ROI is the set of points within distance ϕ of the identified point(s) of interest.

$$ROI_{Optimal} = \{i \in \Omega \mid \left|\frac{perf_i - perf_p}{perf_p}\right| \leq \phi_{perf} \wedge |temp_i - temp_p| \leq \phi_{temp}\} \quad (3)$$

$$ROI_{Pareto} = \{i \in \Omega \mid \forall_{(j \neq i) \in \Omega}\ perf_j \cdot (1 - \phi_{perf}) \leq perf_i \vee (temp_j + \phi_{temp}) \geq temp_i\} \quad (4)$$

4.3 Modeling and Simulation Parameters

The modeling and simulation technique introduced in Section 3 can be parametrized to make trade-offs between simulation time and optimality of the selected design point. In this study we use the following parameters which were found experimentally to offer favorable trade-offs:

- We sample $\eta = 40$ simulation points at random from the design space to build the initial model. This parameter should be large enough to generate an initial model with reasonable accuracy but small enough to avoid degeneration towards random sampling.
- The threshold for accepting new model terms is $\bar{R}^2_{new} - \bar{R}^2_{current} > \theta = 0$. By increasing θ, the model complexity could be reduced at the expense of quality.
- We use ROI radius of $\phi = (8\%, 4°C)$ for discovery metric "Optimal" and $\phi = (5\%, 3°C)$ for discovery metric "Pareto". Larger values of ϕ reduce the probability of convergence to local minima, but generally increase simulation time.
- We iteratively simulate chosen design points in increments of $\chi = 5$. Smaller values of χ inefficiently increase the number of times model building is performed. However excessively large values of χ over-invest simulation resources into a potentially inaccurate intermediate estimation of ROI.
- We use a nominal stopping criteria of $\zeta = 200$ simulations. The trade-off of optimality vs. number of simulations is investigated in Section 5.

4.4 Evaluation Metrics

The goal of the experiment is to identify the ROI defined by the discovery metric, while minimizing the total number of simulations performed. Thus the primary metrics used to evaluate the quality of our technique will be accuracy of identification, number of simulations and run-time overhead of the model building.

When the discovery metric is "Optimal", the distance between the identified point and the true solution is quantified as optimality,

*Equation (4) presents a ϕ-relaxed definition of Pareto optimality that includes all points such that no other point is better by a degree of ϕ in all metrics of interest.

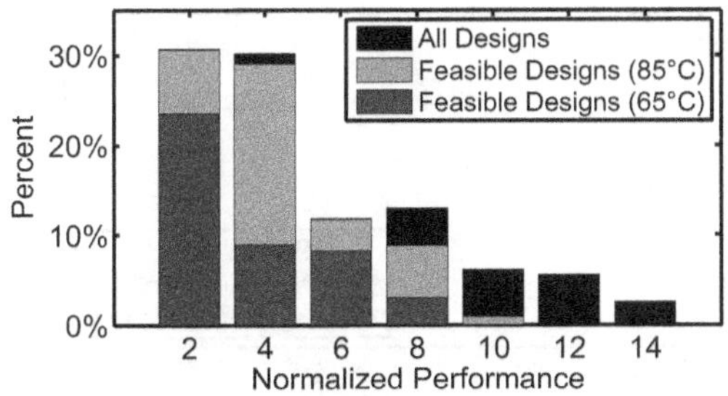

Figure 3: Thermally feasible performance distribution under different thermal constraints

which is the ratio $^{perf_p}/_{perf_o}$ where p is the predicted optimal feasible point and o is the true optimal feasible point (determined by exhaustive simulation for evaluation).

When the discovery metric is "Pareto", the distance between the identified points and the true Pareto set is quantified as accuracy, which is the average Pareto optimality of the predicted Pareto set. The Pareto optimality of design point k is determined by finding the smallest value of ϕ such that k is included in the ROI. Specifically, the Pareto optimality of k is α_k and the smallest value of ϕ that includes k in the ROI is $\phi = (1 - \alpha_k)(100\%,\ 60°\mathrm{C}^{\dagger})$.

In general the optimality/accuracy of the predicted point(s) will increase as more simulations are performed, eventually degenerating into the exhaustive simulation . The net speedup of our technique consists of the reduction in total number of simulations minus the run-time overhead of building the models.

4.5 Comparison to Other Techniques

The rudimentary technique to which our technique is compared is a random sampling methodology where some portion of the solution space is sampled at random and the best design amongst the sampled designs is selected[‡]. Additionally we could consider modeling-only version of our proposed technique that uses SS-ANOVA model building to predict the design point(s) of interest, but simply uses random sampling to provide data to the model builder. The modeling-only approach is representative of design space modeling techniques proposed in past work [8, 7, 11, 9]. In Section 5 we compare the trade off curves of simulation count vs. quality for the three aforementioned techniques:

- **Proposed**: modeling and directed simulation
- **Modeling-Only**: modeling and random simulation[§]
- **Random Sampling**: random simulation (no modeling)

5. RESULTS

In this section we first provide some characterization of the design space explored in our study, and then compare the quality of the investigated methodologies (Section 4.5) for the "Optimal" and "Pareto" discovery metrics.

5.1 Design Space Characterization

We begin by examining the properties of the design space. Exhaustive simulation was performed for the purpose of evaluation. Exhaustive simulation took weeks to perform using university servers with over 100 cores, further motivating the strong need for techniques such as the one proposed in this paper in order to reduce simulation time. We provide some statistics of the design space properties in order to give context for the results of this study.

Figure 3 shows the distribution of normalized performance across all architectural design points. We can see that the design space is biased heavily towards the low-performance region. Furthermore, thermal feasibility constraints bias the design space even further as the constraints tighten (*i.e.* $T_{violation}$ is reduced). This implies that random sampling is not a very good technique for discovering the "Optimal" design point since the probability of randomly sampling a high-performance thermally-feasible design point is low.

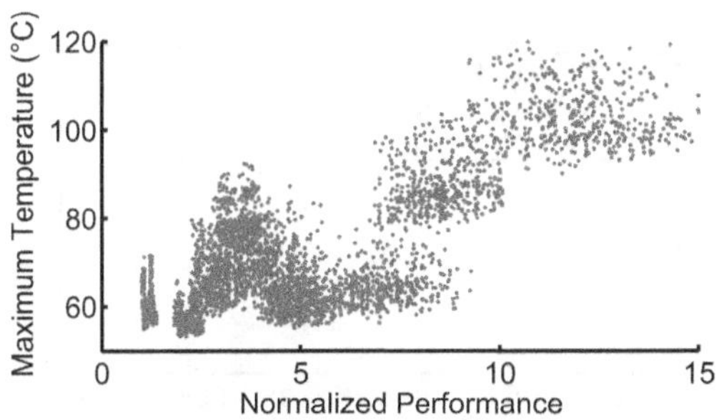

Figure 4: Temperature vs. performance of entire design space

Figure 4 shows a scatter plot of the performance and temperature of each design point in the design space. We can see that identification of both the optimal feasible design point and the Pareto optimal design set without exhaustive simulation is non-trivial. The vast majority of design points in the design space are far from the point(s) of interest using either discovery metric. Moreover the correlation between performance and temperature is weak, motivating the need for independent models of each design property.

5.2 "Optimal" Discovery

There exists a fundamental trade-off between the number of simulations and the quality of the identified solution. We compare the random sampling and modeling-only technique to our proposed modeling and simulation technique and show that our technique significantly reduces the number of simulations required to discover the region of interest in the design space. First we evaluate the techniques using the "Optimal" discovery metric.

Figure 5 plots the number of simulations required to identify a design point of interest with a specified optimality. We observe that modeling alone is a large contributor to the optimality of the identified point. With less than 1% of the solution space sampled (40 points), the two modeling techniques can already identify a solution within 90% of the optimal. However the true power of the proposed technique becomes clear as the optimality target increases. Optimality can be improved significantly for both modeling techniques by adding only a nominal amount of additional simulation samples. However the modeling-only technique begins to degenerate towards random sampling for optimality targets beyond 98% whereas the proposed technique shows no such degredation. By using models to direct simulation effort on each iteration towards the ROI, the technique is able to make roughly linear improvements to prediction accuracy for each additional simulation. Our proposed technique is able to identify the optimal feasible design point while simulating less than 2% (roughly 80 points) of the entire design space, saving 100s of simulation hours compared to the other two techniques.

Robustness to Constraint Tightness: The previous results were evaluated at $T_{violation} = 85°\mathrm{C}$. However as Figure 3 shows, reducing $T_{violation}$ to $65°\mathrm{C}$ significantly reduces the size of the thermal feasibility region. It is expected that a smaller feasibility region will reduce the quality of the random sampling technique significantly, but it is unclear how it would affect the techniques that use model building. We exercise the robustness of the investigated techniques to constraint tightness by lower the thermal constraint. However, the resulting observations would be extendable to analogous situations such as using a lower quality heatsink or a more power-dense manufacturing technology.

Figure 6 plots the number of additional simulations required to accommodate the reduced thermal constraint. We notice that the number of additional simulations required for our proposed method is less than 30 (<1% of the entire design space) and moreover, remains roughly constant as the optimality target is tightened. On the other hand random sampling and modeling-only both require su-

[†] 60 °C was roughly the thermal range of the design space considered in this work as shown in Figure 4.

[‡] Exhaustive simulation is a degenerative case of random sampling.

[§] Representative of past work [8, 7, 11, 9].

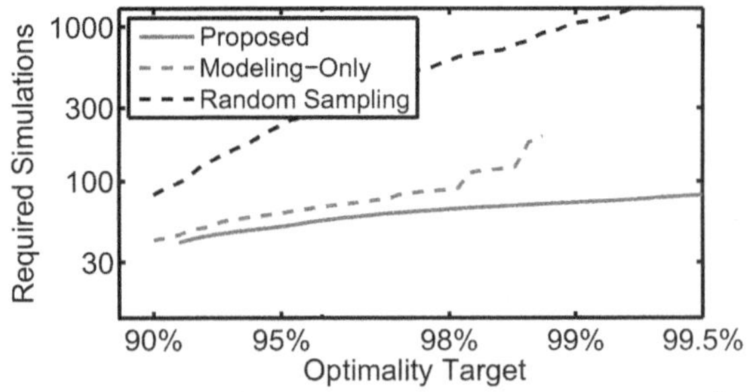

Figure 5: Number of simulations vs. optimality of design¶

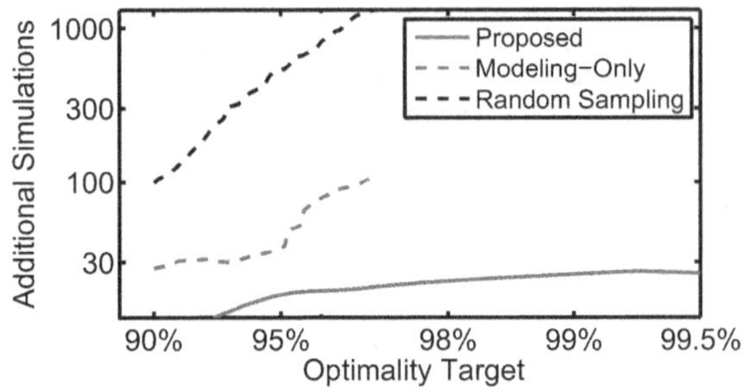

Figure 6: Additional simulations required for 65°C vs. 85°C constraint¶

perlinearly increasing amounts of additional simulations in order to meet optimality targets. Although modeling-only scales reasonable well for small optimality targets, the point at which the technique begins to degenerate is significantly reduced to roughly 95%. Thus we show that compared to a modeling-only technique, our directed simlation technique is significantly more robust to design space feasibility constraints.

5.3 "Pareto" Discovery

Figure 7 shows the accuracy of the considered methods when the "Pareto" discovery metric is applied. Although the general trends and relative ordering of the method results are similar to the "Optimal" case, there are some significant differences. The quality of both model-based techniques is reduced because identification of a set of Pareto points is a more challenging problem which inherently requires more simulation. However the relative improvement of our proposed technique vs. the modeling-only technique is substantially more obvious under this discovery metric. This indicates that, similar to constraint tightness, the proposed technique is significantly more robust to increased problem complexity.

Likewise, the modeling-only technique degenerates into random sampling at an even lower accuracy target than was observed in the previous studies. The conclusion here is that models built with random sampling can approximating a single design much better than the relative ordering of all design points. Directed simulation towards the ROI is of utmost importance for estimation of the Pareto design set, even for rather loose accuracy targets.

5.4 Overhead of modeling approach

There is obviously some run-time overhead associated with model-building in the investigated modeling approaches. We observed that the time consumed building models in our proposed approach was less than the time consumed to simulate a single design point ($< 0.025\%$ of the design space). Our results clearly show that such overhead is negligible compared to the savings in number of required simulations compared to random sampling.

6. CONCLUSIONS

In this paper we propose a comprehensive technique for 3D CPU architectural design space exploration subject to physical constraints. We use smoothing spline regression modeling to efficiently direct our simulation effort. We demonstrate out technique using two case studies. Our technique identifies the optimal feasible design point (Pareto optimal design set) with 100% (98%) accuracy while simulating less than 2% (5%) of the design space.

¶Data is plotted on a log-log axis, so polynomial relationships appear as a straight lines with slope proportional to degree.

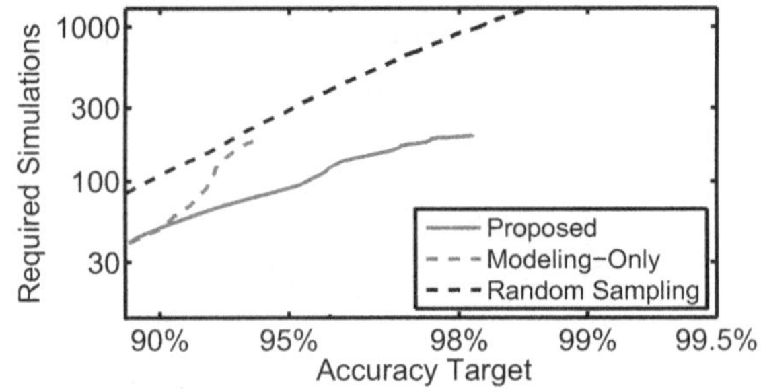

Figure 7: Number of simulations vs accuracy of Pareto set¶

7. ACKNOWLEDGEMENTS

The authors would like to acknowledge that this work has been funded by NSF grant CCF1302375 and DARPA ICECool Project.

8. REFERENCES

[1] C. Bienia, et al. The PARSEC Benchmark Suite: Characterization and Architectural Implications. In *PACT*, 2008. ACM.

[2] D. Gandhi, et al. FastSpot: Host-compiled thermal estimation for early design space exploration. In *ISQED*. IEEE, 2014.

[3] D. Genbrugge and L. Eeckhout. Chip multiprocessor design space exploration through statistical simulation. *IEEE Transactions on Computers*, 2009.

[4] C. Gu. Smoothing Spline ANOVA Models: R Package gss.

[5] C. Gu. *Smoothing spline ANOVA models*, volume 297. Springer Science & Business Media, 2013.

[6] F. E. Harrell. *Regression modeling strategies: with applications to linear models, logistic regression, and survival analysis*. Springer Science & Business Media, 2013.

[7] E. İpek, et al. Efficiently Exploring Architectural Design Spaces via Predictive Modeling. In *ASPLOS*, 2006. ACM.

[8] W. Jia, et al. Stargazer: Automated regression-based GPU design space exploration. In *ISPASS*. IEEE, 2012.

[9] P. Joseph, et al. Construction and use of linear regression models for processor performance analysis. In *HPCA*. IEEE, 2006.

[10] D. H. Kim, et al. 3D-MAPS: 3D Massively parallel processor with stacked memory. In *ISSCCl*. IEEE, 2012.

[11] B. C. Lee and D. M. Brooks. Accurate and efficient regression modeling for microarchitectural performance and power prediction. In *ACM SIGPLAN Notices*, volume 41. ACM, 2006.

[12] S. Li, et al. McPAT: an integrated power, area, and timing modeling framework for multicore and manycore architectures. In *MICRO*. IEEE/ACM, 2009.

[13] Y. Li, et al. CMP design space exploration subject to physical constraints. In *HPCA*. IEEE, 2006.

[14] G. H. Loh. 3D-Stacked Memory Architectures for Multi-core Processors. In *ISCA*, 2008. IEEE.

[15] J. Meng, et al. Optimizing Energy Efficiency of 3-D Multicore Systems with Stacked DRAM Under Power and Thermal Constraints. In *DAC*, 2012. ACM.

[16] R. H. J. M. Otten and R. K. Brayton. Planning for Performance. In *DAC*, 1998. ACM.

[17] B. D. Ripley. The R project in statistical computing. *MSOR Connections*, 2001.

[18] C. Serafy, et al. Unlocking the True Potential of 3-D CPUs With Microfluidic Cooling. *IEEE TVLSI*, 2015.

[19] C. Serafy, et al. Design Space Exploration of 3D CPUs and Micro-Fluidic Heatsinks with Thermo-Electrical-Physical Co-Optimization. In *InterPACK*. ASME, 2015.

[20] B. Shi, et al. Non-uniform Micro-channel Design for Stacked 3D-ICs. In *DAC*, 2011. ACM.

[21] P. Shivakumar and N. P. Jouppi. Cacti 3.0: An integrated cache timing, power, and area model. Technical report, Compaq Computer Corporation, 2001.

[22] R. Ubal, et al. Multi2Sim: a simulation framework for CPU-GPU computing. In *PACT*. ACM, 2012.

[23] S. C. Woo, et al. The SPLASH-2 Programs: Characterization and Methodological Considerations. In *ISCA*, 1995. ACM.

Automated Design of Stable Power Delivery Systems for Heterogeneous IoT Systems

Inna Partin-Vaisband
University of Illinois at Chicago
Department of Electrical and Computer Engineering
Chicago, Illinois, 60607
vaisband@uic.edu

ABSTRACT

Efficiently and reliably managing high quality power is a primary challenge in Internet of Things (IoT) systems. Based on current projections, future IoT will provide vast interconnectedness of embedded devices and sensors, many of which will be powered up wirelessly from spatially distributed power supplies or locally from energy harvesting sources. The energy budget, constrained by inherently lower quality of power of these non-traditional power sources, will become a critical system resource and a primary limiting factor for scalability of future IoT systems. Distributed on-chip power regulation is necessary for efficiently delivering high quality power to high performance heterogeneous integrated circuits (ICs). A multi-feedback system with distributed on-chip power supplies delivering current to billions of non-linear circuits is characterized by complex interactions among the heterogeneous power supplies and loads. These modern multi-feedback systems exhibit high design complexity and degraded stability. No straightforward method exists to efficiently design a stable multi-feedback power delivery system. An automated design and analysis flow for stable, high quality power delivery is proposed in this work based on the passivity of heterogeneous integrated systems. The algorithm is evaluated based on ISPD benchmark circuits and shows that the generated power delivery system addresses both the quality of power (QoP) and stability requirements. A distributed power delivery system is designed based on the passivity criterion and fabricated in 28 nm CMOS technology. The system is tested under a wide range of load, voltage, and temperature variations that are typical for modern heterogeneous ICs. The system exhibits high performance and stable response.

Keywords

On-chip power delivery; distributed system; LDO regulators; power conversion; stability; IoT; wireless power transfer; energy harvesting

Permission to make digital or hard copies of all or part of this work for personal or classroom use is granted without fee provided that copies are not made or distributed for profit or commercial advantage and that copies bear this notice and the full citation on the first page. Copyrights for components of this work owned by others than ACM must be honored. Abstracting with credit is permitted. To copy otherwise, or republish, to post on servers or to redistribute to lists, requires prior specific permission and/or a fee. Request permissions from permissions@acm.org.

GLSVLSI '17, May 10-12, 2017, Banff, AB, Canada
© 2017 ACM. ISBN 978-1-4503-4972-7/17/05. . . $15.00
DOI: http://dx.doi.org/10.1145/3060403.3060497

1. INTRODUCTION

Emerging IoT systems exhibit a wide spectrum of power requirements and switching activity patterns induced by billions of non-linear loads within numerous voltage domains of the individual interconnected IoT devices. Many of these edge devices are expected to be powered by means of energy harvesting (EH) from ambient energy sources and/or by means of wireless power transfer (WPT). Quality of the power supplied by these non-conventional energy sources is significantly lower compared with the traditional power supplies (e.g., batteries and power cords) and poses a critical challenge on efficiently delivering power in heterogeneous IoT systems. A segment of IoT system with interconnected devices powered by heterogeneous, traditional and alternative power sources, is illustrated in Fig. 1. The underlying

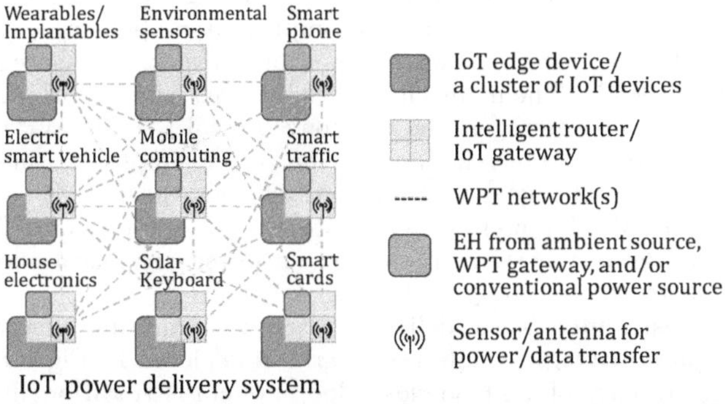

Figure 1: IoT power delivery system with interconnected edge devices powered by heterogeneous (EH, WPT, conventional) energy sources.

heterogeneous power delivery system of a single edge device (e.g., smartphone) is illustrated in Fig. 2.

The quality of power (QoP) in modern high performance systems is typically addressed with a point-of-load (POL) power delivery [6, 5, 4, 9]. Modern distributed power delivery system of a multi-core IC typically comprises a power management module, efficient power converters, global power distribution networks (PDNs), and on-chip voltage regulators distributed within local power grids, all delivering power to billions of non-linear loads within multiple power domains, as shown in Fig. 2. The distributed nature of modern power delivery system with many thousands of on-chip electrical components significantly increases design complexity of next generation IoT edge devices. To cope with the design

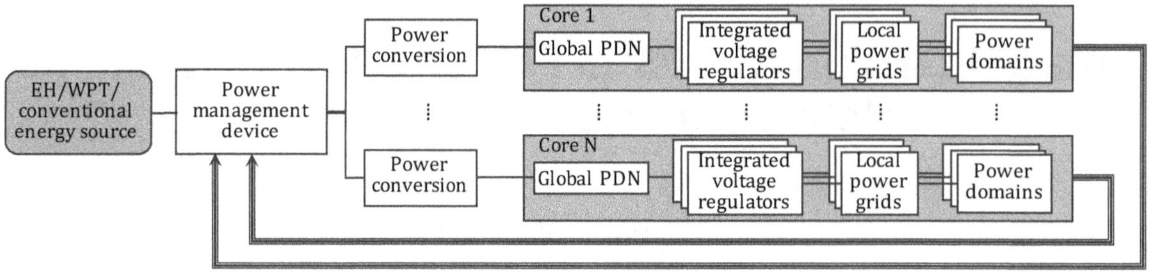

Figure 2: A typical power delivery system of a multi-core IoT edge device (e.g., smartphone)

complexity in complex analog circuits, automated modeling, optimization, and synthesis techniques are typically considered [8]. To automate the design of a power delivery system in future IoTs, accurate methods to evaluate performance metrics (*e.g.*, quality of transient response and stability) are required.

In a heterogeneous IoT system, the total load of a single power domain within a IoT edge device is shared among all of the parallel connected power supplies. The greatest portion of the total current is supplied by those voltage regulators in close proximity with the current load. This supplied current can be significantly higher than the average current supplied by a single regulator [4]. The current load of each regulator is therefore a strong function of the characteristics of the power delivery system (e.g., PDN impedance, load activity, and number and location of power supplies). A distributed system with multiple low-dropout (LDO) regulators delivering power to a single grid can exhibit degraded stability due to complex interactions among the LDO regulators, power distribution network, and shared current loads. The many challenges involved with absorbing energy from heterogeneous non-conventional EH and WPT sources reduce the reliability of the power supplies within the individual edge devices, further reducing the stability of multi-feedback power delivery systems. The stability of IoT power delivery systems is therefore a primary concern and needs to be accurately evaluated.

A distributed power delivery system with multiple power supplies driving a single power grid is depicted in Fig. 3. The stability of a single closed loop system is traditionally determined by the phase margin of the open loop response. In systems with multiple dependent loops, the open loop approach is not practical because no straightforward method exists to identify the unstable loop. An alternative stability criterion has recently been proposed that imposes a passivity condition on the power grid impedance [10]. Based on this passivity-based stability criterion (PBSC), accurate system requirements for evaluating exponential and marginal stability in distributed power delivery systems are provided. Automation of the design process of a power delivery system is proposed in this work based on the PBSC and parametric circuit performance modeling technique.

The rest of the paper is organized as follows. The stability criterion for distributed power delivery is reviewed in Section 2. Automated design of a stable distributed IoT power delivery system is described in Section 3. Experimental results are presented in Section 4. The paper is concluded in Section 5.

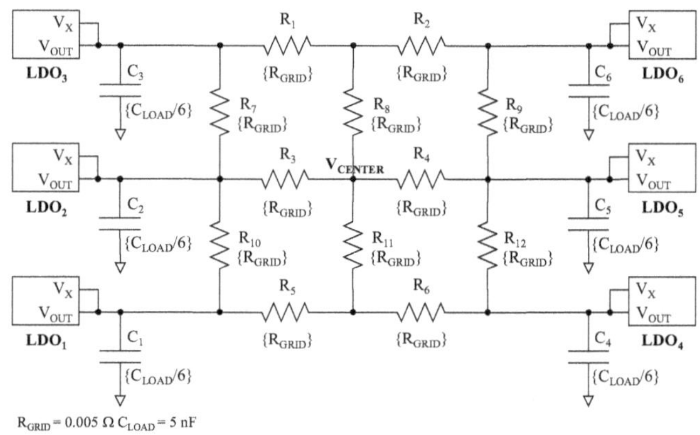

Figure 3: Model of distributed LDO regulators and power distribution network.

2. PASSIVITY-BASED STABILITY OF DISTRIBUTED SYSTEMS

Understanding the effects of the frequency domain parameters on the time domain characteristics provides significant insight into the transient behavior of complex systems. Traditionally, the phase margin of the output response determines the transient stability of a single LDO regulator. Similarly, a criterion is required for determining the stability of a *distributed* power delivery system.

A distributed power delivery system with two or more power supplies driving a single power grid is depicted in Fig. 4(a). In this distributed system, the power supplies can be combined into a single power delivery system, yielding an equivalent single port network, as shown in Fig. 4(b). Note that the output impedance of the equivalent single port network, Z_{TOT} in Fig. 4(b), is the parallel combination of all

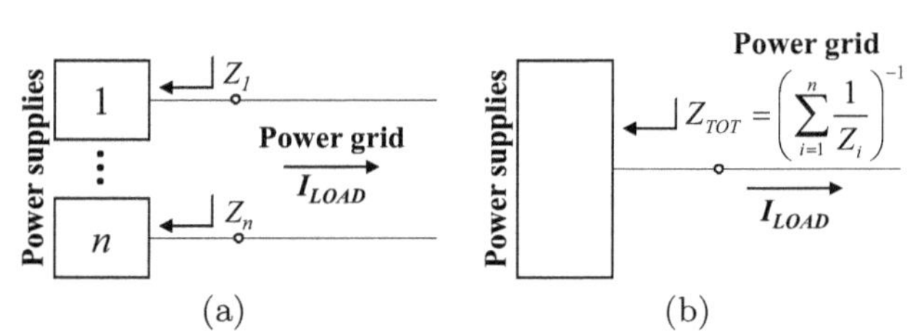

Figure 4: Power delivery system (a) with two or more distributed power supplies, and (b) reduced single port network.

of the output impedances $Z_i, i = 1, \ldots, N$ of the individual power supplies shown in Fig. 4(a). Similarly, the output impedance of a distributed power delivery system is based on the individual output impedance of the parallel connected elements. The open loop transfer function, traditionally used to determine the stability of a lumped power delivery system, cannot be applied to a distributed power delivery system with multiple control loops. An alternative criterion for evaluating the stability of a multi-feedback path system composed of distributed power regulators has recently been proposed [10] that describes sufficient conditions for stability of a distributed power delivery system. These conditions are based on the observation, that a linear, time-invariant (LTI) system is stable when coupled to an arbitrary passive environment if the driving point impedance is a passive system. A distributed power delivery system is therefore stable if the equivalent output impedance Z_{TOT} satisfies passivity requirements, yielding the following passivity-based stability conditions:

- $Z(\omega)$ has no right half plane (RHP) poles.
- The phase of $Z(\omega)$ is within the $(-90°, 90°)$ range.

A distributed system is, therefore, exponentially stable (converges within an exponential envelope) if the impedance of the system satisfies these passivity requirements, marginally stable (oscillates with constant amplitude) if the voltage and current phasors are shifted by precisely 90°, and unstable otherwise. The phase of the output impedance is an efficient alternative to determine the stability of these distributed systems, since the traditional phase margin approach is not practical due to the multiple control loops.

3. CIRCUIT PERFORMANCE MODELING

Existing automated techniques for designing analog circuits are based on numerical optimization and evaluation engines [8]. Parametric models characterize the performance of an analog circuit (*e.g.*, gain, bandwidth (BW), slew rate (SR), or phase margin (PM)) based on circuit design variables (*e.g.*, device sizes and voltage biases) [8]. The performance of an individual power supply is typically determined by a set of parameters, such as the DC gain, phase margin, DC offset, slew rate, and power. Alternatively, a distributed power delivery system should be evaluated based on both the performance of the individual power supply and additional performance metrics of the combined system, such as the *passivity of the output impedance.* To reduce the design complexity of modern distributed power delivery systems, the proposed PBSC is integrated within an automated design methodology.

An automated flow for designing a stable distributed power delivery system is shown in Fig. 5. The first stage of the proposed flow is based on a standard parametric performance modeling technique [8]. During this stage, an LDO regulator is synthesized based on the specific LDO topology and design objectives. The output of the first stage is used during the second stage to determine the number and location of the parallel connected power supplies in the proposed distributed power delivery system. During this second stage, a distributed power delivery system with a different number and location of voltage regulators is iteratively evaluated based on the proposed PBSC and distributed power

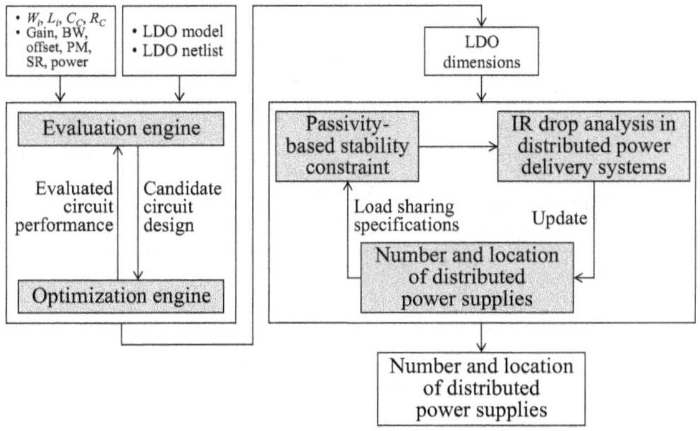

Figure 5: Automated PBSC-based design flow for a distributed power delivery system.

supply placement algorithms [4]. During each iteration, the worst case load sharing scenario is determined for the specific power delivery system. The PBSC of the distributed system is evaluated based on the individual current loads. If required, the number and location of the power supplies are updated. Finally, the number and location of the parallel connected power supplies that satisfies both the QoP and stability requirements of the distributed power delivery system are determined.

The operation of the second stage of the automated PBSC-based design flow is demonstrated here based on the ISPD placement benchmark suite circuits [2]. The floorplan of the superblue5, superblue10, superblue12, and superblue18 circuits is illustrated in Fig. 6. Each of the circuits is composed

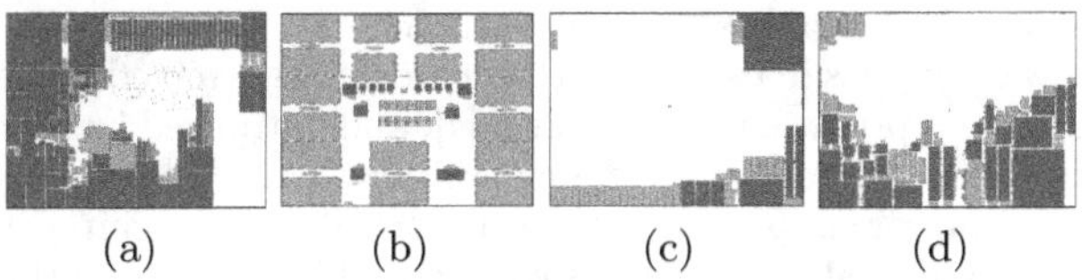

Figure 6: Floorplan of ISPD circuits [2] (a) superblue5, (b) superblue10, (c) superblue12, and (d) superblue18.

of thousands of fine grain rectangular shapes. To reduce the complexity of the circuit evaluation, the fine grain shapes are combined into larger rectangular nodes. Out of the combined nodes only the largest nodes are considered, exhibiting a reduced floorplan. Magnitude of the distributed load currents is determined proportionally to the size of these nodes with a total load current of 1 A. The location of each of the current loads is determined in the center of the corresponding rectangular node. The number of the fine grain shapes, large nodes, coverage of reduced floorplan, and power grid data is listed in Table 1. Note, that the nodes in the reduced floorplan occupy more than 85 % of the total active circuit area.

Ideally, a constant voltage is distributed to all of the current loads within a circuit. Practically, the QoP is degraded in modern circuits due to parasitic on-chip impedance. The voltage drop map of the superblue5 circuit without on-chip power supplies is shown in Fig. 7, yielding a maximum voltage drop of 23.4 %, assuming off-chip voltage supply of 1 V.

Table 1: Properties of ISPD benchmark circuits.

circuit	Number of fine grain shapes	Number of large combined nodes	Coverage of reduced floorplan	Power grid size	Number of nodes in the power grid
superblue5	29,736	129	85.0 %	774 × 713	551,862
superblue10	2,318	30	89.2 %	638 × 968	617,584
superblue12	3,578	15	98.4 %	444 × 518	229,992
superblue18	6,776	71	99.5 %	381 × 404	153,924

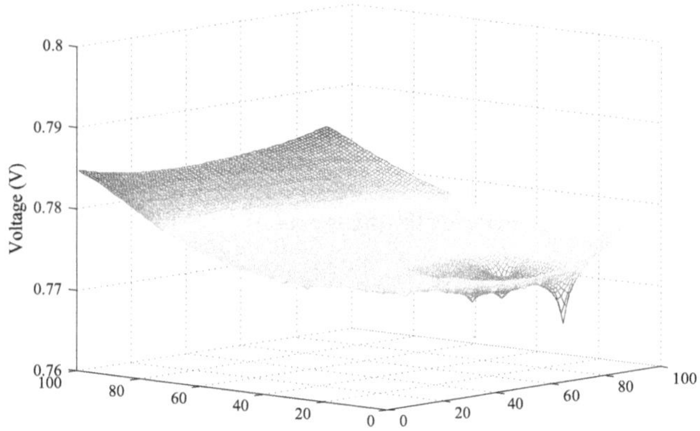

Figure 7: Voltage drop map of the superblue5 circuit.

To address the quality of on-chip power supply, power delivery systems with a single on-chip power supply (case 1), six on-chip power supplies (case 2), and twelve on-chip power supplies (case 3) are considered. For each of the three cases, *IR* drop of the distributed power delivery system is analyzed based on the *IR* drop algorithm for a power grid with multiple power supplies and current loads [3]. The location of power supplies in cases 1 and 2 is modeled as a mixed integer nonlinear programming problem [4], and optimized based on the general algebraic modeling system (GAMS) [1]. In case 3, the power supplies are uniformly distributed on-chip. Stability and quality of power are evaluated in each of the three cases based on, respectively, the PBSC and voltage drop.

The map of the voltage drops and phase of the output impedance within superblue5 with different number of on-chip power supplies is shown in Fig. 8. A distinct peak for the case with a single LDO regulator corresponds with the physical location of the LDO, pulling up the supply voltage locally in the network. The voltage peaks that correspond with the physical locations of the LDO regulators are reduced in cases 2 and 3. The QoP is therefore efficiently enhanced with increasing number of power supplies, exhibiting maximum voltage drop of, respectively, 9.17 %, 3.11 %, and 1.11 % with a single, six, and twelve on-chip power supplies.

The output load of the individual regulators also changes with the number of power supplies, affecting the phase of the output impedance and stability characteristics of the distributed system. Based on the proposed stability criterion, the superblue5 circuit with the evaluated power delivery system is stable with a single power supply and six power supplies (the phase of the output impedance is within the $(-90°, 90°)$ range), and unstable with twelve power supplies (the minimum phase of the output impedance is $-95.1° < -90°$), as shown in Fig. 8(b). While the distributed power delivery system with twelve power supplies exhibits higher QoP than systems with fewer power supplies, this system

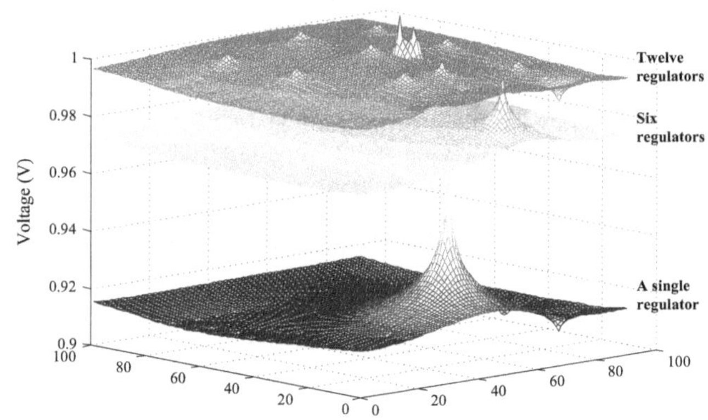

(a)

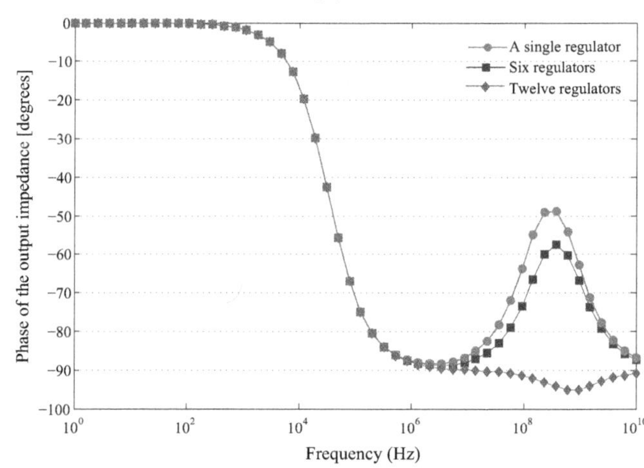

(b)

Figure 8: Superblue5 circuit with a single, six, and twelve on-chip power supplies, (a) map of voltage drops, and (b) phase of the output impedance.

is shown to be unstable under step response. Thus, a stable system with smaller number of power supplies should be preferred to deliver power to the superblue5 circuit while addressing both QoP and stability challenges.

The second stage of the automated PBSC-based design flow, shown in Fig. 5, is implemented in Matlab. Pseudocode of the Matlab algorithm is summarized in Algorithm 1. A typical LDO model [7] is used to describe a small signal response of the on-chip power supplies, and evaluate the output impedance of the power supplies and overall power delivery system.

Power delivery systems for the ISPD benchmark circuits superblue5, superblue10, superblue12, and superblue18 have been generated and evaluated based on this algorithm. The

Algorithm 1 Automated PBSC-based design flow.

```
LDOModel; // A typical LDO model [7]
CircInfo; // Supply voltages, load currents and locations
CircNodes; // All nodes in the evaluated circuit
NumRegsList; // List of numbers of LDOs to evaluate
PreferredNumRegs ← 0; // Preferred number of LDOs
PreferredLocs ← N/A; // Preferred location of LDOs
PreferredIRDrop ← 1; // Maximum allowed IR drop

for all NumRegs ← NumRegsList do
  for all RefNode ← CircuitNodes do
    // Find optimal LDO locations [1]
    OptLocs ← OPT_LOC(CircInfo, NumRegs);

    // Analyze IR drop in a power grid [3]
    IRDrop(RefNode) ← CALC_IRDROP(CircInfo, ...
                                  OptLocs, ...
                                  RefNode);

    // Calculate the output impedance of the LDOs
    for all LDO ← LDOs do
      ISupply ← Current delivered by the LDO;
      Z_OUT^LDO(LDO) ← CALC_ZOUT(LDOModel, ...
                                 ISupply);
    end for

    // Calculate the output impedance of the system
    Z_OUT^SYS ← ( Σ_{LDOs} 1 / Z_OUT^LDO(LDO) )^(-1);

    if max{|∠Z_OUT^SYS|} < 90° then
      if max{IRDrop} < PreferredIRDrop then
        PreferredIRDrop ← max{IRDrop};
        PreferredNumRegs ← NumRegs;
        PreferredLocs ← OptLocs;
      end if
    end if
  end for
end for
```

maximum *IR* drop and stability results are listed in Table 2. Based on the evaluated benchmark circuits, the maximum voltage drop is significantly reduced with the increasing number of on-chip power supplies. Alternatively, stability of the distributed power delivery system is a function of specific load distribution and changes with number of parallel connected power supplies. The proposed automated PBSC-based design flow generates a distributed power delivery system that addresses both the QoP and stability requirements.

4. EXPERIMENTAL RESULTS

A distributed system with six LDO regulators has been designed for IoT power delivery and evaluated based on the proposed PBSC. The system has been fabricated in an advanced 28 nm CMOS technology. The area occupied by the LDO with all capacitors is 85 µm × 42 µm. The regulators are distributed around the perimeter of the on-chip circuits, as shown in Fig. 3, regulating the power grid at reference voltage of 0.7 volts with an input voltage of 1.0 volt and maximum load current of 788 mA. The on-chip regulators simultaneously drive a power network, delivering current to the on-chip loads of an IoT edge device. To evaluate the system response under different load conditions, controllable current loads are integrated onto the test circuit. These current loads can be activated separately or simultaneously, exhibiting different current loads at individual LDO regulators. A die microphotograph of the LDO, and measured transient response for an aggressive load current ramp (from 52 mA to 788 mA in 5 ns) and nominal input and output voltages at 25 °C is illustrated in Fig. 9.

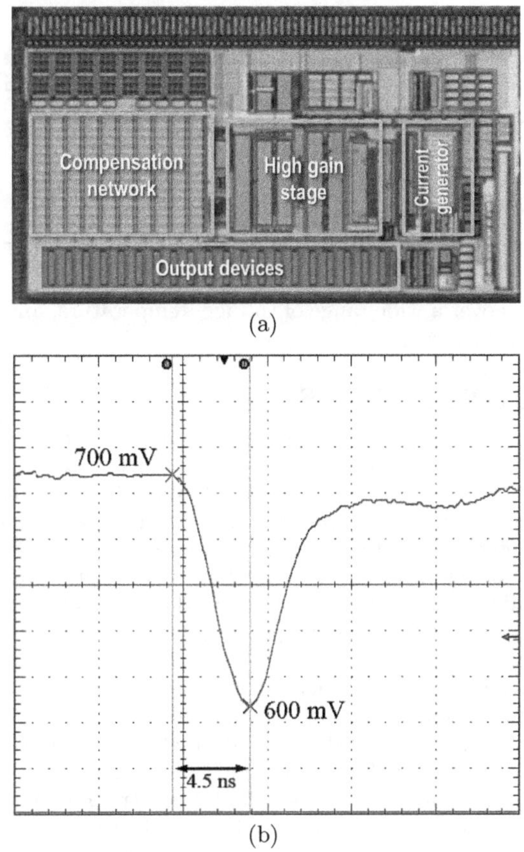

Figure 9: Experimental results, (a) die microphotograph of a single LDO regulator and current generating circuit, and (b) measured transient response for a load current step from 52 mA to 788 mA in 5 ns.

The load current of a single LDO regulator significantly varies in different configurations as compared to the nominal current. To evaluate the effect of voltage, temperature, and load sharing variations on the stability of a power delivery system, the system is measured with different line, load, and temperature configurations. The total load current of the distributed power delivery system with six LDO regulators is aggressively ramped in 5 ns from 17 mA to 309 mA (slow corner), from 52 mA to 441 mA (typical corner), and from 420 mA to 900 mA (fast corner) for, respecttively, −25 °C, 25 °C, and 125 °C. In the typical corner, the system is also evaluated under ±10% line variations. The DC voltages and voltage droop for a transient response of the experimental distributed system are listed in Table 3. Based on these experimental results, the system of six parallel LDO regulators yields a stable response and voltage droop of less than

Table 2: **Properties of ISPD benchmark circuits.**

	No regulators		A single regulator		Six regulators		Twelve regulators	
circuit	*IR* drop	Stability	*IR* drop	Stability	*IR* drop	Stability	*IR* drop	Stability
superblue5	23.4%	N/A	9.17%	Stable	3.11%	Stable	1.11%	Not stable
superblue10	23.0%	N/A	10.8%	Stable	4.75%	Stable	2.43%	Not stable
superblue12	23.6%	N/A	10.7%	Stable	6.39%	Stable	4.88%	Not stable
superblue18	22.7%	N/A	10.7%	Stable	4.43%	Stable	1.54%	Not stable

Table 3: Transient step response at the load under line and temperature variations.

Type of variations		V_{OUT} (mV)		Voltage droop
$V_{IN}(V)$	Temperature (°C)	Max	Min	(mV)
1.0	25	700.8	698.9	64.9
1.1	25	701.1	699.0	61.4
0.9	25	698.3	696.0	71.1
1.0	125	692.3	690.0	55.0
1.0	-25	704.3	702.4	63.3

0.1 volts over a wide range of voltage, temperature, and load sharing variations.

5. CONCLUSIONS

loT have emerged as a powerful technology that creates valuable networked connections among a wide variety of locally intelligent electronic devices. Novel, IoT based market segments, such as intelligent transportation, revolutionary health care, sophisticated security systems, and smart energy applications are emerging that fundamentally change our daily experience and reshape world economy. Many of the IoT edge devices will be powered from non-conventional energy sources (e.g., harvested piezo/thermoelectric, wind flow, solar, photovoltaic energy and/or wireless power transfer). While quality of power in the future IoT edge devices can be addressed with distributed point-of-load power supplies, the stability of the distributed power delivery systems fed by these inherently less reliable, non-traditional power sources, is becoming a primary limiting factor for scalability of future IoT systems. A passivity-based stability criterion has recently been proposed for evaluating the stability of parallel voltage regulators, driving a single power grid. Based on this criterion, a distributed power delivery system is stable if the total output impedance of the parallel connected LDOs is passive.

A design automation flow for stable power delivery in IoT edge devices is proposed in this work based on passivity-based stability criterion. The proposed design flow is demonstrated on a set of ISPD benchmark circuits with different number of parallel connected voltage regulators. A system with few LDO regulators is shown to violate quality of power requirements. Alternatively, a system with large number of distributed LDO regulators designed for maximum quality of power is shown to be unstable under step load response. A tradeoff therefore exists between the stability and quality of power in distributed power delivery systems. A preferred number of power supplies should be determined based on both the PBSC and voltage drop characteristics to simultaneously address the quality of power and stability requirements complex IoT systems.

A distributed power delivery system with six LDO regulators is designed based on the results of the stability analysis. The system is fabricated in 28 nm CMOS technology, and tested under aggressive load ramp transition, exhibiting high performance and stable response over a wide range of voltage, temperature, and load sharing variations. The proposed design automation flow provides an efficient means for designing stable, high quality power delivery system for heterogeneous IoT edge devices.

6. REFERENCES

[1] A. Brooke, D. Kendrick, and A. Meeraus. *GAMS: A User's Guide.* The Scientific Press, 1992.

[2] N. V. *et al.* The ispd-2011 routability-driven placement contest and benchmark suite. In *Proceedings of the ACM International Symposium on Physical Design*, pages 141–146, March 2011.

[3] S. Kose and E. G. Friedman. Fast algorithms for ir voltage drop analysis exploiting locality. In *Proceedings of the IEEE/ACM Design Automation Conference*, pages 996–1001, June 2011.

[4] S. Kose and E. G. Friedman. Distributed on-chip power delivery. *IEEE Journal on Emerging and Selected Topics in Circuits and Systems*, 2(4):704–713, December 2012.

[5] R. J. Milliken, J. S.-Martinez, and E. S.-Sinencio. Full on-chip cmos low-dropout voltage regulator. *IEEE Transactions on Circuits and Systems I: Regular Papers*, 54(9):1879–1890, September 2007.

[6] P. Hazucha *et al.* Area-efficient linear regulator with ultra-fast load regulation. *IEEE Journal of Solid-State Circuits*, 40(4):933–940, April 2005.

[7] I. P.-Vaisband, R. Jakushokas, M. Popovich, A. V. Mezhiba, S. Kose, and E. G. Friedman. *On-Chip Power Delivery and Management, 4th Edition.* Springer, 2016. ISBN-13: 978-3319293936, ISBN-10: 3319293931.

[8] R. A. Rutenbar, G. G. E. Gielen, and J. Roychowdhury. Hierarchical modeling, optimization, and synthesis for system-level analog and rf designs. *Proceedings of the IEEE*, 95(3):640–669, March 2007.

[9] I. Vaisband and E. G. Friedman. Heterogeneous methodology for energy efficient distribution of on-chip power supplies. *IEEE Transactions on Power Electronics*, 28(9):4267–4280, September 2013.

[10] I. Vaisband and E. G. Friedman. Stability in distributed power delivery networks. *IEEE Transactions on Power Electronics*, 31(28):5625–5633, August 2016.

Work Load Scheduling For Multi Core Systems With Under-Provisioned Power Delivery

Divya Pathak
Drexel University
divya.pathak@drexel.edu

Houman Homayoun
George Mason University
hhomayoun@gmu.edu

Ioannis Savidis
Drexel University
isavidis@coe.drexel.edu

ABSTRACT

An energy efficient power delivery method for multi-core systems with under-provisioned on-chip voltage regulators has been proposed in literature. The power delivery network is reconfigurable at run-time to meet the varying current demands of the cores exceeding the maximum output current rating of the voltage regulators. In this paper, a real-time workload scheduling heuristic is developed that assigns the tasks to the cores such that the total load current consumption of the cores is always less than the total current capability of the under-provisioned on-chip voltage regulators. In addition, the energy-efficient scheduling of the tasks on to the cores ensures that the reconfiguration of the power delivery network is minimized. The heuristic includes DVFS management based on the unique constraints of the under provisioned voltage regulators. The work load scheduler is evaluated on homogeneous and heterogeneous multi-core platforms based on the Exynos 5410 big.LITTLE architecture. The proposed workload scheduler along with the run time voltage regulator clustering algorithm proposed in the literature provides a robust cross-layer power management technique for under-provisioned on-chip power delivery.

Keywords

low power scheduling, real-time scheduling, on-chip voltage regulation, under-provisioned power delivery, low-power design, power-aware systems.

1. INTRODUCTION

Energy efficiency has emerged as a critical design parameter in multi-core or chip multi-processor (CMP) systems. Apart from increased energy efficiency, power delivery through on-chip voltage regulators (OCVRs) offers several benefits such as reduced latency to apply DVFS, point of load power delivery with minimal power supply noise, and reduced I/O pin count devoted to power and ground signals [1, 2]. The peak power consumption and worst case power supply noise transient in a CMP determine the design of the power delivery system. Conventionally, the power rating and the design topology of the OCVR is selected based on the maximum possible power consumption of the load circuit. The work done in [3, 4] demonstrates that the conventional method to design the power delivery network is over-provisioned by at least an order of magnitude of the maximum output current rating of the OCVRs. By under-provisioning the OCVRs to meet the typical or average need of the load circuits, the energy efficiency of the CMP system is increased by upto 44% [3]. A reconfigurable power delivery network with run-time clustering of the outputs of the OCVRs is proposed in [3] (refer to Fig. 1). The algorithm developed in [3] for run-time OCVR clustering is an example of supply side load management. The on-chip power management unit reconfigures the connections between the OCVRs and the cores to meet the changing load current demands of the cores. The run-time reconfiguration of the power delivery network operates under a power constraint. The total power demanded at any time instant by the cores is less than the total power delivery capability of the OCVRs. The power constraint is expressed mathematically in (1) for a CMP with N cores and N OCVRs. I_{sense_x} and V_x are, respectively, the sensed load current and the operating voltage of each core x. I_{avg} and V_{dd_m} are, respectively, the maximum output current and the maximum supported power supply voltage level of each OCVR.

$$\sum_{i=1}^{N} V_x \cdot I_{sense\_x} < N \cdot V_{dd\_m} \cdot I_{avg} \tag{1}$$

In this paper, an energy optimized work load scheduling technique is developed which relaxes the power constraint (1) on the run-time OCVR clustering algorithm developed in [3]. Low power workload scheduling on heterogeneous processors is a widely researched field [5, 6], albeit the workload schedulers in literature are oblivious of the power lost in the DC-DC converters delivering regulated power supply to the cores. The workload scheduler described in this paper is a demand side load management technique. Workload schedulers are classified into three categories [7]: best effort scheduling, with acceptance test, and robust scheduling. The proposed heuristic imposes an acceptance test on each incoming task in the system and schedules it on to one of the cores only if it meets the power constraint of the under-provisioned power delivery system. Workloads running on a CMP system are either controllable loads with soft deadlines or non-controllable loads with hard deadlines. The rescheduling of controllable tasks reduces the energy consumption of the CMP system for a given scheduling cycle. Real time applications fall under the category of non-controllable loads as they impose a hard or firm deadline. In the case of non-real time tasks with soft

Permission to make digital or hard copies of all or part of this work for personal or classroom use is granted without fee provided that copies are not made or distributed for profit or commercial advantage and that copies bear this notice and the full citation on the first page. Copyrights for components of this work owned by others than ACM must be honored. Abstracting with credit is permitted. To copy otherwise, or republish, to post on servers or to redistribute to lists, requires prior specific permission and/or a fee. Request permissions from permissions@acm.org.

GLSVLSI '17, May 10-12, 2017, Banff, AB, Canada.
© 2017 ACM. ISBN 978-1-4503-4972-7/17/05...$15.00.
DOI: http://dx.doi.org/10.1145/3060403.3060498

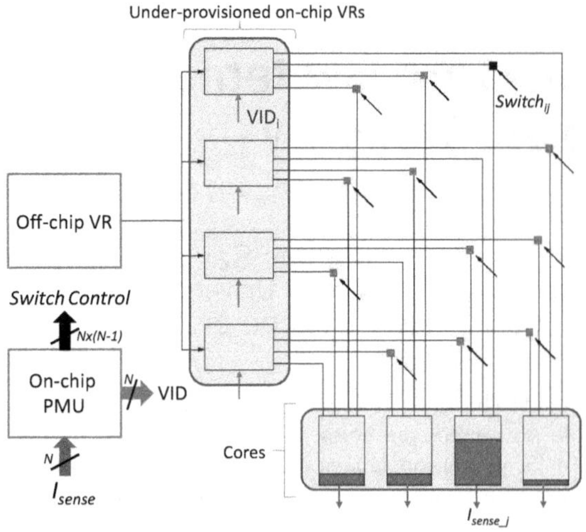

Figure 1: Proposed interconnected on-chip power delivery network in [3]. The on-chip voltage regulators are designed for a maximum output current equal to the average load current demand of workloads executed on the cores (I_{avg}). An algorithm for run-time voltage regulator clustering through a switching fabric is proposed in [3] to meet greater than I_{avg} load current demand.

deadlines and fixed priority, the tasks which violate the power constraint given by (1) are executed in the next scheduling cycle, leading to a performance penalty.

The energy consumed by a taskset on a processing element is a convex function of the computational capacity of the processing element and the task execution time. A convex energy optimization problem is solved to ensure the reliability of the proposed reconfigurable power delivery system with underprovisioned on-chip voltage regulators in [3]. The optimization problem is constrained by the total power budget of the CMP and is limited to the peak current rating of the OCVRs. The feasibility of the solution, determined by solving the optimization problem, is demonstrated through a real time workload scheduling heuristic. The scheduler is applicable to homogeneous and heterogeneous CMPs.

The rest of the paper is organized as follows: The models developed for the CMP system, OCVRs, real time periodic taskset and power consumption of the cores are described in Section 2. The convex energy optimization problem for workload scheduling is described in 3. An energy efficient workload scheduling heuristic is described in Section 4. The evaluation of the workload scheduling heuristic on homogeneous and heterogeneous CMP platforms is provided in Section 5. Concluding remarks are provided in Section 6.

2. SYSTEM MODEL AND NOTATIONS

The under-provisioned CMP system includes a set of processing elements or cores and per-core on-chip voltage regulators. The models constructed for the core architecture, CMP platform, voltage regulators, real time periodic tasks, and the power consumption of the cores are described in Subsections 2.1 through 2.4.

2.1 CMP models

CMP systems with homogeneous core configurations as well as heterogeneous configuration are developed to analyze the work load scheduler. The homogeneous CMP includes processing elements based on the ARM A15 core integrated in the Samsung Exynos 5410 platform [8, 9]. The parameters used in constructing a 16 core homogeneous CMP platform are listed in Table 2. An eight core heterogeneous CMP with four ARM A15 and four A7 cores from the Exynos 5410 platform is also evaluated. The DVFS levels applied to the cores are listed in Table 1. The variation in the power consumption of the core with frequency, based on the power model given by (2) and validated in [10], is shown in Fig. 2.

Table 1: Frequency (MHz) and Voltage (V) pairs used by the DFVS procedure in *Algorithm 1*. The bold values listed in the table are the nominal voltages and frequencies.

big core (A15)	LITTLE core (A7)
1800/1.250	**1200/1.225**
1700/1.200	1100/1.125
1600/1.162	1000/1.100
1500/1.137	900/1.037
1400/1.100	800/0.987
1300/1.062	700/0.950
1200/1.025	600/0.950
1100/1.000	500/0.950
1000/0.962	400/0.950
900/0.925	300/0.950
800/0.900	200/0.950

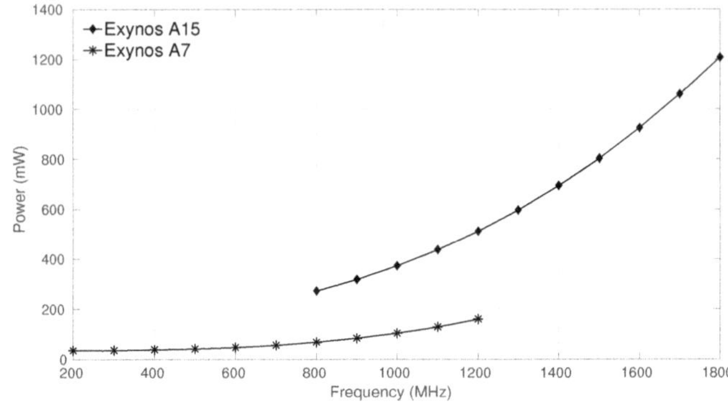

Figure 2: The power consumption of the Exynos big.LITTLE cores with frequency based on the model given by (2). The power model parameters are validated in [10].

2.2 Power model

The power consumption of a processing element π_j is approximated as a function of frequency, similar to work done in [10]. The power consumed by any processing element is given by (2). The $\kappa * f^{\alpha}$ and β terms in (2) represent, respectively, the dynamic and static power consumption of the cores. The model parameters κ, α, and β for the Samsung Exynos A15 and A7 processors [10] are used to validate *Algorithm 1*. The power consumption with frequency using the estimated model parameters is shown in Fig. 2.

$$P(f) = \kappa * f^{\alpha} + \beta \tag{2}$$

2.3 Voltage regulator models

An on-chip power delivery network with per core voltage regulation is considered for the CMP platform. The on-chip

Table 2: Parameters of the CMP cores derived from the Samsung Exynos 5410 big.LITTLE architecture.

Parameter	big core (A15)	LITTLE core (A7)
Nominal voltage (V)	1.16	1.225
Nominal frequency (MHz)	1600	1200
OCVR maximum current rating (I_{avg} in mA)	800	110
Power model parameters [α_j, κ_j (mW/MHz^3), β_j (mW)]	[2.63, 2.91× 10^{-6}, 146.49]	[3.28, 1.00× 10^{-8}, 34.24]
Number of cores in homogeneous CMP system	16	0
Number of cores in heterogeneous CMP system	4	4

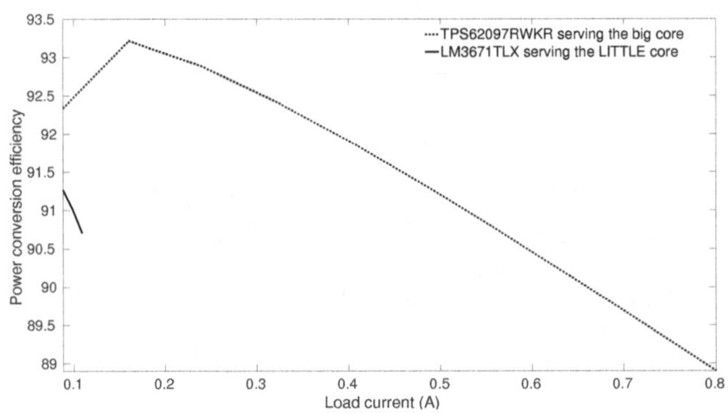

Figure 3: The power conversion efficiency of the voltage regulators serving the Exynos A15 (big) and Exynos A7 (LITTLE) cores [12].

voltage regulators (OCVRs) are modeled as DC-DC switching buck converters [11]. Buck converters with optimum power conversion efficiency based on the power consumption of the A15 and A7 cores (shown in Fig. 2) are developed using [12]. The important parameters of the buck converters for both the big and LITTLE cores are listed in Table 3. The variation in power conversion efficiency with load current is shown in Fig. 3.

2.4 Real-time periodic task model

The real-time workloads are modeled as a set of independent periodic tasks $\tau_i \in \mathcal{T}$ to be scheduled on a subset of cores of a many-core system $\pi_j \in \Pi$ [10]. Each task τ_i, has a hard deadline of D_i. Each core π_j supports distinct DVFS levels $V_x \in [V_{dd\_1}, V_{dd\_2}, ..., V_{dd\_m}]$ and $f_x \in [f_1, f_2, ..., f_m]$. A task τ_i with a hard deadline D_i requires at most $C_{i,j}$ cycles to execute on a core π_j at the highest supported voltage V_{dd_m} and frequency f_m. The context switching overhead and overhead due to resource sharing amongst tasks which remain unresolved after task partitioning is included in $C_{i,j}$. The computational capacity required by task τ_i on core π_j is defined as $u_{i,j} = \frac{C_{i,j}}{D_i}$. The subset of tasks T_j that are executed on core π_j therefore require a total computational capacity of $U_j = \sum_{\tau_i \in T_j} u_{i,j}$ cycles per second.

3. OPTIMAL WORKLOAD SCHEDULING

An optimization problem is defined to partition and schedule real time workloads on a many-core platform. A specific set of constraints unique to the proposed reconfigurable PDN are considered, which account for the use of underprovisioned on-chip voltage regulators. The objective of the optimization problem is to minimize the energy consumption of the many core platform, including the power consumed by the OCVRs. The energy consumed by the system in a given scheduling period T_{epoch} is given by (3), where P(U_j) is the power consumed by the core π_j with computational capacity U_j to execute the scheduled task set, and PCE_{U_j} is the combined power conversion efficiency of the OCVR(s) supplying current to the core π_j. The workload scheduling is constrained by the total computational capacity available to execute the taskset U_j on π_j, where the total capacity must exceed the computational demand of the taskset as given by (4). In addition, the operating frequency must fall within the supported frequency range of the cores as given by (5). The total power consumed by the cores at any time instant must be less than the combined maximum power supported by all OCVRs in the system as described by (6).

$$\min_{U_j} \sum_{\pi_j \in \Pi} \frac{P(U_j)}{PCE_{U_j}} \cdot T_{epoch} \tag{3}$$

$$\text{s.t.} \quad \sum_{\pi_j \in \Pi} U_j \geq \sum_{\tau_i \in T} u_i \tag{4}$$

$$f_{1,j} \leq U_j \leq f_{m,j} \qquad \forall \pi_j \in \Pi \tag{5}$$

$$\sum_{\pi_j \in \Pi} P(U_j) < N \cdot V_{dd\_m} \cdot I_{avg} \tag{6}$$

4. WORKLOAD SCHEDULING HEURISTIC

A heuristic is described in this section, which performs the real time workload scheduling on the cores for the optimization problem developed in Section 3. The heuristic consists of three procedures: *PARTITION*, *DVFS*, and *SCHEDULE*. The *PARTITION* procedure is an evolution of the *Marginal-Power Heuristic (M-PWR)* developed in [10]. Optimal workload partitioning is achieved by incrementing the load on each core such that the constraint given by (5) is not violated. The tasks $\tau_i \in \mathcal{T}$ are first sorted in decreasing order of the maximum computational demand $u_{i,j}$ on cores $\pi_j \in \Pi$. A task is assigned to a core if the scheduling of the task results in the least increase in the power consumption. The output from the procedure is a scheduled taskset Θ_j on each core.

The *DVFS* procedure reduces the operating frequency and the voltage of the cores until the constraint given by (6) is satisfied. The right hand side of (6) is a constant value equal to the total power P_{total} of the CMP. Expressing the total power consumed by the cores with the power model given by (2) in constraint (6) provides a limit to the operating frequency of the cores raised to the power α (refer to constraint (8)). The use of the *DVFS* procedure results in the optimal frequency of operation for each core by solving the bounded knapsack problem. The deadline of each task in the taskset Θ_j is analogous to the value of the item in the knapsack. The required computational demand at a given frequency f_j

Table 3: Operating values of the switching DC-DC buck converters [12] serving the ARM A15 and A7 cores.

Device	LM3671TLX	TPS62097RWKR
Input voltage (V)	2.5	2.5
Output voltage range (V)	0.9 to 1.3	0.9 to 1.3
Maximum output current (mA)	110	800
Efficiency at maximum output current	90.7	88.9
Peak to peak inductor ripple current (mA)	146.93	357.24
Switching frequency (MHz)	2	1.69
Duty cycle (%)	46.18	47.44
Peak-to-peak output ripple voltage (mV)	1.322	3.215
Total power dissipation (mW)	12.4	109.88
Footprint (mm^2)	37	93

Algorithm 1 Real time workload partitioning and scheduling on a many-core system with underprovisioned OCVRs.

Inputs:
Set of real time tasks: $\mathcal{T}$
Set of N cores in the many-core system: Π
Outputs: Schedulable taskset (Θ_j) on each core $\pi_j \in \Pi$ with assigned voltage $V_j \in [V_{dd\_1}, V_{dd\_2}, ..., V_{dd\_m}]$ and frequency $f_j \in [f_1, f_2, ..., f_m]$
procedure PARTITION($\mathcal{T}$, Π)
  for each $\pi_j \in \Pi$ **do**
    $\Theta_j \leftarrow \emptyset$, U $\leftarrow$ 0
  end for
  $\mathcal{T}^{'} \leftarrow$ SORT($\mathcal{T}$ by descending $max_j\ u_{i,j}$)
  for each $\tau_i \in \mathcal{T}^{'}$ **do**
    $\Pi^{'} \leftarrow$ j: $U_j + u_{i,j} < f_{m,j}$ ▷ Cores on which τ_i is schedulable
    if $\Pi^{'} = \emptyset$ **then return** Failed to schedule
    end if
    k $\leftarrow$ arg $min_{j \in \Pi^{'}}\ P_j(U_j + u_{i,j})$ ▷ core id on which τ_i consumes least power
    $\Theta_k \leftarrow \Theta_k \bigcup \tau_i$ ▷ Θ_k is the schedulable set of tasks on π_k
    $U_k \leftarrow U_k + u_{i,j}$
  end for
return Θ
end procedure
procedure DVFS(Θ)
  while $\sum_{\pi_j \in \Pi} f_j^{\alpha} > (P_{total} - N \cdot \beta)/\kappa$ **do**
    for each $\pi_j \in \Pi$ **do**
      while $\sum_{\tau_i \in \Theta_j} u_{i,f_j} \leq f_m$ **do**
        $f_j \leftarrow (f_x \mid f_x \in$ F and $f_x \leq f_j)$ ▷ lower the operating frequency to one of the supported DVFS levels $F = (f_1, f_2, ..., f_m)$
      end while
    end for
  end while
end procedure
procedure SCHEDULE(Θ_j, f_j)
  $k \leftarrow$ arg $min_{\tau_i \in \Theta_j}\ D_i$
  $\pi_j \leftarrow \tau_k$
end procedure

Table 4: Parameters to generate real time periodic tasksets.

Parameter	Value
Number of tasks (N_t)	[32, 48, 64, 80]
Task utilization range	[0.1 to 0.9]
Task period range in seconds (T_i)	[10 to 100]
Taskset utilization factor (ρ)	[0.1 to 1]

on processor π_j is u_{i,f_j}. The weight added to the knapsack is analogous to u_{i,f_j}. The objective of the knapsack problem is to maximize the number of tasks executed on a core, without violating the task deadline. The procedure lowers the operating frequency of each task until constraints (7) and (8) are satisfied. Once the operating frequency of each task in Θ_j is determined, the *SCHEDULE* procedure schedules the tasksets on each core based on an earliest deadline first policy.

$$\sum_{\tau_i \in \Theta_j} u_{i,f_j} \leq f_m \tag{7}$$

$$\sum_{\pi_j \in \Pi} f_j^{\alpha} \leq (P_{total} - N \cdot \beta)/k \tag{8}$$

5. SIMULATION RESULTS

Real time periodic tasks with implicit deadlines are considered to determine the efficacy of the proposed task scheduler. The task scheduling is performed for one hyperperiod of the taskset T_{epoch}, which is the least common multiple of the implicit deadlines of all tasks $\tau_i \in \mathcal{T}$. The tasks are generated with the parameters listed in Table 4. The computational capacity (u_{ij}) of the tasks is selected as a random variable with a uniform distribution between 0.1x to 0.9x the maximum supported operating frequency of the cores in the CMP (maximum frequency f_m of 1800 MHz). The total computation time requested by the taskset in a hyperperiod is less than the available time on the processing elements to prevent system overload. This ensures that the taskset utilization factor or the system load is less than 1 ($\rho < 1$).

The resulting task schedule, from execution of *Algorithm 1* on a homogeneous CMP platform with 16 cores configured as Exynos 5410 A15s, is shown in Fig. 4. The task scheduling is constrained due to the limited power budget of the under-provisioned voltage regulators. For a maximum output current I_{avg} of 1 A, the percentage of tasks scheduled by

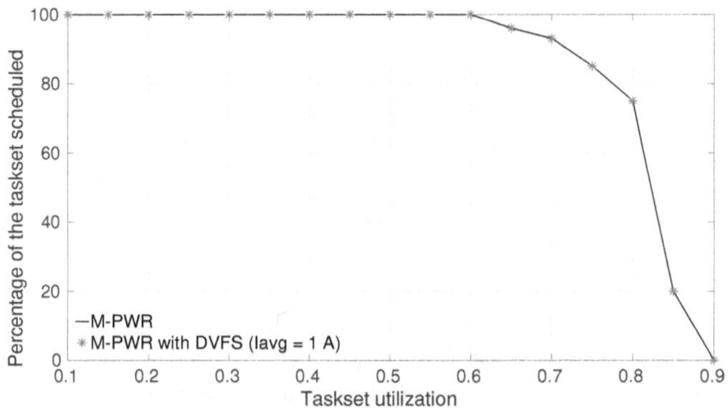

Figure 4: Percentage of tasks successfully partitioned by the M-PWR heuristic [10] and successfully scheduled by *Algorithm 1* in a 16 core homogeneous CMP. Task scheduling through *Algorithm 1* matches the M-PWR heuristic with the maximum output current rating of the voltage regulator set to 1 A.

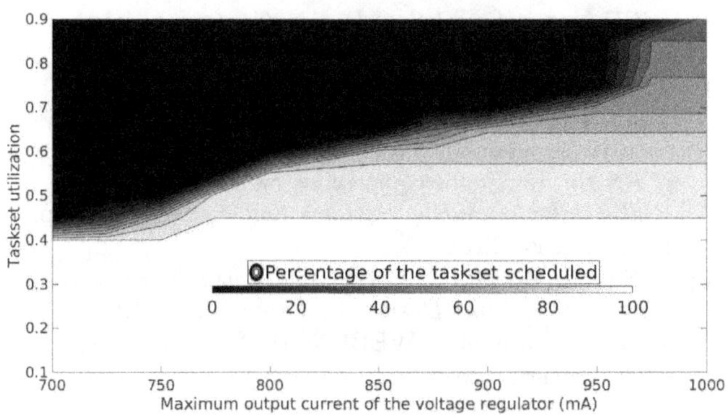

Figure 5: A contour plot of percentage of tasks successfully scheduled by *Algorithm 1* with varying taskset utilization and maximum output current of the voltage regulators in a homogeneous CMP with 16 cores.

Algorithm 1 is identical to the M-PWR heuristic in [10]. The execution of *Algorithm 1* is further characterized on a homogeneous platform with voltage regulators of varying maximum output current I_{avg}. The results are shown through the contour plot in Fig. 5. The percentage of tasks scheduled for a given taskset utilization factor decreases as the maximum output current of the voltage regulators is reduced. For a voltage regulator designed with a maximum output current I_{avg} of 0.7 A, the percentage of tasks scheduled matches the M-PWR heuristic [10] upto a taskset utilization factor ρ of 0.65.

The workload scheduler is also evaluated on a heterogeneous CMP platform with four Exynos A15 (big) and four Exynos A7 (LITTLE) cores. For a randomly chosen taskset hyperperiod, the task distribution and corresponding computational demand ($u_{i,j}$ of each task) is shown in Fig. 6. There are 11 tasks assigned to the big core cluster and five to the LITTLE core cluster. The maximum output current of the voltage regulators serving each of the big cores is set to 800 mA and the voltage regulators serving each of the LITTLE cores to 110 mA. The frequency assigned to each core to meet the constraint given by (8) is determined and shown

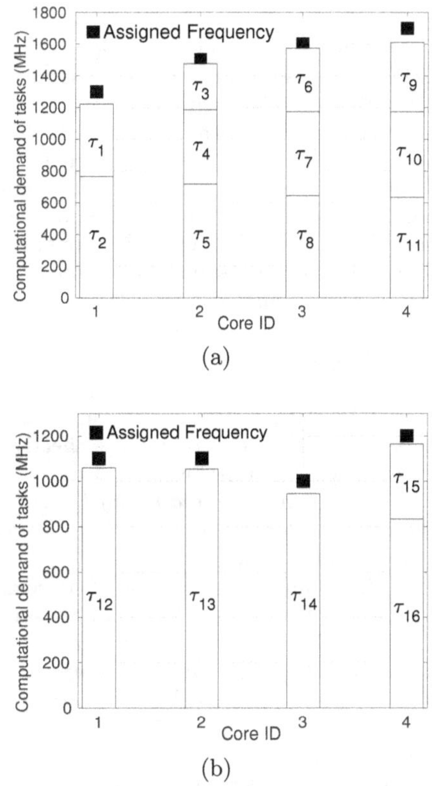

Figure 6: A snapshot of the task assignment on a heterogeneous CMP platform with (a) big cores modeled on A15 parameters, and (b) LITTLE cores modeled on A7 parameters. The maximum output currents of the voltage regulators serving each of the big cores and LITTLE cores are, respectively, 800 mA and 110 mA.

in the Fig. 6. Depending on the total computational demand of the tasks assigned to each core, the frequency is lowered from the maximum supported frequency of 1800 MHz for the big cores and 1200 MHz for the LITTLE cores. The task partitioning performed by the *PARTITION* procedure further improves power efficiency by preferentially assigning tasks to the LITTLE cores, which meet the task utilization constraint given by (4). Consequently, for an identical scaling factor of the peak output current of the OCVRs (I_{avg}/I_{peak}) serving the LITTLE core and the big core, the percentage of tasks scheduled through the *DVFS* procedure is lower for the LITTLE cores as compared to the big cores. As the LITTLE core cluster has a load current range of 100 mA, the scaling factor of the maximum output current of the voltage regulators serving the LITTLE cores is set to a larger value than that for the big cores to achieve a high task schedulability on the heterogeneous platform.

The task scheduling results on the homogeneous and heterogeneous CMP platform demonstrate that the proposed workload scheduler in tandem with the runtime on-chip voltage regulator clustering algorithm developed in [3], offer an efficient and robust cross layer energy optimization mechanism for CMPs with underprovisioned on-chip voltage regulators.

6. CONCLUSIONS

A real-time workload mapping heuristic is developed to minimize the reconfiguration of the power delivery network with under-provisioned on-chip voltage regulators. The scheduled tasks are assigned optimum DVFS levels for each core. The heuristic is evaluated on homogeneous and heterogeneous CMP platforms with real time periodic tasks. The schedulability of the tasks with varying taskset utilization is compared against M-PWR, an energy efficient workload scheduler. The workload mapping heuristic in conjunction with the run-time reconfiguration of the power delivery network ensure reliable and energy efficient operation of the CMP with on-chip voltage regulators designed for only the typical or average load current demand.

7. REFERENCES

[1] M. Tavana, D. Pathak, M. Hajkazemi, I. Savidis, and H. Homayoun, "Realizing Complixity-Effective On-Chip Power Delivery for Many-Core Platforms by Exploiting Optimized Mapping," *Proceedings of the IEEE International Conference on Computer Design*, pp. 581–588, October 2015.

[2] W. Kim, M. S. Gupta, G. Wei, and D. Brooks, "System Level Analysis of Fast, Per-Core DVFS Using On-chip Switching Regulators," *Proceedings of the International Symposium on High Performance Computer Architecture*, pp. 123–134, February 2008.

[3] D. Pathak, M. Hajkazemi, M. Tavana, H. Homayoun, and I. Savidis, "Load Balanced On-Chip Power Delivery for Average Current Demand," *Proceedings of the Great Lakes Symposium on VLSI*, pp. 439–444, May 2016.

[4] D. Pathak, M. Hajkazemi, M. Tavana, H. Homayoun, and I. Savidis, "Energy Efficient On-Chip Power Delivery with Run-Time Voltage Regulator Clustering," *Proceedings of the IEEE International Symposium on Circuits and Systems*, pp. 1210–1213, May 2016.

[5] T. Li, D. Baumberger, D. A. Koufaty, and S. Hahn, "Efficient Operating System Scheduling for Performance-Asymmetric Multi-Core Architectures," *Proceedings of the ACM/IEEE conference on Supercomputing*, , No. 53, November 2007.

[6] S. Ghiasi, T. Keller, and F. Rawson, "Scheduling for Heterogeneous Processors in Server Systems," *Proceedings of the Conference on Computing Frontiers*, pp. 199–210, May 2005.

[7] G. Buttazzo, *Hard Real-Time Computing Systems: Predictable Scheduling Algorithms and Applications*, Vol. 24, Springer Science & Business Media, 2011.

[8] H. Chung, M. Kang, and H. Cho, "Heterogeneous Multi-Processing Solution of Exynos 5 Octa with ARM® big.LITTLE Technology," *Samsung White Paper*, 2012.

[9] Y. Shin, H.J. Lee, K. Shin, P. Kenkae, R. Kashyap, D. Seo, B. Millar, Y. Kwon, R. Iyengar, M. Kim, *et al.*, "28nm high-K Metal Gate Heterogeneous Quad-Core CPUs for High-Performance and Energy-Efficient Mobile Application Processor," *Proceedings of the IEEE International SoC Design Conference*, pp. 198–201, November 2013.

[10] A. Colin, A. Kandhalu, and R. Rajkumar, "Energy-Efficient Allocation of Real-Time Applications onto Heterogeneous Processors," *Proceedings of the IEEE International Conference on Embedded and Real-Time Computing Systems and Applications*, pp. 1–10, August 2014.

[11] E. Salman and E. G. Friedman, *High Performance Integrated Circuit Design*, McGraw Hill, 2012.

[12] Texas Instruments, "WEBENCH Design Center," http://webench.ti.com.

Bio-inspired Programming of Resistive Memory Devices for Implementing Spiking Neural Networks

Elisa Vianello, Thilo Werner,
Alessandro Grossi, Etienne Nowak,
Barbara De Salvo, Luca Perniola,
CEA, LETI, Minatec Campus,
Grenoble, France
+33.4.38.78.90.92
elisa.vianello@cea.fr

Oliver Bichler
CEA, LIST,
Saclay, France

Blaise Yvert
INSERM, Clinatec,
UA01, France

ABSTRACT
In this work, we will focus on the role that non-volatile resistive memory technologies (RRAM) can play for modeling key features of biological synapses. We will present an architecture and a reading/programming strategy to emulate both Short and Long Term Plasticity (STP, LTP) rules using non-volatile OxRAM arrays. A visual-pattern extraction application is discussed using spiking neural networks. We demonstrated that Long-Term plasticity allows the neural networks to learn patterns and the Short Term plasticity allows to improve accuracy (reduction of the false positive events generated by white noise in the input data) in presence of significant background noise in the input data.

Keywords
RRAM; Artificial synapses; Unsupervised learning; Long-term plasticity; Short-term plasticity; Spiking Neural Networks.

1. INTRODUCTION
Resistive memory devices (RRAM), or small RRAM-based circuits, are a promising candidate to emulate the behavior of synapses in artificial Neural Networks, and in particular to reproduce their learning abilities. The pattern detection and classification are the result of a learning phase, the synaptic connections among neurons (RRAM devices) are created, modified and preserved according to a learning model. The learning methods can be divided into two classes: (1) machine-learning algorithms (as for example backpropagation [1] and extreme learning machine [2]) that are inspired by the biological brain to some extent, but do not strictly mimic the brain, and (2) bio-inspired synaptic plasticity rules (as for example Spike Time Dependent Plasticity, STDP) [3-5].
Thanks to their high density, high speed, good endurance and integration in the Back End Of Line (BEOL), RRAM technologies have been developed to replace Flash memories for both storage class applications [6] and embedded products [7]. The fabrication of large RRAM arrays enables the construction of dense large scale synaptic connections among the CMOS-based neurons. Note that the RRAM array requires a selector element in series to the resistive switch, a transistor (1T1R), a two terminal selector (1S1R) or a complementary resistive switch configuration (1CRS). In this paper we describe the potential that 1T1R OxRAM arrays offer to emulate different bioinspired plasticity rules. Plasticity typically operates on very long time scales, ranging from milliseconds to days, weeks or longer. Biological synapses exhibit both short-term plasticity (STP) and long-term plasticity (LTP) [8, 9]. Long-term plasticity produces stable modifications of the synapses according to the timing of pre- and postsynaptic spike events, also known as spike-timing-dependent plasticity (STDP). Along with long-term plasticity, cortical synapses undergo short-term plasticity which is the dynamic modulation of the synaptic strength as a function of input stimulations and shows retrievable dynamics in short time scales (typically in the range of milliseconds) [9].
A visual-pattern extraction application based on a Fully Connected Network of Leaky-Integrate and Fire (LIF) neurons and OxRAM-based synapses organized into 1T1R arrays is adopted to demonstrate that long term plasticity is the responsible of the learning process, while short-term plasticity allows to improve signal detection in highly noisy input data.

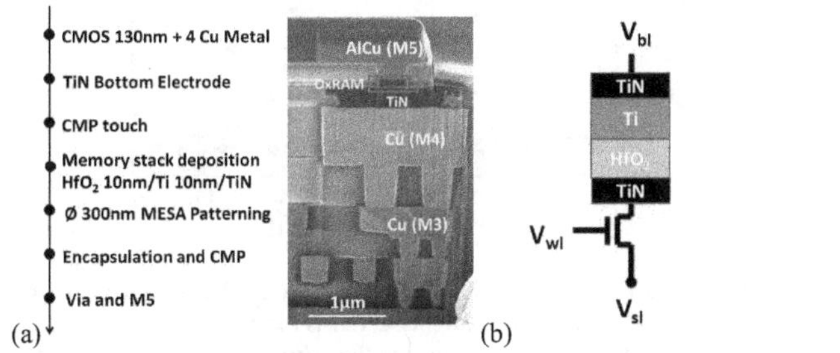

Figure 1 – (a) Description of the integration flow and SEM image of CMOS stack including the OxRAM cell between M4 and M5. (b) Schematic view of the 1T1R cell configuration.

2. ARRAY TEST VEHICLE AND KEY FEATURES OF OXRAM
A 4kb OxRAM array was fabricated using a 130nm CMOS front-end (Fig.1) [10]. The Memory Element integration starts on top of the fourth metal layer (Cu). The OxRAM active stack is composed by a 10nm-thick ALD HfO_2 resistive switching layer sandwiched between PVD TiN and PVD Ti(10nm)/TiN bottom- and top-electrodes. The array is logically organized in 64 rows (WL) and 64 columns (BL). The cell configuration is 1T1R (Fig.1 (b)).

Permission to make digital or hard copies of all or part of this work for personal or classroom use is granted without fee provided that copies are not made or distributed for profit or commercial advantage and that copies bear this notice and the full citation on the first page. Copyrights for components of this work owned by others than ACM must be honored. Abstracting with credit is permitted. To copy otherwise, or republish, to post on servers or to redistribute to lists, requires prior specific permission and/or a fee. Request permissions from Permissions@acm.org.
GLSVLSI '17, May 10-12, 2017, Banff, AB, Canada
© 2017 ACM. ISBN 978-1-4503-4972-7/17/05…$15.00
DOI: http://dx.doi.org/10.1145/3060403.3066871

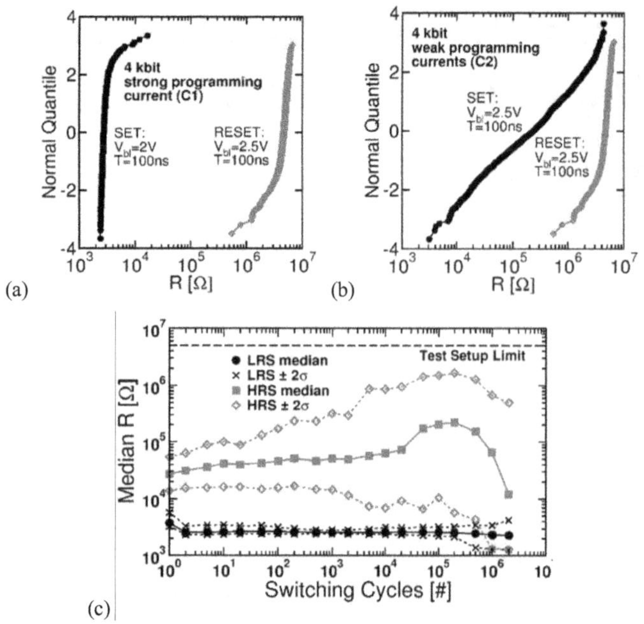

Figure 2 - (a) 4-kbit resistance distributions for strong (Iset~400μA) and (b) weak (Iset~40μA) programming currents. 5MΩ is the resistance measurement limit. (c) Endurance corresponding to the strong progrmming current (Iset~400μA) presented in (a).

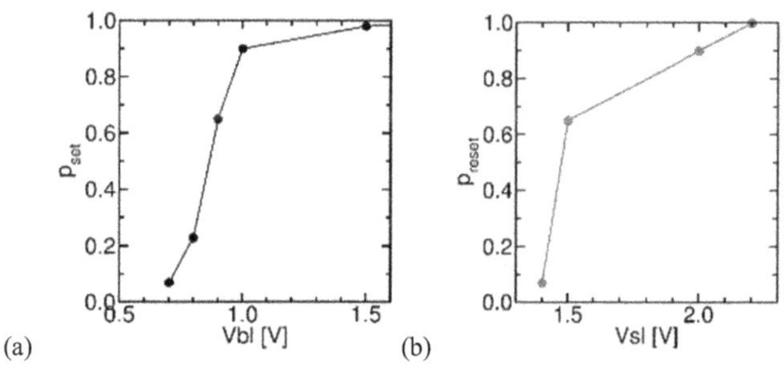

Figure 3 - Set (a) and reset (b) switching probabilities extracted from 4-kbit array (switching being considered succesful if LRS<10 kΩ and HRS>100 kΩ) using low BL and SL voltages during set and reset, respectively. Iset=400μA.

The word line (WL) is connected to the NMOS gate, setting the programming current, Iset. Forming and Set operations are performed by applying a positive voltage pulse on the bit line (BL) that is connected to the OxRAM top electrode, whereas Reset is performed by applying a voltage pulse on the source line (SL) which contact is on the transistor side (bottom electrode). OxRAM devices switch between two distinct resistance states, a Low Resistance State (LRS) and a High Resistance State (HRS), when Set and Rest conditions are applied respectively. Figs.2 (a) and (b) present the 4-kbit LRS and HRS distributions for strong (Iset~400μA) and weak (Iset~40μA) programming currents, respectively. The higher programming current strongly reduces the low resistance state variability (black curve). Fig.2 (c) demonstrates the programming stability of the low and high resistance states during endurance for the strong programming current of Fig.2 (a).

When a low bit line voltage is applied during set immediately after a reset, a probabilistic switching of the device may appear, the set operation fails (LRS>10 kΩ) in several cycles as the set-programming conditions are not strong enough to switch the device in those cycles. A similar behavior has been observed when low source line voltage is applied during reset after a set operation (HRS<100 kΩ). Figs.3 (a) and (b) show the percentage of switched

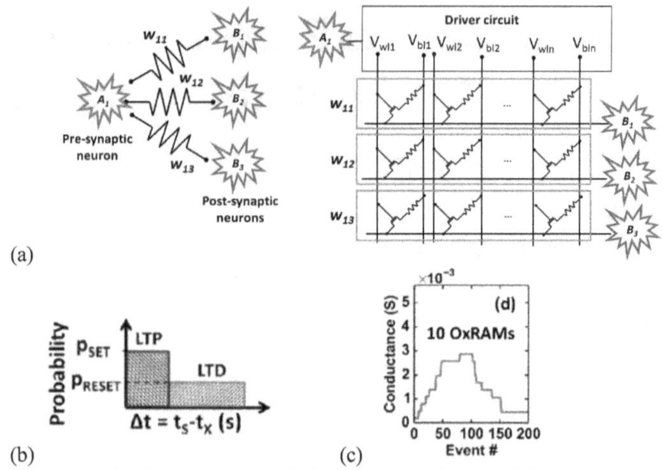

Figure 4 – (a) Schematic of an OxRAM synapse into a 1T1R array, devices on the same row build one equivalent synapse (*n*T*n*R structure). Driver circuit is used to individually program OxRAM devices and propagate spikes to next neuron layer. (b) Simplified probabilistic STDP used in our work. (c) 100 consecutive potentiation (Set) and depression (Reset) events, with p_{SET}=0.02 and p_{RESET}=0.04 on a synapse composed of 10 OxRAM devices. The use of multiple devices allows to implement a multilevel equivalent synapse.

cells as a function of the applied BL and SL voltages, respectively. Set and Reset conditions can be identified to control the probability to switch the memory state.

3. NANOELECTRONIC IMPLEMENTATION

Our implementation of neural architectures is based on a network of Leaky-Integrate and Fire (LIF) neurons and OxRAM synapses, which can learn to detect and classify complex patterns. The information is coded using a spike-based approach, *i.e.* neurons communicate with each other using trains of electrical spikes, which can be characterized as discrete events, with a well-defined time and fixed amplitude.

3.1 Long-term plasticity based on stochastic STDP

The ideal RRAM synapse presents an analog switching under identical pulses in both programming directions: the conductance gradually increases (decreases) when a train of set (reset) pulses is applied. However, in most RRAM devices, both directions of programming are non-cumulative. As shown in Fig.2, HfO_2 based OxRAM are intrinsically binary devices: they switch between two distinct states, LRS and HRS. It is possible to provide multilevel memory by carefully choosing the programming current or the reset voltage [11], while applying the same programming pulse multiple times has no further effect. The use of only two resistance levels per synapse, with respect to the multi-level approach, can be insufficient to achieve good performances in neuromorphic systems designed for some complex applications, as for example image recognition [12, 13]. To emulate synaptic conductance, a single synapse composed of *n* multiple binary OxRAM cells operating in parallel can be adopted (Fig.4 (a)) [14]. Since parallel conductances sum up, the conductance of the equivalent synapse ranges from the sum of the *n* conductance values in the HRS to the sum of all the *n* conductance values in the LRS. Note that for the OxRAM array configuration we adopted a *bit line connected matrix scheme*, the cells in the active matrix are gate connected together following the bit lines. This configuration is ideal in reading mode to perform automatically the Multiply Accumulate (MAC) operation between input data (x_i) and

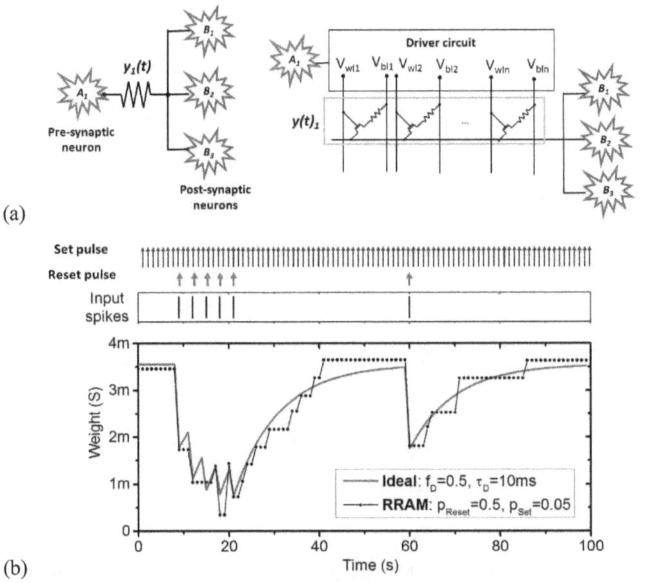

Figure 5 – (a) Schematic of the proposed STP synapse ($y_i(t)$) using n OxRAM cells. (b) Programming strategy to reproduce the STP. The synaptic weight is decreased (reset pulse) at each presynaptic spike and periodically increased (every ΔT=1ms, set pulse) in absence of spikes. The green line represents the theoretical Tsodyks and Markram biological model [9], while the black line is the experimental result obtained on a synapse composed of 10 cells in parallel with p_{Reset}=0.5 and p_{Set}=0.05.

their associated weights (w_{ij}) in a given receptive field (which can be the full input matrix for a fully connected Neural Network or a sub-matrix matching the kernel size in a convolution). When an input neuron spikes, the signal is propagated simultaneously to all the output neurons through different synapses [15].

Concerning the implementation of the learning rule, we adopted a simplified probabilistic Spike Time Dependent Plasticity (Fig.4 (b)) [3]. When a programming event occurs, each OxRAM cell of the synapse has a given probability to have a Set (synaptic potentiation) or Reset (synaptic depression) operation. The synaptic weight changes only when post synaptic spike occurs. If the presynaptic neuron was active recently, the synapse is potentiated, in any other case, it is depressed. The major benefit of this approach is that only square set and reset pulses are necessary simplifying the programming circuitry. Using multiple OxRAM devices in parallel allows to obtain multilevel conductance modulation. The number of OxRAM devices per synapse can be defined as a function of the application. Complex image recognition applications are more demanding in terms of number of devices per synapse [12, 13]. The switching probability can be governed by the OxRAM itself (internal switching probability): Set and Reset conditions can be tuned to control the probability to switch the memory as shown in Fig.3. Another possibility, that allows a finer tuning of the switching probability, at the expense of small increase of the circuit complexity, consists in using stronger programming conditions (i.e. switching probability is equal to one) and extrinsic stochasticity. Extrinsic stochasticity is obtained using an external Pseudo Random Number Generator (PRNG) circuit block, which provides tunable switching probabilities p_{Sest} and p_{Reset}. In order to validate the functionality of the proposed synapse design and learning rule, we carried out simulations of synaptic potentiation and depression operations on an OxRAM synapse composed by 10 OxRAM devices connected in parallel. Fig.4 (c) shows the evolution of the conductance when 100 potentiation events (Set) followed by 100 depression events (Reset) were applied with p_{Set}=0.02 and p_{Reset}=0.04.

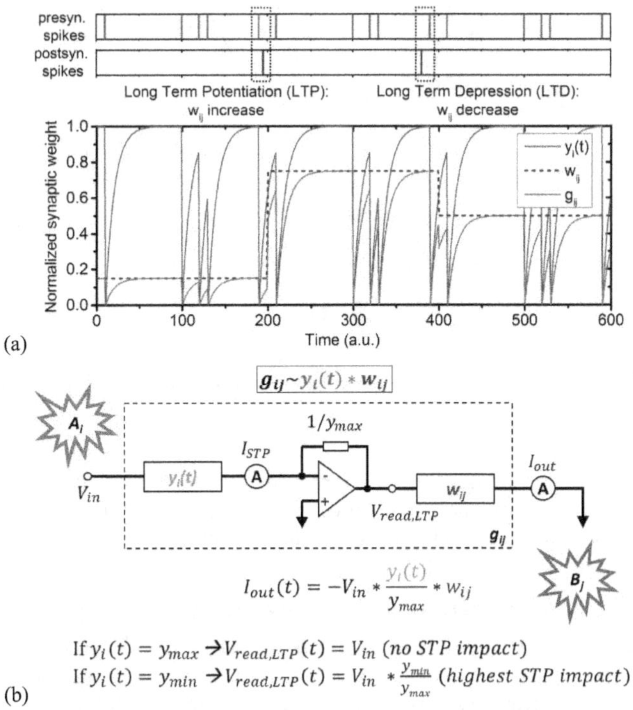

Figure 6 – (a) Example of synaptic evolution, the total synaptic weight is w_{ij}*$y_i(t)$, where w_{ij} is the strength modulated according to the LTP rule and $y_i(t)$ is a scaling factor that describes the STP rule (b) Circuit proposed to reproduce both the STP and the LTP rules. The conductance multiplication during the read operation is performed by means of a buffer which modulates the read voltage for the LTP synapse w_{ij}, as a function of the STP conductance value $y_i(t)$.

3.2 Short-term Plasticity and programming methodology

The main characteristic feature of Short-term plasticity (STP) is that the synaptic change depends only on the history of pre-synaptic spike events and it recovers quickly toward its initial state. It was found in biological synapses that the synaptic weight during a regular spike train would begin to decrease in proportion to the presynaptic spiking frequency [8, 9]. A phenomenological model for this STP effect has been developed by Tsodyks and Markram [9]. Fig.5 (a) shows the core circuit of the proposed OxRAM compound to emulate STP [16]. Ten binary devices in parallel configuration represent a STP synapse, the presynaptic spike is applied to the bit lines of all devices and the postsynaptic current enters the postsynaptic neuron from the source line. Fig.5 (b) describes the programming strategy and the corresponding conductance evolution. Each pre-synaptic event corresponds to a reset operation (conductance decrease). In order to gradually recover the initial value in absence of input spikes, a series of set operations is applied after every time slot ΔT=1ms. The *strength* of the set and reset operation is modulated by switching probability. The black symbols correspond to an example of the Short Term Depression synaptic weight evolution, measured on the OxRAM synapse structure with p_{Reset}=0.5 and p_{Set}=0.05. The green line is obtained with the Tsodyks and Markram model. Higher presynaptic spiking frequency lower synaptic weight. The degree of depression, and the recovery time, is modulated by tuning the set and reset probabilities, respectively. The switching probability can be governed by the internal OxRAM switching probability, Set

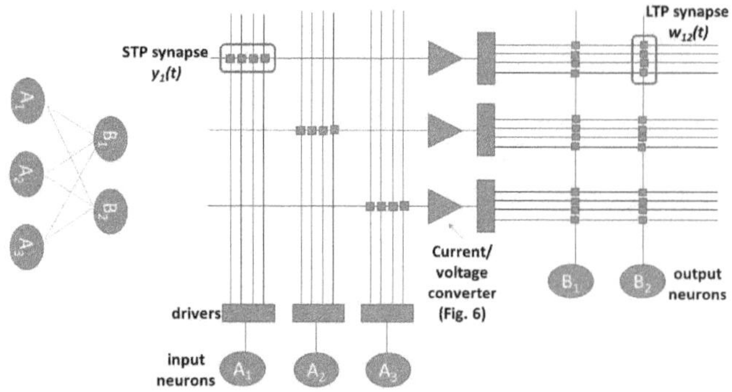

Figure 7 – Architecture for a Fully Connected Neural Network (FCNN). The input neurons (A_i) drive the output neurons (B_j) through weights $y_i(t)$ (STP) and w_{ij} (LTP).

and Reset conditions can be tuned to control the probability to switch the memory as shown in Fig.3, or using extrinsic stochasticity (external Pseudo Random Number Generator circuit block).

3.3 Architecture and reading/programming strategy to emulate both STP and LTP rules

In the previous sections, we described how to implement the short- and long-term plasticity rules into two separate OxRAM based synapses (Figs.4 and 5, respectively). However, in biology there is only one synaptic connection between two neurons, which obeys both STP and LTP. During the reading operation, the strength of the synaptic connection (or synaptic conductance) between the input neuron, A_i, and the output neuron, B_j, is $w_{ij}*y_i(t)$, where w_{ij} is the strength modulated according to the LTP rule and $y_i(t)$ is a scaling factor that describes the STP rule (Fig.6 (a)). Fig.6 (b) shows the circuit proposed to reproduce both the short-term and long-term plasticity rules, when the LTP and STP synaptic weights are stored in two separate resistive elements w_{ij} and $y_i(t)$, respectively. w_{ij} obeys the LTP rule as described in Fig.4, while $y_i(t)$ undergoes the STP rule according to the model presented Fig.5. The conductance multiplication during the reading operation is performed by means of a buffer that modulates the read voltage for w_{ij} as a function of the conductance value $y_i(t)$, the lower $y_i(t)$ the lower the read voltage. When an input neuron receives an incoming event, it generates a small voltage pulse (V_{in}) that propagates to the output neuron though $y_i(t)$, the buffer and w_{ij}. The resulting postsynaptic current (I_{out}) is proportional to $y_i(t)*w_{ij}$.

Fig.7 presents the array implementation of a Fully Connected Neural Network (FCNN) topology, the input neurons (A_i) drive the output neurons (B_j) through the STP and LTP synaptic weights ($y_i(t)$ and w_{ij}) and the buffer. Since the STP depends only on the presynaptic frequency the total number of STP synapses (and corresponding buffers) is equal to the number of input neurons, each $y_i(t)$ synapse is shared by all the output neurons. The total number of LTP synapses w_{ij} is equal to the number of input neurons times the number of output neurons.

4. SYSTEM LEVEL ANALYSIS

We performed full system-level simulations with our special purpose event-based N2D2 simulator tool [17, 18]. The neuron circuits are modeled with behavioral equations as in [18]. Both long- and short term synapses are modeled by fitting data of Fig. 2 with a log-normal distribution, to consider the experimental spread in the conductance parameters. Effect of both device-to-device and cycle-to-cycle variations are captured in the synapse model. We

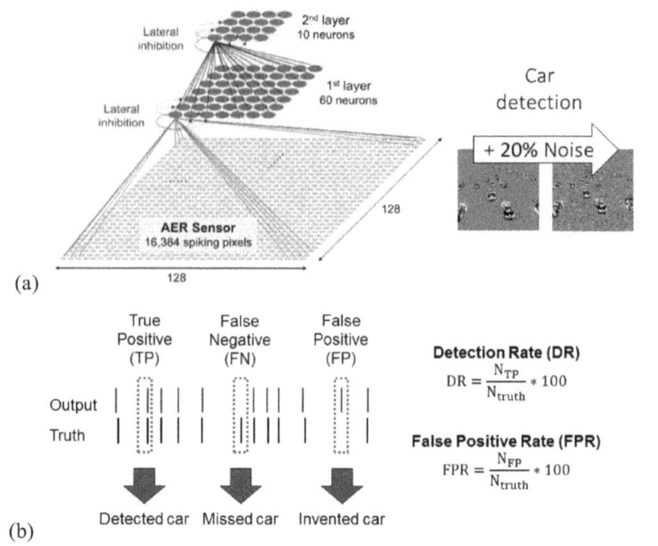

Figure 8 – Two-layer SNN used for car detection and example of unsupervised detection of cars in different traffic lanes. The reference activity (truth) is compared to the activity of the corresponding output neurons (output) to calculate the number of missed events and false positive events.

simulated a Fully Connected Neural Network to process highly noisy temporally encoded video data. A video of cars passing on a 6-lanes freeway is recorded in Address Event Representation format [19]. AER sensors take inspiration from biology, each pixel sends an event (spike) when light changes by a given relative amount (increment or decrement). The event-driven representation can have a strong reduction in terms of computational power, time and energy with respect to frame-based representation, where each frame is passed through the entire processing chain. The simulated architecture is composed of 60 neurons in the first layer and 10 neurons in the second one (Fig.8). The bottommost layer represents a 128 × 128 pixel AER vision sensor. Every input pixel requires two synapses, to send the increase and decrease illumination events. The total number of long-term synapses in this system is thus 2 × 128 × 128 × 60 + 60 × 10 = 1 966 680, while the total number of short-term synapses is 2 x 128 x 128 + 60=32 768. A similar network has been implemented in [20] and [3] exploiting multi-level Phase-Change Memory and binary Conductive Bridge RRAM synapses to capture the long-term plasticity rule only. After unsupervised learning, each output neuron becomes sensitive to one traffic lane. In Fig.8, the reference activity (truth) is compared to the output neuron activity of the corresponding traffic lane (output). False positive (FP), false negative (FN) and true positive (TP) are put in evidence. The metrics to evaluate the network performances (the detection rate, DR, and the false positive rates, FPR) are presented. The false positive estimation is fundamental for highly noisy input data, due to the increased spiking activity of the input neurons in presence of input noise. Fig. 9 reports the false positive rate and the detection rate obtained using the strong and the weak programming conditions (Fig. 2) for the LTP synapse as a function of the number of OxRAM cells per synapse, i.e. the number of resistance levels that can be achieved (see Fig. 4). The detection performances do not improve increasing the number of cells (levels) per synapse, therefore we adopt one OxRAM per LTP synapse in the following. Weak programming conditions (blue) allow to reduce the power consumption by 26% and improve the detection rate about 5%. However, the weak conditions slightly increases (less than 2%) the false positive rate.

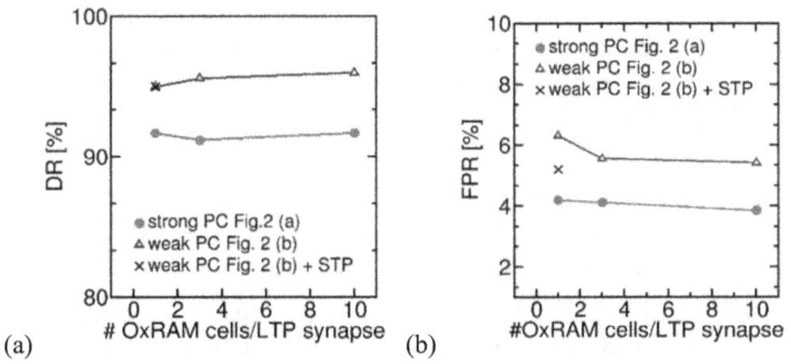

(a) (b)

Figure 9 – Detection rate (a) and false positive rate (b) as a function of the number of cells per long-term potentiation synapse. Only LTP is considered. Results have been obtained on a bench of 20 simulations (no added noise).The parameters used to implement the LTP are p_{set}=0.133, p_{reset}=0.250 and ΔT=16ms (Fg.4 (b)).

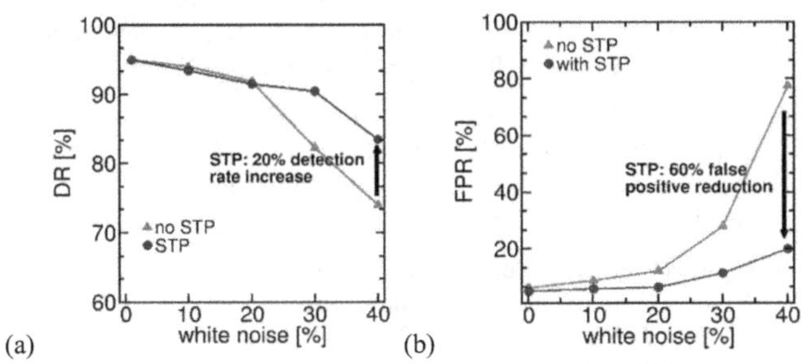

(a) (b)

Figure 10 – Detection rate and false positive rate as a function of the noise level artificially introduced in the Address Event Representation (AER) input data. The STP parameters for each noise level are reported in Table I. STP maintains the functionality of the SNN for high noise levels.

The introduction of the short-term plasticity rule (black cross) allows to reduce the false positive rate without degrading the detection rate. To better investigate this result, we artificially introduced white noise to the already noisy data recorded from the AER sensor. Simulations with added noise (up to 40% of the total amount of spikes in the sequence are random) are presented in Fig.10. The noise introduction strongly increases the false positive events, the network is not able to distinguish between real input stimuli and noise. For a noise level of 40% the system does not work, the false positive rate is about 80%. The short-term plasticity learning rule is fundamental to maintain functionality of the network for the highest noise levels. Thanks to the STP the network learns to stop responding to noise stimulus, thus allowing a 60% reduction of the false positive rate for a noise level of 40%. Therefore, STP implementation enables the network to be used in highly noisy environments (light reflections, fog, rain etc.). Tab. II reports some statistics and energy estimation obtained during a video of 680s.

5. CONCLUSIONS

In this paper, we showed how 1T1R OxRAM arrays can be used to implement bio-inspired learning rules for reliable unsupervised learning in Spiking Neural Networks. An OxRAM-based synaptic compound and a programming methodology to implement simplified short- and long-term learning rules, were presented. We demonstrated that thanks to the introduction of the short-term plasticity, the network learns to stop responding to noise stimulus. A visual-pattern extraction application based on Fully Connected Network is presented. Thanks to the short-term implementation, despite highly noisy input data (noise level of 40%), the demonstrated application exhibits very high performances (detection rate of 83% and false positive rate lower than 20%), while systems without STP would no longer deliver valid results (false positive rate ~80%).

white noise	p_{set}	p_{reset}	ΔT [ms]
0	0.1	0.1	0.3
10%	0.1	0.1	1
20%	0.5	0.1	1
30%	1	0.1	1
40%	0.5	0.1	3

Table I – STP parameters used in the simulations as a function of noise level in the input data in Fig.10.

Statistics	
Duration of video (s)	680
LTP synapses (#)	2 M
STP synapses (#)	32 k
Devices/LTP synapse (#)	1
Devices/STP synapse (#)	10
LTP programming events (#)	39 x10^6
STP programming events (#)	1.16 x10^{10}
Total Read events (#)	4.14 x10^9
Power	
Energy (J)	1.1
Power (mW)	1.7

Table II – Statistics and energy estimation.

6. ACKNOWLEDGMENTS

This work has been partially supported by the h2020 NeuRAM[3] project and by the by the European 621217 PANACHE project.

7. REFERENCES

[1] G.W. Burr, R.M. Shelby, C. di Nolfo, J. Jang, R. Shenoy, P. Narayanan, K. Virwani, E. Giacometti, B. Kurdi, H. Hwang "Experimental demonstration and tolerancing of a large–scale neural network (165,000 synapses), using phase–change memory as the synaptic weight element" *IEDM Technical Digest,* p. 29.5 (2014).

[2] M. Suri and V. Parmar "Exploiting Intrinsic Variability of Filamentary Resistive Memory for Extreme Learning Machine Architectures", *IEEE Trans. on Nanotechnology* vol. 14, no. 6 , p. 963 (2015).

[3] M. Suri, D. Querlioz, O. Bichler, G. Palma, E. Vianello, D. Vuillaume, C. Gamrat, B. De Salvo, "Bio-Inspired Stochastic Computing Using Binary CBRAM Synapses", *IEEE Trans. on Electron Device* vol. 60, issue 7 , p. 2402 (2013).

[4] V. Milo, G. Pedretti, R. Carboni, A. Calderoni, N. Ramaswamy, S. Ambrogio and D. Ielmini "Demonstration of hybrid CMOS/RRAM neural networks with spike time/rate-dependent plasticity", *IEDM Technical Digest,* p. 16.8 (2016).

[5] D. Querlioz, O. Bichler, A. F. Vincent, C. Gamrat, "Bioinspired Programming of Memory Devices for Implementing an Inference Engine", *Proceedings of the IEEE* vol.103, issue 8 (2015).

[6] S. Sills, S. Yasuda, J. Strand, A. Calderoni, K. Aratani, A. Johnson, N. Ramaswamy "A copper ReRAM cell for Storage Class Memory applications", *VLSI Technical Symp.* (2014).

[7] Z. Wei, K. Eriguchi, S. Muraoka, K. Katayama, R. Yasuhara, K. Kawai, Y. Ikeda, M. Yoshimura, Y. Hayakawa, K.

Shimakawa, T. Mikawa, S. Yoneda "Distribution projecting the reliability for 40 nm ReRAM and beyond based on stochastic differential equation", *IEDM Technical Digest,* p. 7.7 (2015).

[8] G.Q. Bi, M.M. Poo "Synaptic modifications in cultured hippocampal neurons: dependence on spike timing, synaptic strength, and postsynaptic cell type", *J Neurosci.* Vol. 18, issue 24 (1998).

[9] M. V. Tsodyks and H. Markram, "The neural code between neocortical pyramidal neurons depends on neurotransmitter release probability", *in Proc. Natl. Acad. Sci.* vol. 94 no. 2 (1997).

[10] A. Grossi, E. Nowak, C. Zambelli, C. Pellissier, S. Bernasconi, G. Cibrario, K. El Hajjam, R. Crochemore, J. F. Nodin, P. Olivo, L. Perniola, "Fundamental variability limits of filament-based RRAM", *IEDM Technical Digest,* p. 4.7 (2016).

[11] E. Vianello, O. Thomas, G. Molas, O. Turkyilmaz, N. Jovanović, D. Garbin, G. Palma, M. Alayan, C. Nguyen, J. Coignus, B. Giraud, T. Benoist, M. Reyboz, A. Toffoli, C. Charpin, F. Clermidy, L. Perniola, "Resistive Memories for Ultra-Low-Power embedded computing design", *IEDM Technical Digest,* p. 6.3 (2014).

[12] D. Garbin, E. Vianello, O. Bichler, M. Azzaz, Q. Rafhay, P. Candelier, C. Gamrat, G. Ghibaudo, B. DeSalvo, L. Perniola "On the impact of OxRAM-based synapses variability on convolutional neural networks performance", *NANOARCH* p.193 (2015).

[13] J. Bill, R. Legenstein "A compound memristive synapse model for statistical learning through STDP in spiking neural networks", *Front. Neurosci.* 8, 412 (2014)

[14] D. Garbin, E. Vianello, O. Bichler, Q. Rafhay, C. Gamrat, G. Ghibaudo, B. De Salvo and L. Perniola "HfO_2-Based OxRAM Devices as Synapses for Convolutional Neural Networks", *IEEE Trans. on Electron Device* vol. 68, issue 8 , p. 2494 (2015).

[15] D. Roclin, O. Bichler, C. Gamrat, J.-O. Klein " Sneak paths effects in CBRAM memristive devices arrays for spiking neural networks", *NANOARCH* (2014).

[16] T. Werner, E. Vianello, O. Bichler, A. Grossi, E. Nowak, J. - F. Nodin, B. Yvert, B. De Salvo, L. Perniola "Experimental demonstration of short and long term synaptic plasticity using OxRAM multi k-bit arrays for reliable detection in highly noisy input data", *IEDM Technical Digest,* p. 16.6 (2016).

[17] O. Bichler, D. Querlioz, S. Thorpe, J. Bourgoin, and C. Gamrat, "Unsupervised features extraction from asynchronous silicon retina through spike-timing-dependent plasticity", in Proc. IJCNN, pp. 859–866 (2011).

[18] O. Bichler, D. Querlioz, S.J. Thorpe, J.-P. Bourgoind and C. Gamrat, "Extraction of temporally correlated features from dynamic vision sensors with spike-timing-dependent plasticity", *Neural Networks* 32 (2012).

[19] P. Lichtsteiner, C. Posch, and T. Delbruck, "A 128 × 128 120 dB 15 μs latency asynchronous temporal contrast vision sensor", *IEEE J. SolidState Circuits*, vol. 43, no. 2, pp. 566–576, (2008)

[20] M. Suri, O. Bichler, D. Querlioz, O. Cueto, L. Perniola, V. Sousa, D. Vuillaume, C. Gamrat, B. DeSalvo "Phase change memory as synapse for ultra-dense neuromorphic systems: Application to complex visual pattern extraction", *IEDM Technical Digest,* p. 4.4 (2011).

A Maze Routing-Based Algorithm for ML-OARST with Pre-Selecting and Re-Building Steiner Points

Kuen-Wey Lin[1,a], Yeh-Sheng Lin[1,b], Yih-Lang Li[1,c] and Rung-Bin Lin[2,d]
[1]Institute of Computer Science and Engineering, National Chiao Tung University, Hsinchu 300, Taiwan
[2]Department of Computer Science and Engineering, Yuan Ze University, Taoyuan 320, Taiwan
[a]kuenweylin.cs99g@nctu.edu.tw, [b]victor181@gmail.com, [c]ylli@cs.nctu.edu.tw, [d]csrlin@cs.yzu.edu.tw

ABSTRACT

The benefits of applying maze routing algorithm over non-maze routing based methods include the feasibility of imposing various additional constraints on routing graphs. However, the much higher complexity of a multi-layer routing graph than that of a single-layer routing graph significantly increases the required runtime of conducting maze routing to solve the multi-layer obstacle-avoiding rectilinear Steiner tree (ML-OARST) problem, making applying maze routing to this problem infeasible. In this paper, we present a maze routing-based algorithm with the proposed Steiner point pre-selection to guide the construction of a ML-OARST. This can achieve a favorable balance between quality and runtime. The quality of routing is determined by total cost, that is, the summation of wire-length and via cost. To improve the flexibility of routing tree generation, we also propose a rip-up and re-building strategy for altering Steiner points and tree topology. Compared with a multi-layer multi-terminal maze routing algorithm, our algorithm can reduce the total cost by 4.8% on average and achieve 45× runtime speed-up averagely; moreover, our algorithm outperforms the state-of-the-art ML-OARST method using computational geometry techniques in terms of wire-length. With additional costs on routing graph, the proposed maze routing-based method can be further enhanced to solve VLSI routing constraints, such as layer-specific costs, scenic control, and layer directive.

Keywords

Layout; Physical Design; Routing; Steiner Tree.

1. INTRODUCTION

Multi-layer obstacle-avoiding rectilinear Steiner tree (ML-OARST) construction is crucial for a router or a placer to approximate or simply complete the routing of a net. Nevertheless, the rectilinear Steiner minimum tree (RSMT) problem has been proven to be NP-complete [4] even without consideration of obstacles and multiple layers.

There are a variety of approaches to the single-layer obstacle-avoiding RSMT (SL-OARSMT) problem [1], [3], [6], [7], [8], [11]-[14]. Lin *et al.* [9] firstly formulated the multi-layer obstacle-avoiding RSMT (ML-OARSMT) problem. Then, Liu *et al.* [10] applied computational geometry techniques, which identifies the best routing quality with minimum required runtime for the ML-OARST problem. However this approach is hard to tackle the routing problem with additional routing constraints. On the contrary maze routing algorithm is very flexible to impose additional constraints on a routing graph. However the runtime for pure maze routing algorithm can be up to several hundred times, or even worse, of that for [10] according to our experiments. To overcome these shortcomings, this work develops a maze routing-based ML-OARST algorithm. The proposed Steiner point pre-selection strategy guides the ML-OARST generation. With the proposed bounded maze routing algorithm, the time-consuming exploration is reduced. The proposed Steiner point rip-up and re-building scheme can alter the tree topology to escape from local optimality. Our method is the first attempt to solve the ML-OARST problem with pre-selecting and re-building Steiner points. Experimental results for the academic and industrial test cases show that our algorithm is competitive in wire-length and runtime.

The rest of this paper is organized as follows. Section 2 provides preliminaries and formulates the ML-OARSMT problem. Section 3 presents our ML-OARSMT approach. Section 4 presents experimental results. Section 5 draws conclusions.

Permission to make digital or hard copies of all or part of this work for personal or classroom use is granted without fee provided that copies are not made or distributed for profit or commercial advantage and that copies bear this notice and the full citation on the first page. Copyrights for components of this work owned by others than ACM must be honored. Abstracting with credit is permitted. To copy otherwise, or republish, to post on servers or to redistribute to lists, requires prior specific permission and/or a fee. Request permissions from Permissions@acm.org.

GLSVLSI '17, May 10-12, 2017, Banff, AB, Canada

© 2017 ACM. ISBN 978-1-4503-4972-7/17/05…$15.00.

DOI: http://dx.doi.org/10.1145/3060403.3060448

2. PROBLEM FORMULATION

Definition 1. An ***obstacle*** is a rectangle or a rectilinear polygon on a layer. Any two obstacles can point-touch at their corners or line-touch at the boundaries, but they cannot overlap each other.

Definition 2. A ***pin*** is a vertex on a layer. A pin can be on the boundary or at the corner of an obstacle, but it cannot be inside any obstacle.

Definition 3. A ***via*** between two adjacent layers is an edge that connects two points (vertices) with the same x and y coordinates on two adjacent layers. Any of its two endpoints must not be located inside an obstacle.

Note that an edge can point-touch at the corner or line-touch on the boundary of an obstacle; moreover, it can pass through the boundary between two line-touching obstacles or the corner of two point-touching obstacles.

Let C_v be the cost of a via, N_l be the number of layers, $P = \{p_1, p_2, \ldots, p_n\}$ be a set of pins for an n-pin net, and $O = \{o_1, o_2, \ldots, o_k\}$ be a set of k obstacles. Throughout this paper, distances/edges/paths are obstacle-avoiding and measured by the L_1 metric (rectilinear distance). For two vertices u and v, let $dist(u, v)$ be the distance of a minimum-cost path between them. The ML-OARSMT problem is formulated as follows:

Given C_v, N_l, P, and O, construct a multi-layer rectilinear Steiner tree T that connects all the pins in P possibly through some additional points, called Steiner points, using rectilinear edges on layers and vias between layers, such that no edge or via intersects an obstacle in O and the cost of T is minimized.

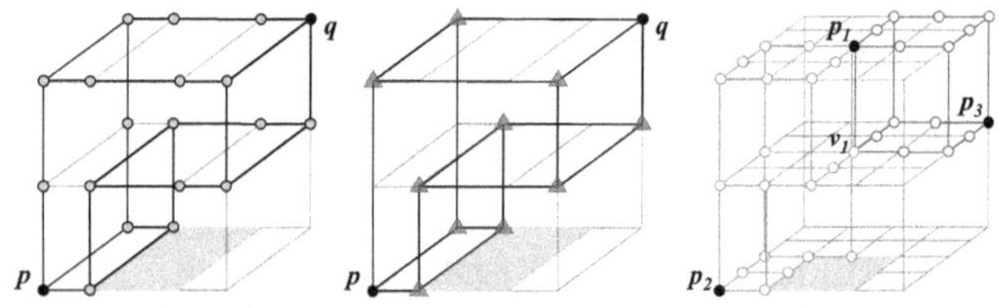

(a) (b) (c)

Figure 1. (a) BMRS. (b) Corner vertices. (c) Selecting Steiner.

A Steiner point is used to reduce the cost of connecting pins; it is a non-pin vertex of degree 3, 4, 5, or 6 in the ML-OARST problem. Let Q be a set of Steiner points. Q can be empty.

3. ALGORITHM

At first (Section 3.1), a routing graph is constructed and the fitness of each vertex is evaluated. The fitter vertices is selected to form the set Q of Steiner points. An initial ML-OARST can be constructed by connecting all the vertices in Q and P. Then, we rip-up and re-build Q to grow the final ML-OARST (Section 3.2).

3.1 Steiner Point Pre-Selection

3.1.1 *Construction of Routing Graph*

An enhanced Hanan grid graph [5], called the three-dimensional (3D) Hanan grid graph, $G(V, E)$, is developed. Note that, the cost of the edges (via edges) that connect two adjacent layers is set to C_v; however, the cost of an edge passing through an obstacle is set to a very large constant.

3.1.2 *Steiner Point Evaluation*

Based on the ideas of determining Steiner point locations from [10] and [11], a method is proposed to locate better Steiner points.

Definition 4. A ***bounded maze routing space*** (BMRS), denoted as $BMRS(p, q)$ for two vertices p and q in a 3D Hanan grid graph $G(V, E)$, is the set of vertices on the boundary of the subgraph bounded by all **minimum-cost paths** between p and q identified by maze routing in G. Note that maze routing is performed with the routing constraints given in the problem formulation.

Definition 5. A ***boundary segment*** of a BMRS is a union of maximum connected graph edges along a direction on the boundary of a BMRS. A ***boundary path*** of a BMRS is a union of connected boundary segments linking two vertices on the grid graph. A ***corner vertex*** of a BMRS is a vertex that is the common endpoint of two perpendicular boundary segments of the BMRS. Fig. 1(a) shows $BMRS(p, q)$; Fig. 1(b) shows its corner vertices.

Here, we develop a Steiner point evaluation (SPE) approach for identifying a set S of **Steiner point candidates** and assigning a score $s(v)$ to each vertex $v \in S$. Based on our observations, a vertex v is likely to be used as a Steiner point if: (1) the vertex v is a corner vertex of a BMRS; and (2) the vertex v is in more than one BMRS. For example, the vertex v_1 in Fig. 1(c), a Steiner point of the optimal ML-OARST, is a corner of both $BMRS(p_1, p_2)$ and $BMRS(p_1, p_3)$. Accordingly, the set S of Steiner point candidates consists of the vertices of the BMRS of each pair of pins.

To determine which vertex is a fitter Steiner point, based on the above two observations we develop a function as shown in equation (1) to calculate a score of each non-pin vertex $v_i \in S$.

$$s(v_i) = \alpha \times \sum_{k_a \in K} isOnCorner(v_i, k_a) + \beta \times \sum_{k_b \in K} isOnBoundary(v_i, k_b) \quad (1)$$

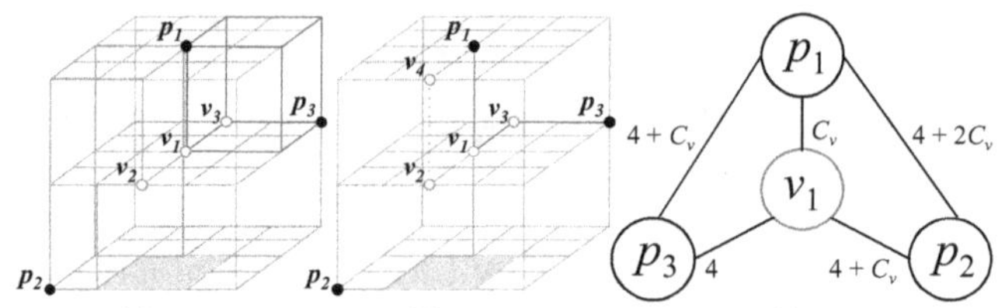

(a) (b) (c)

Figure 2. (a)(b) Steiner point evaluation. (c) Tree construction for p_1, p_2, p_3, and v_1.

where K is the set of BMRSs; P is the set of pins; k_a (k_b) denotes a BMRS in K. α and β are user-defined positive constants. Function $isOnCorner(v_i, k_a)$ returns one if v_i is a corner vertex of BMRS k_a; otherwise, it returns zero. Function $isOnBoundary(v_i, k_b)$ returns one if v_i is on the boundary of k_b; otherwise, it returns zero. Note that, the corner vertices are not considered as the vertices on the boundary of a BMRS. v_i with higher $s(v_i)$ is a fitter candidate.

The two terms in equation (1) account for the above two observations respectively. For example, in Fig. 2(a), vertices v_1, v_2, and v_3 are all on the corners of a BMRS. With respect to the first term, vertex v_1 is on the common corner of two BMRSs while vertices v_2 and v_3 are not. If vertex v_1 is selected as a Steiner point, wire sharing between p_1 and v_1 can be realized as shown in Fig. 2(b). However, if vertex v_2 is selected as a Steiner point, the path marked by dotted lines that connects p_1 and p_2 will be included into the Steiner tree as shown in Fig. 2(b) and thus the Steiner tree is not optimal. Based on the experimental observations, the ratio of α to β is 2:1 in order to favor a corner vertex. Then, two techniques are proposed to mitigate the runtime overhead of maze routing.

3.1.2.1 *Feasible BMRS identification*

The size of the BMRS set K determines the runtime. For a design with n pins, the size of K is $O(n^2)$ which is equal to the total number of pairs of pins. To reduce the size of the set K from $O(n^2)$ to $O(n)$, feasible BMRS is introduced in the following.

Definition 6. For a vertex u being the center, a 3D Hanan grid graph can be divided into eight quadrants. In each quadrant, a vertex v which is nearest to u (in other words, no other vertex w in that quadrant makes $dist(u, w) < dist(u, v)$) is regarded as the ***satellite vertex*** of u. Let $N(u)$ be the set of satellite vertices of u.

Definition 7. For two pins p_x and p_y, $BMRS(p_x, p_y)$ is regarded as a ***feasible BMRS*** (FB) if p_x is a satellite pin (a pin is a vertex on a 3D Hanan grid graph) of p_y.

We propose a feasible BMRS identification (FBI) algorithm which needs only be performed once per pin. Given a pin p, FBI finds the FB that is defined by p and each pin in $N(p)$ and scores the vertices of the found FBs using equation (1). FBI conducts maze routing starting from pin p and expands the wave-front until all the pins of $N(p)$ are reached. Then, FBI obtains a set of minimum-cost paths that enclose p and $N(p)$ in the back-tracing phase. These minimum-cost paths are the boundary paths mentioned earlier (See Definition 5). The vertices on these chosen paths form the BMRS of a pin pair. For each pin, at most eight FBs are processed, thus the number of FBs is $O(n)$. Finding out FBs is in order for obtaining the set S of Steiner point candidates.

3.1.2.2 *Path database for BMRS*

For the two-pin pairs whose BMRSs have been explored by FBI, their optimal costs and optimal paths (boundary paths) are reserved in a path database. That is, all maze routing requests after Section 3.1.2 are replaced by the queries to path database.

3.1.3 Steiner Point Selection

The size of Q will be at most n-2 because an n-pin Steiner tree contains no more than n-2 Steiner points and a Steiner point can be on a pin in some cases. The vertices of S are sorted in order of descending score. Then, these vertices are added to Q in order until the size of Q is n-2 or all the vertices in S are inspected.

3.1.4 Construction of Tree

We construct a routing graph with a vertex set that unites P and Q (Fig. 2(c)), and then employ Prim's algorithm [2] to find a minimum spanning tree (MST). Given a pair of pins, if its BMRS is feasible, we create an edge between them. If a Steiner point is located on a minimum-cost path connecting two pins, two edges are created respectively to connect the Steiner point to the two pins. The costs of these edges can be queried from the path database. Note that there is no edge between p_2 and p_3 because $BMRS(p_2, p_3)$ is redundant.

3.2 Steiner Point-Based Rip-Up and Re-Building

3.2.1 Re-Building Steiner Points

In the section, we rebuild the set S of Steiner point candidates and creates a new set Q of Steiner points.

Definition 8. Let p and q be the two terminals of an edge of an initial tree T; p and q can be a pin or a Steiner point. The BMRS of p and q is called the ***essential BMRS*** (EB).

Each EB can be constructed using the path database because all the selected Steiner points are on the BMRSs identified by FBI. After all EBs have been established, the set S is re-built; that is, the new set S consists of the vertices of all EBs. Then, each vertex of S is re-evaluated using equation (2).

$$s'(v_i) = \sum_{k_j \in K'} isOnEB(v_i, k_j) \quad (2)$$

where v_i is a vertex in S; $s'(v_i)$ is the new score of v_i; K' denotes the set of EBs; k_j is an EB of K', and $isOnEB(v_i, k_j)$ will return one if v_i is on the boundary or the corner of k_j, and zero otherwise. After re-evaluation, v_i will be added to Q if $s'(v_i)$ exceeds one.

Fig. 3(a)-(c) show an example of using the proposed re-building strategy to identify a fitter Steiner point that was not selected before. The initial tree, T, constructed in the preceding step, contains six pins p_1~p_6 and two Steiner points s_1 and s_2 as shown in Fig. 3(a); this tree can be further optimized. First, all EBs of T are identified, as shown in Fig. 3(b). s_3 and s_4 are then added to Q because $s'(s_3)$ and $s'(s_4)$ exceed one. Finally, the improved ML-OARST T' with shorter wire-length can be generated after mapping a new MST into the 3D Hanan grid graph, as shown in Fig. 3(c). Notably, in the proposed Steiner point evaluation (Section 3.1.2), vertex s_1 is selected as a Steiner point to favor growing a good Steiner subtree for the cluster of pins p_1, p_2, and p_5. However, the cluster of p_3 and p_4 demands a Steiner point for growing a high-quality Steiner tree. Hence, Steiner point s_4 is included into Q.

3.2.2 Pruning Redundant Steiner Points

A vertex in Q whose degree is not greater than two should be removed. Notably, the pruning strategy may worsen the quality of a Steiner tree. As shown in Fig. 3(d), vertex s_3 is a redundant Steiner point and can be removed from Q; however, removal of Steiner points may yield a worse Steiner tree as shown in Fig. 3(e) (where redundant Steiner points s_3, s_4, s_5, and s_6 have been removed).

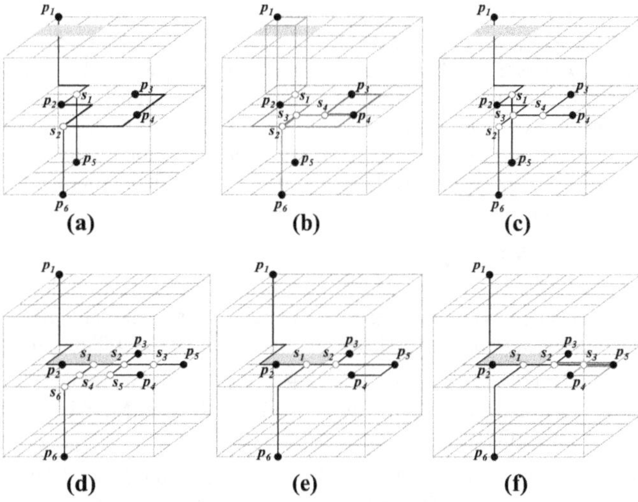

Figure 3. (a)-(c) Example of re-building Steiner points. (d)-(f) Example of escaping from a local optimum.

Re-building Steiner points can yield a better Steiner tree with the introduction of Steiner point s_3 (Fig. 3(f)) because s_3 is on the boundaries of both $EB(p_4, p_5)$ and $EB(s_2, p_5)$.

3.2.3 Adding Turning Points as Steiner Points

For a Steiner tree, we identify its turning points and add these turning points into Q. Note that, we re-grow a new MST after invoking each strategy of this section (that is, Section 3.2.1-3.2.3). The three strategies are repeatedly invoked one by one until the total cost of the ML-OARST cannot be reduced any further.

4. EXPERIMENTAL RESULTS

The proposed algorithm was implemented in C/C++ language. We requested binaries from Liu *et al.* [10]. All experiments were conducted on a 3.4GHz Intel machine with 16GB of memory and the CentOS 7 operating system. There are totally ten benchmark circuits, five industrial ones (ind1-ind5) from Synopsys and five random ones (rt1-rt5) from [10]. Table 1 gives the characteristics of the benchmark circuits and the corresponding 3D Hanan grid graphs.

Table 2 gives the total cost, number of vias (#Via), and runtime for the cases of $C_v = 3$ and $C_v = 5$. Compared with [10], clearly, our maze routing-based algorithm spends more runtime than Liu *et al.* [10] in large test cases and similar runtime in small test cases. The FBI conducting maze routing consumes the majority of the total runtime, and the Steiner point rip-up and re-building step converges in at most five rounds and uses 28.19% of the runtime on average. Our algorithm spends more runtime for rt4 than that for the largest case rt5 because the runtime of our maze routing-based algorithm is determined by the pin territory.

To compare the efficiency of the proposed algorithm with traditional maze routing algorithm, we crafted a multi-layer multi-terminal maze router. A 3D Hanan grid graph is also used. Initially each pin is considered as a sub-tree. In each iteration, all grids on the smallest sub-tree are regarded as sources while no specific sub-tree is set as the target, i.e., the wave propagation stops as any sub-tree is reached. The procedure continues until all sub-trees are connected together. The routing results are listed in the third column for each case of C_v. The proposed algorithm improves the total cost by 4.87% and 4.74% on average for $C_v = 3$ and $C_v = 5$ respectively and achieves about 50× and 40× runtime speed-up on average for $C_v = 3$ and $C_v = 5$ respectively.

5. Conclusions

In this work we develop a maze routing-based algorithm for the ML-OARSMT problem with Steiner point pre-selection and Steiner point-based rip-up and re-building. Experimental results show that our approach can generate a high-quality result. We plan to impose more routing constraints on the routing graph such that it can tackle practical routing problems such as timing, the scenic control or layer directives constraints.

6. REFERENCES

[1] G. Ajwani, C. Chu, and W.-K. Mak, "FOARS: FLUTE based obstacle-avoiding rectilinear Steiner tree construction," *IEEE Transactions on CAD*, vol. 30, no. 2, pp. 194-204, Feb. 2011.

[2] T.H. Cormen, C.E. Leiserson, R.L. Rivest, and C. Stein, *Introduction to Algorithms*, 3rd ed. Cambridge, MA: MIT Press, 2009.

[3] Z. Feng, Y. Hu, T. Jing, X. Hong, X. Hu, and G. Yan, "An O(*n*log*n*) algorithm for obstacle-avoiding routing tree construction in the lambda-geometry plane," in *Proc. ISPD*, 2006, pp. 48-55.

[4] M.R. Garey and D.S. Johnson, "The rectilinear Steiner tree problem is NP-Complete," *SIAM Journal on Applied Mathematics*, vol. 32, no. 4, pp. 826-834, Jun. 1977.

[5] M. Hanan, "On Steiner's problem with rectilinear distance," *SIAM Journal on Applied Mathematics*, vol. 14, no. 2, pp. 255-265, Mar. 1966.

[6] T. Huang and E.F.Y. Young, "ObSteiner: An exact algorithm for the construction of rectilinear Steiner minimum trees in the presence of complex rectilinear obstacles," *IEEE Transactions on CAD*, vol. 32, no. 6, pp. 882-893, Jun. 2013.

[7] L. Li and E.F.Y. Young, "Obstacle-avoiding rectilinear Steiner tree construction," in *Proc. ICCAD*, 2008, pp. 523-528.

[8] C.-W. Lin, S.-Y. Chen, C.-F. Li, Y.-W. Chang, and C.-L. Yang, "Obstacle-avoiding rectilinear Steiner tree construction based on spanning graphs," *IEEE Transactions on CAD*, vol. 27, no. 4, pp. 643-653, Apr. 2008.

[9] C.-W. Lin, S.-L. Huang, K.-C. Hsu, M.-X. Lee, and Y.-W. Chang, "Multilayer obstacle-avoiding rectilinear Steiner tree construction based on spanning graphs," *IEEE Transactions on CAD*, vol. 27, no. 11, pp. 2007-2016, Nov. 2008.

[10] C.-H. Liu, C.-X. Lin, I-C. Chen, D.T. Lee, and T.-C. Wang, "Efficient Multilayer Obstacle-Avoiding Rectilinear Steiner Tree Construction Based on Geometric Reduction," *IEEE Transactions on CAD*, vol. 33, no. 12, pp. 1928-1941, Dec. 2014.

[11] C.-H. Liu, S.-Y. Kuo, D.T. Lee, C.-S. Lin, J.-H. Weng, and S.-Y. Yuan, "Obstacle-Avoiding Rectilinear Steiner Tree Construction: A Steiner-Point-Based Algorithm," *IEEE Transactions on CAD*, vol. 31, no. 7, pp. 1050-1060, Jul. 2012.

[12] J. Long, H. Zhou, and S.O. Memik, "EBOARST: An efficient edge-based obstacle-avoiding rectilinear Steiner tree construction algorithm," *IEEE Transactions on CAD*, vol. 27, no. 12, pp. 2169-2182, Dec. 2008.

[13] Y. Yang, Q. Zhu, T. Jing, X. Hong, and Y. Wang, "Rectilinear Steiner minimal tree among obstacles," in *Proc. ICASIC*, 2003, pp. 348-351.

[14] S.-Q. Zheng, J.S. Lim, and S.S. Iyengar, "Finding obstacle-avoiding shortest paths using implicit connection graphs," *IEEE Transactions on CAD*, vol. 15, no. 1, pp. 103-110, Jan. 1996.

Table 1. Characteristics of the ten benchmark circuits and their corresponding 3D Hanan grid graphs.

Test Cases	Pins	Obstacles	Layers	X	Y	Z	Number of Grids	Pin Territory
rt1	25	10	10	45	44	10	19,800	792
rt2	100	20	10	136	131	10	178,160	1,782
rt3	250	50	10	294	285	10	837,900	3,352
rt4	500	50	10	458	449	10	2,056,420	4,113
rt5	1,000	100	5	702	707	5	1,985,256	1,986
ind1	50	6	5	33	28	4	3,696	74
ind2	200	85	6	83	191	5	79,265	397
ind3	250	13	10	221	223	9	443,547	1,775
ind4	500	100	5	206	499	3	308,382	617
ind5	1,000	20	5	1,008	1,022	3	3,090,528	3,091

† #Number of Grids = X*Y*Z.

Table 2. Comparisons of total cost (wire-length and via cost) and runtime (second).

Test Case	$C_v = 5$									$C_v = 3$								
	[10]			Ours			Maze routing			[10]			Ours			Maze routing		
	Total Cost	#Via	Runtime	Total Cost	#Via	Runtime	Total Cost	#Via	Runtime	Total Cost	#Via	Runtime	Total Cost	#Via	Runtime	Total Cost	#Via	Runtime
rt1	4,300	68	0.01	4,294	69	0.01	4,484	51	0.07	4,169	70	0.01	4,180	66	0.01	4,382	52	0.07
rt2	9,601	209	0.06	9,689	215	0.31	10,108	215	3.26	9,132	209	0.06	9,220	220	0.31	9,669	226	3.28
rt3	15,663	487	0.29	15,912	432	1.94	16,486	503	28.21	14,750	478	0.27	14,912	488	1.97	15,462	530	39.019
rt4	22,965	934	0.44	23,153	873	5.99	24,095	1,010	224.74	21,013	936	0.41	21,207	961	6.25	22,029	1,049	252.413
rt5	28,707	818	0.7	28,811	797	4.51	29,954	965	174.17	26,970	814	0.56	27,201	872	4.5	27,980	1,006	311.425
ind1	53,480	44	0.02	54,750	50	0.02	60,120	44	0.02	54,207	49	0.02	54,313	51	0.02	60,032	44	0.02
ind2	12,397	202	0.06	12,740	208	0.19	13,614	197	1.38	12,008	206	0.06	12,229	219	0.2	13,231	207	1.06
ind3	11,253	349	0.06	11,291	343	1.09	11,825	375	17.92	10,555	348	0.06	10,600	373	1.13	11,071	386	16.74
ind4	76,299	0	0.04	76,511	0	0.21	78,902	0	2.21	77,292	0	0.03	76,511	0	0.21	78,902	0	2.23
ind5	14,525,429	0	0.07	14,501,530	0	1.96	15,257,145	0	247.49	14,599,961	0	0.07	14,501,530	0	1.97	15,257,145	0	248.27
Norm	1		1	0.999		9.274	1.051		399.696	1		1	0.993		10.690	1.045		564.211

An Integrated Optimization Framework for Partitioning, Scheduling and Floorplanning on Partially Dynamically Reconfigurable FPGAs

Xiaodong Xu[1], Qi Xu, Jinglei Huang, Song Chen[2]
University of Science and Technology of China
[1]xxd0210@mail.ustc.edu.cn, [2]songch@uste.edu.cn

ABSTRACT

This paper proposes an integrated optimization framework for task partitioning, scheduling, and floorplanning on partially dynamically reconfigurable FPGAs. In the framework, three problems are represented by a partitioned sequence triple (PS, MS, RS), where (PS, MS) is a hybrid nested sequence pair for floorplanning and RS is a reconfiguration sequence for scheduling. The floorplan and schedule of tasks can be computed from the sequence triple in $O(n^2)$ time. To integrate the exploration of the scheduling and floorplanning design space, a fast perturbation method is elaborated with a simulated annealing-based search engine, where a randomly chosen task is removed from the sequence triple and then inserted back into a proper position selected from all the n^3 possible combinations of partitions, schedule and floorplan. The experimental results demonstrate the efficiency and effectiveness of the proposed framework.

Keywords

Partitioning, Scheduling, Floorplanning, Partially Dynamically Reconfigurable FPGAs

1. INTRODUCTION

FPGAs can change their functionality during operation, which is called dynamical reconfiguration (DR). However, significant reconfiguration overhead would be incurred when transferring the configuration information [1] and tasks are forced into running serially because of the alternate configuration and execution. To hide configuration latency and increase task parallelism, partial dynamic reconfiguration (PDR) are proposed, which can reconfigure the part of a FPGA while retaining normal operation of the rest [2].

When synthesizing a design composed of some tasks with PDR, the schedule and floorplan of tasks on FPGA must be determined, which is a multi-objective optimization problem. Some studies have focused on the task scheduling algorithms for FPGAs. Y. Jiang et al. [3] proposed a network flow-based partitioning algorithm, which partitioning is simplified without considering the partial reconfiguration. R. Cordone et al. [4] proposed an ILP formulation and a greedy heuristic in scheduling phase. However, the former has low efficiency and the latter is a local optimization. A. Purgato et al. [5] proposed a fast task scheduling heuristic algorithm. This work focuses on generating reconfigurable regions to satisfy the resource requirements, which will easily cause the final result failed to be floorplanned. Many works only focused on the floorplanning and the resource reuse, which the tasks have been scheduled or partitioned. L. Singhal et al. [6] improved a multi-layer sequence pair (MLSP) for temporal floorplanning. Given a scheduled task graph, A. Montone et al. [7] proposed a three-step floorplanning approach based on simulated annealing. And P. Barnerjee et al. [8] exploited a partition-slicing tree to generate a global floorplan for the resource reuse.

The PDR-oriented design, generally, involves partitioning, scheduling, and floorplanning of the tasks, which are interdependent considering the communication costs and the performance. Therefore, three problems have to be solved in an integrated framework to effectively explore the design space. However, the aforementioned works either solve three problems sequentially, where a simple iterative refinement between the scheduling and the floorplanning is included, or solve only two of the three problems.

In this paper, our contributions are as follows:

1) A sequence triple (PS, MS, RS) is proposed to represent the partitioning, scheduling, and floorplaning, where PS, MS and RS are the sequences for tasks. (PS, MS) is regarded as a hybrid nested sequence pair (HNSP) for representing the floorplan with spatial and temporal partition, and RS is the partitioned configuration ordering. The schedule of tasks can be solved in $O(n^2)$ time with reconfiguration constraints graph (RCG) constructed from RS and task dependence graph.

2) To integrate the exploration of the design space, an elaborated perturbation method is used in a SA-based search engine, which are efficiently evaluated in $O(n^3)$ time based on a position enumeration procedure.

The remainder of the paper is organized as follows. Section 2 describes the target hardware architecture and the problem definition. Section 3 discusses the representation of sequence triple. Section 4 shows the perturbation method. The experimental results and conclusions are shown in Section 5 and Section 6, respectively.

2. PROBLEM DESCRIPTION

The PDR is subject to the technology limitation of reconfigurable architectures. In reconfigurable system, tasks are stored in the external memory in the form of bitstreams. According to the scheduling sequence and floorplanning lo-

Permission to make digital or hard copies of all or part of this work for personal or classroom use is granted without fee provided that copies are not made or distributed for profit or commercial advantage and that copies bear this notice and the full citation on the first page. Copyrights for components of this work owned by others than ACM must be honored. Abstracting with credit is permitted. To copy otherwise, or republish, to post on servers or to redistribute to lists, requires prior specific permission and/or a fee. Request permissions from permissions@acm.org.

GLSVLSI '17, May 10-12, 2017, Banff, AB, Canada
© 2017 ACM. ISBN 978-1-4503-4972-7/17/05...$15.00
DOI: http://dx.doi.org/10.1145/3060403.3060447

cations, the host processor deploys tasks on the chip. However, the configuration process of a task must not disrupt the execution of other tasks [7]. Thus, dynamical reconfigurable regions (DRRs), where the tasks are dynamically reconfigured in a manner similar to that of a context (time layer) switching mode, are generally used for implementing partial reconfiguration. Moreover, the DRR should be a rectangle region because irregular shapes (such as T or L shape) could introduce routing restriction issues [9]. And a task can be implemented as a rectangular module located in some rows and columns on the FPGA.

The design is composed of some pre-synthesized tasks whose resource usage and internal routing have determined. Let $M = \{m_i | 1 \le i \le n\}$ be a set of n tasks. A task m_i, has a physical attribute vector, (r_i, c_i, ct_i, et_i), where variables r_i, c_i, ct_i, and et_i denote the required rows and columns of CLBs, configuration span, and execution span, respectively.

The data dependencies between these tasks are given as a task dependence graph, $TG = (V_{TG}, E_{TG})$, where $V_{TG} = \{v_i | 1 \le i \le n\}$, vertex v_i denotes the task m_i and $E_{TG} = \{(v_i, v_j) | 1 \le i, j \le n, i \ne j,\ m_i$ must terminate before m_j starts$\}$. The weight of v_i is the execution time et_i of m_i.

The partitioning, scheduling and floorplanning problem of PDR are formulated as follows:

(1). In the spatial domain, the n tasks are partitioned into DRRs. Let N be the number of DRRs.

Definition 1. *The DRRs are denoted as* $RR = \{rr_i | 1 \le i \le N, rr_i \subseteq M, \bigcup_{i=1}^{N} rr_i = M\}$, *where* $\forall i \ne j$, $rr_i \cap rr_j = \emptyset$. *We also denote the DRR of* m_k *as* $rr(m_k)$.

(2). In the temporal domain, the n tasks are partitioned into time layers. A time layer is configured as a whole. And in the same DRR, a new time layer can only reuse the resources after the executing completion of all tasks in the old time layer. Let t_i be the number of time layers in rr_i.

Definition 2. *The time layers are denoted as* $TL = \{tl_j^i | \forall 1 \le i \le N, 1 \le j \le t_i, tl_j^i \subseteq rr_i, \bigcup_{j=1}^{t_i} tl_j^i = rr_i\}$, *where* $\forall j_1 \ne j_2$, $tl_{j1}^i \cap tl_{j2}^i = \emptyset$. *We also denote the time layer of* m_k *as* $tl(m_k)$. *The total number of time layers is denoted as* T.

For convenience, $C[tl_j^i]$ is defined as the configuration order of time layer tl_j^i, $1 \le C[tl_j^i] \le T$ and stipulate that $C[tl_j^i] < C[tl_{j+1}^i]$, $1 \le j < t_i$.

The following constraints are considered during the partitioning, scheduling and floorplanning:

(1). A task can be executed if and only if it was configured and the data dependencies were satisfied simultaneously.

(2). All partitioned time layers are configured sequentially and each time layer can start to execute after configured.

(3). There are no spaces overlapping between DRRs and between tasks which is partitioned into the same time layer.

Thus, the partitioning problem is to determine RR and TL, the scheduling problem is to determine the start configuration time and start execution time of the tasks (time layers), and the flooprlanning problem is to determine the floorplan of DRRs and the floorplan of tasks inside the DRRs.

3. SEQUENCE TRIPLE

3.1 Representation

In this paper, a sequence triple (ST) is proposed specially to represent the partitioning, scheduling, and floorplanning of tasks for the partially dynamically reconfigurable designs.

Definition 3. *The sequence triple is a 3-tuple of task sequences, (PS, MS, RS). (PS, MS), which can be regarded as an HNSP, represents the spatial and temporal partition and the floorplan of the tasks. RS defines partitioned configuration order of the time layers.*

The partitioning of tasks is implied in the ST as follows: all the tasks in a DRR occur in the sequence of PS and MS, consecutively; all the tasks in a time layer occur in all the three sequences, i.e., PS, MS, and RS, consecutively.

In HNSP, the topological position relation among tasks is defined as follows:

Definition 4. *if* $tl(m_i) = tl(m_j)$ *or* $rr(m_i) \ne rr(m_j)$, $(<\ldots m_i \ldots m_j \ldots>, <\ldots m_i \ldots m_j \ldots>) \rightarrow$ *m_i is left to m_j;* $(<\ldots m_j \ldots m_i \ldots>, <\ldots m_i \ldots m_j \ldots>) \rightarrow$ *m_i is below m_j.*

All tasks in a time layer are configured as a whole, and the configuration order in RS is defined as follows:

Definition 5. *Given an RS sequence,* $(<\ldots m_i \ldots m_j \ldots>)$, *the configuration constraints are defined as follows:*
1) if $tl(m_i) = tl(m_j)$, *m_i and m_j are configured along with the same time layer;*
2) if $tl(m_i) \ne tl(m_j)$, $tl(m_i)$ *is configured before* $tl(m_j)$, *and the relation of configuration order is* $C[tl(m_i)] < C[tl(m_j)]$.

Notice that the relationship between the tasks from different time layers in the same DRR is undefined because of the overlap in the spatial domain. Without loss of generality, the tasks in the same time layer is required to occur consecutively, in PS and MS, for clarity in representing different time layers. And the configuration order of tasks in the same time layer also makes no sense in RS.

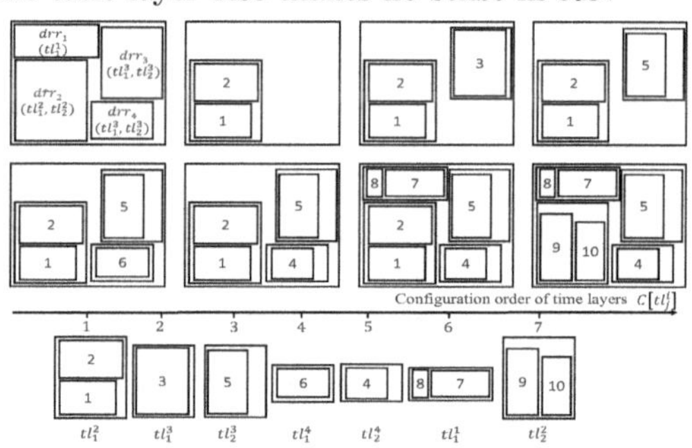

Figure 1: Floorplan of DRRs as well as tasks in time layers and configuration ordering of time layers

In ST, $(\cdot)_j^i$ denotes the sequence of tasks in the time layer tl_j^i and $[\cdot]_i$ is the sequence of tasks in the DRR rr_i. For example, a sequence triple is given as follows:

$< [(1\ 2)_1^2\ (9\ 10)_2^2]_2\ [(8\ 7)_1^1]_1\ [(6)_1^4\ (4)_2^4]_4\ [(3)_1^3\ (5)_2^3]_3 >$,
$< [(8\ 7)_1^1]_1\ [(2\ 1)_1^2\ (9\ 10)_2^2]_2\ [(3)_1^3\ (5)_2^3]_3\ [(6)_1^4\ (4)_2^4]_4 >$,
$< (1\ 2)_1^2\ (3)_1^3\ (5)_2^3\ (6)_1^4\ (4)_2^4\ (7\ 8)_1^1\ (9\ 10)_2^2 >$.

The floorplan of DRRs as well as tasks in time layers and configuration ordering of time layers are shown in Fig. 1. Considering Def. 4, task 2 is below task 1 because they are in the same time layer ($tl(m_1) = tl(m_2) = tl_1^2$), and task 2 is below task 7 because they are in different DRR ($rr(m_7) = rr_1$ and $rr(m_2) = rr_2$). According to Def. 5, the first configuring time layer is tl_1^2 and then the next time layer tl_1^3 can be configured during the execution of task m_1 and m_2.

3.2 Calculating Floorplan and Schedule

With the dimension of tasks, the floorplan can be computed from the HNSP in $O(n^2)$ time by solving the longest weighted common subsequence in PS and MS, denoted as $lcs(PS, MS)$, hierarchically. That is, firstly compute the floorplan of tasks within every DRR to obtain the occupied resource arrays of DRRs, and then compute the floorplan of DRRs to determine the total resource usage.

Combining the partitioning, configuration ordering C in RS and the original task dependence graph (TG), RCG is constructed to model the reconfiguration process. And the schedule time of a task m_c, including configuration and execution, can be computed in $O(n^2)$ time by solving a vertex-weighted single source longest path problem in RCG. The longest path to a vertex v in RCG is denoted as $lpt(v)$.

A RCG (V_{RCG}, E_{RCG}) is a direct acyclic graph (DAG) by adding a new vertex set V_{LTG} and three new edge sets E_{cr}, E_{ce}, and E_{ec} to the task dependence graph TG. That is, $V_{RCG} = V_{TG} \cup V_{LTG}$ and $E_{RCG} = E_{TG} \cup E_{cr} \cup E_{ce} \cup E_{ec}$. $V_{LTG} = \{v_j^i | 1 \le i \le N, 1 \le j \le t_i\}$. v_j^i denotes the time layer tl_j^i. The weight of v_j^i is the total configuration time of tl_j^i.

$E_{cr} = \{(v_{j1}^{i1}, v_{j2}^{i2}) | C[tl_{j2}^{i2}] = C[tl_{j1}^{i1}]+1\}$. E_{cr} represents the configuration constraints of time layers.

$E_{ce} = \{(v_j^i, v_k) | v_j^i \in V_{LTG}, v_k \in V_{TG}$, and $tl(m_k) = tl_j^i\}$. E_{ce} represents m_k can be executed only after the configuration of time layer $tl(m_k)$ is finished.

$E_{ec} = \{(v_k, v_j^i) | v_j^i \in V_{LTG}, v_k \in V_{TG}, tl(m_k) = tl_{j-1}^i, 1 < j \le t_i\}$. E_{ec} represents the time layer tl_j^i can be configured after the execution of task m_k as the previous time layer tl_{j-1}^i is end. We also denote any vertex in V_{TG} pointing to v_j^i as v_{ij}.

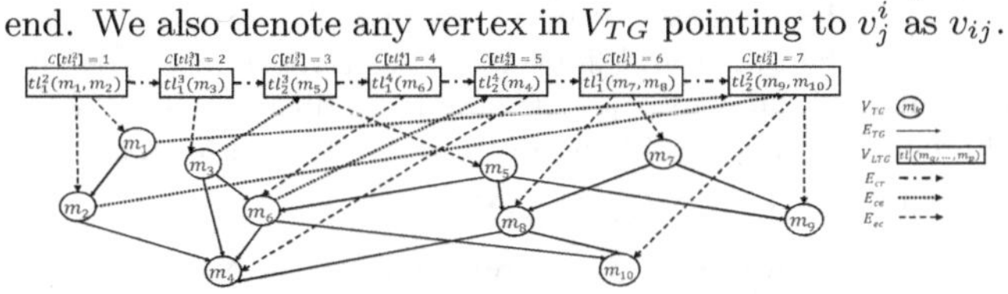

Figure 2: An example of RCG

To compute the schedule of tasks, there must be no inductive cycles in RCG. That is, not all partitions and configuration orderings in RS can be a feasible schedule. The simplest configuration order is the topological sorting of TG. The RCG of the example ST is shown in Fig. 2.

4. PERTURBATION

To integrate the exploration of the design space, a perturbation is elaborated , which is used in a simulated annealing based search engine. The basic idea is to remove a randomly chosen task from the ST, and then the task is inserted back into the three sequences at a proper position selected from all the n^3 possible combinations of partitions, schedule and floorplan, which are efficiently evaluated in $O(n^3)$ time based on a position enumeration procedure.

4.1 Enumerating Positions in Sequence Triple

At the beginning of enumeration, each task is partitioned into an individual time layer in a common DRR. After a task m_c is removed from the ST, the following three types of optional partition are chosen to insert back m_c depending on the spatial partition, DRR $rr(m_c)$, and temporal partitioning, time layer $tl(m_c)$.

Type(1). a single DRR is created for m_c, that is, $rr(m_c)$ is a new DRR and $tl(m_c)$ has to be a new time layer in $rr(m_c)$. The positions locate in the boundary of different partitioned DRRs in ST.

Type(2). a single time layer in an DRR is created for m_c, that is, $tl(m_c)$ is a new time layer in an existing DRR. The positions locate in the boundary of different partitioned time layers in ST. Also, $rr(m_c)$ can be determined.

Type(3). m_c belongs an existing time layer in an existing DRR. The positions locate inside sequences of time layers.

Notice that inserting back m_c cannot introduce cycles in RCG, which will cause infeasible solutions. The cost function is defined as the linear combination of the dimensions of the whole occupied resources, total schedule time and the communication costs:

$$Cost = \alpha \times Col \times Row + \beta \times Time + \gamma \times Comm. \quad (1)$$

The $Comm$ is evaluated by the Manhattan distance and the time interval of execution between tasks. The evaluation of Col, Row and $Time$ will be discussed in next Subsection.

4.2 Evaluating Positions in Sequence Triple

To efficiently evaluate insertion points in ST, a fast method is employed. For floorplanning, it is similar to that in [10]. That is, before the selected task m_c is inserted back, coordinates (x, y) from left-bottom and coordinates (x^r, y^r) from right-top can be calculate by the remained PS and MS.

For scheduling, after the selected task m_c in tl_q^p is deleted from the RS, the RCG is modified accordingly with the partition of m_c. For Type(1), the time layer vertex v_q^p in V_{LTG} along with its incoming and outgoing edges in E_{cr}, and the edge (v_q^p, v_c) in E_{ce} are deleted from the RCG. For Type(2), additional incoming edges of v_q^p and an outgoing edge of v_c, such as (v_{pq}, v_q^p) and (v_c, v_{q+1}^p) in E_{ec}, are also removed except the deletion in Type(1). For Type(3), the weight of vertex v_q^p in V_{LTG} will subtract the configuration time of task m_c, ct_c, and only the edge (v_q^p, v_c) in E_{ce} is deleted. Then the longest path to each vertex in the modified RCG and its reverse graph, rRCG, will be calculated in $O(n^2)$. When enumerating one feasible position in RS, the DRR and the time layer of m_c are determined and the new longest path (total schedule time) after inserting can be evaluated using previous calculated paths in $O(1)$ time. Thus, the complexity of whole enumeration procedure is still $O(n^3)$.

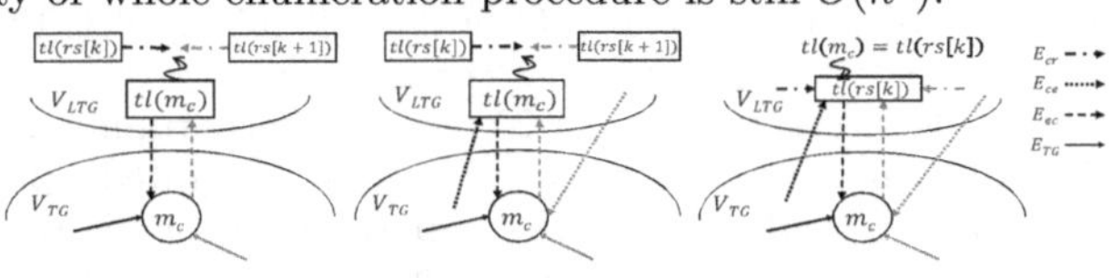

Figure 3: Evaluating $Time$ in RCG for three types

As shown in Fig. 3, the black and red lines display the edges and reverse edges, respectively. $rs[k]$ represents the $k{-}th$ task in RS. Suppose that $v_{ltg}(k)$ is the vertex in V_{LTG} for representing time layer $tl(m_c)$ in the position after $rs[k]$. The required incoming edges of $v_{ltg}(k)$, such like edges in E_{cr} and E_{ec}, are added into modified RCG to decide the earliest start configuration time $tc(k)$, and the edge from $v_{ltg}(k)$ to v_c in E_{ce} are also added to decide the earliest start execution time $te(k)$. In rRCG, the required corresponding reverse incoming edges of $v_{ltg}(k)$ and v_c are added to decide the least time of configuration and execution to the end, denoted as $tc^r(k)$ and $te^r(k)$, respectively. The longest path to a vertex v in rRCG is denoted as $lpt_r(v)$. And the total schedule time $Time$ after inserting can be evaluated as follows:

$$Time = \max(t, tc(k) + tc^r(k) + ct_c, te(k) + te^r(k) + et_c) \quad (2)$$

Where t is the longest path of the RCG before inserting. After adding edges, the $tc(k)$, $te(k)$, $tc^r(k)$and $te^r(k)$ are the $lpt(v_{ltg}(k))$, $lpt(v_c)$,$lpt_r(v_{ltg}(k))$ and $lpt_r(v_c)$, respectively.

5. EXPERIMENTS AND RESULTS

The input of our integrated optimization framework is a design including a set of tasks, whose dependencies are given in a task graph (TG), and also the resource requirements, configuration time and execution time of each task. The proposed method has been implemented in C-language on a linux 64-bit workstation (Intel 2.0GHz, 62G RAM).

Table 1: Experiments and Results

BM	TG				NORES	TWP					PROF								
	Res	imp	CPT (ms)	*para*	*Time* (ms)	#succ	%*Time*	N	COM	RT(s)	#succ	NOCOM				FULL			
												%*Time*	N	COM	RT(s)	%*Time*	N	COM	RT(s)
t50	5.2	1	244.0	9.7	378.2*	50%	+28.2%	2.9	317015	20.8	100%	+25.3%	3.2	433706	9.4	+25.4%	3.1	308448	23.6
		2	464.9	8.4	470.0	20%	+58.1%	3.0	3877344	21.5	100%	+52.6%	3.8	5086958	9.5	+53.2%	3.7	4122234	24.7
		3	595.4	4.0	607.7	70%	+2.9 %	3.6	636327	23.1	100%	+2.1%	4.2	852707	10.6	+3.0%	3.7	662044	25.8
t100	4.7	1	703.1	12.1	707.2	60%	+10.1%	8.9	6814878	110.6	100%	+5.3%	10.9	10046347	43.3	+11.2%	7.7	6645307	124
		2	1265.6	6.7	1266.5	100%	0.0%	8.0	7109259	121.2	100%	0.0%	12.7	13362578	48.5	0.0%	7.4	7210772	133.3
		3	580.5	14.6	581.6	50%	+18.9%	6.3	14188792	105.9	100%	+13.8%	10.9	17925197	40.9	+17.0%	8.1	13390629	121.5
t200	4.6	1	3556.2	9.0	3557.8	100%	0.0%	19.8	51695633	568.7	100%	0.0%	35	91214030	258.5	0.0%	18.9	51415631	602.8
		2	436.4	21.9	437.0	95%	+1.6%	16.4	3156808	524.0	100%	+5.4%	28.8	4603678	215.5	+1.2%	16.6	3156108	558.6
		3	1482	21.7	1483.6	100%	+7.8%	16.8	91239012	516.4	100%	+6.7%	29.1	125680795	238.7	+8.7%	17.3	91712271	570.1
t300	7.1	1	943.4	26.5	944.7*	45%	+27.9%	18.2	38504812	1543.4	100%	+27.4%	28.1	55748853	458.9	+28.7%	16.4	38793827	1598.4
		2	1051.5	23.8	1053.2*	40%	+10.8%	18.5	43888491	1536.9	100%	+10.9%	28.1	63077509	556.7	+10.7%	17.9	44247360	1644.4
		3	2814.7	8.9	2814.4	90%	+0.6 %	15.4	80817250	1532.1	100%	+0.0%	31.7	116284497	461.0	+0.7%	15.5	80186489	1602.5
Avg.	-	-	-	-	-	68.3%	1	1	1	1	100%	-1.5%	+53.8%	+46.4%	-59.8%	-0.6%	+2.3%	+0.14%	+9.6%

The target architecture is XC7VX485T FPGA. There are about 37950 CLBs and ratio of row and coluccmn is about 3:1. So the CLB array in XC7VX485T is about 337 rows and about 112 columns. The configuration time is proportional to the synthesized bitstreams of a task. It will take about 50.7ms to configure the whole resources of XC7VX485T with the maximum bandwidth 3.2Gb/s through interface ICAP [9]. Thus, the overhead of reconfiguring one CLB is 0.0013ms.

Tab. 1 shows the experiments and results. The benchmark (BM) includes t50, t100, t200 and t300, which have three different task graphs with each 50, 100, 200 and 300 tasks, respectively. Res is the resource requirements, (sum of CLBs that all task required)/(total CLBs of target FPGA). CPT is the critical path length of the task graph. *para* is the parallelism of the task graph, (sum of all task execution time)/(critical path length). *RT* is the run time of the program. *#succ* is the success rate of floorplanning. *N* is the number of DRRs. *COM* is the communication costs. All data are the average results in 20 independently running.

In order to verify the efficiency of our integrated optimization framework, a two-phases approach (TWP) is running for the same optimization problem. In the first phase, tasks are partitioned considering optimization of schedule time and satisfying the resource requirements only. In the second phase, the program attempts to find a reasonable floorplan based on previous partitioning. And the full optimization framework (FULL) is also compared to the version without communication cost (NOCOM). For exploring the performance of design using PDR, the optimal schedule time without resource constraints (NORES) is approximated using an integer linear programming model which is solved by Gurobi. That is, *Time* in Tab. 1 is a possible lower bound of the schedule time in each design, and %*Time* is the increasing proportion comparing to *Time* in different experiments.

Due to a larger design space when combining scheduling and floorplanning, the integrated optimization framework has 100% success rate compared to 68.3% in TWP even if its *RT* increases 9.6%. And their schedule time and communication costs are almost similar.

Because of multiplied decrease of resources comparing to NORES, the performance becomes bad for the design whose task graph has long CPT and high parallelism. Such as the schedule time of imp.2 in t50 is obviously worse.

The comparisons between FULL and NOCOM show that about 46.3% communication cost is reduced. And the number of DRRs is also reduced about 51.5%, which means the requirements of I/O ports among DRRs is less. Because there is no need to recalculate coordinates of space and time when evaluating communication cost, its *RT* will be less.

6. CONCLUSIONS

In this paper, we propose an integrated framework for partitioning, scheduling, and floorplanning on partially dynamically reconfigurable FPGAs. A set of methods, e.g. sequence triple, RCG, are used to solve the critical problem for partial and dynamic reconfiguration. Based on the proposed framework, we integrate the exploration of spatial and temporal design space to find the optimal solution of partitioning, scheduling and floorplanning. Experimental results demonstrate the proposed framework can effectively solve the floorplanning problem and improve the performance.

7. ACKNOWLEDGMENTS

This work was partially supported by the National Natural Science Foundation of China (NSFC) under grant No. 61674133 and No.61404123. The authors would like to thank Information Science laboratory Center of USTC for hardware and software services.

8. REFERENCES

[1] S. Hauck and A. DeHon. Reconfigurable computing: the theory and practice of FPGA-base computation. *Morgan Kaufmann*, 2010.

[2] D. Koch. Partial Reconfiguration on FPGAs: Architectures, Tools and Applications. *Springer*, 2012.

[3] Y. C. Jiang and J. F. Wang. Temporal partitioning data flow graphs for dynamically reconfigurable computing. *IEEE Trans. Very Large Scale Integr. (VLSI) Syst.*, 2007.

[4] R. Cordone, F. Redaelli, M. A. Redaelli, M. D. Santambrogio, and D. Sciuto. Partitioning and scheduling of task graphs on partially dynamically reconfigurable FPGAs. *IEEE Trans. Comput. Aided Des. of Integr. Circuit Syst.*, 2009.

[5] A. Purgato, D. Tantillo, M. Rabozzi, D. Sciuto, and M. D. Santambrogio. Resource-efficient scheduling for partially reconfigurable FPGA-based systems. in *Proc. IEEE Int. Parallel Distrib. Proc. Symp. Workshops*, 2016.

[6] L. Singhal and E. Bozorgzadeh. Multi-layer floorplanning on a sequence of reconfigurable designs. in *Proc. Int. Conf. Field Programmable Logic and Appl.*, 2006.

[7] A. Montone, M. D. Santambrogio, D. Sciuto, and S. O. Memik. Placement and floorplanning in dynamically reconfigurable FPGAs. *ACM Trans. Rconfigurable Technol. Syst.*, 2010.

[8] P. Banerjee, M. Sangtani, and S. Sur-Kolay. Floorplanning for partially reconfigurable FPGAs. *IEEE Trans. Comput. Aided Des. of Integr. Circuit Syst.*, 2011.

[9] Xilinx Inc. Vivado Design Suite User Guide Partial Reconfiguration, 2016.

[10] S. Chen and T. Yoshimura. Fixed-outline floorplanning: Block-position enumeration and a new method for calculating area costs. *IEEE Trans. Comput. Aided Des. of Integr. Circuit Syst.*, 2008.

Communication-aware Partitioning for Energy Optimization of Large FPGA Designs

Kalindu Herath, Alok Prakash, Jiang Guiyuan, Thambipillai Srikanthan
Nanyang Technological University, Singapore
kalindub001@e.ntu.edu.sg, {alok, gyjiang, astsrikan}@ntu.edu.sg

ABSTRACT

Modern FPGAs integrate multi-million logic resources that allow the realization of increasingly large designs. However, state-of-the-art simulated annealing based CAD tools for FPGA suffer from long runtime, poor performance and sub-optimal routing and placement decisions, especially for large applications, leading to less energy efficient designs. In this paper, we present a partitioning methodology that divides large application into smaller subsystems based on the communication frequency between these subsystems. We leverage the existing CAD tools to compile the large design, which is now annotated with their subsystems, to obtain the final bitstream. Experiments show that the proposed strategy can lead to a performance gain of over 60% while still achieving more than 20% reduction in energy consumption.

Keywords

CAD; communication-aware partitioning; energy-efficient

1. INTRODUCTION

The continuous scaling of transistor has enabled Field Programmable Gate Array (FPGA) manufacturers such as Xilinx [4] and Altera [1] to integrate millions of logic resources into modern FPGAs, providing opportunities for designers to develop increasingly complex FPGA designs. At the same time, the incorporation of FPGA in the latest iPhone 7 smartphone from Apple [15] bears true testament to the increasing popularity and usefulness of FPGAs. However, FPGAs are still less energy-efficient than their ASIC counterparts and hence their integration in battery powered devices can prove to be detrimental. This issue can be alleviated, to some extent, by extensive power-conscious application-specific customization of FPGA designs [6]. The current Computer-Aided Design (CAD) tools, however, are not sophisticated enough to cater for such customizations. Specially, compiling large applications typically results in very long compilation times, poor placement and routing decisions that inevitably leads to degradation in circuit performance, area and energy consumption [5].

Among CAD steps, scalability of placement step has been discussed recently [10] [5]. An extensive search in literature shows that the widely popular Simulated Annealing (SA) based placement tools poorly scale for larger applications [5] [9] despite being capable of producing high-quality placement for smaller designs [10]. Partitioning based placement tools [12] show faster runtime, but, this comes at the cost of degraded quality of result. Analytical placement tools [10] have been known to achieve better balance between scalability and quality of results. There have also been attempts to lower the runtime of placement by introducing pre-compiled macro block based design flow [8] [7]. But these techniques introduce large degradation in placement quality. The commercial FPGA vendors have also improved the scalability of their placement tools. For instance, Altera uses parallel SA techniques [11] whereas Xilinx relies on scalable analytical placement techniques [10]. These research endeavors, however, mostly focus on optimizing performance, leaving an inadequacy for an energy efficient CAD tools for large applications. In addition, these approaches have not considered runtime characteristics of the application during compilation. Existing work has also identified that the FPGA interconnect resources consumes most of its dynamic power[14][16]. Hence, reducing the usage of these interconnect resources can effectively lead to power and energy-efficient FPGA designs.

In this paper, we propose a communication-aware design mapping technique that is especially targeted towards large and complex FPGA designs. *The proposed technique partitions such FPGA designs into smaller subsystems such that the intra-subsystem communication frequency is maximized, while the inter-subsystem communication frequency is minimized.* This strategy minimizes the energy consumption in the interconnects by reducing the frequency of long distance communication. Additionally, the partitioning of the large design into smaller subsystems also aids the CAD tools during compilation since it already excels in placement for smaller designs [10]. We rely on the existing CAD tools for the entire compilation process and only annotate the input design with the partitioning information using pragmas.

2. MOTIVATION

The main modes of power dissipation in FPGAs are transistor leakage current (static power), short circuit current and the charging/discharging of capacitive loads. Amongst these modes of power dissipation, charging/discharging of capacitive loads contributes the most to the overall power dissipation, and is modelled as [14];

$$P = \frac{1}{2}\Sigma_{i \in nets} C_i.\alpha_i.v^2 \quad (1)$$

where *nets* are all the connections and respective components in the design, P is the average power consumption, C_i is the capacitance of net i, α_i is the average toggle rate of net i and v is the supply voltage. In a typical application, some code sections are executed more frequently than the rest. Hence, the data flow rate of the interconnect links between such frequently executed computation units and the corresponding memory blocks is relatively higher, leading to higher toggle rate α and consequently higher intercon-

Permission to make digital or hard copies of all or part of this work for personal or classroom use is granted without fee provided that copies are not made or distributed for profit or commercial advantage and that copies bear this notice and the full citation on the first page. Copyrights for components of this work owned by others than ACM must be honored. Abstracting with credit is permitted. To copy otherwise, or republish, to post on servers or to redistribute to lists, requires prior specific permission and/or a fee. Request permissions from permissions@acm.org.

GLSVLSI '17, May 10-12, 2017, Banff, AB, Canada
© 2017 ACM. ISBN 978-1-4503-4972-7/17/05...$15.00
DOI: http://dx.doi.org/10.1145/3060403.3060441

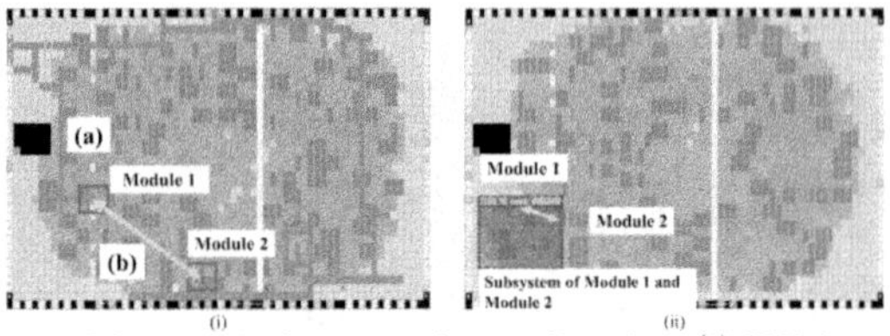

Figure 1: Floorplan for sample application (i) Without Subsystems (ii) With Subsystems

nect power consumption. Additionally, as discussed in the previous section, dynamic power dissipation of FPGAs are dominated by the power consumed by the interconnect resources. This is due to its higher capacitive loads which typically increases with increase in the length of the interconnect[14]. Hence, *it is essential to have shorter routing paths and even more so for the nets with high toggle rate to have overall lower power consumption.*

In order to observe the extent of degradation in power and performance of a large application on an FPGA, we performed a case study using the commercial Quartus CAD flow. An application is considered to be 'large' if it consumes above 80% device logic, memory and routing resources. We developed a hand-coded application, which contains N number of computation units (CU) and memory units (MU). Each CU is connected to n number of MUs. We tuned the parameter N and n to satisfy the above requirement of a large application. Figure 1 shows the floorplan of a Quartus mapping of a sample large application. The high demand for routing resources for the application in Figure 1 has exhausted the routing resources in the central region of the FPGA floorplan. Hence, 2 modules as shown in the floorplan have been connected via an unusually long interconnect path 'a', instead of a far more preferable interconnect path, 'b'. Additionally, since the tool does not consider the communication frequency between the modules during the routing phase, the problem is exacerbated if these two modules communicate frequently, thereby resulting in high power consumption. We observe the maximum allowable frequency (F.Max) for the resulting design, as well as its total energy consumption after running the design on the target FPGA.

Next, we partition this large application into a set of subsystems such that highly communicating computation and memory nodes become part of a single subsystem. We will discuss in detail regarding the subsystems and the exact algorithm for the partitioning step later in Section 3. Next, we use pragmas to instruct the Quartus to place the identified subsystem RTL components as a group. After the mapping is done by the Quartus, we again observe the F.Max and the total energy consumption for this partitioned design.

We observed that the F.max increased from 50.61 MHz to 89.17 MHz while the total energy consumption reduced by over 17%, by using the proposed partitioning strategy. This example proves that the Quartus is unable to optimally map large application into the FPGA. It also shows the suitability of the proposed communication-aware partitioning strategy, explained in the next section, for large application to improve the quality of the final mapping.

3. PARTITIONING FRAMEWORK

The proposed algorithm takes an RTL design, represented as a graph, as input and produces a network of subsystems. A subsystem refers to a group of computation and memory modules with high intra-group communication, which we identify to be placed in close proximity to each other.

3.1 Problem Statement

An FPGA RTL level design can be represented as a graph $G(V, E)$ where V is a set of nodes where each node represents a RTL module; i.e. computation unit or a memory units, and E is a set of edges where each edge represents a connection between two RTL modules. Each design unit node has an area requirement on the FPGA floorplan. The minimum area needed by the unit (vertex) v_i is noted as a_i (l_i, m_i) where l_i and m_i represent number of CLBs and number of Block RAMs (BRAMs) respectively. The communication frequency between two modules (nodes) is analogous to the toggle rate α in the equation 1 and is represented by the cost value of each connection (edge) e_j. The total available number of CLBs and BRAMs in the device can be noted as A_l and A_m respectively. Maximum allowed wires per unit FPGA area (also referred to as connection density) is represented by C and is assumed to be a constant for the entire FPGA area. Given the design graph $G(V, E)$, area requirement of design units $a(l, m)$, communication frequency of each connection between design units α and the FPGA parameters A_l,A_m, and C, the communication-aware design partitioning problem can be thought of as dividing the graph into n ($\leq N$) number of subgraphs (referred to as subsystems), where N is the upper bound of number of subgraphs. The optimization goal for the partitioning problem is to minimize the total inter-subsystem communication activity, and is subjected to the following constraints.

1. Area Constraint: Total number of CLBs and BRAMs required by each subgraph must be less than a predefined value $A_{l'}$ and $A_{m'}$ respectively
2. Congestion Constraint: Ratio of Area and the corresponding connections in each subgraph must be less than C

3.2 Algorithm

Algorithm 1 presents our greedy clustering strategy for the partitioning step. We start the clustering process by treating each computational module and memory module as a subsystem with only one element. The algorithm maintains a list *edge_list* of all the edges and respective communication frequency of the connection in Line 1 of Algorithm 1. In Line 3 through 6, each iteration of the *while* loop, an edge is first selected from this list using the *get_valid_edge*(*edge_list*) procedure. Then, the associated two subsystems of the selected edge are merged to form one (larger) subsystem using the *merge*(*edge*) procedure. This selection of edges and their merging process is repeated until all the edges are exhausted.

3.2.1 *Valid Edge Identification*

An edge can be identified as a valid candidate for *merging operation* if the associated subsystems (nodes) of the edge satisfy the Area and Congestion constraints, as identified above, upon merging. Hence, in Line 8 through 18 of Algorithm 1, if there exists any valid edge, we choose the most profitable edge among them for the *merging operation*.

3.2.2 *Merge Operation*

Line 20 through 31 of Algorithm 1, present the *merge*(*edge*) procedure. Nodes a and b, associated to the edge e are merged to form a new subsystem a', and the edge is removed from *edge_list*. There can be other nodes, e.g. c, adjacent to both a and b that should now maintain a single edge from a'. Other edges associated with nodes a and b are added to the subsystem without modifying their communication frequency. The changes of the graph due to new merged node a' are handled by *update_edge_list*() procedure on Line 30.

Algorithm 1 Communication-aware partitioning algorithm

```
edge_list ← communication activity α for all e ∈ E

while has_valid_edge do
    edge ← get_valid_edge(edge_list)
    merge(edge)
end while

procedure GET_VALID_EDGE(edge_list)
    e_max_profit ← first_edge(edge_list)
    for each e ∈ edge_list where e ∉ marked_edges do
        if meet_constraints(e) then
            if profit(e) > profit(e_max_profit) then
                e_max_profit ← e
            end if
        end if
    end for
    return e
end procedure

procedure MERGE(edge)
    {a, b} ← get_connecting_nodes(edge)
    a′ ← merge of {a, b}
    remove(edge)
    for each node c where c ∼ a and c ∼ b do
        e_c1 ← get_associated_edge(c, a)
        e_c2 ← get_associated_edge(c, b)
        x ← merge of e_c1, e_c2
        α_x ← α_ec1 + α_ec2
    end for
    update_edge_list()
end procedure
```

3.2.3 Calculating the profit

We consider two factors to evaluate profit of merging two nodes (subsystems) a and b, connected by edge e, into $a\prime$. First is the communication between all the RTL modules in a and b. The higher the communication between modules, the better the quality of the resultant subsystem $a\prime$. We term this communication as *intra-subsystem communication*. The other factor is the communication between resultant subsystem $a\prime$ and the nodes outside, which we call as *inter-subsystem communication*. The clustering process strives to increase the *intra-subsystem communication* and decrease the *inter-subsystem communication*. Hence, the profit of merging subsystems (a, b) which is connected by edge e is:

$$profit_{e(a,b)} = \frac{\textit{intra-communication}}{\textit{inter-communication}} \quad (2)$$

3.2.4 Constraints

The partitioning strategy, discussed above, can lead to a trivial solution in extreme cases, where all the nodes are clustered together into a single subsystem so that the inter-communication is zero and intra-communication is maximum. Even in a less than extreme situation, it is not always beneficial to have lesser number of partitions that only satisfy the intra- and inter-subsystem communication goals and maximize the profit term expressed in Equation 2. To avoid such trivial solution, we control the maximum area of a subsystem during merging RTL components by setting area constraint $A_{l\prime}$ and $A_{m\prime}$ for LUTs and BRAMs respectively.

Regarding the congestion constraint, it is noteworthy that while restricting high communication links in a relatively small area improves the intra-communication, merging more nodes into subsystems also involves having more internal edges in the subsystem. These edges ultimately map to physical routing wire of the FPGA. Hence, many connections within a subsystem may cause high routing congestion regions after getting mapped to FPGA. Therefore, to avoid such regions, we control number of connection per unit area by introducing a term called *connection density*.

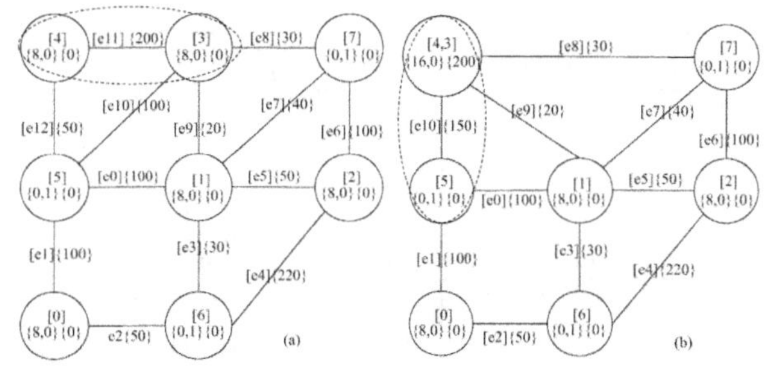

Figure 2: Execution of the algorithm a) Initial condition b) After the first execution

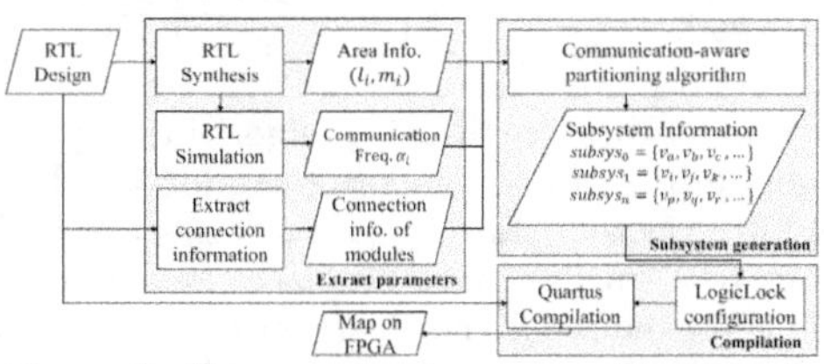

Figure 3: Communication-aware Partitioning

We explain our algorithm using a sample application shown in Figure 2(a). Each circle represents nodes within the subsystem, area consumption of the subsystem(LUTs,BRAMs) and intra-communication in the notation $[node\_list]$ $\{l, m\}\{\alpha_{intra}\}$. The edges in the graph are annotated with edge-id and inter-communication value as a tuple $[edge\_no]$ $\{\alpha_{inter}\}$. From Figure 2 (a), $e11$ is selected for merging as it shows a greater profit than $e4$, although $\alpha_{e11} < \alpha_{e4}$. Merging respective connecting subsystems of $e11$, subsystems $[4]$ and $[3]$, make a new subsystem $[4, 3]$ of area $(l, m) = (16, 0)$, as shown in Figure 2 (b). Since the edge $e11$ is now internal to the subsystem $[4, 3]$, the α_{intra} of the subsystem is now 200. In the next iteration, merging $e10$ is profitable, as it makes $\alpha_{intra} = 350$ and $\alpha_{inter} = 250$, resulting in a profit of 1.4 according to the Equation 2.

3.3 Communication-aware Partitioning

Figure 3 shows our communication-aware FPGA design partitioning methodology. We take an RTL design as the input. From a given RTL design code, the following parameters are extracted to execute the partitioning algorithm:

i) Area of modules: Typical RTL synthesis step of CAD flow estimates area of design modules. Since the runtime of RTL synthesis is minimal as compared to the runtime of placement and routing steps, we obtain area $a(l, m)$ of each node in $G(V, E)$ by performing a quick RTL Synthesis step.

ii) Communication Frequency of Edges: Next, we perform a RTL simulation where each edge $e \in E$ is treated as signal. Simulation signal dump files are then used to obtain communication frequency of each edge e, α_e.

iii) Graph Connectivity: We need a netlist of a given RTL design in order to build the graph $G(V, E)$. However, since commercial CAD tools like Quartus do not allow users to read generated netlist, we perform text processing on design code to extract the relevant information.

Table 1: Performance ($F.Max$) Improvement

App.	Without subsys. F.Max(MHz)	With subsys. F.Max(MHz)	F.Max Imp. (%)
Synth1	50.61	89.17	76.19
Synth2	50.61	69.26	36.85
Synth3	52.43	93.9	79.10
Atax′	51.91	90.23	73.82
Bicg′	57.8	81.01	40.16

Table 2: Power and Energy reduction using subsystems

App.	Total Power Reduction(%)	Routing Power Reduction(%)	Total Energy Reduction(%)
Synth1	6.51	19.80	41.77
Synth2	2.05	9.47	18.00
Synth3	0.56	1.31	18.67
Atax′	3.12	8.47	16.06
Bicg′	0.76	1.64	7.37

After the extraction, these parameters are input to our communication-aware partitioning algorithm. The output of the algorithm is subsystem pragmas for the LogicLock feature in Quartus tool. Each LogicLock is set of RTL modules belongs to a subsystem to be placed in a square region on FPGA. However, we do not instruct the size of the LogicLock and its physical placement of FPGA, and let Quartus compiler decide them. An application with its subsystems identified is then compiled using Quartus.

4. RESULTS AND DISCUSSION

We used the proposed communication-aware partitioning algorithm on various applications and observed their performance in terms of F_{max} and energy consumption. Altera's Quartus toolchain[2] was used for our experiments. For both, traditional and the proposed approaches, Quartus compiler optimizes for the performance of the mapping solution (rather than optimize on area).

After the Quartus compilation finishes for both cases, with and without subsystems, the performance (maximum running frequency - F_{max}) of each case is obtained from the compilation report. We also use the Quartus PowerPlay feature [3] by performing a gate level simulation to obtain an accurate power estimation in each case. Total Energy consumption is also derived from these parameters.

To evaluate our approach, we created three hand-coded applications, as described in section 2, to exhaust the logic and memory resources on a Altera EP2C35 FPGA device. We also modified and experimented with *Atax* and *Bicg* applications from Polybench [13] benchmark suite. Since, these application kernels are relatively small-scale design, we duplicated them multiple times with minor modifications to the kernel itself, to fully utilize the logic and memory resources of a Altera EP2C70 series FPGA device with 70K logic elements. We refer to them as *Atax′* and *Bicg′*.

The three hand-coded applications are mapped to the Altera EP2C35 FPGA device while *Atax′* and *Bicg′* are mapped to the Altera EP2C70 FPGA device, without and with subsystems generated from the proposed technique. Table 1 shows performance of these five applications in terms of maximum achievable frequency, F_{max}. As evident from this table, partitioning the large applications into subsystems, has significantly increased the performance of mapped solution with an average of over 61% in their F_{max}.

Next, Table 2 shows the percentage reduction in overall power consumption as well as for the interconnect resources only. It is evident that the proposed approach can lead to a significant reduction in the interconnect power consumption. Even the total power consumption is reduced while achieving higher performance, when compared to the traditional compilation method without communication-aware design partitioning. Applications such as Synth3 and *Bicg′* do not show significant reduction in power. However, they still show a significant improvement in their performance as seen in Table 1. After careful investigation of these applications, we observed that the CAD tools kept the communicating modules in close proximity for these applications even without partitioning the application into subsystems. Hence, these application do not show a significant reduction in power after the proposed communication-aware partitioning. However, this behavior of the CAD tools is not guaranteed for every application as evident by the significant improvement in power consumption for other applications.

Finally, as shown in Table 2, there is a significant reduction in the overall energy consumption when using the proposed partitioning strategy, especially for applications where both the performance and power consumption improve significantly when compared to the existing tools.

5. CONCLUSION

In this paper, we presented our communication-aware partitioning approach for large FPGA designs, that not only reduces the energy consumption, but also improves the maximum achievable operating frequency (F.Max) of the resulting design significantly. Experimental results on 2 FPGA devices show an average of over 61% improvement in F.Max and more than 20% reduction in energy consumption when compared to the traditional design flow.

6. REFERENCES

[1] Altera. https://www.altera.com/.

[2] Intel FPGA Development Tools - Quartus Prime. https://goo.gl/3kMRQN.

[3] PowerPlay Power Analyzer Support Resources. https://goo.gl/1fE7NI.

[4] Xilinx. https://www.xilinx.com/.

[5] H. Bian et al. Towards scalable placement for FPGAs. In *FPGA*, 2010.

[6] D. Chen et al. Low-power high-level synthesis for FPGA architectures. In *ISLPED*, 2003.

[7] J. Coole et al. BPR: fast FPGA placement and routing using macroblocks. In *CODES+ISSS*, 2012.

[8] C. Lavin et al. HMFlow: accelerating FPGA compilation with hard macros for rapid prototyping. In *FCCM*, 2011.

[9] M. Lin et al. Improving FPGA Placement with Dynamically Adaptive Stochastic Tunneling. *IEEE TCAD*, 2010.

[10] T.-H. Lin et al. An efficient and effective analytical placer for FPGAs. In *DAC*, 2013.

[11] A. Ludwin et al. Efficient and deterministic parallel placement for FPGAs. *ACM TODAES*, 2011.

[12] P. Maidee et al. Timing-driven partitioning-based placement for island style FPGAs. *IEEE TCAD*, 2005.

[13] L.-N. Pouchet. Polybench: The polyhedral benchmark suite. https://goo.gl/t4dm3U, 2012.

[14] L. Shang et al. Dynamic power consumption in Virtex-II FPGA family. In *FPGA*, 2002.

[15] A. Tilley. This Mysterious Chip In The iPhone 7 Could Be Key To Apple's AI Push. https://goo.gl/ZVBgUH, 2016.

[16] T. Tuan et al. A 90Nm Low-power FPGA for Battery-powered Applications. In *FPGA*, 2006.

Combined Centralized and Distributed Connection Allocation in Large TDM Circuit Switching NoCs

Yong Chen, Emil Matus, Gerhard P. Fettweis
Technische Universität Dresden, Vodafone Chair for Mobile Communications Systems
{yong.chen, emil.matus}@ifn.et.tu-dresden.de

ABSTRACT

The centralized methods for connection allocation in a circuit-switched network-on-chip (NoC) based on time-division multiplexing (TDM) may pose serious performance and scalability issues in large-scale networks due to the 1) limited path search speed, 2) increasing allocation request rate at central unit and 3) the increasing communication cost between the central unit and NoC nodes. This paper tackles this problem by proposing a combined centralized-distributed approach that splits the original NoC into multiple non-overlapping logical partitions, each of them served by a dedicated NoC-Manager unit. The NoC-Manager employs fast trellis-search shortest path algorithm enabling local path search inside the associated NoC partition, while a set of NoC-Managers jointly combine the partial results in a distributed manner in order to find the most likely global path. This approach attempts to combine the benefits of distributed and centralized systems, whilst the experimental results demonstrate its high potential regarding performance and scalability improvement.

Keywords

TDM-NoCs; Connection Allocation; Scalability

1. INTRODUCTION

Network-On-Chips (NoCs) can provide Guaranteed Services (GSs), such as minimum throughput or bounded latency. Circuit Switching (CS) is frequently adopted to support GS, which allocates exclusive links to form a dedicated connection for each flow. However, since the resources (link and buffer) are occupied exclusively for the duration of a connection, it is inflexible and may block other communications. Therefore, an extension, Time-Division Multiplex (TDM) CS, was proposed to share the resource. In TDM CS NoCs, the link is split into time slots and shared through TDM scheme, with the allocation information stored in a slot allocation table of particular router [1].

The TDM CS is characterized by contention-free and low latency communication with setup connection overhead, which has to find the shortest contention-free path between the two given modules and allocates the time slots along the path. Due to the global knowledge of this system, the previous centralized approaches [2–5] for connection allocation (i.e. connection setup) provide good performance for small and moderate NoCs. However, the more the NoC size grows, the more allocation requests are received by the central unit per cycle, and the more communication cost is risen between the central unit and the NoC nodes. Consequently, the central unit can become a serious bottleneck in the hotspot traffic. In this paper, we propose a scalable mechanism to address the dynamic connection allocation problem in large systems. The hardware connection allocator 'NoCManager', is presented to solve this allocation problem, whilst the partitioned architecture (i.e. spatial partitioning technique) is used to overcome the scalability problem in traditional centralized systems. NoCs are divided into small logical non-overlapped partitions containing local NoCManagers. This partitioning technique keeps the request load of the manager and manager-node communication overhead moderately. Inside each partition, the path search problem is solved by a local manager with trellis-search algorithm. To establish a path that crosses the different partitions, the managers communicate with others in distributed manner to converge the global path.

2. BACKGROUND AND RELATED WORK

There are two categories of dynamic connection allocation techniques i) centralized [2–5] and ii) distributed allocation [1, 6]. In centralized systems, a central manager is responsible for the allocation of connection. Since the central manager has the global knowledge of the system, it can achieve global optimal results. The central manager can be either an embedded processor or a dedicated hardware accelerator. HAGAR [4] is a hardware accelerator, which supports basic CS and allows to speed up the allocation with two orders of magnitude against Microblaze processor based software methods [3]. The TrElliS-Search Allocation (TESSA) approach [2] proposes a high speed dedicated allocator for TDM CS based on the adapted Viterbi algorithm. In paper [5], a centralized hardware unit that uses breadth-first searching algorithm, is proposed with excellent performance. Though the centralized system has the advantages of global knowledge and high performance, as the network grows with increasing allocation request rate at central unit, the central unit might become the bottleneck due to the drawbacks of centralism in computation and communication. This paper is motivated by TESSA, but we proposed the partitioned architecture that divides the large system into small logi-

Permission to make digital or hard copies of all or part of this work for personal or classroom use is granted without fee provided that copies are not made or distributed for profit or commercial advantage and that copies bear this notice and the full citation on the first page. Copyrights for components of this work owned by others than ACM must be honored. Abstracting with credit is permitted. To copy otherwise, or republish, to post on servers or to redistribute to lists, requires prior specific permission and/or a fee. Request permissions from permissions@acm.org.

GLSVLSI '17, May 10-12, 2017, Banff, AB, Canada

© 2017 ACM. ISBN 978-1-4503-4972-7/17/05...$15.00

DOI: http://dx.doi.org/10.1145/3060403.3060414

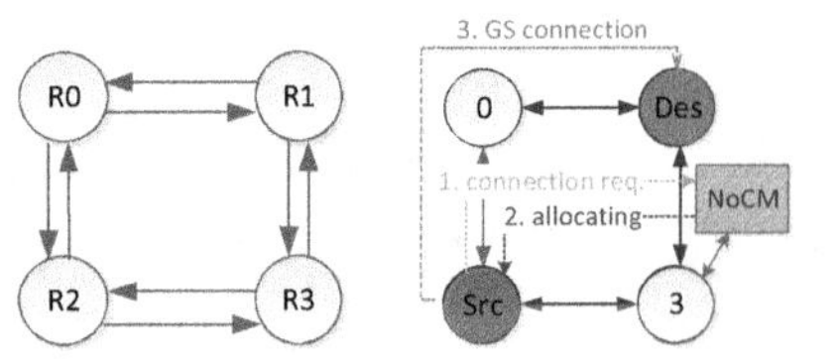

(a) Example NoC (b) System Model

Figure 1: System Model of the NoCManager based NoC platform.

cal partitions with multiple dedicated local managers to enhance the scalability.

3. SYSTEM MODEL

The system model of central allocator (i.e. NoCManager) based 2x2 mesh NoC architecture is illustrated in Fig. 1. The NoCManager (NoCM) is the dedicated unit that attempts to allocate the appropriate connections when it receives GS connection requests. The messages between NoCM and NoCs are delivered over a light-weight dedicated control network.

As soon as a module needs a connection to another module, it sends the request of connection reservation to the NoCM. When NoCM receives the request, it attempts to allocate the appropriate path and slots according to the request requirements. When the allocation succeeds, NoCM sends the results on allocating information to the relevant routers in order to set up the connection. In the NoC, when the data transfer phase is finished, the source node sends deallocate flit to delete the connection, and informs NoCM to free the corresponding allocated links.

4. NOCMANAGER ARCHITECTURE

The NoCManager has to search and allocate connections between two modules. In our system, the connection allocation problem is solved as the shortest path problem in a trellis graph description of the NoC.

4.1 TESSA Approach

The TESSA (non-partitioned TESSA) was initially presented in [2] but without analysis on the performance in large systems. The successive NoC traversal from source to destination node for path searching can be represented by trellis graph (Fig. 2). In general, the path search in trellis graph comprises two steps:

- **Forward search** i.e. traverse the NoC from source to find the best free path to target node.
- **Backtracking** i.e. when target node is reached, the backtrack starts from target node to read out the stored survivor path hop by hop.

The trellis graph in Fig. 2a is defined to represent a traversal through the network of single hop. Normally, iterative traversals are necessary as the distance between the source and destination nodes is more than one hop. Hence, there is 'iteration link' from second stage to first stage and additional registers in order to hold the values of intermediate results(Fig. 2b). Each iteration consumes a clock cycle. The search will be stopped in two cases: i) either the target node has been reached or ii) after certain iterations (i.e. $2N-2$ iterations for NxN mesh NoC, which equals the longest minimal path in the network). Hence, the livelock is avoided. As in Fig. 2b, the forward search starts from Src (node 0), and activates node 2 and node 1. At the next cycle, node

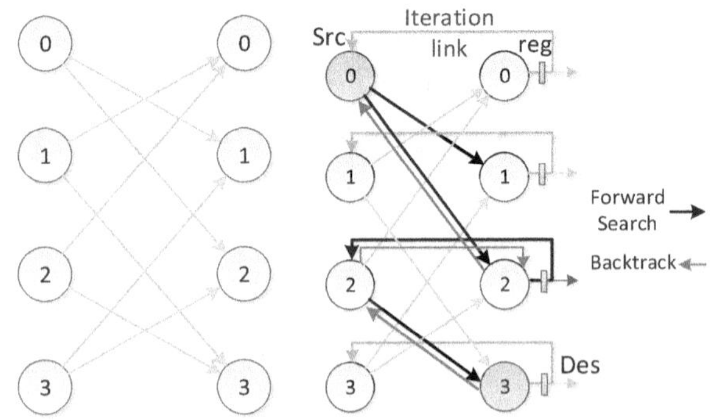

(a) Trellis of single hop (b) Iterative trellis search

Figure 2: The trellis search graph for the example NoC

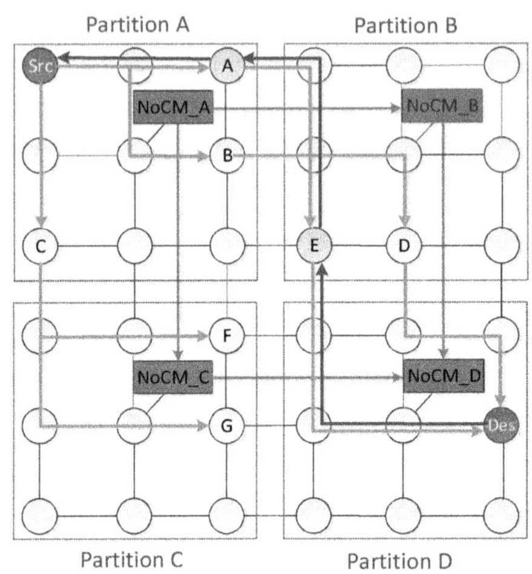

Figure 3: The original NoC is divided into 4 partitions with 4 dedicated NoCMs. The border nodes A and E are backtracked as survivor path. The cross-partition search is along $NoCM\_A \rightarrow (NoCM\_B, NoCM\_C) \rightarrow NoCM\_D$.

2 travels back to its first stage, and activates node 3. Then backtrack starts from Des (node 3) to select path sequence as {0, 2, 3}. The link $1 \rightarrow 3$ is assumed already occupied by previous allocation.

4.2 Partitioned TESSA

To address the scalability issue, we proposed the partitioned architecture that divides the original system into multiple small logical partitions with a local dedicated NoCM per partition. Each local manager only has the state of nodes in its region, and is responsible for searching path in its local region. The NoCMs are connected with each other in 2D-mesh topology via dedicated links. The dedicated link width is $2 \cdot \log_2 M + N \cdot S + 2$ bits, where M is the NoC size (for Des and Src address), $N \cdot N$ is partition size (for border nodes) and S is slot table size, and 2 bits for control signals. These NoCMs can work simultaneously.

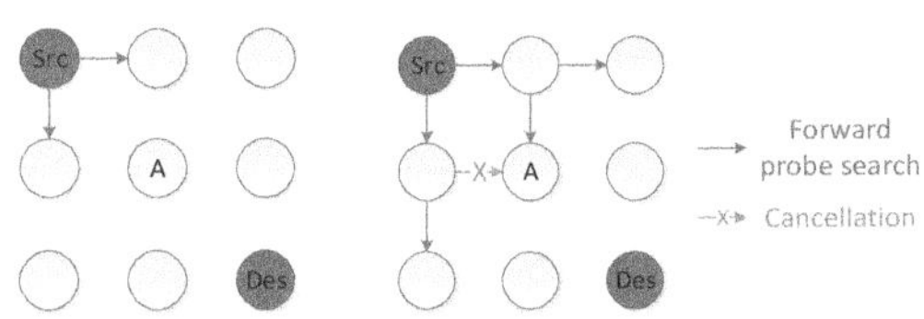

(a) A node doubles the probe. (b) When two probes meet, one is canceled.

Figure 4: The probe search among NoCMs. Each node is a NoCM.

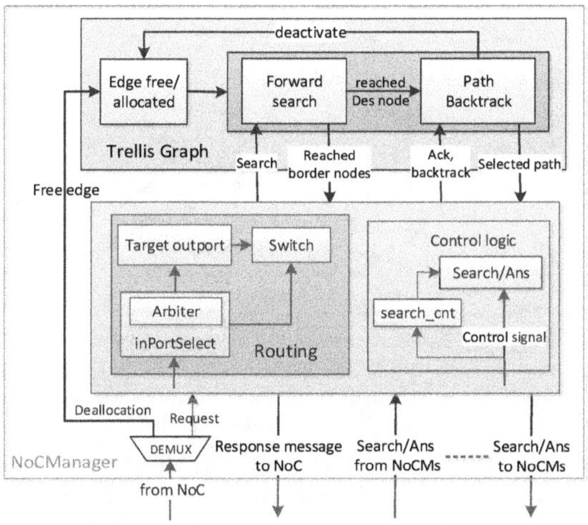

Figure 5: Block diagram of the NoCManager

Table 1: The usage of control signals

Signals	Usage
00	Idle
01	Search comes in
10	Nack (Path search failed)
11	Ack (Path established)

4.2.1 *Partitioned TESSA search algorithm*

If the source and destination nodes of the request are both at the same partition, this request will be handled by the local manager only. Otherwise, as illustrated in Fig. 3, firstly, the local NoCM (NoCM_A) starts to search path in its trellis graph from source node (Src) to reach the border nodes (node A,B and C), and then forwards the search message to its neighbor NoCMs (NoCM_B and NoCM_C), continually until reaches the destination (NoCM_D). When destination (Des) node is reached, backtrack starts from Des to select the survivor path.

The basic search idea among NoCMs is similar to parallel probe search [6], as shown in Fig. 4. The Src NoCM requests search to its neighbor NoCMs, which can lead closer to the destination. The reached neighbor performs trellis search in its partition, and then forwards the message to its reached neighboring NoCMs. Hence, the search is forwarded to the Des along all possible minimal paths. If two searches meet at one NoCM, then one of them will be canceled based on RoundRobin arbitration. If the downstream NoCM is not available, then that probe search will be canceled immediately without waiting.

4.2.2 *Detailed partitioned NoCM architecture*

The block diagram of the NoCM is shown in Fig. 5 and comprises trellis graph and control modules (routing module and control logic).

Control signals: There are 2 bits control wires for 4 control signals for probe search among NoCMs, as listed in table I.

The 'Search comes in' indicates a new probe search comes in, and Nack/Ack are backward answer signals (Ans). The detailed control signals usage during probe search is illustrated in Fig. 6. For each NoCM, if it accepts a search, it will become busy and reject any later search until becomes free again. Since each search may have two productive output directions and may send out two searches, a counter (search_cnt) is used to record the number of sent

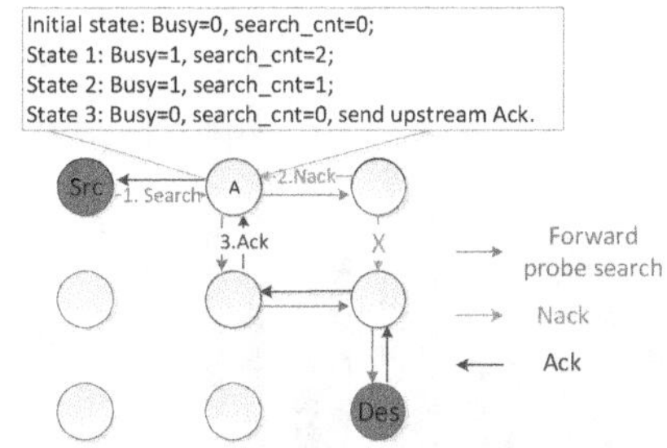

Figure 6: At the beginning, NoCM A is free. At state 1, probe search comes, NoCM A becomes busy. At state 2, Nack comes. At state 3, Ack comes.

out searches. Hence, the value of the counter will be decreased when it receives an Ans signal from the downstream NoCM. The NoCM sends Ack to its upstream NoCM as long as a Ack signal from downstream NoCM is sent back, while sending out Nack only when received all Ans signals (search_cnt=0) and they are all Nack. The busy NoCM will become free again in two cases: i) either receives the Ack or ii) receives all Ans signals (search_cnt=0).

Control trellis graph for search in each partition: If the NoCM is reached by a probe search, it will start the path search in its trellis graph to search the path inside its region. The path backtrack in trellis will start in two cases: i) either an Ack is sent back, or ii) the Des node is reached in this trellis graph. In forward probe search, message of the reached border nodes will be sent to the corresponding downstream NoCMs; and in backtrack, only that of the backtracked border node needs to be sent to the upstream NoCM. Each NoCM sets up the connection in its region.

Ensure the destination only be activated once for one request: The searches belong to the same request but along different directions might reach the Des at different time. The request ID can guarantee the Des is activated only by the first search. Each Des NoCM has a table that stores the ID of last request from each Src NoCM. So when the Des NoCM receives a search, the ID of the received search is compared to the ID of last search from that Src NoCM. If these two IDs are the same, it means they belong to the same request and the newly received one will be rejected. Otherwise, the new search is accepted and the ID table is updated.

Since the forward probe search is along minimal paths and does not wait, the livelock and deadlock are avoided.

5. PERFORMANCE EVALUATION

5.1 Synthesis Results

Using Synopsys DesignCompiler, the NoCM was synthesized with TSMC 65 nm technology. For partitioned TESSA, in 18x18 mesh, it is divided into 4 partitions (four 9x9 mesh partitions) or 9 partitions (nine 6x6 mesh partitions); in 16x16 and 20x20 meshes, it is divided into 4 partitions or 16 partitions.

The area consumption is illustrated in Fig. 7. It might be surprising that the total area of partitioned TESSA is less than non-partitioned TESSA. The reason is that in non-partitioned TESSA, single trellis graph contains the whole network, so its trellis is much larger than that of partitioned architecture, which requires more effort for wiring and more flip-flops to distinguish different nodes. On the other side, in partitioned TESSA, the more partitions we have, the more

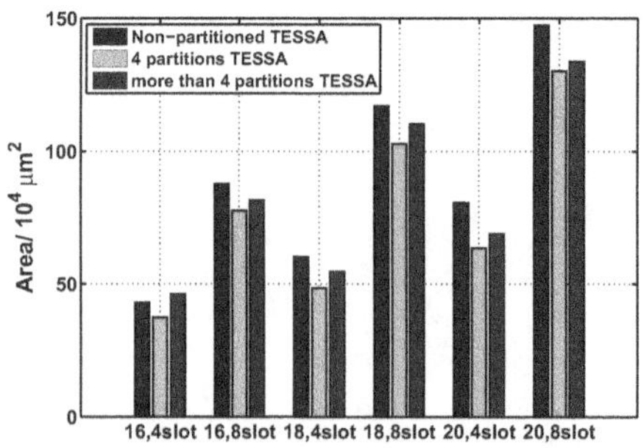

Figure 7: Total area of NoCMs. The x label'16, 4slot' indicates 16x16 mesh with 4slots.

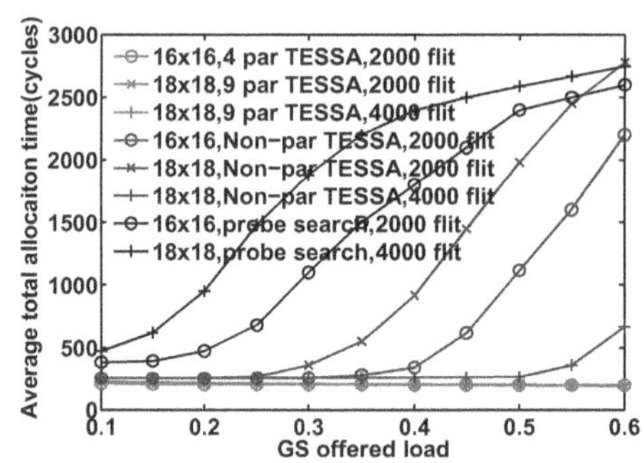

Figure 8: Comparison of allocation speed of two TESSA and probe search.

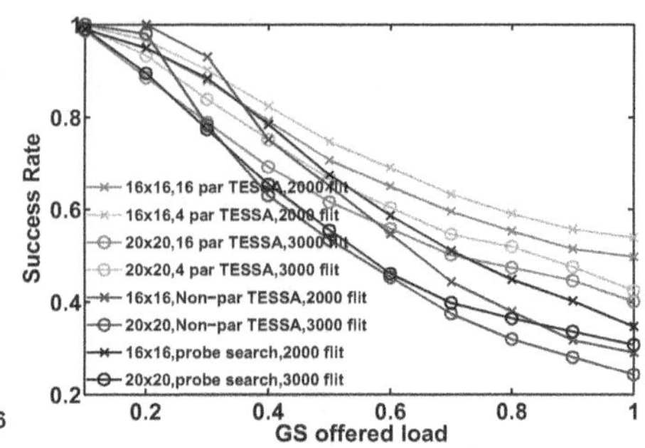

Figure 9: Comparison of Success Rate of two TESSA and probe search.

control logic is required, so using more partitions brings the increase of logic area. Therefore, the partitioned TESSA with 4 partitions cost the least area.

5.2 Simulation Results

The allocation speed and success rate of partitioned NoCMs are compared to the centralized and distributed allocation techniques under uniform random traffic. We re-implemented a distributed parallel probe connection setup approach according to Liu's work [6] for comparison. The request queue sizes of non-partitioned NoCM, single 9-partition NoCM and single 4-partition NoCM are 64, 7 and 16, respectively.

For evaluation several performance metrics are used:

success rate denotes the ratio of successful requests with established paths to the total requests. The incoming requests will be dropped out if the request queue is full.

total allocation time denotes the number of clock cycles for single request that the algorithms need to set up the path or to determine the allocation is impossible, additionally the waiting time for a request in the queue.

GS offered load refers to the ratio of the GS traffic each master offered to its maximum capacity.

In the simulation, half nodes are GS masters and half are slaves. These nodes are uniformly randomly distributed in the system. The connection lifetime, i.e. the number of flits that each connection delivers, is set as 2000 flits, 3000 flits and 4000 flits. The retry deadline of parallel probe search [6] is set to 3000 cycles.

5.2.1 Comparison of allocation speed

In parallel probe search, multiple trials might be needed before the eventual success of search due to the investigation of single slot at once. On the contrary, in TESSA, all slots are being searched simultaneously. As shown in Fig. 8, compared to parallel probe search, the partitioned TESSA offers 7X to 71X higher allocation speed and, furthermore, 48% to 72X higher speed in comparison to non-partitioned TESSA. We can see in non-partitioned TESSA with low request rate, e.g. lower offered load (from 0.1 to 0.2) or longer connection lifetime (4000 flits), the allocation time is reduced significantly. In high request rate, the non-partitioned NoCM is too busy, so the incoming requests have to wait longer in the queue in order to get their turn. However, in partitioned TESSA, since there are multiple NoCMs working in parallel, the requests are usually processed on time without waiting, thereby the allocation speed is much higher.

5.2.2 Comparison of Success Rate

The success rate of simulation results is illustrated in Fig. 9. For partitioned TESSA, the systems that are divided into 4 partitions achieve the best success rate than those with 9 or 16 partitions. Compared to parallel probe search, the 4 partitions TESSA can offer up to 55% higher success rate in 16x16 mesh. In non-partitioned TESSA with high offered load, many incoming requests must be rejected as failure immediately because of the full request queue even though there might be free paths for these requests. Hence, compared to non-partitioned TESSA, the 4-partition TESSA can provide up to 85% higher success rate in 16x16 mesh and up to 75% higher in 20x20 mesh. However, when offered load is very low, e.g. lower than 0.3 in 16x16 mesh, the single NoCM can handle all the requests in time, so the success rate of non-partitioned TESSA becomes the best.

6. CONCLUSION

To address the scalability problem of traditional centralized systems for CS connection allocation, we proposed the partitioned architecture, which divides the original system into multiple partitions with multiple local managers. Since the managers work simultaneously, the computation capacity is increased. As the NoC nodes only communicate with their local managers, the communication overhead is mitigated. The evaluation results also suggest how to divide the system. As long as the managers can handle the requests in time, the system with less partitions (i.e. larger size per partition) will offer better performance.

Acknowledgment

This research work was funded by EuroServer project (FP7-ICT-610456) from the European Union 7th Framework Program and partially supported by China Scholarship Council.

7. REFERENCES

[1] Goossens K, Hansson A. The Aethereal network on chip after ten years: Goals, evolution, lessons, and future, in DAC, 2010.

[2] Chen Y, Matus E, Fettweis G. Trellis-search based Dynamic Multi-Path Connection Allocation for TDM-NoCs, in GLSVLSI. 2016: 323-328.

[3] Stefan R, et al. Online allocation for contention-free routing NoCs,in INA-OCMC. ACM, 2012.

[4] Winter M, Fettweis G P. Guaranteed service virtual channel allocation in NoCs for run-time task scheduling,in DATE, 2011: 1-6.

[5] Pakdaman F, et al. Integrated circuit-packet switching NoC with efficient circuit setup mechanism. The Journal of Supercomputing, 2015.

[6] Liu S, et al. Parallel probe based dynamic connection setup in TDM NoCs. in DATE,2014.

Random Forest Architectures on FPGA for Multiple Applications

Xiang Lin
Department of Electrical and Computer Engineering
Carnegie Mellon University
Pittsburgh, PA 15213
xianglin@andrew.cmu.edu

R. D. (Shawn) Blanton
Department of Electrical and Computer Engineering
Carnegie Mellon University
Pittsburgh, PA 15213
rblanton@andrew.cmu.edu

Donald E. Thomas
Department of Electrical and Computer Engineering
Carnegie Mellon University
Pittsburgh, PA 15213
dthomas@andrew.cmu.edu

ABSTRACT

A random forest is a widely used machine learning classifier. An FPGA is a good platform for performance acceleration of random forests due to their inherent concurrent memory accesses and computational parallelism. Amortizing the cost of an FPGA implementation among different applications is desirable, but the context switch time between applications significantly influences the forest architecture. Several architectures for random forests implemented within an FPGA are described, and the area-reconfiguration tradeoffs that determine the suitability of each for multiple applications are characterized. We show that each architecture can maximize the area utilization efficiency of an FPGA given a constraint on the context switch time.

CCS Concepts

•Computing methodologies → Classification and regression trees; •Hardware → Reconfigurable logic and FPGAs;

Keywords

FPGA; Machine Learning; Reconfigurable Computing

1. INTRODUCTION

A random forest is a well-known, widely used machine learning classifier [1]. It is an ensemble method [2] that uses decision trees, each trained independently on a common data set. To improve their performance, researchers have explored hardware implementations of a random forest accelerator, investigating both training and evaluation phases [3,4]. In this work, we focus on accelerating the evaluation phase of a random forest classifier.

Each internal node in a decision tree of a forest is responsible for a comparison test, consisting of a comparison attribute and a comparison value. Each leaf node has an output class label. The comparison attributes, comparison values of each internal node and the class labels of each leaf node are known collectively as the parameters of a given decision tree, all of which constitute what is learned from the training phase. A large degree of parallelism can be exploited in the forest algorithm, between levels of a tree and between trees. The demand for concurrent accesses to the parameters in a forest is well met by the memory resources of an FPGA, which tend to be the limiting factor in an FPGA implementation of a random forest [3].

Because machine learning is being increasingly used to solve a wide range of problems, the capability to context switch between different applications is an attractive approach to amortize the cost of a random forest (or any machine-learning capability implemented in hardware). Fault detection and tolerance systems such as the work presented in [5] demand moderate switch times between tasks on the order of milliseconds. A system that only uses learning for a single, unchanging task (e.g., a system with a machine learning JTAG security scheme [6]) can be implemented minimally since there is no need for context switching. On the other hand, a system that employs multiple machine learning applications may require fast switch times. Various design scenarios have different constraints on how quickly switches need to be performed between or within applications, which therefore demands a spectrum of architectures that aim for efficient implementation while meeting constraints on context switch time.

This work explores three different architectures: memory-centric, comparator-centric, and synthesis-centric. The optimal choice of architecture depends on the needs of the design scenario which include: forest prediction accuracy, size of the reconfigurable fabric available, and the maximum switch time allowed. To the best of our knowledge, this is the first work to examine the tradeoff between machine learning context switch time and design performance.

The rest of this paper is organized as follows: Section 2 describes related work performed in the field of hardware implementations of decision tree/random forest classifiers, and section 3 describes in greater detail the architectures developed in this work. Section 4 describes example applications for various design scenarios, and section 5 compares the architectures. We conclude with a short summary in section 6.

2. RELATED WORK

In [3], a comparison of various forest classifier implementations on multi-core CPU, GP-GPU, and FPGA platforms

Permission to make digital or hard copies of all or part of this work for personal or classroom use is granted without fee provided that copies are not made or distributed for profit or commercial advantage and that copies bear this notice and the full citation on the first page. Copyrights for components of this work owned by others than ACM must be honored. Abstracting with credit is permitted. To copy otherwise, or republish, to post on servers or to redistribute to lists, requires prior specific permission and/or a fee. Request permissions from permissions@acm.org.

GLSVLSI '17, May 10-12, 2017, Banff, AB, Canada
© 2017 ACM. ISBN 978-1-4503-4972-7/17/05...$15.00
DOI: http://dx.doi.org/10.1145/3060403.3060416

is performed. For the FPGA, a memory-centric architecture is used, balancing the use of BRAMs and distributed flip-flops to store decision tree parameters. The forest is trained using the Compact Random Forest algorithm [3], resulting in a compact forest determined by a maximum depth parameter. The focus in [3] is on tradeoffs between hardware platforms, rather than different architectures on an FPGA. The work of [7] creates a decision tree classifier on an FPGA and examines different architectures that are either pipelined or parallel in nature. These implementations vary classification latency, throughput, and area, but all parameters are stored in memory (distributed and block RAMs). The work in [8] demonstrates an accelerated decision tree classifier by combining architectural techniques and a lightweight addressing scheme for tree nodes. The work of [4, 9] explores FPGA implementations that accelerate the training processes of a decision tree and a random forest respectively, using efficient parallel structures to accelerate the key computational step of determining the optimal comparison value for each internal node of a decision tree.

The aforementioned prior work focuses on the training phase [4, 9], or examines the evaluation phase but relies only on memory elements to store parameters [3, 7, 8]. The work here explores alternative options for storing parameters and the trade-offs incurred in area and context switch time.

3. FOREST ARCHITECTURES

Three different architectures are explored in this work. A conventional memory-centric architecture uses distributed and block RAMs to store the parameters of the random forest. A novel but straightforward synthesis-centric architecture allows a larger forest to be implemented on a given FPGA than the memory-centric approach, at the cost of much higher switch time. Additionally, a novel comparator-centric architecture resides in the middle of the spectrum, balancing switch time and area efficiency.

The implementations of random forests in this work use the same majority vote unit, with the emphasis of variation in the implementations of the individual decision trees within the forest.

3.1 Memory-centric

Figure 1 illustrates a memory-centric random forest architecture. Each tree predicts an output class label, and the predictions of all trees are processed by a majority vote unit

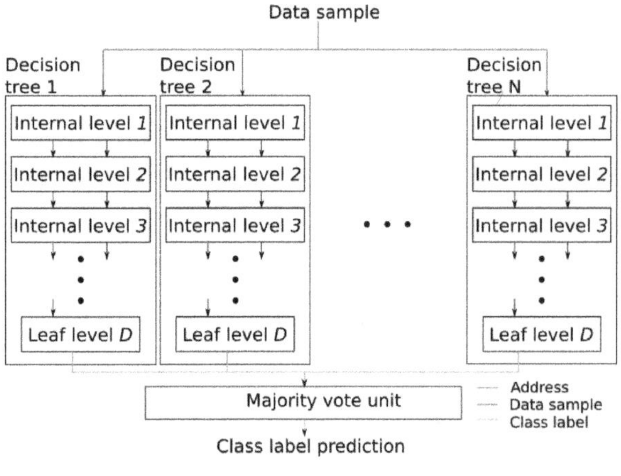

Figure 1: The memory-centric system architecture consists of $D-1$ internal levels and a leaf level D per decision tree.

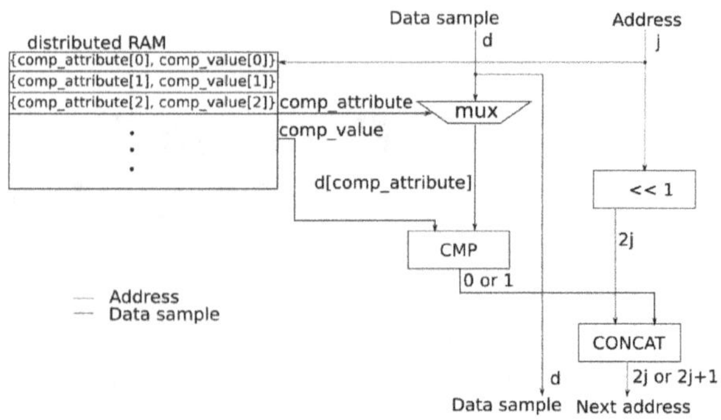

Figure 2: An internal level of a tree in the memory-centric architecture uses the current address to read a comparison attribute and comparison value, which are used to perform the comparison test of the corresponding node.

to produce a final result. Each binary D-level tree has $D-1$ levels of internal nodes and a terminal leaf node. For most applications, very few trees are full binary trees. As a result, each decision tree obtained from training is expanded as follows: each leaf node residing at a depth $i < D$ is converted to an internal node with the comparison bypassed, and has two identical child nodes. Each child node has the class label of the original parent node. This allows the architecture to support any decision tree of up to depth D.

For each internal level, the comparison attributes and comparison values for every node in a given decision tree are stored in memory. A natural choice for storing this information is within BRAM or distributed RAM. Because each data sample being classified can only traverse one node per level in a given decision tree, only a single memory read, and hence memory element (distributed RAM or BRAM), per level is required. The internal levels use distributed RAM, and the leaf levels use BRAM, which results in an approximately equal proportion of utilization of FPGA resources.

Figure 2 illustrates each internal level of a tree. Data samples to be classified are passed through each decision tree from the first level, along with an initial address of 0. The current address is used to read the appropriate node parameters from the memory element, which are then used to test the data sample, determining the address for the next level. The leaf level contains a BRAM, where a look up using the final address received results in the class-label prediction.

Context switching from one forest to another is performed by loading new parameters into the distributed and block RAMs. However, because of the heavy reliance on memory elements, this architecture also demands the largest amount of FPGA resources for a D-level forest.

3.2 Comparator-centric

The comparator-centric architecture reduces the reliance on memory elements, as shown in Figure 3. Note that the parameters for a given forest are static. "Custom comparators" can use LUTs to implement parameter storage and perform the comparison for each internal node, eliminating the ability to change parameters quickly but with the benefit of lower area cost. Conceptually, a custom comparator is a direct representation of an internal node, which is possible only if it assumes the comparison attribute and comparison value are static constants. For example, a 'CC-A2-5' comparator checks whether the second attribute of its input sample is less than 5. Thus, each custom comparator re-

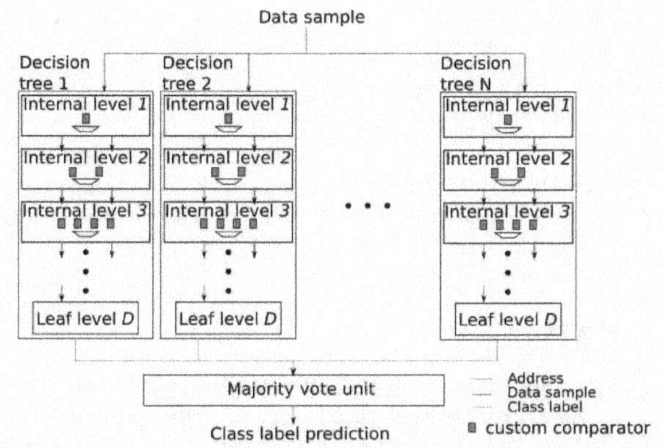

Figure 3: The comparator-centric architecture implements a custom comparator, represented as a gray box, for each internal node in a decision tree.

places the need for a memory element if the parameters are static.

Each internal level $i, (1 \leq i \leq D-1)$ contains 2^{i-1} custom comparators, and a multiplexer to select the output from the custom comparator being used at that level. The leaf levels remain unchanged: a single BRAM contains the class labels of all the leaf nodes per tree. The data flow is similar to the memory-centric architecture: each internal level i processes data sample d in the same way as in the memory-centric architecture, but with addresses of custom comparators instead of memory elements.

To context switch between forests, partial reconfiguration is used to modify each individual custom comparator as needed. An exhaustive library of all possible custom comparators for a given number of attributes and attribute value size can be pre-designed and stored off chip, or designed on-the-fly by a host processor. When context switching, once the parameters of the new application are known, the architecture can switch to the new application by using partial reconfiguration to redefine the custom comparators. While not as fast at switching as in the memory-centric architecture, the comparator-centric architecture makes more efficient use of LUTs to store parameters.

3.3 Synthesis-centric

The synthesis-centric architecture takes the concept of substituting memory elements with combinational logic one step further. Note that a decision tree is essentially a stateless boolean function which takes a data sample as input and returns a class label as output. This boolean function can be optimized by a synthesis tool, eliminating the need for a tree structure and the need for memory storage elements (Figure 4). The resulting boolean function is then implemented using LUTs as logic elements, resulting in a decision tree that has the smallest area footprint.

Data samples to be classified are provided as inputs to the boolean function, with a class label as the output. This design uses almost no memory elements, using only the minimal required for the majority vote unit. However, this architecture has a significant drawback in context switch time. To context switch to a different forest, synthesis of the new forest has to be performed, which can take substantial time depending on the size of the new forest. If the parameters of the new forest are known a priori, the alternative configuration can be synthesized offline and loaded onto the FPGA.

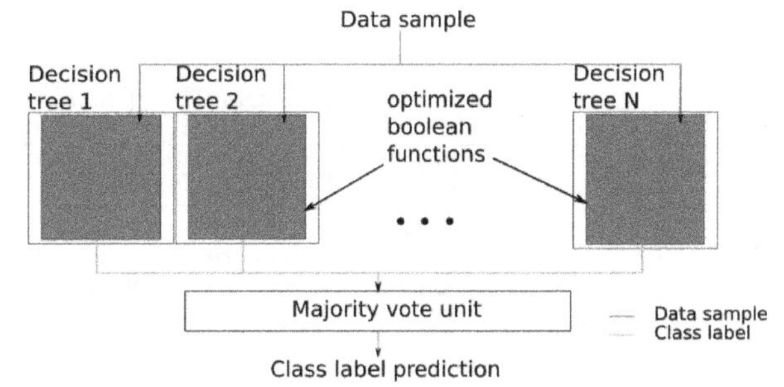

Figure 4: The synthesis-centric architecture implements each decision tree as an optimized boolean function (shown as gray boxes).

However, if this is not the case, then the lengthy process of synthesis will dominate the context switch time.

4. ARCHITECTURE APPLICATIONS

To explore the applicability of forest architectures described in Section 3, this section examines various design scenarios, each of which is characterized by a different switch time constraint. These scenarios include the JTAG security application, the on-chip diagnosis application, and a combination of both. Each architecture is implemented and verified on a Xilinx ZYNQ-7 ZC706 Evaluation Board, which has 218,600 LUTs and 545 36Kb BRAMs.

4.1 JTAG Security

JTAG is an ubiquitous IEEE standard for an on-chip test access port. While primarily targeted for improving testability and post silicon debugging, JTAG also establishes an easily-accessible channel for security attacks [6]. To prevent these attacks, a classifier integrated with existing JTAG hardware is trained to accept JTAG instructions as inputs to determine if the test port is under attack [6].

The nature of JTAG attacks do not change frequently [6]. This implies that changes to the port monitoring hardware are neither frequent nor time-critical, requiring infrequent updates, if any. Therefore, the synthesis-centric architecture is a good match for this design scenario because (i) context switches are infrequent due to the relatively static nature of the test port hacks, and (ii) the performance maximization and area minimization means JTAG operation can be classified quickly at little cost.

Each instance in the dataset represents a series of JTAG instruction sequences, and the goal of classification is to distinguish legitimate and illegitimate use of the JTAG test port. A random forest of ten trees with a maximum depth of 15 levels is trained from this dataset, and ten bits are used as the data width for the hardware implementation.

4.2 On-Chip Diagnosis

In this scenario, on-chip diagnosis [10] uses a classifier to predict the location of a faulty sub-circuit from a group of locations when self-test of a sub-system fails. Different classifiers are needed for each sub-system. It is too costly to simultaneously implement all the required classifiers to cover all of the sub-circuits, especially if only one sub-circuit fails at a time. It is therefore better to have a configurable classifier that can switch based on which sub-system requires diagnosis. Furthermore, while a fast context switch is desirable, it is not extremely critical. These characteristics of on-chip diagnosis suggest that the comparator-centric architecture is a good match.

	Area utilization					Context switch time (s)
	Total LUTs	LUTs as logic	LUTs as memory	Flip-flops	BRAM	
Security (synthesis-centric)	5700 (2.61%)	5700	0	39 (<0.01%)	0 (0.0%)	1.615
Diagnosis (comparator-centric)	88594 (40.53%)	88594	0	88 (0.02%)	10 (1.85%)	0.295
Security and diagnosis (memory-centric)	97720 (44.70%)	10000	87720	83 (0.02%)	320 (58.71%)	0.00164

Table 1: The memory-centric architecture has the lowest context switch time but uses the most FPGA resources, the comparator-centric architecture achieves a middle ground among the architectures, and the synthesis-centric architecture uses the least resources.

Diagnosis data for the L2B cache controller circuit [11] is used in the implementation of the comparator-centric architecture. The goal of this classification problem is to identify which sub-circuit in the failed circuit (the L2B in this case) contains the failure. A random forest of ten trees with a maximum depth of 15 is trained from this dataset, and 12 bits are used for the data width for the hardware implementation.

4.3 Security and Diagnosis

Now consider a design scenario that requires JTAG monitoring and implements on-chip test and diagnosis. For this case, a fast context switch time is necessary. For example, consider the situation where a failure has been detected and on-chip diagnosis is being performed. If JTAG operation begins while diagnosis is being performed, then it will be necessary for the system to quickly context switch to protect the JTAG from potentially being attacked. Such a situation necessitates a fast switch time, which makes the memory-centric architecture a natural choice.

A memory-centric random forest that can switch between on-chip diagnosis and security must support the larger of the parameters of either application. Hence, the implemented architecture can support forests of up to ten trees with a maximum depth of 15, and a data width of 12 bits.

5. ARCHITECTURE COMPARISONS

Table 1 summarizes the implementation results for each architecture, reporting area utilization and context switch time. While area utilization comparisons are straightforward, comparing context switch times is less so. For the synthesis-centric architecture, synthesis of the forest requires significant compute time (~300 seconds). Assuming however that synthesis is accomplished off-line for the classifier or any update to the classifier, the time needed for switching to an updated JTAG classifier is the time to completely re-program the FPGA, which is 1.62 seconds. The context switch time for the comparator-centric architecture depends on the speed of partial reconfiguration. The worst case assumes the use of an external host processor as the partial reconfiguration controller and a JTAG port operating at 66 Mbps to program the FPGA. Partial reconfiguration for all nodes requires 59 seconds if only a single node is reconfigured per reconfiguration cycle. However, the smallest partial reconfiguration frame is 50x1 CLBs, which implies that 200 LUTs can be reconfigured in a single partial reconfiguration cycle. Thus, the ideal reconfiguration latency for this architecture is 0.295 seconds. Context switch time for the memory-centric architecture is measured by the time required to load new values into each of the memory elements. Assuming the worst case, loading one memory value per clock cycle for each of the 10×2^{14} nodes in the random forest would require 1.64 ms at the given clock frequency.

6. SUMMARY

Different machine learning applications have solutions that result in various design scenarios with different constraints on context switch time and area utilization. We explore three random forest architectures that cater to different design scenarios, and suggest examples of applications that represent these design scenarios. Furthermore, we demonstrate the tradeoffs between area utilization and context switch time between architectures, and show how each architecture maps well to a different design scenario.

7. ACKNOWLEDGMENTS

This work was funded in part by the National Science Foundation under contract no. 1314876.

8. REFERENCES

[1] L. Breiman, "Random Forests," in *Machine learning*, vol. 45, pp. 5–32, 2001.

[2] T. G. Dietterich, "Ensemble Methods in Machine Learning," in *Multiple classifier systems*, pp. 1–15, Springer, 2000.

[3] B. Van Essen, *et al.*, "Accelerating a Random Forest Classifier: Multi-core, GP-GPU, or FPGA?," in *Field-Programmable Custom Computing Machines*, pp. 232–239, 2012.

[4] C. Cheng and C. Bouganis, "Accelerating Random Forest Training Process Using FPGA," in *Field Programmable Logic and Applications*, pp. 1–7, 2013.

[5] S. Shreejith, *et al.*, "Accelerated Artificial Neural Networks on FPGA for Fault Detection in Automotive Systems," in *Design, Automation & Test in Europe*, pp. 37–42, 2016.

[6] X. Ren, *et al.*, "Detection of Illegitimate Access to JTAG via Statistical Learning in Chip," in *Design, Automation & Test in Europe*, pp. 109–114, 2015.

[7] J. Struharik, "Implementing Decision Trees in Hardware," in *International Symposium on Intelligent Systems and Informatics*, pp. 41–46, 2011.

[8] F. Saqib, *et al.*, "Pipelined Decision Tree Classification Accelerator Implementation in FPGA (DT-CAIF)," in *IEEE Transactions on Computers*, vol. 64, pp. 280–285, 2015.

[9] R. Narayanan, *et al.*, "An FPGA Implementation of Decision Tree Classification," in *Design, Automation & Test in Europe*, 2007.

[10] X. Ren, *et al.*, "Improving Accuracy of On-chip Diagnosis via Incremental Learning," in *VLSI Test Symposium*, 2015.

[11] "OpenSPARC T2." http://www.oracle.com/technetwork/systems/opensparc/opensparc-t2-page-1446157.html, Oracle.

Exploring Heterogeneous-ISA Core Architectures for High-Performance and Energy-Efficient Mobile SoCs

Wooseok Lee[1], Dam Sunwoo[2], Christopher D. Emmons[2],
Andreas Gerstlauer[1], and Lizy K. John[1]
[1]The University of Texas at Austin, [2]ARM Research

ABSTRACT

In this paper, we explore opportunities to increase energy efficiency by providing cores with restricted functionality, but without necessarily impacting performance. We aim to achieve this by removing support for complex but less frequently executed instructions since instruction mixes used by real-world workloads are often heavily biased. We investigate which instructions are worthwhile to remove by analyzing a subset of instructions in the ARM ISA and their corresponding logic burden in the microarchitecture. We propose a heterogeneous-ISA system to achieve energy efficiency without performance degradation using a system architecture that combines both full- and reduced-ISA cores. Results show that by providing the flexibility of heterogeneous-ISA cores, the proposed system can improve energy efficiency by 12% on average and up to 15% for applications that do not require NEON support, all without performance overhead.

1. INTRODUCTION

Current mobile systems-on-chips (SoCs) take advantage of heterogeneity at the system level by switching between high-performance and energy-efficient cores [1]. These heterogeneous systems match application demands with core types to maximize energy efficiency. In such systems, the heterogeneity lies in the microarchitecture. In bigger cores, more transistors are spent on components that improve performance, such as branch predictors and out-of-order processing capabilities. In smaller cores, reducing the amount of performance-relevant resources can, however, be detrimental to some workloads.

An alternate approach is to implement energy-efficient cores by restricting functionality instead of giving up performance. Specifically, by reducing resources that have less impact on performance, power dissipation can be alleviated without losing significant performance. The benefit of implementing certain features in the Instruction Set Architecture (ISA) is highly dependent on workloads. Not all instructions are frequently used by every workload. If a particular workload favors specific instructions that are not directly supported by the hardware, performance dramatically decreases. By contrast, there is little performance degradation if those instructions are not frequently used.

In this paper, we explore opportunities for systems comprised of heterogeneous reduced-ISA cores to improve energy efficiency. We identify candidate instructions that are complex to implement in state-of-the-art ARM-based systems. We further evaluate performance degradations if candidate instructions are removed. If performance degradation is large, it is not worthwhile to consider removing them despite the potential power benefit. We evaluate system performance with a reduced instruction set running several benchmarks. Results show that some subsets of instructions are critical to performance while others are not essential since in most cases, their usage frequency is low enough to not impact performance significantly.

We propose a heterogeneous-ISA architecture to obtain energy benefits while maintaining performance across a wide range of workloads. In our proposed system architecture, reduced-ISA cores remove hardware support for complex instructions, which increases energy efficiency but requires trapping and emulating of non-supported instructions. When unsupported instructions are infrequent, a workload runs on the reduced-ISA core to reduce energy. By contrast, when unsupported instructions are prevalent, the workload is migrated to a traditional full-ISA core. This dynamic core switching allows the system to avoid the performance degradation and energy inefficiency of software-emulated instructions. As long as they are not performance-critical, a compiler can thereby optimize binaries to remove unsupported instructions and thus maximize residency on the reduced-ISA core. Our results show that workloads without performance critical instructions spend most of their execution time on reduced-ISA cores, achieving energy savings of up to 15%. Workloads with frequent use of unsupported instructions execute exclusively on full-ISA cores with no change in performance or energy consumption. On average, 12% energy savings at little to no performance cost are observed across a variety of benchmarks, where applications migrate between reduced- and full-ISA cores depending on dynamically varying instruction usage.

2. REDUCED-ISA CORE DESIGN

We first identify the instructions that greatly impact logic complexity for reduced-ISA core design and evaluate the performance impact after removing them. As a case study, we select the ARM V7 ISA, and one of the performance-oriented ARM processors, Cortex-A15, as a baseline. We find that the overall number of instructions in an ISA is not as crucial for logic reduction as would be expected. Our study instead focuses on the specific semantics required by particular instructions that contribute to large logic within the microarchitecture. Since the processor is unaware of the instruction until decoded, we regard the fetch stage as an irrelevant block. We analyze the logic burdens of various instructions and provide the instruction distribution of both Android applications and SPEC benchmarks. The details of our ISA analyses can be found in [12]. Based on these analyses, we identify four sets of candidate instructions for removal as follows:

- NEON instruction set extensions including floating-point (FP) and SIMD operations.
- Load and store multiple (LDM/STM) instructions.

Permission to make digital or hard copies of all or part of this work for personal or classroom use is granted without fee provided that copies are not made or distributed for profit or commercial advantage and that copies bear this notice and the full citation on the first page. Copyrights for components of this work owned by others than ACM must be honored. Abstracting with credit is permitted. To copy otherwise, or republish, to post on servers or to redistribute to lists, requires prior specific permission and/or a fee. Request permissions from permissions@acm.org.

GLSVLSI '17, May 10-12, 2017, Banff, AB, Canada
© 2017 ACM. ISBN 978-1-4503-4972-7/17/05...$15.00
DOI: http://dx.doi.org/10.1145/3060403.3060408

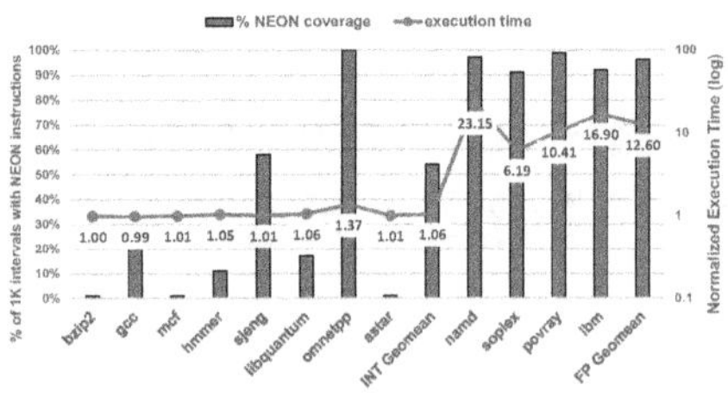

Figure 1: Performance of ISA without NEON instructions.

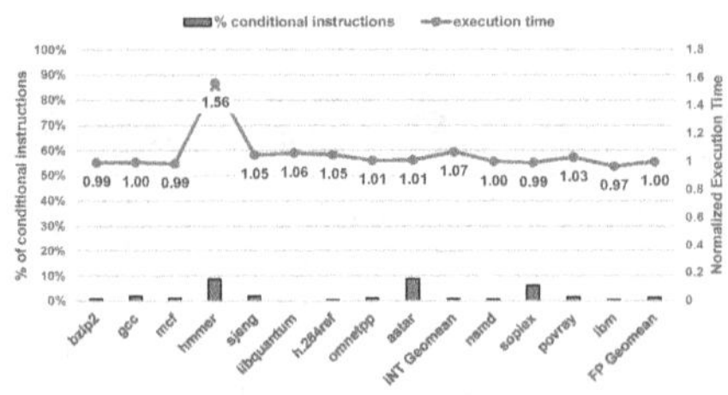

Figure 2: Performance of ISA without conditional instructions.

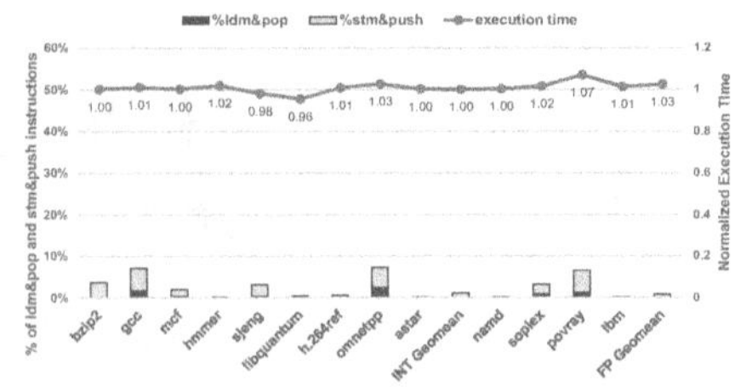

Figure 3: Performance of ISA without Load/Store Multiple instructions.

- Predicated instructions [2].
- DSP-like instructions (QADD, SSAT, etc.).

Reduced-ISA Performance Impact: We define reduced instruction sets as case studies and observe the performance overhead of each with SPEC CPU2006 benchmarks (bzip2, gcc, mcf, hmmer, sjeng, libquantum, omnetpp, astar, namd, soplex, povray, and lbm). We modify LLVM to generate binaries in which candidate instructions are removed. The execution time was measured on an Arndale board [3].

NEON instructions are a large source of logic to sustain performance. In other words, the performance loss from removing NEON instructions is also large if they are heavily used. To measure the performance impact of NEON instructions, we compare the execution time of SPEC benchmarks with and without NEON instructions. Note that since we could not fully remove all NEON code from some of the pre-compiled libraries, there still exist a negligible number of NEON instructions. Figure 1 shows the detailed performance loss and original NEON instruction usage for each benchmark along with NEON coverage.

For floating-point benchmarks, the performance slowdown is significant, ranging from about 6 to 23 times. When removing floating-point support in the ISA, there is no other choice for the compiler than to resort to soft-float emulation. By contrast, for integer benchmarks, which sporadically use NEON instructions, the performance degradation is less than 7% with the exception of *omnetpp*. Since *omnetpp* contains a large number of NEON instructions, the 37% performance degradation is understandable. These profiling result match prior work [5].

Figure 2 shows results for a reduced ISA that excludes predicated instructions. Avoiding to use of conditional instructions is done by disabling the *SimplifyCFG* optimization pass in LLVM. When removing this optimization pass, the compiler also loses the chance to generate optimal code. Thus, the slowdown is not solely from removing conditional instructions. However, since we observed that only a very small number of instructions are changed compared to full-ISA binaries, we regard such effects as negligible.

Overall, the performance loss is less than 5% except for *hmmer*. Removing conditional instructions results in an increased amount of branches in the code. Results indicate that the branch predictor of a modern high-performance mobile processor is good enough to handle the removal of predicated instructions. In case of *hmmer*, further analysis showed that the single hot loop in which most of the execution time is spent shows significantly worse branch predictor performance, causing the severe performance degradation.

Load and store multiple instructions provide a way to reduce a number of consecutive load/store operations. However, since modern instruction prefetch/fetch and out-of-order logic can hide such an increase in instruction count, the penalty of replacing them with separate load/store instructions is somewhat mitigated. Figure 3 shows the detailed performance with and without load/store multiple instructions. The performance loss is negligible across benchmarks.

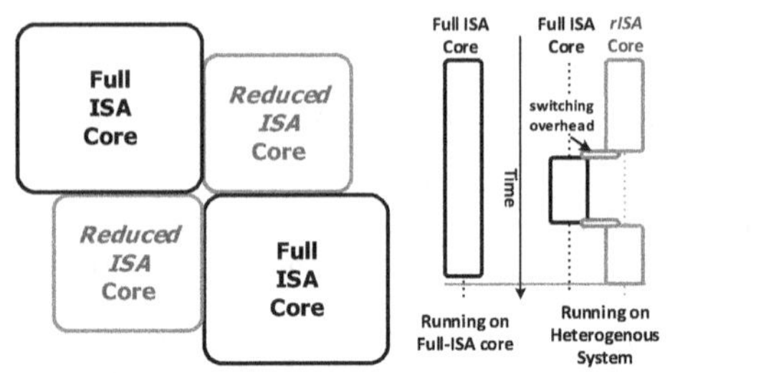

Figure 4: Full- and reduced-ISA core heterogeneous system.

We find that current compilers hardly use DSP-like instructions for most types of workloads. Some of them are never used by the LLVM compiler back-end in the first place. Consequently, it is meaningless to conduct performance comparison with or without these DSP-like instructions. However, despite the fact that we skipped the performance evaluation, a reduced ISA without DSP-like instructions to reduce the logic burden is still valid.

3. HETEROGENEOUS-ISA SYSTEM

We propose a heterogeneous system that contains a combination of both full- and reduced-ISA cores (Figure 4). Traditional full-ISA cores execute applications with no change in performance or energy consumption. By contrast, by cutting down on the instructions supported by the underlying microarchitecture, the logic complexity of reduced-ISA cores is decreased. This allows such cores to achieve lower power consumption. At the same time, unsupported instructions need to be trapped and software-emulated. A compiler can create binaries that are optimized for execution on the reduced-ISA core. Nevertheless, if removed instructions are critical, as is the case with NEON instructions for floating-point workloads, performance suffers severely. In the remainder of the paper, we define *rISA* as the reduced ISA with all the previously mentioned instructions removed.

For workloads with unsupported instructions that are sensitive to performance, a heterogeneous-ISA system can alleviate the performance degradation. When running an application in which performance-sensitive instructions are not prevalent, it is better to run it on reduced-ISA cores. However, when the application is in a phase where it includes performance-sensitive instructions, the application switches to the full-ISA core where it does not lose any performance. The core switching overhead depends on the granularity and subsequent frequency of switching. We present evaluation results for varying core switching granularities in Section 4.

Dynamically monitoring the instruction streams and switching cores based on performance is the best way to maximize energy savings. In this approach, the process scheduler can dynamically map applications to an appropriate ISA core based on the information from hardware performance counters, such as the number of NEON instructions executed during the current scheduling period. As mentioned above, we assume that unsupported instructions are executed using emulation after undefined instruction exceptions

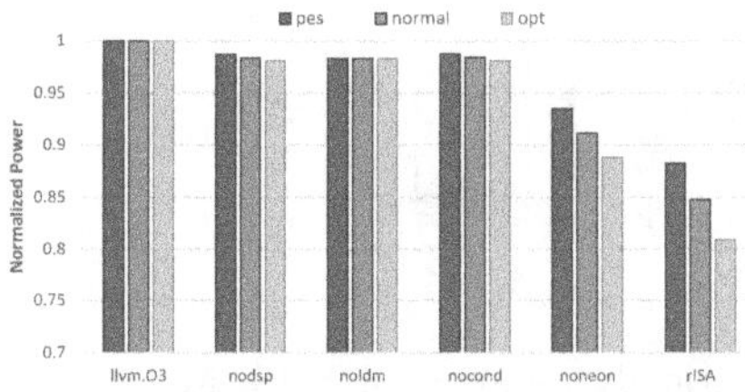

Figure 5: Power estimation of reduced ISA (SPEC CPU2006 INT).

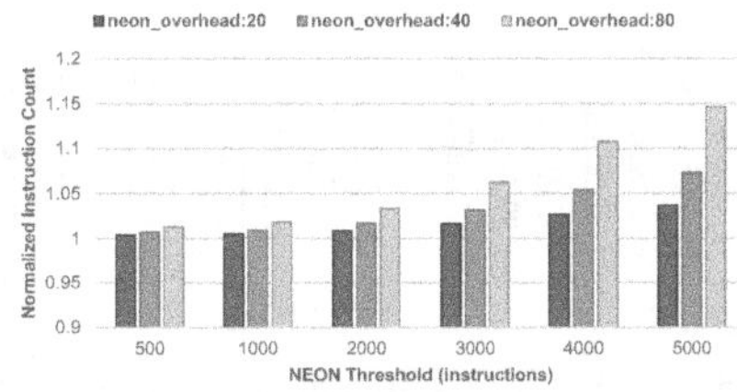

Figure 6: Runlength of SPEC CPU2006 bzip2 with various NEON overheads.

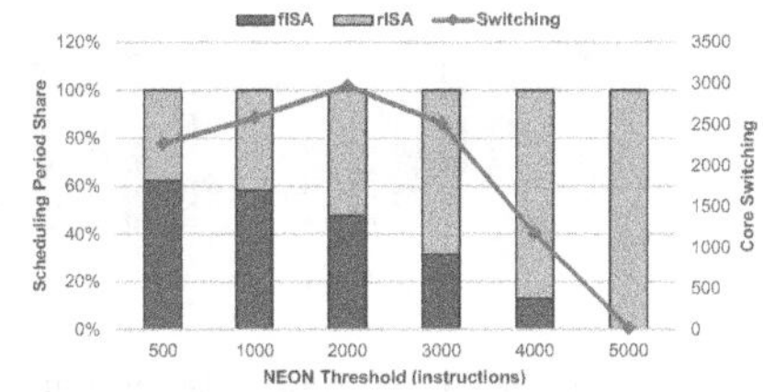

Figure 7: Core residency of SPEC CPU2006 bzip2.

in the reduced-ISA core. This will only be acceptable for infrequent use of the software-emulated instructions. Once the number of software-emulated instructions exceeds a certain threshold within a certain time period, the application should be migrated to a full-ISA core to avoid further performance degradation. On a full-ISA core, on the other hand, the same instructions are also monitored. If the instructions are not used during a certain time period, the application is migrated back to the reduced-ISA core.

For optimal energy and performance balance, we implement a dynamic core scheduling strategy. At the end of each scheduling period, the scheduler determines which core the application should run on based on NEON instruction counts. If there are more NEON instructions than a predetermined threshold, it is better to run the application on a full-ISA core to reduce performance loss. In the opposite case, it is better to run the application on a reduced-ISA core for energy efficiency. Core switching happens when there are consecutive periods where NEON instructions are above or below a pre-defined *neon_threshold*. In this paper, we assume that there are two cores, full- and reduced-ISA, respectively, and no other programs are running. The detailed algorithm can be found in [12].

4. EXPERIMENTS AND RESULTS

Power Estimation: We use McPAT [10] to estimate power consumption. We estimate the logic reduction effects resulting from the removal of the candidate instructions by adjusting numbers under certain assumptions about physical and implementation details. The power estimation details can be found in [12].

As accurately quantifying power consumption is challenging, we give a range of power estimates: *opt* (optimistic) indicates that the effect of the logic reduction is assumed to be relatively large while *pes* (pessimistic) means the opposite (Figure 5). The power reduction for removing most instruction types is about 2% each, except for NEON instructions, which show about 9% improvement. Due to the orthogonality of removed instructions, we assume that the logic related to each instruction is independent, and, thus, those power reductions are additive. Our rISA core shows about 15% power reduction compared to the full-ISA one.

Performance Evaluation: To observe the performance degradation based on the core switching scenario, we evaluate SPEC CPU2006 integer benchmarks using QEMU [4] while collecting a trace of all NEON instructions. We focus on NEON instructions as other removed instructions have little impact on performance as previously shown. We simulate core switching using the previously shown scheduling algorithm that accounts for the number of NEON instruction in each scheduling period. Since switching is not free, each core switching is assumed to incur a fixed instruction overhead. Furthermore, since emulating NEON instructions leads to additional instructions, every time a NEON instruction is executed, an associated instruction penalty is added to the total instruction counts.

Reducing the emulation penalty is crucial for removing instructions. Ideally, it is desirable for an application to entirely run on the reduced-ISA core. However, we find that the penalty to emulate NEON instructions is critical to performance (Figure 6). We estimate the NEON instruction penalty in increments of 20 instructions corresponding to the maximum 20x performance degradation of FP benchmarks. An increase in the penalty per NEON instruction from 20 to 80 directly affects overall performance.

Figure 7 details the fraction of scheduling periods *bzip2* is running on each core and the corresponding number of core switches. The higher the NEON threshold for scheduling, the longer the *bzip2* can run on the reduced-ISA core. This, however, results in more NEON instructions requiring emulation, and, thus, an increase in instruction counts. However, the increase is relatively small. In addition, the number of core switches is low. As such the switching overhead is not crucial for overall performance, and a large switching overhead does not result in significant performance loss. In other words, lowering the penalty allows more NEON instructions to run on the reduced-ISA core.

System Evaluation: Based on the performance and energy evaluation results, we estimate the overall efficiency of our heterogeneous system. The estimated average power of each benchmark is multiplied by the total number of instructions and the square of total instructions to compute energy and energy delay product (EDP), respectively, assuming a constant CPI per benchmark. Furthermore, the computed energy is normalized to the energy and EDP for the full-ISA core in order to observe how much energy savings our system can achieve. These experiments are conducted with a 20-instruction NEON penalty and a core switching overhead of 3000 instructions.

Figure 8(a) shows the estimated performance and energy for SPEC CPU2006 benchmarks. Among the integer benchmarks, we exclude *omnetpp* and *sjeng*; given their high portion of NEON instructions. It is evident that they will run mostly on the full-ISA core. Since dynamic scheduling determines which core to run on next, other applications show diverse scheduling behavior. The *hmmer* benchmark runs on the full-ISA core most of the time due to having more NEON instructions than the threshold for each period, resulting in no performance degradation with no energy benefit.

At the opposite end of the spectrum, *mcf*, *astar*, and *libquantum* run most of the time on the reduced-ISA core with negligible performance degradation, but significant energy benefits. Interestingly, *bzip2* and *gcc* show unbiased behavior. In these workloads, due to the broad range of NEON instructions that vary between 500 and 5000 per period, our scheduling algorithm switches cores frequently depending on the NEON threshold. This aggravates the performance loss with higher NEON penalties and thresholds, thus reducing energy efficiency.

Compiler Optimizations: To optimize energy efficiency, it is better to run applications on the reduced-ISA core as much as possible without losing any performance. This suggests that reducing the amount of NEON instructions is

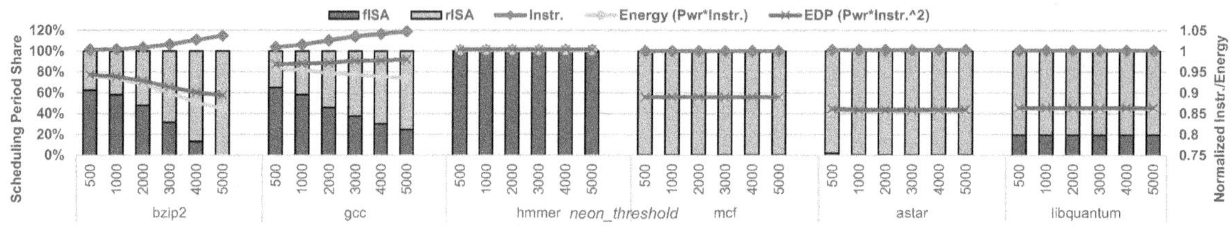

(a) SPEC CPU2006 integer benchmarks with NEON instructions. Compiler statically removes LDM/STM, DSP-like, and conditional instructions

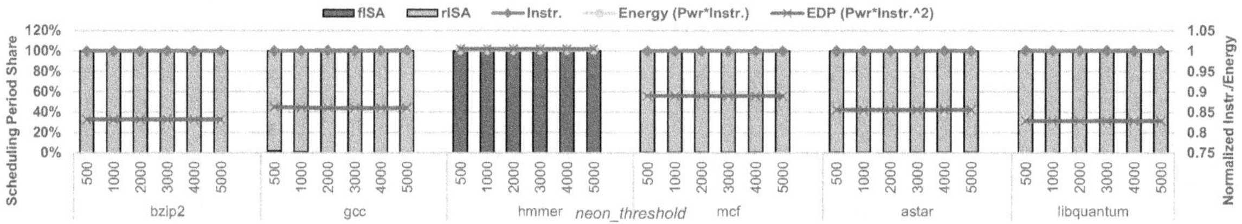

(b) SPEC CPU2006 integer benchmarks. Frequently used NEON load/store instructions are replaced to integer load/store instructions

Figure 8: Performance evaluation and energy estimation.

beneficial not only to maximize residency of workloads on reduced-ISA cores, but also to reduce performance degradation. Thus, we further limit the generation of NEON instructions by modifying the LLVM back-end. Since we observe that vector load/store instructions are frequently used in instruction optimizations, blocking such optimizations leads to less NEON instructions. We measure the performance of the two binaries on full-ISA cores on the real board and confirm that performance differences of blocking such optimizations are negligible.

Figure 8(b) shows the performance and estimated energy of the modified binaries. The amount of time *bzip2* and *gcc* run on the full-ISA core is reduced to zero. This leads to a total energy efficiency equivalent to running solely on the reduced-ISA core. The *hmmer* benchmark still incorporates quite a few NEON instructions, causing it to stay on the full ISA core. Experimental results show that energy savings of up to 15% are achieved for benchmarks that have negligible NEON instructions. On average, about 12% energy savings are achieved across all evaluated benchmarks. Interestingly, with the manipulation of the compiler, core switches are completely avoided, further increasing energy efficiency. This suggests that if a system has control over the compiler, it is possible to prefer and only use the limited set of instructions available on the energy-efficient reduced-ISA core.

5. RELATED WORKS

Kumar et al. first suggested the possibility of increasing energy efficiency by proposing a single-ISA heterogeneous system [9]. ARM's big.LITTLE architecture [1] subsequently implemented this approach for mobile systems. All of these approaches, however, only focused on the high-performance components in the microarchitecture.

Recently, several notable approaches investigated heterogeneous ISA architectures. Blem et al. revisited the debate about RISC versus CISC, comparing x86 and ARM ISAs [6]. Their research quantifies each ISA and argues that there is not much difference between x86 and ARM ISAs. DeVuyst et al. [8] and Venkat et al. [7] proposed a way of harnessing heterogeneous ISAs. However, their research only focused on the diversities of each ISA and argued the benefits when finding the right ISA depending on the workloads. Several prior works [11, 5] investigated OS and software support for task migration between cores with overlapping ISAs. However, their work does not discuss detailed trade-offs in designing actual architectures for such heterogeneous-ISA systems.

6. SUMMARY AND CONCLUSIONS

A reduced ISA core opens up a chance to run high-performance tasks with better energy efficiency. In this paper, we explore and demonstrate the potential with a case study of a heterogeneous system that includes both full- and reduced-ISA cores. Results show that certain complex instructions can be removed with little performance overhead. We argue that in a heterogeneous system that effectively migrates applications to match ISA requirements, significant benefits in energy efficiency can be obtained. Providing heterogeneity in functionality rather than performance can improve energy efficiency with virtually no performance degradation. Results show that our proposed system can improve energy by up to 15% and by 12% on average, all with little to no performance overhead.

7. ACKNOWLEDGEMENTS

This research was supported in part by SRC grant 012-HJ-2317. We would like to thank the anonymous reviewers for their many insightful comments and suggestions.

8. REFERENCES

[1] ARM big.LITTLE Processing. http://www.arm.com/products/processors/technologies/biglittleprocessing.php.

[2] ARMv8 Instruction Set Overview. http://infocenter.arm.com/help/index.jsp?topic=/com.arm.doc.genc010197a/index.html.

[3] Arndale Board. http://www.arndaleboard.org.

[4] Qemu. http://www.qemu.org.

[5] A. Aminot et al. FPU Speedup Estimation for Task Placement Optimization on Asymmetric Multicore Designs. In *MCSoC*, 2015.

[6] E. Blem et al. Power Strugles: Revisiting the RISC vs. CISC Debate on Contemporary ARM and x86 Architectures. In *HPCA*, 2013.

[7] A. V. et al. Harnessing ISA Diversity: Design of a Heterogeneous-ISA Chip Multiprocessor. In *ISCA*, 2014.

[8] M. D. et al. Execution Migration in a Heterogeneous-ISA Chip Multiprocessor. In *ASPLOS*, 2012.

[9] R. K. et al. Single-ISA Heterogeneous Multi-Core Architectures: The Potential for Processor Power Reduction. In *Micro*, 2003.

[10] S. Li et al. McPAT: An integrated power, area, and timing modeling framework for multicore and manycore architectures. In *Micro*, 2009.

[11] T. Li et al. Operating System Support for Overlapping-ISA Heterogeneous Multi-core Architectures. In *HPCA*, 2010.

[12] W. Lee et al. Exploring Opportunities for Heterogeneous-ISA Core Architectures in High-Performance Mobile SoCs. Technical Report UT-CERC-17-01, The University of Texas At Austin, 2017.

An FPGA Coarse Grained Intermediate Fabric for Regular Expression Search

Thomas Luinaud
Polytechnique Montréal
Canada
thomas.luinaud@polymtl.ca

Yvon Savaria
Polytechnique Montréal
Canada
yvon.savaria@polymtl.ca

J.M. Pierre Langlois
Polytechnique Montréal
Canada
pierre.langlois@polymtl.ca

ABSTRACT

Deep Packet Inspection systems such as Snort and Bro express complex rules with regular expressions. In Snort, the search of a regular expression is performed with a Non-deterministic Finite Automaton (NFA). Traversing an NFA sequentially with a CPU is not deterministic in time, and it can be very time consuming. The sequential traversal of an NFA with a CPU is not deterministic in time consequently it can be time consuming. A fully parallel NFA implemented in hardware can search all rules, but most of the time only a small part is active. Furthermore, a string filter determines the traversal of an NFA. This paper proposes an FPGA Intermediate Fabric that can efficiently search regular expressions. The architecture is configured for a specific NFA based on a partial match of a rule found by the string filter. It can thus support all rules from a set such as Snort, while significantly reduce compute resources and power consumption compared to a fully parallel implementation. Multiple parameters can be selected to find the best tradeoff between resource consumption and the number and types of supported expressions. This architecture was implemented on a Xilinx® XC7VX1140 Virtex-7. The reported implementation, can sustain up to 512 regular expressions, while requiring 2% of the slices and 16% of the BRAM resources, for a throughput of 200 million characters per second.

1. INTRODUCTION

Regular expressions are used in a variety of applications such as Network Intrusion Detection Systems (NIDSs). With future 5G telecommunication systems, NIDS will have to support data growth while reducing power consumption. NIDS are thus subject to three constraints : fast search and updates with high energy efficiency. These contradictory requirements pose significant challenges to general purpose processors; thus specialized hardware can be a solution.

In Snort [1], rules are represented as strings and Perl Compatible Regular Expressions (PCREs). Packet payloads are compared to them as per the process shown in Fig. 1. First,

Permission to make digital or hard copies of all or part of this work for personal or classroom use is granted without fee provided that copies are not made or distributed for profit or commercial advantage and that copies bear this notice and the full citation on the first page. Copyrights for components of this work owned by others than ACM must be honored. Abstracting with credit is permitted. To copy otherwise, or republish, to post on servers or to redistribute to lists, requires prior specific permission and/or a fee. Request permissions from permissions@acm.org.

GLSVLSI '17, May 10-12, 2017, Banff, AB, Canada
© 2017 ACM. ISBN 978-1-4503-4972-7/17/05...$15.00
DOI: http://dx.doi.org/10.1145/3060403.3060429

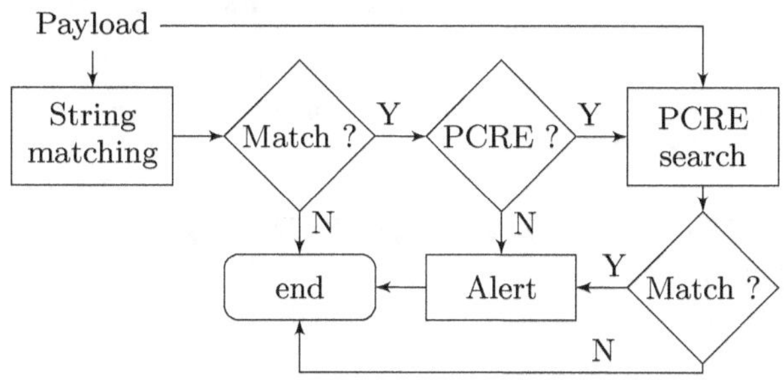

Figure 1: Snort flow

an exact string match is executed. When a match occurs and a PCRE is associated with the rule, the PCRE engine is launched. Finally, an alert is raised when a rule is verified.

Sidhu and Prasanna proposed a VHDL compiler for regular expressions [10]. The resulting system consumes each input character in $O(1)$ by using the high parallelization intrinsic to FPGAs. Mitra et al. proposed to compile Snort rules and integrate them into hardware [9]. Both solutions achieve good performance, but suffer from slow updates. To solve this issue, a re-configurable architecture was proposed by Divyasree et al. [5]. This architecture allows dynamic reconfiguration, but is still time consuming due to the Xilinx partial reconfiguration mechanism. Moreover, this architecture implies that all engines are simultaneously active. Thus, it is not using the Snort string matching result to avoid unnecessary regular expression search so it is not optimal.

The implementation of finite state machines and, consequently, Non-deterministic Finite Automatons (NFAs) on fine-grained FPGAs is often not optimal [3]. NFAs are implemented using multiple-hot encoding, which means that an element can have connections to all other elements. The reconfiguration time for fine-grained reconfigurable architectures is much greater than for coarse grained reconfigurable architectures [7]. In addition, the synthesis time is faster on coarse grained devices due to a fixed placement and routing [6]. A proposed solution consists of integrating a coarse-grained reconfigurable architecture on a FPGA [2]. This concept is also called an Intermediate Fabric (IF) that consists of virtualizing the resources of the FPGA [4].

These observations suggest the use of a coarse-grained architecture. To support the filter, a coarse-grained multiple context architecture is proposed to allow the search of an expression when needed and support fast updates.

The paper is organized as follows. Section 2 introduces the proposed architecture. Then, Section 3 analyzes key ele-

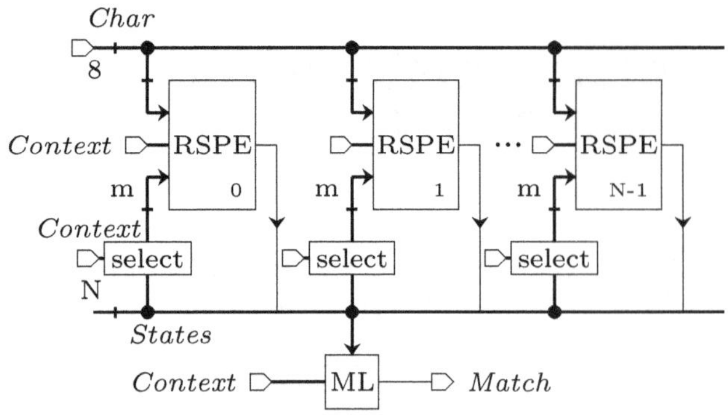

Figure 2: Proposed FPGA intermediate fabric

ments of the architecture, and Section 4 presents the results. Finally, Section 5 concludes the paper.

2. PROPOSED ARCHITECTURE

This section presents the proposed regular expression search IF. It gives an overview of the global architecture and describes its basic elements.

2.1 Global architecture

The proposed architecture, which is presented in Fig. 2, takes as input a character *Char*, and the context number *Context*, from which it generates an output *Match* that indicates if a match has occurred. All the inputs are connected to N Reconfigurable State Processing Elements (RSPEs) described in the next section. Each RSPE output is connected to the bus *States* of size N. This bus is connected to N N-to-m selectors that select the input states for each RSPE. Finally, the *States* bus is used as input by the Match Logic (ML) block to determine if there is a match.

Up to C contexts can be preloaded in each RSPE and each selector. The activation of a context is based on the input *context* and takes a single clock cycle.

2.2 RSPE

Two types of RSPEs are proposed, and presented in this section. The generic architecture of RSPEs is explained below. Types I and II are respectively presented in sections 2.2.2 and 2.2.3.

2.2.1 RSPE generic architecture

A RSPE takes as input an 8-bit character *Char*, the context number *context* and an m-bit state value *States* with $m \leq N$. Thus, each RSPE can receive as input the current state from a number m of other RSPEs. Finally, the size of the input bus *context* is equal to $log_2(C)$. The output of each RSPE is a one bit value representing its state.

The internal representation of a generic RSPE is given in Fig. 3. It is composed of two main blocks: *CVal* and *CMem*. The *CVal* block contains the logic to match the input character. The memory block *CMem* stores the context. In the state validation, *CMem* contains C words of width m. A bit-to-bit AND operator is applied on the output of *CMem* and the input *States* to select the states of interest. An OR operation is then applied on the output to determine if the needed states are active. The complexity of this part is $O(C \times m)$ as it will be shown later. The generic RSPE

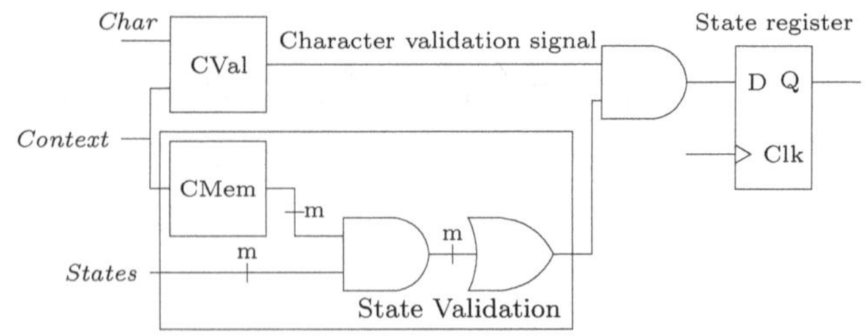

Figure 3: Generic structure of a RSPE

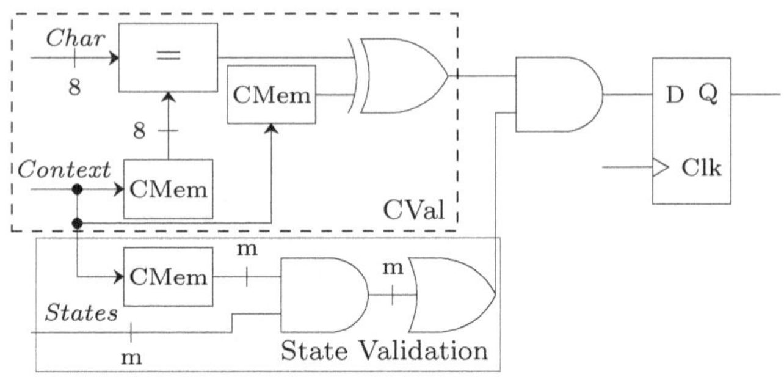

Figure 4: Architecture for the type I RSPE

is adapted in the following sections to obtain two distinct types of RSPE. The difference between those two types is associated with the support of multiple characters.

2.2.2 RSPE type I

The type I RSPE internal representation is shown in Fig. 4. As some regular expressions must ignore one character, this type possesses two modes for character comparison. One verifies if it is the specified character, the other verifies if it is not. This operation can be summarized by: $\bar{A} \wedge B + \bar{B} \wedge A = A \oplus B$, with B a configuration bit and A the comparator output. The character validation logic is composed of a comparator, an XOR gate and two context memories. The comparator compares the input *Char* with the output of the first context memory. The XOR is connected to the output of the comparator and to a 1-bit context memory as expressed in Equation 1, where CM_{out} is the character context memory output.

$$CVal_{out} = (\overline{char} + CM_{out}).(char + \overline{CM_{out}}) \oplus B \qquad (1)$$

The size of the character validation block depends on the size of the memories, which is equal to $C \times (8 + 1)$ bits, so the hardware complexity only depends on the number of contexts C. Finally, the complexity C_{T1} for the type I RSPE is given by Equation 2.

$$C_{T1} = CVal_{out} + C \times m \qquad (2)$$

2.2.3 RSPE type II

The second type of RSPE improves the support of character lists. This type, which is shown in Fig. 5, is configurable to compare up to 256 characters. The character validation is performed through a 256:1 multiplexer. The input of the multiplexer comes from a context memory. The character validation unit has a complexity of $C \times (256 + Cmux)$. Finally, the complexity C_{T2} of the type II RSPE is given by Equation 3.

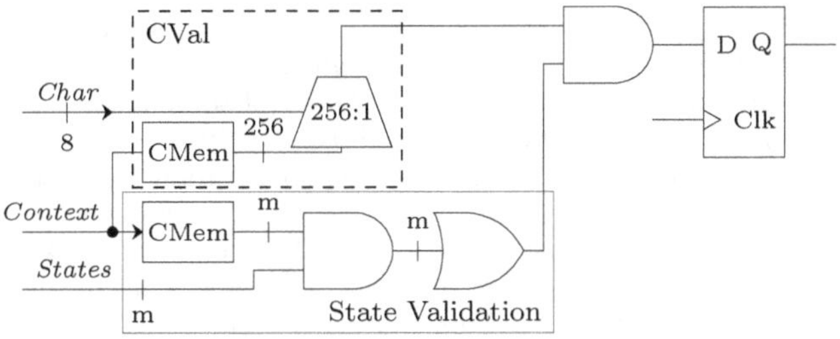

Figure 5: Architecture for the type II RSPE

$$C_{T2} = C \times (256 + Cmux) + C \times m \quad (3)$$

A type I RSPE has $O(mC)$ complexity as shown in Equation 2. Because a list can be separated into multiple states, multiple type I RSPE can be used to implement a list. Thus a type II RSPE requires less logic when a target list covers more than $\frac{256+Cmux+m}{m+1}$ characters.

3. ARCHITECTURE ANALYSIS

This section analyzes the efficiency of the proposed architecture as a function of its configuration parameters. First, a cost estimation of some elements of the design is presented, and then the proposed IF architecture is analyzed.

3.1 Cost of the elements

This section characterizes the hardware cost of some elements of the architecture.

Based on Section 2.2.3, type II RSPEs are preferable to match lists with more than a certain number of characters. It was also shown that the cost depends on m. Therefore, the value m determines when the type II RSPE is preferable to the type I.

The cost of RSPE state validation is determined by $m = N_{T1} + N_{T2}$, where N_{T1} and N_{T2} denote the number of type I and type II RSPEs, respectively. Three elements are considered for this calculation: the size of *CMem*, the number of AND gates that are needed, and the OR gate cost. Since the target platform is an FPGA, the logic cost and the memory cost have to be separated. The cost vector function is expressed with Equation 4.

$$C_{StateSel} = m \times \begin{pmatrix} C_{andGate} + C_{orInput} \\ C_{MemBitCost} \end{pmatrix} \quad (4)$$

Equation 4 shows that the overall cost of state selection is proportional to m. Although in theory up to N states can be required to evaluate the state activation, in practice only a few have to be considered. So, an analysis of the regular expression set must be performed to determine the required number of states.

For an FPGA implementation, the logic cost for the state validation unit can be expressed in terms of number of LUTs with Equation 5 that gives an approximation of the number of 6-input LUTs needed to perform the state validation.

$$N_{LUT} = \left\lceil \sum_{k=1}^{\lceil log_6(m \times 3) \rceil} \frac{m \times 3 + 1}{6^k} \right\rceil \quad (5)$$

Table 1: LUTs and BRAMs consumption after the implementation of the state validation unit.

	$m = 50$		$m = 116$		$m = 200$	
C	LUT	BRAM	LUT	BRAM	LUT	BRAM
2	31	1	70	2	121	3
512	31	1	70	2	121	3

3.2 Intermediate fabric advantages

Using an FPGA instead of an Application-specific integrated circuit (ASIC) allows two levels of reconfiguration. The first one is the IF described previously. The second level, which consists of reconfiguring the FPGA, allows users to adapt the IF to their requirements. In fact, regular expression databases change regularly, the required number of each type of RSPEs may change. In addition, new specialized modules can be proposed. Even if the configuration of the new overlay may require a long time, this type of reconfiguration is manageable because it does not happen often.

4. RESULTS

This section presents implementation results for the two proposed RSPEs and for a specific case of the global architecture. The architecture cost is measured with the number of LUTs and BRAMs. Because the number of BRAMs and LUTs is fixed inside an FPGA, the two metrics are considered independently. The resources consumption after the implementation is given for each type in Table 2

4.1 Tools and methods

Implementations were done for a Xilinx® Virtex-7 vx1140 FPGA using the Vivado 2015.4 tool. Resource usage was obtained after placement and routing. The clock constraint was set to 5 ns. Behavioural simulations were performed with the GHDL software [8].

To determine the design parameters, 394 regular expressions were extracted from the Snort database and adapted to a future IF synthesizer. After compilation, it was determined that 116 RSPEs were needed, five of type II and 111 of type I. The number of configurations was arbitrarily defined to $C = 512$.

4.2 Cost of the state validation unit

Both RSPE types use the same validation unit presented in section 3.1. To validate Equation 5, three values of m were used 50, 116 and 200. Each one was implemented with values of C equal to 2 and 512 to determine the impact of the number of context. The results are given in Table 1. Those results perfectly match the theoretical expectations. They also demonstrate that the number of available context, and thus the number of supported regular expressions, does not affect the logic cost but only the number of memory blocks.

One bit of memory is required for each state in each context. However, the selected FPGA has 67-Mbit BRAMs that can be configured as 512 words of 72 bits. Therefore, to optimize the BRAM usage m should be adapted considering the bus size of each BRAM.

4.3 Cost of a RSPE type I

The type I RSPE is composed of a state and a character validation unit. Based on Equations 1 and 5, the character validation unit is composed of 19 inputs and requires four

Table 2: Resources consumption of the different RSPEs after implementation with $m = 116$

	LUTs	BRAMs	Mux 2-to-11
RSPE Type I	73	2.5	0
RSPE Type II	139	6	49
Global Design	12 827	307.5	250

6-input LUTs. As a result, based on Table 1 with $m = 116$, type I RSPEs requires 74 LUTs.

The difference between the results in Table 2 and the expected ones comes from the fact that some LUTs are shared between the state validation and character validation units. However, those results are close to the theoretical expectations.

In comparison, a specialized unit would consume at least one LUTs for character comparison and state validation, while the proposed architecture uses $73/512 = 0.14$ LUTs per regular expression, that is one order of magnitude smaller.

4.4 Cost of a type II RSPE

The character validation unit of a type II RSPE comprises a 256-to-1 bit multiplexer. This multiplexer is implemented with LUTs to have the same latency because BRAMs require a minimum of 1 clock cycle on the target FPGA. Section 2.2.3, discussed when a type II is preferable to a type I. In light of the results in Table 2, this RSPE type is preferable when at least $\lfloor 6/2.5 \rfloor = 2$ characters are considered. This value is extracted from the BRAM usage of the two types.

4.5 Cost of the global architecture

The global architecture consumes $N_{T2} \times C_{T2} + N_{T1} \times C_{T1}$ resources without the logic to configure the contexts and the ML block. The logic that is needed to write context data is composed of a counter and a multiplexer. An OR gate is used fo the ML block.

With those elements, the cost for all the architecture represents 2% of FPGA slices and about 16% of the FPGA's BRAMs with a clock frequency of 200 MHz which correspond to a throughput of 200 million characters per second.

4.6 Discussion

The presented results are for the case $m = N$, which implies that all states can depend on all the others. However, in most regular expression NFAs, the expression for a given state does not depend on all the other states. Since the state validation unit memory consumption and logic depend on m, correctly defining this value will lead to a reduction of required resources. In any case, the value of m should take into consideration the possible BRAM data bus width.

5. CONCLUSION

This paper proposed a fast re-configurable architecture to implement NFAs generated from regular expressions. Compared to existing solutions implementing NFAs into FPGAs, the proposed solution reduces the reconfiguration time to implement such engines. The proposed solution leverages pre-filters integrated into the Snort Intrusion Detection System. It also considers the constraint of high frequency updates, which is needed in some network applications, by reducing the reconfiguration time.

The paper also presented and validated equations to approximate the logic cost of the architecture. Because it has been demonstrated that the complexity of some elements of the architecture can be minimized, this analysis can be used for the evaluation of tradeoffs between performance and cost. Finally, looking at ways to split regular expressions or NFAs is of great interest due to the ability of the engine to change the context in a single clock cycle. Therefore, it can allow the support of larger expressions with a small overhead on the search efficiency.

Acknowledgements

The authors would like to thank Ericsson Research for their financial support and technical guidance on the project. They also thank the Natural Sciences and Engineering Research Council of Canada and Prompt Quebec for their financial support.

6. REFERENCES

[1] Snort - network intrusion detection and prevention system. https://snort.org/.

[2] N. W. Bergmann, S. K. Shukla, and J. Becker. Quku: A dual-layer reconfigurable architecture. *ACM Trans. Embed. Comput. Syst.*, 12(1s):63:1–63:26, Mar. 2013.

[3] K. Compton and S. Hauck. Reconfigurable computing: A survey of systems and software. *ACM Comput. Surv.*, 34(2):171–210, June 2002.

[4] J. Coole and G. Stitt. Intermediate fabrics: Virtual architectures for circuit portability and fast placement and routing. In *International Conference on Hardware/Software Codesign and System Synthesis*, pages 13–22, Oct 2010.

[5] J. Divyasree, H. Rajashekar, and K. Varghese. Dynamically reconfigurable regular expression matching architecture. In *International Conference on Application-Specific Systems, Architectures and Processors*, pages 120–125, July 2008.

[6] R. Ferreira, J. G. Vendramini, L. Mucida, M. M. Pereira, and L. Carro. An FPGA-based heterogeneous coarse-grained dynamically reconfigurable architecture. In *14th International Conference on Compilers, Architectures and Synthesis for Embedded Systems*, pages 195–204, 2011.

[7] R. Hartenstein. Coarse grain reconfigurable architecture (embedded tutorial). In *Asia and South Pacific Design Automation Conference*, pages 564–570, 2001.

[8] W. J. Landaker. GHDL. https://github.com/tgingold/ghdl/tree/v0.33, 2015.

[9] A. Mitra, W. Najjar, and L. Bhuyan. Compiling PCRE to FPGA for Accelerating Snort IDS. In *Proceedings of the 3rd ACM/IEEE Symposium on Architecture for Networking and Communications Systems*, pages 127–136, Orlando, Florida, USA, 2007. ACM.

[10] R. Sidhu and V. K.Prasanna. Fast Regular Expression Matching Using FPGAs. In *The 9th Annual IEEE Symposium on Field-Programmable Custom Computing Machines*, pages 227–238, Mar. 2001.

Deadline-Aware Joint Optimization of Sleep Transistor and Supply Voltage for FinFET Based Embedded Systems*

Huimei Cheng, Ji Li, Jeffrey Draper,
Shahin Nazarian
University of Southern California
Los Angeles, CA, USA
huimeich@usc.edu, jli724@usc.edu,
draper@isi.edu, shahin@usc.edu

Yanzhi Wang
Syracuse University
Syracuse, NY, USA
ywang393@syr.edu

ABSTRACT

Leakage power consumption has recently become a great concern for modern embedded systems. FinFET technologies, power gating, and near- and super-threshold regimes can significantly reduce the power consumption. However, there lacks a comprehensive analysis of jointly applying the aforementioned power saving techniques. In this paper, we investigate the application of power gating to FinFET circuits operating in near- and super-threshold voltage regimes for embedded system applications. A joint optimization algorithm is proposed to determine the width/length, position and threshold type of the sleep transistor together with the operating voltage constrained to a certain deadline, and with the goal of minimizing energy per operation. Experimental results demonstrate that the proposed algorithm achieves up to 99.9% energy reductions when compared to the near-threshold approach without power gating and 95.3% when compared to deadline-free optimization.

1. INTRODUCTION

Nanoscale CMOS technology, together with wireless communication and sensing technologies, has made it possible to develop ubiquitous embedded systems [1]. Nevertheless, conventional CMOS technology suffers from high leakage power due to short-channel effects [2, 3]. Hence, FinFET structures, which offer lower leakage power and superior scalability, are promising candidates for bulk CMOS structures beyond the 22nm technology nodes [3].

Besides device innovation, Super-Threshold (ST) and Near-Threshold (NT) regimes have proved effective for CMOS and FinFET devices in reducing both dynamic and static energy consumption [4, 5, 6]. ST circuits, for which V_{dd} is much higher than the threshold voltage (V_t) of transistors but lower than the standard V_{dd}, have been reported to attain up to 41% energy reduction compared with the circuits using standard V_{dd} [7]. If V_{dd} is further reduced to the level of V_t, the circuits operate in the NT regime and can achieve more power savings [8]. However, if the V_{dd} is too small, the leakage energy can be significantly increased, as reducing V_{dd} below V_t extends the leaking time exponentially. Hence, there exists a minimal energy point (MEP) [9].

*H. Cheng and J. Li contributed equally to this work.

Permission to make digital or hard copies of all or part of this work for personal or classroom use is granted without fee provided that copies are not made or distributed for profit or commercial advantage and that copies bear this notice and the full citation on the first page. Copyrights for components of this work owned by others than ACM must be honored. Abstracting with credit is permitted. To copy otherwise, or republish, to post on servers or to redistribute to lists, requires prior specific permission and/or a fee. Request permissions from permissions@acm.org.

GLSVLSI '17, May 10–12, 2017, Banff, AB, Canada.

© 2017 ACM. ISBN 978-1-4503-4972-7/17/05...$15.00.

DOI: http://dx.doi.org/10.1145/3060403.3060424

Another effective low power technique is power gating (PG) where idle gates are shut down. In a PG structure, a header (or footer) *sleep transistor* controls the connection between the supply voltage (or ground) and the virtual supply voltage (or virtual ground). The selection between header and footer sleep transistor is one design choice, considering the reduced performance gap between NMOS and PMOS in advanced technology nodes [10]. Additionally, both channel length and width of the sleep transistor should be carefully determined, since a sleep transistor with a larger channel width provides more voltage swing but less energy saving, whereas the channel length significantly affects the threshold voltage (V_t) of the sleep transistor.

Many circuit level low-power techniques such as dynamic voltage scaling, NT and ST operations, clock gating and power gating [11, 12] have been applied to embedded systems. However, there lacks a comprehensive PG optimization method specifically for embedded systems that are dedicated to certain tasks, which jointly optimizes the supply voltage and the sleep transistor parameters (including position, V_t, and channel length/width) while meeting the deadline requirement of the task.

In this paper, we investigate the efficiency of PG in ST/NT regimes for embedded systems, and the objective of the optimization problem is minimizing energy per operation without deadline violation. Simulation results show that significant energy savings can be achieved after applying PG in ST/NT regimes, and the energy per operation is affected by both the sleep transistor parameters and the supply voltage. Based on the analysis, we propose an efficient deadline-aware optimization algorithm, which jointly considers the sleep transistor parameters, the supply voltage, and the deadline requirement, and automatically optimizes the parameter settings in an iterative manner. Experimental results exhibit that the proposed deadline-aware joint algorithm achieves energy reductions up to 99.9% when compared to near-threshold approach without power-gating structures and 95.3% when compared to deadline-free optimization.

2. POWER GATED EMBEDDED SYSTEMS IN ST/NT REGIMES

2.1 Basics of Power Gating Technique

Power gating is an efficient way to reduce static leakage. Such energy reduction is achieved by adding sleep transistors in series with the pull-up or the pull-down of the logic blocks to shut off the power supply when the circuits are idle.

There are typically two operating modes in a PG circuit, namely, *active mode* and *sleep mode*. In the active mode, the voltage drop (V_X) that is induced by the sleep transistor degrades the driving capability (V_{swing}) from V_{dd} to $V_{dd} - V_X$. After the circuit has completed the required calculation, it

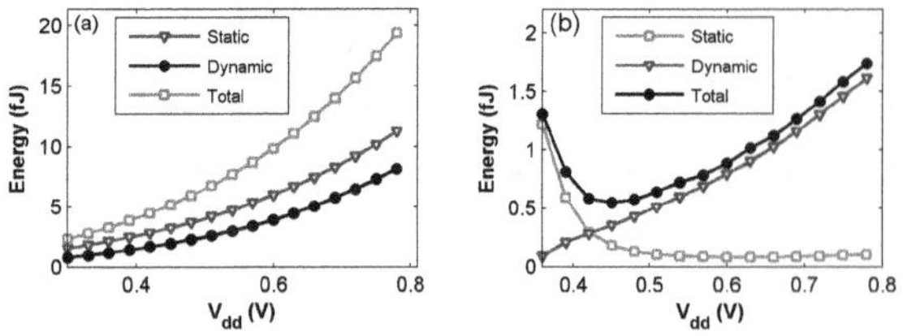

Figure 1: Energy of a 20-stage FO4 inverter chain with different supply voltages: (a) without PG, (b) with PG

enters the sleep mode, where the header or footer operates in the cutoff region and the leakage consumption of the circuit is reduced significantly.

There exists a fundamental tradeoff between performance and energy consumption. Width/length, position, V_t of the sleep transistor should be decided and optimized while meeting the performance requirement of the embedded system application.

For the convenience of the following discussion, we label the sleep transistor selection space as SS, as shown in Table 1. Note that the proposed method can accommodate single threshold library as well. The proposed sleep transistor design method leverages all the aforementioned parameters of sleep transistor (i.e., width, length, position, and V_t) and considers the performance requirement of the embedded application (i.e., T_{ddl}), in order to achieve the maximum energy efficiency while meeting the performance requirement.

2.2 Embedded Systems Optimization

Embedded systems are present in most of the electronic devices and instruments used in daily life. In these systems, the time period during which the circuit is computing a useful transaction is referred to as *active time*. In each operation, the circuit stays idle beyond the active time until T_{ddl} before the next transaction.

Given a relaxed timing requirement (T_{ddl}), ST/NT operation can be applied to save the total energy consumption per operation (both dynamic and static) as long as the active time does not extend over T_{ddl}. The *idle time* is referred to as the idle period when the circuits are shut down between active times. In the case of long idle time, the static energy can be further reduced by using the PG technique.

As mentioned in Section 2.1, during active time, a sleep transistor introduces a voltage drop to the circuit in the active mode, which leads to an increased active time for computation and reduced total power consumption as the operating voltage swing is reduced. The major part of energy saving comes from idle time since PG can significantly reduce the leakage power consumption during idle time.

3. IMPACTS OF OPTIMIZATION PARAMETERS ON EMBEDDED SYSTEMS

Impact of Supply Voltage. It is well known that supply voltage V_{dd} has a significant impact on both the power and timing performance of the circuit. The impacts of V_{dd} on the dynamic, static, and total energy consumptions of the 20-stage in with/without PG are shown in Fig. 1.

The timing constraint is set to $T_{ddl} = 20ns$ (approximately 20 times the propagation delay of 20-stage inverter chain with $V_{dd} = 0.3V$) and the activity factor is 20%.

To be more specific, Fig. 1 (a) illustrates that in the original circuits without PG, both dynamic and static energy decrease drastically as the supply voltage scales down, con-

Table 1: Transistor Selection Space (SS)

SS	(1,1)	(1,2)	(2,1)	(2,2)
Threshold	High V_t	Low V_t	High V_t	Low V_t
Position	Header	Header	Footer	Footer

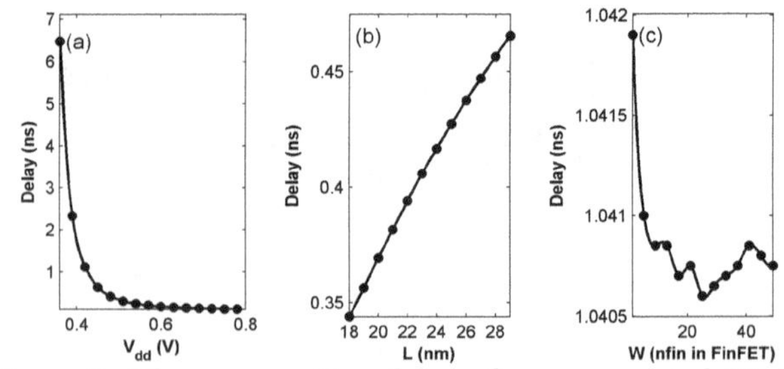

Figure 2: The propagation delay of a power-gated 20-stage inverter chain, with different (a) V_{dd}, (b) L, and (c) W

firming the effectiveness of ST/NT operations. Fig. 1 (b) illustrates the significantly improved static energy performance after applying PG to the inverter chains. With V_{dd} scaling down from the standard operating point 0.8V to the ST regime, the dynamic energy component decreases approximately quadratically. As the supply voltage falls near the V_t of the devices, the delay increases exponentially (as shown in Fig. 2 (a)), leading to a rapid increase in the leakage energy. Hence, there exists a minimal energy point (MEP) for the power gated circuit

Impact of Sleep Transistor Length. The channel length directly affects the capacitance and the threshold voltage of the sleep transistor. Fig. 3 (a) and (b) show the impact of sleep transistor length on the energy per operation E_{total} in a 20-stage FO4 inverter chain without and with PG, respectively.

As the channel length of sleep transistor increases from 18nm to 30nm, static energy can be reduced significantly thus improves total energy efficiency by 80% and 33%, respectively. One can observe from Fig. 3 (a) and (b) that as channel length approaches 30nm, the decrease of static leakage slows down. This is because longer channel length of sleep transistor results in larger propagation delays (as shown in Fig. 2 (b)) and penalizes the overall static energy. Considering this diminished return effect and substantial Engineering Change Order (ECO) problem, we limit the upper bound of gate length to 60% of the nominal value.

Impact of Sleep Transistor Width. We investigate the impact of sleep transistor width on the energy performance and propagation delay using a 20-stage FO4 inverter chain, as shown in Fig. 4 and Fig. 2 (c), respectively. In the inverter chain of interest, gates are charged or discharged mutually exclusively. Hence, the on-current is relatively small, and a very small width can save energy without much performance degradation, as shown in Fig. 4. However, one should be aware of the significantly increased delay for small width (as shown in Fig. 2 (c)) that can potentially erode the energy efficiency gain for a large circuit where gates are not charged or discharged mutually exclusively.

Impact of Sleep Transistor Type. Fig. 5 plots the comparison diagram of energy-per-operation in four SS w.r.t supply voltage, length and width adjustment of the sleep transistors. One can observe that a footer sleep transistor tends to outperform the header for the 20-stage inverter chain of interest (refer to Fig. 5 (a), (b), (c)). In addi-

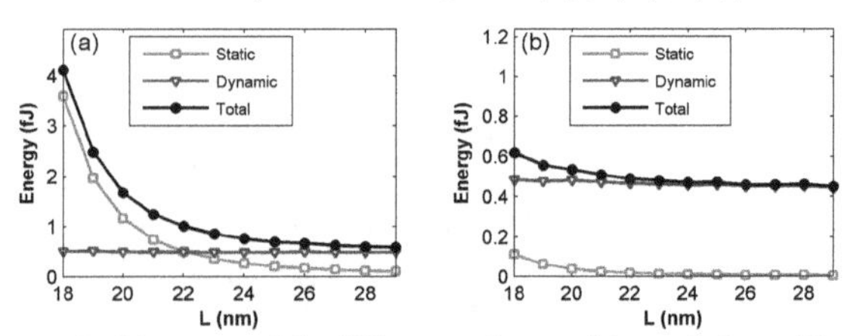

Figure 3: Energy with different channel length in a 20-stage FO4 inverter chain (a) without PG and (b) with PG

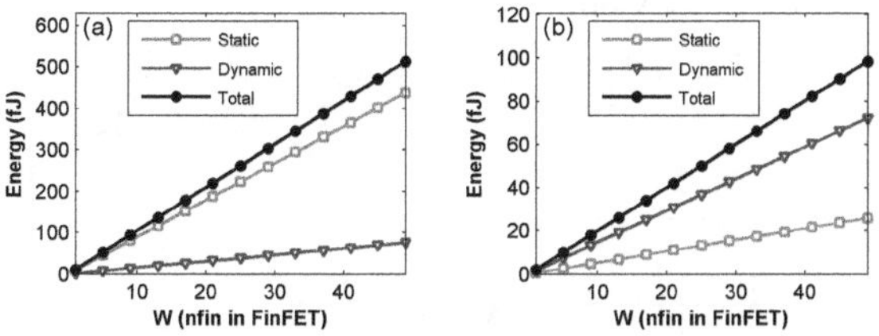

Figure 4: Energy using different channel width in a 20-stage FO4 inverter chain (a) without PG and (b) with PG

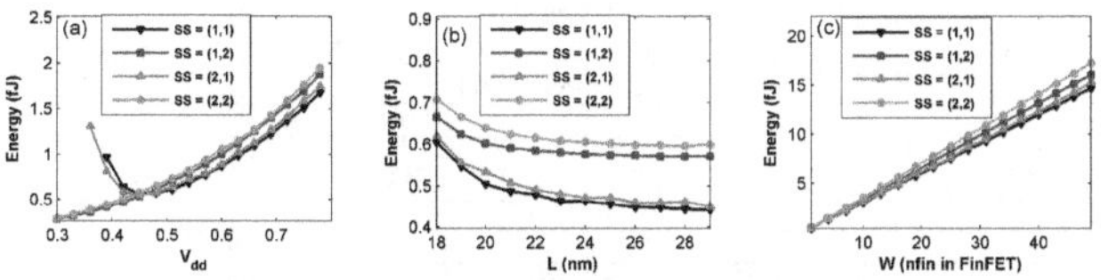

Figure 5: Energy under four SS in the inverter chains of 20-stage with (a) V_{dd} (b) L (c) W adjustment

tion to positions, the high-V_t transistor introduces a large IR drop, leading to a decreased voltage swing for the logic blocks and increased active time for computation. Hence, as shown in Fig. 5 (a), the minimum supply voltage point for high V_t sleep transistors is about 0.43V and it cannot be lower than 0.36V, whereas the low V_t version can reach to approximately 0.3V as the minimum supply voltage. Based on the above analysis, a low V_t footer is a better choice in the NT regime, whereas a high V_t footer achieves higher rate of energy savings in above-threshold regime.

3.1 Formulation of the Optimization Problem

For an embedded system application, the objective is to design and optimize the sleep transistor for the circuit of interest, in order to achieve the minimum energy per operation (E_{total}) while meeting the deadline requirement.

The energy per operation (E_{total}) stands for the total energy consumption during one operation that lasts T_{ddl} and is composed of one active time and one idle time. Dynamic energy (E_{dyn}) comes from switching energy and short-circuit energy in active time, whereas the static energy is the leakage energy (E_{leak}) in active time (E_{leak}^{act}) and idle time (E_{leak}^{idle}). Thus, E_{total} is calculated as

$$\begin{aligned} E_{total} &= \alpha_f \cdot E_{dyn} + E_{leak}^{act} + E_{leak}^{idle} \\ &= \alpha_f \cdot E_{dyn} + P_{leak}^{act} \cdot t_d + P_{leak}^{idle} \cdot (T_{ddl} - t_d) \end{aligned} \quad (1)$$

where α_f is the input activity factor; P_{leak}^{act} and P_{leak}^{idle} represents the leakage power consumption in active mode and sleep mode, respectively; and t_d is the active time, i.e., the total time for the logic circuits in active mode to complete an operation. The term E_{dyn} depends on the supply voltage V_{dd} and V_t of the sleep transistor and can be calculated as

$$E_{dyn} = \frac{1}{2} \cdot C_{load} \cdot V_{dd} \cdot V_{swing} = \frac{1}{2} \cdot C_{load} \cdot V_{dd} \cdot (V_{dd} - V_t) \quad (2)$$

In a power gated circuit, the term P_{leak}^{idle} in Eqn. (1) is much smaller than P_{leak}^{act}, and the energy during idle time E_{leak}^{idle} is negligible if T_{ddl} is small. However, E_{leak}^{idle} plays an increasingly important role when T_{ddl} gets relaxed to more than two orders of magnitude of t_d [13]. The active time t_d is another important factor of E_{total}. According to "alpha-law" [14], t_d is dependent on the supply voltage V_{dd} and the threshold voltage V_t of the sleep transistor, and it can be calculated as $t_d = \frac{C_{load} V_{dd}}{k(V_{dd} - V_t)^{\alpha}}$, where k and α are fitting parameters, and C_{load} is the total load capacitance. Considering the aforementioned factors, the energy minimization problem for an embedded system application is formulated as follows:

Energy Minimization Problem for Embedded Systems.
Given circuit design, deadline T_{ddl}, operation patterns, and the FinFET technology library,
Find the optimal supply voltage V_{dd}, sleep transistor width W, length L, and type from SS.
Minimize the energy per operation E_{total} in Eqn. (1).
Subject to $t_d \le T_{ddl}$.

3.2 Solution Method

Finding the optimal solution using brute-force search takes extremely long time and is impractical for a large circuit. In order to achieve that in a reasonable amount of time, an optimization algorithm is proposed as the solution method, which jointly optimizes the width W, length L and type (from SS) of the sleep transistor together with the supply voltage V_{dd} in an iterative manner based on the analysis in Section IV.

First of all, since the four types of sleep transistors have quite different performance tradeoffs, the proposed algorithm searches for the optimal configuration of each sleep transistor type from the selection space SS separately, and then selects the one that generates the minimum E_{total} among the four configurations. For each type of sleep transistor, the remaining three parameters (i.e., W, L and V_{dd}) are refined iteratively so as to achieve the near optimal performance. Within each iteration, the order of refinement is V_{dd}, L, and then W, which is based on the degree of impact on the performance. The deadline T_{ddl} is provided as input, and the algorithm won't select those settings that violate the deadline constraint.

Algorithm 1: Deadline-Aware Joint Optimization

Initial:

$V_{dd}^{(0)}$	$0.5V$	$\Delta^{(0)}(V_{dd})$	$0.1V$
$L^{(0)}$	$18nm$	$\Delta^{(0)}(L)$	$5nm$
$W^{(0)}$	$1\% \cdot \sum^{allgates} W$	$\Delta^{(0)}(W)$	$10\% \cdot W^{(0)}$
ΔE_{total}	$0.001\% \cdot E_{total}^{(0)}$	T_{ddl}	deadline

```
foreach sleep transistor type in SS do
    Set iteration counter k = 0;
    repeat
        k = k + 1;
        Fix L^(k), W^(k), and test 5 discrete cases of (−2, 2) ×
            Δ^(k)(V_dd) around V_dd^(k). Pick the optimal to be
            V_dd^(k+1);
        Fix V_dd^(k+1), W^(k), and optimize over L^(k) differing by
            (−2, 2)×Δ^(k)(L). Let L^(k+1) be the optimal value ;
        Fix V_dd^(k+1), L^(k+1), and optimize over W^(k) with 5
            discrete test cases around the value of W^(k) by
            differing Δ^(k)(W). Let W^(k+1) be the optimal value;
        if no improvement in the current iteration then
            Reduce Δ^(k+1)(V_dd), Δ^(k+1)(L), Δ^(k+1)(W);
        end
    until E_total^(k) - E_total^(k+1) < ΔE_total;
end
Pick the setting that gives the minimal E_total among the four of
    SS;
return Optimal setting: (SS, V_dd, W, L);
```

For each type of sleep transistors, we denote the supply voltage, length and width of the sleep transistor in the k-th iteration by ${V_{dd}}^{(k)}$, $L^{(k)}$, and $W^{(k)}$, respectively. In each iteration, the proposed algorithm first searches the five neighboring values around the V_{dd} from the previous iteration with fixed L and W. It then refines L and W with fixed other parameters. The varying steps Δ are large initially and narrowed down by half if there is no improvement in the current iteration. This enables a wide range of parameter search at the beginning without the loss of a detailed adjustment after a few iterations. Besides, the search continues until the reduced E_{total} is less than a certain value, i.e., ${E_{total}}^{(k)} - {E_{total}}^{(k+1)} < \Delta E_{total}$, where ${E_{total}}^{(k)}$ denotes the energy per operation achieved in the k-th iteration and ΔE_{total} is the termination value. In this paper, we set $\Delta E_{total} = E_{total}{}^{(0)} \times 0.001\%$. Algorithm 1 provides the pseudo code of the proposed algorithm.

4. EXPERIMENTAL RESULTS

In order to validate the effectiveness of the proposed algorithm, we examine several ISCAS'85 benchmarks, 20-stage inverter chain, and 8-bit Carry Look-ahead Adder (CLA), which are synthesized using Synopsys Design Compiler with 15nm NanGate FinFET library [15]. We extract 20 critical timing paths using Synopsys Design Compiler, and the delays and energy consumptions are measured in HSPICE based on 15nm FinFET technology.

Table 2 concludes the results generated by the proposed deadline-aware joint optimization algorithm. All benchmarks are tested with the timing constrained by 10, 100, 1000 times of D_{org}, which stands for propagation delay of the circuits at 0.3V. The input patterns are generated randomly with an activity factor of 0.2 ($\alpha_f = 0.2$). We compare the energy-per-operation E_{total} optimized by our algorithm with E_{PG}^{bl} and E^{org}. E_{PG}^{bl} is measured under the initial setting of a footer with high-V_t, $L = 18nm$, $W = 1\% \sum^{allgates} W$, and $V_{dd} = 0.5V$. E^{org} is the total energy consumption of the original benchmark circuits operating at 0.3V without PG. Table 2 results confirm that our algorithm-optimized E_{total} can achieve up to 99.9% energy-per-operation reduction compared to E^{org}, and 95.3% E_{PG}^{bl} reduction.

One observation is that a larger sleep transistor (W) is assigned to control a benchmark circuit with more gates. This is because a large sleep transistor introduces only a small voltage drop to the logic block, which helps large circuits gain high peak on-current, finish transactions fast, and enter sleep mode quickly. On contrary, a large sleep transistor is usually not assigned to a small circuit because upsizing the sleep transistor introduces larger load capacitance, logic effort, and the leakage of the sleep transistor itself.

The optimal channel length of the sleep transistor is higher than the setting of the library technology thus benefits V_t increasing and the leakage energy savings, but smaller than the maximum value, which degrades the current sinking capability and propagation speed.

In the tight performance requirement situation, a footer is selected to provide more current capability. As the timing performance become less critical, a benchmark has the freedom of setting SS according to the input patterns and internal transactions. In benchmarks with high V_{dd} to meet the tight timing requirement, a high-V_t sleep transistor that is less leaky can be used to save leakage. Whereas a low-V_t sleep transistor need be applied to support the circuits with high current capability in NT voltage regime.

5. CONCLUSION

This paper has addressed energy optimization in embedded systems in FinFET technologies, by jointly optimizing power gating and supply voltage parameters. An effective heuristic for finding near-optimal solutions under different constraints was presented, and experimental results demonstrated significant reductions in energy per operation.

Table 2: Optimal Configuration under Different Deadlines

T_{ddl}/D_{org}	V_{dd}(V)	SS	L(nm)	W	E_{total}(fJ)	E_{PG}^{bl}(fJ)	E^{org}(fJ)
20-stage FO4 inverter chain							
10	0.30	(1,2)	24	2	0.78	1.06	1.47
100	0.30	(1,2)	22	1	0.98	2.15	7.62
1000	0.30	(1,2)	28	1	1.49	9.07	69.19
8-bit CLA							
10	0.40	(1,1)	25	1	1.12	4.50	1.56
100	0.30	(1,2)	25	1	1.47	7.43	8.12
1000	0.30	(1,2)	24	1	1.53	11.57	63.81
ISCAS-85 c432							
10	0.30	(1,2)	29	1	3.44	35.60	49.38
100	0.30	(1,2)	18	2	5.31	296.77	466.10
1000	0.30	(1,2)	19	3	5.99	1775.87	4635.17
ISCAS-85 c499							
10	0.30	(1,2)	28	9	12.12	57.27	24.12
100	0.39	(1,2)	30	26	14.56	53.42	151.82
1000	0.40	(1,2)	29	2	15.35	60.00	1428.90
ISCAS-85 c880a							
10	0.30	(1,2)	18	37	19.64	42.75	276.43
100	0.30	(1,2)	18	24	23.23	111.96	2726.70
1000	0.30	(1,2)	18	6	32.11	115.64	27228.10
ISCAS-85 c1355							
10	0.32	(1,2)	29	5	7.20	28.59	14.22
100	0.30	(1,2)	28	26	13.71	51.77	47.85
1000	0.30	(1,2)	28	26	14.13	299.83	382.76
ISCAS-85 c1908							
10	0.32	(2,2)	29	3	8.06	57.83	16.88
100	0.30	(2,2)	29	9	11.82	149.92	86.85
1000	0.30	(2,2)	29	9	12.14	160.78	786.43
ISCAS-85 c2670							
10	0.30	(1,2)	20	100	126.45	385.27	1937.57
100	0.30	(1,2)	28	124	140.57	490.31	19285.64
1000	0.30	(1,2)	27	152	169.24	1009.55	192766.34

6. REFERENCES

[1] S. C. Mukhopadhyay, "Wearable sensors for human activity monitoring: A review," *Sensors Journal, IEEE*, vol. 15, no. 3, pp. 1321–1330, 2015.

[2] M. Alam, "Reliability-and process-variation aware design of integrated circuits," *Microelectronics Reliability*, vol. 48, no. 8, pp. 1114–1122, 2008.

[3] J. Li, Q. Xie, Y. Wang, S. Nazarian, and M. Pedram, "Leakage power reduction for deeply-scaled finfet circuits operating in multiple voltage regimes using fine-grained gate-length biasing technique," in *Proceedings of the 2015 Design, Automation & Test in Europe Conference & Exhibition*. EDA Consortium, 2015, pp. 1579–1582.

[4] T. Cui, J. Li, S. Nazarian, M. Pedram *et al.*, "An exploration of applying gate-length-biasing techniques to deeply-scaled finfets operating in multiple voltage regimes." *IEEE Transactions on Emerging Topics in Computing*, 2016.

[5] H. Kaul, M. Anders, S. Hsu, A. Agarwal, R. Krishnamurthy, and S. Borkar, "Near-threshold voltage (ntv) design: opportunities and challenges," in *Proceedings of the 49th Annual Design Automation Conference*, 2012, pp. 1153–1158.

[6] T. Cui, J. Li, A. Shafaei, S. Nazarian, and M. Pedram, "An efficient timing analysis model for 6t finfet sram using current-based method," in *Quality Electronic Design (ISQED), 2016 17th International Symposium on*. IEEE, 2016, pp. 263–268.

[7] J. Hu, Y. Zhang, C. Han, and W. Zhang, "An investigation of super-threshold finfet logic circuits operating on medium strong inversion regions," *Open Electrical & Electronic Engineering Journal*, vol. 9, pp. 22–32, 2015.

[8] N. Pinckney, L. Shifren, B. Cline, S. Sinha, S. Jeloka, R. G. Dreslinski, T. Mudge, D. Sylvester, and D. Blaauw, "Near-threshold computing in finfet technologies: opportunities for improved voltage scalability," in *Proceedings of the 53rd Annual Design Automation Conference*, 2016, p. 76.

[9] X. Lin, Y. Wang, and M. Pedram, "Joint sizing and adaptive independent gate control for finfet circuits operating in multiple voltage regimes using the logical effort method," in *Proceedings of the International Conference on Computer-Aided Design*. IEEE Press, 2013, pp. 444–449.

[10] A. E. Shapiro, F. Atallah, K. Kim, J. Jeong, J. Fischer, and E. G. Friedman, "Adaptive power gating of 32-bit kogge stone adder," *Integration, the VLSI Journal*, vol. 53, pp. 80–87, 2016.

[11] Y.-H. Lee, S.-C. Huang, S.-W. Wang, W.-C. Wu, P.-C. Huang, H.-H. Ho, Y.-T. Lai, and K.-H. Chen, "Power-tracking embedded buck–boost converter with fast dynamic voltage scaling for the soc system," *IEEE Transactions on Power Electronics*, vol. 27, no. 3, pp. 1271–1282, 2012.

[12] Y. Zhou, X. Peng, L. Hou, P. Wan, and P. Lin, "Clock gating-a power optimization technique for smart card," in *Solid-State and Integrated Circuit Technology (ICSICT), 2014 12th IEEE International Conference on*, 2014, pp. 1–3.

[13] M. Seok, S. Hanson, D. Sylvester, and D. Blaauw, "Analysis and optimization of sleep modes in subthreshold circuit design," in *Proceedings of the 44th annual Design Automation Conference*. ACM, 2007, pp. 694–699.

[14] X. Cui, K. Ma, K. Liao, N. Liao, D. Wu, W. Wei, R. Li, and D. Yu, "A dynamic-adjusting threshold-voltage scheme for finfets low power designs," in *2013 IEEE International Symposium on Circuits and Systems (ISCAS2013)*, 2013, pp. 129–132.

[15] Nangate 15nm Open Library, Nangate Inc., 2009. [Online]. Available: http://www.nangate.com/

Energy Savings and Performance Improvement in Subthreshold Using Adaptive Body Bias

Rajsaktish Sankaranarayanan
University of California Santa Cruz
rsankara@ucsc.edu

Matthew R. Guthaus
University of California Santa Cruz
mrg@ucsc.edu

ABSTRACT

In subthreshold operation, circuits are more sensitive to the impact of parametric variation due to reduced supply voltages. To meet timing specification and ensure reliable operation, circuits require compensation techniques that mitigate variation. We developed a design methodology to use adaptive forward body bias and reduce worst-case 3σ active energy, delay and standby energy caused by threshold voltage variation. We validated this methodology on the ISCAS85 benchmarks and improved the worst-case metrics in each case, with no loss of performance. Our approach reduces worst-case standby energy and worst-case active energy by up to 21.06% and 18.80%, respectively, on average.

1. INTRODUCTION

Designing circuits for subthreshold operation is challenging as the impact of process variation is more significant at reduced voltages due to the exponential dependence of drain current on gate voltage. Variation in analog circuits like current mirrors and voltage reference circuits is minimized by using large geometry devices. In subthreshold digital design, however, minimum sized devices are optimal for energy efficiency [3]. For a low target frequency, body biasing was more energy efficient than supply voltage scaling in mitigating process and temperature variation [9]. Reverse bias was found to worsen drain current mismatch and forward bias reduced the mismatch [5]. Gate-level clustering with cluster specific body bias was found to improve leakage power [7]. However, these techniques do not adapt to variation, which could limit their effectiveness. Threshold voltage variation could affect transistor delays on critical paths, which in turn affects active energy, circuit performance and thus overall energy efficiency. Critical path replication [4] or approaches like block-based and path-based statistical analyses [10] have been used to measure this. To accurately determine the impact of variation, the exact critical path and its delay need to be estimated.

In this work, we reduce standby energy caused by threshold voltage variation. We developed a design methodology to use forward bias with a body bias regulator [1]. We use a previous regulator, but, develop a digital design methodology to mitigate the impact of variation. This paper presents the methodology of: finding the optimal number of regulators, determining their placement and assigning cells to be biased by these regulators.

The rest of this paper is organized as follows: We present an overview of proposed approach along with a motivational example in Section 2. In Section 3, we describe details of our design methodology and LP formulation. We discuss experimental methods including variation model, static timing analysis and energy measurement in Section 4. We present results in Section 5 and conclusions in Section 6.

Permission to make digital or hard copies of all or part of this work for personal or classroom use is granted without fee provided that copies are not made or distributed for profit or commercial advantage and that copies bear this notice and the full citation on the first page. Copyrights for components of this work owned by others than ACM must be honored. Abstracting with credit is permitted. To copy otherwise, or republish, to post on servers or to redistribute to lists, requires prior specific permission and/or a fee. Request permissions from permissions@acm.org.

GLSVLSI '17, May 10-12, 2017, Banff, AB, Canada
© 2017 ACM. ISBN 978-1-4503-4972-7/17/05...$15.00
DOI: http://dx.doi.org/10.1145/3060403.3060421

2. METHODOLOGY OVERVIEW

We use the regulator circuit shown in Figure 1 which has an NMOS and PMOS transistor in diode-connected mode that are connected at the drains with their wells shorted. This improves device matching in a circuit (an inverter in this case) by producing an output voltage at which the leakage currents match. Even small variations in the doping profile of FETs can lead to exponentially mismatched drain currents. By shorting the wells, a pathway for the minority carriers exists between wells.

2.1 Variation-aware Adaptive Regulation

Consider an inverter with equal rise and fall times, biased by an equal sized regulator as shown in Figure 1. The regulator is designed to output a voltage of $V_{dd}/2$ since the two FETs in cutoff act like a voltage divider. In the presence of threshold voltage variation, the actual regulator output voltage will be higher or lower than $V_{dd}/2$ depending on the specific FET threshold voltages.

We assume the threshold voltages of NFETs (and PFETs) of both circuits to be normally distributed around the nominal value. According to Pelgrom's model the variance of the parameter mismatch between transistors is directly proportional to the distance between them and inversely proportional to the area of the devices [8]. Given the distance between two transistors, variance of threshold voltage mismatch can be computed using Pelgrom's model. Using variance of mismatch, variance of threshold voltage distribution and uncorrelated random samples from this distribution, we determine the correlation between random variables.

In Figure 2, we compare the worst-case 3σ standby energy of an inverter biased by the regulator, and an inverter biased by a voltage source at $V_{dd}/2$. Well-biases and offsets between wells can have many possible combinations to meet target performance and power. Instead, a simple way to mitigate

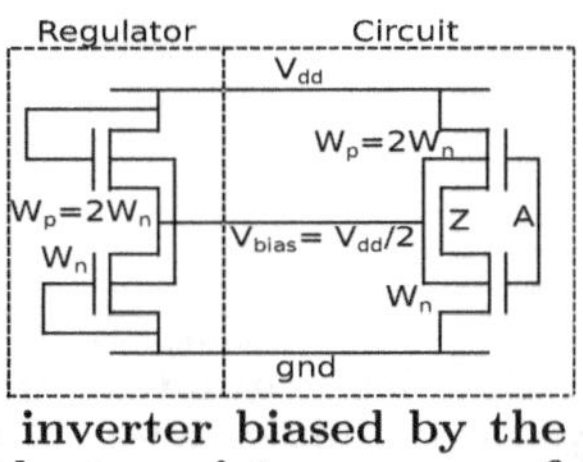

Figure 1: An inverter biased by the bias regulator circuit when the transistors are perfectly matched.

impact of variation is biasing both wells by the same amount. For this work, we use $V_{dd}/2$ because, the substrate current is much smaller than drain current and thus scalable to deep subthreshold voltages. In the case of the inverter biased by the regulator, we see the inverter worst-case standby energy decreases over a range of correlation values which changes over distance between inverter and regulator.

3. ON-CHIP REGULATOR METHODOLOGY

Standard cell design flows use a set of pre-designed library of cells. From Figure 2, we see savings in worst-case 3σ energy when the regulator is nearby and thus correlates better with the cell. The regulator circuit consumes standby energy and incurs area. Our methodology makes a trade-off in the number of regulators and the performance of the circuit. We target filler cell locations for regulator insertion.

3.1 Regulator Design

We use the Nangate Open Cell Library implemented using 45nm FreePDK process technology. The library cells were redesigned for equal rise and fall times in the worst case switching condition. The impact of variation can vary between a cell and its associated regulator, which in turn could affect the leakage current match and hence energy savings. For improved matching, the transistor dimensions of the regulator need be similar to that of the library cells. So, we custom designed a set of regulators based on the functionality and transistor dimensions of the library cells.

3.2 Cell Characterization

The worst-case standby energy of the inverter follows a linear trend over distance between inverter and regulator. So, to use this methodology in a standard cell based flow targeting worst-case energy savings, we characterized all cells in Nangate Open Cell Library for power and performance using cell specific regulators and with the variation model that was used to characterize the inverter circuit described earlier. Using the characterization data, we fit linear models for the worst-case standby energy savings of each cell in the library, as a function of distance.

3.3 Design Implementation

We developed a CAD flow with industry standard tools for synthesis and placement of standard cells and a separate regulator placement and assignment tool. The regulator assignment is formulated as a Linear Program (LP), which is described in the next section. In Figure 3, we show the CAD flow of our proposed design and verification methodology. Starting with Verilog description of the benchmarks, we synthesized them using Synopsys Design Compiler and Nangate Open Cell Library to obtain gate level netlists. These netlists were placed using Synopsys IC Compiler. The placement contains filler cells in the unused areas. Our LP optimizer reads in the placed netlists containing geometric coordinates of the cell and filler instances. Because the regulators consume standby power, we do not want to replace all of the filler cells, but they are candidate locations for regulator instances. Our optimizer solves for the optimal clustering of cells biased by regulators, using LP_Solve [2].

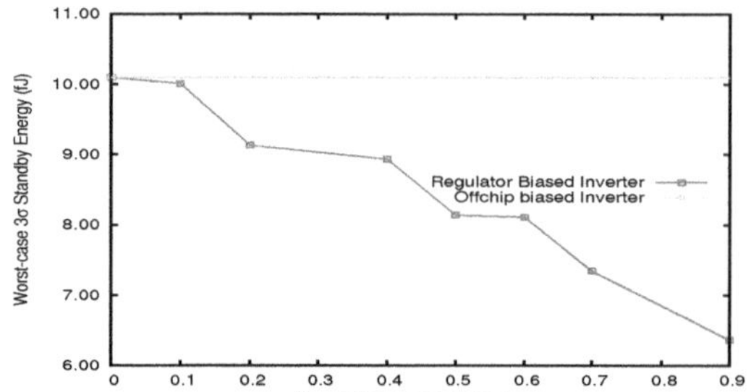

Figure 2: On-chip bias regulators improve worst-case 3σ standby energy better when they are nearby, and more correlated, with the circuit they bias.

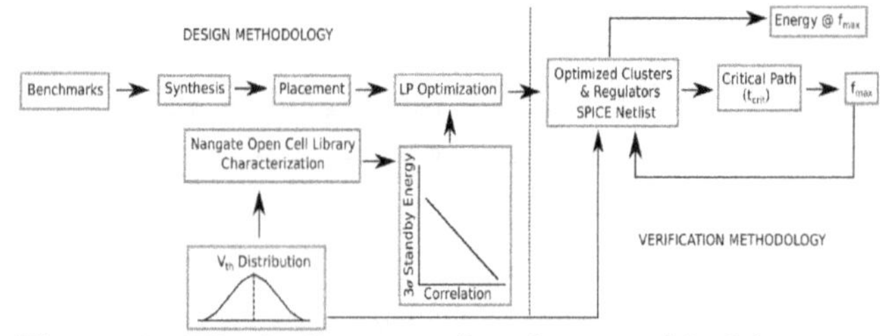

Figure 3: Block diagram showing on-chip bias regulator design and verification methodology.

3.4 Regulator Placement and Assignment

Insertion of each regulator incurs a standby energy cost. To achieve worst-case energy savings at the circuit level we determine the optimal number of regulators, the placement of these regulators and the cell(s) assigned to a regulator.

We model the problem of assigning regulators to one or more groups of standard cells as an LP. We demonstrate two algorithms to solve this LP problem. The first is an exhaustive approach yielding the optimal solution, while the second is a faster, heuristic solution. The two approaches differ in the number of LP constraints formulated and how they generate the constraints.

In the optimal solution, we consider all filler cells as candidate locations for regulators, each of which can be paired with any cell on chip.

In the heuristic approach, we derive candidate subsets of filler locations from the set of all filler locations, for regulator insertion. We then proceed to determine the regulators to make clusters with cell instances. For these subsets, we consider only rows immediately adjacent to a cell, for each cell in the design. Using this row adjacency constraint, we build LP constraints and attempt to solve the LP. If the LP does not converge, we increase the set of rows from which we derive the subset of filler cells, for each cell in the design. Again we attempt to solve the LP. The goal of the heuristic is to determine the smallest number of rows from which the subsets can be derived leading to a solvable LP. The goal of the LP formulation is to identify a subset of regulators from the available regulators and determine the grouping of standard cells to be assigned to those selected regulators.

The LP formulations of both algorithms have identical cost functions and differ only in the number of constraints. So, for brevity we present the equations of the optimal formulation and indicate the areas where they differ.

Both algorithms have similar inputs, namely, placed file containing fillers and cells and the cell-specific characterization data. The output from both algorithms is the gate clustering and regulator assignment. For brevity, we present the heuristic and indicate where it differs from the optimal solution. Lines 2,5 and 6 constitute the iterative part of the heuristic solution only and are not applied in the optimal solution. All other aspects are common to both algorithms.

To physically implement our methodology we leverage features available in place and route tools. We first create relative placement groups for each cell cluster connected to a regulator and associate a power domain with that group. We then designate the output net of each regulator as a supply net and connect those nets to cell bias pins.

- Let m be the number of cell instances in the design.
- Let i be an index variable such that i = *0,1,......(m-1)*.
- Let C represent the set of all cells indicated by C_i where i = *0,1,...(m-1)*.
- Let n represent the number of regulators in the design.
- Let j be an index variable such that j = *0,1,.......(n-1)*.

Algorithm 1: Heuristic algorithm finds clustering of cells and assigns bias regulators

Define : RSS = Row Search Space,
$RSS_{min} = 1$, $RSS_{curr} = RSS_{min}$,
RSS_{max} =Number of rows in placed chip
Input : Placed File, Cell characterizing information
Output: Gate clustering, Regulator assignment

```
while RSS_curr ≤ RSS_max do
    write ILP constraints using RSS_curr;
    solve_ILP() ;
    RSS_curr + +
end
```

- Let R represent the set of regulators indicated by R_j where j = *0,1,...(n-1)*.
- Let a be a constant representing the standby energy cost of a single regulator.
- Let X_{ij} represent a decision variable taking values $\{0, 1\}$ indicating whether a specific cell C_i is assigned to a specific regulator R_j.
- Let Y_i represent an auxiliary variable denoting the cost of a specific cell being assigned a specific regulator from the available regulators.
- Let e_{ij} represent the energy savings coefficient for a given cell C_i regulator R_i assignment. This is obtained from the linear energy savings model discussed earlier, with distance of a fixed regulator to a given cell as input to this model.

The LP solver solves for decision variables X_{ij} which determines the optimal grouping of cells biased by regulators. Our formulation is described below:

$$\text{Minimize} \sum_{i=1}^{m} Y_i + m \cdot a \quad \text{such that} \tag{1}$$

$$\sum_{j=1}^{n} [e_{(i \cdot n)+j} \cdot X_{(i \cdot n)+j}] \leq Y_{(i+1)} \ \ \forall i = 0, 1, 2...(m-1) \tag{2}$$

$$\sum_{j=1}^{n} X_{(i \cdot n)+j} = 1 \quad \forall i = 0, 1, 2...(m-1) \tag{3}$$

$$X_p = \{0, 1\} \quad \forall p = 1, 2, ...(m \cdot n) \tag{4}$$

The cost function in Eq.1 describes the goal of this formulation, which is to minimize the number of clusters into which all standard cells can be grouped, such that each cluster is connected to a regulator. Here Y_i denotes the linearized worst-case 3σ standby energy cost of a cell i from amongst the set of all cell instances C, when biased by a regulator. Summed over the set of all cell instances, our goal is to minimize the cost of clustering all the cell instances in the design. The second term indicates the standby energy cost of the regulators needed to cluster all the cell instances.

The set of constraints denoted by Eq.2 determine which of the cells get clustered together to be biased by a common regulator and get assigned a regulator. The coefficient term is the energy cost of driving a particular cell with a particular regulator. This term is obtained by precharacterizing the cells of the standard cell library and the distance between the regulator and the cell.

The LHS of constraint Eq.2 represents the energy cost of biasing a given standard cell by each of the available regulators. The RHS of constraint Eq.2 ensures this cell is biased by one of the available regulators only.

The constraint Eq.3 ensures each cell has to be driven by a regulator and enables grouping of cells to a common regulator. The constraint Eq.4 indicates X_{ij} is a binary decision variable taking values {0,1}.

The above described constraints apply to the Algorithm-1. For Algorithm-2, the indices of the variables and the limits of the summation are not constant n and instead take variable values based on the number of regulator candidates available in the rows adjacent to each cell.

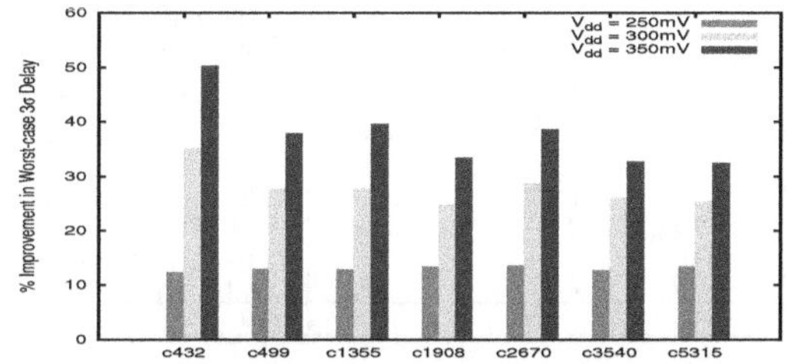

Figure 4: On-chip regulator methodology improves worst-case 3σ delay compared to an unbiased circuit.

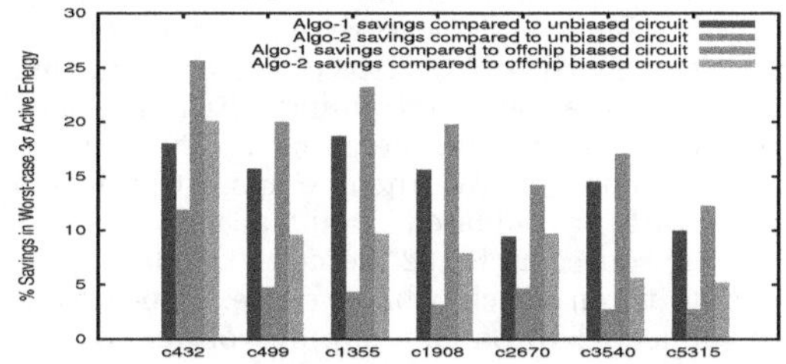

Figure 5: On-chip regulator methodology improves worst-case 3σ active energy using V_{dd}=350mV

4. EXPERIMENTAL METHODS

We use Nangate Open Cell Library implemented using the 45nm FreePDK process as our standard cell library. We designed the bias regulators using this process. The nominal threshold voltages of the transistor models in this process were $V_{th0_N} = 0.4106$ V and $|V_{th0_P}| = 0.3842$ V.

4.1 Variation Model

We consider parametric variation of threshold voltage caused by Random Dopant Fluctuation (RDF). Our input variation model is based on Pelgrom's model given by,

$$\sigma^2 (V_{th}) = (S^2_{V_{th}} \cdot Distance^2) + (\frac{A^2_{V_{th}}}{W \cdot L}) \cdot \tag{5}$$

$S^2_{V_{th}}$ and $A^2_{V_{th}}$ are technology specific constants in the range of 0.01 mV/μm and 0.001 mV respectively. We assume the threshold voltage is normally distributed around the nominal value, with 1σ variance of 20 mV [11]. All instances of standard cells and regulators are subject to threshold voltage variation from the distribution. Given spatial separation between a cell instance and regulator instance and the variance of mismatch between them, we proceed to find the respective threshold voltages of the FETs. For a given mismatch variance, which is a function of the spatial separation, and the threshold voltage distribution, the correlation between the random variables is computed. Two randomly picked threshold voltage values are transformed into correlated values using the computed correlation coefficient, by applying Cholesky decomposition [6].

4.2 Optimized Circuit

Our optimizer reads in placed netlists containing coordinates of cell and filler instances. Considering filler cells as candidate locations for regulator insertion, our optimizer solves for the clustering of cells biased by regulators and the locations of regulators, using LP_Solve [2]. Using the results of optimization and placed netlists, we obtain SPICE netlists containing clusters of cells biased by regulators. We apply our variation model on these netlists.

4.3 Timing and Energy Measurement

Circuit timing paths are affected when threshold voltage variation causes delay variation in transistors. This affects circuit performance and energy consumption. So, we find the exact critical path delay by performing transistor level static timing analysis using Synopsys Nanotime and find the maximum operating frequency f_{max} of the circuit. Using

Table 1: Savings in worst-case 3σ standby energy using on-chip regulator assignment at V_{dd}=350mV

Circuit	Unbiased vs On-chip biased					Offchip biased vs On-chip biased				
	Unbiased (fJ)	Optimal (fJ)	Savings (%)	Heuristic (fJ)	Savings (%)	Offchip bias (fJ)	Optimal (fJ)	Savings (%)	Heuristic (fJ)	Savings (%)
c432	0.92	0.60	41.95	0.87	5.70	1.04	0.60	42.30	0.87	17.12
c499	1.15	0.98	1.64	1.24	-8.13	1.32	0.98	25.75	1.24	6.41
c1355	1.16	0.90	3.30	1.26	-8.61	1.29	0.90	30.23	1.26	2.69
c1908	1.67	1.35	12.52	1.65	1.41	1.74	1.35	22.41	1.65	5.50
c2670	2.00	1.96	4.07	1.98	1.15	2.04	1.96	3.92	1.98	3.06
c3540	1.94	1.80	5.21	1.95	-0.82	2.04	1.80	11.76	1.95	4.03
c5315	2.34	2.16	3.15	2.36	-0.57	2.43	2.16	11.11	2.36	2.97
Avg.			10.26		-1.41	-		21.06		5.96

critical path delay, we then simulate the circuit at f_{max} using random input stimuli and measure active and standby energy per cycle using Synopsys Hspice. We perform this process of applying variation, determining critical path, finding f_{max} and using it to compute energy using 1000 iterations of Monte Carlo simulation. We then compare the benchmark performance with an unbiased circuit and a circuit biased using a voltage source at $V_{dd}/2$, described earlier in Section 2, comparable to an off-chip bias source. Since the regulators are connected to on-chip supply voltage, our results include the energy overhead of the regulators.

5. RESULTS

In this section, we present the results of our optimization process and the impact of optimization driven body bias on energy and performance of ISCAS85 benchmarks.

The run time of our optimization process was measured for several benchmarks using the optimal and heuristic approaches. Across the benchmarks, the improvement in runtime of the heuristic solution, was 68% on average. This is due to the reduced subset of candidate regulators considered for each cell by our optimizer.

We found the active energy, standby energy and delay following log-normal distributions. So, we evaluate the distributions using typical parameters namely mean (μ) and worst-case 3σ. The regulator bias method provides improvement by delivering a forward bias which is adapted to the cell variation in that spatial vicinity. This locally relevant forward bias offers a better matching of the FET off-currents and lowers the cell threshold voltage, thus improving its performance. This increased performance enables scaling the circuit to lowered supply voltages, thus saving worst-case active energy and standby energy.

Since each regulator could output a bias voltage different from another regulator, we consider inter-well spacing for wells at different potential to measure the impact on circuit area. This area overhead spans a range of 17.5% at the minimum to 24.5% at the maximum across all benchmarks with an average of 19.4%.

From Figure 4, we see the regulator method offers improvement in worst-case delay of the circuit for all benchmarks compared to an unbiased circuit. The improvements decrease as the supply voltage is scaled down. This is because, at lower operating voltages, the impact of variation is much higher than the applied bias compensation. The improvement in delay spans a range of 10.89% at the minimum to 50.16% at the maximum. Considering all benchmarks, the average improvement in worst-case delay is 36.93%, 27.85% and 12.74% at 350mV, 300mV and 250mV respectively using Algorithm-2, compared with an unbiased circuit.

From Figure 5, we see the regulator method offers savings in worst-case active energy of the circuit for all benchmarks when compared against an unbiased circuit and an offchip biased circuit. We have verified this using both our algorithms. The active energy savings on average compared to an unbiased circuit across all benchmarks include 14.52% and 4.50% for Algorithm-1 and Algorithm-2 respectively. Compared to an offchip biased circuit, the savings are 18.84% and 9.20% using Algorithm-1 and Algorithm-2 respectively. We can see Algorithm-1 slightly outperforms Algorithm-2 in both cases of comparison, namely against an unbiased circuit and offchip biased circuit. This is because, the optimal solution algorithm offers a wider choice of regulators to choose from, resulting in improved savings.

In Table 1 we list the savings in worst-case 3σ standby energy using our methodology. We compare this against unbiased circuits and with offchip biased circuits using both algorithms. Algorithm-1 offers savings across all benchmarks, while Algorithm-2 offers savings in some cases. In other cases there is a slight increase in the worst-case standby energy. This corresponds to the cases where the active energy savings are also at the lowest, due to the reduced

6. CONCLUSION

In this work we developed a design methodology to use forward bias and reduced the impact of threshold voltage variation. We formulated optimal assignment of forward bias as a LP optimization in this methodology. We reduce worst-case standby energy and active energy by up to 21.06% and 18.80% on average respectively and reduce worst-case delay by up to 37.8% on average. The improvements are available over a range of deep subthreshold voltages.

7. REFERENCES

[1] Andres Bryant et al. "Low Power CMOS at Vdd = 4kT/q". In *Device Research Conference Proceedings*, 2001.

[2] M. Berkelaar, K. Eikland, and P. Notebaert. lp_solve 5.5. *Open source (Mixed-Integer) Linear Programming System, GNU LGPL*, 2004.

[3] B. H. Calhoun, A. Wang, and A. P. Chandrakasan. "Device Sizing for Minimum Energy Operation in Subthreshold Circuits". In *CICC Proceedings*, 2004.

[4] I. J. Chang, S. P. Park, and K. Roy. "Exploring Asynchronous Design Techniques for Process-Tolerant and Energy-Efficient Subthreshold Operation". *IEEE JSSC*, 45(2), February 2010.

[5] M. J. Chen, J. S. Ho, and T. H. Huang. "Dependence of Current Match on Back-Gate Bias in Weakly Inverted MOS Transistors and Its Modeling". *IEEE JSSC*, 31(2), February 1996.

[6] P. E. Gill, W. Murray, and M. H. Wright. *Numerical Linear Algebra and Optimization*, volume 1. Addison-Wesley Publishing Company, 1991.

[7] S. Kulkarni, D. Sylvester, and D. Blaauw. A Statistical Framework for Post-Silicon Tuning through Body Bias Clustering. In *ICCAD Proceedings*, 2006.

[8] M. J. M. Pelgrom, A. C. Duinmaijer, and A. P. Welbers. "Matching Properties of MOS Transistors". *IEEE JSSC*, 24(5), October 1989.

[9] Scott Hanson et al. "Exploring Variability and Performance in a Sub-200mV Processor". *IEEE JSSC*, 43(4), April 2008.

[10] A. Srivastava, D. Sylvester, and D. Blaauw. *Statistical Analysis and Optimization for VLSI: Timing and Power.* Springer, 2005.

[11] Yun Ye et al. "Statistical Modeling and Simulation of Threshold Variation Under Random Dopant Fluctuations and Line-Edge Roughness". *IEEE TVLSI*, 19(6), June 2011.

Low Voltage Stochastic Flash ADC with Front-end of Inverter-based Comparative Unit

Xuncheng Zou, Bo Liu, and Shigetoshi Nakatake
1-1 Hibikino, Wakamatsu, Kitakyushu, Fukuoka 808-0135, Japan
naka-lab@is.env.kitakyu-u.ac.jp

ABSTRACT

This paper presents a low supply voltage design of stochastic flash ADC, introducing an inverter-based comparative unit which is used as the front-end. A stochastic flash ADC has a significant advantage in reducing the supply voltage, while it needs a large number of comparators even for middle-level resolution. A key of our design is in the simplicity of the structure, and it enables us to decrease the number of transistors by replacing a comparator with a chain of inverters. Plus, the supply voltage can go down to 0.6V on 65nm process, as well as it can be designed with fully digital standard cells. We introduce a latch circuit combining with the chain of inverters for the signal stability, and discuss about an appropriate circuit structure for the resolution by analyzing three different structures. In the simulation, we demonstrate fundamental but promising results for a low voltage ADC design.

Keywords

low voltage, analog-to-digital converter, stochastic flash ADC, inverter-chain

1. INTRODUCTION

An analog signal comes into the ADC, and a digital result would be generated. Accomplishing this transformation needs comparator generally, which plays an important role in transformation from analog signal to digital signal. However, a device mismatch induced by the process variation results in a comparator offset, and produces input-referred offsets which would affect the linearity of conversion function of ADC. As the process becomes finer, the comparator offset is becoming one of critical factors for designer to design a good ADC. To deal with issues of the comparator offset, some of researches had been done to reduce or cancel the comparator offset using special techniques [1, 2, 3], but would cost a larger design overhead. [4] has proposed a stochastic ADC, which aggressively makes use of the comparator offset variability rather than leaving nothing to do.

Permission to make digital or hard copies of all or part of this work for personal or classroom use is granted without fee provided that copies are not made or distributed for profit or commercial advantage and that copies bear this notice and the full citation on the first page. Copyrights for components of this work owned by others than ACM must be honored. Abstracting with credit is permitted. To copy otherwise, or republish, to post on servers or to redistribute to lists, requires prior specific permission and/or a fee. Request permissions from permissions@acm.org.

GLSVLSI '17, May 10-12, 2017, Banff, AB, Canada

© 2017 ACM. ISBN 978-1-4503-4972-7/17/05...$15.00

DOI: http://dx.doi.org/10.1145/3060403.3060466

Targeting a flash architecture based on the idea of the stochastic ADC, [5] has analyzed a cumulative distribution function (CDF) of offsets among a lot of comparators induced by the process variation, and presented a stochastic flash ADC, proposing a conversion mechanism to employ an approximately linear section of the cumulative distribution function as the conversion function. As shown in Fig. 1(a), in a stochastic flash ADC, an input signal line and a common reference voltage are connected to the inputs of comparators. Plus, following on the heels of a group of comparators, a Wallace Tree adder [6] is used to sum up the number of logic '1' from all comparator outputs. Note that this architecture has no resistor-ladder, and the cumulative distribution of comparator-offsets plays a role of a series of trip points by the resistor-ladder. It means we can aggressively decrease the supply voltage.

[7] proposes a 3-input NAND-based comparator to replace an analog comparator, and realizes a digital synthesized stochastic flash ADC. In [5] and [7], however, both of their single comparators cost 24 transistors, and it could be a fatal defect to large-scale adoption of comparators and would increase the area of design. In [8], a fully differential comparator circuit is introduced to the stochastic ADC but capacitors of which would increase the power consumption and design area.

This paper introduces an inverter-based comparative unit to a stochastic flash ADC, substituting for an analog comparator. The unit is composed of a chain of inverters and a latch circuit, and total number of transistors is only 8 to 12. A latch circuit is designed combining with the chain of inverters for the signal stability. Besides, providing different circuit structures of the unit, we discuss about an appropriate structure for the resolution by observing the simulation results on 65nm process. Plus, the supply voltage can go down to 0.6V on 65nm process, as well as it can be designed with fully digital standard cells.

The rest of the paper is organized as follows. Section 2 is devoted into describing our proposed inverter-based comparative unit and Section 3 discusses about an appropriate circuit structure of our unit based on the simulation results. Section 4 concludes this work.

2. INVERTER-BASED COMPARATIVE UNIT

In this section, we attempt to find a simpler circuit which can be used instead of a conventional comparator in the front-end of a stochastic flash ADC.

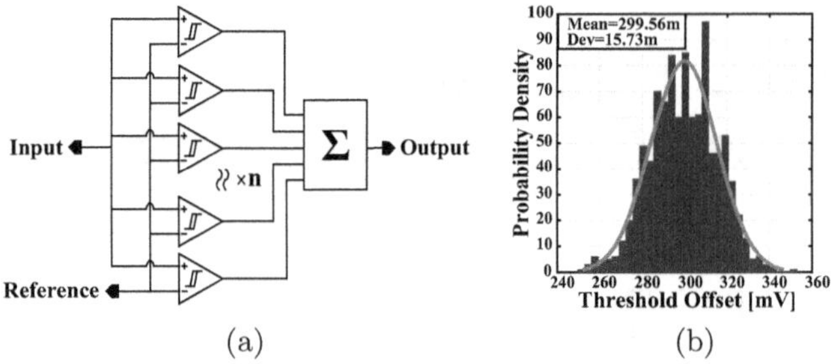

Figure 1: (a) Stochastic flash ADC and (b) Probability density function (PDF) of the threshold voltage of an inverter.

2.1 Inverter and Inverter-chain

In terms of an ideal comparator, when an input is connected to a negative port as well as a reference is connected to a positive port, it has a similar function of an ideal inverter, if regarding the reference voltage of the comparator as the inverter's threshold voltage.

Fig. 1(b) shows the 1000 times Monte Carlo simulation results on 65nm process. The supply voltage is set to 0.6V. Here, a ramp signal is given to an inverter, and the input voltage is regarded as the threshold voltage when the input is equal to the output. Obviously, a set of the threshold voltages are also distributed according to a Gaussian distribution due to the process-induced variation.

In addition, tuning the transistor size of the inverter can adjust the mean and deviation of the threshold voltages. Hence, an inverter could be a substitution for a comparator in a stochastic flash ADC in terms of theory.

However, some of comparators include regenerative latch, and it helps comparator quickly judge the magnitude between input signal and reference voltage, and then outputs a logic level, but an inverter can not do when the input voltage is in the transitional region.

It is well known that, when input signal comes into an inverter chain, it would be pulled up or pulled down according to the number of inverters, and converges to a logic level. It is called a regenerative function of inverter-chain and can be used to compensate the defect of a single inverter. See Fig. 2(a) and (b).

However, even if employing an inverter-chain, the output of the inverter is unable to keep a signal state when the input signal changes, which influences to an additive operation in Wallace Tree adder.

Thus, only inverter or inverter-chain is not sufficient to replace a comparator yet.

2.2 D-latch

Since the output of the inverter-chain cannot latch a signal state when the input signal changes, we introduce a D-latch combining with the inverter-chain. Fig. 3 shows the schematic of D-latch, which consists of two inverters (INV) and two transmission gates (TG). Two inverters inside the D-latch work as an inverter-chain.

Furthermore, we introduce two clocks, CA and CB for controlling the two transmission gates to strongly keep the state. In our design, CB lags 20ns behind CA, so that the D-latch mainly works at the following three stages.

Stage 1: When CA and CB are high, TG1 is open and TG2 is closed. An input signal is pulled up or pulled down by the regenerative function of inverter-chain.

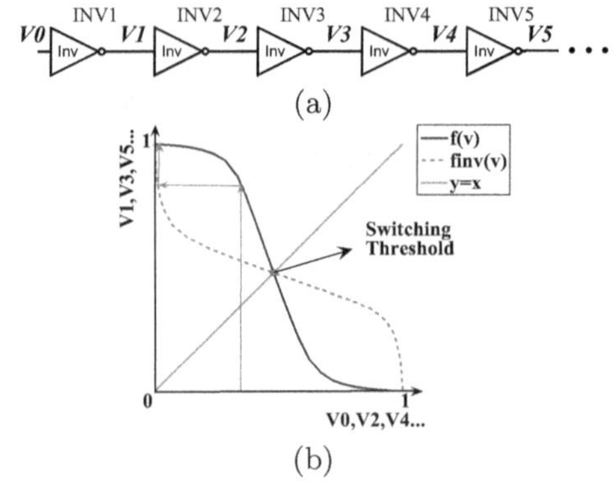

Figure 2: (a) Inverter-chain and (b) Regenerative function of an inverter-chain.

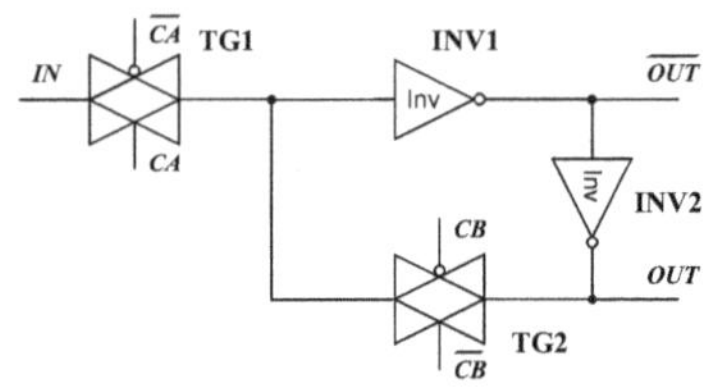

Figure 3: D-latch (structure-1).

Stage 2: CA becomes low but CB is still high due to the lag of CB in a short period. Both of TG1 and TG2 are closed. Signal keeps almost invariant in the meanwhile even if TG1 has been closed.

Stage 3: When both of CA and CB are low, TG1 is closed and TG2 becomes open. INV1 and INV2 configure a loop circuit. The signal is converged into a state in the loop analogously to the behavior at Stage 1.

As mentioned above, an analog signal is converted to a digital signal through three stages. We illustrate the signal transient analysis result in Fig. 4. As seen in the figure, however, a hopping on signal happens and is magnified by two inverters when CA at the transmission gate changes. The loop circuit responds to the hopping swiftly and might lead to a wrong logic value, which would deteriorate the resolution in the conversion.

In this design, a dual clocking constitutive of CA and CB is used to avoid errors by the hopping to some extent. The magnifying hopping is pulled to wrong logic voltage swiftly, but it gives a sufficient time to a signal so that signal can return almost to primary voltage level. Without doubt, suitably tuning transistor sizes of TG1 and TG2 is also necessary. Here, a tuning of TG1 is for keeping the signal almost at the same voltage level before and after the hopping. The transistor size of TG2 is adjusted for distinguishing a logic of a signal correctly at Stage 3.

3. DESIGN CASES AND SIMULATION RESULTS

The middle voltage nearby the switching threshold is more difficult for the D-latch to distinguish an appropriate logic.

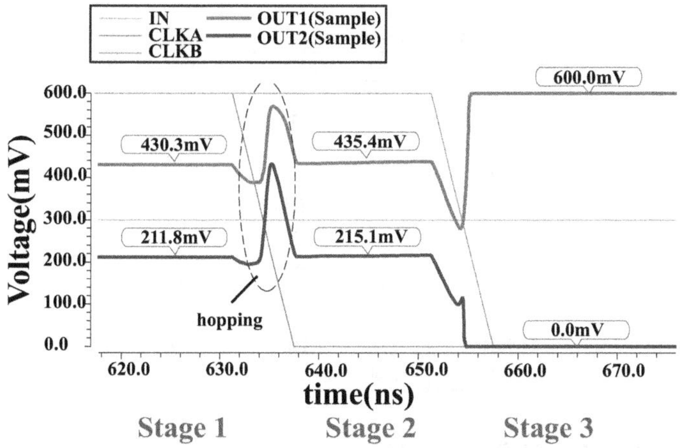

Figure 4: Transient analysis of inverter-based comparative unit.

Hence, we try to improve the structure of the D-latch to enhance the accuracy of conversion.

3.1 Improved D-latch Structures

Utilizing the regenerative effect of inverter-chain, one or two more inverters are added in front of D-latch to play a role of pre-amp before the conversion. We show the schematics of D-latch improvement in Fig. 5(a) and (b). To distinguish the structures, the original D-latch is 'structure-1'; the improved version adding one inverter shown in Fig. 5(a) is 'structure-2'; the version adding two inverters in Fig. 5(b) is 'structure-3'.

In the design of structure-2, INV1 has the same transistor sizes as those of INV3 so that the switching threshold built by INV1 and INV2 is totally same as the one built by INV3 and INV2. Although a mismatch between INV1 and INV3 would affect the consistency of the switching threshold, the effect in the conversion would hide under 1 LSB and could be ignored. For the same reason, in the design of the structure-3, INV1 and INV2 must match INV3 and INV4, respectively.

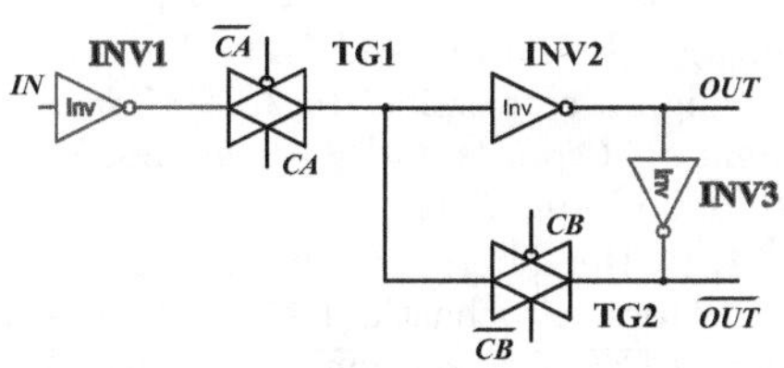

(a) structure-2

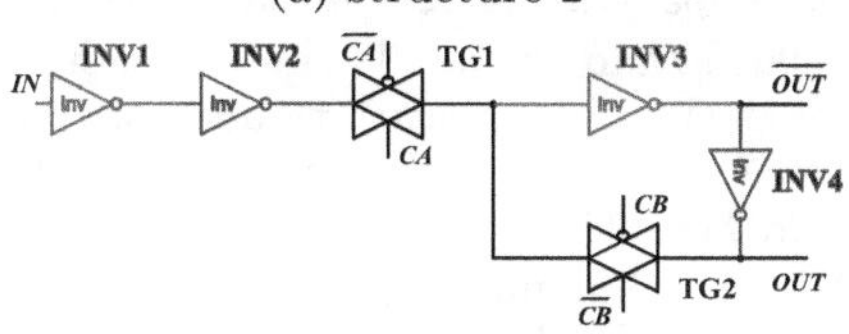

(b) structure-3

Figure 5: Improved D-latch Structures.

3.2 Comparison of D-latch Structures

We verify the relationship between the inputs and the outputs of our different D-latch structures by Monte Carlo simulation on 65nm process. Here, 200 times simulations are applied to each input, and we test 97 input voltages in total from 252mV to 348mV, corresponding to -3σ to $+3\sigma$ of switching threshold, and step is 1mV.

All of three structures are simulated under a supply voltage of 0.6V. Fig. 6(a),(c),(e) respectively demonstrate three structures' PDF curves of the switching threshold offset in 1000 times Monte Carlo simulation. Plus, Fig. 6(b),(d),(f) correspondingly show the input-output plotted points, and the fitting CDF curves, and the ideal CDF curves, which are generated according to the means and deviations in the PDF results. It can be observed that the conversions through comparative units are close to the ideal CDF curves of the switching threshold. And the fitting CDF curves in structure-2 and structure-3 are closer to the respective ideal CDF curves than structure-1. It means the added inverters in front of D-latch improve the accuracy of the conversion.

We can evaluate the amount errors in terms of RMS for a pair of the plotted points and the ideal CDF curve. Table 1 summarizes the resultant data. Structure-1 results in the worst for RMS, while structure-2 makes a better performance for RMS than structure-3. It means structure-2 generates least errors, because of less match requirement of inverters in the structure-2 than structure-3.

Table 1: Comparison among three structures. RMS: root mean square of difference.

	RMS of plotted points to ideal CDF curve	# transistors
structure-1	3.7186	8
structure-2	1.9805	10
structure-3	2.3723	12

3.3 Discussion in Conversion Accuracy

Table 2 shows 200 times Monte Carlo simulation results with different input voltages in structure-1. The column of 'before' shows the number of samples of which the signal voltage is greater than the switching threshold in Stage 1. The column of 'after' does the number of samples of which the signal voltage is recognized as the high voltage in Stage 3. Ideally, the signal voltage which is greater than the switching threshold must result in the high voltage after the conversion. 'Error rate' shows an error rate in the conversion. As seen in the table, the error rate for each input is small enough, and acceptable.

3.4 Low Supply Voltage

This inverter-based comparative unit is appropriate for design of low voltage stochastic flash ADC. In this paper, the design of the unit has been achieved with 0.6V supply voltage based on 65nm process.

Restricted by drain-source voltage drop, as the number of transistors along a current path from VDD to VSS increases, the supply voltage has to increase to ensure each transistor works on an appropriate region. Accordingly, fewer transistors from VDD to VSS have a big advantage in the low voltage design. In designs of [5] and [7], both have four transistors, as well as [8] has three transistors. In our design, only two levels of transistors are used to realize comparative function. Obviously, it greatly contributes to reduce the supply voltage than others.

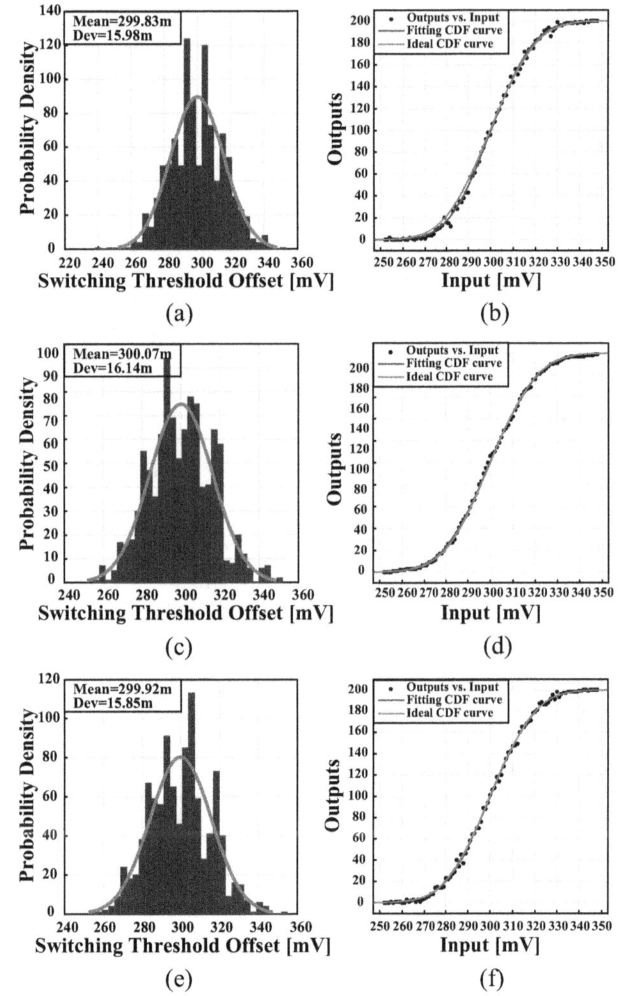

Figure 6: (a), (c) and (e) are PDFs of structure-1, -2 and -3, respectively. (b), (d) and (f) are CDFs of structure-1, -2 and -3, respectively.

Theoretically, under a low supply voltage, the switching threshold of inverter-chain still exists even though both of PMOS and NMOS in inverter are working on the subthreshold region. However, for no loss of the threshold voltage when a signal passes through a transmission gate, the precondition that supply voltage is greater than $|V_{thp}| + |V_{thn}|$ must be satisfied. In addition, as the supply voltage decreases, a hopping irregularity starts to appear on a transmission gate at a clocking edge, which would have a bad influence in distinguishing the logic. As a result, these conditions make the supply voltage of the comparative unit unable to decrease without limits.

Each structure of D-latch introduced in this paper has significant advantages to replace a comparator in the design of stochastic flash ADC. The first one is to decrease the number of transistors, resulting in saving the total area and power consumption of design. The second is that the D-latch can work under a low supply voltage such as 0.6V, which contributes to a possibility to overall design of low voltage stochastic flash ADC. The third is to make use of a digital standard cell library to replace analog comparator, so that the circuit can be digitally synthesized.

Table 2: Error rate at supply voltage 0.6V.

input(mV)	before	after	error rate(%)
250	0	0	0
260	1	1	0
270	4	3	0.5
280	20	17	1.5
290	53	51	1
300	97	94	1.5
310	153	152	0.5
320	181	184	1.5
330	196	196	0
340	199	199	0
350	200	200	0

4. CONCLUSION

This paper presents a low voltage stochastic flash ADC, introducing a inverter-based comparative unit which is used as the front-end. For the sake of the simplicity of the structure in the unit, we attain less than half number of transistors compared to a conventional comparator. We discuss three different structures about the correctness for distinguishing a logic, and propose an appropriate circuit structure from the viewpoint of the resolution. Furthermore, we demonstrate the supply voltage can be reduced to 0.6V on 65nm process, as well as it can be built with fully digital standard cells. In future work, we will design a layout of our stochastic flash ADC, and evaluate the fabricated chip.

5. REFERENCES

[1] Behzad Razavi and Bruce A. Wooley. Design techniques for high-speed, high-resolution comparators. 1992.

[2] Daihong Fu, K. C. Dyer, S. H. Lewis, and P. J. Hurst. A digital background calibration technique for time-interleaved analog-to-digital converters. *IEEE Journal of Solid-State Circuits*, 33(12):1904–1911, Dec 1998.

[3] J. Doernberg, P. R. Gray, and D. A. Hodges. A 10-bit 5-msample/s cmos two-step flash adc. *IEEE Journal of Solid-State Circuits*, 24(2):241–249, April 1989.

[4] J. L. Ceballos, I. Galton, and G. C. Temes. Stochastic analog-to-digital conversion. In *48th Midwest Symposium on Circuits and Systems, 2005.*, pages 855–858 Vol. 1, Aug 2005.

[5] S. Weaver, B. Hershberg, P. Kurahashi, D. Knierim, and U. K. Moon. Stochastic flash analog-to-digital conversion. *IEEE Transactions on Circuits and Systems I: Regular Papers*, 57(11):2825–2833, Nov 2010.

[6] Sakshi Sharma and Pallavi Thakur. Design of high speed power efficient wallace tree adders. *International Journal of Exploration in Engineering and Technology*, 1(5):18–22, May 2016.

[7] Skyler Weaver, Benjamin P. Hershberg, and Un-Ku Moon. Digitally synthesized stochastic flash adc using only standard digital cells. *IEEE Trans. on Circuits and Systems*, 61-I:84–91, 2014.

[8] Nguyen Ngoc Mai Khanh, Rimon Ikeno, Takahiro J. Yamaguchi, Tetsuya Iizuka, and Kunihiro Asada. Experimental demonstration of stochastic comparators for fine resolution adc without calibration. In *ICECS*, 2016.

Switched Capacitor and Infinite Impulse Response Summation for a Quarter-Rate DFE with 4Gb/s Data Rate

Gyunam Jeon
Electrical and Computer Engineering
Northeastern University
Boston, MA, United States
gjeon@ece.neu.edu

Yong-Bin Kim
Electrical and Computer Engineering
Northeastern University
Boston, MA, United States
ybk@ece.neu.edu

ABSTRACT

This paper presents a novel area effective 2-tap speculative Decision Feedback Equalizer (DFE) with one switched-cap and one IIR summation for data recovery in standard CMOS 180nm technology node. The conventional first-tap speculative quarter rate DFE is composed of eight different paths, which have exactly same hardware. By using the switched-cap method, it is possible to get rid of the duplicated paths. Instead of having a large number of feedback taps in conventional DFE, one single Infinite Impulse Response (IIR) tap in the DFE can compensate the effects of the multiple post-cursors. An input of the second tap is fed back from Infinite Impulse Response (IIR) filter with self-adjusted time constants ($\tau 1$). Less number of taps is used in the proposed scheme. The eight summers with two taps in conventional scheme are changed to four current integrating summers and one speculative tap and one general tap by using switched capacitor and IIR filter, respectively. The proposed DFE consumes 12.76mW with 1.8V supply when equalizing 4Gb/s data passed over a channel with 28 dB loss at 2GHz.

Keywords

Decision feedback equalizer (DFE); current-integrating summer; high-speed serial link; quarter-rate receiver: switched capacitor; signal integrity; infinite impulse response (IIR).

1. INTRODUCTION

As the data rate of chip-to-chip communication over high loss channel increases dramatically, the data require a compensation of the loss at receivers. Thus, achieving high-success data rate from transmitters (TXs) to receivers (RXs) is mainly concentrated to improve higher data transmission through long wire channels. Consequently, the transceiver faces challenges to improve the data transmission rate through channels in the multi Giga-bits per second range. The reason to have loss through channels is that the high frequency signal is degraded by skin effect, reflection, and dielectric loss [1] when a transmission line such as coaxial line or printed-circuit-board (PCB) trace is used to transmit a high-speed signal. In addition, when data is transmitted through a dispersive channel in the high-speed serial interface, inter-symbol interference (ISI) can cause bit detection errors at the RX. Various numbers of compensation techniques [2]-[3] have been demonstrated for the equalization with higher data rate of chip-to-chip links on the PCB substrates or coaxial cable links which have between 20-30dB loss at one-half the bit rate [1]. There is a continuous time linear equalizer (CTLE), which is used to compensate channel loss at high frequency by boosting the high-frequency components of the attenuated input signal by the channel. For this reason, the CTLE effectively works to broaden the bandwidth of the channel. The CTLE, however, has a critical drawback that it amplifies not only noise but also crosstalk. Although the transmitted swing of several hundred mV can overcome the noise enhancement, it can also increase crosstalk [1]. On the other hand, a decision feedback equalizer (DFE) has become popular for the equalization because DFEs also achieve higher signal-to-noise ratio (SNR) compared with linear equalizer and its prior decision is noise-free and the subtraction of the ISI does not add noise to the equalizer signal [2]. In the DFE implementation, post-cursor ISI is suppressed by feeding back the transmitted previous samples. The DFE has an advantage that signal distortion can be reduced without amplifying noise or crosstalk, making it appropriately to equalize channels where the loss exceeds 20 dB [4]. DFEs are used as main equalizer in the high-speed serial interface design.

This paper presents a novel area effective DFE architecture composed of the switched-capacitor-based discrete-time tap and the infinite-impulse-response-based (IIR) continuous-time tap to achieve area efficiency, higher data rate with less power dissipation, and relaxing feedback time by having speculative tap summation and quarter-rate architecture. The proposed circuit is designed using an 180nm CMOS technology at 1.8V supply voltage.

This brief is organized as follows. Section II describes the architecture of the conventional half-rate DFE with feedback dependent taps and the details about the operation of each component. In addition, section III gives the details about the operation theory of the switched-capacitor and the IIR filter in the proposed design. Section IV presents the circuit simulation results, followed by the conclusion of the paper in Section V.

2. DFE ARCHITECTURE REVIEW

The DFE has been widely used to get rid of the post-cursors generated by ISI. In case of a digital data transmission on a specific channel, the bits from n-UI (unit interval) ago produce the stable post-cursor ISI in the received current data bit [4]. Since the first post-cursor dominates the overall ISI in a medium-loss channel (~10dB), the DFE can only have the first post-tap for power saving [5]. However, more than 20dB high-loss channel at

Permission to make digital or hard copies of all or part of this work for personal or classroom use is granted without fee provided that copies are not made or distributed for profit or commercial advantage and that copies bear this notice and the full citation on the first page. Copyrights for components of this work owned by others than ACM must be honored. Abstracting with credit is permitted. To copy otherwise, or republish, to post on servers or to redistribute to lists, requires prior specific permission and/or a fee. Request permissions from Permissions@acm.org.
GLSVLSI'17, May 10–12, 2017, Banff, AB, Canada.
© 2017 ACM. ISBN 978-1-4503-4972-7/17/05...$15.00.
DOI: http://dx.doi.org/10.1145/3060403.3060427

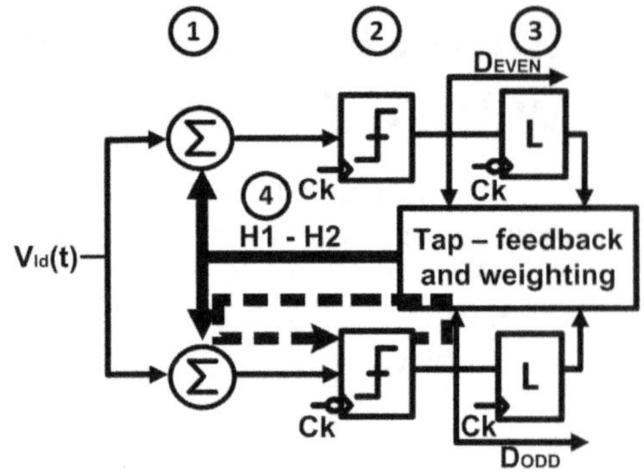

Figure. 1. Conventional half-rate DFE with 2 taps

high frequency requires more than 1 taps to attenuate the ISI in the input signals. The tap numbers directly affect the power consumption and feedback timing constraint of the DFE architecture in the high loss channel. For this reason, the number of taps should be optimized and decreased. To cancel the accumulated ISI in a current bit one by one, some proper coefficients will be added and fed back to the previous digital bits that have been already generated by the DFE. To convert a current bit into a digital signal, the slicer in the DFE can make an appropriate decision for it.

Fig. 1 shows the conventional half-rate DFE with 2 taps that are fed back from either delayed D_{EVEN} or D_{ODD} of the architecture. The DFE mainly consists of four parts: First, a current-integrating summer is designed as resistor-based one in general. The current integration operation is performed in the block. Second, a component that makes decision of the current bit by using the output signals of the summer is called a slicer. Third, the decision by the slicer will be fed back to the tap-feedback and weighting block, which is composed of a current digital to analog converter to supply a current weight to the current-integrating summer to eliminate ISI. Finally, feedback taps that get rid of the accumulated ISI by subtracting coefficients depending on previous bit are presented. In particular, the DFE has a critical path (dashed line) that is a time constraint of feedback time, which corresponds roughly to less than 1 UI.

Fig. 2 (a) shows full-rate DFE with 2 taps that are fed back from the output (D_{OUT}) of the architecture. But the architecture has a continuous tap that the weight of voltage is varied by a time constant, $\tau 1$. In other words, a discrete-time-based tap which is described Fig. 1 dissipates static current dissipation during 1 UI. For high loss channel, the DFE is required more than 2 taps in order to cancel ISI effectively. The number of taps in the current-integrating summer causes excessively large amount of power because of additional latches. And n-taps require n-delayed time

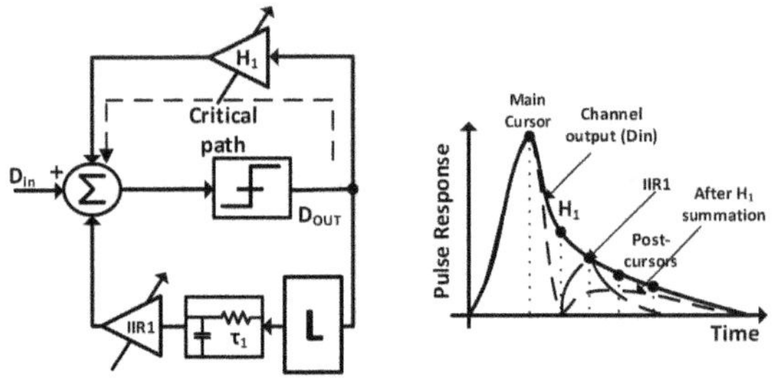

Figure. 2 IIR based DFE (a) architeture (b) pulse resoponse with post-cursor elimination

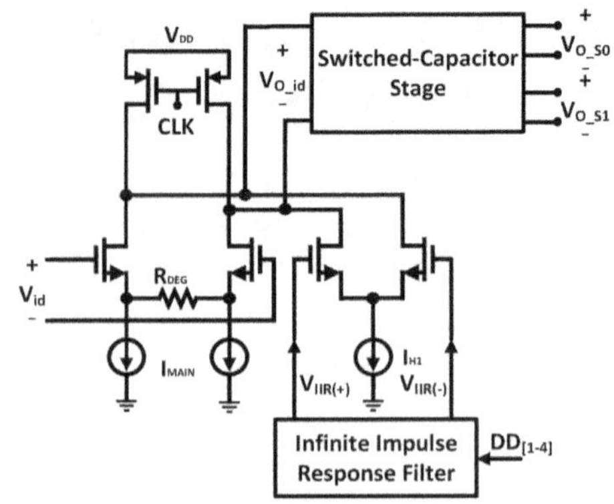

Figure 3. Proposed design of current-integrating summer with discrete-tap and continuous-tap

to feedback to the current-integrating summer. Fig. 2 (b) shows a pulse response that describes bit 'one' after the channel passes through the channel and steadily attenuates for one-UI. For the input signal with severe post-cursor, an exponentially decaying function can be utilized to represent the long "tail" after main cursor [4]. By using the feedback dependent taps, H1 and IIR1, the ISI can be cancelled easily. The taps help to determine the current bit without any crosstalk. The feedback coefficients, H1 and time constant $\tau 1$, can be adjusted by current DACs and capacitor arrays, respectively. Instead of involving a large number of feedback taps in the conventional DFE, one single Infinite Impulse Response (IIR) tap in this new DFE can compensate the effects of multiple post-cursors [5]-[8]. Therefore, this DFE architecture combined with IIR filter is a good candidate for lower power dissipation and low complexity.

3. PROPOSED DECISION FEEDBACK EQUALIZER

The half-rate DFE architecture consisting of the speculative first tap and the second discrete tap from the feedback requires paralleled two paths which are called strong-one and strong-zero paths in the even or odd paths in general. Subtracting or adding of the first speculative tap coefficient is an operation which occurred in those paths described above. The main part of the conventional current-integrating summers used in two speculative paths is exactly same and redundant hardware [9]. In addition, to cancel the ISI generated by high loss channel effectively, numbers of unspeculative taps are desirable. The numerous number of taps, however, accompany with high power dissipation by a data-delaying block, a latch. Therefore, to improve the quarter rate speculative DFE architecture in terms of area and performance, the DFE architecture is very strongly required to reduce the duplicated speculative taps with the increasing unspeculative tap number. Therefore, we propose a novel area effective quarter rate DFE which is designed not only to save area by combining the first speculative of the duplicated coefficient-tap but also to reduce the number of unspeculative taps. Therefore, the DFE architecture has less number of taps with much less ISI effect by using the IIR as the second tap to save power dissipation.

Fig. 3 describes the proposed current-integrating summer with a switched-cap stage and an infinite impulse response filter stage in the proposed DFE. The current-based stage is same operation as the conventional one. At the same time of current integrating, the IIR filter generates a continuous time signal (elimination of second post-cursor) that depends on a 1-UI

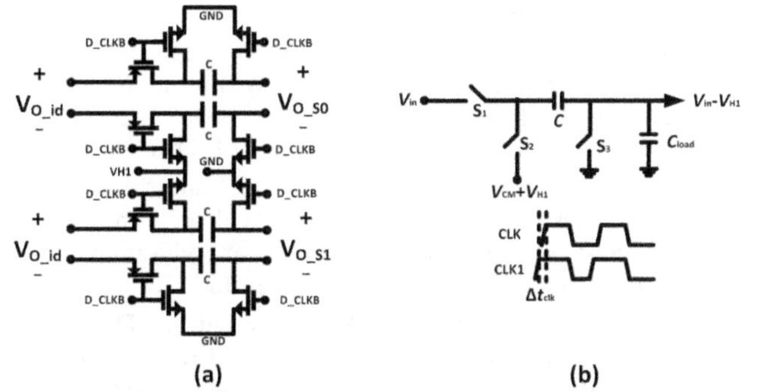

Figure. 4. Proposed DFE components (a) switched-capacitor stage (b) simplified model and delayed clock timing for the stage

delayed signal to cancel post-cursors. After the operation of storing the current into the switched capacitor, the output of the current-integrating stage, Vo_id, becomes the input of the switched-capacitor stage for the first speculative tap to cancel the first post-cursor only. The amount of the voltage cancelled ISI from the first tap depends on either strong one or strong zero path.

The detailed circuit of switched-capacitor stage in the current-integrating summer is shown in Fig. 4 (a). The switched capacitor stage and the current integration stage are distinguished by the switches that are controlled by the delayed clock, D_CLKB to isolate and prevent leakage from the current integration stage. The clock timing for the switched capacitor is shown in Fig. 4 (b). There are two different clocks in the stage to control either the current integration to the capacitor or discharging the current for first post-cursor from the capacitors. The timing is extremely critical in the switched capacitor stage. Since each block of the proposed DFE is operated by lower frequency in the quarter rate DFE, the timing margin for the operation of the switched capacitor stage is much relaxed than half-rate and full-rate DFEs. Two speculative paths for +H1 and –H1 are split at the output of the first stage by using four switched-capacitors [10]-[11]. The operation of the charge sharing effect can be emphasized between C_{load} and the capacitor C [9]. Due to this effect, the output voltage of the summer cannot be exactly V_{in}-V_{H1} but can be shown as the following equation.

The output voltage is attenuated by the factor of $C/(C+C_{load})$, which will be significant if C is comparable to C_{load}. To eliminate this attenuation, C_{load} needs to be minimized and a proper value of capacitor C larger than C_{load} is needed [12]. In this paper, the capacitance in the current-integrating summer is set as 130fF and the input capacitance of the slicer is set to 23fF for the simulation. In addition, by using the speculative tap, the architecture can relax the critical path timing from 1UI to 2UI.

Without the sacrifice of the DFE accuracy, the reduction of number of taps helps decrease the DFE complexity due to the adaptation of only one coefficient (1-pole) in IIR tap shown in Fig. 5 (a). The tunable MOSFET capacitor array at the differential outputs as shown in Fig. 5 (b) controls the time constant, τ1, which depends on post-cursors from the input signals. The IIR tap provides the same amount of ISI cancellation as 10 finite impulse response (FIR) feedback taps. In addition, the reason why it becomes difficult to cancel the first post-cursor ISI tap using only IIR filters is the delays of the feedback path [4, 7]. The discrete tap is not only added to cancel the first post cursor on the design, but it can also alleviate the timing issues in the proposed design. The capacitance array of the IIR circuit is changeable depending on the feedback signal of either even or odd paths.

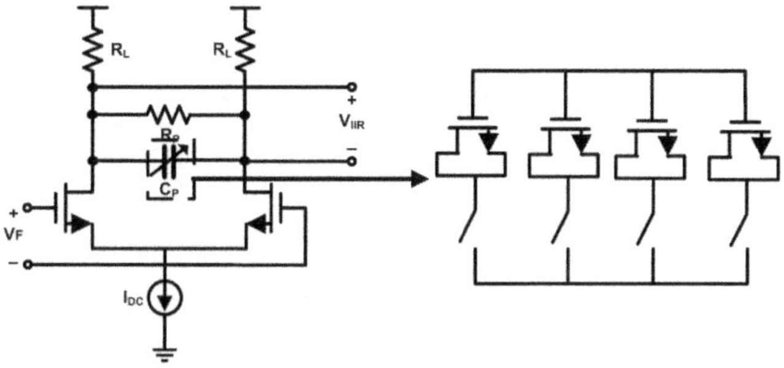

Figure. 5. Circuits of (a) infinite impulse response (b) MOSFET capacitor array

4. SIMULATION RESULTS

The proposed DFE is simulated using an 180nm CMOS technology node with 1.8V power supply. The channel loss of the input signal through the cascaded B1 channel between the transmitter and the receiver is shown in Fig. 6 to show the distorted input signal at the DFE. It is about 28dB loss at 4Gbps data rate of the DFE.

Fig. 7 shows eye diagrams of the input signal and the recovered output data of the DFE. We can see that the eyes are opened widely after the equalization. Table. 1 describes how much power is consumed by sample and hold, comparator, IIR, current-integrating summer, multiplexer, and current and voltage source blocks. The total power consumption is 12.76mW with 1.8V power supply. The proposed design has less power dissipation (3.19mW/Gb/s) than [7] which proposed 3-IIR tap DFE with 17.2mW power consumption at 1.2V of power supply on 130nm technology node with 3.7Gb/s data rate (4.65mW/Gb/s). Fig. 8 presents a pass and fail diagram of with the DFE to examine the equalization performance of the proposed design with adjusting differential amplitude of the input signal from the transmitter and shifting the UI from -0.3 to 0.3. The range of the UI corresponds from -150ps to 150ps at the operating frequency of the DFE.

5. CONCLUSION

This paper demonstrates the proposed DFE with a switched capacitor as the 1st speculative tap and an IIR as the 2nd tap. The improved circuit effectively corrects the distorted input signal that arises from the ISI through the channel using standard 180nm CMOS technology node with 1.8V power supply. The proposed

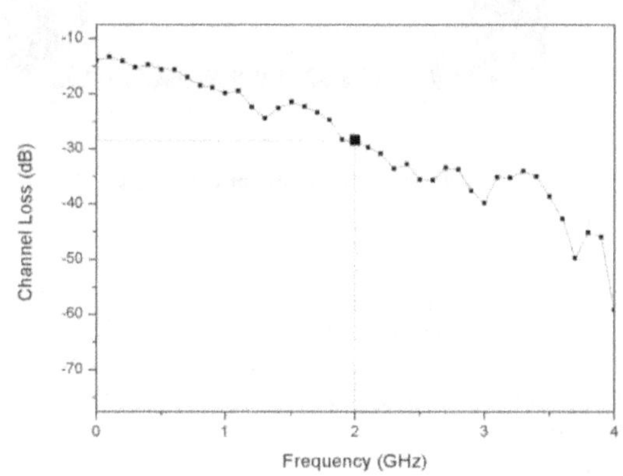

Figure. 6. Channel loss

Table 1. DFE power consumption details

	Block	Power (mW)
DFE core	Summers	4.52
	Pre-amplifier	3.62
	SR latch	1.09
	DFFs	0.38
	IIR	1.62
	Mux	0.52
	S/H	0.15
Peripherals	Voltage and current source	0.86

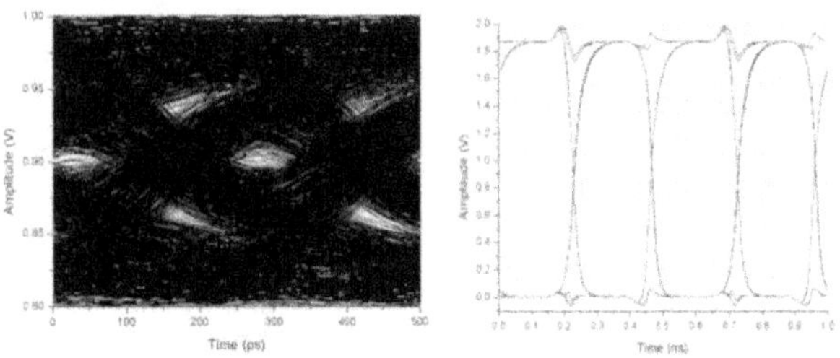

(a) (b)

Figure. 7. Eye diagram (a) before the DFE (b) after recovery by the DFE

CMOS technology node with 1.8V power supply. The proposed design can achieve relaxed critical timing path to 2UI compared

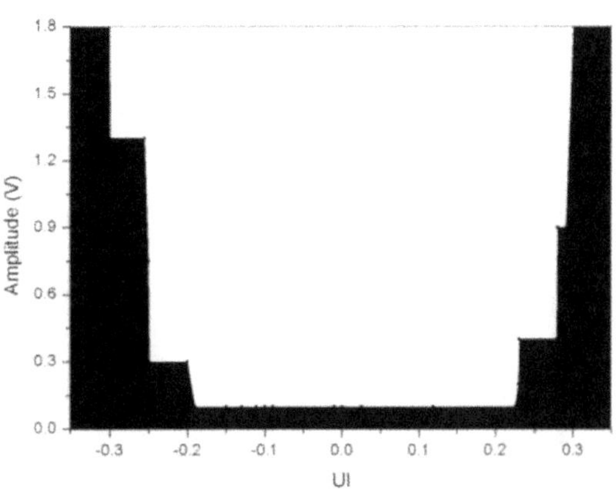

Figure 8. Pass/fail diagram with the DFE

with 1UI of the conventional IIR-based DFE. Since the duplicated summer is reduced to two, it takes less area than the conventional DFE. Moreover, it is possible to compensate high channel loss at high operation frequency with less number of IIR taps. Finally, the switched-capacitor stage has much larger timing margin by operating at lower frequency in the quarter rate DFE. Therefore, the proposed DFE turns out to be a viable solution to correct the transmitted data at lower area and less power overhead comparing with the conventional approach.

6. REFERENCES

[1] Bob Alverson. 1993. Book Review: High-Speed Digital Design: A Handbook of Black Magic by Howard W. Johnson and Martin Graham. *ACM SIGARCH Computer Architecture News SIGARCH Comput. Archit. News* (1993), 85–86.

[2] K. L. J. Wong, A. Rylyakov and C. K. K. Yang, "A 5-mW 6-Gb/s Quarter-Rate Sampling Receiver With a 2-Tap DFE Using Soft Decisions," in IEEE Journal of Solid-State Circuits, vol. 42, no. 4, pp. 881-888, April 2007.

[3] Park, M.; Bulzacchelli, J.; Beakes, M.; Friedman, D., "A 7Gb/s 9.3mW 2-Tap Current-Integrating DFE Receiver," in *Solid-State Circuits Conference, 2007. ISSCC 2007. Digest of Technical Papers. IEEE International*, vol., no., pp.230-599, 11-15 Feb. 2007.

[4] Alireza Sharif-Bakhtiar, Anthony Chan Carusone, "A 19.6-Gbps CMOS optical receiver with local feedback IIR DFE", VLSI Circuits (VLSI Circuits) 2015 Symposium on, pp. C116-C117, 2015.

[5] Dickson, T.O.; Bulzacchelli, J.F.; Friedman, D.J., "A 12-Gb/s 11-mW half-rate sampled 5-tap decision feedback equalizer with current-integrating summers in 45-nm SOI CMOS technology," inVLSI Circuits, 2008 IEEE Symposium on , vol., no., pp.58-59, 18-20 June 2008

[6] B. Kim, Y. Liu, T. O. Dickson, J. F. Bulzacchelli, and D. J. Friedman, "A 10-gb/s compact low-power serial i/o with dfe-iir equalization in 65-nm cmos," in IEEE Journal of Solid-State Circuits, December 2009.

[7] S. Shahramian, H. Yasotharan and A. C. Carusone, "Decision Feedback Equalizer Architectures With Multiple Continuous-Time Infinite Impulse Response Filters," in IEEE Transactions on Circuits and Systems II: Express Briefs, vol. 59, no. 6, pp. 326-330, June 2012

[8] Beukema, T.; Sorna, M.; Selander, K.; Zier, S.; Ji, B.L.; Murfet, P.; Mason, J.; Woogeun Rhee; Ainspan, H.; Parker, B.; Beakes, M., "A 6.4-Gb/s CMOS SerDes core with feed-forward and decision-feedback equalization," in *Solid-State Circuits, IEEE Journal of*, vol.40, no.12, pp.2633-2645, Dec. 2005.

[9] S. Saeedi and A. Emami, "A 10Gb/s, 342fJ/bit micro-ring modulator transmitter with switched-capacitor pre-emphasis and monolithic temperature sensor in 65nm CMOS," 2016 IEEE Symposium on VLSI Circuits (VLSI-Circuits), Honolulu, HI, 2016, pp. 1-2.

[10] C. Zhang, G. Jeon, Y. Choi, Y. B. Kim and K. K. Kim, "An Area Efficient 4Gb/s Half-Rate 3-Tap DFE with Current-Integrating Summer for Data Correction," 2016 IEEE 25th North Atlantic Test Workshop (NATW), Providence, RI, 2016, pp. 6-11.

[11] Emami-Neyestanak, A.; Varzaghani, A.; Bulzacchelli, J.F.; Rylyakov, A.; Yang, C.-K.K.; Friedman, D.J., "A 6.0-mW 10.0-Gb/s Receiver With Switched-Capacitor Summation DFE," in *Solid-State Circuits, IEEE Journal of*, vol.42, no.4, pp.889-896, April 2007.

[12] Toifl, T.; Menolfi, C.; Ruegg, M.; Reutemann, R.; Dreps, D.; Beukema, T.; Prati, A.; Gardellini, D.; Kossel, M.; Buchmann, P.; Brandli, M.; Francese, P.A.; Morf, T., "A 2.6 mW/Gbps 12.5 Gbps RX With 8-Tap Switched-Capacitor DFE in 32 nm CMOS," in *Solid-State Circuits, IEEE Journal of*, vol.47, no.4, pp.897-910, April 2012

An Energy Combiner Design for Multiple Microbial Energy Harvesting Sources

Ridvan Umaz
University of Connecticut
371 Fairfield Road
Storrs, CT 06269, USA
ridvan.umaz@uconn.edu

Lei Wang
University of Connecticut
371 Fairfield Road
Storrs, CT 06269, USA
lei.3.wang@uconn.edu

ABSTRACT

Multiple renewable energy sources, such as microbial fuel cells (MFCs), can greatly improve the energy output to drive loads for prolonged operation time. However, even designed with exactly the same material, size and structure, the generated voltages at their outputs are different due to the nonlinear effects of microorganisms. Simply combining these sources degrades the overall efficiency and excludes some source contributions. A conventional energy combining platform is not suited for low-voltage energy sources and has limited overall efficiency. In this paper, a new energy combiner circuit is proposed. The proposed circuit can be either power up a load or charge an energy storage such as a rechargeable battery or a supercapacitor. Simulation results are carried out in a 0.13μm CMOS process and demonstrate the effectiveness of the proposed design.

Keywords

Energy harvesting, energy combining, energy scavenging, boost converter, regulation circuit, microbial fuel cell, energy management.

1. INTRODUCTION

The issues related to power supply and autonomy for a wide set of applications, such as wireless sensor networks and remote devices, have gained great attentions. Self-powering over a full lifetime by extracting energy from the surrounding environment is currently under active study. Due to impractical use of other energy harvesting systems, microbial fuel cells (MFCs) [1] are developed for energy harvesting in deep oceans, lakes and other aquatic environments.

One critical issue of energy harvesting with MFCs is the inherently low output power density and voltage. As such, MFCs might not be able to directly connect to the load [2, 3]. An interface circuit is usually required to manage the low output voltage in a way compatible with the load. Driving an external load through a power converter by single energy harvesting system might not be an efficient case. Efforts of placing multiple energy harvesting systems can help to either power up the load or minimize the limitation of load operation. Multiple energy harvesting systems combined can increase the overall output power and improve the functionality of the load (e.g., sensor duty cycles) [4], [5], [6].

As the power output of MFCs strongly depends on the environment, even identically designed MFCs (i.e. same size and physical structure) will generate different output voltages [7], [8], [9]. The discrepancy at MFC outputs can be explained by the nonlinear effects of microorganisms during inoculation [8], [9]. As a result, while combining multiple energy sources such as MFCs improves overall reliability and functionality, it also triggers other issues; for example, the highest generated output voltage constrains or excludes the contributions from other generated voltages. Therefore, multiple MFC outputs might not be combined to the load directly through multiple power converters.

Some previous studies have discussed the combining of multiple MFCs for enhanced power output [10], [11], [12], but they did not considered the variations in different output voltages and how this will affect the power transfer cycle, i.e., synchronizing the output power cycles of different MFCs simultaneously. As a result, the overall efficiencies of these designs are limited by the highest generated voltage, whereas the lower generated voltages are not exploited at their best efficiencies. A basic energy combiner design for other energy harvesting systems [4, 5, 6] (e.g., solar cell, thermoelectric generator and wind), so-called power ORing, is shown in Fig. 1a. This design requires more than 1V input voltage, but the output voltage of MFCs is typically a few hundreds millivolts. Therefore, conventional power combiner design with power ORing is not suited for MFCs. In addition, the power loss associated with the diode voltage drop affects overall efficiency negatively. To overcome these problems, this work develops a more efficient method for combining multiple microbial energy harvesting systems, as shown in Fig. 1b. Simulation results in a 0.13μm CMOS process demonstrate the effectiveness of the proposed energy combiner circuit.

2. SYSTEM ARCHITECTURE

As illustrated in Fig. 1b, the proposed energy combiner system consists of a number of power converters associated with the energy sources, an energy combiner circuit, a rechargable battery, and a load. The energy combiner circuit is not directly connected to the energy sources due to the following reasons: (1) the inherent low output voltage from the MFCs (e.g. a few hundreds millivolts) is not sufficient to

Permission to make digital or hard copies of all or part of this work for personal or classroom use is granted without fee provided that copies are not made or distributed for profit or commercial advantage and that copies bear this notice and the full citation on the first page. Copyrights for components of this work owned by others than ACM must be honored. Abstracting with credit is permitted. To copy otherwise, or republish, to post on servers or to redistribute to lists, requires prior specific permission and/or a fee. Request permissions from permissions@acm.org.

GLSVLSI '17, May 10-12, 2017, Banff, AB, Canada

© 2017 ACM. ISBN 978-1-4503-4972-7/17/05...$15.00

DOI: http://dx.doi.org/10.1145/3060403.3060434

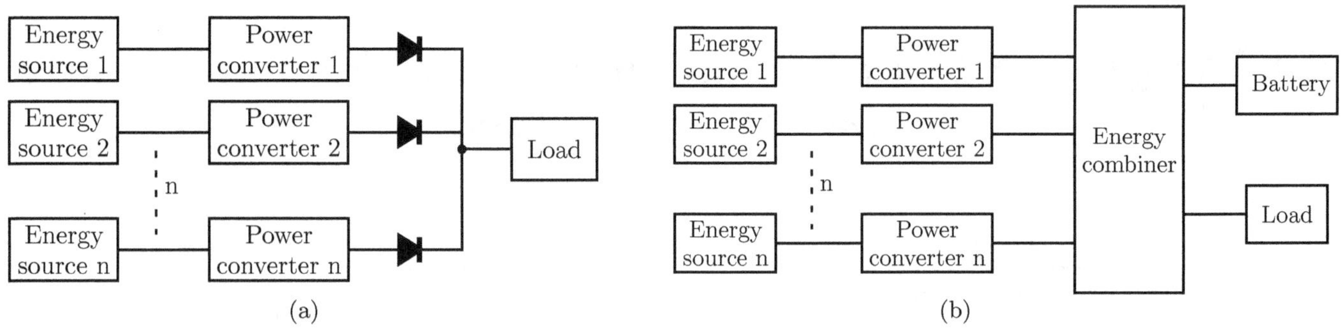

Figure 1: (a) The block diagram of a conventional energy combiner circuit. (b) The block diagram of the proposed energy combiner circuit.

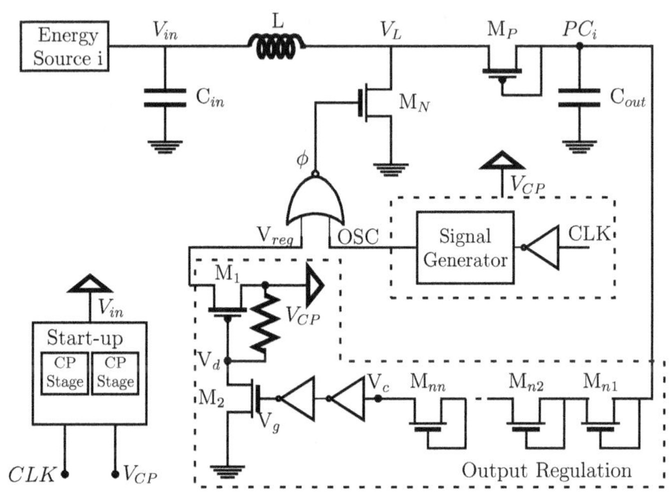

Figure 2: Implementation of the power converter circuit.

power up a load, and (2) the system should be self-powered. Therefore, an interface circuit (i.e. power converter) between the energy sources and the energy combiner circuit must be placed. A switching inductor converter is employed as the power converter, as shown in Fig. 2. The converter includes a start-up circuit, output regulation, signal generator, power transistors and other external components. The start-up circuit designed with a two-stages charge pump boosts the output (V_{cp}) from a low voltage at the output of the energy source (V_{in}) to power up the signal generator and to regulate the output of the converter for a desired load voltage.

The energy combiner provides a more efficient sequentially connected outputs of power converters (e.g. PC_i) to either load or battery, which depends on the output of the regulation circuit (V_{reg}) in the power converter. More detailed explanation of the energy combiner circuit will be given in the following section.

3. THE PROPOSED ENERGY COMBINER

Variations in the voltage at the output of each identically designed MFCs cause different frequencies in the converter to control the switch M_N on/off behaviors. This results in different times to discharge the current stored on inductor L to the output PC_i ($i = 1$ to n), which reduces the overall efficiency. Therefore, the outputs of the power converters PC_i cannot be directly connected to the load.

An energy combiner circuit is placed between the power converters and the load\battery to efficiently manage the stored energy at the PC_i, either to power up the load or to charge the battery. The energy combiner allows all energy sources to simultaneously operate and connect to the power converters. However, each converter is not allowed to connect concurrently to the load\battery. The energy combiner circuit operates in a time-multiplexed manner to manage the energy distributed to either load or battery. For n energy sources, the power converter output PC_1 to PC_n connect sequentially to either load or battery, thereby leading to a n time-multiplexing operation.

An energy transfer cycle defines a time (T_{ci}), in which the stored energy at the output of each power converter is transferred in order of connection (e.g., PC_1 first and then PC_2 and so on). They can be expressed as

$$T_{c1} = T_{c2} = ... = T_{cn} = T_c \tag{1}$$

$$T_{off} = (n-1) \times T_{ci} \tag{2}$$

where T_{off} is the time duration that no energy is transferred and n is the number of energy sources and converters. This results in

$$T = T_{ci} + T_{off} \tag{3}$$

Subsituting (1) and (2) into (3), we obtain

$$T = T_{ci} + (n-1) \times T_{ci} = n \times T_c \tag{4}$$

Due to variations in output voltages, different amount of charges are fed into the output capacitor C_{out_i} by each converter, resulting in leakage from the highest (i.e. Load) to the lowest (power converter output) even with the well-designed energy combiner once time-multiplexing allows the output converter connection. Thus, it is needed to reduce the leakage and direct the stored energy to somewhere else to keep overall efficiency nearly constant. To achieve this, energy can be directed either to the load or to the battery. If the connected converter output voltage is higher than the load, direction toward to the load, otherwise toward to the battery.

3.1 Energy Combiner Control Flow

The energy combiner circuit performs in the order of connection and directs the corresponding converter output to ei-

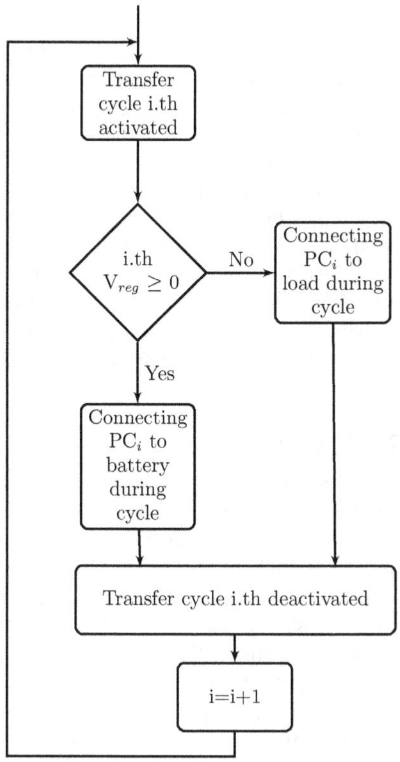

Figure 3: Control flow of the proposed energy combiner.

ther the load or the battery, as described in Fig. 3. Once the ith transfer cycle is activated, the output is ready to transfer. The corresponding converter output regulation voltage V_{reg_i} (see Fig. 2) is checked to see whether it is zero or not. If it is equal to zero, the converter output PC_i is connected to the load in the time of T_{ci}. Otherwise, it is connected to the battery. At the end of the energy transfer cycle T_{ci}, the stored energy at the converter output stops to transfer, i.e., transfer cycle i^{th} is deactivated. Next, the following transfer cycle $(i+1)^{th}$ is activated and the above process is repeated.

3.2 Implementation of the Combiner Circuit

Fig. 4 shows the circuit implementation of the proposed energy combiner where $n = 4$ for illustration. The outputs of converters PC_1 to PC_4 are connected to transistors M_{c1} to M_{c4} which are controlled by a switch matrix generated by a digital control unit (DCU). Once the output converter PC_i is connected, the power of the corresponding switch EH_i goes low, but others switches keep high, pulling the switch M_{ci} to the ON status while leaving others in the OFF status. Thus, the output connected to the energy direction distributer decides the next connection, either the load or the battery. The same steps are repeated for others converter outputs. Note that while four energy sources are used in this paper, it is straightforward to extend to more energy sources. More detailed explanation of the circuit implementations for the DCU and energy direction distributor is given in the following subsections.

3.2.1 Digital control circuit (DCU)

A clock signal is generated from the start-up circuit output CLK signal (see Fig. 2) of one of the energy sources. The

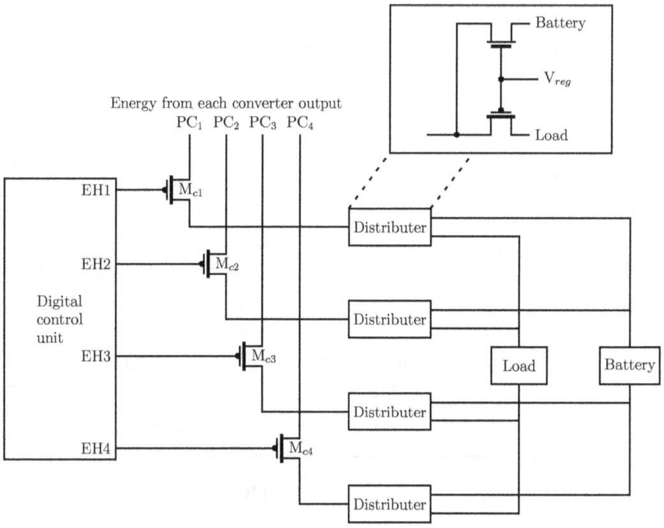

Figure 4: Implementation of the energy combiner circuit with four energy sources.

clock is used by a 4-bit counter as a clock source. The output of the counter feeds into a 4-bit serial-in parallel-out shift register to generate transistor control signals EH1 to EH4.

3.2.2 Energy direction distributer

The energy distributer is designed with single input and dual outputs, which are the battery and the load. The implementation of the energy distributer is shown in Fig.4 at the right top of the figure. The circuit is based on two transistors controlled by the output of the regulation circuit (see Fig. 2).

4. SIMULATION RESULTS

The proposed energy combining system was designed and simulated using a 0.13μm CMOS process. Four identical sediment MFCs [12] are deployed as the energy sources. The variations on the output voltages were simulated with an analytical model of MFCs [9], which also simulates the output power/voltage of the MFCs. The power converter parameters are as follows: a $20\mu H$ inductor L, a $4.7\mu F$ output capacitor C_{out}, and a $470\mu F$ input capacitor C_{in} were used. These parameters are also kept the same for the other converters used in the platform (e.g., additional three converters used in this paper).

The simulation was carried out for the energy combining system to show all system operation. Here, for demonstration purpose, the load used is a resistance of 1kΩ in parallel with a capacitor of 18.8μF, and a capacitor of 20μF is used as an energy storage (which could also be a rechargeable battery). The simulation results for all converter output voltages (V_{outc1}-V_{outc4}), load voltage (V_{out}) and capacitor voltage (V_{bat}) are shown in Fig. 5. Some parameters observed from these results are shown in Table 1. It is obvious that the small variations in the input voltage of converters generate different switching frequencies. In addition to the switching frequencies for the power converters, different output voltages (V_{outci}) are generated. Simple combination of all output voltages without the energy combiner leads to energy losses and affect the voltage outputs contribution.

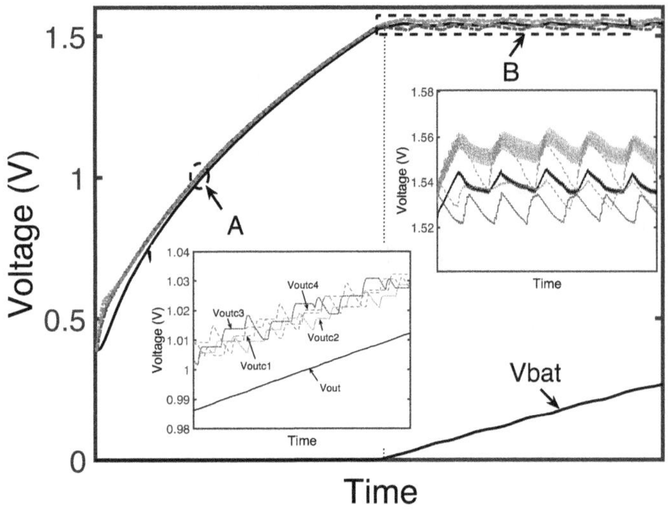

Figure 5: Voltage waveforms of four power converters V_{outc1} to V_{outc4}, load output voltage V_{out} and energy storage voltage V_{bat}. Bottom inset zooms in area shown at the circle A. Top inset zooms in area shown at the rectangular B.

Table 1: Some parameters are observed from Fig. 5.

Converter	Input voltage Vin	Output voltage Voutci	Frequency fsi
PC1	405mV	1.54V	194.93kHz
PC2	440mV	1.56V	263.852kHz
PC3	400mV	1.536V	185.185kHz
PC4	420mV	1.557V	223.713kHz

Thus, the proposed energy combiner design is an efficient way to improve energy harvesting outputs.

It can be seen from Fig. 5 that the output voltage initially starts from zero till some power converter energy is directed to the output, before that all power converter energy is transferred to the load (see Fig. 4). After that, some power converter energy is directed either to the load or to the energy storage, which depends upon the output voltage of the regulation circuit (see Fig. 2).

The inset figure at the bottom zooms in the circle A of Fig. 5. In this figure, each output voltage increases by the time of energy transfer cycle being off, which is T_{off} in (3), and the voltage decreases by the time of the energy transfer cycle being on, which is T_{ci} . The circle A is shown for demonstration purpose, these scenarios are identical for all voltage levels till the output voltage starts to increase from zero.

The inset figure at the top zooms in the rectangular B of Fig. 5. It can be seen that some output voltages are higher than the load output voltage (e.g., V_{outc2}, V_{outc4}). Therefore, these converters output energy is directed to the load. However, some output voltages are lower than the load output voltage (e.g. V_{outc3}), and these converters output energy is routed toward the energy storage whose voltage is gradually increased.

5. CONCLUSIONS

Multiple microbial fuel cells (MFCs) designed with exactly the same materials, size and structure generate different voltages at their outputs due to the nonlinear effects of microorganisms. Combinations of these sources introduce some issues, degrade to the overall efficiency, and excluded some source contributions. In this paper, an energy combining system was developed to overcome these issues. The combiner circuit connecting the converter outputs is based on an in-order connection and has equal time of the connection T_{ci}. The stored energy at the output converter are fully transferred without loss of the energy by routing the output to a load or an energy storage such as a rechargeable battery or a supercapacitor. The energy combiner circuit can either power up the load or charge the energy storage. Simulation results demonstrate the effectiveness of the proposed energy combining system.

6. REFERENCES

[1] Rabaey, K., Verstaete, W., "Microbial fuel cells: novel biotechnology for energy generation," *Trends in Biotechnol*, 23(6), 291-298, 2005.

[2] A. Meehan, H. Gao and Z. Lewandowski, "Energy Harvesting With Microbial Fuel Cell and Power Management System," *Power Electronics, IEEE Transactions on*, Volume 26, Issue 1, Jan. 2011.

[3] G. Guoxian et al.,"A biomass based marine sediment energy harvesting system," in Proceedings of the IEEE International Symposium on Low Power Electronics and Design (ISLPED), 2013, pp. 359-364.

[4] D. Carli D. Brunelli L. Benini M. Ruggeri, "An effective multisource energy harvester for low power applications" *Proc. DATE* pp. 1-6 2011.

[5] J. Colomer-Farrarons P. Miribel-Catala A. Saiz-Vela J. Samitier, "A multiharvested self-powered system in a low-voltage low-power technology" *EEE Trans. Ind. Electron.* vol. 58 no. 9 pp. 4250-4263 Sep. 2011.

[6] Y. K. Tan S. K. Panda, "Energy harvesting from hybrid indoor ambient light and thermal energy sources for enhanced performance of wireless sensor nodes" *IEEE Trans. Ind. Electron.* vol. 58 pp. 4424-4435 Sep. 2011.

[7] G. Huang et al., "A power management integrated system for biomass-based marine sediment energy harvesting," *International Journal of High Speed Electronics and Systems*, vol. 23, March 2014.

[8] F. Khaled, O. Ondel, and B. Allard, "Microbial fuel cells as power supply of a low-power temperature sensor. *J. Power Sources* 306, pp.354-360 2016.

[9] U. Karra et al., "Stability characterization and modeling of robust distributed benthic microbial fuel cell (DBMFC) system," *Elsevier Bioresource Technology*, Volume 144, pp. 477-484, September 2013.

[10] R. Umaz et al., "A power management system for multianode benthic microbial fuel cells" *IEEE Trans. on Power Electronics*, Volume 32, Issue 5, May. 2017.

[11] F. Qian et al., "Design of a shared-stage charge pump circuit for Multi-anode Microbial Fuel Cells," *IEEE International Symposium on Circuits and Systems (ISCAS)*, 2016

[12] T. Ewing, P. Ha, J. Babauta, N. Tang, D. Heo, and H. Beyenal, "Scale-up of sediment microbial fuel cells," *Journal Power Sources*, vol. 272, pp. 311-319, 2014.

LUTOSAP: Lookup Table Based Online Sample Preparation in Microfluidic Biochips*

Lingxuan Shao[1†], Yibin Yang[1†], Hailong Yao[1], Tsung-Yi Ho[2], and Yici Cai[1]
1. Tsinghua University 2. National Tsing Hua University
shao-14@mails.tsinghua.edu.cn, yyb15@mails.tsinghua.edu.cn, hailongyao@tsinghua.edu.cn
tyho@cs.nthu.edu.tw, caiyc@tsinghua.edu.cn

ABSTRACT

Existing sample preparation algorithms are either based on NP-style problem formulations, e.g., using integer linear programming (ILP), which runs very slowly, or based on heuristic algorithms, which cannot obtain optimal solutions regarding different objectives. This paper proposes the first online sample preparation algorithm based on the lookup table method, named LUTOSAP. LUTOSAP enables fast query response for online sample preparation requirements with the solution where the weighted sum of sample consumption, buffer consumption, and the number of mix-split operations is optimized. Experimental results show that LUTOSAP obtains optimal sample preparation solutions in microseconds within the accuracy tolerance of 0.2% for both single and double concentration values, which is orders of magnitude faster than existing algorithms. For multiple concentration values, the multiple-target sample preparation algorithm in LUTOSAP obtains near-optimal solution based on the constructed lookup table in microseconds, which well meets the critical fast-response requirements in online sample preparation.

1. INTRODUCTION

In the past decade, tremendous advances in microfluidic technologies have boosted automation of the traditional laboratory procedures in molecular biology and biochemistry. With specific fundamental driving technologies and working mechanisms, different microfluidic platforms have been developed, including two major types of microfluidic biochips supporting large-scale integration: (1) droplet-based (digital) microfluidic biochips using the *electrowetting* technology, and (2) flow-based microfluidic biochips based on the *multilayer soft lithography* technology. Compared with traditional laboratory procedures, a microfluidic biochip, also called *Lab-on-a-Chip* (*LoC*), greatly reduces both analysis time and sample/reagent consumption. Therefore, LoC has many promising applications including point-of-care diagnosis, drug discovery, protein and DNA analysis, sample preparation, cell-based assays and immunoassays. LoC is also used for multiplexed assays simultaneously for significantly enhanced flexibility and throughput.

Automatic *sample preparation* is a crucial preprocessing step in biochemical applications, which accounts for 60% of the work in analytical tests [1]. In molecular diagnosis, sample preparation dominates 90% of cost and 95% of the analysis time in biochemical experiments [2]. In the sample preparation process, sample droplets are typically mixed with buffer droplets in an appropriate way to produce droplets of a target concentration value. Both digital and flow-based microfluidic biochips are suitable for performing sample preparation tasks.

There has been a large body of research works on sample preparation algorithms [3–8], either using the digital microfluidic biochips or the flow-based digital microfluidic biochips. All previous works proposed heuristic/optimal algorithms for computing the sample preparation solutions, with the objective of either minimizing sample consumption, minimizing buffer (i.e., water for dilution) consumption, or the number of mix-split operations. However, for optimizing the weighted sum of all these objectives, only methods based integer linear programming (ILP) are suitable, which run slowly in real applications [8]. We propose the first lookup-table-based sample preparation method LUTOSAP, which simultaneously optimizes the sample consumption, buffer consumption, and number of mix-split operations. Moreover, LUTOSAP runs in microseconds and thus is orders of magnitude faster than existing methods. Major contributions of the paper are summarized as follows.

- The first lookup-table-based sample preparation method is proposed, where lookup tables are constructed for both single and double concentration values, and it takes microseconds to obtain optimal sample preparation solution.
- The constructed lookup tables are utilized in the proposed multiple-target sample preparation algorithm to obtain the near-optimal solution.
- Effective table construction algorithm is proposed based on the depth-first search (DFS) strategy, which guarantees the low memory consumption and fast construction of all the table entries.

*The work of H. Yao was supported in part by the National Natural Science Foundation of China (61674093) and Tsinghua University Initiative Scientific Research Program (20141081203). The work of T.-Y. Ho was supported in part by the Ministry of Science and Technology of Taiwan, under Grant MOST 105-2221-E-007-118-MY3 and 104-2220-E-007-021 and in part by the Technical University of Munich-Institute for Advanced Study, funded by the German Excellence Initiative and the European Union Seventh Framework Program under grant agreement no 291763. The work of Y. Cai was supported by the National Natural Science Foundation of China (61274031).

†Indicates equal student contribution.

Permission to make digital or hard copies of all or part of this work for personal or classroom use is granted without fee provided that copies are not made or distributed for profit or commercial advantage and that copies bear this notice and the full citation on the first page. Copyrights for components of this work owned by others than ACM must be honored. Abstracting with credit is permitted. To copy otherwise, or republish, to post on servers or to redistribute to lists, requires prior specific permission and/or a fee. Request permissions from permissions@acm.org.

GLSVLSI '17, May 10-12, 2017, Banff, AB, Canada
© 2017 ACM. ISBN 978-1-4503-4972-7/17/05...$15.00
DOI: http://dx.doi.org/10.1145/3060403.3060446

- The proposed method can optimize the weighted sum of (1) buffer consumption, (2) sample consumption, and (3) the number of mix-split operations. Moreover, the obtained accuracy tolerance is within 0.2%.

2. PRELIMINARIES AND PROBLEM FOMULATION

2.1 Preliminaries

For sample preparation in digital microfluidic biochips, the $1:1$ mixing model is naturally supported, i.e., two droplets of same volume can be mixed into a larger one, and then split into two equal-volume droplets. Whereas in flow-based microfluidic biochips, there are no droplets but fluids of certain volume. Therefore, using the $1:1$ mixing model in flow-based microfluidic biochips, two unit-volume fluids are mixed into a two-unit-volume fluid, and then split into two parts of fluids of unit volume. For simplicity, we use droplets to represent both the above two cases. Unless otherwise specified, a droplet is of a unit volume.

In sample preparation process for a target concentration value, the initial input includes sample droplet with 100% concentration value and buffer/water droplet with 0% concentration value, respectively. Both digital and flow-based microfluidic biochips support the 1:1 mixing model, i.e., two different droplets can be mixed and then split with equal volume. Using the $1:1$ mixing model, after mixing a sample droplet with a buffer droplet, and then splitting the mixture into two droplets, we have two droplets with the same concentration value 50%. We call the mixing operation followed by a splitting operation as *mix-split* operation, which is also called as a *dilution operation*. Formally, in a single mix-split operation, for droplet i with concentration value p_i ($0\% \leq p_i \leq 100\%$) and droplet j with concentration value p_j ($0\% \leq p_j \leq 100\%$), the output are two droplets of concentration value $\frac{p_i+p_j}{2}$.

2.2 Problem Formulation

This paper presents the lookup-table-based sample preparation method to address the following problem:

Given: (1) The sample fluid with certain concentration value, (2) the number of targets and the target concentration values, and (3) the required accuracy tolerance.

Find: Constructed lookup table along with the queried table entry of optimal or near-optimal sample preparation steps for the target concentration values.

Objective: Minimize the cost function of sample consumption, buffer consumption, and the number of mix-split operations.

Subject to: The accuracy tolerance must be observed.

Let c_v denotes the concentration value of the input sample, and let c_t denotes the target concentration value (suppose there is only one target). Then we define $p_t = c_t/c_v$ as the ratio of the two concentration values. After the transformation, we still call p_t as the target concentration value. Because of the transformation, we may assume that the concentration value of input sample fluid is 1, and that of the buffer fluid is 0.

The objective cost function, which is the cost for sample preparation, is defined as $f(c_s, c_b, s_o)$, where c_s means the cost for sample droplet consumption, c_b is the cost for buffer consumption, and s_o is the number of mix-split operation steps. Here, the cost function can be either linear or nonlinear combinations of c_s, c_b, and s_o. For example, the cost function can be defined as

$$f(c_s, c_b, s_o) = \alpha_1 c_s + \alpha_2 c_b + \alpha_3 s_o$$

where α_1, α_2, and α_3 are user-defined coefficients. It is easy to understand that the number of mix-split operation steps should be minimized for reduced number of mixers and assay execution time. Besides, the sample/reagent droplets are so expensive that minimizing the sample consumption reduces the total cost. Therefore, these two factors are usually considered in the cost function.

With the $1:1$ mixing model, the available concentration values that can be obtained are in the form of $\frac{m}{2^n}$, where $n, m \in \mathbb{N}$. Therefore, the required accuracy tolerance needs to be provided in sample preparation, which is defined as σ. Let $\overline{p}$ denote the concentration value that can be obtained using the proposed sample preparation method. For any target concentration value $p_t \in \mathbb{R}$, $0 \leq p_t \leq 1$, we expect that there exists $\overline{p}$ such that the following constraint is satisfied:

$$|\overline{p} - p_t| \leq \sigma$$

Let ε denote accuracy tolerance of the proposed sample preparation method, i.e., for any target concentration value $p_t \in \mathbb{R}$, $0 \leq p_t \leq 1$, the proposed method obtains the sample preparation solution with concentration value of $\overline{p}$, satisfying

$$|\overline{p} - p_t| \leq \varepsilon$$

Therefore, as long as the user-specified σ is less than ε, our method can always obtain the target concentration value within the required accuracy tolerance. Now we only have to focus on how to find the way to produce the droplet with the concentration value $\frac{m}{2^{n_0}}$, where $0 \leq m \leq 2^{n_0}$, and n_0 is a fixed constant. The value of n_0 depends on the accuracy tolerance we could reach. For different sample preparation methods, the tolerance is related to the number of target concentration values. Therefore, n_0 is different in different cases, e.g., $n_0 = 11$ in single-target problem and $n_0 = 10$ in double-target and multiple-target problems.

The proposed sample preparation method can obtain every concentration value $\frac{m}{2^{n_0}}$, where $0 \leq m \leq 2^{n_0}$, and every droplet can be produced within the accuracy tolerance $\varepsilon = \frac{1}{2^{n_0}}$. Taking single-target problem as an example, if we get the target concentration value p_t and the required accuracy tolerance σ, we find out every m_0 satisfying $|\frac{m_0}{2^{n_0}} - p_t| \leq \sigma$. Then we define the set $\mathcal{M} = \{m_0 : |\frac{m_0}{2^{n_0}} - p_t| \leq \sigma\}$. For typical values of σ (i.e., σ is greater than ε), m_0 exists. When multiple m_0 values are available, we choose the m_0 value with the minimum cost. Then we present sample preparation solution for the concentration value $\frac{m_0}{2^{n_0}}$. This way guarantees the accuracy tolerance $\varepsilon = \frac{1}{2^{n_0}}$.

3. PHASE I

3.1 Table Construction

In this section we adopts the depth first search (DFS) strategy to search every way to produce the droplets with every available concentration value. Since we only care about the ratio of concentration values, we extract a common denominator from these fractions of concentration values and omit the denominator. This can be obtained by multiplying $\lambda = 2^n$ to all the fractions, where n is number of mix-split operations.

The number of mix-split operations n is limited within 10 in LUTOSAP. From the following results, the accuracy tolerance of 0.1% can be achieved within 10 mix-split operations. So we assume there are 10 sample droplets and 10 buffer droplets at the beginning for constructing the lookup table. We recursively compute every possible concentration values within 10 operations. Let *state* denote the set of droplets together with some essential information for each scenario. $state(n,s)$ is defined as

$$\begin{cases} (n,s) \\ (p_1,q_1)),(p_2,q_2),(p_3,q_3),\ldots,(p_{l_{n,s}},q_{l_{n,s}}) \\ (pre_n, pre_s, pre_{p_1}, pre_{p_2}) \end{cases}$$

where n means the number of mix-split operations that have been conducted, p_i means the concentration value of the droplets, and q_i

means the number of droplets with the concentration value p_i. We assume that $q_i > 0, q_i \in \mathbb{N}$. So q_i satisfies $\sum_{i=1}^{l_{n,s}} q_i = 20$, where $l_{n,s}$ means the number of different concentration values in $state(n,s)$. Except the initial state, the current state is always induced from a previous state. (pre_n, pre_s) means that $state(n,s)$ is induced from the previous state $state(pre_n, pre_s)$, and (pre_{p_1}, pre_{p_2}) means the concentration values of the droplets used in the previous mix-split operation. Obviously, $pre_n = n-1$.

Let $state(n)$ denotes the set $state(n) = \{states(n,s) : n\ is\ a\ fixed\ constant\}$. And let $|state(n)|$ denote the number of states in $state(n)$. We use s $(1 \le s \le |state(n)|)$ to number those different states, which have all experienced n mix-split operations.

If we do a mix-split operation on the $state(n,s)$, then

$$\begin{cases} (n,s) \\ (p_1,q_1),(p_2,q_2),(p_3,q_3),\ldots,(p_{l_{n,s}},q_{l_{n,s}}) \\ (pre_n, pre_s, pre_{p_1}, pre_{p_2}) \end{cases}$$

Let i_0, j_0 $(1 \le i_0, j_0 \le l_{n,s})$ denote the subscripts of the concentration values during mix-split operations. We define an *effective operation* as the operation where the two droplets for mixing have different concentration values. So an effective operation means $p_{i_0} \neq p_{j_0}$. If the mix-split operation is effective, the state $state(n,s)$ will induce $state(n+1, s_k)$ in 1 : 1 mix-split model.

$$\begin{cases} (n+1, s_k) \\ (p_1,q_1),\ldots,(p_{i_0},q_{i_0}-1),\ldots,(p_{j_0},q_{j_0}-1),\ldots, \\ \quad (p_{l_{n,s}},q_{l_{n,s}}),(\frac{1}{2}p_{i_0}+\frac{1}{2}p_{j_0},2) \\ (n,s,p_{i_0},p_{j_0}) \end{cases}$$

If $q_{i_0} - 1 = 0$, we omit $(p_{i_0}, q_{i_0} - 1)$.

4. PHASE II

4.1 Single Target

Lookup tables for single and double target concentration values are constructed by the previous searching procedure. We can query the table to obtain the optimal solution when the number of target concentration values is less than or equal to 2. The single-target lookup table is constructed as followings. First we fix $\lambda = 1024$, which means we multiply all the concentration values by 1024. The concentration value $\overline{p}$ that can be obtained satisfies $0 \le \overline{p} \le 1024$, $\overline{p} \in \mathbb{N}$.

The *flag-array* is defined for describing the sample preparation method.

$$\{(j, f_o(j))|(p1_j^1, p2_j^1),(p1_j^2, p2_j^2),\ldots,(p1_j^{n_j}, p2_j^{n_j})\}_{j=0}^{1024}$$

where j is the concentration value that can be obtained and other notations will be explained later. After we obtain the $state(n)$, $(n \le 10)$, we record every concentration value that has been computed, as long as the value of cost function and the mix-split operations to obtain the concentration value. For example, once $state(n,s)$ have been computed, we have

$$\begin{cases} (n,s) \\ (p_1,q_1),(p_2,q_2),(p_3,q_3),\ldots,(p_{l_{n,s}},q_{l_{n,s}}) \\ (pre_n, pre_s, pre_{p_1}, pre_{p_2}) \end{cases}$$

Now we have found a way to obtain one concentration value $p_i, 1 \le i \le l_{n,s}$. Suppose that $p_i = j$. Then since $(pre_n, pre_s, pre_{p_1}, pre_{p_2})$ is recorded, the previous state $state(pre_s, pre_p)$ and the corresponding mix-split operations can be traced. Therefore, we can trace back to the original $state(0,1)$, and thus the n operations can be obtained. Thus, $(p1_j^1, p2_j^1),(p1_j^2, p2_j^2),\ldots,(p1_j^n, p2_j^n)$ denote the concentration values of droplets used in the n operations. We set $n_j = n$ to show that n is specific for j to distinguish the different concentration values.

For a particular j and the relative $state(n_j, s)$, the cost function could be evaluated and the state with lower cost could be identified. Then, the optimal concentration value along with the cost and mix-split steps is stored for future query. *flag-array* shows the minimum cost function for each concentration value, from which we guarantee the accuracy tolerance of 0.1% in 10 steps. This lookup table is also utilized to solve the multiple-target problem. For 11 mix-split operations, a lookup table with accuracy tolerance of 0.05% can also be constructed. In the experimental results, the $n = 11$ case is also achieved (see Section 6).

Algorithms 1 and 2 present the lookup table construction algorithm based on depth first search (DFS) strategy. The main idea is to recursively mix-split the droplets and store the intermediate states for all droplets with different concentration values. Then the lookup table could be constructed according to the different states with different concentration values.

```
Input: Number of mix-split operations n_max.
Output: Constructed lookup table.
Let cost denote the value of given cost function;
Let Q(i) denote the number of droplets with concentration
  value i;
Let state denote the set of droplets;
Let |state| denote the number of different concentration values;
Let state(i) denote the i^th concentration value in the state;
Let f(state(i)) denote the value of cost function for state(i);
Set Q(0) <- n_m ax, and set Q(1) <- n_m ax;
Call function ConstructTable(0, 0, Q);
```

Algorithm 1: Lookup table construction algorithm.

```
Input: n, cost, and state.
Output: Constructed table by depth first search.
for i = 1 to |state| do
    if cost < f(state(i)) then
        Set f(state(i)) <- cost;
        Record how concentreation value state(i) is obtained;
if n == n_max then
    return;
for i = 1 to |state| do
    for j = i+1 to |state| do
        Compute new state state_new by mix-split operation on
          the two droplets of concentration values state(i) and
          state(j);
        Compute Q_new[state_new] and the new cost f_new;
        Call function ConstructTable(n+1, f_new,
          Q_new[state_new]);
```

Algorithm 2: Algorithm *ConstructTable*.

4.2 Double Target

The idea in solving the double-target problem is similar to the single-target case. We define *flag-array*2 for double-target sample preparation to record the minimum number of mixing operations:

$$\{i, j, f_o(i,j))|(p1_{i,j}^1, p2_{i,j}^1),\ldots,(p1_{i,j}^{n_{i,j}}, p2_{i,j}^{n_{i,j}})\}_{i=0,j=0}^{1024}$$

Here, (i, j) is the concentration value obtained, and $f_o(i, j)$ is the minimum cost function for the double-target concentration pair (i, j).

$(p1_{i,j}^1, p2_{i,j}^1),(p1_{i,j}^2, p2_{i,j}^2),\ldots,(p1_{i,j}^{n_{i,j}}, p2_{i,j}^{n_{i,j}})$ means the concentration values of droplets used in the $n_{i,j}$ mix-split operations. *flag-array*2 is computed with the same algorithm as that in the single-target sample preparation method. Using *flag-array*2 we can obtain the double-target sample preparation solution. And from the experimental results, the accuracy tolerance is limited in 0.2% (see Section 6). Except the double-target sample preparation, this lookup table is also utilized to solve the multiple-target problem.

5. MULTIPLE TARGET

After the lookup tables in both simple-target and double-target problems have been successfully constructed, the multiple-target table can be theoretically achieved in the same way. But the issue is that the size of the lookup table increases exponentially as the number of targets increases. Therefore, we propose a fast multiple-target sample preparation algorithm denoted by LUTOSAPm relying on the single-target and double-target lookup tables. Algorithm 3 presents the proposed method that utilizes the lookup tables to obtain the near-optimal solution for the multiple-target problem.

Suppose that there are k target concentration values $p_1, p_2, \ldots, p_k$, which are reordered by their denominators. The fraction value with larger denominator is sorted to the front of the list. The list is sorted in such a way because the concentration value with larger denominator is more difficult to produce. Such difficult concentration values should be produced earlier.

Input: k and $\{p_1, p_2, \ldots, p_k\}$
Output: Multiple-target solution
for $i = 2$ *to* k **do**
  Query the double-target lookup table to find the solution $chain_i$ to produce (p_1, p_i);
  Simulate the mix-split process by $chain_i$ and obtain state $state_i$;
  Calculate the number of concentration values c_i in set $\{p_j\}_{j=1}^{k}$ included in $state_i$;
  Record the value of minimal cost function f_i in $state_i$;
Choose i_0 so that $state_{i_0}$ has (a) the largest c_{i_0} and (b) the lowest f_{i_0}, where Condition(a) has higher priority than (b);
Print the solution $chain_{i_0}$;
Call function $LUTOSAPm(k-2; p_2, \hat{p}_{i_0}, \ldots, p_k)$ with p_1 and p_{i_0} removed;

Algorithm 3: Multiple-target sample preparation algorithm *LUTOSAPm*.

From the proposed method the k target concentration values $p_1, p_2, \ldots, p_k$ can be realized by a series of mix-split operations, and the runtime is in microseconds according to the experimental results (see Section 5). This proposed method does not guarantee to obtain the optimal solution, but we claim that it is near-optimal with the lookup tables.

6. EXPERIMENTAL RESULTS

6.1 Single and Double Target

We have implemented the proposed sample preparation method, LUTOSAP, in C++ programming language on a 2.60GHz 32-core Intel Xeon Linux workstation with 132GB memory. For single-target sample preparation, the accuracy tolerance is 0.05% ($\varepsilon = 0.05\%$). And for double-target sample preparation, the accuracy tolerance is 0.2% ($\varepsilon = 0.2\%$). Table 1 shows the runtime to query the table for both single-target and double-target values, which is in microseconds.

Table 1: The runtime for querying lookup table.

Cases	Average time(μs)	Max time(μs)	Standard Deviation(μs)
Single Target	8.6403	21	1.32
Double Target	4.17	28	3.93

6.2 Multiple target

The lookup tables are constructed, where the mix-spit operation steps n equals 10. So the single and double concentration values are in the form of $\frac{m}{1024}$. Therefore, the proposed LUTOSAPm can obtain the multiple target solution within the accuracy tolerance $\varepsilon = 0.1\%$. We take minimizing the number of mix-split steps as an example. In this case, the test program has the following 3 steps (suppose that there are k targets).

- Step 1: generate k random uniform variables in the form of $\{\frac{m}{1024}\}$ denoted by $T_1, T_2, \ldots, T_k$.
- Step 2: use the proposed algorithm to search the solution of the k target concentration value $T_1, T_2, \ldots, T_k$, and record the number of operation steps n and the runtime rt.
- Step 3: repeat Step 1 and Step 2 for 1000 times, and calculate the average number of operation steps $\overline{n}$ and the average runtime $\overline{rt}$.

Table 2: The mix-split operation steps and the runtime using LUTOSAPm.

k	100	50	20	10	5
$\overline{n}$	492	251	110	60	34
$\overline{rt}$	44.198ms	8.242ms	0.801ms	0.273ms	0.105ms

The average number of mix-split steps $\overline{n}$ and the average runtime $\overline{rt}$ in different cases are presented in table 2. From the table, the runtime for searching the multiple-target solution is in microseconds. To verify the effectiveness of LUTOSAPm, we implemented the simulate annealing algorithm (SAA) to optimize the multiple-target solution. The input of target concentration values of SAA are exactly the same as that of LUTOSAPm. From the results, the number of mix-split operation steps in the two algorithms are very close. However, the runtime for searching the near-optimal solution by SAA is 492 times of LOUSAPm on average. The experimental results show that LOUSAPm is very effective and efficient.

7. CONCLUSION

We have proposed a fast online sample preparation algorithm, called LUTOSAP, based on lookup table method. LUTOSAP enables fast query response with (near-)optimal solution minimizing weighted sum of sample consumption, buffer consumption, and number of mix-split steps. From the experimental results, LUTOSAP obtains optimal sample preparation solution for both single- and double-target sample preparation problems, and near-optimal solution for multiple-target sample preparation problem within the required accuracy tolerance. Moreover, the runtime of LUTOSAP is in microseconds, which is orders of magnitude faster than existing multiple-target sample preparation algorithms.

8. REFERENCES

[1] J. Ducrée, R. Zengerle, and J. Newman, "FlowMap: Microfluidics Roadmap for the Life Sciences", FlowMap Consortium, 2004. *Online*. Available: https://microfluidics-roadmap.com

[2] P. R. C. Gascoyne, and J. V. Vykoukal, "Dielectrophoresis-based sample handling in general-purpose programmable diagnostic instruments", *Proc. IEEE*, vol. 92, no. 1, 2004, pp. 22-42.

[3] C. Kim, K. Lee, J. H. Kim, K. S. Shin, K. J. Lee, T. S. Kim, and J. Y. Kang, "A serial dilution microfluidic device using a ladder network generating logarithmic or linear concentrations", *Lab-on-a-Chip*, vol. 8, no. 3, pp. 473-479, 2008.

[4] S. Roy, B. B. Bhattacharya, and K. Chakrabarty, "Optimization of dilution and mixing of biochemical samples using digital microfluidic biochips", *IEEE Trans. on CAD*, vol. 29, no. 11, pp. 1696-1708, 2010.

[5] C.-H. Liu, K.-C. Shen, and J.-D. Huang, "Reactant minimization for sample preparation on microfluidic biochips with various mixing models" *IEEE Trans. on CAD*, vol. 34, no. 12, pp. 1918-1927, 2015.

[6] D. Mitra, S. Roy, S. Bhattacharjee, K. Chakrabarty, and B. B. Bhattacharya, "Onchip sample preparation for multiple targets using digital microfluidics," *IEEE Trans. on CAD*, vol. 33, no. 8, pp. 1131-1144, 2014.

[7] C.-Y. Lee, C.-L. Chang, Y.-N. Wang, and L.-M. Fu, "Microfluidic mixing: A review" *Int. J. Mol. Sci.*, vol. 12, no. 5, pp. 3263-3287, 2011.

[8] T. A. Dinh, S. Yamashita, and T.-Y. Ho, "A Network-Flow-Based Optimal Sample Preparation Algorithm for Digital Microfluidic Biochips," *Proc. ASP-DAC*, pp. 225-230, 2014.

Throughput Optimization for Lifetime Budgeting in Many-Core Systems

Liang Wang[1,2,3,4], Xiaohang Wang[2,4,5], Ho-fung Leung[1] and Terrence Mak[3,4,5]

[1] Department of Computer Science and Engineering, The Chinese University of Hong Kong, Hong Kong
[2] School of Software Engineering, South China University of Technology, China
[3] School of Electronics and Computer Science, University of Southampton, United Kingdom
[4] Guangzhou Institute of Advanced Technology, Chinese Academy of Sciences, China
[5] Shenzhen Institute of Advanced Technology, Chinese Academy of Sciences, China
lwang@cse.cuhk.edu.hk, xiaohangwang@scut.edu.cn, lhf@cuhk.edu.hk, tmak@ecs.soton.ac.uk

ABSTRACT

Due to technology scaling, lifetime reliability is becoming one of major design constraints in the design of future many-core systems. In this paper, we propose a novel runtime mapping scheme which could dynamically map the applications given a lifetime reliability constraint. A *borrowing strategy* is adopted to manage the lifetime in a long-term scale, and the lifetime constraint could be relaxed in short-term scale when the communication performance requirement is high. The throughput could be improved because the communication performance of communication intensive applications is optimized, and meanwhile the waiting time of computation intensive application is reduced. Furthermore, an improved neighborhood allocation method is proposed for the runtime mapping scheme. The experimental results show that compared to the state-of-the-art lifetime-constrained mapping, the proposed mapping scheme could have over 20% throughput improvement.

Keywords

Many-core systems; lifetime reliability constraint; runtime mapping; throughput

1. INTRODUCTION

Due to technology scaling, aging issue is becoming a major design challenge of a chip. To improve the mean time to failure (MTTF) of many-core systems, various techniques such as dynamic voltage and frequency scaling (DVFS) [9], task mapping [1, 7], etc. have been proposed. The lifetime reliability could also be taken as a design constraint to meet a target MTTF [6, 8]. However, existing lifetime-constrained runtime task mapping algorithms [6] try to map the incoming application to a near-square area to reduce the communication overhead, which possibly incurs lower throughput of the system. Fig. 1 presents an example. The left diagram shows that when the application is mapped to a square region, the high-aged core is also occupied. If the lifetime constraint of the high-aged core is not satisfied, the application needs to wait until the core recovers from high-aged status. The long waiting time leads to low throughput of the system. Moreover, since the applications have various communication characteristics, mapping all applications to a near-square region is not necessary. Therefore, as shown in the right diagram of Fig. 1, the computation intensive applications could be mapped to a non-square area. Despite of slightly increase of the average communication distance, the system throughput could be improved due to shorter waiting time.

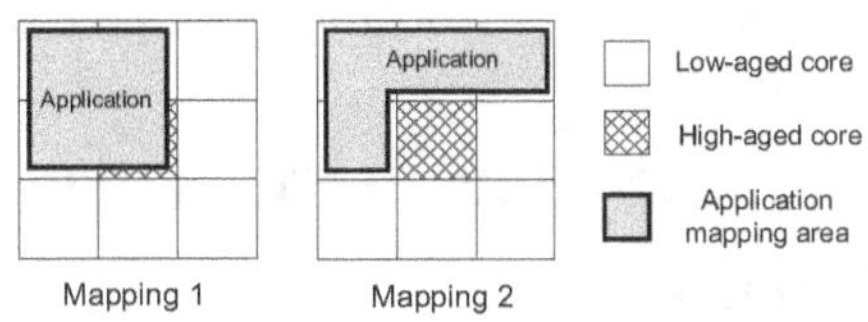

Figure 1: Motivation example

In this paper, we propose a runtime task mapping scheme with lifetime reliability as a constraint. The aim is to improve the global throughput of the system by dynamically mapping applications with various communication characteristics. The *borrowing strategy* [9] is adopted to meet the lifetime constraint in a long-term scale. In other words, if the incoming application is communication intensive, it is mapped to a near-square area with lifetime constraint locally relaxed because of higher communication performance requirement in local time window. Meanwhile, the computation intensive applications are mapped to an area with higher dispersion to free the high-aged cores. The global throughput is improved because the communication performance of communication intensive applications is optimized, and meanwhile the waiting time of computation intensive application is reduced.

2. RELATED WORK

Task mapping algorithms have been widely exploited to improve the lifetime reliability of many-core systems. The lifetime reliability could also be taken as a design constraint to meet a target MTTF [8, 4, 6]. Huang et al. [8] proposed to use simulate annealing to minimize the energy consumption under lifetime reliability constraint for the task scheduling problem on MPSoCs. However, the mapping and scheduling problem is solved offline. Gnad et al. [4] proposed a run-

Permission to make digital or hard copies of all or part of this work for personal or classroom use is granted without fee provided that copies are not made or distributed for profit or commercial advantage and that copies bear this notice and the full citation on the first page. Copyrights for components of this work owned by others than ACM must be honored. Abstracting with credit is permitted. To copy otherwise, or republish, to post on servers or to redistribute to lists, requires prior specific permission and/or a fee. Request permissions from permissions@acm.org.
GLSVLSI '17, May 10-12, 2017, Banff, AB, Canada
© 2017 ACM. ISBN 978-1-4503-4972-7/17/05...$15.00
DOI: http://dx.doi.org/10.1145/3060403.3060419

time aging management system which harnesses dark silicon to decelerate aging, and improves the overall system performance for a given lifetime. However, their method targets at malleable applications, not applicable for task graph based applications. The method in [6] takes the aging information into consideration when selecting the first node, and a runtime mapping given lifetime constraint is proposed. However, the method neglects that the lifetime reliability could be managed in a long-term scale. The *borrow strategy*, proposed in [9], indicates that the lifetime constraint can be locally relaxed for better performance in local time window while still meeting the lifetime constraint over the large time window. DVFS is adopted to control the performance and reliability. However, the *borrow strategy* is less exploited to manage lifetime reliability by runtime task mapping. In this paper, the proposed runtime mapping scheme incorporates the *borrow strategy* to take performance in local time window as the first priority to optimize, and manages the lifetime in a large time window.

3. MODELS AND PROBLEM STATEMENT

3.1 Relevant Models

3.1.1 Reliability Model

The lifetime reliability can be modeled according to Weibull distribution [7]. Considering the runtime variation of operating conditions, an aging effect for a processor is also defined as $A = \sum \Delta t_i/\alpha_i$ [7], where Δt_i is the duration of the i-th time interval. α_i is the scale parameter. The aging effect integrates all operating conditions including temperature, voltage, frequency and utilization into a single value. To satisfy the pre-defined lifetime constraint, the aging effect should be less that the target aging effect. We define a lifetime budget in Eq. 1.

$$\Delta A(t) = A_{target}(t) - A(t) > 0 \qquad (1)$$

A positive lifetime budget value means the lifetime constraint is satisfied and vice versa. For lifetime reliability management, the lifetime could be regarded as a resource consumed over time. $A_{target}(t)$ indicates the given resource, and $A(t)$ indicates the consumed resource. As soon as the consumed resource is less than the given resource, the lifetime constraint is satisfied.

3.1.2 Application Model and Platform Model

Each application can be modeled as a directed task graph $AG = (T, E)$, where T is the set of tasks, and E is the set of directed edges. Each task $t_i \in T$ has a worst-case execution time when mapped to a core. Each edge $e_{i,j} \in E$ represents data dependency between the source task t_i and destination task t_j. The weight $w_{i,j}$ represents the communication volume from task t_i to task t_j.

The many-core system is assume homogeneous. The system could be represented as a directed graph $G(P, L)$, where P represents the set of cores n_i and $l_{i,j} \in L$ represents the physical channel from n_i to n_j. The application mapping and resource management are controlled by a centralized resource manager. The task mapping scheme determines how an application is mapped on a set of cores. In this paper, it is assumed the maximum number of tasks running on a core is 1. The mapping function $map(t_i)$ defines which core that the task t_i is mapped on.

3.2 Problem Statement

In this paper, the throughput is defined as the average number of applications finished within a time period, at the end of which the lifetime constraint of the system is satisfied. To improve the throughput, the problem is formulated as

$$\begin{aligned} \text{maximize} \quad & \textbf{Throughput} = \frac{N}{t - t^1_{\text{arrive}}} \\ \text{subject to} \quad & t \geq t^N_{\text{finish}} \\ & \Delta A_j(t) > 0, \forall n_j \in P \end{aligned} \qquad (2)$$

where t^1_{arrive} is the arrival time of the first application. Eq. 2 defines the constraint that the all N applications should have finished at time t. For each application, the finishing time is related to the execution time and the waiting time. Eq. 2 also defines the lifetime constraint which should be satisfied at time t, otherwise the high-aged cores should be kept free until the lifetime constraint is met.

4. PROPOSED APPROACH

4.1 Aging Map Update and First Node Selection

For runtime lifetime management, the aging effect can be calculated given operating conditions by an on-line reliability estimation framework which is similar as [10]. The manager records the ΔA values for all cores. Because aging is a slow process, aging map is updated periodically.

Recent runtime mapping algorithms generally include two steps [3, 6] (1) selecting a first node (2) allocating the tasks around the first node. The state-of-the-art method incorporates lifetime reliability metric, status of the cores and the range of the square into a single value when selecting the first node [6]. In this paper, the first node selection is based on a similar reliability factor defined in [6], but the metric for lifetime is replaced as the lifetime budget defined in this paper.

4.2 Lifetime Constraint Satisfaction

To satisfy the lifetime constraint, the applications are grouped in batches. Each batch contains at most N applications. When a new application arrives, the application is put in current batch if the current batch is not full. Otherwise, it is put into the next batch. In the mapping process, only when the lifetime budget of the system becomes positive after mapping all applications in previous batch, the application of next batch could be mapped. Within each batch for the next application to map, the mapping scheme first determines if the application is put into the waiting queue or mapped immediately according to the lifetime budget of the first node.

4.3 Mapping Algorithm

After the first node is selected, the tasks of the application are allocated to the neighborhood cores around the first node. The applications are classified into communication intensive applications and computation intensive applications according to their communication to computation ratio (CCR), which is defined as the average data volume to be sent in one application divided by the average computation workload. The *borrowing strategy* is adopted to meet the lifetime constraint in a long-term scale. In other words, if the incoming application is a communication intensive applications, it is mapped to a near-square area with lifetime

Algorithm 1 Neighborhood allocation for an application

Input n_f: First node;
$\Delta A_i, i \in [1, |N|]$: Aging map of all cores.
AG_i: the application to be mapped;
Output Mapping function $T \to P$
Definition Ω: the tasks that are not mapped;
1: $\Omega \leftarrow T$
2: $r \leftarrow 1$ ▷ Radius of square around the first node
3: Take the first task t_f from Ω in breadth-first order of AG_i
4: Map t_f on n_f
5: $S_r \leftarrow$ The set of cores that are unoccupied within current square, which is with radius r around n_f
6: **while** $\Omega \neq \varnothing$ **do**
7: Take the next task t_n in Ω in breadth-first order
8: **if** $S_r = \varnothing$ **then**
9: $r \leftarrow r + 1$
10: S_r is expanded
11: **end if**
12: **if** CCR > Threshold **then**
13: $n_m \leftarrow$ the unoccupied core within S_r and with the minimum number of weighted hops with all predecessors of task t_n
14: **else**
15: $n_m \leftarrow$ the unoccupied core with $\Delta A_m > 0$ and within S_r and with the minimum number of weighted hops with all predecessors of task t_n
16: **end if**
17: Map t_n on n_m
18: Remove n_m from S_r, and remove t_m from Ω
19: **end while**

constraint locally relaxed. This is because the communication performance requirement in local time window is higher, the performance is the first priority to optimize. However, the computation intensive applications are mapped to an area with higher dispersion to free the high-aged cores.

4.3.1 Mapping Communication Intensive Application

For communication intensive applications, the communication distance is a more important metric to optimize. One of important metrics to evaluate the area selection is Average Weighted Manhattan Distance (AWMD) [3]. A lower AWMD value indicates lower communication overhead in terms of communication time and power. To mitigate the internal and external congestion, a near-square region is preferred [3]. The widely adopted method for neighborhood allocation is CONA [3], which selects the node that fits the smallest square when mapping next task. However, the communication distance with predecessors of current task is not considered, which possibly leads to high communication cost with predecessors. In this paper, we propose an improved method for neighborhood nodes allocation named aging-aware neighborhood allocation (ANA), which takes both task communication overhead and aging information into consideration. The algorithm for the method is presented in Algorithm 1. Compared to CONA, the major improvement is that the proposed method maps the next task to the core that is with the minimum weighted communication with predecessors of the task. The weighted hops with all predecessors of task t_n could be represented as $\sum w_{i,n} MD(map(t_i), map(t_n)), \forall e_{i,n} \in E$.

Since the maximum possible number of cores in S_r is $|P|$ and the maximum possible number of predecessors is $|T|$, the complexity of the algorithm is $O(|T|^2|P|)$, showing that the algorithm has low complexity.

4.3.2 Mapping Computation Intensive Application

Compared to communication intensive application, the execution time of computation intensive application is less affected by the communication distance. This creates the opportunities to map the application to a more dispersed area to avoid high-aged cores. The cores with negative lifetime budget can also recover from high-aged status. The mapping algorithm for computation intensive application is also presented in Algorithm 1 (line 15-17). Compared to mapping for communication intensive applications, the communication distance increases because some high-aged cores are avoided and the mapping area is more dispersed.

5. EXPERIMENTAL RESULTS

5.1 Simulation Setup

In this paper, the experiments are performed in an event-driven many-core simulator. A modified CALIPER [2] is integrated to model the lifetime reliability of many-core system. We assume that the MTTF of the many-core system is determined by the minimum MTTF of all cores. Synthetic applications are adopted in the experiments. The synthetic task graphs are generated by DAGGEN [11] with configurations shown in Table 1.

The proposed lifetime-constrained mapping schemes, which incorporate CONA and ANA, are named *LBRM-CONA* and *LBRM-ANA* respectively. The mapping scheme is also compared with the state-of-the-art lifetime-constrained scheme [6], named as *DSRM*. A thermal design power (TDP) constrained mapping named *PAM* [5] and a state-of-the-art non-lifetime-aware runtime mapping named *MAPPRO* [6] are also compared in the experimental results.

5.2 Throughput Comparisons

The proposed mapping algorithm is evaluated in terms of throughput and AWMD under various lifetime constraints. There are 100000 application generated in the simulation, and the arrival rate of application is 0.001 application/cycle. The threshold to classified the applications is 1Kbit/cycle. In this paper, we do not evaluate how this threshold affects the results. It is left a future work to study how to select a threshold for higher throughput.

In the experiments, the metric for lifetime reliability is aging effect. First we assume that there is no lifetime constraint, i.e. $\Delta A > 0$ for all cores. The reference aging effect

Table 1: Configurations of synthetic applications and platform

Synthetic graph parameters	
Number of tasks	[15, 35], [45, 65]
Task execution time	[1000, 4000] (cycles)
Load of task	[0.5, 1]
CCR	[0, 2] (Kbit/cycle)
Network Parameters	
Size & Topology	$8 \times 8, 12 \times 12, 16 \times 16$ 2D mesh
Bandwidth	256 bits
Routing algorithm	XY routing
Base topology	8× 8
Latency	2 cycles per hop

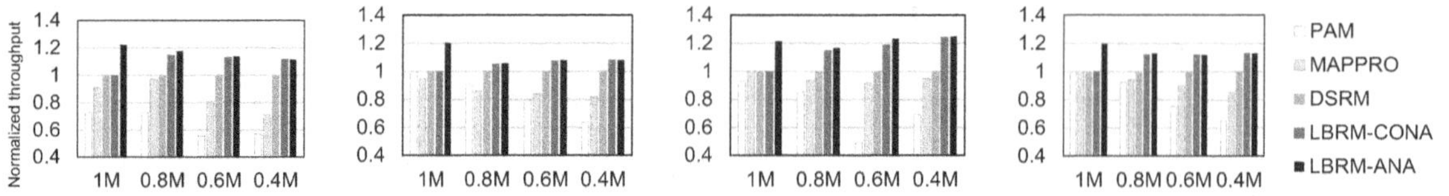

(a) Platf. size: 8×8, App. size: [15, 35] (b) Platf. size: 12 × 12, App. size: [15, 35] (c) Platf. size: 12 × 12, App. size: [45, 65] (d) Platf. size: 16 × 16, App. size: [45, 65]

Figure 2: (a)-(d) are the results under various platform sizes and application sizes. The results are normalized throughput under various lifetime constraints. M is the reference aging effect value of the system when there is no lifetime constraint.

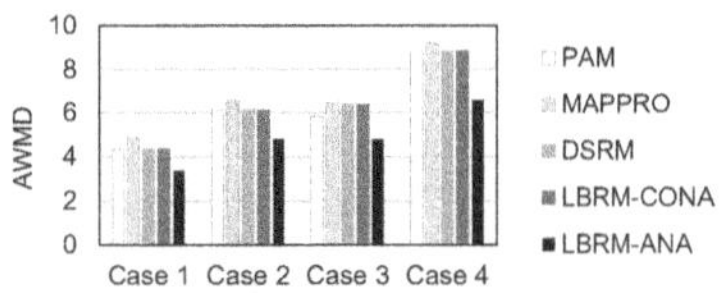

Figure 3: AWMD

value M of the system is obtained by running the proposed mapping algorithm without lifetime constraint. Then the target aging effect, i.e. lifetime constraint is set from $1M$ to $0.4M$, which means that the lifetime constraint imposed on the many-core system is from loose to tight. The experimental results are demonstrated in Fig. 2(a)-Fig. 2(d), which present the normalized throughput of the mapping schemes under various platforms and application sizes. The throughput is normalized to *DSRM*. The results show that when there is no lifetime constraint, *LBRM-CONA* has almost the same throughput as *DSRM*. However, when the lifetime constraint becomes tighter, *LBRM-CONA* has more that 20% throughput improvement that *DSRM*. For application size [15, 45], the improvement under 12 × 12 is less compared to 8 × 8 because the relative size of an application is smaller, creating less chances for avoiding high-aged cores in the neighborhood allocation. When there is no lifetime constraint, *LBRM-ANA* has around 20% higher throughput than others because an improved neighborhood allocation method is adopted, which leads to less communication time. When the lifetime constraint becomes tighter, *LBRM-CONA* and *LBRM-ANA* incur similar throughput. This is because they lead to similar aging effect distribution, and the recovery time from high-aged status is also counted in the calculation of throughput. Although the applications in a batch finish earlier for *LBRM-ANA*, the recovery time is longer.

The proposed neighborhood allocation is compared with CONA in terms of AWMD, shown in Fig. 3. Case1-case4 correspond to the configurations of Fig. 2(a)-Fig. 2(d) respectively. For each case, the AWMD is the average value among the 4 lifetime constraints. The results show that the proposed area selection method *ANA* reduces the AWMD by over 20% compared to CONA, indicating that the communication overhead is significantly lower than CONA.

6. CONCLUSION

In this paper, we propose a lifetime-constrained runtime mapping algorithm, which could dynamically map the incoming applications on the many-core system under a lifetime constraint. A *borrowing strategy* is adopted to manage the lifetime in long-term scale, while the lifetime constraint is locally relaxed to satisfy communication performance requirement in short-term scale. Compared to state-of-the-art lifetime-constrained mapping scheme, the proposed scheme has more than 20% throughput improvement on synthetic applications.

Acknowledgment

This research program is supported by CUHK Global Scholarship Programme for Research Excellence, Natural Science Foundation of China No. 61376024 and 61306024, Natural Science Foundation of Guangdong Province No. S2013040014366 and 2015A030313743, Basic Research Programme of Shenzhen No. JCYJ20140417113430642 and JCYJ20140901003939020, Special Program for Applied Research on Super Computation of the NSFC-Guangdong Joint Fund (the second phase), and the Science and Technology Research Grant of Guangdong Province No. 2016A010101011.

7. REFERENCES

[1] C. Bolchini and et al. Run-time mapping for reliable many-cores based on energy/performance trade-offs. In *Proc. of DFTS*, pages 58–64, 2013.

[2] C. Bolchini and et al. A lightweight and open-source framework for the lifetime estimation of multicore systems. In *Proc. of ICCD*, pages 166–172, 2014.

[3] M. Fattah and et al. Cona: Dynamic application mapping for congestion reduction in many-core systems. In *Proc. of ICCD*, pages 364–370, 2012.

[4] D. Gnad and et al. Hayat: Harnessing dark silicon and variability for aging deceleration and balancing. In *Proc. of DATE*, pages 180:1–180:6, 2015.

[5] M. H. Haghbayan and et al. Dark silicon aware power management for manycore systems under dynamic workloads. In *Proc. of ICCD*, pages 509–512, 2014.

[6] M. H. Haghbayan and et al. A lifetime-aware runtime mapping approach for many-core systems in the dark silicon era. In *Proc of DATE*, pages 854–857, 2016.

[7] L. Huang and et al. Lifetime reliability-aware task allocation and scheduling for mpsoc platforms. In *Proc. of DATE*, pages 51–56, 2009.

[8] L. Huang and et al. Energy-efficient task allocation and scheduling for multi-mode mpsocs under lifetime reliability constraint. In *Proc. of DATE*, pages 1584–1589, 2010.

[9] P. Mercati and et al. Workload and user experience aware dynamic reliability management in multicore processors. In *Proc. of DAC*, pages 1–6, 2013.

[10] P. Mercati and et al. An on-line reliability emulation framework. In *Proc. of EUC*, pages 334–339, 2014.

[11] F. Suter. Daggen: A synthethic task graph generator. https://github.com/frs69wq/daggen.

A Test Pattern Quality Metric for Diagnosis of Multiple Stuck-at and Transition faults *

Sarmad Tanwir
Virginia Polytechnic Institute and State University
Blacksburg, VA, USA
sarmadt@vt.edu

Michael Hsiao
Virginia Polytechnic Institute and State University
Blacksburg, VA, USA
hsiao@vt.edu

Loganathan Lingappan
Intel Corporation
Folsom, CA, USA
loganathan.lingappan@intel.com

ABSTRACT

The test patterns computed for detecting the manufacturing defects in the electronic circuits are generally insufficient for diagnosis. The test set compaction and failure log truncation lead to loss of critical failure observations that diagnosis might depend on. In this context, it is beneficial to know the diagnostic usefulness of failures so that we can log the more useful failures instead of logging the initial failures. In this paper, we evaluate three metrics to gauge such diagnostic usefulness in real-time by observing the circuit responses on the tester. We implement a pattern selection framework for failure logging and compare the results with those achieved by logging the initial failures. Using one of our proposed metrics, we were able to improve the diagnosis quality for a significant number of faulty instances of ISCAS'89 and IWLS'05 benchmarks having 1-7 inserted stuck-at and transition faults.

Keywords

Diagnosis, failure data, failure sampling, real-time, transition faults, stuck-at faults, metric, pattern selection

1. INTRODUCTION

Diagnosis of defective VLSI circuits plays an important role in improving the yield of the chip manufacturing processes. During diagnosis, we analyze the test, layout and design data to identify suspect locations of manufacturing defects, to reduce the cost of the physical failure analysis (PFA).

Figure 1 provides a simplified overview of the test and diagnosis process. A test suite consisting of a good mix of random and deterministic patterns targeted at stuck-at and transition faults is applied to the manufactured chips and the failures are logged. These failures that are mismatches with the good circuit response are then analyzed by offline diagnosis software tools to find a set of suspect locations. In

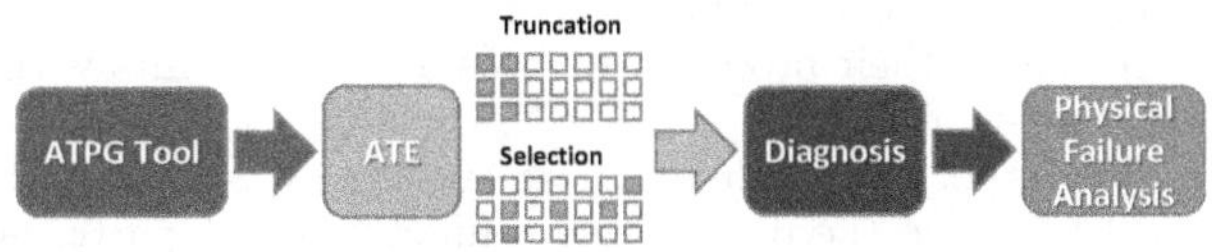

Figure 1: Testing and Diagnosis Process Flow

an ideal scenario, we will uncover the real defects by physically analyzing a small number of suspect locations. However, during the low yield regime, we observe a large number of failures in most of the faulty circuits, all of which cannot be logged due to memory limitations. Therefore, we must discard a significant portion of the log which likely includes information that is critical for diagnosis.

Recently, the test data explosion due to the increasing design complexity and continual technology scaling has sparked interest in methods that can minimize the failure data without a large trade-off on diagnosis quality. The authors of [6] have used machine learning techniques to predict a termination point for failure data collection. Using their proposed method, they could achieve a data reduction of 30.4% while ensuring about 90% accuracy. The main drawback of their method is that a large population of full failure data is needed for learning. In their implementation, they learnt from 90% of initial full failing data to minimize about 10% of the remaining data by 30%. Their method only improves the accuracy (not the resolution) and is not practical for adoption by the industry.

In [4] and subsequent papers, the authors propose saving a predetermined subset of response bits. They rank the output bits on the basis of the single stuck-at and transition fault detection counts and log the top ones that cover all modeled faults. Their ranking is predetermined and cannot be changed according to the observed failures. Moreover, fault model changes requires re-ranking, which is computationally expensive for real-time. Also, one particular output response ranking may not work for all failing chips that fail differently.

The authors of [3] have used rule mining to reduce failure log sizes. Their method is dependent on available diagnosis results and circuit design; however, during the low yield regime, the diagnosis data is usually not good enough to support such learning. In [2] and [1] the authors have proposed a static and dynamic N-cover algorithm for failure data minimization. They compute an N-cover requirement corresponding to the total failing frequency of an output,

*Supported in part by NSF Grant 1422054 and Intel Corp.

Permission to make digital or hard copies of all or part of this work for personal or classroom use is granted without fee provided that copies are not made or distributed for profit or commercial advantage and that copies bear this notice and the full citation on the first page. Copyrights for components of this work owned by others than ACM must be honored. Abstracting with credit is permitted. To copy otherwise, or republish, to post on servers or to redistribute to lists, requires prior specific permission and/or a fee. Request permissions from permissions@acm.org.

GLSVLSI '17, May 10-12, 2017, Banff, AB, Canada

© 2017 ACM. ISBN 978-1-4503-4972-7/17/05...$15.00

DOI: http://dx.doi.org/10.1145/3060403.3060450

which is a monotonically increasing function computed by repeating diagnosis on a small sample of failing chips. Once this function is available, the authors use it and the total failing frequencies of the outputs to find the actual number of instances to be logged. A concern with this method is that a single N-cover curve may not be applicable to all failing outputs of the circuit. Secondly, it is highly dependent on the population of defects in the initial sample. Also, the fact that different chips fail differently presents a challenge to the generalization of the technique.

In another recent paper [5], the authors have experimented with various metrics for the online selection of failure logs, some of which require additional meta-data. Their best techniques may be computationally expensive and may not be suitable for making log selection decisions in real-time for large circuits. Another limitation of their work is that they have evaluated their proposed metrics only on circuits with single stuck-at faults.

In this paper, we evaluate three such metrics that may be used to gauge the diagnostic usefulness of test patterns in real-time. In order to reduce the cost, we don't use any internal signals and rely only on the scan and primary outputs. In our experiments, using one of our proposed metrics, we could improve the diagnosis quality for 29 and 25 benchmark circuits having multiple stuck-at and transition faults respectively.

The paper is organized as follows. In Section II, we explain in detail the evaluated metrics. In Section IV and V, we explain our evaluation framework and the results of our experiments. Finally, we present our conclusions in Section VI.

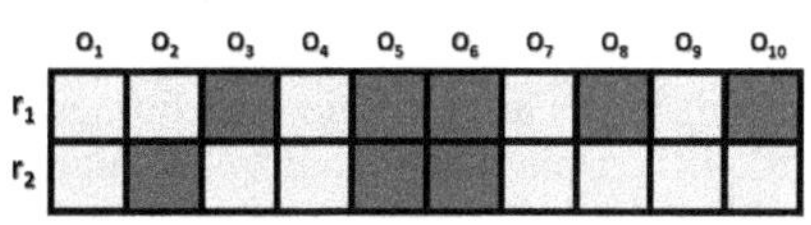

Figure 2: Counting total and unique output responses

2. THE EVALUATED METRICS

We evaluate and compare three different metrics on faulty circuits having one or more stuck-at and transition faults:

2.1 Total Number of Failing Outputs

When using this metric, we intend to maximize the total number of failing outputs in the selected failing responses logged. Figure 2 shows two output responses of a hypothetical circuit to failing test patterns p_1 and p_2. These responses r_1 and r_2 consist of the failing outputs $\{o_3, o_5, o_6, o_8, o_{10}\}$ and $\{o_2, o_5, o_6\}$ respectively. The total number of failing outputs in these two responses is $|r_1|+|r_2| = 5+3 = 8$. The motivation for this metric is that a larger number of failing outputs offers a larger set of observable points.

2.2 Number of Unique Failing Outputs

When using this metric, we intend to keep as many unique failing outputs in the log as possible. Using the same responses r_1 and r_2, the number of unique failing outputs is the size of their union i.e $|r_1 \cup r_2| = |\{o_2, o_3, o_5, o_6, o_8, o_{10}\}| = 6$. The motivation for this metric is that a larger number of unique failing outputs offers a greater opportunity to prune the search among failing vectors.

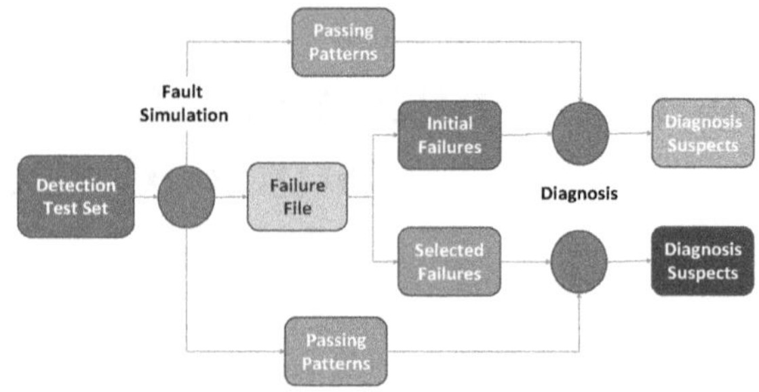

Figure 3: Overall Evaluation Process

2.3 Sum of Total and Unique Failing Outputs

This is a hybrid metric, where we try to maximize both the total and unique failures. For the above example responses r_1 and r_2, the sum of total and unique failing outputs is $|r_1| + |r_2| + |r_1 \cup r_2| = 5 + 3 + 6 = 14$.

2.4 Algorithm for Log Selection

We use a greedy algorithm for selecting failing responses on the basis of the metrics enumerated above. First, we let the log fill up with the initial failing responses. Then, with each new failing pattern, we determine how much the metric would improve when its response replaces each of the existing responses. We replace an existing response with the new response such that we achieve the maximum gain. In case of no gain, we discard the new response.

3. EVALUATION FRAMEWORK

We use 29 full scan circuits from the ISCAS'89 benchmarks and 8 full scan circuits from the Opencores library in the IWLS'05 benchmarks to test the effectiveness of the considered metrics.

3.1 Test Generation

We use a state-of-the-art commercial tool to generate two separate test sets for stuck-at and transition faults. For the transition faults, we generate double-capture or broadside patterns. Table 1 lists the characteristics of the generated tests. Column 1 lists the benchmark names. Columns 2 and 3 list the number of generated tests and fault coverages for stuck-at faults respectively. Columns 4 and 5 list the same for the transition faults.

3.2 Generation of Faulty Circuits

For our evaluation experiments, we create two sets of faulty circuits each for stuck-at and transition fault models. The first set consists of 300 circuits with a single stuck at fault each. The second set also consists of 300 faulty circuits except that each circuit has 2 to 7 inserted faults. We determine at random the faults and the number of faults inserted in these circuits.

3.3 Test Application and Response Collection

We apply the computed tests to the generated faulty circuits. The commercial tool is used to compute the responses that make up the failure files. From the full failure files, we create two shortened failure files. In the first file, we keep

Table 1: Test Statistics

Bench	Stuck-at		Transition	
	# Tests	FC	# Tests	FC
s00027	6	100.00%	8	100.00%
s00208	34	100.00%	37	89.71%
s00298	28	100.00%	33	85.65%
s00344	19	100.00%	39	95.55%
s00349	18	99.91%	43	95.39%
s00382	29	100.00%	38	83.76%
s00386	69	100.00%	55	84.12%
s00400	28	98.50%	40	82.33%
s00420	71	100.00%	87	86.79%
s00444	31	98.54%	43	82.36%
s00510	61	100.00%	80	91.80%
s00526	62	100.00%	68	70.48%
s00641	37	100.00%	65	96.89%
s00713	36	99.01%	73	93.60%
s00820	104	100.00%	125	84.76%
s00832	104	99.20%	128	83.65%
s00838	148	100.00%	183	85.61%
s01196	129	100.00%	204	99.94%
s01238	145	97.37%	216	97.16%
s01423	59	99.26%	91	91.11%
s01488	116	100.00%	143	93.43%
s01494	115	99.57%	143	93.07%
s09234	196	94.63%	381	90.14%
s13207	288	99.28%	437	91.50%
s15850	184	98.32%	310	89.07%
s35932	55	91.06%	85	89.33%
s38417	165	99.78%	267	98.90%
s38584	198	96.89%	423	92.47%
aes_core	377	99.95%	658	99.96%
des3_area	128	100.00%	263	99.98%
des3_perf	128	99.99%	206	100.00%
spi	339	99.97%	761	99.15%
sysc_aes	154	99.39%	361	95.16%
sysc_des	92	99.97%	155	99.35%
wb_dma	190	99.41%	1994	99.01%

the failing outputs corresponding to the initial $k = 5$ failing patterns. In the second file, we store the failing outputs of the selected k failing patterns, using the proposed metrics.

3.4 Diagnosis

We perform diagnosis on the truncated and selected failure files. A definitive improvement in accuracy and resolution in a large number of benchmarks would imply that the metric is good for improving diagnosis. In our comparison, we look at two measures.

3.4.1 Accuracy

We define accuracy as the number of actual (inserted) faults reported by the diagnosis tool among the suspects divided by the total number of actual faults existing (inserted) in the circuit. For example, if 6 faults were inserted in a circuit and only 2 of those ended up in the list of suspects. The accuracy of diagnosis is $2/6 \times 100\% = 33.33\%$.

3.4.2 Average Inverse Hit Index

In the context of our experiments, the hit index is the index of an inserted fault in the ranked list of suspects. If a fault does not end up in the suspects, we assign it a hit index of ∞. For each faulty circuit instance, we take the reciprocal of the hit indices and calculate the average. The higher this average, the higher is the diagnosis quality. For example if three faults were inserted in the circuit and their corresponding hit indices were $\{1, \infty, 9\}$. The average inverse hit index would be $\frac{1/1+1/\infty+1/9}{3} = \frac{1+0+0.11}{3} = 0.37$.

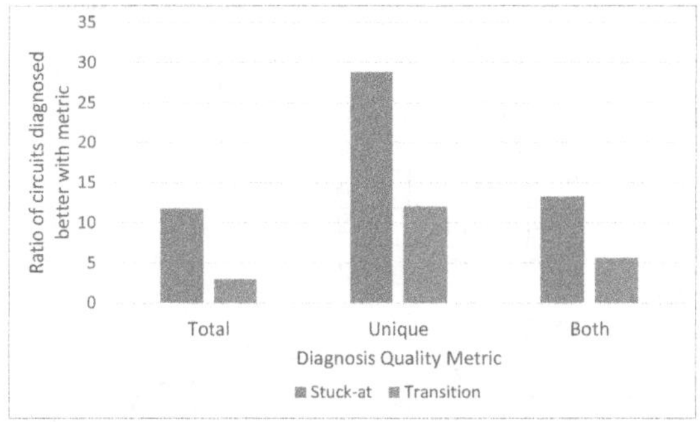

Figure 4: Comparison for diagnosis quality for circuits with single stuck-at faults

4. EXPERIMENT RESULTS

Tables 2 and 3 provide the results for about 300 faulty instances for each benchmark having 2-7 stuck-at and transition faults respectively. Column 1 of Table 2 lists the benchmark circuits. Column 2 and 6 list the average accuracy and inverse hit index for the baseline results obtained using the 5 initial failing patterns (and all passing patterns from the test set). Columns 3, 4 and 5 state the diagnosis accuracy achieved when we optimized the log by total failing outputs, unique failing outputs and both total and unique failing outputs respectively. Whereas, columns 7, 8 and 9 provide the average inverse hit index for these three cases.

As can be seen from the table, optimizing the total number of failures did improve the accuracy and resolution for some benchmarks. However, for most benchmarks, we see a drop in the diagnosis quality. On the other hand, when we optimize the number of unique failing outputs, we see an improvement in diagnosis quality for 29 out of 35 benchmarks for stuck-at faults and 25 out of 28 benchmarks for transition faults. When we optimize both, the result is not as good because we see a deterioration in diagnosis quality for more number of benchmarks.

Fig 4 depicts the improvement in diagnosis resolution for circuits having single faults using the three metrics. It shows the ratios of the number of circuits that were diagnosed better with the application of the metric to the circuits diagnosed better using the initial failures. As may be observed, the most significant improvement in diagnostic resolution was achieved by optimizing the unique failing outputs that yielded better diagnosis for **28x**, and **12x** more circuits having single stuck at and transition faults respectively.

5. CONCLUSION

In this paper, we evaluated three log selection metrics for improving VLSI diagnosis. Using the metric that optimizes the number of unique failing outputs in the failure log, we

Table 2: Metric Comparison for Circuits with Multiple Stuck-at Faults

Bench	Avg Accuracy				Avg Inv Hit Index			
	Init	Selective			Init	Selective		
		T	U	B		T	U	B
s00027	36.8	38.1	37.8	38	0.3	0.3	0.3	0.3
s00208	28.4	30.7	30.2	30.6	0.2	0.2	0.2	0.2
s00298	33.8	30.9	32.4	31.6	0.3	0.3	0.3	0.3
s00344	40	35.5	39.9	37	0.3	0.3	0.3	0.3
s00349	38.9	34.6	38.7	34.7	0.3	0.3	0.3	0.3
s00382	30.6	32.4	34.5	32.5	0.2	0.2	0.2	0.2
s00386	35.8	32.9	38.8	36.1	0.3	0.3	0.3	0.3
s00400	34.2	33.1	34.9	34.1	0.2	0.2	0.2	0.2
s00420	26.8	31.7	30.5	31.7	0.2	0.2	0.2	0.2
s00444	32.2	32.9	34	32.7	0.2	0.2	0.3	0.2
s00510	33.5	32.4	35.6	33.6	0.3	0.3	0.3	0.3
s00526	33.3	32.3	34.6	32.4	0.3	0.3	0.3	0.3
s00641	41.7	37.2	43.5	39.4	0.4	0.3	0.4	0.3
s00713	40.5	34.2	42.7	37.1	0.3	0.2	0.3	0.2
s00820	31.7	31.8	33.2	32.9	0.3	0.3	0.3	0.3
s00832	30.8	32.9	33.9	33.2	0.3	0.3	0.3	0.3
s00838	34.8	35.7	38.1	36.8	0.3	0.2	0.3	0.3
s01196	40.8	35.8	44.3	37.3	0.4	0.3	0.4	0.3
s01238	38.3	35	40.9	36.8	0.3	0.3	0.3	0.3
s01423	43.2	36	44.1	36.6	0.3	0.3	0.3	0.3
s01488	34	32.6	34.2	32.8	0.3	0.3	0.3	0.3
s01494	34.2	33	37.1	36.4	0.3	0.3	0.3	0.3
s09234	39.5	35.8	44.5	38.9	0.3	0.3	0.3	0.3
s13207	40.4	43.7	46.6	43.8	0.3	0.3	0.3	0.3
s15850	41.9	38.4	45.6	39.4	0.3	0.2	0.3	0.3
s35932	36.5	34.8	35.7	34.7	0.3	0.2	0.2	0.2
s38417	43.2	37.4	46.6	39.3	0.4	0.3	0.4	0.3
s38584	42.5	40.6	47.7	41.8	0.3	0.3	0.4	0.3
aes_core	45.9	38.8	54.3	42.7	0.4	0.3	0.5	0.4
des3_area	35.3	28.8	34.7	29.9	0.3	0.2	0.3	0.2
des3_perf	46	40.8	50.5	41.4	0.4	0.3	0.5	0.3
spi	35.6	39.9	39.5	39.1	0.3	0.3	0.3	0.3
sysc_aes	42.8	37.1	43.6	38.7	0.4	0.3	0.4	0.3
sysc_des	36.7	34.3	36.6	35.1	0.3	0.3	0.3	0.3
wb_dma	43.6	42.5	46.8	41.2	0.3	0.3	0.3	0.3

were able to achieve a significant improvement in both accuracy and resolution for a majority of ISCAS'89 and IWLS'05 circuits having single and multiple stuck-at and transition faults. Increasing the number of unique failing outputs is effective because the internal signals explaining those are likely to be different. Especially for circuits with multiple faults, different unique failing outputs may correspond to different activated faults. This helps us capture a greater number of symptoms, thus improving the accuracy.

Table 3: Metric Comparison for Circuits with Multiple Transition Faults

Bench	Avg Accuracy				Avg Inv Hit Index			
	Init	Selective			Init	Selective		
		T	U	B		T	U	B
s00027	23.9	23.5	23.9	23.3	0.16	0.16	0.16	0.16
s00208	15.4	16.3	14.4	15.4	0.10	0.10	0.09	0.09
s00298	23.4	23.1	25.0	22.9	0.15	0.16	0.17	0.16
s00344	30.0	29.9	34.7	30.3	0.19	0.19	0.22	0.20
s00349	26.6	27.1	30.1	27.1	0.17	0.17	0.19	0.17
s00382	29.9	29.6	31.6	31.0	0.20	0.20	0.21	0.21
s00386	24.1	24.3	24.3	25.0	0.15	0.16	0.16	0.16
s00400	25.4	24.5	26.3	25.5	0.18	0.17	0.18	0.18
s00420	19.1	18.6	18.5	17.6	0.11	0.10	0.10	0.10
s00444	24.2	24.8	25.2	25.5	0.16	0.16	0.16	0.17
s00510	20.4	22.5	22.2	22.5	0.12	0.14	0.14	0.14
s00526	22.8	22.7	23.4	24.0	0.14	0.14	0.14	0.15
s00641	40.4	29.6	40.6	32.0	0.20	0.15	0.21	0.17
s00713	38.7	33.3	41.2	35.0	0.16	0.15	0.19	0.17
s00820	21.8	22.1	23.7	22.2	0.12	0.12	0.14	0.13
s00832	20.9	20.7	21.4	21.2	0.12	0.13	0.13	0.13
s00838	15.2	17.0	15.9	16.7	0.09	0.09	0.09	0.09
s01196	40.5	34.0	41.0	36.8	0.23	0.21	0.25	0.22
s01238	41.5	38.1	46.4	40.6	0.25	0.23	0.28	0.25
s01423	28.1	24.1	30.6	26.1	0.17	0.15	0.19	0.16
s01488	24.1	25.1	24.0	24.6	0.14	0.15	0.15	0.15
s01494	24.4	24.5	26.3	25.0	0.13	0.14	0.14	0.14
s09234	35.9	31.8	43.5	34.5	0.16	0.16	0.19	0.17
s13207	35.3	31.6	41.1	30.9	0.15	0.15	0.18	0.15
s15850	38.4	32.8	43.0	33.4	0.18	0.15	0.20	0.16
s38417	42.6	32.5	43.9	34.3	0.21	0.17	0.22	0.17
s38584	37.3	33.0	45.3	35.2	0.21	0.18	0.24	0.19

6. REFERENCES

[1] S. Bodhe, M. E. Amyeen, C. Galendez, H. Mooers, I. Pomeranz, and S. Venkataraman. Reduction of diagnostic fail data volume and tester time using a dynamic n-cover algorithm. In *2016 IEEE 34th VLSI Test Symposium (VTS)*, pages 1–6. IEEE, 2016.

[2] S. Bodhe, M. E. Amyeen, I. Pomeranz, and S. Venkataraman. Diagnostic fail data minimization using an-cover algorithm. *IEEE Transactions on Very Large Scale Integration (VLSI) Systems*, 24(3):1198–1202, 2016.

[3] C. Bolchini, E. Quintarelli, F. Salice, and P. Garza. A data mining approach to incremental adaptive functional diagnosis. In *2013 IEEE International Symposium on Defect and Fault Tolerance in VLSI and Nanotechnology Systems (DFTS)*, pages 13–18. IEEE, 2013.

[4] K.-J. Lee, W.-C. Lien, and T.-Y. Hsieh. Test response compaction via output bit selection. *Computer-Aided Design of Integrated Circuits and Systems, IEEE Transactions on*, 30(10):1534–1544, 2011.

[5] S. Tanwir, S. Prabhu, M. Hsiao, and L. Lingappan. Information-theoretic and statistical methods of failure log selection for improved diagnosis. In *Test Conference (ITC), 2015 IEEE International*. IEEE, 2015.

[6] H. Wang, O. Poku, X. Yu, S. Liu, I. Komara, and R. D. Blanton. Test-data volume optimization for diagnosis. In *Design Automation Conference (DAC), 2012 49th ACM/EDAC/IEEE*, pages 567–572. IEEE, 2012.

Reducing Microfluidic Very Large Scale Integration (mVLSI) Chip Area by Seam Carving

Brian Crites, Karen Kong, Philip Brisk
University of California, Riverside
900 University Ave
Riverside, CA
bcrit001@ucr.edu, kkong006@ucr.edu, philip@cs.ucr.edu

ABSTRACT

This paper introduces a technique based on seam carving to reduce the area of microfluidic very large scale integration (mVLSI) chips. Seam carving repeatedly identifies small slices of the device that can be safely removed (carved) and patched without adversely affecting device functionality. Using non-linear seam carving we achieve an average improvement of $4.28x$ in area utilization and an average reduction in fluid routing channel length of 53%.

Keywords

Microfluidics, Seam Carving, mVLSI

1. INTRODUCTION

Laboratories-on-a-chip (LoCs) based on continuous fluid flow microfluidics are widely used for a variety of biochemical applications. Through automation and miniaturization, LoCs offer the benefits of higher throughput, lower sample/reagent usage, and reduced likelihood of human error compared to traditional benchtop chemistry methods.

The primary component of modern LoCs is the microvalve. This device is fabricated using multi-layer soft lithography with two layers of flexible polymer, polydimethylsiloxane (PDMS), mounted on top of a rigid substrate, typically a glass slide. The two logical layers of these devices are the "flow layer," which transports biological fluids of an assay, and the "control layer," which provides actuation capabilities. A microvalve forms where a control channel crosses a flow channel. By default, all microvalves are open; pressurizing a control channel closes all of the microvalves that it drives. Components, such as pumps, mixers, switches, etc. can be built from microvalves [6].

As *microfluidic Very Large Scale Integration (mVLSI)* densities increase [1], designers will require CAD tools to cope with increasing device complexity. Like integrated circuits, an mVLSI chip can be viewed as a netlist, which must be placed and routed, with the restriction that each layer must be planar. Optimal mVLSI physical design has been achieved using integer linear programming [10], however, it is unlikely that this approach will scale to large devices. Meanwhile, tractable heuristics based on planar graph embedding [5] yield solutions that are far from optimal.

Permission to make digital or hard copies of all or part of this work for personal or classroom use is granted without fee provided that copies are not made or distributed for profit or commercial advantage and that copies bear this notice and the full citation on the first page. Copyrights for components of this work owned by others than ACM must be honored. Abstracting with credit is permitted. To copy otherwise, or republish, to post on servers or to redistribute to lists, requires prior specific permission and/or a fee. Request permissions from permissions@acm.org.

GLSVLSI '17, May 10-12, 2017, Banff, AB, Canada

© 2017 ACM. ISBN 978-1-4503-4972-7/17/05...$15.00

DOI: http://dx.doi.org/10.1145/3060403.3060461

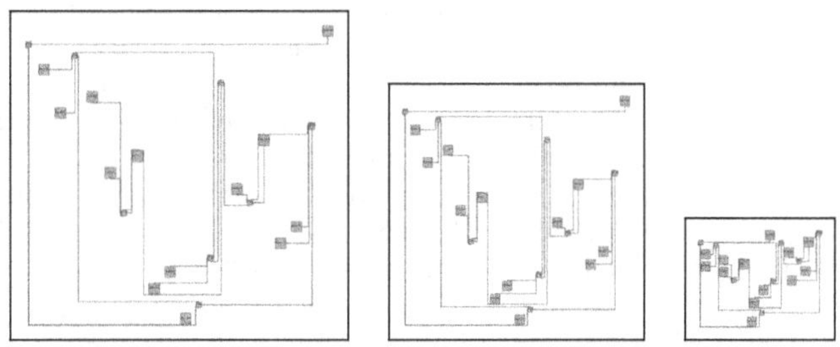

(a) (b) (c)

Figure 1: (a) Shows the benchmarks Synthetic 1 after the baseline placement and routing [5] has completed. (b) is the same benchmark after linear seam carving has been applied, while (c) is after non-linear seam carving has been applied.

This paper adapts seam carving [2], an image size reduction technique, to improve the area utilization of low-quality mVLSI layouts. The basic premise is to identify seams (paths) through the chip which can be removed without adversely affecting device functionality, shortening fluid channels that may be cut. Fig. 1 shows a motivating example. Fig. 1a shows a low quality initial layout [5]. Fig. 1b shows an improved layout, which was derived using linear seam carving, which we introduce in Section 4; on average, linear seam carving improves area utilization by $1.4x$ and reduces the average fluid routing channel length by 13%. Fig. 1c shows a better result which was obtained with a more aggressive technique, nonlinear seam carving, which we introduce in Section 5; non-linear seam carving improves area utilization by $4.28x$ on average, while reducing average fluid routing channel length by 53%

2. RELATED WORK

2.1 Seam Carving

A seam is a path of pixels through an image whose removal minimally degrades image quality. Seams can be identified by converting an image into a weighted graph, where each vertex represents a pixel and each vertex's weight represents its relative importance to image quality [2]. Seam carving then finds the lowest-cost path from one perimeter edge to its opposite and removes it from the image. The process repeats until the desired reduction in size is achieved.

2.2 mVLSI Placement

Seam carving can reduce the area of mVLSI chips designed manually, or laid out using sub-optimal heuristic methods such as simulated annealing [7], incremental cluster expansion [9] and extensions to planar graph embedding [5]. Seam carving will not be able to improve an optimal placement result [10] because the existence of a removable seam contradicts the optimality of the result.

3. PRELIMINARIES

The input to seam carving is a placed and routed mVLSI architecture $A = (C, R, n, m)$, where C is a set of placed components, R is a set of routed channel segments, and n and m are the respective height and width of the layout. We represent each microfluidic component $c_i = (x_i, y_i, w_i, h_i)$ using a bounding box: point (x_i, y_i) is the upper-left corner of the component, and h_i and w_i are its respective height and width. Each routed channel segment $r_i = (x_{i,t}, y_{i,t}, x_{i,l}, y_{i,l})$ is a straight-line connection between points $(x_{i,t}, y_{i,t})$ and $(x_{i,l}, y_{i,l})$; multiple segments may comprise a longer channel with twists and bends. The physical layout process may include an additional parameter, Δ, which adds white space around each component to improve routability.

In microfluidic devices all space in an architecture can be classified into three categories. Components, which have a fixed height and width; we assume that component dimensions are fixed by fluidic IP designers and cannot be reduced without adversely affecting chip functionality. Fluidic channels, which can be of any length as long as they provide a continuous flow of fluid between source and sink components; channel length can be reduced without altering chip functionality. Free space, which is superfluous, except for the buffer space surrounding each component.

A seam is a path through the architecture that connects one perimeter edge to its opposite and contains no points that are invalid for removal; this ensures that correct device functionality is maintained when the seam is removed. Invalid points include any part of a component (including its buffer space) or a switch at a channel intersection. In the latter case, removal of a switch would require the post-processor to re-place the switch and reroute its incident fluid channels accordingly; it is preferable to avoid this overhead. Valid points for removal include free space and channel segments that are not part of a switch and would not break the route connection between connected components.

4. LINEAR SEAM CARVING

Linear seam carving restricts seams to be horizontal or vertical straight lines that do not bend. Fig. 2a shows an example mVLSI chip with a loose placement and ample white space. Fig. 2b shows four horizontal seams, two of which intersect fluid channels in the center of the chip. Fig. 2c shows the smaller chip after the four seams are removed. Device functionality is not altered, and the channel connecting the two components is shortened but not disrupted.

4.1 Seam Identification

Linear seam carving employs two Boolean arrays, B_x and B_y, which respectively represent removable vertical and horizontal seams. Without loss of generality, as we move along the x-axis, $B_x[i]$ represents a vertical line containing all points within the component having i as the x-coordinate.

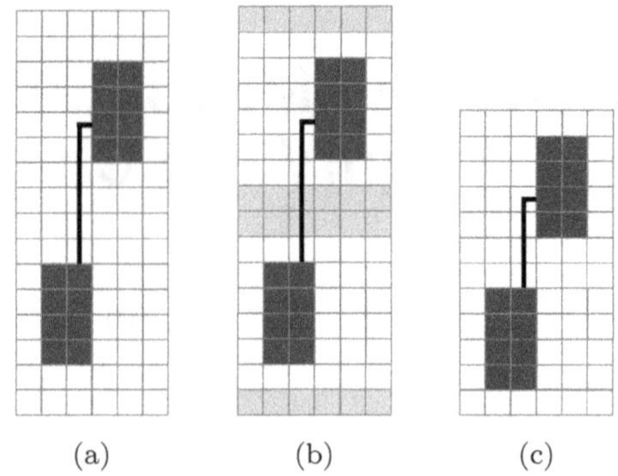

Figure 2: (a) A laid out mVLSI chip; (b) seam identification ($\Delta = 1$); (c) the chip after seam removal.

Both arrays are initialized to $B_x[0:m] = B_y[0:n] = True$.

The algorithm identifies vertical and horizontal seams for removal separately. To identify vertical seams, the algorithm iterates through all components $c_i \in C$ setting $B_x[x_i : x_i + w_i] = False$; this disallows any seam that cuts through a component. For each route $r_i \in R$ the algorithm sets $B_x[x_{i,t}] = False$ and $B_x[x_{i,l}] = False$ to disallow the removal of switches at channel intersections. Any index i for which $B_x[i] = True$ represents a vertical seam that could be removed. Horizontal seams are identified similarly, using B_y and the y-coordinates of components and channel segments.

Seams are permitted to cut through channel segments, effectively shortening them. If a channel segment of a prespecified length is required (e.g., to achieve a chemical separation), then it should be characterized as a component.

4.2 Seam Carving

Each index $j \in \{0, ..., m\}$ where $B_x[j]$ is $True$ is a removable vertical seam. Each component $c_i \in C$ such that $x_i > j$ is shifted left to fill the space removed by the seam; the height and width of c_i remain unchanged. Channel segments completely to the right of the removed seam are shifted left by one grid point. For channel segments that cross the seam, the right endpoint is shifted left by one grid point. Seam carving cannot completely remove a channel because seams cannot contain channel endpoints. The final step is to reduce the length of the guide B_x by one grid point by setting $B_x[k] = B_x[k+1], j \leq k \leq m$, and decrementing m.

This process then repeats similarly for all vertical seams, $0 \leq j \leq n$ where $B_y[j]$ is $True$.

5. NON-LINEAR SEAM CARVING

Non-linear seam carving eliminates the restriction that seams are exclusively horizontal or vertical segments. Seams are still required to begin at one perimeter edge and end at the opposite edge. This increases opportunities for seam removal and can lead to substantially smaller chip designs.

5.1 Seam Identification

Seam identification employs an $m \times n$ Boolean grid G to determine if a given point is a candidate for seam carving. All grid entries are initialized to $True$. For each component $c_i \in C$ at position (x_i, y_i) we set $G[j][k] = False$, $x_i \leq j \leq x_i + w_i, y_i \leq k \leq y_i + h_i$, rendering these points invalid for inclusion in a seam. For each routed channel segment $r_i \in R$ we set $G[x_{i,t}][y_{i,t}] = G[x_{i,l}][y_{i,l}] = False$ to disallow seam carving through switches at channel in-

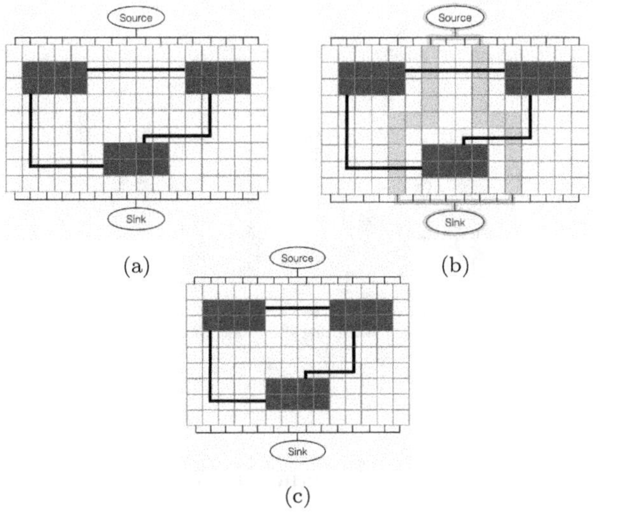

Figure 3: (a) A placed and routed mVLSI netlist (b) two nonlinear seams identified for removal ($\Delta = 1$); (c) the smaller chip after seam removal.

tersection points. A seam S is a collection of straight line segments $s_i = (a_i, b_i, c_i, d_i)$, where (a_i, b_i) and (c_i, d_i) are the (x, y)-coordinates of the two endpoints.

Non-linear seam carving retains the directional approach of its linear counterpart. Seams are first identified along the x-axis, with an artificial *source* connected to all grid positions $G[j][0], 0 \leq j \leq m$ and and artificial *sink* connected to all grid positions $G[j][n], 0 \leq j \leq m$, as shown in Fig. 3a. Lee's Algorithm [3] is repeatedly called to identify seams from *source* to *sink*, until no valid paths remain. Fig. 3b shows two non-linear seams, whose removal yields the smaller chip depicted in Fig. 3c. This process then repeats along the y-axis.

5.2 Perpendicular Channel Segments

Non-linear seam carving requires special handling of channel segments that run perpendicular to the carving direction. Without loss of generality, assume that we are carving in the y-direction and consider a horizontal channel segment r_i having $y_{i,t} = y_{i,l}$. A seam can be identified that cuts through r_i in such a way that its removal causes $y_{i,t} \neq y_{i,l}$; the updated channel would require a diagonal connection, or a small bend (necessitating three new channel segments), neither of which is problematic, per se.

Perpendicular carving, however, can cause a component to shift and collide with the perpendicular channel. For example, Fig. 4a shows a laid out mVLSI chip. Fig. 4b shows multiple seams that cross perpendicular channel segments; in Fig. 4c, carving these seams causes a component to shift and collide with the perpendicular channel. To prevent this, non-linear carving may not carve through perpendicular channel segments by setting $G[x_{i,t}][z] = False$ for $y_{i,t} < z < y_{i,l}$; Fig. 4d depicts a valid set of seams, and Fig. 4e shows the resulting collision-free mVLSI chip after carving.

5.3 Seam Carving

Non-linear seam carving must choose whether to move a component or channel segment endpoint based on the opposite axis along the seam. When carving along the x-axis, any component $c_i \in C$ that exists to the right of a seam

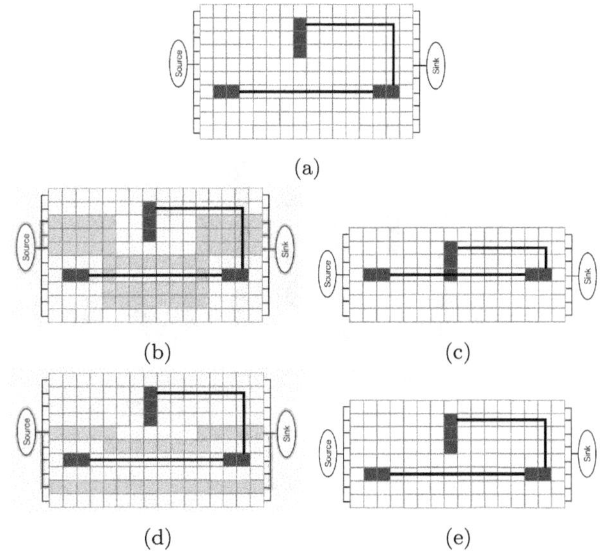

Figure 4: (a) A placed and routed mVLSI chip; (b) when carving along the y-axis ($\Delta = 1$), a set of non-linear seams are found that cross a perpendicular (horizontal) segment; (c) removal of the preceding seams yields an invalid layout; (d) non-linear seams are prevented from crossing the perpendicular segment; (e) removal of non-linear seams that do not cross the perpendicular segment yields a legal layout.

with $x_i > a_j$ between $b_j \leq y_i \leq d_j$ for any segment $s_j \in S$ will be shifted left to fill the the space that has been carved; to do this, set $x_i = x_i - 1$. All channel segments $r_i \in R$ with a source to the right of the seam with $x_{i,t} > a_j$ and $b_j \leq y_{i,t} \leq d_j$ will be shifted left to $x_{i,t} = x_{i,t} - 1$; all segments with a sink to the right of the seam with $x_{i,l} > a_j$ and $b_j \leq y_{i,l} \leq d_j$ will be shifted left to $x_{i,l} = x_{i,l} - 1$.

This process then repeats similarly along the y-axis.

6. EXPERIMENTAL RESULTS

Our Baseline algorithm is the mVLSI flow layer placer and router described by McDaniel et al. [5]. We implemented the Baseline algorithm in C++, along with linear and non-linear seam carving as post-processing steps. All experiments were run on a 2015 MacBook Pro Laptop with a 2.9GHz Processor and 8GB of RAM. For evaluation, we use a suite of nine benchmarks: AquaFlex-3b and AquaFlex-5a (proprietary netlists provided by Microfluidic Innovations LLC), a bead-based HIV1 immunoassay (Li et al. [4]), a molecular gradients generator (Rhee & Burns [8]), and five synthetic netlists. Our implementation uses a "unitless grid" with a standard buffer size $\Delta = 5$ for all benchmarks. We report the area utilization, (the percentage of the chip area consumed by components; Fig. 5), average channel routing length (Fig. 6), and the average algorithmic runtimes across five runs per algorithm/benchmark (Fig. 7).

Compared to the Baseline placement, linear seam carving marginally improved area utilization and average wirelength, while non-linear seam carving yielded far more significant improvements. The Baseline placer is ineffective because its underlying planar graph embedding algorithm does not try to minimize area, and further loses efficiency as vertices (points) are expanded into 2D components, which necessitates further shifting of components and re-routing of flow channels to eliminate overlap. Seam carving can effec-

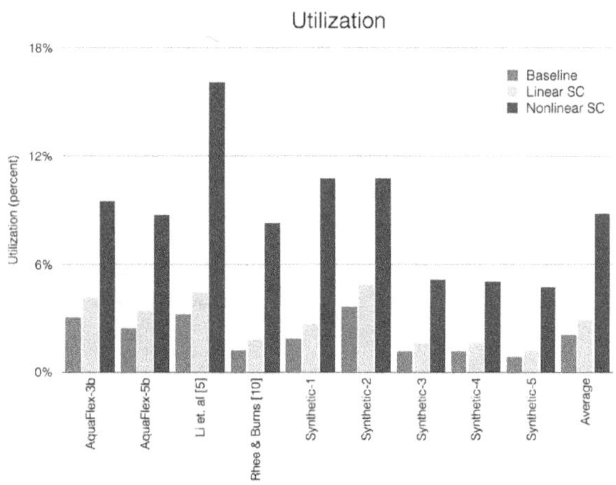

Figure 5: Area utilization (larger is better)

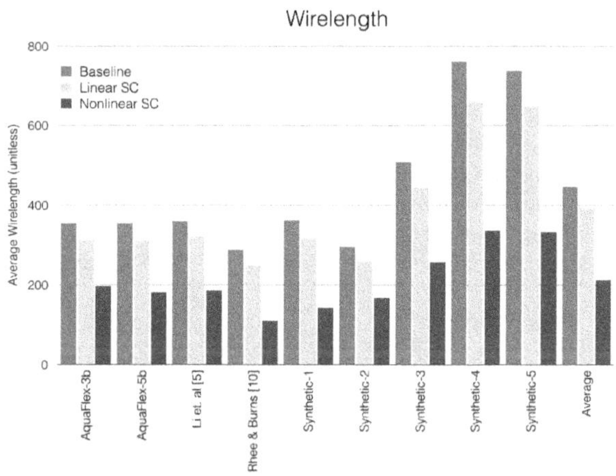

Figure 6: Average wirelength (smaller is better)

tively counteract these inefficiencies, and the results clearly show that there are far more non-linear seams available for removal than linear seams.

The runtimes reported in Fig. 7 include the Baseline placer in all cases. Although its effectiveness is limited, linear seam carving imposes negligible runtime overhead; in contrast, the runtime of non-linear seam carving is inversely proportional to the density of the design, and, as a post-processing step, it often runs longer than the Baseline placer (e.g., Synthetic-1 and -2).

7. CONCLUSION AND FUTURE WORK

Linear and non-linear seam carving can reduce the amount of unused space in an mVLSI chip. Linear seam carving is more conservative and runs faster, improving area utilization by by $1.4x$ and reducing the average wirelength by 13% on average; non-linear seam carving is far more aggressive, improving average area utilization by $4.28x$ while reducing average wirelength by 53%. Compared to the baseline placer however, this comes at a much greater runtime cost.

Acknowledgement

This work was support in part by NSF Awards #1351115, #1536026 and #1640757.

8. REFERENCES

[1] Araci, I. E., Pop, P., and Chakrabarty, K. Microfluidic very large-scale integration for biochips: Technology, testing and fault-tolerant design. In *20th IEEE European Test Symposium, ETS 2015, Cluj-Napoca, Romania, 25-29 May, 2015*, pp. 1–8.

[2] Avidan, S., and Shamir, A. Seam carving for content-aware image resizing. *ACM Trans. Graph. 26*, 3 (2007), 10.

[3] Lee, C. Y. An algorithm for path connections and its applications. *IRE Trans. Electronic Computers 10*, 3 (1961), 346–365.

[4] Li, B., Li, L., Guan, A., Dong, Q., Ruan, K., Hu, R., and Li, Z. A smartphone controlled handheld microfluidic liquid handling system. *Lab Chip 14* (2014), 4085–4092.

[5] McDaniel, J., Crites, B., Brisk, P., and Grover, W. H. Flow-layer physical design for microchips based on monolithic membrane valves. *IEEE Design & Test 32*, 6 (2015), 51–59.

[6] Melin, J., and Quake, S. R. Microfluidic large-scale integration: The evolution of design rules for biological automation. *Annual Review of Biophysics and Biomolecular Structure 36*, 1 (2007), 213–231. PMID: 17269901.

[7] Minhass, W. H., Pop, P., Madsen, J., and Blaga, F. S. Architectural synthesis of flow-based microfluidic large-scale integration biochips. In *Proceedings of the 15th International Conference on Compilers, Architecture, and Synthesis for Embedded Systems, CASES 2012, Tampere, Finland, October 7-12, 2012*, pp. 181–190.

[8] Rhee, M., and Burns, M. A. Microfluidic assembly blocks. *Lab Chip 8* (2008), 1365–1373.

[9] Tseng, K., You, S., Liou, J., and Ho, T. A top-down synthesis methodology for flow-based microfluidic biochips considering valve-switching minimization. In *International Symposium on Physical Design, ISPD'13, Stateline, NV, USA, March 24-27, 2013*, pp. 123–129.

[10] Tseng, T., Li, M., Li, B., Ho, T., and Schlichtmann, U. Columba: co-layout synthesis for continuous-flow microfluidic biochips. In *Proceedings of the 53rd Annual Design Automation Conference, DAC 2016, Austin, TX, USA, June 5-9, 2016*, pp. 147:1–147:6.

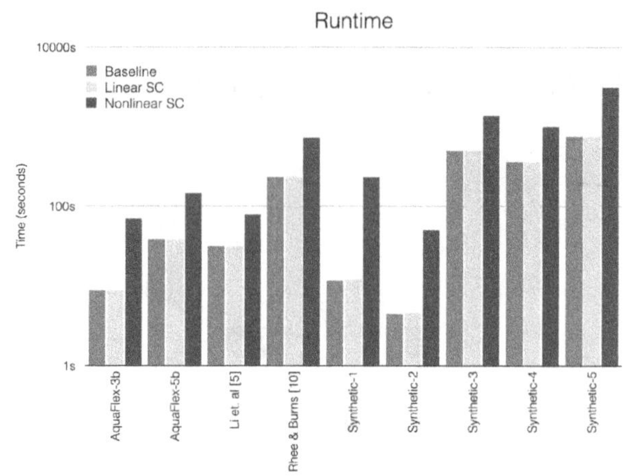

Figure 7: Algorithmic runtime in seconds (log. scale)

ProACt: A Processor for High Performance On-demand Approximate Computing

Arun Chandrasekharan[1] Daniel Große[1,2] Rolf Drechsler[1,2]
[1]Group of Computer Architecture, University of Bremen, Germany
[2]Cyber Physical Systems, DFKI GmbH, Bremen, Germany
{arun,grosse,drechsle}@cs.uni-bremen.de

ABSTRACT

We present ProACt, a *Processor for high performance on-demand Approximate Computing.* ProACt is a general purpose processor that can dynamically approximate floating point operations. In ProACt, the approximations are done in hardware, but the software can directly enable, disable or control the accuracy of approximations. In addition, ProACt offers a complete open-source development framework consisting of a hardware processor and associated software tool chain. ProACt uses functional approximations and is proven in FPGA. Further, we show performance improvements of about 30% on case studies in image processing and scientific computing.

1. INTRODUCTION

Approximate computing can deliver significant performance benefits (e.g. in speed or energy) over conventional computing by relaxing the precision of results. In order to harness the full potential of approximations, both hardware and software need to work in tandem [18, 16, 10]. However, in a general application, there are program segments that can be approximated and others which should not be approximated. In addition, it has become good strategy to perform approximation in certain situations, e.g. when the battery goes low. Also, decisions such as the duration and degree of approximations may depend on external factors and input data set of the application, which may not be fully known at system design time. All these calls for an on-demand, rapidly switchable hardware approximation scheme that can be fully controlled by software. This software-control may originate from the application itself or from a supervisory software like the operating system [12, 6].

In this work, we present ProACt, a *Processor for high performance on-demand Approximate Computing* which fullfills all the above requirements. The core idea of ProACt is to functionally approximate floating point operations using previously computed results from a cache thereby relaxing the requirement of having the exact identical input values for the current floating point operation. To enable on-demand approximation we add a *custom instruction* to the *Instruction Set Architecture* (ISA) of the used processor which essentially adjusts the input data for cache look-up and by this controls the approximation behavior. Overall we have devised a ProACt development framework. Our framework consists of the extended hardware processor[1] and the software tool chain (cross-compiler, linker etc) to build a complete system for on-demand approximate computing.

In ProACt we target floating point operations for approximation. These operations are essential to modern multimedia and signal processing engines, and form the basis of several industry standards [2]. However, complex floating point operations such as division and square-root are computationally expensive, and usually span over multiple clock cycles [8, 11]. With ProACt we aim to reduce the number of clock cycles spent on floating point operations with our on-demand approximation scheme. Therefore, these operations and results are stored in an approximation look-up table. This look-up table is checked first before executing a new floating point operation. In this step, *approximation masks* are applied to the operands before the cache look-up. These masks are set by the new custom approximation control instruction (assembly mnemonic `SXL`[2]), and they define the degree of approximation. The `SXL` instruction also controls additional flags for approximation behavior such as enable/disable the cache look-up table. Thus ProACt functions as a normal processor when the approximation look-up table is disabled.

The custom approximation control instruction `SXL` is designed as an *immediate* instruction resulting in very little software overhead and run-time complexity. `SXL` is fully resolved at the *decode* stage of the processor pipeline, and therefore situations such as *control* and *data hazards* [15] are reduced to a minimum. This is significant in a multithreaded, multi-process execution environment, and in atomic operations. Being able to rapidly switch between approximation and normal modes is an important factor affecting the throughput of the processor in such contexts.

We have prototyped ProACt in a Xlinix FPGA. Experimental results show the benefits in terms of speed for different applications.

To summarize, we make the following key contributions:

- High performance general purpose processor hardware for on-demand floating point approximation
- Dynamic control of approximation from software
- Complete development framework including processor hardware and software tool set

Permission to make digital or hard copies of all or part of this work for personal or classroom use is granted without fee provided that copies are not made or distributed for profit or commercial advantage and that copies bear this notice and the full citation on the first page. Copyrights for components of this work owned by others than ACM must be honored. Abstracting with credit is permitted. To copy otherwise, or republish, to post on servers or to redistribute to lists, requires prior specific permission and/or a fee. Request permissions from permissions@acm.org.

GLSVLSI '17, May 10-12, 2017, Banff, AB, Canada
© 2017 ACM. ISBN 978-1-4503-4972-7/17/05...$15.00
DOI: http://dx.doi.org/10.1145/3060403.3060415

[1]ProACt is based on RISC-V [17], a state-of-the-art open-source 64 bit RISC architecture

[2]`SXL` stands for *Set approXimation Level.*

The remainder of this paper is structured as follows. In Section 2 related work is discussed. The ProACt architecture is introduced in Section 3 and details on ProACt evaluation is provided in Section 4. Finally, the paper is concluded in Section 5.

2. RELATED WORK

There are several works in approximate computing for hardware and software approximations that range from dual voltage hardware units, to dedicated programming languages (see for e.g., [18], [9]). In particular [10] explains a generalized set of architectural requirements for an approximate ISA with a dedicated programming language. The authors discuss approximation variants of individual instructions that can be targeted to a dual voltage hardware showing the benefits, though only in simulation. Similarly significant progress has been made on custom designed approximation processors such as [14], targeted for one particular area of application. In contrast, ProACt is a general purpose processor with on-demand approximation capabilities. Approximations can be even completely turned off in ProACt. Moreover, our work is focused on functional approximations, rather than schemes like dynamic voltage/frequency scaling (DVFS), that involve fabrication aspects, and are tedious to design, implement, test and characterize. We refer to [18] for a detailed overview of such techniques.

Several schemes have been presented so far to approximate a floating point unit. Hardware look-up tables are used in [8] to accelerate multi-media processing. This technique called *memoing* has been shown to be very effective. Work of [3] extends this further to *fuzzy memoization* using approximations. However, none of these approaches use custom instructions for software controlled approximations and are limited to the scope of the application it is designed for. In addition, they do not offer direct support to treat the critical program segments differently. An example from image processing is the JPEG image header which contains critical information, and should not be approximated, whereas the pixel data content of the image is relatively safe to approximate.

A detailed overview on the ProACt architecture is given next.

3. ProACt ARCHITECTURE

The ProACt system overview is shown in Fig. 1 on the left hand side. As can be seen it consists of the processor hardware and the software units working together to achieve approximation in computations. To operate the approximations in hardware we have added the *Approximate Floating Point Unit* (AFPU) (a zoom is given on the right hand side of Fig. 1 and its details are described in the next section). In normal mode (i.e. approximations disabled), ProACt floating point results are IEEE 754 compliant.

The AFPU is explained next, followed by the ISA extensions for approximation. The ISA and the assembly instructions are the interface between ProACt hardware and the applications targeting ProACt. Other details on the processor architecture and compiler framework is deferred to the end of this section.

3.1 Approximate Floating Point Unit (AFPU)

The AFPU in ProACt consists of an approximation look-up table, a pipelined *Floating Point Unit* (FPU) and an approximation control logic (see Fig. 1, right hand side). The central approach used in this work is that the results of the FPU are stored first, and further operations are checked in this look-up table, before invoking the FPU for subsequent computation. The input arguments to the FPU are checked in the look-up table and when a match is found, the results from the table are fed to the output, bypassing the entire FPU. The FPU will process only those operations which do not have results in the table. This look-up mechanism is much faster, resulting in significant savings in clock cycles. Approximation masks are applied to the operands before checking the look-up table. Thus, the accuracy of the results can be traded-off using these masks. These approximation masks are set by the software (via the custom approximation control instruction `SXL`, details see next section) and varies in precision. The mask value (or alternatively called *approximation level*) denotes the number of bits to be masked from the LSB, before checking for an entry in the look-up table.

These approximation levels are fully configurable and provide a bit level granularity to the approximations introduced. The look-up table stores the last N floating point operations in a round robin fashion. Software controls the approximation mask, look-up table mechanism, and all these units can be optionally turned off. This is achieved by extending the ISA with a custom instruction for approximation. This ISA extension is presented in the next section.

3.2 ProACt ISA Extension

The software compiler relies on the ISA to transform a program to a binary executable. Hence the ISA is extended with a single assembly instruction `SXL` (*Set approXimation Level*) for the software control of approximations. `SXL` is designed as an immediate instruction that takes a 11-bit immediate value. The LSB, when set to '1' enables the hardware approximations. The remaining bits are used to set the approximation level and other special flags. The software can also enable the approximation unit but set the level as 0. Here it will simply act as a result caching and look-up mechanism without any approximation.

3.3 ProACt Processor Architecture

The ProACt processor is based on RISC-V architecture [17]. RISC-V is a modern, general purpose, high quality, instruction set architecture based on RISC principles. Besides, RISC-V is distributed open source; thus making it well suited for academic and research work. Moreover several implementations of this ISA are publicly available. ProACt is based on one such implementation called Rocket chip [5]. ProACt uses 64-bit addressing scheme with 32 general purpose registers. The pipeline used is a 64-bit, 5-stage, in-order pipeline. As shown in Fig. 1, the processor has separate L1 and L2 cache memories.

3.4 Compiler Framework and System Libraries

The ProACt compiler framework consists of cross-compiler, linker, and associated tools based on *GNU Compiler Collection* (GCC) [1].

In addition to this compiler framework, a set of system library routines and macros are provided with the distribution for the convenient use of on-demand approximations in software programming. The need for approximations could be due to a variety of reasons. Architectural choice, external and run-time factors, nature of the algorithm, quick iterations for initial results, power savings due to approximations, are only some of these. Moreover, the impact of approximations may depends on the nature of input data, as can be seen from the experimental results in Section 4.2. Thus, by providing a compact set of software routines all these scenarios are addressed.

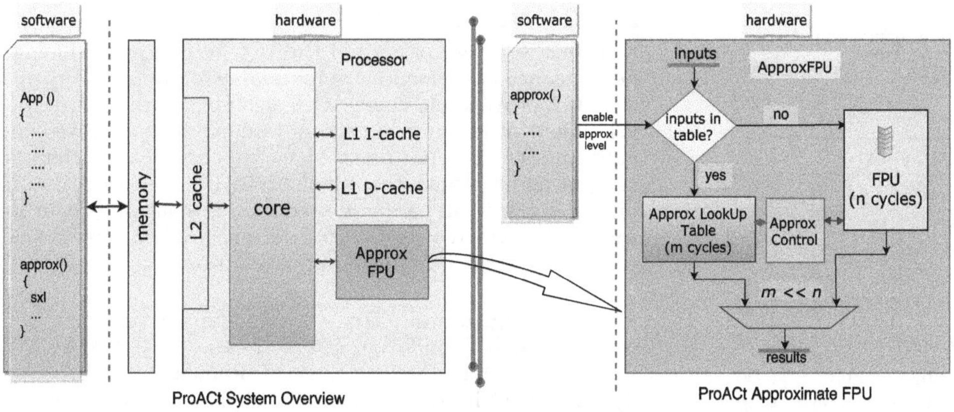

Fig 1: ProACt system overview: SW controlled HW approximations

Table 1: ProACt FPGA hardware prototype details

Platform and Tools:	
FPGA: Xilinx Zynq-XC7Z020	
Prototype Board: Digilent ZedBoard	
FPGA Tools: Xilinx Vivado 2016.2	
Hardware Implementation:	
Frequency:	100MHz*
LUTs:	42527
Power/MHz:	18.66 mW/MHz

⋆ provided by ZedBoard

4. ProACt EVALUATION

In this section we present the experimental evaluation of ProACt. First, we give a brief overview of the ProACt FPGA implementation. The experimental results for different applications using ProACt hardware are presented afterwards.

4.1 FPGA Implementation Details

We have implemented a ProACt prototype in hardware using Xilinx Zynq FPGA. We use a fixed 128 entry approximation look-up table throughout our experiments. The table size is set to 128 mainly to utilize the FPGA resources for hardware implementation efficiently. In general, as the table size increases, the hit-rate and thereby the speed-up resulting from approximations increases. The general impact has already been observed by others [3, 8]. Hence, due to page limitation we do not repeat the underlying experiments here. The hardware details of the evaluation prototype is given in Table 1. This FPGA prototype implementation is the basis of all experimental results and benchmarks presented in the subsequent sections.

4.2 Experimental Results

We have used two different categories of applications to evaluate ProACt. The first one is an image processing application and the second set consists of mathematical functions from scientific computing. These experiments evaluate the performance of ProACt and also tests the on-demand approximation switching feature. All applications are written in C, compiled using ProACt GCC compiler and executed in the ProACt FPGA hardware prototype. All programs have a computationally expensive *core algorithm* which is the focus of evaluation. A top level supervisor program controls the approximations and invokes this core algorithm. Thus, the same algorithm is run with different approximation schemes set by the supervisor program. The scope of approximations in this experimental evaluation is restricted to floating point division only. We next discuss the experiments performed in the two categories:

4.2.1 *Image edge detection*

Table 2 shows the results from a case study on edge detection [13] using ProACt. Image processing applications are very suitable for approximations since there is an inherent human perceptual limitation in processing image details.

The top row of images (Set 1) in Table 2 are generated with approximations disabled by the supervisory program. The middle row (Set 2) are generated with approximations

Table 2: Edge detection with approximations

Lena	IEEE-754	Barbara	Building

Set 1: Images with approximation disabled *(reference)*

Set 2: Images with approximation enabled (20-bit)

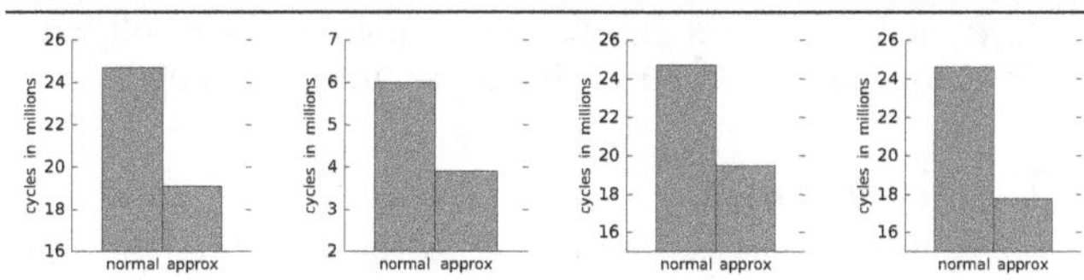

speed-up: 23%	speed-up: 35%	speed-up: 21%	speed-up: 28%

Hardware cycles taken and speed-up with approximations

Images generated from ProACt FPGA hardware
Set 1 reference images are with normal processing
Set 2 images are with approximation enabled (20-bit)

enabled, and the last row shows bar plots for the hardware cycles taken by the core algorithm, along with the speed-up obtained. As evident from Table 2, ProACt is able to generate images with negligible loss of quality with performance improvements averaging more than 25%. Furthermore, the speed-up is much higher in images with more uniform pixels, as evident from the second image, *IEEE-754* (35% faster). This has to be expected since such a sparse input data set has higher chances of computation reuse.

4.2.2 *Scientific functions*

We have also evaluated ProACt with several scientific functions as the core algorithm. A subset of the results is given in Table 3. The first row (non-shaded) in each set is the high accuracy version of the algorithms, i.e. with hardware approximations disabled. The second row (shaded)

Table 3: Math functions with approximations

appx level (a)	cycles n (b)	$\|\Delta y\|$ x10^{-3} (c)	speed up% (d)	appx level (a)	cycles n (b)	$\|\Delta y\|$ x10^{-3} (c)	speed up% (d)
$y = sinh(x)$				$y = sinh^{-1}(x)$			
-1	11083	0.00	0.00	-1	76899	0.00	0.00
20	7791	0.15	29.70	20	72506	3.91	5.71
$y = cosh(x)$				$y = cosh^{-1}(x)$			
-1	10820	0.00	0.00	-1	78616	0.00	0.00
20	7501	0.14	30.67	20	73843	2.14	6.07
$y = tanh(x)$				$y = tanh^{-1}(x)$			
-1	10848	0.00	0.00	-1	7698	0.00	0.00
20	7505	0.10	30.82	20	6135	0.93	20.30

Functions $y = f(x)$ evaluated in ProACt FPGA hardware
Shaded rows are results with approximations enabled.
(a) Approximation level (set with **SXL** instruction)
-1: high accurate result (approximation fully disabled)
20: 20-bit approximation in float division.
(b) Number of machine cycles (n) taken for computation.
(c) Accuracy, $|\Delta y| = |y_{-1} - y_{20}|$ x 10^{-3}
(d) Speed up from approximation $= \frac{n_{-1} - n_{20}}{n_{-1}}$ x 100 %

shows the result with approximations turned on. The absolute value of the deviation of the results ($|\Delta y|$) with approximation from the high accurate version is given in the third column, along with respective speed-up obtained in fourth column (column d).

The speed-up (d column) and the accuracy loss (c column) in Table 3 show that on-demand approximations can significantly reduce the computation load with an acceptable loss in accuracy. The accuracy loss is only in the 4th decimal place, or lower in all the experiments. Functions such as *cosh* and *tanh* can be approximated very well with a speed-up more than 30% with an accuracy of 0.0001

4.3 Discussion

There is a substantial reduction in the run-time and machine cycles in ProACt with approximations enabled. About 25% speed-up, on an average, is obtained with approximations in the image edge detection applications shown in Table 2. This is also reflected in Table 3, where some of the mathematical functions are more than 30% faster. The dynamic power consumption of the system also decreases when approximations are enabled since this speed-up directly corresponds to a reduction in the whole hardware activity.

The throughput and performance of a system, taken as a whole, is largely governed by Amdahl's law [4]. I/O read and write are the main performance bottleneck in our ProACt system prototype. Consequently we have implemented all the algorithms to read the input data all at once, process, and then write out the result in a subsequent step. To make a fair comparison, the costly I/O read-write steps are not accounted in the reported speed-up.

It is worth mentioning that all experimental results presented in Tables 2, 3 are compiled with GCC flag `-ffast-math` [1]. This flag enables multiple compiler level optimizations such as constant folding for floating point computations, rather than offloading every operation to the FPU hardware. Thus, it potentially optimizes the floating point operations while generating the software binary itself, and the speed up due to ProACt approximation adds on top of that.

5. CONCLUSIONS

In this work, we presented ProACt - a Processor for high performance on-demand Approximate Computing. ProACt is FPGA proven, and comes with a complete open-source development framework. Further, we have demonstrated the advantages of ProACt using image processing and scientific computing programs, that show up to 30% performance improvement with dynamic approximation control. In future we aim to extend ProACt with formal methods such as [7] to guarantee the bounds of approximation.

Acknowledgments:. This work was supported by the German Research Foundation (DFG) in the project MANIAC (DR 287/29-1), by the University of Bremen's graduate school SyDe, funded by the German Excellence Initiative and by the German Academic Exchange Service (DAAD).

ProACt repository: *https://gitlab.com/arunc/proact-processor*

6. REFERENCES

[1] GCC - the GNU Compiler Collection 6.1, 2016.
[2] International Telecommunication Union, 2016.
[3] C. Alvarez, J. Corbal, and M. Valero. Fuzzy memoization for floating-point multimedia applications. *IEEE Trans. Comput.*, 54(7), 2005.
[4] G. M. Amdahl. Validity of the single processor approach to achieving large scale computing capabilities, reprinted from the AFIPS conf. *IEEE Solid-State Circuits Society Newsletter*, 12(3):19–20, 2007.
[5] K. Asanovic et al. The Rocket Chip Generator. *Technical Report UCB/EECS-2016-17, EECS Department, University of California, Berkeley*, 2016.
[6] M. Carbin, S. Misailovic, and M. C. Rinard. Verifying quantitative reliability for programs that execute on unreliable hardware. In *OOPSLA*, pages 33–52, 2013.
[7] A. Chandrasekharan, M. Soeken, D. Große, and R. Drechsler. Precise error determination of approximated components in sequential circuits with model checking. In *DAC*, 2016.
[8] D. Citron, D. Feitelson, and L. Rudolph. Accelerating multi-media processing by implementing memoing in multiplication and division units. In *ASPLOS*, ASPLOS VIII, pages 252–261. ACM, 1998.
[9] J. Constantin, L. Wang, G. Karakonstantis, A. Chattopadhyay, and A. Burg. Exploiting dynamic timing margins in microprocessors for frequency-over-scaling with instruction-based clock adjustment. In *DATE*, pages 381–386, 2015.
[10] H. Esmaeilzadeh, A. Sampson, L. Ceze, and D. Burger. Architecture support for disciplined approximate programming. *SIGPLAN Not.*, 47(4):301–312, 2012.
[11] J. R. Hauser. Handling floating-point exceptions in numeric programs. *ACM Trans. Program. Lang. Syst.*, 18(2):139–174, 1996.
[12] H. Hoffmann, S. Sidiroglou, M. Carbin, S. Misailovic, A. Agarwal, and M. Rinard. Dynamic knobs for responsive power-aware computing. In *ACM SIGPLAN Notices*, volume 46, pages 199–212. ACM, 2011.
[13] R. P. Johnson. Contrast based edge detection. *Pattern Recogn.*, 23(3-4):311–318, 1990.
[14] G. Karakonstantis, A. Sankaranarayanan, M. M. Sabry, D. Atienza, and A. Burg. A quality-scalable and energy-efficient approach for spectral analysis of heart rate variability. In *DATE*, pages 1–6, 2014.
[15] D. A. Patterson and J. L. Hennessy. *Computer Organization and Design, Fourth Edition: The Hardware/Software Interface.* Morgan Kaufmann.
[16] A. Sampson, W. Dietl, E. Fortuna, D. Gnanapragasam, L. Ceze, and D. Grossman. Enerj: Approximate data types for safe and general low-power computation. In *PLDI*, PLDI '11, pages 164–174. ACM, 2011.
[17] A. Waterman, Y. Lee, D. A. Patterson, and K. Asanovic. The RISC-V instruction set manual, volume i: Base user-level ISA. *EECS Department, UC Berkeley, Tech. Rep. UCB/EECS-2011-62*, 2011.
[18] Q. Xu, T. Mytkowicz, and N. S. Kim. Approximate computing: A survey. *IEEE Design Test*, 33(1):8–22, 2016.

Softmax Regression Design for Stochastic Computing Based Deep Convolutional Neural Networks

Zihao Yuan, Ji Li,
University of Southern California
Los Angeles, CA, USA
zihaoyua@usc.edu,
jli724@usc.edu

Zhe Li, Caiwen Ding, Ao Ren,
Syracuse University
Syracuse, NY, USA
zli89@syr.edu, aren@syr.edu,
cading@syr.edu

Bo Yuan
City University of New York
New York, NY, USA
byuan@ccny.cuny.edu

Qinru Qiu
Syracuse University
Syracuse, NY, USA
qiqiu@syr.edu

Jeffrey Draper
University of Southern California
Los Angeles, CA, USA
draper@isi.edu

Yanzhi Wang
Syracuse University
Syracuse, NY, USA
ywang393@syr.edu

ABSTRACT

Recently, Deep Convolutional Neural Networks (DCNNs) have made tremendous advances, achieving close to or even better accuracy than human-level perception in various tasks. Stochastic Computing (SC), as an alternate to the conventional binary computing paradigm, has the potential to enable massively parallel and highly scalable hardware implementations of DCNNs. In this paper, we design and optimize the SC based Softmax Regression function. Experiment results show that compared with a binary SR, the proposed SC-SR under longer bit stream can reach the same level of accuracy with the improvement of 295X, 62X, 2617X in terms of power, area and energy, respectively. Binary SR is suggested for future DCNNs with short bit stream length input whereas SC-SR is recommended for longer bit stream.

1. INTRODUCTION

Nowadays, Deep Convolutional Neural Network (DCNN) is the dominant approach for classification and detection tasks for images, video, speech as well as audio [1]. DCNNs implement the backpropagation algorithm, which points out the parameters that should be updated. These parameters are used to compute the representation in each layer from the output of the previous layer. Clearly, the huge amount of computation power of DCNNs prevents their widespread applications in wearable and Internet of Things (IoT) devices [2, 3, 4].

Compared to the studies using conventional binary arithmetic computing, Stochastic Computing (SC) is a fascinating solution to the above issues due to its superior performance in terms of area and power consumption as well as high tolerance to soft errors [5, 6, 7]. SC represents a number by the probability of 1s in a random bit stream. Many complex arithmetic operations can be implemented with very simple hardware logic in the SC framework, which alleviates the extensive computation complexity [6, 8]. On this account, a mass of research efforts have been put into designing neural networks using SC [2, 6, 8, 9]. Both of the recent designs [2, 9] successfully implement the SC-based neuron cells and the layerwise structure of neural networks. Nevertheless, there is no existing design flow for Softmax Regression (SR) function after the fully-connected layer for DCNNs. SR is the generalization of logistic regression function when multiple categories need to be classified. It is one of the most significant part in deep learning networks due to the fact that it directly affects the final result.

In this paper, we first propose a SC-based Softmax Regression function block. The design parameters are optimized in order to achieve best performance for accuracy. After that we conduct a comprehensive comparison between binary ASIC SR function and SC-based SR function under different input sizes and stochastic bit stream lengths. Moreover, we further construct and investigate the network performances between the conventional binary SR design and the proposed SC-based SR design in a practical DCNN.

Permission to make digital or hard copies of all or part of this work for personal or classroom use is granted without fee provided that copies are not made or distributed for profit or commercial advantage and that copies bear this notice and the full citation on the first page. Copyrights for components of this work owned by others than ACM must be honored. Abstracting with credit is permitted. To copy otherwise, or republish, to post on servers or to redistribute to lists, requires prior specific permission and/or a fee. Request permissions from permissions@acm.org.

GLSVLSI '17, May 10-12, 2017, Banff, AB, Canada
© 2017 ACM. ISBN 978-1-4503-4972-7/17/05...$15.00
DOI: http://dx.doi.org/10.1145/3060403.3060467

2. DCNN ARCHITECTURE AND SOFTMAX REGRESSION FUNCTION

2.1 Deep Convolutional Neural Network

A general DCNN architecture consists of a stack of convolutional layers, pooling layers, and fully connected layers. A convolutional layer is associated with a set of learnable filters (or kernels), and common patterns in local regions of inputs are extracted by convolving this kind of filter over the inputs [10]. A feature map is built to store the convolution result. After that, a subsampling step is applied to aggregate statistics of these features in the pooling layer for the sake of reducing the dimensions of data and alleviating over-fitting issues. In addition, a nonlinear activation function is applied here to generate the output of the layer [11]. After several convolutional and pooling layers, the high-level reasoning fully connected layer is applied in order to further aggregate the local information learned in previous layers. After that, a Softmax Regression function should be applied for classification.

2.2 Stochastic Computing (SC)

Stochastic computing is a technology that represents a numeric value $x \in [0, 1]$ by counting the number of 1s in a bit stream, e.g., the value of a 4-bit sequence "0100" is $x = P(X = 1) = 0.25$. In addition to this unipolar format, another widely used format is bipolar format. In this coding scheme, a value $x \in [-1, 1]$ is processed by $P(X = 1) = \frac{x+1}{2}$. With SC, addition, multiplication, and division can be implemented using significantly smaller circuits, compared to the conventional binary arithmetic [6] as shown in Figure 1 (a), (b) and (c).

To be more specific, multiplications are executed using XNOR gates in bipolar format. The stochastic number of C is calculated as $c = 2P(C) - 1 = 4P(A)P(B) - 2P(A) - 2P(B) + 1 = (2P(A) - 1)(2P(B) - 1) = a \times b$. Multiplexers (MUXes) are used to processed addition in SC [6]. In order to achieve a better accuracy with little deficit in terms of power, area and energy, we adopt the Approximate Parallel Counter (APC) proposed in [12]

Division can only be accomplished in an approximate form in the stochastic number representation schemes [6]. Given input X and Y, output $Q = \frac{Y}{X}$ is represented as

$$Q = -\alpha(XQ - Y) \quad (1)$$

where α is a positive parameter which controls the rate change for the counter state. A SC-based unipolar division circuit is implemented by adopting the gradient descent technique with a saturated counter as an integrator. Division is implemented by incrementing the counter when Y is 1 and decrementing the counter when both X and Q are 1s.

2.3 Softmax Regression (SR) Function

Softmax Regression (SR) is a generalization of logistic regression for the sake of classifying multiple mutually exclusive classes. SR is placed after fully connected layer in order to assign probabilities to an object being one of several different things. SR is composed of two parts, i.e., summation and softmax. Summation is used to add up the pixel intensities. It is quite similar to normal neuron cell operation except the activation function. Given input x, output Z in class i is calculated as

$$Z_i = \sum_j W_{i,j} x_j + b_i \quad (2)$$

where $W_{i,j}$ is the weight and b_i stands for extra parameter called bias of class i. These parameters are adjusted during the backpropagation process. The subsequent softmax step acts like an activation function which changes the linear function into different nonlinear shapes. In this scenario, the summation result is shaping into a probability distribution function over different classes. Given input x, output P for class i is defined as

$$P_i = \frac{exp(x_i)}{\sum_j exp(x_j)} \quad (3)$$

The exponential function means little increase in input x_i will result in dramatically growth in result $exp(x_i)$ and indeed increase the probability in class i. This enables SR to

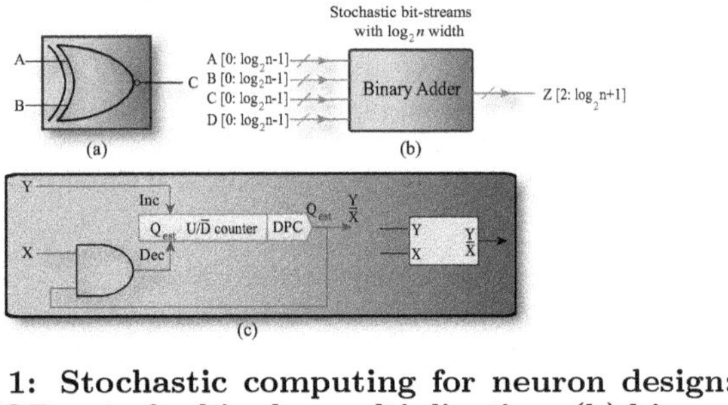

Figure 1: Stochastic computing for neuron design: (a) XNOR gate for bipolar multiplication, (b) binary adder, and (c) unipolar division.

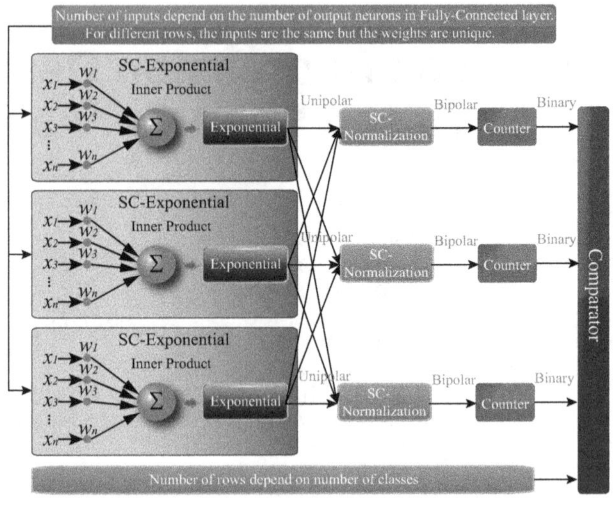

Figure 2: Structure for SC based Softmax Regression function.

Table 1: Naming Conventions in a SC based SR

m	the length of bit stream
q	number of classes
n	input size: the number of input bit streams (or the number of input and weight pairs) in each convolution block
x_i^j	the i-th input bit of the j-th convolution block ($i \in [0, n-1]$, $j \in [0, q-1]$)
w_i^j	the i-th weight bit of the j-th convolution block ($i \in [0, n-1]$, $j \in [0, q-1]$)
t_j	the sum calculated by the j-th convolution block, which is a $log_2 n$-bit binary number

distinguish among different categories and select the most similar result.

3. SC-SOFTMAX REGRESSION DESIGN

3.1 Overall Structure

The proposed structure of SC-SR is shown in Figure 2, which is composed of SC-exponential, SC-normalization, SC-comparator and counter blocks. Bipolar encoding scheme is employed. The proposed SC-SR design adopt XNOR gates and APCs for addition and multiplication (same as convolution), respectively. Note that the outputs of APCs are binary. In addition, SC-exponential accomplishes a binary input to unipolar stochastic bit stream conversion. After that, the SC-normalization step converts the unipolar output from exponential block to bipolar stochastic bit stream. For the convenience of discussions, we follow the naming conventions in Table I.

3.2 SC-exponential

The author in [2] use a saturated up/down counter to implement a binary hyperbolic tangent function. We adopt the saturated counter idea and implant in our design. Algorithm 1 presents the proposed SC-exponential function where step 8-11 correspond to convolution using XNOR gates and APCs and step 12-16 are the adopted saturated counter. The counted binary number generated by APC is taken by the saturated up/down counter which represents the amount of increase and decrease. Besides, we also use a history shift register H[0:α-1] in order to count the last α bits of output stochastic bit stream. By using the sum of the α bits, which is denoted by δ, we can predict the next stochastic output bit. To be more specific, if the sum of last α bits falls in range of $[0.3\alpha, 0.4\alpha]$, the output is predicted as 0 because the possibility of this value being large is small. On the other hand, if it falls into $[0.6\alpha, 0.7\alpha]$, this output is predicted to be a 1.

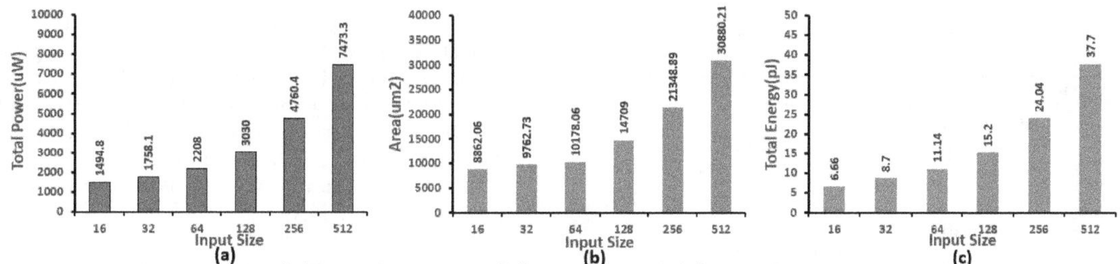

Figure 3: Input size versus (a) total power, (b) area, and (c) total energy for the proposed SC-SR.

Another reason for this is that the normalization block in our proposed design is created by adopting the unipolar division method in [6]. Note that the outputs of our SC-exponential block are in unipolar encoding scheme.

Algorithm 1: Designated Softmax Regression SC-Exponential $(m, n, x_i^j, w_i^j, \alpha, e)$

```
   input  : q indicates number of classes
   input  : α is the number of registers in the temporary array
   input  : e is internal FSM state number
   output: z_k is the k-th stochastic output bit for the SC-exponential
1  S_max ← e − 1 ;                                          /* max state */
2  S ← e/2 ;                                                /* current state */
3  r ← α − 1 ;                                              /* r is an iterator */
4  H[0 : α − 1] ← 0 ;                                       /* initialize history array */
5  δ ← α/2 ;                                                /* initialize shadow counter */
6  for k ← 1 to m do
7      for i ← 1 to n do
8          p_i^j = x_i^j ⊙ w_i^j ;                          /* XNOR multiplication */
9      end
10     t_j = 2 · Σ_{i=0}^{n} p_i^j − n ;                    /* APC addition */
11     S ← S + t_j
12     if S < 0 then                                        /* saturated counter */
13         S ← 0
14     else if S > S_max then
15         S ← S_max
16     end
17     if S < n/4 then                                      /* output logic */
18         if 0.4 × α > δ > 0.3 × α then
19             z_k ← 0
20         else if S > S/2 then
21             z_k ← 1
22         else
23             z_k ← 0
24         end
25     else
26         if 0.7 × α > δ > 0.6 × α then
27             z_k ← 1
28         else if S > S/2 then
29             z_k ← 1
30         else
31             z_k ← 0
32         end
33     end
34 end
35 while r ≥ 1 do
36     H[r] ← H[r − 1];                                     /* update the history array */
37     r ← r − 1
38 end
39 H[0] ← z_k
40 δ ← Σ_{r=0}^{α−1} H[r];                                  /* update the shadow counter */
41 r ← α − 1
```

3.3 SC-normalization

Since the output from previous SC-exponential block is in unipolar encoding format. In Algorithm 2, We adopt the unipolar division circuit from [6]. Step5-17 correspond to the summation of all the previous outputs and determine the divisor value by using an AND gate. We create designated SC-exponential and SC-normalization for each class. Therefore, the dividend is just the output of previous SC-exponential block for corresponding class. We have 4 different conditions to control the amount of increase and decrease in the implanted saturated counter as shown in step19-30. Since the output is a non-negative bipolar stochastic number, a history shift register H[0:α-1] is also implemented in this algorithm in order to eliminate negative value. To be more specific, if the sum δ is less than $\frac{\alpha}{2}$, the current value is predicted to be negative. Since each negative value will raise

Table 2: Network Accuracy

	input size	bit stream	validation(%)	test(%)
software	256	-	99.03	99.10
	512	-	98.96	99.04
binary	256	-	99.04	99.10
	512	-	98.96	99.07
SC	256	16	59.04	59.75
		32	78.26	77.23
		64	98.80	98.91
		256	99.02	99.08
		1024	99.00	99.14
	512	16	19.72	19.53
		32	98.85	99.00
		64	98.04	98.29
		256	98.93	99.09
		1024	98.78	99.06

an error, we mitigate such error by outputting a 1 instead of a 0.

4. EXPERIMENTAL RESULTS

4.1 Performance analysis for SC-SR

For SC-SR, the accuracy depends on the bit stream length m and input size n. Hence, in order to consider the aforementioned factors, we create and analyze the inaccuracy of SC-SR using LeNet-5 [14] classification method based on the wide range of input size and bit stream length as shown in Figure 4. The corresponding hardware costs of proposed SC-SR are shown in Figure 3 (a), (b) and (c). The SRs and DCNNs are synthesized in Synopsys Design Compiler with the 45nm Nangate Library [13] using Verilog. Note that the inaccuracy here is calculated by comparing with the software results. It is obviously that SC-SR will be less accurate provided that the input size increases and it will be precision if the bit stream length increases. we further test the proposed design under different number of classes using AlexNet [15] classification method, the classification accuracies for different input size and bit stream length are all 100 % which means there is no accuracy degradation.

4.2 Comparison with Binary ASIC SR

We further compare the performance of the proposed SC-based Softmax Regresion block with the binary ASIC hardware SR. The input is set to 800 and the number of classes is set to 10. The binary exponential function is built us-

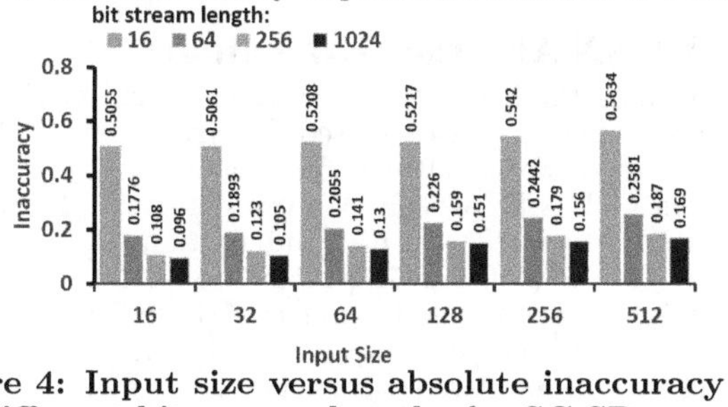

Figure 4: Input size versus absolute inaccuracy under different bit stream lengths for SC-SR.

Algorithm 2: Designated Softmax Regression SC-Normalization (m, x_j, α, e)

```
input : f is rate change for the FSM
input : x_j is the input bit of the j-th exponential block
input : e is number of different classes
output: z_k^j is the k-th stochastic output bit of class j for the
        SC-normalization
Algorithm 1 step 1-4
δ ← 0 ;                                   /* initialize shadow counter */
for k ← 1 to m do
    p = Σ_{j=1}^{e} x_j ;   /* summation of output bits from exponential blocks */
    if p > e/2 then                       /* nomralize summation result */
        h ← 1
    else
        h ← 0
    end
    if S > e/2 then                       /* Divisor */
        X ← h
    else
        X ← 0
    end
    Y = x_j;                              /* Dividend */
    if X == 1&&Y == 1 then                /* Next state logic */
        S = S − p + f × e
    end
    if X == 0&&Y == 1 then
        S = S + f × e
    end
    if X == 1&&Y == 0 then
        S = S − p
    end
    if X == 0&&Y == 0 then
        S = S
    end
    if S < 0 then                         /* saturated counter */
        S ← 0
    else if S > S_max then
        S ← S_max
    end
    if δ < α/2 then                       /* compensate for negative value */
        z_k^j ← 1
    else
        if 0.7 × α > δ > 0.6 × α then     /* output logic */
            z_k^j ← 1
        else if S > e/2 then
            z_k^j ← 1
        else
            z_k^j ← 0
        end
    end
end
Algorithm 1 step 35-41
```

Table 3: Performance Comparison with 8 Bit Fixed Point Binary Design when $n = 800$ and $q = 10$

	SC-800bits	binary 800bits	improvement
dynamic power(uW)	10981	3503800	319X
leakage power(uW)	1078	58986	55X
total power(uW)	12058	3562100	295X
area(um2)	50083	3094968	62X
delay(ns)	5.05	44.74	8.8X
energy(pJ)	61	159368	2617X

ing LUTs, whereas the normalization block is built using divider. Clearly, the number of bits in fixed-point numbers affect both the hardware cost and accuracy. To make the comparison fair, we adopt minimum fixed point (8 bit) that yields a DCNN network accuracy that is almost identical to the software DCNN (with < 0.0003 difference in network test error). Table 3 shows the performance comparison between binary SR and SC-SR. Compared with binary ASIC SR, the proposed SC-SR achieves up to 295X, 62X, and 2617X improvement in terms of power, energy and area, respectively, indicating significant hardware savings.

4.3 DCNN Accuracy Evaluation

To evaluate the network accuracy, we construct a LeNet-5 DCNN, which is a widely-used DCNN structure, by replacing the software Softmax function with the proposed SC-SR as well as binary SR. We evaluate two SR configurations, i.e., the LeNet-5 with configurations of 784-11520-2880-3200-800-256-10 and 784-11520-2880-3200-800-512-10. The DCNNs are evaluated using the MNIST handwritten digit image dataset [16]. we apply the same amount of training time in software for these two DCNN architectures. Table 2 summarizes the accuracy of DCNNs using SC-SR and binary SR. One can observe that with a long input bit stream length ($m >= 64$), SC-SR reaches the same precision level as binary SR and software SR. As we discuss above, compared to binary SR, SC-SR has better performance in terms of power, area and energy. Hence, binary SR is suggested for future DCNNs when bit stream length is short (e.g., $m = 64$), whereas SC-SR is recommended for long bit stream length DCNNs.

5. CONCLUSION

In this paper, we present a novel SC based Softmax Regresion function design. We test the proposed SC-SR under different input size and bit stream length as well as output classes. In addition, we implant the proposed design into LeNet-5 DCNN. Experimental results on the MNIST dataset demonstrate that compared to the binary SR, the proposed SC-SR under long bit stream length input were able to significantly reduce the area, power and energy footprint with nearly no accuracy degradation.

6. REFERENCES

[1] Y. LeCun, Y. Bengio, and G. Hinton, "Deep learning," *Nature*, vol. 521, no. 7553, pp. 436–444, 2015.

[2] K. Kim, J. Kim, J. Yu, J. Seo, J. Lee, and K. Choi, "Dynamic energy-accuracy trade-off using stochastic computing in deep neural networks," in *Proceedings of the 53rd Annual Design Automation Conference.* ACM, 2016, p. 124.

[3] J. Li, A. Ren, Z. Li, C. Ding, B. Yuan, Q. Qiu, and Y. Wang, "Towards acceleration of deep convolutional neural networks using stochastic computing," in *Asia and South Pacific Design Automation Conference (ASP-DAC). IEEE*, 2017.

[4] Y. Xue, J. Li, S. Nazarian, and P. Bogdan, "Fundamental challenges towards making iot a reachable reality: A model-centric investigation," *ACM Transactions on Design Automation of Electronic Systems (TODAES)*, 2017.

[5] J. Li and J. Draper, "Accelerating soft-error-rate (ser) estimation in the presence of single event transients," in *Proceedings of the 53rd Annual Design Automation Conference.* ACM, 2016, p. 55.

[6] B. D. Brown and H. C. Card, "Stochastic neural computation. i. computational elements," *IEEE Transactions on computers*, vol. 50, no. 9, pp. 891–905, 2001.

[7] J. Li and J. Draper, "Joint soft-error-rate (ser) estimation for combinational logic and sequential elements," in *VLSI (ISVLSI), 2016 IEEE Computer Society Annual Symposium on*, 2016, pp. 737–742.

[8] Z. Li, A. Ren, J. Li, Q. Qiu, Y. Wang, and B. Yuan, "Dscnn: Hardware-oriented optimization for stochastic computing based deep convolutional neural networks," in *Proceeding of IEEE International Conference on Computer Design*, 2016.

[9] A. Ren, J. Li, Z. Li, C. Ding, X. Qian, Q. Qiu, B. Yuan, and Y. Wang, "Sc-dcnn: Highly-scalable deep convolutional neural network using stochastic computing," *arXiv preprint arXiv:1611.05939*, 2016.

[10] Z. Li, A. Ren, J. Li, Q. Qiu, B. Yuan, J. Draper, and Y. Wang, "Structural design optimization for deep convolutional neural networks using stochastic computing."

[11] J. Li, Z. Yuan, Z. Li, C. Ding, A. Ren, Q. Qiu, J. Draper, and Y. Wang, "Hardware-driven nonlinear activation for stochastic computing based deep convolutional neural networks," in *Neural Networks (IJCNN), 2017 International Joint Conference on.* IEEE, 2017.

[12] K. Kim, J. Lee, and K. Choi, "Approximate de-randomizer for stochastic circuits," in *SoC Design Conference (ISOCC), 2015 International.* IEEE, 2015, pp. 123–124.

[13] Nangate 45nm Open Library, Nangate Inc., 2009. [Online]. Available: http://www.nangate.com/

[14] Y. LeCun, L. Bottou, Y. Bengio, and P. Haffner, "Gradient-based learning applied to document recognition," *Proceedings of the IEEE*, vol. 86, no. 11, pp. 2278–2324, 1998.

[15] A. Krizhevsky, I. Sutskever, and G. E. Hinton, "Imagenet classification with deep convolutional neural networks," in *Advances in neural information processing systems*, 2012.

[16] L. Deng, "The mnist database of handwritten digit images for machine learning research," *IEEE Signal Processing Magazine*, vol. 29, no. 6.

Computing Polynomials with Positive Coefficients using Stochastic Logic by Double-NAND Expansion *

Sayed Ahmad Salehi, Yin Liu, Marc D. Riedel, Keshab K. Parhi
University of Minnesota
200 Union Street SE, Minneapolis, MN, 55455
{saleh022, liux1394, mriedel, parhi}@umn.edu

ABSTRACT

This paper proposes a novel method, referred to as *double-NAND expansion*, to implement polynomials with all positive coefficients using unipolar stochastic logic. The proposed double-NAND expansion leads to implementations of polynomials using no more than $2n$ NAND gates where n represents the degree of the polynomial. The proposed implementations are compared with those based on multiplexers, Bernstein polynomial method, finite state machine method and factorization. The paper also considers implementations of several functions expressed as polynomials using truncated Mclaurin series based on the proposed approach. The experimental results show that the proposed method outperforms the prior methods in terms of accuracy, hardware complexity, and critical path.

Keywords

Stochastic logic; double-NAND expansion

1. INTRODUCTION

This paper presents a novel method for implementing polynomials with all positive coefficients such that the sum of all coefficients is less than or equal to 1 by using stochastic logic circuits that require only two NAND gates for each term of the polynomial.

Stochastic logic circuits can be realized by simple combinational logic gates [2]. In this paper we only use AND and NAND gates for polynomial computations. Using unipolar representation, the AND gate computes the multiplication of its two inputs, $z = xy$ and the NAND gate computes $z = 1 - xy$. Although the proposed circuits are primarily based on NAND gates, for computation of some polynomials, AND gates also may be required only at the beginning and end of the circuits.

*This research is supported by the National Science Foundation Grants CCF-1423407 and CCF-1319107.

Permission to make digital or hard copies of all or part of this work for personal or classroom use is granted without fee provided that copies are not made or distributed for profit or commercial advantage and that copies bear this notice and the full citation on the first page. Copyrights for components of this work owned by others than ACM must be honored. Abstracting with credit is permitted. To copy otherwise, or republish, to post on servers or to redistribute to lists, requires prior specific permission and/or a fee. Request permissions from permissions@acm.org.

GLSVLSI '17, May 10-12, 2017, Banff, AB, Canada.
© 2017 ACM. ISBN 978-1-4503-4972-7/17/05...$15.00.
DOI: http://dx.doi.org/10.1145/3060403.3060410

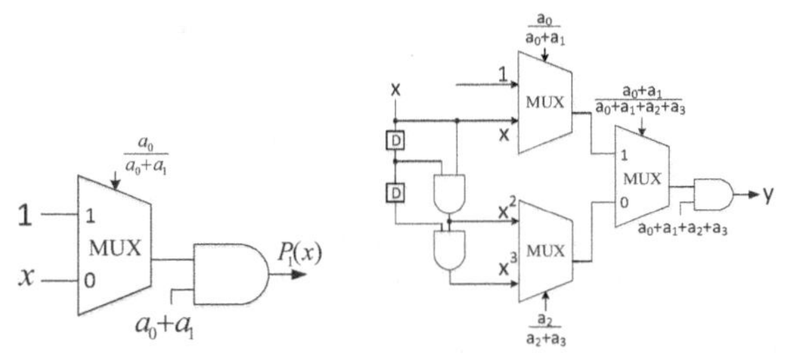

(a) (b)

Figure 1: Multiplexer-based Stochastic logic circuits for computing (a) first-order polynomial and (b) third-order polynomial.

This paper considers a polynomial of degree n, i.e., $P_n(x)$, represented in power form as:

$$P_n(x) = a_0 + a_1x + a_2x^2 + a_3x^3 + ... + a_nx^n. \quad (1)$$

All a_i's are assumed to be positive or zero, and sum of a_i's is assumed to be less than or equal to 1.

A multiplexer-based stochastic logic circuit for implementation of FIR digital filters was proposed in [1]. We can adapt this circuit for the purpose of computing polynomials with all positive coefficients. Figure 1(a) shows the multiplexer-based circuit for computation of $P_1(x) = a_0 + a_1x$. Similarly, $P_2(x) = a_0 + a_1x + a_2x^2 + a_3x^3$ can be implemented by the circuit shown in Figure 1(b). The delay elements are used for decorrelation [5]. Factorization method, presented in [4], is another approach to synthesize stochastic logic circuits for computing polynomials.

This paper proposes a new approach that can map polynomials having all positive coefficients to a hardware-efficient circuit composed of NAND gates. For the proposed method, each term of the polynomial is implemented by two two-input NAND gates and the proposed expansion of polynomials is referred to as *double-NAND* expansion.

This paper is organized as follows. Section 2 presents the proposed method for computing a class of polynomials and certain functions. Section 3 presents the experimental results for the proposed method and comparisons with prior work.

2. PROPOSED DOUBLE-NAND METHOD

Using stochastic logic circuits composed of simple two-input NAND gates, this section presents the proposed method for computing polynomials with all positive coefficients, i.e.,

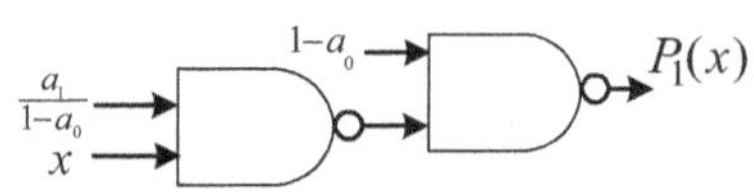

(a)

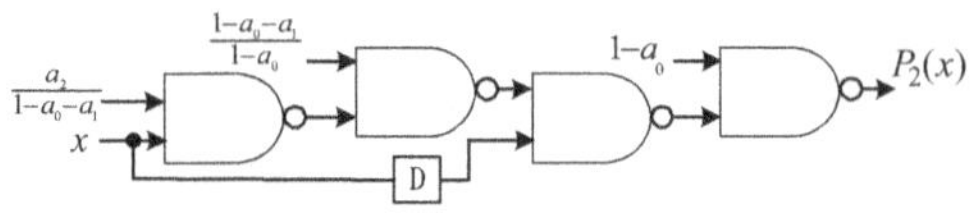

(b)

Figure 2: The proposed Stochastic logic circuits for computing (a) first-order polynomial and (b) second-order polynomial.

$0 \leq a_i < 1$ for $i = 0, ..., n$. Each term of the polynomial has the form of $a_i x^i$ and is monotonically increasing. Therefore, the polynomials considered in this paper are monotonically increasing in the interval [0,1). It is important to note that not all monotonically increasing polynomials satisfy the all positive coefficient property as considered in this paper.

First Consider the simple example of the first-order polynomial given by:

$$P_1(x) = a_0 + a_1 x = 1 - (1 - a_0)(1 - \frac{a_1}{(1 - a_0)} x) \quad (2)$$

For $a_0, a_1 \in [0, 1)$, Equation (2) can be mapped to the stochastic logic circuit shown in Figure 2(a). Similarly, the second-order polynomial, $P_2(x)$, with all coefficients in the unit interval can be expressed as (3), and implemented as shown in Figure 2(b).

$$\begin{aligned} P_2(x) &= a_0 + a_1 x + a_2 x^2 \\ &= 1 - (1 - a_0)[1 - x(1 - \tfrac{1 - a_0 - a_1}{1 - a_0}(1 - \tfrac{a_2 x}{1 - a_0 - a_1}))] \end{aligned} \quad (3)$$

This approach can be extended for the general case of a polynomial of degree n, $P_n(x)$, with all positive coefficients. $P_n(x)$ can be represented as a sum of its first term, a_0, and the other terms, $xP_{n-1}(x)$, as given by:

$$P_n(x) = a_0 + \underbrace{a_1 x + a_2 x^2 + a_3 x^3 + ... + a_n x^n}_{xP_{n-1}(x)} = a_0 + xP_{n-1}(x) \quad (4)$$

Equation (4) can be rewritten as:

$$\begin{aligned} P_n(x) &= a_0 + xP_{n-1}(x) = \\ 1 - (1 - a_0)&(1 - x(\underbrace{\frac{a_1 + a_2 x + a_3 x^2 + ... + a_n x^{n-1}}{1 - a_0}}_{P_{n-1}(x)})) \end{aligned} \quad (5)$$

Equation (5) shows that $P_{n-1}(x)$ has a form similar to the original $P_n(x)$; however, its degree is reduced by one and the coefficients are divided by $(1 - a_0)$. Thus, the above mentioned step can be repeated for $P_{n-1}(x)$ and the procedure can be continued as required. Using this approach $P_n(x)$ can be reformatted as

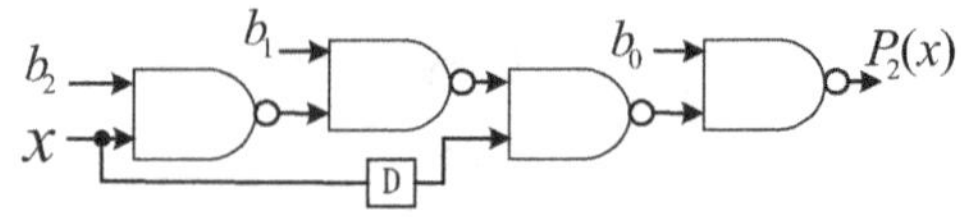

Figure 4: Stochastic logic circuit for Equation (7).

$$\begin{aligned} P_n(x) &= 1 - (1 - a_0)(1 - x(1 - \frac{1 - (a_0 + a_1)}{1 - a_0}(1 - x(\\ &...(1 - \frac{1 - \sum_{i=0}^{k-1} a_i}{1 - \sum_{i=0}^{k-2} a_i}(1 - x(... \\ &(1 - \frac{1 - \sum_{i=0}^{n-1} a_i}{1 - \sum_{i=0}^{n-2} a_i}(1 - \frac{a_n x}{1 - \sum_{i=0}^{n-1} a_i})))))))) \end{aligned} \quad (6)$$

THEOREM 1. *All the coefficients for the representation of $P_n(x)$ in Equation (6) are greater than 0 and less than 1.*

PROOF. We know that the sum of all a_i's for $i = 0, ..., n$ is less than or equal to one, i.e., $\sum_{i=0}^{n} a_i \leq 1$. All of the coefficients in Equation (6), except the one in the innermost parentheses, have the form of $\frac{1 - \sum_{i=0}^{k} a_i}{1 - \sum_{i=0}^{k-1}}$ for $k = 0, ..., n - 1$. It is clear that for these coefficients the numerator is less than the denominator. Thus, the values of the coefficients are less than 1. Since $\sum_{i=0}^{n} a_i \leq 1$ we have $a_n + \sum_{i=0}^{n-1} a_i \leq 1$ or equivalently $a_n \leq 1 - \sum_{i=0}^{n-1} a_i$. Thus, the coefficient inside the innermost parentheses is also less than one, i.e., $\frac{a_n}{1 - \sum_{i=0}^{n-1} a_i} \leq 1$. Moreover, the the numerator and denominator of all the coefficients in Equation (6) are greater than 0. Therefore, these coefficients are greater than 0. □

Equation (6) can be mapped to a stochastic logic circuit containing cascaded NAND gates as shown in Figure 3. Note that the delay elements are used for decorrelation [5].

In the proposed circuits, for the first-order polynomial, $P_1(x)$, two NAND gates are required, and for each additional term another two NAND gates are needed. Thus, $2(n_t - 1)$ NAND gates are required to implement a polynomial that has n_t terms. For example, $P_n(x)$ represented in Equation (1) requires $2n$ two-input NAND gates.

We now show that for any stochastic logic circuit implemented by cascaded double-NAND gates, the coefficients add to less than 1. To illustrate this, consider the circuit shown in Figure 4. The second-order polynomial implemented by this circuit is given by:

$$\begin{aligned} P_2(x) &= 1 - b_0(1 - x(1 - b_1(1 - b_2 x))) \\ &= (1 - b_0) + b_0(1 - b_1)x + b_0 b_1 b_2 x^2. \end{aligned} \quad (7)$$

Therefore, $a_0 = 1 - b_0$, $a_1 = b_0(1 - b_1)$, and $a_2 = b_0 b_1 b_2$. For this example, $\sum_{i=0}^{2} a_i = 1 - b_0 b_1 (1 - b_2) < 1$.

For a polynomial of degree n, stochastic logic circuit in Figure 5 implements $P_n(x)$ shown in Equation (8).

$$P_n(x) = 1 - b_0(1 - x(1 - b_1(1 - x(...(1 - b_{n-1}(1 - b_n x)))))) \quad (8)$$

The polynomial represented in Equation (8) can be expressed in power form in Equation (9).

$$\begin{aligned} P_n(x) &= (1 - b_0) + b_0(1 - b_1)x + b_0 b_1 (1 - b_2) x^2 + ... \\ &+ b_0 b_1 .. b_{n-2}(1 - b_{n-1}) x^{(n-1)} + b_0 b_1 .. b_{n-1} b_n x^n \end{aligned} \quad (9)$$

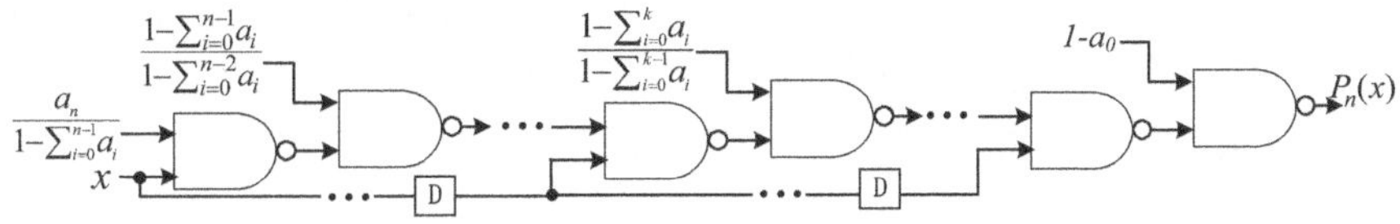

Figure 3: General double-NAND structure for polynomial of degree n. Based on the proposed approach we change the form of Equation (4) to the form of Equation (6) and map it to a cascade of NAND gates.

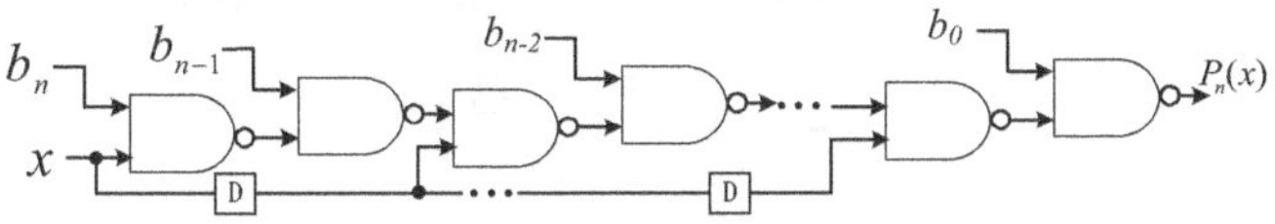

Figure 5: Stochastic logic circuit for implementation of polynomial in Equation (8).

The sum of the coefficients in Equation (9) is equal to $1 - b_0 b_1 ... b_{n-1}(1-b_n)$. Considering $0 \leq b_i \leq 1$ for $i = 0, ..., n-1$ and $0 < b_n \leq 1$, it is easy to show that this sum is less than or equal to 1 and greater than 0.

Example 1: Consider the polynomial $P(x) = \frac{4}{5} + \frac{x}{15} + \frac{x^2}{10}$. Using Equation (6), it can be rewritten as:

$$P(x) = 1 - \frac{1}{5}(1 - x(1 - \frac{2}{3}(1 - \frac{3}{4}x))) \qquad (10)$$

This equation can be implemented by the circuit in Figure 4 with $b_0 = \frac{1}{5}$, $b_1 = \frac{2}{3}$ and $b_2 = \frac{3}{4}$.

The proposed approach can be used to implement certain arithmetic functions using stochastic logic. For this purpose, first the target functions are approximated by truncating their Maclaurin series expansions [5].

We consider three functions whose Maclaurin series expansions are listed below.

$$e^{(x-1)} = \frac{1}{e}\sum_{n=0}^{\infty}\frac{(x)^n}{n!} \approx \frac{1}{e} + \frac{1}{e}x + \frac{x^2}{2e} + \frac{x^3}{6e} = 1 - \frac{e-1}{e}(1- x(1 - \frac{e-2}{e-1}(1 - x(1 - \frac{2e-5}{2(e-2)}(1 - \frac{x}{6e-15})))))$$

$$\begin{aligned}\sec x - 1 &= \sum_{n=1}^{\infty}\tfrac{(-1)^n E_{2n}}{(2n)!}x^{2n} \approx \tfrac{x^2}{2} + \tfrac{5}{24}x^4 + \tfrac{61}{720}x^6 \\ &= x^2(1 - \tfrac{1}{2}(1 - x^2(1 - \tfrac{7}{12}(1 - \tfrac{61}{210}x^2))))\end{aligned}$$

$$\begin{aligned}\cosh x - 1 &= \sum_{n=0}^{\infty}\tfrac{x^{2n}}{(2n)!} \approx \tfrac{x^2}{2} + \tfrac{x^4}{24} + \tfrac{x^6}{720} \\ &= x^2(1 - \tfrac{1}{2}(1 - x^2(1 - \tfrac{11}{12}(1 - \tfrac{x^2}{330}))))\end{aligned}$$

where E_n is an Euler number.

Notice that, since all the terms of the Maclaurin series of these three functions have coefficients that are less than one, are positive, and have sums less or equal to 1, they can be mapped to stochastic logic circuits using the proposed method. Note that because approximations for $\sec(x) - 1$ and $\cosh(x) - 1$ are polynomials in x^2 with no constant term, they require two AND gates in addition to the NAND gates. The implementations are shown in Fig. 6.

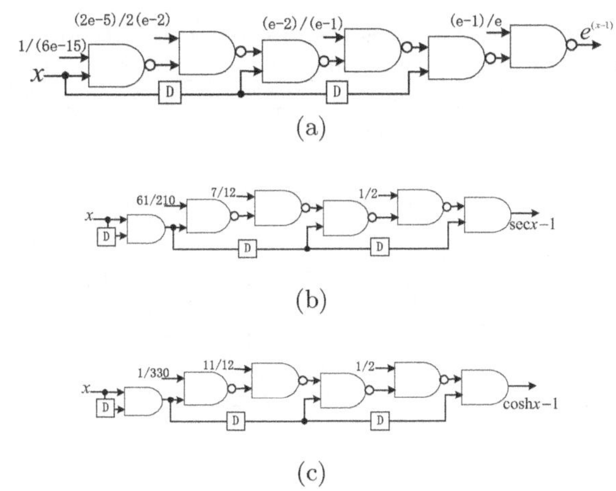

Figure 6: Stochastic implementations of (a) $e^{(x-1)}$, (b) $\sec x - 1$ and (c) $\cosh x - 1$ by mapping Maclaurin series to double-NAND circuits.

3. EXPERIMENTAL RESULTS

In our experiments, we compare accuracy and hardware complexity of the proposed circuits with those of prior work. With respect to the performance, we compare our approach with four other alternative approaches: multiplexer-based [1], Bernstein polynomial [6], finite-state-machine (FSM) using a 2-dimensional FSM with 8 states [3], and factorization [4]. For the factorization method, the scale factors of $e^{(x-1)}$, $\sec(x) - 1$, and $\cosh(x) - 1$ are, respectively, given by $\frac{1}{e}$, $\frac{1}{2}$, and $\frac{1}{2}$.

Table 1 presents the mean absolute error (MAE) of different approaches for computing the target functions. The errors are computed using Montecarlo simulation for each of the 101 inputs, between 0 and 1, i.e., $x = 0, 0.01, 0.02..., 1$. The length of the stochastic bit streams is 1024 bits. Note that stochastic logic circuits of approximate Maclaurin polynomials implemented by the proposed method outperform other methods.

The implementation of double-NAND expansion requires $2n$ NAND gates, $(n+1)$ coefficients and $(n-1)$ delay units needed for decorrelation. The structure presented in [1] requires $3n$ gates to implement n multiplexers, $(n-1)$AND gates and $(n-1)$ delays to calculate x^i for $i = 2$ to n, one AND gate to scale the computed output, and $(n+1)$ coefficients. We assume that each delay unit can be implemented by 10 gates. For the coefficients, we assume that one LFSR is used to generate all coefficients and each coefficient uses a unique comparator and delay unit. A 10-bit LFSR can be realized using 160 gates. Although the number of gates

Table 1: The mean absolute error (MAE) for computing polynomials in Example 1, $e^{(x-1)}$, $\sec(x)-1$ and $\cosh(x)-1$ functions using the proposed method and previous methods.

Function		Proposed			Multiplexer			Bernstein Polynomial			Factorization			FSM
Example 1			0.0040			0.0040		-	-	-		0.0040		-
$e^{(x-1)}$	degree	2	3	4	2	3	4	2	3	4	2	3	4	8-state
	error	0.0197	0.0042	0.0011	0.0199	0.0050	0.0015	0.0253	0.0164	0.0122	0.0199	0.0074	0.0032	0.0163
$\sec(x)-1$	degree	4	6	8	4	6	8	4	6	8	4	6	8	8-state
	error	0.0172	0.0053	0.0027	0.00175	0.0068	0.0034	0.0505	0.0330	0.0245	0.0175	0.0068	0.0061	0.1200
$\cosh(x)-1$	degree	4	6	8	4	6	8	4	6	8	4	6	8	8-state
	degree	0.0016	0.0008	0.0005	0.00017	0.0008	0.0005	0.0235	0.0154	0.0113	0.0017	0.0008	0.0006	0.0399

Table 2: The synthesis results for area in terms of two-input NAND gates and critical path (ns) for different stochastic logic polynomial and functions using 5 approaches.

Function		Proposed			Multiplexer			Bernstein Polynomial			Factorization			FSM
Example 1	area		488.8			494.5		-	-	-		494.5		-
	delay		2.42			2.71		-	-	-		2.71		-
$e^{(x-1)}$	degree	2	3	4	2	3	4	2	3	4	2	3	4	8-state
	area	488.8	559.5	634.4	494.5	569.4	648.9	496.1	569.4	664.0	494.5	563.9	641.2	1144.0
	delay	2.42	2.68	3.02	2.71	2.94	3.16	2.59	2.96	2.90	2.71	2.78	3.11	2.76
$\sec(x)-1$	degree	4	6	8	4	6	8	4	6	8	4	6	8	8-state
	area	463.3	530.9	612	466.4	541.3	626.6	664.0	872.0	1153.2	466.4	541.3	623.5	1144.0
	delay	2.43	2.84	3.03	2.47	3.04	3.47	2.90	4.01	3.98	2.47	3.04	3.44	2.76
$\cosh(x)-1$	degree	4	6	8	4	6	8	4	6	8	4	6	8	8-state
	area	463.3	530.9	612	466.4	541.3	626.6	664.0	872.0	1153.2	466.4	541.3	623.5	1144.0
	delay	2.43	2.84	3.03	2.47	3.04	3.47	2.90	4.01	3.98	2.47	3.04	3.44	2.76

required for the comparators varies for each coefficient, we estimate that an average of 30 gates is required for each comparator. These numbers are taken from our synthesis results. Hence, for $(n+1)$ coefficients $160+30(n+1)+10(n+1)$ gates are used. Collecting these values together, computation of $P_n(x)$ based on the stochastic logic in [1] requires $54n+190$ gates while the double-NAND method requires $52n+190$ gates, leading to saving 4% of the number of gates for a large n.

With respect to the critical path, for the double-NAND circuits the critical path is in the order of n. Since the structure in [1] has $\log_2 n$ levels of multiplexers and the critical path for each multiplexer is about two gates, the critical path for the multiplexer levels is $\mathcal{O}(\lceil \log_2 n \rceil)$. When we consider $(n-1)$ AND gates at the input and 1 AND gate at the output the total critical path for multiplexer-based stochastic logic circuit is $\mathcal{O}(\lceil \log_2 n \rceil + n)$. One should note that, while for small values of n the critical paths for the two methods are close, the difference is remarkable for higher values of n. Table 2 compares area and critical path for all 4 polynomials using discussed methods. The architectures are implemented using 65nm libraries and synthesized using Synopsys Design Compiler. All required SNGs including 10-bit LFSRs as random number generators are considered in our synthesis. The operating conditions for each implementation are specified by a supply voltage of 1.05 V and a temperature of 25 degree Celsius. It can be observed from Table 2 that the proposed stochastic circuits have less hardware complexity compared to prior approaches.

4. CONCLUSIONS

A novel double-NAND expansion approach has been presented to expand any polynomial with positive coefficients where the sum of coefficients is less than or equal to one. Note that the coefficients need not be either increasing or decreasing, but can be in any arbitrary order. The proposed expansion leads to stochastic logic implementations of these polynomials using cascaded two-input NAND gates. The reader is referred to [5] for stochastic logic implementation of polynomials with alternating signs and decreasing magnitude.

5. REFERENCES

[1] Y.-N. Chang and K. K. Parhi. Architectures for digital filters using stochastic computing. In *Proc. of IEEE International Conference on Acoustics, Speech and Signal Processing (ICASSP)*, pages 2697–2701. IEEE, May 2013.

[2] B. R. Gaines. Stochastic computing. *in Proceedings of AFIPS spring joint computer conference, ACM*, pages 149–156, 1967.

[3] P. Li, D. J. Lilja, W. Qian, K. Bazargan, and M. Riedel. The synthesis of complex arithmetic computation on stochastic bit streams using sequential logic. *in Proceedings of the International Conference on Computer-Aided Design*, pages 480–487, 2012.

[4] Y. Liu and K. K. Parhi. Computing complex functions using factorization in unipolar stochastic logic. In *Proceedings of the 26th edition on Great Lakes Symposium on VLSI*, pages 109–112. ACM, 2016.

[5] K. K. Parhi and Y. Liu. Computing arithmetic functions using stochastic logic by series expansion. *IEEE Transactions on Emerging Technologies in Computing (TETC)*, DOI: 10.1109/TETC.2016.2618750.

[6] W. Qian, X. Li, M. D. Riedel, K. Bazargan, and D. J. Lilja. An architecture for fault-tolerant computation with stochastic logic. *IEEE Transactions on Computers*, 60(1):93–105, 2011.

On the Role of Sequential Circuits in Stochastic Computing

Paishun Ting and John P. Hayes
Department of Electrical Engineering and Computer Science
University of Michigan, Ann Arbor, MI 48109, USA
{paishun, jhayes}@umich.edu

ABSTRACT

Interest in stochastic computing (SC) has been growing due to the need for low-cost circuitry in areas like image processing and machine learning. While combinational stochastic circuits are relatively easy to design, their limitations such as having few implementable functions and inaccuracies due to correlation, call for sequential components and design methods. The theory underlying sequential stochastic circuits is not fully understood, however. Almost all existing sequential SC circuits fall into the up/down-counter-based (UCB) class. In this paper, we identify and investigate a new SC circuit class: shift-register-based (SRB). We focus on the properties of SRB circuits and demonstrate their central role in stochastic computing. This leads to an algorithm MOUSE for sequential design optimization. By exploiting sequential stochastic equivalence, MOUSE can reduce SRB circuit cost without compromising performance or accuracy.

Keywords

Stochastic computing; sequential circuits; correlation and decorrelation; approximate computing

1. INTRODUCTION

Stochastic computing (SC) has recently shown considerable potential in applications such as image processing [1], artificial neural networks [4], and ECC decoding [8]. It processes data in the form of clocked (pseudo) random sequences of 0s and 1s, referred to as stochastic numbers (SNs). SC's key advantages are very small arithmetic circuits and high tolerance of soft errors compared with conventional "binary" computing. Its drawbacks are low accuracy and complex design needs.

In SC, a set of SNs $\mathfrak{X} = \{\mathbf{X}_1, \mathbf{X}_2, \ldots, \mathbf{X}_n\}$ with probability values $\{X_1, X_2, \ldots, X_n\}$ is typically applied to a combinational logic circuit C realizing some Boolean function $f(x_1, x_2, \ldots, x_n)$. Viewed as a stochastic circuit, C computes an arithmetic function $F(X_1, X_2, \ldots, X_n)$ determined by f and the joint probability distribution of $\mathfrak{X}$ [3]. For example, the AND gate of Fig. 1*a* has $f(x_1, x_2) = x_1 \wedge x_2$ and $F(X_1, X_2) = X_1 \cdot X_2$, assuming bit-streams $\mathbf{X}_1$ and $\mathbf{X}_2$ are independent, and so serves as a unipolar stochastic multiplier. Despite its use of bit *sequences,* it is tempting to treat C as part of a combinational rather than a sequential digital system. Indeed, the SC literature focuses on "combinational" design, except where sequential elements such as D flip-flops (DFFs) and feedback are explicitly added to C. It is clear, however, that the random number sources (RNSs) and the stochastic number generators (SNGs) driving the input bit sequences of C are inherently sequential. Although they are usually the costliest part of the system [11], RNSs and SNGs are often overlooked. Here, we examine stochastic circuit behavior focusing on its overall sequential nature. This viewpoint reveals unexpected costs, as well as design limitations and opportunities.

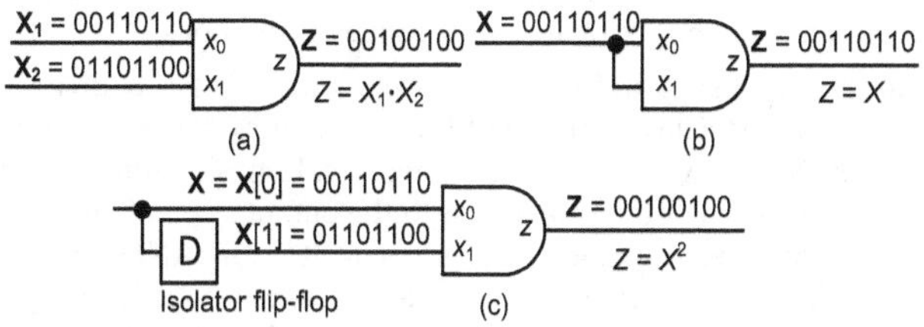

Figure 1. Stochastic circuits that serve as: (a) a multiplier; (b) a bad combinational squarer; (c) a good sequential squarer.

While "pure" combinational stochastic circuits are relatively easy to design, they have the big drawback of implementing very few functions. To see why, consider the class of single-input, single-output logic functions. It has only two members $f(x) = x$ and $g(x) = x'$, corresponding to $F(X) = X$ and $G(X) = 1 - X$ in the stochastic domain. Thus, no single-input/output functions except F and G can be implemented exactly by a combinational stochastic circuit!

Another problem is that undesired correlation among bit-streams cannot be handled by combinational circuits alone. Suppose we want to use an AND gate to compute $X \cdot X = X^2$. This requires two independent, i.e., uncorrelated, bit-streams to represent X. If the naïve scheme in Fig. 1*b* with two identical copies of $\mathbf{X}$ is used, the circuit computes X instead of X^2, and so is a bad approximation to a squarer. This problem is resolved either by using two RNSs to generate two independent copies of $\mathbf{X}$, or else by decorrelation, a process that eliminates the effect of correlation [14]. Fig. 1*c* shows how the AND squarer is decorrelated by a DFF which acts as a 1-bit delay element called an isolator [6]. Assuming that each bit of the SN $\mathbf{X}$ is independently generated, i.e., $\mathbf{X}$ is a Bernoulli sequence, then consecutive bits of $\mathbf{X}$ are also independent. Thus, the delayed version of $\mathbf{X}$, namely $\mathbf{X}[1]$, applied to x_1 and the original version $\mathbf{X} = \mathbf{X}[0]$ applied to x_0 are independent in every clock cycle. Hence, $Z = X[0] \cdot X[1] = X^2$, as desired. This highlights the fact that decorrelation makes a combinational circuit sequential.

Combinational synthesis methods for SC [2][11] expand the class of implementable functions by generating multiple independent copies of the input variable SNs, and by introducing constant SNs as ancillary inputs. The synthesis process can then focus on combinational arithmetic design. However, generation of the variable and constant inputs requires sequential elements, which make the final circuit sequential. For example, the ReSC synthesis method [11] implements functions expressed as Bernstein polynomials. A Bernstein polynomial of degree n takes the form

$$F(X) = \sum_{i=0}^{n} c_i \binom{n}{i} X^i (1 - X)^{n-i} \quad (1)$$

Given n independent versions of $\mathbf{X}$ to represent X, the probability that there are i 1s in the SNs is $\binom{n}{i} X^i (1 - X)^{n-i}$. If this event occurs, an SN of a constant value c_i is selected to be sent to the

Permission to make digital or hard copies of all or part of this work for personal or classroom use is granted without fee provided that copies are not made or distributed for profit or commercial advantage and that copies bear this notice and the full citation on the first page. Copyrights for components of this work owned by others than ACM must be honored. Abstracting with credit is permitted. To copy otherwise, or republish, to post on servers or to redistribute to lists, requires prior specific permission and/or a fee. Request permissions from Permissions@acm.org.
GLSVLSI '17, May 10–12, 2017, Banff, AB, Canada.
© 2017 ACM. ISBN 978-1-4503-4972-7/17/05…$15.00.
DOI: http://dx.doi.org/10.1145/3060403.3060453

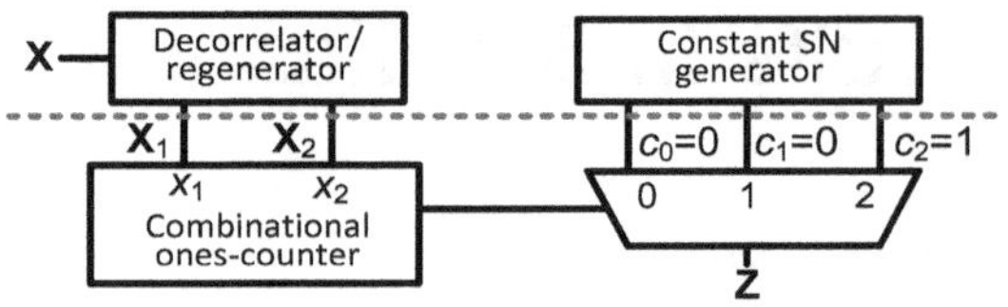

Figure 2. ReSC implementation of a squarer [11]. The sequential components above the dotted line provide independent copies of SNs needed by Eq. (1).

output. By adjusting the values of the c_i's, ReSC uses Bernstein polynomials to approximate a wide range of functions.

Example 1. Using ReSC to synthesize $F(X) = X^2$ with $n = 2$ results in the stochastic circuit of Fig. 2 where $c_0 = c_1 = 0$ and $c_2 = 1$. When $\mathbf{X}_1^{(t)} = \mathbf{X}_2^{(t)} = 1$, the combinational ones-counter outputs "2", which selects $c_2 = 1$ to be sent to the output z. In this case, the ReSC structure is logically equivalent to an AND-gate SC multiplier. This is because $z = 1$ if and only if $x_1 = x_2 = 1$. In Fig. 2, while the arithmetic components below the dotted line are combinational, the pre-processing units above the dotted line are not. To generate independent copies of SNs, sequential elements are needed.

Despite the prominent role of sequential components in SC, the literature on explicitly sequential stochastic circuits is small. Much of it, going back to early ADDIE designs [6], concerns *up/down-counter-based* (UCB) circuits. We will point out some limitations of the UCB approach, and explore a new class of sequential stochastic circuits that we call *shift-register-based* (SRB), which turn out to be widespread in SC and have some distinct advantages.

2. BACKGROUND

Sequential elements overcome the limitations of combinational SC designs by providing multiple states that implement different stochastic functions [4][6]. These depend on two factors: (1) the frequency or probability $\pi_i = p(S = s_i)$ for the circuit to visit a state s_i, and (2) the corresponding output function F_i, which is the stochastic function implemented in state s_i.

A sequential circuit is a finite-state machine (FSM) whose behavior is defined by a state-transition graph (STG). The state behavior is probabilistic due to the randomness of the input SNs, and may be viewed as a Markov chain [7]. The long-term probability π_i for the FSM to visit state s_i is obtained from the chain's steady-state probability distribution. The overall stochastic function realized is $F = \boldsymbol{\pi}^{\mathrm{T}} \cdot \mathbf{F}$, where $\boldsymbol{\pi} = [\pi_0\, \pi_1 \dots \pi_{n-1}]^{\mathrm{T}}$ and $\mathbf{F} = [F_0\, F_1 \dots F_{n-1}]^{\mathrm{T}}$.

Only a few FSM types have been studied in the SC context, notably Moore-type UCB circuits [4][6]. As depicted in Fig. 3, the STG of a UCB circuit has a "linear" structure [6], where each state can only transition to two adjacent states. Prior work has led to many variants of the basic UCB structure. Gaines studied an element called an ADDIE, which works with an up/down counter and a global feedback loop to approximate non-linear functions [6]. Brown and Card use UCB circuits with ancillary inputs to implement functions for artificial neural networks [4]. They restrict the members of the function set $\mathbf{F}$ to binary constants. More recent work extends the range and efficiency of UCB designs [10] [13].

It is noteworthy that none of the above UCB models apply to the circuit for $F(X) = X^4$ in Fig. 4*a*, where three DFFs are used to generate three independent copies of $\mathbf{X}$ [5]. Observe that its STG (Fig. 5) does not have a UCB STG's linear structure. The designs in Fig. 4 represent a large class of stochastic circuits formed by

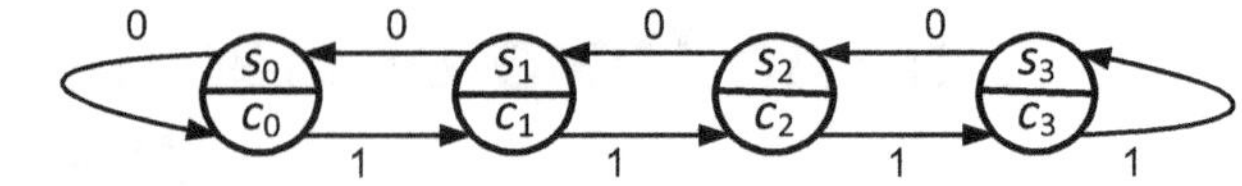

Figure 3. State transition graph (STG) for a 4-state Moore-type UCB circuit.

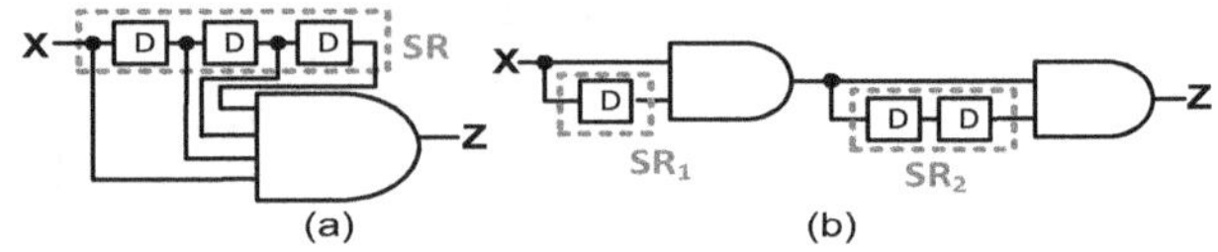

Figure 4. Implementations of $F(X) = X^4$: (a) canonical SRB design, and (b) non-canonical SRB design.

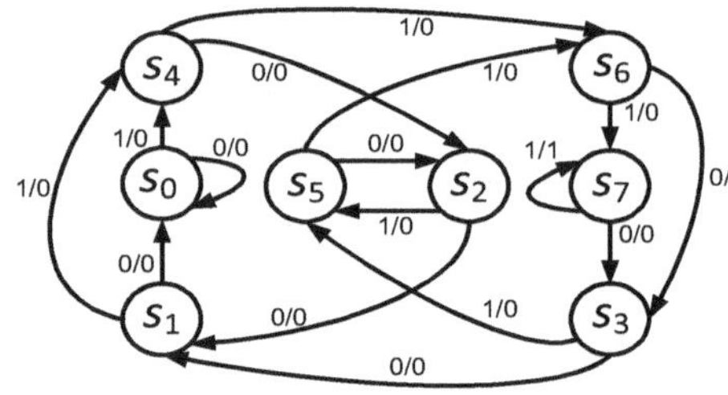

Figure 5. STG for the SRB circuit of Fig. 4*a*.

inserting DFFs into combinational logic for decorrelation purposes [5][14]. These DFFs create feed-forward shift registers, so we refer to the resulting sequential stochastic circuits as *shift-register based* (SRB). Besides enabling decorrelation, SRB circuits enrich the class of implementable stochastic functions by producing multiple independent copies of an SN. In the squarer of Fig. 1*c*, the shift register shifts the input SN $\mathbf{X}$ by 1 bit, thereby creating the independent copy of $\mathbf{X}$ the multiplier needs to function as a squarer.

Example 2. The circuit in Fig. 6 designed by the STRAUSS synthesizer [2] computes the (inverted) bipolar stochastic function $F(X) = 0.4375 - 0.25X - 0.5625X^2$. Although $F(X)$ is a single-input function, its combinational part requires two independent copies of $\mathbf{X}$ and four independent constant SNs $\mathbf{c}_1$, $\mathbf{c}_2$, $\mathbf{c}_3$, $\mathbf{c}_4$, each of value 0.5. The constant SNs can be generated by a 4-bit LFSR, as is done in [2], or they can be produced by a chain of three DFFs if a random source $\mathbf{c}$ is available, as in Fig. 6. Generation of all six independent inputs can be done by two shift registers as indicated in the figure. Taken together, they make the final circuit highly sequential.

While shift registers are a powerful tool for decorrelation, they have only been used in ad hoc fashion in SC, as in Example 2 and in some examples in [5][14]. In this work, we identify these circuits as members of a well-defined class of sequential stochastic circuits and investigate their role in SC. The rest of the paper systematically examines the properties of SRB circuits and the stochastic functions they implement. It also describes a Monte-Carlo algorithm that explores opportunities for optimizing SRB designs.

3. SRB CIRCUITS

It turns out that SRB circuits implement a classical form of FSM called a *definite* or *finite-input-memory machine* [9, Sec. 14.2]. The name reflects the fact that the current state is determined by the most recent m inputs for some fixed m. This implies that for a definite machine, every length-m input sequence is a synchronizing sequence. For example, the SRB circuit with three DFFs in Fig. 4*a* has an input memory of $m = 3$. As Fig. 5 shows,

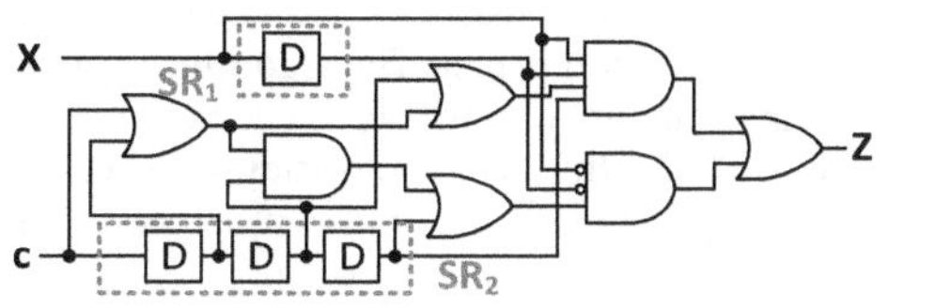

Figure 6. Circuit [2] requiring two copies of variable SN **X** and four independent constant SNs generated by shift registers SR_1 and SR_2.

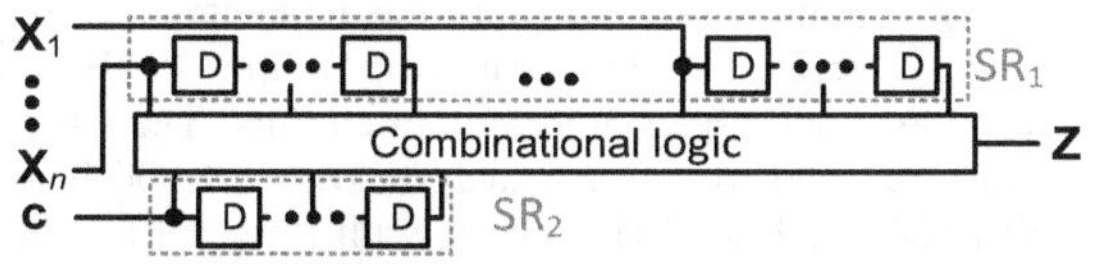

Figure 7. A general canonical single-output SRB circuit taking $\mathbf{X}_1$, $\mathbf{X}_2$, …, $\mathbf{X}_n$ as variable inputs and **c** as a constant input.

applying a 3-bit sequence like 101 leads it to s_5, regardless of the initial state.

While a definite FSM can have different implementations, it has a canonical form which is an SRB circuit with each shift register taking its input directly from a primary input [9]. Fig. 7 shows a canonical SRB circuit for SC purposes, where the shift registers generate multiple independent copies of the variable and constant inputs. The circuits in Figs. 4*a* and 6 are in canonical form. The SRB circuit in Fig. 4*b* is a non-canonical definite circuit since the internal shift register SR_2 has an internal signal as its input. We will focus on the canonical SRB forms of definite machines.

Definiteness has a useful role in SC design. As noted in [4], sequential components can introduce autocorrelation into SNs, which may reduce overall accuracy. Further, when its input SNs change value, a sequential circuit cannot respond completely until steady state is reached. While such warmup delays can be of indefinite length in general circuits, the warmup delay of an SRB circuit is bounded by its finite input memory—a definite advantage.

Fig. 8 shows two SC designs realizing a complex single-input function $tanh(2X)$. One is a UCB design from [4]; the other is a new SRB design of similar accuracy. Fig. 8*c* compares the errors of the two circuits as the input changes. Both are fed with a bipolar SN of value $X = 0.9$ for a warmup period, then X is changed to 0.3. The figure plots the average errors against the number of clock cycles after the value transition takes place. The SRB design reaches steady state 4 cycles after the input transition, while the UCB design takes about 12 cycles. The short response time of the SRB design is due to its definiteness property, which is important in delay-sensitive applications like ECC decoding. The above observations lead directly to the following result.

Theorem 1. The number of clock cycles required by an SRB circuit to reach a steady state is at most m, the input memory length.

4. SRB FUNCTIONS

Next, we examine the stochastic functions implemented by SRB circuits. We consider circuits containing a single shift register; the multiple shift-register case is similar. A shift register SR composed of m DFFs has 2^m states. Let s_i denote the state when SR stores b_i, the radix-2 form of i. For example, when SR is composed of three DFFs and is in state s_6, the DFFs are storing $b_6 = 110$. SR's STG structure is a binary, directed de Bruijn graph, where two nodes s_i and s_j are connected if b_j is a shifted value of b_i, with the empty position filled with 0 or 1. For example, the 8-node de Bruijn graph in Fig. 5 has an outgoing edge from s_7 to s_3, because $b_3 = 011$ is obtained by shifting a 0 into $b_7 = 111$.

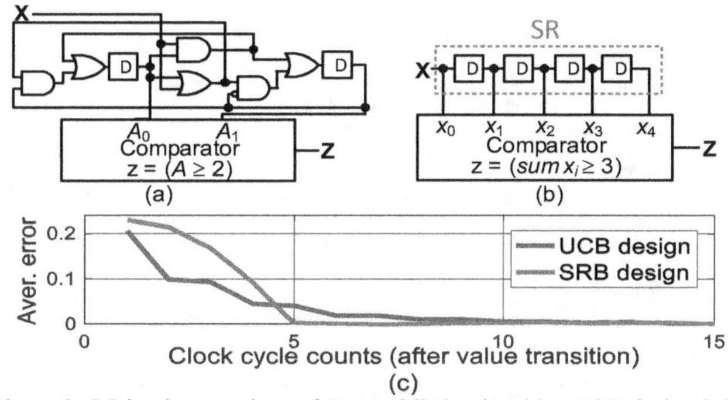

Figure 8. SC implementations of $Z = tanh(2X)$ using (a) a UCB design [4], and (b) an SRB design. (c) Error comparison between the two designs when input X changes from 0.9 to 0.3.

While standard methods [7] can be used to obtain the steady-state distribution of an SRB circuit, an intuitive approach is the following. With a shift register composed of m DFFs, associate a set of state groups G_0, G_1, …, G_m, where state s_i belongs to group G_j, if the number of 1s in b_i is j. For example, s_3, s_5 and s_6 in the STG of Fig. 5 belong to G_2 because $b_3 = 011$, $b_5 = 101$ and $b_6 = 110$ all contain two 1s. Since the FSM has an input memory of $m = 3$, the current state is determined by the most recent three inputs, which are stored in the DFFs. This implies that π_i, the probability of visiting s_i, depends only on the most recent three inputs. Since the probability of seeing a 1 in the input SN **X** is X, the probability of receiving a 3-bit pattern with j 1s is $X^j(1 - X)^{3-j}$. For example, the probability of receiving the pattern 101 is $X^2(1 - X)$, which is π_5, the probability of visiting s_5. It follows that in a shift register with m DFFs, the steady-state probability distribution of $s_i \in G_j$ is $\pi_i = X^j(1 - X)^{m-j}$. This leads immediately to the next result.

Theorem 2. A single-input SRB circuit having m DFFs implements the stochastic function

$$F(X) = \boldsymbol{\pi}^{\mathrm{T}}\cdot\mathbf{F} = F_0\cdot(1 - X)^m + F_1\cdot X(1 - X)^{m-1} + F_2\cdot X(1 - X)^{m-1} + F_3\cdot X^2(1 - X)^{m-2} + \ldots + F_{n-1}\cdot X^m \quad (2)$$

which is a polynomial in X.

For example, the circuit in Fig. 4*a* has $F_0 = F_1 = \ldots = F_6 = 0$, $F_7 = X$ and $m = 3$. From Eq. (2), we know immediately that it computes $F(X) = F_7\cdot X^3 = X^4$, as expected. Eq. (2) is essentially equivalent to the Bernstein polynomial implemented by ReSC [11]; see Eq. (1). This is because by setting $F_i = c_j$ for all $s_i \in G_j$, $F(X)$ becomes $c_0\cdot(1 - X)^m + c_1\cdot X(1 - X)^{m-1} + c_1\cdot X(1 - X)^{m-1} + \ldots + c_m\cdot X^m = \sum_{i=0}^{n} c_i \binom{n}{i} X^i (1-X)^{n-i}$. Hence, all ReSC-implementable functions can be realized by an SRB circuit. Eq. (2) can be easily extended to handle multi-variate Bernstein polynomials.

It is helpful to view a sequential stochastic circuit in terms of its state transition probabilities. The circuit's overall state behavior is given by $\boldsymbol{\pi}^{\mathrm{T}}\cdot\mathbf{F} = \sum_{i=0}^{n}\sum_{\mathbf{b}} \pi_i p(\mathbf{x} = \mathbf{b}) f_i(\mathbf{b})$. The term $\pi_i\cdot p(\mathbf{x} = \mathbf{b})$ is the probability that the machine is in state s_i and the current input is $\mathbf{x} = \mathbf{b}$. This is the probability of a state transition from s_i given input $\mathbf{b}$, which we denote by $p(T_i^{(\mathbf{b})})$. For example, in the STG of Fig. 5, $\pi_2\cdot p(x = 0) = T_2^{(0)}$ is the probability of being in s_2 with input 0; this is also the probability of a transition from s_2 to s_1. We can now describe the stochastic function of a (Mealy) sequential circuit using $p(T_i^{(\mathbf{b})})$ and the corresponding output value $f_i(\mathbf{b})$ as follows:

$$\boldsymbol{\pi}^{\mathrm{T}}\cdot\mathbf{F} = \sum_{i=0}^{n}\sum_{\mathbf{b}} p(T_i^{(\mathbf{b})}) f_i(\mathbf{b}) \quad (3)$$

An interesting and useful fact is that many state transitions in an SRB circuit occur with the same probability, a phenomenon

```
Input:      Target SRB circuit: Ckt
Output:     Result SRB circuit with reduced cost: Ckt_out
  While iteration limit is not exceeded
    For each stochastically equivalent transition class S in Ckt
      w = sum over all f(a_i) associated with S
      Randomly pick w f(a_i)'s and assign them value 1
      For the unpicked f(a_i)'s, assign them value 0
    End For
    Ckt_cur = STAMINA(Ckt), Cost = state count of Ckt_cur
    If Cost < Cost_Low
      Cost_Low = Cost, Ckt_out = Ckt_cur
    End If
  End While
```

Figure 9. Pseudo-code for optimization algorithm MOUSE.

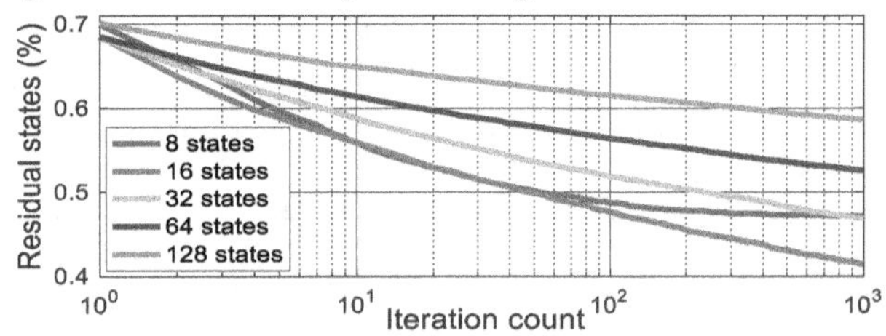

Figure 10. Percentage of residual states vs. iteration count for single-input SRB circuits with various initial state counts.

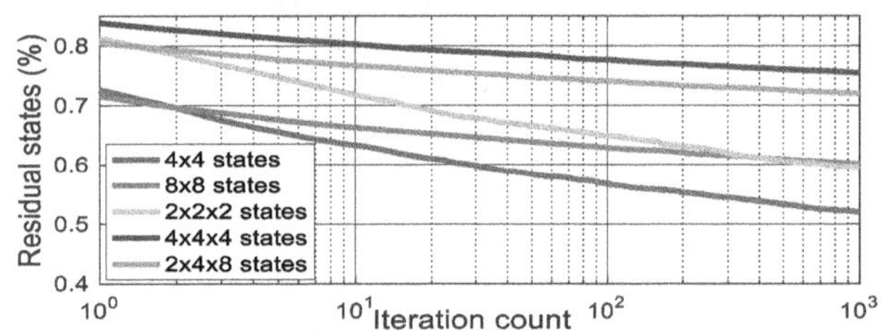

Figure 11. Percentage of residual states vs. iteration count for multi-input SRB circuits with various initial state counts.

seldom seen in UCB circuits. For example, in Fig. 5, $p(T_7^{(0)}) = p(T_5^{(1)})$, i.e., the transition from s_7 to s_3, has the same probability as that from s_5 to s_6. We define state transitions as *stochastically equivalent* if they have the same probability. Eq. (3) implies that the output values $f_i(\mathbf{a})$ and $f_j(\mathbf{b})$ of two stochastically equivalent transitions $T_i^{(\mathbf{a})}$ and $T_j^{(\mathbf{b})}$ can be switched without changing the overall stochastic function. This leads to the following easily-proven result.

Theorem 3. Suppose a sequential stochastic circuit has state transitions with output values $f_i(\mathbf{a}) \neq f_j(\mathbf{b})$. These values can be switched without changing the underlying stochastic function if and only if $p(T_i^{(\mathbf{a})}) = p(T_j^{(\mathbf{b})})$.

As Theorem 3 suggests, in sequential stochastic circuit design, especially in the SRB case, a set $\mathfrak{F}$ of distinct FSMs can implement the same stochastic function, but with potentially different costs. This raises an interesting new design question: Find an FSM in $\mathfrak{F}$ that, when standard optimization techniques are applied, results in the greatest hardware cost reduction. In the following section, we devise a Monte-Carlo algorithm to achieve this goal.

5. DESIGN OPTIMIZATION

We now outline an algorithm *MOUSE* (**M**onte-Carlo **O**ptimization **U**sing **S**tochastic **E**quivalence) for optimizing SRB designs. Given an SRB circuit, MOUSE randomly searches for a better design by switching state function values based on Theorem 3. The cost metric used is state count. In each iteration, MOUSE explores the space of stochastically equivalent transitions of a target circuit, and generates a new circuit implementing the same stochastic function by randomly switching equivalent state function values. A fast state reduction procedure STAMINA [12] assesses the new circuit's cost. MOUSE keeps the best design it finds until a stop criterion is met. The algorithm is summarized in Fig. 9. The final circuit, which may implement a very different FSM, preserves all the stochastic properties of the original design, including its output function and the property of finite input memory.

Since SRB circuits are a new concept in SC and hence no suitable benchmarks are available, we assess MOUSE's performance using random circuits. Fig. 10 plots the percentage of residual states against iteration count for single-input SRB circuits produced by averaging over 500 random circuits. The state count is frequently reduced by more than 50% within 1,000 iterations. For small FSMs such as SRB circuits with three DFFs, the state reduction process slows down and reaches its optimal value within 1,000 iterations. This is because with a small FSM, few possibilities exist for function value switches, so MOUSE can usually find a good solution after just a few iterations. Similar phenomena are observed for multi-input SRB circuits, as shown in Fig. 11.

MOUSE can also be applied to existing SRB designs for hardware cost reduction. For example, the multi-input SRB in Fig. 6 has 16 states. Applying STAMINA directly to this circuit results in 13 states—a 19% decrease in state count. MOUSE, on the other hand, reduces the number of states from 16 to seven after about 90 iterations. Hence, in this particular case, MOUSE enables one of the original circuit's four DFFs to be eliminated.

6. CONCLUSIONS

We examined the role of sequential components in SC, and identified two key classes of sequential stochastic circuits, UCB and SRB. Some basic properties of SRB circuits were determined, and an optimization method MOUSE for them was given. We showed that MOUSE can effectively reduce the state count by exploiting the property of sequential stochastic equivalence.

7. ACKNOWLEDGEMENT

This work was supported by Grant CCF-1318091 from the U.S. National Science Foundation.

8. REFERENCES

[1] Alaghi, A. et al. "Stochastic circuits for real-time image-processing applications." *Proc. DAC*, pp.136, 2013.

[2] Alaghi, A. and Hayes, J.P. "STRAUSS: spectral transform use in stochastic circuit synthesis." *IEEE Trans. CAD*, 34, pp. 1770-1783, 2015.

[3] Alaghi, A. and Hayes, J.P. "On the functions realized by stochastic computing circuits." *Proc. GLSVLSI*, pp.331-336, 2015.

[4] Brown, B. D. and Card, H. "Stochastic neural computation I." *IEEE Trans. Computers*, 50, pp.891-905, 2001.

[5] Chen, T.-H. and Hayes, J.P. "Analyzing and controlling accuracy in stochastic circuits." *Proc. ICCD*, pp.367-373, 2014.

[6] Gaines, B.R. "Stochastic computing systems." *Adv. Inform. Syst. Sci.* 2, pp.37-172, 1969.

[7] Gallager, R.G. *Discrete Stochastic Processes*. Springer, 1996.

[8] Gaudet, V.C. and Rapley, A.C. Iterative decoding using stochastic computation. *Electon. Letters*, 39, pp.299-301, 2003.

[9] Kohavi, Z. and Jha, N.K. *Switching and Finite Automata Theory*, 3rd ed. Cambridge Univ. Press, 2010.

[10] Li, P. et al. "The synthesis of linear finite state machine-based stochastic computational elements." *Proc. ASP-DAC*, pp. 757-762, 2012.

[11] Qian, W. et al. "An architecture for fault-tolerant computation with stochastic logic." *IEEE Trans. Comp.*, 60, pp.93-105, 2011.

[12] Rho, J.-K. et al. "Exact and heuristic algorithms for the minimization of incompletely specified state machines." *IEEE Trans. CAD*, 13, pp. 167-177, 1994.

[13] Saraf, N. and Bazargan, K. "Polynomial arithmetic using sequential stochastic logic." *Proc. GLSVLSI*, pp.245-250, 2016.

[14] Ting, P.-S. and Hayes, J.P. "Isolation-based decorrelation of stochastic circuits." *Proc. ICCD*, pp.88-95, 2016.

Circuit Techniques for Online Learning of Memristive Synapses in CMOS-Memristor Neuromorphic Systems

Sagarvarma Sayyaparaju, Gangotree Chakma, Sherif Amer and Garrett S. Rose
Department of Electrical Engineering & Computer Science
University of Tennessee, Knoxville
1520 Middle Drive, Knoxville, Tennessee
{ssayyapa, gchakma, samer1, garose}@utk.edu

ABSTRACT

Memristors are widely leveraged in neuromorphic systems for constructing synapses. Resistance switching characteristics of memristors enable online learning in synapses. This paper addresses a fundamental issue associated with the design of synapses with memristors whose switching rates in either direction differ up to two orders of magnitude. A twin-memristor synapse that uses memristors with identical switching rates is first presented. It is shown this design fails in the case of disproportionate switching times. To circumvent this issue, a quad-memristor synapse is also considered. The scheme used for online learning of the synapse circuit implementation, and simulation results are also presented. To compare the two synapses, their area, clock frequency, dynamic power and energy per spike values are provided.

Keywords

Memristors, Online learning, Switching rate, Synapse

1. INTRODUCTION

Neuromorphic systems are brain-inspired computing systems, wherein synapses are utilized as the medium of communication. Synapses are responsible for the adaptability of any system which mimics the brain. Learning is that characteristic of the synapse which enables it to update itself depending upon the relative timing of the occurrence of input and output spikes. The learning mechanism is mainly classified into two types: online learning and offline learning. Online learning is often based on unsupervised learning such as Spike Time Dependent Plasticity (STDP), Long Term Potentiation (LTP), and Long Term Depression (LTD) [9,10]. Memristors are widely utilized to construct synapses in neuromorphic computing systems [5] owing to the analog programmability of their resistance, which represents the synaptic weight. In addition, memristors are nano-scale devices, hence paving the way for low power designs. During the online learning of these memristive synapses, the weight of the synapse is altered by the application of voltage pulses across the memristors.

Memristors can be made to switch between several resistance states. For a given voltage across the memristor, the specific switching mechanism in the device determines the time it takes to switch from the Low Resistance State (LRS) to the High Resistance State (HRS) or vice-versa. However, due to the disparate nature of the switching mechanism for opposite polarities, the switching rates could differ significantly [1–3]. Failure to acknowledge this difference in the switching rates leads to functional errors in the operation of memristive systems. Specifically, with same voltage applied in both the directions, the memristor switches in a single step in one of the directions (to attain LRS or HRS), but attains an intermediate resistance state (due to slower switching rate) in the other direction. In this paper, we present two different mechanisms for online learning, to cater to this dichotomy of the symmetric and asymmetric switching rates possible in memristive devices. We also describe the advantages and disadvantages associated with each learning technique depending on the above-mentioned switching mechanism and the available memristor models.

The remainder of the paper is organized as follows. Section 2 details the construct of the twin-memristor synapse that uses memristors with symmetric switching rates. Section 3 delineates the quad-memristor approach for designing with memristors with asymmetric switching rates. Section 4 illustrates some results to compare the two synapses and details some thoughts that emerge from this discussion from the perspective of both circuit designers and device personnel. Section 5 concludes the paper.

2. TWIN-MEMRISTOR SYNAPSE

The twin-memristor synapse structure is comprised of two memristors connected with opposite polarity. The synaptic weights are represented using memristors, where the memristance is proportional to the desired weight. This approach follows that of several other memristor-based neural network designs where voltage inputs across memristive weights yields a weighted sum in the form of a current [4,6–8].

Negative weights are achieved through the use of a pair of memristors (Figure 1) for every synaptic weight. This approach is similar to that presented in [4] where a pair of memristive crossbar arrays are used to represent the negative and positive components of the weights. In the memristor pair for each synapse, one memristor is used to drive positive current while the other drives negative current (pulls current from the integrator). If the memristance of both

Permission to make digital or hard copies of all or part of this work for personal or classroom use is granted without fee provided that copies are not made or distributed for profit or commercial advantage and that copies bear this notice and the full citation on the first page. Copyrights for components of this work owned by others than ACM must be honored. Abstracting with credit is permitted. To copy otherwise, or republish, to post on servers or to redistribute to lists, requires prior specific permission and/or a fee. Request permissions from permissions@acm.org.

GLSVLSI '17, May 10-12, 2017, Banff, AB, Canada
© 2017 ACM. ISBN 978-1-4503-4972-7/17/05...$15.00
DOI: http://dx.doi.org/10.1145/3060403.3060418

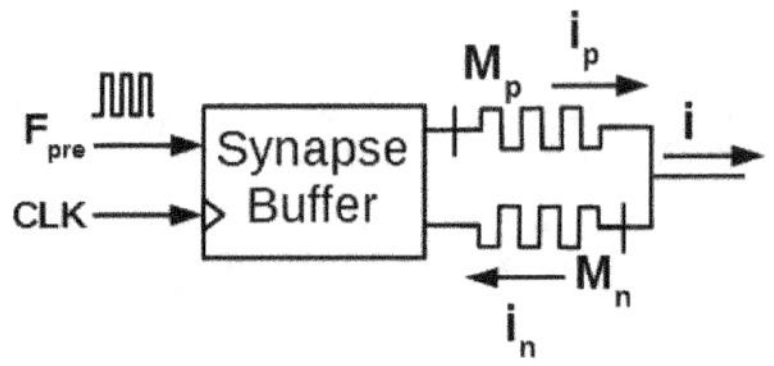

Figure 1: Schematic of the twin-memristor synapse structure showing two memristors used to provide both positive and negative weights.

memristors in the pair are equal then the currents will cancel each other for any given input spike and the effective weight is zero. From this point, where the memristance values are equal, one memristance can be increased (decreased) to change the weight while the other memristance decreases (increases) by a complementary amount. The weight of the synapse is proportionate to the effective conductivity of the pair of memristors, given by:

$$G_{eff} = \frac{1}{M_p} - \frac{1}{M_n}. \quad (1)$$

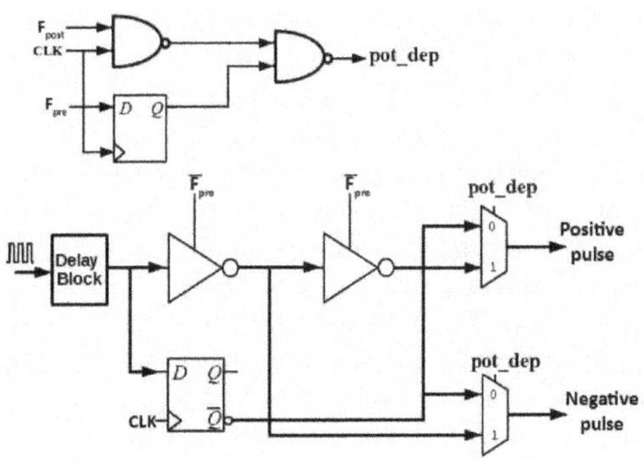

Figure 2: Detailed view of the synaptic buffer.

The synaptic buffer (Figure 2) is used to generate driving currents for both memristors in a synapse. It contains a delay block (chain of shift registers) which represents the delay of a synapse and it also handles the online learning mechanism. The synaptic buffer generates a signal "*pot_dep*" in itself which determines the potentiation or depression of a synapse. This signal becomes low whenever there is a post-synaptic fire caused by the pre-synaptic spike, otherwise it remains high such that online learning is inactive during that period. The condition for potentiation or depression is determined by the occurrence of both pre and post synaptic fires. If the pre-synaptic fire causes a post-synaptic firing spike, the synapse associated with the firing is potentiated or the weight of the synapse is increased (Figure 3). Likewise, if the pre-synaptic fire arrives simultaneously with the post-synaptic signal, the synapse is depressed.

3. QUAD-MEMRISTOR SYNAPSE

During the learning process in the twin-memristor synapse, both memristors switch in opposite directions with voltage pulses of opposite polarity and of the same duration. However, switching rates are rarely equal for both increasing and decreasing memristance. In this paper, we consider the

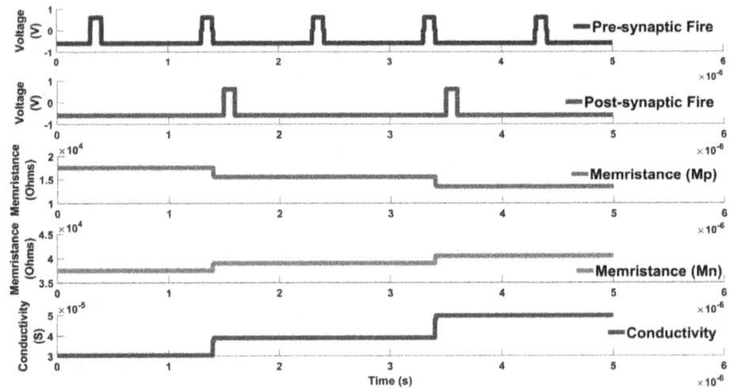

Figure 3: Basic LTP operation on the twin-memristor synapse.

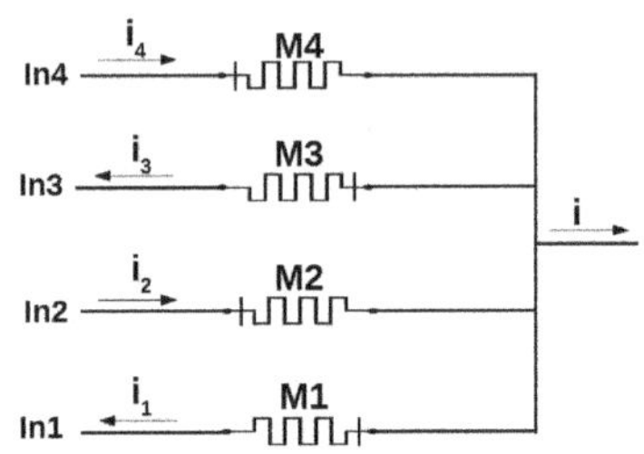

Figure 4: Simplified view of the quad-memristor synapse.

HfO_2 device described in [1]. Based on experimental results reported therein, we conservatively assume that the time taken for switching from LRS to HRS is 1μs whereas switching from HRS to LRS takes only 10ns. In the case where a voltage pulse greater than the switching threshold and of duration larger than or equal to 10ns is applied, the memristor switches from HRS to LRS in a single step. Thus, for such voltage pulses, the memristor is unable to display analog programmability, making LTP/LTD infeasible.

To be able to perform LTP/LTD in the face of asymmetric switching rates of memristors, we propose a quad-memristor synapse structure as follows.

3.1 Working Scheme

A simplified view of this synapse is shown in Figure 4. Currents through M1 and M3 flow in the negative direction, whereas those through M2 and M4 flow in the positive direction. The total current flowing out of the synapse is proportional to its weight and its direction determines if the weight is positive or negative. The current through the synapse is proportional to the effective conductivity of the memristor cluster, given by:

$$G_{eff} = \frac{1}{M2} + \frac{1}{M4} - \frac{1}{M1} - \frac{1}{M3}. \quad (2)$$

.

The learning mechanism for this synapse abides by the following set of rules:

1) A memristor switching during LTP/LTD is always from LRS to HRS.

2) Only one of the memristors switches during LTP/LTD. Either of M1 and M3 is selected for potentiation while one of M2 and M4 is used for depression.

3) Any pair of memristors, whose memristances are equal and both higher than LRS, are both reset to LRS. The possible combinations being (M1, M2), (M2, M3) and (M1, M4).

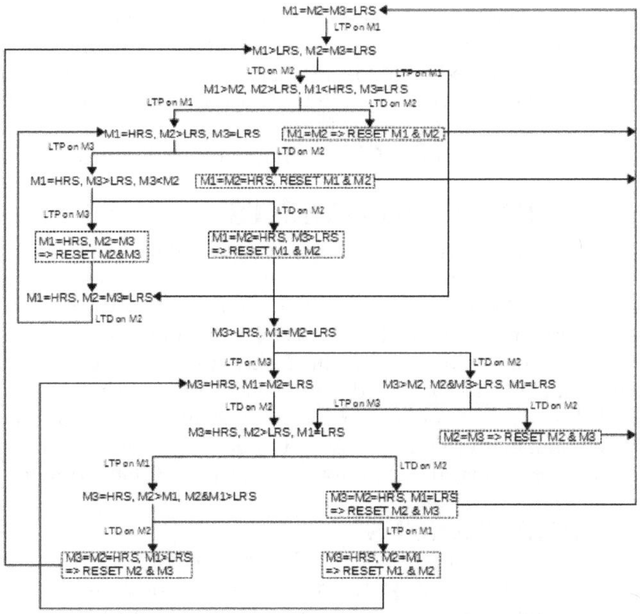

Figure 5: State change diagram for the quad-memristor synapse showing all the operational and transitional states.

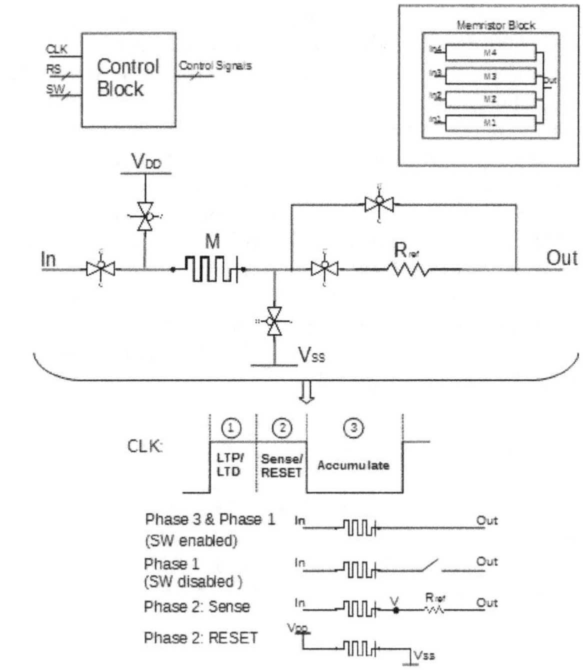

Figure 6: A single memristor circuit in the memristor block.

Starting with an initial weight, when an LTP/LTD is performed on the synapse, it can have several states as shown in Figure 5. Here, starting with a positive weight, the state diagram shows which of the memristors is to be selected for an LTP/LTD event. After a weight change operation, a new state results and a new pair of memristors are to be selected for LTP/LTD. In this process, whenever the memristances of two devices (*not* in their LRS state) are equal, they are $RESET$ to LRS. This leads the synapse into one of the other "Operational States." The states on which a $RESET$ operation is performed are named the "Transitional States." Figure 5 shows the transitions for positive weights. An analogous diagram can be drawn for negative weights.

3.2 Circuit for the quad-memristor synapse

Figure 6 shows a single memristor circuit inside the memristor block. Four such memristor circuits make up the memristor block as shown in the inset to the figure. As shown in Figure 6, the operation of the synapse is split into three phases. The control block for the memristor is used to enable the appropriate transmission gates of the memristor circuit so as to form the various circuit configurations as needed for the three phases of operation.

LTP/LTD phase: In this phase, the synapse's weight changes. Each memristor is assigned a signal SW, to determine if its state should change during this phase. Only those devices whose SW signal is enabled have their state changed.

Sense and RESET: This phase is used to ascertain the state of the synapse and determine which pair of devices to use in case of a weight change operation. In this phase, a voltage divider network is formed as shown in Figure 6. The sensed voltage V, from the divider of all the four memristors drives the main control block. The control block compares these voltages against reference voltages V_{ref0} and V_{ref1}, which represent LRS and HRS states for the memristor, respectively. This comparison is accomplished using a differential voltage-mode comparator.

Using the digital outputs of the analog comparators, the control block ascertains the state of the synapse and outputs SW, to assert the memristors to be used for the next LTP/LTD phase. If the main control block senses the current state of the synapse to be a transitional state, it enables the appropriate RS signal to $RESET$ the pertinent pair of memristors to LRS. A $RESET$ operation is again followed by a sensing phase to sense the new operational state that the synapse has attained (after the $RESET$ operation).

Accumulation: In this phase no state change occurs. Current flows through the synapse proportionate to its weight and accumulates charge on the post-synaptic neuron.

3.3 Simulated Synaptic Operation

In this section, we present some simulations of the synapse's weight change scheme described thus far.

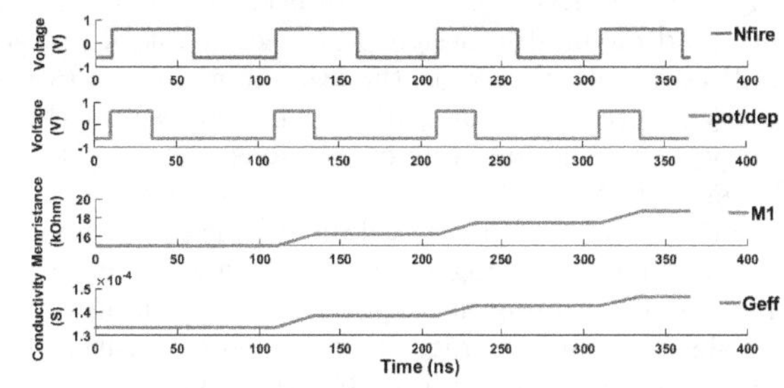

Figure 7: Basic LTP operation on the quad-memristor synapse.

Figure 7 shows the basic LTP operation being performed on the synapse. Here, the signal $Nfire$ indicates the firing event of the post-synaptic neuron and the signal pot/dep indicates LTP/LTD. When pot/dep is asserted HIGH, it indicates potentiation and when it is LOW the weight is depressed. The synapse here is in the initial state of $M1 > LRS$ and $M2 = M3 = M4 = LRS$. With each $Nfire$ event, the pot/dep is asserted HIGH, indicating potentiation. Therefore, M1 is used for weight change.

Figure 8 shows the case when the synapse is initially in the state $M1, M2 > LRS$, $M1 > M2$ and $M3 = M4 = LRS$. In this case, when repeated LTD is performed on the synapse, at a certain stage, M2 attains the same memristance as that of M1. This is a transitional state, hence both M1 and M2 go to LRS, as shown in Figure 8. Further LTD operations result in the switching of M2.

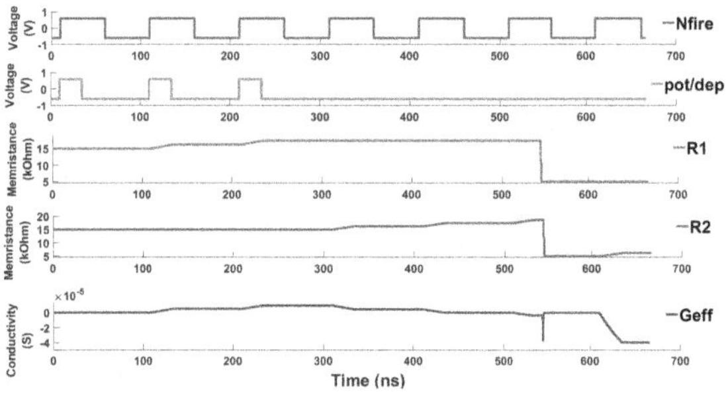

Figure 8: Reset operation performed when a transitional state is encountered.

Table 1: Metrics for comparison of the two synapses.

Metric	Twin-memristor	Quad-memristor
No. of MOS devices	80	1481
No. of memristors	2	4
Clock frequency used	10 MHz	10 MHz
Phases of operation	2	3
Average Power	45.35 μW	306.2 μW
Energy per Spike	4.558 pJ	30.6 pJ

4. COMPARISON AND DISCUSSION

Table 1 shows some metrics for the two synapses. Obviously, the quad-memristor synapse has a higher silicon footprint, consumes more power and has an extra phase of operation (the sense/$RESET$ phase). However, it may be noted that the quad-memristor design addresses a major (often neglected) issue with respect to the switching of some memristors: asymmetric switching rates. The analysis of these synapses provokes the following conclusions:

1) Better memristive device stacks need to be engineered to reduce the mismatch in the switching times.

2) In the wake of having to design synapses with contemporary devices having disproportionate switching rates, circuit designers could leverage our scheme of operation for the quad-memristor synapse to realize such synapses.

5. CONCLUSION

In this paper, we have considered an issue that is fundamental to the physics of switching in the memristor, the mismatch in the switching rates in opposite directions. Starting with the design of a twin-memristor synapse suited for online learning using memristors with identical switching rates, we have presented a quad-memristor synapse structure for use with devices whose switching rates differ by a margin as large as two orders of magnitude. We have also shown and compared the metrics of their circuit implementations.

6. ACKNOWLEDGMENTS

This material is based in part on research sponsored by Air Force Research Laboratory under agreement number FA8750-16-1-0065. The U.S. Government is authorized to reproduce and distribute reprints for Governmental purposes notwithstanding any copyright notation thereon. The views and conclusions contained herein are those of the authors and should not be interpreted as necessarily representing the official policies or endorsements, either expressed or implied, of Air Force Research Laboratory or the U.S. Government.

7. REFERENCES

[1] K. Beckmann, J. Holt, H. Manem, J. Van Nostrand, and N. C. Cady. Nanoscale hafnium oxide rram devices exhibit pulse dependent behavior and multi-level resistance capability. *MRS Advances*, pages 1–6, 2016.

[2] Y. H. Do, J. S. Kwak, Y. C. Bae, K. Jung, H. Im, and J. P. Hong. Hysteretic bipolar resistive switching characteristics in tio2/tio2-x multilayer homojunctions. *Applied Physics Letters*, 95(9):093507–093507, 2009.

[3] N. Hashem and S. Das. Switching-time analysis of binary-oxide memristors via a nonlinear model. *Applied Physics Letters*, 100(26):262106, 2012.

[4] M. Hu, H. Li, Y. Chen, Q. Wu, G. S. Rose, and R. W. Linderman. Memristor crossbar-based neuromorphic computing system: A case study. *IEEE Trans. Neural Netw. Learning Syst.*, 25(10):1864–1878, October 2014.

[5] S. H. Jo, T. Chang, I. Ebong, B. B. Bhadviya, P. Mazumder, and W. Lu. Nanoscale memristor device as synapse in neuromorphic systems. *Nano letters*, 10(4):1297–1301, 2010.

[6] I. Kataeva, F. Merrikh-Bayat, E. Zamanidoost, and D. Strukov. Efficient training algorithms for neural networks based on memristive crossbar circuits. In *2015 International Joint Conference on Neural Networks, IJCNN*, pages 1–8, July 2015.

[7] C. E. Merkel and D. Kudithipudi. A current-mode cmos/memristor hybrid implementation of an extreme learning machine. In *Great Lakes Symposium on VLSI 2014, GLSVLSI '14, Houston, TX, USA - May 21 - 23, 2014*, pages 241–242, 2014.

[8] G. S. Rose, H. Manem, J. Rajendran, R. Karri, and R. Pino. Leveraging memristive systems in the construction of digital logic circuits. *Proceedings of the IEEE*, 100(6):2033–2049, June 2012.

[9] T. Serrano-Gotarredona, T. Masquelier, T. Prodromakis, G. Indiveri, and B. Linares-Barranco. Stdp and stdp variations with memristors for spiking neuromorphic learning systems. *Frontiers in neuroscience*, 7:2, 2013.

[10] G. S. Snider. Spike-timing-dependent learning in memristive nanodevices. In *2008 IEEE International Symposium on Nanoscale Architectures*, pages 85–92. IEEE, 2008.

Mitigating Control Flow Attacks in Embedded Systems with Novel Built-in Secure Register Bank

Sean Kramer, Zhiming Zhang , Jaya Dofe, and Qiaoyan Yu
<sdq46, zz1017, jhs49> @wildcats.unh.edu, qiaoyan.yu@unh.edu
Department of Electrical and Computer Engineering
University of New Hampshire, Durham, NH 03824

ABSTRACT

Embedded systems are prone to security attacks from their limited resources available for self-protection and unsafe language typically used for application programming. Attacks targeting control flow is one of the most common exploitations for embedded systems. We propose a hardware-level, effective, and low overhead countermeasure to mitigate these types of attacks. In the proposed method, a *Built-in Secure Register Bank (BSRB)* is introduced to the processor micro-architecture to store the return addresses of subroutines. The inconsistency on the return addresses will direct the processor to select a clean copy to resume the normal control flow and mitigate the security threat. This proposed countermeasure is inaccessible for the programmer and does not require any compiler support, thus achieving better flexibility than software-based countermeasures. Experimental results show that the proposed method only increases the area and power by 3.8% and 4.4%, respectively, over the baseline OpenRISC processor.

1. INTRODUCTION

Embedded systems are widely used for the security-critical systems in military, government, banking applications, and many household applications. Nowadays, various embedded systems are connected with the outside world, and hence the system may be remotely subverted by controlling their software behaviors. A common way to conduct control flow attacks (CFAs) is to perform a buffer overflow [1–3], through which the program deviates from its original routine and disrupts the normal control flow. Unfortunately, as embedded systems are typically hardware constrained, there may not be sufficient computation power and memory space available to protect themselves from these types of attacks [4–7].

The countermeasures to defeat CFAs are studied extensively including software- and hardware-based defenses. Limitations of software-based countermeasures require programmers to inspect their source codes and frequently update them. Furthermore, some necessary modifications on compilers or operation systems are needed to support software-based countermeasures. As mentioned in [8], software defenses increase the complexity and consume extensive resources, but do not guarantee the security of embedded systems. Thus, it is imperative to explore hardware-based methods to improve the embedded system's resistance against CFAs.

In this work, we propose a new hardware-based countermeasure to mitigate CFAs from software exploitations. The proposed *Built-in Secure Register Bank (BSRB)*, located in the microprocessor, is used to save the return address for each subroutine. When our subroutine epilogue checker triggers, the BSRB pops a return address for the detection of CFAs induced by software exploitations. The BSRB further assists the microprocessor to thwart buffer overflow and function pointer corruption attacks.

The rest of the paper is organized as follows. Section 2 summarizes the related work and contributions of our work. The proposed method is presented in Section 3. Section 4 provides our experimental setup and results. We conclude the paper in Section 5.

Permission to make digital or hard copies of all or part of this work for personal or classroom use is granted without fee provided that copies are not made or distributed for profit or commercial advantage and that copies bear this notice and the full citation on the first page. Copyrights for components of this work owned by others than ACM must be honored. Abstracting with credit is permitted. To copy otherwise, or republish, to post on servers or to redistribute to lists, requires prior specific permission and/or a fee. Request permissions from Permissions@acm.org.

GLSVLSI '17, May 10 - 12, 2017, Banff, AB, Canada

© 2017 Copyright held by the owner/author(s). Publication rights licensed to ACM.

ISBN 978-1-4503-4972-7/17/05... $15.00
DOI: http://dx.doi.org/10.1145/3060403.3060433

2. RELATED WORK & CONTRIBUTIONS OF THIS WORK

2.1 Related Work

High-level languages, like C/C++, are prone to CFAs, such as stack buffer overflows and pointer corruptions [1, 5, 9]. Enhancements to the compiler, altered system libraries, or static analysis all provide methods to protect source codes from CFAs. The methods StackGuard [9] and StackGhost [10] utilize the concept of canaries to encrypt the return address. In encryption-based countermeasure [11], the data is XORed with a special key before storing to the memory. If the encrypted data is fetched from memory by a CFA, that data cannot be decrypted correctly. However, if the encryption key is leaked, this method will lose all defense capability. Compiler enhancements/alterations [12] are another type of technique towards the protection against CFAs. These approaches require the recompiling or rewriting of source code, and increase the size of the binary file for array bounds checking. The work [13] protects the control flow by creating a separate stack to save every return address. Although this method incurs minor performance degradation, the complexity of shadow stack design dramatically increases when the program is large. In [14], the original stack is divided into two separate ones, one for normal data and one for return addresses which is located in a different area than the normal stack. Our preliminary work was first presented at CSAW 2016 [15] competition, with emphasis on the attack side.

2.2 Contributions of This Work

This work makes three major contributions as below.

- To thwart CFAs, we propose a processor micro-architecture enhancement method implemented entirely in hardware. The complexity of our method is less the existing works [4, 13, 16] that require a collaborative support from software and hardware.

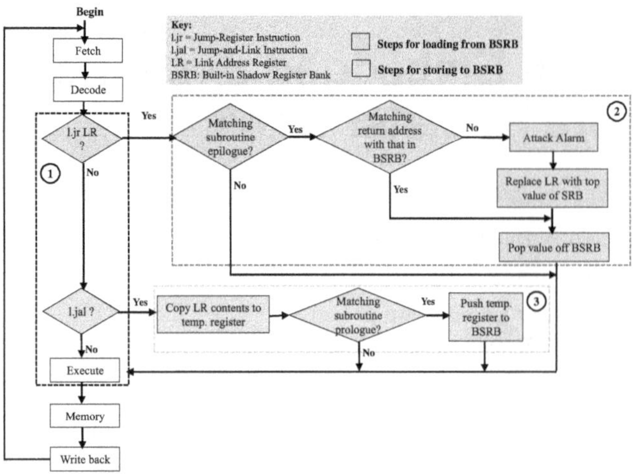

Figure 1: Flowchart for the proposed control flow attack mitigation.

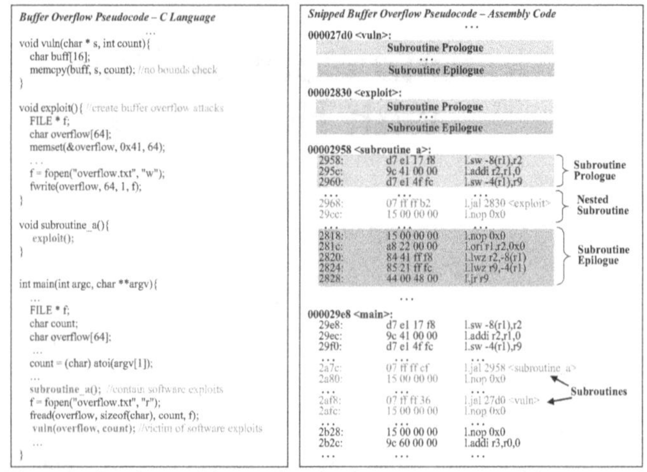

Figure 2: C and assembly pseudocodes for a program containing a control flow attack.

- We propose to use a built-in secure register bank to save the return address for each subroutine in a C program, rather than reserving a new stack or a block of memory. Thus, the CPU is unable to be manipulated by the compiler and developer through software exploits, and achieves a better isolation capability.
- The proposed method exploits the resource available in the microprocessor pipeline stages and eliminates the need of extending the stack size and data memory space as required in existing software-based countermeasures.

3. PROPOSED METHOD AGAINST CONTROL FLOW ATTACKS

3.1 Method Overview

To prevent a microprocessor from CFAs, we propose a processor micro-architecture enhancement method. Our method uses a Built-in Secure Register Bank (BSRB) to save the return address for each subroutine in the program. The function of the BSRB is a last-in-first-out (LIFO) stack which containing a number of entries (specified by users). The BSRB is written when the subroutine prologue checker is active high,and read when the subroutine epilogue checker is active high. The return address provided by the normal branch address computation path is compared with the return address popped from the BSRB. This comparison can indicate the presence of an attack.

3.2 Flowchart for Proposed Method

To implement the proposed countermeasure, we modify the typical Fetch/Decode/Execute/Memory/Write back instruction cycle of the microprocessor. Changes are highlighted in the flowchart, shown in Fig. 1. The instruction cycle now contains three paths. One path ① is to perform the standard instruction cycle, ignoring all modifications done by the BSRB. This means, the execution of these instructions do not pose any security threat to the embedded systems. The other two paths ② and ③, hinge on whether the incoming instruction is either a jump-and-link (*l.jal*) or jump-register (*l.jr*) call.

3.2.1 Storing Return Addresses to Register Bank

During the execution of the *l.jal* instruction, the Link Address Register (LR) saves the value of the current return address, which is the current Program Counter (PC) address plus eight. When nested subroutines occur, the LR value is overwritten with the most recent return address and previous return address values is moved to the program stack. This is prone to software exploitation. To eliminate the security threat, we utilize the BSRB in the microprocessor to store the LR contents. As not every *l.jal* instruction leads to the beginning of a subroutine, the proposed flowchart checks whether the three consecutive instructions following the instruction *l.jal* matches to the typical prologue of a subroutine. The *prologue* represents a special instruction sequence, which is unique for subroutines. We initially copy the return address from the LR to a temporary register. Only when the next three instructions proceeding a *l.jal* matches to the subroutine prologue, the register contents are pushed to the BSRB.

3.2.2 Retrieving Return Addresses from Register Bank

Subroutines are exited after retrieving the return address from the LR using a *l.jr* instruction. At execution, the contents of the LR is placed into the PC and the program will return to the memory address stored previously held by the PC before entering the subroutine. During execution of a *l.jr* instruction, we detect a CFA by checking the consistency between the return addresses reloaded from the stack and the BSRB. Any mismatch between the addresses will raise an alarm. The proposed flowchart also incorporates an epilogue to determine the arrival of the *l.jr* instruction specifically for a subroutine returning. The *epilogue* is composed of a microprocessor instruction sequences, which are used to retrieve the contents of the LR and guide the control flow jumping back to the upper level.

3.2.3 A Case Study

In this subsection, we use a simplified C program that is executable in the embedded system to further explain the proposed method. The pseudocode written in C is shown in the left side of Fig. 2 with an assembly listing on the right side. In that example, we take advantage of the function *memcpy*, which does not provide a boundary check before copying a number of bytes from location A to location B. A nested subroutine is executed in the main function. The first subroutine, *subroutine_a*, calls another subroutine, *exploit*, which creates a variable meant to overflow the allocated buffer size defined in function *vuln*. Analyzing the disassembled code, we can further distinguish the prologue, epilogue, and jump instructions which are of most importance.

Beginning in the main procedure of the assembly code, we encounter the first subroutine, *subroutine_a*. Moving to the location

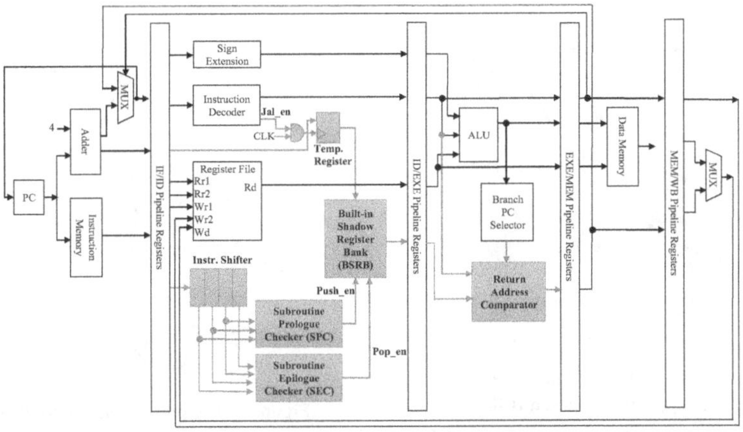

Figure 3: Architectural review of the OpenRISC 1000 micro-architecture with proposed method. The highlighted modules belong to the proposed countermeasure. IF: instruction fetch, ID: instruction decode, EXE: execution, MEM: read/write memory, and WB: write back.

specified by the *l.jal* instruction, we enter the start of *subroutine_a*. Here we notice that the subroutine prologue is performed through the first three instructions. Following the prologue, a second subroutine (*exploit*) takes place. The final five instructions in *subroutine_a* comprise the subroutine epilogue. Regardless of the location or which subroutine, the prologue and epilogue will retain the same instruction sequences as shown in Fig. 2.

3.3 Architectural View of Proposed Method

The proposed countermeasure against CFA mainly consists of return address store, load, and comparison steps. The first two steps focus on pushing/popping the key block to/from BSRB. The hardware implementation for return address storing and loading is located in the instruction decode stage, as shown in Fig. 3. The current instruction fetched is saved in the *instruction (instr.) shifter*. By analyzing the prologue and epilogue of the subroutine assembly codes for OpenRISC, we find that the minimum number of instructions for prologue and epilogue detection are three and four, respectively. Thus, the depth of the instruction shifter is four and the shifter width is equal to the width of each microprocessor instruction. The *subroutine prologue checker (SPC)* and *subroutine epilogue checker (SEC)* are comparators, in which one of the input is hard wired to the binary presentation of the instruction sequences for prologue and epilogue, respectively. The positive value of SPC output (*Push_en*) indicates to push the return address to BSRB. Similarly, the SEC output, *Pop_en*, notifies BSRB to pop off a value for the return address comparator in the execution stage. The data input for the BSRB is from a temporary register, which stores the next PC predicted in the IF stage. As only the next PC after the *l.jal* instruction is the return address for the subroutine, we apply the clock-gating technique to the temporary register using the signal of *Jal_en*. The Jal_en signal goes high as soon as the *l.jal* instruction opcode is detected.

The CFA detection is physically performed by the *Return Address Comparator* module in the execution stage, as shown in Fig. 3. The *Branch PC Selector* module prepares the next PC using the return addressed provided by the normal stack, which may be compromised by a CFA. Our return address comparator examines the consistency between the computed next PC with the return address saved in the BSRB. The difference between the two PCs will raise a system alarm and meanwhile the copy from the BSRB will be used for the subroutine return. Because the BSRB is located inside the microprocessor like the register file, attackers cannot access it to change the return address through buffer overflow, for instance.

4. EXPERIMENTAL RESULTS

4.1 Experimental Setup

A Terasic DE0-Nano embedded system was the primary hardware used for the implementation and evaluation of our countermeasure. An OpenRISC embedded processor is implemented and emulated in an Altera Cyclone IV EP4CE22F17C6N FPGA running a form of Linux that unique to the OpenRISC1000. We developed small programs, written in the C language, that cause a buffer overflow attack to occur [15]. We applied the proposed countermeasure to the register transfer level of the OpenRISC microprocessor. Our design was tested by uploading the examples containing the malicious codes to the development board and executing it. We compared the results with the baseline of the OpenRISC processor. To report the area, performance, and power overhead of the proposed method, we synthesized the Verilog HDL codes for the OpenRISC using the Synopsys Design Compiler with a TSMC 65nm CMOS technology. According to the worst-case delay on the critical path of each pipeline stage, we set up the clock period as 3.2ns for baseline and proposed countermeasure implementations.

4.2 Comparison of Area, Delay, and Power

The baseline OpenRISC and the source code are from the website [15]. We chose a moderate depth, 32, for the proposed BSRB. The BSRB depth represents the maximum number of nested subroutines in the program that can be supported by our method. Increasing the BSRB depth can allow the C program to use more nested subroutines. Table 1 compares the total synthesized area for the OpenRISC microprocessor. As shown, for the BSRB with a depth of 32, the proposed countermeasure only increases the microprocessor area by 3.8%.

The worst-case delay of a pipelined OpenRISC is determined by the execution stage. As the proposed countermeasure is mainly located in the instruction decode stage, our method does not lead to an increase on the worst-case delay of the microprocessor. This is shown in Table 1.

Next, we swept the BSRB depth in the proposed countermeasure. Figure 4 shows that the area cost increases with the depth of the BSRB design which is a user-define parameter. A larger built-in secure register bank can support more nested subroutines, but will result in more area overhead. For a rough estimation, when the BSRB depth grows to 128, the total area overhead will be around 14%.

The proposed countermeasure also leads to an increase on power consumption of the OpenRISC microprocessor. As listed in Ta-

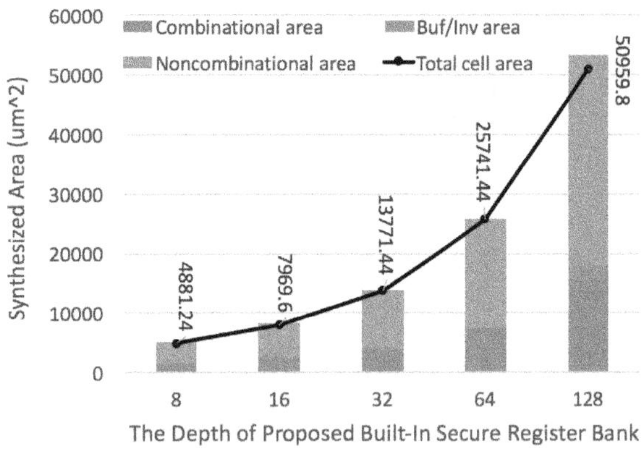

Figure 4: The area cost of different depths for proposed BSRB.

Table 1: Comparison of Area and Delay.

Design	Processor Area (μm^2)	Worst-case Delay (ns)
Baseline	377170.19 (100%)	2.80
Proposed	391358.15 (103.8%)	2.80

Table 2: Power Increase Caused by Countermeasure. Power Unit: mW.

Design	Dynamic Power	Leakage Power	Total Power
Baseline	69.31 (100%)	1.72 (100%)	71.02 (100%)
Proposed	72.37 (104%)	1.80 (104%)	74.16 (104%)

ble 2, our BSRB based method incurs 4.4% dynamic power increase. The overhead on the leakage power is 4.2%. We further break down the power consumption of each pipeline stage. As shown in Fig. 5, the major power overhead is on the instruction decode stage; however, the increased power is relatively small compared to the MEM and WB pipeline stages. That is why the total power overhead of our method is small and acceptable.

5. CONCLUSION

In this work, we propose a hardware-level method, which enhances the microprocessor architecture to transparently perform the control flow attack (CFA) detection at the microprocessor chip level. A built-in secure register bank (BSRB) is introduced to the microprocessor instruction decode stage to keep a clean copy of return addresses. The proposed countermeasure eliminates the need of a reserved memory space for a shadow stack. Furthermore, our method detects and mitigates CFAs in parallel with the normal operations. The area, delay and power overhead of the proposed countermeasure were assessed in Synopsys Design Compiler. Experimental results show that, for the BSRB with a depth of 32, our method increases the processor area by 3.8% and the total power consumption by 4.4% than the baseline OpenRISC 1000 microprocessor. As our countermeasure is not located in the critical path of the microprocessor, the worst-case delay of the microprocessor protected with our method is same with that of the baseline microprocessor. The limitation of this method is, when the depth of the BSRB increases to a larger number, the area and power overhead will increase accordingly.

6. REFERENCES

[1] C. Cowan *et al.*, "Buffer overflows: attacks and defenses for the vulnerability of the decade," in *Proc. of Foundations of Intrusion Tolerant Systems*, pp. 227–237, 2003.

[2] B. G. Roth and E. H. Spafford, "Implicit Buffer Overflow Protection Using Memory Segregation," in *Proc. of Availability, Reliability and Security*, pp. 175–182, 2011.

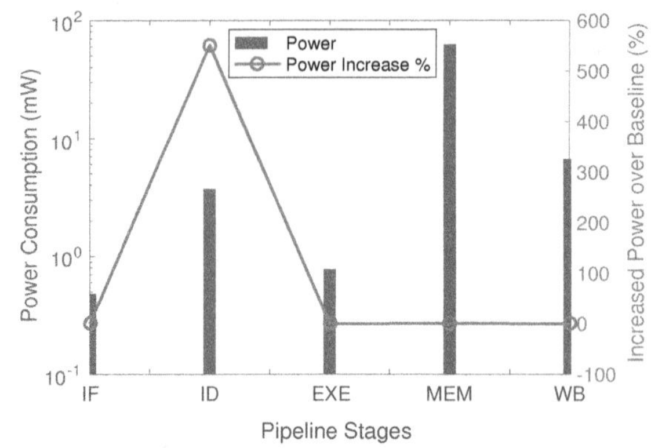

Figure 5: The power consumption comparison for pipeline stages.

[3] X. Wang, C. C. Pan, P. Liu, and S. Zhu, "Sigfree: A signature-free buffer overflow attack blocker," *IEEE Trans. on Dependable and Secure Computing*, vol. 7, no. 1, pp. 65–79, 2010.

[4] F. A. T. Abad *et al.*, "On-chip control flow integrity check for real time embedded systems," in *Proc. of CPSNA'13*, pp. 26–31, 2013.

[5] L. Davi, P. Koeberl, and A. R. Sadeghi, "Hardware-assisted fine-grained control-flow integrity: Towards efficient protection of embedded systems against software exploitation," in *Proc. of 2014 51st ACM/EDAC/IEEE Design Automation Conference (DAC)*, pp. 1–6, June 2014.

[6] M. Payer, A. Barresi, and T. R. Gross, "Fine-grained control-flow integrity through binary hardening," in *Proc. of DIMVA'15*, pp. 144–164, 2015.

[7] M. Conti *et al.*, "Losing control: On the effectiveness of control-flow integrity under stack attacks," in *Proc. of CCS'15*, pp. 952–963, 2015.

[8] K. Piromsopa and R. J. Enbody, "Secure bit: Transparent, hardware buffer-overflow protection," *IEEE Trans. on Dependable and Secure Computing*, vol. 3, no. 4, pp. 365–376, 2006.

[9] C. Cowan *et al.*, "StackGuard: Automatic Adaptive Detection and Prevention of Buffer-overflow Attacks," in *Proc. of USENIX*, pp. 5–5, 1998.

[10] M. Frantzen and M. Shuey, "StackGhost: Hardware Facilitated Stack Protection," in *Proc. of USENIX*, pp. 13–17, 2001.

[11] N. Tuck, B. Calder, and G. Varghese, "Hardware and binary modification support for code pointer protection from buffer overflow," in *Proc. of MICRO'04*, pp. 209–220, 2004.

[12] C. Tice *et al.*, "Enforcing Forward-edge Control-flow Integrity in GCC & LLVM," in *Proc. of USENIX*, pp. 941–955, 2014.

[13] S. Groh, M. Pizka, and J. Rudolph, "Shadow Stacks-a hardware-supported DSM for objects of any granularity," in *Proc. of ICA3PP'97*, pp. 225–238, 1997.

[14] A. Francillon, D. Perito, and C. Castelluccia, "Defending embedded systems against control flow attacks," in *Proc. of SecuCode'09*, pp. 19–26, 2009.

[15] "CSAW Embedded Security Challenge Exploits." https://github.com/nekt/csaw_esc_2016.

[16] S. W. Boyd *et al.*, "On the general applicability of instruction-set randomization," *IEEE Trans. on Dependable and Secure Computing*, vol. 7, no. 3, pp. 255–270, 2010.

Using Security Invariant to Verify Confidentiality in Hardware Design

Shuyu Kong
Northwestern University
shuyukong2020@u.northwestern.edu

Yuanqi Shen
Northwestern University
yuanqishen2020@u.northwestern.edu

Hai Zhou
Northwestern University
haizhou@northwestern.edu

ABSTRACT

Due to the increasing complexity of design process, outsourcing, and use of third-party blocks, it becomes harder and harder to prevent Trojan insertion and other malicious design modifications. In this paper, we propose to deploy security invariant as carried proof to prevent and detect Trojans and malicious attacks and to ensure the security of hardware design. Non-interference with down-grading policy is checked for confidentiality. Contrary to existing approaches by type checking, we develop a method to model-check a simple safety property on a composed machine. Down-grading is handled in a better way in model-checking and the effectiveness of our approach is demonstrated on various Verilog benchmarks.

1. INTRODUCTION

Design and manufacture of complex semiconductor circuits and systems requires many steps, and one design could involve hundreds of engineers, typically distributed across multiple locations and organizations worldwide. Moreover, the deployment of IP blocks from different sources has become a common practice. The conventional processes and tools for design and manufacture of semiconductors at most ensure the correctness. However, to date, these processes do not provide confidence about whether the chip is altered such that it provides illegal sensitive information leakage. Such undesirable behavior can be due to a weakness in the design that results in an unintentional side channel or due to maliciously inserted Trojan hardware.

Existing protections from hardware Trojan insertion and side-channel attacks are mostly based on testing or circuit analysis that are passive, ad hoc, and afterthoughts based on individual designs. In this paper, we propose a proactive approach based on a novel design framework called *Invariant-Carrying Machine* that will increase the confidentiality and trustworthiness of hardware. It leverages the current practice of verification in hardware design, and is based on lightweight formal methods that are scalable for large designs.

Permission to make digital or hard copies of all or part of this work for personal or classroom use is granted without fee provided that copies are not made or distributed for profit or commercial advantage and that copies bear this notice and the full citation on the first page. Copyrights for components of this work owned by others than ACM must be honored. Abstracting with credit is permitted. To copy otherwise, or republish, to post on servers or to redistribute to lists, requires prior specific permission and/or a fee. Request permissions from permissions@acm.org.

GLSVLSI '17, May 10-12, 2017, Banff, AB, Canada

© 2017 ACM. ISBN 978-1-4503-4972-7/17/05...$15.00

DOI: http://dx.doi.org/10.1145/3060403.3060456

The idea of carrying proof in hardware has been proposed in some recent work on "Proof-Carrying Hardware" [3, 7]. Drzevitzky 's approach only applies on configuration bit stream for FPGA. Even though Love 's approach can handle general designs in HDL, it requests the design being translated into another formal language, and a proof being constructed based on required security properties. Such requests incur extra workloads on designers and the scalability of formal methods could be a concern. Contrarily, ICM will use the native Verilog directly as the hardware model, and only add the inductive invariant in the Verilog description. Similar to the Proof-Carrying Code (PCC) for software security, Invariant-Carrying Machine (ICM) requests that each hardware design carries with it an inductive invariant. The invariant constitutes an assurance of the design, that is, it implies the security property or policy. The invariant must also be inductive.

In this paper, we mainly focus on one of the most important security property, confidentiality. We uses the notion of noninterference as a means to specify and prove hardware confidentiality. Noninterference requests the low confidential output will not be affected by the high confidential input. Based on the allowed amount of information leakage, noninterference can be further categorized into pure noninterference and relaxed noninterference. We develop strategies to handle both types and leverage state of the art formal verification tools to extract the inductive invariant held in state machine of the hardware system that can imply the noninterference property. In the experiment, we verify our approach on six small and median-sized behavioral verilog benchmarks revised from standard design.

2. ICM FRAMEWORK

In this paper, we are going to develop a hardware design framework called ICM (Invariant-Carrying Machine) for hardware assurance. As illustrated in Figure 1, the framework consists of a library of security policies and properties that are agreed among all parties, tools to aid the generation of inductive invariant for a given hardware design, and tools to check the validity of the invariant-carrying machine under the given security properties. If the hardware is an in-house design, the inductive invariant will be maintained through the whole design process and its validity will be checked after each big design step. If the hardware is an IP block, the user needs to check the validity of the inductive invariant before deploying the block. Hardware Trojans will be detected when validity checking fails. The whole approach is based on formal methods and follows the principles of the

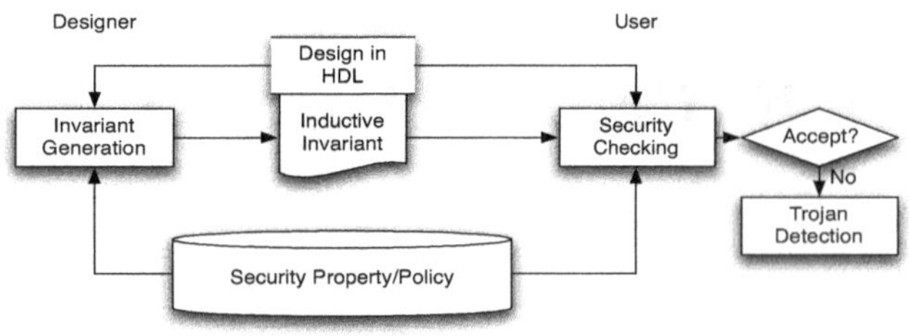

Figure 1: The Process Flow of Invariant-Carrying Machine for Hardware Assurance

famous and successful PCC (Proof-Carrying Code) [8] with modification for hardware design. An inductive invariant is used as the proof of hardware security. One critical observation is that the most expensive part of hardware correctness verification is the computation of an inductive invariant from the target property. With the request of inductivity, the checking of the invariant only requires three validations: the initial states satisfying the invariant, any state satisfying the invariant only going to states satisfying the invariant, and the invariant satisfying the security policy. None of the checks requests state unrolling, thus avoids the state explosion problem.

3. HARDWARE MODELED AS STATE MACHINE

Lamport [5] has shown and advocated that any computing system can be better modeled as a state machine. The behavior of a state machine is given by a subset of state changing sequences, each of which gives the sequence for a specific input. Therefore, we can specify the properties of state machine by temporal logic [5]. In temporal logic, we can use conventional logic to specify facts in one state (as in the initial condition), and use conventional logic with primed and non-primed variables to specify facts in two consecutive states (as in the transition relation).

In practice, it is unrealistic to implement a parser that can translate the hardware description language (HDL) like verilog of a large-scale design into state machine expressed in temporal logic because this would require the parser to handle the logical relation between executions of the complex behavioral hardware description. More specifically, the blocking assignments in always@ blocks happen sequentially as in the software programming language. This means that parser may have to compute the net effect of all the executions within the block to generate next state logic expression for each state variable. The cost and complexity could be very large. Therefore, a more realistic strategy is to borrow the idea of execution control flow from PCC and treat the set of blocking assignments as sequence of state transitions. Instead of generating the real hardware state transition, the clockwise transition, the parser will produce a statement-wise state transition. As a result, the original one-cycle state transition is divided into multiple state transition steps. Thus, it is necessary to introduce an extra state variable to represent and control the execution flow, e.g. PC. In addition, not only all the registers are treated as state variables, all the intermediate wires originally representing the netlists of the circuit may become state variables as well. In this way, each statement of execution can be regarded as one step transition.

The transition encoded with the execution flow actually represents a different hardware system. Due to many intermediate states generated from the revised transition, the property held in the original state machine is no longer an invariant in the state machine with parsed transition relation. It is meaningful to check the property only in the state which represents the end/start of one clock cycle computation in the original state machine because only these states exist in the original system. To make the invariant proof consistent, any original invariant *Inv* should be replaced by a new invariant *NInv* in the following way assuming PC is the state variable representing the execution flow and the state with $PC = 0$ indicates the start/end of the one clock cycle computation (we make this assumption by default in the rest of the paper).

$$NInv \triangleq (PC = 0 \Rightarrow Inv)$$

The statement-wise transition relation is obviously much easier to generate since Verilog parser can treat one HDL statement as a step of transition and avoids handling the complex logical relation between multiple executions within a sequential always block. It is important to realize that when there are multiple combinational **always** blocks and **assign** statements, it is necessary to topologically sort all the blocks before translating the design.

4. VERIFICATION OF CONFIDENTIALITY

In this section, we discuss our specification of confidentiality property and our strategies of handling the transition relation parsed from the HDL in order to leverage formal verification methodologies to verify the confidentiality of the given hardware design.

4.1 Noninterference

Only a small subset of hardware requests confidentiality. However, these hardware are probably more important to protect than others. Intuitively, it requests that no secrecy is leaked to the attacker. The first question is how confidentiality can be specified and proved in our logic. A recent breakthrough in security research was the discovery by Clarkson and Schneider [2] that many security properties such as *noninterference* and *average response time* are not properties of a computational trace, but properties of a set of traces, called "hyperproperties". They have shown that hyperproperties need second-order logic to express, which is out of the scope of conventional first-order logic.

Noninterference, in variety of forms, has been thoroughly studied for confidentiality. Generally speaking, a computing system may have both high and low confidential inputs and outputs, noninterference requests that the low confidential output will not be affected by the high confidential input. Formally, we can use a function $(O_l, O_h) = F(I_l, I_h)$ to represent the computing system, with O_l, O_h representing low and high outputs, and I_l, I_h low and high inputs. Then, noninterference means that for any $(O_l, O_h) = F(I_l, I_h)$ and $(O_l', O_h') = F(I_l', I_h')$, if $I_l = I_l'$ then $O_l = O_l'$.

Even though the plain noninterference is a security policy that is easy to express, it never has been widely enforced in real systems. The reason is that the plain noninterference is too strict to make a computing system satisfying this property. Even a simple prototype of the login process,

$$\text{IF } H = g \text{ THEN } l = 1 \text{ ELSE } l = 0,$$

where H representing the high confidential password, g the low guess, and l the low output, violates the property. However, in this example, even though the low output l depends on H, unless the domain of H is small, it will be almost impossible to learn H from (g, l) pairs.

One possible way to evaluate the confidentiality level is through quantitative information flow analysis that uses probabilistic analysis to calculate the amount of leaked information. However, such probabilistic analysis is very expensive and heavily depends on the specifics of the target system. Alternatively, we decide to use relaxed noninterference with downgrading policies [6] as the confidentiality policies in our framework. *Downgrading* is used to specify allowed information flow from a high security level to a low security level, which is also called *declassification* for confidentiality. Intuitively, *relaxed noninterference* is the same as noninterference that forbids information flow from high security to low security, with the exception of the given downgrading. A security policy can be modeled as a *downgrading function F* which involves at least one high-security input.

4.2 Self-composition

After settling on the relaxed noninterference with downgrading policies for confidentiality, we need to consider how to specify them and how to prove them. We come to an approach based on *self-composition* [1,9]. Intuitively, noninterference means that for any computational trace of the system, there must exist another trace where even the high security inputs have different values, the low security behavior is the same. *Self-composition* composes two copies of the original system (with input and variable renaming). Therefore, any property about two possible traces in the original system can be stated as a property about one trace in the composed system.

Formally, a state machine $M = (\bar{X}, \bar{I}, \bar{O}, Init, TR)$ can be described by propositional logic formulas: $\bar{X}$ is all the internal state variables, $\bar{I}$ and $\bar{O}$ are all the inputs and outputs, $Init(\bar{X})$ is the initial condition and $TR(\bar{I}, \bar{X}, \bar{O}, \bar{X}')$ is the transition relation where $\bar{X}'$ represents the next state. Meanwhile, inputs and outputs are categorized by their security sensitivity such that $\bar{I} = \bar{I}^l \vee \bar{I}^h$ and $\bar{O} = \bar{O}^l \vee \bar{O}^h$.

Given M, we can characterize self-composed state machine $M_{comp} = (\bar{X}_{comp}, \bar{I}_{comp}, \bar{O}_{comp}, Init_{comp}, TR_{comp})$ as follows:

$$\bar{X}_{comp} \triangleq \bar{X} \vee \bar{X}_c, \quad \bar{O}_{comp} \triangleq \bar{O} \vee \bar{O}_c, \quad \bar{I}_{comp} \triangleq \bar{I}_l \vee \bar{I}_h \vee \bar{I}_h^c$$

$$Init_{comp} \triangleq Init \wedge Init_c \bigwedge\nolimits_{x \in X} (x = x_c),$$

$$TR_{comp} \triangleq TR \wedge TR_c$$

The pure noninterference can also be specified by the following propositional logic.

$$Inv \triangleq \bigwedge\nolimits_{o \in O_l} (o = o_c)$$

Then, the proof obligation is to show that every reachable state in the transition state machine M satisfies Inv, which is symbolically represented as $M \models Inv$. Now, the noninterference proof problem is reduced to a model checking problem. Ideally, we can take advantage of formal verification tools and apply state-of-the-art model checking algorithm to verify the query $M \models Inv$ and compute the fixed point as our inductive invariant. Note the above self-composition is for the clock-wise transition relations. If execution flow is encoded and TR is statement-wise, TR_{comp} should be revised to support synchronization at the end of one clock cycle executions since one copy may run faster than the other copy. Besides, $Init_{comp}$ and Inv should be revised as follows:

$$Init_{comp} \triangleq Init \wedge Init_c \bigwedge\nolimits_{x \in X} (x = x_c) \wedge (PC = PC_c = 0)$$

$$Inv \triangleq (PC = PC_c = 0) \Rightarrow \bigwedge\nolimits_{o \in O_l} (o = o_c)$$

4.3 Transition Relation With Downgrading

The proof obligation presented in Section 4.2 does not take downgrading policy into consideration. Our next step is to show how to revise the composed transition relation to prove the relaxed noninterference of a given design.

Intuitively, relaxed noninterference verification is equivalent to the strong noninterference verification if the sensitive information is never leaked through the downgrading function. Accordingly, our goal is to encode this condition into the state transition relation. This requires the same output value of any corresponding computation blocks in both copies that perform the downgrading function. For the sake of simplicity in demonstration but without loss of generality, we assume only one downgrading function is provided and is performed by at most one execution block only once. We make this assumption default in the rest of the paper. It is trivial to extend the idea to more complex cases.

Firstly, we have the observation that it is relatively straightforward to incorporate the downgrading function into the proof obligation if the transition relation is coarse-grained without execution flow. In order to build the state transition TR_F with downgrading policy F, we only need to revise the transition relation to force the output of the downgrading function of one copy(minor copy) equal to that of the other copy(major copy) instead of minor copy's own downgrading function output. On the other hand, when the transition relation is generated by a parser and has execution control flow, the two copies may not be synchronous during the execution. So it is relatively hard to enforce the same output of the downgrading function from two copies. To solve this problem, we introduce an extra boolean state variable, *flag* to indicate whether the major copy has already performed the downgrading function or not. The transition for *flag* is as follows assuming *dp* and $cond^F$ are the execution point and corresponding branch condition under which the downgrading is performed respectively.

$$\begin{aligned} TR^{flag} \triangleq \quad & PC = 0 \Rightarrow \neg flag' \wedge (PC = dp \wedge cond^F) \Rightarrow flag' \\ \wedge \quad & \neg(PC = 0 \vee PC = dp) \Rightarrow flag' = flag \end{aligned}$$

To construct the new composed transition relation TR^F_{comp} from TR_{comp} to support downgrading function F, the transition logic of the control state variable from the minor copy PC_c should be changed. If the minor copy is about to perform the downgrading, it first needs to check whether the flag is raised, meaning the major copy has already been through the downgrading in the same clock cycle. If the flag is raised, it will take the output value of the downgrading function from the major copy and proceed forward. If the flag is not raised, it will wait until either the flag is raised or the major copy reaches the end of a clock cycle computation. Denote *Fvar* as the variable assigned to the output value of the downgrading function F. Accordingly, new PC_c and *Fvar* transition wil be as follows:

$$cond1 \triangleq PC_c = dp \wedge cond_c^F \wedge \neg flag \wedge PC \neq maxPC + 1$$

$$cond2 \triangleq PC_c = dp \wedge cond_c^F \wedge flag = TRUE$$

$$PC'_c = \begin{cases} PC_c & cond1 \\ same\ as\ in\ old\ TR_{comp} & otherwise \end{cases}$$

$$Fvar'_c = \begin{cases} Fvar & cond2 \\ same\ as\ in\ old\ TR_{comp} & otherwise \end{cases}$$

where $maxPC$ is the original last execution point in one clock cycle and $maxPC{+}1$ is the extra execution point to synchronize two copies at the end of a clock cycle.

To summary, the final desired version of transition relation, initial condition and relaxed noninterference property

Table 1: experiment results for both strict and relaxed noninterference verification

benchmarks	# of clauses in inductive invariant		# of sat queries		model checking time (s)	
	strict	relaxed	strict	relaxed	strict	relaxed
updown-cntr.v	46	27	1090	1447	1.56	3.73
LFSR.v	114	44	5513	6728	14.24	68.62
fib.v	148	157	7059	12025	72.2	132.39
multiplier.v	209	218	12431	12891	187.62	199.47
gcdEuclid.v	176	198	9787	10017	104.42	158.05
crc.v	208	242	17875	20242	230.45	257.86

are expressed as:

$$TR_{final} \triangleq TR^F_{comp} \wedge TR^{flag}$$

$$Init_{final} \triangleq Init_{comp} \wedge \neg flag \wedge (PC = PC_c = 0)$$

$$Inv_{final} \triangleq (PC = 0 \wedge PC_c = 0) \Rightarrow \bigwedge_{o \in O_l} (o = o_c)$$

Our approach to enforce the same downgrading function output of two copies can avoid false negative, that is, report secure when the hardware is actually insecure under the given downgrading policy. This guarantees the baseline security checking criterion. However, we can not avoid false positive, that is, report insecure when the hardware is actually secure under the given downgrading policy. In this sense, our approach to verify the relaxed noninterference is over conservative and it is necessary to conduct further security checking when the a result of "insecure" is reported.

5. EXPERIMENT RESULTS

We have implemented a Verilog parser that currently can translate a behavioral specification into a state machine given by its initial condition and transition relation. We leverate the state-of-art model checking tool CTIGAR (Counterexample To Induction-Guided Abstraction-Refinement) [4] to verify and compute the inductive invariant of the confidentiality property from the state machine. CTIGAR is an SMT-based model checker which extracts the inductive invariant by finding counterexamples and incrementally refining the property. CTIGAR is more efficient than many other model checking algorithms because it avoids unnecessary state unrolling.

We verify our approach on 6 small and median-sized behavioral verilog benchmarks revised from standard design. We first have a short description of each of our benchmarks:

- **updown-cntr.v**: 8-bit bidirectional counter and the direction is depending on a 1-bit input.
- **LFSR.v**: 8 bit linear-feedback shift registers.
- **fib.v**: sequentially compute the nth fibonacci number, where n is an 8-bit input.
- **multiplier.v**: sequentially compute the multiplication of two 16-bit inputs.
- **gcdEuclid.v**: compute greatest common divisor between two 16-bit inputs using Euclid Algorithm.
- **crc.v**: serial cyclic redundancy check $x^{16}+x^{15}+x^2+x^0$.

In all the benchmarks, we define the downgrading function as well as the security level of each input and output. Experimental results are shown in table 1. Compared with small-scale designs like **updown-cntr.v**, larger designs like **crc.v** require more sat queries and longer model checking run time to generate inductive invariants with more clauses. This is because larger designs have more execution blocks and will be translated into longer transition relations.

6. CONCLUSION

In this paper, we have introduced the framework of Invariant Carrying Machine for hardware assurance and investigated one of the most important security policy, confidentiality. We focused on relaxed noninterference with downgrading policies that could be proved by inductive invariant on self-composition of the machine. Experimental results on small- and median-sized designs have demonstrated the effectiveness of our approach.

7. ACKNOWLEDGEMENT

This work is partially supported by NSF under CNS-1651695 and CNS-1441695, and by SRC under 2014-TS-2559.

8. REFERENCES

[1] BARTHE, G., D'ARGENIO, P. R., AND REZK, T. Secure information flow by self-composition. In *Proceedings of the 17th IEEE Workshop on Computer Security Foundations* (Washington, DC, USA, 2004), CSFW '04, IEEE Computer Society, pp. 100–.

[2] CLARKSON, M. R., AND SCHNEIDER, F. B. Hyperproperties. *J. Comput. Secur. 18*, 6 (Sept. 2010), 1157–1210.

[3] DRZEVITZKY, S., KASTENS, U., AND PLATZNER, M. Proof-carrying hardware: Towards runtime verification of reconfigurable modules. In *Reconfigurable Computing and FPGAs, 2009. ReConFig '09. International Conference on* (Dec 2009), pp. 189–194.

[4] J. BIRGMEIER, A. R. B., AND WEISSENBACHER, G. Counterexample to induction-guided abstraction-refinement. *CAV* (2014).

[5] LAMPORT, L. *Specifying Systems: The TLA+ Language and Tools for Hardware and Software Engineers.* Addison-Wesley Publishing Company, 2002.

[6] LI, P., AND ZDANCEWIC, S. Downgrading policies and relaxed noninterference. In *Proceedings of the 32Nd ACM SIGPLAN-SIGACT Symposium on Principles of Programming Languages* (New York, NY, USA, 2005), POPL '05, ACM, pp. 158–170.

[7] LOVE, E., JIN, Y., AND MAKRIS, Y. Proof-carrying hardware intellectual property: A pathway to trusted module acquisition. *IEEE Transactions on Information Forensics and Security 7*, 1 (2012), 25–40.

[8] NECULA, G. C. Proof-carrying code. In *ACM Symposium on Principles of Programming Languages* (1997).

[9] TERAUCHI, T., AND AIKEN, A. Secure information flow as a safety problem. In *Proceedings of the 12th International Conference on Static Analysis* (Berlin, Heidelberg, 2005), SAS'05, Springer-Verlag, pp. 352–367.

Leveraging All-Spin Logic to Improve Hardware Security

Qutaiba Alasad, Jiann Yuan, and Deliang Fan
Department of Electrical & Computer Engineering, University of Central Florida, Orlando, FL 32816 USA
qutaibaeng@knights.ucf.edu, yuanj@ece.ucf.edu, dfan@ucf.edu

ABSTRACT

Due to the globalization of Integrated Circuit (IC) design in the semiconductor industry and the outsourcing of chip manufacturing, third Party Intellectual Properties (3PIPs) become vulnerable to IP piracy, reverse engineering, counterfeit IC, and hardware trojans. A designer has to employ a strong technique to thwart such attacks, e.g. using Strong Logic Locking method [1]. But, such technique cannot be used to protect some circuits since the inserted key-gates rely on the topology of the circuit. Also, it requires higher power, delay, and area overheads compared to other techniques. In this paper, we present the use of spintronic devices to help protect ICs with less performance overhead. We then evaluate the proposed design based on security metric and performance overhead. One of the best spintronic device candidates is the All Spin Logic due to its unique properties: small area, no spin-charge signal conversion, and its compatibility with conventional CMOS technology.

1. INTRODUCTION

Since the complexity of the design becomes very large and needs modern manufacturing equipment, several fabless companies only design the chips and then outsource the chips to semiconductor foundry for fabrication to reduce the fabricating costs. Thus, ICs might be imitated by an untrusted foundry or reversed engineering to be sold in markets illegally [1]. Consequently, IP owners do not have full control over untrusted foundries to protect their designs, where they are susceptible in front of many attacks, such as reverse engineering, IP piracy and IC counterfeiting [2].

Many researchers tend to develop emerging devices (such as spintronic device) as an alternative to traditional CMOS methodology in several applications to achieve lower power dissipation, smaller area and better performance. In spintronic device, a magnet could be switched by taking advantage of the current induced Spin-Transfer Torque (STT). The current induced STT is more power efficient and easier to control than the use of an external magnetic field. The main advantages of spintronic device over CMOS technology are listed: (1) stored data are not lost when power is turned off, and (2) its leakage power consumption is zero [3].

To summarize, protecting ICs from IP piracy, counterfeiting, and reverse engineering has been experimentally implemented using prevalent traditional CMOS technology but with some limitations and highly performance overhead. A more practical technique on protecting IC is Strong Logic Locking (SLL) method [1], but it has some limitations as follows: (1) this approach requires high performance overhead, (2) the inserted key-gates depend on the topology of the circuit. In some cases, the algorithm of SLL will terminate without inserting sufficient number of key-gates, and (3) the complexity of the algorithm is really high. Orthogonal to this technique, the unique characteristics of the emerging devices can give a better secure circuit with less performance overhead than CMOS technology if these characteristics utilize properly. In this paper, we present a case study of how spintronic device, e.g. All Spin Logic Device (ASLD), can protect ICs from different attacks without adding extra hardware resources by only replacing the traditional CMOS circuit with ASL device. We also evaluate and compare the delay, energy, and area of our proposal with previous works.

Permission to make digital or hard copies of all or part of this work for personal or classroom use is granted without fee provided that copies are not made or distributed for profit or commercial advantage and that copies bear this notice and the full citation on the first page. Copyrights for components of this work owned by others than ACM must be honored. Abstracting with credit is permitted. To copy otherwise, or republish, to post on servers or to redistribute to lists, requires prior specific permission and/or a fee. Request permissions from permissions@acm.org.

GLSVLSI '17, May 10-12, 2017, Banff, AB, Canada
© 2017 ACM. ISBN 978-1-4503-4972-7/17/05...$15.00
DOI: http://dx.doi.org/10.1145/3060403.3060471

2. FUNDAMENTAL OF ASL DEVICE

The first proposal for spin-based logic in semiconductors was introduced by Dery et al. [4]. The proposed design contains non-local spin signals, which require a high amplification circuit to enlarge these signals and produce a sufficient current to switch the nanomagnets. An improvement on this work [5], namely All Spin Logic device, was achieved to switch a nanomagnet, which could be an input for the next stage, by employing the non-local spin signal without any extra hardware (amplification circuit).

Figure 1 shows the All Spin Logic device in details; Figure 1 (a) represents the nanomagnetic unit, which is used to store the binary data, an isolation layer between the input (with low spin polarization factor) and output (high spin polarization factor) ports, and one non-magnetic channel. Figure 1 (b) shows a simple ASL with two magnets. These two magnets are polarized in the same direction and connected with each other through a non-magnet channel. The channel is made from nickel or copper due to high spin-flip length. The maximum length of the channel is relied on spin-flip length, which is used to identify the maximum distance that the spin current can be traveled (more details about the channel length is described in [6]). On applying negative VDD, the spin current will flow from M1 (where M is magnet) through the channel. The charge current will flow from GND to VDD, and the electrons will flow from VDD to GND. Spins with the same direction of M1 will pass while spins with opposite direction will not pass M1 (electrons get filtered). Since the output of M1 has high spin polarization and the input of M2 has low spin polarization, M1 will dominate the spin current and the passed spins will accumulate in the channel. Meanwhile, M2 will receive large spin current from M1. The direction of M2 will not be changed because both of M1 and M2 have the same

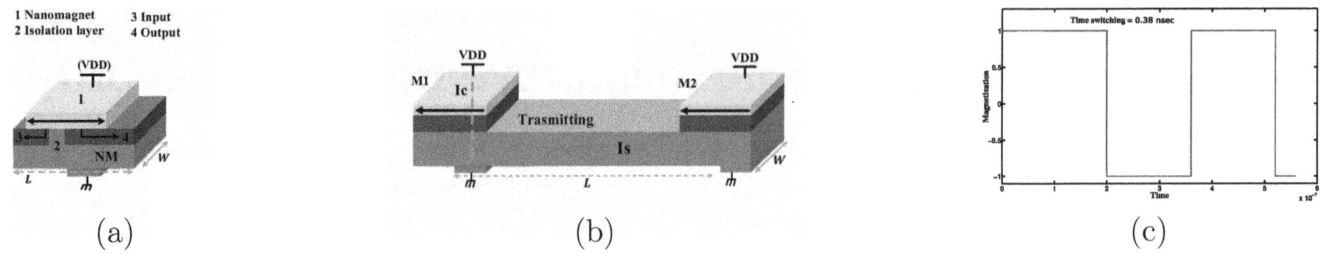

Figure 1: ASL device technique (a) Scheme (layout) of ASL device (b) a simple scheme of ASL with two magnets (c) Simulation results of inverter switching diagram.

magnetization direction. Therefore, the whole design will work as a buffer. In contrast, on applying positive VDD, the electrons will flow from the ground to the M1. As a consequence, spins with opposite direction of the magnet will accumulate in the channel. Meanwhile, only the spins with the same direction of M1 will pass out of M1 while the spins with opposite direction will be moved through the channel to switch the direction of M2, therefore, the device will work as inverter [6].

Based on this phenomena, we leverage the Current-In-Plane non-local spin valve modular model in [7] to simulate the all spin logic. We design a simple ASL with two magnets to get a simple polymorphic gate (inverter/buffer), as shown in Figure 1 (b). We can easliy switch the functionality from buffer to inverter (by supplying positive VDD) or from inverter to buffer (by supplying negative VDD). We apply input voltage 50 mV (positive VDD) to invert the direction of M2. Figure 1 (c) shows our simulation result to invert the magnetization direction of M2 using this model. The delay to completely switch the signal is 0.38 nsec. It is worth noting that the designer can easily improve the switching speed by increasing the input voltage at the expense of increased power dissipation. So it is trade-off between the delay and energy consumption (more information regarding the trade-off is clarified in [8]).

3. ASLD IN HARDWARE SECURITY

The features of ASL device, shown in Figure 1, might provide robust IP protection against several attacks with less performance overhead. In this section, we will present the circuit structure for IP protection purposes using ASL device.

The main idea of using the polymorphic gates is to obtain different logic gates with the same structure. For instance, a polymorphic gate in [9] using CMOS technology can perform as an AND or OR gate when the VDD is 3.3 V or 1.5 V, respectively, which is useful in many applications, such as aerospace purposes and intelligent system. For IP protection, the designer can conceal the functionality of the circuit by inserting polymorphic gates. The functionality will not be exposed even if an assailant can get the encrypted design by reverse engineering because only the designer knows the correct configuration signals for the polymorphic gates.

The ASLD can naturally perform as a majority gate (MG) operation. The principle of the MG is that the value of the primary output relies on the values of the majority inputs. Based on this phenomena, the ASLD can implement any logic gate. For instance, a designer can easily get N-inputs NOR gate by making the value of the fixed magnet as '1' (signified by left pointing arrow, as shown in Figure 1 (b)). By changing the magnetization direction of the fixed magnet (making the value of the fixed magnet as '0'), the design can perform as an N-inputs NAND gate. To get AND and OR gates, one more magnet layer has to be added at the primary output [10].

Based on this analysis, we propose ASL device as a polymorphic gate by employing its unique feature. The device gives us an opportunity to change the functionality of the circuit with the same structure and without any extra hardware by making one of the primary input as an external key. As shown in Figure 2 (a), the structure of ASL can provide four different gates with the same circuit; AND, OR, NAND, and NOR using only 4 magnets. Where A and B are the primary inputs, Key and VDD are used to change the functionality of the circuit. We make the third input of magnet (C) as an external key input. The circuit can be switched from AND to OR or OR to AND gate by only exchanging the value of the key from '0' to '1' or '1' to '0', respectively, when the VDD is positive. On applying negative VDD, the design can work as a NAND or a NOR gate if the value of the key is '0' or '1' respectively. There is another way to get a NAND or a NOR gate. A designer can apply only positive VDD and add one more magnet at the output of an AND or an OR gate, respectively.

Two options have already be introduced by Augustine et al. [6] to design a universal Full Adder (FA). The first one requires 44 magnetic units (using many NAND gates as majority gates), which is very expensive. While the second way needs to employ only 5 magnets to implement 3-inputs XOR gate as a sum of FA. The idea that the authors used to implement the sum of the FA is to make the distance (the channel length) from the primary input magnet (A, B, or C) to the output magnet (F1 in Figure 2 (b)) twice the distance from the output magnet (F1) to the primary output (F2 in Figure 2 (b)). As demonstrated in Figure 2 (b), the circuit will work as three-inputs XOR gate (sum of FA) if the distance from the primary input (A, B, or C/Key) to the output (F1) is twice the distance from the output (F1) to the primary output (F2). We realize that the structure can also function as an XOR or an XNOR gate by only making one of the primary input as an external input key, in which it will be an XOR gate if the key is '0' or an XNOR gate when the key is '1'. The summarization of our simulation results for the six different gates based on polymorphic gates is described in Table 1.

4. SECURITY ANALYSIS

In this section, we briefly discuss attacks and defenses methodologies based on logic locking approaches. An attacker can perform different techniques to get either the secret key of an encrypted circuit or the original IC, as in the following:

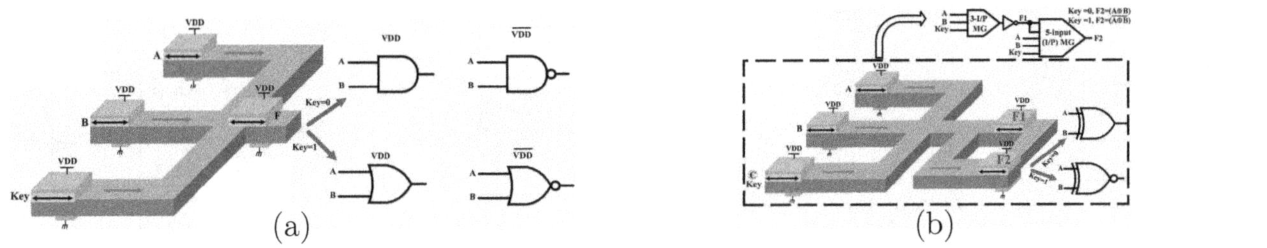

Figure 2: ASL technique as polymorphic gates (a) Layout of AND/OR/NAND/NOR gates (b) Layout of XOR/XNOR gates.

Table 1: Implementing AND, OR, NAND, and NOR gates and implementing XOR/XNOR gate with same structure

VDD	C/Key	A	B	AND/OR	VDD'	NAND/NOR	XOR/XNOR
1	0	0	0	0	-1	1	0
1	0	0	1	0	-1	1	1
1	0	1	0	0	-1	1	1
1	0	1	1	1	-1	0	0
1	1	0	0	0	-1	1	1
1	1	0	1	1	-1	0	0
1	1	1	0	1	-1	0	0
1	1	1	1	1	-1	0	1

4.1 Applying brute force search

A secret key of a locked IC can be revealed via an attacker on supplying all key combinations if the length of the key is not large enough. However, one can easily prohibit such offense by enlarging the size of the secret key. In conventional CMOS technology, increasing the size of the secret key requires more inserted key-gates (because one of each inserted-gate input has to be a key-bit). This will largely increase the performance overhead, especially for small scale benchmarks, where the total overhead of a small encrypted circuit might override the original circuit-size. Interestingly, implementing a circuit using ASL can give a designer a key-bit for any 2-inputs logic gate without any extra hardware. More specifically, a designer can freely increase the size of a valid key to a maximum N times, where N is the number of gates in the original circuit. Note that an attacker needs 2^N and 4^M number of attempts to recover the secret key from a circuit implemented using ASLD, where N is the number of Buffer/Inverter and XOR/XNOR gates, and M is the number of AND/NAND/OR/NOR gates in the encrypted circuit.

4.2 Propagating the secret key

Yasin et al. [1] proved that inserted XOR/XNOR randomly or without interference graph between key-gates is vulnerable because the value of the secret key-bits can easily be propagated to outputs by applying special input patterns on the locked IC, such as using Automatic Test Pattern Generation (ATPG) algorithm if an attacker gets the unlocked IC illegally. For instance, the circuit shown in figure 3 (a), Key1 and Key2 are two secret key-bits for the encrypted circuit storing in a tamper-memory and cannot be accessed by an attacker. On applying input pattern "111X", the values of both Key1 and Key2 will be revealed on the primary outputs (O1 and O2), respectively. Then the authors proposed a new technique to solve the weakness of the random insertion method by making a relationship between the inserted key-gates, in which muting a key-bit will not expose the value of other key-bits. This technique is named Strong Logic Locking. Even though using SLL can protect the circuit from reverse engineering, the SLL has also some limitations (as mentioned in Section 1). On the other hand, designing a circuit using ASL will naturally prevent such an attack from propagating the value of the secret key in an encrypted circuit because each key-bit has exactly the same characteristic of the other primary inputs (a designer can specify any primary input as a key-bit) , which means propagating the value of the key is impossible.

4.3 Applying golden input-output pairs

An assailant can acquire an unlocked chip from either an untrusted company or open market. Accordingly, he can expose the structure of the circuit and also observe the outputs by supplying input test patterns. By procuring unlocked IC and observing outputs via supplying distinguished input patterns, the attacker can extract the value of the secret key leveraging satisfiability solver (SAT) tools in a while for a large locked circuit [11], where the value of the secret key will be formalized in SAT formula. More specifically, attacker can use SAT solver, namely SAT based-attack, carefully choose distinguishing input patterns, and monitor their correct corresponding outputs. Each discriminating input/output (I/O) pair will rule out a bunch of the invalid key-bits from the locked IC. After supplying all of the discriminating I/O pairs, only one combinational correct key-bits will satisfy all of these golden I/O pairs, which ensures that this key must be the correct key of the encrypted circuit [11].

It is worth noting that SAT based-attacks break all existing logic locking techniques. Yasin et al. [1] added AES cryptography algorithm with fixed 32 bit key size to mitigate the effectiveness of SAT-attack since SAT algorithm cannot break AES cryptography. Even though this technique can increase the execution time of the SAT attack exponentially, implementation of AES algorithm demands large number of gates. Interestingly, SAT-attack is vulnerable against a tree of AND gates between the distinguishing inputs of the encrypted circuit and external key-bits (as the authors of SAT-attack reported) [11]. Based on this limitation, a designer can add a small circuit having several XOR gates (between primary inputs and key-bits) with many AND gates as a tree to increase the execution time of SAT-attack exponentially with much less performance overhead, but the key will be vulnerable in front of propagating secret-key attack.

In ASL, this technique can easily be implemented with more secure circuit and less performance overhead. For instance, the circuit shown in Figure 3 (b) is the SAT-resilient circuit using sufficient amount of XOR/XNOR and AND/NAND gates, which can be designed using ASL device. Where X is the distinguishing input-bits, and K1, K2, and K3 are the external input key (Key II) and $\mid K1 \mid = \mid K2 \mid = \mid K3/2 \mid$. The final output of SAT-resilience (S-O/P) can be either '0' or '1' (based on the designer's configuration) on applying the correct key, and the last inserted key-gate (between original output of the encrypted

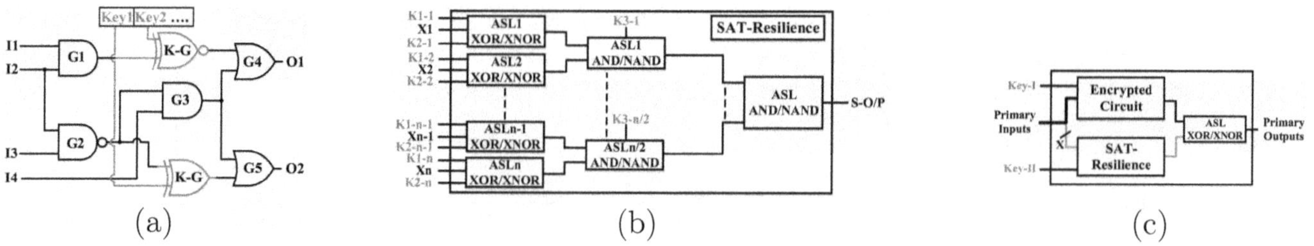

Figure 3: (a) encrypted circuit using random insertion approach (b) Scheme of SAT-resilient design. (c) Encrypted IC with SAT-resilience.

circuit and SAT-resilient output (S-O/P)) has to be XOR or XNOR, respectively, in order to get correct output. As demonstrated in Figure 3 (c), it shows the encrypted circuit combined with SAT-resilience. SAT-attack algorithm will fail if the length of Key II is long enough (larger than 32 bits). As a result, the design requires less number of inserted key-gates and is more secure against propagating-key attack.

5. SIMULATION RESULTS

In this section, we present the simulation results demonstrating the ASL device area, energy, and delay performance.

5.1 Simulation Setup

We use the non-local lateral spin valve modular model based on Current In-Plan (CIP) to implement three different categories of polymorphic gates; buffer/inverter, AND/OR/NAND/NOR, and XOR/XNOR gates. The Synopsys HSPICE simulator is adopted for circuit-level simulation to characterize ASL based polymorphic gates.

5.2 Performance and Device Parameters

It is not surprising that CMOS can outperform spintronic device in terms of speed, but the truth is that the ASL can be very fast if we increase the amount of the supply input voltage. However, that leads to an increase in power dissipation as well. So, it is a trade-off between the delay and power. In this work, we use ASL supply input voltage of 50 mV. The energy, delay, and area of all polymorphic gates are evaluated and compared with previous works. We summarize different types of polymorphic gates with their performance for our work and other previous works using traditional CMOS, DWM, and ASL, respectively, as shown in Table 2. The detailed setup parameters of non-local lateral spin valve are illustrated in Table 3. Designing IC using ASL device provides naturally protection from serious attacks without any extra hardware. Also, one can freely enlarge the size of the secret key without any additional hardware (in CMOS technology, each new key needs new inserted key-gate) since the ASL device can provide a key for any simple 2-inputs gate. A designer can implement a large scale circuit using ASL device, and then he or she can randomly specify the locations of the key-bits, where all other extra inputs (each gate has one more input) have to fixed to VDD or GND based on the type of the gate.

Table 2: Comparison between this work and previous works

Publication	# functions	# Tran/MTJ	Energy	Speed
[12] CMOS	XOR/XNOR	21/-	4pJ	224 ps
[12] DWM	XOR/XNOR	17/4	20.9pJ	219 ps
[13] CMOS	AND/OR	8/-	6.69 fJ	62 ps
[13] DWM	AND/OR	-/6	67.72 fJ	1.12 ns
This work	NAND/NOR/AND/NOR	-/4	0.58 pJ	1.65 ns
This work	XOR/XNOR	-/5	1.16 pJ	3.3 ns
This work	Inverter/Buffer	-/2	0.13 pJ	0.38 ns

Table 3: Simulation results of ASL parameters

ASL parameters	Value
Alpha (α)	0.01
Resistivity of interconnect (ρ)	7 Ω-nm
Spin-flip length (λ)	1 μ m
Area of magnet(A)	10×10 nm^2
H_K	4 KOe
M_S	780 emu/cm^3
Magnet volume (V)	$170\times80\times4\times e^-21$ m^3
Polarization (P)	0.1/0.95

6. CONCLUSION

In this paper, we have investigated the usage of spintronic device, i.e. All Spin Logic (ASL), that can help improve in hardware security. We extract and evaluate the unique properties of ASL device, which can naturally be used to protect an IC from various attacks. We first build different polymorphic gates that can be used to implement a highly secure combinational logic circuit without adding additional hardware and provide lower power and smaller area overheads. Based on our analyses with the simulation results, ASL can outperform conventional CMOS in terms of providing fully secure designs with low performance overhead.

7. REFERENCES

[1] M. Yasin et al. On improving the security of logic locking. *IEEE Trans. CAD*, 2015.
[2] J. Rajendran et al. Regaining trust in vlsi design: Design-for-trust techniques. *Proceedings of the IEEE*, 2014.
[3] X. Fong et al. Spin-transfer torque devices for logic and memory: Prospects and perspectives. *IEEE Trans. CAD*, 2016.
[4] H. Dery et al. Spin-based logic in semiconductors for reconfigurable large-scale circuits. *Nature*, 447:573–376, 2007.
[5] B. Behin-Aein et al. Proposal for an all-spin logic device with built-in memory. *Nature*, 5:266–270, 2010.
[6] C. Augustine et al. Low-power functionality enhanced computation architecture using spin-based devices. In *IEEE/ACM International Symposium on NANOARCH*, 2011.
[7] Kerem Camsari, Samiran Ganguly, and Supriyo Datta. Modular approach to spintronics. In *2015 Scientific Reports*, volume 5.
[8] Mrigank Sharad et al. Ultra-high density, high-performance and energy-efficient all spin logic. *Cornell University Library*, 2013.
[9] A. Stoica et al. Taking evolutionary circuit design from experimentation to implementation: some useful techniques and a silicon demonstration. *IEE P-COMPUT DIG T*, 2004.
[10] J. Kim et al. Spin-based computing: Device concepts, current status, and a case study on a high-performance microprocessor. *Proceedings of the IEEE*, 2015.
[11] P. Subramanyan et al. Evaluating the security of logic encryption algorithms. In *IEEE International Symposium on HOST*, 2015.
[12] Shoun Matsunaga et al. Fabrication of a nonvolatile full adder based on logic-in-memory architecture using magnetic tunnel junctions. *Applied Physics Express*, 1(9):091301, 2008.
[13] K. Huang et al. Magnetic domain-wall racetrack memory-based nonvolatile logic for low-power computing and fast run-time-reconfiguration. *IEEE Trans on VLSI Systems*, 2016.

Author Index

www.ingramcontent.com/pod-product-compliance
Lightning Source LLC
LaVergne TN
LVHW082023200926
848481LV00010B/2911
* 9 7 8 1 4 5 0 3 5 4 7 0 7 *